MAKING A NATION

The United States and Its People

Volume II

Jeanne Boydston
University of Wisconsin

Nick Cullather
Indiana University

Jan Ellen Lewis
Rutgers University, Newark

Michael McGerr
Indiana University

James Oakes
The Graduate Center, The City University of New York

Prentice Hall

Upper Saddle River, New Jersey 07458

Library of Congress Cataloging-in-Publication Data

Making a nation : the United States and its people / Jeanne Boydston . . . [et al.].
    p. cm.
  Includes bibliographical references and index.
  ISBN 0-13-033771-4
    1. United States—History. 2. United States—Economic conditions. I. Boydston, Jeanne.
  E178.1 .M22 2001
  973—dc21

2001034375

Use the Internet and eliminate mail time and postage costs
http://cip.loc. gov/cip

Editorial Director: Charlyce Jones Owen
Senior Acquisitions Editor: Charles Cavaliere
AVP, Director of Production and Manufacturing:
    Barbara Kittle
Editor in Chief of Development: Susanna Lesan
Development Editors: Barbara Muller, Robert Weiss
Senior Production Editor: Barbara DeVries
Prepress and Manufacturing Manager: Nick Sklitsis
Prepress and Manufacturing Buyer: Tricia Kenny
Marketing Manager: Claire Rehwinkel
Creative Design Director: Leslie Osher
Interior and Cover Design: Maria Lange
Chapter Opener Art Creation: Bruce Killmer

Line Art Supervisor: Gary Ruggiero
Electronic Art Coordinator: Mirella Signoretto
Copy Editor: Martha Francis
Editorial Assistant: Adrienne Paul
Photo Research: Linda Sykes
Photo Permission Manager: Kay Dellosa
Photo Permission Specialist: Tara Gardner
Cartographer: CartaGraphics
Cover Photos: Scott Barrow/International Stock
    Photography Ltd.; WallaceGarrison/Index Stock
    Imagery, Inc.; Aiello Productions, Inc.; CORBIS;
    Aiello Productions, Inc.

This book was set in 10/12 Stempel Garamond Regular by Carlisle
Communications and was printed and bound by Courier Companies, Inc.
The cover was printed by Phoenix Color Corporation.

 © 2002 by Pearson Education
Upper Saddle River, New Jersey 07458

Printed in the United States of America
10 9 8 7 6 5 4 3 2

ISBN 0-13-033996-2

PEARSON EDUCATION LTD., London
PEARSON EDUCATION AUSTRALIA PTY. Limited, Sydney
PEARSON EDUCATION SINGAPORE, Pte. Ltd.
PEARSON EDUCATION NORTH ASIA LTD, Hong Kong
PEARSON EDUCATION CANADA, LTD., Toronto
PEARSON EDUCATION DE MEXICO, S.A. de C.V.
PEARSON EDUCATION—Japan, Tokyo
PEARSON EDUCATION MALAYSIA, Pte. Ltd.
PEARSON EDUCATION, Upper Saddle River, New Jersey

BRIEF CONTENTS

CONTENTS

16
Reconstructing a Nation, 1865–1877 448

17
The Triumph of Industrial Capitalism, 1850–1890 480

18

Cultural Struggles of Industrial America: 1850–1895   512

19

The Politics of Industrial Society, 1870–1892   540

20

Industry and Empire, 1890–1900 566

21

A United Body of Action, 1900–1916 596

27

The Consumer Society, 1950–1960   770

28

The Rise and Fall of the New Liberalism, 1960–1968   800

MAPS

FIGURES and TABLES

SPECIAL FEATURES

WHERE THEY LIVED, WHERE THEY WORKED

ON TRIAL

GROWING UP IN AMERICA

PREFACE

Every human life is shaped by a variety of different relationships. Cultural relations, diplomatic relations, race, gender, and class relations, all contribute to how an individual interacts with the larger global community. This was as true in the past as it is today. *Making a Nation* retells the history of the United States by emphasizing the relationships that have shaped and defined the identities of the American people. For example, to disentangle the identity of a Mexican American woman working in a factory in Los Angeles in the year 2000 is to confront the multiple and overlapping "identities" that define a single American life. *Making a Nation* assumes that the multiplicity of cultures, classes, and regions, the vast changes as well as the enduring elements of our past, can nonetheless be told as the story of a single nation, always in the making. There are many ways to explore these relationships. *Making a Nation* views them through the lens of political economy. This is an especially appropriate way to approach American history.

In March of 1776, Adam Smith published his masterpiece, *The Wealth of Nations,* a few months before American colonists declared their independence from Great Britain. The imperial crisis had been building for some time and was a topic of international discussion. Smith delayed publication of his work for a year so that he could perfect a lengthy chapter on Anglo-American relations. Thus *The Wealth of Nations,* one of the most important documents in a new branch of knowledge known as *political economy,* was written with a close eye to events in the British colonies of North America, the colonies that were soon to become the United States. The fact that a large portion of Smith's book was framed as a history of England is equally important. Smith believed that history was one of the best ways to approach the study of political economy. *Making a Nation* shares that assumption; it takes political economy as an organizing theme for the history of the United States.

What did Smith and his many American followers mean by "political economy?" They meant, firstly, that the economy itself is much broader than the gross national product, the unemployment rate, or the twists and turns of the stock market. They understood that economies are tightly bound to politics, that they are therefore the products of history rather than nature or accident. And just as men and women make history, so to do they make economies—in the way they work and organize their families as much as in their fiscal policies and tax structures.

The term "political economy" is not commonly used any more, yet it is a way of thinking that is deeply embedded in American history. To this day we casually assume that different government policies create different "incentives" shaping everything from the way capital gains are invested to how parents raise their children, from how unmarried mothers on welfare can escape from poverty to how automobile manufacturers design cars for fuel efficiency and pollution control. This connection between government, the economy, and the relationships that shape the daily lives of ordinary men and women is the essence of political economy. But that connection points in different directions. Politics and the economy do not simply shape, but are in turn shaped by, the lives and cultural values of ordinary men and women.

In short, political economy establishes a context that allows students to see the links between the particular and the general, between large and seemingly abstract forces such as "globalization" and the struggles of working parents who find they need two incomes to provide for their children. *Making a Nation* shows that such relationships were as important in the seventeenth and eighteenth centuries as they are today.

So, for example, we begin this history of our nation by stepping back to view an early modern "world in motion." Every chapter in the book opens with a vignette that captures the chapter's theme, but each of the first six vignettes focuses on a different traveler whose life was set in motion by the European expansion across the Atlantic: an explorer, a settler, a young mother, a slave, a Native American. In a sense, globalization has been a theme in American history from its earliest beginnings. Europe, Africa, and the Americas were linked to each other in an Atlantic world across which everything was exchanged, deadly diseases along with diplomatic formalities, political structures and cultural assumptions, African slaves and European servants, colonists and commodities.

In subsequent chapters *Making a Nation* traces the development of the newly formed United States by once again stressing the link between the lives of ordinary men and women to the grand political struggles between Alexander Hamilton and Thomas Jefferson, between Andrew Jackson's Democrats and Henry Clay's Whigs. Should the federal government create a centralized bank? Should it promote economic development by sponsoring the construction of railroads, turnpikes, and canals? At one level, such questions exposed competing ideas about what American capitalism should look like and what the implications of those ideas were for

American democracy. But a closer look suggests that those same political quarrels were propelled by the concerns that farmers, workers, and businessmen were expressing about the pace and direction of economic change. A newly democratic politics had given many ordinary Americans a voice, and they immediately began speaking about the way the policies of the government affected the basic elements of their daily lives. They have been speaking the same way ever since.

Similarly, the great struggle over slavery and freedom—a struggle that literally tore the nation apart in the middle of the nineteenth century—is told as the story of dramatic political maneuvers and courageous military exploits, as well as the story of women who created the modern profession of nursing by caring for civil war soldiers and of runaway slaves who helped push the United States government into a policy of emancipation. The insights of political economy frame the way *Making a Nation* presents the transition from slave to free labor in the South after the Civil War. A new labor system meant an entirely new pattern of gender relations between freedmen and freedwomen whose marriages were legalized for the first time.

In the twentieth century, as America became a global power, the demands of the new political economy of urban and industrial America inform our examination of both U.S. diplomacy and domestic affairs. It was no accident, for example, that the civil rights leader A. Philip Randolph took advantage of the crisis of the Second World War to threaten Franklin Roosevelt's administration with a march on Washington. For Randolph, the demand for racial equality was inseparable from the struggle for a more equitable distribution of the rewards of a capitalist economy.

The United States victory in World War II, coupled with the extraordinary burst of prosperity in the war's aftermath, gave rise to fantasies of omnipotence that were tested and shattered by the American experience in Vietnam. Presidents, generals, and ordinary soldiers alike shared in the illusion of invulnerability. America's was the greatest democracy and the most powerful economy on earth. Thus did Americans in Southeast Asia in the late twentieth century find themselves in much the same place that Christopher Columbus had found himself centuries before: halfway around the world, face to face with a people whose culture he did not fully understand.

Student Learning Aids

To assist students in their appreciation of this history, we have added several distinctive features.

Chapter Opening Vignettes
The vignettes that open each chapter have already been mentioned; they are intended to give specificity as well as humanity to the themes that follow. From the witchcraft trials in Salem to the Trumps' American dream, students are drawn into each chapter with interesting stories that illustrate the organizing factor of political economy.

"Where They Lived, Where They Worked" sections, such as the story of the company-owned town of Pullman, Illinois, featured in Chapter 20 help students see the connections between home and work that are obscured in most accounts of American history.

"Growing Up In America" includes the history of young people in a systematic way. Instead of just concentrating on famous people in history, these sections look particularly at one or a group of younger people and relate their experiences to the larger movements of their day. By providing students insights into the lives of ordinary people like themselves, such as Jarena Lee presented in Chapter 9, this special feature makes the text inherently more interesting .

"On Trial" highlights a series of cases, such as the Scottsboro trial in Chapter 24, that show how personal, social, and even political struggles are often played out as dramatic and illuminating courtroom battles.

Web Connection
Making a Nation is the first text to integrate Web-based activities into each of its chapters. Tied closely to the themes of the text, each Web Connection combines text, audio, and visuals to explore provocative topics in depth.

Maps
The study of history has always been enhanced by maps. To help students understand the relationships between places and events, *Making a Nation* provides extensive map coverage. With over 120 full color maps devoted to such topics as "Exploring the Trans-Mississippi West," "Patterns of Global Migration," and "The Globalization of the U.S. Economy," students can more readily place events in their geographic context. To capture the element of globalization, almost every chapter contains at least one map dedicated to that theme.

Pedagogical Aids
Each chapter has numerous aids to help students read and review the information. Chapter outlines, listing of key topics, chapter chronologies, review questions, further readings and a collection of related Internet sites are found in every chapter.

Additional Study Aids
In addition to providing several key documents in United States history, the Appendix presents demographic data reflecting the 2000 census figures. A Glossary explains important terms highlighted in the book, and an extended Bibliography offers an expanded compilation of literature, arranged by chapter.

Themes and Coverage

Because *Making a Nation* was written from the very beginning with an organizing theme in mind, we have been able to incorporate many topics relatively smoothly within the larger narrative. For example, this textbook includes some of the most extensive coverage of Indian and western history available, but because our coverage is integrated into the larger narrative, there is no need to provide a separate chapter on either topic. At the same time, the theme of political economy allows us to cover subjects that are often missed in standard texts. For example, *Making a Nation* includes more than the usual coverage of environmental history, as well as more complete coverage of the social and cultural history of the late twentieth century than is available elsewhere. And in every case the *politics* of globalization and environmentalism, of capitalist development and democratic reform, of family values and social inequality are never far from view. *Making a Nation* also provides full coverage of the most recent American history, from the end of the Cold War to the rise of a new information economy and on to the terrorist attacks against the World Trade Center and the Pentagon in September 2001. Here, again, the organizing theme of political economy provides a strong but supple interpretive framework that helps students understand developments that are making a nation in a new century.

Supplementary Instructional Materials

Making a Nation comes with an extensive package of supplementary print and multimedia materials for both instructors and students.

PRINT SUPPLEMENTS

Instructor's Resource Manual

Prepared by Laura Graves, South Plains College
Contains introduction to instructors, chapter outlines, detailed chapter overviews, discussion questions, lecture strategies, essay topics, suggestions for working with Web resources, and tips on incorporating Penguin titles in American history into lectures.

Test Item File

Prepared by Bruce Caskey, Herkimer County Community College
Includes over 1000 multiple-choice, true-false, essay, and map questions, organized by chapter. A collection of blank maps can be photocopied and used for map testing or other class exercises.

Study Guide (Volumes I and II)

Prepared by Laura Graves, South Plains College
Contains introduction to students, chapter overviews,

chapter outlines, map questions, sample exam questions, analytical reading exercises, collaborative exercises, and essay questions.

Documents in United States History (Volumes I and II)

Prepared by Paula Stathakis, University of North Carolina, Charlotte, and Alan Downs, Georgia Southern University
Edited specifically for *Making a Nation*, the Documents Set brings together over 200 primary sources and scholarly articles in American history. Headnotes and review questions contextualize the documents and prompt critical inquiry.

Transparencies

This collection of over 150 full-color transparencies provides the maps, charts, and graphs from the text for classroom presentations.

Retrieving the American Past 2001 Edition (RTAP)

RTAP enables instructors to tailor a custom reader whose content, organization, and price exactly match their course syllabi. Edited by historians and educators at The Ohio State University and other respected schools, RTAP offers instructors the freedom and flexibility to choose selections of primary and secondary source readings—or both—from 73 (14 new) chapters. Contact your local Prentice Hall representative for details about RTAP. Discounts apply when copies of RTAP are bundled with *Making a Nation*.

Themes of the Times

 This special newspaper supplement is prepared jointly for students by Prentice Hall and the premier news publication, the *New York Times*. Issued twice a year, it contains recent articles pertinent to American history, which connect the classroom to the world. Contact your Prentice Hall representative for details.

Reading Critically about History

Prepared by Rose Wassman and Lee Rinsky, DeAnza College, this brief guide provides students with helpful strategies for reading a history textbook and is available free when packaged with *Making a Nation*.

Understanding and Answering Essay Question

Prepared by Mary L. Kelley, San Antonio College, this helpful guide provides analytical tools for understanding different types of essay questions and for preparing well-crafted essay answers. It is available free when packaged with *Making a Nation*.

MULTIMEDIA SUPPLEMENTS

Companion Website™

The access code protected *Companion Website™* for *Making a Nation* is available at *www.prenhall.com/boydston* and offers students one of the most comprehensive Internet resources available. Organized around the primary subtopics of each chapter, the *Companion Website*™ provides detailed summaries, multiple-choice, true-false, essay, identification, map labeling, and document questions and Web Connection activities based on the text. Overview tables in each chapter facilitate quick review. Hyperlinks to other Web resources provide students with access to screened sites. Chat rooms and message boards allow students to share their ideas about American history with their own class or with colleges across the country.

The *Faculty Module* contains a wealth of material for instructors, including Microsoft PowerPoint™ presentations with maps, charts, and graphs that can be downloaded.

History on the Internet

This guide focuses on developing the critical-thinking skills necessary to evaluate and use online resources. It provides a brief introduction to navigating the Internet and outlines the many references to history Websites. Available free when packaged with *Making a Nation*.

PowerPoint™ Images CD-ROM

Available in Windows and Mac formats for use with Microsoft PowerPoint™, this CD-ROM includes the maps, charts, tables, and graphs from *Making a Nation*. These resources can be used in lectures, for slide shows, and printed as transparencies.

COURSE MANAGEMENT SYSTEMS

As the leader in course-management solutions for teachers and students of history, Prentice Hall provides a variety of online tools. Contact your local Prentice Hall representative for a demonstration, or visit *www.prenhall. com/demo*

Acknowledgements

We would like to express our express our thanks to the reviewers whose thoughtful comments and insights were of great value in finalizing *Making a Nation:*

Tyler Anbinder, George Washington University
Debra Barth, San Jose City College
James M. Bergquist, Villanova University
Robert Brandfon, College of the Holy Cross
Stephanie Camp, University of Washington
Mark T. Carleton, Louisiana State University
Jean Choate, Northern Michigan University
Martin B. Cohen, George Mason University
Samuel Crompton, Holyoke Community College
George Daniels, University of South Alabama
James B. Dressler, Cumberland University
Elizabeth Dunn, Baylor University
Mark Fernandez, Loyola University of New Orleans

Willard B. Gatewood, University of Arkansas
James Gilbert, University of Maryland at College Park
Richard L. Hume, Washington State University
Frederic Jaher, University of Illinois at Urbana-Champaign
Glen Jeansonne, University of Wisconsin-Milwaukee
Constance Jones, Tidewater Community College
Laylon Wayne Jordan, University of Charleston
Peter Kirstein, St. Xavier University
John D. Krugler, Marquette University
Mark V. Kwasny, Ohio State University-Newark
Gene D. Lewis, University of Cincinnati
Glenn Linden, Southern Methodist University
Robert McCarthy, Providence College
Andrew McMichael, Vanderbilt University
Dennis N. Mihelich, Creighton University
Patricia Hagler Minter, Western Kentucky University
Joseph Mitchell, Howard Community College
Reid Mitchell, University of Maryland Baltimore County
Carl Moneyhon, University of Arkansas at Little Rock
James M. Morris, Christopher Newport University
Earl Mulderink III, Southern Utah University
Alexandra Nickliss, City College of San Francisco
Chris S. O'Brien, University of Kansas
Peter Onuf, University of Virginia
Annelise Orleck, Dartmouth College
Richard H. Peterson, San Diego State University
Leo R. Ribuffo, George Washington University
Kenneth Scherzer, Middle Tennessee State University
Sheila Skemp, University of Mississippi
Kevin Smith, Ball State University
Michael Topp, University of Texas at El Paso
Gregory J. W. Urwin, University of Central Arkansas
Paul K. Van der Slice, Montgomery College
Jessica Weiss, California State University of Hayward
James A. Wilson, Southwest Texas State University
John Wiseman, Frostburg State University

The authors would like first to acknowledge their co-authors: Without the patience, tenacity, and intellectual support we received from each other, we could scarcely have continued to the end. And we are grateful of course to our families, friends, and colleagues who encouraged us during the planning and writing of *Making a Nation*.

Jeanne Boydston would like to thank Joy P. Newmann for her enduring patience. I dedicate my work here to my father, Donnell B Boydston, who probably would have quarreled with much of what I've written, but would have loved reading it.

Jan Lewis expresses special thanks to Andy Achenbaum, James Grimmelmann, Warren F. Kimball, Ken Lockridge, and Peter Onuf, who either read portions of the manuscript or discussed it with me. And I am grateful to Barry Bienstock for his enormous library, his vast knowledge, and his endless patience.

Michael McGerr: This is for Frances Asbach and Edward McGerr, Grace Sarli and Joseph Fanelli, and Pauline Tornay and Michael Tuoti, who helped make a nation, and for Katie and Patrick McGerr who will help remake it.

The authors would like to thank Bruce Nichols for helping launch this textbook many years ago, and the editors and staff at Prentice Hall, especially our acquisitions editor, Charles Cavaliere, editorial director and vice president, Charlyce Jones Owen, development editor Barbara Muller, Susanna Lesan, editor in chief of development, senior production editor, Barbara DeVries, marketing manager, Claire Rehwinkel, and designer, Maria Lange. We have benefited at each stage from their patience, their experience, and their commitment to this project. Thanks also to Linda Sykes who managed the photo research, Mirella Signoretto who formatted the line art, Nick Sklitsis, manufacturing manager, Tricia Kenny, manufacturing buyer, and Jan Stephan, managing editor, and many other people behind the scenes at Prentice Hall, for helping make the book happen.

ABOUT the AUTHORS

Jeanne Boydston is Professor of History at the University of Wisconsin-Madison. She is the author of *Home and Work: Housework, Wages, and the Ideology of Labor in the Early American Republic*, coauthor of *The Limits of Sisterhood: The Beecher Sisters on Women's Rights and Woman's Sphere*, co-editor of *The Root of Bitterness: Documents of the Social History of American Women* (second edition), as well as author of articles on the labor history of women in the early republic. Professor Boydston teaches in the areas of early republic and antebellum United States history and United States women's history to 1870. Her BA and MA are from the University of Tennessee, and her PhD is from Yale University.

Nick Cullather is Associate Professor at Indiana University, where he teaches courses on the history of United States foreign relations. He is on the editorial boards of *Diplomatic History* and the *Encyclopedia of American Foreign Policy,* and is the author of *Illusions of Influence* (1994), a study of the political economy of United States-Philippines relations, and *Secret History* (1999), which describes a CIA covert operation against the government of Guatemala in 1954. He received his AB from Indiana University and his MA and PhD from the University of Virginia.

Jan Ellen Lewis is Professor of History and Director of the Graduate Program at Rutgers University, Newark. She also teaches in the history PhD program at Rutgers, New Brunswick and was a Visiting Professor at Princeton University. A specialist in colonial and early national history, she is the author of *The Pursuit of Happiness: Family and Values in Jefferson's Virginia* (1983), and co-editor of *An Emotional History of the United States* (1998) and *Sally Hemings and Thomas Jefferson: History, Memory, and Civic Culture* (1999). She is currently completing an examination of the way the Founding generation grappled with the challenge presented to an egalitarian society by women and slaves and a second volume of the Penguin History of the United States. She received her AB from Bryn Mawr College, and MAs and PhD from the University of Michigan.

Michael McGerr is Associate Professor of History and Associate Dean for Graduate Education in the College of Arts and Sciences at Indiana University-Bloomington. He is the author of *The Decline of Popular Politics: The American North, 1865–1928* (1986). With the aid of a fellowship from the National Endowment for the Humanities, he is currently writing a book on the rise and fall of Progressive America. Professor McGerr teaches a wide range of courses on modern American history, including the Vietnam War, race and gender in American business, John D. Rockefeller, Bill Gates, and the politics of American popular music. He received his BA, MA, and PhD degrees from Yale University.

James Oakes is Graduate School Humanities Professor and Professor of History at the Graduate Center of the City University of New York, and has taught at Purdue, Princeton, and Northwestern. He is author of *The Ruling Race: A History of American Slaveholders* (1982) and *Slavery and Freedom: An Interpretation of the Old South* (1990). In addition to a year-long research grant from the National Endowment for the Humanities, he was a fellow at the Center for Advanced Study in the Behavioral Sciences in 1989–90. His areas of specialization are slavery, the Civil War and Reconstruction, and the history of American political thought. He received his PhD from Berkeley.

MAKING A NATION
THE UNITED STATES AND ITS PEOPLE

Just as men and women make histories, so do they make nations. By showing the links between the specific and the general, and between large and seemingly abstract forces such as globalization and political conflict with the daily struggles of ordinary women and men, *Making a Nation* provides students with a rich and compelling perspective on American history. Carefully crafted by a team of leading scholars and experienced teachers, *Making a Nation* gets behind the facts to reveal the many stories that made—and continually remake—American history.

A focus on the relationships that shape and define human identity.
Making a Nation returns again and again to the concept that everyone's life is formed by many different relationships. Whether it be Indians negotiating with colonists in the 18th century, newly-freed slaves in the 19th century, or immigrant garment workers in the present century, *Making a Nation* confronts the multiple and overlapping identities that define American life.

The Varieties of Colonial Experience

Although the eighteenth-century industrial and consumer revolutions tied the peoples of the North Atlantic world together and gave them many common experiences, factors such as climate, geography, immigration, patterns of economic development, and population density made for considerable variety. Although the vast majority of Americans lived in small communities or on farms, an increasing number lived in cities, and urban centers played a critical role in shaping colonial life. At the same time, farming regions, both slave and free, were maturing, changing the character of rural life. The growing colonial population continued to push at the frontiers of settlement, leading to the founding of a new colony in Georgia.

Political economy approach establishes a context for seeing the links between the particular and the general.

Making a Nation traces the development of the United States to show the connections between government, the economy, and the relationships that shape daily life. The insights of political economy allow students to understand that economies and politics are the products of history rather than nature or accident.

Conceptions of Political Economy in the New Republic

Most free Americans believed that the success of the republic depended ultimately on the political virtue of its citizens. By "political virtue," they meant the essential characteristics of good republican citizens. In an age of breathtaking economic expansion, it is unsurprising that Americans associated those qualities with economic life. When people grew too wealthy and accustomed to luxury, many Americans believed, they grew lazy

A global perspective on American history.

More than any other text, *Making a Nation* highlights the ties between seemingly abstract forces and the struggles of ordinary men and women. It shows that globalization has been a theme of American history from its earliest beginnings—profoundly affecting human relationships on many different levels.

The Political Economy of Global Capitalism

The economic history of the late nineteenth century was sandwiched between two great financial panics, one in 1873 and the other in 1893. Both were followed by prolonged periods of high unemployment. Both led directly to tremendous labor unrest. The years between the two panics were marked by a general decline in prices that placed a terrible burden on producers. Farmers found that their crops were worth less at harvest time than they had been during planting season. They responded by expanding their enterprises to meet the worldwide demand for American agriculture.

OUTLINE

Chapter outlines **at the beginning of each chapter list primary topics that follow.**

Tituba Shapes Her World and Saves Herself

Her name was Tituba. Some say she was African, a Yoruba. Others believe that she was an Arawak Indian from Guyana. Had she not been accused of practicing witchcraft in Salem, Massachusetts, in 1692, she surely would have been forgotten by history. Now, more than three centuries later, the record is dim. Her name appears on a list of slave children owned by a Barbados planter in 1677. Whether she came from South America or Africa, she had been torn away from her home and sent to work on a sugar plantation on the Caribbean Island that the English had colonized almost fifty years before. In those years, the English were enslaving small numbers of Arawaks from the northern coast of South America. The peaceful habits of the Arawaks and their domestic skills made them good house servants, while their alliance with the Dutch, who were at war with the English, made them vulnerable to English raiders. Sugar planters preferred African slaves, however, and by the 1670s they were importing 1,300 of them each year onto the tiny island in order to feed Europe's insatiable appetite for sugar. By 1680, the African population of Barbados, at 37,000, was more than twice that of the European. Whatever her origins, Tituba lived in an African-majority society and absorbed African customs.

Tituba was still young, probably a teenager, when she was taken, once again as a slave, to a new home in Massachusetts in 1680. She had been purchased by a young, Harvard-educated Barbadian, Samuel Parris. Parris' father had failed as a planter, and now his son was about to meet the same fate as a merchant in Boston. Both planting and commerce were risky ventures, at the mercy of both the market and luck. Tituba found herself in Salem because of the market: Barbados planters wanted field hands and house servants, and now a failed merchant, Samuel Parris, abandoned commerce for the ministry. In 1689 Parris moved his

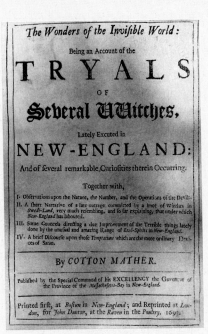

Opening vignettes **capture each chapter's theme. Each chapter in *Making a Nation* briefly narrates the experiences of a person whose life embodies the key themes of the chapter.**

Where They Lived, Where They Worked sections help students see the connections between home and work, which are obscured in most accounts of American history.

WHERE THEY LIVED, WHERE THEY WORKED

The Chesapeake Plantation Village

The eighteenth-century Chesapeake plantation village linked the worlds of Europe, Africa, and North America. The plantation itself was a hub of production, producing tobacco to sell in the markets of Europe, as well as many of the manufactured goods used on the plantation, such as nails, bricks, and cloth. All were produced by slave labor.

The plantation's architecture combined English and African elements. After about 1720, the most affluent planters began building large brick homes, copying Georgian styles then popular in England. The wooden buildings on the plantation, however, including the homes of less prosperous planters, slave cabins, and other "out" buildings, were constructed with African techniques. Their frames were much lighter, more like those of central African houses than of contemporary English

ones. Winding paths that followed the natural contours of the land and raised burial plots also reflected African influences. Plantation villages themselves bore an uncanny resemblance to an African king's village, in which smaller homes were arrayed behind the chieftain's main house.

Whites borrowed from African culture in other ways. The barbecue at which "a great number of young people met together with a Fiddle and Banjo played by two Negroes" represented a melding of European (the fiddle) and African (the banjo) music. The ecstatic shouting and visions of African worship services also made their way into Baptist and Methodist church services. These borrowings were usually silent. Black influences quietly made their way into white culture, in the process creating a culture that was neither fully African nor fully European.

Notice the similarities in construction between the Zaire home (top) and the Virginia cabin (bottom left). Although the photo of the Zaire home is from c. 1910 and the Virginia cabin from 1897, they suggest how African homes and Virginia slave cabins looked in the late eighteenth century. The planter's "big house" and the slave cabins and other out buildings made a small village, similar in layout to that of an African chieftain's. The photo (bottom right) is of the plantation community at Green Hill Plantation, built in the late eighteenth century.

Growing Up in America features spotlight the history of young people, showing how American youth have always been part of a larger political economy.

GROWING UP IN AMERICA

Jane Addams at College

Jane Addams became a successful activist while still in school, long before she became famous for her social work among Chicago's poor. In 1877, at the age of 17, Addams enrolled in a seminary at Rockford, Illinois, to begin her college education. The fact that the school still called itself a seminary rather than a college was one indication that it had yet to transform its curriculum along the lines of Johns Hopkins, Cornell, or Harvard. Nevertheless, over the next several years, Jane and her contemporaries brought the struggle over the modern curriculum to Rockford. "So much of our time is spent in preparation, so much in routine . . . ," Addams complained while at the seminary. She and her companions therefore made "various and restless attempts" to challenge the "dull obtuseness" of the college curriculum.

In one of those "various attempts" Jane and her friends took opium in an effort to stimulate their imaginations; it didn't work. They fell in love with the grand themes of Greek philosophy and Romantic literature, but in the end they yearned for a more practical course of study in history and economics. More than the others in her group, Jane resisted the "evangelical" pressure to become a missionary. Instead, she threw herself into the movement to upgrade Rockford's curriculum so that it could join the growing number of colleges that awarded bachelor's degrees to women. She and her friends studied mathematics. They represented Rockford at the state intercollegiate oratory competition, the first time a women's college in Illinois was represented at such an event.

Above all, Jane and her colleagues were fascinated by science. In it they saw the unvarnished search for truth, freed from all dogmatism. They were inspired by the example of Charles Darwin. They were frustrated by those teachers who had yet to accept the theory of natural selection and also by the meager scientific holdings in the school's library. "I used to bring back in my handbag books belonging to an advanced brother-in-law who had studied medicine in Germany," Addams wrote some years later, "and who was therefore quite emancipated."

By studying mathematics, science, history, and economics, Addams had taken it upon herself to step outside the

A young Jane Addams was one of a new generation of college-educated women who committed themselves to social reforms.

boundaries of the traditional seminary curriculum. In so doing she and her friends transformed Rockford. A year after she had left college, Addams and a classmate returned "to receive the degree we had so eagerly anticipated." Together with two new graduates, they "were dubbed B.A. on the very day that Rockford Seminary was declared a college in the midst of tumultuous anticipations."

ON TRIAL

The Supernatural on Trial—Witchcraft at Salem

The eruption of accusations had begun in the household of Salem Village's minister, Samuel Parris, a dissatisfied and bitter man, often at odds with the members of his congregation, when his daughter Betty and her cousin Abigail Williams tried to foresee their future husbands. These young women and the others who became accusers were among the most powerless segment of New England's white population, and they must have enjoyed these outbursts against order and authority and the attention they drew to themselves.

When questioned by those in authority, curses and shouts

guilty by at least two witnesses who had observed a particular act of malice. As Tituba discovered when she confessed and pointed the finger at others, in Salem all those who confessed were ultimately released, while all those who were executed maintained their innocence, even when they were tortured. Richard Carrier, age 28, and his brother Andrew, 16, confessed only when they were "tyed ... Neck and Heels till the Blood was ready to come out of their Noses." They said their mother had recruited them. Their lives were spared; their mother, Martha Carrier, however, was executed.

Although it soon became evident that a confession was the

On Trial sidebars illuminate courtroom battles that profoundly affected the political, social, and cultural issues of the day.

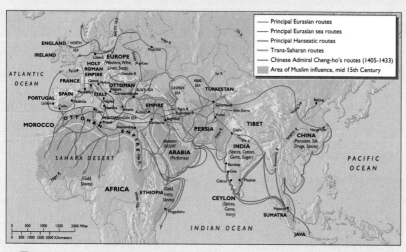

Map 1-1 World Trade on the Eve of Discovery.
For a thousand years, world trade centered on the Mediterranean. European, Arab, and Asian traders criss-crossed much of the Eastern Hemisphere, carrying spices, silks, and cottons from Asia; linens, woolens, and wine from Europe; and gold and slaves from Africa.

Global Maps vividly illustrate the global context of American history.

web connection

Stamping out Stamps

www.prenhall.com/boydston/stampact

In 1765, in the wake of its great victory in the Seven Years' War (known as the French and Indian War in the American colonies), Great Britain set about putting its imperial house in order. Retiring the debt was a major priority, and the Stamp Act was one of several revenue measures designed to force the colonies to pay a greater share of the costs of empire. Colonists refused to pay the new stamp tax. Instead they organized a boycott of British goods and proclaimed that Parliament lacked the power to tax them, something only their own colonial legislatures could legitimately do. Use the materials here to explore how Americans forged their own peculiar notions of representation.

Web Connection boxes in each chapter, prepared by John McClymer of Assumption College and Eileen Walsh of Bemidji State University, provide a direct link to Web-based learning activities that drill down to explore the impact of key episodes in American history. Combining primary sources, visuals, graphs, audio clips, and interactive maps, Web Connections provide opportunities for further exploration of important topics presented in *Making a Nation*.

Conclusions tie together the chapter's themes, review main topics, and set the stage for developments ahead.

Conclusion

At the middle of the seventeenth century, the New England and Chesapeake colonies could hardly have appeared more different. Although the forces of capitalism shaped each region, other factors left their distinctive imprint: the objectives of the founders, disease environment, demographic patterns, and relations with local Indians. In 1660, both regions had about 35,000 inhabitants, but the colonies of New England were much more settled. As much as anything else, the early history of New England was shaped by the extraordinary energy and cohesiveness of Puritan society. In fact, the cohesiveness of the New England colonies, their early success, and their great economic and social stability make them almost unique in the history of colonial ventures throughout the world. If New England achieved settlement within a few years, unsettlement was the norm. That surely was the case in New Spain, New France, and New Netherland, which all bore the marks of rough, frontier societies for many decades. It was particularly true of the Chesapeake colonies, which were still raw colonial outposts, disproportionately populated by aggressive young men long after New England had achieved a secure and gratifying order.

All of the North American colonies were outposts in the global political economy, created to enrich their mother countries and enhance their power. The New England colonies were the striking exceptions. Indeed, had the Virginia Company known that the founders of Massachusetts wanted to create a religious refuge rather

---

Review Questions in each chapter ask students to consider the central problems of each chapter.

Review Questions

1. What were the objectives of the founders of Virginia? Why did the colony survive, in spite of poor planning?

2. What were the objectives of the founders of the Puritan colonies at Plymouth and Massachusetts Bay? Compare the early years of these colonies to those of the Virginia colony?

3. What place did gender play in the social order of the Chesapeake and New England colonies? Compare and contrast family life in the two regions.

4. Compare and contrast relations with the Indians in the Chesapeake and New England.

Chronologies found at the end of each chapter provide a review of key events.

CHRONOLOGY

1838	Frederick Douglass escapes from slavery	1848	Zachary Taylor elected president
1844	Samuel F. B. Morse invents the telegraph	1851	The "Maine Law" enacts temperance reform
1846	David Wilmot introduces his "proviso"	1852	*Uncle Tom's Cabin* published in book form Franklin Pierce elected president
1847	Treaty of Guadalupe Hidalgo	1854	Gadsden Purchase Ratified Kansas-Nebraska Act

---

Further Readings and **History on the Internet** sections at the end of each chapter provide annotated lists of suggested print and Web resources.

Further Readings

Kathleen M. Brown, *Good Wives, Nasty Wenches, and Anxious Patriarchs* (1996). A provocative interpretation of Colonial Virginia that puts gender at the center.

William Cronon, *Changes in the Land: Indians, Colonists, and the Ecology of New England* (1983). A comparison of the ways that Indians and New Englanders used, lived off, and changed the land.

John Demos, *A Little Commonwealth: Family Life in Plymouth Colony* (1970). Brief and beautifully written, this book helped revolutionize the writing of American social history by showing how much could be learned about ordinary people from a sensitive reading of a wide variety of sources.

Jack P. Greene, *Pursuits of Happiness: The Social Development of Early Modern British Colonies and the Formation of American Culture* (1988). An interpretive overview of Colonial development that argues that the Chesapeake was the most American region of all.

Ivor Noël Hume, *The Virginia Adventure: Roanoke to James Towne: An Archaeological and Historical Odyssey* (1994). A detailed and well-written history of the early Chesapeake settlements with a focus on archaeology.

History on the Internet

"Religion and the Founding of the American Republic. America as a Religious Refuge: The Seventeenth Century"

http://lcweb.loc.gov/exhibits/religion/rel01.html

Through this Library of Congress website, discover the role of religion in the founding of the New England colonies. This site details the religious persecution religious "nonconformists" experienced in their European homelands and the promise of religious freedom the New World held out to these men and women.

"From Indentured Servitude to Racial Slavery"

http://www.pbs.org/wgbh/aia/part1/1narr3.html

Read about Virginia's recognition of slavery, slave codes, and the need for African slave labor. The site also contains scholarly commentary on the earliest African Americans and their experiences.

SUPPLEMENTS THAT MAKE A DIFFERENCE

Making a Nation comes with an extensive package of supplementary print and multimedia materials for both instructors and students.

PRINT SUPPLEMENTS

Instructor's Resource Manual

Prepared by Laura Graves, South Plains College

Contains introduction to instructors, chapter outlines, detailed chapter overviews, discussion questions, lecture strategies, essay topics, suggestions for working with Web resources, and tips on incorporating Penguin titles in American history into lectures.

Test Item File

Prepared by Bruce Caskey, Herkimer County Community College

Includes over 1000 multiple-choice, true-false, essay, and map questions, organized by chapter. A collection of blank maps can be photocopied and used for map testing or other class exercises.

Study Guide (Volumes I and II)

Prepared by Laura Graves, South Plains College

Contains introduction to students, chapter overviews, chapter outlines, map questions, sample exam questions, analytical reading exercises, collaborative exercises, and essay questions.

Documents in United States History (Volumes I and II)

Prepared by Paula Stathakis, University of North Carolina, Charlotte, and Alan Downs, Georgia Southern University

Edited specifically for *Making a Nation*, the Documents Set brings together over 200 primary sources and scholarly articles in American history. Headnotes and review questions contextualize the documents and prompt critical inquiry.

Transparencies

This collection of over 150 full-color transparencies provides the maps, charts, and graphs from the text for classroom presentations.

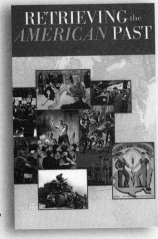

Retrieving the American Past 2001 Edition (RTAP) gives instructors the opportunity to tailor a custom reader whose content, organization, and price exactly match the their course syllabi. Edited by historians and educators at The Ohio State University and other respected schools, RTAP offers instructors the freedom and flexibility to choose selections of primary and secondary source readings—or both—from 73 (14 new) chapters. Contact your local Prentice Hall representative for details about RTAP. Discounts apply when copies of RTAP are bundled with *Making a Nation*.

Themes of the Times

This special newspaper supplement is prepared jointly for students by Prentice Hall and the premier news publication, the *New York Times*. Issued twice a year, it contains recent articles pertinent to American history, which connect the classroom to the world. Contact your Prentice Hall representative for details.

Reading Critically about History

Prepared by Rose Wassman and Lee Rinsky, DeAnza College, this brief guide provides students with helpful strategies for reading a history textbook and is available free when packaged with *Making a Nation*.

Understanding and Answering Essay Question

Prepared by Mary L. Kelley, San Antonio College, this helpful guide provides analytical tools for understanding different types of essay questions and for preparing well-crafted essay answers. It is available free when packaged with *Making a Nation*.

MULTIMEDIA SUPPLEMENTS

Companion Website

The access code protected *Companion Website*™ for *Making a Nation* is available at www.prenhall.com/boydston and offers students and instructors of American history one of the most comprehensive Internet resources available. The passcode to access the site is included with all new copies of the text. Organized around the primary subtopics of each chapter, the *Companion Website*™ provides detailed summaries, multiple choice, true-false, essay, identification, map labeling, and document questions and Web Connection activities based on the text. Overview tables in each chapter facilitate quick review. Hyperlinks to other Web resources provide students with access to screened sites. Chat rooms and message boards allow students to share their ideas about American history with their own class or with colleges across the country.

The *Faculty Module* contains a wealth of material for instructors, including a downloadable Microsoft PowerPoint™ presentation with maps, charts, and graphs that can be customized to an instructor's specific needs, and easy-to-follow directions for creating, posting, and revising a syllabus online.

History on the Internet — This guide focuses on developing the critical-thinking skills necessary to evaluate and use online resources. It provides a brief introduction to navigating the Internet and outlines the many references to history Websites. Available free when packaged with *Making a Nation*.

PowerPoint™ Images CD-ROM — Available in Windows and Mac formats for use with Microsoft PowerPoint™, this CD-ROM includes the maps, charts, tables, and graphs from *Making a Nation*. These resources can be used in lectures, for slide shows, and printed as transparencies.

COURSE MANAGEMENT SYSTEMS

As the leader in course-management solutions for teachers and students of history, Prentice Hall provides a variety of online tools. Contact your local Prentice Hall representative for a demonstration, or visit www.prenhall.com/demo

Powered by Blackboard 5, CourseCompass fuses the content of *Making a Nation* with Blackboard's powerful course-management tools to provide pre-loaded content, refined navigation, and national hosting to make it easier for instructors and students to create their own customized learning environments.

With a powerful menu of communication tools, testing options, and design tools, Blackboard makes creating, managing, and using online materials easy.

With such robust course-management tools as page tracking, progress tracking, and reporting tools, WebCT saves instructors valuable time in managing their courses.

For qualified adopters, Prentice Hall is proud to introduce Instructors 1st—the first integrated service program committed to meeting customization, support, and training needs. Contact your local Prentice Hall representative for details.

PRENTICE HALL AND PENGUIN BUNDLE PROGRAM: MAKING AN IMPACT ON HISTORY

Prentice Hall and PenguinPutnam are pleased to provide adopters of *Making a Nation* with an opportunity for their students to receive significant discounts when orders for *Making a Nation* are bundled together with Penguin titles in American history.

PENGUIN CLASSICS

BARTOLOME DE LAS CASAS
A SHORT ACCOUNT OF THE DESTRUCTION OF THE INDIES

PENGUIN CLASSICS

OLAUDAH EQUIANO
THE INTERESTING NARRATIVE
AND OTHER WRITINGS

Signet Classic

DEMOCRACY IN AMERICA
ALEXIS DE TOCQUEVILLE

Edited and abridged by
RICHARD D. HEFFNER

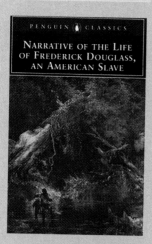

PENGUIN CLASSICS

NARRATIVE OF THE LIFE OF FREDERICK DOUGLASS, AN AMERICAN SLAVE

The Anti-Federalist Papers and the Constitutional Convention Debates
RALPH KETCHAM

THE CLASHES AND THE COMPROMISES THAT GAVE BIRTH TO OUR FORM OF GOVERNMENT

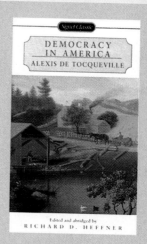

Signet Classic

Nobel Peace Prize-Winner
Martin Luther King, Jr.

WHY WE CAN'T WAIT
With an afterword by Reverend Jesse L. Jackson, Sr.

"Freedom is never voluntarily given by the oppressor; it must be demanded by the oppressed."

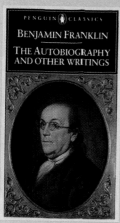

PENGUIN CLASSICS

BENJAMIN FRANKLIN
THE AUTOBIOGRAPHY AND OTHER WRITINGS

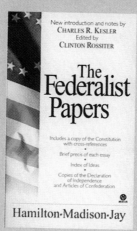

New introduction and notes by
CHARLES R. KESLER
Edited by
CLINTON ROSSITER

The Federalist Papers

Includes a copy of the Constitution with cross-references
Brief precis of each essay
Index of Ideas
Copies of the Declaration of Independence and Articles of Confederation

Hamilton·Madison·Jay

PENGUIN CLASSICS

UPTON SINCLAIR
THE JUNGLE

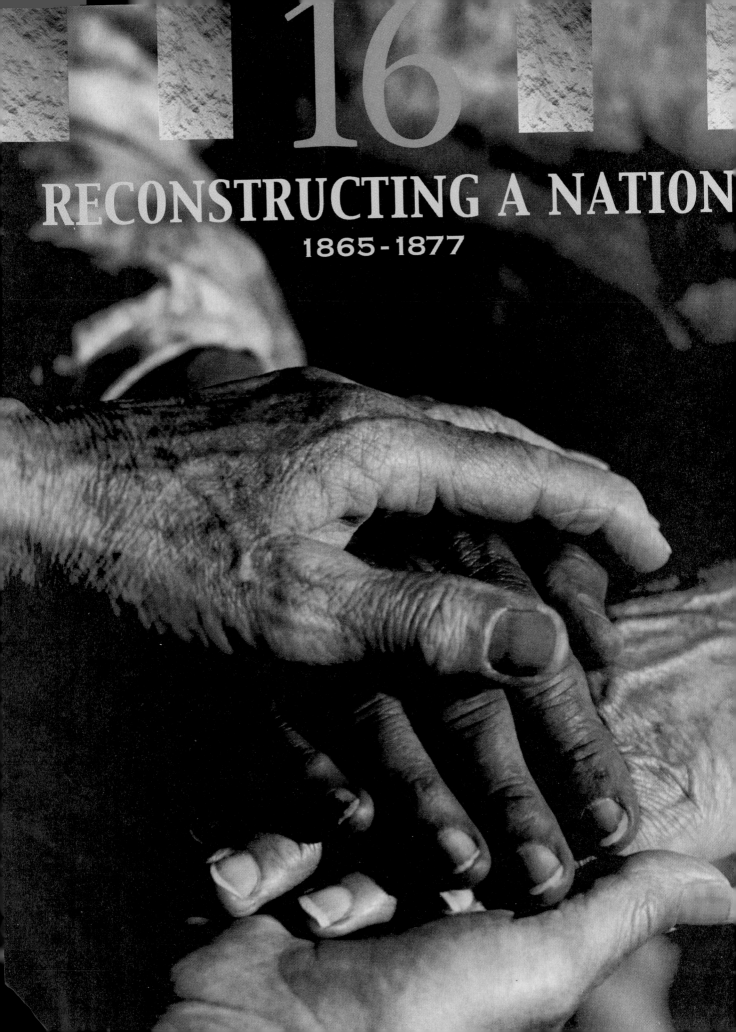

16

RECONSTRUCTING A NATION
1865-1877

OUTLINE

John Dennett Visits a Freedmen's Bureau Court

John Richard Dennett arrived in Liberty, Virginia, on August 17, 1865 as part of a tour of the South during which he sent back weekly reports for publication in a new magazine called *The Nation*. The editors wanted accurate accounts of conditions in the recently defeated Confederate states and Dennett was the kind of man they could trust. He grew up in Massachusetts, graduated from Harvard, and became a firm believer in the sanctity of the Union. Dennett moved comfortably within a class of elite Yankees who thought of themselves as the "best men" the country had to offer.

After he stepped from the train at Liberty, Dennett was accompanied by a Freedmen's Bureau agent. The Freedmen's Bureau was a branch of the U. S. Army that had been established by Congress to assist the freed people in the transition from slavery to freedom. Dennett and the agent were going to the courthouse because one of the Freedmen's Bureau's functions was to adjudicate disputes between the freed people and southern whites. Dennett listened to the cases that came to the agent that day.

The first to arrive was an old white farmer who complained that two of the African Americans who worked on his farm were "roamin' about and refusin' to work in any shape or manner." He wanted the agent to help find the men and bring them back. Both men had wives and children living on his farm and eating his corn, the old man complained.

"Have you been paying any wages?" the Freedmen's Bureau agent asked. "Well, they get what the other niggers get," the farmer answered. "I a'n't payin' great wages this year," he went on, "makin' a little corn's about all." There was not much the agent could do. He had no horses and very few men, but one of his soldiers volunteered to go back to the farm with the old man and tell the blacks that "they ought to be at home supporting their wives and children."

After the farmer left, a well-to-do planter came in to see if he could fire the African Americans who had been working on his plantation since the beginning of the year. The planter complained that his workers were unmanageable now that they were free and he could no longer punish them. The sergeant warned the planter that he could not beat his workers as if they were still slaves. In that case, the planter responded, "will the Government take them off our hands? I'm sure I don't want mine any longer. They are free, and the Government ought to take them, or it ought to give the employers such power as would enable them to control the Negroes and make them work." The Freedmen's Bureau agent suspected that the planter was looking for an excuse to discharge his laborers at the end of the growing season, after they had finished most of the work but before they had been paid their wages. "If they've worked on your crops all the year so far," the agent told the planter, "I guess they've got a claim on you to keep them a while longer." When the planter left the agent told Dennett that there were lots of those cases now.

Next came a "good-looking mulatto man" representing a number of African Americans living in the countryside. They were worried by rumors that they would be forced to sign five-year contracts with their employers. "No, it a'n't true," the agent said. "You can hire yourselves out for as long as you want to." They also wanted to know if they would be allowed to rent or buy land so that they could work for themselves. "Yes, rent or buy," the agent said. But the African Americans had no horses, mules, or ploughs to work the land. So they wanted to know "if the Government would help us out after we get the land. We could rent a place up here if we had some horses to plough, and so on." But the agent had no help to offer.

This engraving shows a typical trial in a Freedmen's Bureau Courtroom.

"The Government hasn't any ploughs or mules to give you," he said. In the end the African Americans settled for a piece of paper from the Freedmen's Bureau authorizing them to rent or buy their own farms.

The last case involved a field hand who came to the agent to complain that his master was beating him with a stick. "What did you do to him? You've been sassy?" the agent asked. But the field hand insisted that he had done nothing. "Well, I suppose you were lazy," the agent said. "Boss, I been working all de time," the man answered. The agent was unsympathetic. He told the field hand to go back to work. "Don't be sassy, don't be lazy when you've got work to do; and I guess he won't trouble you." The field hand left "very reluctantly," but came back a minute later and asked for a letter to his master "enjoining him to keep the peace, as he feared the man would shoot him, he having on two or three occasions threatened to do so." The agent sent him away and then told Dennett that there were "any quantity of those cases," but that his office was scarcely equipped to hear a quarter of them.

It is not surprising that most of the cases Dennett witnessed centered around labor relations. The southern economy had been devastated by the war, and everyone agreed that a successful reunion depended on the swift creation of a new political economy based on free labor. There was, however, little agreement about what kind of free labor system should replace slavery in the postwar South. What John Dennett saw in the courthouse in Liberty, Virginia, was a good indication of how difficult the labor problem was. The freed people preferred to work their own land, but they lacked the resources to rent or buy farms for themselves. Black workers and white owners who had negotiated wage contracts had trouble figuring out the limits of each other's rights and responsibilities. The former masters wanted to retain as much of their old authority as possible, including the right to physically punish their workers. The former slaves wanted as much

autonomy as possible and clearly resented the continued use physical punishment.

The Freedmen's Bureau was placed in the middle of thes conflicts. Most agents thought it was their job to get the free people back to work, much to the dismay of many of the former slaves. But the agents also tried to ensure that the free people were paid for the lab they performed and that the were not brutalized the way they had been as slaves. Southern whites resented thi intrusion, and their resentme filtered all the way up to sympathetic politicians in Washington, D. C. As a resu the Freedmen's Bureau beca a lightning rod for the politi conflicts of the years immed ately following the Civil Wa period known as Reconstruc tion.

Reconstruction raised a number of challenging questions for Americans. Wh conditions should the federal government impose on the southern states before they could readmitted to the Union? Should these conditions be set by t president or by Congress? How far should the federal gover ment go to protect the economic well-being and civil rights o the freed people? Politicians in Washington disagreed violent on these questions. At one extreme was Andrew Johnson wh as president, thought it was his responsibility to shape Recon struction policy. Because he believed in small government an speedy readmission of the southern states, Johnson looked upon the Freedmen's Bureau with deep suspicion. At the oth extreme were the Radical Republicans, men like Congressma Thaddeus Stevens and Senator Charles Sumner. The Radicals believed that the federal government should redistribute confiscated land to the former slaves, guarantee their civil rights, and give African-American men the power of the vote They viewed the Freedmen's Bureau as too small and weak to do the necessary job. Between the Radicals and the president supporters were the moderate Republicans who controlled Congress. The moderates tried to work with the president, b when the president became obstreperous they shifted toward the Radical position.

Regardless of where they fell on the political spectrum, however, policymakers in the nation's capital were always responding to what went on in the South. Events in the Soutl were shaped in turn by the policies emanating from Wash ington. What John Dennett saw in Liberty, Virginia, was a good example of this. The Freedmen's Bureau agent listened t the urgent requests of former masters and their former slaves of small white farmers and wealthy planters. His responses were shaped in part by the policies established by his superio in Washington. But his superiors shaped their policies in response to reports on conditions in the South sent back by Freedmen's Bureau agents like him and by journalists like Jol Dennett. From this interaction the political economy of the "New South" slowly emerged. ▪

Wartime Reconstruction

Long before the Civil War was over Republicans in Congress and the White House had already considered a number of questions concerning the reconstruction of the southern states. What system of free labor would replace slavery? What were the political conditions under which the southern states would be readmitted to the Union? What civil and political rights should the freed people receive? Such questions were inescapable once emancipation became Union policy. Until the southern armies actually surrendered, however, politicians in Washington put most of their energies into winning the war. As a result, no official reconstruction policy emerged before 1865. Instead, Congress and the Lincoln administration responded piecemeal to developments in those regions of the South under Union control. From these experiences a variety of approaches to the political and social reconstruction of the South emerged. Some were utopian experiments confined to particular regions or specific plantations. But other approaches, notably those developed in Louisiana, established precedents that shaped Reconstruction for many years.

Experiments With Free Labor

Classical theories of political economy taught the Republicans to believe that once the benefits of free labor were unleashed the South was bound to prosper. But two interesting wartime experiments left very differ-ent clues about what African-American workers would do after emancipation. At Davis Bend, Mississippi, a group of highly motivated slaves established a wage labor system on the lands they purchased from Confederate president Jefferson Davis and his brother Joseph. Once in control of production, the freed people produced a highly profitable cotton crop, even before the war was over. The Davis Bend experience suggested that if left to their own devices, and given autonomy over their own lands, the freed people would produce cotton for the market. But on the Sea Islands off South Carolina, the former slaves behaved very differently. Early in the war the masters had abandoned their low-country plantations to the slaves and the Union Army. With the owners gone, the freed people abandoned the production of cash crops and focused almost exclusively on subsistence agriculture. They showed little interest in producing cotton for the market. Neither the Sea Island experience nor the community at Davis Bend established a pattern for Reconstruction across the South. Far more important were events in Louisiana.

Southern Louisiana came under Union control early in the war. The sugar and cotton plantations of the low country around New Orleans therefore provided a site for the first major experiments in the transition from slave to free labor. The Union commander of the area, General Nathaniel Banks, hoped to stem the flow of African-

Slaves in parts of coastal South Carolina were freed early in the Civil War. Here the freed people on Edisto Island in 1862 are shown planting sweet potatoes rather than cotton. In other parts of the South the former slaves returned to the cultivation of cash crops.

Charlotte Forten, born to a prominent African-American family in Philadelphia, was one of many northern women who went to the South to become a teacher of the freed slaves. Forten helped found the Penn School on St. Helena's Island in South Carolina.

Before the Civil War it was illegal in most southern states to teach a slave how to read. With emancipation, the freed people clamored for schools and teachers, such as the one pictured here. Within a few years hundreds of thousands of former slaves became literate.

American refugees running to Union lines. Unsympathetic to the wishes of the former slaves, Banks issued a series of harsh labor regulations designed to put the freed people back to work as quickly as possible. The Banks Plan required African Americans to sign year-long contracts to work on their former plantations, often for their former owners. Workers would be paid either five percent of the proceeds of the crop or three dollars per month. The former masters would provide the freed people with food and shelter. Once they signed their contracts, African-American workers were forbidden to leave the plantations without permission. So stringent were these regulations that to many critics Banks had simply replaced one form of slavery with another. "Our freedmen, on the plantations, at the present time, could more properly be called, mock freedmen," a black newspaper in New Orleans complained. Nevertheless, the Banks Plan was implemented throughout much of the lower Mississippi Valley, especially after the fall of Vicksburg in the summer of 1863. Eventually, Banks' labor regulations were applied to tens of thousands of freed people and hundreds of plantations in Louisiana and Mississippi.

The Banks Plan touched off a political controversy that stretched from New Orleans to Washington, D. C. Established planters had the most to gain from the general's plan. It allowed them to acknowledge the abolition of slavery while preserving as much as possible of the prewar labor system. But Louisiana Unionists, who had remained loyal to the government in Washington, formed a Free State Association to press for more substantial changes. In August 1863 Lincoln publicly supported the Free State movement. Five months later, hoping to speed things along in Louisiana, the president issued a Proclamation of Amnesty and Reconstruction. With the war still going on, Lincoln issued the proclamation in an effort to undermine the Confederacy by cultivating the support of southern Unionists. It contained the outline of the so-called Ten-Percent Plan, which turned out to be not much of a plan at all.

Lincoln's Ten-Percent Plan *Versus* the Wade-Davis Bill

The Ten-Percent Plan promised full pardons and the restoration of civil rights to all those who swore their loyalty to the Union. It excluded from amnesty only a few high-ranking Confederate military and political leaders. When the number of loyal whites in any of the former Confederate states reached 10 percent of the 1860 voting population, they could organize a new state constitution and set up a new government. The only stipulation was that they recognize the abolition of slavery. Abiding by these conditions, Free State whites met in Louisiana in the spring of 1864 and produced a new constitution for the state. By traditional standards it was a progressive charter. It provided for a free system of public education, a minimum wage, a nine-hour day on public works projects, and a graduated income tax. However, although it abolished slavery in Louisiana, it also denied all African Americans the right to vote.

By the spring of 1864 such denials were no longer acceptable to Radical Republicans, either in Louisiana or in Congress. The Radicals were a small but vocal wing of the Republican Party. They were active in many parts of the

South immediately after the war, and they developed strong ties to leading Radicals in Congress such as Thaddeus Stevens of Pennsylvania and Charles Sumner of Massachusetts. Despite their differences, most Radicals favored some plan for distributing land to the former slaves. Most of them also favored federal guarantees of the civil rights of the former slaves, as well as the right to vote. All Radicals were prepared to use the full force of the federal government to enforce congressional policy in the South. Although the Radicals never formed a majority in Congress, they gradually succeeded in winning over the moderates to many of their positions. As a result, when Congress took control of Reconstruction away from the president after the elections in 1866, the process became known as Radical Reconstruction.

The Radicals were particularly strong in New Orleans thanks to the city's large and articulate community of African Americans who had been free before the Civil War. In the spring of 1864 they sent a delegation to Washington, D. C. to meet with President Lincoln and press the case for voting rights. The day after their visit Lincoln wrote a letter to the acting governor of Louisiana suggesting a limited suffrage for the most intelligent blacks and for those who

had served in the Union Army. The delegates to Louisiana's constitutional convention completely ignored Lincoln's suggestion. Shortly thereafter free African Americans in New Orleans organized a coalition with the former slaves demanding civil and political rights and the abolition of the Banks labor regulations. Radicals complained that Lincoln's Ten-Percent Plan was too kind to former Confederates and that the Banks Plan was too harsh on former slaves.

Moved largely by events in Louisiana, congressional Radicals rejected the Ten-Percent Plan. In July 1864 Congressmen Benjamin F. Wade and Henry Winter Davis proposed a different plan for reconstructing the southern states. Under the terms of the Wade-Davis Bill, Reconstruction could not begin until a majority of a state's white men swore an oath of allegiance to the Union. This "Iron-clad Oath" was far more restrictive than Lincoln's Ten-Percent Plan. In addition, the Wade-Davis Bill guaranteed full legal and civil rights to African Americans, but not the right to vote. Lincoln pocket vetoed the bill, less because he disagreed with it than because the war was going on and he was still interested in cultivating southern Unionists. By the spring of 1865, however, Lincoln had shifted toward

Because slave marriages had no legal standing, many freed people got married as soon as they could. Pictured here is one such wedding, performed at the Freedmen's Bureau.

the Radical position. In his last speech Lincoln publicly supported voting rights for some freedmen as part of the Reconstruction process.

The Louisiana experience had made several things clear. The radical wing of the Republican Party was determined to press for more civil and political rights for African Americans than moderates were initially willing to support; however, the moderates showed a willingness to move in a more radical direction. Equally important, the Louisiana experience showed that any Reconstruction policy, whether congressional or presidential, would have to consider the wishes of southern blacks.

The Freed People's Dream of Owning Land

Freedom meant many things to the millions of former slaves. It meant they could move about their neighborhoods without passes. It meant they did not have to step aside to let whites pass them on the street. It meant that their marriages would be secured by the law, without fear that a master could separate husbands from wives or parents from children. Following emancipation southern African Americans almost immediately withdrew from white churches and established congregations with their own ministers. During Reconstruction the church emerged as a central institution in the southern African-American community. Freedom also meant literacy. Even before the war ended northern teachers poured into the South to set up makeshift schools for the freed people. The American Missionary Association organized hundreds of such northern teachers. When the fighting stopped, the U. S. Army helped recruit and organize thousands more northern women who volunteered their services as teachers. "So anxious are they to learn," Edmonia Highgate reported from Lafayette Parish, Louisiana, that children from as far as eight miles away walk to school early each morning determined "never to be tardy." The graduates of the missionary schools sometimes became teachers themselves, setting up classrooms in rundown churches and dilapidated barns, if necessary. As a result, hundreds of thousands of southern blacks became literate in the space of a few years.

But even more than churches of their own and schools for their children, the freed people wanted land. Without land, the former slaves saw no choice but to return to work for their old masters on their old farms and plantations.

An African-American church in Virginia in 1880. With emancipation, the former slaves withdrew from their masters' churches and formed their own congregations.

"The sole ambition of the freedmen at the present time appears to be to become the owner of a little piece of land," one northerner observed, "there to erect a humble home, and to dwell in peace and security at his own free will and pleasure." As the war ended many African Americans had reason to believe that the government would assist them in their quest for independent landownership.

Marching through the Carolinas in early 1865, Union General William Tecumseh Sherman discovered how important land was to the freed people on the Sea Islands. They did not want to go to work for the speculators who paid fire-sale prices to scoop up the plantations of their runaway masters. A delegation of local blacks went to Sherman to express their wishes. "The way we can best take care of ourselves is to have land," they declared, "and turn it out and till it by our own labor." Persuaded by their arguments, Sherman issued Special Field Order No. 15 granting captured land to the freed people. By June of 1865, 400,000 acres had been distributed to 40,000 former slaves.

Congress seemed to be moving in a similar direction. In March 1865, the Republicans established the Bureau of Refugees, Freedmen and Abandoned Lands, commonly known as the Freedmen's Bureau. Although designed as an emergency measure to provide newly freed slaves with food and clothing at the end of the war, the Freedmen's Bureau quickly became involved in the politics of land redistribution. As part of its mandate, the Freedmen's Bureau controlled the disposition of 850,000 acres of confiscated and abandoned Confederate lands. In July 1865, General Oliver Otis Howard, the head of the Bureau, issued Circular 13, directing his agents to rent the land to the freed people in forty-acre plots that they could eventually purchase. Some Bureau agents believed firmly that the land should be distributed to the former slaves, but more were either uncertain about the idea or openly hostile. These agents believed that slavery had taught African Americans to avoid work and ignore the future. To re-educate them in the values of thrift and hard work, the freed people should be encouraged to save up their wages and buy land for themselves. From the perspective of most Freedmen's Bureau agents, redistributing land was like giving it away to people who had not actually paid for it.

From the perspective of the former slaves, however, black workers had more than earned a right to the land. "The labor of these people had for two hundred years cleared away the forests and produced crops that brought millions of dollars annually," H. C. Bruce explained, remembering his first months of freedom. "It does seem to me that a Christian Nation would, at least, have given them one year's support, forty acres of land and a mule each." Even Abraham Lincoln seemed to agree. In March 1865 he declared in his second inaugural address that all of the South's wealth had come from the slaves' two hundred and fifty years of unrequited toil. But a month later Lincoln was dead and Andrew Johnson became president of the United States.

Presidential Reconstruction, 1865–1867

When Andrew Johnson took the oath of office in April 1865, it was still unclear whether Congress or the president would control Reconstruction policy, and whether that policy would be lenient or harsh. To the delight of Radical Republicans, Johnson had spoken sharply of punishing southern "traitors." His political roots lay in the old Jacksonian Democratic Party. He blamed the Civil War on aristocratic planters and viewed their defeat as a victory for the common people of the South. But it turned out that the new president disliked Radical Republicans as much as planter aristocrats. As a Jacksonian he was committed to limited government and therefore resisted Republican plans to use federal power to help the freed people. Like so many Democrats, Johnson's sympathy for the common man did not extend to African Americans. As a politician, Johnson lacked the flexibility and good humor that had allowed Lincoln to work constructively with his political opponents. Determined to reconstruct the South in his

AWKWARD COLLISION ON THE GRAND TRUNK COLUMBIA R. R.

In this satirical cartoon, Andrew Johnson and Congress square off against one another. The political struggle over who should control Reconstruction policy led to Congress' impeachment and trial of the president.

own way and blind to the interests of the freed people, Johnson grew increasingly bitter and resentful of the Republicans who controlled Congress. As a result, Presidential Reconstruction was a monumental failure.

The Political Economy of Contract Labor

In the mid-nineteenth century Congress was normally out of session from March until December. Having assumed the presidency in April 1865 Johnson hoped to take advantage of the long congressional recess to complete the entire Reconstruction process and present the finished product to the lawmakers when they returned in December. At the end of May the president offered amnesty and the restoration of property to white southerners who swore an oath of loyalty to the Union. He excluded only high-ranking Confederate military and political leaders and very rich planters, whom he despised. At the same time Johnson named provisional governors to the seceded states and instructed them to organize constitutional conventions elected from all those who took the loyalty oaths. To earn readmission to the Union, the seceded states were required to nullify their secession ordinances, repudiate their Confederate war debts, and ratify the Thirteenth Amendment abolishing slavery. These terms were far more lenient than Lincoln and the congressional Republicans had contemplated. They did nothing to protect the civil rights of the former slaves.

Johnson's leniency encouraged a mood of defiance among white southerners. Although they had been willing to succumb to northern directives in the spring, they were no longer willing to do so by the fall of 1865. Secessionists had been barred from participating in the states' constitutional conventions. But they participated openly in the first elections held late in the year because Johnson issued thousands of pardons to ex-Confederates and the wealthy planters he claimed to despise. Leading Confederates were thus able to assume public office in the southern states. Restored to power, white southerners promptly demanded the restoration of all properties confiscated or abandoned during the war. President Johnson quickly obliged their request. In September 1865 he ordered the Freedmen's Bureau to return all confiscated and abandoned lands to their former owners.

A few Bureau agents tried to stall the evictions until Congress came back into session in December, but when white southerners complained Johnson had the agents removed. In late 1865 thousands of African-American families were ordered to give up their plots of land. On Edisto Island off South Carolina, for example, the freed people had carved farms of their own out of the former plantations. But in January 1866 General Rufus Saxton restored the farms to their previous owners and encouraged the freed people to sign wage contracts with their old masters. "I told the people that they could take it or leave it," Sax-

ton reported, "and that if they declined to work the plantation the houses must be vacated." The blacks unanimously rejected his offer, whereupon the general ordered them to evacuate their farms within two weeks. By the end of 1865 former slaves were being forcibly evicted from the forty-acre plots they had been given by the Union Army or the Freedmen's Bureau. With this crucial turning point in the evolution of a new political economy in the South, the freed people's hopes of independent landownership were dashed. Thereafter, they would be compelled to sign contracts to work for the whites who still owned the land (see Map 16-1).

Besides ending all hopes of land redistribution, the Johnsonian state governments enacted a series of "Black Codes" severely restricting the civil rights of freed people. The Black Codes were often thinly disguised attempts to coerce African Americans to sign labor contracts with white landowners. Vagrancy statutes, for example, allowed local police to arrest and fine virtually any African-American man. If he could not pay the fine, as was the case with most recently emancipated slaves, the "vagrant" was put to work on a farm, often the one owned and operated by his former master. Even more disturbing to the former slaves were the apprenticeship clauses of the Black Codes. These laws allowed local white officials to remove children from their homes, against their parents' will, and put them to work as "apprentices" on nearby farms.

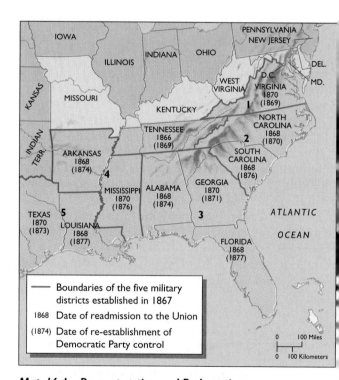

Map 16-1   Reconstruction and Redemption.
By 1870 Congress readmitted every southern state to the Union. In most cases the Republican Party retained control of the "reconstructed" state governments for only a few years.

TABLE 16-1

Cotton Prices in New York (cents per pound)	
Year	Real Price (1880 $)
1864	52.59
1865	45.07
1866	24.83
1867	19.50
1868	15.73
1869	19.21
1870	17.76
1871	13.04
1872	15.06
1873	13.65
1874	13.49
1875	12.71
1876	11.82
1877	11.07

The price of cotton fell sharply and almost continuously between 1864 and 1879. But this masks the fact that the purchasing power of a pound of cotton was about the same in the 1870s and 1880s as it had been in the boom years of the 1850s.
Source: M. B. Hammond, The Cotton Industry (Macmillan, 1897), reproduced in Gavin Wright, "Cotton Competition and the Post Bellum Recovery of the American South," Journal of Economic History, 34 (Sept., 1974), p. 611.

Presidential Reconstruction left the freed people with no choice but to sign labor contracts with white landlords. The contracts restricted the personal as well as the working lives of the freed people, and employers still provided their black workers with food and shelter. In one case, a South Carolina planter contractually obliged his African-American workers to "go by his direction the same as in slavery time." In the cotton South contracts often required blacks to work in gangs, just as they had before the war. Owners sometimes prohibited their workers from leaving the plantation without permission. Former masters often continued the practice of whipping and brutalizing their workers. Contracts required African Americans to work for wages as low as one-tenth of the crop, and cotton prices were steadily falling (see Table 16-1). Even those meager wages would be forfeited by anyone who changed jobs before the end of the year. Blacks who moved into towns and cities in search of alternative employment discovered that the tax laws were designed to send them back onto farms and plantations. It is no wonder that contract labor struck the freed people as little different from slavery.

Resistance to Presidential Reconstruction

In September 1865 a group of African Americans in Virginia issued a public appeal for assistance. They began by declaring that they lacked the means to make and enforce legal contracts. The Black Codes denied African Americans the right to testify in court in any case involving a white person. "So far as legal safeguards of our rights are concerned, we are defenseless before our enemies." Their former masters had returned to their homes "with all their old pride and contempt for the Negro transformed into bitter hate for the new made freeman." In many areas organized planters blocked the development of a free labor market by agreeing among themselves to hire only their former slaves and by fixing wages at a low level. In the more remote regions, the freedmen went on, planters "still refuse to recognize their Negroes as free, forcibly retaining the wives and children of their late escaped slaves." Finally, there were numerous incidents in which black workers who had faithfully obeyed the terms of their contracts were "met by a contemptuous refusal of the stipulated compensation." As the first year of freedom drew to an end, the complaints mounted. Across the South whites reported a growing number of recalcitrant freed people who would not abide by the humiliating conditions of the contract labor system. Some African Americans refused to perform specific tasks while others were accused of being "disrespectful" to their employers or to whites in general. Some African Americans refused to answer to their slave names or insisted that they be addressed as Mr. or Mrs. As 1865 came to a close thousands of freedmen declined to renew their contracts for another year.

As black defiance spread, reports of a violent white backlash flooded into Washington in late 1865 and 1866. A former slave named Henry Adams claimed that "over two thousand colored people" were murdered around Shreveport, Louisiana, in 1865. Near Pine Bluff, Arkansas, in 1866 a visitor arrived at an African-American community the morning after whites had burned it to the ground. "24 Negro men woman and children were hanging to trees all around the cabins." African Americans were assaulted for not speaking to whites with the proper tone of submission, for disputing the terms of labor contracts, or for failing to work up to the standards white employers expected. Through relentless intimidation, whites prevented blacks from buying their own land or attending political meetings to press for civil rights. "With us the death of slavery is recognized," a former master explained, "but we don't believe that because the nigger is free he ought to be saucy; and we don't mean to have any such nonsense as letting him vote. He's helpless and ignorant, and dependent, and the old masters will still control him."

Northerners read these reports as evidence that "rebel" sentiment was reviving in the South. When Congress came back into session in December 1865, moderate Republicans were already suspicious of Presidential Reconstruction. The Radicals were the most upset. They pointed to the number of defiant secessionists in the Johnsonian governments. They argued that the contract system made a mockery of their party's commitment to free labor. They claimed that by denying basic civil rights to the freed people the Black Codes made emancipation meaningless. Finally, the

Radicals insisted that the only way to protect the interests of the freed people was to grant them the right to vote.

Congress Clashes With the President

Increasingly distressed by events in the South, Republican moderates in Congress moved toward the Radical position of active government force in the South and of voting rights for African-American men. President Johnson, meanwhile, abandoned all thought of using Reconstruction to empower ordinary southern whites at the expense of the planter aristocracy. Instead Johnson became obsessed with fears of "negro rule" in the South. When he insisted on the swift readmission of southern states that were clearly controlled by unrepentant Confederates, Congress refused. Instead, the Republicans formed a Joint Committee on Reconstruction to review conditions in the South and propose the terms for the readmission of the seceded states. Established in December of 1865, the Joint Committee reflected Congress' determination to follow its own course on Reconstruction. A sharp break between Congress and the president came a few months later.

In February 1866 Congress voted to extend the life of the Freedmen's Bureau. Concerned by widespread reports that blacks could not get justice in the South, Congress also empowered the Bureau to set up its own courts, which would supersede local jurisdictions. The Bureau's record during its first year had been mixed. It provided immediate relief to thousands of individual freed people, and it assisted in the creation of schools that taught basic literacy skills to thousands more. But in the crucial area of labor relations, the Bureau too often sided with the landowners and against the interests of the freed people. Many agents were concerned that the labor contracts were unfair or that landowners themselves showed little inclination to abide by their terms, but those same agents were usually more concerned with getting the former slaves back to work, even if that meant making them sign contracts with their former masters. "It is therefore perfectly useless for the poor laborer to look at the Freedmen's Bureau for relief," an African-American newspaper editor concluded. "He will not be assisted to get his pay or to get redress but will be told to go back and do his work."

Nevertheless the understaffed and overworked Bureau agents often acted under very difficult circumstances to protect the freed people from racist violence, unfair employers, and biased law-enforcement officials. For this reason, thousands of freedmen and freedwomen looked to the Bureau as their only hope for justice. For the same reason, however, thousands of southern whites resented the Bureau's presence, and they let Andrew Johnson know it.

To the amazement of moderate Republicans, Johnson vetoed the Freedmen's Bureau Bill. In his veto message the president complained that the legislation would increase the power of the central government at the expense of the states. By interfering in the process of Reconstruction, he claimed, Congress kept African Americans "in a state of uncertain expectation and restlessness." He invoked the Jacksonian political economy of the free market, insisting that the "laws that regulate supply and demand" were the best way to resolve the labor problem. Republicans fell just short of the two-thirds vote they needed to override the president's veto. Johnson reacted to his narrow victory with an intemperate public speech attacking the Republicans in Congress and questioning the legitimacy of the Joint Committee on Reconstruction.

Origins of the Fourteenth Amendment

A few weeks later, in March of 1866, Congress passed a landmark Civil Rights Act. It overturned the Dred Scott decision by granting United States citizenship to Americans regardless of race. This marked the first time in American history that the federal government intervened in the states to guarantee due process and basic civil rights. But as he had with the Freedmen's Bureau renewal, President Johnson vetoed the Civil Rights Act of 1866. In addition to the usual Jacksonian rhetoric about limited government, Johnson made an overtly racist argument to justify his veto. He doubted that African Americans "possess the requisite qualifications to entitle them to all the privileges and immunities of citizens of the United States." He hinted darkly that the civil rights bill would invalidate southern laws against racial intermarriage, thus legalizing sexual relations between whites and African Americans.

Johnson's two veto messages, plus his unrestrained public remarks, forced the moderate Republicans to confront the president. In short order the Republican Congress overrode the president's veto of the Civil Rights Act. At the same time the Republicans passed another Freedmen's Bureau bill. Once again Johnson vetoed it, but this time Congress overrode his veto.

To ensure that the civil rights of the freed people would be impervious to future presidential or congressional interference, the Joint Committee on Reconstruction proposed a Fourteenth Amendment to the United States Constitution. The most powerful and controversial of all the Constitution's amendments, the fourteenth guaranteed national citizenship to all males born in the United States, regardless of color. Although the amendment did not guarantee African Americans the right to vote, it based representation in Congress on the voting population of the state. This effectively punished southern states by reducing their representation if they did not allow blacks to vote.

By the summer of 1866, Congress had refused to recognize the state governments established under Johnson's plan, and it had authorized the Freedmen's Bureau to create a military justice system in the South to supersede the local courts. Congress thereby guaranteed the former slaves the basic rights of due process. Finally, it made rati-

Led by President Andrew Johnson, attacks on the Freedmen's Bureau became more and more openly racist in late 1865 and 1866. This Democratic Party broadside was circulated during the 1866 election.

fication of the Fourteenth Amendment by the former Confederate states a requirement for their readmission to the Union. Congress and the president were now at war, and Andrew Johnson went on a rampage.

Race Riots and the Election of 1866

A few weeks after Congress passed the Civil Rights Act white mobs in Memphis rioted in the streets for three days. They burned hundreds of homes, destroyed churches, and attacked schools of the city's African Americans. When the rioters finished, five women had been raped and 46 blacks were dead. "Thank heaven the white race are once more rulers in Memphis," a local newspaper declared. Three months later, white mobs in New Orleans rioted in the streets as well. Unlike the Memphis riot, however, the New Orleans massacre appears to have been an organized affair. The rioters focused their fury on a convention of Radical leaders who were demanding constitutional changes that would give African-American men in Louisiana the right to vote. Disciplined squads of white police and firemen marched to the Mechanics' Institute where the convention was in session and proceeded to slaughter the delegates. Thirty-four blacks and three whites were killed. The massacre made front-page news in papers across America, just as the 1866 election campaign was getting underway.

The Memphis and New Orleans massacres quickly became political issues in the North, thanks in large part to

Andrew Johnson's disturbing reaction to them. In late August the president undertook an unprecedented campaign tour designed to stir up the voters' hostility to Congress, but this "swing around the circle," as Johnson's tour was called, backfired. Unable to control his temper, the president blasted congressional Republicans, blaming them for the riots. At one point he suggested that Radical Congressman Thaddeus Stevens should be hanged. Republicans charged in turn that Johnson's own policies had revived the rebellious sentiments in the South that led directly to the massacres at Memphis and New Orleans.

The elections of 1866 became a popular referendum on Presidential Reconstruction. The results were "overwhelmingly against the President," the *New York Times* noted, "clearly, unmistakably, decisively in favor of Congress and its policy." Johnson's supporters suffered humiliating losses. The Republicans gained a veto-proof hold on Congress. Republican moderates were pushed further to the Radical position by the spectacle of defiant white southerners goaded by an intemperate president. Congressional Reconstruction was about to begin.

Congressional Reconstruction

Johnson's outrageous behavior during the 1866 campaign, capped by a Republican sweep of the elections, brought Presidential Reconstruction to an end. Congressional Reconstruction would be a far different affair. The Republican Congress threw out the state constitutions drawn up under the president's guidelines and replaced them with an entirely new set of state charters. Congress placed the South under direct military rule. For the first time in American history, the Senate put the president on trial. Two more amendments were added to the Constitution. African-American men finally won the right to vote, and hundreds of them assumed public office across the South. It was an extraordinary series of events, second only to emancipation in its revolutionary impact on the history of the United States.

Origins of the African-American Vote

The Congress that reconvened in December 1866 was far more Radical than the Congress that had adjourned earlier in the year. Nothing demonstrated this as clearly as the emerging consensus among moderate Republicans that southern blacks should be allowed to vote. Radical Republicans and African-American leaders had been calling for such a policy for two years. Shortly after the war ended, black men in North Carolina, some of them veterans of the Union Army, petitioned the president for "the privilege of voting." When the white backlash began in late 1865, Virginia blacks argued that if they were given the right to vote "you may rely upon us to secure justice for ourselves."

Moderate Republicans initially resisted the idea. They had hoped to build a Republican Party in the postwar South by courting the loyalty of white Unionists. At most, moderates like Abraham Lincoln contemplated granting the vote to black veterans and to educated African Americans who had been free before the war. As late as the summer of 1866 the Republican majority was prepared to do no more than punish southern states that excluded black voters. Not until early 1867 did moderates conclude that the only way to avoid a lengthy military occupation of the South was to put political power into the hands of all male freedmen. This was an extraordinary decision: Slavery was abolished everywhere in the hemisphere during the nineteenth century, but only in the United States was emancipation followed by full legal and political rights for the freedmen.

It was none other than Andrew Johnson who finally pushed the moderate Republicans over the line. All but ignoring the results of the 1866 elections, Johnson urged the southern states to defy Congress by rejecting the Fourteenth Amendment. Frustrated moderates thereupon joined with Radicals and repudiated Presidential Reconstruction. On March 2, 1867, Congress assumed control of the entire process by passing the First Reconstruction Act. It reduced the southern states to the status of territories and divided the South into five military districts directly controlled by the U. S. Army. Before the southern states could be readmitted to the Union they had to draw up new "republican" constitutions and ratify the Fourteenth Amendment. In addition, they had to allow African-American men to vote. The Second Reconstruction Act, passed a few weeks later, established the procedures to enforce African-American suffrage by placing the military in charge of voter registration. Johnson vetoed both acts, and in both cases Congress immediately overrode the president. "Congress has finally given us the means of relief," an African-American newspaper in Louisiana declared. "After governments of minorities, we are at last enabled to organize a government of the people." This was Congressional Reconstruction at its most radical, and for this reason it is often referred to as Radical Reconstruction.

Radical Reconstruction in the South

Beginning in 1867, the constitutions of the southern states were completely rewritten, thousands of African Americans began to vote, and hundreds of them assumed public office (see Table 16-2). Within six months 735,000 blacks and 635,000 whites had registered to vote across the South. "We'd walk fifteen miles in wartime to find out about the battle," a prospective black voter in Alabama explained in the spring of 1867. "We can walk fifteen miles and more to find out how to vote." African Americans formed electoral majorities in South Carolina, Florida, Mississippi, Alabama, and Louisiana. In the fall these new voters elected delegates to conventions that drew up some of the most progressive state constitutions in America. They guaran-

TABLE 16-2

	Reconstruction Amendments, 1865–1870		
Amendment	Main Provisions	Congressional Passage (2/3 majority in each house required)	Ratification Process (3/4 of all states including ex-Confederate states required)
13	Slavery prohibited in United States	January 1865	December 1865 (twenty-seven states, including eight southern states)
14	1. National citizenship 2. State representation in Congress reduced proportionally to number of voters disfranchised 3. Former Confederates denied right to hold office 4. Confederate debt repudiated	June 1866	Rejected by twelve southern and border states, February 1867 Radicals make readmission of southern states hinge on ratification Ratified July 1868
15	Denial of franchise because of race, color, or past servitude explicitly prohibited	February 1869	Ratification required for readmission of Virginia, Texas, Mississippi, Georgia Ratified March 1870

teed universal manhood suffrage, mandated public-education systems, and established progressive tax structures.

The Republican governments elected under congressional authority were based on a new and unstable political coalition. Northern whites occupied a prominent place in the southern Republican Party. Stereotyped as greedy **carpetbaggers,** they were in fact a varied group that included Union veterans who stayed in the South when the war ended, idealistic reformers, well-meaning capitalists, and opportunistic Americans on the make. More important to the Republican coalition were southern whites. Derided as **scalawags** by their opponents, white Republicans in the South supported their party for many reasons. Some of them lived in upcountry regions where slavery had been unimportant and where resistance to secession and the Confederacy had been strongest. Other white Republicans had been Whigs before the war and hoped to regain some of the influence they had lost in the sectional crisis. But new African-American voters were the Republican Party's core constituency in the South. Like the Carpetbaggers and Scalawags, African-American voters were a varied lot. There were important differences between those who had been free before the war and those who had been slaves. Elite black artisans and professionals did not always share the same interests as poor black farmers and farm laborers (see Figure 16-1). Nevertheless, most African Americans were drawn together by a shared interest in securing their basic civil rights.

In the long run the class and race divisions within the southern Republican coalition would weaken the party's ability to resist the powerful forces arrayed against it. But

for a brief moment in the late 1860s and early 1870s the southern Republicans launched an impressive experiment in interracial democracy in the South. Racist legend paints these years as a dark period of "negro rule" and military domination. In fact, military rule rarely lasted more than a year or two in most places. In only one state, South Carolina, did African Americans ever control a majority of seats in the legislature. Whites outnumbered blacks in every other Republican government elected in the South during Congressional Reconstruction. Those blacks who did hold office came largely from the ranks of the prewar free African-American elite. Teachers, ministers, and small businessmen were far more common among black elected officials than were field hands and farmers. Nevertheless, these Reconstruction legislatures were more democratic, more representative of their constituents, than most legislatures in nineteenth-century America.

Achievements and Failures of Radical Government

Once in office, southern Republicans had to cultivate a white constituency and at the same time serve the interests of the African Americans who were the party's main supporters. In an effort to strengthen this bi-racial coalition in

One of the greatest achievements of Congressional Reconstruction was the election of a significant number of African Americans to public office. Only in South Carolina, however, did African Americans ever form a legislative majority.

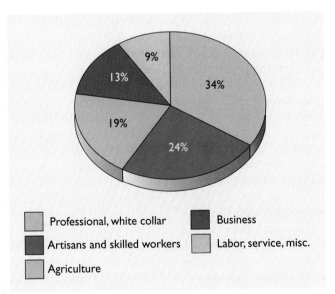

Figure 16-1 Occupations of African-American Officeholders During Reconstruction.
Source: Eric Foner, Freedom's Lawmakers: A Directory of Black Officeholders during Reconstruction, 2d. ed. (Baton Rouge, LA), p. xxi.

the late 1860s, white Republican leaders emphasized a policy of active government support for economic development. Republican legislatures granted generous tax abatements for corporations and spent vast sums to encourage the construction of railroads. They preached a "Gospel of Prosperity" that promised to bring the benefits of economic development to ordinary white southerners who had been held back by the slaveholders' regime. Return the South to the Union, one Republican editor predicted, and "her levees will be rebuilt, her railroad grants restored, the mouths of the Mississippi opened, sandbars and snags removed, canals dug, marshes drained, taxes taken off cotton and sugar, emigration directed southward instead of westward, and all the material interests of the state spring into robust vigor and healthful activity." It was an exciting vision of a new political economy, but it never materialized.

In the long run the "Gospel of Prosperity" did not hold the Republican coalition together. Outside investors were unwilling to risk their capital on a region marked by so much political instability. As long as Congress and the president were at war, investment in the South was too risky. By the early 1870s, African-American politicians questioned the diversion of scarce revenues to railroads and tax breaks for corporations. Instead, they demanded more public services, especially universal education. But more government services meant higher property taxes at a time of severe economic hardship for most ordinary southerners. Many small white farmers had been devastated by the Civil War. Unaccustomed to paying high taxes and strong believers in limited government, they grew increasingly receptive to Democratic appeals for the restoration of "white man's government." Thus southern Republicans failed to develop a program around which to unite the diverse interests of their party's constituents.

Despite such powerful opposition from white majorities at home and lukewarm support from Washington, D. C., Radical governments in the South boasted several important achievements. They funded the construction of hospitals, insane asylums, prisons, and roads. They introduced homestead exemptions that protected the property of poor farmers. One of their top priorities was the establishment of universal public education. In the short time since the war ended the importance of basic literacy became clear to poor southern blacks. They had entered a world of contracts and calculations, a world where the ability to read English and add up figures was critical to a farmer's livelihood. Motivated by such concerns, Republican legislatures established public school systems that were a major improvement over their antebellum counterparts. The literacy rate among southern blacks rose steadily, thanks in large part to a cadre of newly trained African-American teachers who began staffing the classrooms within a few years of their establishment.

Nevertheless, public schools for African Americans remained inadequately funded and sharply segregated. In Savannah, Georgia, for example, the school board allocated less than five percent of its 1873 budget to support the African-American schools, although white children were in the minority in the district. Pointing to similar inequities in his own state of Florida, Congressman Josiah T. Walls called for the federal government to create a nationwide system of public schools, but there was virtually no chance that the Congress would undertake such a measure. As a result, in states like South Carolina, fewer than one in three school-age children were being educated in 1872.

The Political Economy of Sharecropping

Congressional Reconstruction made it a little easier for the former slaves to negotiate the terms of their labor contracts. Republican state legislatures in the South abolished the Black Codes, for example. By 1868 they had also passed "lien" laws, statutes giving African-American workers more control over the crops they grew. Workers with grievances had a better chance of securing justice, as southern Republicans became sheriffs, justices of the peace, and county clerks, and as southern courts accepted the testimony of African-American witnesses and allowed blacks to sit on juries.

The strongest card in the hands of the freed people was a severe shortage of agricultural workers throughout the South. After their emancipation thousands of African Americans left the countryside looking for better opportunities in towns and cities. Others left the South entirely. And even though most African Americans remained as farmers when the war ended, they reduced their working hours in several ways. African-American women withdrew from field work in significant numbers, for example. At the same time public education drew thousands of black children away from agricultural work. The resulting labor shortage forced white landlords to renegotiate their labor arrangements with the freed people.

The contract labor system that had developed during the war and under Presidential Reconstruction collapsed. It was replaced with a variety of arrangements that differed from region to region. On the sugar plantations of southern Louisiana the freed people became wage laborers. In low country South Carolina, by contrast, a large number of former slaves became independent farmers. But across the tobacco and cotton regions of the South, where the vast majority of freed people lived and worked, negotiations between workers and landlords gradually led to a new system of labor called sharecropping. The sharecropping system had a number of variations, but in most cases an agricultural worker and his family agreed to work for one year on a particular plot of land. The landowner often provided the tools, seed, and the work animals. At the end of the year the sharecropper and the landlord split the crop, perhaps one-third going to the

The free labor system that replaced slavery took different forms in different parts of the South. On the Grove plantation, in South Carolina, the freed slaves were required to sign the contracts being read to them in the picture above. In most cases, the freed people were eventually paid wages in the form of a share of the crop they produced.

sharecropper and two-thirds to the owner. If the "cropper" had his own animals and tools he might negotiate to keep a larger share.

Sharecropping shaped the political economy of the postwar South by transforming the way cash crops were produced and marketed in much of the region. Most dramatically, it required landowners to break up their plantations into family-sized plots. Under slavery, most African Americans worked in gangs under the direct supervision of a master, an overseer, or a driver. By contrast, sharecroppers worked in family units with no direct supervision. Before the Civil War, slaveholders relied on "factors" (agents in port cities) to sell their crops and supply their plantations. With the breakup of the plantations after the war, each sharecropping family established its own relationship with local merchants and creditors. Merchants became crucial to the southern credit system because during the Civil War the Congress had established nationwide banking standards that most southern banks could not meet. Local storekeepers were usually the only people who could extend credit to sharecroppers. The result was a dramatic proliferation of merchants within the South. In the 1870s the number of stores grew by perhaps 300 percent. Local merchants soon became essential to the postwar southern economy. They provided sharecroppers with food, fertilizer, animal feed, and other provisions over the course of the year, until the crop was harvested.

These same developments had important consequences for small white farmers in many parts of the South. As the number of merchants grew, they fanned out into "upcountry" areas inhabited mostly by ordinary whites. Recon-

web connection

Did Reconstruction Work for the Freed People?

www.prenhall.com/boydston/reconstruction

Lincoln's assassination led to a power struggle between President Andrew Johnson, former Democratic senator from Tennessee, and the Republican Congress over how to "reconstruct" the South. The two sides agreed on the abolition of slavery but on little else. Often overlooked in the struggles over national policy were the everyday experiences of the newly freed slaves. How did they attempt to build lives for themselves? What were the principal obstacles they faced?

struction legislatures meanwhile sponsored the construction of railroads in many of those same upcountry districts. The combination of merchants offering credit and railroads offering transportation made it easier than ever for small farmers to focus on the production of cash crops. Thus Reconstruction accelerated the process by which the southern yeomen abandoned self-sufficient farming in favor of cash crops. Up through the 1870s, however, most white farmers continued to own their own land.

By contrast, sharecropping spread quickly among African-American farmers in the cotton South. By 1880 80 percent of cotton farms had fewer than 50 acres, the

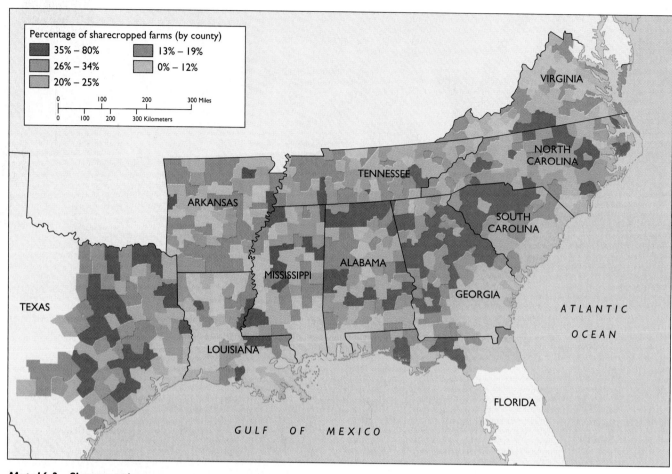

Map 16-2 Sharecropping.
By 1880 the sharecropping system had spread across the South. It was most common in the inland areas where cotton and tobacco plantations were most common before the Civil War.

majority of which were operated by croppers (see Map 16-2). A white landowner in the South complained that sharecropping was "the universal plan; negroes prefer it and I am forced to adopt it. Can't choose your system. Have to do what negroes want. They control this matter entirely." In fact, sharecropping had several advantages for landlords. It reduced their risk when cotton prices were low, it encouraged workers to increase production without costly supervision, and if sharecroppers changed jobs before the crop was harvested they would lose a whole year's pay. But the system also had advantages for the workers. For freed people who had no hope of owning their own farms, sharecropping was the next best thing. In principle it rewarded those who worked hard. The bigger the crop, the more they earned. It gave the former slaves more independence than contract labor.

Sharecropping also allowed the freed people to work in families rather than in gangs. Freedom alone had rearranged the powers of men, women, and children within the families of former slaves. Parents gained newfound control over the lives of their children. They could send sons and daughters to school; they could put their sons to work in the fields and

their daughters to work in the house. Successful parents could give their children an important head start in "the race of life." Similarly, African-American husbands gained new powers that shaped the lives of their wives. Slave marriages had no legal standing, so when the former slaves got married their relationships changed. The laws of marriage in the mid-nineteenth century defined the husband as the head of the household. Once married, women often found that their property belonged to their husbands.

The sharecropping system also assumed that the husband was the head of the household and that he made the economic decisions for the entire family. Men signed most labor contracts, and most landlords assumed that the husband would take his family to work with him. Shortly after the war Laura Towne, a teacher from the North, observed that African-American men in the South Carolina low country were claiming "the right . . . to have their own way in their families and rule their wives."

Sharecropping thereby shaped the entire political economy of the postwar South: It influenced the balance of power between men and women within cropper families; it established the balance of power between landowners

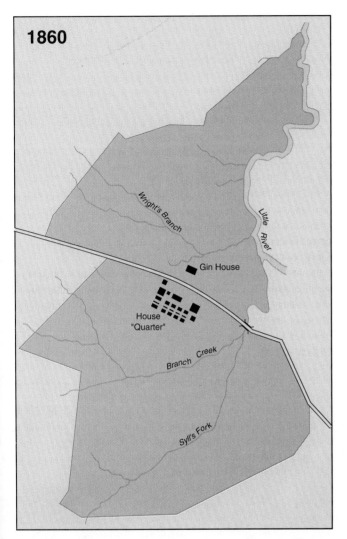

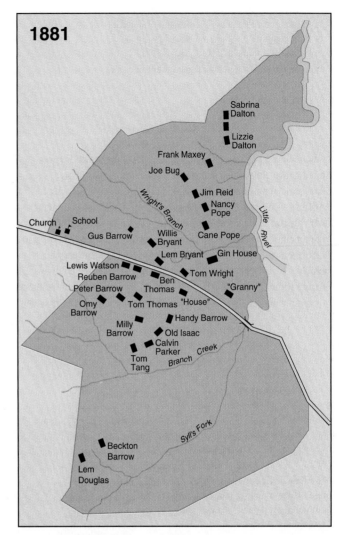

Map 16-3   *Effect of Sharecropping in the South: The Barrow Plantaton in Oglethorpe County, Georgia.*
Sharecropping cut large estates into small landholdings worked by sharecroppers and tenants, changing the landscape of the South.

and sharecroppers; and it tied the southern economy to agriculture, in particular to cotton production, in a way that seriously impeded the region's overall economic development (see Map 16-3). Yet even as this new way of life was taking shape, the Republican Party was retreating from its commitment to the freed people.

The Retreat From Republican Radicalism

By the late 1860s the Republican coalition was splintering in ways that weakened the party's continued commitment to Radical Reconstruction. In 1867 the Radicals led a drive to impeach President Johnson, but they failed to remove him from office. The fall elections suggested that northern voters were already tiring of Radical Reconstruction. By

1868 the Republicans were presenting themselves to voters as the party of moderation. They pointed out that the Democrats represented extremism and continued disruption of the southern political system and that the Democrats relied on terrorist organizations such as the Ku Klux Klan. The Republican appeal to moderation succeeded, bringing in its wake the last major achievements of Reconstruction.

The Impeachment and Trial of Andrew Johnson

Throughout 1866 and much of 1867 President Johnson waged a relentless campaign against Congress and the Radicals. When Congress began to override the president's repeated vetoes, Johnson stepped up his campaign. The conflict between Congress and the president led to a struggle over control of the military in the South. The First Reconstruction Act placed the entire South under direct military control, and the Freedmen's Bureau was a branch of the

ON TRIAL

Andrew Johnson

"Didn't I tell you so?" Thaddeus Stevens asked upon hearing the news that Johnson had ordered Stanton's dismissal. "If you don't kill the beast, it will kill you." But Radicals like Stevens had been prepared for some time to "kill the beast" by removing Andrew Johnson from office. More telling was the reluctant conclusion among moderate Republicans that the president had to be put on trial for a positive violation of the law. On February 24, 1868, the House Judiciary Committee voted nearly a dozen articles of impeachment against the president. They charged him with violating the Tenure of Office Act, of replacing a cabinet officer without the advice and consent of the Senate even though Congress was in session, of devising means to obstruct the execution of various Reconstruction laws, and of ridiculing and disrespecting Congress. The strongest case for a technical breach of the law was Johnson's attempted removal of Stanton in violation of the Tenure of Office Act, but behind that charge lay widespread disgust with the president's undignified behavior, his abusive public pronouncements, and his obstreperous interference with Congressional Reconstruction.

It was an extraordinary thing to put a president on trial. No Congress had ever done so before. By March 4, when the Senate presented the articles of impeachment, the atmosphere in Washington, D. C. was understandably agitated. Congressmen were besieged with requests for tickets to the Senate gallery. It was reported that Stanton

Court proceedings were held in the Senate chambers during the impeachment trial of President Andrew Johnson. It was an extraordinary thing to put a president on trial.

Congressmen were besieged with requests for these tickets to the Senate Gallery by constituents who wanted to observe the impeachment proceedings.

had barricaded himself in his office and was sleeping on a sofa, protected by armed guards. Yet for all the electricity surrounding the impeachment, the trial itself turned out to be a rather dull affair. For a moment Republican Senator Ben Butler lost his reserve and, citing the horror stories pouring out of the South, announced in heated tones that "We want these things stopped!" Stevens at one point referred to the president as "this offspring of assassination." For the most part, however, the participants maintained the dignity befitting so solemn an occasion.

There were, after all, serious legal questions that had to be considered. The House managers argued that a president could be removed not only for violating the Constitution or the law, but also for abusing his powers, breaking his oath of office, or neglecting his duties "without violating a positive law." In response, Johnson's lawyers argued that a president had to actually violate the law. Indeed, one of the president's attorneys went so far as to claim that the violation had to be especially severe before he could be removed. Thus even if Johnson did violate the Tenure of Office Act, it was not a serious enough breach of the law to justify removal from office. In any case the Tenure of Office Act was unconstitutional, Johnson's lawyers argued, making his violation of it

meaningless. To this argument Johnson's accusers shot right back that only the Supreme Court could decide whether or not a law was constitutional. Otherwise the president would be free to break any laws he felt like breaking.

Still, some of Johnson's sharpest critics wondered about the constitutionality of the Tenure of Office Act. They wondered whether the standards for conviction by the Senate had to be as strict as those for conviction in a court of law. And they were not sure whether the Tenure of Office Act even applied to Secretary of War Stanton, since he had been appointed by President Lincoln rather than President Johnson. Nor were constitutional questions and legal technicalities the only issues to consider. Several senators were wary of the man who stood next in line to replace Johnson in the event of a conviction. That man was Benjamin Wade, president *pro tem* of the Senate and an outspoken Radical from Ohio. The prospect of a Wade presidency disturbed both Republican moderates and the New York financial markets. Finally, Johnson behaved himself during the trial, and his lawyers quietly hinted that if the president was acquitted he would continue his good behavior. In the end, thanks to the votes of seven Republicans who sided with the president, the Senate fell one vote short of the two-thirds required to remove Johnson from office.

The Radicals were thwarted in their efforts to convict Johnson, but in other ways they had gained a victory. Hoping to avoid conviction, President Johnson had promised to abide by the law. On the advice of his supporters, Johnson at last forwarded to the Congress the new state constitutions submitted by Arkansas and South Carolina. Finally, the president stopped interfering with the Reconstruction Acts by removing Army officers who enforced the law in the South. "Andrew Johnson has been a changed man," the *Chicago Tribune* declared during the impeachment trial. "The great obstruction to the law has been virtually suspended; the President . . . has been on his good behavior." Thus Johnson was acquitted, but the Reconstruction of the South went forward anyway.

U. S. Army. Judicial authority was vested in the provost marshals. The military also oversaw the process of voter registration. But the president was the commander in chief of the military, and Andrew Johnson made clear his determination to interfere with Congress' wishes as much as he possibly could. Exercising his authority over the military, Johnson removed dozens of Freedmen's Bureau officials who acted to protect the freed people by enforcing the Civil Rights Act of 1866. He replaced Republican provost marshals with men who were hostile to Congress and contemptuous of the former slaves. In short, President Johnson went out of his way to undermine the law.

Radicals called for Johnson's impeachment, but Republican moderates and conservatives resisted such a move. Instead, the Congress hoped to restrain the president in two ways—first by refining the Reconstruction Acts, and then through the Tenure of Office Act of March 2, 1867. This act prohibited the president from removing any official whose appointment required congressional approval. One purpose of the law was to prevent Johnson from firing Secretary of War Edwin M. Stanton, who was sympathetic to the Republicans. A related statute required that all presidential orders to the military pass through General Ulysses S. Grant. Republicans hoped that this would prevent the president from systematically removing military officials who enforced the Reconstruction Acts in the South.

Congress' actions only served to provoke the president. In his veto messages and in his public pronouncements, Johnson indulged in some of the most blatant racist pandering in the history of the executive office. He played on fears of "amalgamation," "miscegenation," and racial "degeneration." He claimed that the Republicans were attempting to "Africanize" the South. He expressed fear for the safety of white womanhood. In the off-year elections of 1867 northern Democrats played the race card relentlessly and with considerable success. Democratic victories erased many of the huge Republican gains of 1866 and inspired the president to defy the restraints Congress had imposed upon him. As a test of his power, and as a deliberate provocation, Johnson asked Secretary of War Stanton to resign on August 5, 1867. Stanton refused, and a week later the president appointed General Grant as interim secretary of war. Still Stanton would not budge, so in February 1868 Johnson at last fired him outright.

Republicans Become the Party of Moderation

While Andrew Johnson was on trial in the Senate, voters in Michigan went to the polls and overwhelmingly rejected a new state constitution that granted African Americans the right to vote. Coming on the heels of Democratic victories in late 1867, Republicans read the Michigan results as another rejection of Radical Reconstruction. When Senator Charles Sumner submitted a bill confiscating the land of ex-Confederates, his fellow Republicans rebuffed him. Congressman Thaddeus Stevens was similarly thwarted when he proposed the distribution of 40 acres and a mule to the families of freed slaves. Republican moderates also rejected Radical proposals to guarantee educational opportunities for freed people and to deny voting privileges to large numbers of ex-Confederates. The Republican Party was backing away from radicalism.

During the 1868 elections Republicans continued to cultivate a moderate image. They rejected the Radicals' demand that the party platform endorse nationwide African-American suffrage. Moderates argued that African-American suffrage was a uniquely southern solution to a uniquely southern problem. The northern states should be free to decide for themselves whether to grant African-American men the vote. With plenty of time before election day, Congress readmitted six southern states to the Union, thereby demonstrating that Republican policies had successfully restored law and order to the South. By nominating General Ulysses Grant as their presidential candidate, the Republicans confirmed their retreat from radicalism. "Let Us Have Peace," was Grant's campaign slogan.

In sharp contrast, the Democrats nominated Horatio Seymour, who had been New York's governor during the Civil War. Seymour ran a vicious campaign of relentless race baiting. The Democratic platform denounced the Reconstruction Acts and promised to restore white rule to the South. The loose-tongued Seymour openly suggested that a Democratic president might nullify the governments organized under Congressional Reconstruction. Where the Republicans ran on a platform promising order and stability, the Democrats seemed to promise only continued disruption. Northern fears were confirmed by the horrendous violence that swept through the South during the election.

Southern Democrats relied on such violence to keep African-American voters from the polls on election day. At the height of the 1868 campaign an Alabama sharecropper named William Ford was visited by several members of the Ku Klux Klan. The Klansmen whipped Ford in an effort to "convince" him to vote for the Democratic presidential candidate. "They asked me who I was going to vote for: Grant or Seymour." Knowing that the Klan had whipped one of his neighbors "for talking politics," Ford claimed to be ignorant of the campaign. The Klan visit had the desired effect. "When the election came off I didn't vote," Ford testified. "I was afraid to. I thought if I couldn't vote the Republican ticket I would not vote at all." Vigilantes made similar visits in many parts of the South during the 1868 election campaign.

The Ku Klux Klan was only one of several secretive organizations dedicated to the violent overthrow of Radical Reconstruction and the restoration of white supremacy. They went by various names, including the Knights of the White Camelia, Red Shirts, and Night Riders. Some of these white vigilantes tried to force African Americans to

The Ku Klux Klan was one of a number of racist vigilante groups trying to restore the Democratic Party to power in the postwar South.

go back to work for white landlords. Some attacked African Americans who refused to abide by traditional codes of racial etiquette. But in the main, organizations such as the Klan worked to restore the political power of the Democratic Party in the South. They rampaged through the countryside intimidating white Republicans, burning African-American homes and lynching blacks who showed signs of political activism. In Arkansas alone there were 200 murders. It is fair to say that in 1868 the Ku Klux Klan served as the paramilitary arm of the southern Democratic Party.

But as a means of restoring white supremacy, the Klan's strategy of violence backfired. A wave of disgust swept across the North in late 1868. The Republicans regained control of the White House, along with 25 of the nation's 33 state legislatures. The victorious Republicans quickly seized the opportunity to preserve the achievements of Reconstruction.

The Grant Administration and Moderate Republicanism

The Republicans reinforced their moderate image by attempting to restore law and order in the South. A lengthy series of dramatic congressional hearings produced vivid evidence of the Klan's violent efforts to suppress the African-American vote in the South. Congress responded with a series of Enforcement Acts, designed to "enforce" the recently enacted Fifteenth Amendment (see the fol-

lowing section for more information). After some initial hesitation, the Grant administration used the new laws to suppress Klan violence. By the end of 1871, the anti-Klan prosecutions had effectively diminished political violence throughout the South. As a result the 1872 presidential elections were relatively free of disruption. The successful prosecution of the Ku Klux Klan helped reinforce the Republican Party's image as the voice of moderation.

Further evidence of this moderate trend was the Republican shift to an aggressive foreign policy. Before the Civil War, Republicans associated expansionism with the "slave power" and the Democratic Party. But with the triumph of nationalism, the Republicans equated American overseas expansion with the spread of liberty. They went on the offensive: In 1867 Secretary of State William Seward successfully negotiated the purchase of Alaska from Russia. For the first time, the United States claimed territory that did not border on any other state. The administration was equally adroit in its negotiations with Great Britain over the settlement of the so-called *Alabama* claims. In 1872 the English accepted responsibility for having helped equip the Confederate Navy during the Civil War. They agreed to pay over 15 million dollars in claims for damage done to American shipping by the *Alabama* and other southern warships built in England.

But Grant's aggressive foreign policy did not go uncontested. In 1869 the president set his sights on Santo Domingo (now the Dominican Republic), but the administration bungled the entire effort. Grant's private secretary negotiated a treaty without letting the cabinet, including the secretary of state, know what he was doing. Once Grant sent the treaty to Congress in 1870 it aroused the suspicions of several prominent Republican senators, including Charles Sumner and Carl Schurz. Grant then tried to bulldoze the treaty through Congress, but succeeded only in alienating more members of his own party. The Senate rejected the annexation of Santo Domingo, and the Republicans were weakened still further by the debacle.

Reconstruction in the North

Although Reconstruction was aimed primarily at shaping the transition from slavery to freedom in the South, the North was affected by the process as well. Because most northern states restricted voting to whites, the struggle over the black vote spilled beyond the borders of the defeated Confederacy. As Republicans moved toward prohibiting the use of race as a qualification for voting rights, for example, northern feminists began to raise objections. Why should African-American men recently released from slavery be guaranteed the right to vote, feminists asked, when educated northern women were still denied the privilege? Thus Reconstruction politics disrupted a long-standing alliance between abolitionists and feminists in the North. At the same time, northern workers were inspired by the radical promises of Reconstruction to launch a new wave of organized protest. Although not as dramatic as developments in the South, the transformation of the North was still an important chapter in the history of Reconstruction.

The Fifteenth Amendment and Nationwide African-American Suffrage

Before the Civil War African Americans in the North were segregated in theaters, restaurants, cemeteries, hotels, streetcars, ferries, and schools. Most northern blacks lived in states that denied them the vote. The Civil War galvanized the northern black community to launch a full-scale assault on racial discrimination, with some success. In 1863 California removed the ban on African-American testimony in the criminal courts. Two years later Illinois did the same. During the war, many northern cities abolished streetcar segregation. But when they considered black voting, northern whites retained their traditional racial prejudices. In 1865 voters in three northern states (Connecticut, Wisconsin, and Minnesota) soundly rejected constitutional amendments to enfranchise African-American men. "Slavery is dead, the negro is not, there is the misfortune," the Democratic *Cincinnati Enquirer* declared. "For the sake of all parties, would that he were." Two years of Presidential Reconstruction changed little. In 1867, even as the Republican Congress was imposing the black vote on the South, African-American suffrage was defeated by voters in Ohio, Minnesota, and Kansas.

But the shocking electoral violence of 1868 persuaded many northerners that, given the chance, southern whites would quickly strip African Americans of the right to vote. This latest shift in northern public opinion was expressed most dramatically in Iowa and Minnesota, where voters finally approved black suffrage. Emboldened by their victory in the 1868 elections, the following year Republicans took one last, deep breath and exhaled a Fifteenth Amendment to the Constitution. It prohibited the use of "race, color, or previous condition of servitude" to disqualify voters anywhere in the United States. This was nationwide black suffrage, just as the Radicals had asked for in 1868. But by 1869 the Radicals wanted more. They complained that the Fifteenth Amendment did not guarantee the vote to all adult males in the United States. Nor did it ban literacy tests and educational requirements for voting. Yet by outlawing voter discrimination on the basis of race, the Fifteenth Amendment protected the most radical achievement of Congressional Reconstruction.

The Fifteenth Amendment brought Reconstruction directly into the North by overturning the state laws that still discriminated against African-American voters. The Republicans could pass the amendment after the 1868 elections because they now controlled three-fourths of the state legislatures, allowing the Republicans to ratify the Fifteenth Amendment without popular referendums. In addition, Congress required ratification of the amendment in those southern states still to be readmitted to the Union. Virginia, Mississippi, and Texas did so and were restored to the Union in early 1870. After several irregularities were cleared up, Georgia followed suit. On March 30, 1870, the Fifteenth Amendment became part of the Constitution. For the first time in American history, racial criteria for voting were banned everywhere in the United States, North as well as South.

Women and Suffrage

The issue of African-American voting divided northern Radicals who had long been allies in the struggle for emancipation. Before the Civil War, feminists and abolitionists had forged a strong progressive coalition. They appeared on each other's platforms and gave speeches advocating both abolition and women's equality. But signs of trouble appeared as early as May 1863 when a dispute broke out at the National Convention of the Woman's National Loyal League in New York City. One of the convention's resolutions declared that "there never can be a true peace in this Republic until the civil and political rights of all citizens of African descent and all women are practically established." For some of the delegates, this resolution went too far. The Loyal League had been organized to assist in bringing about northern victory in the war against the slave South. Some delegates argued that it was inappropriate to inject the issue of women's rights into the struggle to restore the Union.

By the end of the war, Radicals were pressing for African-American suffrage in addition to emancipation. This precipitated an increasingly rancorous debate among reformers. Abolitionists argued that while they continued to support women's suffrage, the critical issue at that moment was the immediate protection of the freed people of the South. This, abolitionist Wendell Phillips argued, was "the Negro's Hour." As he explained to Elizabeth Cady Stanton in May 1865, "I would not mix the movements. . . . I think such a mixture would lose for the negro far more than we should gain for the woman." Phillips' position sparked a powerful sense of betrayal among leading women's rights activists. For 20 years they had pressed their claims for the right to vote. They had organized to support the Union in the struggle for emancipation. They were loyal allies of the Republican Party, and now the Republicans abandoned them. "Some say, 'Be still, wait, this is the negro's hour,'" Stanton complained in December 1865. It would be better, she argued, to press for "a vote based on intelligence and education for black and white,

Elizabeth Cady Stanton, a leading advocate of women's rights, was angered when Congress gave African-American men the vote without also giving it to women.

Not all feminists agreed with Stanton. Abby Kelley Foster pointed to the urgent needs of African Americans in the South at that moment. "He is treated as a slave today in the several districts of the South. Without wages, without family rights, whipped and beaten by thousands, given up to the most horrible outrages, without that protection which his value as property formerly gave him. . . . Have we any true sense of justice, are we not dead to the sentiment of humanity if we shall wish to postpone his security against present woes and future enslavement till woman shall obtain political rights?" As racist violence erupted in the postwar South, abolitionists argued that African-American suffrage was simply more urgent than women's suffrage. The African-American vote "is with us a matter of life and death, and therefore can not be postponed," Frederick Douglass argued. "I have always championed women's right to vote; but it will be seen that the present claim for the negro is one of the most *urgent* necessity. . . . The negro needs suffrage to protect his life and property."

Stanton was unmoved by such arguments. For her the Fifteenth Amendment barring racial qualifications for voting was the last straw. She complained that by granting African-American men the right to vote Republicans had subjected African-American women to a new and oppressive form of male domination. Supporters of women's suffrage therefore opposed the Fifteenth Amendment on the ground that it subjected elite, educated women to the rule of base and illiterate males, especially immigrants and African Americans. "Think of Patrick and Sambo and Hans and Yung Tung who do not know the difference between a Monarchy and a Republic," Stanton declared, "who never read the Declaration of Independence or Webster's spelling book, making laws for Lydia Maria Child, Lucretia Mott, or Fanny Kemble." Abolitionists were shocked by such remarks. They favored universal suffrage, not the "educated" suffrage that Stanton was calling for. The breach among reformers weakened the coalition of Radicals pushing to maintain a vigorous Reconstruction policy in the South.

The Rise and Fall of the National Labor Union

In the late 1860s the Boston Labor Reform Association called for a dramatic change of "the whole Social System." Just as southern society was being transformed, "so too must our dinner tables be reconstructed." Inspired by the radicalism of the Civil War and Reconstruction, industrial workers across the North organized dozens of craft unions, Eight-Hour Leagues, and workingmen's associations. The general goal of these associations was to protect northern workers who were overworked and underpaid. They called strikes, initiated consumer boycotts, and formed consumer cooperatives. In 1867 and 1868 workers in New York and Massachusetts launched impressive cam-

man and woman." Voting rights based on "intelligence and education" amounted to literacy tests that would have excluded virtually all the freed slaves as well as many immigrants, particularly the working-class Irish, Germans, and Chinese. Thus, Stanton's remarks revealed a strain of elitism that would further alienate abolitionists.

In 1866 the struggle for the Fourteenth Amendment widened the rift between feminists and abolitionists. The amendment reduced a state's congressional representation in proportion to the number of *males* who were denied the ballot. Indeed, with the passage of the Fourteenth Amendment the word "male" appeared in the Constitution for the first time. In the same year conservative Democrats cynically added women's suffrage amendments to congressional legislation securing the African-American vote, knowing that the amendments would thereby fail. But women's rights advocates sided with the conservatives. Stanton argued in May 1867 that the voting power of "unlettered" and "unwashed" men threatened the interests of women. The only thing that could "outweigh this incoming tide of ignorance, poverty and vice," she concluded, was "the virtue, wealth and education of the women of the country."

paigns to enact laws restricting the workday to eight hours. Shortly thereafter workers began electing their own candidates to state legislatures. The Knights of St. Crispin sent two dozen of its candidates to the Massachusetts state legislature in 1869.

The National Labor Union (NLU) was the first significant postwar effort to organize all "working people" into a national union. William Sylvis, an iron molder, founded the NLU in 1866 and became its president in 1868. Like most of the worker organizations of the time, the NLU subscribed to "producers ideology." It sought to unify all those who produced wealth through their own labor and skill. Hostile to anyone who made money from money, the NLU targeted bankers, financiers, and stockbrokers as the enemies of the producing classes. These sentiments were most powerful among farmers, craftsmen, and small shopkeepers, but the NLU welcomed a broader range of working people including women's rights advocates and wage earners.

Under Sylvis' direction the National Labor Union advocated a wide range of political reforms, not just bread-and-butter issues of interest to working people. Nevertheless, the NLU was thwarted by the limits of producer ideology. Sylvis believed that through successful organization American workers could take the "first step toward competence and independence." Thus Sylvis' NLU clung to the Jeffersonian vision of a society of independent petty producers. By the 1860s this vision was an outdated relic of an earlier age. Many small businessmen and factory owners took pride in their own "independence" and still considered themselves "producers." Meanwhile wage labor rather than economic independence had become the permanent condition for the majority of American workers. Sylvis showed little interest in organizing women, African Americans, rural workers, and most unskilled wage laborers. Sylvis died in 1869 and, after a miserable showing in the elections of 1872, the NLU fell apart. By then Reconstruction in the South was also coming to an end.

The End of Reconstruction

National events had as much to do with the end of Reconstruction as did events in the South. A nationwide outbreak of political corruption in the late 1860s and 1870s provoked a sharp reaction everywhere. When the corruption was exposed in the South, however, it diminished popular support for continuing Reconstruction. A group of influential northern "Liberals," previously known for their support for Reconstruction, abandoned the Republican Party in disgust in 1872. The following year a major depression turned the nation's attention away from the social and political problems of the South. The end of Reconstruction finally came after a new round of electoral vi-

olence corrupted the results of the 1876 elections. Republican politicians in Washington, D. C., responded not with renewed determination to enforce Reconstruction but with a sordid political bargain that came to symbolize the end of an era.

Corruption as a National Problem

Postwar Americans witnessed an extraordinary display of public dishonesty, from the scandals in the Grant administration to the notorious swindles of the Tweed Ring in New York City. Democrats were as prone to thievery as Republicans. Northern swindlers looted the public treasuries from Boston to San Francisco. In the South black legislators took bribes, but so did whites. Indeed, some of the most prominent whites in the South paid some of the most spectacular bribes. Corruption, it seemed, was endemic to postwar American politics.

Few Americans stopped to recall the corruption scandals of the 1850s. Nor did the opponents of Reconstruction bother to notice that the corruption of the Republican legislatures in the South was part of a nationwide trend. If corruption was everywhere to be seen in the late 1860s and 1870s, it was largely because there were more opportunities for it than ever before. The Civil War and Reconstruction had swollen government budgets at the state and national levels. Never before was government so active in collecting taxes and disbursing vast sums for the public good. Under the circumstances, many government officials proved unable to refrain from accepting bribes for votes, embezzling public funds, or using insider knowledge to defraud the taxpayers.

The federal government set the tone. In the most notorious case, the directors of the Union Pacific Railroad set up a dummy corporation called the Crédit Mobilier, awarded it phony contracts, and protected it from inquiry by bribing several influential congressmen. The Grant administration was eventually smeared with scandal as well. Though personally honest, the president surrounded himself with rich nobodies and army buddies rather than respected statesmen. Grant's own private secretary was exposed as a member of the "Whiskey Ring," a cabal of midwestern distillers and revenue agents who cheated the government out of millions of tax dollars every year.

State and city governments in the North were no less corrupt. Wealthy businessmen and local elites curried favor with politicians whose votes would determine where a railroad would be built, which land would be allocated for rights of way, and how many government bonds had to be floated to pay for such projects. Henry Demarest Lloyd, a prominent social critic, declared that Standard Oil could do anything with the Pennsylvania legislature except refine it. State officials regularly accepted gifts, received salaries, and sat on the boards of corporations whose fortunes were directly affected by their votes. Cities were

William Marcy Tweed, the boss of New York's notoriously corrupt, "Tweed Ring" was parodied by the great cartoonist, William Nast. Nast's portrayal of the bloated public official became an enduring symbol of governmental corruption.

rocked by scandal as well. The spectacular growth of urban centers created a huge new demand for public services. Municipalities awarded lucrative contracts for the construction of schools, parks, libraries, water and sewer systems, and mass-transportation networks. Every such contract created apparently irresistible temptations for corruption. The Tweed Ring alone bilked New York City out of tens of millions of dollars. By these standards the corruption of the southern Reconstruction legislatures was relatively small.

But corruption in the South was real enough, and it had particular significance for the politics of Reconstruction. Southern Republicans of modest means depended heavily on the money they earned as public officials. These same men found themselves responsible for the collection of unusually high taxes; the construction of schools, hospitals, and prisons; and the award of land grants and bond issues for railroads, river improvements, and other economic-development projects. As elsewhere in industrializing America, the lure of corruption proved overwhelming. The Republican governor of Louisiana grew rich while in office by "exacting tribute" from railroads seeking state favors. The Littlefield "ring" in North Carolina spent hundreds of thousands of dollars in bribes to win huge state appropriations for a railroad that was

never built. Corruption on a vast scale implied petty corruption as well. Individual legislators sold their votes for as little as 200 dollars.

Nevertheless, the charges of corruption leveled against southern Republican governments were often unfair. As Reconstruction legislatures established basic public services, they were forced to impose taxes at far higher rates than anything antebellum voters were accustomed to. Simply extending public-school education to African Americans would have been an enormous burden on the devastated southern economy. But several Republican governments also had to build entirely new public-school systems, not to mention hospitals, roads, canals, and rail lines. Had they done all of this without so much as a dime's worth of corruption, the Reconstruction governments still would have created a tax burden that would have caused white voters to shudder in horror. Inevitably, the whites blamed their woes on corruption.

In many cases opponents of Reconstruction used attacks on corruption to mask their contempt for Republican policies. Their strategy helped galvanize opposition to the Republican Party, destroying its hopes of attracting a loyal core of white voters. Realizing that corruption only weakened their cause, black Republicans grew increasingly critical of the politics of economic development.

Finally, corruption in the South helped provoke a backlash against active government nationwide, weakening northern support for Reconstruction. The intellectual substance of this backlash was provided by a group of influential Liberal Republicans many of whom had once been ardent supporters of Radical Reconstruction.

Liberal Republicans Revolt

The term "Liberal Republicans" embraced a loosely knit group of intellectuals, politicians, publishers, and businessmen from the northern elite. These "best men" of American society were discouraged by the failure of Radical Reconstruction to bring peace to the southern states. They were even more disgusted by the pervasive corruption of postwar politics. Although small in number, Liberals exercised important influence in northern politics. They spoke through the pages of magazines like *The Nation* and newspapers such as the Springfield *Republican*. As Liberals tired of the seemingly perpetual strife aroused by Reconstruction they increasingly urged resistance to growing demands by women, African Americans, and workers.

At the heart of Liberal philosophy was a deep suspicion of democracy itself. Liberals argued that any government beholden to the interests of the ignorant masses was doomed to corruption. They did not oppose active government in general; rather, Liberals worried that democracy threatened to undermine "good" government. Public servants should be chosen on the basis of intelligence, as measured by civil-service examinations, rather than by patronage appointments that sustained corrupt party machines. Indeed, party politics itself was the enemy of good government, Liberal reformers believed.

Liberals therefore grew increasingly alienated from the Republican Party in general and from President Grant in particular. Above all they resented the fact that the Republican Party had changed. Its idealistic commitment to free labor was waning by the 1870s. Its Radical vanguard was fast disappearing. The rising generation of Republican leaders was committed primarily to keeping the party machinery well oiled. Getting and holding office had become an end in itself for Republican stalwarts.

As Republicans lost their identity as moral crusaders, Liberal reformers proposed a new vision of their own. In 1872 they left their party to support Horace Greeley, who took up the Liberal banner as the Democratic presidential candidate. The Liberal plank in the Democratic platform proclaimed the party's commitment to the principles of universal equality before the law, the integrity of the Union, and support for the Thirteenth, Fourteenth, and Fifteenth Amendments to the Constitution. At the same time, however, Liberals demanded "the immediate and absolute removal of all disabilities" imposed on the South as well as a "universal amnesty" for all ex-Confederates. Finally, the Liberals declared their belief that "local self-government" would "guard the rights of all citizens more securely than any centralized power." In effect, the Liberals were demanding the immediate end of all federal efforts to protect the former slaves.

In the long run, the Liberal view would prevail, but in 1872 it did not go over well with the voters. The Liberals' biggest liability was their own presidential candidate. Horace Greeley's erratic reputation and Republican background were too much for Democrats to swallow. In record numbers Democrats refused to go to the polls and vote for him. Grant was easily re-elected, but he and his fellow Republicans saw the returns as evidence that Reconstruction was becoming a political liability for the Republican Party.

The 1874 elections confirmed the lesson. Democrats made sweeping gains all across the North, and they maintained their electoral strength for decades. An ideological stalemate developed. For a generation, neither party would clearly dominate American politics. The Republicans would take no more risks in support of Reconstruction.

During his second term, therefore, Grant did little to protect African-American voters from the revival of violence during elections in the South. Not even the Civil Rights Act of 1875 undid the impression of waning Republican zeal. Ostensibly designed to prohibit racial discrimination in public places, the Civil Rights Act was a toothless law that had no meaningful enforcement provisions. The bill's most important clause, prohibiting segregated schools, was eliminated from the final version. Southern states ignored even this watered-down statute, and in 1883 the Supreme Court declared it unconstitutional. Thus the Civil Rights Act of 1875, the last significant piece of Reconstruction legislation, was an ironic testament to the Republican Party's declining commitment to equal rights.

A Depression and a Deal "Redeem" the South

Angered by corruption and high taxes, white Republicans across the South succumbed in growing numbers to the Democratic Party's appeal for a restoration of white supremacy. As the number of white Republicans fell, the number of black Republicans holding office in the South actually increased, even as the Grant administration backed away from the active defense of African-American civil rights. But the persistence of African-American officeholders only reinforced the Democrats' determination to "redeem" their states from Republican rule. In fact, Democrats had taken control of Virginia in 1869, sparing the state from any experience of Republican rule. North Carolina was redeemed in 1870, Georgia in 1871, and Texas two years after that. Then depression struck.

In September 1873 America's premier financial institution, Jay Cooke, went bankrupt after wildly overextend-

The severe depression that followed the financial panic of 1873 drew the nation's attention away from the problems of Reconstruction.

cans away from the polls on election day, 1875. Republicans were beaten, forced to flee the state, and in several cases murdered. Washington turned a deaf ear to African-American pleas for military protection. In the end enough blacks were kept from the polls and enough scalawags voted their racial prejudices to put the Democrats in power. Mississippi was redeemed.

The tactics tried out in Mississippi were repeated elsewhere the following year, only this time they had dramatic consequences for the presidential election of 1876. Amidst a serious economic depression, and with an electorate tired of the politics of Reconstruction, the Democrats stood a good chance of taking the presidency away from the Republicans. In fact, the Democratic candidate, Samuel J. Tilden, won 250,000 more votes than his Republican rival Rutherford B. Hayes (see Map 16-4). But outrageous electoral fraud

ing itself on investments in a second railroad to the West Coast, the Northern Pacific. Within weeks hundreds of banks and thousands of businesses, including 89 railroads, went bankrupt as well. The country sank into a depression that lasted five years and saw unemployment rise to 14 percent. Corporations responded to hard times and growing competition by slashing wages. To protect their incomes, railroad workers tried to organize a nationwide union and attempted to strike in protest several times. Their employers, however (armed with spies and court orders and backed up by an army of private policemen as well as government troops), repeatedly thwarted such efforts. A series of railroad strikes in the early and middle 1870s failed.

As the nation turned its attention to labor unrest and economic depression, the Republican Party's commitment to Reconstruction all but disappeared. By the middle of the 1870s, the Republican Party in most parts of the South was almost exclusively African American. Democrats regained control of the governments of Alabama and Arkansas in 1874. In the few southern states where black Republicans clung tenaciously to their political power, white "redeemers" turned to violent methods to overthrow the last remnants of Reconstruction.

Mississippi established the model in 1875. Confident that authorities in Washington, D.C., would no longer interfere in the South, Democrats launched an all-out campaign to regain control of the state government by any means necessary. The Democratic campaign was double edged. Crude appeals to white supremacy further reduced the dwindling number of scalawags. But the redeemers launched more powerful weapons against black Republicans. White Leagues organized a blatant campaign of violence and intimidation designed to keep African Ameri-

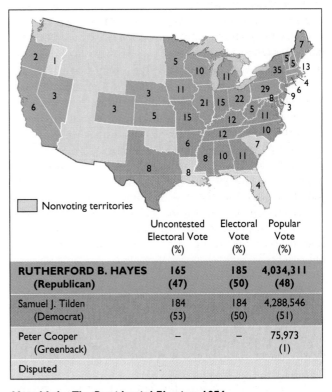

	Uncontested Electoral Vote (%)	Electoral Vote (%)	Popular Vote (%)
RUTHERFORD B. HAYES (Republican)	**165** **(47)**	**185** **(50)**	**4,034,311** **(48)**
Samuel J. Tilden (Democrat)	184 (53)	184 (50)	4,288,546 (51)
Peter Cooper (Greenback)	–	–	75,973 (1)
Disputed			

Nonvoting territories

Map 16-4   The Presidential Election, 1876.
In 1876 the Democratic presidential candidate, Samuel Tilden, won the popular vote but was denied the presidency because the Republicans who controlled Congress chose to interpret voting irregularities in Louisiana, South Carolina, Oregon, and Florida in a way that gave their candidate, Rutherford B. Hayes, all of the disputed electoral votes.

in South Carolina, Louisiana, Florida, and Oregon threw the results into doubt.

If all of the electoral votes from those states had gone to Hayes, he would have won. But if even a single electoral vote had gone to Tilden, a Democrat would have won election to the presidency for the first time in 20 years. The outcome was determined by an electoral commission with a Republican majority, and the commission awarded every one of the disputed electoral votes to the Republican candidate. Ever since then the odor of corruption has hovered about the 1876 presidential election. When Hayes was inaugurated on March 4, 1877, the legitimacy of his presidency was already in doubt. But what he did shortly after taking office made it appear as though he had won the presidency thanks to a sordid "compromise" with the Democrats to bring an end to Reconstruction in the South. There is no solid evidence that such a deal was ever actually made. Nevertheless, the new president almost immediately ordered the federal troops guarding the Republican statehouses in South Carolina and Louisiana to return to their barracks. This order marked the formal end of military occupation of the South and the symbolic end of the Reconstruction process. By late 1877, every southern state had been redeemed by the Democrats.

The following year the Supreme Court began to issue a series of rulings that further undermined the achievements of Reconstruction. In *Hall v. DeCuir* (1878) the Supreme Court invalidated a Louisiana law that prohibited racial segregation on railroads, steamboats, streetcars and other "common carriers." In 1882, the justices declared unconstitutional a federal criminal statute that was most often used to protect southern African Americans against racially motivated murders and assaults. More importantly, in the Civil Rights Cases of 1883, the Supreme Court sharply narrowed the significance of the Fourteenth Amendment by declaring that it did not pertain to discriminatory practices by private persons. This series of decisions paved the way for the Court's landmark ruling, in *Plessy v. Ferguson* (1896), that the Constitution permitted

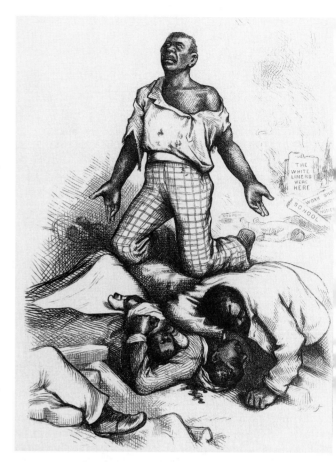

By the mid-1870s the Republican Party lost its zeal to sustain Reconstruction. In many parts of the South, violent repression left African Americans feeling abandoned by the Republican Party to which they had been so loyal.

"separate but equal" facilities for African Americans and whites on America's railroads. The Supreme Court thus put the finishing touches on the national retreat from Reconstruction.

Conclusion

Inspired by an idealized vision of a political economy based on free labor, Republicans expected emancipation to bring about a dramatic transformation of the South. Freed from the shackles of the "slave power," they thought, the entire region would soon become a shining example of democracy and prosperity. If the results were less than Republicans expected, the achievements of Reconstruction were nonetheless impressive. Across the South, African-American men and women carved out a space in which their families could live more freely than

CHRONOLOGY

1863 Lincoln's Proclamation of Amnesty and Reconstruction

1864 Wade-Davis Bill

1865 General Sherman's Special Field Order No. 15
Freedmen's Bureau established
Lincoln's second inaugural
Lincoln assassinated. Andrew Johnson becomes president.
General Howard's Circular 13
President Johnson orders the Freedmen's Bureau to return confiscated lands to former owners
Joint Committee on Reconstruction established by Congress.

1866 Congress renews Freedmen's Bureau; Johnson vetoes renewal bill
Civil Rights Act vetoed by Johnson
Congress overrides presidential veto of Civil Rights Act
Congress passes Fourteenth Amendment
Congress passes another Freedmen's Bureau Bill over Johnson's veto
Johnson begins "swing around the circle"
Republicans sweep midterm elections

1867 First and Second Reconstruction Acts
Tenure of Office Act

1868 Johnson fires Secretary of War Stanton
House of Representatives impeaches Johnson
Senate trial of Johnson begins
Acquittal of Johnson
Fourteenth Amendment ratified
Ulysses S. Grant wins presidential election

1869 Congress passes Fifteenth Amendment

1870 Fifteenth Amendment ratified

1872 "Liberal Republicans" leave their party
Grant re-elected

1873 Financial "panic" sets off depression

1875 "Mississippi Plan" succeeds
Civil Rights Act of 1875 enacted

1876 Disputed presidential election

1877 Electoral commission awards presidency to Rutherford B. Hayes

ever before. They established their own churches, sanctified their marriages by law, and educated their children. African-American men by the tens of thousands registered to vote and elected to office some of the most Democratic state legislatures of the nineteenth century. Voting with their feet, thousands more African-American workers repudiated an objectionable contract labor system in favor of an innovative compromise known as sharecropping. Furthermore, Reconstruction added three important amendments to the Constitution, amendments that transformed civil rights and electoral laws not only in the South but throughout the nation.

Nevertheless, the Republicans washed their hands of Reconstruction with unseemly haste. Instead of a shining example of prosperity, the political economy of sharecropping held the South in poverty and colonial dependency. Unable to attract capital investment from without, the "New South" was too poor to sustain an economic boom on its own. The Republicans also left the former slaves unprotected in a hostile world. Sharecropping offered them a degree of personal autonomy but little hope of real economic independence. Democratic redeemers excluded African Americans from the substance of power. Tired of the whole Reconstruction process, Americans turned their attention to the new and difficult problems of urban and industrial America.

Review Questions

1.   Why was the "Banks Plan" in Louisiana so controversial?

2.   What was the fate of the various efforts to redistribute southern land among the freed people?

3.   What was so "radical" about Radical Reconstruction?

4.   Why was Andrew Johnson impeached?

5.   How did Reconstruction affect the North?

6.   What were the major causes for the decline of Radical Reconstruction?

Further Readings

Michael Les Benedict, *The Impeachment and Trial of Andrew Johnson* (1973). Especially strong on the constitutional issues and highly critical of Andrew Johnson.

Dan T. Carter, *When the War Was Over: The Failure of Self-Reconstruction in the West* (1985). Reveals the weaknesses of Presidential Reconstruction.

W. E. B. DuBois, *Black Reconstruction in America, 1860–1880* (1935). This classic is one of the greatest American history books ever written.

Eric Foner, *Reconstruction: America's Unfinished Revolution.* The best one-volume treatment of the period.

John Hope Franklin, *Reconstruction: After the Civil War* (1961). The first modern treatment of African-American politics in the South.

Jacqueline Jones, *Labor of Love, Labor of Sorrow: Black Women, Work, and the Family from Slavery to the Present* (1985). This text includes a pioneering treatment of women's experience of Reconstruction.

Leon Litwack, *Been in the Storm So Long* (1979). This is a detailed and poignant treatment of the former slaves' first experience of freedom.

Roger Ransom and Richard Sutch, *One Kind of Freedom* (1977). The authors provide a clear picture of the breakup of the plantation system and the emergence of sharecropping.

Kenneth M. Stampp, *The Era of Reconstruction* (1965). Stampp gives a lucid overview of events in Washington, D.C.

Mark W. Summers, *The Era of Good Stealings* (1993). *Good Stealings* is a lively treatment of the corruption issue.

History on the Internet

"Finding Precedent: The Impeachment of Andrew Johnson"

http://www.andrewjohnson.com/

By examining the impeachment of President Andrew Johnson, this website explores the major issues behind the impeachment debate and describes the political factions vying to determine Reconstruction policy. The site employs the use of Reconstruction-era editorials and provides biographical sketches and portraits of many of the key figures involved.

"The Black Codes and Reaction to Reconstruction"

http://chnm.gmu.edu/courses/122/recon/code.html

This site contains the text of the Mississippi Black Code and other Reconstruction policies. The site also chronicles citizens' reactions to these policies through contemporary newspaper editorials, magazine articles, and congressional testimony, and it discusses the impact of these reforms on African Americans.

"Civil War and Reconstruction, 1861–1877: Reconstruction and Rights"

http://lcweb2.loc.gov/ammem/ndlpedu/features/timeline/civilwar/civilwar.html/recontwo/recontwo.html

In addition to a good overview of the Civil War and Reconstruction eras, read transcripts of oral histories from whites who actually experienced Reconstruction in the South. Their stories include eyewitness accounts of racially motivated violence in regard to African-American voting.

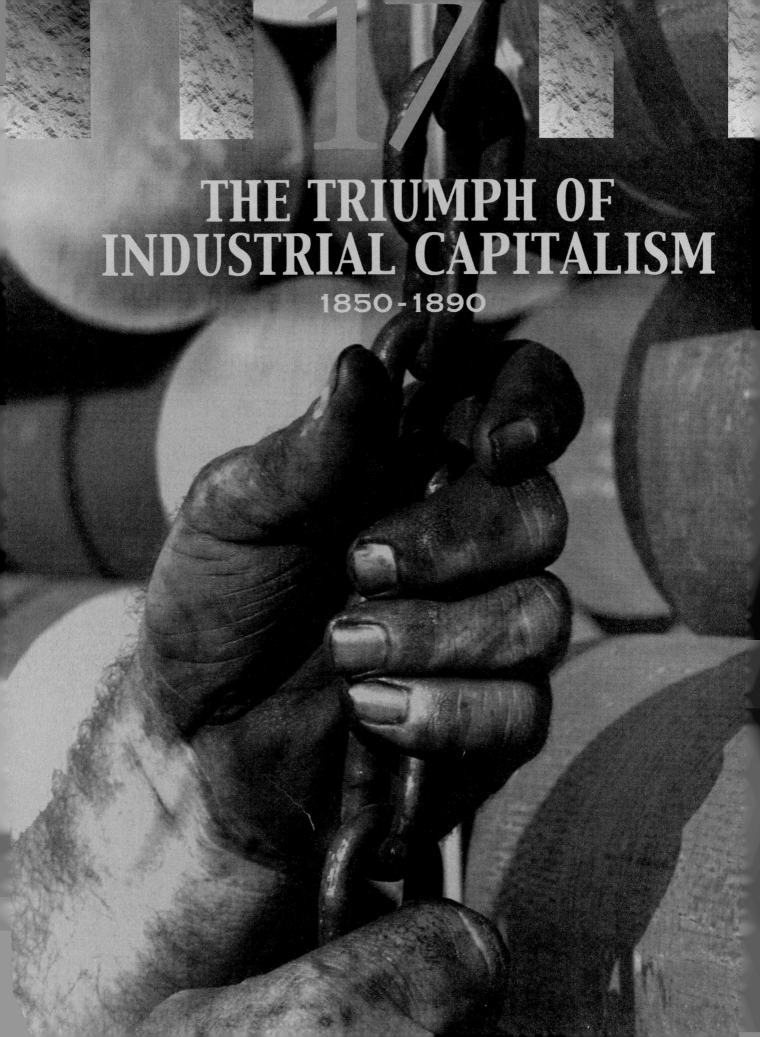

THE TRIUMPH OF
INDUSTRIAL CAPITALISM

1850-1890

OUTLINE

Rosa Cassettari

In 1884 Rosa Cassettari left her home in the Italian village of Cugiono, near Milan. Her mother had arranged for Rosa to marry a man named Santino, who was then working as a miner in Union, Missouri. Rosa was reluctant to go, especially because she had to leave behind her infant son. "It is wonderful to go to America even if you don't want to go to Santino," Rosa's friends told her at the train station in Milan. "You will get smart in America. And in America you will not be so poor." Along with millions of others, Rosa entered a swirling stream of migrants coming from the far corners of the European continent. She traveled first to Paris, then to Le Havre, where she waited six days before embarking on a ship for America. "All us poor people had to go down through a hole to the bottom of the ship," she remembered.

"There was a big dark room down there where we were going to sleep—the Italian, the German, the Polish, the Swede, the French—every kind." Rosa's ship hit a storm on its fourth day at sea, and the passengers in the hold were closed in for three days waiting for the weather to clear. By the time the doors were opened many of the passengers were sick, and two of them had died. Despite the difficulties of the voyage, the passengers dressed in their best clothes and stood silently on deck as the land of their dreams came into sight. "*America!* The country where everyone would find work! Where wages were so high that no one had to go hungry! Where all men were free and equal and where even the poor could own land!"

But Rosa's first taste of America did not live up to such dreams. In New York she was cheated out of her few dollars and was forced to make the long trip to Missouri with nothing to eat. When she arrived at the town of Union she found a shabby collection of tents and shacks occupied largely by fellow immigrants. She had known many of them since her childhood in Cugiono, and they made her entry into American culture a good deal easier than it might have been. Nevertheless, life in the mining camp lived up to her fears rather than her hopes. With no doctors or midwives available, Rosa gave birth to a premature child while she was all alone on the floor of her cabin. Santino turned out to be an abusive husband and a cruel father. Rosa had to supplement her husband's earnings by cooking meals for twelve additional miners.

Yet as she struggled to learn a new language and new customs, Rosa was impressed by many things about America. She noticed, for example, that poor people did not behave humbly in the presence of the rich. They sat in railroad cars together; they spoke to one another as "equals." Even in the difficult circumstances of the mining camp, Rosa became accustomed to wearing decent clothing and eating meat every day, things she could never do back in Europe. When she returned to Italy a few years later Rosa's family and friends were amazed by the changes in her. She was assertive in the presence of the authorities. She kept the oil lamps lit in the dark. She insisted on having rice for

dinner each night. "Whoever heard of such extravagance!" her relatives would cry. "The people in America make pigs of themselves. They are like pigs!" Rosa soon went back to America, but when she discovered that her husband planned to spend all their savings to open a house of prostitution, she separated from Santino. With the help of her immigrant friends from Missouri, Rosa moved to Chicago with her two children. She took a job at a place called Hull House where the social workers were so impressed by her life story that they wrote it down and published it as *Rosa Cassettari's Autobiography.*

Rosa was one of millions of men and women who were moving around the world in the late nineteenth century. This great human migration stretched from Japan and China to Brazil and Argentina, from Syria and Sicily to Hungary and Poland. Many migrants never left their native lands. They moved from the countryside to the city or from town to town in Europe, Asia, and Latin America. They moved from less developed regions to places where industrialization was well under way. But the nerve center for all of the movement was a powerful core of industrial capitalist societies, and at the center of the core was the United States of America. Migrants were on a worldwide trek, but more of them came to the United States than any other nation on earth.

Perpetual human migration, global in its extent, had become a hallmark of the political economy of industrial capitalism. Even within the United States there was

extraordinary movement. Common laborers moved from place to place because jobs were insecure and unsteady. Railroads hired armies of construction workers who had to move as the track was laid and had to find other work when the line was finished. African-American sharecroppers in the South moved from place to place at year's end. Over time they moved out of upcountry areas into cotton-growing districts, into towns and cities, or out of the South altogether. White tenant farmers moved into the mill towns that grew up along the southern Piedmont plateau. Native Americans were pushed off their lands throughout the trans-Mississippi West, making room for a dramatic flood of white settlers. And all across America the children of farmers abandoned the rural life: They went to small towns, to mill villages, and to huge cities like New York, Chicago, and Philadelphia—each of which had more than a million people by 1890.

They went looking for work. For many that meant buying a farm or opening a small shop. But for the majority of the people who moved around the world, finding a job meant going to work in the novel ways created by industrial capitalism. It meant working in cities and mill towns rather than the countryside and rural villages. It meant working in a bureaucracy under professional managers who controlled the work process. It meant working with new and ever more complicated machines. It meant working with polluted air, dirty rivers, or spoiled land. Most of all industrial capitalism meant wage labor. Working people had been freed from the political constraints that held them in place in earlier times and in different worlds. Feudal dues, slavery, even independent farming had tied people to the land in one way or another. But wage labor released men and women to move about from community to community, from country to country, and finally from continent to continent. In principle, wage earners could sell their labor power to the employer of their choice, changing jobs as they saw fit, or they could lose their jobs at the drop of a dime and find themselves back in the migratory stream. To watch Rosa Cassettari as she traveled from the factories of Cugiono to the mining camps of Missouri and the streets of Chicago is to witness one small part of a global process set in motion by the triumph of wage labor. ∎

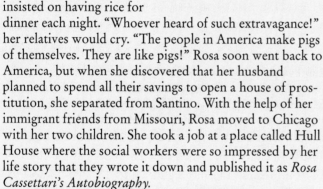

Immigrants arriving in America through New York harbor were often awed by the sight of the Statue of Liberty.

The Political Economy of Global Capitalism

The economic history of the late nineteenth century was sandwiched between two great financial panics, one in 1873 and the other in 1893. Both were followed by prolonged periods of high unemployment. Both led directly to tremendous labor unrest. The years between the two panics were marked by a general decline in prices that placed a terrible burden on producers. Farmers found that their crops were worth less at harvest time than they had been during planting season. They responded by expanding their enterprises to meet the worldwide demand for American agricultural products, only to find themselves vulnerable to the fierce competition of a global marketplace. Manufacturers fell into a vicious cycle of their own. To maintain profits they increased production, but the more they produced the lower their prices fell. In search of an inexpensive work force that could produce more for less, industrialists turned to an international labor market. Immigrants poured into America from around the world. So it was that amidst financial panics and nationwide strikes, severe depressions and sustained deflation, Americans passed through one of the most dramatic economic transformations in the history of the world. When it was over, the United States had become the leading capitalist nation on earth.

The "Great Depression" of the Late Nineteenth Century

On July 16, 1877, workers for the Baltimore and Ohio Railroad struck at Martinsburg, West Virginia. Within days the strike spread to the Pennsylvania Railroad, the New York Central, the Great Western, and the Texas Pa-

cific. The governors of ten states issued orders for the strikers to disperse. Four governors asked for federal assistance. The president issued two emergency proclamations. Federal troops were sent to Philadelphia, Baltimore, Chicago, and New York, but confrontations between workers and armed forces only fanned the flames of insurrection, until the entire economy seemed about to collapse. "Other workingmen followed the example of the railroad employees," explained Henry Demarest Lloyd, a prominent social critic. "At Zanesville, Ohio, fifty manufactories stopped work. Baltimore ceased to export petroleum. The rolling mills, foundries, and refineries of Cleveland were closed. . . . The grain and cattle of the farmer ceased to move to market, and the large centres of population began to calculate the chances of famine. . . . Merchants could not sell, manufacturers could not work, banks could not lend. The country went to the verge of a panic. . . ." Every part of the economy seemed connected to every other part, so that a strike by workers in one key industry now threatened the entire nation.

The railroad strike of 1877 was fueled by an economic depression that began in the United States with the Panic of 1873 (see chapter 16) and which spread throughout the developed world. As the U. S. economy slumped, German stocks fell by 60 percent. The number of immigrants who had arrived in New York—200,000 every year between 1865 and 1873—fell to under 65,000 in 1877. Although employment recovered in the 1880s, prices and wages continued to fall throughout most of the developed world. Then in 1893 another panic struck. Once again several major railroads went bankrupt. Before the year was out more than 500 banks and 15,000 businesses shut their doors. Once again the economic collapse was not confined to the United States. Indeed, from 1873 to 1896 a "Great Depression" blighted much of the globe. "Its most noteworthy peculiarity has been its universality," one observer pointed out. "It has been grievous in old communities like England and Germany, and equally so in Australia, South Africa and California which represent the new."

The world was shrinking, and most Americans knew it. Their economic well-being had become linked more closely than ever to global patterns of trade and migration. In 1866 a telegraph cable was laid across the Atlantic Ocean. From that moment on, Americans could read about events in Europe in the next morning's newspaper. Railroads seemed to slash the distances that separated eastern from western Europe, the East Coast from the West Coast of the United States. Steamships brought the far reaches of the world into swift and regular contact. Midwestern farmers sold their wheat in Russia. Florida growers sold their oranges in Italy. Chinese workers laid the tracks of the Union-Pacific Railroad. Eastern Europeans worked the steel mills of Pittsburgh. President Grant saw the hand of God at work. The "telegraph and steam have changed everything," he declared in 1873. "I rather believe

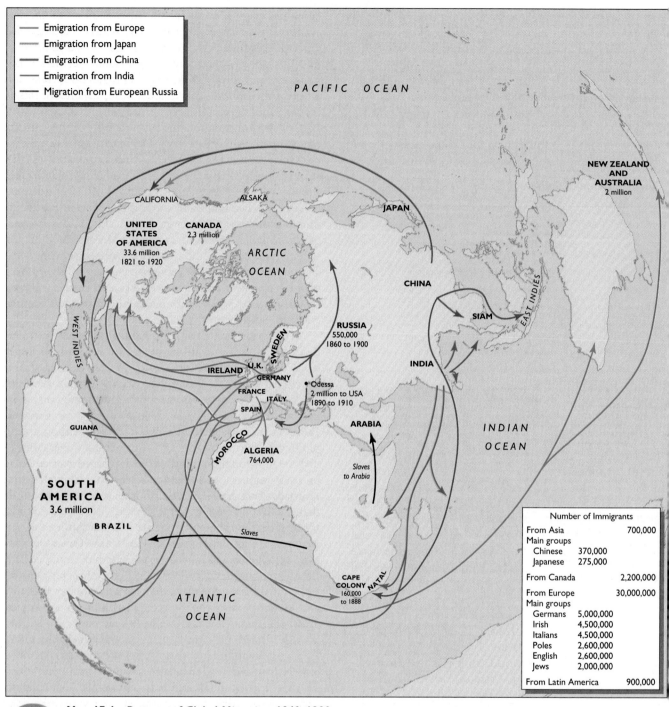

Number of Immigrants		
From Asia		700,000
Main groups		
Chinese	370,000	
Japanese	275,000	
From Canada		2,200,000
From Europe		30,000,000
Main groups		
Germans	5,000,000	
Irish	4,500,000	
Italians	4,500,000	
Poles	2,600,000	
English	2,600,000	
Jews	2,000,000	
From Latin America		900,000

Map 17-1   Patterns of Global Migration, 1840–1900.
Emigration was a global process by the late nineteenth century. But more immigrants went to the United States than to every other nation combined.
Source: London Times Atlas.

that the great Maker is preparing the world to become one nation, speaking one language. . . ." The Lord may not have been making one nation of the world, but the political economy of capitalism was certainly tying the world's nations together.

The clearest sign of this linkage was the emergence of an international labor market. As economic change swept through the less developed parts of the world, men and women were freed from their traditional ties to the land. Sicilian peasants and Plains Indians, Russian Jews and Chinese farmers were all hurled into a global stream of wage laborers. Irish women went to work as domestic servants of the new middle class. African Americans took jobs as porters on the expanding network of railroads. Wage laborers built and maintained the transportation network, the steel mills, and the petroleum refineries. Wage laborers slaughtered beef in Chicago and sewed ready-made clothing in factories along the southern Piedmont. Wage laborers stood behind the sales counters at department stores in Boston, New York, and Philadelphia. One measure of the triumph of wage labor was the way the "Great Depression" of the late nineteenth century was recognized. In earlier centuries economic collapse was registered in levels of starvation. After 1850 depression was measured in statistics on unemployment. It was also measured in the rates at which wage laborers moved from one place to another.

The Political Economy of Immigration

For most immigrants, setting foot in the United States was not the first experience of capitalism. On the contrary, nineteenth-century migrants tended to leave areas already in the grip of social and economic change. Rosa Cassettari, for example, had worked in a silk-weaving factory in Italy. At first, the largest numbers emigrated from the most developed nations, such as Great Britain and Germany. Later in the century, as industrial or agricultural revolution spread into eastern and southern Europe, growing numbers of immigrants came from the so-called "periphery": Scandinavia, Russia, Italy, and Hungary (see Map 17-1). As capitalism developed in these areas, small farmers were forced to produce for a highly competitive international market. The resulting upheaval eventually sent millions of rural folk into the worldwide migratory stream.

Improvements in transportation and communication were a sign that capitalism was spreading across the globe; they also made migration easier than ever. In 1856, more than 95 percent of immigrants came to America aboard sailing vessels. By the end of the century, more than 95 percent came in steamships. It became almost as easy to get to the United States from Eastern Europe as from England. The Atlantic crossing took one to three months on a sailing ship, but only 10 days on a steamship. The voyage was also far less painful. There was much less disease, and it was a lot cheaper. Beginning in the 1880s fierce competition among steamship lines dramatically lowered the cost of a transatlantic ticket. The quick voyage and the low prices made two-way movement easier. Like Rosa, increasing numbers of immigrants went back and forth across the Atlantic, particularly workers in seasonal trades like construction.

But economics alone will not explain the great migrations of the late nineteenth century. Economic change was often related to political upheaval. In China, for example, the Taiping rebellion of 1848 was accompanied by an economic disaster rivaling the Irish potato famine of the same decade. This combination of economic and political disruption sent some 300,000 Chinese to the Pacific Coast of North America between 1850 and 1882. They labored in mines and panned for gold, and large numbers of Chinese workers helped build the transcontinental railroad. The more successful Chinese immigrants settled their own farms or set up restaurants and other small businesses. But mostly the Chinese survived as poorly paid wage laborers. Desperate for employment and willing to work at miserably low rates, the Chinese soon confronted a wave of racist hostility from American and European workers. Union organizers in San Francisco argued that the Chinese threatened the "labor interests" of white workers. "They can never assimilate with us . . . their civilization is demoralizing to our people." In 1882 the U. S. Congress responded to such pressures by passing the Chinese Exclusion Act banning further immigration from China. But this did not stop Asian immigration completely. In 1885, the Japanese emperor lifted the ban on emigration from his country. A steady stream of Japanese migrated to Hawaii beginning in the late 1880s and 1890s. When the U. S. annexed the islands in 1898 Hawaii already had a substantial population of Japanese immigrants.

A similar combination of economic and political forces lay beneath European immigration to America. The revival of employment in the 1880s brought with it a revival of movement, particularly from Germany, Great Britain, and Scandinavia. After 1890 immigration from northern and western Europe fell off sharply, in large part because rapid capitalist development made labor scarce in those areas. But by then a familiar mixture of agrarian crisis and political disruption had set off a wave of emigration from eastern and southern Europe. In Austria-Hungary, for example, the revolution of 1848 brought with it basic economic and political changes that resulted, by the 1880s, in a profound agrarian crisis. A similar sequence of events took place in southern Italy. Once again political revolution sparked an economic transformation, leaving southern Italian farmers vulnerable to an increasingly global economy. Citrus fruits from Florida and California arrived on the international market in the 1880s. Protective tariffs thwarted the sale of Italian wines abroad. Late in the same decade, desperate farmers from southern Italy started coming to the United States.

Jewish immigration was propelled by a somewhat different combination of politics and economics. The catalyst for the great Jewish migration was the assassination of Czar Alexander II in 1881, which was followed by a surge of Russian nationalism. Anti-Jewish riots (called "pogroms") erupted in 1881–1882, 1891, and 1905–1906, during which countless Jews were viciously massacred. Anti-Semitic laws forced Russian Jews to live within the so-called "Pale of Settlement" along Russia's western and southern borders. The "May Laws" of 1882 severely restricted the ability of Russian Jews to worship, to own land, to work in industry and the professions, to get an education, or to work in government. In the 1880s, Russian Jews began moving to America in significant numbers.

They were joined by smaller groups of Syrians, Armenians, Greeks, Portugese, and Canadians.

Not all immigrants came to America intending to stay. Some hoped to make money and return to their homeland. But whether they intended to stay or not, most immigrants came to America looking for work. Some came with education and skills; some were illiterate. Most came with little more than their ability to work, and they usually found their jobs through a network of families, friends, and fellow immigrants. Letters from America told of high wages and steady employment. Communities of immigrant workers already in the United States provided the information and the connections that smoothed the entry of newcomers. As a result, immigrants clustered unevenly in different parts of the country. Large Scandinavian communities settled the upper Midwest, for example, whereas the Chinese were concentrated on the West Coast. Some immigrants settled directly on farms, but the overwhelming number lived in cities. To a very great extent, cities and immigrants were synonymous in the late nineteenth century. In 1890, when one in three Americans lived in a big city, two out of three immigrants were city dwellers.

America Moves to the City

"In the essentials of life," the writer Henry Adams wrote, "the boy of 1854 stood nearer the year one than to the year 1900." Adams was thinking in large part about cities. Between 1850 and 1900 the map of the United States was redrawn thanks to the appearance of dozens of new cities (see Figure 17-1). Of the 150 largest cities in the United States in the late twentieth century, 85 were founded in the second half of the nineteenth century. In 1850 the largest

city in the United States was New York, with a population of just over half a million. By 1900 New York, along with Philadelphia and Chicago, had more than a million residents. The people of the world were moving, and most of them were moving to cities. Chicago in the 1880s was "a giant magnet," Theodore Dreiser wrote in his novel, *Sister Carrie,* "drawing to itself from all quarters the hopeful and the hopeless."

The industrial city was different from its predecessors. By the middle of the nineteenth century the modern "downtown" was born, a place where people shopped and worked but did not necessarily live. Residential neighborhoods not only separated city dwellers from the downtown districts, they also separated the classes from one another. Streetcars and commuter railroads brought middle-class clerks and professionals from their homes to their jobs and back, but the fares were beyond the means of the working class. The rich built their mansions uptown, but working men and women had no choice but to remain within walking distance of their jobs.

As cities became more and more crowded they become notorious for being unsanitary and unsafe. Yellow fever and cholera epidemics were among the scourges of urban life in the nineteenth century. Fires periodically wiped out entire neighborhoods. For several days in October of 1871 much of the city of Chicago went up in flames. Along with fires and epidemics urban life was marred by poverty and crime. Beginning in New York in the 1880s, immigrants lived in a new kind of apartment building—the "dumb bell" tenement, five- or six-story walkups housing huge concentrations of city dwellers. Immigrant slums appeared in most major cities of America, as well as mill towns and mining camps from New England to Colorado. In 1890 Jacob Riis published *How the Other Half Lives,* his famous exposé of life in the immigrant slums of New York. He described a dark three-room apartment inhabited by six people. The "closeness and smell are appalling," Riis wrote. The two bedrooms were tiny, the beds nothing more than boxes filled with "foul straw." Such conditions were a common feature of urban poverty in the late nineteenth century.

Yet during these same years urban reformers set about to make city life less dangerous and more comfortable. Professional fire departments were formed in most big cities by the 1860s. Professional police departments appeared around the same time, greatly reducing the amount of urban violence. In 1866 New York City set up the first board of health. Ten years earlier, in the same city, a great urban landscape architect named Frederick Law Olmsted was given the job of creating a huge park in the center of Manhattan island. Central Park, Olmsted explained, would function as the "lungs of the city," providing New Yorkers with a respite from the trials of urban life.

Electricity changed city life almost as much as philanthropic reform projects. Thomas Edison, working out of

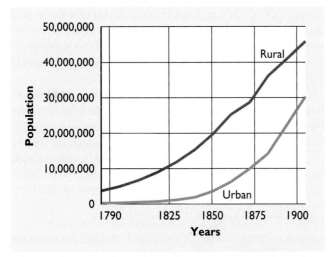

Figure 17-1   Proportion of Population Living in Cities, 1790–1900.
A growing proportion of Americans lived in cities. But not until the twentieth century did city dwellers outnumber rural Americans.

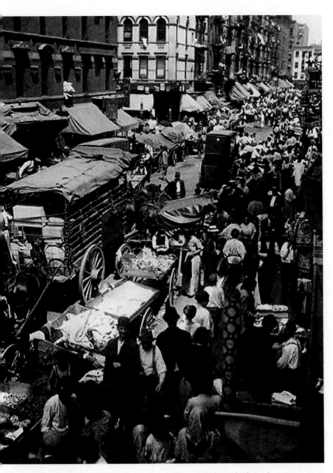

The lower east side of Manhattan, swollen with largely Jewish immigrants.

Whitman was not the only American to find hope in the American city. Annie Aitken, for example, moved from Scotland to Pittsburgh, Pennsylvania, in 1840 and almost immediately began urging her sister Margaret to join her. America is "far better for the working man," Aitken wrote. "In fact you seem to breathe a freer atmosphere here." The depression of the 1840s put a strain on Aitken's enthusiasm, and she sometimes warned her sister "not to come to America this soon." But by 1848 Aitken was prospering in the United States while her sister Margaret's family back in Scotland was sinking fast. Margaret's husband, Will, had been a traditional handloom weaver whose livelihood was destroyed by the rise of textile mills. "I can't get nae mair work," Will told his son in 1847. So the next year Will and Margaret Carnegie and their two sons, Tom and Andrew, left their home in Dunfermline, Scotland. With money borrowed from friends, the Carnegies moved to Pittsburgh. Annie Aitken let her sister's family live rent-free in a small house she owned. Her nephew, Andrew, took a job as a bobbin boy in a textile mill where he earned $1.20 a week. Fifty years later, Andrew Carnegie sold his steel mills to J. Pierpont Morgan for $480 million.

The Rise of Big Business

Before the Civil War very few businesses in the United States had more than one or two dozen employees. The largest factories in New England were not valued at even a million dollars. The only enterprises that could be called "big businesses" were the railroads. Indeed, railroads became the model for a new kind of business—big business—that emerged with startling speed after the Civil War, especially during the 1880s. In addition to railroads, the manufacturing and banking industries of the late nineteenth century produced businesses that were so huge that they dwarfed their largest antebellum counterparts. The massive, complex bureaucracies of big business were managed by professionals rather than owners. They were financed through a national banking system centered on Wall Street. They marketed their goods and services across the nation and around the world. Finally, big business generated wealth in staggering concentrations, giving rise to a class of men whose names—Carnegie, Rockefeller, Morgan, Vanderbilt, and others—became synonymous with American capitalism.

The Rise of Andrew Carnegie

Andrew Carnegie's career was hardly typical. He was an immigrant where most businessmen were native born. His childhood in Scotland was marked by something close to poverty, whereas most of America's leading men of business were born and raised in relative prosperity. Certainly

his laboratory in Menlo Park, New Jersey, had perfected the incandescent light bulb. He quickly established the Edison Illuminating Company, and in September 1882 electric lights generated by coal-burning power plants lit up several office buildings in New York City for the first time. Electricity eventually lit up the homes of ordinary urbanites as well, replacing dirty and dangerous gaslights and candles. And, of course, electricity lit up cities at night, giving them their recognizably modern signature.

In the second half of the nineteenth century American cities undertook the colossal task of making urban life decent and safe. To a large degree they succeeded: Cities provided their citizens with clean drinking water, transported them efficiently between home and work, and built great museums, impressive public libraries, and beautiful urban parks. And so the city, which the Jeffersonian tradition had long associated with corruption and decay, was increasingly defended as an oasis of diversity and excitement. Walt Whitman embraced "the splendor, picturesqueness, and oceanic amplitude and rush of these great cities." He welcomed the crowds, the colors, the noise of the city as "a continued exaltation and absolute fulfilment."

few working families in the late nineteenth century could hope to match Carnegie's spectacular climb from rags to riches. Even the company Carnegie built was unusually large. As late as 1900 the majority of American businesses were still small, family-owned concerns, and they generally catered to local or regional clients. Nevertheless, Andrew Carnegie was the perfect reflection of the most spectacular feature of American capitalism in the late nineteenth century, the rise of big business. In the course of his career Carnegie mastered the telegraph, railroad, petroleum, iron, and steel industries. He introduced modern management techniques and strict accounting procedures to American manufacturing. There were other great industrialists and financiers who made their mark in the last half of the nineteenth century—Henry Clay Frick, Collis P. Huntington, George M. Pullman, John D. Rockefeller, Cornelius Vanderbilt—but none of their careers touched as many aspects of big business as did Andrew Carnegie's. Also, none of their lives took on the mythic proportions of that of the poor young Scots lad who came to America at the age of twelve and ended up "the richest man in the world."

"I have made millions since," Carnegie once wrote, "but none of these gave me so much happiness as my first week's earnings." Young Andrew may have been happy to earn a wage, but he was not content with his job as a bobbin boy. Carnegie found the mill work difficult and tedious. He enrolled in a night course to study accounting, and a year later his uncle got Andrew a job as a messenger boy in a local telegraph office. So astute and hard working was Andrew that by 1851 he was promoted to a full time telegraph operator. In his dealings with the other operators Carnegie soon displayed the remarkable leadership ability that served him throughout his career. He recruited talented, hard-working men to the telegraph office and organized them with stunning efficiency.

The most successful businessmen in Pittsburgh were beginning to notice Carnegie's talents. One of them was Tom Scott, a superintendent for the Pennsylvania Railroad. In 1853, Scott offered Carnegie a job as his secretary and personal telegrapher. Carnegie accepted, and he stayed with the Pennsylvania Railroad for 12 years. It was a good time to work for the industry. Railroad construction

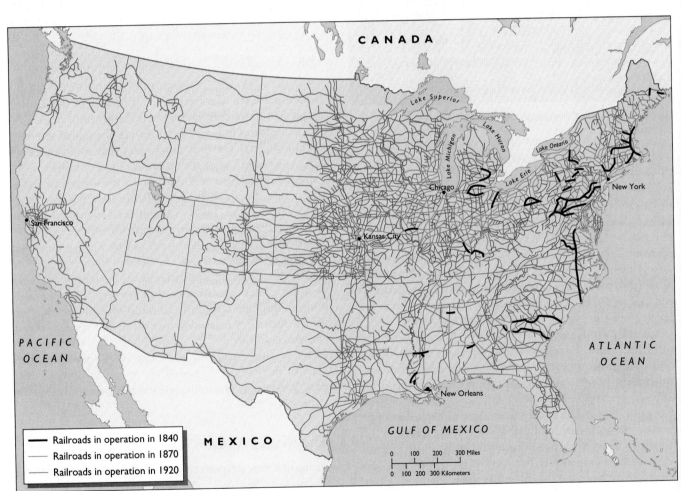

Map 17-2   The Growth of Railroads, 1850–1890.
Railroads were more than a means of transportation; they were also America's first "big business." Railroad management established the model for running huge industrial corporations, and the growth of railroads sustained the initial growth of the iron and steel industries.

oared during the 1850s, and it continued almost without interruption for several decades (see Map 17-2).

Railroads stood at the center of the booming industrial economy. They would become the steel industry's biggest customer. Petroleum refiners shipped their kerosene by rail. Mining corporations needed railroads to ship their coal and iron to power and steel plants. Ranchers shipped their cattle by rail to the slaughterhouses of Chicago, and from there meatpackers distributed butchered carcasses in refrigerated railroad cars. Thus his position at the Pennsylvania Railroad gave Carnegie an unrivaled familiarity with the structure and workings of big business.

By the mid-1850s no companies in America were as big as the railroads. By way of comparison, the largest factory in the country, the Pepperell Mills in Biddeford, Maine, employed 800 workers. In those same years the Pennsylvania Railroad had over 4,000 employees spread out over 3,500 miles of track. If the men who maintained the track fell down on the job, if an engineer arrived late, if a fireman came to work drunk, if a switchman missed his cue, if the telegrapher failed to dispatch the proper information, trains were wrecked, lives were lost, and business failed. So the railroads borrowed the disciplinary methods and bureaucratic structure of the military to ensure that the trains ran safely and on time. "What is required," explained David McCallum, the principal founder of the modern management system for the Erie Railroad, "is a rigid system of personal accountability through every grade of service."

The man who introduced this organizational discipline to the Pennsylvania Railroad was Tom Scott, the same man who hired Andrew Carnegie. Indeed, Scott hired Carnegie after concluding that the company needed to have its own telegraph system if it was to run reliably. J. Edgar Thomson, the Pennsylvania's president, was a pioneer of a different sort. He established an elaborate and efficient bookkeeping system that gave him and his superintendents detailed knowledge of every aspect of the Pennsylvania's operations. Scott used the statistics Thomson collected to reward managers who improved the company's profits and to eliminate those who failed.

Carnegie succeeded. After Scott was promoted to vice president in 1859, Carnegie took Scott's place as superintendent of the western division. Well versed in the Thomson-Scott methods of management, Carnegie helped make the Pennsylvania Railroad into a model of industrial efficiency. Even critics of the railroads were impressed. Charles Francis Adams conceded that the Pennsylvania was a "superb organization." By 1865 the Pennsylvania had 30,000 employees and a capital stock worth over $60 million. It had expanded its line east into New York City and west all the way to Chicago. It was the largest private company in the world.

Carnegie's experience at the Pennsylvania Railroad gave him a keen understanding of the modern financial system. Railroads dwarfed all previous business enterprises in the amount of investment capital they required and in the complexity of the financial arrangements that kept the railroads in business. Railroads benefited from direct subsidies by state and local governments and from huge land grants by the federal government. But these government resources served chiefly as collateral for private funding. Railroads were the first corporations to issue stocks through sophisticated trading mechanisms that attracted investors from around the world. To organize the market in such vast numbers of securities the modern investment house was developed. J. Pierpont Morgan joined with Drexel to form Drexel, Morgan and Company. It grew rich selling railroad stocks. The House of Morgan also prospered greatly from its close association with Andrew Carnegie, for there was no shrewder investor in all of America.

Carnegie Becomes a Financier

Carnegie began making money from money in 1856. On Tom Scott's advice Carnegie borrowed 600 dollars and invested it in Adams Express Company stock, which soon began paying handsome dividends. "It gave me the first penny of revenue from capital," Carnegie remembered, "something that I had not worked for with the sweat of my brow." He had become a successful capitalist, and for the next 15 years he made a series of financial moves that earned him several more fortunes.

Carnegie invested in the Woodruff Sleeping Car Company in the late 1850s and, a decade later, used his shares and his influence to help win George Pullman near-monopoly control of the industry—and make Carnegie millions in the bargain. Carnegie had brokered a similar deal that created the Western-Union monopoly of the nation's telegraph industry. He invested in an Oil Company in western Pennsylvania and demonstrated that strict management would produce steadier profits than reckless speculation. He made shady deals playing the international financial markets in London; he made millions selling worthless bonds to naïve German investors. More substantially, he created the Keystone Bridge Company, which built the first steel arch bridge over the Mississippi River and provided the infrastructure for the Brooklyn Bridge over New York's East River. With Keystone's success Carnegie perfected a model of managerial organization that was the envy of the industrial world.

"I have never bought or sold a share of stock speculatively in my life," Carnegie later wrote. It was not the first time he lied about his business dealings. Nevertheless, by 1872, Carnegie was tired of financial speculation and ready for something new. He was 37 years old and had proven himself a master of the railroad industry, a brilliant bureaucratic manager, and a shrewd financial manipulator. He had made unheard-of sums of money trading telegraph

The steel arches of the St. Louis Bridge across the Mississippi River were both an engineering marvel and a triumph of Andrew Carnegie's managerial skills.

lines, digging oil wells, and building bridges. Now Carnegie wanted to create an industry of his own. "My preference was always for manufacturing," he explained. "I wished to make something tangible." He would make iron and steel.

Carnegie Dominates the Steel Industry

Carnegie had been investing in the iron business since 1861, but he did not become actively involved until 1865, when he acquired a controlling interest in the Union Iron Company. Carnegie's first goal was to speed the flow of materials to his Keystone Bridge Company. This was an important innovation. Iron manufacturing in America had always been decentralized. Each stage of the production process was handled by a different manufacturer. Merchants moved the product at every stage of its development, from recently mined ore to the final sale of the finished iron. But Carnegie forced Union Iron and Keystone Bridge to coordinate their operations, thereby eliminating middlemen and making the production process more efficient.

More important, Carnegie forced Union Iron to adopt the managerial techniques and accounting practices he had learned at the Pennsylvania Railroad. By keeping a strict account of all costs, Carnegie was able to locate the most wasteful points in the production process and to isolate and reward the most efficient workers at his plant. Because he knew exactly what his costs were, Carnegie figured out that his iron mill would be more profitable if he invested in the most expensive new equipment. He shocked his British

competitors by running his furnaces at full blast, wearing them out after only a few years, and replacing them with still more modern machines. The managers and workers at Union Iron resented and resisted Carnegie's innovations. But Carnegie's will was stronger than the iron he produced. In the end his great achievement as an entrepreneur was his introduction of modern management techniques to American industry, but it was in steel rather than iron that Carnegie would prove the worth of those techniques.

As with so many industries, the development of steel was driven by the development of railroads. Traditional iron rails deteriorated rapidly, and as trains grew larger and heavier, iron withered under the load. J. Edgar Thomson, Carnegie's ultimate boss at the Pennsylvania Railroad, began experimenting with steel rails in 1862 and was soon persuaded of their superiority. Steel was also a better material with which to construct locomotives, boilers, and railroad cars themselves. In the 1860s two developments cleared the path for the transition from iron to steel. First, Henry Bessemer's patented process for turning iron into steel became available to American manufacturers. Second, iron ore began flowing freely onto the American market from deposits in northern Michigan.

Andrew Carnegie was uniquely situated to take advantage of these developments. His experience with Union Iron taught him how to run a mill efficiently, and he had access to the substantial investment capital that steel manufacturing required. So in 1872 Carnegie organized his wealthy friends around Pittsburgh and came up with the money to build a brand new steel mill, the Thompson Works. Within a few years Carnegie bought out most of his original partners and had a controlling interest in the company. Despite a worldwide depression the steel mill was profitable from the start.

One of the great sources of Carnegie's success was his personal acquaintance with the presidents of nearly every railroad in America. In the past, for example, Carnegie had helped out Collis P. Huntington, president of the Southern Pacific Railroad, and Huntington returned the favor with orders for Carnegie steel. When the Union-Pacific opened up bidding for 70,000 tons of steel rails, Carnegie got the company's president, another friend, to promise Carnegie the order at the lowest bid that came in.

Carnegie knew he could make a profit on the lowest bid because he was fanatic about controlling costs. He did this in two ways. First, he continually reinvested the company's profits into the most modern equipment and the most efficient techniques. Before anyone else in the busi-

Andrew Carnegie won the bid to provide much of the steel for the construction of the Union-Pacific railroad. Here Chinese workers are pictured laying the tracks at Promontory Point, Utah, in 1869.

ness, for example, Carnegie scrapped all of his Bessemer furnaces, knowing that in the long run the lower cost of the open-hearth process would prove more profitable. Second, Carnegie subjected every operation and every employee, from the highest-paid manager to the lowest-paid worker, to constant scrutiny of his productivity. "There goes that _____ bookkeeper," one worker complained. "If I use a dozen bricks more than I did last month, he knows it and comes round to ask why." As a result, when the Thomson Works opened, it was able to produce steel at lower prices than any other mill in the world. Because Carnegie knew exactly how much a ton of steel cost, he knew exactly how low he could price his products. "Watch the costs," he said, "and the profits will take care of themselves."

Big Business Consolidates

Not all enterprises became "big businesses" in the late nineteenth century. Businesses that sold their products locally (such as flour mills, sawmills, bakers, and brickmakers) remained small-scale operations. In other industries, such as textiles and agricultural equipment, the average size of the factory got much bigger with no major change in manufacturing technique or administrative structure. But "big businesses" were different. They sold their goods and services nationally and even internationally. They were so

big that they required huge investments of capital that could only be managed by big new investment houses.

In the late nineteenth century the names of a handful of wealthy capitalists became closely associated with different industries: Gustavus Swift in meatpacking, John D. Rockefeller in oil refining, Collis P. Huntington in railroads, J. P. Morgan in financing, and of course Andrew Carnegie in steel (see Map 17-3). These powerful individuals, sometimes called "Robber Barons," were actually part of a passing phase in the history of American enterprise. Most big businesses were so big that no single individual or family could own them, much less run them. Thus one of the things that made big business different (even from most factories) was that they were run by a growing army of professionally trained managers who did not actually own the companies they ran. With big business the highest profits went to those companies that maintained the most efficient bureaucracies. And because they were so big, because the equipment was so expensive, they had to be kept in operation continuously. Railroads never shut down. Blast furnaces were never turned off.

An average factory could respond to an economic slowdown by closing its doors for a while, but big businesses could not afford to do that. There was too much expensive equipment, too much sunk capital, too many trained professionals. Beginning in the 1880s big businesses developed several strategies designed to shield them

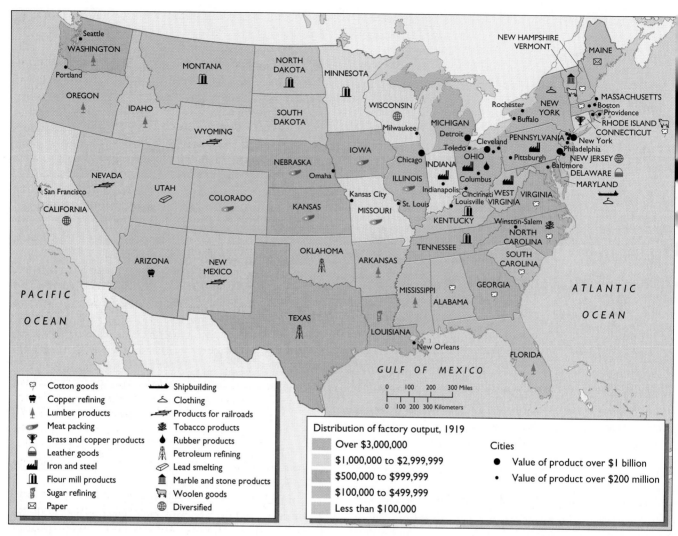

Map 17-3 *Major American Industries c. 1890.*
An industrial map of the late nineteenth century America shows regions increasingly defined not by their crops but by their major industries.

from the effects of ruinous competition. The most common strategy was "vertical integration," the attempt to control as many aspects of a business as possible, from the production of raw materials to the sale of the finished product. One of the most spectacular examples of this was Gustavus Swift's integration of the production and distribution of fresh meat to American consumers. Swift integrated the meatpacking business from the point of slaughter *forward* to the point of sale. Carnegie integrated the steel industry from the point of production forward to the distribution of steel but also *backward* to the extraction of iron ore. He bought iron mines to produce his own ore and railroads to ship the ore to his mills and the finished product to market. His Keystone Bridge Company then purchased the steel. In 1881 Carnegie formed a partnership with Henry Clay Frick, the nation's leading producer of coke, thus assuring Carnegie of a steady supply of the fuel needed to heat his furnaces.

In 1882 John D. Rockefeller devised a new solution to the problem of ruinous competition by forming the Standard Oil Trust. Rockefeller had entered the oil business in Cleveland, Ohio, in 1863, founding Standard Oil four years later. Like Carnegie, Rockefeller surrounded himself with the best managers and financiers to build and run the most efficient modern refineries, but he was more willing than Carnegie to use ruthless tactics to wipe out his competitors. Having extracted preferential shipping rates from the railroads, Rockefeller gained a critical advantage in the savagely competitive oil business. In 1872 Rockefeller began trying to impose over the national oil refining industry the same order and control that he had already achieved in Ohio. As president of the National Refiner's Association he formed cartels with the major operators in New York and Pennsylvania as well as Ohio. But the cartels were too weak to keep independent producers and refiners from going it alone.

Rockefeller set out to take control of the entire oil industry by merging all of the major companies together under the control of Standard Oil. By 1879 the Standard Oil monopoly was largely in place, but it was not until 1882 that it was formalized as a trust. The "trust" was an elaborate legal device by which different producers came together under the umbrella of a single company which could police competition internally. In 1889 the New Jersey legislature passed a general incorporation law that made it possible for corporations based in that state to form holding companies that basically controlled companies in other states. Thus the trust gave way to the "holding company," with Standard Oil of New Jersey as its most prominent example. Within a decade many of the largest industries in America were dominated by one or two massive holding companies.

Rockefeller's Standard Oil monopoly became one of the most notorious examples of how big business had changed the face of the American economy. Rockefeller himself came to represent a powerful new class of extraordinarily wealthy businessmen and financiers. Their names—Carnegie, Rockefeller, Morgan, Harriman, and others—soon became associated with the wealthy families that formed the upper class of the new social order of industrial America.

A New Social Order

Classes were not supposed to exist in the United States the way they existed in Europe, as many Americans continued to believe in the late nineteenth century. "It is commonly asserted that there are in the United States no classes, and any allusion to classes is resented," wrote the prominent sociologist William Graham Sumner in 1883. And yet, he pointed out, the reality of class divisions was so obvious that it had become a normal part of public discussion. "We constantly read and hear discussions of social topics in which the existence of social classes is assumed as a simple fact." Indeed, it was hard not to notice the conspicuous gap between the astonishing wealth of men like Andrew Carnegie and the daily struggles of women like Rosa Cassettari.

Lifestyles of the Very Rich

When Cornelius Vanderbilt died in 1877 he was 10 times as wealthy as John Jacob Astor, who had been the wealthiest man in America before the Civil War. Between 1850 and 1890 the 4,000 richest families in America grew richer than ever. Their proportion of the nation's wealth nearly tripled. At the very top of the social pyramid rested some 200 families worth more than 20 million dollars each. Their names became synonymous with the biggest industries of the late nineteenth century: Carnegie Steel, Huntington's South-

ern Pacific, Rockefeller's Standard Oil, and the House of Morgan. Concentrated in the Northeast, especially in New York, these families were known throughout America and the world for their astonishing wealth. Spread more evenly across America were the several thousand millionaires whose investments in cattle ranching, agricultural equipment, mining, commerce, and real estate boosted them into the ranks of wealthy capitalists.

As a group America's millionaires had a lot in common. Most traced their ancestry to Great Britain. Most were Protestant, usually Episcopalians, Presbyterians, or Congregationalists. By the standards of their day they were unusually well educated. Half of Baltimore's business elite had been to college, at a time when fewer than one in 10 Americans reached high school. Except in the South, America's upper class voted Republican.

After 1850 the upper class began shipping its sons off to elite boarding schools. St. Paul's, which opened its doors in Concord, New Hampshire, in 1856, became the model. It combined Protestant piety and a classical curriculum with rigorous physical education and rural splendor. St. Paul's set the standard to be copied or repudiated. By 1900 a host of similarly elite boarding schools (among them Lawrenceville, Groton, Deerfield Academy, Hotchkiss, and Choate) sprang up all across the Northeast. Yet for all their training in the Victorian virtue of rigorous self-discipline, wealthy Americans moved away from the middle-class restraint of their parents. By the turn of the century social critics were denouncing the "conspicuous consumption" of the very rich.

The upper classes lived in spectacular houses in neighborhoods that became famous for their wealthy residents. Elaborate mansions lined Fifth Avenue in Manhattan, ran up and down Nob Hill in San Francisco, surrounded Rittenhouse Square in Philadelphia, and filled in Boston's Back Bay. Wealthy suburbs (Brooklyn Heights, Philadelphia's Main Line, and Brookline, Massachusetts) acquired similar reputations as privileged retreats. Further away from the cities, the richest families built rural estates that rivalled the country homes of England and the chateaus of France. Newport, Rhode Island, had long been a watering hole for America's wealthy, but in the late nineteenth century the richest families built a string of spectacular summer homes along the Newport shoreline.

Fine homes and impressive mansions were merely the showcases for some of the more conspicuous acts of consumption undertaken by the upper class of the late nineteenth century. For several years leading figures in New York's high society competed with one another to see who could stage the most lavish costume balls and the most expensive dinner parties, with the largest and most elite list of invited guests. The competition reached a climax of sorts on March 26, 1883, when Mrs. William Vanderbilt staged a stupendous costume ball that challenged Mrs. William Astor's long-standing position as the queen of New York's upper class. Mrs. Astor, who had previously snubbed the

The homes of the industrial rich were huge by comparison with their predecessors. Pictured here is the immense Biltmore Estate outside Asheville, North Carolina. Constructed by railroad titan Cornelius Vanderbilt in the late 1800s, Biltmore had 255 rooms and required a railroad of its own to bring the construction materials to the building site.

newly rich Vanderbilt, made a tactful retreat. The ball was a great success. All of New York society turned out at the magnificent Vanderbilt mansion where the hostess made a grand entrance dressed as a Venetian princess.

It was left to the new middle class to preserve the traditional virtues of thrift and self-denial.

The Consolidation of the New Middle Class

In 1889 *The Century Dictionary* introduced the phrase "middle class" for the first time in the United States. Americans had talked for generations of "the middling sort" and "the middle ranks" of society. But *middle class* was a modern term. Its appearance in 1889 reflected a novel awareness that American society had become permanently divided in a way that earlier generations had stoutly denied. Yet even as the middle class grew increasingly aware of its own existence, defining the boundaries of the middle class world became increasingly difficult. One reason was that the boundaries were shifting.

For many Americans, professionals were the backbone of the new middle class that emerged in the nineteenth century. Architects, teachers, and lawyers followed a path familiar to most professions after 1850. They defined what it meant to be a member of their tribe, organized themselves into professional associations, and set educational standards for admission. By these means professionals could command high salaries and enjoy a

standard of living and a level of prestige unavailable to most Americans. Scholarly journals established new standards of professional respectability, as did professional organizations like the American Medical Association (1847) and the American Bar Association (1878). Between 1870 and 1890 some 200 societies were formed to establish the educational requirements and maintain the credentials of their members. In 1870 a single year of study was considered adequate to practice law in most places. Thirty years later it took three years to earn a law degree. In colleges and universities the Ph. D. became the new standard of excellence for training the leading scholars in various fields. Even the management of corporations became a professional occupation. Business schools appeared in the late nineteenth century to train professionals in the science of accounting and the fine art of management. Sometimes professionals succeeded in having their standards written into law. In most states by 1900 a doctor without a license could no longer treat patients and lawyers who had not passed the bar exam could no longer take clients.

Behind the professional managers who ran the industrial and financial bureaucracies of the late nineteenth century marched an expanding white-collar army of cashiers, clerks, and government employees. They were overwhelmingly men; women did not yet dominate the sales forces in department stores or the secretarial staffs of business and government bureaucracies. Through the end of the century these white-collar workers earned annual incomes far beyond those of independent craftsmen and factory workers. And they enjoyed much better opportunities for upward mobility. A beginning clerk might make only $100 a year, but within five years the salary could be closer to $1,000 annually. In Boston, a quarter of the people who were clerical workers in 1870 would become independent businessmen by 1885. At a time when the average annual income of a skilled factory worker in Philadelphia was less than $600, over 80 percent of the male clerks in the Treasury Department earned over $1,200 a year.

As if to clarify matters, the middle class withdrew from the messy uncertainties of the central city. As cities improved their roads and built mass-transit systems, they made it easier than ever for middle-class families to move away. These families initially fled the central cities to escape the extremes of great wealth and miserable poverty. As the decades passed, however, the suburbs took on a lure of their own. Middle-class residents idealized the physical advantages of trees, lawns, and gardens, as well as the comfortable domestic life that suburbs afforded. By 1900, one of the sharpest markers of middle-class status was a home in a respectable neighborhood or suburb, away from the rigors of life in the central city.

Only the most successful craftsmen matched the incomes and suburban lifestyles of white-collar clerks.

Butchers might earn over $1,600 annually, for example, but shoemakers averaged little more than $500 a year. A shoemaker who owned his own tools and ran a small shop maintained the kind of independence that was long cherished among middle-class Americans, yet his income scarcely distinguished him from skilled factory workers. The manual crafts were therefore a bridge between the remnants of the independent middle class and the growing industrial working class made up of men and women like Rosa Cassettari.

The Industrial Working Class Comes of Age

"When I first went to learn the trade," John Morrison told a congressional committee in 1883, "a machinist considered himself more than the average workingman; in fact he did not like to be called a workingman. He liked to be called a *mechanic*." Morrison put his finger on one of the great changes in the political economy of nineteenth-century America. Before the Civil War urban workingmen were most often referred to as artisans and mechanics. "Today," Morrison explained, the mechanic "is simply a laborer." Big businesses often replaced mechanics with semi-skilled or unskilled factory laborers. Andrew Carnegie, for example, made his steel mills so productive by using

In the hierarchy of industrial wage laborers, women were the lowest paid and the least skilled. Pictured here are female workers welding metal parts in a crowded factory.

WHERE THEY LIVED, WHERE THEY WORKED

Mining Camps of the West

Rosa Cassettari's experience in the mining camps of Missouri was not unique. But it is overshadowed by the more famous mining camps of California and the Far West. Mining fever began in 1848 when James Marshall discovered gold close to John Sutter's mill on the American River near what is now Sacramento, California. Thousands of prospectors poured into California during the 1850s, panning for gold wherever rumors of a vein hit, pulling up stakes and generating boomtowns and ghost towns with dizzying speed. "Every few days news would come of the discovery of a brand-new mining region," Mark Twain wrote from California. "Immediately the papers would teem with accounts of its richness, and away the surplus population would scamper to take possession." Eventually word of new discoveries pulled prospectors eastward from California. Tens of thousands of miners flooded into Colorado in 1859. Meanwhile prospectors in Nevada discovered the largest single vein in American history, the Comstock Lode,

which would yield 350 million dollars worth of gold and silver during the 1860s and 1870s alone. Similar rushes transformed parts of Idaho in 1862 and Montana in 1864.

Western mining camps were extraordinary places. They were peopled by settlers from a variety of different backgrounds. In the gold country camps on the western slope of the Sierra Nevada, native-born Yankees lived among British subjects, Chinese immigrants, Mexicans, Spaniards, and African Americans. This was a male-dominated world of violence, vigilantism, and multicultural interaction. Alone or in small groups they would pan for gold in the beds of the rivers and streams that poured out of the Sierra Nevada Mountains. This was known as placer mining. Once the surface gold had been captured, miners would shovel dirt into boxes or sluices to capture gold and silver by running water over it. Only a few miners struck it rich this way, although their stories captured the imaginations of thousands.

An idealized image of mining country as a paradise. In time, the individual miners shown here were displaced by huge mining corporations.

Marcus Daly, for example, came to America as a penniless Irish immigrant and struck it rich in the gold fields of California. But his biography says less about the prospects for success among individual miners than it does about the larger transformation in the mining frontier. With the wealth he accumulated on his own, Daly persuaded a group of San Francisco investors to back his plans to dig a silver mine deep into the ground at Butte, Montana. They did not find silver, but they did strike one of the largest veins of copper in the world. The Anaconda mine made Daly and his partners rich, but it also symbolized the changes that had taken place in western mining. Daly became the supervisor of a large group of engineers and wage laborers. Anaconda extracted and smelted its own ore then shipped its high-grade copper around the world to cities and industries anxious to harness the power of electricity that was transmitted across copper wires. By 1883 the United States was the largest producer of copper on earth.

The world of the placer miners disappeared almost as quickly as it arose. As the years passed the miners moved from west to east, into and then across the Sierra Nevada, following the news of new strikes in Idaho, Montana, Nevada, and Colorado. But as the surface riches were quickly snapped up, the remaining veins of gold and silver proved too deep for any one prospector to reach. It took heavy machines to get at the ore buried deep underground, and machinery required capital investments beyond the means of most miners. Most of the wealth taken from the Comstock mines, for example, was extracted by corporations using powerful tools to dig deep into the earth. So mining corporations steadily bought up the settlers' claims and created a more permanent industrial presence in the western states. Mark Twain's experience was typical: Having gone out to prospect for gold on his own, he ended up selling his labor for wages. "I went to work as a common laborer in a quartz mill," he explained, "at ten dollars a week and board."

A mining crew drifting for gold in Deadwood, Dakota Territory, 1876.

more-sophisticated machines and less-skilled workers. For traditional mechanics, this felt like downward mobility. The mechanic once "felt he belonged in the middle class," Morrison explained, "but today he recognizes the fact that he is simply the same as any other ordinary laborer, no more and no less."

Yet few of the men and women who worked in the factories and mills of industrial America had ever been artisans or mechanics. Most factory operatives and common laborers entered the workplace as migrants (or children of migrants) from the small towns and farms of the American or European countryside. Few, therefore, experienced automated shoemaking or the mass production of clothing as a degradation of their traditional skills, the way John Morrison did. But most migrants did experience industrial labor as a harsh and disciplined existence. Factory operatives worked long hours in difficult conditions performing repetitious tasks with little security that the job would be there the next day.

Within the working class factory operatives were more fortunate than most, although their working lives were neither secure nor prosperous. The clothing industry is a good example. The introduction of the sewing machine in the 1850s gave rise to sweatshops where work was radically subdivided into simple, repetitive tasks. Operatives were organized into distinct units. One group produced collars for men's shirts, another produced cuffs, and yet another stitched the parts together. Each group had its own internal hierarchy, and the entire unit operated within a larger bureaucracy. In all such industrial organizations, jobs were defined to ensure that anyone occupying a position could be easily replaced by someone else. Factory operatives learned this lesson quickly in the late nineteenth century. They were young; often they were women or children who moved into and out of different factory jobs with astonishing frequency. But even among men, factory work was at best unsteady. The business cycle swung hard and often in the late nineteenth century, leaving few factory operatives with the luxury of secure, long-term employment.

At the bottom of the hierarchy of wage earners were the common laborers. Their trademark was physical exertion rather than carefully honed skills or the ability to operate complicated machinery. Their numbers grew throughout the century until by 1900 common laborers accounted for perhaps a third of the industrial work force. Most often they found work in the businesses that were becoming the most highly bureaucratized. Hundreds of thousands of common laborers went to work for railroads and steel companies. Before Andrew Carnegie and his competitors revolutionized their industry, for example, no more than 20 percent of iron and steel workers were common laborers. By the 1890s 40 percent of steel workers were common laborers. In the construction industry the number of common laborers rose by over 400 percent between 1870 and 1910.

Common laborers were the most difficult to organize into effective unions. A large proportion of them were immigrants and African Americans, and ethnic differences and language barriers often frustrated the development of workers' alliances. Even the kind of work common laborers performed inhibited the growth of effective unions. It was rarely steady work. Women often toiled in low-paying jobs for a few years before they married and had children. The men who laid the railroad tracks or dug the canals and subway tunnels generally moved on when they finished. Common labor was often seasonal: Work on the docks slowed down during the winter months, as did construction. As a result many unskilled workers had to change jobs over the course of a typical year. Common laborers were unusually mobile and easily replaceable, and they increasingly came from parts of the world where the idea of organized labor was unknown. They benefited most from labor unions, but they had the most trouble organizing. They often had shallow roots in the community, while community support was crucial to successful labor organization. Even when they did organize, common laborers faced the biggest, most powerful, most effectively organized corporations in the country.

A great deal of the wage work done by women fell into the category of common labor. In 1900 women accounted for nearly one of every five gainfully employed Americans. They stood for hours behind the counters at fancy new department stores; young Irish women went to work as domestics in northern middle-class homes. In the South, servants were so common in middle-class homes that at the turn of the century there were more African-American domestics working in the city of Atlanta than there were white households. A smaller proportion held white-collar jobs, often as teachers and nurses but more commonly as low-paid clerical workers and sales clerks.

The same hierarchy that favored men in the white-collar and professional labor force existed in the factories and sweatshops of industrial America. In the clothing industry, for example, those units dominated by male workers were higher up the chain of command than those dominated by women. Indeed, as the textile industry became a big business, more and more jobs went to men. During the second half of the nineteenth century the proportion of women working in textile mills steadily declined. The reverse trend was beginning to appear among white-collar workers. As department stores like R. H. Macy & Company expanded in the 1870s and 1880s, they hired a growing number of low-paid women, often Irish immigrants, with none of the prospects for promotion still available to men. White-collar work was not a signal of middle-class status for women, as it was for most men in the late nineteenth century.

The story was somewhat different for married women and their children. In the decades after the Civil War as few as one in 50 working-class wives and mothers took jobs outside the home. Women periodically supplemented the family income by taking in boarders or doing laundry. Most often, however, working-class families survived by sending their children into the workplace. Even in the families of the highest paid industrial workers, 50 percent of the children went to work. Among the poorest working-class families, three out of four children earned wages to supplement the father's income. Child labor was one of the clearest class distinctions of the late nineteenth century. The rich sent their daughters to finishing schools and their sons to elite boarding schools; middle-class parents sent their children to public schools. By contrast, working-class families sent their sons and daughters to work. This was especially true in the South, where sharecropping was becoming a form of wage labor.

Sharecropping Becomes Wage Labor

As the southern economy had recovered from the devastation of the Civil War many observers predicted a bright future for the region. Optimists saw a wealth of untapped natural and human resources, a South freed from the constraints of an inefficient slave labor system ripe for investment, brimming with opportunities, and ready to go. Edward Deleon, one of the region's greatest boosters, argued in 1870 that a "New South" had taken "the seat of the dethroned king, exhibiting a lustier life, and the promise of greater growth and strength, than did its predecessor." Spokesmen for this "New South" rejected any nostalgia for antebellum slave society. Occasionally they even argued that, in retrospect, the destruction of slavery was a good and necessary thing for the South. Everywhere they looked they saw compelling evidence that southerners stood on the threshold of unprecedented prosperity.

Talk of this sort was not complete fantasy. In an age when Americans were building railroads at an exuberant clip, southerners built them faster, laying tracks so enthusiastically that by 1890 nine out of 10 southerners lived in a county with a railroad. By then impressive steel mills were coming to life in Birmingham, Alabama. The Piedmont plateau (running along the eastern foothills of the Appalachian Mountains from Virginia to Georgia) was dotted with textile mills bigger and more efficient than any of New England's. Southerners were on the move, migrating from the countryside to the towns, expanding the production of cotton into new areas, bringing the rich soil of the Mississippi Delta under cultivation. All of this impressed people like Henry W. Grady, the preeminent spokesman for the New South. "What a pull it has been!" he declared in 1889. Having passed "through the ashes and desolation of war.... The ground has been prepared—the seed put in—the tiny shoots tended past the danger-point—and the day of the mighty harvest is here!" For ordinary southerners, especially African Americans, there was no mighty harvest to be found amidst the general poverty of the New South.

After the war African Americans had to return to work on land they did not own (see chapter 16). The master-slave relationship had been destroyed, but in its place emerged a new labor relationship between landlords and sharecroppers. Between the landlords and croppers, supplying the credit that kept the system alive, there arose a new and powerful class of merchants. At the beginning it was unclear how much power the landlords, the merchants, and the sharecroppers each had. The most important question was who owned the cotton crop at the end of the year. Was it the sharecropper who produced it? Was it the landlord who owned the farm? Or was it the merchant who loaned the supplies needed to survive until the crop came in? The answer would be decided in the state legislatures where the credit laws were written and in the state courts where the laws were interpreted. In such laws and cases the political economy of the New South was defined.

By the late 1870s, the Republican Party had collapsed in much of the South. Democrats had taken power in most of the former Confederate states, and they would resolve the labor question in the courts and legislatures they dominated. The resolution came swiftly and was legally complete by the middle of the 1880s. First the courts defined a sharecropper as a wage laborer. The landlord therefore owned the crop and simply paid his workers a wage in the form of a share of what was produced. Landlords also won a stronger claim on the crop than the merchant creditors. The three-way struggle between landlords, sharecroppers, and merchants was therefore settled in favor of the landlord. Sharecropping had become a form of wage labor in which the employers had the most power.

Under the circumstances, merchants were reluctant to loan money to sharecroppers. Many of them left the plantation districts and moved instead into the upcountry where they established commercial relations with white yeomen farmers. Increasingly trapped in their own cycle of debt, white farmers in the 1880s began losing their land and falling into tenancy. Meanwhile in the "black belt" (where most African Americans lived and most of the cotton was produced) successful landlords became merchants while successful merchants often purchased land and hired sharecroppers of their own. A new landlord-merchant class developed and with it an entirely new labor relationship. By the mid-1880s African-American sharecroppers worked as wage laborers for the landlord-merchant class across much of the South.

Sharecropping differed in two critical ways from the wage work more common to industrial America. First, sharecropping was family labor. In industrial factories men, women, and children received wages for the time they worked. By contrast, sharecropping depended on a husband and father who signed the contract and thereby delivered the labor of his wife and children to the landlord. Second, wage earners in urban and industrial America

After the Civil War southern African Americans migrated in several patterns: from the upcountry districts into the cotton belt, from farms to cities, and, in the picture above, from the South to the West. They moved in part to escape racist violence and in part for economic opportunity.

did not sign long-term contracts. They were always vulnerable to layoffs and firings, but sharecropping contracts were year long. This restricted the labor market in the rural South to a few weeks at the end of each year. If croppers left before the end of the year, they risked losing everything they had worked for up to that point.

The political economy of sharecropping impoverished the South by binding the region to a single crop—cotton—that steadily depleted the soil even as it fell lower and lower in price. Yet for most southern blacks there were few alternatives to sharecropping. Over time a small percentage of black farmers managed to purchase their own land, but their farms were generally tiny and the soil of poor quality. The skilled black artisans who had worked on plantations before the Civil War largely disappeared: Many of them moved to southern cities where they took unskilled, low-paying jobs, the only ones they were offered. Industrialization was not much help for African Americans. Northern factories were segregated, as were the steel mills of Birmingham, Alabama. Textile mills were completely restricted to whites. In towns and cities African-American women worked increasingly outside the home, most commonly as domestic servants, to supplement their husbands' meager incomes. As the number of black domestics grew, they changed the way they worked. At the end of the Civil War, most domestic servants lived in the homes of their employers. By 1900, most of them lived at home with their families and commuted to work each day. Wage labor had transformed the lives of southern blacks, but it had not brought them prosperity.

Hoping to escape the poverty and discrimination of southern life, a number of former slaves did what millions of other Americans did: They packed up and moved west. One particular group, known as Exodusters, began moving out to the Kansas prairie during the mid-1870s. By 1880 more than 6,000 African Americans had joined them, searching for cheap land on which to build independent farms. The Exodusters found themselves locked in the same battles with cattlemen that troubled white farmers, and blacks who settled in cowtowns like Dodge City and Topeka found the same pattern of discrimination that had worked against them back in Birmingham and Atlanta. Nevertheless, some of the Exodusters did manage to buy their own land and build their own farms in the West. In this respect, the African-American exodus was similar to the movement of Americans headed west for relief from the constraints of urban and industrial America.

Clearing the West for Capitalism

In 1860 Senator James R. Doolittle of Wisconsin declared his support for a homestead act "because its benign operation will postpone for centuries. . . . All serious conflict between capital and labor in the older free states." The Homestead Act, passed by Congress during the Civil War, was designed to ensure that the trans-Mississippi West would be settled by small, hard-working, independent farmers. And millions of farmers actually did settle in the West during the second half of the nineteenth century. Their movement has become the stuff of legend. By migrating west, the story goes, Americans could escape the limitations of the urban and industrial East. Beyond the Mississippi River lonesome cowboys and sturdy pioneers kept the dream of American individualism alive. The new social hierarchy of the East gave way to the rough equality of the West. In the West hard work and a determination still shaped a person's fate in life more than powerful banks, big corporations, and rigid bureaucracies.

But the realities of daily life in the American West challenged this enduring legend. Hardy individuals did not settle an empty prairie. Waiting for them in the West were various native peoples, some of them helpful and many of them hostile. The settlers came in families, and the families generally came as part of a larger community of friends and relatives. Far from escaping the social hierarchy of industrial capitalism, the settlers brought it with them. By the time the director of the U. S. census declared the frontier "closed" in 1890, the political economy of the American West was composed of railroad tycoons and immigrant workers, commercial farmers and impoverished Native Americans, industrial magnates and choking miners.

The Overland Trail

"Left home this morning," Jane Gould wrote in her diary on April 27, 1862. Along with her husband, Albert, and their two sons, Jane loaded a covered wagon in Mitchell, Iowa, and joined a group of migrants on the Overland Trail to California (see Map 17-4). It would be a long and difficult journey. By the Fourth of July Jane was homesick, wondering in her diary "what the folks at home are doing."

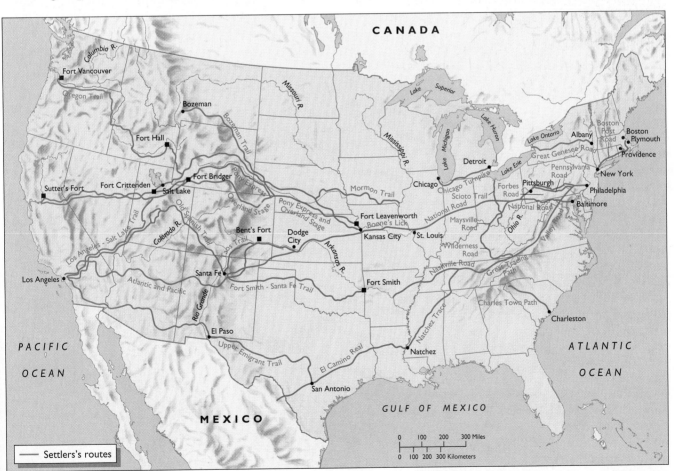

Map 17-4   The Overland Trail.
There was no transcontinental railroad until the late 1860s. Before then, and even thereafter, most settlers moved west on a series of well-developed overland trails.

Albert had begun to get sick shortly after they left, and Jane had to nurse him, drive the wagon, and care for the children. Another woman in the group lost her infant to sickness and then died herself after being run over by a wagon. The farther they traveled the more distressed Jane became. The Overland Trail was increasingly littered with the remnants of wagon trains that had gone before, including discarded furniture, dried bones, and lonely graves. "It is now almost four months since we have slept in a house," Jane wrote. "I do so want to get there." In early October the Goulds at last reached their new home in the San Joaquin Valley. Five months later Jane's husband died.

A popular image pictures the West as a haven for rugged men who struck out on their own, but Jane Gould and her family were far more typical. Most migrants went in family groups, and the families were mostly middle class. Few poor people could afford the expense of the long journey and still hope to buy a plot of land and set up a farm in the West. No single reason drove so many Americans to move West. As he watched a group of families prepare for the westward journey in Independence, Missouri, the historian Francis Parkman tried "to divine the various motives that give impulse to this strange migration." Some,

he thought, were driven by "an insane hope of a better condition in life." Others seemed to be "shaking off restraints of law and society." Still others moved out of "mere restlessness."

The journey across the Overland Trail changed over the years. In 1843 the newspaper editor, Horace Greeley, thought there was "an aspect of insanity" about the mass movement. In a few years, however, Greeley was trumpeting the virtues of westward migration. One reason was that the journey became safer. In the late 1840s the U. S. government began building a string of forts along the various overland routes. Besides protecting migrants from Indians, the forts became stopping points for wagon trains, places where travelers could rest for days and even months at a time. By the 1850s Mormon settlers in Utah had built Salt Lake City into a major stopping point, about halfway between the Mississippi River and the West Coast. Despite the tensions between Mormons and Christians, thousands of migrants came to rely on the facilities at Salt Lake City to substantially ease the journey across the Overland Trail. It was also during the 1850s that the government began to pursue a long-term solution to the growing problem of Native American-white relations in the trans-Mississippi West.

As more and more whites migrated west, Native Americans felt increasing pressure to abandon their lands to the settlers. The result was a dramatic series of plains wars that lasted for nearly thirty years.

The Origins of Indian Reservations

In 1851 more than 10,000 Native Americans from across the Great Plains converged on Fort Laramie in Wyoming Territory. All the major Indian peoples were represented: Sioux, Cheyenne, Arapaho, Crow, and many others. They came to meet with officials of the United States government who hoped to develop a long-term solution to the growing problem of Indian-white relations. Ever since the discovery of gold a few years earlier, a growing number of white migrants had been crossing through Indian territory on their way to California, most of them already prejudiced against the Indians. "We are disgusted with the wretched creatures," Jane Gould wrote of the Native Americans who traded with the migrants. U. S. officials wanted to prevent hostility between whites and Indians from breaking out into violence and also to restrain the conflicts among Indians themselves. They proposed the creation of a separate territory for each Indian tribe, along with government subsidies to entice the Indians to stay within their territories. This was the beginning of the "reservation" system, and for the rest of the century the U. S. government struggled to force the Indians to accept it (see Map 17-5).

From the start the reservation system was riddled with corruption and difficult to enforce. Agents for the Bureau of Indian Affairs cheated Indians and the government alike, sometimes reaping huge profits. But mostly the reservations failed because not all Indians agreed to restrict themselves to their designated territories. The flaws in the system were revealed in western Minnesota during the Civil War. In the summer of 1862 the Dakota Sioux demanded that government officials distribute the food and supplies that had been promised to the Indians. Let them "eat grass or their own dung," one white trader responded. The comment enraged some of the Dakotas, and on August 17 they attacked and killed a family of white farmers. Hysterical government officials called in the U. S. Army, which swiftly rounded up 1,500 Indians and sentenced 300 to die. President Lincoln, distracted by the Civil War, commuted most of the death sentences but allowed 38 Indians to hang.

Minnesota was not the only place where Indians and whites came to violence during the Civil War. Late in 1864 Cheyenne chief Black Kettle brought his people to Sand Creek, Colorado, to begin peace negotiations with Colorado's territorial authorities. But on November 29, instead of talking peace, the Colorado militia launched a murderous attack upon the unsuspecting Cheyennes. Most of the warriors were hunting elsewhere, and the Indian women and children were in no position to defend themselves. The militia slaughtered over 100 Indians, mutilating many of the bodies and carrying their scalps back to Denver as trophies. The Sand Creek Massacre cemented an alliance between the Sioux, the Arapaho, and the Cheyennes, against white settlers and the government. War broke out across the northern and central plains. The alliance proved too powerful for the U. S. forces. Led by Red Cloud and other warriors, thousands of Plains Indians attacked and killed a column of 80 U. S. soldiers at the Battle of One Hundred Slain in December 1866.

By the late 1860s the tensions between Indians and whites were at a fever pitch, as Senator James R. Doolittle of Wisconsin soon discovered. Hoping to devise an Indian policy that would bring peace to the Great Plains, Doolittle went on a fact-finding mission through the West. In Denver he asked an audience of whites whether they preferred outright

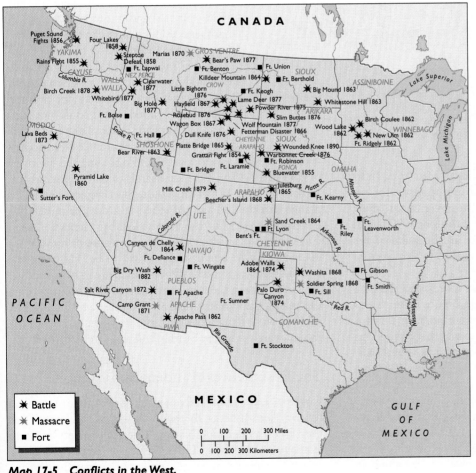

Map 17-5   Conflicts in the West.
In the late nineteenth century, battles between whites and Native Americans erupted all across the western half of the continent.

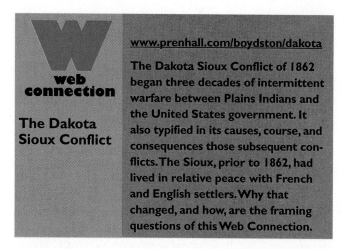

www.prenhall.com/boydston/dakota

web connection

The Dakota Sioux Conflict

The Dakota Sioux Conflict of 1862 began three decades of intermittent warfare between Plains Indians and the United States government. It also typified in its causes, course, and consequences those subsequent conflicts. The Sioux, prior to 1862, had lived in relative peace with French and English settlers. Why that changed, and how, are the framing questions of this Web Connection.

The Ghost Dance of the Ogallala Sioux. The Ghost Dance swept across the plains among Native Americans threatened with destruction by white settlement.

extermination of the Indians to a policy of restricting Indians to reservations. The crowd roared its approval for extermination. Army officers agreed. The government "must act with vindictive earnestness against the Sioux," General William Tecumseh Sherman declared in the wake of the Battle of One Hundred Slain, "even to their extermination, men, women, and children."

Senator Doolittle and his colleagues resisted the calls for extermination, opting instead for a more comprehensive reservation policy. The government pursued this approach by means of two important treaties that divided the Great Plains into two huge Indian territories. The Medicine Lodge Treaty, signed in Kansas in October 1867, organized thousands of Indians across the southern plains. In return for government supplies of food, clothing, and ammunition, most of the southern plains peoples agreed to restrict themselves to the reservation. The northern Plains Indians did not sign onto the reservation so readily. A treaty was initially formulated at Fort Laramie in Wyoming, but a band of holdouts demanded further gov-

ernment concessions. Inspired by Red Cloud, the leader at the Battle of One Hundred Slain, the Indians insisted that U. S. forces abandon their forts along the Bozeman Trail. When the government at last agreed, Red Cloud signed the Fort Laramie Treaty in November 1868.

Red Cloud respected the treaties for the rest of his life, but the treaties nevertheless failed. Most white settlers still preferred extermination to reservations, and they continually poached on Indian reservations. And not all the Plains Indians approved of the treaties. Those Indian leaders who agreed to the reservations were "rascals," Sitting Bull declared, who "sold our country without the full consent of our people." Nor did the U. S. Army abide by the policy made in Washington. Within weeks of Red Cloud's signature on the Fort Laramie Treaty, for example, the Seventh Cavalry led by Colonel George Armstrong Custer massacred Black Kettle's people yet again, this time at Washita, Kansas, on November 27, 1868. Thus the treaties failed to restore peace to the Great Plains. As long as the U. S. Army sustained the settlers' hunger for extermination, Indian "policy" was made on the battlefields of the West rather than in the government offices of Washington, D. C. For General Sherman, the Indians were "the enemies of our race and of our civilization." As far as General Philip Sheridan was concerned, "the only good Indians I ever saw were dead."

By 1870 it was clear that western Indians would not voluntarily retire to government reservations and that the military might of the United States could not force the Indians into surrender. If any further evidence of the Indian resistance were needed, it came in South Dakota in 1876. Following the discovery of gold in the Black Hills, thousands of whites poured onto Indian territory. When the Lakota Sioux rejected white demands that the Indians cede their lands to the miners, the government sent in the Army led by General Custer. Custer was an arrogant man, far more sure of himself and his men than he could safely afford to be. He made two critical mistakes. First he divided his army in two, and then he failed to keep them in communication with each other. Outmanned and outmaneuvered, Custer and hundreds of his men were slaughtered at Little Bighorn by some 2,000 Indian warriors led by Sitting Bull and Crazy Horse.

The Destruction of Indian Subsistence

Custer's "Last Stand" did not signal any change of fortunes for the Plains Indians. By the 1870s whites had learned that they could undermine Native-American society most effectively by depriving Indians of their sources of subsistence. The most dramatic example of this was the destruction of the buffalo. "Kill every buffalo you can," a U. S.

Army colonel urged one hunter, "every buffalo dead is an Indian gone." Federal authorities did not actually sponsor the mass killing of the buffalo; they merely turned a blind eye to the slaughter, knowing that it would destroy the capacity of the Indians to resist white settlement. In the words of Texas congressman James W. Throckmorton, "so long as there are millions of buffaloes in the West, so long the Indians cannot be controlled. . . ." Railroads joined the process, sponsoring mass kills from slow-moving trains as they crossed the prairies. The destruction was as vast as it was swift. Some 13 million bison in 1850 were reduced, by 1880, to a few hundred.

With their subsistence thus destroyed, the Indians' surrender was only a matter of time. In 1881, Chief Sitting Bull and his starving men finally gave up. The Sioux war ended at last in 1890 with a shocking massacre of 200 Native-American men, women, and children at Wounded Knee, South Dakota. In the Northwest in 1877 the Nez Percé, fleeing from Union troops, set out on a dramatic trek across the mountains into Yellowstone in an attempt to reach Canada. Unable to find refuge among the Crows or the Sioux, the Nez Percé nevertheless eluded government troops and nearly made it over the Canadian border.

Hunger and the elements did what the Union Army had failed to do. "I am tired of fighting," Chief Joseph finally concluded. "It is cold and we have no blankets. The little children are freezing to death. . . . Hear me, my chiefs! I am tired. My heart is sick and sad. From where the sun now stands, I will fight no more forever." Chief Joseph and his exhausted people agreed to go to their reservations.

Reformers who advocated reservations over extermination always believed that the Indians should be absorbed into the political economy of capitalism. By "confining the Indians to reservations," explained William P. Dole, Lincoln's Commissioner of Indian Affairs, "they are gradually taught and become accustomed to the idea of individual property." This, Dole added, "is the best method yet devised for their reclamation and civilization." Most white settlers considered Native Americans an inferior race worthy of destruction. By contrast, Dole believed it was "a demonstrated fact that Indians are capable of attaining a high degree of civilization." But reformers like Dole equated civilization with the cultivation of "individual property." Accordingly, reformers set out to destroy Native-American family structures, political institutions, and economic relationships. They introduced government schools on Indian reservations to teach children the virtues of private property, individual achievement, and social mobility.

The reformers' influence peaked in 1887 when Congress passed the Dawes Severalty Act. It was the most important piece of Indian legislation in the entire century. The Dawes Act was designed to destroy what remained of Native American political and social organization. Under the terms of the Dawes Act land within the reservations was broken up into separate plots of land and distributed among individual Indian families on the reservation. The goal (and effect) was to undermine the traditional political hierarchy among Native Americans and to force Indians to live like stereotypical white farmers. But the lands allotted were generally so poor, and the plots so small, that their owners sold them as soon as they were allowed. Four out of five Indian landowners eventually lost their property, and by the early twentieth century there were virtually no reservations left except for a few parcels in the desert Southwest. With the Indians subdued, the path was cleared for the capitalist transformation of the West.

Location.	Acres.	Average Price per Acre.	Location.	Acres.	Average Price per Acre.
Colorado	5,211.21	$7.27	Oklahoma	34,664.00	$19.14
Idaho	17,013.00	24.85	Oregon	1,020.00	15.43
Kansas	1,684.50	33.45	South Dakota	120,445.00	16.53
Montana	11,034.00	9.86	Washington	4,879.00	41.37
Nebraska	5,641.00	36.65	Wisconsin	1,069.00	17.00
North Dakota	22,610.70	9.93	Wyoming	865.00	20.64

FOR THE YEAR 1911 IT IS ESTIMATED THAT 350,000 ACRES WILL BE OFFERED FOR SALE

For information as to the character of the land write for booklet, "INDIAN LANDS FOR SALE," to the Superintendent U. S. Indian School at any one of the following places:

CALIFORNIA: Hoopa.	MINNESOTA: Onigum.	NORTH DAKOTA: Fort Totten. Fort Yates.	OKLAHOMA—Con. Sac and Fox Agency. Shawnee. Wyandotte.	SOUTH DAKOTA: Cheyenne Agency. Crow Creek. Greenwood. Lower Brule. Pine Ridge. Rosebud. Sisseton.	WASHINGTON: Fort Simcoe. Fort Spokane. Tekoa. Tulalip.
COLORADO: Ignacio.	MONTANA: Crow Agency.	OKLAHOMA: Anadarko. Cantonment. Colony. Darlington. Muskogee. Pawnee.	OREGON: Klamath Agency. Pendleton. Roseburg. Siletz.		WISCONSIN: Oneida.
IDAHO: Lapwai.	NEBRASKA: Macy. Santee. Winnebago.				
KANSAS: Horton. Nadeau.					

WALTER L. FISHER, Secretary of the Interior.   **ROBERT G. VALENTINE,** Commissioner of Indian Affairs.

Within a couple of decades of the passage of the Dawes Act, most Native-American lands were sold to white settlers.

The Economic Transformation of the West

A few hundred civilians died in Indian attacks during the late nineteenth century. Over 5,000 died building the railroads. There were cowboys, and there were Indians, but there were also railroads and mining corporations. Lawless violence and wild speculation were very much a part of the western experience in the late nineteenth century, but so were struggling families, temperance reformers, and hard-working immigrants. Mark Twain captured the diversity of the American West: The Nevada Territory, he wrote in the 1860s, "is fabulously rich in gold, silver, lead, coal, iron, quicksilver, ... thieves, murderers, desperadoes, ladies, children, lawyers, Christians, Indians, Chinamen, Spaniards, gamblers, sharpers, coyotes, poets, preachers and jackass rabbits." Yet despite such bewildering diversity, an astute observer could detect a larger pattern. The trans-Mississippi West of the late nineteenth century was being drawn rapidly into the political economy of global capitalism. Wealthy cattle barons sent tons of beef to the stockyards of Chicago, where it was butchered, refrigerated, and distributed nationwide. Great corporations stripped the timber from the virgin forests of the Pacific Northwest and dug the gold, silver, and copper ore from deep below the ground in California, Nevada, Colorado, and South Dakota. And tens of thousands of ordinary farm families, having braved a difficult trek across the Great Plains, conquered a forbidding climate to force from the earth the produce that found its way back to the markets of the Midwest and the East. By 1900 the West provided Americans with the meat and bread for their dinner tables, the wood that built their homes, and the gold and silver that backed up their currency.

Cattlemen: From Drovers to Ranchers

The cowboy is the great mythic figure of the American West. He was a rugged individual, a silent loner, a man who scorned the attractions of society for the independence of the trail. Like many myths, this one has elements of truth in it. Cowboys were usually unattached men. They worked hard, but when their work was over they played just as hard, spending their earnings on a shave, a new suit of clothes, and a few good nights in town. But there was a lot about the cowboy's life that rarely makes it into the romantic accounts. Driving cattle was hard work, but it was often dangerous, and even more often it was boring. Nor does the legend tell of the diversity of the men who became cowboys. Civil War veterans, emancipated slaves, displaced Indians, and Mexican *vaqueros*—all became cowboys at various times and for various reasons. But those who became cowboys in search of the independent life, freed from the constraints of wage labor, were bound to be disappointed. Cowboys were poorly paid, their work was unsteady, and their chances of reaching real independence were slim.

Longhorn cattle were as much a part of western legend as the cowboys who drove them. Longhorns were common in Texas during the 1850s, but the Civil War

The romantic image of the western cowboy is captured here in James Walker's 1877 painting, Vaqueros in a Horse Corral. In reality, the cowboy's life was difficult and uncertain. Over time, cowboys became wage laborers for large cattle barons.

closed off any expansion of the cattle industry into the North. With the end of the war, the destruction of the buffalo, and the westward spread of the railroads, it became possible to drive huge herds of Texas longhorns north onto the Great Plains. The longhorns had the great advantage of being able to travel long distances on very little water and to feed on the plains grasses during the winter. Thus with relatively little capital, cattle herders could make substantial profits. Cowboys drove gigantic herds, sometimes numbering half a million longhorns, until they reached a town with a railroad connection from which the cattle could be shipped. The first such "cow town" was Abilene, Kansas, but others (Wichita and Dodge City, for example) were quickly established. Cattlemen sold half of their stock to eastern markets and the other half in the West, to Californians or to the U. S. government, which purchased beef to feed its soldiers and the Indians on reservations.

But the Texas longhorn had several drawbacks that eventually led to its replacement. Most seriously, it carried a tick that devastated many of the grazing animals that came into contact with the longhorn on its annual drive. Beginning in 1867, farm-state legislatures succeeded in banning the longhorn drives in many parts of the West. In addition, the longhorn took a long time to fatten up and never really produced much good beef. Wealthy investors began to experiment with hybrid breeds of cattle that did not carry the deadly tick, fattened up quickly, and produced higher-quality meat. This was the first of several dramatic changes in the cattle industry. By the early 1880s eastern and European investors were pouring their capital into mammoth cattle-herding companies. At the same time it was becoming clear that the Great Plains were seriously overstocked. The grazing lands were depleted, leaving the cattle weak from malnutrition. In 1885 a severe winter devastated the sickly herds on the lower plains. The same thing happened on the northern plains a year later. The winter of 1889–1890 worked similar devastation on the cattle herds of the Nevada desert.

Open-range herding eventually became so environmentally destructive that it was no longer economically feasible. In addition, long drives became increasingly difficult as farmers settled the plains states and fenced in their lands. By the 1890s huge cattle companies were giving way to smaller ranches on which farmers raised feed for hybrid cattle. The western railroad network was by then so extensive that it was no longer necessary to drive large herds hundreds of miles to reach a railhead. Cowboys became ranch hands who worked for regular wages, like miners and factory workers throughout industrializing America.

In the mid-1880s, more than 7,000,000 head of cattle roamed the Great Plains, but their numbers declined rapidly thereafter, and in place of the cattlemen came sheepherders. Sheep survived without water even better than longhorns, and they fed on the growths that cattle would not eat. In fact, the sheep ate so many grasses that they proved even more ecologically destructive than the cattle. Nevertheless, by 1900 sheepherding had largely replaced the cattle industry in the northern plains states of Wyoming and Montana and was spreading onto Nevada's upper desert as well. Sheepherding had one other crucial advantage. It did not interfere with small farmers as much as cattle driving did.

Commercial Farmers Subdue the Plains

Between 1860 and 1900, the number of farms in America nearly tripled, largely thanks to the economic development of the West. On the Great Plains and in the desert Southwest, farmers took up lands of which Native Americans had been dispossessed. From San Francisco to Los Angeles, white settlers poached on the estates of Spanish-speaking landlords, stripping them of their natural resources and undermining their profitability. The legal costs of maintaining Spanish titles (remnants of California's days as a colony of Spain) eventually overwhelmed the landlords, and so over time Hispanic ranchers gave way to Euro-American farmers. The Hispanic population of Los Angeles fell from 82 percent in 1850 to 19 percent in 1880. A similar pattern of white poaching and legal expenses displaced the Mexican-American landowners in New Mexico and Texas during the same decades. Throughout the late nineteenth century, therefore, western agriculture changed hands, from Native-American buffalo hunters and Hispanic ranchers to white cattlemen and farmers.

This ethnic shift signaled more profound changes in the ecology and political economy of the West, for driving these transformations was the exploding global demand for western products. Cattle ranchers were feeding eastern cities. Lumber from the Pacific Northwest found its way to Asia and South America. By 1890 western farmers produced half of the wheat grown in the United States, and they shipped it across the globe, from Australia to Eastern Europe.

But farming in the arid West was different from farming in the humid East. To begin with, the one-hundred-and-sixty-acre homesteads envisioned by eastern lawmakers bore little relationship to the actual pattern of agricultural settlement in the trans-Mississippi West. Farms of that size were simply too small for the economic and ecological conditions of western agriculture. From the very beginning, western farmers were commercial farmers. To produce wheat and corn that could be sold at a profit on the international market they had to use heavy steel plows, costly mechanical equipment, and extensive irrigation. To make these capital investments, western farmers had to

A farm family poses in front of its sod house on the dusty Nebraska plains.

mortgage their lands. For mechanized, commercial agriculture to succeed on mortgaged land, western farms had to be much bigger than 160 acres. Settlers therefore conspired with speculators to evade the limit imposed by the Homestead Act.

In practice the bulk of western agricultural settlement took place not on government-sponsored homesteads but through the private land market. As with mining and cattle driving, speculation initially prevailed before giving way to more enduring economic enterprises. By some estimates land speculators bought up nearly 350 million acres of western lands from state or federal governments or from Indian reservations. Railroads gobbled up another 200 million acres granted to them by the federal government. The railroads quickly took the lead in promoting settlement. The more farmers railroads planted in the West, the more agricultural produce they could regularly ship back East. Railroads set up immigration bureaus and advertised throughout Europe and on the East Coast. They offered settlers cheap transportation, credit, and agricultural assistance. In effect, the railroads created their own clientele by filling up the Great Plains with settlers from the East Coast and from Ireland, Germany, and Scandinavia.

More dramatic than the steady immigration was the series of "land booms" that swept across the region, generally following the rail lines. Railroads often deliberately provoked such booms. When the tracks reached western Kansas and Nebraska in the 1870s, a land boom suddenly settled much of the region. A series of "Dakota booms" quickly settled the northern Plains in the mid-1880s. West Texas filled in at the same time. And beginning in 1889, the U. S. government chased the Indians off their territories in Oklahoma and opened up millions of acres to settlers. In 1890 the director of the Bureau of the Census reported that the frontier had at last been filled.

Changes in the Land

The trans-Mississippi West was no Garden of Eden waiting for lucky farmers to move in and reap the land's abundant riches. The climate of much of the region, particularly the Great Plains and the desert Southwest, was notoriously forbidding. It was too dry for most kinds of farming. The sod on the plains was so thick and hard that traditional plows ripped like paper; only steel would do the job. With little wood or stone to build houses farmers lived first in dugouts carved from the sides of hills or sodhouses that were damp and infested. The weather was atrocious: Fierce blizzards gave way to blistering summers, each rocked by harsh winds. Yet settlers seemed determined to overcome, and to overwhelm, nature itself. To build fences where wood was scarce, manufacturers invented barbed wire and for a long time shipped every foot of it they could produce out to the Plains. Windmills dotted the prairie to pump water up to the surface from hundreds of feet below ground. New and powerful agricultural machinery tore through the earth, and new strains of wheat from Europe and China were cultivated to withstand the brutal climate.

In these and other ways the western environment was transformed. The wolves, elk, and bear of the Pacific Northwest were exterminated as farmers brought in pigs, cattle, and sheep. Tulare Lake, covering hundreds of square miles of California's central valley, was sucked dry by 1900. Hydraulic mining sent tons of earth and rock cascading down the rivers flowing out of the Sierra Nevada, raising water levels to the point where entire cities became vulnerable to periodic flooding. The skies above Butte, Montana, turned grey from the pollutants released by the copper smelting plants. Sheepherding undermined the vegetation on the eastern slopes of the Rocky Mountains and the Sierra Nevada. In the waters off California the sea otters were all but eliminated, leading to a dramatic increase in the number of sea urchins and abalone. The abalone and urchins in turn fed on the kelp, the supply of which soon dwindled. Since fish fed on kelp, fish supplies decreased as well.

By the turn of the century, the West had been dramatically transformed. Drawn into the whirlwind of a global political economy, the very landscape of the region was changed forever. The buffalo had all but disappeared, and the Indians had been confined to reservations. Even the grass that grew on the Great Plains was different. Industrial mining corporations, profitable cattle ranches, and mechanized farms now dominated the economy and society of the West. The frontier was gone, and in its place were commercial farmers whose lives were shaped by European weather, eastern mortgage companies, commodity brokers, and railroad conglomerates. Cowboys sold their labor to cattle companies owned by investors in Boston and Glasgow. Mining corporations like Anaconda Copper and lumber corporations like Crown-Zellerbach employed tens of thousands of wage laborers to exploit the West's natural resources.

Big cities sprang up almost overnight. San Francisco had 5,000 inhabitants in 1850, but by the time the Gold Rush was over, in 1870, there were 150,000 people living there. Denver was incorporated in 1861 but its population hovered at just below 5,000 until the railroad came in 1870. Twenty years later Denver had over 100,000 inhabitants. Railroads connected these cities to one another, to mining towns, cow towns, and the major cities of the Midwest and the East. Those same railroads hired thousands of wage laborers to help transport the cattle, the ore, the wheat, and the wood across the region, the nation, and around the world.

Conclusion

Rosa Cassettari and Andrew Carnegie never met, but together their lives suggest the spectrum of possibilities in industrializing America. Both were immigrants. Caught up in the swirling political economy of industrial capitalism in the late nineteenth century, both made their way to the United States. Yet the same grand forces touched the two immigrants in very different ways. Cassettari grew up in Italy and moved to a mining camp west of the Mississippi River before making her way to Chicago—the city that opened the west to the dynamism of industrial capitalism. Carnegie was born in Scotland and migrated, almost overnight, from the pre-industrial world of his father to the very heart of the industrial revolution in America—Pittsburgh, with its railroads, oil refineries, and steel mills. Cassettari struggled all her life and in the end achieved a modest level of comfort for herself and her children. She did as well as most immi-

grants could hope for, and in that sense her biography reflects the realities of working-class life in industrial America. Carnegie's life, by contrast, embodies the fantastic dream of the struggling young immigrant who made his way from rags to riches. Cassettari's experience with failure—the harsh life of the mining camp and a bad marriage—impelled her to move on in search of something better. It was success, however, that made Carnegie itch for something different. By 1890, having made his millions, he decided to remake himself by becoming a patron of culture. He moved to New York. He traveled throughout the world, especially in Great Britain. There he befriended some of the leading intellectuals of his day. He contemplated ways of giving his money away and decided to build libraries and endow universities. He had helped create an industrial nation. Now he set out to recreate American culture.

CHRONOLOGY

1848	Taiping Revolution spurs Chinese emigration to U.S.	**1871**	October: Great Chicago fire
	Revolution in Austria-Hungary	**1872**	Edgar Thompson Steel Works open near Pittsburgh
	Andrew Carnegie emigrates to U.S.	**1873**	Financial panic, followed by depression
1851	Fort Laramie Treaty establishes Indian reservations	**1876**	Custer's "Last Stand" at Little Big Horn
1856	St. Paul's boarding school opens	**1877**	"Great Strike" of railroad workers begins
1857	Henry Bessemer develops process for making steel	**1878**	American Bar Association founded
1862	Pacific Railroad Act	**1881**	Czar Alexander II of Russia assassinated
	Homestead Act	**1882**	Chinese Exclusion Act
	Rebellion of Dakota Sioux in Minnesota		John D. Rockefeller forms Standard Oil "Trust"
1864	Sand Creek Massacre		Edison Electric Company lights up New York buildings
1865	First transatlantic telegraph cable begins operation	**1887**	Dawes Severalty Act
1866	Battle of One Hundred Slain	**1890**	Jacob Riis publishes *How the Other Half Lives*
1867	Medicine Lodge Treaty		Massacre at Wounded Knee, South Dakota
1868	Second Fort Laramie Treaty		Director of U.S. Census declares frontier "closed"
	Washita Massacre	**1893**	Financial panic, followed by depression

Review Questions

1. Why did so many immigrants come to the United States in the late nineteenth century?

2. What were Andrew Carnegie's major contributions to the development of American industry?

3. Describe the new social hierarchy of industrial America.

4. Trace the development of Indian "reservations."

5. What were the major changes in the American West in the second half of the nineteenth century?

Further Readings

Alfred D. Chandler, *The Visible Hand: The Managerial Revolution in American Business* (1977) is the standard account of the rise of corporate bureaucracy.

William Cronon, *Nature's Metropolis: Chicago and the Great West* (1991) meticulously charts the way Chicago's influence stretched across much of the West.

Eric Hobsbawm, *The Age of Empire: 1875–1914* (1987) establishes the global context for the industrial transformation of the United States.

Maldwyn Jones, *American Immigration*, 2d ed. (1992) is unusually sensitive to the political and economic background to global migration.

Harold Livesay, *Andrew Carnegie and the Rise of Big Business* (1975) does an unusually fine job of placing Carnegie in historical context.

David Montgomery, *The Fall of the House of Labor: The Workplace, the State and American Labor Activism, 1865–1925* (1987) shows how the rise of Big Business changed the daily labor of the American working class.

Gregory Nobles, *American Frontiers: Cultural Encounters and Continental Conquest* (1997) is a brief survey reflecting the latest scholarship in western history.

Henry Nash Smith, *Virgin Land: The American West as Symbol and Myth* (1950) the premier example of the much-maligned "myth and symbol" approach to American studies, this is a classic account of the "image" of the West in the nineteenth century.

C. Vann Woodward, *Origins of the New South, 1877–1913* (1951) is one of the great works of American historical literature.

Richard White, '*It's Your Misfortune and None of My Own': A History of the American West* (1991) is a comprehensive survey by a leading historian of the West.

History on the Internet

"How the Other Half Lives"

http://www.yale.edu/amstud/inforev/riis/title.html

Explore the world of immigrants in New York in the late nineteenth century by viewing the full text and illustrations of Jacob Riis' work. To see a collection of over a dozen photographs depicting tenement life, see http://www.masters-of-photography.com/R/riis/riis.html.

"The Gilded Age and the Titans of Industry"

http://www.pbs.org/wgbh/amex/carnegie/gildedage.html

On PBS' The American Experience website, learn about the experience of Americans during the so-called gilded age. Timeline features and a picture gallery provide links to a biography of industrialist Andrew Carnegie and photos of the industrialists' New York homes known by many as "Millionaires' Row."

"African American Mosaic—Migrations"

http://www.loc.gov/exhibits/african/intro.html

Maps, illustrations, genealogical charts, and photos depict the African-American quest of the "Exodusters" who migrated West, especially to Kansas, in search of a better life.

"Still Livin' Under the Bonds of Slavery"

http://historymatters.gmu.edu/text/1563a-whitney.html

Download and listen to the audio recording of Minnie Whitney who describes sharecropping in the late nineteenth century. Hear tales of hard times and oppression as well as agency and self-sufficiency.

18

CULTURAL STRUGGLES OF INDUSTRIAL AMERICA

1850-1895

OUTLINE

Anthony Comstock's Crusade Against Vice

Anthony Comstock was a driven man. He devoted most of his adult life to putting out of business the owners of brothels, gambling dens, abortion clinics, and dance halls. "You must hunt these men as you hunt rats," Comstock declared, "without mercy." There was little in his background to foreshadow such zeal. While still a young man Comstock had moved from his home in rural Connecticut to New York City, where he began working as a clerk in a dry goods store. White-collar careers of this sort were a familiar path for native-born Protestant men in the middle of the nineteenth century. Anthony Comstock would never abandon his middle-class roots, but he was destined for greater things. Fame came to him in 1873 when the United States Congress enacted a statute that would forever bear his name, although Comstock himself never served in any legislature. The Comstock Law, as it was known, banned the production, distribution, and public display of obscenity. Thereafter, Comstock spent much of his life chasing down and prosecuting pornographers, prostitutes, and stripteasers.

Comstock and like-minded citizens were disturbed by the municipal corruption that kept police departments from enforcing obscenity laws. To overcome this obstacle reformers established a series of private organizations with quasi-official authority to enforce the law. Their model was the British Society for the Prevention of Cruelty to Animals and its American counterpart, the ASPCA, founded in 1866. The ASPCA spawned a host of imitators, including the Society for the Prevention of Cruelty to Children, the Society for the Prevention of Crime, and the Civil Vigilance League. Among the most influential was Anthony Comstock's very own New York Society for the Suppression of Vice, commonly known as the SSV. Founded in 1873, the SSV was dedicated to "the enforcement of laws for the suppression of the trade in, and circulation of, obscene literature and illustrations, advertisements, and articles of indecent or immoral use."

As head of the SSV Comstock was appointed a special agent of the U. S. Post Office. This gave him the power to prosecute his own antiobscenity statute. Along with other

SSV leaders Comstock proceeded to disregard the rights of due process by entrapping their victims. But they always defended their actions by claiming that the established legal procedures of the police and the judiciary were ineffective in preventing the sale of smut. As proof, the SSV pointed to its own success. Before his career was over Comstock claimed that he had destroyed 160 tons of pornography.

Comstock maintained that his chief concern was the protection of children. "From infancy to maturity the pathway of the child is beset with peculiar temptations to do evil," Comstock explained. He called his most famous book *Traps for the Young* (1883). In it he warned that American youngsters were being enticed into deviant ways before their emotions had been effectively controlled. Obscenity was artificially nourishing youthful appetites and passions until they exerted "a well-nigh irresistible mastery over their victim." Parents were of no help. Their "incontinence," along with their children's "morbidly susceptible natures," produced young people who were "ready to fall into shame at the slightest temptation."

The evils that trapped America's children were thought to be concentrated in cities. The vice crusades thus perpetuated a long-standing view of cities as dangerous and disreputable places. Thomas Jefferson had likened cities to "sores on the body politic." In the late nineteenth century, as millions of young people abandoned the rural life, the guardians of American morality revived Jefferson's concerns. Young men and young women were leaving small towns and villages where everyone recognized them. A vice-society speaker in Boston warned that in the city "that whole bulwark is swept away. They are lost in the crowd." In large part, the vice crusades were driven by this renewed fear of cities.

Comstock was not simply imagining that the cultural standards of small-town America were loosening up. Huge cities had indeed freed millions of Americans from the watchful eyes of the neighbors they left behind in the village and the countryside. Not only was urban life relatively anonymous, it was also a world driven by vast amounts of cash. In the last third of the nineteenth century the income of nonfarm employees in America rose steadily, while prices just as steadily declined. Except for the very poorest workers, urban Americans had more money to spend and more time to spend it than ever before. "A workingman

wants something besides food and clothes in this country," a compositor explained to a Senate committee in 1883. "He wants recreation." And if industrial workers enjoyed more leisure time, the growing numbers of white-collar employees enjoyed even more. The big city offered Americans a new variety of entertainments that frequently provoked the ire of those determined to defend the traditional standards of middle-class respectability.

Anthony Comstock's crusade was part of a larger debate swirling through the late nineteenth century over what counted as "culture." American cities gave rise to a "popular culture" that included baseball games, minstrel shows, and world's fairs. For Comstock urban culture was a cesspool of vice and corruption, where traditional standards of sexual decency and self-restraint threatened to disappear. For modern historians a great deal of urban culture resided in its immigrant neighborhoods, with their distinctive family structures and religious practices. But at the time many Americans looked at immigrant slums as utterly devoid of culture. They assumed yet another definition of "culture," one that referred only to the great works of western art, literature, and music. High culture, in this sense, was seen as an alternative to the sordid realities of urban and industrial America. Ironically, the best artists and writers of the late nineteenth century were "realists." While Anthony Comstock tried to suppress the vices of the city, realists embraced the city, translating it into compelling fiction and dramatic canvases.

Thus Comstock's crusade was only one of several major cultural battles spawned by the rapid growth of cities and industry in the second half of the nineteenth century. Cultural clashes were as much a part of the political economy of industrial capitalism as were class conflict and political upheaval. Thus rural America reacted defensively to the culture of the city. Native-born Protestants struggled against the cultures of immigrants. The defenders of high culture launched a campaign against the rise of popular culture. Amateur sportsmen sniffed at the emergence of spectator sports. Victorian moralists were shocked by the apparent collapse of traditional gender distinctions. Yet each of these struggles reflected the nervous efforts of Americans to absorb, in different ways, the dramatic social transformations that accompanied the rise of industrial capitalism. ∎

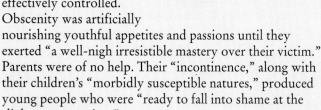

An 1897 cartoon in Life magazine made fun of Anthony Cornstock's crusade against pornography.

KEY TOPICS

- New forms of popular culture generated by the city

- Conventional and unconventional gender distinctions in Victorian America

- The cultural significance of immigration

- The difference between "high" culture and "popular" culture

- The flowering of artistic realism

The Varieties of Urban Culture

Americans both loved and hated the cities they lived in, and their mixed feelings showed up in the varieties of entertainment they embraced during the second half of the nineteenth century. They indulged in romanticized recreations of the Plains wars on the western frontier, and they paid good money to watch nostalgic minstrel shows about plantation life in the Old South. As the political economy changed, however, the nation's love affair with the countryside gave way to popular entertainments that idealized

the city as never before. These new entertainments rested more than ever on the technological marvels of American industry. Beginning in the 1880s electricity lit up the big city after dark, thus making it possible to create new forms of urban "night life." By 1900 electricity was powering the trollies and subways that brought tens of thousands of Americans into new "downtown" districts (see Figure 18-1). Stores, businesses, and factories were the hallmarks of the older downtowns. But leisure activities attracted tens of thousands to the new city centers. In unprecedented numbers Americans went to theaters, music halls, concert saloons, baseball stadiums, and sports arenas. City life, long associated with poverty and crime, now came to mean fun and excitement as well.

Minstrel Shows as Cultural Nostalgia

Beginning in the late nineteenth century the western frontier became one the most popular themes in American show business. As rugged pioneers gave way to wage earners, commercial farmers, and industrialists, the mythology of the West grew. The most spectacular example of this was Buffalo Bill Cody's hugely successful *Wild West Show*. Cody and company toured the country parading live Indians before delighted spectators in New York, Philadelphia, and Chicago. Audiences watched displays of horsemanship interspersed with bloodless, highly stylized re-enactments of the Plains wars. America's fascination with a romanticized frontier was one example of a popular nostalgia for ways of life that were thought to have been simpler and yet more interesting than the life of the city. Nowhere was this nostalgia more obvious than in the minstrel shows.

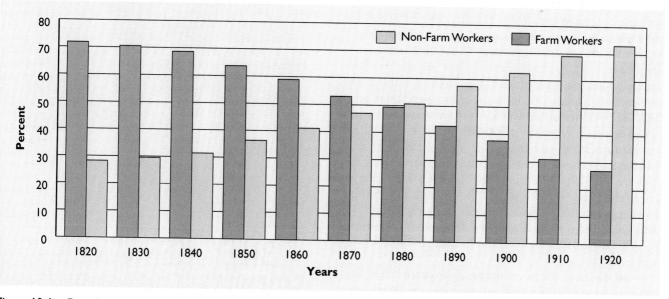

Figure 18-1   *Growth of the Non-Farm Sector.*
Underpinning the rise of urban culture was the emergence of a wage-earning labor force. Concentrated in cities, wage earners had cash at their disposal to spend on the amusements cities had to offer.

Source: Historical Statistics of the United States, From Colonial Times to the Present, 2d. ed. (1975), Part I, D-75-84.

Minstrel shows were the most significant form of public entertainment for most of the nineteenth century. Their popularity skyrocketed in northeastern cities during the 1830s and 1840s. In those years minstrel shows were dominated by white performers in blackface. Although the minstrels stereotyped plantation slaves as happy and carefree, the earliest performances were not as viciously racist as they became in later decades. In the mid-1850s, however, the tone of blackface minstrel shows changed. As the slavery controversy forced white northerners to take sides on an issue many would have preferred to avoid, popular troupes like New York's Christy Minstrels took the side of the slaveholders. During the Civil War and Reconstruction, minstrel shows continued to attack white reformers in the North who supported emancipation and African-American rights. They removed all remaining antislavery sentiments from their performances and any remnants of realistic African Americans. Thereafter blacks were portrayed only in the grossest racial stereotypes, and abolitionists were subjected to withering ridicule. Minstrel troupes staged corrupted versions of *Uncle Tom's Cabin:* They stripped the novel of its abolitionist theme and reduced the plot to a simplistic story of beleaguered southern whites. The black characters were portrayed as hopelessly incompetent fools who were led to devilish acts under the evil influence of Yankee radicals. Yet throughout the period, minstrel shows continued to poke fun at the aristocratic pretensions of cultural elites. Indeed, minstrel shows commonly combined their racism with their populism. They lampooned elites by playing them in blackface wearing fancy clothes and putting on airs.

In the 1870s minstrel shows grew larger and more elaborate as they sought to compete with new forms of popular entertainment. J. H. Haverly led the way. His plan was to build a minstrel troupe "that for extraordinary excellence, merit, and magnitude will astonish and satisfy the most exacting amusement seeker in the world." Haverly hired the most players, dressed them in the gaudiest costumes, placed them in the most spectacular sets, and had them perform the widest variety of numbers. He toned down the emphasis on blackfaced singers and plantation themes and added large numbers of scantily clad women and off-color routines. Haverly expanded his audiences with extensive newspaper advertisements, large colorful posters, and effective publicity stunts. By 1881 he had theaters in New York, Brooklyn, Chicago, and San Francisco, three national minstrel troupes, four touring comedy theaters, and heavy investments in mills, mines, and stocks.

Of Haverly's three companies, two were white and one was exclusively black. There were other black companies as well. As national minstrel shows abandoned their earlier commitment to authentic representations of southern life, blacks often took to the stage and kept the plantation theme alive. In some cases African Americans formed minstrel troupes of their own. More often they were owned and financed by whites. Indeed, black minstrels operated within the racial stereotypes established by prewar whites in blackface. The most famous African-American minstrel of the nineteenth century, Billy Kersands, drew huge audiences with his portrayals of ignorant and comical characters. His grossly exaggerated lips, thick dialect, and shuffling walk brought howls of laughter from white and black audiences alike. Yet as the plantation theme became the preserve of African-American players, some of the early criticism of slavery crept back into the productions. When black minstrels romanticized the Old South, their nostalgia was reserved for slaves. The kind mistress and good Massa' fell out of their performances. The most important change, however, was the introduction of religious songs that had been so important to slave culture. Black minstrels, often advertising themselves as former slaves, were more concerned with the authenticity of their performances than black-*faced* minstrels had been.

BILLY KERSANDS.
CALLENDER'S (GEORGIA) MINSTRELS.

African-American minstrels such as Billy Kersands moderated the racism characteristic of the extremely popular white minstrels.

Meanwhile, the largest and most successful minstrel shows retained their exclusively white casts and their heavy-handed racism. They did not retain their local character and their raucous tone. In the wake of Haverly's success, competing show-business entrepreneurs put smaller local troupes out of business or swallowed them up into national companies; productions had grown too ornate and expensive. From more than 60 troupes in the late 1860s, the number of minstrel troupes fell to just 13 by the early 1880s. Carefully orchestrated to maintain the widest possible appeal, the minstrel show lost many of its rough edges. Differences from one company to the next diminished as minstrel shows became uniform and somewhat more bland. Yet they were more popular than ever. National companies expanded their audiences into the far West and the deep South. By 1890 a handful of huge entertainment moguls had taken control of the minstrel shows. They never lost their nostalgic appeal to rural, pre-industrial America, but by the late nineteenth century minstrel shows looked more and more like vaudeville, an art form that was born and bred in the big city.

The Origins of Vaudeville

Unlike the minstrels, vaudeville shows did not rely on nostalgia for the rural life or the western frontier. Rather, vaudeville and its cheaper cousins (concert saloons and dollar theaters, for example) flourished in American cities after elites succeeded in distinguishing serious theater from variety shows. As the cost of a ticket to a Shakespeare production rose beyond the means of most working people, urban audiences turned instead to less expensive houses that offered music, singing, sketches, and variety acts. At first the audiences in such theaters were generally rowdy and exclusively male. Theater and saloon owners used variety shows to attract patrons who spent money on food and liquor. Tobacco smoke filled the air, and peanut shells littered the floors. Yet these concert saloons and variety theaters attracted a range of patrons from up and down the social scale. The men at Harry Hill's famous New York saloon "represent all classes of society," one observer noted in 1882. A year later a Chicago guidebook claimed that the city's variety theaters were patronized not only by "the lower class of society, but [by] journalists, professional men, bankers, railroad officials, politicians, and men of rank in society." Even so, there were no blacks.

Increasingly, however, there were women. The presence of women made all the difference between a rowdy and a "respectable" audience. Beginning in the 1880s, a handful of show-business entrepreneurs tried to capitalize on this gender distinction by developing variety theaters that openly appealed to "mixed" audiences, that is, audiences with both males and females. The respectability of a mixed audience was one of the distinguishing signs of a new form of popular entertainment known as vaudeville.

Like the concert saloons and dollar theaters, vaudeville producers booked a variety of acts to appeal to a broad audience. They also developed continuous performances, which allowed patrons to come to a vaudeville show any time of the day or evening.

Continuous performances kept the prices down, thereby increasing the size of the potential audience. And by locating downtown in the heart of the city, vaudeville widened its appeal still further. Theater owners also regulated smoking and, over time, banned alcohol consumption, thus promoting the image that their houses were fit for entertaining the entire family. Finally, they booked great opera singers or distinguished musicians for brief appearances, in a conscious effort to enhance vaudeville's reputation for respectability. "By winning over to the varieties some who have acted only in serious drama the distinctions between theaters of various quality have been lessened," the *Dramatic Mirror* declared in 1897.

Growing audiences made it possible for vaudeville producers to construct huge theatrical "palaces" that housed ever more elaborate productions. B.F. Keith's New Theatre in Boston was advertised at its opening in 1894 as "the handsomest, most solidly constructed, most elaborately decorated, and most sumptuously appointed amusement established on the face of the earth." The high cost of such theaters kept the number of competitors down. As a result, a handful of major companies came to dominate the vaudeville theater industry in much the same way that minstrel companies had become concentrated in the hands of a few owners. Nevertheless, by the turn of the century, vaudeville theater was one of the most popular forms of public entertainment in American cities. But minstrel shows and vaudeville theaters were not the only places Americans went during their leisure time.

Sports Become Professional

As growing numbers of Americans went to the theater to be entertained, still more of them went to the baseball park or the sports arena. For a significant segment of the urban population, sports was becoming something to watch rather than something to do. In the second half of the nineteenth century Americans started paying to attend professional prizefights. They went in even larger numbers to the many professional baseball stadiums that appeared suddenly in most major cities across the country.

As the number of spectators increased, baseball and prizefighting became professionalized. Prizefighting, for example, had long been a disreputable amusement of shady bars and lower-class streets, but during the 1880s, it became a professionally organized sport attracting a huge national audience. Richard Kyle Fox, owner of the *National Police Gazette,* used his popular magazine and his considerable financial resources to transform the sport of boxing. The *Gazette* skillfully drummed up excitement about forthcoming fights by promoting personalities like John L. Sullivan, the most popular prizefighter of the age. Because Fox put up the prize money himself, he had the power to reform the sport. He made it both more profitable and more respectable. For example, Fox introduced rules that required boxers to wear gloves, limited rounds to only three minutes, and established that 10 seconds on the mat constituted a knockout.

As the sport grew in popularity, entrepreneurs sponsored fights at indoor rings where they could control unruly audiences with police and security guards. Thereafter, as Sullivan himself explained in 1892, professional prizefights took place "under police supervision, and the price of admission is put purposely high so as to exclude the rowdy element, and a gentleman can see the contest, feeling sure that he will not be robbed of any of his valuables or in any way be interfered with." Although professional prizefighting never completely lost its aura of disrepute, by the 1890s it was one of the most popular spectator sports in America, second only to baseball.

Like prizefighting, baseball was professionalized in the last half of the nineteenth century. The popularity of pro teams rested on an earlier groundswell of enthusiasm for baseball at the local level. By the 1860s baseball had become tremendously popular among city dwellers, particularly immigrants and their children. They formed hundreds of leagues in urban neighborhoods all across the country. But not until 1869, when the Cincinnati Red Stockings went on tour and charged admission, did baseball become a professional spectator sport. Soon thereafter standardized rules required overhand pitching, established the distance of the mound from the plate, and set the number of "balls" that would constitute a "walk."

Within a decade the owners of eight ball clubs had formed a National League that had all the earmarks of a corporate cartel. It restrained the power of players, restricted the number of teams to one per city, prohibited Sunday games, banned the sale of alcohol at ballparks, hired umpires, and set schedules and admission prices. Chafing under these restrictions, many players jumped to a new American Association that was formed in 1882. The owners regrouped, however, and within a year the two leagues merged and quickly reinstated the caps on player salaries and the "reserve clause" that prevented players from moving from team to team. In reaction the players formed a league of their own but were unable to match the wealth and power of the owners. By the mid-1890s the National League was in complete control of professional baseball.

Baseball idealized the principle of success based purely on merit. Objective statistics identified the best players without respect to any individual's personal background. A model of ordered competition, the baseball meritocracy provided a useful lesson in the way capitalist society was supposed to work. Professional players became working-class heroes, many of them having risen from factories and slums to achieve national success. But professional baseball reflected the realities as well as the ideals of American capitalism. The players would have been the first to point out that the owners had formed a cartel that was carefully designed to prevent professional athletes from taking advantage of the market. In addition, baseball's meritocracy had no place for the merits of African-American ball players, all of whom were rigidly excluded from the professional sport. And right from the start, baseball was very much a man's game, particularly a young man's game. Even the seating arrangements in ballparks reflected America's social divisions. Working-class fans sat in the bleachers, the middle class occupied the stands, and elites took the box seats. All the while baseball's popularity soared: In 1887, 51,000 fans watched the championship game.

The popularity of sports was reflected in the growing numbers of participants as well as spectators. As daily work became more sedentary, especially for the expanding army of white-collar workers, Americans spent more and more time engaged in physical recreation. During the late nineteenth century, the sporting life became an American pastime. The popularity of bicycling exploded, for example, particularly after the invention of the modern "safety bike" in 1888. Within a decade there were 10 million bicycles in the United States. In towns and cities across America men joined the YMCA or organized local baseball teams. The sporting life seemed democratic because it attracted Americans from very different social backgrounds. At Harvard, Yale, and Princeton young men took up football, basketball, and rowing. At Smith, Vassar, and Berkeley young women played baseball, basketball, and tennis. In urban neighborhoods ethnic groups organized Irish, Italian, and German baseball teams. Women began riding bicycles, swimming, and playing golf and croquet.

But appearances were deceptive. As the sports craze spread in the late nineteenth century, it mirrored the inequalities and anxieties of industrial America. Men who were raised to believe that independence was a sign of masculinity became concerned by the triumph of wage labor, fearing that it would make them soft and "feminine." A vocal segment of the American elite turned to athletic activities as an antidote to the supposedly feminizing tendencies of industrial capitalism. Theodore Roosevelt, the product of an old and wealthy New York family who went on to become president of the United States, believed that "commercial civilization" placed too little stress on "the more virile virtues." There is, Roosevelt argued, "no better way of counteracting this tendency than by encouraging bodily exercise and especially the sports which develop such qualities as courage, resolution and endurance."

As baseball and prizefighting became both popular and professional, elites reacted by glorifying the amateur ideal. Sports should not be a profession from which an accomplished athlete made money, they argued. Nor were sports something you should pay to observe. Rather, the

Prosperity and shorter working hours gave many middle-class Americans more leisure time than ever before. Bicycling was only one of the many physical activities that became wildly popular in the late nineteenth century.

amateur ideal embraced vigorous athletic activity for its own sake. This was a principle most easily upheld by the well-to-do. In the late nineteenth century wealthy Americans pursued the sporting life at elite colleges, exclusive race tracks, and private athletic clubs, country clubs, and yacht clubs. The posh New York Athletic Club opened its doors in 1866. At Saratoga, New York, and Newport, Rhode Island, the rich gathered for thoroughbred races and annual regattas. Lawn tennis, croquet, and yachting kept the wealthy entertained. At the same time, football emerged as a favorite sport at elite private schools. The first Harvard-Yale game was played in 1875. By the turn of the century, some of the most exclusive colleges in the Northeast had come together to form football's Ivy League, a designation that has long since become synonymous with elite private universities.

By embracing the sporting life, the American elite threw off the image of idleness and femininity long associated with wealth, commerce, and city life. The rigors of sport taught men how to face the rigors of business competition. Strenuous activity weeded out the weak and pre-

pared society's leaders for the contest of daily life. Thus the elite's attraction to rugged sports reinforced a self-serving view of American society. In the political economy of competitive capitalism the best nations, like the best men, would rise to the top. "If you are rich and worth your salt," Theodore Roosevelt explained, "you will teach your sons that though they may have leisure, it is not to be spent in idleness." Men who pursued "timid peace" were not the proper role models, he insisted. Rather, "we admire the man . . . who has those virile qualities necessary to win in the stern strife of actual life."

The most significant attempt to spread such values more widely through the population was the founding of the Young Men's Christian Association in 1851. By 1869 there were YMCAs in San Francisco, Washington, D. C., and New York City. Twenty-five years later there were 261 scattered across the nation. A strong reform impulse sustained the YMCA movement. Its founders hoped that organized recreational activity would distract workers from labor radicalism and that classes and games would help assimilate dangerous immigrants into the laws, customs, and language of the United States. In many ways the YMCA was an extension of Anthony Comstock's movement to suppress vice. The founders of the "Y" hoped to provide wholesome amusements to young men who might otherwise succumb to the temptations of city life.

World's Fairs: The Celebration of the City

To celebrate the accomplishments of urban and industrial society, the city of London hosted a spectacular world's fair at the Crystal Palace in 1851. It was a huge success. Over the next 50 years the great cities of the western world became showcases for the technological and cultural achievements of industrial capitalism. The city of Paris alone hosted five world's fairs between 1855 and 1900. By then there had been similar expositions in Vienna, Brussels, Antwerp, Florence, Amsterdam, Dublin, and even Sydney, Australia. Most of them featured the achievements of the host countries and the civic pride of their sponsoring cities. But nearly all of them celebrated the triumph of technology and the progress of humanity. American fairs were no exception. Anxious to show off the United States to an increasingly curious world, a dozen major cities sponsored world expositions in the late nineteenth and early twentieth centuries.

The first major world's fair in the United States took place in Philadelphia in 1876, timed to commemorate the centennial of American independence. It was an enormous undertaking. Machinery Hall alone required 14 acres to pay tribute to the technological marvels of industrial civilization. In keeping with the theme of global interaction, the fair's sponsors asked the nations of the world to build pavilions of their own. The pavilions were arranged to reflect not the harmony of nations but the differences among the world's "races." Americans were only beginning to develop such ideas in 1876, but the broad outlines of the racial categories were already evident. France and its colonies, "representing the Latin races," were grouped together. In a different spot England and its colonies, "representing the Anglo-Saxon races," were also placed together. So were "the Teutonic races," represented by Germany, Austria, and Hungary. Within 20 years, these racial categories would harden into an elaborate hierarchy that embraced all the peoples of the world.

Nowhere was this hierarchy more visible than at the greatest fair of the century, the World's Columbian Exposition held in Chicago in 1893. Built on Lake Michigan several miles south of the downtown "loop," the Chicago fair outdid its Philadelphia predecessor in every way. It had twice as many foreign buildings, it covered 686 acres,

and it attracted 25 million visitors. The exposition itself was divided between the fabulous White City and the Midway Plaisance. The White City was the premier showcase for American industrial might. Immense steam engines and the latest consumer goods were among its biggest attractions. But the Midway Plaisance was much more popular. It featured carnivals, the first Ferris wheel, games, and sideshows. It also featured an extraordinary ethnographic exhibit providing millions of Americans with a popular rendition of principles of scientific racism. The exhibit portrayed the "races" of the world in a hierarchy from the most to the least civilized. Sophisticated Europeans stood atop the ladder of civilization, while mysterious Asians and "savage" Africans were relegated to the lowest levels.

Where earlier forms of popular entertainment had romanticized pre-industrial society and the rural life, the world's fairs openly celebrated the new political economy of cities and industry. Native Americans and African Americans no longer functioned as props in a romantic evocation of the Old South or the western frontier. Instead, they represented the savage peoples who were the antithesis of urban and industrial society. The White City, the heart of the World's Columbian Exposition in Chicago, was an idealized vision of urban life. A marvel of Beaux-Arts architecture and a masterful example of urban planning, the White City reflected the dramatic changes that had overtaken American culture. Rural simplicity had given way to the majestic city as the model for civilized life. American culture was beginning to embrace the idea of urban civilization.

The World Columbian Exposition in Chicago was the largest of the world's fairs that became popular in the late nineteenth century. Among other things, they were celebrations of the technology and city life that were becoming the characteristics of modern, industrial civilization.

The Elusive Boundaries of Male and Female

Anthony Comstock saw the city as a place where traditional morality broke down. He was particularly disturbed by the fact that standards of sexual propriety were apparently loosened in the city. In fact, the political economy of industrial capitalism posed a serious challenge to long-standing ideals concerning the proper roles of men and women. For men who had been reared in the Jeffersonian tradition, masculinity was associated with economic independence. Wage labor, by contrast, was viewed as a form of "dependency" and was therefore associated with women. But with the triumph of wage labor, men and women were compelled to rethink traditional conceptions of masculinity and femininity. As they did so, spectacular new cities and new-found leisure time offered Americans unprecedented opportunities to test the conventional boundaries of sexual identity.

The Victorian Construction of Male and Female

Until the mid-1700s most European doctors believed that there was only one sex: Females were simply inferior, insufficiently developed versions of the males. On the inside of their bodies women had everything that men had, in more developed form, on the outside. Sometime after 1750, however, scientists and intellectuals began to argue that males and females were fundamentally different, that they were "opposite" sexes. For the first time it was possible to argue that women were naturally less interested in sex than men or that men were "active" while women were "passive." Nature itself seemed to justify the infamous double standard that condoned sexual activity among men but punished women for the same thing.

In the nineteenth century Victorians drew even more extreme differences between men and women. Victorian boys were reared on moralistic stories of heroes who overcame their fears in battle and in everyday life. In this way boys were raised to prepare themselves for the competitive worlds of business and politics, worlds from which women were largely excluded. To be a "man" in industrial America was to work outside the home, in the rough-and-tumble world of the capitalist market. Men proved themselves by their success at making a living and therefore at taking care of a wife and children. A cult of male bonding developed. Men's clubs sprang up in cities across America. Certain leisure activities, from smoking to sporting, were defined as distinctively male, and male companionship was elevated to unprecedented heights of cultural significance.

Victorian men defined themselves as supremely rational creatures whose reason was nevertheless threatened by their overwhelming sexual drives. Physical exertion was an important device for controlling a man's powerful sexual urges. In Victorian America masturbation was an unacceptable outlet for these drives. Thus men were urged to channel their sexual energies into strenuous activities such as hunting, sports, the "outdoor" life, and, conveniently enough, wage labor. Masculinity was thereby defined as the ability to leave the secure confines of the home and to compete successfully in the capitalist labor market.

Where masculinity became a more rigid concept, femininity became less certain. Women's schools established their own sports programs. Thousands of women took up bicycling, tennis, and other physical activities. Yet at the same time the stereotype persisted that women were too frail to leave the home and engage in the hurly burly of business and enterprise. Lacking the competitive instinct of the male animal, the female was destined to remain as wife and mother within the protective confines of the home. There she would be provided for by the man of the house. Just as men congregated in social clubs and sports teams, a "female world of love and ritual" developed as well. Middle-class women often displayed among themselves a passionate affection that was often expressed in nearly erotic terms. But genuinely passionate female sexuality was even more disturbing to the Victorian culture than the oversexed male. Evidence of sexual passion among women was increasingly diagnosed, mostly by male doctors, as a symptom of a new disorder called "neurasthenia."

Over time the differences between men and women were defined in increasingly medical terms. After 1850 doctors replaced ministers as the authoritative voices on matters of sex, reproduction, and morality. Victorian doctors redefined homosexuality as a medical abnormality, a perversion, and urged the passage of laws outlawing sexual relations between consenting adults of the same gender. The new science of gynecology powerfully reinforced popular assumptions about the differences between men and women. But rather than attribute sexual differences to divine providence, medical experts attributed them to the power of the body, and in the case of women, the power of the womb. As one male expert explained in 1871, woman is "what she is in health, in character, in her charms, alike of body, mind and soul because of her womb alone." Distinguished male physicians argued that the energy women expended in reproduction left them unable to withstand the rigors of higher education. This medicalization of gender differences led some doctors to mutilate women's bodies to cure mental "disorders." In extreme cases physicians would excise a woman's clitoris to thwart masturbation or remove her ovaries to cure nurasthenia.

On the assumption that motherhood was a female's natural destiny, doctors pressed to restrict women's access to contraception and to prohibit abortion. Before the Civil War abortion in the first three months of pregnancy was tolerated, although not necessarily approved. This began to change as the medical profession organized itself and claimed control over the regulation of female reproduction. Asserting its professional authority, the American Medical Association (founded in 1847) campaigned to restrict the activities not only of quacks and incompetents, but also of female midwives and abortionists. Most doctors were males, and most of them accepted prevailing assumptions about the maternal destiny of women. Hence doctors opposed almost anything that would allow women to interfere with pregnancy. The AMA supported passage of the Comstock Law, which outlawed the sale of contraception. Doctors also pushed successfully to criminalize abortion. Between 1860 and 1890, 40 state legislatures made abortion illegal.

Victorians Who Questioned Traditional Sexual Boundaries

One reason Victorians struggled so mightily to maintain traditional sex roles and to suppress their emotions was that all around them men and women seemed to be indulging

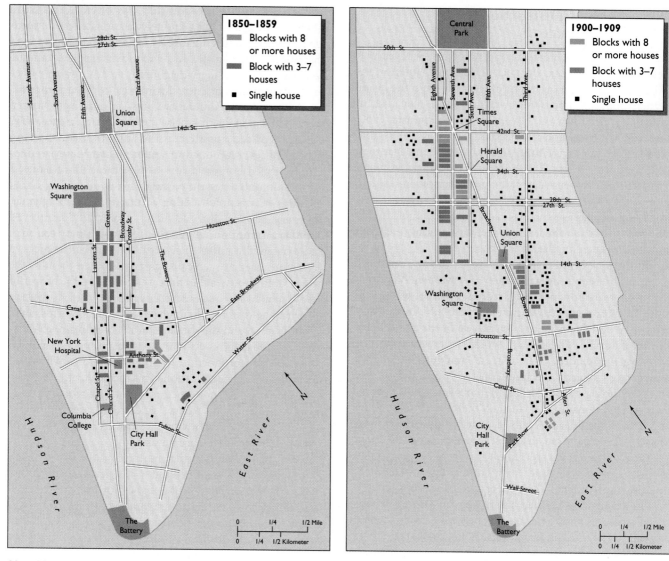

Map 18-1   Houses of Prostitution, 1850–1859 and 1900–1909.
One measure of the sexual freedom characteristic of city life was the explosive increase in prostitution. As the demand for prostitution rose, so did attempts to suppress it.

Source: Timothy J. Gilfoyle, City of Eros (New York: WW Norton, 1992), p. 33.

their passions and abandoning the strict division between male and female. In a new political economy based on wage labor large numbers of Americans, especially young men, now found themselves with cash and leisure time. The anonymity of huge cities gave them the opportunity to defy established standards of sexual behavior. Freed from the constraints of parents and the scrutiny of small-town life, wage earners began to pay for various forms of sexual amusement. They frequented prostitutes in unprecedented numbers (see Map 18-1). They attended shows that increasingly featured sexually provocative entertainers. They read erotic novels, and they purchased pornographic prints. Thousands, perhaps millions, of Americans began to explore unconventional sexual practices.

The major venues of popular entertainment increasingly displayed a looser, more relaxed attitude toward sex.

Can-can girls, off-color jokes, and comedy skits focusing on the war of the sexes—all of these contradicted the Victorian embrace of extreme propriety and familial harmony. Even the styles of clothing that consumers purchased in mass quantities were a rejection of the stifling conventions of the Victorian middle class. Trousers got looser, starched collars disappeared, women's dresses were simplified and rendered considerably more comfortable.

The sensuous human body became an object of fascination in much of the popular culture. Minstrels, musical variety shows, and the vaudeville theater all glorified female sexuality. For the first time male sports heroes were openly admired for their physiques. Eugene Sandow made a career out of touring the country to show off his well-developed body to large audiences. After his public performances, Sandow often offered smaller showings in a special room offstage. There he lectured to intimate groups of about 15 people. "As I step before you," he would say, "I want each of you to pass the palm of your hand across my chest." Men touched his pectorals with astonishment and admiration. During one showing Sandow had to coax a woman who hesitated to participate. "These muscles, madam, are hard as iron itself, I want you to convince yourself of the fact." He ran her hand slowly across his chest. "It's unbelievable," she cried, and then fainted.

Female impersonation, one of the major innovations of the minstrel show in the late nineteenth century, pushed the boundaries of convention even further. According to actress Olive Logan, some of the female impersonators were "marvelously well fitted by nature for it, having well-defined soprano voices, plump shoulders, beardless faces, and tiny hands and feet." The most famous female impersonator was Francis Leon, who billed himself simply as "Leon." According to one critic, Leon was "more womanly in his by-play and mannerisms than the most charming female imaginable." Leon apparently relished his reputation. He explained, "with real feminine pride," that he never wore "costumes." He dressed only in authentic women's clothing.

Much of the literature of the day was infused with the theme of homosexual relations. Walt Whitman's poems sometimes celebrated sexual attraction among men, and some scholars see elements of homoeroticism in Huckleberry Finn's relationship with Jim in Mark Twain's famous novel. A more obvious case is Horatio Alger. In the late nineteenth century he wrote a series of books about young boys who lived on the streets of New York and made their way out of poverty. Alger's heroes thus earned a reputation as embodiments of the American dream of upward mobility. Alger began his own career as a Unitarian minister in Brewster, Massachusetts, but in 1866 he was expelled from his pulpit for "the revolting crime of unnatural familiarity with boys." Alger left New England in disgrace and made his way to New York. There he developed a keen interest in the problems of young boys who roamed loose and in increasing numbers on the city streets.

Alger's charity work became the basis of his fiction. In most of his novels, the young heroes shared the same physical attributes. They were dirty but handsome. "In spite of his dirt and rags," Alger wrote of one of his most famous characters, "there was something about Dick that was attractive. It was easy to see if he had been clean and well dressed he would have been decidedly good looking." In most cases it was the boy's good looks that first attracted the attention of the wealthy male patron. Alger's novels depicted the relationships between men and boys in terms reminiscent of a seduction. Once rescued from rags and gainfully employed, the most common pattern in Alger's novels was for the hero to set up house with a roommate. These households had all the earmarks of Victorian respectability. They were fastidiously neat, and their inhabitants were thrifty and sober. The only differ-

ence from an ideal middle-class household was that both inhabitants were male. In one case, two male roommates, having both been saved and made respectable, actually "adopted" a little boy, a street urchin named "Mark the Matchboy."

Few readers saw Horatio Alger's novels as experiments in unconventional sexuality, but the homoeroticism of his stories was consistent with the increased sexual frankness of urban life in the late nineteenth century. In the big city it was possible to experiment as never before, and an individual could, quite literally, get lost in the crowd. It was not surprising that reformers like Anthony Comstock looked at the city and saw an explosion of vice. Others, however, were struck less by urban sexuality than by the profusion of immigrants who were transforming the culture of the city.

Immigration as a Cultural Problem

When the novelist Henry James returned to the United States in 1907 after having lived a quarter of a century in Europe, he was stunned and disgusted by the pervasive presence of immigrants in New York City. On the streetcars he confronted "a row of faces, up and down, testifying, without exception, to alienism unmistakable, alienism undisguised and unashamed." His walks through Central Park were disturbed by the "babel" of foreign languages. The Jewish immigrants on the Lower East Side reminded him of "animals . . . snakes or worms." The tenements occupied by the city's immigrants seemed like a zoo to James,

Jacob Riis, who included this photo in his classic study of immigrant slums, How The Other Half Lives, believed that immigrant neighborhoods were plagued by the absence of culture.

"a little world of bars and perches for human squirrels and monkeys." Immigrants had transformed James' city, and he clearly disapproved. He was one of the many native-born Americans who assumed that their culture was Protestant, democratic, and English-speaking. They were deeply disturbed, therefore, by the arrival of vast numbers of immigrants who were Catholic or Jewish, who came from nations with little or no democratic tradition, and who spoke Chinese, Italian, or Yiddish. Native-born Americans were even more disturbed by the way ethnic subcultures seemed to flourish in the United States, particularly in the big cities. Yet among immigrants and their children, an ethnic identity was often a sign of assimilation into a broader American culture.

Josiah Strong Attacks Immigration

"Every race which has deeply impressed itself on the human family has been the representative of some great idea," Josiah Strong wrote in *Our Country*. Greek civilization was famed for its beauty, he explained, the Romans for their law, the Hebrews for their purity. The Anglo-Saxon race had two great ideas to its credit, Strong argued. The first was the love of liberty, and the second was "pure *spiritual* Christianity." Published in 1885, Strong's book was a bestseller by the standards of the day. By the time it was revised and reprinted in 1891, *Our Country* had been serialized in newspapers across America and had sold over 130,000 copies as a book. Strong spoke to the concerns of

vast numbers of native-born Americans who saw themselves as the defenders of Anglo-Saxon culture. The time was coming, Strong warned them, when the pressures of population would be felt across the entire globe. "Then will the world enter upon a new stage of its history—*the final competition of races, for which the Anglo-Saxon is being schooled.*" Strong was optimistic. As representatives of "the largest liberty, the purest Christianity, the highest civilization," the powerful Anglo-Saxon race "will spread itself over the earth."

But there was a problem. To Strong and his readers, the Anglo-Saxon in America was threatened by the arrival of vast numbers of immigrants. "During the last ten years we have suffered a peaceful invasion by an army more than four times as vast as the estimated number of Goths and Vandals that swept over Southern Europe and overwhelmed Rome." The typical immigrant, he warned, was not a freedom-loving Anglo-Saxon Protestant but a "European peasant." Narrow-minded men and women "whose moral and religious training has been meager or false," immigrants brought crime to America's cities and convicts to America's jails. And they undermined the nation's politics just as they undermined its morals. Immigrants voted in blocks, as Mormons, as Catholics, and increasingly as socialists. Furthermore, the influence of immigrants was enhanced by the fact that they were concentrated in big cities. "[T]here is no more serious menace to our civilization," Strong warned, "than our rabble-ruled cities."

At the core of the problem was the fact that immigrants could not be assimilated into the American way of life. "Our safety demands the assimilation of these strange populations," Strong wrote. But they were coming in such huge numbers that assimilation was becoming impossible (see Map 18-2). Politicians encouraged them to retain their alien identities by voting, for example, as Germans or as Irish. Worst of all, the Catholic Church held millions of immigrants in its grip, filling their heads with superstition rather than "pure Christianity." It did not help that immigrants had large numbers of children. Through its elaborate network of parochial schools, the Catholic Church was training new generations to love tyranny rather than liberty. The future of Anglo-Saxon civilization and with it the future of the world was, according to Strong, thereby thrown into doubt.

Strong and his readers need not have worried. The millions of immigrants who came to the United States adapted with surprising speed to American society. Indeed, Strong misread much of his own evidence. By cultivating the German vote or the Irish vote, for example, politicians went far toward assimilating immigrants into American political culture. Nor were immigrants as slavishly subservient to the Catholic Church as Strong made them out to be. In the end, the Church played an ambiguous role in the cultural history of American immigrants.

web connection

The French Canadian Controversy

www.prenhall.com/boydston/frenchcanadian

In 1880 Colonel Carroll D. Wright, head of the Massachusetts Bureau of the Statistics of Labor, founder of the scientific collection of data in the U.S., and a tireless advocate for causes such as temperance, shorter working hours, and an end to child labor, wrote in an official report that the "Canadian French are the Chinese of the Eastern States." Outraged French Canadians demanded an opportunity to prove "we are a white people." The controversy occasioned by Wright's remarks provides a window on the ways various groups of Americans thought about who was and was not "white." How did the French Canadians set about proving they were "a white people"?

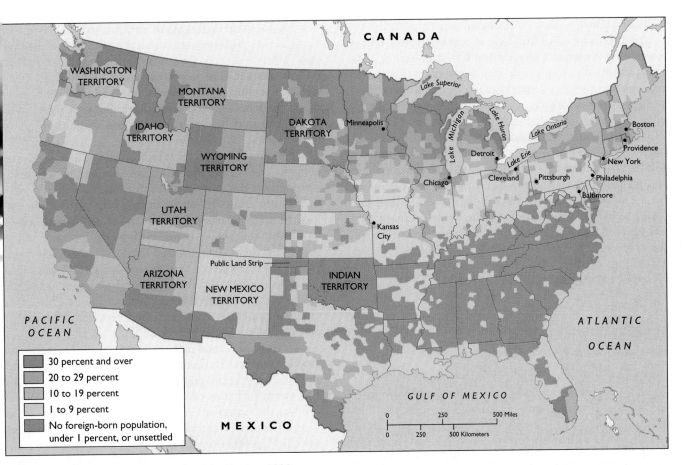

Map 18-2   Population of Foreign Birth by Region, 1880.

Source: Clifford L. Lord and Elizabeth H. Lord, Lord & Lord Historical Atlas of the United States (New York: Holt, 1953).

From Immigrants to Ethnic Americans

Critics like Strong scarcely noticed the regional and class differences that immigrants brought with them from their homelands. In the middle of the nineteenth century, most immigrants came to America with loyalties to their regions and villages, but not to their nationality. In New York City German-speaking immigrants thought of themselves primarily as Bavarian or Prussian rather than as German. In San Francisco, Italians from Genoa fought with immigrants from Sicily over control of the city's fishing industry. Irish immigrants long identified with their home counties more than their native country. Immigrant churches across America were torn by such regional conflicts. In Gary, Indiana, Serbs from Lika fought with Serbs from Montenegro. In Chicago, Greeks from Sparta would not associate with Greeks from Arcadia.

After immigrants arrived in the United States, however, regional differences began to decline. One reason for this was the spectacular growth of secular fraternal organizations. Many immigrants were accustomed to joining voluntary associations in their homelands—there were

over 6,000 such organizations in southern Italy by 1894, for example—but as they were transplanted to the United States, fraternal organizations quickly lost their regional identities. They often began as mutual-aid societies designed to help newcomers find jobs and housing. In 1893 mineworkers formed the Pennsylvania Slovak Catholic Union to help workers cover burial expenses for those killed in the mines. Most often, however, middle-class immigrants took the lead in forming fraternal organizations; in other cases local priests played prominent roles. Regardless of their leadership, about half of all immigrants eventually joined ethnic fraternal societies.

As they grew, fraternal organizations became national in their scope. In place of the older, local identity, immigrant associations constructed a new "ethnic" identity that united all members under a single national rubric. In some cases immigrant businessmen led the drive toward the development of a unified ethnic identity. Marco Fontana, who ran the Del Monte company in California, encouraged the growth of an "Italian" identity among his workers. He found that regional loyalties hindered the efficient operation of his enterprises. German businessmen like

William Steinway, the piano manufacturer, actually attempted to bring all of his German workers together in a town of their own at College Point on Long Island, New York. Eventually, immigrants began to think of themselves as ethnic groups who shared the same national ancestry.

It was not merely coincidental that immigrants developed "national" identities in the United States. Nationalism was spreading throughout the western world during the nineteenth century. While immigrants in America were coming to see themselves as Irish or Italian, the same thing was happening back home in Ireland, Italy, and Germany, for example. In the United States the Civil War had unleashed a wave of nationalistic fervor, while a series of liberal revolutions did the same thing in many European nations. It is not surprising, therefore, that as the decades passed immigrants brought to America an increasingly powerful sense of their ethnic identities.

The Catholic Church and Its Limits in Immigrant Culture

The Roman Catholic Church played a complicated role in the development of ethnic cultures among immigrants. In some cases churches were established to preserve Old World traditions rather than encourage adjustment to American ways. In 1841, for example, the Reverend Johann Raffeiner collected the money to build Holy Trinity, a German-speaking Catholic church designed to preserve the language and traditions of the Old World. In other ways the church smoothed the transition into American life by performing the functions of a mutual-aid society. In 1864 the Sisters of Mercy established the Magdalen Asylum to assist the San Francisco Irish, for example. Polish churches in Chicago and German parishes in Milwaukee used their women's groups and youth clubs as mutual-aid societies for their local immigrants.

Yet the church meant different things to different immigrant groups, and in that way it unintentionally sped the development of ethnic identities. The Irish became more devout in America as they came to rely on the church to assist them in resisting the pressures of an overwhelmingly Protestant culture. Germans also gravitated toward the church and in the process overcame their regional differences. But the more they came to equate their German identity with Catholicism, the more they resented Irish domination of the church hierarchy. Thus German Catholics worked hard to establish their own churches and their own parish schools or to have sermons preached in German. By contrast, the Italians were largely alienated from the official church. By the late nineteenth century North American bishops were making strenuous efforts to standardize Catholicism in America. They published uniform catechisms and established powerful bureaucratic systems of control. But the hierarchy was largely Irish, and

it tried to suppress many of the folk rituals of Italian Catholicism. Bishops particularly disapproved of the Italians' practice of processions and their heavy reliance on statues. Thus Italians were ironically united in their suspicion of the church. They would not send their children to parochial schools, they were more likely to worship at home, and they held their processions without priests in attendance.

The church's power was reinforced by the struggle for control over the education of immigrant children. Throughout the nineteenth century public schools were heavily Protestant. Josiah Strong and other native-born reformers tried to use public education to "Americanize" immigrant children in a number of ways. They taught the Protestant *Bible*. They shifted the focus in the classroom away from the classics and toward "practical" education and language training. The reformers' goal was to turn immigrants into reliable workers and patriotic citizens. But immigrants fiercely resisted such efforts, and the bulwark of their resistance was the church.

During the second half of the nineteenth century both the Catholic and Lutheran Churches established systems of parochial schools designed to protect immigrant children from the biases of public education. So comprehensive was the Catholic Church's effort that by 1883 all but two parishes in the city of Chicago had their own parochial schools. The Missouri synod of the Lutheran Church set up its own system of church schools, for similar reasons. And immigrants from smaller groups often set up their own folk schools.

Ironically, parochial education contributed to the breakdown of cultural identities among immigrants. Catholic or Lutheran schools in Irish or German parishes reinforced the growth of distinctively American ethnic identities. They also bound ethnicity to an increasingly standardized and characteristically American Catholicism or Lutheranism. But assimilation is only part of the story of immigrant culture in America. What repelled Henry James and others were the genuinely distinctive aspects of immigrant life.

The Political Economy of Immigrant Culture

Despite assimilation, the ethnic identities that immigrants developed in America remained distinctive. Irish Americans, for example, fused together songs from various parts of Ireland and then added piano music to accompany the singing. Similarly, Polish immigrant bands expanded beyond the traditional violin of their homelands by adding accordions, clarinets and trumpets. But the results were still distinctively Polish-American or Irish-American musical forms. Hundreds of immigrant theaters sprang up across the country offering productions that adjusted traditional story lines to the needs of the New World. Jewish plays told of humble peddlers who outwitted their prosperous patrons. Italian folk tales emphasized the impor-

Despite the concerns of conservatives, immigrants brought rich cultural traditions with them to America and readily adapted their cultures to their new surroundings. Pictured here is a German immigrant band from Glen Lyon, Pennsylvania.

tance of the family. In these ways distinctive ethnic identities developed but they did so in ways that were suited to the needs of urban and industrial America.

One of the most distinctive features of immigrant culture was the family. At a time when the number of children in middle-class families had declined to two or three per household, immigrant families remained large. There were sound economic reasons for this. In the late nineteenth century there were no child-labor laws restricting the employment of minors and few compulsory-education laws requiring all children to attend school. Working-class families relied heavily on the incomes of their children, particularly their teenage children. "When you work," one immigrant recalled, you "bring your pay home and give it to your parents. And whatever they feel they want to give you, they decide. There was no disagreement." Children in the immigrant working class were expected to contribute to the economic well-being of their families.

Thus economics and culture combined to encourage large families among many immigrants. At the turn of the century, Italian mothers in Buffalo, New York, had an average of eleven children. Among Polish wives the average was closer to eight, which was still large by the standards of the native-born middle class. In Pennsylvania's coal-mining district,

working-class immigrant women had 45 percent more children than native-born women. But the death rate among immigrant children was also very high. In 1900, one out of three Polish and Italian mothers had seen one of their children die before his or her first birthday. Nevertheless, when Anglo-Saxons like Josiah Strong turned their attention to immigrants, one of the first things they noticed was the large size of their families.

Finally, many of the most noticeable distinctions of ethnic subcultures were grounded in the fact that immigrants were disproportionately working class. Indeed, as ethnicity developed in the late nineteenth century, class divisions were increasingly difficult to isolate from cultural distinctions. The middle class, for example, was overwhelmingly native born, white, Anglo-Saxon, and Protestant. The working class was, by contrast, African American, foreign born, Catholic, or Jewish. By 1900, 75 percent of the manufacturing workers in the United States were immigrants or the children of immigrants (see Figure 18-2). In cities like New York, five out of six new manufacturing jobs were filled by immigrants and their children. In the South, wage laborers were overwhelmingly African-American sharecroppers, and landlords were overwhelmingly white, Anglo-Saxon Protestants. It was in this context that educated elites worked

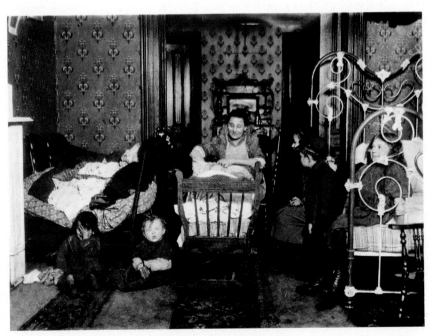

Immigrants often crowded into "tenements," a new form of apartment building that actually improved living conditions for many of America's poor city dwellers.

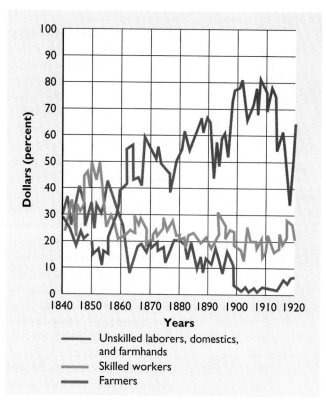

Figure 18-2 Working-Class Immigration, 1840–1920.
Source: U.S. Bureau of the Census.

strenuously to construct a definition of "high culture" that would distinguish the sober middle classes from the allegedly uncultivated and uncultured working classes.

The Creation of High Culture

During the second half of the nineteenth century many leading intellectuals sought to isolate and define a tradition (high culture) that stretched through western history all the way back to ancient Greece and Rome. This tradition looked to the secular intellect as a source of moral guidance. The eternal truths of art and literature, many intellectuals argued, would allow anxious men and women to navigate the uncertainties of urban and industrial society. At the same time, the natural and social sciences claimed to have located the immovable bedrock of truth. High culture also assured Americans that they stood atop the hierarchy of the world's peoples. Biologists placed white men at the pinnacle of the evolutionary scale. Political scientists declared the superiority of western European forms of government. Humanists found transcendent beauty and absolute truth in the art, literature, and music of the western world. By the 1890s these principles of social, cultural, and political hierarchy were firmly installed in museums, li-

braries, and universities across the United States. A high culture had been created.

High Culture Becomes Sacred

The leading advocate of high culture was an Englishman named Matthew Arnold. In *Culture and Anarchy,* published in 1869, Arnold promoted the study of "the best which has been thought and said in the world" as an antidote to the "anarchy" of capitalist society. He looked to culture as "the great help out of our present difficulties." But Arnold was not alone. Similar views about high culture were already spreading on both sides of the Atlantic. "Certain things are not disputable," *Harper's* Magazine declared in 1867; authors such as Homer, Shakespeare, and Dante "are towering facts like the Alps or the Himalaya. . . . It is not conceivable that the judgment of mankind upon those names will ever be reversed." American elites looking for firm moral guidelines were turning to a canon of great cultural achievements the way earlier generations had looked to holy scripture. Secular culture thereby assumed sacred qualities. The artist's vocation, Edward Baxter Perry wrote in 1892, "is, or should be, a religion."

Lurking beneath the sacred view of culture was the fear that the modern world had undermined traditional values, especially religious values. "Organizations are splitting asunder, institutions are falling into decay, customs are becoming uncustomary," one observer complained in 1865. Particularly troubling was the apparent decline in religious fervor. Middle-class men and women often confessed to a loss of their own faith. In 1887 Frederick Law Olmsted, the social critic and landscape architect, commented on the religious enthusiasm he had felt 40 years earlier as a Yale undergraduate. "I only think it is queer that I could ever have thought myself to have such ideas as I did," he wrote, "and queer that anyone else can continue to have them."

The middle class never lost its faith entirely. On the contrary, Victorians retained their overwhelmingly Protestant orientation and their deep suspicion of Roman Catholicism. What they lost was a strong theology and the zeal that had marked the Second Great Awakening of the 1820s. Victorians moved restlessly from one denomination to another, but few found the spiritual satisfaction or moral guidance they sought. "I find I am living an objective life with almost no introspection," James Garfield, the future president, wrote in 1857. "I fear I am losing spirituality of soul." As religious fervor waned, the Victorian middle class looked for comfort in more secular pursuits.

Thomas Wentworth Higginson typified this shift. Nurtured in the reform movements of antebellum New England, Higginson had been an abolitionist and a supporter of women's rights. During the Civil War he commanded a regiment of African-American troops that earned fame thanks to Higginson's postwar memoir of their experience. Fully engaged in the politics of his day, Higginson was equally at home in the literary culture of his native New England. He had known Emerson and Thoreau as a young man, and he sustained a long friendship with Emily Dickinson after the war. During those postwar years many men of his class grew disenchanted by capitalist greed and political corruption. Like them, Higginson turned to culture for relief from the sordid realities of capitalist political economy.

In 1871, two years after Matthew Arnold published *Culture and Anarchy,* Higginson made a strikingly similar case. Higginson wrote as if culture had a life of its own. Culture, he explained, "pursues" art and science for their intrinsic worth. It "places the fine arts above the useful arts." It sacrifices "material comforts" for the sake of a "nobler" life. He even worried that the unrestrained pursuit of culture could result in "a reactionary distrust of the whole spirit of the age." But at its best, Higginson believed, culture reminds men and women that there is more to life "than meat." It "supplies that counterpoise to mere wealth which Europe vainly seeks to secure by aristocracies of birth." Like Matthew Arnold, Higginson saw culture as a defense against the materialism of the age.

Despite his contempt for the European aristocracy, Higginson could write just as condescendingly about ordinary people. He thus shared the Victorian conviction that culture was an attribute of the middle classes. At the top of the social order stood an increasingly dissolute and unrestrained capitalist class. At the bottom, poor working men and women were thoroughly consumed by the grubby need to find adequate food, clothing, and shelter. They lived lives utterly devoid of gentility and refinement, and they were jammed into cities that mushroomed to enormous sizes. To many progressive intellectuals, therefore, saving America from barbarism required an infusion of culture into the lives of ordinary city folk. "Tenement houses have no aesthetic resources," Jacob Riis argued in his 1890 exposé of the slums of New York City, *How the Other Half Lives.* "If any are to be brought to bear on them, they must come from the outside."

Yet these very classes, the greedy capitalists at the top and the ignorant masses below, seemed to grow in influence as cities grew in size. To counteract this threat, American elites joined forces to transform American cities into centers of high art and cultural distinction. They built great museums and impressive public libraries to expose the common people to the canon of great works.

The Creation of a Cultural Establishment

In the early nineteenth century Shakespeare was the most popular playwright in America. Traveling through the country in the 1830s Alexis de Tocqueville encountered Shakespeare even in "the recesses of the forests of the New World. There is hardly a pioneer's hut that does not contain a few odd volumes of Shakespeare. I remember that I

read the feudal drama of *Henry V* for the first time in a log cabin." In established theaters, Shakespearean plays were performed more than any others, and the repertoire was not limited to a few classics. American audiences were familiar with a substantial body of Shakespeare's work. The American consul in England declared that Shakespearean dramas were "more frequently played and more popular in America than in England." Nor were such performances restricted to big eastern cities. Small western cities such as Louisville, Natchez, and Cincinnati rushed to set up theater companies in which Shakespeare was performed more than any other playwright. Traveling troupes of Shakespearean actors appeared in the mining camps of California and Nevada, in hotel dining rooms, and above saloons in small towns and villages across America.

A Shakespearean play was rarely performed alone. It was most often the centerpiece of an entire evening's entertainment that included music and dancing along with acrobats, magicians, and comedians. The show generally ended with a short humorous skit, or farce. Audiences attending these shows came from all walks of life, and they often made a noisy crowd. "The more they like a play, the louder they whistle," a French reporter observed in San Francisco in 1851. They were even less reserved in their

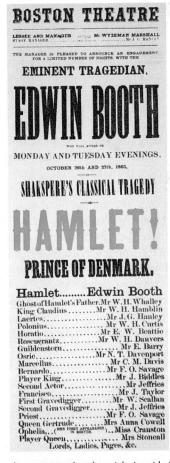

Shakespeare was the most popular playwright in mid-nineteenth-century America. This 1863 playbill advertised the appearance of one of the most popular Shakespearean actors of the times.

criticism. When an audience in Sacramento disapproved of a performance of *Richard III*, "cabbages, carrots, pumpkins, potatoes, a wreath of vegetables, a sack of flour and one of soot, a dead goose, with other articles . . . made their appearance upon the stage." Often what the audiences objected to was not the acting or the production but the content of the play. Americans preferred highly melodramatic renditions of Shakespeare. It was best if the moral ambiguities were smoothed out, the lessons made sharp and clear. Ideally the ending was always satisfying. Good always triumphed over evil. Instead of committing suicide, Romeo and Juliet lived happily ever after. Nevertheless, by 1850 Americans were so familiar with Shakespeare that politicians could safely make allusions to his plays without fear of losing an audience.

All of this changed in the second half of the nineteenth century. Shakespeare was redefined as high culture. Performances of his plays were separated from other features of popular entertainment. This shift was evident as early as the 1850s, when a San Francisco theater announced that its production of *A Midsummer Night's Dream* would be performed by itself, with "NO FARCE." The various entertainments that had once accompanied Shakespearean performances were separated out and became the basis of the vaudeville theater. Theater audiences also became segregated. The respectable classes retreated from the boisterous houses into quieter theaters where the prices rose beyond the means of ordinary working people. Acting styles changed as well. Shakespeare was performed more quietly, less melodramatically. Audiences became spectators who were no longer engaged with the actors on stage. By the end of the century, Shakespeare had entered the canon of great works, best appreciated by the educated elite.

The same thing happened to opera. In the first half of the nineteenth century opera was an eclectic and highly popular art form in the United States. Performances were often mixed with popular songs and music, as in "The Traviata Quickstep." Most opera was sung in English before engaged, boisterous audiences. After 1850, however, elite critics registered their complaints. They insisted that opera be sung in the original Italian, German, or French. By the twentieth century, in the words of one observer, opera was "controlled by a few rich men who think it a part of the life of a great city that there should be an opera house with a fine orchestra, fine scenery, and the greatest singers obtainable. It does not exist for the good of the whole city, but rather for those of plethoric purses." Opera had become associated with high fashion and elite culture. In several cities the opening of the opera season became synonymous with the opening of the "social season" among the very rich.

So it went with orchestral music as well. In the first half of the nineteenth century, local bands sprang up in thousands of communities across America (3,000 of them by 1860) with a repertoire that included a mixture of popular and classical pieces. But beginning in the 1840s and continuing through the end of the century, classical music

Orchestra Hall in Chicago was one of many stately auditoriums built to house America's major symphony orchestras in the second half of the nineteenth century.

became the preserve of elite symphony orchestras in Boston, New York, Chicago, Philadelphia, and other large cities.

To sound their best, orchestras like the New York Philharmonic and the Chicago Symphony needed expensive new halls. Opera companies needed endowments. Serious theater needed generous patrons. To support the arts in the manner to which they were becoming accustomed, great infusions of private wealth were necessary. In the late nineteenth century, the rich formed an alliance with leading performers and intellectuals to create a cultural establishment that endures to this day. The great opera houses and symphony halls were built with and sustained by the patronage of the wealthiest citizens. They were the architectural embodiment of the "high culture" that developed after the Civil War.

Great cities required great museums as well. Along with the symphony halls and the opera houses Americans built a stunning array of secular temples devoted to the inspired creations of the world's great artists. In 1870 New York's Metropolitan Museum of Art and the Boston Museum of Fine Arts were established. The Philadelphia Museum of Art was founded in 1876 and the Art Institute of Chicago in 1879. Spectacular new public libraries appeared in the same cities around the same time. By 1900 many Americans had come to associate "culture" with impressive institutions lodged in major cities. By this reasoning, for example, the cultural life of Chicago was embodied not in the immigrant neighborhoods or the popular theaters but in the Art Institute, Symphony Hall, and the Chicago Public Library.

The Emergence of the Modern University

At the same time that American elites were endowing cities with great museums and libraries they stepped up their commitment to the establishment of distinguished private universities. Cornell, Johns Hopkins, Vanderbilt, Stanford, and the University of Chicago all appeared between the late 1860s and the 1890s. Wealthy businessmen had good reason to endow great universities. The political economy of industrial capitalism rested more than ever on technological developments, which in turn depended on the most up-to-date scientific learning. Research universities increasingly played a central role in such developments. In addition, large corporations demanded an educated elite trained in the art of management and the science of engineering. Universities provided the training for this new elite. And finally, corporate philanthropists agreed with many Americans that a great western nation required great universities. Hence the proliferation of richly endowed colleges in the late nineteenth century.

Not only were there more great American centers of higher education than ever, the colleges themselves reflected a new conception of how universities should be organized. In 1876 Daniel Coit Gilman became the first president of the newly established Johns Hopkins University in Baltimore. Gilman was strongly influenced by German methods of scholarship and teaching. He created specialized departments of History, English, and the various sciences. He gave the departments primary responsibility for recommending appointments and promotions and for developing their own courses. He encouraged the publication of academic journals and he established the first university press in 1878. Gilman had created the modern university with a faculty of specialists dedicated to research and the training of other scholars. His innovations spread quickly to other colleges during the 1870s and 1880s. Out of this reform movement came the undergraduate major, the system of numbered courses, unit requirements, electives, and Ph. D programs with research seminars and dissertations based on original research. The antebellum college teacher, grounded in the ministry, gave way to the modern professor who was a highly trained specialist and a secular professional.

In this new setting, the study of modern literature entered the college curriculum for the first time. Some professors, influenced by German scholarship, emphasized sentence structures, word roots, and forms of publication. This approach appealed to those who sought to make the study of literature into a science, as demanding as was the older study of Greek and Latin. But beneath the surface was a set of assumptions about the intrinsic superiority of western European languages. A leading Oxford scholar, Friedrich Max Muller, used his linguistic skills to isolate what he called the "great Aryan brotherhood." Muller saw "an unbroken chain between us and Cicero and Aristotle." In this way, Muller and his American followers created a canon of great works that they believed defined culture of the "West." They also defined the study of literature as the preserve of highly trained specialists.

Leading scholars in the new "social sciences" of sociology, anthropology, and political science also divided the world into great and inferior nations. Best of all were the so-called "Teutonic" nations of western Europe and North America. John W. Burgess, a founder of political science in the United States, declared in 1884 that "the creation of Teutonic political genius stamps the Teutonic nations as the political nations *par excellence*, and authorizes them, in the economy of the world, to assume the leadership in the establishment and administration of the states." Anthropologists, sociologists, and professional economists also claimed that the human hierarchies they constructed were grounded in the objective methods of pure science. Science was becoming the model for the production of all human knowledge.

Social Darwinism and the Growth of Scientific Racism

In 1859 Charles Darwin published his masterpiece of evolutionary theory, *On the Origin of Species*. Several scientists had already suggested that human life was not created at one moment but rather evolved over a long period of time. But Darwin offered the first persuasive theory of how this evolution might have taken place. He argued that a process of "natural selection" favored those genetic changes that were most suited to the surrounding environment. In Darwinian theory, natural selection was the single most important explanation for the vast array of life forms on earth. American scientists were remarkably receptive to Darwinism. By 1880 the Presbyterian *Observer* was frustrated that it could find only two working naturalists who did not believe in evolution. Asa Gray at Harvard and Joseph LeConte at the University of California spread the evolutionary word in their influential textbooks on botany and geology. By 1900 virtually all the science textbooks used in American high schools embraced evolution.

Darwin's remarkable influence did not stop with the natural sciences. The evolutionary hierarchy he outlined, from the lowest to the highest forms of life, also intrigued social scientists. They were particularly interested in applying the theory of natural selection to social as well as biological evolution. This combination of social theory with evolutionary science was known as **social Darwinism.** The leading theorist of social Darwinism was an Englishman named Herbert Spencer. In the United States Spencer's most influential follower was William Graham Sumner, who taught sociology at Yale. Social Darwinists argued that human inequality was the outcome of a struggle for survival in which the fittest rose to the top of the social

GROWING UP IN AMERICA

Jane Addams at College

Jane Addams became a successful activist while still in school, long before she became famous for her social work among Chicago's poor. In 1877, at the age of 17, Addams enrolled in a seminary at Rockford, Illinois, to begin her college education. The fact that the school still called itself a seminary rather than a college was one indication that it had yet to transform its curriculum along the lines of Johns Hopkins, Cornell, or Harvard. Nevertheless, over the next several years, Jane and her contemporaries brought the struggle over the modern curriculum to Rockford. "So much of our time is spent in preparation, so much in routine . . . ," Addams complained while at the seminary. She and her companions therefore made "various and restless attempts" to challenge the "dull obtuseness" of the college curriculum.

In one of those "various attempts" Jane and her friends took opium in an effort to stimulate their imaginations; it didn't work. They fell in love with the grand themes of Greek philosophy and Romantic literature, but in the end they yearned for a more practical course of study in history and economics. More than the others in her group, Jane resisted the "evangelical" pressure to become a missionary. Instead, she threw herself into the movement to upgrade Rockford's curriculum so that it could join the growing number of colleges that awarded bachelor's degrees to women. She and her friends studied mathematics. They represented Rockford at the state intercollegiate oratory competition, the first time a women's college in Illinois was represented at such an event.

Above all, Jane and her colleagues were fascinated by science. In it they saw the unvarnished search for truth, freed from all dogmatism. They were inspired by the example of Charles Darwin. They were frustrated by those teachers who had yet to accept the theory of natural selection and also by the meager scientific holdings in the school's library. "I used to bring back in my handbag books belonging to an advanced brother-in-law who had studied medicine in Germany," Addams wrote some years later, "and who was therefore quite emancipated."

By studying mathematics, science, history, and economics, Addams had taken it upon herself to step outside the

A young Jane Addams was one of a new generation of college-educated women who committed themselves to social reforms.

boundaries of the traditional seminary curriculum. In so doing she and her friends transformed Rockford. A year after she had left college, Addams and a classmate returned "to receive the degree we had so eagerly anticipated." Together with two new graduates, they "were dubbed B.A. on the very day that Rockford Seminary was declared a college in the midst of tumultuous anticipations."

ladder. This theory made the rich seem more fit than the poor; it made blacks seem less fit than whites.

Naturally, social Darwinists opposed government policies designed to help the poor or to compensate for racial discrimination. For them social inequality was the natural order of things, not something that had to be changed. Darwin himself seemed resigned to this apparent law of nature. "At some future period," he wrote in 1871, "the civilized races of man will almost certainly exterminate and replace the savage races throughout the world." In this way Darwinism was put to use in defense of the political economy of industrial capitalism.

From the moment he published *On the Origin of Species* in 1859 Darwin's theory of natural selection was taken up by social scientists in support of the theory of African racial inferiority. Racists had argued that emancipation would force blacks to compete with their white superiors and that this competition could only end in the disappearance of the African race. Over the course of the late nineteenth century racists pored over the census returns for evidence that blacks were reproducing more quickly or slowly than whites, in accordance with Darwinian theory. When the 1890 census seemed to confirm the view that blacks were withering under the strain of competition with whites, racial theorists unleashed a volley of influential studies.

In 1892 Joseph LeConte weighed in with an article on "The Race Problem in the South." A distinguished biologist, LeConte offered a complex Darwinian exploration of the "struggle for life and the survival of the fittest." In conditions of free competition with whites, he argued, blacks faced either "extinction" or permanent subordination. Only the protection of whites could shield African Americans from their natural fate.

Far more influential than the LeConte article was Frederick L. Hoffman's full-length treatise, *Race Traits and Tendencies of the American Negro*, published in 1896. Where LeConte gave racism the blessing of professional biology, Hoffman's book was published under the auspices of the American Economic Association. It quickly established itself as one of the most important studies of race relations written in the nineteenth century. Hoffman himself was a statistician, and the tables and figures scattered throughout *Race Traits* gave his book the authoritative air of the new social sciences. Yet from beginning to end the book was an ideological rant. Hoffman dismissed African Americans as "a vanishing race," comparing them to the recently defeated Indians. "Constitutional weaknesses" left blacks vulnerable to diseases that whites could resist. A racial tendency toward sexual immorality compounded the problem of African-American physical deterioration. Ever since they had left the protective cover of slavery, Hoffman argued, blacks had shown clear signs of moral degeneration. Genetically predisposed to laziness and criminality, African Americans were doomed to poverty and social inferiority. Hoffman brought together the new insights of professional biology, sociology, anthropology, and statistics. Organizing those insights around social Darwinist theory, he produced the most influential racist tract of the late nineteenth century.

Social scientists like Hoffman prided themselves on their realism, their commitment to the unvarnished truth as it was revealed in facts and statistics. Just as the advocates of high culture elevated the moral truths of the art and literature of western history, sociologists and anthropologists claimed to have isolated the definitive truths of human society. But not all "realists" sought solace in the past or justified the inequalities of the present. Some sociologists, like Lester Ward, openly attacked the antidemocratic thrust of social Darwinism. At the same time, the best American artists of the late nineteenth century openly embraced the realities of urban and industrial America.

Artistic Realism Embraces Urban and Industrial America

"This is the age of cities," the writer Hamlin Garland declared. "We are now predominantly urban and the problem of our artistic life is practically one of city life." Garland was expressing a view common among artists and writers in the second half of the nineteenth century. They embraced the world that Anthony Comstock wanted to suppress and that Matthew Arnold wanted to escape. They called themselves realists, because they hoped to implant the realities of urban and industrial America into great works of literature and painting. Writers like Henry James and Kate Chopin and painters like Winslow Homer and Thomas Eakins rejected the romanticized view of the world that prevailed in the art of pre-Civil War America. Even photographers like Mathew Brady and architects like Louis Sullivan claimed to be a part of this realist aesthetic. To be sure, not all realists focused on the city. Garland, for example, emphasized the harsh realities of rural life while Sarah Orne Jewett wrote realistically about small-town America. But most of those who called themselves realists saw themselves as part of the first major artistic movement that was grounded in urban and industrial America. As writer Fanny Bates put it, the people of the cities "live more in realities than imagination."

The Triumph of Literary Realism

In April of 1861 the *Atlantic Monthly* published a powerful story called "Life in the Iron Mills" by a writer named

Rebecca Harding. Her story created a sensation. Rarely had the dreary lives of ordinary working men and women been presented in such relentless detail. Yet Harding was only one of a number of writers who rejected the sentimental approach to fiction that had prevailed during the previous generation. In the decades to come, the best writers in America joined in the crusade to make fiction realistic. "The public demands realism," Willa Cather explained, "and they will have it."

For Mark Twain, the central idea behind literary realism was the creation of characters who were "exactly true to the originals, in even the minutest particulars." But the leading spokesperson for realistic fiction was not Twain but William Dean Howells. A formidable literary critic, Howells was himself the author of one of the best realist novels, *The Rise of Silas Lapham.* Howells was also editor of the *Atlantic Monthly,* one of a handful of influential magazines, which championed the cause of literary realism. He had grown up believing that in fiction "persons and things should be nobler and better than they are in sordid reality." But this "romantic glamour," Howells came to realize, "veiled the world to me, and kept me from seeing things as they are."

Realists tried to bridge the gap between "high" and "popular" culture by making great literature out of the ordinary details of everyday life. To "enjoy the every-day life," Sarah Orne Jewett explained in *Deephaven,* one must "find pleasure in thought and observation of simple things, and have an instinctive, delicious interest in what to other eyes is unflavored dullness." By writing about failed businessmen or runaway slaves, writers like Howells and Twain hoped to reveal both courage and cowardice in the lives of ordinary men and women. "Let fiction cease to lie about life," Howells declared. "Let it portray men and women as they are . . . let it speak the dialect, the language, that most Americans know—the language of unaffected people everywhere." This was the great achievement of *Huckleberry Finn.* Twain wrote it entirely in the dialect of ordinary people in the Mississippi Valley.

The characters in realistic novels were far from the saintly heroes and coarse villains of sentimental fiction. Realistic figures were flawed men and women who struggled with the moral dilemmas they encountered in their daily lives. In Howells' greatest novel, Silas Lapham had to decide whether to mislead the men who wanted to buy his failing paint company. Huck Finn had to decide whether to turn in a runaway slave. Yet neither Lapham nor Finn was "heroic" in the way that Dickens' heroes were. Lapham was an ill-educated social climber who talked too much, especially when he drank. Huck Finn was a barely literate seeker of adventure who played hooky, spoke improper English, and spun absurd fantasies. In the end both Silas Lapham and Huck Finn made the right moral decisions. But neither found their decisions easy to make, and Lapham suffered for having done so.

Some realists hoped that their approach to writing would advance the cause of social reform simply by shining the light of "truth" on American society. "Realism is the tool of the democratic spirit," Thomas Sergeant Perry declared, "the modern spirit by which the truth is elicited." But not all realists were engaged by such democratic sentiments. Henry James, perhaps the greatest and certainly the most sophisticated of the realist novelists, rejected all attempts to use fiction as a sounding board for moral or political criticism. Like other writers of his generation, James believed that the "real is the most satisfactory thing in the world." But for James realism had little to do with the lives of ordinary men and women. "The multitude has absolutely no taste," he once wrote. So instead of writing about "the multitude," James wrote about the lives of well-heeled men and women in New York City, Boston, London, and Paris. What made James a great writer was his novels' realistic detail of the physical and psychological worlds inhabited by the upper crust of urban America.

Even if James was no radical, the realist movement he embraced was greeted with shock by the defenders of the genteel tradition of American letters. In March of 1885 the public library committee of Concord, Massachusetts, banned *Huckleberry Finn* from its shelves, denouncing Twain's novel as "the veriest trash." Members of the committee characterized Twain's masterpiece as "rough, coarse and inelegant, dealing with a series of experiences not elevating, the whole book being more suited to the slums than to intelligent, respectable people." The Springfield *Republican* supported Concord's library committee in an editorial attacking Twain's taste for the "grotesque." The Huck Finn stories, the editors complained, "are no better in tone than . . . dime-novels . . ., their moral level is low, and their perusal cannot be anything less than harmful."

Realists dismissed such criticism as evidence of the "feminine" taste that prevailed in American letters. They saw realism as a "masculine" alternative to the sentimental writing that appealed to the women who read most of the fiction published in America. In their commitment to the unvarnished truth, realists thought of themselves as "virile and strong." Even Elizabeth Barstow Stoddard, a New England author, vowed to write her fiction "with a masculine pen." Female realists such as Kate Chopin rejected the assumption, common to sentimental fiction, that women's lives should be bounded exclusively by the needs of their husbands and children. Ellen Glasgow complained about the "colored spectacles of tradition and sentiment" that produced unrealistic female characters. Louisa May Alcott wanted her female characters to be "strong-minded, strong-hearted, strong-souled, and strong-bodied." Realistic writers thus challenged the sentimental depiction of women as nervous, frail, and destined only for the domestic life.

Other authors, most notably Walt Whitman, pushed the radical possibilities of realism even further. Like most

Walt Whitman, one of America's greatest poets, was a champion of the diversity and excitement of city life.

realists, Whitman aspired to "manly" writing. Through his poems, he said, he hoped "to exalt the present and the real, to teach the average man the glory of his daily walk and trade." Away with romance, he declared, "I am the poet of reality!" He was also the poet of the city; Whitman loved New York, and he filled his poems with vivid details of urban life in all its variety. For Whitman that meant he would embrace the "goodness" as well as the "wickedness" of modern America. Just as minstrel shows and vaudeville flirted more and more openly with sexual titillation, Whitman wrote more and more openly about the joys of eroticism. Thus Whitman, like so many realists, fused the themes of popular culture with the forms of "high" art.

Painting Reality

In 1878 the New York artist John Ferguson Weir declared that "art, in common with literature, is now seeking to get nearer the reality, to 'see the thing as it really is.'" Throughout the nineteenth century painters continued to produce romantic canvases that glorified nature and idealized the family. But like the best writers of the post-Civil War era, the finest painters rejected romanticism in favor of realism. Winslow Homer and Thomas Eakins, Childe Hassam and Mary Cassatt, together shifted the emphasis of American painting from sentiment to **realism,** from unspoiled nature to the facts of social life in urban and industrial America. Realists did not always paint the city, but

even when they depicted rural life, or in Winslow Homer's case the life of the seafarer, realists generally avoided romanticism.

Homer was, in the words of one critic, a "flaming realist—a burning devotee of the actual." Some likened his painting to Whitman's poetry, particularly because of Homer's "healthy and manly" manner of painting. He left several important bodies of work, all realistic in different ways. A series of Civil War studies, notably *Prisoners from the Front* (1866), presented ordinary soldiers with ragged uniforms and worn, tired expressions on their faces. This was a sharp departure from a tradition of painting military men in heroic poses and glorious battle. As an illustrator for *Harper's Weekly*, the first successful mass-circulation magazine in America, Homer also drew realistic scenes of New England factories, railroad workers, and other aspects of industrial life.

Homer's two most enduring contributions were his sensitive depictions of African Americans and his remarkable portrayals of seafaring men struggling against nature. From his extraordinary representation of a female slave in *Near Andersonville* (1866) to his poetic study of an African-American fisherman in *The Gulf Stream* (1899), Homer sharply distanced himself from the prevailing racism of his era. At a time when intellectuals were perfecting theories of African-American racial inferiority and minstrel shows and world's fairs presented blacks in the grossest stereotypes, Winslow Homer represented African Americans as varied men and women who worked hard and struggled with dignity against the difficulties of everyday life. In the process, Homer produced some of his finest paintings.

Beginning in the 1880s, Homer's subject matter focused more and more on New England fishermen, often in battle with the sea. In paintings such as *The Life Line* (1884), Homer combined the romantic's interest in heroism with the realist's concern for ordinary people. Mark Twain had used a similar combination in *Huckleberry Finn*, as Walt Whitman did in *Democratic Vistas*. Like the novelist and the poet, Homer saw heroism in ordinary lives and with it created made fine art.

Thomas Eakins was a more thoroughgoing realist. Unlike Homer, Eakins was determined to drain his paintings of all romantic sentiment. He wielded his paintbrush with the precision of a scientist in a laboratory. Indeed, in his determination to represent the human body with perfect accuracy, Eakins attended medical school, where he mastered the details of human anatomy. The *Nation* reported in 1874 that Eakins wanted to be known in the art world as a "realist, an anatomist and a mathematician." After studying for several years in Europe, Eakins returned to his native Philadelphia in 1870 and was soon shocking viewers with warts-and-all portraits of his own sisters. Eakins, one critic sniffed, "cares little for what the world of taste considers beautiful."

Though never as popular as Winslow Homer, Eakins was a more formidable artist. He established his reputation with a series of lifelike paintings of rowers. *Max Schmitt in a Single Scull* (1871), for example, was almost photographic in its accuracy and spontaneity. Even then, at the beginning of his career, Eakins could render scenes with startlingly three-dimensional effects. A few years later, in 1875, he shocked the art world once again with *The Gross Clinic,* a large canvas depicting the gruesome details of a surgical procedure being performed under the direction of Eakins' former teacher, Dr. Samuel David Gross. The selection committee for the 1876 Philadelphia Centennial Exposition rejected *The Gross Clinic* on the grounds that "the sense of actuality about it was more than impressive, it was oppressive."

Eakins was undaunted; in the 1870s he began teaching at the Pennsylvania Academy of Fine Arts, becoming its director in 1881. There he demanded that his students learn how to draw the human form with painstaking accuracy by working from nude models. Eakins was fascinated by the human form. He photographed dozens of naked men and women and used some of them as the basis for full-scale paintings. *The Swimming Hole* (ca. 1884) was clearly based on a photograph Eakins had taken the year before. By 1886 the directors of the Academy had had enough. Eakins was fired after he pulled the loin cloth from a male model posing before a group of female students.

Critics complained that Eakins was obsessed with nudity, but for Eakins himself the exact details of the human body were merely the entryway into a deeper exploration of the characters and personalities of his subjects. In the late 1880s and 1890s Eakins produced a number of portraits that were stunning both for their physiological accu-racy and their psychological penetration. He painted his friend, Walt Whitman, so honestly that the poet's admirers objected. Whitman, however, thought the portrait was a masterpiece. Eakins was especially good at painting women. Like Winslow Homer's portrayals of African Americans, Eakins' women were thoughtful and dignified. *Miss Amelia C. van Buren* (1891) conveys its subject's intelligence and complexity with no sacrifice of accuracy. Eakins thereby did for painting what Henry James did for literature. Both demonstrated that distinguished works of art could be impressively realistic and at the same time deeply insightful.

By showing that accuracy did not preclude interpretation, Eakins revealed the links between realism and impressionism. Mary Cassatt, the Philadelphia-born impressionist painter who spent most of her career in Paris, had thoroughly absorbed the assumptions of artistic realism. Cassatt wanted her paintings "to achieve force, not sweetness," she said, "truth, not sentimentality or romance." But for impressionists near-photographic accuracy could be an obstacle to genuine realism. Nevertheless, the best American impressionist, Childe Hassam, revealed his affinities with realism by painting unsentimental scenes of city life. Hassam's *Rainy Day, Boston* (1885), for example, is "realistic" in its evocation of the loneliness of life in the big city.

Is Photography Art?

As city life became the subject matter for painters and writers, a major technological development—photography—created an entirely new medium of artistic expression. In the fall of 1862 Mathew Brady mounted an exhibit of Civil War photographs in his New York gallery. The pictures

Thomas Eakins was a pioneer in the artistic use of photography. By using photography as the basis for painting, and by using scenes of ordinary life as the basis of high art, Eakins demonstrated his commitment to artistic realism in paintings such as "The Agnew Clinic" (left) and "The Swimming Hole" (right).

Civil War photography, pioneered by Mathew Brady's New York studio, was part of a larger artistic movement toward realism. The photos were not simply graphic; the best of them were works of art.

were taken by Brady and a small army of associates, many of them extremely talented photographers. This was the first time a large viewing public was able to see realistic pictures of the most gruesome facts of war. The camera had been invented scarcely a generation earlier, in 1839, by a Frenchman named Louis Daguerre. By the early 1860s photographic technology had improved dramatically, and Mathew Brady knew how to take advantage of it. His 1862 exhibition had electrifying effects. The *New York Times* declared that Brady had exposed "the terrible realities" of war. "If he has not brought bodies and laid them in our door-yards and along [our] streets, he has done something very like it."

The photograph soon became an integral part of most journalistic efforts at documentary accuracy, despite the fact that pictures could distort and conceal as often as they exposed the truth. By the 1880s journalists used photographs to heighten the reality, the sense of "truth," conveyed by their stories. The effect of Jacob Riis' *How the Other Half Lives*, published in 1890, was enhanced by the fact that he included a series of dramatic photographs documenting the misery of the urban poor. The public "wants facts, not theories," Riis explained in his introduction, "and facts I have endeavored to put down in these pages." What was different was that photography had become part of the body of factual evidence.

The ability of the camera to capture reality inevitably fascinated realistic writers and artists. In the second half of the nineteenth century photography set the standard for accurate representation to which many artists aspired. Thomas Eakins, for example, used the camera to freeze images that he intended to paint on canvas. He photographed horses in motion to guide him as he painted *A May Morning in the Park* (1879), one of the first paintings to capture accurately the position of animals' legs as they moved. Eakins soon became a skilled photographer, producing hundreds of portraits of his subjects. He took numerous photos of the naked human form, and not always as a basis for later paintings. Eakins was thus one of the first artists to recognize the artistic element of photography itself. His work thereby raised a question that troubled many of his contemporaries. Is photography art?

Some writers applauded the camera's capacity to capture the "truth." One painter praised photographer William Chase for revealing "the beauty of the commonest and humblest subjects." Writers as varied as Walt Whitman and Harriet Beecher Stowe used photographic metaphors to describe the effects they hoped to achieve with their words. But others were not persuaded that the photograph could ever be a genuine work of art. The camera captures only "the external facts, *The Galaxy* magazine declared, it "does not tell the whole truth."

Anthony Comstock worried a great deal about the difference between art and photography. Millions of copies of great and not-very-great works of art flooded the market in the late nineteenth century. Photographs of naked men and women suddenly became a new form of readily accessible pornography. Comstock was forced to consider the issue. "Is a photograph of an obscene figure or picture a work of art?" he asked. "My answer is emphatically, No." Humans rise above savages by clothing their nakedness, Comstock reasoned. Artists who paint nude portraits use lines, shadings, and colors in ways that "seem to clothe the figures." Their artistry thus diverts the viewers' attention from the nudity which "if taken alone, is objectionable." Photographers have no such artistic devices at their disposal, Comstock explained. "A photograph of a nude woman in a lewd posture, with a lascivious look on her face," was to Comstock no work of art, for it lacked "the skill and talent of the artist."

CHRONOLOGY

1851 YMCA is founded
First world's fair is held at Crystal Palace in London

1859 Charles Darwin publishes *On the Origin of Species*

1861 Rebecca Harding publishes "Life in the Iron Mills"

1862 Mathew Brady exhibits Civil War photos at his New York studio

1866 New York Athletic Club opens
Horatio Alger expelled from his pulpit in Brewster, Massachusetts
Winslow Homer paints *Prisoners from the Front* and *Near Andersonville*

1869 Cincinnati Red Stockings charge admission to watch baseball games
Matthew Arnold publishes *Culture and Anarchy*

1870 Metropolitan Museum of Art and Boston Museum of Fine Arts are founded

1870s National League is formed; baseball becomes professional

1871 Walt Whitman publishes *Democratic Vistas*
Thomas Eakins paints *Max Schmitt in a Single Scull*

1873 New York Society for the Suppression of Vice (SSV) founded
Congress enacts the Comstock Law

1875 First Harvard-Yale football game is played
Thomas Eakins paints *The Gross Clinic*

1876 World's Fair held in Philadelphia
Philadelphia Museum of Art founded
Daniel Coit Gilman becomes first president of Johns Hopkins University

1877 Jane Addams enrolls at Rockford Seminary

1878 Johns Hopkins establishes the first university press

1879 Art Institute of Chicago founded

1880s Richard Kyle Fox professionalizes boxing

1883 Anthony Comstock publishes *Traps for the Young*

1884 Mark Twain publishes *The Adventures of Huckleberry Finn*
Winslow Homer paints *The Life Line*
Thomas Eakins paints *The Swimming Hole*

1885 William Dean Howells publishes *The Rise of Silas Lapham*
Childe Hassam paints *Rainy Day, Boston*
Josiah Strong publishes *Our Country*

1888 Modern "safety" bike invented

1890 Jacob Riis publishes *How the Other Half Lives*

1891 Thomas Eakins paints *Miss Amelia C. van Buren*

1893 World's Columbian Exposition held in Chicago

1894 Vaudeville producer B. F. Keith opens the New Theatre in Boston

1896 Frederick L. Hoffman publishes *Race Traits and Tendencies of the American Negro*

1899 Winslow Homer paints *The Gulf Stream*

Conclusion

When Comstock questioned whether photography could be art he was participating in a larger debate about what counted as American culture in the new political economy of industrial capitalism. Did it include the popular culture of the city, with its bawdy minstrels, its immigrant neighborhoods, its baseball stadiums, and its department stores? Or was American culture restricted to the nation's great libraries, universities, museums, and opera houses? And what was culture supposed to do for Americans? Did it provide a refuge from the chaos and competition of industrial life, an alternative to the business values of capitalist society? Or were business and industry, cities and factories themselves the subject matter of truly great art? Americans argued over whether culture should maintain traditional values or boldly face up to the realities of the new political economy.

Cultural struggles easily spilled over into American politics. Urban reformers proposed public policies to elevate the cultural level of slum dwellers. Elites convinced politicians to subsidize the construction of huge public libraries. Nevertheless, American politics in the late nineteenth century had not yet become cultural politics. The issues that brought Americans into the streets and into the voting booths remained, for the most part, economic issues. Just as American culture was transformed by the rise of cities and industry, the problems of capitalist political economy became the focus of American politics in the late nineteenth century.

Review Questions

1. What motivated Anthony Comstock's crusade against vice?

2. How did minstrel shows change over time?

3. Did urban life transform sexuality in nineteenth-century America?

4. How accurate was Josiah Strong's view of immigrant culture?

5. Did "high culture" offer an escape from urban, industrial America?

6. What was the philosophy behind artistic realism?

Further Readings

John D'Emilio and Estelle Freedman, *Intimate Matters: A History of Sexuality in America* (1988). This text is an innovative overview with important chapters on the late nineteenth century.

Elliot J. Gorn and Warren Goldstein, *A Brief History of American Sports* (1993). True to its title, this provides a brief but intelligent introduction to the subject.

John Higham, *Strangers in the Land: Patterns of American Nativism, 1860–1925* (1955). Higham has prepared a classic study of the response of native-born Americans to immigrants.

Lawrence Levine, *Highbrow/Lowbrow: The Emergence of Cultural Hierarchy in America* (1988). Levine, a leading cultural historian, has effected a masterful study.

Roy Rosenzweig, *Eight Hours for What We Will: Workers and Leisure in an Industrial City, 1870–1920* (1983). Rosenzweig demonstrates the importance of leisure time to industrial workers.

David Shi, *Facing Facts: Realism in American Thought and Culture, 1850–1920* (1995). Refer to this for a broad introduction to the topic.

Robert Toll, *Blacking Up: The Minstrel Show in Nineteenth-century America* (1974). *Blacking Up* is very good at tracing changes over time.

Alan Trachtenberg, *The Incorporation of America: Culture and Society in the Gilded Age* (1982). Trachtenberg gives us a brief, spirited overview of the topic.

History on the Internet

"Metropolitan Lives"

http://nmaa-ryder.si.edu/collections/exhibits/metlives/index.html

See the Ashcan artists' scenes of the realism of the city. Informative essays that discuss class relations, immigration, and changing gender norms accompany the paintings.

"Forms of Variety Theatre"

http://lcweb2.loc.gov/ammem/vshtml/vsforms.html#ms

Through this online exhibit on popular entertainment from 1870–1920 read about variety shows, vaudeville, minstrel shows, and musical reviews. Browse through a collection of online playbills and programs and listen to sound recordings.

"The Victorian Web"

http://landow.stg.brown.edu/victorian/gender/genderov.html

While this site addresses issues of gender in Victorian Great Britain, it provides valuable insight for those studying the period. Nineteenth-century images of women in contemporary art and literature, essays on gender theory, and numerous links to additional information are also available.

THE POLITICS OF
INDUSTRIAL SOCIETY

1870-1892

O U T L I N E

The "Crusade" Against Alcohol

A few days before Christmas in 1873 Dr. Diocletian Lewis arrived in Hillsboro, Ohio, to speak on the evils of alcohol. He had given the speech many times before, but on this occasion the women who were present proved unusually responsive. Lewis told them the story of how, when he was a young boy, his mother saved his father from drink by persuading a local saloon keeper to stop selling liquor. The next morning a group of Hillsboro women met at the home of Eliza Jane Thompson, a leading citizen of the town and a devout Protestant. After praying to God for guidance, Thompson and the other women marched through the winter streets to the various drugstores in town where alcohol was sold. Three of the four druggists agreed to stop selling liquor. The next day the women marched on the town's hotels and saloons, singing hymns as they went. Inspired by their success, the women kept up the pressure through the winter of 1873–1874. When they were not marching on saloons, they held prayer meetings at the Methodist Episcopal church. The women eventually persuaded several of Hillsboro's merchants to suspend the sale of alcohol.

The Crusade, as it came to be called, quickly spread beyond Hillsboro and beyond Ohio. First hit were the neighboring states of Indiana, Michigan, and Pennsylvania. By the end of the Crusade, women had marched in over 900 towns and cities in 31 states and territories. They closed down thousands of liquor stores and saloons. They secured written pledges from hundreds of druggists and hotel keepers not to sell alcohol. With the dramatic success of the Crusade of 1873–1874 the temperance movement was reborn. But unlike its pre-Civil War counterpart, the postwar drive to suppress alcohol was dominated by women. The Woman's Christian Temperance Union, organized in late 1874 in the wake of the Crusade, formally restricted its membership to females. Before the century was out, the WCTU would bring tens of thousands of women directly into the political arena.

The WCTU dwarfed all other women's political organizations in the late nineteenth century. By the early 1890s, for example, the National American Woman Suffrage Association claimed 13,000 dues-paying members. Another 20,000 women joined the less-radical General

541

Federation of Women's Clubs. The WCTU was mammoth by comparison. In 1890 it had 150,000 adult members and another 50,000 in its young women's auxiliary. The WCTU was the largest women's protest movement in American history up to that time.

Much of this success could be attributed to the WCTU's powerful and charismatic president, Frances Willard. Willard was born in Churchville, New York, near Rochester, in 1839. The child of well-educated parents, she attended college in Milwaukee and completed further studies in Rome and Berlin and in Paris at the College de France and the Sorbonne. While in Europe, she settled on the question that would guide her life: "What can be done to make the world a wider place for women?" By her early thirties Willard was already a renowned public speaker. In 1871 she was appointed president of the Woman's College in Evanston, Illinois. In 1874 Willard attended the founding convention of the WCTU and was appointed its corresponding secretary. At first the organization was dominated by "conservatives" who wanted to restrict its activity to the suppression of liquor. But Willard had grander visions, and so, apparently, did the WCTU's members. In 1879 they elected Willard their national president, a position she held until her death in 1898.

Led by Willard, the temperance movement broadened its interests and grew steadily more radical. It embraced women's suffrage, workers' rights, and finally "Christian socialism." And as it grew more radical it also grew more popular. By the 1890s the WCTU was the largest and most powerful association of women in the United States. Nevertheless, the WCTU's appeal, and its radicalism, were restricted by its predominantly middle-class membership. The middle-class Protestant bias of the WCTU was consistent with its disdain for most of the forms of party politics.

To be sure, the WCTU convened huge rallies, but Willard carefully contrasted them to party conventions. WCTU gatherings were depicted as clean, well-disciplined

affairs. The female delegates were restrained. Their oratory was substantive rather than bombastic. And unlike the major parties, the WCTU embarked on a series of campaigns that combined education with interest-group pressure. Willard and her associates gave speeches, wrote articles, and published books on the evils of drink. By 1890, some 150 newspapers regularly published WCTU columns. The WCTU's own publication reached a circulation of 100,000, making it the bestselling women's newspaper in history up to that time. The WCTU organized petition campaigns and lobbied officeholders. Thus did the crusade against the evils of alcohol grow into a broad-ranging political campaign to alleviate the problems of a new industrial society. In this sense the WCTU was typical of American politics in the late nineteenth century.

After the Civil War the temperance movement revived, beginning with a "crusade" by women against liquor stores and saloons.

The political economy of industrial capitalism had thrown into doubt long-standing beliefs about the limited role of government in the regulation of the economy. Mainstream politicians, Democrats and Republicans alike, railed against the evils of big government, but the spectacular growth of big business worried their constituents even more. So politicians responded with the first tentative steps toward government regulation of American commerce. For a growing number of Americans small steps were not enough. Middle-class reformers, labor activists, and aggrieved farmers stepped outside the two-party system to propose more radical solutions to the social problems of industrial America. Dissatisfied with party politics itself, many activists turned to wholesale political reforms. The WCTU tried all of these approaches, imitating the tactics of party politics while positioning itself outside the political mainstream. The effect of these competing styles was a dramatic increase in the number of politically active Americans. And most of them, like the members of the WCTU, demanded more and more that their government actively confront the problems of industrial society. ∎

Two Political Styles

There were two distinct political styles in late nineteenth-century America. One was partisan, the other was voluntary. Partisan politics included all the eligible voters who counted themselves as Democrats or Republicans, attended party parades and electioneering spectacles, and cast their ballots in record numbers. This was very largely a world of men. The second political style, voluntarism, embraced a vast network of organizations, including women's assemblies, reform clubs, labor unions, and farmers' groups. A small but vocal band of critics decried the American rage for politics, especially party politics. They advocated measures to reduce the influence of parties in government and of immigrant voters in parties. Critics of popular politics supported a nonpartisan style that became increasingly influential in the twentieth century.

The Triumph of Party Politics

In 1884 the *Philadelphia Inquirer* compared political parties to "religious sects." A voter "did not merely entertain opinions, he had convictions." American men voted along very strict party lines. Indeed, political parties themselves printed and distributed their own ballots. Loyal Republicans and Democrats voted by simply dropping a party ballot in the appropriate box. So fierce were party allegiances that campaigns seemed more like religious wars, both in "bitterness and the distinctiveness with which partisans were ranged upon sides." Party discipline was strict, and campaigns were carefully organized. But discipline was not imposed from the top. Instead, party organization took root in local towns and cities across the country. At no other time in American history did voters ally themselves so tightly to the two major parties.

And never again would so large a proportion of American men participate in presidential elections. During the second half of the nineteenth century, American men voted in record numbers. From the 1840s through the 1860s an average of 69 percent of eligible voters cast their ballots in presidential elections. During the final quarter of the century, the average rose to 77 percent, a record high. The figures were less impressive in the South, although they followed the same general pattern. Between 1876 and 1892, nearly two out of three southern men cast ballots in presidential elections. In the North men voted in truly astounding numbers. Eighty-two percent of them went to the polls every four years between 1876 and 1892. And in the next two presidential elections, 1896 and 1900, northern voter turnout peaked at 84 percent (see Figure 19-1).

Newspapers played a critical role in maintaining this level of political participation. Most editors were strong party advocates, partly from conviction and partly from need. Papers survived with the help of official advertisements and contracts to print ballots and campaign documents. Strong-willed editors such as Horace Greeley of the *New York Tribune* and William Cullen Bryant of the *New York Evening Post* became influential party leaders. Papers editorialized relentlessly in favor of their candidates and their party. There were no editorial pages to distinguish opinion from news. Editors consistently slanted stories to show their party in the most favorable light. During campaigns they sometimes printed their candidates' names on the masthead. Other papers printed logos boasting of their partisan affiliation. "Republican in everything, independent in nothing," the *Chicago Inter Ocean* declared. "Democratic at all times and under all circumstances," the La Crosse, Wisconsin, *Democrat* announced. Newspapers thus presented to their readers a starkly partisan world in which the difference between Democrats and Republicans was the same as the difference between good and evil. "Editors assailed their opponents as if they were villains of the most depraved sort," one observer noted.

Spectacular political campaigns reinforced the partisan attachments promoted by newspapers. The parties organized thousands of political clubs around the country to drum up enthusiasm for upcoming elections. Military marching companies organized the party foot soldiers as well. The clubs and marching groups in turn organized an endless series of competing party parades. "You can hardly go out after dark without encountering a torchlight procession," remarked a visitor to Maine during the 1880 election. "In the larger places not a night passes without a demonstration of some sort." Marchers rang bells, set off cannons, raised banners, and unfurled flags. At night they lit Chinese lanterns, carried torches, and set off fireworks. They marched to mass rallies where they listened to bands, sang party songs, heard speeches, and cheered their political and military heroes. Millions of American men, perhaps a fifth of all registered voters, participated in these huge spectacles.

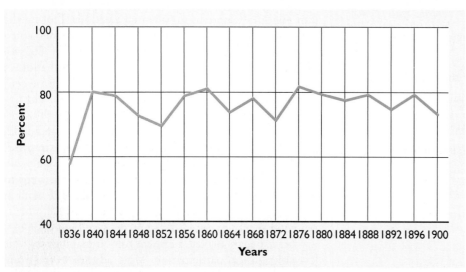

Figure 19-1   Percent of Eligible Voters Casting Ballots.

Conspicuously absent from these events were the candidates themselves, particularly in presidential contests. Throughout the nineteenth century presidential candidates who campaigned for office were the exception rather than the rule. It was considered unseemly for presidential candidates to stump for votes. It was also dangerous. With the Democrats and Republicans closely matched in their national popularity, presidential candidates learned that the safest course was to accept a party's nomination and then gracefully retire from the public scene until the election was over. Those who did campaign—for example, Stephen Douglas in 1860, Horace Greeley in 1872, or James G. Blaine in 1884—were notoriously prone to losing the election. As the *Philadelphia Inquirer* explained in 1884, "It is better that the country should make its choice between the two candidates from what they know of their public records rather than from what they may learn of their personal appearance."

Masculine Partisanship and Feminine Voluntarism

Party politics was a largely masculine activity in the late nineteenth century. Both major parties functioned like fraternal organizations. Political marches were increasingly saturated with masculine icons. Local militia companies, Civil War veterans, rail-splitters, and brawny workingmen all marched in public to demonstrate both their partisan allegiances and their masculinity. Voting was increasingly referred to as a "manly" or a "manhood" right. Denying a man his right to vote was like denying him his masculinity.

If the electoral sphere of campaigns and voting was a man's world, the private sphere of home and family was widely understood as a world of women. In actual practice, women always participated in the background of popular politics. They sewed the banners, decorated the meeting halls, and prepared the food for mass rallies and party picnics. Although women were largely excluded from rallies and marches, they found ways to express their partisan preferences. They often illuminated their windows during torchlight parades to show their support of the passing marchers, or they darkened their windows to show their opposition. Women frequently joined the parades dressed as symbolic representations of the Goddess of Liberty or some similarly feminine icon. Nevertheless, as a result of politics' increasing masculinity, politically active women opted for a different style of politics altogether.

The stereotypes of the public man and the private woman rested on the assumption that women were destined by nature to remain at home as protectors of the family's virtue. By the middle of the century, increasing numbers of women used that female stereotype to develop their own form of political activism. Female virtuousness justified women's support for various moral reform movements. Abolitionist women attacked slavery for its disruption of the family. Temperance reformers claimed that men who drank became unsteady providers for their wives and children. Thus many women entered the public sphere in order to protect the private sphere. By defining "the family" in broad terms, women expanded the horizons of political activity beyond the confines of the two-party system. "Woman's place is in the home," Retha Childe Dorr explained, but "home" for her included public schools and nurseries. Even "the city full of people is the Family," Dorr wrote in the early twentieth century. Thus a stereotype that initially restricted feminine political activity had turned into a justification for women's increasing participation in a host of public crusades.

Women rarely entered public life as individuals or as party spokespersons. Instead, they pursued politics as representatives of voluntary associations that were dedicated to a host of specific reforms. Some fought for Sabbatarian laws that would prohibit working and drinking alcohol on the Sabbath. Other voluntary associations brought women into the struggles against slavery, prostitution, and poverty. Most women entered the public arena under the auspices of organizations such as the Female Moral Reform Society, the National American Woman Suffrage Association, and most importantly, the Woman's Christian Temperance Union. Because it grew out of voluntary associations rather than political parties, this style of political activity has come to be known as **voluntarism.**

A satirical cartoon from 1869 belittled the campaign for women's suffrage. Entitled "Women on Top," the image reflected the common assumption that electoral politics was a strictly masculine activity.

The vast majority of those who joined voluntary associations came from the educated middle class. Although they were often quite radical in their politics, voluntary associations inevitably reflected the class biases of their members. By upholding the home as the special preserve of feminine authority, for example, reformers ignored the fact that working-class families depended heavily on the labor of children. The domestic ideal was something few working-class women could reproduce in their own lives. As a result, working women did not join voluntary associations in large numbers.

Sometimes women's associations copied the style of partisan politics. The Woman's Christian Temperance Union staged mass marches and convened huge rallies. But in important ways women's politics pioneered an entirely new style of public activity. Along with a growing number of elite men, many politically active women were critical of the emotional style of mass politics. Voluntary associations concentrated less on rousing the voters than on educating the public and lobbying elected officials. Although men also joined voluntary associations, they were dismissed by mainstream politicians as "namby-pamby, goody-goody gentlemen." In the late nineteenth century, voluntarism was associated with feminine politics in the same way that party politics was associated with masculinity.

The Critics of Popular Politics

The combination of partisanship and voluntarism made American politics more "popular" than ever before. Women and men, blacks and whites, immigrants and those native born, working class and middle class all found a place somewhere in the popular politics of the late nineteenth century. But not all Americans appreciated popular politics. After the Civil War a small but influential group of conservatives reacted with disgust to the American rage for politics. Contemptuous of partisanship, they advocated a new style of *non*partisan politics. Suspicious of the large number of voters, they began to question the principle of universal suffrage. Horrified by the arrival of millions of politically active immigrants, they supported unprecedented immigration restrictions. In the late nineteenth century the critics of popular politics were a distinct minority. Nevertheless, they laid the groundwork for a new style of politics that would prevail in the twentieth century. In important ways, the critics were ahead of their time.

"Universal suffrage can only mean in plain English the government of ignorance and vice," Charles Francis Adams complained in 1869. "It means a European, and especially Celtic, proletariat on the Atlantic coast; an African proletariat on the shores of the Gulf, and a Chinese proletariat on the Pacific." Adams spoke for a traditional American elite that saw popular politics not as a democratic triumph but as a degradation of public life. Such men were the heirs of a tradition that saw economic independence as the precondition for political virtue, among voters and public officials alike. Naturally, they were horrified by the specter of a working-class electorate. The fact that the American working class was made up largely of African Americans, Asians, and Catholic immigrants only made matters worse.

But blatantly antidemocratic rhetoric was a losing proposition in the late nineteenth century. Elites who retained any hope of maintaining political influence learned to avoid direct assaults on the principle of universal suffrage. Instead they became advocates of good government, government run by professionals rather than party bosses and staffed by civil servants rather than party favorites. They became, in short, the advocates of *nonpartisan* politics. In a nonpartisan world, they reasoned, political parties would have less power and voting itself would be less meaningful.

Nonpartisan politics was a reaction against the upheavals associated with the political economy of industrial capitalism. Many elites were haunted by what they saw as the twin evils of radicalism and immigration. In the wake of the nationwide strikes of 1877, *Nation* magazine, a reliable barometer of elite opinion, asked whether an "alien" proletariat had transformed universal suffrage from a democratic blessing into a frightful nightmare for the "well-to-do and intelligent" classes. A few years later, in 1881, supporters of good government organized the National Civil Service Reform League. Its goal was to prevent political parties from filling government positions with their supporters. Victory came two years later with the establishment of a Civil Service Commission that would assign federal jobs on the basis of merit rather than patronage.

But civil service reform would not stop the phenomenal growth of a working-class electorate made up largely of recent immigrants. Hostility to immigrants deepened after the Haymarket bombing in Chicago in 1886, to be described later in this chapter. Political opposition to immigration, known as nativism, had enjoyed some success in the 1850s, and in 1882 nativists had secured a congressional ban on the further immigration of Chinese. But it was not until the Haymarket bombing that the movement to restrict immigration generally gained ground in the United States. Thereafter the press was filled with tales of the threat to liberty and property posed by the growing numbers of immigrants coming to America.

Anti-Catholicism spread across the country, especially in the Midwest in the late 1880s. Immigrants were Catholic *and* working class, and so Yankee Protestants often saw working-class radicalism as a double threat. One nativist pointed to the "two lines" of foreign influence that were threatening the American republic. One line led to the radical politics of "agrarianism" and "anarchy." The second line tended toward Catholic "superstition." Both led "by different roads to one ultimate end, *despotism!*"

By the mid-1890s, as the newer sources of immigration from eastern and southern Europe became more evident, nativist rhetoric grew more racist. It was no longer merely radicals and Catholics who were swarming into the United States, but darker skinned peoples from Italy, Russia, and Eastern Europe. Social scientists wrote treatises on the inherent intellectual inferiority of such peoples. They gave the imprimatur of science to the most vicious stereotypes. Italians were said to be genetically predisposed to organized violence. Jews supposedly had inherited tendencies toward thievery and manipulation. Whether from custom or makeup, all lacked the ability to live in a free society. Thus as the working class became more heavily immigrant and more organized, native-born Protestants became more xenophobic. Anti-immigrant parties sprang up. Nativist societies appeared across America. By the 1890s a generation-long campaign to close immigration was in full swing, a campaign that culminated after World War I with the virtually complete restriction of all immigration into the United States.

Throughout most of the nineteenth century, however, the critics of popular politics remained a vocal minority. During the so-called "Gilded Age" of the 1870s and 1880s Americans participated actively in the political arena, either as loyal party voters or voluntary activists. In most cases they entered the political arena with deep concerns over the problems of a society that was rapidly becoming more urban and more industrial. Thus did the political economy of industrial capitalism generate the issues that dominated American public life in the late nineteenth century.

Economic Issues Dominate National Politics

By the late nineteenth century Americans were accustomed to the idea that government should oversee the distribution of the national wealth. After the Civil War federal officials sold public lands to homesteaders and doled out huge parcels to railroads. The Interior Department granted mining, ranching, and timber companies the right to exploit the nation's natural resources. But distribution and regulation were not the same; the idea that government should actively regulate the economy was alien to the traditions of Jeffersonian and Jacksonian democracy. The Federalist and Whig Parties had always advocated active government, but before the Civil War those traditions were tainted with elitism. By the late nineteenth century, however, the rise of big business led growing numbers of Americans to believe that the government should at least regulate the currency and protect American commerce and workers from ruinous foreign competition. With the growth of large concentrations of corporate power, Americans hesitantly accepted that government should regulate interstate commerce and restrain the power of monopolies. To undertake these new responsibilities fairly and professionally, government employees had to be freed from the hold of political parties. Thus the reform of civil service became a political football tossed back and forth by a generation of American politicians. These issues, all of them touching on the government's role in the regulation of the economy, dominated party politics in the late nineteenth century.

Weak Presidents Oversee a Stronger Federal Government

The slow growth of the federal government was presided over by a succession of weak presidents. Abraham Lincoln had dramatically expanded the powers of the presidency, largely because of the Civil War. During the subsequent era of Reconstruction, the Congress struggled ferociously with the president and won most of its traditional power back from the chief executive. By the mid-1870s the nearly equal electoral strength of Democrats and Republicans restrained both parties from acting very aggressively. From 1876 through 1896, not a single president enjoyed a full term during which both houses of Congress were controlled by his own party. Nor did any of the presidents who served during these years take office with an overwhelming mandate from the voters. The late nineteenth century witnessed a string of razor-thin victories in presidential elections. In two cases, the victorious candidate actually won fewer votes than his opponent. After Grant's re-election in 1872, no president was re-elected to two consecutive terms until 1900.

In some cases, a president took office already tainted by the process that put him there, as was certainly true of Rutherford B. Hayes' election in 1876. Hayes' fellow Republicans were annoyed by his inexplicable efforts to conciliate the same southern Democrats who were conducting congressional investigations of his election. Republicans were further frustrated by the president's contradictory position on civil service reform. Hayes spoke warmly of reform. He forbade his party from raising money by assessing Republican officeholders, and he wrestled with the

mighty Roscoe Conkling, Republican boss of New York City, for control of the New York Customs House—the most lucrative source of patronage in America. But although Hayes spoke for civil service reform, he acted the role of the party patron. He denied patronage to the Conkling faction, but he lavishly rewarded his own supporters. Soon enough the disgusted supporters of civil service reform turned away from Hayes.

In 1877 Hayes took one important step toward reviving the power of the presidency. When railroad workers went on strike to protest wage reductions, Hayes dispatched federal troops to suppress the workers. This was an important precedent. Later presidents would often exercise their authority to intervene directly in disputes between workers and employers. But except for calling out the troops, Hayes' policy was to do nothing whatsoever to relieve the distress caused by the depression of the 1870s. "Let it be understood," the president declared in December of 1878, "that during the coming year the business of the country will be undisturbed by governmental interference with the laws affecting it." Millions of Americans were suffering from the sharp fall in wages and prices. Yet against the advice of his own secretary of the Treasury, Hayes vetoed a bill that would have counteracted the general deflation by modestly inflating the currency. By 1880 the president was so unpopular that his fellow Republicans happily took him up on his offer not to run for re-election.

The results of the 1880 election were perfectly typical of the era. Republican James A. Garfield won the presidency by a tiny margin. He received 48.31 percent of the votes; Hancock received 48.23 percent. As usual, the Republicans did best in New England, the upper Midwest, and the West. The Democrats swept the South but also took New Jersey, Nevada, and California. Had the Democrats taken New York, where Tammany Hall provided the party with a reliable block of immigrant votes, the election would have gone to Hancock. As a general rule, the Republicans appealed to southern blacks and to a northern middle class that was native born and overwhelmingly Protestant. The Democrats could count on strong support from working-class immigrants and southern whites. But there were countless variations from these general rules.

Economic issues dominated the 1880 campaign, as they did in most other presidential elections. But this did not mean that the Democrats and Republicans could be easily distinguished on matters of economic policy. Both parties were equally addicted to the patronage system, so neither pressed very strongly for civil service reform. In theory the Democrats favored lower tariffs than the Republicans. In practice, neither party advocated free trade, and both parties had strong "protectionist" blocks (those who supported high tariffs to *protect* American business) as well as significant numbers who favored

As the number of immigrants to America swelled, so did opposition to it. This 1891 cartoon blames immigration for causing a host of social and political evils.

lower tariff rates. The Democrats were more likely to support inflationary monetary policies than the Republicans, but Republican mining interests also pressed for a more liberal coinage of silver. Neither party, however, reversed the deflationary policies that prevailed. Finally, while Republicans made periodic gestures in support of southern blacks, they had pretty much abandoned the freed people of the South to the domination of the virulently racist Democrats. Thus Garfield's victory for the Republicans in 1880 did not foreshadow any major shifts in government policy.

On July 2, 1881, the president was shot by a lunatic who claimed to be a disappointed office-seeker. Garfield died two months later, and Chester A. Arthur assumed the office of chief executive. Arthur was the product of one of the most powerful patronage machines in America. Accordingly, he doubted whether passing a civil service exam demonstrated anyone's ability to hold down a government job. But the assassination that put him in office made it dangerous for the president to resist the swell of popular support for civil service reform. The Republicans in control of Congress did resist, however, and they paid the price in the elections of 1882. Democrats swept into office on a tide of resentment against Republican corruption and

patronage. The following year the Congress passed, and President Arthur signed, the landmark Pendleton Civil Service Act.

The Pendleton Act prohibited the practice of requiring patronage officeholders to contribute to the party machine that gave them their jobs. More importantly, the law authorized the president to establish a civil service commission to administer competitive examinations for "classified" federal jobs. Initially only about 12 percent of federal jobs were so classified, but over the next several decades succeeding presidents gradually increased the proportion. Before the century ended, the majority of federal jobs were classified and thereby removed from the reach of the patronage machines. The Pendleton Act was a major turning point in the creation of a stable and professional government bureaucracy.

Although Arthur signed the Pendleton Act, he squandered any chance of gaining popular credit as a civil service reformer by lavishly distributing patronage to his supporters in a shameless bid for re-election in 1884. He likewise threw away a golden opportunity to lead the way on tariff reform. With the return of prosperity in the late 1870s and early 1880s, government coffers were bulging with surplus revenues from import taxes. Cries for lower

On July 2, 1881 a deranged assassin named Charles J. Guiteau shot President James Garfield to death in a Washington, D.C., train station.

tariffs grew louder, and Arthur at first seemed to hear them. But in the end the president succumbed to the political manipulations of the high-tariff forces in Congress. The so-called "Mongrel Tariff" he signed in 1883 was noteworthy chiefly for doing nothing. Arthur was no more successful in his attempts to strengthen the Navy. And when he turned in desperation to an aggressive foreign policy, he likewise fumbled. To make matters worse, the economy began to slow down again. As a result, Arthur approached the 1884 elections a tainted man with no record of presidential accomplishments. His fellow Republicans would not even renominate him.

The Democrats rose to the occasion by nominating and electing the eminently respectable Grover Cleveland. In his brief career as mayor of Buffalo and governor of New York, Cleveland had developed a reputation as an honest man of moderate principles. Cleveland became the first Democrat elected to the presidency in nearly 30 years. Not surprisingly, sectional reconciliation between the North and the South was a major theme of his administration. In this effort Cleveland represented the spirit of the times. During the middle and late 1880s, American readers devoured the memoirs of Ulysses S. Grant, with their conciliatory tone toward the South. Major magazines pub-

lished the recollections of Union and Confederate soldiers. And across the South, monuments to the fallen heroes of the "Lost Cause" began to appear. The public celebration of the memory of civil war thus became an ironic emblem of sectional reconciliation.

Cleveland's conviction that the federal government should defer to southern whites derived in part from his principled commitment to limited or local government. Accordingly, Cleveland was not an activist president. During his first two years in office he initiated no bold new programs, but neither did he thwart congressional moves to strengthen the authority of the central government. Cleveland approved legislation that raised the Agriculture Department to the status of a cabinet office. He also signed into law the Dawes Severalty Act of 1887, which placed the federal government in direct control over the lives of most Native Americans (see chapter 17). In the same year, Cleveland also signed the Interstate Commerce Act. This was the first important piece of federal legislation designed to regulate big business. It empowered a five-member Interstate Commerce Commission to curb monopolistic and discriminatory practices by American railroads. For many years the ICC was weak and ineffective in controlling the railroads, but it was one of the federal government's first

This Republican campaign poster from the 1888 presidential election assails the Democratic candidate, Grover Cleveland, on both personal and ideological grounds. Cleveland supported lower tariffs, and is therefore derided as an advocate of free trade. He has also fathered a child out of wedlock, hence the image of the infant.

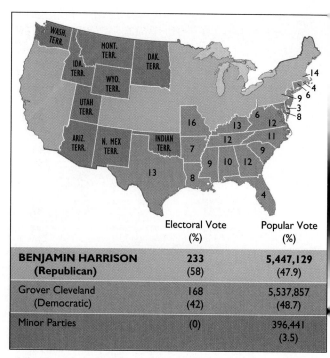

	Electoral Vote (%)	Popular Vote (%)
BENJAMIN HARRISON (Republican)	233 (58)	5,447,129 (47.9)
Grover Cleveland (Democratic)	168 (42)	5,537,857 (48.7)
Minor Parties	(0)	396,441 (3.5)

Map 19-1   The Election of 1888.

important responses to growing demands for the democratic regulation of the economy.

President Cleveland earned few points for merely signing laws passed by Congress, no matter how important the laws were. When his fellow Democrats lost control of the House of Representatives in the 1886 elections, Cleveland decided it was time to take the lead on some important issue. The issue he chose was the tariff. In December 1887, shortly before his re-election campaign was about to get underway, Cleveland devoted his annual message to Congress almost entirely to an argument for sharp reductions in the tariff. He insisted that he was not an advocate of free trade; he simply thought that the tariff was too high and should be reduced.

But having staked so much on tariff reduction, the president dropped the ball. He watched passively as Congress produced a doomed bill that was flagrantly biased in favor of southern interests. When powerful forces in his own party saw to it that the 1888 Democratic platform included only a weak endorsement of tariff reform, Cleveland did nothing. And throughout his campaign for re-election, the president spoke not one word on the subject. Outmaneuvered by the Republicans in Congress, Cleveland went before the voters with no tariff reform, and little else, to show for his four years in office.

Running a skillful campaign on an overtly protectionist platform, the Republicans succeeded in winning back the White House in 1888 (see Map 19-1). A Republican president, Benjamin Harrison, at last presided over a Republican majority in Congress. Making good on their campaign promises, Republicans enacted new tariff rates that were higher than ever. But the Harrison-McKinley Tariff of 1890 was also important for giving the president the authority to raise or lower tariffs with nations that opened their markets to American businesses. This was known as the principle of "reciprocity." Thus the 1890 legislation gave the president important new authority in the conduct of foreign affairs. Republicans also tried to counteract the prevailing deflation by authorizing a more liberal coinage of silver. And in 1890 the Republicans passed the Sherman Anti-Trust Act, declaring it illegal for "combinations" to enter into arrangements that would restrain competition. By failing to define precisely what constituted a "restraint of trade," the Sherman Act left it to the courts to decide. And because the courts were largely pro-business, the law proved less effective at curbing monopoly than many of its supporters had hoped. Still, the Sherman Anti-Trust Act was yet another indication of the federal government's increasing involvement in the regulation of the economy.

The Republicans received little credit for their efforts, and part of the problem was the president himself. Nicknamed "the human iceberg," Harrison was too stiff and pompous to rally the people behind an aggressive legislative agenda. But the larger problem was the rising discontent among voters nationwide. Nothing the two major parties did seemed to satisfy the voters. In 1890 they put the

TABLE 19-1

Electoral Margins in the Gilded Age

Year	Popular Vote	% of Popular Vote	Electoral Vote
1876	4,036,572	48.0	185
	4,284,020	51.0	184
1880	4,453,295	48.5	214
	4,414,082	48.1	155
	308,578	3.4	
1884	4,879,507	48.5	219
	4,850,293	48.2	182
1888	5,477,129	47.9	233
	5,537,857	48.6	168

Democrats back in control of the House of Representatives, and in 1892 brought Grover Cleveland out of retirement and re-elected him president. Once again, however, a president took office without having won a popular majority. Cleveland was the last of a string of relatively weak presidents (see Table 19-1).

But the weakness of the executive did not indicate a completely inactive central government. National politicians during the late nineteenth century could boast of several important achievements. With the Pendleton Act they laid the groundwork for a professional civil service. The Interstate Commerce Act asserted the government's authority to regulate interstate trade. The Sherman Anti-Trust Act established the principle that the federal government could regulate monopolistic corporations. Hoping to counteract the debilitating effects of long-term deflation, the government tried to inflate the currency by modestly increasing the amount of silver in circulation. By maintaining high tariffs politicians effectively protected the wage rates of millions of workers and the economic security of countless American businesses. The Sherman Act was therefore a small but important move toward the regulation of business. Nevertheless, the weakness of the federal government left growing numbers of Americans with the impression that the political system had failed to deal effectively with the problems associated with the political economy of industrial capitalism.

Government Activism and Its Limits

There are two standard themes in the political history of the late nineteenth century. The first theme stresses that government in this era was little more than a swamp of corruption. Capitalists bribed senators with impunity. Ward bosses pocketed vast sums. Entire state legislatures were beholden to corporate fatcats. Glittering wealth masked thoroughly corrupted politics and a hopelessly inept government. No wonder Mark Twain and Charles Dudley Warner called their novel of late-nineteenth-century politics *The Gilded Age*. The second theme emphasizes that the late nineteenth century was the great age of limited government and unregulated markets. After incurring the vast expenses of the Civil War, national politics entered a period of "retrenchment." With the retreat from Reconstruction, the government stepped back and allowed the new industrial economy to grow at its own rapid pace. There is a kernel of truth in each of these themes. Corruption was a very real problem in late-nineteenth-century American politics, and the government's regulatory powers were trivial compared to what would come later. Nevertheless, despite all the talk of limited government, and despite all the bribes and shady political deals, government in the late nineteenth century did become more centralized and somewhat more involved in the regulation of the economy. The conflicting impulses toward limited and active government can be seen most clearly in one of the most disruptive issues of late-nineteenth-century American politics, the regulation of the currency.

Greenbacks and Greenbackers

For as long as governments have produced money there have been fights over how much money governments should produce and how they should produce it. During the eighteenth century American colonists complained that there was not enough money in circulation to sustain their economic needs. In the first half of the nineteenth century Americans fought over how much power the government should give to banks to regulate the amount of money in circulation. Currency battles broke out yet again after the Civil War, as Americans struggled through dramatic and disruptive economic changes. Once again capitalist development sparked a political debate over the role of government in the organization of the economy. Unfortunately, neither politicians nor their constituents had clear or consistent ideas about what the proper monetary policy should be.

The problem began during the Civil War itself, when the U. S. government printed 450 million dollars worth of "greenbacks" to help support the Union effort. Greenbacks were paper bills that were backed up by the government's word, but not by the traditional reserves of gold or silver. When the war ended most Americans agreed that the greenbacks should be withdrawn from circulation. But the depression of the 1870s and the deflationary spiral caused by industrialization created a strong constituency for an inflationary policy. To prime the pump of economic activity, and to keep prices from falling further, a growing number of Americans demanded that the government keep the greenbacks in circulation. Those who wanted to return to the gold standard by making greenbacks convertible for "specie"—gold or silver—were called "resumptionists," that is, they wanted the government to resume specie payments. Those who wanted the government to keep greenbacks in circulation to help inflate the currency were called **greenbackers.**

The struggle between resumptionists and greenbackers reached a fever pitch during the late 1870s. The supporters of the gold standard associated sound money with sound religion. In 1878, for example, the *Christian Advocate* compared greenbackers to atheists. And in fact, greenbackers were often radical critics of the new political economy. They formed a Greenback-Labor Party, which garnered over a million votes in the 1878 congressional elections. Fourteen Greenbackers were elected to Congress that year. But the sound money forces won out, and in 1879 the 300 million dollars in greenbacks that were still in circulation were made convertible into gold.

This cartoon belittles those who advocated a more inflationary policy by using silver as well as gold as the basis of the money supply. The implication of the image is that "bimetallism"—the use of both gold and silver—would create economic instability.

Although "sound money" was generally the conservative position and greenbackers were often radicals, it was hard to predict who would support inflation and who would support deflation. As one voter complained in 1878, it was "difficult to know where the *right* is" on the currency question. Farmers, for example, generally favored inflation to make sure their crops were worth more and their loans less at the end of each year, but farmers were also traditionally suspicious of paper money. Industrial workers benefited from the steady decline in prices but not from the decline in wages. Every president from Grant onward supported resumption, but in Congress there were no stable divisions between Republicans and Democrats on currency questions, and presidents often found themselves repudiated by their own parties.

Once Congress made greenbacks convertible into gold, supporters of inflation took up the issue of "free silver." To counteract the deflationary trend, they argued, the government should add to the amount of money in circulation by allowing the unlimited coinage of silver. In 1878 the inflationists and sound money forces in Congress compromised and passed the Bland-Allison Act. The law authorized the Treasury to purchase silver and mint it in amounts tied to the amount of gold being minted. But with the return of prosperity in the 1880s the currency question died down. Not until the 1890s, with the arrival of another severe depression, did the supporters of inflation resume their crusade for the free coinage of silver.

Foreign Policy and Commercial Expansion

Capitalist development reshaped American foreign policy just as it dominated domestic politics. Indeed, the com-

mercially oriented tone of late-nineteenth-century diplomacy was established soon after the Civil War. In the 1860s William Henry Seward shifted the emphasis of American foreign policy from the acquisition of more territory to the expansion of American commerce. As the secretary of state for Abraham Lincoln and Andrew Johnson, Seward argued for foreign and domestic policies that consistently promoted American industrial expansion. Before the Civil War Seward had been a vigorous advocate of continental expansion, and even in the late 1860s it was Seward who skillfully negotiated the purchase of Alaska from the Russians. But prewar southern expansionism had dampened Seward's enthusiasm for the acquisition of more land. He came to believe that "political supremacy follows commercial supremacy," and so he shifted his attention to the opening of American markets in Latin America, Canada, and the Pacific Ocean, including Asia. The "real empire," Seward declared, was "the empire of the seas."

Seward did not always get what he wanted. In the late 1860s, as congressional Republicans struggled with President Johnson over Reconstruction policy in the South, many of Seward's plans got caught in the crossfire. His biggest success came on April 9, 1867, when the Senate ratified the treaty purchasing Alaska for $7.2 million. A few months later, however, the Senate blocked a similar treaty Seward had negotiated with Denmark for the purchase of the Virgin Islands. Seward likewise failed to win congressional approval for a naval base in Santo Domingo and a treaty with Colombia giving the U. S. exclusive rights to build a canal across the isthmus of Panama. Protectionists thwarted passage of a reciprocity treaty with Hawaii until after Seward's death. Yet most of his failures foreshadowed the future of American diplomacy. The treaty with Hawaii eventually passed, Americans eventually built their canal through Panama, and in 1917 the Virgin Islands became American territories. Most importantly, Seward had established the principle that American foreign policy would be driven by American commercial interests.

Those commercial interests were increasingly global. Between 1860 and 1897 American exports tripled, surpassing a billion dollars every year. After 300 years of trade deficits, in 1874 America's exports began to surpass its imports. Nearly 85 percent of those exports were agricultural commodities. "Southern mills are now exporting more cotton fabrics to China than to all New England," one Bostonian declared. But the growth of industrial exports was even more spectacular. Iron and steel exports jumped by 230 percent between 1888 and 1898, as Andrew Carnegie began shipping steel rails to Russia for the construction of the Trans-Siberian railway. John D. Rockefeller's Standard Oil corporation, the largest oil refining company in the world by 1870, shipped three-quarters of its kerosene overseas between the 1860s and the 1880s. William Herbert Libby directed Standard Oil's foreign operations, shipping kerosene all over Latin America, the South Pacific, China, Japan, Europe, and Africa. In the 1880s U. S. multinational corporations became a fixture of international commerce.

This expansion of overseas commercial interests did not mean that the U. S. had abandoned its territorial ambitions. Angered by England's failure to support the Union during the Civil War, for example, President Grant and Senator Charles Sumner revived long-standing American hopes of annexing Canada. But the Canadians seemed intent on cementing their ties to Great Britain. When the Washington Treaty of 1871 settled the *Alabama* claims (see chapter 16), tension between England and the United States subsided. Nevertheless, until the twentieth century many Americans cherished the dream of absorbing Canada into the United States.

European powers similarly thwarted U. S. territorial ambitions in Latin America, but so did racist concerns about bringing large numbers of nonwhites into the United States. A rebellion in Cuba in 1868 heightened American interest in annexing the island, for example. But Secretary of State Hamilton Fish had long resisted the idea of absorbing half a million Cubans of "every shade and mixture of color." Similar inhibitions led the Senate to reject President Grant's 1869 treaty with Santo Domingo, and so Grant had to be satisfied with a vigorous reassertion of U. S. supremacy in the hemisphere.

Despite the territorial restraints imposed by European power and racial ideology, a succession of aggressive

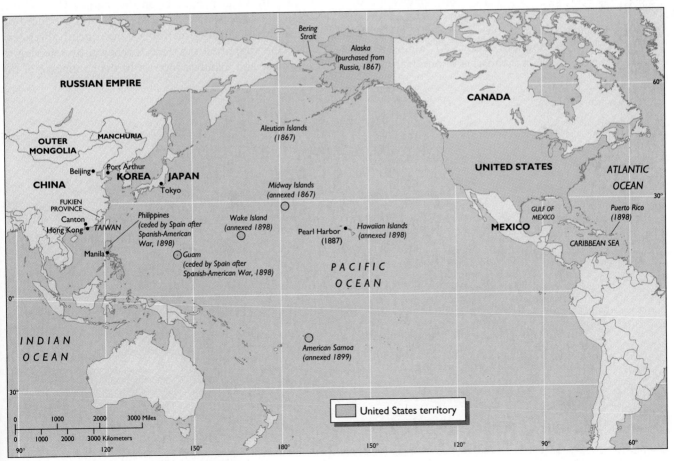

Map 19-2 *American Expansion, 1857–1898.*

secretaries of state reaffirmed Seward's commitment to commercial expansion. In 1886, for example, James G. Blaine worried openly that rapidly industrializing European nations were diverting Latin American commerce away from the United States. "We want the $400,000,000 annually which to-day go to England, France, Germany, and other countries," Blaine declared. "With these markets secured new life would be given to our manufactories, the product of the Western farmer would be in demand." This abiding concern for access to foreign markets pushed successive administrations to assert America's exclusive right to build a canal across central America (see Map 19-2). The canal, President Harrison argued in 1891, "is the most important subject now connected with the commercial growth and progress of the United States." Hoping to thwart European commercial expansion by forging ties of friendship with Latin America, the United States convened the first Pan-American Conference in 1889.

Mexico provided the most vivid demonstration of the nature of U. S. commercial expansion. Although Americans had been buying up property in Mexico since before the Civil War, political instability limited Mexico's attractiveness as an investment. In 1876, however, Porfirio Diaz seized power in Mexico and began a reign of 35 years that proved a boon to American commercial interests. The United States soon recognized the Diaz regime, and by 1880 the dictator had silenced all his opponents. American investors quickly swarmed into Mexico. In 1883 the *Chicago Tribune* pronounced Mexico an "almost virgin outlet for the extension of the market of our overproduc-

ing civilization." United States businessmen began building railroads, selling life insurance, and digging oil wells throughout Mexico. So extensive was this American commercial invasion that by 1910 Americans owned 43 percent of all the property in Mexico, more than Mexicans themselves owned. The advantage of such commercial expansion, as Secretary of State Thomas F. Bayard saw it, was that Mexicans did not become Americans. "We don't want them," Bayard explained in 1888, until "they are fit."

Latin America loomed large in the vision of American commercial expansionists, but neither Asia nor even Africa escaped their notice. In 1870, for example, the *New York Herald* sent Henry M. Stanley off to Africa in search of the presumably lost Dr. David Livingstone. During the same decade several U. S. officials began to speak of Africa as "the great commercial prize of the world."

But far more United States attention was turned toward Asia and the islands of the South Pacific. In the 1880s the United States nearly went to war with England and Germany over disputed claims to Samoa. During the same decade American commercial interests in Hawaii were becoming even more entrenched. An 1876 reciprocity treaty gave Hawaiian sugar favored treatment on the American market, prompting a huge influx of Hawaiian sugar into the U. S. market (along with a backlash against the treaty's renewal by sugar producers on the mainland). By 1886, however, two-thirds of Hawaiian sugar was produced on plantations owned by Americans. Consequently, President Cleveland supported the treaty's renewal by referring to "our close and manifest interest in the commerce of the

Extensive foreign control of Mexico's natural resources eventually helped provoke the Mexican Revolution, one of whose leaders, Pancho Villa, is shown in this 1914 photograph.

Pacific Ocean" and more specifically to the "essential importance" of "the Hawaiian group."

By the 1890s American power in Hawaii had grown so great that it provoked among native Hawaiians a backlash that culminated in the ascension of Queen Liliuokalani to the throne in January 1891. The Queen then did herself in by grabbing for absolute power, and two years later she was dethroned by Hawaiians favorable to the United States. Taking advantage of the situation, President Harrison sent a treaty of annexation to the Senate in February 1893.

The United States treaded somewhat more cautiously in East Asia, where European powers had long-established ties. United States diplomats negotiated with Japan and Korea a series of commercial treaties that substantially increased American access to Asian markets.

For 25 years after 1865 Congress kept a close watch on the executive branch, with important consequences for American foreign policy. The Senate, for example, repeatedly rejected treaties negotiated by the President's emissaries. But a succession of powerful secretaries of state compensated for a succession of weak presidents: Following the lead of William H. Seward, men such as Hamilton Fish, William M. Evarts, and James G. Blaine transformed American diplomacy into a spearhead of commercial expansion. By the late 1880s America's global interests were so extensive that they began to shape the nation's military policy. Spy agencies, under the control of the president, were created as adjuncts to diplomatic and commercial policy. In 1890 Congress approved the construction of the first modern warships, and in the same year the Supreme Court extended the president's control over "our international relations." The growing links between commercial and diplomatic interests were thereby reviving the powers of the American presidency.

Growth of the Central Government

The Civil War established the supremacy of the nation over the states, but it did not create many of the institutions needed for a permanent federal government bureaucracy. There was no civil service to manage the federal government's day-to-day operations. Political parties filled government offices with patronage appointments. Courts as much as legislatures established the central government's rules and procedures, most of which favored economic development. The presidency had been weakened by the Reconstruction-era battles between the executive and the legislature. But even Congress, especially the House of Representatives, was badly organized. The speaker of the house had little power. The seniority and committee systems could not yet discipline debate. Disappearing quorums and filibusters often blocked legislation. Woodrow Wilson called the House of Representatives a "disintegrate mass of jarring elements."

Despite its archaic rules and outdated structure, the central government grew steadily after 1860. Even after the inevitable retrenchment that followed the Civil War, the government continued to grow. Congress passed more and more legislation, from an average of 430 bills a year between 1855 and 1865 to more than 700 a year in the 1870s. In addition, a number of new bureaucracies were created between the end of the Civil War and 1890. Congress consolidated the United States Geological Survey in 1879. The Interstate Commerce Commission was established in 1887. As the attorney general's workload ballooned, Congress created the Department of Justice in 1870. The Interior Department's responsibilities grew steadily, especially after it assumed control of the territories in 1873. In 1889 the Department of Agriculture was created.

More impressive than the reorganization of the bureaucracy was the spectacular growth of the Post Office. The dramatic increase in the number of postal employees was a measure of the rising importance of long-distance communication in the rapidly developing industrial economy. Led by the Post Office the number of civilian employees on the federal payroll rose from 53,000 in 1871 to 256,000 in 1901.

The growth of the civil service provides the clearest evidence of the emergence of a permanent government bureaucracy. In 1883, when Congress passed the first civil service law, 13,780 federal jobs were "classified," meaning that applicants had to pass an exam to qualify. Fifteen years later, 89,306 federal positions were classified, amounting to nearly half of the jobs in the national government. This expansion of the number of civil service jobs substantially weakened the power of the Democratic and Republican Parties. For generations they had maintained their strength by awarding thousands of patronage positions to loyal party regulars. By a system of "rotation," the jobs were vacated every four years, thus allowing the parties to distribute their patronage even more widely. By contrast, civil service positions were awarded on the basis of merit, and they did not rotate. As the proportion of "classified" federal jobs swelled, the patronage well dried up.

By the turn of the century the rudiments of a permanent federal bureaucracy were in place, but they were only the rudiments. The Interstate Commerce Commission lacked the power to enforce its own rulings. It was forced to rely on the courts, which were dominated by supporters of big business. The Sherman Anti-Trust Act was even weaker. Few monopolies were broken up, much less threatened, by it. Not until the first decades of the twentieth century would the federal government learn to regulate monopolies effectively. Finally, only about 15 percent of the wage labor force was actually protected by the high tariffs. Far from representing a rational government attempt to nurture a young industrial economy, the tariff policies of the late nineteenth century were constructed by a hodgepodge of special interests. By 1900 the federal government had developed in important ways, yet it remained small and weak by later standards. Indeed, it was not the federal, but rather the state and municipal governments that responded most aggressively to the problems of the new political economy.

States Regulate; Municipalities Reform

Even as Americans called upon their government to do more and more, politicians proclaimed their opposition to the taxes and bureaucracies that active government required. The result was a jarring contradiction. At the state level, politicians across America enacted policies of retrenchment. In contrast to the federal government, for example, late-nineteenth-century state legislatures passed fewer and fewer laws. Many state governments lowered their taxes and balanced their budgets.

But the same state politicians established a host of powerful new regulatory bodies to govern the exploding municipalities of urban and industrial America. Because the structure of local government is determined by the states, municipal reform was usually implemented in statehouses. During the late nineteenth century state officials often transferred municipal power from elected officials and party politicians to experts and specialists on unelected boards. Mayors, city council members, and aldermen lost much of their authority over budgets, schools, police, and parks. For example, reformers shifted budgetary authority to unelected controllers. They handed control of the police to commissions staffed by upright middle-class citizens rather than by working-class immigrants. Parks commissions, sanitation commissions, public health commissions, and transportation commissions all went the same way. These boards were generally staffed by middle-class professionals who were appointed to their posts. They prided themselves on their "nonpartisan" approach to government. The results of municipal reform were impressive by almost any standard. The quality and professionalism of police and fire services increased dramatically over the course of the nineteenth century.

At least as important for the proper functioning of city government was the willingness of municipalities to raise taxes. As states retrenched, cities increased their property taxes to pay for an unprecedented array of public services. Municipal governments paved streets, built sewers and reservoirs, and established practical and efficient systems of public transportation. In the late nineteenth century city governments produced some of the great urban achievements of American history. Huge public parks, such as Central Park in New York and Golden Gate Park in San Francisco, sprang up across the country. Urban residents paid for the construction of magnificent public libraries. At the same time cities sponsored a host of spectacular feats of urban engineering and architecture. New Yorkers built the Brooklyn Bridge; Chicagoans literally reversed

San Francisco's Golden Gate Park, designed by Frederick Law Olmsted, was one of the most impressive of the great municipal parks built in cities across America in the late nineteenth century.

the flow of the Chicago River. Despite their reputation for corruption and inefficiency, municipal governments went a long way toward enhancing the civility and decency of urban life in America.

Yet more and more Americans grew dissatisfied with their governments. Some were disgusted by corruption and inefficiency, others were offended by the hoopla of popular politics. But a significant number of citizens were concerned that government policies seemed inadequate to the demands of a new political economy. The powers of government grew slowly and steadily, but they were dwarfed by the private power of huge new corporations. Frustrated by piecemeal government reforms, increasing numbers of middle-class Americans turned to more radical campaigns for social and economic transformation.

Middle-Class Radicalism

In the late nineteenth century a number of middle-class radicals gained notoriety by arguing that the political economy of industrial capitalism had undermined the American values of individual liberty and equality. Henry George, Edward Bellamy, and Frances Willard gained both fame and a following. They inspired thousands of Americans to organize in support of their proposals. Yet while heir attacks on capitalism were severe, their assumptions were surprisingly traditional. They were usually frightened, not motivated, by socialism. They often worried that if substantial reforms were not undertaken, a discontented working class would overthrow the reign of private property. Not surprisingly, the followers of George, Bellamy, and Willard were drawn chiefly from the prosperous northern middle class. Yet despite the limits of their appeal, their radical critiques of industrial society exposed deep wells of discontent among tens of thousands of American men and women.

Henry George and the Limits of Producers' Ideology

Henry George was born in Philadelphia in 1839, the son of middle-class parents of Scottish and English descent. Although his formal education was limited, George traveled extensively and read widely. Like many middle-class Americans of his generation, he was shocked by the fact that as the United States grew richer the number of poor people grew as well. The "great enigma" of capitalism, George wrote, was that "the tramp comes with the locomotive." He studied the problem for many years, and in 1879, he published his conclusions in a bestselling book called *Progress and Poverty*. George was soon lecturing throughout the United States and Europe, explaining to his listeners how technology and economic growth had given rise to both progress *and* poverty.

George's explanation rested on what historians have called **producers' ideology.** It started from the assumption that only human labor could create legitimate wealth. Anything of real value, such as food, clothing, or even steel rails, came from the world's producing classes. By contrast, stockbrokers, bankers, and speculators made money from money rather than from the goods they produced. Producers' ideology therefore deemed their wealth illegitimate. Starting from these premises, Henry George divided the world into two great classes, producers and predators. His critique of industrial capitalism harkened back to Thomas Jefferson's vision of a society of small farmers and independent shopkeepers. "There is no luxury" in such a society, George argued, "but there is no destitution." Life was not easy in the society of producers, he admitted, but no one who was "able and willing to work is oppressed by the fear of want."

The harmony of capital and labor was a central theme of producers' ideology. Henry George dreamed of recovering a lost world in which working people owned their own farms and shops, making them both capitalists and laborers. America used to be that way, George believed, but as society "progressed," he complained, the land was monopolized by a wealthy few. Producers were forced to give up their independence and go to work for wealthy landholders. Employers then invested in technology designed to increase the productivity of their workers, but they kept the added wealth for themselves. Increasingly complex technology thus multiplied the wealth of the predators at the expense of the producers.

George's solution for the inequities of industrial society was a "Single Tax" on rents. Because all wealth derived from labor applied to land, he reasoned, rents amounted to an unnatural transfer of wealth from the producing classes to the landlords. To thwart that transfer, George suggested taxing rents and improvements on land at prohibitive levels. This Single Tax would discourage the accumulation of land by the landowning class. All other taxes would be abolished, including the tariffs that protected big business. Gradually, the Single Tax would return the land to the producers themselves. A Jeffersonian republic of small farmers would be restored.

George's radical critique of capitalist "selfishness" was made acceptable by the traditional Jeffersonian goal of his proposal. Indeed, he presented his Single Tax as an alternative to the dangerous socialist doctrines that he thought were spreading among the working class. George attacked as "faulty" the socialist idea that there was an inherent conflict between labor and capital. He opposed government regulation of the economy, and he was a fiscal conservative, suspicious of radical proposals to counteract deflation by putting more money in circulation. "Such ideas," he

John F. Weir's 1877 painting, Forging the Shaft: A Welding Heat, *graphically depicts the forms of industrial wage labor that Henry George feared. His response was to propose the restoration of a Jeffersonian economy of small, independent producers.*

warned, "bring great masses of men, the repositories of political power, under the leadership of charlatans and demagogues." Despite his apparent radicalism, George's popularity actually testified to the strength of middle-class concerns about the political power of the working class.

Edward Bellamy and the Nationalist Clubs

In 1888 Edward Bellamy, a thirty-eight-year-old Massachusetts editor, published a bestseller with a critique of capitalism even more powerful than Henry George's. Bellamy's book, *Looking Backward,* was a utopian novel set in the future. The plot revolves around Julian West, who goes to sleep in Boston in 1887 and wakes up in the same city in the year 2000. His host, Doctor Leete, introduces West to the miraculous changes that have taken place. Technological marvels have raised everyone's standard of living. Boston has become a clean and orderly city, like all the other cities of the future. The great problems of industrial civilization have been solved. This was possible, Doctor Leete explains, because Americans had overcome the "excessive individualism" of the late nineteenth century, which "was inconsistent with much public spirit."

What about "the labor question?" Julian West asks. It had been "threatening to devour society" in 1887 when West fell asleep. Bellamy's critique of capitalism is contained in Doctor Leete's answer to West's question. In the early years of the American republic, the doctor explains, workers and employers lived in harmony. Upward mobility was common. "Workingmen were constantly becoming employers and there was no hard and fast line between the two classes." All of this changed when "great aggregations of capital" arose. A worker was "reduced to insignificance and powerlessness against the great corporation, while at the same time the way upward to the grade of employer was closed to him." Like Henry George's, Bellamy's criticism of capitalism was grounded in traditional Jeffersonian ideals. For both authors the triumph of wage labor led to concentrations of wealth that undermined the harmony of capital and labor.

But there were important differences between George and Bellamy. Where *Progress and Poverty* proposed the restoration of the simple virtues of Jeffersonian society, *Looking Backward* imagined a high-tech future in which all the creature comforts of consumer capitalism were provided in abundance. Henry George reasserted the values of hard work and self-restraint. By contrast, Edward Bellamy embraced the modern cult of leisure. In his futuristic utopia, labor fell lightly on the shoulders of working men and women. Machines produced most of life's necessities. Gourmet meals were served in sparkling communal kitchens. Live concert music was pumped directly into every home. For Henry George technology led only to misery and inequality, but for Edward Bellamy machines would free mankind from the burdens and inequities of the modern world.

In spite of these differences, Bellamy and George were both motivated by a profound fear of militant workers. *Looking Backward* catered to a middle class craving for order amidst the chaos of industrial society. In Bellamy's utopian political economy the harmony of capital and labor was restored. Strikes were eliminated, along with crime and filth, and political turmoil did not exist. Superficially, Bellamy's futuristic Boston appeared to be a socialist utopia. Decisions about what to produce were made collectively, and society as a whole owned the means of production. Yet Bellamy was contemptuous of socialism and insisted on calling his vision "nationalism." Under nationalism, the restoration of social peace was so complete that there was little or no need for government. Thus, like Henry George, Edward Bellamy imagined a world without corrupt politicians, without political parties, and without patronage appointments. This vision of social peace inspired thousands of middle-class Americans to form "Bellamy Clubs" or "Nationalist Clubs," particularly in New England.

The Woman's Christian Temperance Union

"Edward Bellamy's wonderful book" likewise inspired Frances Willard, president of the Woman's Christian Temperance Union. She called nationalism "the fulfillment of man's highest earthly dream." Another WCTU leader, Zerelda Wallace, considered *Looking Backward* "the greatest book of its kind of the century." Fifteen years earlier such support would have been impossible. The temperance movement that had revived in the early 1870s had initially restricted itself exclusively to the suppression of alcohol.

Even under Frances Willard's direction the WCTU never lost sight of its central goal. Although its tactics were not always successful, numerous states as well as hundreds of towns and cities buckled under WCTU pressure. All across America, new laws established prohibitive license fees for the sale of liquor. Others banned the sale of liquor on Sunday. Various states passed "local option" laws giving communities the power to regulate the sale of alcohol in their own jurisdictions. But to temperance purists such victories presented a problem. Liquor licenses implied the government's endorsement of alcohol, local option meant that towns were free to permit the consumption of liquor, and laws prohibiting the sale of liquor on Sundays or to minors implied that drinking on weekdays by adults was acceptable. Thus the ultimate goal of the WCTU became a complete prohibition on the manufacture and sale of alcohol throughout the United States.

But under Frances Willard's direction, temperance became the springboard to a wide range of political and social reforms. In 1881 the WCTU endorsed women's suffrage. By the end of the decade, Willard had formed an alliance with the largest labor union in the country. She supported laws restricting the workday to eight hours and prohibiting child labor. Even the WCTU's attitude toward alcohol changed. By the 1890s Willard viewed drunkenness as a public health problem rather than a personal sin, a problem of political economy rather than individual failure. Accordingly, temperance advocates moved steadily into reforms designed to relieve poverty, improve public health, raise literacy, alleviate the conditions of workers, reform prisons, suppress public immorality, and preserve peace. In the end, Willard attributed the evils of liquor to the inequities of corporate capitalism. The WCTU newspaper declared that human progress was impossible in a situation where the "great wealth producing interests are in the hands of individuals or private corporations." Despite this increasing radicalism, or perhaps because of it, the WCTU grew into the most powerful women's reform organization of the century.

Three factors explain the WCTU's success. The first was Frances Willard's paradoxically conservative approach to radical reform. Her justification for female political activism always came back to women's distinctive calling as protectors of the home. The National Home Protection Party, which Willard tried to launch in 1881, endorsed women's suffrage "in order to give those who suffer most from the drink curse a power to protect themselves, their homes, and their loved ones." The second reason for the WCTU's success was its decentralized structure. Willard left the local chapters of the Union free to adjust their activities to suit their particular needs. In the southern unions there was little talk of women's suffrage, for example, while more radical locals advocated a variety of reforms that the national union ignored. Willard called this the "Do Everything" policy. Finally, the WCTU succeeded by appealing to middle-class women who felt isolated by a culture that restricted them to the narrow confines of the home. In hundreds of towns and cities women found in the WCTU a source of camaraderie that was also a wellspring of political activism. Willard called the WCTU a "mutual admiration society" that helped women develop "an *esprit de corps*" among themselves.

For all its success, however, temperance remained a narrowly middle-class reform movement. The WCTU's leadership was almost exclusively Protestant and native born. In most towns the WCTU hierarchy was drawn directly from the leading Protestant denominations. Outside the prosperous professional and commercial classes few women had the leisure time to pursue the WCTU's active agenda. The organization's vitality rested on a constituency that was concentrated in cities, especially in the North. Thus farm women were scarcely touched by the WCTU.

Although Willard made repeated trips to drum up support in the South, she met with only limited success. The southern unions that did survive accommodated themselves to the spreading practice of racial segregation. Although the WCTU's official policy preached openness and toleration, the reality was something quite different.

For example, Rebecca Felton, a WCTU leader in Georgia, was also one of the South's most notorious racists. As the number of African-American lynchings skyrocketed in the 1890s, Felton publicly defended the practice. "If it takes lynching to protect woman's dearest possession from drunken, ravening human beasts," she declared in 1897, "then I say lynch a thousand a week if it becomes necessary." Not surprisingly, the WCTU had few African-American members.

Nor did the WCTU attract many immigrants. Once again, the official policy of toleration was undermined by the prejudices of the WCTU's middle-class members. For many temperance advocates immigrants were the Union's targets rather than its constituents. While drunken husbands made life difficult and dangerous for all classes of women and their children, the strong Protestant identity of the WCTU limited its appeal among working-class Catholics. One of its first major campaigns in the 1870s was aimed at replacing altar wine with grape juice in Christian services, a switch that Catholics and Lutherans were unwilling to make. When Frances Willard first suggested that the WCTU include women's suffrage in its platform, she claimed that the vote was necessary to combat the influence of "the infidel foreign population of our country." Almost 20 years later, in 1892, she urged the WCTU to pressure Congress for laws "prohibiting the influx into our land of more of the scum of the Old World." As radical as it was, the WCTU would never reflect the interests of black sharecroppers, white tenant farmers, or immigrant workers. Nevertheless, like the Single-Taxers and the Bellamy Clubs, WCTU reformers reflected a growing sense that the American political system was unable to deal effectively with the problems of an industrial political economy.

Discontent Among Workers

Radicalized workers shared the conviction that mainstream politics could not confront the problems of industrial capitalism. Employers were frightened by the upsurge of labor radicalism, especially the railroad strikes of 1877. Workers were turning to violence, and employers were demanding that government use its police powers to forcefully put down strikes. Labor radicals began to question one of the premises of producers' ideology, that American democracy was secured by a unique harmony between capital and labor. "Our social system is not better than that of Europe," labor activist J. P. McDonnell declared in 1879. "Labor in this Republic, as in the European monarchies, is the slave of capitalism, instead of being the master of its own products." But if the harmony of capital and labor had been destroyed, advocates of the producers' ideology continued to search for a political solution to the labor problem.

The Knights of Labor and the Haymarket Disaster

Not all workers had benefited equally from the dramatic growth of the economy, and after the Civil War a growing number of American wage earners turned to government for help. Between 1860 and 1890 wages overall grew by 50 percent, but the bulk of the growth was confined to an elite of skilled and semiskilled workers in a handful of industries, such as printing and metal working. The vast majority of workers suffered directly from the deflation and economic instability of the late nineteenth century. By 1880 40 percent of industrial workers lived at or below the poverty line. The average industrial worker was unemployed for 15 or 20 percent of the year. More than a third of industrial firms were closed down for part of the year. Except for the very largest factories, seasonal unemployment was a normal part of life among wage earners after the Civil War. To relieve their plight, American workers sought political solutions to economic problems.

The most important labor organization to emerge from the crisis of the 1870s was the Noble and Holy Order of the Knights of Labor. Founded in 1869, the Knights of Labor was originally a secret society known for its elaborate rituals. Inspired by the producers' ideology, the Knights of Labor admitted everyone from self-employed farmers to unskilled factory workers. It appealed to a nostalgic vision of a lost world dominated not by big corporations and powerful financiers, but rather by ordinary working people. Nevertheless the Knights of Labor advocated a host of progressive reforms, including the eight-hour day, equal pay for men and women, the abolition of

child and prison labor, inflation of the currency to counteract the deflationary spiral, and a national income tax.

The Knights of Labor grew slowly during its first decade. By the late 1870s its leaders realized that they needed a stronger national organization to hold various locals together. A new constitution, drawn up in 1878, required all members to pay dues. This allowed the Knights of Labor's national organization to support local boycotts and thereby boost its credibility among workers. But the tradition of secrecy inhibited many workers from joining, since the Catholic Church prohibited membership in the Knights. So beginning in 1881, under the leadership of Terence Powderly, the Knights of Labor eliminated most of their quasi-religious rituals. Thereafter the organization grew rapidly, from 19,000 members in 1881 to 111,000 in 1885. True to the producers' tradition, Powderly favored the consumer boycott over the strike. His approach proved most successful during the sharp recession of 1884, a time when trade union strikes were being broken. By 1886 membership in the Knights skyrocketed to over 700,000.

But the more the Knights of Labor grew the more the strains among its members began to show. Rhetoric proclaiming the unity of the producing classes could not mask the fact that the interests of shopkeepers and small factory owners were often very different from those of wage laborers. The critical issue dividing self-employed producers from wage-earning producers was the use of the strike as a weapon of organized labor. For obvious reasons, strikes were of no use to self-employed producers. They preferred the

The Knights of Labor grew into the largest union in America up to that time in large part because it was open to all workers, including the women delegates (pictured above at an 1886 convention of the Knights of Labor).

ON TRIAL

Anarchism

In the days following the Haymarket bombing the police made a spectacular roundup of Chicago radicals. In the homes of anarchists they found bombs and bomb-making equipment. Within a few weeks a grand jury had indicted 10 anarchists on 69 different counts. On June 21, 1886, less than two months after the rally, eight of those indicted were put on trial.

The proceeding quickly degenerated into a spectacle. The presiding judge, Joseph E. Gary, was blatantly hostile to the defendants. He refused to dismiss potential jurors who proclaimed in advance their belief in the defendants' guilt. He rejected the defense demands that the eight defendants be tried separately. His insistence on trying them together reinforced public fears that the city of Chicago was in the grip of a dangerous anarchist conspiracy, although there was no evidence that such a conspiracy existed.

The prosecutors took full advantage of the leeway Judge Gary gave them. They paid for the testimony of some of their key witnesses in a botched attempt to prove that one defendant had been seen throwing the bomb. When the suspicious testimony fell apart under cross examination, prosecutors switched tactics. They focused instead on the inflammatory rhetoric of the anarchists before and during the Haymarket rally. In effect, the anarchists were tried for being anarchists. State's Attorney Julius Grinnell argued that the radicals' fiery language had caused the bomb to be thrown, whether or not any of the defendants had actually thrown it or even contemplated throwing it.

To make his case Grinnell quoted from anarchist articles and letters advocating the use of violence. He presented jurors with an array of explosive devices found in the homes of various radicals. And throughout the courtroom Grinnell hung anarchist banners bearing incendiary anarchist slogans. The defendants were no less aware of the theatrical possibilities of the trial. But while Judge Gary allowed prosecution tremendous latitude, he suppressed all defense attempts to turn the trial into a showcase for radical ideas. Nevertheless, the defendants took every opportunity to exploit their newfound fame. They turned the witness stand into a platform, and they used their closing statements to rehearse at length their radical philosophy. "*I despise you,*" one defendant spat at the court. "*I despise your order; your laws, your force-propped authority. HANG ME FOR IT!*"

The jury did just that, sentencing seven of the eight defendants to death. The convictions were upheld by the Illinois Supreme Court, and in November 1887 the U. S. Supreme Court refused to hear the case. In the meantime a huge inter-

In this image published in Harper's Weekly (September 4, 1886), cartoonist Thomas Nast depicted a massive female Liberty crushing the Haymarket defendants in her hands, presumably rescuing the republic in the process.

national movement had developed, demanding that Governor Richard Oglesby commute the harsh death sentences. Pressed on one side by the forces of law and order demanding the executions and on the other by 41,000 signatures on a petition for clemency, Oglesby took a middle course. He commuted the sentences of the two defendants who had pleaded for mercy. A third defendant committed suicide in his jail cell. On the morning of November 11, 1887, four anarchists went to their deaths, still shouting defiance at the forces of law and order. "Let the voice of the people be heard," one of them yelled from under his hood as the trap door opened beneath his feet.

consumer boycott, and so did the leadership of the Knights of Labor. By contrast, wage laborers were coming to see the strike as their most powerful weapon.

With the return of prosperity, trade unions around the country called for a nationwide strike for the eight-hour day. On May 1, 1886, hundreds of thousands of workers across the country walked off their jobs. It was one of the largest and most successful labor walkouts in American history. In the city of Chicago alone 80,000 workers went out on strike. The Chicago job action was largely peaceful until May 4. At an Anarchist rally at Haymarket Square near downtown Chicago, someone from the crowd tossed a bomb into the nearby line of police. One policemen was killed instantly, and seven more died within then next several days. The number of civilians killed and wounded was never determined. Although the bomb thrower was never identified, eight anarchists were tried for inciting violence, and four of them were put to death.

Anarchism is a doctrine that questioned the legitimacy of all government power. A small group of anarchists had been active in Chicago for several years before the Haymarket riot. Although they had little influence on the labor movement in general, the anarchists' fiery rhetoric advocating the use of violence made them conspicuous. "Dynamite is a peace-maker," declared one anarchist newspaper, "because it makes it unsafe to wrong our fellows." At the Haymarket rally on the evening of May 4 anarchist speakers used the same violent rhetoric. Samuel Fielden, for example, urged his listeners to "throttle" and "kill" the legal system or else, he warned, "it will kill you." It was this remark that provoked Captain James Bonfield to rush 170 policemen to the dwindling rally, and it was into this crowd of policemen that someone threw a bomb. Inevitably, the fiery words of the anarchists were used by prosecutors to convict those who had organized and spoken at the Haymarket rally. It was one of the most spectacular trials of the nineteenth century.

Haymarket was a turning point in the history of American labor politics. With the support of its president, Terence Powderly, the Knights of Labor had tried to prevent its own locals from supporting the May Day walkouts. Powderly had put himself into a bind. Within the Knights workers resented his failure to support the strikes for the eight-hour day. Outside the union a wave of revulsion against labor agitation swept the country. The Knights of Labor never recovered from the Haymarket disaster. Thereafter worker agitation split dramatically into two competing wings. Petty producers, especially farmers, formed their own organizations, while wage laborers organized separately into industrial trade unions.

Agrarian Revolt

The late nineteenth century was a desperate time for many American farmers, especially in the West and South. To compete they had to buy expensive agricultural equipment, often from manufacturers who benefited from tariff protections. Then they had to ship their goods to market on railroads that charged higher rates to small farmers than to big industrialists. When their goods finally made it to market, farmers faced steadily declining prices. Cotton fell from more than 15 cents a pound in the early 1870s to 6 cents a pound in the mid-1890s, and wheat prices did pretty much the same thing.

As the economy became global, American farmers faced stiff new competitors. Southern cotton had to compete against cotton from India and the Near East, especially after the opening of the Suez Canal in 1869. Western wheat farmers entered the world market in competition with Russians and Eastern Europeans. To keep up with the competition, farmers went further and further into debt, and in a deflationary spiral the money they borrowed to plant their crops was worth more when it came time to pay it back, while their crops were worth less. More and more farmers mortgaged their homes and land. The proportion of owner-occupied farms declined while the number of tenants rose.

Farmers were traditionally opposed to active government, but in the desperate conditions of the late nineteenth century they began to press for a host of government policies, beginning with inflation of the currency. Inflation lowered the value of the money farmers borrowed while it raised the value of the crops they produced. Farmers also sought railroad regulations to end the rate discrimination that favored big industrial concentrations over scattered farming districts. They sought to reform a tariff system that protected manufacturing interests but left farmers exposed to the insecurities of an international market. Eventually, militant farmers began to press for antitrust legislation to break up the emerging concentrations of wealth in the steel, oil, and railroad industries.

But farmers were notoriously hard to organize. They were scattered over large sections of the country, they were committed to an ideology of economic independence that was suspicious of collective organization, and they were traditionally hostile to government intervention in the economy. In American politics the principle of limited government was originally an agrarian ideal. It was associated not with the defense of economic development but rather with hostility to economic development. If American farmers were to pursue their political agenda effectively, they needed to overcome these and many more obstacles.

One of the first attempts to organize farmers was the Patrons of Husbandry, generally called the Grange. Founded in 1867, the Grange began to attract large numbers of farmers during the depression of the 1870s. Its chapters claimed 1.5 million members by 1874. Consistent with producers' ideology, the Grange organized cooperatives designed to eliminate the role of merchants and creditors. By storing grain collectively, farmers held their products back from the market in the hopes of gaining some measure of control over commodity prices. But inexperience made the Grange cooperatives difficult to organize efficiently and sustain over time. After 1875 their membership dwindled.

The National Farmers' Alliance and Industrial Union, known simply as the Farmers' Alliance, was much more effective than the Grange. Founded in Texas in 1877, the Farmers' Alliance began to grow rapidly after 1886. Through effective organization and charismatic leadership, the Farmers' Alliance spread rapidly across the South. Its potency was demonstrated at a huge meeting at Ocala, Florida, in 1890. The Ocala Platform supported a host of reforms, many of which had been staples of radical politics for a generation. The Farmers' Alliance advocated currency inflation through the free coinage of silver, lower tariffs, and a constitutional amendment providing for direct election of senators. The Ocala Platform also demanded that the government establish a system of "subtreasuries." These were public warehouses in which farmers could store their crops until they could get the best prices. In return the subtreasuries would loan farmers money for subsistence at low rates of interest. Finally, the Alliance called for strict government regulation, and if necessary direct government ownership, of the nation's railroad and telegraph industries.

Even though the Farmers' Alliance demanded a host of political reforms and government projects, it steered clear of independent politics. Instead, members vowed to judge political candidates by the degree to which they supported the reforms advocated in the Ocala Platform. But very little such support was forthcoming from either of the two major parties. A handful of Farmers' Alliance members therefore formed their own third parties, with some success on the Great Plains in the election of 1890. Out of these initial forays into politics came the most significant third party of the late nineteenth century, the People's Party, otherwise known as the Populists.

The Rise of the Populists

On February 22, 1892, a huge coalition of reform organizations met in St. Louis. Among those present were Single Tax advocates inspired by Henry George, greenbackers who wanted an inflationary currency policy, representatives of the Knights of Labor, and members of the Farmers' Alliance. Together they founded the People's Party and called for a presidential nominating convention to meet in Omaha, Nebraska, on the fourth of July. There they nominated General James B. Weaver of Iowa for President, and there they drew up the famous Omaha Platform. "We meet in the midst of a nation brought to the verge of moral, political, and material ruin," the platform began. It depicted the government as thoroughly corrupted by corporate interests: Ballot boxes were stuffed; voters were intimidated. Capitalists hired private "standing armies" to shoot down urban workers in the streets. From this

Kansas farmers organizing to attend a Populist Party gathering.

unholy alliance of capitalists and crooked politicians, the Populists declared, "we breed the two great classes—tramps and millionaires."

Inspired by the producers' ideology, the People's Party called for the unity of all working people and for the restoration of the harmony of interests between small property holders and wage earners. "Wealth belongs to him who creates it, and every dollar taken from industry without an equivalent is robbery. 'If any will not work, neither shall he eat.' The interests of rural and civic labor are the same; their enemies are identical." The Populist platform was a vigorous restatement of the proposals laid out two years earlier by the Farmers' Alliance. Like the Ocala Platform, the Omaha Platform demanded an inflationary currency policy and subtreasuries. The Populists called for a graduated income tax, direct government ownership of the railroad and telegraph industries, and the redistribution of all lands owned by the railroads.

In the 1892 elections the Populist presidential candidate won about a million votes. The People's Party succeeded in electing several senators, representatives, and governors, as well as quite a few state legislators. But it was clear that this could never be the basis of a national party. There was no evidence of substantial support among wage earners outside the South and West. The producers' ideology, for all its talk of the unity of working people, remained the ethos of small farmers and shopkeepers rather than of urban wage laborers. In many ways the Populist platform was frankly incompatible with the interests of industrial workers. Workers had little reason to oppose protective tariffs that shielded the industrial economy. Inflation would only undermine the value of their wages and raise the price of commodities, and income taxes would shift the tax burden from landowners and importers to wage laborers. Conversely, farmers had every reason to oppose the eight-hour day and laws restricting child labor. In short, Populism was grounded in a rural society of independent farmers and craftsmen, a world that was rapidly disappearing. The growing majority of American workers lived by selling their labor for wages.

CHRONOLOGY

1867	U. S. purchases Alaska from Russia
	Patrons of Husbandry (the Grange) founded
1869	Noble and Holy Order of the Knights of Labor founded
	Suez Canal opened
1870	Department of Justice created
1871	Washington Treaty settles *Alabama* claims
1872	Grant re-elected
1873	"Crusade" against alcohol begins in Hillsboro, Ohio
1874	WCTU is formed
1876	Rutherford B. Hayes elected president
	Porfirio Diaz seizes power in Mexico
1877	Farmers' Alliance founded
1878	Bland-Allison Act
1879	Frances Willard becomes president of the WCTU
	Henry George publishes *Progress and Poverty*
1880	James Garfield elected president
1881	Garfield assassinated; Chester Arthur becomes president
	WCTU endorses women's suffrage

1883	Pendleton Civil Service Act
	"Mongrel Tariff"
1884	Grover Cleveland elected president
1886	Nationwide strike for eight-hour day
	Riot at Haymarket Square in Chicago
1887	Interstate Commerce Act
	Four Haymarket anarchists executed
	Dawes Severalty Act
1888	Benjamin Harrison elected president
	Edward Bellamy publishes *Looking Backward*
1889	U. S. convenes first Pan-American Conference
	Department of Agriculture created
1890	Harrison-McKinley Tariff
	Sherman Anti-Trust Act
	Ocala Platform
1891	Queen Liliuokalani assumes the Hawaiian throne
1892	Omaha Platform of the People's Party
	Grover Cleveland re-elected
1893	Queen Liliuokalani overthrown
1898	Frances Willard dies

Conclusion

After the Civil War the problems of industrial capitalism placed increasing strain on the political system. The two major parties were so closely matched in electoral strength that neither could risk bold new programs to meet the needs of a new political economy. So restless workers, desperate farmers, and an anxious middle class began to look beyond the Democratic and Republican Parties. They turned in increasing numbers to voluntary organizations, labor unions, and farmers' alliances.

The politics of industrial society reached a dramatic turning point in the 1890s. During that decade American voters went to the polls in greater numbers than ever before or ever after. Organized farmers made their most radical demands, labor agitation reached a violent climax, and conservatism began to triumph. Potent movements to restrict the number of voters emerged, particularly in the South. Opponents of immigration made significant strides. The Supreme Court declared constitutional one of history's greatest social experiments, systematic racial segregation. In short, radicalism and reaction reached their peak in the 1890s. During the closing decade of the nineteenth century, Gilded Age politics came to an end and a recognizably modern America was born.

Review Questions

1. Who was Frances Willard, and what was significant about her political career?
2. Why were Gilded Age presidents so weak?
3. In what ways did the federal government become more active after the Civil War?
4. What was "producers' ideology," and how did it influence American politics in the late nineteenth century?
5. In what way was the Haymarket riot a turning point in the history of organized labor?
6. What was "partisan politics" and how did conservatives respond to it in the late nineteenth century?

Further Readings

Paul Avrich, *The Haymarket Tragedy* (1984). This is an exhaustive account by the leading historian of American anarchism.

Ruth Bordin, *Woman and Temperance: The Quest for Power and Liberty, 1873–1900* (1981). *Women and Temperance* is the best single volume available on the subject.

Leon Fink, *Workingmen's Democracy: The Knights of Labor and American Politics* (1983). This case study, with broad implications, shows the connections between political mobilization and labor organization.

Lawrence Goodwyn, *Democratic Promise: The Populist Moment in America* (1976). Goodwyn traces the roots of populism to the Farmers' Alliance.

Walter LaFeber, *The New Empire: An Interpretation of American Expansion, 1860–1898* (1963). LaFeber ties American foreign policy to commercial expansion.

Michael McGerr, *The Decline of Popular Politics: The American North, 1865–1928* (1986). This text is particularly strong on the culture of popular politics in the late nineteenth century.

John L. Thomas, *Alternative America: Henry George, Edward Bellamy, Henry Demarest Lloyd, and the Adversary Tradition* (1983). Thomas' work is a sensitive examination of middle-class radicalism and its limits.

History on the Internet

"1896: The Presidential Campaign, Cartoons, and Commentary—The Populists"

http://www.iberia.vassar.edu/1896/populists.html

This site provides extensive information about the Populist Party, including explanations about dueling Populist factions, the party's platform and primary news accounts.

"Looking Backward"

http://xroads.virginia.edu/~HYPER/BELLAMY/toc.html

This site provides access to the full text of Edward Bellamy's famed 1888 utopian novel *Looking Backward.*

"The Dramas of Haymarket"

http://www.chicagohistory.org/dramas/overview/main.htm

Produced by the Chicago Historical Society, this site details the events leading up to the Haymarket riot, including the radicalization of many American workers and class tensions in America. The site includes both essays and primary-source material.

20

INDUSTRY AND EMPIRE

1890-1900

OUTLINE

Dealmaking in the White House

It was a short distance from the Arlington Hotel to the White House, and although it was an icy, dark February morning J. Pierpont Morgan chose to walk. He pulled his scarf up around a scowling face known to millions of newspaper readers. He had not wanted to come to Washington. There were "large interests" that depended on keeping the currency of the United States sound, he told a Treasury Department official, and those interests were now in jeopardy. The commander in chief of the nation's bankers was going to meet the president in order to keep the United States from going bankrupt.

The events leading up to this urgent meeting stretched back five years, to 1890, when business failures in Argentina toppled London's venerable Baring Brothers investment house and triggered a collapse in European stock prices. Depression spread through Britain, Germany, and France. Anxious European investors began selling off their substantial American holdings. For two years, good harvests staved off the inevitable, but in early 1893 the panic reached the United States. The Philadelphia and Reading Railroad folded in February, followed by another giant trust, the National Cordage Company. Fourteen thousand businesses soon followed, along with more than 600 banks.

Summer brought more bad news from abroad. The government of India stopped minting silver, causing U. S.

silver dollars to lose one-sixth of their value. Wall Street went into another tailspin. In New York 55,000 men, women, and girls in the clothing industry were thrown out of work. Banks refused to cash checks, and coins of all kinds vanished from circulation. The governor of Nebraska instructed the police to deal leniently with the thousands of homeless poor people on the roads. Breadlines formed. "For thorough chaos I have seen nothing since the war to compare with it," the historian Henry Adams observed. "The world surely cannot remain as mad as it is."

For the administration of President Grover Cleveland the madness was only starting. The anger of workers and farmers, which had been simmering for decades, was about to boil over. The president called Congress into special session and pledged to keep the dollar on the gold standard, but it was not enough. A wave of strikes swept the country. Unemployed workers battled police on the Capitol grounds. By January 1895 so many panicky investors were cashing government bonds that the Treasury's gold reserve was half gone, and it looked as if the remainder might last only two weeks. Reluctantly, President Cleveland asked his aides to open negotiations with Morgan.

Admired and reviled, Morgan was known as the preeminent financial manipulator of the late nineteenth century. Born to wealth in Hartford, Connecticut, he had been a Wall Street fixture since before the Civil War. Like his contemporaries, steelmaker Andrew Carnegie and oil magnate John D. Rockefeller, Morgan's skill lay in organization. He restructured railroads, rooting out corruption, waste, and competition and driving down wages. Instead of taking risks, he eliminated them. His style was to gather the leaders of warring firms for a meeting aboard his mammoth yacht, the *Corsair*, and strike a bargain that allowed everyone to profit. Cleveland was about to place the Treasury in this man's hands.

The president opened the meeting by suggesting that things might not be so bad; perhaps a new bond issue would stabilize the Treasury. No, Morgan replied flatly, the run on gold would continue until European investors regained confidence. As things stood, they had more faith in the house of Morgan than in the government. If the president agreed, Morgan would arrange a private loan and personally guarantee the solvency of the U. S. Treasury. After a stunned silence, the two men shook hands. News of the deal instantly calmed the bond markets. The crisis was over. The New York *Sun* reported that the deal struck between the country's political and economic chief executives "revived a confidence in the wealth and resources of this country," but Populist newspapers denounced it as a conspiracy and a "great bunco game."

Morgan's vast fortune enabled him to collect art and antiquities from Europe, Africa, and Asia. He visited Italy with the art critic Roger Fry, who remarked that Morgan "loves to go to the churches to see things that he can't buy."

Culminating two decades of economic turbulence, the Panic of 1893 and the depression that followed it permanently transformed the American political economy. Businessmen like Morgan created even larger corporate combinations and placed them under the control of professional managers. They used technology and "scientific management" to take control of the workplace and push laborers to work faster and harder. Workers resisted, and the 1890s witnessed brutal clashes between capital and labor. Looking for jobs and schools, country people moved to the city and found both promise and danger. Social mobility among African Americans aroused fears in whites, and southerners created a system of formal segregation, enforced by law and terror. Amid growing violence, industrial workers, Native Americans, and African Americans debated how best to deal with the overwhelming forces ranged against them.

The 1890s were also a turning point in American political history. After the 1896 election, many Americans voluntarily withdrew from the electoral process. Others were systematically removed from the voter rolls through a process known as "disfranchisement." African-American leaders and union organizers urged their followers to turn away from politics in favor of "bread and butter" economic issues. Torchlight parades and flag raisings became scarce, and the masculine, public spectacle of nineteenth-century politics died out. Patriotism, once synonymous with partisanship, now became identified with the United States' global military and economic ambitions. Civic events featured army bands and cannon salutes. Newspapers conjured up foreign threats. As Americans became more conscious of their military power, they watched the horizon, fearing that well-being at home could hinge on events as far away as China.

Americans began to feel that their economy's links to the world—and the changes manufacturing and rapid communications brought to politics and daily life—separated the events of their times from everything that had happened before. Morgan's rescue required transactions on two continents, instantaneously coordinated by telegraph. The speed of industry, trade, and information, the ability of machines and technology to span distance and time created a sense that the environment and the future could be controlled. Many felt that the peoples who possessed this newfound control—the modern countries—stood apart from those living in other lands whose thought and action were not guided by science and the streams of information issuing from transoceanic cables.

Between 1890 and 1900 Americans made their country recognizably modern. Those with the means to do so enlarged, accelerated, and rationalized the settings of work and daily life. Financiers and giant corporations assumed control of a vast portion of the American economy. Huge cities complemented the huge corporations. The significance of voting declined, and a decade that opened with a global economic catastrophe ended with a dramatic display of the global reach of U. S. power. ∎

The Crisis of the 1890s

Financial convulsions, strikes, and the powerlessness of government against wealth rudely reminded Americans of how much their country had changed since the Civil War. When Illinois sent Abraham Lincoln to Congress, Chicago's population was less than 5,000; in 1890 it passed the one million mark. Abraham Lincoln's son, Robert Todd Lincoln, presided over the Pullman Palace Car Company, whose 5,000 workers lived in company-owned houses, shopped in company stores, and received funerals in company churches before being buried in the company graveyard.

As the turn of the century approached, Americans saw signs that a threshold had been crossed. Gone was the America of myth and memory, where class tensions were slight and upward (or at least westward) mobility seemed easy. Foreclosures reversed the achievements of the pioneers, as independent farmers lost their land and became tenants on industrial farms or moved east to factories. With population, money, and misery all concentrating in large cities, social conflict seemed likely, perhaps unavoidable. Many Americans, a British diplomat noted, predicted the imminent collapse of civilization: "They all begin with the Roman Empire and point out resemblances." Others, however, felt that the United States was passing into a new phase of history that would lead to still greater trials and achievements.

Hard Times

The depression of the 1890s assumed many faces. In the West, the ranching and mining industries were scarred by fierce battles between workers and owners. In the South, sharecroppers and tenants scrambled for survival as the price of cotton plunged. Although no single place captured the varied experiences of the depression, the city of Chicago exemplified its complexity; although no one event epitomized the social tensions created by the depression, the cross-country march of Coxey's Army struck many Americans as a symbol of what had gone wrong.

Chicago in 1893 captured the hopes and fears of the new age. To celebrate the 400th anniversary of Columbus' discovery of America, the city staged the World's Columbian Exposition, transforming a lakefront bog into a gleaming vision of the past and the future, but just outside the exposition's gates lay the city of the present. By December 1893 Chicago had 75,000 unemployed, and the head of a local relief committee declared that "famine is in our midst." The nation's second largest metropolis had few paved streets and even fewer sewers. The Chicago River flowed from the stockyards to Lake Michigan under a shimmering layer of grease. Thousands lived in shacks huddled close to factories or shared rooms in high-rise tenements in which each floor had only a single bathroom. One out of 10 of the city's factory workers was younger than 16, earning wages as low as 40 cents a week. Jobs were hard to find, and when groups of men gathered at the exposition's gates to beg for work, the police drove them away.

"Industrial armies" of unemployed workers, such as the one led by Jacob Coxey, demanded national action against the economic crisis.

As the depression deepened, the Cleveland administration ordered special troops to guard Treasury branches in New York and Chicago. Groups of jobless people began banding together, forming "industrial armies," many with decidedly revolutionary aims. "It is part of our religion to seize the government of the United States," declared the leader of a San Francisco contingent. Hundreds heeded the call of Jacob Coxey, a prosperous Ohio landowner and Populist. Coxey appealed in 1894 to the unemployed to march on Washington and demand free silver and a public road-building program that would hire half of a million workers. When Coxey set out on Easter Sunday with 100 followers, reporters predicted the ragged band would disintegrate as soon as the food ran out, but the march struck a chord of sympathy in towns along the way, and well-wishers turned out by the thousands to greet the Coxeyites and offer coffee and canned goods for the trip.

Industrial armies set out from Boston, St. Louis, Chicago, Portland, Seattle, and Los Angeles. In Montana, 200 laid-off miners hijacked a train and rode the length of the state before federal troops stopped them. The miners surrendered peaceably, but eastern newspapers sensationalized the event. "Blood Flows From Coxeyism" headlined the *New York Times*. When Coxey arrived in Washington on May 1 with 500 marchers, Cleveland put the U. S. Army on alert. The march ended ignominiously. In front of the Capitol, police wrestled Coxey into a paddy wagon. His disillusioned army dispersed. Still, after the march no one could deny that something was seriously wrong. Ray Stannard Baker, a reporter for the *Chicago Record*, acknowledged that "the public would not be cheering the army and feeding it voluntarily without a recognition, however vague, that the conditions in the country warranted some such explosion."

The Overseas Frontier

At noon on September 16, 1893, thousands of settlers amassed along the borders of the Cherokee Strip, a six-million-acre tract in northwestern Oklahoma. In the next six hours, the population of Wharton, Oklahoma, grew from zero to 10,000, and the last great land rush came to an end. The line of settlement that had been marked on census maps throughout the nineteenth century had ceased to exist.

Frederick Jackson Turner, a historian at the University of Wisconsin, explained the implications of this event to a solemn gathering at the Columbian Exposition in 1893. Steady westward movement had placed Americans in "touch with the simplicity of primitive life," he explained, and allowed the nation to renew the process of social development continuously. The frontier furnished "the forces dominating the American character," and without its rejuvenating influence, democracy itself might be in danger. Turner's thesis resonated with Americans' fears that modernity had robbed their country of its unique

strengths. Theodore Roosevelt congratulated Turner for putting "into shape a good deal of thought that has been floating around rather loosely." For the previous 10 years, Populists and financiers had worried that the end of free lands would signal trials for free institutions. "There is no unexplored part of the world left suitable for men to inhabit," Populist writer William "Coin" Harvey claimed, "and now justice stands at bay."

That assertion turned out to be premature. More homesteaders claimed more western lands after 1890 than before, and well into the twentieth century new "resource frontiers"—oilfields, timber ranges, Alaskan ore strikes—were explored. Irrigation technology and markets for new crops created a bonanza for dry-land farmers. Nonetheless, the economic and social upheavals of the 1890s seemed to confirm Turner's contention that the energies of the American people could not be safely confined and that new frontiers would have to be found. Americans looked overseas.

While farmers had always needed to sell a large portion of their output abroad, until the 1890s manufactured goods had sold almost exclusively through domestic distribution networks. As the total volume of manufactured goods increased, the composition of exports changed as well. Oil, steel, textiles, typewriters, and sewing machines made up a larger portion of overseas trade. American consumers still bought nine-tenths of the output of domestic factories, but by 1898 the extra tenth was worth more than one billion dollars (see Figure 20-1). Standard Oil, International Harvester, New York Life, and other large companies depended heavily on foreign sales, as did textile mill towns in the South and mining camps in the West.

As American firms entered European, South-American, and Asian markets they ran into stiff competition from British, German, and Japanese goods. Overseas states and colonies did not always welcome American products. Some used restrictive tariffs just as the United States did, to promote domestic manufacturing. Others discriminated in favor of one industrial country with which it had an imperial or strategic relationship. Many frankly feared American economic influence. Government and business leaders acknowledged that to gain a larger share of world trade, the United States might have to use political or military leverage to pry open foreign markets. Their "social Darwinist" view of the world—as a jungle in which only the fittest nations would survive—justified engaging in global competition for trade and economic survival. The State Department warned that "we can no longer afford to disregard international rivalries now that we ourselves have become a competitor in the world-wide struggle for trade."

Recognizing that naval power could extend economic influence, and wanting to find a use for surplus steel, Congress authorized the construction of three large battleships in 1890. In 1894, Congress sent a commission to Nicaragua to study the feasibility of a canal across Central America. In 1895 industrialists organized the National Association of Manufacturers to urge the government to help open foreign

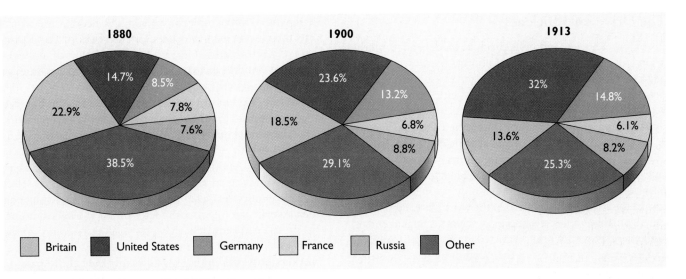

Figure 20-1   Relative Shares of World Manufacturing.
The United States was a significant industrial power by 1880, but by the turn of the century it moved into a position of dominance.

markets. The administration responded by creating a Bureau of Foreign Commerce and urging U. S. consuls abroad to seize opportunities to extend sales of American industrial products. Congress took the lead in expanding the Navy, exploring a canal route between the Atlantic and Pacific oceans, and adjusting the tariff to capture foreign markets.

Congress also knew that **tariff** rates could influence the expansion of trade. Before 1890 taxes on imports had been set high for two reasons: to raise revenue for the national government and to help domestic manufacturers by making foreign goods unaffordable. The Harrison-McKinley Tariff of 1890 did something different. It allowed the president to use the tariff to punish countries

that closed their markets to U. S. goods or reward them for lifting customs barriers. This "bargaining tariff" exposed some domestic producers to foreign competition for the first time, but it also put the full weight of the U. S. economy behind the drive to open markets around the world.

To deal with the apparent closing of the domestic frontier, the United States began to reorganize itself to compete in a global marketplace. The struggle required the executive branch to enlarge the military and take on additional authority. It also meant that domestic industries had to produce higher quality goods at less cost to match those being turned out in Germany or Japan. Employers and workers had to gear up for the global contest for profits.

U.S. firms created a global demand for their goods and global sales and manufacturing networks to fill it. The Singer Sewing Machine Company printed instruction booklets in 54 languages. Of the 15 factories making the machines, 7 were in the United States.

The Drive for Efficiency

In mines, factories, and mills production depended on the knowledge of skilled workers. Laborers used their knowledge to rationalize their work, to set work routines that made sense to them, and to bargain with managers who wanted to change the pace or conditions of work. As profits stagnated and competition intensified, however, managers tried to prevent labor from sharing control over production. To increase output, employers wanted to make specialized skills the property of management, allowing supervisors to seize the initiative that now belonged to workers. In the struggle for control in the workplace, employers relied on three allies: technology, scientific management, and federal power. Workers resisted, organizing themselves and enlisting the support of their communities. The struggle was still unresolved at the beginning of the twentieth century, but new battle lines had been drawn.

Advances in the techniques of management enabled employers to break routines favored by laborers and to dictate new methods. Frederick Winslow Taylor, the first "efficiency expert," devised a system that reduced each occupation to a series of simple, precise movements that could be easily taught and endlessly repeated. To manage time and motion scientifically, Taylor explained, employers should collect "all of the traditional knowledge which in the past has been possessed by workingmen" and reduce "this knowledge to rules, laws, and formulae." The goal was to take control of the processes of work from mechanics and skilled workers and give it to management.

Taylor's stopwatch studies determined the optimal load of a hand shovel (21.5 pounds), how much pig iron a man could load into a boxcar in a day (75 tons), and the amount the man ought to be paid (3.75 cents per ton). Such matters, Taylor said, were not "to be theorized over, settled by boards of directors, . . . nor voted upon by trade unions." This was a job for science. Even office work could be separated into simple, unvaried tasks. Secretaries turned into file clerks, recordkeepers, or members of the typing pool. "Taylorization" created a new layer of college-educated "middle managers" who supervised production in offices and factories.

While **Taylorism** accelerated production, it boosted absenteeism and job turnover as well. Telephone operators, who answered hundreds of inquiries an hour out of a manual of prearranged responses, had a 100 percent yearly turnover rate. Another new technique, "personnel management," promised to solve this problem with tests to select suitable employees, team sports to ward off boredom, and social workers to regulate the activities of workers at home.

In the early nineteenth century, laborers could set the pace of work and leisure. As the century ended, fewer workers possessed indispensable skills they could pass on to their children. Management was establishing a monopoly on expertise and using it to set the rhythms of work and play, but workers did not easily relinquish control of their craft or the factory floor. In the 1890s, the labor struggle entered a new phase that pitted laborers' mutualistic culture against management's drive to impose its will in the workplace. New unions confronted corporations in bloody struggles that forced the federal government to decide whether communities or property had more rights. Skilled workers asserted leadership over the labor movement, and they rallied to the cause of retaining control of the conditions of work.

Progress and Force

To accelerate production, employers aimed to seize full control over the workplaces they owned. They had private detective agencies at their disposal, the courts on their side, and federal troops ready for any emergency. Managers believed this struggle would set the future course of the economy and the nation. In Pennsylvania and Chicago this antagonism led to some bloody confrontations.

In 1892 Andrew Carnegie's mill at Homestead, Pennsylvania, on the Monongahela River was the most modern steel works in the world. The plant turned out armor plating for American warships and steel rails for shipment to Mexico, Manchuria, and Siberia. In June Carnegie's partner, Henry Clay Frick, broke off talks with the plant's AFL-affiliated union and announced that the plant would close on July 2 and reopen a week later with a nonunion work force. The union contended that Frick's actions constituted an assault on the community, and the town agreed. On the morning of July 6, as 300 armed detectives hired by Frick tried to land from barges in the river, they were raked by gunfire from shore. Townspeople turned out with what weapons they had, which included a cannon, and forced the detectives to surrender.

The victory was short lived. A week later the governor of Pennsylvania sent in the state militia, and under martial

A TAYLOR SYSTEM MACHINIST "UP-TO-DATE"

An argument without words

Corporations used stopwatches and social workers to stretch each machine and worker to full capacity. The method was called "Taylorism."

law strikebreakers reignited the furnaces. The violence temporarily stirred nationwide sympathy for the locked-out workers, but Carnegie, traveling in Europe, cabled to "congratulate all around—improve works—go ahead—clear track." Homestead became one of labor's most celebrated battles, but it broke the union and showed that corporations, backed by government, would defend their prerogatives at any cost.

The Pullman strike paralyzed the nation's railroads for two weeks in the summer of 1894. It pitted the American Railway Union, which welcomed all railroad workers, against a confederation of 24 railroads. As at Homestead, local officials sympathized with the strikers. The governor urged the president not to send troops and appealed to the company to negotiate. The calm at the center of the strike was Eugene V. Debs, president of the ARU. A charismatic figure who urged strikers to obey the law, avoid violence, and respect strikebreakers, he spoke quietly but firmly for the dignity of labor. Violence did not erupt until after the Army arrived in Chicago. Enraged crowds blocked tracks and burned railroad cars. Police arrested hundreds of strikers. Debs went to jail for six months and came out a Socialist. Pullman and Homestead showed that the law was on the side of the proprietors. For Debs, a fair deal for workers would require a change of government.

Newspapers, magazines, and novels portrayed Pullman and Homestead as two more battles in an unending war against the savage enemies of progress. Frederic Remington, famous for his reporting on wars against the Navajo and Apache Indians, covered the Pullman strike for *Harper's Weekly*. In his account, roughhewn cavalrymen, having defeated the Sioux, now came to rescue civilization from itself. "There is a big foreign population here in Chicago that isn't American in any particular," he reported. "Eventually this unlicked mob will have to be shot up a little, or else washed, before it will get into a mental calm."

Business executives, too, labeled union members a primitive tribe. "Organized labor know but one law," the president of the National Association of Manufacturers insisted, "and that is the law of physical force—the law of the Huns and Vandals, the law of the savage." The business elite's influence over cultural expression (see chapter 18) allowed it to define the terms of this contest, to label its enemies as enemies of progress. Workers did not object to efficiency or modernization, but they wanted a share of its benefits and some control over the process of change. With state and corporate power stacked against them, these goals appeared beyond reach, at least for the moment.

Just as the massacre at Wounded Knee in 1890 had ended the armed resistance of Native Americans, the violence at Homestead and Chicago signified that the struggle of industrial workers had entered a new phase. Workers and Native Americans would each have to find ways to adjust to the new alignment of power.

Corporate Consolidation

In a nationwide wave of mergers between 1897 and 1904, investment bankers consolidated leading industries under the control of a few corporate giants. More than 4,000 companies merged to form 257 corporations, and J. P. Morgan led the movement. His goal was to take industry away from the industrialists and give it to the bankers. He created Northern Securities, a 400-million-dollar "holding company," which controlled the Northern Pacific Railroad, because, he explained, "I wanted the Northern Pacific stock put where nothing could interfere with the policy I had inaugurated."

Industrial companies were so secretive about their earnings, assets, and liabilities that stockholders had little knowledge of the companies they owned. Uncertainty often fed wild speculation on the stock exchange, creating the kind of "turbulence" Morgan wanted to avoid. Bankers, he felt, had better information about the true worth of an industry, and they could make better decisions about its future. Financiers could create the larger and leaner firms needed to take on foreign competitors.

Morgan's greatest triumph was the merger of eight huge steel companies, their ore ranges, rolling mills, railroads, and shipping lines into the colossal U. S. Steel. Announced in March 1901, the merger instantly created the world's largest corporation. Its capital amounted to seven percent of the total wealth of the United States (by comparison, Microsoft's total assets in 1998 amounted to less than one-third of one percent of the gross national product). Andrew Carnegie bet against U. S. Steel's success, taking his proceeds in bonds and planning to buy back his factories when Morgan's scheme collapsed. It was a bad bet. U. S. Steel's investors (Morgan especially) earned profits "greatly in excess of reasonable compensation," according to one government report.

Bankers outnumbered steelmakers on U. S. Steel's board, and they controlled the company. *McClure's* magazine reported that the new company had a "republican form of government, not unlike that of the United States," and that it was "planning the first really systematic effort ever made by Americans to capture the foreign steel trade." Others worried that democracy and law were no match for the power of a mammoth corporation. Morgan's son wrote to his stepmother that "Father is in the same category with Queen Victoria." He did not say what category U. S. Steel's employees and customers fell into.

A Modern Political Economy

Grover Cleveland's bargain with Morgan revived the industrial economy, but farm prices, wages, and the president's

WHERE THEY LIVED, WHERE THEY WORKED

Pullman, Illinois

When economist Richard T. Ely saw the industrial town of Pullman, Illinois, in 1885 he thought he beheld the future. A planned suburb entirely owned by one company and inhabited by its employees, Pullman "aims to be a forerunner of better things for the laboring classes." On broad streets named for famous inventors—Watt, Fulton, Morse, and of course Pullman—mechanics, shopkeepers, and company officials lived side by side in tidy homes supplied with gas and indoor plumbing. Pullmanites shopped under the glass roof of The Arcade, the first indoor shopping mall, and benefited from a library, a theater, and a school provided by their employer. Surrounded by culture and natural beauty, Pullman workers, the company estimated, were 40 percent more refined, thrifty, and wholesome than "any corresponding group of work-ingmen which could be assembled elsewhere in the country."

The town sprang from the mind of George Mortimer Pullman, whose name meant luxury. With the help of Andrew Carnegie (see chapter 17) he had become the preeminent maker of passenger railroad cars. By the 1880s every railroad in the country used Pullman sleeping cars, dining cars, and observation cars.

In 1880 Pullman decided to centralize his scattered factories into a single facility on Lake Calumet, south of Chicago. He asked Solomon S. Beman, a young architect, and Nathan Barrett, a landscape designer, to build a model town around the plant. By the following year there were 1,400 dwellings, public parks and gardens, a hotel, a school, and a church, all designed in a gracious "secular Gothic" style. In three years the town had 8,000 residents, and by 1893 the population topped 12,000.

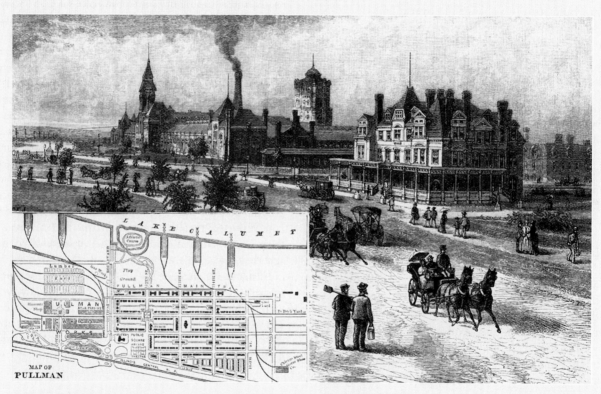

Residents of the company town of Pullman on Lake Calumet in northern Illinois were, according to the company, exactly 40 percent more refined than other workers.

The town of Pullman was not designed as art or charity, but rather for business. Happy, healthy workers were expected to produce more, and in Pullman's estimate, they did. Modern sewers and plumbing made the air and water safe. The death rate in Pullman was less than half that of nearby neighborhoods. There were no saloons. Drinkers had to walk several miles to one of the 30 taverns lining Kensington Avenue on the town's southern edge. The theater's management screened out any "immoral pieces." An exhibit at the 1893 Columbian Exposition claimed that Pullman was making a new kind of worker, "distinct in appearance, in tidiness of dress, in fact in all the external indications of self respect."

Others rushed to copy Pullman's success. Hershey, Pennsylvania, was built by and for chocolate makers, and near Cincinnati the producers of floating soap colonized the model town of Ivoryville. Some observers noticed that the residents of Pullman were not as enthusiastic as the town's founder. Despite the low rents and spacious homes, most Pullmanites moved out within a year or two. Even those who stayed saw the arrangement as temporary. "We call it camping out," one woman told Ely. Workers acknowledged that the town was nicer than any they had lived in before, an observer noted, but "the general complaint seemed to be that they were too much under Mr. Pullman's thumb."

Pullman had no newspaper, no clubs, no elected officials. The school board was entirely filled by company executives. When a group of women tried to organize a charity, the company disapproved. Political activity, especially on behalf of Democrats, was discouraged. When shopkeeper John P. Hopkins campaigned for Grover Cleveland, his lease was revoked.

The company ran the town with an eye on the bottom line. The public library charged admission, 3 dollars a year, more than twice the average laborer's daily wage. Rent on the town's only church was so high that no congregation could afford it, and so it stood empty. Pullman, the Socialist magazine *The Call* remarked, "wasn't a man to let you pray for free." Pullman valued the appearance of harmony over the real thing. The church, he said, "was not intended for the moral and spiritual welfare of the people, as it was for the artistic effect of the scene."

After staying for several weeks, Ely concluded that "the idea of Pullman is un-American." It was impossible for the residents to escape the overshadowing power of the company, which owned the houses, the shops, even the streets. There was not a single piece of property that was privately owned, and tenants' leases could be terminated in 10 days. Workers built sumptuous railroad cars that only reminded them of the unattainable wealth belonging to their employer.

When the Panic of 1893 hit, wealthy customers canceled orders for lavishly appointed cars. Pullman laid off 2,000 of his 5,000 employees and cut wages for the others by 25 percent. Rents dropped in Chicago, but not in Pullman. Many residents could not afford rent or food, but there were no charities and no municipal government to help them. There was only the company, which seemed not to care.

Desperate workers organized in the spring of 1894 and joined Eugene V. Debs' American Railway Union. On May 11, they struck. Mr. Pullman cut off credit for workers at the stores in The Arcade and then went on vacation. In June, Pullman workers asked the entire American Railway Union to join the strike. "We struck because we were without hope," one worker told the union convention. The ARU voted to make the strike national. ARU switchmen would refuse to switch Pullman cars onto trains.

The strike shut down 20 railroads in the West and Midwest. Almost no traffic moved through Chicago, the nation's hub. The U. S. attorney general vowed to meet the strike with force, and President Cleveland sent 2,000 troops to Chicago. Fighting between workers and soldiers broke out at the stockyards and in the Illinois Central switchyard. Troops fired into crowds of workers, killing 20 and wounding 60 others. Debs was jailed for interfering with the mails; the union was broken. The town of Pullman remained peaceful, but residents saw, over the tops of their houses, a column of smoke rising from the Columbian Exposition where the White City burned.

Three years later George Pullman died of a heart attack. His obituaries mixed praise for his achievements with criticism of his stubborn refusal to head off one of the bloodiest labor conflicts in U. S. history. The next year, the city of Chicago absorbed Pullman and turned the company town into a neighborhood. A writer for *The Nation* noted that what working people wanted most was a chance to own a place of their own. "Mr. Pullman in his scheme for a model community for American workmen overlooked this peculiar American characteristic. Hence, in my humble opinion, these tears."

popularity remained flat. Cash-strapped farmers in the West and South grumbled against the president's hard-money policies and cozy relationship with plutocrats like Morgan. Calling out troops to crush the Pullman strike cost Cleveland the support of northern workers. The escalating cycle of economic and political crises, farmer and labor insurgencies, middle-class radicalism, and upper-class conservatism fractured political parties. Democrats, Republicans, and Populists all called for stronger government action, but each party split over what action to take. In 1896 the "currency question" dominated a watershed election that transformed the two major parties and destroyed the third.

1896 was the last time presidential candidates openly debated great economic questions in terms that had been familiar to nineteenth-century voters since Thomas Jefferson ran for president in 1800; 1896 was also the first recognizably modern presidential election. It was the first time a successful candidate fully employed the advertising and fundraising techniques of twentieth-century political campaigns. Spectacular and dramatic on its own terms, the presidential election of 1896 was also a turning point in the history of national politics.

Currency and the Tariff

The soundness of the dollar, which Morgan and Cleveland worked so hard to preserve, was a mixed blessing for Americans. Based on gold, the dollar helped sell American goods in foreign markets, especially in Europe, where the franc, the mark, and the pound were also based on gold. Using the same standard allowed these currencies to be exchanged easily, and it allowed American manufacturers to predict the price their products would fetch on the global market. The United States traded on a much smaller scale with countries—like Mexico or China—that used silver. "Without exception," Cleveland's secretary of commerce explained, "prices are fixed in the markets of countries having a gold standard." Gold, however, was valuable because it was scarce, and many Americans suffered from that scarcity. Few farmers in Nebraska or Texas had ever seen a 20 dollar gold piece. The low prices and murderous interest rates that made Populists complain were a result of the gold standard.

Increasing the money supply would reduce interest rates and make credit more available. There were two ways to put more money in circulation: The government could print paper "greenbacks," or it could coin silver (see chapter 19). "Free silver" advocates generally favored coining a ratio of 16 ounces of silver for each ounce of gold. Populists initially wanted greenbacks but later found silver an agreeable compromise. Western mining interests pushed silver as well. The Republican and Democratic Parties were committed to the gold standard, but by 1896 each party harbored a renegade faction of silverites. To Americans in the 1890s, the crucial political issues—jobs, foreign trade,

the survival of small farms, and the prosperity of big corporations—boiled down to one question: Would the dollar be backed by gold or silver? The election of 1896 was "the battle of the standards."

The Cross of Gold

A dark mood hung over Chicago as delegates arrived at the Democratic Convention in July 1896. They had come to bury Cleveland and the party's commitment to the gold standard along with him. When a photographer asked Senator David Hill to say cheese, he scowled, "I never smile and look pleasant at a funeral." The draft platform denounced Cleveland for imposing "government by injunction" during the Pullman strike and condemned the gold standard "which has locked fast the prosperity of an industrial people in the paralysis of hard times." When the platform came before the full convention, delegates had to decide whether the party would stand for silver or gold and who would replace Cleveland as the candidate for president.

Both questions were decided when a former congressman from Nebraska, William Jennings Bryan, mounted the stage. Handsome, and only 36 years old, he was known as an electrifying speaker. "You come and tell us that the great cities are in favor of the gold standard," he said in a deep but restrained voice. "Destroy our farms, and the

Victor Debreuil, The Cross of Gold (c. 1896). Debreuil was known for his realistic still lifes of coins, greenbacks, and photographs. Artists and citizens in the 1890s used the "money question" to ask what was valuable, true, and real in the modern age.

ass will grow in the streets of every city in the country!" he audience was on its feet, and Bryan delivered his lines the rhythmic cadence of a camp preacher. "We will answer their demand for a gold standard by saying to hem"—he paused stretching out his arms in an attitude of ucifixion—"You shall not press down upon the brow of bor this crown of thorns. You shall not crucify mankind pon a cross of gold!" The hall exploded with cheers. ryan won the nomination handily.

Two weeks later the Populists, meeting in St. Louis, so named Bryan as their presidential nominee. The delegates, jubilant that a major party had finally seen the light n the money question, nonetheless had misgivings about eing absorbed into the Democratic ticket. The Ocala and Omaha platforms, which imagined comprehensive hanges in the money system and American institutions, ad been reduced to a single panacea: silver. Republicans olit on the currency issue, but after a walkout by the silver faction, the convention overwhelmingly adopted a ro-gold plank drafted with the approval of J. P. Morgan. he delegates nominated William McKinley, the governor f Ohio, a nondescript but loyal supporter of industry. he parties could hardly have offered two more different andidates, or two more different visions of the future.

he Battle of the Standards

n one of the most exciting contests since the Civil War he candidates each employed creative new techniques in adically different ways. McKinley ran like an incument. During the campaign he never left his home in Canon, Ohio. Instead, delegations came to him. Some 0,000 people from 30 states trampled McKinley's grass nd listened to speeches affirming the candidate's comitment to high tariffs and sound money. In offices in New York and Chicago the speeches were set in type and istributed as newspaper columns, fliers, and pamphlets hroughout the country. The campaign used sophisticated public-relations techniques to educate the electorate on the virtues of the gold standard. Posters reduced he campaign's themes to pithy slogans like "Prosperity r Poverty," or "Vote for Free Silver and be Prosperous Like Guatemala."

The genius behind the campaign was a Cleveland coalnd-oil millionaire named Marcus Hanna. Hanna ankrolled his publicity blitz with between 3 and 7 million ollars raised from industrialists who well knew what was t stake in this election. Leaving nothing to chance, he asessed a fair share of the campaign's expenses from corpoations and banks based on calculations of the profitability nd net worth of each. The combination of big money and dvertising revolutionized presidential politics. "He has dvertised McKinley as if he were a patent medicine," Theodore Roosevelt crowed.

With only $300,000 to spend, Bryan ran like a challenger even though his party occupied the White House.

Rejecting McKinley's front-porch tactics, he hit the road, logging 29,000 miles by rail and buggy and making more than 500 speeches in 29 states. Oratorical ability had won Bryan the nomination, but audiences were unaccustomed to hearing a candidate speak for himself during a campaign. Many considered it undignified. "The Boy Orator has one speech, but he makes it twice a day," wrote an unsympathetic Republican, John Hay. "He simply reiterates the unquestioned truths that . . . there is no goodness or wisdom except among the illiterate and criminal classes, that gold is vile, that silver is lovely and holy."

Despite the scorn of eastern newspapers, industrialists genuinely feared the prospect of a Bryan presidency. "He has succeeded in scaring the gold bugs out of their five wits," Hay remarked. Factory owners threatened to close shop if Bryan won. Just before election day, the global markets that McKinley prized returned the favor. Crop failures abroad doubled the price of wheat in the Midwest. In the final tally, Bryan won the South and West decisively, but McKinley won the populous states of the industrial Northeast, as well as several farm states in the upper Midwest, capturing the electoral college by a majority of 271 to 176 (see Map 20-1).

The election of 1896 changed the style of political campaigns and shifted the political positions of both major parties. By pushing currency policies to improve the lives of workers and farmers, Bryan's Democrats abandoned a commitment to minimal government that stretched back to Andrew Jackson. The Republicans recognized that the

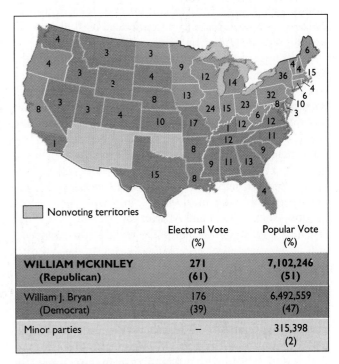

	Electoral Vote (%)	Popular Vote (%)
WILLIAM McKINLEY (Republican)	**271** **(61)**	**7,102,246** **(51)**
William J. Bryan (Democrat)	176 (39)	6,492,559 (47)
Minor parties	–	315,398 (2)

Map 20-1 The Election of 1896.
William McKinley's "front porch campaign" carried the northern industrial states, along with the key farm states of Iowa and Minnesota, securing a narrow victory over Bryan.

electorate would judge the president on his ability to bring prosperity to the country. As president, McKinley asserted his leadership over economic policy, calling Congress into special session to pass the Dingley Tariff Act, which levied the highest taxes on imports in American history. He extended the reach of presidential power even more dramatically through an expansionist foreign and military policy.

In the election of 1896 fundamental economic questions—Who is the economy supposed to serve? What is the nature of money?—were at stake in a closely matched campaign. No wonder voter turnout hit an all-time high. Administrative agencies and expert panels took over those issues after the turn of the century, but Americans long remembered that raucous campaign when America's economic future was up for grabs. In the 1960s, schoolchildren still recited the Cross of Gold speech.

The Retreat From Politics

The economy improved steadily after 1895 but this latest business panic and its aftermath left lasting marks on corporate and political culture. Industrial workers made a tactical retreat in the face of a new political and legal climate. In the South, depression, urbanization, and the modernizing influence of railroads accelerated the spread of legalized racial segregation and disfranchisement. Increasingly, a system of repression imposed by custom and terror became a system enforced by law and terror. Racial segregation or "Jim Crow" laws became a fact of life throughout the South in the 1890s, and states devised legal pretexts to prohibit African Americans from voting.

Although an extreme case, what was happening in the South was part of nationwide decline of participatory politics. The rituals of citizenship—voting, electioneering, partisanship—had once provided a means to understand and discuss relationships between power, wealth, and the rights of persons and groups in a democracy. With the slackening of agrarian unrest and the exhaustion of resistance to corporate capitalism, politics lost some of its value. Voter participation declined, and Americans felt less of a personal stake in election campaigns. Disaffected groups—such as labor and African Americans—had to devise new ways to build community and express resistance.

The Lure of the Cities

In the South as in the North people left the countryside and moved to villages, towns, and cities. Thousands of small towns sprang into existence between 1880 and 1910, and cities like Charlotte, Montgomery, Mobile, and Charleston swelled with newcomers from the country. By 1900 one out of six southerners lived in town. With the lone exception of Birmingham, Alabama, southern cities were not devoted to manufacturing but to commerce and services. Doctors' offices, haberdasheries, dry goods stores, and groceries could be found near warehouse where cotton was stored, ginned, and pressed and near th railway station where it was loaded for shipment to distan textile mills. Families from outlying farms visited thes main streets to sell crops and do the weekly marketing.

The growth of villages and towns in the South was no the product of urban prosperity, but rather of rural deca Crop liens, which gave bankers ownership of a crop befor it was planted, and debt drove people from the country side. "There is absolutely nothing before them on th farm," George Henry White, an African-American con gressman, explained, "and they lose hope and go into th cities." Work and wages were often only slightly bette but families still went, in the words of one migrant, "as on instinctively moves from a greater toward a lesser pain. The young and the ambitious left first, while older an poorer residents stayed behind. In urban areas the new mi grants found more activity and excitement, chances to g to school and join organizations, and a different set o challenges.

While white newcomers settled on the outskirts o towns, African Americans moved into industrial district along the railroad tracks. Cities became more segregated a they grew, and by 1890 most blocks in the larger cities wer either all African American or all white. Still, towns offere things that were missing in the country, such as schools. I rural areas, children worked as field hands and went t school only a few weeks a year. A Little Rock, Arkansas resident noted that newly arrived African-American parent were "very anxious to send their children to school." Job were often available, too, although more frequently fo women than for men. African-American women could fin work cooking or doing laundry in small towns and villages but there were few positions for carpenters, teamsters, o porters. Men usually had to look for seasonal labor at farm or lumber camps some distance from town. This mean families faced a tough choice between poverty and separa tion. A quarter of the urban African-American household between 1880 and 1915 were headed by women, more than twice the number in rural areas.

Despite setbacks, the newcomers gained a place fo themselves in urban life. By 1890 every southern city had an African-American business district with its ow churches, insurance companies, lawyers, doctors, under takers, and usually a weekly newspaper. Benevolent an reform organizations, sewing circles, and book clubs en riched community life. Mary Church Terrell founded the National Association of Colored Women in 1896 unde the motto, "lifting as we climb." However, there were lim its to how high educated African Americans could ascend Professionals like lawyers, doctors, and nurses had t work within their community. Jobs on the bottom rung o the corporate ladder—clerk, salesman, telephone operator

Mary Church Terrell (1863–1954). Activist, suffragist, and educator, Terrell tried to unite the struggles for women's rights and civil rights. "A white woman has but one handicap to overcome," she wrote. "I have two—both sex and race."

stenographer, railroad conductor—were reserved for whites. In towns and cities, African-American southerners faced a frustrating mix of opportunities and obstacles.

Inventing Jim Crow

In June 1892 Homer Plessy boarded the East Louisiana Railway in New Orleans for a trip to Covington, Louisiana. Having purchased a first-class ticket, he attempted to board the whites-only car and was arrested under a Louisiana law that required African Americans and whites to ride in "equal but separate accommodations" on trains. Before Judge John H. Ferguson could try the case, Plessy's lawyer, Albion W. Tourgée, appealed on the grounds that the separate car law violated the Constitution's Fourteenth Amendment, which requires that all citizens receive equal protection of the law.

When *Plessy v. Ferguson* came before the Supreme Court in April 1896, lawyers for the state of Louisiana argued that the law was necessary to avoid the "danger of friction from too intimate contact" between the races. In separate cars, all citizens enjoyed equal privileges. Tourgée

replied that the question was not "the equality of the privileges enjoyed, but the right of the state to label one citizen as white and another as colored." In doing so, the government gave unearned advantages to some citizens and not to others. "How much would it be *worth* to a young man entering upon the practice of law, to be regarded as a white man rather than a colored one?" he asked. "Nineteen-twentieths of the property of the country is owned by white people. Ninety-nine hundredths of the business opportunities are in control of white people." The issue for Tourgée was not racial conflict or even prejudice, but whether the government should be allowed to divide people arbitrarily.

In a seven-to-one decision the court upheld the "separate but equal" doctrine. The decision provided legal justification for the system of official inequality that expanded in the twentieth century. Southern whites served notice that law and force were on their side. "I want to give you niggers a few words of plain talk and advice," Alabama governor William C. Oates told an audience of African-American businessmen and officials, "You might as well understand that this is a white man's country, as far as the South is concerned, and we are going to make you keep your place."

The Plessy decision was handed down as a formal system of racial discrimination was being put in place across the South. Informal segregation had existed for some time. Soon after the Civil War, African Americans and whites formed separate churches, schools, and hospitals. People associated with members of their own race when they could, and when they could not—at work, in business, or when traveling—unwritten local customs usually governed their interaction. By the 1890s those informal customs were being codified in law.

In 1885 T. McCants Stewart, a correspondent for an African-American newspaper in New York, found that on trains from Maryland to the Gulf of Mexico a white passenger "would be compelled to ride with a Negro, or walk." But five years later, Booker T. Washington traveled the same roads and discovered that "the Negro is forced to ride in railroad coaches that are inferior in every way to those given the whites." The systematic separation of the races by law, later known as segregation, began during this period, and railroads, as symbols of progress, were a chief point of contention. The whistle of an approaching train forewarned of a segregated future.

The political and economic tensions created by the depression helped turn racist customs into a rigid caste division. Competition for jobs fed racial antagonisms, as did the migration into cities and towns of a new generation of African Americans, born since the war, who showed less deference to whites. New notions of "scientific" racism led intellectuals and churchmen to regard racial hostility as natural and to see separation as a humane alternative to extermination. The depression created political opportunities

Lynchings were public spectacles. When 17-year-old Jesse Washington was killed in Waco, Texas in 1916, a crowd of several thousand, including the mayor, police chief, and students from Waco High, attended the event on the lawn of city hall. Afterwards, the murderers posed for a photograph and sold their victim's teeth for $5 apiece.

for segregationists. Angry voters in many southern states deposed the coalitions of landowners and New South industrialists that had governed since Reconstruction and replaced them with Populist "demagogues."

James K. Vardaman of Mississippi and Pitchfork Ben Tillman of South Carolina reshaped the politics of their states. They appealed to poor white farmers and workers by attacking African Americans and the railroads. Segregation hurt both, since it forced national railroads to conform to local customs. Between 1887 and 1891 nine states in the South passed railroad segregation laws. Trains began pulling separate cars for African Americans, called "Jim Crow" cars after the name of a character in a minstrel show. Soon Jim Crow laws were extended to waiting rooms, drinking fountains, and other places where African Americans and whites might meet.

Segregation was also enforced by terror. The threat of lynching poisoned all relations between the races, and African Americans learned at a young age that they could be tortured and killed for committing a crime, talking back, or simply looking the wrong way at a white woman. Lynchings occurred most frequently in areas thinly populated by whites and where African Americans worked seasonally at lumber camps or cotton farms, but killings and mob violence against African-American neighborhoods also occurred in the largest cities. Between 1882 and 1903, nearly 2,000 African-American

southerners were killed by mobs, and lynchings became more savage during this period. Victims were routinely tortured, flayed, castrated, gouged, and burned alive, and members of the mob often took home grisly souvenirs like a piece of bone or a severed thumb. Lynching revealed the barbarity at the core of southern racism, but many whites saw it as a justification for racial separation. If contact between blacks and whites provoked violence, they reasoned, the government should try to reduce interaction as much as possible.

Many African-American southerners fought segregation with boycotts, lawsuits, and disobedience. Ida Wells-Barnett, a Nashville journalist, organized an international anti-lynching campaign (see chapter 21). Segregation never became fixed or uniform throughout the South. It was constantly negotiated and challenged, but after 1896 it was backed by the U. S. Supreme Court.

The Atlanta Compromise

When Atlanta invited the African-American educator, Booker T. Washington, to address the Cotton States Exposition in 1895, northern newspapers concluded that a new era of racial progress had begun. "Had anyone predicted twenty-five years ago that the South would so honor a Negro," the *Philadelphia Telegram* reported, "he would have been looked upon as a madman." The speech made Wash-

With voting rights denied to African Americans, Booker T. Washington urged vocational education, such as this cooking class at Tuskegee, as the surest route to economic advancement.

...ngton the most recognized African American. Starting with 40 students and an abandoned shack, Washington had built Tuskegee into a nationally known institution, the preeminent technical school for African Americans. Northern philanthropists took an interest in Tuskegee, impressed by Washington's industriousness and by his policy of avoiding politics and encouraging his students to do likewise. Washington was a guest in the stately homes of Newport and at Andrew Carnegie's castle in Scotland. When Atlanta, inspired by Chicago's success, staged an exposition to showcase the region's industrial and social progress, the organizers asked Washington to speak.

Washington's address stressed racial accommodation. He stated that relations had not always been smooth and that his own race was partly to blame. After the Civil War, African Americans had tried to attain equality by asserting their civil and political rights. "The wisest among my race understand that agitation of questions of social equality is the extremest folly," he said, "and that progress in the enjoyment of all the privileges that will come to us must be the result of severe and constant struggle rather than artificial forcing." He urged white businessmen not to rely on immigrant labor, but rather to employ African-American southerners "who have, without strikes and labor wars, tilled your fields, cleared your forests, built your railroads and cities." Raising his hand above his head, stretching out his fingers and then closing them into a fist, he delivered the line that summarized his approach to race relations: "In all things that are purely social, we can be as separate as the fingers, yet one as the hand in all things essential to mutual progress."

The largely white audience, which had murmured uneasily as Washington approached the podium, erupted into applause. Women threw flowers. President Grover Cleveland congratulated him, and the editor of the *Atlanta Constitution* declared that "That man's speech is the beginning of a moral revolution in America." Enthusiastic well-wishers accompanied him to the depot, where he boarded a Jim Crow car bound for Tuskegee.

Washington's "Atlanta Compromise" stressed the mutual obligations African Americans and whites had to each other. African Americans would give up the vote and stop insisting on social equality if white leaders would keep violence in check and allow African Americans to succeed in agriculture and business. White industrialists welcomed this arrangement, and African-American leaders felt that for the moment it might be the best that could be achieved. "Here might be the basis of a real settlement between whites and blacks in the South," a young professor named W. E. B. Du Bois wrote in the *New York Age*, "if the South opened to the Negroes the doors of economic opportunity, and the Negroes cooperated with the white South in political sympathy."

Disfranchisement and the Decline of Popular Politics

After the feverish campaign of 1896 elections began to lose some of their appeal. Attendance fell off at the polls. Some 79 percent of voters cast ballots in the battle of the standards; four years later the figure was down to 73 percent and fell to 65 percent four years after that. More visibly, the public events surrounding campaigns drew thinner crowds. Fewer people turned out for parades, speeches, or pig roasts. Organizers fretted about "apathy," which seemed to have become a national epidemic.

Many commentators and politicians were unworried, interpreting the electorate's quietude as a sign of political maturity, and it took several decades for voter turnout to sink far enough to seem unhealthy. However, an unmistakable trend had begun.

In the South, the disappearance of voters was easy to explain. For much of the electorate, voting was illegal. As Jim Crow laws multiplied, southern states disfranchised African Americans (and one out of four whites) by requiring voters to demonstrate literacy, property ownership, or knowledge of the Constitution before they could register. Louisiana added the notorious "grandfather clause," which denied the vote to men whose grandfathers were prohibited from voting. While voter participation declined voluntarily throughout the country after the 1890s, it declined in the South by law and force (see Table 20-1).

Whites saw **disfranchisement** and segregation not as throwbacks to Reconstruction-era racism but as modern,

TABLE 20-1

The Spread of Disfranchisement

	State	Strategies
1889	Florida	Poll tax
	Tennessee	Poll tax
1890	Mississippi	Poll tax, literacy test, understanding clause
1891	Arkansas	Poll tax
1893, 1901	Alabama	Poll tax, literacy test, grandfather clause
1894, 1895	South Carolina	Poll tax, literacy test, understanding clause
1894, 1902	Virginia	Poll tax, literacy test, understanding clause
1897, 1898	Louisiana	Poll tax, literacy test, grandfather clause
1899, 1900	North Carolina	Poll tax, literacy test, grandfather clause
1902	Texas	Poll tax
1908	Georgia	Poll tax, literacy test, understanding clause, grandfather clause

managed race relations, products of an urbanized and sophisticated New South. Whites-only facilities and quiet, orderly polling places were seen by whites as signs that government rested in the proper hands. Demonizing African Americans enforced solidarity among white voters, who might otherwise have voted on local or class interests. Turnout fell most sharply in the South, averaging just 32 percent from 1900 to 1916.

No new legal restrictions hampered voting in the North and West, but participation fell there too. This withdrawal from politics reflected the decline of political pageantry as an element of cultural and social life, but it also reflected the disappearance of the intense partisanship that made such spectacles exciting. For American men in the nineteenth century, party membership provided a sense of identity that matched and strengthened ethnic, religious, and neighborhood identities. Rallying together with party members from the same lodge, parish, or homeland filled campaigns with a personal meaning and excitement that was heightened by cliffhanger contests against equally committed opponents.

A developing economy with new patterns of recreation, class relations, and community participation undermined the habits of partisanship, but so did the new style of campaigns. The new emphasis on advertising, education, and fundraising took away the aspects of electioneering that thrilled voters. Educated middle- and upper-class voters liked the new style, feeling that raucous campaigns were no way to decide important issues. They sought to influence policy more directly, through interest groups

rather than parties. Without knowing it, they discarded traditions that unified communities and gave voters a feeling of connection to their country and its leaders.

Organized Labor Retreats From Politics

Workers also withdrew from politics as organized labor turned away from political means and goals and redefined objectives in economic terms. As traditional crafts came under attack, skilled workers grew impatient with the political aspirations of the Knights of Labor and created new organizations that addressed immediate issues: wages, hours, and the conditions of work. The American Federation of Labor, founded in 1886, built a base around skilled trades—miners, printers, molders, carpenters, longshoremen, brewers, and machinists—growing from 150,000 members to more than two million by 1904. While the Knights sought to reform the underlying political economy, the AFL focused on more immediate goals that would improve the working lives of its members. Its founder, Samuel Gompers, promised a practical "bread and butter" unionism. Born in London's East End, Gompers apprenticed as a cigar maker at the age of 10. Three years later his family moved to New York, where Gompers joined the International Cigar Makers Union.

Although affiliated with the Knights, the cigar makers were more interested in getting higher wages than in remaking the economy to benefit producers. They concentrated on shortening work hours, increasing pay, and establishing the union as a permanent concern. High dues and centralized control allowed the union to offer insurance and death benefits to members while holding a strike fund in reserve. Gompers applied the same practices to the AFL. In industry after industry, Federation unions compelled corporations to accept collective bargaining. Gompers' "pure and simple unionism" made modest demands, but it still encountered fierce resistance from corporations, which were backed by the courts.

In the 1895 case of *In re Debs*, the Supreme Court allowed the use of injunctions to criminalize strikes. The court then disarmed one of the few weapons left in labor's arsenal, the boycott. In the 1908 case of *Loewe v. Lawlor*, popularly known as the Danbury Hatters case, the court ruled that advertising a consumer boycott was illegal under the Sherman Anti-Trust Act. In 1911, the court upheld a contempt conviction against Gompers, who had violated an injunction by publicizing another boycott.

Gompers believed that industrial unions, associations that drew members from all occupations within an industry, lacked the discipline and shared values needed to face the combined power of corporations and government, and that unions organized around a single trade or craft would break less easily. However, because the AFL was organized by skill, it was often indifferent to those with less training, as well as to women or recent immigrants. Because employers used unskilled newcomers to break strikes or to run machinery that replaced expert hands, Gompers allowed practices that excluded a large part of the labor force. Organizers recruited Irish and German workers through their fraternal lodges, clubs, and saloons while ignoring similar opportunities in Italian, African-American, Jewish, and Slavic neighborhoods. Instead of drawing female workers in as members, the union attacked them for stealing jobs that rightfully belonged to men. "Every woman employed," said the Federation's newspaper, "displaces a man and adds one more to the idle contingent that are fixing wages at the lowest limit." Although it represented mainly privileged workers, the AFL's size and influence made it the voice of organized labor.

Other leaders rejected Gompers' philosophy and strategy, but they too built unions into institutions representing the immediate interests of their members. Under the leadership of Eugene V. Debs, railroad workers merged the old railroad brotherhoods into an industry-wide association, the American Railway Union (ARU) in 1893. The United Mine Workers (UMW) unionized the bituminous (soft coal) mines of Pennsylvania, Ohio, Indiana, and Michigan but had a harder time in the anthracite region of eastern Pennsylvania. The ARU and the UMW, founded in 1890, were "industrial unions," which tried to organize all of the workers in an entire industry in order to match the size and power of the corporations they bargained with. These new unions faced determined opposition from business and its allies in government. "Our government cannot stand, nor its free institutions endure," the National Association of Manufacturers declared in a pamphlet distributed to schools, "if the Gompers-Debs ideals of liberty and freedom of speech and press are allowed to dominate."

American Diplomacy Enters the Modern World

The Republican victory in 1896 gave heart to proponents of prosperity through foreign trade. Before the turn of the century, the new president announced, the United States would control the markets of the globe. "We will establish trading posts throughout the world as distributing points for American products," Senator Albert Beveridge forecast. "Great colonies, governing themselves, flying our flag and trading with us, will grow about our posts of trade." McKinley sought neither war nor colonies, but many in his party wanted both. Called "jingoes," they included Assistant Secretary of the Navy Theodore Roosevelt, John Hay, the ambassador to London, and Senators Beveridge and Henry Cabot Lodge. Britain, France, and Germany were seizing territory around the world, and jingoes believed the United States needed to do the same for strategic, reli-

gious, and economic reasons. Spain was the most likely target. Madrid clung feebly to the remnants of its once-vast empire, now reduced to Cuba, the Philippines, Guam, and Puerto Rico. Under Cleveland, the United States had moved away from confrontation with Spain, but McKinley, at first reluctantly but later enthusiastically, pushed for the creation of an American empire that stretched to the far shores of the Pacific.

Sea Power and the Imperial Urge

Few men better exemplified the jingoes' combination of religiosity, martial spirit, and fascination with the laws of history than Alfred Thayer Mahan. A naval officer and strategist, he told students at the Naval War College that since the Roman Empire, world leadership had belonged to the nation that controlled the sea. Published in 1890, his book *The Influence of Sea Power upon History, 1660–1783,* became an instant classic.

In his first paragraph, Mahan connected naval expansion and empire to the problem of overproduction that the United States faced. A great industrial country needed trade; trade required a merchant fleet; and merchant shipping needed naval protection and overseas bases. Colonies could provide markets for goods and congregations for Christian missionaries, but more importantly they offered a springboard for naval forces that could protect sea lanes and project power into the great land masses of Asia, Latin America, and Africa.

Mahan urged the United States to build a canal across Central America, allowing manufacturers on the Atlantic coast to "compete with Europe, on equal terms as to distance, for the markets of eastern Asia." He felt that naval bases should be established along routes connecting the United States with markets in Latin America and the Far East. Congress and the Navy Department began implementing these recommendations even before McKinley took office (see Figure 20-2).

Mahan was not the only prophet who saw resemblances to the Roman Empire. Brooks Adams' *The Law of Civilization and Decay* (1895) spelled out the implications of the closing of the frontier: greater concentration of wealth, social inequality, and eventually collapse. To repeal this "law" the United States needed to seek a new frontier in Asia where it could regenerate itself through combat. Sharing the social Darwinist belief (see chapter 18) that nations and races were locked in a savage struggle for survival, Mahan and Adams expected the United States to prevail and benefit from the approaching conflict.

If subduing continents with cross, Constitution, and gatling gun appealed to anyone, it was Theodore Roosevelt. As a politician and strategist, Roosevelt paid keen attention to new ideas and forces that were magnifying the power of some nations and diminishing others. **Imperialism** seemed to him the essential characteristic of modernizing countries. He was the image of the modern frontiersman, a

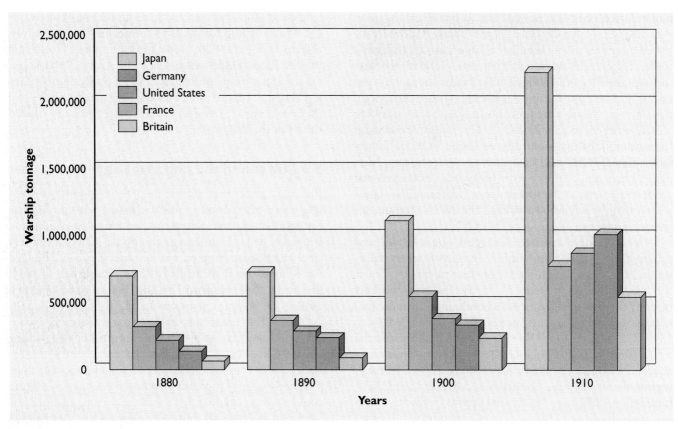

Figure 20-2   Warship Tonnage of the World's Navies.
Naval strength was the primary index of power before World War I. The United States held onto third place in the naval arms race, while Germany and Japan made significant gains.
Source: Paul Kennedy, Rise and Fall of the Great Powers (New York: Random House, 1987), p. 203.

writer, soldier, and politician (see page 618). Between stints in the state assembly and as New York City police commissioner, he raised cattle in the Dakota Territory, reading books by the campfire at night to the amusement of his fellow cowpunchers. Roosevelt was acutely conscious of how modern forces—globalized trade, instant communications, the reach of modern navies, and imperialism—had altered the rules of domestic and international politics. He sought to position the United States at the center of these modernizing currents, a place that would have to be earned, he felt, both on foreign battlefields and at home, where the material and technological gains of the nineteenth century had not yet been translated into the social and moral advancement that marked a true civilization.

The Scramble for Empire

For jingoes, China was the ultimate prize to be won in the global contest for trade and mastery. It had more people than any other country, hence more customers and more souls to be brought to Christ. The number of American missionaries in China doubled in the 1890s. Many of them came from the Student Volunteer Movement, which promised "the evangelization of the world in this generation" and had chapters on nearly every college campus. Even

though no more than one or two percent of U. S. exports had ever gone to Chinese ports, manufacturers believed that if any country could absorb the output of America's overproductive factories, it was China. James B. Duke founded the British-American Tobacco Company based on "China's population of 450 million people, and assuming that in the future they might average a cigarette a day." In 1890 Standard Oil began selling kerosene in Shanghai. Fifteen years later, China was the largest overseas market for American oil. Mahan had predicted that China would be the arena for the coming struggle for industrial and military supremacy, and by 1897 he appeared to be right.

In 1894 Japan declared war on China, and within months it occupied Korea, Manchuria, and China's coastal cities. When the fighting was over, western powers seized slices of Chinese territory. In November 1897, German troops captured the port of Qingdao on the Shandong Peninsula. An industrial area on the northeast coast, Shandong was the center of American missionary activity, investment, and trade. To Americans, the invasion of Shandong presaged the beginning of an imperial grab for territory and influence. In the 1880s European powers had carved up Africa. Now it appeared that the same thing was about to happen in China. "It is felt," the *Journal of Commerce* declared, "that we stand at the dividing of the ways,

Thanks to the work of missionaries in China, Mark Twain observed, "the people who sit in darkness . . . have become suspicious of the blessings of civilization."

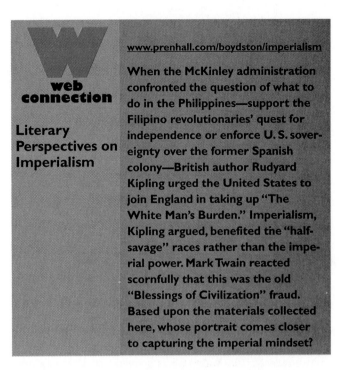

web connection

Literary Perspectives on Imperialism

www.prenhall.com/boydston/imperialism

When the McKinley administration confronted the question of what to do in the Philippines—support the Filipino revolutionaries' quest for independence or enforce U. S. sovereignty over the former Spanish colony—British author Rudyard Kipling urged the United States to join England in taking up "The White Man's Burden." Imperialism, Kipling argued, benefited the "half-savage" races rather than the imperial power. Mark Twain reacted scornfully that this was the old "Blessings of Civilization" fraud. Based upon the materials collected here, whose portrait comes closer to capturing the imperial mindset?

between gaining or losing the greatest market which awaits exploitation." The McKinley administration watched the events unfolding in China carefully, but in the winter of 1897–1898 the Departments of State and War had more pressing concerns closer to home.

War With Spain

While other European powers were expanding their empires, Spain was barely hanging on to the one it had. Since the 1860s its two largest colonies, Cuba and the Philippines, had been torn by revolution. Between 1868 and 1878 Cuban nationalists fought a prolonged war of independence, financed by contributions from New York. Spain ended the war by promising reforms, but the McKinley Tariff (see chapter 19) and the Panic of 1893 ruined the island's chief export industry, sugar. Groaning under a crushing debt, Spain reneged on its promise. The rebellion resumed in 1895 and quickly overran two-thirds of the island. The rebels practiced a "scorched earth" policy, dynamiting trains and burning plantations in an attempt to force Spain to withdraw or the United States to intervene.

Spain retaliated with a brutal campaign of pacification. General Valeriano Weyler herded civilians into reconcentration camps enclosed by barbed wire. Nearly 100,000 died, many of them women and children. William Randolph Hearst's *New York Journal* and other newspapers provided readers with lurid details of "Butcher" Weyler's atrocities. Cuba's story sold newspapers. "Is there no nation," one editorialist asked, "wise enough, brave enough, and strong enough to restore peace to this bloodsmitten land?"

Cleveland had tried to minimize U. S. involvement in Cuba, but McKinley moved quickly toward confrontation. In June 1897 he protested Weyler's actions, and a month later he demanded that Spain withdraw from Cuba. The government in Madrid retreated, and McKinley breathed a sigh of relief. Despite his bluster, he realized that he could pay for a war only by coining silver. The Treasury's gold reserve was still precariously low, but events in Havana were soon outracing policy. Riots erupted in the Cuban capital, and American expatriates demanded protection. The president asked the Navy to send a warship to Havana, and Theodore Roosevelt selected the *Maine,* one of the new battleships that had been built at Mahan's urging.

The arrival of the *Maine* reduced tensions for a while, but on February 15 an explosion ripped through the ship and sent it to the bottom of Havana harbor. Almost the entire crew of 266 perished. Navy investigators later concluded that the explosion had been internal, probably in the new oil-fired boilers, but the newspapers had already blamed Spanish treachery. Hearst printed a full-page diagram showing the ship being destroyed by a "sunken torpedo." A New Orleans newspaper claimed that "no explanation by the Spanish Government, no offer to make reparation, could prevent a declaration of war."

McKinley hesitated, mindful of the budget and the unfolding events in China, but Roosevelt ordered Commodore George Dewey's Asiatic Squadron to steam for Hong Kong: "Keep full of coal. In the event of declaration of war with Spain, your duty will be to see that the Spanish squadron does not leave the Asiatic coast, and then offensive operations in the Philippine Islands." Congress appropriated 50 million dollars for arms. Secretary of War Russell A. Alger warned that the president was out of step with the country. "Congress will declare war in spite of him. He'll get run over." Spanish emissaries tried to gain support from other European countries, but they were rebuffed. "Nobody wants to arouse America's anger," the German foreign minister explained. "The United States is a rich country."

In March the economic picture took a turn for the better, and McKinley sent Spain an ultimatum demanding independence for Cuba. On April 11 he asked Congress for authorization to use force, and Congress responded by passing a declaration of war. Expansionists such as Roosevelt, Mahan, and Adams would not have had their way if war had been less popular. Corporate interests favored it, immigrants and southerners saw it as a way to assert their patriotism, and newspapers found it made good copy. "We are all jingoes now," declared the *New York Sun*.

Neither side had many illusions about how the fighting would turn out. Going to war with Spain, novelist Sherwood Anderson wrote, was "like robbing an old gypsy woman in a vacant lot at night after the fair," but the war opened with a cliffhanger that even Hearst could not have invented. On May 1 news arrived that Dewey's Asiatic Squadron was in battle against the Spanish fleet in Manila Bay in the Philippines. The war had begun not in Cuba, but instead half a world away on the far edge of the Pacific Ocean. There the information stopped. The telegraph cable connecting Manila to the outside world had been cut. Official Spanish reports were vague, but they alleged that the Americans had suffered a "considerable loss of life." Dewey's squadron contained only two modern cruisers, but all of its ships were steel hulled in contrast with Spain's wooden vessels. For six anxious days the American public awaited word from the Far East.

It arrived in the early morning hours of May 7, interrupting a poker game in the newsroom at the *New York Herald*. The paper's Hong Kong correspondent had been at the battle. Dewey destroyed Spain's entire fleet of 12 warships without suffering a single serious casualty. The country went wild with relief and triumph. New York staged a parade on Fifth Avenue. A Dewey-for-president movement began. In Washington, McKinley consulted a map to see where the Philippines were. Roosevelt quit his job and ordered Brooks Brothers to make him a uniform.

The war in Cuba unfolded less spectacularly. The Navy bottled up Spain's Atlantic fleet in the Bay of Santiago de Cuba. When the ships attempted to escape, American warships cut them to pieces. "Don't cheer, men," an officer ordered the gun crews, "Those poor devils are dying." A bit of drama was provided by the voyage of the *U. S. S. Oregon*, which left its West-Coast base and traveled at top speed around the southern tip of South America in 68 days to join the Atlantic fleet too late for the fighting. Its journey, tracked by newspapers around the country, dramatized the need for a canal connecting the Atlantic and the Pacific.

In the years before the war, Congress had poured money into the Navy but not the Army, and it took some time before soldiers could be trained and equipped. Recruits were herded into camps in Florida without tents, proper clothing, or latrines. There were few medical supplies or doctors. In unsanitary camps in Florida, soldiers in woolen uniforms died of dysentery and malaria. Of the 5,462 U. S. soldiers who died in the war with Spain, 5,083 succumbed to disease, a scandal that forced the government to elevate the status of the surgeon general and to regard sanitation and disease prevention as important to national defense.

The Army landed on the Cuban coast and marched inland to engage Spanish defenders. A cavalry general, Joseph Wheeler, an ex-Confederate from Alabama, urged his men on, yelling "The Yankees are running! Damn it, I mean the Spaniards!" Roosevelt came ashore with the First Volunteer Cavalry, known as the "Rough Riders." He recruited, trained, and publicized the regiment, and afterwards he wrote its history, all with an eye to symbolism. Comprised of outlaws, cowboys, Ivy League athletes, New York City policemen, a novelist, and a Harvard Medical School graduate, its membership combined frontier heroism with Eastern elite leadership. The regiment traveled with its own film crew and a correspondent from the *New York Herald*.

Spanish forces stubbornly resisted around the city of Santiago. Their Mauser rifles had a longer range and a faster rate of fire than American weapons. At San Juan Hill, 500 defenders forced a regiment of the New York National Guard to retreat. The all-African-American 9th and 10th Cavalry took their place along with the Rough Riders, with Roosevelt cautiously waiting until gatling guns could be brought up from the rear. "The negroes saved that fight," a white soldier reported. The capture of Santiago effectively ended Spanish resistance. When fighting ended in August, U. S. troops occupied Cuba, Guam, Puerto Rico, and the city of Manila. The war had lasted only four months.

As American and Spanish diplomats met in Paris to conclude a peace treaty, McKinley had to decide which occupied territories to keep as colonies. Congress, not wanting to inherit the island's 400 million dollars in debt, had already resolved not to annex Cuba. McKinley decided that Guam and Puerto Rico would make ideal naval bases.

The president also seized the opportunity to annex the island nation of Hawaii. In 1893 American sugar planters, led by Sanford Dole, overthrew the islands' last queen, Liliuokalani, and petitioned for annexation (see chapter 19). They were motivated by the Harrison-McKinley Tariff, which would ruin the planters financially unless they could somehow reconnect Hawaii's trade to the United States. Annexation was their best chance, and they had a powerful ally in the U. S. Navy. Mahan had identified the deep-water anchorage at Pearl

Harbor, on Oahu, as a vital base. McKinley now decided to take up Dole's annexation offer.

The Philippines presented more of a problem. Its 7,000 islands were far from the United States and had a population of several million. What the United States needed was a naval base and a coaling station close to the China coast, but holding just one island would be impossible if another power controlled the others. Shortly after Dewey's victory, British and German warships anchored in Manila Bay, clearly intending to divide up whatever territory the United States did not claim. McKinley felt trapped. "The United States, whatever it might prefer as to the Philippines, is in a situation where it cannot let go," he advised his negotiators.

One consideration McKinley did not take into account was that the United States did not actually control the Philippines, and in Manila it was increasingly clear that it would take a war to do so. Before Dewey's fleet sailed from Hong Kong, naval intelligence officers had sought help from Philippine rebel leader Emilio Aguinaldo. Two years earlier, Aguinaldo had led an uprising that fought Spain to a draw. When Spain began employing the same brutal policies used in Cuba, Aguinaldo accepted surrender and exile. Shortly after Dewey's victory in Manila Bay, an American warship delivered Aguinaldo to his native Cavite. Within five days, Filipino insurgents liberated the entire province and marched on Manila. The rebellion spread throughout the islands, and Aguinaldo soon controlled most of the main island of Luzon. His troops laid siege to Manila, but rather than surrender to the Filipinos, the Spanish in the city surrendered to the Americans on August 13, 1898. At Malolos, 25 miles north of Manila, Aguinaldo proclaimed himself president of the independent Philippines and issued a constitution modeled on that of the United States. When the U. S. Army finally arrived, American troops filled Spanish trenches just opposite the Philippine lines. At the end of 1898, the two armies still faced each other across a no-man's land.

Spanish negotiators recognized Cuban independence and surrendered most of the Spanish empire to the United States for free, but they gave up the Philippines only after the United States agreed to pay 20 million dollars, or as an American satirist calculated, $1.25 for every Filipino. The treaty was signed December 10, 1898.

The Anti-Imperialists

Many prominent Americans opposed both the annexation of new colonies and the approaching war with the Philippines. During the treaty fight in Congress in January 1899, they tried to mobilize opinion against the treaty. The movement included ex-presidents Grover Cleveland and Benjamin Harrison, William Jennings Bryan, labor unionists including Samuel Gompers and Eugene Debs, writers such as Mark Twain and Ambrose Bierce, and industrialists including Andrew Carnegie. The anti-imperialists advanced an array of moral, economic, and strategic arguments. Filipinos and Hawaiians, they said, had sought American help in good faith and were capable of governing themselves. The islands could not be defended. Instead of using the Pacific Ocean as a barrier, U. S. forces would be exposed to attack at Pearl Harbor or Manila. Carnegie argued that imperialism distracted attention from domestic problems and took tax money that could be spent at home. White supremacists asked whether Filipinos would become citizens or be allowed to vote and emigrate to the mainland.

The most moving objections came from those who believed imperialism betrayed America's fundamental principles. "Could there be a more damning indictment of the whole bloated ideal termed 'modern civilization' than this amounts to?" William James asked. To Mark Twain imperialism was only the newest form of greed. "There is more money in it, more territory, more sovereignty, and other kinds of emolument, than there is in any other game that is played." Opponents of annexation organized an Anti-Imperialist League and lobbied for the rejection of the Paris Treaty.

Congress whittled away at anti-imperialist objections, banning Philippine immigration, placing the colonies outside the tariff walls, and promising eventual self-government. Jingoes had the momentum of military victory and public acclaim on their

Kansas volunteers under Col. Frederick Funston move through Caloocan, a suburb of Manila, February 1899.

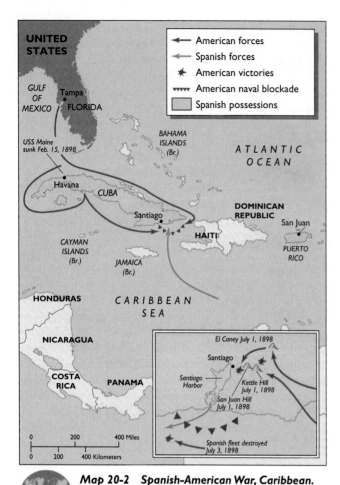

Map 20-2 *Spanish-American War, Caribbean.*

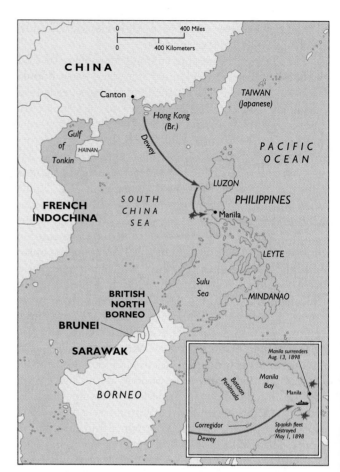

Spanish-American War, Pacific.

side. Anti-imperialists could not offer a vision comparable with naval supremacy, the evangelization of the world, or the fabled China market. On February 6, 1899, the U. S. Senate ratified the Paris Treaty and annexed the Philippines. A day earlier, on the other side of the world, the Philippine-American War began.

The Philippine-American War

McKinley believed he had annexed islands full of near savages "unfit for self-rule," but the Philippines by 1899 had an old civilization with a long tradition of resistance to colonialism. When Magellan discovered the islands in 1521, he found a literate population linked by trade ties to India, Japan, and China. The Spanish converted most Filipinos to Catholicism and established schools and a centralized government. Manila's oldest university was older than Harvard. By 1898 much of the upper class, the *illustrados,* had been educated in Europe. Aguinaldo convened a national assembly comprised of doctors, lawyers, professors, and writers.

Dewey had given Aguinaldo his word that America desired no colonies. Aguinaldo continued to have faith in that word long after the occupation of Manila made it clear that the United States intended to stay. On February 4 an argument between American and Filipino sentries ended in gunfire, and shooting erupted along the line. Aguinaldo was despondent: "No one can deplore more than I this rupture. I have a clear conscience that I endeavored to avoid it at all costs . . . despite frequent humiliation and many sacrificed rights."

By mid-summer the Filipino armies fell back into the mountains and abandoned conventional warfare for guerilla ambushes. The new tactics were effective. Some 4,000 Americans were killed during the war and another 3,000 wounded out of a total force of 70,000. Frustrated by guerilla conflict, American soldiers customarily executed and tortured prisoners, looted villages, and raped Filipino women. An American general on the island of Samar ordered his soldiers to kill everyone over the age of 10. One soldier wrote home, "No cruelty is too severe for these brainless monkeys, who can appreciate no sense of honor, kindness, or justice. I am in my glory when I can sight some dark skin and pull the trigger."

Letters like this and newspaper accounts of torture and massacres fueled opposition in the United States to the war, but just as the anti-imperialist movement gained steam, U. S. forces scored some victories. Recognizing that they were fighting a political war, U. S. officers took pains to win over dissidents and ethnic minorities. In early 1901 this strategy began to pay off. When American troops intercepted a messenger bound for Aguinaldo's secret headquarters, Brigadier General Frederick Funston came up with a bold (and under the rules of war, illegal) plan. He dressed a group of Filipinos loyal to the American side in the uniforms of captured Filipinos, and posing as a prisoner, Funston entered Aguinaldo's camp and kidnapped the president.

After three weeks in a Manila prison, Aguinaldo issued a proclamation of surrender. "Enough of blood, enough of tears and desolation," he pleaded. Resistance continued in Batangas province, south of Manila, for another year. The U. S. Army increased the pressure by imposing the same reconcentration policies the United States had condemned in Cuba, and produced the same result. Perhaps as much as a third of the province's population died of disease and starvation. On July 4, 1902, President Theodore Roosevelt declared the war over.

The American flag flew over the Philippines until 1942, but the colony never lived up to its imperial promise. Instead of defending American trade interests, U. S. troops were pinned down in Philippine garrisons, guarding against sporadic uprisings and the threat of Japanese invasion. The costs of occupation far exceeded the profits generated by Philippine trade. The colony chiefly served as an outlet for American reformers and missionaries, who built schools, churches, and agricultural colleges. A small group of colonists sought statehood, but as the Philippines became more closely tied to the United States, Americans liked their colonial experiment less and less. Labor unions feared a flood of immigration from the islands, and farmers resented competition from Philippine producers; in 1933 Congress voted to phase out American rule.

The Open Door

As Americans celebrated their victories, European powers continued to divide China into quasi-colonial "concessions." An alarmed imperial court in Beijing began a crash program of modernization, but reactionaries within the government overthrew the emperor and installed the conservative "dowager empress" Ci Xi. In the countryside, western missionaries and traders came under attack from local residents led by street-corner martial artists known as Boxers. In 1899, a British author, Charles Beresford, lectured across the United States promoting his book *The*

A FAIR FIELD AND NO FAVOR.
UNCLE SAM: "I'm out for commerce, not conquest."

With the Open Door policy, the United States set out to capture markets rather than colonies.

Breakup of China. Large audiences turned out to hear what they already feared, that the approaching disintegration of China would mean the exclusion of U. S. trade. Just as the United States arrived at the gateway to the Orient, the gates were swinging closed.

Secretary of State John Hay watched events in China with growing apprehension. "The inherent weakness of our position is this," he wrote McKinley, "we do not want to rob China ourselves, and our public opinion will not allow us to interfere, with an army, to prevent others from robbing her. Besides, we have no army." Casting about for some means to keep China's markets open, McKinley turned to William Rockhill, a legendary career foreign service officer who had lived in China and had been the first westerner to visit Tibet. He, in turn, consulted his friend Alfred Hippisley, an Englishman returning from service with the British-run Chinese imperial customs.

Together, Rockhill, Hippisley, and Hay drafted an official letter known as the Open Door Note. Sent to each of the imperial powers, it acknowledged the partitioning of China into spheres, and it observed that so far none of the powers had closed its areas to the trade of other countries. The note urged each of the powers to continue this policy and to declare publicly their intention to keep their concessions open to the trade of the other powers (see Map 20–3).

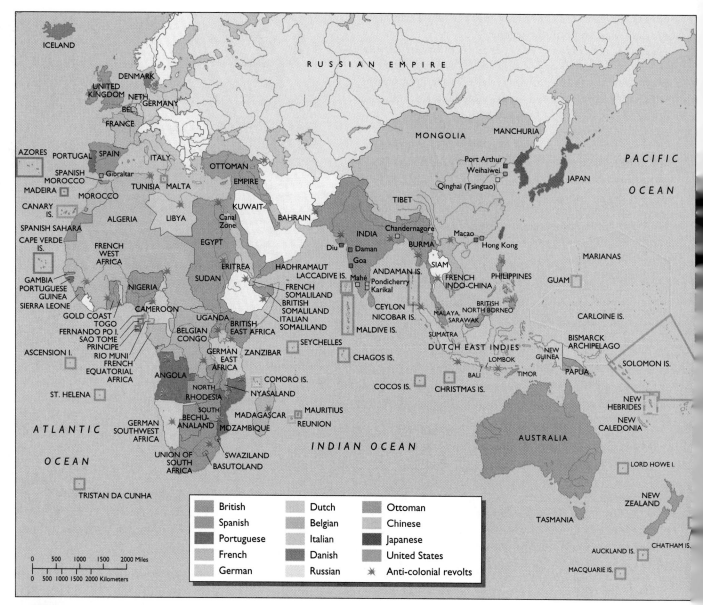

Map 20-3   The Imperial World.

Modern imperialism reached its apex between 1880 and 1945. Most of Africa, the Middle East, and Asia, a third of the world's population, was absorbed into global empires linked by telegraph and steamship to centers of government and commerce in London, Paris, Tokyo, and Washington, D.C.

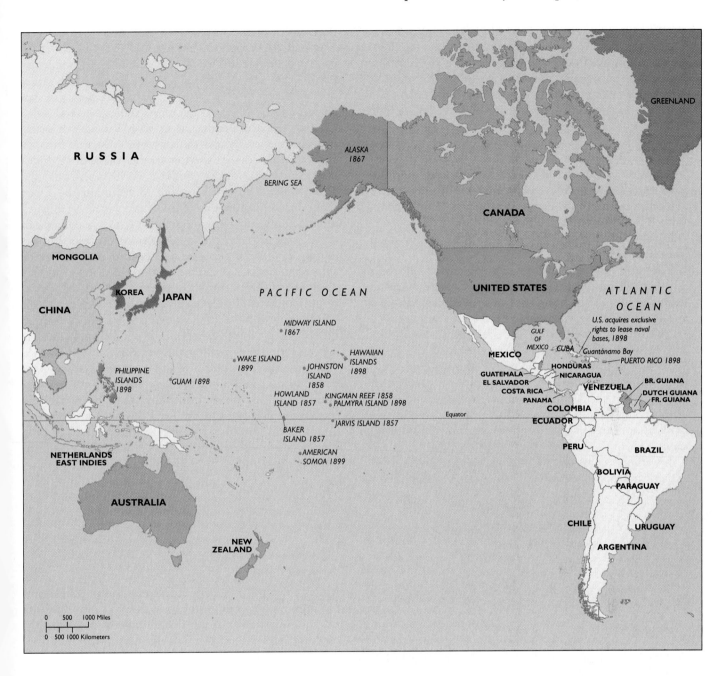

The Open Door was mostly bluff. The United States had no authority to ask for such a pledge and no military power to enforce one. The foreign ministers of Germany, Japan, Russia, Britain, and France replied cautiously at first, agreeing to issue a declaration when the others had done so, but Hay adroitly played one power off another, starting with Britain and Japan, whose trade interests gave them a stake in the Open Door. Once the two strongest powers in China had agreed, France reluctantly acquiesced. Russia and Germany, rather than challenge the other powers, did likewise. Hay proclaimed the Open Door as a diplomatic watershed on the order of the Monroe Doctrine. The United States had secured access to China without war or partition, but the limits of Hay's success soon became apparent.

In early 1900, the antiforeign Boxer movement swept through Shandong province. Armed Chinese attacked missions and foreign businesses, destroyed railroads, and massacred Chinese Christians. Empress Ci Xi recruited 30,000 Boxers into her army and declared war on all foreign countries. The western powers rushed troops to China, but before they could arrive Chinese armies laid siege to western embassies in Beijing. An international force of British, Russian, Japanese, and French troops gathered at Tianjin to march to the rescue. European powers appeared all too eager to capture the Chinese capital.

Without consulting Congress, McKinley ordered American troops into battle on the Asian mainland. Five thousand soldiers rushed from Manila to Tianjin. John Hay issued a second Open Door Note, asking the allied countries to pledge to protect China's independence. Again, the imperial powers reluctantly agreed rather than admit their secret plans to carve up China. On August 15, 1900, U. S. cavalry units under General Adna Chaffee reached Beijing along with Russian cossacks, French zouaves, British-Indian sepoys, German hussars, and Japanese dragoons. After freeing the captive diplomats, the armies of the civilized world looted the city. The United States was unable to maintain the Open Door in China for long. Russia and Japan established separate military zones in northeast China in defiance of the Beijing government and American protests, but the principle of the Open Door, of encouraging free trade and open markets, guided American foreign policy throughout the twentieth century. It rested on the assumption that, in an equal contest, American firms would prevail, spreading manufactured goods around the world, and American influence with them. Under the Open Door, the United States was better off in a world without empires, a world where consumers in independent nations could buy what they wanted. Just one year after the Spanish-American War, Hay's notes rejected imperial expansion in favor of trade expansion. This bold new strategy promised greater gains, but it placed the United States on a collision course with the great empires of the world.

Conclusion

In the turbulent 1890s the social and economic divisions among Americans widened, and old ways of imposing and mediating authority passed away. The hope that a solution to these divisions could be found outside the United States was short-lived. Imperialism promised new markets and an end to the wrenching cycle of depression and labor strife. The United States conquered an overseas empire and challenged other empires to open their ports to free trade, but the goal of prosperity and peace at home proved elusive.

In many ways social Darwinism became a self-fulfilling prophecy, and competition rather than compromise prevailed. Workers and businessmen, farmers and bankers, middle-class radicals and conservatives, whites and African Americans saw each other as enemies. In some cases this meant defeat for one side or point of view. Native Americans withdrew to reservations, and mechanics surrendered the factory floor to middle managers. Racial segregation acknowledged that middle ground, where whites and African Americans could meet on equal terms had grown scarce, but for the most part widening divisions among Americans narrowed but did not eliminate the range of negotiation. Workers, farmers, African Americans, radicals, and reformers had to decide what was politically possible and devise new bargaining strategies.

The strength of the economic recovery and victory in global conflict closed the decade on a note of high optimism. Prosperity, power, and the new force of technology seemed to have rewritten the rules of human affairs to America's advantage. Henry Adams, standing in the American exhibit at the Paris Exposition of 1900 contemplated a forty-foot dynamo—a "huge wheel, revolving within arm's-length at some vertiginous speed, and barely murmuring"—and felt as if he had crossed a "historical chasm." The machine's silent immense force, scarcely understood or controlled and emanating from "a dirty engine-house carefully kept out of sight," seemed a metaphor for the invisible power of the modern age.

CHRONOLOGY

1890   Global depression begins
United Mine Workers founded
Battle of Wounded Knee ends Indian wars
Harrison-McKinley Tariff passed
Alfred T. Mahan publishes *The Influence of Sea Power Upon History, 1660–1783*
Standard Oil markets kerosene in China

1892   Homestead strike

1893   Financial crisis leads to business failures and mass unemployment
World's Columbian Exposition, Chicago
Cherokee Strip land rush
American sugar planters overthrow Queen Liliuokalani of Hawaii

1894   Coxey's Army marches on Washington
Pullman strike
U. S. commission charts canal route across Nicaragua

1895   Morgan agrees to Treasury bailout
National Association of Manufacturers founded
Brooks Adams publishes *The Law of Civilization and Decay*
Booker T. Washington gives "Atlanta Compromise" address
Revolution begins in Cuba
Japan annexes Korea and Taiwan

1896   *Plessy v. Ferguson* declares "separate but equal" facilities constitutional
Mary Church Terrell founds National Association of Colored Women
William McKinley elected president

1897   Germany captures Qingdao, on China's Shandong Peninsula
McKinley issues formal protest to Spain

1898   *Maine* explodes in Havana's harbor
U. S. declares war on Spain
Dewey defeats Spanish fleet at Manila Bay
In the Treaty of Paris, Spain grants Cuba independence, cedes Guam, Puerto Rico, and the Philippines to the United States
Aguinaldo proclaims Philippine independence

1899   Senate votes to annex Puerto Rico, Hawaii, and the Philippines
Philippine-American War begins
Hay issues first Open Door Note

1900   Hay issues second Open Door Note
U. S. Army joins British, French, Russian, German, and Japanese forces in capture of Beijing
Great Exposition of Paris showcases American technology
William McKinley re-elected

1901   Aguinaldo captured
McKinley assassinated; Theodore Roosevelt becomes president

1902   Roosevelt declares Philippine-American war over

Review Questions

1. Business, intellectual, and political leaders in the 1890s had a different view of competition than we have today. Is competition—among workers, companies, or nations—beneficial or harmful to society?

2. Why did workers feel threatened by the kind of efficiency that Frederick W. Taylor promoted?

3. Eugene Debs and Samuel Gompers advocated different agendas and tactics for the American labor movement, just as Booker T. Washington advocated a change in tactics for the movement for racial equality. Would Washington have been more likely to agree with Gompers or with Debs? Why?

4. The election of 1896 hinged on the question of whether the dollar would be backed by gold or by silver. Explain why that issue would matter to a cotton farmer in North Carolina, a factory worker in Milwaukee, or to Andrew Carnegie.

5. Did the United States annex Hawaii and the Philippines for the same reasons that it annexed Oregon or Arizona or for different reasons altogether?

Further Readings

Edward L. Ayers, *The Promise of the New South: Life After Reconstruction* (1992). A study of daily life, work, and politics in the turn-of-the-century South.

H. W. Brands, *The Reckless Decade: America in the 1890s* (1995). A lively look at some of the decade's noteworthy events and characters.

Ron Chernow, *The House of Morgan: An American Banking Dynasty and the Rise of Modern Finance* (1990). The life and business of J. P. Morgan and his heirs, the lions of Wall Street for more than a century.

James B. Gilbert, *Perfect Cities: Chicago's Utopias of 1893* (1991). The fears and dreams that led Chicago's elite to create the World's Columbian Exposition.

Robert Kanigel, *The One Best Way: Frederick Winslow Taylor and the Enigma of Efficiency* (1997). The most famous efficiency expert and how his system changed the world.

Stanley Karnow, *In Our Image: America's Empire in the Philippines* (1989). America's colonial venture in the Philippines from 1898 to 1986.

David L. Lewis, *W. E. B. Du Bois: Biography of a Race, 1868–1919* (1993). The story of the man who "pleaded with a headstrong, careless people to despise not Justice," and the era that produced him.

Ivan Musicant, *Empire by Default: The Spanish American War and the Dawn of the American Century* (1998). A misnamed but thorough account of the war and its meaning.

Nick Salvatore, *Eugene V. Debs: Citizen and Socialist* (1982). From the railroad yards to federal prison, the story of one of America's great labor leaders.

History on the Internet

"The Cross of Gold Speech"

http://www.ukans.edu/~kansite/hvn/articles/b_gold.htm

Read the full text of William Jennings Bryan's speech at the 1896 Democratic National Convention in which he attacks the notion of the gold standard.

"Racial Prejudice"

http://www.iberia.vassar.edu/1896/prejudice.html

This informative website includes many primary-source documents that speak to racial issues in the New South period. These documents include the full text of a public address by Booker T. Washington, African American and white responses to African-Americans' quest for civil rights, and links to African-American pamphlets published from 1880–1920.

Taylorism and Scientific Management

http://www.fordham.edu/halsall/mod/1911taylor.html

Read Frederick Taylor's essays in his work "The Principles of Scientific Management." These principles of work had a dramatic effect on industry, the way work was performed, and the lives of workers.

21

A UNITED BODY OF ACTION

1900-1916

OUTLINE

Alice Hamilton

On an October morning in 1902, three distinguished friends, Maude Gernon of the Chicago Board of Charities, Gertrude Howe, director of the kindergarten at Hull-House, and Dr. Alice Hamilton, a professor of pathology at Northwestern University, stood over two open sewer drains catching flies. The prey was abundant, and as the women bagged bluebottles they carefully placed their trophies in test tubes partly filled with beef broth. Hamilton had organized the expedition to prove a point. Chicago was in the grip of a typhoid epidemic. The disease had ravaged the city's nineteenth ward, a working-class neighborhood where Hull-House stood. To find out why, Hamilton "prowled about the streets and the ramshackle wooden tenement houses," which often had illegal outdoor privies because landlords refused to install plumbing. It was then that she noticed the flies. Army doctors in the Spanish-American War had found a link between flies and poor sanitation and the spread of typhoid. Hamilton incubated her test tubes for several days, examined the broth under a microscope, and confirmed that Chicago's flies carried the typhoid bacillus.

When her findings appeared in the *Journal of the American Medical Association* a few months later, they touched off a furor in Chicago. Hull-House attacked the Board of Health for failing to enforce the sanitary codes, and an inquiry discovered that landlords bribed sanitation inspectors to overlook the outdoor privies. Further investigations found that tap water was pumped straight from Lake Michigan, without any purification, and that broken pumping equipment had channeled raw sewage into the water mains. Through a chain of bribery, neglect, and malfeasance, Chicago's city government was directly responsible for an epidemic that killed hundreds of people.

Hamilton, who grew up in affluent surroundings in Fort Wayne, Indiana, chose medicine because "as a doctor I could go anywhere I pleased . . . and be quite sure that I could be of use anywhere." She attended the Fort Wayne College of Medicine and in 1892 entered the University of Michigan, later going on to do advanced work in bacteriology and pathology at Leipzig and Munich. Despite her training, she was not able to find work anywhere she pleased, but in Chicago she found a university position and

597

a supportive environment in Hull-House, a "settlement house" founded by women who wanted to live among the poor and avoid patronizing forms of charity. Hamilton lived there for 22 years. Her work concerned occupational disease, which she began studying in Germany where there was a large medical literature on job-related hazards. In the United States she noticed a "strange silence on the subject." Her early research linked the working conditions of Jewish garment workers in the neighborhoods near Hull-House to the tuberculosis that frequently claimed their lives.

After the typhoid scandal, Hamilton began looking into stories about poisoning among workers at the National Lead Company. Clouds of metallic dust filled the plant, and employees came home from work glistening with lead. The company refused to admit that the high rates of absenteeism had anything to do with the work. Hamilton interviewed workers' wives and priests in the neighborhood surrounding the plant. One foreman told her that lead workers "don't last long at it. Four years at the most, I should say, then they quit and go home to the old country." "To die?" she asked. "Well," he replied, "I suppose that is about the size of it." Searching through hospital records, she documented a pattern of disability and death resulting from chronic lead poisoning. Confronted with these findings, the president of the company agreed to install ventilators and create a companywide medical department with a doctor in each plant. Hamilton pushed for state laws on occupational disease, and in 1911 Illinois became the first state to pass legislation giving workers compensation for job-related disability. By the 1930s, all major industrial states had similar laws.

Alice Hamilton's activism was noteworthy but not unique. She was one of millions of people in the early twentieth century who reshaped government and business

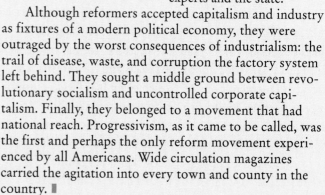

Dr. Alice Hamilton discovered that many industrial occupations were associated with diseases. Textile workers who did "piece work" suffered from tuberculosis, and lead workers from respiratory ailments.

by intervening in politics in new ways. Responding to the challenges of immigration, industrialization, and urbanization, Americans agitated for change on a broad variety of issues. Members of both major parties participated, but they also worked from outside the two-party system, forming their own organizations. Women, who did not have the vote, took the lead and created a new style of political activism.

Some reformers feared the uncontrolled wealth and power of corporations, while others feared losing wealth and power to the uncontrolled political passions of the poor. Both called themselves progressives. Although they disagreed on many of their goals and methods, these reformers shared certain characteristics. They saw politics and economics, according to W. E. B. Du Bois, as "but two aspects of a united body of action and effort." They optimistically believed in people's ability to improve their environment through work and persuasion, but they were pessimistic about the ability of people, particularly nonwhite people, to improve themselves. Science and evangelical Protestantism, as progressives understood them, supported both of these beliefs and justified the supervision of human affairs by qualified experts and the state.

Although reformers accepted capitalism and industry as fixtures of a modern political economy, they were outraged by the worst consequences of industrialism: the trail of disease, waste, and corruption the factory system left behind. They sought a middle ground between revolutionary socialism and uncontrolled corporate capitalism. Finally, they belonged to a movement that had national reach. Progressivism, as it came to be called, was the first and perhaps the only reform movement experienced by all Americans. Wide circulation magazines carried the agitation into every town and county in the country. ∎

- The new conditions of life in an urban, industrial society and the new political problems they created

- A new style of politics emerges from women's activism on social issues

- Nationally organized interest groups and the decline of partisan politics

- Interventionist programs and new forms of administration in cities and states

- Progressivism at the federal level and the power of the executive to regulate the economy and make foreign policy

Toward a New Politics

The political and economic crises of the 1890s contributed to the strength of progressivism. Politics became less participatory, and millions of Americans lost the strong loyalties they once had to traditional parties. "People got mighty sick of voting for Republicans and Democrats when it was a 'heads I win tails you lose' proposition," a Schenectady, New York, man explained. A growing Socialist movement threatened to lead Americans in a more radical direction if moderate reform failed. Protestant churches became outspokenly critical of capitalism's abuses, and new interpretations of Christian ethics lent a moral urgency to reform. The mounting dangers of urban life, some of which Alice Hamilton encountered, gave educated, affluent Americans a sense that civic problems needed to be dealt with immediately. Convinced that masculine politics created or at least tolerated the worst evils, women took leading and public roles, using pressure groups to extend their influence while also seeking the vote.

Egged on by a national press, progressives organized at the local, state, and national levels to solve the problems of the new industrial world. Although they sometimes pined for the security small-town shopkeepers of an earlier (and probably imaginary) era enjoyed, progressives recognized that large-scale industrial capitalism was here to stay. They worked as troubleshooters, laboring to make an erratic and brutal system more predictable, efficient, and humane. In pushing for reform, however, they were willing to enlarge the authority of the state and to use state power to tell people what was good for them and then make them do

it. As reform gained momentum, mayors, governors, and presidential candidates identified themselves and their agendas as progressive. The movement rewrote the Democratic and Republican platforms and gave politics a new purpose.

The Insecurity of Modern Life

Most people who lived in cities at the turn of the century had grown up in the country or in smaller towns. They remembered living in communities where people knew each other, where many of the foods they ate and clothes they wore were made locally. These communities were less dependent on outsiders or big corporations. For many Americans, living in a modern metropolis, connected by rail, telephone, and telegraph to other cities and the world beyond meant depending on strangers. Meat and bread came not from a familiar butcher or baker, but from packinghouses and producers located hundreds or thousands of miles away. Tap water, gas for heating and lighting, and transportation to work were all supplied by large, anonymous corporations. Unknown executives made decisions that affected the livelihoods, savings, and safety of thousands of people. "Under our present manner of living, how many of my vital interests must I entrust to others!" declared Richard Ely, an economist. "Nowadays the water main is my well, the trolley car is my carriage, the banker's safe is my stocking, and the policeman's billy is my fist." City dwellers felt more sophisticated than their parents but also less secure.

It was clear to anyone who read the newspapers that city living carried risks. In Chicago marketplaces journalist Upton Sinclair found milk preserved with formaldehyde, peas colored green with copper salts, and smoked sausage doctored with toxic chemicals. Druggists sold fraudulent cures for imaginary diseases. Dozens of patent medicines advertised themselves as the remedy for "catarrh," a diagnosis that included everything from hay fever to cancer. Cures available over the counter included wood alcohol, cocaine, heroin, and other dangerous substances.

Simply finding a place to live could involve hazards. Tenement blocks housing hundreds of people often had no fire escapes or plumbing. Unscrupulous bankers and real estate brokers could hoodwink families out of their savings. Consumers were at the mercy of unrestrained monopolies and hucksters. "The challenge of the city," Frederic Howe, a New York reformer, observed, "has become one of decent human existence."

Tragedy reminded New Yorkers of these dangers on March 25, 1911, when fire engulfed the Triangle Shirtwaist Company just as its employees were preparing to leave work. In the company's rooms on the top three floors of a ten-story building on Washington Square, 500 Jewish and Italian women manufactured blouses with heavy sewing and cutting equipment. When fire broke out, they raced

Employers had locked the emergency exits when fire broke out at the Triangle Shirtwaist Factory. The death toll provoked state and federal investigations and a public clamor for regulation.

for the exits, which had been locked by their employer to discourage employees from taking breaks. Women plunged to their deaths in a desperate attempt to escape the flames, many jumping from ledges in groups, holding hands. Others dove into empty elevator shafts. In all, 146 died. "This is not the first time girls have been burned alive in this city," Rose Schneiderman, a union official, declared, "Every year thousands of us are maimed. The life of men and women is so cheap and property is so sacred." Such episodes demonstrated to many Americans that they could no longer console themselves with thoughts about the larger benefits of an unregulated *laissez-faire* economy. The political economy was enormously productive, but it was also deadly.

Government not only failed to address these problems, it contributed to them. Regulation by legislature or elected city officials often only supplied a pretext for kickbacks and bribery. City and state machines were riddled with graft. In 1895 the president of Cornell University declared American cities to be "the worst in Christendom— the most expensive, the most inefficient, and the most corrupt." In 1904 and 1905, journalists and investigators uncovered corruption in state after state. In New York insurance companies paid off state representatives and even a U. S. senator in return for favorable legislation. Trials in San Francisco disclosed that Boss Abraham Ruef ruled the

city with a slush fund donated by public utilities. The Vermont railroad commission accused state legislators of being on the take, and later investigations charged the commission itself with corruption. The Minneapolis police, with the connivance of the mayor's office, protected brothels and gambling dens in return for bribes. Elections made the system less accountable, not more. By creating a demand for campaign contributions and jobs for loyal party officials, elections became invitations to graft. Politics, journalist Lincoln Steffens complained, merely amplified the power of big corporations; "it was natural, inevitable, and possibly right that business should—by bribery, corruption, or—somehow" take control of the government.

The rising middle class of professionals and managers found public and corporate irresponsibility particularly infuriating. Around many urban centers a ring of "street car suburbs" grew in the latter years of the nineteenth century, filled with Victorian homes belonging to business managers, accountants, engineers, lawyers, doctors, and highly skilled workers. For these people, loyalties to ethnic groups or political parties had less importance than their identity as members of an occupation, and through their respect for one another's professional skills they became conscious of themselves as a class, with common interests. By virtue of their education and experience, they had their own ideas on how organizations, like cities, should run. Modern corporations had to have clear lines of authority, an emphasis on efficiency, and reliable sources of information. Yet these virtues were frustratingly absent from civic life. Government needed to become more responsive, accountable, and vigilant against dangers to the public.

The Decline of Partisan Politics

In the early years of the twentieth century many Americans, particularly among the middle and upper classes, began seeking new ways to compel government to deal with the problems of industrial, urban society. Frustrated with traditional politics, they created new organizations and political tactics. They demanded civil service reform, the regulation of monopolies, and an end to the rule of party machines. They voted not as members of a party but as independents.

As the new activism increased, popular party politics declined. Participation in national and state elections dropped off sharply. Nationally, 79 percent of the electorate voted in 1896, but four years later only 73 percent voted, and in 1904 the total fell to 65 percent. Literacy tests accounted for much of the decline in the South, but in all regions the old spectacular style of electioneering, with torchlight parades, mass rallies, and flagpole raisings gave way to campaigns that were more educational and less participatory. "Listless" was how one observer described the 1904 turnout. "There is much apathy on the part of the public as regards the campaign—more than I have ever seen before," a political operative noted. Worse from the parties' point of view, more of the voters who did turn out split their tickets. The ethnic and sectional loyalties that led people to vote a straight party ballot in the late nineteenth century seemed to be weakening (see Figure 21-1).

Increasingly, Americans participated in politics through voluntary associations. Pressure groups took over important functions that formerly belonged to the parties: educating and socializing voters and even making policy. Journalist Herbert Croly noted in 1914 that "A large number of voluntary groups have sprung up during the past twenty years" devoted to "special political and social ideas." Some were concerned with public morals, others with urban corruption, restraining monopolies, or caring for the poor. A few functioned almost as parties did. New York's Citizen's Union ran its own candidates for city offices in 1897 and 1901, but most worked outside the system to gather support for a particular cause or proposal. Many voluntary organizations were patterned after corporations, with a board of directors, administrators, and state and local chapters. Built on the idea that reform was a continuous process, they strove for permanence. Some, like the National Association for the Advancement of Colored People (NAACP), the Salvation Army, and the Sierra Club, remain prominent after a century.

Social Housekeeping

The growing clamor for social change aroused latent political strength in unexpected places. Women's social clubs had been nonpolitical before the turn of the century. Clubwomen, generally white and upper or middle class, enjoyed sufficient freedom from housework to attend weekly or monthly meetings dedicated to developing public talents like art, speaking, reading, and conversation. They met "without some work of benevolence or reform in view," but were nonetheless highly organized, with local, state, and national chapters. The General Federation of Women's Clubs was formed in 1890. Within ten years the urgency of social problems led many clubs to launch campaigns on behalf of free kindergartens, civil service reform, and public health. "Ladies," Sarah P. Decker announced at her inauguration as head of the Federation in 1904, "Dante is dead. He has been dead for several centuries, and I think that it is time that we dropped the study of his inferno and turned attention to our own." Following her advice, clubwomen turned from developing public skills to exercising them.

Clubwomen explained that activism was a natural outgrowth of their domestic responsibilities as wives and mothers. One could hardly keep a safe, comfortable home in the midst of a dangerous and corrupt community. "We have

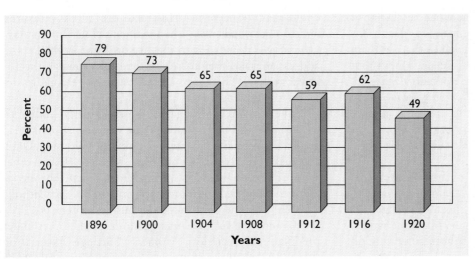

Figure 21-1   Voter Participation, 1896–1920.
After the intense partisanship and high-stakes elections of the 1890s, campaigns became more "educational" and voters lost interest.

Source: Michael E. McGerr, The Decline of Popular Politics (New York: Oxford University Press, 1986), pp. 185–86.

Suffragists on parade, Long Island, New York, 1913. Women's groups campaigned simultaneously for the vote and for social reforms. Five states extended the vote to women after 1910, but resistance remained strong.

no platform unless it is the care of women, children, and the home," a federation leader declared, "the latter meaning the four walls of the city as well as the four walls of brick and mortar." Club membership grew alongside activism. The federation's 50,000 members in 1898 expanded by 1914 to well over a million, and the organization became a powerful lobby at all levels of government. In some communities the women's club was the only organized voice for civic improvement.

By the turn of the century, more women than ever before had attended college. The first generation of graduates from the new women's colleges had reached adulthood—and some, like Alice Hamilton, had gone on to attain advanced professional degrees—at a time when few men had a college education. These "new women," as historians have called them, had ambitions and values that set them apart from women of their mothers' generation. About half of the female college graduates did not marry. Since the career paths their male classmates followed were closed to them, educated women inadvertently joined a reserve army available for service in voluntary organizations. Reform politics allowed them to use their talents for a larger purpose.

Educated women found careers by finding problems that needed solving. Florence Kelley, trained as a lawyer, became Illinois' first state factory inspector and later directed the National Consumers' League. Margaret Sanger, a New York public health nurse, distributed literature on birth control and sex education when it was illegal to do so. Sophonisba Breckinridge, who had a doctorate in political science from the University of Chicago, led the struggle for legislation restricting child labor. Female activists "discovered" problems, publicized them, lobbied for new

laws, and then staffed the bureaus and agencies created to administer the solutions.

The sudden growth of women's professional associations, labor unions, business clubs, ethnic and patriotic societies, and philanthropic foundations testifies to the new women's handiwork. Many of these—such as the National Association of Collegiate Women (1896), the National Council of Jewish Women (1893), and the National Congress of Mothers (1897)—had local, state, and national organizations, while some, such as the World YWCA (1894) and the International Council of Nurses (1899) had a global reach. Through interlocking national networks, like-minded women gave one another encouragement, advice, and political support.

Middle-class women remained concerned with the welfare of women and children and with issues related to their homes and neighborhoods. By uniting with others around the country, however, they changed the political culture. Activities that had once been considered charity or volunteer work became political. Through national networks, female activists learned that the problems of their neighborhoods had origins elsewhere and could not be solved at the local level. Individual problems might only be symptoms for larger social evils. Ultimately, to maintain decent and safe homes, women needed the help of the state.

The logic of social housekeeping called for enlarging state powers and increasing women's influence over the state. The experiences of women's clubs and associations taught political activists the importance of cooperation, organization, and expertise. Government could apply these principles better than charities or volunteers could. It could make long-term plans, take preventive measures, and compel obedience. When women's clubs built a playground and donated it to the city or urged lawmakers to address an issue, they increased their own stake in the political system. They gave themselves new reasons to demand full citizenship.

The women's suffrage movement quietly built momentum in the early years of the century. Women had gained the vote in four states—Colorado, Wyoming, Utah, and Idaho—early on, but between 1896 and 1910 no other states adopted a women's suffrage amendment. The movement encountered stubborn opposition from the Catholic Church, machine politicians, and business interests.

Competing suffrage organizations joined forces under the National American Women's Suffrage Association (NAWSA). Led by Carrie Chapman Catt and Anna Howard Shaw, NAWSA developed a strategy based on professional lobbying and publicity. Suffragists appealed to clubwomen and middle-class reformers by cultivating an image of Victorian respectability and linking suffrage to moderate social causes, such as temperance and education. NAWSA eventually narrowed its constituency and became less democratic, but initially its strategy paid off. After 1910, five states adopted suffrage amendments in rapid succession, but the opposition rallied and defeated referendums in three eastern states.

Frustrated with the glacial pace of progress, Alice Paul's National Woman's Party adopted more radical tactics, picketing the White House and staging hunger strikes. Despite setbacks, women led the transformation of politics through voluntary organizations and interest groups and were on the threshold of even greater gains.

Evolution or Revolution?

No group was more buoyantly optimistic about the prospects for revolutionary change than the Socialists. The founders of the Socialist Party of America (SPA) met in Indianapolis in the summer of 1901 and declared their Marxian confidence in the inevitability of capitalism's downfall. The party's swelling membership in the years that followed appeared to confirm the trend. By 1912, Eugene V. Debs, the party's candidate for president, garnered almost a million votes, some six percent of the total. Socialists elected two members of Congress, 56 mayors, and 33 state legislators.

Even more impressive was their influence within the labor movement. A third of the delegates to the AFL's 1912 convention had party cards. The membership was diverse. The party's executive committee translated its minutes into Finnish, Lettish, Italian, Hungarian, German, Slovak, Polish, and Yiddish for distribution to chapters around the country. Jewish workers in New York and Germans in Milwaukee formed powerful urban voting blocs. "Gas and water" Socialists, who demanded public ownership of utilities, captured municipal offices in smaller cities across the country. In the plains states, socialism drew strength from primitive Baptist and Holiness churches and held revival-style tent meetings. The party's stronghold was Oklahoma, where almost one-quarter of the electorate voted Socialist in 1914.

Debs' party dreamed of a peaceful evolution to a kind of economy that rewarded cooperation and valued human labor. Although tinged with religion, Socialists' analysis of modern problems was economic. They maintained that the profit mo-tive distorted human behavior, forcing people to compete for survival as individuals instead of joining together to promote the common good. Driven by the need for profits, corporations could not be trusted to look after the welfare of their customers or workers. Socialists demanded the collective ownership of industries, starting with ones that most directly affected the livelihoods and safety of people, the railroads and city utilities. They realized their ambitions collided with the organizing principles of modern corporate society, but they had faith that America could make the transition through the ballot without violence. Above all, they were sure socialism was coming, "coming like a prairie fire," a socialist newspaperman told his readers, "You can see it in the papers. You can taste it in the price of beef."

"Social Gospel" clergymen combined this socialist millennialism with evangelical zeal. Washington Gladden, a congregational pastor from Columbus, Ohio; Walter Rauschenbusch, a Baptist minister from New York; William Dwight Porter Bliss, who founded the Society for Christian Socialists; and George Herron, an Iowa Congregationalist were among the prominent ministers who interpreted the Bible as a call to social action. Their visions of the Christian commonwealth ranged from vague reformism to revolutionary socialism, but they all believed that corporate capitalism was organized sin, and that the church had an obligation to stand against it.

When the Industrial Workers of the World (IWW), known as the Wobblies, talked about revolution they meant a war not an election. Founded in 1905, the IWW

Socialists ran well-organized national campaigns in 1904, 1908, and 1912, when Eugene Debs, the party's candidate for president, won nearly a million votes.

unionized some of the most rugged individuals in the West: miners, loggers, and even rodeo cowboys (under the Bronco Busters and Range Riders Union). Wobblies gathered unskilled workers into "one big union," challenging both the AFL's elite unionism and the Socialists' gradualism. Membership remained small, fewer than 100,000, but the union's legendary leader, William "Big Bill" Haywood, frightened people by calling for sabotage and a general strike. To Haywood, the IWW was "socialism with its working clothes on." Its members had no use for voting or negotiations with owners. At IWW strikes in Lawrence, Massachusetts, and Paterson, New Jersey, strikers clashed with police and staged parades in which thousands of marchers carried red flags. To sensationalist newspapermen and anxious middle-class readers, these activities looked like signs of approaching class warfare.

Conservatives and reformers alike felt the hot breath of revolution on their necks, and socialism's greatest influence may have been the push it gave conservatives to support moderate reform. Speaking for his branch of government, Justice Oliver Wendell Holmes, Jr., attested that "When socialism first began to be talked about, the comfortable classes of the community were a good deal frightened." Theodore Roosevelt warned that unless something was done the United States would divide into two parties, one representing workers, the other capital.

The failure of the two parties to deal with urgent social problems created a chance to redefine politics and citizenship. Precisely because they had been outside the system, women—particularly middle-class, educated, Protestant women—gained a powerful moral authority and a public voice that enabled them to transform their humanitarian concerns and voluntary activities into a new kind of politics. The harangues of Christian reformers and the glowering danger of revolution aided their efforts and discouraged the opposition. As the new century began, Americans were testing their political ideals, scrapping the old rules, and getting ready to fashion new institutions and laws to deal with the challenges of modern society.

The Progressives

As the old politics declined, a new politics of voluntary organizations and activists arose to take its place. Historians have found it difficult to define the progressives, as they called themselves. Progressives addressed a wide variety of social problems with many different tactics, but for people of the time the connectedness was apparent. A rally to end child labor, for instance, might draw out young lawyers, teachers, labor unionists, woman suffragists, professors, and politicians. "Scores of young leaders in American politics and public affairs were seeing what I saw, feeling what I felt," journalist William Allen White remembered. "All over the land in a score of states and more, young men in

both parties were taking leadership by attacking things as they were in that day." A series of overlapping movements, campaigns, and crusades defined the era from 1890 to 1920.

Progressivism was not a unified movement with a platform or an agreed-upon set of goals. It was more like a political style, a way of approaching problems. Progressives had no illusions that wage labor or industrialism could be eliminated or that it was possible to recreate a rural commonwealth. Big cities and big corporations, they believed, were permanent features of modern life, but they shared an optimistic conviction that modern institutions could be made humane, responsive, and moral.

In choosing solutions, progressives relied on scientific expertise as a way to avoid the clash of interests. The generation raised during the Civil War knew democracy was no guarantee against mass violence. Rival points of view could be reconciled more easily by impartial authority. Like the salaried managers many of them were, progressives valued efficiency and organization. No problem could be solved in a single stroke. Instead, true remedies could be enforced only by repeated actions by institutions dedicated to reform. Instead of organizing a reform party, progressives formed **interest groups** to lobby government and raise public awareness.

Convinced that science and God were on their side, progressives did not balk at imposing their views on other people, even when democracy or individual rights got in the way. Such measures as identifying "born criminals" who could be put on probation for life without ever having committed a crime would be described by advocates as "progressive." To southern progressives "scientific" principles of race justified segregation and paternalism. Reforms could be unpopular—as the drive to ban alcoholic beverages was—but this posed a strategic rather than a philosophical problem. Progressives demanded more democracy when it led to "good government," but if the majority was wrong, in their view, progressives readily handed power to unelected managers. Some progressives acknowledged their belief that reform imposed by the "better classes" was preferable to democratic change, which could easily get out of control. The basic structure of American government and economy, they felt, should not be open to political debate.

More than anything else, progressives shared the conviction that social problems required urgent action. "There are two kinds of people," Alice Hamilton learned from her mother, "the ones who say 'Someone ought to do something about it but why should it be I?' and the ones who say, 'Somebody must do something about it, then why not I?'" Hamilton and other progressives never doubted that they were the second kind.

Social Workers and Muckrakers

Among the first to hear the call to service were the young women and men who volunteered to live among the urban poor in "settlement houses." Stanton Coit established the first on New York's lower east side in 1886, but the most famous was Hull-House, which opened in Chicago three years later. Its founders, Jane Addams and Ellen Starr, bought a run-down mansion that had once been the country estate of Charles J. Hull on Halsted Street. A lot had changed since Hull's day, and the house now stood at the center of an inner-city ward thick with sweatshops, factories, and overcrowded tenements. Poverty, backbreaking labor, and disease blighted life for residents of the Nineteenth Ward. The women of Hull-House attacked these problems with fearless persistence. They opened a kindergarten and a clinic, took sweatshop bosses to court, investigated corrupt landlords, criticized the ward's powerful alderman, and built the first public playground in Chicago. They invited their working-class neighbors to Hull-House for concerts, exhibits, and lectures by notables like architect Frank Lloyd Wright, educator John Dewey, and the renowned trial lawyer Clarence Darrow.

Addams drew together at Hull-House a remarkable group of women with similar backgrounds. Florence Kelley organized a movement that pushed some of the nation's first occupational safety laws through the Illinois legislature. Julia Lathrop headed the state's Children's Bureau. All three women were raised in affluent Quaker homes during or shortly after the Civil War, and their parents were all abolitionists. Like Alice Hamilton, all three attended college and afterward traveled or studied in Europe (see Growing Up in America, chapter 18).

As the fame of Hull-House spread, women (and some men) organized settlement houses in cities across the country. By the turn of the century there were more than 100, and by 1910 more than 400. Reformers often began by using social science techniques to survey the surrounding neighborhoods, gathering information on the national origins, income, housing conditions, and occupations of the local people. Addams released *Hull-House Maps and Papers,* a survey of the Nineteenth Ward, in 1895. One of the progressive era's most ambitious research projects was the Pittsburgh Survey, a massive investigation of living and working conditions in the steel city published in six volumes between 1909 and 1914. By relying on survey data, progressives acknowledged that the causes of poverty were social, not personal. This seemingly simple idea contradicted a common belief that the poor had only themselves to blame. Since economic conditions, not laziness or immorality, caused poverty, progressives did not offer charity; they were social workers.

This outlook motivated settlement workers to attack urban problems across a broad front. "If parks were wanted, if schools needed bettering," Jacob Riis wrote, "there were at the College Settlement, the University Settlement, the Nurses' Settlement, and at a score of other such places, young enthusiasts to collect the facts and urge them, with the prestige of their non-political organization to back them." Social workers labored to improve the urban environment by making food safe, repairing housing, and sponsoring festivals and pageants. Working conditions, especially for women and children, drew special attention, but employers, landlords, and city bosses were not the only targets. The "young enthusiasts" attacked with equal indignation working-class vices—gambling dens, saloons, and brothels. Addams and many of her colleagues were single, educated, independent new women, but they encouraged immigrant women to stick to more traditional roles as wives and mothers.

Settlements touched many lives. Perhaps their greatest achievement was in training a generation of social workers. Harry Hopkins, Eleanor Roosevelt, and Frances Perkins, who would each attain political prominence in the 1930s, acquired a taste for activism in settlement houses. Others participated vicariously by reading *The House on Henry Street, The City Wilderness, Twenty Years at Hull-House,* and other popular books written by settlement workers. Newspaper accounts and memoirs awakened a national readership to the suffering of the urban poor and carried the hopeful message that action and intelligence could change things for the better.

The loudest voice of progressivism came from a new type of journalism introduced on the pages of *McClure's* magazine in 1902. In successive issues, *McClure's* published Lincoln Steffens' investigation of graft in St. Louis, "The Shame of the Cities," and the first installment of Ida Tarbell's "History of the Standard Oil Company," two sensational exposés that disclosed crimes of the nation's political and economic elite. As cities grew and periodicals

Ida Tarbell pored through public records and interviewed Standard Oil's officers, customers, and business partners to learn how the company worked. Her conclusion: Rockefeller played with "loaded dice," defeating competitors with bribery, espionage, and double-dealing.

competed for a mass readership, the old partisan style of journalism declined. Newspapers and magazines enticed readers with promotional stunts, crusades, celebrity correspondents, and "sob sister" features. The new ten-cent magazines, like *Everybody's, Cosmopolitan,* and *McClure's,* had national audiences and budgets big enough to pay for careful, in-depth investigations. The result was a type of reporting Theodore Roosevelt disdainfully called "muckraking." Readers loved it, and an article exposing some new corporate or public villainy could easily sell half a million copies.

Muckrakers named names, and their articles set up targets for crusades. Upton Sinclair described the grisly business of canning beef. Ray Stannard Baker investigated railroads and segregation. Samuel Hopkins Adams cataloged the damage done by narcotics in popular medicines. Some muckrakers, like Sinclair, saw capitalism as the culprit behind these abuses, but most blamed greedy individuals and a system that failed to impose restraint. "We 'muckraked' not because we hated the world, but because we loved it," Baker recalled. Tarbell's family faced ruin when John D. Rockefeller's Standard Oil crushed central Pennsylvania's independent oil producers. Her articles in *McClure's* exposed his methods: camouflaged companies, espionage, sweetheart deals, and predatory pricing. The series ran in 24 straight issues and shattered the notion that industrial giants competed in a free market. Amid a national outcry, the Justice Department sued Standard Oil in 1906 for conspiracy to restrain trade.

The ten-cent magazines reached subscribers in farms and cities across the country, and they projected local problems onto a national canvas. Newspapers had covered municipal corruption before, but Steffen's series in *McClure's* revealed that bribery, influence peddling, and protection rackets operated in nearly every major city, and for the same reason: an insidious alliance between city officials and local monopolies. Magazines also carried news of progressive victories, allowing solutions adopted in Toledo or Milwaukee to spread quickly to other cities. Muckraking declined after 1912, the victim of corporate advertising boycotts and declining readership, but while it lasted, the outrage of millions of readers became "public opinion," a force that could shake politicians and powerful corporations.

Dictatorship of the Experts

For doctors, lawyers, engineers, and members of other licensed occupations, progressive reforms offered a chance to apply their special skills to urgent problems. Experts like Alice Hamilton led crusades and adorned the boards of reform leagues. Not accidentally, the progressive era coincided with the rise in influence of the social sciences and the professions. Much of the reformers' optimism came from their faith in the powers of science and expertise to solve modern problems. Experts could mediate potentially violent conflicts between rival interests and eliminate the un-

Flatiron Building, New York (c. 1910). Rapid advances in engineering, architecture, science, and medicine gave Americans a sense of control over their environment.

certainties of democracy. Science could unify a society that seemed to be disintegrating. Rapid advances seemed to justify this faith. In just a generation, antiseptic techniques and a new understanding of disease transformed medicine from a collection of folk beliefs into a science. In 1909 a cure for syphilis was found. Equally spectacular advances in engineering, architecture, chemistry, and agriculture confirmed science's ability to shape the future (see Figure 21-2).

Crime, education, labor relations, and other problems came under attack from social engineers using scientific or pseudoscientific methods. Social workers copied doctors, diagnosing each case with clinical impartiality and relying on tests and individual histories. Newly professionalized police forces applied the techniques of fingerprinting, handwriting analysis, and psychology to law enforcement. Dietitians descended on school cafeterias, banishing pierogies and souvlaki and replacing them with bland but nutritionally balanced meals. Reformers tried (but failed) to simplify spelling and bring "efficiency" to the English language.

Trust in science sometimes led to extreme measures. One was the practice of **eugenics,** an attempt to rid society of crime, insanity, and other defects through selective breeding. "We know enough about eugenics so that if the

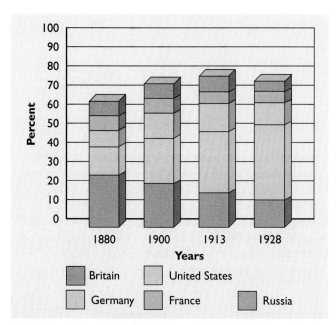

Figure 21-2   Relative Shares of World Manufacturing Output, 1890–1928.
The noticeable success of U.S. corporations in world markets made the corporation—with its stress on organization, efficiency, and expertise—the model for the practice of progressive reform.
Source: Paul Kennedy, Rise and Fall of the Great Powers (New York: Random House, 1987), p. 202.

knowledge were applied, the defective classes would disappear within a generation," the president of the University of Wisconsin predicted. In 1907 Indiana passed a law authorizing the forced sterilization of "criminals, idiots, rapists, and imbeciles." Seven other states followed suit.

Behind progressives' emphasis on expertise lay a thinly veiled distrust of democracy. Education reform was one example. Professional educators took control of the schools away from local school boards and gave it to expert administrators and superintendents. They certified teachers and classified students based on "scientific" intelligence tests. Emphasizing educational excellence, reformers wanted to consolidate schools and extend education beyond the eighth grade. The new "high schools" had courses that prepared students to become experts themselves, but consolidation diluted the power of elected school boards. To reformers, education was far too important to be left to amateurs, like teachers, parents, or voters.

Progressivism created new social sciences, changed the agendas of others, and made universities into centers of advocacy. Sociology was a product of the progressive impulse. The study of government became political science, and "scientific" historians searched the past for answers to modern problems. John R. Commons, Richard Ely, and Thorstein Veblen escaped from the old debates over classical theory and used economics to study how modern institutions developed and functioned. Legal scholars like Louis Brandeis and Roscoe Pound called for revising the law to reflect social realities.

This stress on expertise made progressive-era reforms different from those of the Gilded Age and earlier. Instead of trying to gain success at a single stroke—by passing a law or trouncing a corrupt politician—progressives believed reform had to be a process. There could be no final victories. Corruption, inertia, and injustice had to be balanced against science and reason. When they could, progressives set up permanent organizations and procedures that would keep the pressure on and make progress a habit.

Progressives on the Color Line

In her international crusade against lynching, Ida B. Wells-Barnett pioneered some of the progressive tactics of research, exposure, and organization. A schoolteacher in Memphis, Tennessee, Wells-Barnett had been stung into activism by the unpunished murder of three of the city's leading African-American citizens in 1892. She documented mob violence against African Americans and mobilized opinion in the United States and Britain. Cities that condoned extralegal executions soon faced a barrage of condemnation from church groups and women's clubs. As her Afro-American Council took on national and then international scope, she joined forces with white suffragists, social workers, and journalists, but her cause fell outside of the progressive mainstream. Many reform groups sympathized with white southerners or wanted to avoid dividing their membership over race. The WCTU segregated its meetings; its president, Frances Willard, argued that drunkenness justified disfranchising African Americans. Theodore Roosevelt's Progressive Party refused to seat African-American delegates to its convention or even to hear a resolution that called for equal rights.

Wells-Barnett referred to lynch mobs and their supporters as "barbarians," thus inverting the progressives' code word for the (usually darker-skinned) peoples eligible to be patronized. Reformers debated as to how much progress Native Americans, Puerto Ricans, African Americans and other non-Anglo-Saxons were capable of, but they were inclined to be pessimistic. Eugenics gave white supremacy the endorsement of science. A new technology, the motion picture, showed its power to rewrite American history from a racial viewpoint in D. W. Griffiths' classic *Birth of A Nation* (1915), which romanticized the Ku Klux Klan's campaign of terror during Reconstruction. Following the opinion of educated Americans, public policy incorporated assumptions about the diminished capabilities of various races. Trade schools, not universities, were deemed appropriate for educating Filipinos and Hawaiians. Considering tribal culture unreformable, progressives took Native-American children from their families and placed them in boarding schools. Electoral reform in Texas meant dismantling political "machines" that courted Spanish-speaking voters. The "scientific" racism of the day classified nonwhites as subjects to control rather than citizens.

ON TRIAL

The Eight-Hour Day

The battle to limit working hours for women revealed the progressive strategy for reform based on organization, expertise, and continual vigilance and adjustment. Few causes aroused more general sympathy than the predicament of female laborers. Five million women worked for wages at the turn of the century, a quarter of them in industry. Earning half the pay of men, they filled some of the least desirable occupations. For women, jobs were hard to find, and the ones available offered low pay, long hours, and dangerous work. States began passing laws to protect women in the 1870s. Massachusetts limited the workweek for women and children to 60 hours. Other states limited hours, banned night work, and required meal breaks and a minimum wage.

Women's organizations led the drive to pass these laws. The spearhead of the movement was the National Consumers' League (NCL), headed by Florence Kelley, a Hull-House alumna who rammed Illinois' eight-hour law through the legislature. The NCL allied consumers with women workers, organizing boycotts of stores that sold clothes made in sweatshops and providing expert testimony at legislative hearings on protective laws. It had chapters in 20 states, including Oregon.

The most active lobby for protection, the NCL also had the most radical vision. Kelley saw special laws for women as the first step in a campaign to win occupational protection for all workers. The eight-hour law would open the way for precedents, regulation, and government oversight that would eventually cover the whole industrial work force, and this was precisely what business feared. Protective laws could encourage a paternalistic state to suffocate business with regulations. Soon after Illinois passed its women's eight-hour law in 1893, industrialists joined forces in the National Association of Manufacturers to resist occupational laws in the courts.

It took only a minor incident in a Portland, Oregon, laundry to touch off a legal contest that would challenge the entire structure of protective laws. On Labor Day 1905 a supervisor at the Grand Laundry asked Emma Gotcher to continue working at the end of her ten-hour shift. The request violated Oregon's maximum-hours law. Gotcher reported it to the district attorney, who filed criminal charges against the laundry's owner, Curt Muller. Muller was found guilty and fined 10 dollars. Portland's laundry owners banded together and hired corporate lawyer William Fenton. Fenton had good reasons to be optimistic about Muller's chances on appeal.

Florence Kelley's National Consumers' League led the campaign for shorter working hours for women.

Courts in New York had struck down protective laws on the grounds that they violated workers' and employers' right to enter into contracts freely.

When the Oregon Consumers League notified Kelley that an appeal had been filed, she packed her bags for Portland. An attorney herself, she knew the Muller case could overturn maximum-hours laws nationwide. After talking with women who knew the case, she boarded a train for New York to look for a lawyer who could defeat Fenton. She found Louis Brandeis, an unorthodox Boston lawyer famous for his outspoken criticism of big corporations. Brandeis saw *Muller v.*

By arguing from facts and statistical data rather than precedent, Louis Brandeis pioneered a new form of legal reasoning.

Oregon as an opportunity to force the court to abandon legal fictions like "freedom of contract," and to recognize the social realities that made it impossible for an overworked laundry-woman to refuse her employer's demands.

Brandeis placed these realities before the court, in the form of statistics, case studies, and expert opinion showing that long hours hurt women. Josephine Goldmark, head of the NCL's committee on labor law, led a team of researchers who combed through the New York Public Library looking for official reports, articles, and statements by doctors and social workers. Using social-science evidence in this way was a bold maneuver. In American law, legal briefs traditionally quoted legal precedents. The "Brandeis brief," as it came to be called, put scientific authority on a par with judicial authority.

In the brief's opening pages, Brandeis argued that the state was entitled to interfere if the public's health and safety were in danger. The rest of the brief, some 100 typewritten pages, contained "facts of common knowledge." The facts argued that women had a "special physical organization" that made them more vulnerable than men to heavy labor. Overwork contributed to miscarriage, infant mortality, and to children who were physically and mentally impaired.

The U. S. Supreme Court voted unanimously on February 24, 1908, to uphold the Oregon law. The decision held that laws could be made that applied just to women. For the NCL, *Muller* was a landmark victory. Suffragists and clubwomen rejoiced. "Supreme Court Holds Women Above Men," one headline read, but some advocates for women's rights worried that the decision made women and men legally unequal. *Muller* led to more regulations on female labor, but many employers responded by replacing women with other low-wage workers. Curt Muller fired his female staff and hired Chinese employees.

The NCL continued to fight for protective laws. Goldmark prepared new Brandeis briefs in cases that upheld maximum-hours laws for men and state minimum-wage laws. This persistence was characteristic of progressive reform, as were many of the ingredients of the *Muller* victory: organization, expertise, national reach, and the willingness to carry on the fight at local, state, and federal levels.

Editor of The Crisis *(circulation 103,000), William Edward Burghardt Du Bois was the voice of African-American progressives. "We expect revolutionary changes to come mainly through reason, human sympathy, and the education of children," he wrote.*

Du Bois and Booker T. Washington came to espouse opposing visions of African Americans' place in the political economy of the United States. Both emphasized the importance of thrift and hard work. Du Bois, however, rejected Washington's aloofness from politics and his willingness to accept legal inequality. Gradually, Du Bois came to believe that the Atlanta Compromise (see chapter 20) led only to disfranchisement and segregation. He disliked the way Washington's influence with the national press and his standing with white philanthropists silenced other voices. Five years after the Atlanta speech he opened a sustained attack on Washington's "Tuskegee Machine."

In *The Souls of Black Folk* (1903), Du Bois argued that the strategy of accommodation contained a "triple paradox": Washington had urged African Americans to seek industrial training, build self-respect, and become successful in business, while asking them to stop striving for higher education, civil rights, or political power. How could a people train themselves without higher education or gain self-respect without having any of the rights other Americans enjoyed? How could African Americans succeed in business without having the political power to protect themselves or their property? Economic, political, and educational progress had to move together. Like other progressives, Du Bois insisted on the importance of process and organization. African Americans could not stop demanding the right to vote, civic equality, or education at all levels.

In July 1905, Du Bois and 28 prominent African-American leaders met at the Erie Beach Hotel on the Canadian side of Niagara Falls (hotels on the United States side would not accept African-American lodgers) to declare that "the voice of protest of ten million Americans must never cease to assail the ears of their fellows, so long as America is unjust." The Niagara Movement was one of several organizations formed around the turn of the century to lobby against racial violence, segregation, and disfranchisement. In 1909, Ida Wells-Barnett, Lillian Wald, Jane Addams, and other social reformers and intellectuals formed the National Association for the Advancement of Colored People (NAACP) and named Du Bois as editor of its newspaper, *The Crisis.* The NAACP attacked segregation and disfranchisement in print and the courts. In 1915 it won a Supreme Court decision outlawing the grandfather clause, which denied the vote to descendants of slaves, but it took another 40 years before it succeeded in overturning *Plessy v. Ferguson.*

Barnett was not alone in finding doors through this stone wall of racial ideology. William Edward Burghardt Du Bois upset smug assumptions by documenting the costs of racism in *The Philadelphia Negro* (1898). Modeled on *Hull-House Maps and Papers* and sponsored by settlement workers, the survey spoke the progressives' language, insisting that discrimination was not just morally wrong but *inefficient,* since it took away steady work and encouraged alcoholism and crime. Social activism created new audiences for opponents of the racial status quo, and Du Bois soon transformed the politics of race in America as profoundly as Addams had transformed the politics of the cities.

Raised in Massachusetts in a large family that had been free citizens for three generations, Du Bois learned Latin and Greek in public schools. At 17, he received a scholarship to Tennessee's Fisk University and ventured into the South, where he "came in contact for the first time with a sort of violence that I had never realized in New England." He also had his first encounter with African-American religion and gospel music. The songs he heard in church stirred him deeply with their "bursts of wonderful melody, full of the voices of my brothers and sisters, full of the voices of the past." Du Bois later studied at Harvard and the University of Berlin.

In the towns and modern cities of the South, whites struggled to maintain their system of social and legal supremacy amid changing circumstances, while African Americans fought to fulfill the promise of freedom. Booker T. Washington's strategy of accommodation may have been appropriate for a time when Jim Crow laws were gaining force and starting at the bottom was the only choice African-American southerners had, but by challenging the laws and customs that supported injustice, Du Bois anticipated the struggle against segregation and disfranchisement that would take the next 60 years to complete. "The problem of the Twentieth Century," he predicted, "is the problem of the color line."

Progressives in State and Local Politics

Progressives were of two minds about the public. Walter Lippmann, a journalist and reformer, could write fondly of "the voiceless multitudes," and contemptuously of the "great dull mass of people who just don't care." As reformers engaged in politics, their tactics betrayed this split vision. Their aim was to break political machines into scrap iron, rupture the pipelines connecting politics to business, and increase the influence of reform's supporters. To bring the cities under control, they made city government less democratic. Machine politicians had mastered the arts of electioneering, and reformers found the only permanent solution was to make municipal government less political and more "businesslike." Reforms at the state level, however, expanded the power of individual voters to initiate legislation and remove corrupt officeholders while placing important aspects of policy under the control of unelected expert commissions. In both cases, the changes enlarged the influence of the small-town and urban-middle-class reform constituency while reducing that of immigrants and the working class (see Figure 21-3).

Redesigning the City

Ward heelers, machine aldermen, and the insiders who ran American cities proved remarkably adaptable to the changing political environment. To immigrants and factory workers, the local boss was one of the few people looking out for the interests of the average person. He rushed to fire scenes to offer help to the homeless victims and came always mournful and never empty-handed to funerals. He distributed turkeys in poor neighborhoods at Christmas. When a family member was jailed or thrown out of work, the machine politician stood ready to help. Jane Addams acknowledged that as a benefactor to the city's disinherited, Hull-House had nothing on Johnny Powers, boss of Chicago's Nineteenth Ward: "What headway can the notion of civic purity, of honesty of adminis-

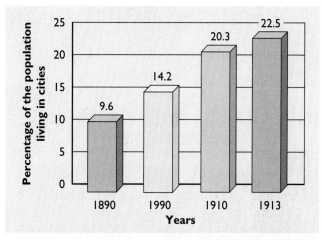

Figure 21-3   Percentage of the Population Living in Cities, 1890–1913.
Cities and towns underwent dramatic growth around the turn of the century. Offices, department stores, and new forms of mass entertainment—from vaudeville to professional sports—drew people to the city center. Railroads and trolleys allowed cities to spread outward, segregating residents by class.
Source: Kennedy, Rise and Fall of the Great Powers, p. 200.

tration, make against this big manifestation of human friendliness, this stalking survival of village kindness?"

Yet Powers and other aldermen also sheltered the brothels, saloons, gambling dens, and petty "boodlers" who, in Addams view, exploited honest workers. Big corporations could do what they liked, so long as they padded the right wallets. "If you want to get anything out of the council," the head of the Chicago chamber of commerce advised, "the quickest way is to pay for it—not to the city, but to the aldermen." Old city governments lost their appeal not by providing too few services, but rather too many. As city budgets and tax burdens grew, voters turned to reform candidates. Decrying the faults and ignoring the merits of machine politics, progressives set out to replace the fatherly generosity of the ward boss with efficient, scientific administration.

After the depression of 1893, scores of city improvement leagues and good government associations sprang up to criticize the "degeneracy of councils and boards of aldermen." The structure of many cities resembled the federal government in miniature. A mayor, elected by the whole city, presided over a council comprised of representatives from each neighborhood, or ward. This system diluted the influence of the "better classes," good government reformers argued, and allowed the chiefs of a few powerful wards to rule the city. In 1899 Louisville's Conference for Good City Government proposed a new model, later known as the "strong mayor" system. It abolished wards, gave more power to the mayor, and required that the council be chosen in citywide elections. Two years later, Galveston, Texas, experimented with an even bolder plan after a tidal wave destroyed the city and killed a sixth of its population. Amid the disaster, a small committee of

"Annual Parade of the Cable Trolley Cripple Club," from The Verdict, *March 20, 1899. Injuries attributed to private firms that ran city transporatation, water, and sewage monopolies led to demands for public supervision or control of essential services.*

businessmen stepped in to manage the cleanup and recovery. Afterward, the city retained the system, placing power in the hands of a nonpartisan commission of five officials, each of whom managed a city department. Des Moines, Iowa, copied and improved on Galveston's design, and by 1911 some 160 cities had commission governments.

The city commission plan imitated the features of the modern business corporation. The commission was comparable to a board of directors. A city was, after all, a type of corporation, reformers argued. Honest, efficient, economical management, the skills that made for business success, could make a city run too. This philosophy led Detroit voters to elect Ford Motor Company's chief efficiency expert, James Couzens, as mayor. Other cities, led by Dayton, Ohio, tried to improve on the city commission plan by placing local government in the hands of an unelected "city manager."

Middle- and upper-class professionals led this revolution in city government, and they gained the most from it. The new city officials could explain where tax money was spent, and they responded to criticisms from leading citizens and newspapers, but there were no turkeys at Christmas. Getting a job or help from the city meant filling out the proper forms. Reform administrations targeted urban "vice," which included prostitution and drugs, but also working-class recreations like drinking and gambling. Voters also learned that businesslike efficiency did not lower taxes. City managers pared back spending where they could, but budgets continued to grow along with the public's demand for services.

Reform Mayors and City Services

While commissioners and managers tinkered in obscurity, a new breed of reform mayors gained heroic reputations by cleaning up and humanizing their cities. Samuel "Golden Rule" Jones, a Welsh immigrant who earned a fortune in the Pennsylvania oilfields, won election three times as the independent mayor of Toledo. He enacted the eight-hour day for city employees, pushed for public ownership of city utilities, built kindergartens and public playgrounds, and staged free concerts in the parks. "Everyone was against him," one of his aides remembered, "except the workers." Like Tom Johnson in Cleveland and Hazen Pingree in Detroit, Jones worried less about inefficiency and saloons and more about public utility magnates, who turned city government into "an instrument of the cunning few for the purpose of plundering the poor." Vice raids and blue laws, they agreed, paled next to the larceny of public contracts, tax breaks, and exclusive franchises for favored businesses. Milwaukee, Schenectady, and other cities bought or regulated the private monopolies that supplied street lighting, garbage removal, water, and streetcars. By World War I Americans enjoyed the highest level of city services in the world.

The reform mayor's efforts to humanize the urban environment were supported by architects, engineers, and planners, who endeavored to improve urban life through the arrangement of public space. Inspired by Chicago's White City of 1893, voluntary art and planning commissions formed a City Beautiful movement that sought to soften the urban landscape with vistas, open spaces, and greenery. If the city environment could degrade, it could also uplift, they believed, and in the visions of planners well-ordered urban scenes would educate and Americanize city dwellers. New York enacted zoning laws in 1916, and city planners (like all self-respecting experts) formed a credentialing association and organized themselves as a profession. Planning became a permanent feature of city administration.

Progressivism and the States

Reform at the state level displayed a distinctly regional character. In the East it mimicked the tactics and agenda of urban reform. New York's progressive governor, Charles Evans Hughes, passed laws prohibiting gambling and creating a state commission to regulate public utilities. In southern states, progressivism often meant refining the techniques of segregation and disfranchisement, freeing white voters to disagree among themselves about ways to improve schools and state administration. Lynching and white mob assaults on African-American neighborhoods were weekly occurrences in the progressive era. White leaders justified segregation and disfranchisement using the same terms that justified urban reform in the North: The "better classes" had an obligation to prevent the disorder and corruption that came from too much democracy.

States in the West and Midwest produced the boldest experiments in governmental reform. In Oregon the drive was led by William S. U'Ren, an itinerant farmer who went into politics after reading Henry George's *Progress and Poverty*. Under U'Ren's guidance, Oregon adopted a series of democratic innovations. The secret ballot and voter registration protected the polls from manipulation. The state passed three measures originally proposed by the Populists: the **initiative, recall** and **referendum.** The initiative allowed voters to place legislation on the ballot by petition; the referen-

dum let the legislature put proposals before the voters for approval; and the recall gave voters the chance to remove officials from office before the end of their terms. In his inaugural address as governor of New Jersey, Woodrow Wilson observed that Oregon had brought "government back to the people and protect[ed] it from the control of the representatives of selfish and special interests." Other states soon adopted all or part of the "Oregon system."

The best known of the progressive governors was Robert M. "Fighting Bob" La Follette, whose model of state government came to be known as the "Wisconsin Idea." La Follette claimed that as a young congressman the offer of a bribe had awakened in him a resolve. "I determined that the power of this corrupt influence, which was undermining and destroying every semblance of representative government in Wisconsin, should be broken." More probably, La Follette responded to his constituents' demands for state action against corporate interests.

Elected governor in 1900, La Follette pushed through a comprehensive program of social legislation. Powerful railway and public-utility commissions placed some of the state's largest corporations under public control. A tax commission designed a "scientific" distribution of the tax burden, including a state income tax. Other commissions regulated hours and working conditions and protected the environment. Wisconsin also implemented the direct primary, which allowed party nominees to be chosen directly by the voters rather than by party caucuses. Professors from the University of Wisconsin manned commissions and traveled through the state lecturing on behalf of the new laws. Defying *laissez-faire* prescriptions, the state's economy prospered under

Robert LaFollette, governor of Wisconsin (1901–1906), U.S. senator (1906–1925). "Where public opinion is free and uncontrolled," he wrote, "wealth has a wholesome respect for the law."

regulation. To conservative reformer Theodore Roosevelt, it was a "lesson of popular self-help and of patient care in radical legislation."

Few machine politicians had as much personal power as the reform governors did. A journalist observed that in Oregon "the state government is divided into four departments—the executive, judicial, legislative, and Mr. U'Ren—and it is still an open question who exerts the most power." Wisconsin papers reserved the term "demagogue" for La Follette, but the demagogic reform governors dispelled much of the public's cynicism and brought policymaking out of the "smoke-filled rooms."

By shaking up city halls and statehouses, progressives made government more responsive to demands for reform, but they knew that social problems did not respect city and state boundaries. National corporations and nationwide problems had to be attacked at the federal level, and that meant capturing the White House.

The Presidency Becomes "The Administration"

If Theodore Roosevelt stood at the center of the two great movements of his age, imperialism and progressivism, it was because he prepared himself for the part. The Roosevelt family was one of the oldest in New York and wealthy enough to afford a life of comfort, but Theodore embarked instead on a series of pursuits that were unusual for a man of his class. After graduating from Harvard in 1880, he married, started law school, wrote a history of the War of 1812 (he would write four other works, including the four-volume *Winning of the West*), bought a cattle ranch in the Dakota Territory, and most surprisingly, ran for the state legislature.

Roosevelt's political bid stunned his family and friends, who believed that government was no place for gentlemen. Roosevelt shared their disdain; he described his colleagues in the legislature as "a stupid, sodden, vicious lot, most of them being equally deficient in brains and virtue." Avoiding the "rough and tumble," he argued, only conceded high offices to those less fit to lead. Albany's politicos hardly knew what to make of the young swell who appeared at the capitol wearing a monocle and carrying "a gold-headed cane in one hand and a silk hat in the other." Roosevelt's flair for publicity got him noticed, and in 1886 the Republican Party nominated him for mayor of New York. He finished a poor third, lagging behind the Tammany nominee and the United Labor Party candidate. Losing to a Socialist gave him a conviction, shared by many progressives, that reform was necessary to keep voters from turning to more radical, even violent, alternatives. "Constructive change," he warned, "offers the best method of avoiding destructive change."

A turn as head of New York's board of police commissioners from 1895 to 1897 deepened Roosevelt's commitment to reform. Created by reformers, the commission supervised an army of 38,000 policemen. Roosevelt made friends with two muckraking journalists, Lincoln Steffens and Jacob Riis, with whom he stalked the dark streets looking for policemen on the take. Riis showed him the dismal tenement neighborhoods that housed Irish and Italian immigrants. Roosevelt's crackdown on saloons and corruption in the police department earned him a reputation as a man who would not be intimidated, even by his own party's bosses, and when McKinley captured the presidency he named Roosevelt assistant secretary of the Navy. The Spanish-American War catapulted him to national fame, and in quick succession he became governor of New York, vice president and then president of the United States. In the White House he rewrote the president's job description, seizing new powers for the executive branch and turning the presidency into "the administration."

The Executive Branch Against the Trusts

Roosevelt approached politics the way Jane Addams approached poverty, studying it, living in its midst, and carefully choosing his battles. His fear that economic desperation could lead to political violence was borne out in September 1901. President William McKinley was shaking hands at the Pan American Exposition in Buffalo, New York, when a man thrust a pistol into his chest and fired twice. The assassin, Leon Czolgosz, came from the slums of Cleveland. He claimed to have done it on behalf of the poor.

Roosevelt entered the White House at the age of 42, the youngest man to attain the presidency. With characteristic vigor, he moved to increase the power of the presidency and bring order and efficiency to governmental administration. He was the first president to call himself a progressive, and the first, according to Lippmann, "who realized clearly that national stability and social justice had to be sought deliberately and had consciously to be maintained. . . . Theodore Roosevelt began the work of turning the American mind in the direction which it had to go in the Twentieth Century."

Unsatisfied to be merely the standard bearer of his party, Roosevelt set out to remake the executive as the preeminent branch of government, the initiator of legislation, molder of public opinion, and guardian of the national interest at home and abroad. "I believe in a strong executive," he explained, "I believe in power." Instead of asking Congress for legislation, he drafted bills and lobbied for them personally. He believed federal administrators should intervene in the economy to protect citizens or to save business from its own shortsightedness. McKinley had already decided that action against the trusts was necessary, but his plans were not as bold as his successor's.

Challenging the megacorporations would be no easy task. Roosevelt took office less than a decade after J. P.

Morgan had saved the federal Treasury. In an 1895 decision, the Supreme Court gutted the Sherman Anti-Trust Act, one of the few laws that allowed federal action against monopolies. The underfunded Interstate Commerce Commission possessed only theoretical powers. Roosevelt admitted to Congress that "publicity is the only sure remedy which we can now invoke." He used it to the limit. Wall Street took notice when in his first inaugural he asserted that trusts "are creatures of the State, and the State not only has the right to control them, but it is duty bound to control them." In 1903 Roosevelt established a Department of Commerce and Labor with a Bureau of Corporations to penetrate the shroud of secrecy surrounding mergers and corporate activities and to put business information before the public.

The Justice Department revitalized the Sherman Act with vigorous prosecutions of the worst offenders. To send a message to corporate boardrooms, Roosevelt selected cases for maximum publicity value. Attorney General Philander Knox took on the "Napoleon of Wall Street" by filing suit against J. P. Morgan's holding company, Northern Securities. Morgan expected that the matter could be settled in the usual way, and his attorney asked how they might "fix it up." "We don't want to fix it up," Knox replied. "We want to stop it." When the court handed Roosevelt a victory in 1904, Americans cheered.

With this case, Roosevelt gained an undeserved reputation as a "trust buster." Although he opposed serious abuses, he considered anyone who wished to destroy all monopolies "at least a quack and at worst an enemy to the Republic." He distinguished between good and bad trusts, and he believed government should restrain the bad and encourage the good. His thinking mirrored that of progressive writers like Herbert Croly, editor of *The New Republic,* who imagined a professionalized, central government staffed by nonpartisan experts who would monitor the activities of big corporations to assure efficiency and head off destructive actions.

Not all progressives agreed. Brandeis and Woodrow Wilson envisioned a political economy of small, highly competitive firms kept in line by regular applications of the Sherman Act. To Roosevelt, there could be no return to an economy of competing small businesses. Large combinations were necessary, even desirable, fixtures of modern life. It was government's obligation not to break them up but to force them to serve the public interest.

To this end, Roosevelt revitalized the Interstate Commerce Commission. He secured passage of the Hepburn Act (1906), which allowed the commission to set freight rates, and banned special deals between carriers and favored clients (such as the one Standard Oil enjoyed). Another piece of legislation, the Elkins Act (1910), gave the ICC authority over telephone, telegraph, and cable communications and allowed the commission to act on its own, without waiting for an injured party to file a complaint. The Pure Food and Drug Act (1906) responded to Upton Sinclair's stomach-turning exposé of the meatpacking industry by making it a crime to ship or sell contaminated or fraudulently labeled food and drugs. Under Roosevelt, the federal government gained authority and tools to counterbalance the power of business. It grew to match its responsibilities. The number of federal employees almost doubled between 1900 and 1916.

The Square Deal

Roosevelt's exasperation with big business reached a peak during the anthracite strike of 1902. The United Mine Workers represented 150,000 miners in the coal fields of eastern Pennsylvania. The miners, mostly Polish, Hungarian, and Italian immigrants, earned less than $6 a week in a dirty, hazardous line of work. Over 400 died underground yearly to supply the kind of soft coal needed to run railroads and heat homes. Seventy percent of the mines were owned by six railroads, which in turn fell under the control of the usual financiers—Morgan, Rockefeller, and George Baer, among others. The owners refused to deal with the UMW, declaring it a band of outlaws. Baer insisted that the miners "don't suffer . . . why, they can barely speak English." When the miners struck in May 1902, they had the public's sympathy. Editorials, even in Republican newspapers, urged the president to take the mines away from the owners.

The "gross blindness of the operators" infuriated Roosevelt. A coal famine might kill hundreds in the cities

Nearly one of every five American children worked full time in 1900. This Pennsylvania coal mine started its workers at age eight.

and lead to class warfare. Rumors spread of a general strike in support of the miners. The mine owners, he fumed, "knew nothing either of the great principles of government or of the feelings of the great mass of our people." Roosevelt exhausted the options his office allowed, publicly and privately urging the two sides to settle. In early October, as schools in New England closed for lack of heat, he invited UMW officials and the operators to Washington for negotiations. John Mitchell, head of the mineworkers, eagerly accepted the president's arbitration, but the owners accused Roosevelt of grandstanding and flatly refused to deal with "criminals" and "anarchists."

For Roosevelt this was the final straw. He drew up plans for the Army to move into the coal fields and place the mines under government control. The secretary of war warned Morgan of the impending move, and the owners capitulated, agreeing to submit the dispute to a federal commission. The commission produced a compromise: Miners received a 10 percent increase in pay and a nine-hour workday, but owners did not have to recognize the union.

Roosevelt's direct action set precedents that made the federal government a third force in labor disputes. For the first time a strike was settled by federal arbitration, and for the first time a union had struck against a strategic industry without being denounced as a revolutionary conspiracy. The government would no longer automatically side with the corporations. Instead, Roosevelt offered an understanding: "We demand that big business give the people a square deal; in return, we must insist that when anyone engaged in big business honestly endeavors to do right, he shall be given a square deal." Part of that deal included acknowledging the legitimacy of labor, farm, and consumer groups who would work to make a corporate economy more congenial to wage earners and families.

Conserving Water, Land, and Forests

When Roosevelt felt important issues were at stake, he seldom accepted the limits of his office. He enraged Congress by stretching the definitions of presidential power, nowhere more so than in the area of conservation. When Congress sent him a bill to halt the creation of new national forests in the West, Roosevelt first created or enlarged 32 national forests then signed the bill (see Map 21-1). To stop private companies from damming rivers, he reserved 2,500 of the best hydropower sites by declaring them "ranger stations." The energy behind his program came from Gifford Pinchot, the chief forester of the United States, who saw conservation as a new frontier. Unsettled, undeveloped lands were growing scarce, and Pinchot convinced the president that hope for the future lay in using the available resources more efficiently. Few words were dearer to progressive hearts than "efficiency," but

among those that came close were "research" and "management," and Pinchot used those too. Preserving nature for its own sake had no place in his plans. Forests, deserts, and ore ranges were to be used, but wisely, scientifically, and in the national interest.

One of the first victories for the new policy of resource management was the Newlands Reclamation Act (1902), which gave the Agriculture Department authority to build reservoirs and irrigation systems in the West. In the next four years, three million acres were "reclaimed" from the desert and turned into farms. To prevent waste, Roosevelt put tighter controls on prospecting, grazing, and logging. Big lumber and mining companies had few complaints about rationalized resource administration, but small-scale prospectors and ranchers found themselves shut out of federal lands. Naturalists, like John Muir, also resisted, pointing out that nature was to be appreciated, not used. When Congress decided to build a reservoir in California's Hetch Hetchy Valley, part of Yosemite National Park, the split between utilitarian and aesthetic conservationists came into the open. Muir and the Sierra Club bitterly opposed the destruction of one of the country's most scenic spots, but Pinchot favored the plan, which supplied water to San Francisco and irrigation projects in the surrounding area.

By 1909, conservation had become a national issue. Hikers, sightseers, and tourism entrepreneurs drawn to the new parks and forest reserves were forming a powerful antidevelopment constituency. By quadrupling the acreage in federal reserves, professionalizing the forest service, and using his "bully pulpit" to build support for conservation, Roosevelt helped create the modern environmental movement.

web connection

An Early Conservation Controversy

www.prenhall.com/boydston/hetchhetchy

A plan to dam the Hetch Hetchy Valley, a portion of Yosemite National Park, to provide water to San Francisco, pitted leaders of the new conservation movement—and competing definitions of conservation—against each other. On the side of the dam was Gifford Pinchot, founder of the National Forest Service and close adviser to Theodore Roosevelt. Leading the opposition was John Muir, founder of the Sierra Club, in whose honor Theodore Roosevelt dedicated Muir Woods just north of San Francisco. What were the arguments for and against the dam?

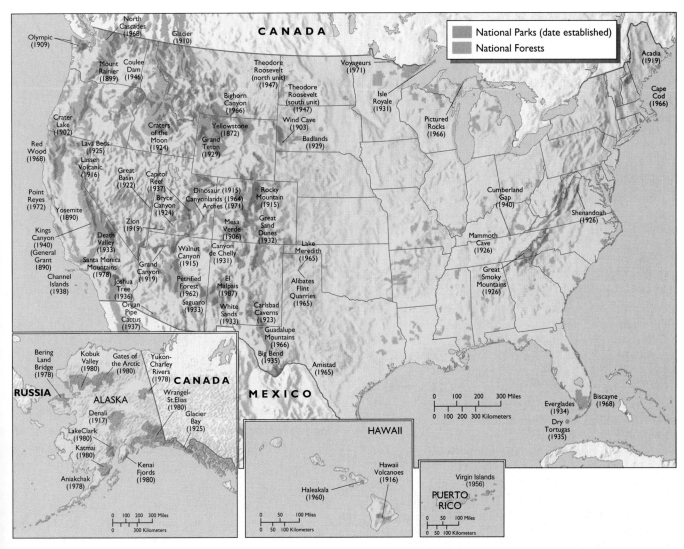

Map 21-1 Growth of Public Lands.
Responding to a national conservation movement, Roosevelt set aside public lands for use as parks and managed-yield forests. The National Park Service was founded in 1916.

TR and Big Stick Diplomacy

The expansion of U. S. overseas investment and new threats to American security placed greater demands on foreign and military policy after the turn of the century. American investors wanted assurances that Washington would use its leverage to protect their overseas factories and railroads against civil wars and hostile governments. The diplomatic and military budgets grew to meet these demands, and the United States staffed permanent embassies in many Latin-American capitals. The State Department replaced political cronies in the diplomatic corps with a trained, professionalized foreign service. Commercial attachés issued reports on foreign business conditions. Conducting foreign relations was no longer a matter of weathering "incidents" but of making policy.

Roosevelt's view of world affairs flowed from his understanding of both history and the future. Global trade and communications, he believed, separated civilized nations moving in the main current of history from savage and barbarian peoples caught outside of it. His foreign policy aimed to keep the United States in the central stream of globalizing processes such as commerce, imperialism, and military (particularly naval) modernization. Roosevelt felt obligated to interfere with "barbarian" governments in Asia, Latin America, or Africa, that blocked the progress of civilization. The United States had a moral duty, he felt, to overthrow governments and even seize territory in such cases because it was acting in the interests of the world as a whole.

Building an interoceanic canal topped Roosevelt's list of foreign-policy priorities. A canal would be a hub of world trade and naval power in the Atlantic and Pacific. Plans had been in the works for a long time, and Roosevelt shoved aside the remaining obstacles. He pressed Britain to drop its claim to joint control over a canal, urged Congress to choose the Colombian province of Panama as the site, and negotiated a deal to buy out a failed French canal venture.

Meanwhile in Colombia, a civil war pitted modernizers led by José Marroquín against Catholic traditionalists who wanted to isolate the country from foreign investment and other outside influences. In 1902 American diplomats brokered a peace that gave Marroquín the presidency and handed the parliament to his fundamentalist opponents. The parliament fiercely opposed the canal, which would thrust Colombia into the crossroads of world trade. Marroquín favored it, but he knew war would erupt again unless the Americans gave Bogotá a substantial sum of money and control over the canal. From Roosevelt's point of view, the canal was a gift and any government that refused it did not deserve to rule. He denounced the "greedy little anthropoids" in Bogotá and accused Marroquín of blackmail. Stymied, Roosevelt pursued another option.

In the Spring of 1903 Panamanian senators, upset by the rejection of the U. S. offer, began conspiring at separation. Panama had declared its independence from Colombia twice in the last century, and a revolutionary movement had been active there as recently as 1900, but the United States had always stepped in to preserve Colombia's sovereignty. Together with Philippe Bunau-Varilla, who represented shareholders in the French canal company, the Panamanians lobbied U. S. officials to support their plot. Sure of American support, Bunau-Varilla forecast a revolution for November 3, thereby assuring that all the participants would be ready: the rebels, the Colombian Army (which had been bribed into surrendering), and most importantly, U. S. warships.

The revolution went off without a hitch, and Roosevelt presented the new Panamanian government a treaty that gave less and took more than the one offered to Colombia. The president was defensive about his behavior, claiming that he had acted "with the highest, finest, and nicest standards of public and governmental ethics." Congress had a different opinion and launched an investigation. "I took the canal and let Congress debate," Roosevelt said, "and while the debate goes on the canal does also." Engineers, led by George W. Goethals, removed a mountain to let water into the isthmus and built another to shore up an artificial lake. Colonel William C. Gorgas defeated malaria and yellow fever, reducing the death rate in Panama to below that of an average American city. The canal, a fifty-mile cut built at a cost of 352 million dollars and more than 5,600 lives, opened in 1914.

Theodore Roosevelt inspects earth-moving equipment at the canal in 1906. The canal was completed in 1914, ahead of schedule and under budget.

Once construction was under way, Roosevelt acted to protect the canal from other imperial powers. Poverty and unrest in the Caribbean states created opportunities for European navies to establish bases on Panama's doorstep. Neighboring nations owed millions to European investors, and imperial practice allowed creditor nations to seize the port cities of defaulting states. In 1902 Germany came close to invading Venezuela over an unpaid debt, but Roosevelt stepped in to mediate. Two years later, a civil war caused the Dominican Republic to renege on its loans. Four European nations laid plans for a debt-collecting expedition.

Roosevelt went before Congress in December 1904 and announced a policy later known as the Roosevelt Corollary. It stipulated that when chronic "wrongdoing or impotence" in a Latin-American country required "intervention by some civilized nation" the United States would do the intervening. Its language captured the president's world-view. White "civilized" nations acted; nonwhite "impotent" nations were acted upon. The following month the United States took over the Dominican Republic's customs offices and began repaying creditors. The economic intervention turned military in 1916, when the United States landed Marines to protect the customs from Dominican rebels. U. S. troops stayed until the early 1920s.

By enforcing order and administrative efficiency in the Caribbean, Roosevelt extended progressivism beyond the borders of the United States; the movement gained footholds in the Far East too. Governor General William H. Taft took municipal reform to Manila. In 1906 the U. S. federal courts took the unusual step of creating a court outside the United States, in Shanghai, China, to control prostitution in the American community there.

Roosevelt extended American stewardship to conflicts in Asia and Africa. He won the Nobel Peace Prize for mediating the end of the Russo-Japanese War in 1905, and he proposed a compromise settlement to the British-French-German dispute over Morocco. Congress objected both times, but in each case Roosevelt used the negotiations to extend open door trade policies and prevent larger wars.

Taft and Dollar Diplomacy

Enormously popular at the end of his second term, Roosevelt chose his friend, William H. Taft, to succeed him. As an Ohio circuit judge, Taft gained national attention with two decisions that enlarged federal power to regulate trusts. Roosevelt made him the first governor general of the Philippines and later his secretary of war. Taft easily defeated William Jennings Bryan in the 1908 election, and as president he began consolidating Roosevelt's programs with the help of a more progressive Congress. He sent to the states constitutional amendments for the direct election of senators and the income tax. His administration increased antitrust enforcement and levied the first tax on corporations. Satisfied that his legacy would continue, Roosevelt left for a tour of Africa.

In the Caribbean, Taft put the Roosevelt Corollary into action (see Map 21-2). The United States bought up the debts of Honduras and Nicaragua, in order to prevent another incident like the one in the Dominican Republic. Taft persuaded four New York banks to refinance Haiti's debt, to prevent German intervention there. Taft intended "dollar diplomacy" to replace force as an instrument of policy, "substituting dollars for bullets," but in most cases, dollars preceded bullets. For Caribbean nations, American financial protection meant allowing the Americans to impose high import taxes, and a revolt usually followed. Marines went into Honduras and Nicaragua in 1912. They stayed in Central America until 1933.

Dollar diplomacy also aimed to harness corporate investment power to foreign policy objectives. Shortly after his inauguration, Taft mobilized a consortium of financiers led by Morgan and Kuhn, Loeb and Company to invest in China's planned Chinchow-Aigun railway. Railroads were instruments of power in North China, and with one railroad Taft felt he could drive a wedge between the imperial powers—Britain, Russia, and Japan—and compel them to resume open door trade. Instead, they joined forces against the United States and the Open Door. In 1910 they signed a protocol opposing U. S. interference in China. Roosevelt criticized the China venture, but Taft believed that he was only taking his mentor's vision of modern diplomacy seriously. Global trends were changing the nature of power. Military force was outmoded, he felt, and soon economic power would be the only kind that mattered.

Taft disappointed both conservatives and progressives in his party. He urged Congress to reduce the tariff, but when protectionists in the Senate put up a fight he retreated and signed the Payne-Aldrich Tariff in 1909, a compromise that lowered rates for some goods but actually raised rates on steel, cotton, silk, and other important imports. Taft's flip flop disgusted La Follette and other midwestern progressives.

Taft's secretary of the interior, Richard Ballinger, sided with ranchers and miners who opposed resource-management policies. Ballinger eliminated Pinchot's fictional "ranger stations," opening water-power sites and a million acres of public land to private development. Pinchot fought back on the pages of Collier's magazine, accusing Ballinger of representing corporate interests. Taft fired Pinchot in 1910, further alienating the progressives. The Ballinger-Pinchot affair had brought the party's divisions into the open.

Taft maintained but did not extend Roosevelt's reforms. To the former Rough Rider, that was not enough. "I was able to hold the Republican Party in power only because I insisted on a steady advance and dragged them along with me," Roosevelt wrote from Africa. "Now the advance has been stopped." Enlarging the president's powers did no good unless the president was willing to use them. Roosevelt began to believe his country needed him back.

Rival Visions of the Industrial Future

After Roosevelt returned in 1910, Pinchot, La Follette, Croly, and others trooped to his home at Sagamore Hill to complain about Taft. The former president denied his interest in the Republican nomination, but a friend acknowledged that "no thirsty sinner ever took a pledge that was harder for him to keep." Roosevelt re-entered politics because his views had evolved, and because politics was what he knew best. Just 54 years old, his energy was undiminished. He took more radical positions on corporations, public welfare, and labor than he had during his

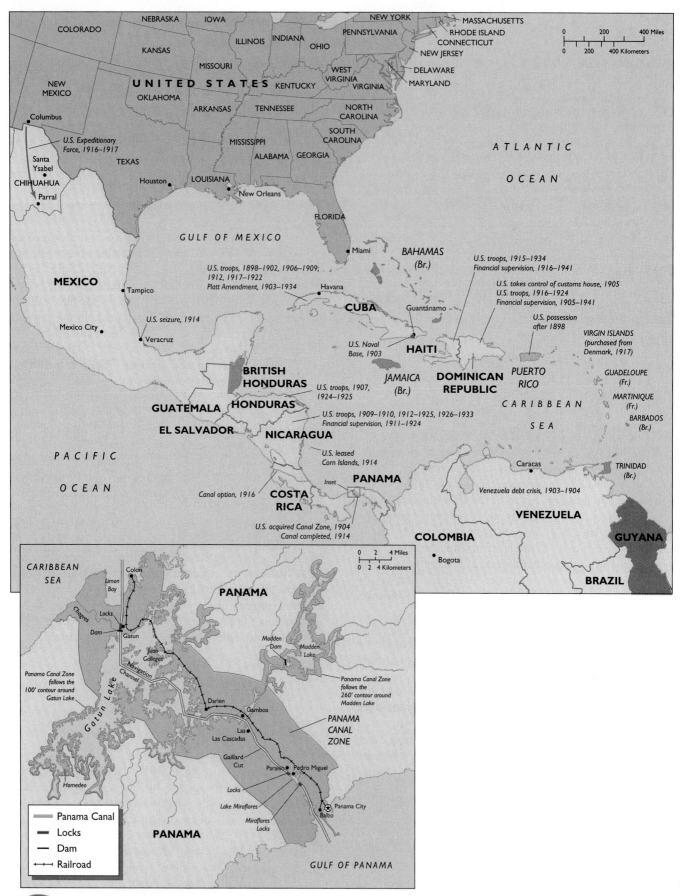

Map 21-2   United States in the Caribbean.

U. S. troops intervened repeatedly in the Caribbean and Central America to protect investments and guard against perceived threats to order. Panama, Nicaragua, Haiti, and the Dominican Republic were under nearly constant U.S. occupation until the mid-1920s.

Source: Thomas Patterson, American Foreign Relations, vol. II (D.C. Heath, 1995), pp. 55, 40.

Main map labels

COLORADO
NEBRASKA
IOWA
NEW YORK
MASSACHUSETTS
RHODE ISLAND
CONNECTICUT
NEW JERSEY
DELAWARE
MARYLAND
KANSAS
ILLINOIS
INDIANA
OHIO
PENNSYLVANIA
MISSOURI
UNITED STATES
KENTUCKY
WEST VIRGINIA
VIRGINIA
NEW MEXICO
OKLAHOMA
ARKANSAS
TENNESSEE
NORTH CAROLINA
SOUTH CAROLINA
Columbus
U.S. Expeditionary Force, 1916–1917
Santa Ysabel
CHIHUAHUA
TEXAS
Parral
Houston
LOUISIANA
New Orleans
MISSISSIPPI
ALABAMA
GEORGIA
FLORIDA

ATLANTIC OCEAN

GULF OF MEXICO
Miami
BAHAMAS (Br.)
MEXICO
Tampico
U.S. troops, 1898–1902, 1906–1909; 1912, 1917–1922 Platt Amendment, 1903–1934
Havana
CUBA
Guantánamo
U.S. troops, 1915–1934 Financial supervision, 1916–1941
U.S. takes control of customs house, 1905 U.S. troops, 1916–1924 Financial supervision, 1905–1941
Mexico City
U.S. seizure, 1914
Veracruz
U.S. Naval Base, 1903
HAITI
U.S. possession after 1898
VIRGIN ISLANDS (purchased from Denmark, 1917)
BRITISH HONDURAS
JAMAICA (Br.)
DOMINICAN REPUBLIC
PUERTO RICO
GUADELOUPE (Fr.)
GUATEMALA
HONDURAS
U.S. troops, 1907, 1924–1925
CARIBBEAN SEA
MARTINIQUE (Fr.)
EL SALVADOR
NICARAGUA
U.S. troops, 1909–1910, 1912–1925, 1926–1933 Financial supervision, 1911–1924
BARBADOS (Br.)
PACIFIC OCEAN
U.S. leased Corn Islands, 1914
Caracas
TRINIDAD (Br.)
PANAMA
Inset
Canal option, 1916
COSTA RICA
Venezuela debt crisis, 1903–1904
VENEZUELA
U.S. acquired Canal Zone, 1904 Canal completed, 1914
COLOMBIA
GUYANA
Bogota
BRAZIL

0 200 400 Miles
0 200 400 Kilometers

Inset map labels

CARIBBEAN SEA
Colon
Limon Bay
PANAMA
Chagres
Locks
Dam
Gatun
Juan Gallegos
Madden Dam
Madden Lake
Panama Canal Zone follows the 100' contour around Gatun Lake
Gatun Lake
Navigation Channel
Panama Canal Zone follows the 260' contour around Madden Lake
Darien
Gamboa
PANAMA CANAL ZONE
Las
Las Cascadas
Gaillard Cut
Homedeo
Paraiso
Pedro Miguel
Locks
Lake Miraflores
Miraflores Locks
Panama City
Balbo
PANAMA
GULF OF PANAMA

0 2 4 Miles
0 2 4 Kilometers

— Panama Canal
— Locks
— Dam
⊢—⊣ Railroad

presidency. The election of 1912 became a race that would define the future of industrial America.

The New Nationalism

At a sunbaked railroad stop in Osawatomie, Kansas, in August 1910, Roosevelt declared that "the essence of any struggle for liberty . . . is to destroy privilege, and give the life of every individual the highest possible value." He laid out a political program he called the New Nationalism. It included the elimination of corporate campaign contributions, regulation of industrial combinations, an expert commission to set tariffs, a graduated income tax, banking reorganization, and a national workers' compensation program. "This New Nationalism regards the executive power as the steward of the public welfare." The message drew cheers. "The West loves and understands Roosevelt," the *Denver Republican* boasted. The East was less understanding. To the *New York Times*, the speech crossed "the ultimate boundary line of radicalism."

From the beginning, Roosevelt had the newspapers while Taft had the delegates. The nomination fight tested the new system of direct primaries. Taft's control of the party machinery gave him an advantage in states that chose delegates by convention, but in a number of key states Roosevelt could take his campaign to the voters. "The professional bread and butter politicians are all for Taft," he told an audience, "at least here in Illinois the plain people have a chance to speak for themselves." Victories in Illinois and New Jersey revived his faltering campaign, but when the convention met in Chicago in June 1912, Taft's slim but decisive majority allowed him to control the platform and win over undecided delegates. Grumbling that he had been robbed, Roosevelt walked out.

Roosevelt returned to Chicago in August to accept the nomination of the newly formed Progressive Party, which La Follette had organized. The delegates were a mixed group. They included Hiram Johnson, the reforming governor of California; muckraking publisher Frank Munsey; imperialist senator Albert Beveridge; and J. P. Morgan's business partner George W. Perkins. "It was a well dressed crowd," newspaperman William Allen White observed. "Judging the delegates by their clothes, I figured there was not a man or woman on the floor who was making less than two thousand a year, and not one . . . who was topping ten thousand." The party platform endorsed the New Nationalism, along with popular election of senators, popular review of judicial decisions (which would allow the voters to second-guess the courts), and women's suffrage. Women served as delegates, and Jane Addams gave the speech seconding Roosevelt's nomination. The gathering had an evangelical spirit. Roosevelt spoke apocalyptically. "Our cause is based on the eternal principles of righteousness," he said. "We stand at Armageddon and we battle for the Lord."

The 1912 Election

Meanwhile in Baltimore the Democratic convention nominated a former college professor and governor of New Jersey. Woodrow Wilson had trained himself for a life in politics. Like Roosevelt, the young Wilson defied his family's expectations by pursuing a political career. At Davidson College, where he had been sent to study for the ministry, he resolved to "acquire knowledge that we might have power." He entered politics by an unusual route, the university. Obtaining a doctorate in government from Johns Hopkins University in 1886, he published his first book, *Congressional Government*, at the age of 28. It advocated reforming the federal structure by enlarging the power of the executive branch. As a professor and later president of Princeton University, he became a well-known lecturer and commentator for the new national political magazines like *Harper's* and *The Atlantic*. In 1910 he won election as governor of New Jersey and enacted a sweeping program of progressive reforms. For Democrats, smarting from a string of defeats under Bryan's leadership, Wilson offered a new image and the ability to unite the South and the East under a progressive program.

With Roosevelt in the race, Wilson had to stake his own claim to the progressive constituency. Competing with the New Nationalism's popular, specific reforms would not be easy, but with the help of Louis Brandeis, Wilson devised a program called the New Freedom. It challenged Roosevelt on his fundamental approaches to the economy and politics. Simply regulating the trusts, Wilson argued, would not make the economy friendly to consumers, workers, or small entrepreneurs. Instead, it would create a paternalistic bureaucracy. Wilson wanted antitrust laws that would allow a lean but powerful government to return competition and economic mobility to the marketplace. Both men agreed on the importance of a strong executive and continual intervention in the economy, but they had different answers to the question of who benefited from the economy. Roosevelt appealed to a collective, national interest, while Wilson stressed the needs of individual consumers and investors. The political philosophy and style of New Nationalism was evangelical, aiming to inspire people to work for the common good. Wilson appealed to reason and self-interest.

On election day, Wilson won fewer votes than Bryan had in any of his races, but the split in the Republican Party gave him a plurality. He won 42 percent of the popular vote, compared to 27 for Roosevelt, 23 for Taft, and 6 for Debs (see Map 21-3). Although his margin was thin, Wilson could interpret Taft's repudiation and the large combined vote for the progressive candidates as a mandate for change. "What the Democratic Party proposes to do," he told his followers, "is to go into power and do the things the Republican Party has been talking about doing for sixteen years."

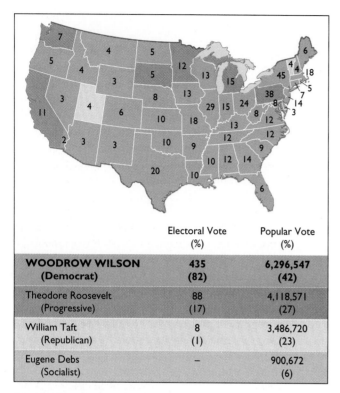

	Electoral Vote (%)	Popular Vote (%)
WOODROW WILSON (Democrat)	**435 (82)**	**6,296,547 (42)**
Theodore Roosevelt (Progressive)	88 (17)	4,118,571 (27)
William Taft (Republican)	8 (1)	3,486,720 (23)
Eugene Debs (Socialist)	–	900,672 (6)

Map 21-3   The Election of 1912.
The 1912 election pitted rival visions of progressivism against each other. Roosevelt's Bull Moose candidacy split the Republican vote, allowing Wilson's victory.

The New Freedom

Within a year and a half of his inauguration, Wilson produced one of the most coherent and far-reaching legislative programs ever devised by a president. Drawing on his long study of congressional politics, he seized the advantage of his party's majority and exercised an unprecedented degree of personal control through the majority leaders in both houses. The New Freedom advocated lower tariffs, increased competition, and vigorous antitrust enforcement. Three monumental bills passed through Congress in rapid succession.

The first bill was the Underwood-Simmons Tariff, which made the first deep cuts in tariff rates since before the Civil War. The bill overturned one of the cornerstones of Republican economic policy, the protectionist tariff, and it helped farmers and consumers by lowering prices and increasing competition, but Wilson argued that its real beneficiaries would be manufacturers. Lower tariffs would help persuade other countries to reduce taxes on imports from the United States, he reasoned, opening new markets for American-made goods. Wilson created an expert Tariff Commission in 1916 to carry tariff bargaining to a new level. The most-favored nation policies it implemented

(and which remain standard practice) induced European powers to open their empires to American goods. The Singer, Ford, and Camel brand names began appearing in bazaars, souks, and godowns from Caracas to Mandalay. The Underwood-Simmons Tariff (1913) also permanently shifted the revenue base of the federal government from taxes on imports to taxes on income.

Wilson's next target was the banking system. When Steffens and Lippmann investigated banking for *Everybody's* magazine in 1908, they found its structure was "strikingly like that of Tammany Hall: the same pyramiding influence, the same tendency of power to center on individuals who did not necessarily sit in the official seats, the same effort of human organization to grow independently of legal arrangements." Money poured into investment houses but scarcely trickled to western farmers. The Federal Reserve Act of 1913 set up a national board to supervise the system and created 12 regional reserve banks in different parts of the country. Banks were now watched to assure that their reserves matched their deposits. The system's real advantage was the flexibility it gave the currency. The Federal Reserve Board could put more dollars into circulation when demand was high and retire them when it subsided. Regional banks could adjust the money supply to meet the needs of different parts of the country. The system broke Wall Street's stranglehold on credit and opened new opportunities for entrepreneurship and competition.

Finally, Wilson attacked the trusts. He established the Federal Trade Commission (FTC), an independent regulatory commission assigned to enforce free and fair competition. It absorbed the functions of Roosevelt's Bureau of Corporations, but it had more far-reaching powers, including the right to subpoena corporate records and issue cease-and-desist orders. The Clayton Antitrust Act (1914) prohibited price fixing, outlawed interlocking directorates, and made it illegal for a company to own stock in its competitor. To enforce these provisions citizens were entitled to sue for triple the amount of the actual damages they suffered. In 1916 Wilson produced another crop of reform legislation, including the first national workers' compensation and child-labor laws, the eight-hour day for railroad workers, and the Warehouse Act, which extended credit to cash-strapped farmers.

These programs furthered Wilson's goal of "releasing the energies" of consumers and entrepreneurs, but they also helped business. Businessmen headed many of the regulatory boards, and the FTC and Federal Reserve Board brought predictability and civility to unruly markets. The New Freedom implemented reform without resorting to the elaborate state machinery that the New Nationalism envisioned or that European industrial nations were assembling. The New Freedom linked liberal reform to individual initiative and the free play of markets.

CHRONOLOGY

1889   Hull-House founded

1890   General Federation of Women's Clubs founded

1893   Illinois passes eight-hour day for women

1895   National Association of Manufacturers organized

1900   Robert La Follette elected governor of Wisconsin

1901   Socialist Party of America founded
Galveston introduces commission government
McKinley assassinated; Theodore Roosevelt inaugurated president

1902   Newlands Reclamation Act funds construction of dams and irrigation systems
Alice Hamilton investigates Chicago's typhoid epidemic
McClure's publishes first episodes of Ida Tarbell's "History of the Standard Oil Company" and Lincoln Steffens' "The Shame of the Cities"
Roosevelt settles anthracite strike

1903   Roosevelt establishes Department of Commerce and Labor
Panama declares independence from Colombia
W. E. B. Du Bois publishes *The Souls of Black Folk*

1904   Justice Department sues Standard Oil under the Sherman Anti-Trust Act
U. S. Supreme Court orders Northern Securities Company dissolved as an illegal combination
Roosevelt elected president
The Roosevelt Corollary announced

1905   U. S. takes over Dominican customs
Industrial Workers of the World founded
Roosevelt mediates end to Russo-Japanese War

1906   Hepburn Act passed, allowing the Interstate Commerce Commission to set freight rates
Pure Food and Drug Act requires accurate labeling

1907   Indiana passes forcible sterilization law

1908   William H. Taft elected president
Supreme Court upholds maximum-hours laws for women in *Muller v. Oregon*

1909   Payne-Aldrich Tariff goes into effect
NAACP founded

1910   Taft fires chief forester Gifford Pinchot
Elkins Act authorizes Interstate Commerce Commission to regulate electronic communications
Roosevelt announces the New Nationalism

1911   Triangle Shirtwaist Company fire

1912   U. S. troops occupy Nicaragua
Woodrow Wilson elected president

1913   Federal Reserve Act reorganizes banking system
Underwood-Simmons Tariff

1914   Panama Canal completed
Clayton Act strengthens antitrust enforcement

1916   New York City enacts zoning laws
Federal workers' compensation, child-labor, and eight-hour-day laws passed

Conclusion

By 1900 America's political economy had outgrown the social relationships and laws that served the rural republic for most of the nineteenth century. Squeezed between the indifference of corporate elites and the large, transient immigrant communities that controlled urban politics, middle-class reformers created a new style of political participation. They experimented with the structure of decision-making at the municipal and state levels and vested the state with responsibility for the quality of life of its citizens. Progressives challenged but never upset the system. Above all, they wanted managed, orderly change. Science and the pressure of informed opinion, they believed, could overcome resistance without open conflict.

The progressive presidents continued this movement on the national stage. Roosevelt and Wilson touted their programs as attacks on privilege, but both presidents helped position the federal government as a broker among business, consumer, and labor interests. "Democracy is now setting out on its real mission," William Allen White observed, "to define the rights of the owner and the user of private property according to the dictates of an enlightened public conscience." In less than two decades, the federal government overcame its reputation for corruption and impotence and adapted to a new role at the center of economic and social life. The concept of a "national interest" that superseded individual and property rights and needed to be protected through continuous action was now firmly ingrained. The president's leadership now extended beyond the administration to Congress and public opinion. These achievements created a modern central government just at the time when military, diplomatic, and economic victories made the United States a global power. The consensus favoring a strong central government and the strength of American influence abroad would both be tested by events unfolding in Europe.

Review Questions

1. Was the political culture that women activists like Jane Addams and Alice Hamilton fought to change a *male* culture?

2. Were the progressives' goals conservative or radical? How about their strategies?

3. Why did reformers feel that contracts between elected city governments and privately owned utilities invited corruption?

4. What were the Oregon system and the Wisconsin Idea?

5. Theodore Roosevelt has been called the first modern president. In what ways did his administration change the presidency?

Further Readings

Jane Addams, *Twenty Years at Hull-House* (1910). In her autobiography, Addams urges respect for the traditions of immigrants and action against the causes of crime and poverty.

John Milton Cooper, Jr., *The Warrior and the Priest: Theodore Roosevelt and Woodrow Wilson in American Politics* (1983). A dual biography of the progressive presidents compares their backgrounds, philosophies, and political styles.

J. Anthony Lukas, *Big Trouble: A Murder in a Small Western Town Sets off a Struggle for the Soul of America* (1997). The anxiety and tension of the progressive-era West comes to the surface in the trial of three labor leaders for the murder of a former governor of Idaho.

Kevin Starr, *Inventing the Dream: California Through the Progressive Era* (1985). The century's first decade in a state that was defining a distinct local identity through planning, art, and reform.

David Thelen, *Robert M. La Follette and the Insurgent Spirit* (1976). The life and philosophy of the progressive governor and senator from Wisconsin.

Robert H. Wiebe, *The Search for Order, 1877–1920* (1967). This classic study of progressivism traces the movement's origins to the middle class's yearning for a lost Eden of small towns and personal relationships.

History on the Internet

"The Triangle Shirtwaist Factory Fire"

http://www.ilr.cornell.edu/trianglefire/

This rich and informative site details this now-infamous workplace disaster. Through the use of an interpretative introductory essay, photographs, oral histories of survivors, and contemporary newspaper accounts, this source explains the impact of the industrial accident on workplace safety reform.

"The Evolution of the Conservation Movement"

http://memory.loc.gov/ammem/amrvhtml/conshome.html

Explore this area of progressive reform through timelines that link to important documents in conservation history, such as Teddy Roosevelt's addresses on the subject and Acts of Congress.

"The Urban Log Cabin"

http://www.wnet.org/tenement/logcabin.html

See what living conditions were like in a 1915 tenement house. This site describes the many conditions progressives were battling, including overcrowding, poor sanitary conditions, and disease.

"How the NAACP Began"

http://www.i/stu.edu/RSO/NAACP/history.htm

This site offers a copy of Mary White Ovington's history of the organization as originally printed in 1914. As a former executive secretary and chairperson of the organization, Ovington outlined in the document the NAACP's original platform, acts of civil injustices against blacks, and the role of W. E. B. DuBois.

22

A GLOBAL POWER

1914-1919

Walter Lippmann

"War in Europe is impending," Walter Lippmann wrote in his diary on July 29, 1914. The twenty-four-year-old journalist was making his way to Switzerland for two weeks of hiking in the Alps. In Belgium, he witnessed the aftershocks of a crisis in the Balkans. Four weeks earlier, the heir to the throne of Austria-Hungary, Archduke Ferdinand, had been shot in his car as he drove through the Serbian city of Sarajevo, touching off a progression of events that plunged Europe into war. Austria threatened war unless Serbia found and punished the conspirators. Russia mobilized to come to Serbia's defense. As stock markets tumbled and banks collapsed, Lippmann found himself caught up in a conflict between the world's most powerful states: Austria and Germany on one side, Russia, France, and Britain on the other. "The railroad stations are crowded with angry, jostling people, carrying every conceivable kind of package," Lippmann wrote, "I am making straight for Switzerland tonight." He never made it. Belgium closed its borders, and unable to leave by train, he crossed the Channel to England.

In the twilight of August 4, as Lippmann stood with an anxious crowd on the terrace outside the House of Commons, Britain's foreign minister, Sir Edward Grey, asked Parliament for a war resolution. Two hours later, in Berlin, the Reichstag declared war on France. "We sit and stare at each other and make idiotically cheerful remarks," Lippmann wrote, "and in the meantime, so far as anyone can see, nothing can stop the awful disintegration now. Nor is there any way of looking beyond it: ideas, books, seem too utterly trivial, and all the public opinion, democratic hope, and what not, where is it today?"

Lippmann had come of age in the progressive era. As a student at Harvard, he came to believe that reason and science would allow his generation to "treat life not as something given but as something to be shaped." He worshiped Theodore Roosevelt, and after graduation he set out to become a political journalist, studying under Lincoln Steffens and helping to start a magazine called *The New Republic.* "It was a happy time, those last few years before the First World War," he remembered many years later; "the air was soft, and it was easy for a young man to believe in the inevitability of progress, in the perfectibility of man and of society, and in the sublimation of evil."

The European war crushed those hopes. Just days after Lippmann left Belgium, German armies sliced through the neutral nation in a great wheeling maneuver that aimed to encircle the French Army, but before the ring could be closed, reserve troops from Paris, many of them rushed to the front in taxicabs, struck the German flank and stopped the advance at the Marne River in northeastern France. By November, the western front had stabilized into the bloody stalemate that would prevail for the next four years, absorbing between 5,000 and 50,000 lives a day. The machine gun defeated all attempts to break through the enemy's trench lines. Colossal artillery, poison gas, submarine warfare, aerial bombardment, and suicide charges would each be used in desperate bids to break the deadlock, and all would fail.

The carnage horrified Americans. German soldiers used terror against Belgian civilians, killing over 5,000 hostages. Two weeks after the invasion began, German troops burned the picturesque medieval city of Louvain in retaliation for a Belgian attack. "We will teach them to respect Germany. For generations people will come here to see what we have done," a commander, standing in the ashes of the city, told an American diplomat.

As a college student in the early years of the century, Walter Lippmann believed technology and reason would conquer social problems. World War I would shatter the optimism of his generation.

"We Americans have been witnessing supreme drama, clenching our fists, talking, yet unable to fasten any reaction to realities," Lippmann told his readers. "We are choked by feelings unexpressed and movements arrested in mid-air." For three years, Americans watched as a civilization they had admired sank into barbarism. They recoiled from the war's violence and the motives behind it, and they debated what, if anything, they could do to stop it.

When the United States entered the fight in 1917, it mobilized its economy and society to send an army of a million to Europe. The war both interrupted and culminated the progressive movement. In the name of efficiency, government stepped in to manage the economy as never before, placing corporations under federal supervision but allowing them to prosper. The war transformed many of the most controversial items on the progressive social agenda—women's suffrage, prohibition of alcohol, restrictions on prostitution—into matters of national urgency. The federal government used its control of the mails to punish political dissenters. On the battlefield, American forces brought swift triumph, but victory failed to impose a new stability. Defeated powers collapsed into revolution and anarchy. New ideologies threatened American ideals. The experience of war brought home the dangers of a modern, interdependent world, but it also revealed the United States' power to shape the global future. ▪

KEY TOPICS

• Wilson's attempt to replace war and revolution with a new order based on free trade and international law

• Wilson's choice between the external danger posed by an allied defeat and the risk of widening political divisions in the United States

• War regimentation accelerates trends started in the progressive era

• Americans' reinforced faith in modernism and the virtues of their own society

• New fears of internal subversion in America

The Challenges of Revolution and Neutrality

The Great War disturbed the American president's sense that order could be imposed on the conduct of foreign relations. Along with other progressives, Wilson saw similar evils assailing the United States from within and without. Revolution, militarism, and corrupt diplomacy threatened democracy and stability outside of the country just as surely as labor wars, reckless corporations, and corrupt officials threatened the republic internally. Imperial powers practiced the same kind of predatory capitalism that the Standard Oil Company did. Wilson opposed revolutionary radicalism at home and abroad, and he tried to fashion "organic" institutions and processes to mediate disputes and foster orderly change. Like reform, stability within a modern, interconnected world was not a goal but a process, but Wilson also believed order had to be forced on those who resisted. Opponents of domestic reform "who will not be convinced," he wrote, deserved to be "crushed." He felt the same about the opponents of international order.

Imposing that order, the president believed, was both a political duty and an economic opportunity for the United States. An expanding commercial power like the United States had talent, technology, and capital to share with the world. "Prosperity in one part of the world ministers to prosperity everywhere," he declared, but it could only do so in markets protected from both economic and political chaos. Imperialism and revolution endangered the free trade that was necessary for world peace and the economic health of the United States. They also threatened to close markets and breed rivalries that could lead to war. It was the government's duty to assure the safety of foreign travel, investments, and markets in order to secure American prosperity and its benefits for the world.

This combination of idealism and self-interest, humanitarianism and force, produced a foreign policy that often seemed contradictory. Wilson renounced "dollar diplomacy," only to use Taft's tactics himself when the open door was threatened in China. He atoned for the imperialism of prior administrations, but he intervened repeatedly in Central America. Secretary of State William Jennings Bryan negotiated a series of conciliation, or "cooling-off" treaties that required arbitration before resorting to war, but Wilson was seldom willing to submit his own policies to arbitration. He believed the United States had a mission to promote democracy, yet he considered many peoples, including Filipinos, unready to govern themselves.

These contradictions are explained by Wilson's view of history. As he saw it, the modernizing forces of commerce and communications were creating a global society with new rules of international conduct. He also felt that forces of the past—militarism and revolution—threatened to "throw the world back three or four centuries." The United States had to "set up a new international psychology," new norms and institutions, at a moment when the past and the future were locked in struggle. In Europe, Wilson's sympathies lay with Britain and France; even so, he felt the United States had to remain out of war. With Europe aflame, the United States remained the sole voice of reason, the hope for the future. "Somebody must keep the great economic processes of the world of business alive," he protested. He was also preoccupied with matters closer at hand. In April 1914 American troops had invaded Mexico in an attempt to overthrow its revolutionary government.

The Mexican Revolution

In May 1911, Francisco Madero's rebels overthrew the dictatorship of Porfirio Díaz, ending over three decades of enforced order and rapid industrialization. Díaz and a clique of intellectuals and planners known as the *científicos* had spanned the country with railroads, built up Mexican industry, and after the discovery of oil at Tampico in 1900, turned Mexico into one of the world's leading exporters of petroleum. Foreign investment poured in, and by 1911 Americans owned 40 percent of the property in the country, more than the share owned by the Mexicans themselves (see chapter 19). As the government relied more heavily on its foreign creditors, it neglected the sources of its power: the army and the state governors. Mexicans grew to resent the privileged colonies of foreign businessmen and the heavy taxes the regime needed to keep industrialization going. When Madero's revolt broke out, the army folded, Díaz fled to Spain, and power changed hands in a nearly bloodless coup.

The fall of Díaz gave the United States little cause for concern: Madero left foreign investments undisturbed and held an election to confirm his presidency, but in February 1913, just two weeks before Wilson's inauguration, General Victoriano Huerta seized power and had Madero shot. Outraged by the army's betrayal of the president and the constitution, Mexican states raised armies and revolted against Huerta's regime, beginning one of the twentieth century's longest and bloodiest civil wars. In the mountains south of Mexico City, Emiliano Zapata led a guerrilla resistance. Meanwhile along Mexico's northern border, Venustiano Carranza organized a constitutionalist army and bought weapons in Texas and New Mexico.

Britain and the U. S. ambassador in Mexico urged Wilson to support Huerta, but to the new president this was a "government of butchers." Wilson denounced Huerta, warning that he would "teach the South American republics to elect good men." He gave arms to Carranza's soldiers and sent 7,000 marines to occupy Mexico's largest port city, Veracruz, in April 1914. The invasion radicalized the revolution, unifying all sides against the United States and its investments and influ-ence in Mexico. When Carranza deposed Huerta a few months later, he promised to nationalize oilfields owned by Americans.

Still determined to "put Mexico on a moral basis," Wilson repeated the mistakes he had made in dealing with Huerta. He pressured Carranza to resign while providing arms to his enemy, Francisco "Pancho" Villa. Joining forces with Zapata, Villa briefly seized the capital at the end of 1914, but Carranza counterattacked, reducing Villa's army to outlaw bands scattered along the northern border. Reluctantly, Wilson recognized the Carranza government and cut off supplies to Villa, hoping that at last the Mexican problem would go away. He was not so lucky. Stung by Wilson's betrayal, Villa crossed the border and attacked the U. S. Thirteenth Cavalry outpost at Columbus, New Mexico, killing 17 Americans and stealing horses and guns.

Furious, Wilson launched a "punitive expedition," sending 10,000 troops under General John J. Pershing into Mexico in pursuit of Villa (see Map 22-1). Like the Veracruz adventure, Pershing's invasion unified Mexicans against the United States. The force penetrated as far as Parral, where it clashed with Carranza's army. Wilson now faced a choice between declaring war on Mexico and giving up the hunt for Pancho Villa. He ordered Pershing home. After three years of trying to bring democracy and stability to Mexico, Wilson had nothing to show for his ef-

In April 1914, Wilson ordered the capture of Mexico's largest port, Veracruz. The Mexican population resisted, and American warships shelled the city before Veracruz was taken in bitter street fighting.

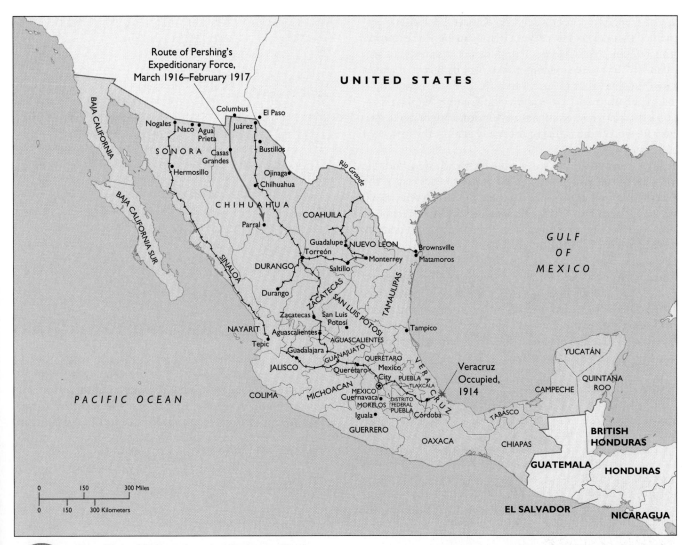

Map 22-1   Mexican Invasion Routes to Veracruz.
General John Pershing led 10,000 troops together with observation aircraft and a convoy of trucks 419 miles into Mexico on a fruitless hunt for Francisco Villa's band. Federal forces loyal to Carranza confronted Pershing near Parral, bringing the U.S. advance to a halt.

forts. Villa was still at large, Carranza was seeking German arms, the civil war still raged, and American lives and property were more in danger than ever.

Bringing Order to the Caribbean

In principle, Wilson opposed imperialism and gunboat diplomacy, but his desire to impose order on neighboring countries led him to use force again and again. During his first year as president he promised that the United States would "never again seek one additional foot of territory by conquest" and that principles would take precedence over material interests. However, Wilson sent the marines into more countries in Latin America than any other president. United States troops quashed a revolution in Haiti in 1915

and stayed on until 1934. Marines landed in the Dominican Republic the following year to supervise an election. The U.S. turned the country into a protectorate and fought a guerilla war there until 1924. Wilson kept in place the marines that Taft had sent to occupy Honduras, Panama, and Nicaragua, and briefly sent troops into Cuba. From each of these countries Wilson obtained the right to intervene if necessary to restore order. These agreements reassured American business that the United States would maintain what Wilson called "orderly processes" in the "markets which we must supply."

Congress had less enthusiasm for treaties that promised to embroil American soldiers in one crisis after another. Progressive senators wondered why Wilson busted trusts and reorganized banks at home but put the marines at their service abroad. Senator Robert La Follette explained that corporations were in the business of exploitation, whether in Wisconsin or Mexico: Business, he explained, "makes so much money out of us that it creates a huge surplus" that must be invested in "weak and undeveloped countries." La Follette and George W. Norris argued that in some countries revolutions might be necessary to protect the rights of the many against the power of the few.

Opponents of Wilson's policies in Mexico and the Caribbean also urged the United States to stay out of the Great War in Europe. On August 29, 1914 some 1,500 women, dressed in black, marched down Fifth Avenue in New York City to oppose the occupation of Veracruz and the war in Europe. In April 1916, progressive writers and social workers met at New York's Henry Street Settlement House to organize the American Union Against Militarism and protest against intervention in Mexico. Jane Addams regarded war as "a throwback in the scientific sense." She and Carrie Chapman Catt founded the Woman's Peace Party, whose 25,000 members supported

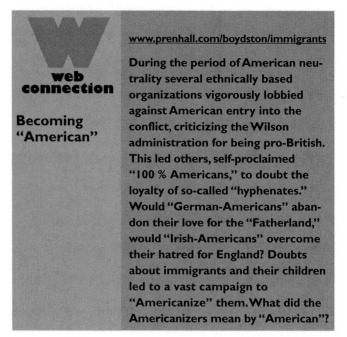

Breaking with other Progressive Era reformers, Jane Addams (left) remained a pacifist even after the declaration of war. In 1919 she founded the Women's International League for Peace and Freedom.

a mediated settlement to the European conflict. Addams, who later won the Nobel Peace Prize for her efforts, traveled through Europe meeting with leaders of the belligerent countries in an attempt to convene a peace conference. Peace advocates supported Wilson's policy of neutrality but saw signs that the United States was being drawn into war.

A One-Sided Neutrality

As German armies crossed Belgium in August 1914, Woodrow Wilson declared a policy of strict neutrality and called on Americans to "be impartial in thought as well as in action." The war took him by surprise, and like Addams he found it "incredible" that civilized nations could display such savagery. His first worry was that America's immigrant communities, filled with people newly arrived from the countries now at war, would take sides. Americans, he worried, "may be divided in camps of hostile opinion, hot against each other."

With 32 million Americans either born abroad or having at least one parent from overseas, and over 10 million with family ties to Germany and Austria-Hungary, Wilson's concern was understandable. Shortly after the crisis began, 450 steelworkers from Gary, Indiana, enlisted in the Serbian Army. Irish Americans, who wanted independence for their homeland, sided with Germany against England. The Allies (Britain, France, Italy, and Russia) and the Central Powers (Germany, Austria-Hungary, and Turkey) did their best to sway opinion. Britain cut the telegraph cable between Germany and the United States, making sure that news had to pass through censors in London. In 1915 a New York City subway policeman found a stack of German documents revealing secret plans to fund peace groups in the United States. Both the president and the press worried that propaganda could push the electorate to demand American intervention.

Wilson did his best to appear completely neutral. He dispatched his closest aide, Colonel Edward House, to Europe with offers to broker a peace agreement. He told Americans that this was a war "whose causes cannot touch us," but privately the president believed that a German victory would be a catastrophe. Protected by Britain's control of the seas, the United States had thrived and expanded its influence during the previous century. If the Allies were defeated, he told his brother-in-law, "the United States, itself, will have to become a military nation, for Germany will push her conquests into South America, if not actually into the United States." With Europe and possibly Asia controlled by a single power, the United States would be vulnerable and alone.

Modern warfare and commerce made true neutrality difficult, and in choosing policies Wilson's bias became clear. The belligerent powers desperately needed everything the United States had to export: food, textiles, steel, chemicals, and fuel. Wilson refused to follow the example Thomas Jefferson set during the Napoleonic Wars and ban trade with all warring countries. The economy rose on a tide of war orders, mainly from the Allies. Factories hired extra shifts. Farm prices rose to an all-time high.

American trade with the Allies grew to more than 3 billion dollars by 1916, while trade with the Central Powers sank from 170 million dollars to less than 1 million dollars. The House of Morgan and other banks generously extended credit to Britain and France and less enthusiastically to Germany. U. S. loans to the Allies grew to 2.5 billion dollars by 1917, but the Central Powers received only 127 million dollars in credit. Although the United States had not formally taken sides, the American economy was already in the war on the side of the Allies.

Wilson's reaction to the British and German naval blockades helped the Allies capture American trade. The British fleet closed European ports and laid mines across the North Sea, preventing American ships from reaching Germany. London's actions violated the "freedom of the seas," which the United States fought to uphold in the War of 1812, but the Wilson administration never strenuously protested or used force to break the blockade. Instead, it acknowledged that Britain's concern for its "national safety" might justify the violation. Wilson reacted differently to Germany's submarine blockade of Britain. On February 4, 1915, Berlin announced a policy of "unrestricted submarine warfare" against ships entering a "war zone" around the British Isles. Britain was able to stop, board, and inspect ships before escorting them into an Allied port. A German *Unterseeboot* or U-boat, a small, fragile submarine with a crew of only 32 men, could not do that without giving up the stealth and surprise that were its only weapons.

The *Lusitania*'s Last Voyage

Germany posted advertisements in American newspapers warning passengers not to travel on ships bound for the war zone; Americans were horrified by the targeting of ships carrying civilian men, women, and children. The State Department was divided. Robert Lansing, the department's counselor, condemned submarine attacks as an offense against law and morality. Secretary of State William Jennings Bryan wanted to bar Americans from traveling on all belligerent ships in order to prevent a tragedy from inflaming **public opinion.** Wilson sided with Lansing and declared that Germany would be held to "strict accountability" for American lives or property destroyed by U-boats.

On the afternoon of May 7, 1915, submarine U-20 sighted the luxury liner *Lusitania* off the coast of Ireland. A torpedo struck the starboard side behind the bridge and exploded. In 18 minutes the massive ship broke apart and sank. Of almost 2,000 passengers aboard, 1,198 drowned, including 94 children. Of these, 124 were Americans. Newspaper headlines accused Germany of savagery. The condemnations, the *Literary Digest* observed, seemed "to be limited only by the restrictions of the English language." To Theodore Roosevelt it was a crime to shame Blackbeard's ghost, "piracy on a vaster scale of murder than the old-time pirates ever practiced." A German in Berlin remarked that the Americans she knew "had always professed to be neutral. But a sudden change now took place. . . . Their rage and horror at the idea that Americans had been killed knew no bounds."

Wilson's advisers again disagreed on how to respond. Bryan wanted to balance an official protest with a simultaneous denunciation of Britain's violation of neutral rights. Wilson ignored him and demanded that Germany pay reparations and stop attacking ships without warning. He hinted that unless these demands were met, the United States would break relations. Accusing Wilson of pushing the country into war, Bryan resigned.

Public opinion was equally divided. Newspapers called for war, but as Lippmann wrote to a friend in England, "the feeling against war in this country is a great deal deeper than you would imagine by reading editorials." In early 1916 antiwar senators introduced resolutions that would have refused passports to Americans planning to travel on belligerent ships. When Germany promised not to attack passenger liners without warning, Wilson accepted this guarantee, known as the *Sussex* Pledge, as a diplomatic triumph. The *Sussex* Pledge restored calm, but official and public opinion had turned against Germany. The *Lusitania*'s sinking made the worst accusations believable. The rules of neutrality, as applied by Wilson, strongly favored the Allies. American involvement no longer seemed impossible.

GROWING UP IN AMERICA

Plattsburg

Dawn rose over Lake Champlain as a special train pulled onto a siding near the old army barracks at Plattsburg, on the lake's New York side. The passengers, young men in their 20s and early 30s, some in civilian clothes, others already in uniform, filed from the cars and stood at attention on the platform. These were no ordinary recruits. They included diplomat and Morgan partner Willard Straight, Thomas Miller, a twenty-nine-year old congressman, Raynal C. Bolling, a top executive at United States Steel, southern plantation owners, Ivy League professors, the editor of *Vanity Fair,* and the mayor of New York.

They were there for four weeks of push-ups, forced marches, and intensive military training, although none had actually enlisted in the Army. Drill sergeants called them "tourists," but the recruits saw themselves as the bearers of a new martial spirit. "This was young America," one observed, "a very decent sort of thing, a thing even thrilling to touch shoulders with for a little time."

The camp was conceived in New York's Harvard Club by an alliance of generals, businessmen, and professors. Leonard Wood, commander of the Army's eastern division, wanted to create an army reserve that could be used in a foreign war. University presidents suggested that he organize a summer military camp for college students. Students needed the discipline and exercise, and the Army needed educated commanders. The president of Harvard explained that the camps would train "a class of men" that would supply "a large proportion of the commissioned officers" in the next war. Private businessmen provided funds, and the first college camps bivouacked at Gettysburg, Pennsylvania, and Monterey, California, in the summer of 1913.

When war erupted in Europe the following summer, young business leaders clamored for a camp of their own. Over a thousand people jammed the Harvard Club on

Theodore Roosevelt and General Leonard Wood helped to organize the Businessmen's Military Training Camp at Plattsburg.

The Drift to War

The *Lusitania* disaster opened an unbridgeable gap between progressives on the issue of the war. Peace advocates like Addams, Bryan, and La Follette urged a stricter neutrality to prevent another tragedy that might require retaliation, and letters to congressmen continued to run heavily against involvement. Others believed war, or preparations for war, were justified. The *Lusitania* incident "united Englishmen and Americans in a common grief and a common indignation" and might "unite them in a common war," Lippmann predicted. Theodore Roosevelt clamored for it. Had he been president, he told a friend, he would make "the Germans either absolutely alter all of their conduct or else put them into war with us." He en-

June 14, 1915, five weeks after the *Lusitania* disaster, to hear Wood announce the Businessmen's Military Training Camp at Plattsburg. Word spread through alumni societies and professional associations, and 1,300 of "the best and most desirable men" signed up. Plattsburg emptied "the whole table at Delmonico's," one organizer beamed. Young men from the wealthiest and most prestigious families shelled out 30 dollars for a khaki uniform and mess kit.

The press sniped at this new fashion for militarism, but Willard Straight replied that the camp's organizers "do not propose to militarize the American nation. They seek rather to civilize the American military." Harvard was out to show West Point how to run an army, but two weeks of close formation drill was enough to give the "tourists" a new respect for professional soldiers. The recruits answered reveille at 5:55 A.M. After breakfast and inspection, calisthenics and drill began at 7:25 and went until supper. Top college atheletes found it gruelling. Regular infantry marched 30 miles in a day, but at the end of four weeks the recruits could barely manage 10.

At evening campfires, recruits discussed politics, war, and what the Plattsburg experience meant. Theodore Roosevelt, who had three sons and a nephew at the camp, came one evening to denounce "the professional pacifist, the poltroon, and the college sissy" who were trying to keep the United States out of the war. Some recruits agreed with Roosevelt that the United States must be prepared for war, but others saw preparedness as a way to avoid war. They agreed that all young Americans could benefit from military drill.

Recruits talked about the wholesome, democratic influence of military training. It instilled "discipline, manliness, and that comradeship in a high common purpose which grows so slack ... in a society governed by purely economic conditions," one observed. A millionaire looked like anyone else in uniform, and a journalist remarked that "each reservist left his worldly goods, his 'pull,' his record of past performances at home." Just as in sports, the only standard was how well one performed now. The camp included a large number of college athletes, including Yale fullback Frank Butterworth; Hamilton Fish, Jr., the captain of Harvard's football team; and his coach, Percy Haughton. Not surprisingly, recruits saw what one described as the "obvious parallel between a football team and an army, and between the training of a fullback and a first-rate squad leader." War, he wrote, was the "real game."

In articles written afterwards, and memoirs many years later, the recruits remembered the emotions stirred by watching the flag lowered at sunset to the solemn strains of a bugle sounding retreat. "There is a fine restraint in military ceremony," Harvard philosophy professor Ralph Barton Perry noted, "that enables the purest product of New England self-repression to *feel*." "I do not believe that anyone in the camp," John J. McCloy, an Amherst college student who would become an adviser to five presidents, told a friend, "no matter how tired or blue he felt, ever 'stood retreat' without having a tiny thrill run up his spine." Like McCloy, many of the young men at Plattsburg fought in World War I, served the federal government in World War II, and ran law firms, industries, embassies, and government agencies during the cold war. For them, Plattsburg was the beginning of America's adventure in world leadership. "Plattsburg was not just a military training camp," historian Kai Bird later wrote, "it was, in a way, a secular retreat for a whole generation. There, amid simple, material surroundings, the upper class elite underwent a conversion experience of patriotism."

dorsed the preparedness campaign mounted by organizations like the National Security League and the American Defense Society. Thousands of preparedness supporters marched down New York's Fifth Avenue under an electric sign declaring "Absolute and Unqualified Loyalty to our Country."

The preparedness leagues, headed by businessmen and conservative political figures, called attention to the pathetic state of the armed forces, which were fit only for garrison duty in far-flung imperial outposts. When Pancho Villa attacked the 13th Cavalry at Columbus, New Mexico, every one of the Americans' machine guns jammed. Pershing's punitive expedition suffered from chronic shortages of trucks, planes, and supplies. The U. S. Army was tiny, smaller than the army of Portugal. The preparedness campaign adopted patriotic rituals once

The sinking of the Lusitania, and artistic dramatizations like this one, encouraged Wilson to abandon neutrality. He insisted that Germany unilaterally cease attacks on liners. Secretary of State Bryan resigned in protest, strengthening the administration's tilt toward the Allies.

reserved for elections. Wilson himself led the parade in Washington in 1916, wearing a red tie, white trousers, and a blue blazer. "What a picture," Mrs. Wilson remembered, "as the breeze caught and carried out the Stars and Stripes!"

The Election of 1916

In campaigning for re-election, Wilson had to reconcile the public's overwhelming desire for peace with his own feeling that the United States could not remain uninvolved for much longer. "I know that you are depending upon me to keep this nation out of war," he reminded a Milwaukee audience, but "that depends upon what others do." Nonetheless he campaigned under the slogan "He kept us out of war." It was a sure vote-getter. One of the year's most popular songs was "I Didn't Raise My Boy to Be a Soldier."

The preparedness issue reunited Theodore Roosevelt with the Republicans. Bringing the Progressive Party with him, he endorsed Supreme Court Justice Charles Evans Hughes, the GOP candidate. Hughes attacked Wilson for failing to defend American honor in Mexico and Europe. The party organizations took a back seat to modern advertising campaigns waged by poster and press release. "This campaign would be won or lost with publicity," a Democratic official forecast (see Map 22-2). Both sides mixed **patriotism** with attacks on "hyphenated" Americans. Democrats charged Hughes with sympathy to Germany, while Republicans accused Wilson of "leniency with the British Empire." Woman suffragists campaigned

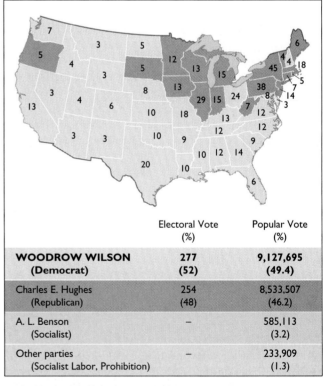

	Electoral Vote (%)	Popular Vote (%)
WOODROW WILSON (Democrat)	**277** **(52)**	**9,127,695** **(49.4)**
Charles E. Hughes (Republican)	254 (48)	8,533,507 (46.2)
A. L. Benson (Socialist)	–	585,113 (3.2)
Other parties (Socialist Labor, Prohibition)	–	233,909 (1.3)

Map 22-2   The Election of 1916.
With Theodore Roosevelt's endorsement, former New York governor Charles Evans Hughes came close to defeating Wilson. The president doubted the country could avoid war much longer, but the war was his best campaign issue.

A national preparedness movement campaigned for compulsory military training and modernization of the U.S. Army, which ranked 17th in the world. Campaigners used parades, such as this one in Mobile, to overcome public doubts. Some residents of Mobile could remember greeting the U.S. Army on different terms.

against Wilson. They whistle-stopped across the country in a train called the *Golden Special* and picketed the White House with signs asking "Mr. President? How long must women wait for liberty?"

Although the country remained strongly Republican, Hughes proved an inept campaigner. He won pivotal states in the North and East—New York, Pennsylvania, and Illinois—but lost in the South and West. Wilson won narrowly; a shift of a few thousand votes in California would have cost him the election. Republicans gained seats in the House and the Senate. Still, re-election freed Wilson to pursue a more vigorous foreign policy. As Lippmann realized, "What we're electing is a war president—not the man who kept us out of war."

The Last Attempts at Peace

After the election, Wilson launched a new peace initiative. Looking for an opening for compromise after years of stalemate, he asked each of the belligerent powers to state its war aims. The results were disappointing. Each side insisted on punishing the other and enlarging its own territories. Moreover, when Wilson pointed out the similarities, British officials reacted testily, calling Wilson an "ass." Going before Congress in January 1917, the president called for a "peace without victory," based on self-determination of all nations and the creation of an international organization to enforce peace.

Germany toyed with accepting Wilson's proposals and decided to wait. Having subdued the Balkans and pushed deep into Russia by February 1917, it could begin shifting armies from the Eastern Front to France. It seemed that the summer of 1917 might bring a German victory. To accelerate that outcome, Berlin ordered the resumption of unrestricted submarine warfare. U-boats torpedoed British passenger liners and American merchant ships. In late February, British naval intelligence officers showed the U. S. ambassador in London an intercepted telegram from the German foreign minister, Arthur Zimmermann, to his ambassador in Mexico City. It instructed the ambassador in Mexico City that if the United States joined the war on the side of the Allies he should invite Carranza to form an alliance with Germany. Together, Germany and Mexico would then fight to regain "lost territories" in Arizona, California, and New Mexico. The Zimmermann Telegram confirmed Americans' darkest fears about the implications of a German victory, and it provoked alarm in the West, where antiwar feeling had been strongest. If Wilson did not declare war now, Roosevelt declared, he would "skin him alive."

Americans disagreed then, as historians do today, on why the United States went to war. Economic and strategic issues were at stake, as was national honor and the ability to shape the peace. Critics pointed to the influence of munitions makers and banks that stood to gain from war.

"Where Morgan's money went, your boy's blood must go, else Morgan will lose his money. That's all there is to it," Georgia politician Tom Watson explained. Publicly and in private, Wilson stressed two considerations that led to his decision: First, attacks on American ships had forced him into a position where he had to retaliate. Second, joining the war was necessary in order for the United States to influence the peace settlement. The treaty conference afterward would settle scores of issues in which American interests would be involved. Unless it took part in the conflict, Wilson told Jane Addams, the United States would have to shout "through a crack in the door."

Wilson's War Aims

Rain was falling on the evening of April 2, 1917, as Wilson, accompanied by cavalry, rode up Pennsylvania Avenue to ask Congress for war. In the crowds lining the curb, some onlookers cheered and waved paper flags while others stared silently at the president's black car. The speaker called the crowded House chamber to order as Wilson made his way to the podium. Wilson expected to have to fight for a declaration of war. He was known for his oratory, and he put all of his skill into this address. The war, he told his audience, was in its last stages. American armies could bring it to a quick, merciful end. The United States had tried to stand apart from the conflict, but it had failed. Neutrality had provided no safety for American travelers or American trade. The only hope for avoiding future wars that might pose even graver dangers to the nation was to place the United States in a position to dictate the peace, to establish a "concert of free peoples as shall bring peace and safety to all nations and make the world itself at last free." This would be a war to end all wars, to make the world safe for democracy.

In urging Congress to vote for war, the president explicitly rejected the war aims of the Allies. "We have no quarrel with the German people," he said of the nation that would soon be at the receiving end of American artillery. "We have no feeling towards them but one of sympathy and friendship." His argument was with the kaiser and all other emperors and autocrats who stood in the way of his plan to rebuild the world on "American principles." Wilson realized, however, that France and Britain, both of which had large colonial empires, did not stand for democracy or self-determination. Roosevelt and Henry Cabot Lodge wanted victory for the Allies and assumed that American war aims would resemble those of Britain and France. Wilson contended that "we have no allies." The United States would be an "associated power."

Allied diplomacy contradicted Wilson's sense of what a progressive foreign policy should be. He knew about secret treaties that would divide the German and Austrian empires among the Allies after victory. He wanted to prevent the kind of peace that would lead to more imperialism, absolutism, and war, and he believed the conclusion of the war would allow only a momentary chance to establish institutions that could enforce a durable peace. He told his adviser Edward House to concentrate on the "*method* of peace rather than the terms of peace."

House assembled a secret committee, known as the Inquiry, and assigned it to draft a peace proposal, based on "American principles," that would be both generous enough to show "sympathy and friendship" to the German people and harsh enough to punish their leaders. Made up of economists, historians, geographers, and legal experts, it met in the cramped offices of the American Geographical Society in New York. House named Lippmann as the group's secretary. Working day and night, the Inquiry produced a set of fourteen recommendations that redrew the boundaries of Europe, created a league of nations, and based peace on the principles of freedom of the seas, open door trade, and ethnic self-determination.

The Fight in Congress

During the ovation after Wilson's speech to Congress, one senator stood silently chewing gum, his arms folded across his chest. Robert La Follette told his colleagues that if this was a war for democracy, it should be declared democratically. He asked for a national referendum on the war. The country had voted only five months earlier for the peace candidate for president, and there were strong reasons to suspect a declaration would fail a national vote. Representatives who polled their districts found that voters opposed American entry, in many places by two to one. Midwestern farmers, William Allen White reported from Iowa, "don't seem to get the war."

Prowar representatives blocked the movement for a referendum and brought the declaration to a vote on April 6, when it passed by a margin of 82 to six in the Senate and 373 to 50 in the House. As debate turned to questions of how to pay for the war and who would fight in it, the divisions resurfaced. Wilson wanted to raise an army by universal conscription, the first draft since the Civil War. The 1917 draft law created a selective service system comprised of 4,000 local boards manned by volunteers. Men between the ages of 18 and 45 were required to register. Both supporters and opponents believed the draft would be used to mold young men. It would be a "melting pot," said one representative, that would "break down distinctions of race and class and mold us into a new nation and bring forth new Americans." La Follette countered that the new Americans would be like the new Germans, militarist "automatons" indoctrinated by the Army.

Congressman Claude Kitchin argued that if young men were to be drafted, profits should be drafted too. He proposed to pay for the war with large increases in taxes on incomes, corporations, and war profits. Business interests wanted to finance the war instead with sales taxes and bonds, passing the cost on to consumers and future generations. "It is not right," an editorial claimed, "that the present generation should bear the whole burden of a conflict fought for the freedom of our children's children." Senator Porter J. McCumber (R-ND) worried that if the rich were taxed heavily it would "dampen their ardor and destroy their war spirit."

Newspapers and politicians denounced the antiwar progressives as traitors who belonged either in jail or in Germany. They had too few votes to stop conscription, but they managed to make an exemption for conscientious objectors and to reduce some of the taxes on sugar, bread, and coffee used to pay for the war. The voices of opposition were soon silenced by patriotic calls for unity at all costs. There was little room in wartime America for dissent or divided loyalties. "I pray God," Wilson avowed, "that some day historians will remember these momentous years as the years which made a single people of the great body of those who call themselves Americans."

Mobilizing the Nation and the Economy

News of the war declaration, carried in banner headlines on Easter Sunday, 1917, set the nation astir with activity. William Percy, a college student from Mississippi, rushed home to Greenville and found women "knitting and beginning to take one lump of sugar instead of two, men within draft age were discussing which branch of the service they had best to enter, men above draft age were heading innumerable patriotic committees and making speeches . . . You could sense the pleasurable stir of nobility and the bustle of idealism." Army units erected camps outside of major cities, and young men lined up to enlist. Businesses converted to war production. Presses at the Government Printing Office began stamping out the necessary forms, and the War Department stockpiled 12,000 typewriters to be used in filling out those forms. Hull-House started a bond drive, eventually raising $50,000 from its neighbors in the Nineteenth Ward.

Wilson recognized that he was asking the nation to undertake an unprecedented effort. Raising an army of over three million men, supplying it with the equipment of modern war, and transporting it across submarine-infested waters to France were herculean feats. By midsummer, there were more men at work building army barracks than had been in the Union and Confederate armies at Gettysburg. Americans would spare from their dinner plates and send to Europe 1.8 million tons of meat, 8.8 million tons of cereals, and 1.5 million tons of sugar. Factories that produced sewing machines, automobiles, and textiles would retool to make howitzers, tanks, and explosives.

Accomplishing these tasks placed tremendous strains on the American people and economy. Wilson and others feared that it could widen political divisions and destroy the achievements progressives had made in the previous 15 years, but others felt that sharing the sacrifices of war would consolidate the progressives' gains. "We shall exchange our material thinking for something quite different," the General Federation of Women's Clubs predicted. "We shall all be enfranchised, prohibition will prevail, many wrongs will be righted, vampires and grafters and slackers will be relegated to a class by themselves." Lippmann hoped the war would bring a new American revolution. "We are living and shall live all our lives now," he predicted, "in a revolutionary world."

Enforcing Patriotism

The summons to a war to end all wars allowed many progressive pacifists to put aside their opposition and join in the task at hand. German and Irish Americans forgot their reservations amid the general outpouring of patriotism. Still, some resistance remained. The Socialist Party, whose presidential candidate polled over half a million votes in 1916, maintained its opposition to "the system of exploitation and class rule which is upheld and strengthened by military power and sham national patriotism." Midwestern farmers continued to grumble. In Oklahoma, a group of poor tenant farmers vowed to march on Washington, D. C., gathering an army of draft resisters along the way, but the Green Corn Rebellion was stopped by a sheriff's posse before it could get started.

Authorities dealt severely with dissent. Suspicions about the loyalties of ethnic communities and fears that pacifists and "slackers" were in league with German saboteurs fed the hysteria. Since 1914, mysterious explosions had disrupted American munitions factories and ports. On July 30, 1916, across the river from New York City, the largest arms storage facility in the country, known as Black Tom, exploded, perforating the Statue of Liberty with shrapnel. Thousands of pounds of shells and guns bound for Russia were destroyed. Four days after Wilson declared war, saboteurs struck again, blowing up a munitions factory outside of Philadelphia and killing 112 workers, mostly women and girls. Federal agents rounded up large numbers of aliens, but the fear of internal enemies persisted.

Congress gave the president sweeping powers to suppress dissent. The Espionage Act (1917) and the Sedition Act (1918) effectively outlawed opposition to the war and used the postal service and the Justice Department to catch offenders. The Post Office banned socialist magazines like *The Masses* and Catholic publications that advocated independence for Ireland. The Justice Department raided the Chicago offices of the Industrial Workers of the World and sent 96 of the union's leaders to prison on charges of sedition. William D. "Big Bill" Haywood was sentenced to 20 years. Eugene V. Debs, leader of the Socialist Party, received 10 years for telling a Cincinnati audience that "You need to know that you are fit for something better than slavery and cannon fodder."

The Justice Department also went after less obvious targets. Moviemaker Robert Goldstein was sentenced to 10 years for producing "The Spirit of '76," a film about the American Revolution, on the grounds that it was anti-British. An Ohio judge sent John White, a farmer, to jail for comparing what German troops did in Belgium to what American soldiers had done in the Philippines. The Justice Department organized a volunteer auxiliary, the American Protective League, with a quarter of a million members who carried secret service IDs, opened mail, wiretapped phones, and conducted searches. In September 1918, the APL conducted a "slacker raid" in downtown Manhattan, arresting suspected draft dodgers in offices, subways, and shops. The dragnet pulled in more than 50,000 people.

States also passed laws criminalizing opposition to the war and deputizing volunteer enforcers. Indiana's Council for Defense licensed citizens to raid German homes, prevent church services in German, and make sure German Americans conserved meat and wheat and bought war bonds. Towns, schools, and clubs with German-sounding names changed them. East Germantown, Indiana, became Pershing. Hamburgers became "liberty sandwiches." School systems in the Midwest that for decades had taught math and science in German stopped teaching the language altogether. Americans who had once proudly displayed their ethnicity now took pains to disguise it.

Mennonites, Jehovah's Witnesses, and other pacifist faiths faced their own ordeals. Some sects had come to America to avoid conscription in Germany or Russia. Many could not comply even with the conscientious objector statute, which required submission to military control. Fifteen hundred Mennonites and Hutterites fled to Canada to avoid being placed in camps. Thirty-four members of a pacifist sect called the Molokans trooped into the courthouse in Phoenix, Arizona, to face martyrdom. Inside, they sang hymns as their families wept. They were turned over to the Army, court-martialed, and sent to Leavenworth.

Advertising the War

Josephus Daniels, the secretary of the Navy, enlisted the new art of mass advertising to overcome the public's indifference and mold the American people into a "white-hot mass" afire with "devotion, courage, and deathless determination." He turned to former muckraker George Creel, who had helped to mastermind Wilson's publicity campaign in 1916. Creel called his propaganda bureau, the Committee on Public Information (CPI), "the greatest adventure in advertising." It made films, staged pageants, dispatched an army of "four-minute men"—trained to make

a pitch in exactly four minutes—on speaking tours, and churned out a river of display ads, billboards, posters, leaflets, and press releases. The CPI sold the war by telling Americans they were fighting to save their own homes. "If you don't come across," liberty bond customers learned, "the Kaiser will." In a famous poster, a fleet of German bombers pass over a shattered, headless Statue of Liberty while New York burns in the background. The inscription reads, "That liberty shall not perish from the earth."

Propaganda images represented Germany as menacing and bestial. An advertisement in the New York University alumni magazine asked "Are you going to let the Prussian python strike at your alma mater?" Another depicted Germany as a gorilla, a club in one hand and "Europa," a partly disrobed white woman, clutched in the other. Like Wilson, however, propaganda distinguished between Germany and the German people, especially the ones who had emigrated to the United States. The CPI distributed leaflets in German offering "Friendly Words to the Foreign Born." A poster showing central Europeans crowding a ship's rail to gaze upon the Statue of Liberty asked immigrants to "Remember your first thrill of American liberty." Billboards

The new business of commercial advertising came to the aid of the war effort, producing memorable images and slogans for mass-circulation magazines.

encouraged the foreign born to think of themselves as Americans.

Creel cast women as symbols of progress and **patriotism.** He drafted Charles Dana Gibson, whose "Gibson Girls" personified glamour in prewar advertisements, to depict women as mothers, nurses, and patriotic consumers. The National Woman's Party seized upon this theme and began highly publicized pickets outside the White House. Wilson endorsed the suffrage amendment in January 1918 in words that might have been lifted from a CPI poster: "We have made partners of the women in this war. Shall we admit them only to a partnership of suffering and sacrifice and toil and not to a partnership of privilege and right?"

Advertising mobilized American thought on behalf of the war effort and, in the process, advanced progressive agendas like assimilation of immigrants, women's suffrage, and reconciliation between labor and management.

Regimenting the Economy

The first prolonged conflict between industrial nations, World War I introduced the public to the term "total war." It was a struggle to protect not just territory or state interests but fundamental values and ways of life. It subordinated all human efforts, ideas, and institutions to the needs of the nation. By 1917 all of the resources, manpower, and productive capacities of the combatants had been mobilized behind massive war machines. Shortly after the War Department laid plans to place a million-man American Expeditionary Force (AEF) in Europe by the spring of 1918, it became clear that the economy of the United States would have to be reorganized, planned, and centralized in ways that had never been experienced before. The government began issuing contracts, enlisting men, and building camps, just as it had during the Civil War and the Spanish-American War, but on a gigantic scale.

To build ships to carry an army across the Atlantic, the United States commissioned the construction of a vast shipyard on Hog Island, just outside Philadelphia. It was to have 250 buildings and 80 miles of railroad track, employ 34,000 workers, and have facilities to build 50 ships simultaneously. When finished it would be larger than Britain's seven largest shipyards combined, but in April 1917, Hog Island was 847 acres of swamp. Wilson asked steelmaker Charles M. Schwab to build the facility, and Schwab signed contracts for the delivery of machinery, cement, steel, and timber. Manufacturers loaded goods on trains headed for Hog Island. The result was the Great Pile Up, the biggest traffic jam in railroad history. Railroads refused to coordinate traffic or to hire enough workers to unload, so cars began to back up on sidings in Philadelphia. Within weeks cars could get no closer than Pittsburgh or Buffalo, and loads were being dumped on the outskirts of cities. Schwab begged the railroads to cooperate, to no avail. The voluntary system for mobilizing the nation's re-sources had failed, and on January 1, 1918, Wilson nationalized the railroads.

The Hog Island fiasco demonstrated the need for national supervision of the economy. Wilson created a War Industries Board (WIB) to set prices, regulate manufacturing, and control transportation. The job was enormous, and the first WIB administrator had a nervous breakdown and quit. Wilson found the overseer he needed in Bernard Baruch, a Wall Street financier, who believed in central control of the economy by "socially responsible" businessmen. He drafted corporate executives to fill the top managerial positions and paid them a salary of a dollar a year. The president of the Aluminum Company of America became chairman of the WIB's aluminum committee, and a former top executive of John Deere and Co. was named to head the agricultural implements section.

The dollar-a-year men regimented the economy and put business at the service of government, but they also guaranteed profits and looked after manufacturers' long-term interests. One of their innovations was the "cost-plus" contract, which assured contractors the recovery of costs plus a percentage for profit. Under these arrangements, the Black and Decker Company used its factories to make gun sights, Akron Tire made army cots, and the Evinrude Company stopped making outboard motors and turned out grenades instead. The contract allowed each of these companies to build up revenues to reconvert or to launch new product lines after the war. One steel executive observed, "We are all making more money out of this war than the average human being ought to."

Not all businesses submitted willingly to "war socialism." The Ford Motor Company had just set up a national dealer network at great expense and effort, and it refused to completely stop making cars as the WIB had ordered. When other automakers followed suit, the board threatened to cut off the industry's supply of coal and steel, amounting to "confiscation of the industry," one carmaker sputtered. After months of negotiations, the auto manufacturers agreed to cut production by three-fourths. The delay hurt. When American troops went into battle they had a grand total of two tanks.

The war economy was a culmination of two movements: Wall Street's drive for corporate consolidation and the progressives' push for federal regulation of giant corporations. Businessmen recognized that the WIB could rationalize the economy. These "New Capitalists" wanted to end cutthroat competition and bring central organization and "scientific management" to the economy, to make the United States competitive overseas, and they saw the war as their chance. They established the National Foreign Trade Council and other trade associations to represent them in government. They worked to control price fluctuations, share technology, and make business predictable. They tried to make workers identify with the company through stock sharing and bonus plans and by working with union leaders.

The WIB prevented economic chaos, held down inflation, and racked up a list of lesser accomplishments. It standardized products and forced manufacturers to pay attention to quality. It changed fashion, making women's shoes smaller and removing metal stays from corsets, saving enough to build two battleships. Its main achievement was to demonstrate how a corporate economy could work for the national interest.

The Great Migration

The war economy gave Americans new choices and opportunities. As factories geared up for war production, corporate managers faced a shortage of labor. The draft took eligible employees from the cities, and the usual source of new workers—Europe—was sealed off behind a screen of U-boats. Elbert Gary, head of U. S. Steel, wanted to import laborers from China, but other employers found a ready supply in the South. In small towns and rural junctions, labor recruiters arrived offering free rides to the North and well-paid employment on arrival. Large manufacturers came to rely on the labor of former sharecroppers. The Westinghouse Company employed about 25 African Americans in 1916, and by 1918 it employed 1,500. The Pennsylvania Railroad recruited 10,000 African-American workers from Florida and Georgia. In some northern cities, African-American migrants were arriving at the rate of a thousand a week. The massive movement of African Americans from the rural South to the urban North and West that began during World War I came to be called the Great Migration.

Almost half a million people came north during the war years, so many that it emptied out some counties in the South and created panic among the whites left behind. Mississippi lost 75,000 African-American workers, leaving farms without tenants and delivery wagons without drivers. "We must have the Negro in the South," the Macon, Georgia *Telegraph* pined. "It is the only labor we have . . . If we lose it, we go bankrupt." Southern states passed laws banning recruiters and free passes on the railroads. In some places, migrants were discouraged by violence, and the number of lynchings increased during the war years, provoking still more migration. "Every time a lynching takes place in a community down south," one observer noted, "you can depend on it that colored people will arrive in Chicago within two weeks."

Memories of discrimination and brutality made the decision to move an easy one for many African Americans, but en-

couragement also came from the Chicago *Defender,* an African-American newspaper available in any county that had a railroad. "Every black man for the sake of his wife and daughters especially should leave," the *Defender* said on September 17, 1917. "We know full well that this would mean a depopulation of [the South] and if it were possible we would glory in its accomplishment." The paper estimated the war would create 1.5 million jobs for African Americans in northern cities. Classified ads promised jobs in factories in Milwaukee, St. Louis, Indianapolis, Cleveland, and other cities. For the price of a 20-dollar ticket, a sharecropper could be at a factory in six hours.

African-American workers moved into jobs at the bottom of the pay scale: janitors, domestics, and common laborers in stockyards, steel mills, and factories. The work was backbreaking and often dangerous, and the migrants faced hostility from employers and unionized white workers. Rent, groceries, and other necessities were substantially more expensive in the cities. Still, African-American workers could earn wages 70 percent higher than what they were used to at home. Almost no one went back.

The new arrivals found apartments and boardinghouses in ghetto neighborhoods and adapted to the rhythms of city life. "South State Street was in its glory then, a teeming Negro street with crowded theaters, restaurants, and cabarets," Langston Hughes wrote of Chicago in 1918. "Midnight was like day. The street was full of workers and gamblers, prostitutes and pimps, church folks and sinners." To Carl Sandburg this vibrant community was "spilling over, or rather being irresistibly squeezed out into other residence districts."

In his painting Black Belt *(1934), Archibald Motley captured the sense of excitement and freedom of Chicago at the height of the Great Migration.*

With new construction stopped by the war, housing was in short supply, and African-American renters found their options limited to overcrowded districts wedged between industrial zones and unfriendly white neighborhoods. W. E. B. Du Bois observed that at the turn of the century African-American residences were scattered throughout Philadelphia, but by the end of the First World War they were concentrated in the city's teeming Seventh Ward. Ghetto neighborhoods were both expensive and decrepit. On Chicago's South Side, rents were 15 to 20 percent higher than in white neighborhoods, and the death rate was comparable to that of Bombay, India.

White property owners and real estate agents worked hard during the war to create the ghettos and define their boundaries. In Chicago's South Side, the Hyde Park-Kenwood Property Owners Association organized to "Make Hyde Park White." A real estate agent explained that African-American homeowners "injure our investments. They hurt our values." When discrimination failed to deter "undesirables" from owning homes, the neighbors used dynamite. From 1917 to 1919 there were 26 bombings of African-American residences in Chicago. On July 2, 1917, in East St. Louis, a squalid industrial town in southern Illinois, competition for housing and jobs and rumors that upstate Republicans were "colonizing" the county with African Americans led a mob of white workers to attack an African-American neighborhood, killing 47 people and leaving 6,000 homeless.

After East St. Louis, white mobs found African-American neighborhoods less easy to attack. Three years later, in Washington, D. C., when a mob invaded the ghetto, residents fought back, using guns and retaliating against white neighborhoods. "New Negroes are determined to make their dying a costly investment for all concerned," an African-American newspaper explained drily, "This new spirit is but a reflex of the Great War, and is largely due to the insistent and vigorous agitation carried on by the younger men of the race." The New Negro, urban, defiant, demanding rather than asking for rights, became the subject of admiring and apprehensive reports. Editorials in African-American newspapers subjected southern politicians, the president, and whites generally to increasingly harsh criticism and urged readers to recognize their own beauty and prowess: "The black man is a power of great potentiality upon whom consciousness of his own strength is about to dawn." Attorney General A. Mitchell Palmer kept a file of such "insolent" remarks for use in identifying militants, but another observer, Alain Locke, warned that such opinions only reflected the realities of American cities, where "the Old Negro had long become more of a myth than a man."

Reforms Become "War Measures"

"Why not make America safe for democracy?" asked the signs carried by marchers protesting racism in New York.

The NAACP, in response to the East St. Louis riots, urged Congress to outlaw lynching as a "war measure." African Americans were not alone in using the president's language and the legal changes required by the war emergency as justifications for immediate reform. Carrie Chapman Catt told Wilson that he could enact women's suffrage "as a 'war measure' and enable our women to throw, more fully and wholeheartedly, their entire energy into work for their country." As Wilson pledged the country to fight for liberty, workers, women, and other advocates of social change demanded that the United States practice at home the ideals it fought for abroad. In return, they offered hard work and the promise of a more genuine patriotism. On a variety of issues, reformers used the war to advance the progressive agenda.

Suffragists hitched their cause to the national struggle. Catt's National American Woman Suffrage Association (NAWSA) abandoned its strategy of lobbying state by state and worked to identify women with the war effort. NAWSA members sold liberty bonds and knitted socks for the Red Cross, making clear to the president and Congress that they expected to be rewarded with a constitutional amendment on suffrage. The tactics of Alice Paul's National Woman's Party (NWP) contrasted the nobility of the administration's war aims with its treatment of American women. A lobbyist for NAWSA, Paul left the organization in 1914 to pursue a more partisan, confrontational strategy. Pickets at the White House gate carried signs insisting, in Wilson's own words, on "the right of those who submit to authority to have a voice in their own governments." When arrested, the protestors refused food and suffered force-feeding and abuse at the hands of prison guards. When Wilson announced his support for suffrage in 1918, he cited women's war service as the reason. The Nineteenth Amendment was finally ratified in 1920, "so soon after the war," according to Jane Addams, "that it must be accounted as the direct result of war psychology."

As it had for African Americans, the wartime shortage of labor increased opportunities for women. Although fewer than one in 20 women workers were new to the labor force, many took jobs previously considered "inappropriate" for their sex. Women replaced men as bank tellers, streetcar operators, mail carriers, and in heavy manufacturing firms that made automobiles, aircraft, and chemicals. Women in low-skilled and low-paid occupations found room for upward movement. Cashiers became sales clerks, file clerks became stenographers, and line workers became supervisors. Most of these opportunities vanished as soon as the war was over, but in rapidly expanding sectors like finance, communications, and office work women made permanent gains. By 1920, more than 25 percent of working women labored in offices or as telephone operators, and 13 percent were in the professions. Meanwhile, the number of women employed in factories and domestic service, previously the leading employers of women, declined. The new opportunities made work a

Members of the National Woman's Party picket outside the White House in 1917. Founded by Alice Paul, the NWP campaigned for suffrage through civil disobedience.

source of prestige and enjoyment for women. Alice Hamilton remarked on the "strange spirit of exaltation among the men and women who thronged to Washington, engaged in all sorts of 'war work' and loving it." War propaganda enhanced the glamour, portraying working women as "our second line of defense." Housewives became "house managers" and "victory canners" whose hard work and careful spending could shorten the war.

The general appreciation for women's sacrifices afforded a chance to revisit the issue of special protection for female workers. Sociologist Mary Van Kleeck and Mary Anderson of the Women's Trade Union League persuaded the Army Ordnance Department to issue General Order 13, which recommended uniform standards for women's work, including an eight-hour day, prohibitions on working at night or in dangerous conditions, and provisions for rest periods, lunchrooms, and bathrooms. The order made it plain that the war emergency required these steps: "Fair working conditions and a proper wage are essential to high production." For military contractors the standards were mandatory, but a number of other firms voluntarily followed them, and several states enacted them into law. The Labor Department created a Women in Industry branch to investigate cases of exploitation.

The shortage of labor and high turnover in industrial jobs—sometimes reaching 100 percent a week—forced the government to realize how important it was to keep work-

ers happy. Strikes in critical industries, like copper and lumber, and an increase in the overall number of labor disputes threatened to slow the war effort to a crawl. Union leaders recognized that the war put labor relations on a different footing. Gompers believed it would lead to a "general reorganization" of the economy that could either help or hurt labor. Workers were prepared to make "any sacrifice which may be necessary to make our triumph sure," he told mineworkers, "but we are not going to make sacrifices that shall fill the coffers of the rich." Conservative unions like the American Federation of Labor supported the war, participated in government commissions, and backed the administration's repression of more radical unions. Gompers participated in a mediation commission that settled the copper and lumber strikes in the West, and he helped the Justice Department investigate the IWW.

In return, Wilson went further than any previous president had in recognizing the interests of labor. He authorized a National War Labor Board to intervene in industries "necessary for the effective conduct of the war." The board set an unofficial minimum wage based on a calculation of the cost of living. For the first time the federal government recognized workers' rights to organize, bargain collectively, and join unions. Unskilled workers earned higher real wages than ever before. Wilson ordered a wage hike for railroad workers after nationalization. When the Smith and Wesson Company refused to acknowledge its workers' right to bargain collectively, the Army seized the factory and recognized the union. There were limits, however, to how far the administration would go to keep workers happy. When skilled machinists at the Remington Arms plant in Bridgeport, Connecticut, made demands the board considered excessive, Baruch threatened to have them drafted and sent to France.

Prohibition did not please workers either, but beer, wine, and spirits were early casualties of war. The Anti-Saloon League and the Woman's Christian Temperance Union had assembled a powerful antiliquor coalition by 1916. Congress would have passed prohibition without war, but in the rush to mobilize, temperance became a patriotic crusade. "Sobriety is the bomb that will blow Kaiserdom to kingdom come," one editorial declared. Temperance groups touted the liquor ban as the cure for slums, insanity, poverty, high taxes, and inefficiency. Alcohol represented a "wasted expenditure of two billion a year." Newspapers alleged a conspiracy between brewers and German agents. "The liquor traffic says 'lager uber alles',," an Anti-Saloon League poster claimed. When the battleship *Tennessee* was christened with a magnum of champagne, the state's dry governor lodged a complaint. "King Alcohol no longer rules th' sea or th' land," Finley Peter Dunne's humorous character, Mr. Dooley, pined. "Take a drink, me boy, whether ye need it or not. Take it now. It may be y'er last."

War measures gradually closed the spigot. Military regulations prohibited the sale of liquor in the vicinity of Army camps and outlawed selling or giving alcohol to men in uniform. Food conservation laws made it illegal to use grain to make liquor. Finally, on December 22, 1917, Congress passed the Eighteenth Amendment, banning the "manufacture, sale, or transportation of intoxicating liquors." The amendment was ratified in 1919, and Congress passed a "bone dry" enforcement act, sponsored by Congressman Andrew J. Volstead, that defined liquor as any beverage containing half a percent of alcohol or more. Wilson opposed the Volstead Act, favoring restrictions on hard liquor only, but Congress overrode his veto. At midnight on January 28, 1920, the Anti-Saloon League celebrated the dawn of "an era of clear thinking and clean living." America was "so dry it couldn't spit," according to Billy Sunday. He overstated the case. By some estimates, after the ban illegal speakeasies in New York outnumbered the legal saloons they replaced. Bootleggers, smugglers, and organized crime slaked American thirsts, but liquor prices rose and consumption declined. Americans never again drank anything like the average two and a half gallons of pure alcohol per person annually imbibed before Prohibition.

The war also lent patriotic zeal to antivice crusaders. During the progressive era, vice commissions attacked gambling dens, brothels, and dime-a-dance parlors while muckrakers exposed the police-protection rackets that allowed them to thrive. Within days of the declaration of war, reformers identified prostitutes as domestic enemies bent on sabotaging the health of American troops. Gonorrhea reportedly afflicted a quarter of the Allied forces in France, and proper middle-class Americans worried what might become of soldiers sent to such a moral wilderness. When French premier Georges Clemenceau offered to furnish licensed brothels for the American Army, his letter stopped on the desk of Newton Baker, the reform mayor of Cleveland who had become secretary of war. "For God's sake, Raymond," he told his assistant, "Don't show this to the president or he'll stop the war."

The administration mobilized against venereal disease. The president formed an Interdepartmental Board of Social Hygiene, which implemented severe restrictions known as the "American Plan." Military police could arrest any woman found within five miles of a military cantonment in the United States and force her to submit to medical tests. If infected, she could be sentenced to a "farm colony" or "detention home" until cured. Authorities confined 15,520 afflicted women during the war, although few were cured. The Army closed vice districts in port cities, including New Orleans' famous Storyville. The plan worked. Soldiers suffered less than half the rate of venereal disease of civilians. Cities and states followed the Army's lead and mounted their own attacks on prostitution and disease. The war permanently changed the nature of the crusade for public morals. Before 1917, reformers targeted commercial vice as a source of political and social corruption, but afterward they directed their efforts at women as carriers of disease.

The Army acted against liquor and prostitution to protect the welfare of soldiers, but it shrank from challenging racial injustice even when lives were at stake. At training camps in the South, it was often unclear who had more authority, uniformed African-American soldiers or white local officials. Clashes could easily turn violent. A riot in Houston in August 1917 began when soldiers from nearby Camp Logan rushed to the aid of an African-American woman being beaten by police. Before it was over, 20 policemen and soldiers were dead and 54 soldiers received life sentences in the largest court-martial in U. S. history.

After the Houston riot, African-American units were dispersed to camps across the country. They were not allowed to assemble in full companies or join their officers until they were in France. Training was continually interrupted by menial assignments like road building or freight handling. The Army remained segregated. Worse, many southern communities used military discipline to strengthen their own Jim Crow laws. Encouraged by the Army's "work or fight" order, which required draft-age men to either enlist or get a job, states and localities passed compulsory work laws that applied to women and older men. The laws were intended to keep laborers in the fields and servants in the kitchens at prewar wages.

In the "war welfare state" created by full mobilization, the government served as a mediator among labor, industry, and other organized interests. Social activism became a matter of lobbying federal agencies who could either dictate sweeping changes from Washington or use wartime powers to maintain the status quo. Success required organization and an ability to tie one's goals to the government's national and international ambitions.

Over There

When the U. S. Senate took up the enormous war budget the president submitted in April 1917, the finance committee questioned Major Palmer E. Pierce about what would be done with all of that money. "Clothing, cots, camps, food, pay," he replied, "and we may have to have an army in France." "Good Lord!" exclaimed Senator Thomas

Martin of Virginia, "You're not going to send soldiers over there, are you?" After the horrors of the Somme and Verdun, where men were fed to the Spandau guns by the tens of thousands, it hardly seemed reasonable to send Americans to such a place. "One would think that, after almost four years of war, after the most detailed and realistic accounts of murderous fighting, . . . it would have been all but impossible to get anyone to serve," one veteran later recalled. "But it was not so, we and many thousands of others volunteered."

Americans went to France optimistically believing they could change the war and the peace. Trench warfare was not for them. They planned to fight a war of movement, sweeping in formations across open fields, as Americans had at Antietam and Gettysburg. The Europe they expected to see would confirm their opinion that their immigrant ancestors had made the right choice. To a remarkable degree, they got the war they wanted. Europeans watched their civilization destroy itself in the Great War, but Americans saw theirs rising. Soldiers, "doughboys," said so in their letters, echoing the words of their leaders, their newspapers, and the volumes of poetry they carried with them into battle. As F. Scott Fitzgerald recognized, soldiers see war through the eyes of their culture. "This western-front business couldn't be done again," explained a character in Fitzgerald's novel, *Tender is the Night.* "You had to have a whole-souled sentimental equipment going back further than you could remember. You had to remember Christmas, and postcards . . . and going to the Derby, and your grandfather's whiskers."

Citizens Into Soldiers

The job of enlisting, training, and transporting soldiers began with a rush of excitement. Camps housing 400,000 recruits went up in the first 30 days. A Wisconsin man found Fort Sheridan "alive with enthusiastic recruits, with an atmosphere somewhat like that of a college campus on the eve of a big game." To Secretary of War Newton D. Baker's surprise, conscription went smoothly, and soon 32 camps were in operation, housing 1.3 million men. Commander John J. Pershing arrived in France in June along with 40,000 men and the first of some 16,000 women who would serve in the American Expeditionary Force (AEF).

Neither the Wilson administration nor the Allies initially anticipated that soldiers would be the United States' main contribution to the war effort. Once Wilson was firmly committed to war, the British government revealed how financially desperate it was. London had been buying 75 million dollars worth of war supplies a week from the United States, and it had only enough dollar reserves to last another two weeks. Wilson advanced 200 million dollars immediately, and loans to the Allies eventually amounted to 10 billion dollars. Wilson planned to "fight with our

dollars to the last Frenchman," Senator Hiram Johnson observed. The Allies agreed that funds, food, and ammunition were needed more urgently than men, but that changed in October 1917, when German and Austrian forces smashed through the Italian lines at Caporetto, capturing 275,000 men and finishing the war on that front. When the Bolshevik Revolution curtailed Russian resistance in the east in November, Britain and France saw that by the next spring Germany would be able to mass its armies on the line between Ostend and Switzerland and break through to Paris. The war became a race between the United States and Germany to see who could place the most men on the western front in 1918.

To get troops to the war the United States needed ships, but the American merchant fleet was smaller in 1917 than it was during the Civil War. For a time the United States had to cut back draft calls because it had scarcely a dozen ships for carrying men. The War Department confiscated 16 German passenger ships docked in U. S. ports, including the *Vaterland*, the largest liner afloat, and the British converted freighters to use as transports. Men shared berths, sleeping in shifts. The Navy, meanwhile, cured the U-boat problem. The addition of the American destroyer fleet allowed the Allies to convoy effectively for the first time, cutting losses dramatically and banishing submarines from the sea lanes. When a torpedo was sighted, destroyers would sprint to the far end of the wake and deploy depth charges in a circle around the U-boat. By July 18, some 10,000 troops a day boarded the "Atlantic Ferry" for the ride to France.

The Fourteen Points

Meanwhile in New York the Inquiry completed its work, sending the president a memorandum titled "The War Aims and the Peace Terms It Suggests" on Christmas Day, 1917. Consulting with Col. Edward House, Wilson redrafted the report and presented it in an address to Congress on January 8, 1918. The Fourteen Points outlined U. S. objectives, but more fundamentally they suggested an entirely different basis for peace than any that had been proposed up to that point. Unlike nineteenth-century wars waged for limited territorial or political objectives, the Great War was a total war, fought for unlimited aims. The principal belligerents—Britain, France, Russia, Germany, and Austria-Hungary—were global empires whose trade and law spanned continents and oceans. Germany hoped not only to defeat Britain, but also to take its empire and its place in the world. France wanted to destroy Germany's future as a great power, economically and militarily. Wilson replaced these imperial visions of total victory with a peace based on limited gains and struck among nations, instead of empires.

The Fourteen Points were grouped around four themes: national self-determination; freedom of the seas;

enforcement of peace by a league of nations; and open, instead of secret, diplomacy. The Inquiry's memorandum included a thick sheaf of maps marked with new European boundaries based on national, ethnic identities. The new state of Poland, for instance, should govern only territories with "indisputably Polish populations." Point III restated the Open Door, urging international free trade. Wilson thus hoped to eliminate what he saw as the two leading causes of war, imperial and commercial rivalry. By calling for open diplomacy and national rights, he aimed to appeal directly to the people of Europe, over the heads of their governments. The expectation was that the hope of a just peace would weaken the enemy nations' will and inspire the Allies to fight harder. Creel printed 60 million copies and had them distributed around the world. Planes dropped copies over Germany and Austria.

Wilson hoped the Fourteen Points would dispel not only the old dream of empire, but also the new one of world socialist revolution. On November 7, two months before Wilson presented the points to Congress, Russian workers overthrew the Provisional Government of Alexander Kerensky. The one-party regime of the Bolsheviks, led by Vladimir Lenin, took its place and summoned workers everywhere to rise against their governments and to make peace without indemnities or annexations. "The crimes of the ruling, exploiting classes in this war have been countless. These crimes cry out for revolutionary revenge." In December, Lenin revealed the contents of the secret treaties, unmasking the imperial ambitions of the Allies. He sued for peace based on the principle of self-determination. The Council of People's Commissars allocated two million rubles to encourage revolutions around the world and called "upon the working classes of all countries to revolt."

Two world leaders—Lenin and Wilson—now offered radically different visions of the new world order, and Lenin was putting his into effect. "The entire strategy of the negotiated peace," American writer Randolph Bourne observed, "has passed out of American hands and into those of Russia." The Bolsheviks' contempt for democracy angered Wilson, but he continued to hope that the revolution would move in a more liberal direction and that Russia would stay in the war. Those hopes ended with the treaty of Brest-Litovsk, signed by Russia and Germany in March 1918. The treaty showed the fearful price of defeat in modern war. Russia lost the Ukraine, Poland, and Finland, three-quarters of its iron and steel, one-quarter of its population, and most of its best farmland. Those assets went to the Germans, who began integrating them into their war machine. With its eastern front secure, Germany began transferring ten divisions a month to the west.

Wilson was the first, but not the last, American president to be haunted by the specter of a German-Russian alliance, uniting the immense war-making resources of Europe and Asia. Wilson's strategic vision replaced Alfred Thayer Mahan's (see chapter 20). Sea power threatened U. S. security less, in Wilson's view, than the great land powers of Eurasia. He refused to recognize the Bolshevik government, and he sent 7,000 American troops to Russia to support anti-Bolshevik forces and to try to restart the war on the eastern front. U. S. troops joined Japanese forces invading Siberia from the east. The Bolshevik government now counted the United States among its enemies. Meanwhile, the battle for the control of Europe was about to begin.

The Final Offensive

The German high command knew the spring offensive would be the last. Their exhausted economy no longer could supply food or ammunition for a sustained effort. Breadlines, strikes, and industrial breakdowns foreshadowed the chaos that would follow defeat. Risking everything, the German commander Erich Ludendorff launched his offensive on March 21, 1918. Specially trained shock troops hurled the British Fifth Army back to Amiens. In May they penetrated French lines as far as Soissons, 37 miles from Paris. As gaps opened in the lines, French General Ferdinand Foch and General Douglas Haig of Britain appealed urgently to Pershing to allow American troops to reinforce trenches under British and French command; raw American recruits could learn from seasoned troops, and the Allies could use the American reserves where needed. Pershing opposed the idea. Born in Missouri six months before the Civil War began, the AEF's commander had attended West Point at a time when cadets learned tactics by studying Shiloh and Chickamauga. He wanted the American Army to play "a distinct and definite part" in the war in order to strengthen the United States' negotiating position and to allow him to try his own strategy for defeating the Germans.

Pershing criticized European commanders for remaining on the defensive when the war could be won only by "driving the enemy out into the open and engaging him in a war of movement." Imagining himself a General Grant replacing European McClellans, he saw trenches not as protection against the murderous efficiency of modern weaponry but as symbols of inertia (see Map 22-3). Pershing favored massed assaults on the main German force in which the sheer numbers of American troops would overwhelm the enemy. Infantry commanders, he decided, "must oppose machine guns by fire from rifles." In envisioning Europe's war as a replay of the American Civil War Pershing revealed a habit of mind that would typify American geopolitical thinking for the next century: the belief that as the most advanced industrial nation the United States was historically "ahead" of other countries. It followed that other nations would follow a similar historical path, and that Americans could understand the world through the prism of their own experience.

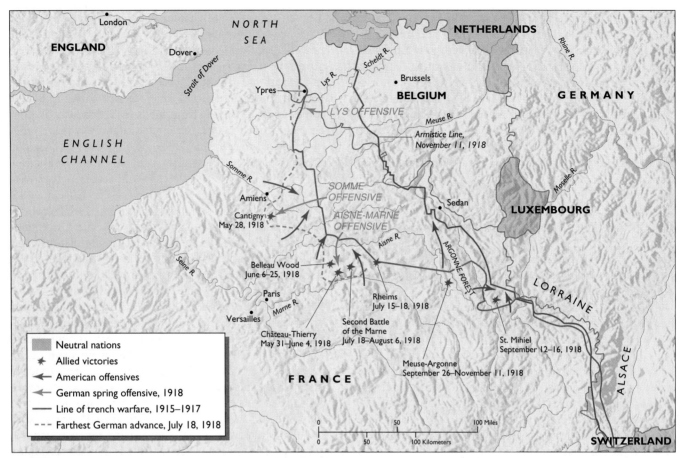

Map 22-3 Western Front, 1918.
On the western front, the opposing armies fought from trenches fortified with earthworks and barbed wire. The parallel trench lines stretched thousands of miles from the North Sea to Switzerland.

The German onslaught interfered with Pershing's plans. On May 27, German divisions pierced French lines at Château-Thierry and began advancing on Paris at a rate of 10 miles a day. The French government considered whether to abandon the capital or surrender. Bowing to urgent requests, Pershing threw the AEF into the breach. It was springtime in France as column upon column of fresh American troops filled the roads from Paris to the front. Photographs show doughboys marching to meet the enemy across fields of wildflowers. "We are real soldiers now and not afread [sic] of Germans," John F. Dixon, an African-American infantryman from New York, wrote home. "Give my love to Claypool, Mary, June, and Grace. Tell them I say war is more than a notion. Our boys went on the battlefield last night singing." Ahead of them lay five German divisions, poison gas, minefields, rolling artillery barrages, and machine guns emplaced in interlocking fields of fire. The Americans stopped the Germans, but at a fearful cost. The Marine brigade that took Belleau Wood suffered 4,600 casualties, half the force. Without artillery or tanks, they assaulted machine gun nests head on,

with rifles. The Americans, with help from a global influenza epidemic that put a million enemy troops on the casualty lists (and killed over 20 million worldwide), stopped the German drive.

By mid-July, the initiative passed to the Allies. On September 12, Foch allowed Pershing to try his tactics against the Saint Mihiel salient, a bulge in the French lines which, unknown to the Allies, the Germans had already begun to evacuate. The doughboys raced behind the retreating enemy past their planned objectives, even outdistancing their own supply wagons. Pershing was delighted. Saint Mihiel had vindicated his strategy, and he yearned for another chance. It came two weeks later, at the battle of the Meuse-Argonne.

Ten miles northwest of Verdun, the Argonne Forest contained some of the most formidable natural and manmade defenses on the western front. Atop parallel ridges lay three fortified trench lines, *stellung*—barriers of concrete pillboxes, barbed wire, artillery, and observation posts—named for Wagnerian witches, Giselher, Kriemhilde, and Freya. Half a million German troops had defended

African-American troops advance toward the sound of gunfire in northern France, 1918. "Our boys went on the battlefield last night singing," one wrote home.

these fortifications for four years. Against this force, Pershing arrayed the American First Army, 1,031,000 men. The average doughboy at the Meuse-Argonne had a total of four months of training, some as little as 10 days. Pershing's battle plan called for overwhelming the German defenses with speed and numbers, breaching the Giselher Stellung, and reaching the second trench line, 10 miles inside the German front, the first day.

"Moving slowly forward, never heeding the bursting shells, nor gas, we followed a road forking to the left . . . into no man's land. It was soon noticed that we were in the bracket of a German barrage," a soldier wrote from the battlefield. Breaking through the first line of German trenches after a day and a half, the battle turned into a deadly crawl up the Romagne heights into the teeth of the Kreimhilde Stellung. "We came to the spot where the fel-

low was hit during the night—he had one boot and leg blown off," Lt. Robert Sawyer of Texas wrote in his diary. "The dead seemed to be in hundreds, though I am quite sure it was my imagination." In two weeks of fighting, 26,277 Americans died. French soldiers reported seeing the American dead lying in rows, cut down by machine guns as they marched in formation. American divisions "suffer wastage out of all proportion to results achieved," a British observer noted. Finally, on November 10, American troops reached their objective and dynamited the rail line connecting the cities of Metz and Sedan. Meanwhile, Germany announced that it would accept the Fourteen Points as the basis for an **armistice** and negotiations. At 11:00 A.M. on November 11, 1918, the guns fell silent.

American intervention had been decisive. The American economy, two and a half times the size of Germany's, lent its immense industrial and agricultural productivity to the Allies at a crucial moment. American naval strength and manpower had also tipped the balance. Pershing failed to transform strategy; it remained a mechanized war of attrition until the end, but by striking the final blow, Americans had the illusion that their way of war had been triumphant. American losses, 116,516 dead, were smaller than the British (908,371), the French (1.4 million), or the Germans (1.8 million), but they still show the colossal destructiveness of the kind of industrial war fought on the western front. In just six months, the United States suffered twice as many combat deaths as in the Vietnam War and almost a third as many as in World War II.

While they fought on the same battlefields, Americans and Europeans fought two vastly different wars. The Americans' war, swift and victorious, bore almost no resemblance to the European experience, a prolonged catastrophe that consumed an entire generation. For Europeans, the mental world of the prewar era, with its optimistic faith in modernity, in the ability of science and democracy to create a better future, vanished forever. War, however, validated Americans' confidence in the virtues of their own civilization, while reinforcing their suspicions of foreign systems and ideas. Doughboys expected victory to reinvigorate their society and economy. "New bonds will draw us together," one private predicted, "New interstate commerce will arise and the fabrics of the nation will be strengthened." Confidence in the inevitability of progress became a distinctive feature of U. S. culture in the postwar era. In much of the world "American" became almost synonymous with "modern," but not everywhere. In the East another political and economic system shouted its claim to the future.

The Black Cloud in the East

Americans celebrated the armistice with bonfires, automobile horns, church bells, and uplifted voices. New York's Metropolitan Opera interrupted a performance to sing the anthems of the Allied nations. Outside the White House a choir from Howard University sang "The Spirit of Victory," a cantata written for the occasion, as army biplanes flew overhead. Wilson told Congress that "everything for which America fought has been accomplished," but he observed that the situation in Russia cast doubt on the durability of peace. Even before the armistice, German revolutionaries took power in Hamburg, Lubeck, and Bremen. Socialists declared the Free State of Bavaria and expelled their doddering king. Over the next months, revolutions broke out throughout eastern Europe. From the trenches of Flanders to the Sea of Japan, not a single government remained intact, and in Moscow the new Soviet state towered above the ruins of the old regimes. Just as diplomats prepared to make peace in Europe, journalist Ray Stannard Baker wrote, there arose a "black cloud of the east, threatening to overwhelm and swallow up the world."

Wilson in Paris

For Wilson, the moment he had planned for in 1917 had arrived: Having joined in the victory, the United States could help set the terms of peace, but the war had exhausted the president. "Those were harrowing days," his attorney general, Thomas Gregory, remembered. Wilson's "nerves were taut and his intellectual sentinels were not on the lookout for danger." Confident that the public would view the nation's victory as his victory, he committed mistakes that undermined his support at home just as he was preparing to deal with the leaders of Europe. First, he tried to turn the victory to political advantage. Republicans in the House and Senate had given the president considerable support during the war, and the spirit of patriotic bipartisanship might have lasted had Wilson not dispelled it with an advertisement in the *New York Times*. "If you have approved my leadership," it read, "I earnestly beg that you will express yourself unmistakably to that effect by returning a Democratic majority to both the Senate and the House." Despite the plaintive tone, Republicans attacked it as an insult to their patriotism. "The president has thrown off the mask," Senator Henry Cabot Lodge fumed.

"The only test of loyalty is loyalty to one man." When the ballots were counted in the 1918 midterm elections, Republican majorities took power in both houses. The defeat could easily be seen in Europe as a repudiation of Wilson's leadership. "Mr. Wilson has no authority whatever to speak for the American people at this time," Theodore Roosevelt attested.

He next decided to go to Paris to lead the American peace delegation. Had he remained at home, some historians have argued, he could have taken credit for the achievements of his negotiators while keeping a close eye on his critics. Instead, he identified himself with the peace agreement, staking its success on his own prestige and popularity. He passed up a chance to include in the delegation a prominent Republican, like Lodge, who could guide the treaty through Congress afterwards. A member of the British cabinet, Winston Churchill, observed that "if Mr. Wilson had been either simply an idealist or a caucus politician, he might have succeeded. His attempt to run the two in double harness was the cause of his undoing."

In December 1918, Walter Lippmann, now an Army captain, stood on the balcony of the Crillon Hotel witnessing Wilson's triumphal entry into Paris. Huge crowds lined the streets, and as the procession crossed the Pont du Concorde into the center of the city, a great cheer went up, echoing off the walls of the Chamber of Deputies. "Never has a king, never has an emperor received such a welcome," *L'Europe Nouvelle* declared. For the next month, Wilson toured France, Italy, and Britain with cries of "Viva Veelson" ringing in his ears. An Italian mayor compared his visit to the second coming of Christ. "They say he thinks of us, the poor people," a workingman remarked, "that he wants us all to have a fair chance; that he is going to do something when he gets here that will make it impossible for our government to send us to war again. If he had only come sooner!"

By the time he arrived for the treaty talks at the Palace of Versailles, two of the Fourteen Points had already been compromised, and Wilson's popularity provided little help at the negotiating table. Britain's David Lloyd George refused to accept the point on freedom of the seas, which would thwart the use of the Royal Navy in a future conflict. Wilson was unable to refute his argument that the United States had already conceded the point by respecting Britain's blockade during the war. Wilson's own actions also undercut his position on point six, respect for Russia's sovereignty, since American troops were occupying Russian territory in the Arctic and Siberia. Wilson was unable to prevent Britain, France, and Japan from dividing Germany's colonies among themselves and imposing harsh peace terms. Germany had to sign a humiliating "war guilt" clause and pay 33 billion dollars in reparations, enough to cripple its economy for decades. "God gave us the ten commandments and we broke them," Clemenceau quipped. "Wilson gave us the Fourteen Points—we shall see."

Wilson "growing grimmer and graver, day by day" concentrated his efforts on creating the League of Nations, which might make up for the treaty's other weaknesses and provide some safety against the rising tide of revolution. He took the lead in drafting the League Covenant, which committed each member to submit disputes to arbitration and pledged them to take action against "any war or threat of war, whether immediately affecting any Members of the League or not." Wilson presented the covenant to the peace delegations and declared "A living thing is born." The president slumped in the car on the way home, causing Edith Wilson to remark on his weariness. "Yes," he said. "I suppose I am, but how little one man means when such vital things are at stake."

The Senate Rejects the League

To many observers in the United States the Treaty of Versailles' imperial land grabs and severe treatment of the vanquished nations betrayed the goals Americans had fought to attain. "This is Not Peace," declared *The New Republic.* Few in Congress and the press shared Wilson's confidence that the League of Nations would prevent future wars. They felt instead that it might only guarantee that the

United States would be involved in the next conflict. Americans were "far more afraid of Lenin than they ever were of the Kaiser," Lippmann wrote. "We seem to be the most frightened lot of victors the world ever saw." To Republican leaders, like Henry Cabot Lodge, the United States' best bet was to look to its own security, keep its options open, and work out its international relations independently rather than as part of an alliance or league.

In early March 1919, before the treaty was concluded, Lodge and 38 other senators—more than enough to defeat the treaty—signed a petition opposing the League of Nations. James A. Reed of Missouri said the covenant would turn American foreign policy over to foreigners "most of whom could not speak the English language." Senator William Borah called it "the greatest triumph for English diplomacy in three centuries of English diplomatic life." Editorialists described scenarios in which American troops would be automatically summoned to settle blood feuds in the Balkans. Wilson knew he would have to fight, but he believed that in the end the Senate would not reject the treaty.

In September, Wilson went "over the heads" of Congress and stumped for the treaty on a nationwide tour. In St. Louis he told crowds that secret treaties would be replaced by agreements registered just like "mortgages on real estate." He assured listeners in Sioux Falls that "the peace of the world cannot be established without America." He promised the citizens of Salt Lake City that China's independence would be respected. Traveling more than 8,000 miles and speaking before large audiences without loudspeakers took a toll on the president's health. After a speech in Pueblo, Colorado, he became so ill that he was rushed back to Washington, where he suffered a stroke that left him paralyzed on his left side and unable to concentrate for more than a few minutes a day. Mrs. Wilson and the president's physician kept his condition a secret and refused to allow anyone to see him.

It was at this moment, with the League of Nations' champion secluded in the White House, that the Senate voted on the treaty. On November 19, the Senate defeated the ratification bill. Down to the end, Wilson refused to allow Senate Democrats to accept any modifications to the treaty. Even Lippmann's *New Republic,* which had been a mouthpiece for the Wilson administration throughout the war, called the treaty's demise "desirable and wholesome." Lodge and the Republicans were not ready to retreat into isolation, but they preferred

The Big Four—Vittorio Orlando of Italy, David Lloyd George of Great Britain, Georges Clemenceau of France, and Woodrow Wilson—gather at the Paris Peace Conference in 1919.

diplomatic strategies that employed the United States' overwhelming economic power, rather than its relatively weak military forces. They also saw Latin America as more critical than Europe to U.S. security. Lodge even toyed briefly with the idea of two leagues, one for each hemisphere.

Meanwhile, European governments organized the League of Nations without delegations from the United States or the Soviet Union. Over the next decade, U. S. influence abroad grew enormously. American automobiles, radios, and movies could be seen in far corners of the globe. However, the United States was cautious in its diplomatic dealings in Europe and Asia, in order to avoid being drawn into what the *New York Tribune* called the "vast seething mass of anarchy extending from the Rhine to the Siberian wastes."

Red Scare

On May 1, 1919, a dozen or more mail bombs were sent to prominent Americans: J. P. Morgan, John D. Rockefeller, senators, cabinet officials, and Supreme Court Justice Oliver Wendell Holmes. None of the explosive packages reached its intended target, but one blew up in the hands of a maid in the home of Senator Thomas Hardwick. A month later a bomb exploded outside the residence of Attorney General A. Mitchell Palmer in Washington, nearly injuring Franklin and Eleanor Roosevelt, who lived next door. Investigations later showed that the bombings were the work of lone lunatics, but many people quickly

concluded that communists were trying to overthrow the government. Since the Russian Revolution, newspapers, evangelists, and government officials had fed fears of Bolshevism. "Is Bolshevism coming to America?" read full-page advertisements paid for by the *Christian Herald.* The answer was yes, according to Attorney General Palmer. "The blaze of revolution was sweeping over every American institution of law and order . . . licking at the altars of the churches, leaping into the belfry of the school bell, crawling into the sacred corners of American homes, seeking to replace marriage vows with libertine laws, burning up the foundations of society."

The **Communist** risings in Europe terrified conservatives in the United States and led them to look for Soviet accomplices, particularly among immigrants and unionized workers. They drew no distinctions among Socialists, anarchists, Communists, and labor unionists; they were all "red." When steelworkers in Gary, Indiana, struck for higher wages and shorter hours in September 1919, Judge Elbert Gary, president of U. S. Steel, denounced them as Bolsheviks. During the war they had worked 12 hours a day, 7 days a week for an average wage of 28 dollars a week. Enlisting the help of local loyalty leagues, Judge Gary broke the strike. Seattle's mayor called in the army when dock workers struck. "Bolshevism, soviets, anarchists, and the red flag will not be tolerated," he declared.

Using the patriotic rhetoric of the war, industry leaders labeled strikers as dangerous aliens bent on destroying the United States. They persuaded allies in the courts to take action, and a series of Supreme Court decisions made union activity virtually illegal. In 1919 the court allowed antitrust suits under the Sherman Act to be filed against unions, and it later declared boycotts illegal and limited stikers' freedom to picket. Then, in January 1920, began a series of crackdowns known as the Palmer raids. Some 250 members of the Union of Russian Workers were arrested and deported to Russia on an Army transport. In one night, 4,000 suspected Communists were arrested in raids across the country; some said this was not enough. "If I had my way with these ornery, wild-eyed Socialists and IWWs," evangelist Billy Sunday allowed, "I would stand them up before a firing squad and save space on our ships."

The most notorious case associated with the "Red Scare" began in May 1920 when Nicola Sacco and Bartolomeo Vanzetti, a shoemaker and a fish peddler, were arrested for robbing a shoe company in South Braintree, Massachusetts. Two

The Sacco and Vanzetti trial, depicted here by Ben Shahn, come to symbolize the arbitrary injustices of the Red Scare. Their trial became an international cause célebre.

men died of gunshot wounds during the robbery, and ballistics experts claimed that the bullets came from Sacco's gun. The trial, however, focused less on the evidence than on the fact that the defendants were Italian and anarchists. The state doctored evidence and witnesses changed testimony, but the judge favored the prosecution. Despite Sacco's corroborated testimony that he was in Boston at the time of the robbery and the sworn confession of another man, Judge Webster Thayer sentenced Sacco and Vanzetti to death. "Did you see what I did with those anarchistic bastards the other day?" he said to an acquaintance at a football game the following weekend. "I guess that ought to hold them for a while."

The appeals lasted six years, during which protests for their release mounted. As the day of the execution approached, Europeans and Latin Americans organized boycotts of American products. Riots in Paris took 20 lives. Uruguayan workers called a general strike. Governments called on the president to intervene, but on August 23, 1927, Sacco and Vanzetti died in the electric chair.

Americans who had talked in 1917 about making the world safe for democracy now seemed ready to throw their own freedoms away out of fear of anarchy. Lippmann found it "incredible that an administration announcing the most spacious ideals in our history should have done more to endanger fundamental American liberties than any group of men for a hundred years." By the end of 1920, the original terror subsided, but labor unions and social radicals would have to fend off the charge of communism for decades to come.

CHRONOLOGY

1911	Mexican Revolution begins
1914	U. S. troops occupy Veracruz, Mexico World War I begins
1915	U. S. troops occupy Haiti (until 1934) *Lusitania* sunk
1916	U. S. forces invade Mexico in search of Pancho Villa U.S. forces enter the Dominican Republic Woodrow Wilson re-elected
1917	Russian czar abdicates; parliamentary regime takes power U.S. declares war on Germany East St. Louis riot Houston riot October Revolution overthrows Russian government; Lenin takes power
1918	Wilson announces U. S. war aims: the Fourteen Points Wilson nationalizes railroads Sedition Act outlaws criticism of the U. S. government Armistice ends fighting on the western front
1919	Eighteenth Amendment outlaws manufacture, sale, and transport of alcoholic beverages Versailles Treaty signed in Paris Mail bombs target prominent government and business figures Gary, Indiana, steel strike U.S. Senate rejects Versailles Treaty
1920	Nineteenth Amendment secures the vote for women Palmer raids arrest thousands of suspected Communists Sacco and Vanzetti arrested on charges of robbery and murder

Conclusion

Wilson tried to lead America toward what he called a new world order, a world where nations and international law would count more than empires and where the United States could light the way toward progress, stability, and peace. What he failed to recognize was that for many Americans this future was filled with terrors as well as promise. The strains of war had introduced new divisions in American society. Progressivism, which had given coherence and direction to social change, was a spent force.

The growth of federal administration, the new powers of big business, internal migrations, and new social movements and values added up to what Lippmann called a "revolutionary world." Many of the changes that began during the war had not fully played out, nor were their consequences apparent, but Americans entered the 1920s with a sense of uneasiness. They were aware that their nation was now the world's strongest, but they were unsure about what that might mean for their lives.

Review Questions

1.   As a progressive, Wilson was committed to order, efficiency, and gradual reform. How did his policies toward Mexico and Europe reflect this commitment?

2.   Both the Philippine-American War of 1899 and U. S. involvement in World War I in 1917 provoked dissent at home. Why did the government tolerate opposition in the first case but suppress it in the second?

3.   Did the war help or hurt the progressive movement?

4.   Allied commanders wanted to use American troops as a reserve, but Pershing wanted his soldiers to enter the battle as an army. Why was that so important to him?

5.   Did Senate Republicans reject the League of Nations because they wanted the United States to withdraw from the world, or because they wanted to deal with the world in a different way?

Further Readings

Nancy K. Bristow, *Making Men Moral: Social Engineering During the Great War* (1996). How government and women's groups used military training to mold men into model citizens.

John Eisenhower, *Intervention! The United States and the Mexican Revolution, 1913–1917* (1993). The story of the U. S. occupation of Veracruz and Pershing's search for Pancho Villa.

Meirion Harries, *The Last Days of Innocence: America at War, 1917–1918* (1997). Lively anecdotal history of the war years.

David M. Kennedy, *Over Here: The First World War and American Society* (1980). The best study of the home front during World War I.

N. Gordon Levin, Jr., *Woodrow Wilson and World Politics* (1968). The progressive president's response to the disorder of world politics. Levin analyzes the idealism and realism of Wilsonian foreign policy.

H. C. Peterson and Gilbert C. Fite, *Opponents of War, 1917–1918* (1957). Still the best study on wartime peace movements and the Wilson administration's attempts to suppress dissent.

Ronald Steel, *Walter Lippmann and the American Century* (1980). More than any other journalist, Lippmann shaped American foreign policy in the twentieth century.

History on the Internet

"The Red Scare"

http://newman.baruch.cuny.edu/digital/redscare/

This site consists of some 300 images, including political cartoons, that depict Americans' distrust of immigrants and radicals following World War I.

"War Message of World War I"

http://www.lib.byu.edu/~rdh/wwi/1917/wilswarm.html

The speech featured on this site was delivered to Congress by President Woodrow Wilson on February 3, 1917. In it, he severed diplomatic relations with Germany, drawing America into the Great War.

"Talking History"

http://www.albany.edu/talkinghistory/archive/goinnorth.ram

Beginning with part 2 of "Goin' North, Great Tales of the Great Migration," hear African Americans talk through audio files about their experiences in going to Philadelphia for jobs during World War I. (This is an audio file and requires the common audio player feature.)

"World War I Document Archive"

http://www.lib.byu.edu/~rdh/wwi/

This archive consists of official primary documents such as conventions and treaties concerning World War I. Also, the site contains personal stories of men and women who were involved with the war.

THE 1920s

OUTLINE

"The Queen of Swimmers"

On the morning of August 6, 1926, Gertrude Ederle walked across the beach at Cape Gris-Nez on the French coastline. Her body and her bright red swim suit were heavily greased. At seven o'clock, the nineteen-year-old American from New York City plunged into the water and began to swim, with a measured crawl stroke, toward the coast of England, miles away.

"Trudy," the daughter of a German immigrant butcher, was a champion distance swimmer who had won medals at the 1924 Olympic games, but no woman had ever completed the long, hazardous swim across the English Channel. In fact, only five men had accomplished the feat. Ederle herself had already tried and failed the year before. Exhausted, she had been pulled from the water by her coach, who rebuked her for playing the ukulele instead of practicing in the preceding weeks.

This time was different. Despite the tides, the chill water, and the threat of sharks, Ederle persevered hour after hour. The swimmer was spurred on by her competi-tive instincts, by her eagerness to please her mother, and by her father's promise to buy her a sporty new car, a roadster, if she succeeded.

Inspired by thoughts of that roadster, Ederle fought the choppy waves as she hunted for a favorable tide. Finally, after 14 hours and 31 minutes in the water, she came ashore in the dark at Kingsdown, England, at 9:40 P.M. Ederle had not only become the first woman to swim the channel, she had also made the crossing faster than any of the men before her. "I am a proud woman," Ederle announced as she walked up the English beach.

Back in the United States, newspapers trumpeted Ederle's stunning achievement in page-one headlines and analyzed it in editorial columns. Ederle came home to a tumultuous ticker-tape parade on the streets of New York. "No President or king, soldier or statesman," reported the *New York Times*, "has ever enjoyed such an enthusiastic and affectionate outburst of acclaim by the metropolis as was offered to the butcher's daughter . . . hailed as the

'Queen of Swimmers.' " President Calvin Coolidge sent Ederle his congratulations. Meanwhile, the swimmer was overwhelmed with "big money" offers to endorse products and to appear on stage and in the movies.

Gertrude Ederle's enormous reception said a great deal about the United States in the decade after World War I. Once again at peace, 1920s America could afford to indulge an interest in the exploits of a long-distance swimmer. The nation's dynamic industrial economy seemed effortlessly to produce plenty of roadsters, movies, and prosperity.

Ederle herself exemplified a new national culture, rooted in the needs of the booming economy, that broke sharply with the forms and conventions of the past. Emphasizing the importance of pleasure, this modern culture celebrated leisure activities such as dancing, channel swimming, and other diversions. The ukulele-playing Ederle loved "all normal pleasures, including a jazzy dance now and then." The new culture glorified the purchase and consumption of material goods such as the roadster Ederle wanted to buy and the merchandise she was eager to advertise. The teenaged swimmer embodied still other aspects of the new culture—its fascination with youth, its endorsement of a more indulgent, child-centered

Gertrude Ederle is greased to keep warm in the cold waters of the English Channel before her record-setting swim on August 6, 1926. Ederle's successful Channel crossing made her a symbol for the emerging culture of 1920s America.

family life, and its infatuation with pleasure-seeking, independent, nontraditional women.

Ederle—the solitary swimmer and enthusiastic consumer—also exemplified the resurgent individualism that shaped the political economy of the 1920s. It was no wonder that President Coolidge, a staunch Republican, congratulated Ederle. She seemed to prove that individuals could still achieve great things and find happiness in an increasingly organized, centralized, bureaucratized society.

In the euphoria of the ticker-tape parade, it might have been easy to conclude that Americans welcomed the emerging cultural and political order as much as they welcomed its heroic symbol, Trudy Ederle. In fact, many people were troubled by the changes that swept across the nation in the 1920s. The new order did not substantially reflect or change the values of millions of Americans. Neither did it speak to some of the most fundamental social and economic inequalities that plagued national life. As a result, the new cultural and political order had to contend with a powerful backlash, just as Ederle had to face a hostile tide in the English Channel. Nevertheless, like the swimmer, the new culture and politics seemed to grow stronger and overcome all opposition as the decade moved to a close. ▮

KEY TOPICS

- The impact of the continuing transformation of the industrial economy on big business, work, organized labor, farmers, and urban growth

- The emergence of a more secular modern culture, dedicated to pleasure, leisure, and consumerism

- The importance of individualism and new individual identities in the modern culture

- The widespread but unsuccessful backlash against the modern culture

- The Republicans' dominance of the emerging system of modern politics

A Dynamic Economy

By and large, the 1920s were a prosperous time for America. After a recession during 1920 and 1921, the economy stabilized and continued to grow. Consumer prices remained fairly steady throughout the decade, and jobs were plentiful. After reaching a high of 11.7 percent during the recession, the unemployment rate went as low as 1.8 percent in 1926. Wages jumped: The nation's net income—the value of its earnings from labor and property—leapt from 64.0 billion dollars in 1921 to 86.8 billion dollars in 1929.

This prosperity was driven by the dynamism of the evolving industrial economy. New technologies, increased efficiency, a maturing automobile industry, and new businesses all contributed to the nation's impressive economic gains in the 1920s. The development of industry contributed as well to the increasing dominance of corporations and other large-scale organizations and to the reshaping of work and the work force.

Despite the general prosperity, economic change was not only a story of gain and progress. The transformation of the economy involved serious defeats for organized labor and wrenching decline for many farmers. For better or for worse, the relative weakness of agriculture and the strength of industry helped to turn the United States, for the first time, into a predominantly urban nation. In the prosperous 1920s, as always, industrial capitalism was a dynamic, transforming force.

The Development of Industry

Several long-term factors shaped the development of American industry in the 1920s. In their continuing quest for more efficient production, businessmen made use of new technologies and other innovations during the decade. The federal government issued more patents for new inventions—421,000 of them—than in any preceding decade. The industrial economy also made greater use of technical expertise. During the 1920s, the number of engineers in the country nearly doubled.

The switch from coal to electricity, underway since the 1910s, was a critically important innovation in the nation's factories. By the end of the 1920s, electricity powered more than two-thirds of American manufacturing plants. New machines, running on electricity, simplified and sped up production. For instance, a new paint machine at the Ford Motor Company did the work of 10 men.

Henry Ford's car company pioneered another critical innovation, the system that became known as Fordism or **mass production.** By the 1910s, Ford, like many other American manufacturers, made extensive use of interchangeable parts, simple and accurate machine tools, and electric power in order to speed output at its giant Highland Park factory complex in Detroit, Michigan. However, auto production was slowed by a traditional manufacturing practice. Frames, transmissions, and other key subassemblies remained in place on stands while teams of workers moved from one stand to another to do their work.

Eager to meet the rising demand for the popular Model T car, Ford's managers reversed the process by "moving the work to the men." Beginning in 1913, one section of the Ford plant after another started using conveyor belts and chains to send subassemblies past groups of stationary workers. Instead of making an entire engine or subassembly, a worker might tighten a few bolts or install a single part. This assembly line led to an astonishing increase in output. In 1914, Ford produced 300,000 Model Ts. In 1923, the company produced more than two million. By that time, other American manufacturers were racing to copy Ford's techniques of mass production.

Mass production, electrification, and other innovations spurred an extraordinary increase in productivity for American industry as a whole in the 1920s. Output per worker skyrocketed 72 percent from 1919 to 1929.

Along with increased productivity, the rise of several industries drove the economy in the 1920s. Auto production now dominated as textiles, railroads, iron, and steel had in earlier decades. In 1921, there were already 9.3 million registered cars on American roads. By 1929, the figure had more than doubled to 23 million. By producing all those cars, auto manufacturers stimulated the development of other industries. The demand for plate glass, oil, gasoline, and rubber surged during the 1920s.

Mass production at work: the assembly line at the Ford Motor Company plant in Dearborn, Michigan, in 1928.

Other sectors of the industrial economy also grew rapidly in the 1920s. The demand for processed foods, household appliances, office machinery, and chemicals increased dramatically. Smaller, emerging industries such as aircraft demonstrated their potential economic importance as well.

Arguably the first powered, fixed-wing flight had occurred in December 1903, when Wilbur and Orville Wright, brothers and bicycle mechanics from Ohio, brought their "Flyer" to the beach at Kitty Hawk, North Carolina. With Orville lying at the controls, the fragile plane flew 120 feet in 12 seconds. But the civilian airplane industry did not really take off for good until the 1920s. Aircraft production rose from less than 300 in 1922 to more than 6,000 in 1929. By then, fledgling airlines were flying passengers on scheduled commercial flights.

The Trend Toward Large-Scale Organization

The development of industry reinforced the trend toward large-scale organization that was so basic to capitalism in the United States. Only big businesses had the financial resources to pay for "Fordism," with its expensive machinery and huge factories. By 1929, corporations produced 92 percent of the nation's manufactured goods.

A wave of mergers contributed to the growth of big business in the 1920s. During the decade, more than 8,000 mining and manufacturing firms disappeared as the result of more than 1,200 mergers. The mergers meant that big businesses controlled more factories and assets than ever.

The largest firms also benefited from new, more efficient organizational structures. When the recession of 1920 and 1921 left big corporations with too many unsold goods, companies such as General Motors and Du Pont chemical company reorganized themselves. Now top managers, aided by staffs of financial, legal, and other experts, oversaw the work of semiautonomous divisions that supplied different markets. At General Motors, for example, the Chevrolet division produced huge numbers of relatively inexpensive cars while the Cadillac division turned out a smaller number of expensive cars. The new organizational system made corporations more flexible, efficient, and responsive to changes in consumer demand.

Corporate growth was not confined to industry. Chains such as A & P grocers and F. W. Woolworth's variety stores increased their share of the nation's retail sales from four to 20 percent during the 1920s. One percent of the nation's banks managed nearly half of the country's financial assets.

Giant firms and their leaders had often been the targets of suspicion, hostility, and reform during the Gilded Age and the Progressive era, but many Americans softened their attitude toward business in the prosperous 1920s. Basking in the glow of public approval, big business confidently forecast a central role for itself in the nation's destiny. "The modern business system, despised and derided by innumerable reformers, will," a businessman predicted, "be both the inspiration and the instrument of the social progress of the future."

The Transformation of Work and the Work Force

Whatever its role in the future, the "modern business system" was certainly changing the nature of work and the work force in the 1920s. Businessmen's quest for productivity had sweeping consequences for American workers. Industrial efficiency was not just a matter of electricity and machines. To speed up production, the managers at Ford and other factories had to control their workers and speed up the labor process.

Accordingly, the spirit of Taylorism—Frederick Winslow Taylor's system of scientific management—continued to sweep through American industry. Laboring under ever tighter supervision, workers were pushed to work faster and harder. In textile mills, workers faced the "stretch-out," the requirement that they tend more looms than before. Ford's system of mass production shared Taylor's determination to simplify and regiment labor. The result was less satisfying work. Instead of making a whole engine, a Ford assembly-line worker might spend his day turning a few nuts on one engine after another. In 1913, the company's labor turnover rate soared to 380 percent as unhappy workers quit their jobs.

The development of industry contributed to the ongoing transformation of the nation's occupational structure. As the economy became increasingly efficient, there was less need for factory operatives and other workers. During the prosperous 1920s, the nation actually experienced a net loss of about a million jobs in manufacturing, coal mining, and railroading. The growth of other kinds of employment more than compensated for this decrease, however. The ranks of the nation's white-collar workers increased 80 percent from 1910 to 1930. By 1930, nearly one worker in three did white-collar work rather than manual labor. Even as American factories flourished in the 1920s, the nation had already begun a long-term evolution from an industrial economy based on manual labor to a postindustrial economy based on white-collar work in sales and service.

The development of the economy also encouraged the continuing, gradual movement of women into the paid work force. By the end of the 1920s, women made up a majority of the growing ranks of clerical workers in the nation's offices. Married women were more likely than ever to find paid work outside the home.

Despite these changes, women still faced discrimination in the workplace. Overwhelmingly concentrated in low-wage occupations such as domestic service, they were paid less than men who did comparable work. Female sales workers, for example, earned between 42 and 63 percent of the wages paid to their male counterparts. Hardly any women held high-level managerial jobs in the 1920s.

Moreover, there was still considerable resistance to the idea that women should work outside the home, let alone have careers. Most men and many women continued to believe that a woman's place was in the home, especially if she had children. Many men feared that paid labor would make women too independent. Apparently, only economic necessities—families' need for income and employers' need for workers—reconciled much of American society to women's employment in the 1920s.

The Defeat of Organized Labor

The American labor movement did not respond effectively to the transformation of work and the work force. In an age of increasing economic organization, workers actually became less organized during the 1920s. At the start of the decade nearly one nonagricultural worker in five belonged to a union. By 1929, little more than one in 10 was a union member. The labor movement was especially weak in the developing mass-production industries such as automobiles and steel. Moreover, unions had barely addressed the growing ranks of clerks and other white-collar workers.

The weak state of organized labor was partly a result of the prosperity of the 1920s. Earning relatively good wages, many workers were less interested in joining unions, and their employers tried hard to convince them that unions were unnecessary. Some corporations promoted welfare capitalism, a broad set of highly publicized programs for workers ranging from lunch-hour movies to sports teams to profit-sharing plans.

While some firms tried to win over their workers with baseball teams and company unions, many employers used tougher tactics in their long-time battle against the labor movement. As during World War I, management crusaded for the "open shop"—a workplace free of labor organization, and as before, employers found an invaluable ally in the judicial system. During the 1920s, rulings by the U. S. Supreme Court made it easier for lower courts to grant injunctions against union picketing and boycotting. State and federal courts issued more injunctions than ever to stop unions from striking and exercising their rights. The courts also allowed businesses to sue unions for damages.

Beset by courts and employers, the labor movement also hurt its own cause. The leadership of the major national organization, the American Federation of Labor (AFL), was increasingly conservative and timid. The heads of the AFL were mainly white males with Western European roots who represented skilled crafts. For the most part, these men had little interest in organizing women workers. The AFL leadership wanted nothing to do with socialists, radical unionists, and African-American workers. The AFL was slow to admit or even pay attention to the Brotherhood of Sleeping Car Porters, the assertive union of African-American workers organized in 1925 under the leadership of socialist A. Philip Randolph. Despite pleas from Randolph and others, the AFL leadership failed to organize unskilled workers, many of whom were African Americans or white immigrants from eastern and southern Europe.

Weakened by internal divisions, welfare capitalism, the open-shop crusade, and the courts, the labor movement did not mount much of a challenge to the ongoing transformation of industrial labor in the 1920s. Nationwide, the number of strikes and lockouts dropped from 3,411 in 1920 to just 604 in 1928. All too often, these work stoppages ended in defeat for workers.

The Decline of Agriculture

Against the backdrop of national prosperity, American agriculture continued its long decline in the 1920s. While the rest of the United States pulled out of the recession of 1920 and 1921, the rural economy failed to rebound. Prices for basic crops such as cotton and wheat fell, and the number of farms dropped.

The larger story of decline obscured important signs of growth and health. Some sectors of American agriculture were as dynamic as the nation's industry, and for the same reasons—above all, the increased efficiency promoted by new technologies and large-scale organization. Mechanization, including the introduction of such tractors as the huge Fordson built by the Ford Motor Company, made farm labor more efficient, as did the increasing development of irrigation systems since the turn of the century. By the 1920s, the irrigated farms of the Southwest were producing bumper crops of cotton, fruits, and vegetables. The Southwest also witnessed the rise of huge farms, with hundreds and even thousands of acres, whose owners could afford to pay for mechanization and irrigation. These innovative "factories in the fields" depended on the old-fashioned exploitation of farm labor, as well as on size and technology. In California's Imperial Valley and elsewhere, migrant workers labored in harsh conditions for low pay in order to create modern, large-scale agriculture.

Ironically, the dynamism of the agricultural economy was part of the problem for many American farmers. Mid-size farms, too big to be run by their owners alone and too small to make mechanization practical, could not compete with the vast "factories in the fields." Increased efficiency, meanwhile, led to bumper crops that did not always find a market at a good price. Farmers were hurt, too, by changes in Americans' diet such as declining consumption of bread and potatoes. They were hurt as well by the rise of competitors overseas. Producing too much, American farmers could not export enough of their surplus crops to foreign countries. The resulting glut kept the price of farm products down. As their incomes lagged behind those of urban workers, farmers yearned for "parity"—the return of high pre-World War I agricultural prices that would restore rural America's buying power.

Farmers' purchasing power did improve as nonagricultural prices dropped and farm prices rose toward the end of the decade, but the basic reality did not change. As a Georgia farmer angrily observed, "The hand that is feeding the world is being spit upon."

The Urban Nation

The woes of agriculture contributed to the climax of a long-term shift in the geographical distribution of the American population. For the first time, according to the federal census of 1920, a majority of Americans—54 million out of 105 million—lived in urban territory. This did not mean the United States had become a nation of big cities. The census defined "urban territory" as places with as few as 2,500 people. Many "urban" areas were really small towns little removed from rural life. Nevertheless, a fundamental shift had clearly occurred. The United States was no longer a predominantly rural society.

The decline of farming spurred this transformation. As agricultural prices fell, millions of Americans fled the nation's farms, and the dynamic growth of the industrial economy helped swell the population of towns and cities. In the 1920s, factory production was still centered in urban areas. Manufacturing gave many cities their identity. Detroit was becoming the "motor city." Akron, Ohio, was the home of the nation's rubber production. Pittsburgh, Pennsylvania, and Birmingham, Alabama, symbolized the American steel industry. Most of the new white-collar jobs were located in cities. The headquarters of the big corporations were concentrated in the cities, especially the two largest, Chicago and New York.

The rise of the automobile also contributed to the emergence of the urban nation. The car made it practical for more Americans to live in suburbs and drive into the city to work and shop. In the 1920s, the suburban lifestyle was still reserved mostly for well-to-do Americans. Elite suburbs, such as Grosse Pointe and Ferndale outside Detroit, and Beverly Hills, Glendale, and Inglewood outside Los Angeles, grew explosively during the decade. The transformation of the countryside into suburban developments was a powerful symbol of the emergence of the urban nation.

A suburban street in the 1920s. Fittingly, automobiles, which did so much to spur the growth of cities and suburbs, dominate the foreground.

A Modern Culture

The 1920s saw the full emergence of a modern culture that had gradually been taking shape for decades. So perfectly symbolized by Gertrude Ederle, the new culture extolled the virtues of modernity and, above all, pleasure, leisure, and consumption. Rooted in the nation's economic development, the new culture reflected the desires of those Americans who had more free time and money than ever. It reflected the needs of an industrial economy that had to sell the many roadsters and other goods rolling off the assembly lines. Supported by advertising and installment buying, the culture of leisure and consumption offered such pleasures as spectator sports, movies, popular music, radio, and sex. The new culture also entailed new views of gender, family life, and youth. At the same time, the modern culture placed renewed emphasis on the importance of individuals and the old values of individualism in an increasingly organized society.

The Spread of Consumerism

By the 1920s, many Americans, encouraged by big business, increasingly defined life as the pursuit of pleasure. Rather than look for happiness in work, people were invited to seek gratification through the consumption of goods and services. This philosophy of **consumerism**, taking shape for decades, saturated American society by the end of the decade.

In addition to higher wages, many workers had more free time. For salaried, middle-class workers, the annual vacation had become a tradition by the 1910s. Although blue-collar workers seldom enjoyed a vacation, they were spending less time on the job. Some employers, including Henry Ford, instituted a five-day workweek during the 1920s. More commonly, businesses shortened their workday. "The shorter work day brought me my first idea of there being such a thing as pleasure," said one young female worker. "Before this time it was just sleep and eat and hurry off to work."

A change in attitude accompanied these changes in wages and workdays. The work ethic seemed less necessary in a prospering economy. Thanks to Fordism and Taylorism, work was less satisfying, too. In these circumstances, people justified pleasure as an essential antidote to labor. As early as 1908, a magazine announced that "Fun Is a Necessity." Many Americans now agreed.

The advertising industry encouraged the new attitude toward pleasure. Although advertising agencies had first appeared in the 1850s and 1860s, the business did not reach maturity until the 1920s. During the decade, ads appeared everywhere in America—in newspapers and magazines, on billboards and big electric signs, and, by the end of

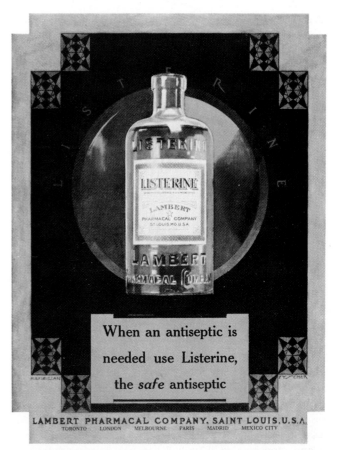

Selling mouthwash and consumerism. An elegant and rather restrained ad was part of the successful campaign to market Listerine to Americans.

the decade, on radio. Major advertising agencies such as J. Walter Thompson and Batten, Barton, Durstine, and Osborn became concentrated in New York City, home to so many corporations. Impressed by successful ad campaigns for such products as Listerine antiseptic and mouthwash and Fleischmann's yeast, big businesses increasingly turned to the agencies to sell goods and services. Expenditures for advertising leaped from 682 million dollars in 1914 to nearly 3 billion dollars by 1929.

All that money paid for ad campaigns deeply influenced by the emerging modern culture of the period. Advertising, like the new culture, optimistically embraced change and innovation. The ad men believed they were bringing the benefits of modernity to Americans. According to advertisements, the purchase of the right products and services would solve people's problems and thereby bring them fulfillment. The advertising of the 1920s presented consumerism as a kind of therapy for Americans trapped in the drudgery of work.

Sure that they were successful, ad men confidently trumpeted the power and importance of their profession. The advertising executive Bruce Barton even described the rise of Christianity as a triumph of advertising. In his best-selling book, *The Man Nobody Knows* (1925), Barton portrayed Jesus Christ as a great salesman, a dynamic businessman who had turned his disciples into an effective sales force "that conquered the world."

Along with advertising, business used installment plans to encourage Americans to buy goods and services. If consumers did not have enough money, companies were increasingly willing to offer them credit. The booming sales of such consumer goods as automobiles, radios, pianos, and washing machines depended on allowing customers to buy "on time," as it was called. Credit buying spread so rapidly that the nation's total consumer debt more than doubled in only seven years from 1922 to 1929.

New Pleasures

The culture of the 1920s offered many pleasures, especially spectator sports, movies, popular music, and radio. Gertrude Ederle was part of a golden age for spectator sports in the 1920s. Although people still avidly played games themselves, they also passively observed other people's games more than ever before. Tennis, boxing, and auto racing flourished during the decade. The American Professional Football Association, which became the National Football League, played its first season in 1920. Although crowds packed stadiums for college football games, baseball remained the most popular American sport, thanks in part to the exploits of the New York Yankees' home-run-hitting outfielder, Babe Ruth.

While spectator sports enthralled millions, another passive pleasure, the movies, was undeniably the most popular consumer attraction of the 1920s (see Figure 23-1). Little more than a novelty when first shown in the mid-1890s, movies had rapidly matured into a big business commanding the loyalty of millions of Americans. Spreading through the cities and into the suburbs, theaters became larger and more elegant. By the 1920s, there were even lavish movie "palaces," such as the Roxy in New York and the Tivoli in Chicago, whose garish decorations evoked the Orient and other exotic faraway places.

The ornate theaters and the features helped to make movies into a big business. Movie attendance doubled from 40 million a week in 1922 to 80 million a week in 1929. That attendance fueled the development of the handful of film companies, including Warner Brothers and RKO, that dominated the industry. By the 1920s, the center of movie production had shifted from New York City to Hollywood, California. As the film industry began to be called "Hollywood," technological innovation promised that this big business would grow still bigger. In 1927, Warner Brothers successfully released the first sound movie, *The Jazz Singer*. The era of "talking pictures" had begun.

It was fitting that the first sound movie was about the impact of a musical genre, jazz. Popular music in general and jazz in particular played an important role in the consumer culture of the 1920s. Created by African Americans in the 1910s, jazz was a rhythmically and harmonically innovative music that featured improvised solos and a hot beat. The new music emerged in various places around the country, but its first great center was the streets, brothels, and dives of New Orleans. The Louisiana city was home to the first major jazz composer, Jelly Roll Morton, and to the first jazz superstar, trumpeter and singer Louis Armstrong. As jazz became nationally popular, Morton, Armstrong, and the focus of jazz moved on, as did so many African Americans, to Chicago and New York City.

The new music quickly attracted white Americans, especially the young, who yearned for something more dar-

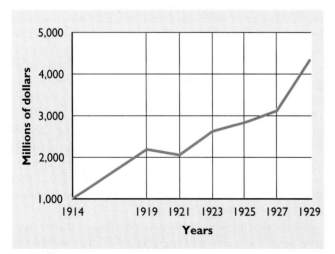

Figure 23-1   Consumer Spending for Recreation, 1914–1929.
Source: Historical Statistics of the United States, I, 401.

Jazz pioneers: The Washingtonians, led by pianist, composer, and arranger Edward Kennedy "Duke" Ellington (seated at right). By the end of the 1920s jazz had swept across the nation, and Ellington had become one of the new music's great stars.

ing than the relatively sedate popular music of the day. For young white people, jazz was the music of outsiders, of African Americans. Even the name—a reference perhaps to speed or sexual intercourse—conjured up pleasure and liberation. Soon white musicians such as the cornet player Bix Beiderbecke were contributing to the evolution of the music. For many whites, jazz summed up a period seemingly dominated by the pursuit of liberating pleasures. The 1920s became known as the "Jazz Age."

The great popularity of jazz and other musical genres was made possible by a relatively new technology, the phonograph. Originated by Thomas Edison in the 1870s and modified by other inventors, the phonograph played shellac platters spinning at 78 revolutions per minute (rpm). In the 1920s, the introduction of the electrical recording microphone dramatically improved the sound quality of these 78 rpm records. Listening to 78s, millions of Americans enjoyed musicians they would otherwise never have heard.

A newer technological innovation, the radio, also allowed Americans to hear the varieties of popular music. After the Italian inventor Guglielmo Marconi transmitted the first radio waves through the air in 1895, a series of innovations made possible the inauguration of commercial radio broadcasting in the United States by 1920. The federal government began licensing radio stations the next year.

Like the movies, radio quickly became a big business. By 1923, there were already more than 500 stations nationwide. In 1926, the first permanent network of stations, the National Broadcasting Company (NBC), took to the airwaves. Americans tuned in to hear broadcasts of live music, news, sports, soap operas, and other programming. To meet the popular demand for radios, American manufacturers turned out more than two million sets a year as early as 1925. By then, radio, like the movies, played a key role in disseminating the values of consumerism. Corporations were already eager to advertise their products by sponsoring radio programs.

A Sexual Revolution

Along with such new pleasures as radio and movies, the modern culture offered a new attitude toward an old pleasure, sex. By the 1920s, Americans' sexual attitudes and behavior were clearly changing. The middle class' discreet silence about sex gave way in the twentieth century. During the progressive era, reformers forced the public discussion of such sexual issues as prostitution and venereal disease. The popular amusements of the 1910s and 1920s inundated Americans with sexual images. From the beginning, the movies explored sexual topics in such films as *The Anatomy of a Kiss* and *A Bedroom Blunder*. As early as 1913, a magazine concluded that "Sex O'Clock" had struck in the United States.

The increased openness about sex reflected the growing belief that sexual pleasure was a necessary and desirable part of human life, particularly of marriage. In the twentieth century, married couples were increasingly allowed to consider intercourse as an opportunity for pleasure as well as procreation.

The new view of marital sexuality helped to change attitudes toward contraception. By the 1910s, an emerging grassroots movement, led by Socialists, members of the Industrial Workers of the World, and other radicals, promoted sex education and access to contraceptives, which were largely illegal. The crusade's best-known figure was the fiery former nurse and socialist organizer, Margaret Sanger. In 1915, Sanger coined the term "birth control" that defined the movement for years to come. Although Sanger temporarily fled the country to avoid prosecution in New York, birth control gradually became respectable—and widely practiced—in the 1920s.

The extent of the change in sexual attitudes and practices should not be exaggerated. The overwhelming majority of Americans still insisted publicly that sexual intercourse should be confined to marriage, and they still condemned homosexuality, but a sexual revolution was underway, as the emergent modern culture insisted that sexual pleasure was an integral aspect of life.

Changing Gender Ideals

The shifting attitude toward sex was closely tied to new gender ideals. By the 1920s, Americans' sense of what it meant to be female was changing markedly. Since the late nineteenth century, Americans had been talking about the independent and assertive "New Woman" who claimed the right to attend school, vote, and have a career. The "New Woman" of the 1920s was now a sexual being, too. An object of male desire, she was also a fun-loving individual with desires of her own.

The most popular image of the American woman of the 1920s was the vivacious young "flapper," with her short skirt, bound breasts, and bobbed hair. The flapper was quite likely to wear cosmetics and to smoke cigarettes—practices once associated with prostitutes rather than respectable middle-class women. An ideal type as much as a reality, the flapper nevertheless said a great deal about changing notions of femininity in 1920s America.

Notions of masculinity were also changing. With the growing emphasis on female needs and desires, men were urged to be more attentive and responsive to women. The more women claimed a public role, the more men were encouraged to focus on the home. As the world of work became less satisfying, experts told men to look for individual fulfillment in family life. The family man of the 1920s, unlike the stereotypical Victorian man of the nineteenth century, was not supposed to be a distant, stern patriarch. Instead, the ideal man of the 1920s was a

Symbols of the fun-loving culture of the "Jazz Age": a flapper and two jazz musicians on the cover of McClure's Magazine.

better companion to his wife and a doting friend to his children.

In practice, many men had trouble living up to the ideal. Along with the rest of society, they still tended to define themselves in terms of their work, rather than their domestic life. Moreover, American society still regarded women as the primary parent in the lives of children. Despite the clear change in domestic values, many men were still relative outsiders in the home.

The Family and Youth

Changing gender ideals were directly related to a reconsideration of family life and youth. In the 1920s, the American family no longer played a critically important direct role in economic production. Although whole families still labored together in California fields and North Carolina textile mills, most Americans did not regard the family as a group of productive workers. The family farm, whose members all pitched in to get the work done, was obviously declining. Around the country, child-labor laws in-

creasingly made sure that boys and girls spent their time in school rather than in the workplace.

Less a unit of production, the family became primarily a unit of leisure and consumption. The home was the place where men, women, and children were expected to find pleasure and fulfillment, where they congregated around the radio and used their Fleischmann's yeast and Listerine mouthwash.

The new view of the family affected youth. Reflecting the values of the modern culture, parents became more likely to indulge their children in the twentieth century. The boys and girls of the 1920s enjoyed more toys, possessions, spending money, and pleasures than had earlier generations of children. Teenagers went out to the movies on their own more often than with their parents. The automobile gave young people more mobility, too. With their new freedom, they could begin to create their own separate culture. One sign was the dramatic spread of petting among high-school youth, newly free from parental control.

Most adults accepted this situation partly because they admired and envied youthfulness more than before. The modern culture, unhappy with work and anxious for fun, glorified youth. After all, vibrant, energetic, unemployed young people seemed capable of having the most fun. "Flaming Youth" became a symbol of the culture of the 1920s.

The Celebration of the Individual

The emphasis on the individual, so evident in changing views of sex, gender, family, and youth, was a fundamental aspect of the modern culture. In addition to Gertrude Ederle and Babe Ruth, Americans admired the feats of a host of individual sports heroes and heroines during the decade, including the tennis player Helen Wills Moody, the boxers Jack Dempsey and Gene Tunney, the golfer Bobby Jones, and the football runningback Red Grange. In the 1920s, the movie industry, which originally had not even bothered to reveal the names of actors and actresses, increasingly focused public attention on the distinctive personalities of individual stars. **Individualism** was basic to the "New Woman," too. Feminism, a feminist explained, "means that woman wants to be an individual."

The resurgence of individualism was not surprising. The belief in the importance of the individual was deeply engrained in the American political economy. The worth of individuals had been fundamental to the Declaration of Independence and the Constitution in the eighteenth century, and to the antislavery crusade of the nineteenth century. Paradoxically, the development of industrial capitalism in the twentieth century intensified the importance of individuals and organizations at the same time. As corporations grew larger and produced ever more goods and services, these giant firms needed to stimulate a form of individualism among the American people. Consumerism

GROWING UP IN AMERICA

"Flaming Youth" on Campus

More than any other places, college and university campuses defined "Flaming Youth" in the 1920s. "The college population might be said to represent the advance guard of the younger generation," wrote two observers. During the decade, male and female college students helped create a distinctive youth culture within the larger modern culture. Their lives embodied two of the central features of twentieth-century American society: the desire for individual freedom and the need to cope with organization.

Colleges and universities played such a large role in the definition of "Flaming Youth" because they afforded students a space to create their own way of life. At school, students were free from the constraints of home and workplace.

Partly because college was still such an unusual experience, campus life attracted a great deal of attention from the rest of society. College students made up a fashionable elite. As late as 1930, only one in five college-age Americans was enrolled in some kind of educational institution. At the same time, college life had become more visible than ever, thanks to the dramatic expansion of enrollments after World War I. As the dynamic economy demanded more educated, white-collar workers, prospering middle-class families found the means to send their sons and daughters to college. In just three years, from 1919 to 1922, enrollments doubled from 3,000 to 6,000 at the University of Illinois and from 4,000 to 8,000 at Ohio State University.

At school, young people created their own version of the new culture of leisure and pleasure. They pushed against the campus limits on individual freedom. "To me the Jazz Age signifies an age of freedom in thought and action," explained a co-ed at the University of Denver. "The average young person of today is not bound by the strict conventions which governed the actions of previous generations."

On campuses across the country, students held "petting parties." They forced college officials to tolerate racy new dances such as the Toddle, the Shimmy, the Charleston, and the Black Bottom. By the end of the decade, about two out of three students defied Prohibition by drinking on and off campus. Public drunkenness was no longer a scandal. Meanwhile, women students had won the right to engage in the "unladylike," sexually suggestive practice of smoking. "College," sniffed a dean at Princeton, "has unfortunately become a kind of glorified playground ... a paradise of the young."

Students' quest for pleasure was allied with a strengthened belief in individualism. The students of the 1920s increasingly regarded sex and other satisfactions as private matters. College newspapers criticized prohibitionists and other moral reformers who wanted to regulate individual behavior.

Even as they reflected the individualist values of the modern culture, the college students of the 1920s also adapted to the growing power of organization in American society. Collegiate life became more bureaucratic as administrators coped with rising enrollments. Students themselves turned to organizations in the 1920s. Nationwide, the number of fraternities and sororities shot up during the decade. By 1930, about one student in three belonged to a fraternity or sorority. On most campuses, the Greek houses included most student leaders and set the tone of campus fashions for the "barbs," the barbarians who made up the rest of the student body.

Fraternities and sororities were places where college students could try out smoking and other freedoms, but the Greek system also forced its members to come to terms with organization. As the campus newspaper at Cornell University explained, the fraternity "crushes individuality." Initiation rites and hazing taught new members that they were expected to conform to the norms of the group. The distinctive culture of "flaming youth," like the new national culture, embraced organization as well as freedom, conformity as well as individualism.

The faces of "Flaming Youth" on campus: Members of the University of Wisconsin class of 1924 pose for the camera. Kneeling fourth from right is Charles Lindbergh who dropped out of college and became a symbol of the era with his solo transatlantic flight in 1927.

depended on Americans' willingness to define life in terms of gratifying their individual needs and desires.

Although many Americans wanted to believe in their own individual power and autonomy, there were serious obstacles to true individualism in the 1920s. Powerful organizations, including corporations, controlled individual life in many ways. Even the most famous individual exploit of the decade depended on organization. On May 20 and 21, 1927, Charles A. Lindbergh successfully flew his monoplane, *The Spirit of St. Louis,* from New York City to Paris. The flight, the first nonstop solo crossing of the Atlantic, made Lindbergh an international hero and a symbol of what an individual could still accomplish, but Lindbergh's solitary feat relied on other people. A group of businessmen put up the money, and a corporation built *The Spirit of St. Louis.* Organization and individualism, the new and the old, were interdependent realities in the 1920s.

The Limits of the Modern Culture

In spite of its rapid growth, the modern culture had clear limits in the 1920s. For millions of Americans, much of the consumer lifestyle was simply out of reach. Despite the general prosperity of the decade, low incomes and poverty persisted across the nation. As late as 1928, six out of 10 American families made less than the 2,000 dollars a year required for just the "basic needs of life." In the 1920s, half the nation's families did not own a car. In the countryside at mid-decade, only about one farm in 10 had running water, gas, or electric lighting.

The spread of the new values was as limited as the spread of cars and running water. Many Americans, among them a new generation of artists and intellectuals, were unwilling to define their lives in terms of the pursuit of pleasure, leisure, consumption, and a narrowly defined individualism. For millions of people, the modern culture represented an unwelcome abandonment of old values and ways of life. The 1920s witnessed a backlash from Americans troubled by the pace and character of change. In different ways, fundamentalist Christians, immigration restrictionists, and the Ku Klux Klan demanded a return to an earlier United States. Other Americans, including some of the targets of the immigration restrictionists and the Klan, found that the new culture did not speak fully to their needs. Mexican Americans and Mexican immigrants discovered that the dynamic economy provided limited opportunity, and modern culture complicated the search for identity. African Americans, meanwhile, realized that the United States had changed very little when it came to issues of racial equality.

The "Lost Generation" of Intellectuals

A good number of artists and intellectuals felt alienated from the United States of the 1920s. For a group of white, mostly male writers and artists who came of age during World War I, the conflict represented a profound failure of western civilization. The war, especially for those who had witnessed it firsthand, was a brutal and seemingly pointless exercise in destruction on an unprecedented scale. Its aftermath left these Americans angry at what the poet Ezra Pound called "an old bitch gone in the teeth . . . a botched civilization." It also left them alienated and rootless. In a nation supposedly devoted to individualism, they did not feel free. They were, as the writer Gertrude Stein described them, a "Lost Generation." Some of them, such as Stein and her fellow writer Ernest Hemingway, left the United States for Paris and other places in Europe. Hemingway's fiction, most notably his 1926 novel *The Sun Also Rises,* dramatized the sense of lost direction for this generation roaming Europe after the war.

However prosperous and peaceful, the postwar years did not reassure the "Lost Generation" about the course

F. Scott Fitzgerald, seen here dancing for the camera with his wife and daughter, explored the lives of quintessential 1920s figures, "Flaming Youth" and the rich, in his stories and novels.

of American life. Some artists and intellectuals argued that the nation had not changed much at all. The dead hand of Victorianism still laid hold of American culture. In such works as *Winesburg, Ohio* (1919), the novelist Sherwood Anderson portrayed a still-repressive society that denied people real freedom and individuality. The acid-tongued critic H. L. Mencken, editor of the magazine *The American Mercury,* excoriated a supposedly provincial and parochial culture still dominated by the "booboisie" and its rural values.

At the same time, other American artists and intellectuals feared that their country had changed too much. Although excited by the potential of the machine, they noted the toll that industrialization exacted in hard, increasingly routinized work. They noted, too, the dangers of a culture devoted to the pursuit of superficial pleasures. In his 1922 novel, *Babbitt,* Sinclair Lewis satirized the life of a midwestern Republican businessman obsessed with consumerism. As the pages of *Babbitt* made amusingly clear, there was no real individualism if the pursuit of objects and pleasures made people all alike. F. Scott Fitzgerald, in such fiction as *This Side of Paradise* (1920) and *The Great Gatsby* (1925), conveyed the sense of loss and emptiness in the lives of fashionable "Flaming Youth" and decadent rich people.

From a different angle, 12 southern intellectuals, including Allen Tate, Robert Penn Warren, Donald Davidson, and John Crowe Ransom, attacked the modern culture in *I'll Take My Stand: The South and the Agrarian Tradition* (1930). Their essays offered a spirited defense of the rural, traditional culture, supposedly embodied by the Old South, that H. L. Mencken had savagely condemned. In turn, the southern Agrarians lamented the defects of an industrial, consumer society that demeaned work and exalted individualism.

The impact of art and ideas in the 1920s was difficult to gauge. The poets, writers, artists, and other creative figures of the decade certainly did not set off a mass rebellion against the modern culture, but they did articulate the ambivalence and uneasiness of many people in the new world of the "Jazz Age." In different and contradictory ways, the artists and intellectuals of the 1920s laid out an agenda for Americans as they came to terms with modern, consumer society in the decades to come.

Fundamentalist Christians and "Old-Time Religion"

For many Americans of faith, the rapid growth of the modern culture promoted a sense of profound and unsettling change. "The world has been convulsed and every field of thought and action has been disturbed," declared *Presbyterian Magazine.* "The most settled principles and laws of society have been attacked." The new culture was all the more troubling because it was so secular. In the 1920s, American society seemed to define life more than ever before in terms of material satisfactions rather than spiritual commitments. Many Protestants also felt that their own churches had betrayed them in this critical time. These Americans resented the influence of the liberal Protestants who had tried to accommodate their faith to the methods and discoveries of science and scholarship since the late nineteenth century. In the 1910s and 1920s, the fundamentalist movement emerged to challenge liberals for control of several denominations.

The opponents of liberalism took their name from *The Fundamentals,* a series of booklets with essays by leading conservative Protestant theologians that began to appear in 1909. Fundamentalists emerged all around the country, but they were strongest in rural areas and in the South and West. By the end of World War I, fundamentalists dominated the Southern Baptist Convention and were fighting liberals for control of the northern churches.

Fundamentalists rejected liberalism on several grounds, but above all for its willingness to question the historical truth of the *Bible.* Sure that the modern world threatened Christianity, the fundamentalist movement urged people to return to biblical, patriarchal, and denominational authority, to what came to be called "old-time" religion.

While the fundamentalist–liberal battle was mainly played out in Protestant denominations, its high point came in a courtroom in Tennessee in 1925. That year, a high school biology teacher, John Scopes, decided to test a new state law banning the teaching of "any theory that denies the story of the divine creation of man as taught in the Bible, and that teaches instead that man has descended from a lower order of animals." After Scopes was arrested for violating the law, his trial became a national media event that illuminated the confrontation between fundamentalism and liberalism. The chief lawyer for the prosecution was William Jennings Bryan of Nebraska, the former Democratic presidential candidate and secretary of state who had become a leading crusader for fundamentalism in general and the legal ban on the teaching of evolution in particular. While Bryan was a long-time champion of rural America, Scopes' attorneys—Clarence Darrow of Chicago and Dudley Field Malone—were representatives of the city and modern culture. Malone, interestingly, had helped to finance Gertrude Ederle's swim across the English Channel. In a dramatic confrontation, Darrow called Bryan to the stand and forced the Nebraskan to concede that the *Bible* might not be literally accurate after all. Although Scopes was convicted and fined, Bryan and the fundamentalists had lost a good deal of credibility.

The defense team in the 1925 trial of school teacher John Scopes for violating Tennessee law by the teaching of evolution. The tense faces and the packed courtroom suggest how much was at stake in this battle over the ongoing cultural transformation of the United States.

Nativists and Immigration Restriction

While fundamentalist Christianity sought a return to old-time religion, a resurgent nativist movement wanted to go back to an earlier, supposedly more homogenous America. As had happened so often in the past, some Americans reacted to stressful change in the 1920s by singling out immigrants. As mass migration from Europe to the United States resumed after World War I, there was a striking revival of nativist feeling among Americans from West European backgrounds. Thanks to the Russian Revolution and the domestic Red Scare, they associated immigrants with anarchism and radicalism. Thanks to the purportedly scientific study of racial and ethnic differences, they viewed southern and eastern Europeans as inferior races that would weaken the nation. Consequently, the nativists called urgently for a return to a simpler, less ethnically diverse nation.

This view quickly and decisively shaped public policy. In 1921, Congress overwhelmingly passed a law temporarily limiting the annual immigration from any European country to just three percent of the number of its immigrants who had been living in the United States in 1910. This quota measure sharply reduced the number of new immigrants from southern and eastern Europe, but nativists wanted even tougher action. Congress responded with the even more restrictionist National Origins Act of 1924. This measure cut unwanted immigration even further by limiting the annual intake from a European coun-

TABLE 23-1

The Impact of Nativism: Immigration, 1921–1929

	(arrivals in thousands)		
	1921	1925	1929
E. Europe & Poland	138	10	14
S. Europe	299	8	22
Asia	25	4	4
Mexico	31	33	40
TOTAL	805	294	280

Source: Historical Statistics of the United States, I, 401.
(Note: itemized groups do not add up to totals.)

try to a mere two percent of the number of its immigrants living in the United States in 1890—a time when there were still relatively few southern and eastern Europeans in America. The National Origins Act also excluded Japanese immigrants altogether. The legislation had the desired effect: Immigration fell from 805,000 arrivals in 1921 to 280,000 in 1929 (see Table 23-1).

The Rebirth of the Ku Klux Klan

Nativism and fundamentalism helped spur another challenge to the new cultural order of the 1920s. In 1915, the

Ku Klux Klan, the secret, vigilante group that had terrorized African Americans in the South during Reconstruction, was reborn in a ceremony on Stone Mountain, Georgia. The revived Klan enjoyed explosive growth after World War I, particularly when Hiram Evans, a dentist from Dallas, Texas, became the new imperial wizard in 1922. Under Evans' leadership, the organization effectively blended old and new. The "Invisible Empire" borrowed the rituals of the nineteenth-century Klan, including its costume of white robes and hoods and its symbol of a burning cross. Like the old Klan, the twentieth-century version was driven by a racist hatred of African Americans, but the new Klan also had new targets, including Jews, Roman Catholics, immigrants, religious liberalism, and change in general.

The reborn Klan had extremist views but a mainstream, national membership. The "Invisible Empire" of the 1920s flourished in every region of the country, in cities as well as the countryside. Its members included farmers, clerks, salesmen, and storeowners; the order included women as well as men. The Klan was an extremist group with surprisingly strong roots in "respectable" America.

The "Invisible Empire" condemned the modern culture. Hostile to the increasing materialism of American society, the Klan charged that the nation now valued "money above manhood." Klan rallies rang with denunciations of big business. Above all, the Klan condemned the new cul-

ture of leisure and pleasure. "Pleasure," announced a Klansman, "has become the god of the young people of America, and a very unwholesome and lascivious pleasure it is." The Klan was hostile to the new gender ideals, to birth control and freer sexuality, and to the independence of youth.

In essence, the Ku Klux Klan lamented the transformations of the twentieth century—what Hiram Evans called "the moral breakdown that has been going on for two decades." Klansmen yearned for an earlier America in which white Protestant males had power over women, youth, and other groups and had nothing to fear from big business.

The Klan's tactics were a blend of old and new. Seeing themselves as an army of secret vigilantes, some Klan members supported the age-old tactics of moral regulation—intimidation, flogging, and sometimes lynching—in order to scare people into good behavior. At the same time, much of the "Invisible Empire" repudiated violence and used the latest advertising techniques to boost its membership.

For several years, the Klan's potent combination of old and new elements proved extraordinarily successful. At its peak, the organization enrolled perhaps three to five million secret members, and its power reached much further. Because so many politicians sympathized with the Klan or feared its power, the organization had considerable political influence in such states as Ohio, Indiana, Kansas, Oklahoma, Georgia, Texas, California, and Oregon. Working with both major parties, the order helped to elect governors, senators, and other officials.

At the height of its power, however, the "Invisible Empire" collapsed under the weight of scandal. Evans' predecessor as imperial wizard was revealed to have drunk alcohol, read pornography, and consorted with prostitutes. Two of Evans' assistants were caught, drunk and nude, in an adulterous tryst. In 1925, David Stephenson, the grand dragon of Indiana kidnapped and attacked a former schoolteacher, who died. Incidents such as these, along with financial scandals, revealed the lawlessness and hypocrisy of the Klan's leadership. It had also become obvious that America had nothing to fear from such Klan targets as Communists and unions. Most basically, millions of Americans, however uneasy about the new culture, had no desire to support prejudice, lawbreaking, and violence in a futile attempt to go back to the past. The Klan's membership dropped precipitously in the late 1920s.

White-robed men, women, and children of the Ku Klux Klan arriving in Cincinnati, Ohio, to celebrate the organization and its defense of "traditional" values.

Mexican Americans

Despite the activities of immigration restrictionists and the Klan, the United States remained a diverse nation at the end of the 1920s. In some ways, in fact, American society was even more diverse than before. After World War I, Mexican immigrants and Mexican Americans became a more visible presence than they had been in many years. The struggle of Chicanos, ethnic Mexicans, to make a life in the United States revealed both the opportunities created by the dynamic economy and the limits of the new culture.

By the late nineteenth century, the ethnic Mexican population of the United States, concentrated in the Southwest, had become less visible as the tide of European and Anglo migration continued to sweep across the region, but in the 1890s the migration of Mexicans began a dramatic, long-term increase. Perhaps a million to a million and a half Mexicans crossed the border into the United States legally or surreptitiously between 1890 and 1929. They left their homeland primarily to escape the transformation of Mexican agriculture that made it impossible for millions of the rural poor to make a living off the land, and to avoid the violence and economic upheaval surrounding the Mexican Revolution of 1910. The construction of railroads across Mexico spurred migration by making travel easier and also, more subtly, by introducing more U. S. culture and goods into Mexican society. More fundamentally, impoverished Mexicans traveled north to take advantage of the opportunities created by the dynamic U. S. economy. Ironically, the restrictionist immigration legislation of the

1920s helped to insure that Mexicans would find work waiting for them in the United States. Unable to get enough European or Asian workers, U. S. employers turned eagerly to Mexico as a source of cheap and often temporary labor willing to move from factory to factory and farm to farm with the change of seasons. By the 1920s, Mexicans labored in the steel mills of Indiana and the auto plants of Michigan. Mexican immigrants even worked as far north as the fishing fleets and canneries of Alaska, but the vast majority of Mexican immigrants stayed closer to the Mexican border in the Southwest. The region's rapidly developing economy needed workers for its mines, railroads, construction gangs, and above all, its vast farms. By the end of the 1920s, Mexican immigrants and Mexican Americans dominated low-wage manual labor in the Southwest.

Like a large number of immigrants from Europe, many Mexican migrants did not plan to stay in the United States. They traveled back and forth to their homeland, or returned permanently. Gradually, however, many chose to stay in the United States as they developed economic and family ties north of the Mexican border. The National Origins Act, which made it costly, time-consuming, and often humiliating for Mexicans to cross the border, also encouraged migrants to remain in the United States. As a result, the Mexican population of the United States more than doubled from 103,000 to 222,000 between 1900 and 1910, and then doubled again to 478,000 by 1920. At the turn of the century, the majority of immigrants lived in Texas and Arizona, and there were large enclaves of Mexicans in the Texas cities of El Paso and San Antonio. However, California, with its booming agricultural economy, rapidly became the center of the Mexican population. The city of Los Angeles, growing phenomenally in the early twentieth century, particularly attracted Mexican migrants. The city's Mexican population, less than 5,000 in 1900, grew to perhaps 190,000 by 1930.

Mexican immigrants and Mexican Americans, like so many other ethnic groups in the United States, wrestled with complex questions about their national identity. Were they still Mexicans or had they become Americans or some unique combination of the two nationalities? Those questions were still more complicated because Mexican immigrants had left one rapidly changing country for another. The meaning of "Mexican" and the meaning of "American" were both very fluid. In the United States, moreover, ethnic Mexicans received a mixed reception from a society that both did and did not want them. While southwestern employers were eager

Mexican immigrant workers, posed on the tracks of a railroad in Texas in the 1900s. It was the railroad that helped disrupt life in Mexico and offered the promise of jobs in the United States.

for labor, they and many other native-born whites tended to assume that migrant Mexican workers should return to Mexico rather than live permanently in the United States. Many white Americans stereotyped Mexicans as a lazy and shiftless race who would take jobs from native-born workers and who could not be assimilated into American life and culture. Immigration restrictionists, not surprisingly, wanted Mexican immigration banned altogether. As one restrictionist congressman asked, "What is the use of closing the front door to keep out undesirables from Europe when you permit Mexicans to come in here by the back door by the thousands and thousands?" Still other white Americans, drawing on the reform techniques of the progressive era, wanted to "Americanize" Chicanos by teaching them English and the middle-class values of thrift and time discipline. Mexican wives were encouraged to learn American home-making practices and had to give up native diets heavy in fried food, rice, and beans.

The economy also presented Chicanos with a mixed message. Like other Americans, Mexicans were surrounded by the products and advertisements of the new consumer culture, but limited education and persistent discrimination prevented most Mexican immigrants and Mexican Americans from earning the larger incomes needed to enjoy American-style consumerism. Largely confined to low-wage, less-skilled work, ethnic Mexicans had a low standard of living. In many towns and cities, they were effectively segregated in certain neighborhoods—barrios—in poor conditions. In Los Angeles, for instance, much of the large Mexican population gradually congregated in East Los Angeles by the end of the 1920s. The Mexicans of Los Angeles had to live in the poorest one- or two-room residences, known as "cholo courts," and had to endure high rates of tuberculosis and infant mortality.

In the face of this ambivalent and often hostile reception, ethnic Mexicans forged their unique identities. There was no single Mexican response to the United States and its new culture. In varying degrees, Chicanos clung to their old national identities and adapted to their new home. Mexican immigrants and Mexican Americans, moreover, often emphasized the differences between the two groups. Mexican Americans, eager to hold onto the advantages they had won by birth and long-time residence in the United States, feared that the immigrants, poor and unused to American ways, would provide competition for jobs and cause native-born whites to denigrate all Mexicans alike. The immigrants, in turn, often derided Mexican Americans as pochos—bleached or faded people—who had lost their true Mexican identity. "I don't have anything against the Pochos," a Mexican immigrant declared, "but the truth of the matter is . . . they pretend that they are Americans. They only want to talk in English . . . ."

Nevertheless, ethnic Mexicans created a distinctive culture in the United States. For all their differences, immigrants and second- and third-generation Mexican Americans shared a sense of common cultural origins and common challenges. In a white-dominated society, they saw themselves as La Raza—the race—set apart by heritage and skin color. Although some became Protestants, the Mexican population was overwhelmingly Catholic. Young Mexican Americans were quite likely to intermarry.

Mexicans' response to the consumer culture helped create a common identity. Like other American workers, Mexicans went into debt to buy cars and other consumer goods. Largely ignored by corporations marketing goods nationwide, the Mexican population supported its own businesses. Similarly, Chicanos listened to their own Spanish-language radio programs and bought records made by Mexican musicians in San Antonio and Los Angeles. Among the most popular forms of Mexican-American music were corridos, the traditional folk ballads from rural Mexico adapted to life in the United States. Singing of things that Mexicans were often reluctant to say, corridos testified both to the distinctiveness of Chicanos' culture and to the uneasiness of their place in the new culture of the United States. In 1926, "El Lavaplatos" ("The Dishwasher"), the very first commercially recorded corrido, told the story of an illegal migrant attracted by American consumerism but unable to make ends meet in low-paying jobs: "I dreamed in my youth of being a movie star/ And one of those days I come to visit Hollywood./ . . . And I, how could I stand it, I was better off washing dishes./ How repentant, how repentant, I am for having come." But hundreds of thousands of Mexicans did stay in the United States and struggled for equal rights and economic progress. In 1928, a farm workers' strike in the Imperial Valley led to the creation of the Federation of Mexican Workers Unions. A year later, Chicano businessmen and professionals in Texas formed the League of United Latin American Citizens (LULAC) in Texas.

African Americans and the "New Negro"

Like Chicanos, African Americans found the new cultural terrain of the United States appealing but unsatisfying. For many African-American people, the United States of the 1920s had changed a great deal and yet hardly changed at all. They enjoyed and helped to create the new culture. It was a largely African-American music, after all, that supplied the name for "the Jazz Age," but modern culture did little to alter discrimination against African Americans. Segregation—by law in the South, by custom in the North—was still the rule. African Americans in the South were effectively disfranchised. Everywhere, African Americans lived with economic inequality.

While discrimination had not changed, many African Americans insisted that they had. The decade that saw the "New Woman," also witnessed the appearance of the "New Negro." This new ideal was partly the product of a fresh sense of freedom as African Americans left the

The gaze of the "New Negro:" One of the great poets of the Harlem Renaissance—Langston Hughes—portrayed in pastel by one of its leading artists, Winold Reiss.

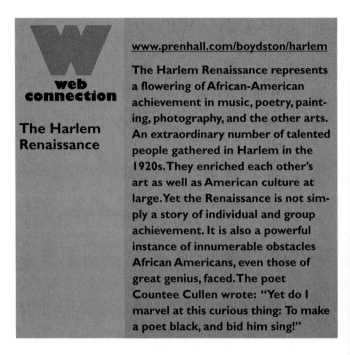

www.prenhall.com/boydston/harlem

web connection

The Harlem Renaissance

The Harlem Renaissance represents a flowering of African-American achievement in music, poetry, painting, photography, and the other arts. An extraordinary number of talented people gathered in Harlem in the 1920s. They enriched each other's art as well as American culture at large. Yet the Renaissance is not simply a story of individual and group achievement. It is also a powerful instance of innumerable obstacles African Americans, even those of great genius, faced. The poet Countee Cullen wrote: "Yet do I marvel at this curious thing: To make a poet black, and bid him sing!"

southern countryside for southern and northern cities. It was also the product of a fresh sense of frustration as African Americans encountered inequality along with opportunity in urban areas. Unlike the stereotype of the "Old Negro," the "New Negro" was more militant and assertive in the face of mistreatment by whites. "The time for cringing is over," said an African-American newspaper.

The "New Negro" was also defined by a profound sense of racial difference. In the 1920s, African Americans investigated and applauded the distinctiveness of their life and culture. The Harlem Renaissance was a major result of this effort. Harlem, the section of upper Manhattan in New York City where so many African Americans had moved since the turn of the century, became the center of a period of great artistic and intellectual creativity in the 1920s. Mostly based in Harlem, novelists such as Zora Neale Hurston, Jessie Fauset, Claude McKay, and Jean Toomer; poets such as Langston Hughes and Countee Cullen; and artists such as Aaron Douglas and Augusta Savage produced a renaissance, a new birth of African-American creativity. In different ways, these women and men explored and celebrated the distinctive nature of

blackness in 1920s America. They also focused attention on Africa, the original home of African Americans.

The militance of the "New Negro" was reflected in the development of the NAACP. While whites still belonged to the organization and helped fund it, the NAACP turned increasingly to African-American leadership in the 1920s. The organization's key figure, W. E. B. Du Bois, became more critical of whites and more determined that white-dominated imperial nations should return Africa to African control. The NAACP also pushed the cause of African-American civil rights more aggressively. The organization attacked the white primary system that denied African Americans any say in the dominant Democratic Party organizations of the South. The NAACP also helped to continue the long-time antilynching campaign in which such women as Mary B. Talbert played a leading role. That campaign bore fruit in the 1920s, as southern whites who once glorified mob violence were increasingly embarrassed by lawless vigilante justice. In 1921, for example, a group of white ministers in Athens, Georgia, condemned the burning of John Eberhardt, an African American accused of murder, as "barbarism . . . subversive of every interest we hold precious."

For a time, the NAACP's efforts were overshadowed by the crusades of Marcus Garvey. A Jamaican immigrant to New York City, Garvey founded the Universal Negro Improvement Association (UNIA), which became the largest African-American political organization of the 1920s. Garvey exalted "a new Negro who stands erect, conscious of his manhood rights and fully determined to preserve them at all times." The founder of the UNIA was not interested in political rights or integration for African

Americans, however. Instead, he focused on African-American self-help and on Africa. Garvey wanted African Americans to develop their own businesses and thus become economically self-sufficient. Like Du Bois, he insisted that the imperial powers give up their colonial control of the African continent. Sure that African Americans could never find freedom and equality in a white-dominated nation, Garvey believed African Americans should ultimately return to their true home in Africa.

The UNIA grew rapidly after the war. While the NAACP attracted mostly middle-class members, Garvey's organization developed a vast following among the African-American working class. In 1919, Garvey launched an economic self-help project, the Black Star Line, which, he promised, would buy ships and transport passengers and cargo from the United States to the West Indies, Central America, and Africa. Many of his followers invested in the Black Star Line, but it collapsed due to mismanagement. Garvey himself was indicted for mail fraud in connection with the project in 1922. By the end of the decade, federal authorities had deported him to Jamaica, and the UNIA had lost its mass following.

As the fate of the UNIA suggested, militance could be costly for African Americans. The NAACP also paid the price for its assertiveness as its membership dropped dramatically during the decade. Nevertheless, African Americans' struggles against the inequities of the 1920s laid the groundwork for more successful struggles in the future. These struggles also underscored the modern culture's inattention to economic and racial inequality.

A "New Era" in Politics and Government

The uneasiness with the modern culture had only a limited impact on American politics and government. Other factors—the resurgence of individualism, the power of organizations, and the spread of consumerism—shaped public life more decisively in the 1920s. The decade witnessed the full emergence of the modern political system characterized by advertising, weak parties, and low voter turnout. As support for progressive reform declined, Republicans dominated the new politics. A succession of Republican presidents—Warren G. Harding, Calvin Coolidge, and Herbert Hoover—monopolized the White House during the decade. Committed to individualist values and corporate interests, the Republican ascendancy brought the return of a political economic vision centered on minimalist government and a less internationalist foreign policy. Republicans called the 1920s a "New Era" in American politics and government. But paradoxically, much of the "New Era" represented the resurrection of older beliefs in a modern context.

The Modern Political System

The 1920s marked the full emergence of a new political system that had been taking shape since the late nineteenth century. The major political parties, weakening since their nineteenth-century heyday, grew still weaker during the decade. Their control over the political culture loosened even more with the emergence of new media. Unlike newspapers, the growing numbers of radio stations and movie theaters had no political affiliations at all. As a result, partisanship no longer engulfed Americans as it once had. The number of independent voters most likely increased during the decade.

As the parties weakened, a new, educational political style flourished. Rather than using emotional appeals to party loyalty, this approach emphasized the objective, nonpartisan presentation of facts to educate voters and policymakers about particular issues or candidates. Pressure groups and other organizations used the educational style to lobby voters and legislators about public policies. In Washington, Congress was besieged by lobbyists from corporations, business groups such as the National Association of Manufacturers, professional organizations such as the American Medical Association, and single-issue pressure groups such as the Anti-Saloon League.

The other dominant political style of the 1920s drew its inspiration from consumerism. Copying big business, politicians put ads in newspapers and magazines and on billboards and subway cars to appeal to voters. Because of the decline of intense partisanship, political advertising campaigns seldom emphasized the parties themselves. Instead, reflecting the individualist focus of the modern culture, the campaigns sold the personality of individual candidates. Criss-crossing the nation by railroad, presidential nominees campaigned more openly and more extensively than ever before.

The educational and advertising styles did a poor job of mobilizing voters on election day. Nationwide, voter turnout fell from 79 percent for the presidential election of 1896 to just 49 percent for the elections of 1920 and 1924. A number of factors helped to account for this drop-off: African Americans in the South had been effectively disfranchised, and newly enfranchised women were less likely to vote than men in the 1920s, but white male turnout dropped dramatically, too. Most strikingly, the new political styles simply did not engage and motivate voters the way the old-style partisanship had in the nineteenth century.

The Republican Ascendancy

The chief beneficiaries of the new politics were the Republicans. Determined to win back the White House in 1920, the Republican Party chose an uncontroversial, conservative ticket. Handsome and charismatic, presidential nominee Warren G. Harding of Ohio had accomplished little during a term in the Senate. His running mate, Governor Calvin Coolidge of Massachusetts, was best known for having taken a firm stance against a strike by the Boston police the year before.

The Republican ticket was not imposing, but neither was the opposition. The Democratic presidential nominee, Governor James M. Cox of Ohio, was saddled with the unpopularity of the Woodrow Wilson administration. His running mate, Franklin Roosevelt of New York, was a little-known cousin of former President Theodore Roosevelt and had served as assistant secretary of the Navy in the Wilson administration.

While the Democrats ran an ineffective campaign, the Republicans made excellent use of advertising. And Harding neatly appealed to the reaction against Wilson's activist government. The country needed, he argued, "not nostrums but normalcy." That is, Harding offered a return to normal after the progressive innovations that had disrupted American society during and after the war.

On election day, Harding won a huge victory with 60.3 percent of the popular vote, a new record. Normalcy was triumphant; Harding won 37 states for a total of 404 electoral votes. Cox carried only 11 southern and border states worth 127 electoral votes. Meanwhile, the Republican Party had substantially increased its majorities in both the House and the Senate.

Launched with a sweeping electoral victory, the Harding administration ended prematurely in scandal and death. The president was plagued by revelations of fraud and corruption, some involving the so-called "Ohio Gang," political cronies from Harding's home state. The director of the Veterans' Bureau, caught making fraudulent deals with federal property, went to prison. One of the "Ohio Gang," fearing exposure of the group's influence-peddling schemes—committed suicide in 1923. The revelations shook the president, who complained about "my damn friends, my God-damn friends."

On a western trip, Harding died suddenly of a misdiagnosed heart attack in August 1923. But the scandals continued. Congressional hearings revealed that former Secretary of the Interior Albert B. Fall had apparently accepted bribes from two businessmen in return for leasing them U. S. Navy oil reserves at Teapot Dome, Wyoming, and Elk Hills, California. Teapot Dome, as the scandal came to be called, eventually earned Fall a fine and a jail term. In 1924, another member of Harding's cabinet, Attorney General Harry Daugherty, had to resign because of his role in the "Ohio Gang."

The parade of scandals permanently damaged the reputation of the dead president, but they did not seriously harm his party or his successor, Calvin Coolidge. The former vice president—so reserved in public that he was called "Silent Cal"—proved well-suited to the political moment. The picture of rectitude, Coolidge restored public confidence in the presidency after the Harding scandals.

An artist's fanciful depiction of a United States Capitol dominated by the Teapot Dome scandal. For a time in the 1920s, revelations of corrupt dealings involving leases of U.S. oil reserves at Teapot Dome, Wyoming, and Elk Hills, California, threatened the image of the federal government and its Republican leadership.

In 1924, Coolidge easily won the presidency in his own right against the Democrat John W. Davis, a colorless, conservative corporate lawyer from West Virginia, and the standard-bearer of the new Progressive Party, Senator Robert M. La Follette of Wisconsin. The choice, insisted Republicans, was either "Coolidge or Chaos." The voters chose Coolidge. Holding onto the White House and to their majorities in Congress, the Republicans continued their ascendancy.

The Politics of Individualism

Once in power, the Republicans practiced the politics of individualism. Eager to serve big business, they wanted a political economy driven by individualist values and minimalist government. Led by Harding and Coolidge, the Republicans of the 1920s denounced the activist, progressive state and called instead for less government and more individual freedom. Critical of government, Harding, Coolidge, and their allies praised business and consumerism. Coolidge declared that "the chief business of the American people is business." Harding bluntly summed up the Republican prescription for America: "Less Government in Business and More Business in Government."

Despite such slogans, Republicans sometimes used money and government power to spur economic development. The Federal Highway Act of 1921 provided federal matching grants to improve the nation's roads. In a return to the policy of protection, the Fordney-McCumber Tariff of 1922 restored high taxes on imports in order to shelter American producers from foreign competition.

These measures were exceptions to the rule of Republican economic policy in the 1920s. Above all, the Harding and Coolidge administrations called for "economy" in government, which meant reduced spending and lower taxes. The Republicans also condemned budget deficits and pledged to reduce the national debt; they succeeded on all counts. Federal expenditures dropped from 6.4 billion dollars in 1920 to 3.1 billion dollars in 1929 (see Figure 23-2). At the urging of Harding and Coolidge, Congress repeatedly cut income and other taxes. Despite the tax cuts, the federal government managed to produce annual budget surpluses and to reduce its debt.

Republicans' commitment to minimal government was obvious in their lax enforcement of key legislation of the progressive era. During the Harding and Coolidge administrations, the federal government made only weak attempts to enforce Prohibition. Congress failed to commit enough money and manpower to stop the production and sale of illegal "bootleg" liquor. Harding himself kept a private stock of liquor in the White House.

If anything, the Republican administrations of the 1920s weakened progressive regulation of the economy even more. Harding and Coolidge allowed the regulatory commissions of the Gilded Age and the progressive era to atrophy. Thanks to weak, pro-business leadership, the Interstate Commerce Commission (ICC) and the Federal Trade Commission (FTC) were effectively controlled by the very businesses they were supposed to regulate.

Herbert Hoover, the secretary of commerce in both the Harding and Coolidge administrations, had a more activist view of the government's role in the economy than either of his bosses. Trained as an engineer, Hoover had become a national hero by supervising the government's effort to relieve famine in Europe during and after World War I. More deeply affected by progressivism than other leading Republicans, the commerce secretary aggressively sought ways to enlarge the size and power of his department. Sensitive to business interests, Hoover wanted to promote "associationalism"—organized cooperation among business trade groups.

Hoover's associational initiatives did not accomplish too much. Businessmen did not trust one another enough to make voluntary cooperation effective, and Hoover did not advocate federal action to force them to cooperate. Critical of socialism and other forms of statism, Hoover believed above all in what he called "American individualism."

Republican Foreign Policy

After America's intense involvement in international affairs during World War I, the 1920s seemed to mark a period of relative withdrawal. During the decade, there was no crisis that thrust foreign policy to the center of American life. As Coolidge declared in his first annual message, "our main problems are domestic problems." Nevertheless, the United States, the world's greatest power, played an active role around the globe in the 1920s. In the aftermath of the First World War, a surging international peace movement wanted to make sure that there would never be a second global conflict. In the United States, a broad range of groups, including women's and religious organizations, supported the peace movement. Their push for disarmament influenced the Harding administration to organize the Washington Naval Conference that began in 1921. Meeting in the U.S. capital, the world's leading naval powers produced the first international arms-reduction agreement. The United States, Great Britain, and Japan agreed to scrap some of their largest navy ships and, along with France and Italy, promised to limit the tonnage of their existing large ships, abandon gas warfare, and restrict submarine warfare.

The peace movement was less successful in achieving its second goal, the outlawing of war. In 1928, the United States and 14 other countries signed the Kellogg-Briand Pact foreswearing war as an instrument of national policy. Enthusiastically received in the United States and elsewhere, the

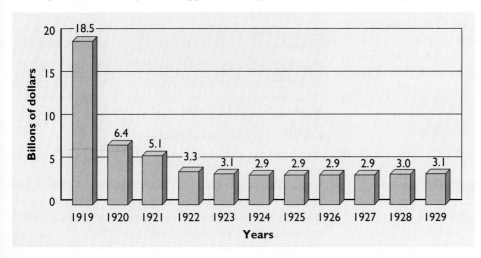

Figure 23-2   Shrinking Federal Spending, 1919–1929.
Source: Historical Statistics of the United States, II, 1104.

measure nevertheless contained no effective mechanism to stop a nation from going to war. U. S. membership in a World Court, the third major goal of the peace movement, was not achieved at all in the 1920s. Too many Americans believed that participation in the court, like participation in the League of Nations, would undermine U. S. sovereignty.

While Americans debated membership in the court, the U. S. economy became increasingly bound up in the world economy. Driven by prosperity at home, American investment grew substantially overseas during the 1920s. American bankers made major loans around the world. Ford, American Telephone and Telegraph, and other American companies exported more of their products around the world, too. And American corporations became multinational firms by building plants overseas.

The growth of American economic activity abroad complicated the foreign-policy priorities of the Harding and Coolidge administrations. In the 1920s, the United States had more interests than ever to protect overseas, but the American people were wary of any government action that might lead to another war. Many Americans were also uneasy about imperialism, the nation's continuing military role in its own possessions and in supposedly sovereign nations.

In these circumstances, the Harding and Coolidge administrations tried to pull back from some old-style imperial commitments. U. S. Marines withdrew from the Dominican Republic in 1924. American Marines also left Nicaragua in 1925 but returned the next year in greater numbers when the Central American nation became politically unstable. It was not so easy to limit America's imperial role.

The Harding and Coolidge administrations also made active efforts to promote a stable world in which Americans would be safe and American business would thrive. During the 1920s, the United States was involved in negotiations to increase Chinese sovereignty and thereby reduce the chances of conflict in Asia. The United States was also active in trying to stabilize Europe in the years after World War I. With the quiet approval of Republican presidents, American businessmen intervened twice to help resolve the controversial issue of how much Germany should be expected to pay in reparation to the Allies. First Charles G. Dawes in 1924 and then Owen D. Young in 1929 chaired international commissions that produced new plans for easier payment of reparations.

Extending the "New Era"

The Republicans' cautious foreign and domestic policies proved popular. Despite the uneasiness over consumerism and other aspects of the new culture, there was no serious challenge to the Republican ascendancy as the decade came to a close.

The backlash against the modern culture actually hurt the Democrats more than the Republicans. The Democratic Party depended on support not only from rural na-

The two major candidates in the 1928 presidential election—Republican Herbert Hoover and Democrat Al Smith—get a lecture on politics from Uncle Sam. Hoover apparently learned his lessons better: he won the election.

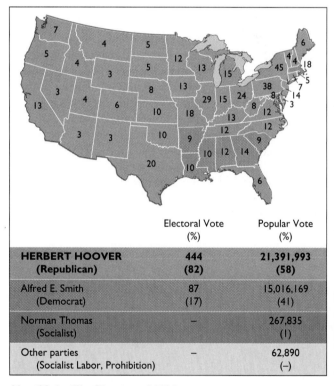

	Electoral Vote (%)	Popular Vote (%)
HERBERT HOOVER (Republican)	444 (82)	21,391,993 (58)
Alfred E. Smith (Democrat)	87 (17)	15,016,169 (41)
Norman Thomas (Socialist)	–	267,835 (1)
Other parties (Socialist Labor, Prohibition)	–	62,890 (–)

Map 23-1   The Election of 1928.

tivists, fundamentalists, and Klansmen, but also from their frequent targets—urban Catholics and Jews. By the mid-1920s, these constituencies had split the party with battles over such issues as immigration restriction, Prohibition, and the Klan. The antagonism helped doom the Democrats' chances in the 1924 elections, and it did not help the party's fortune four years later.

In 1928, the Democrats nominated Al Smith, the governor of New York, for president. The first Irish Catholic presidential nominee of a major party, Smith displeased fundamentalists and nativists. Moreover, his brassy, urban style—his campaign theme song was "The Sidewalks of New York"—alienated many rural Americans. Smith represented a new generation of urban, ethnic Democrats who were ready to use activist government to deal with social and economic problems. Their brand of urban liberalism would be greatly influential in just a few years, but in 1928, Smith's politics and background could not galvanize a majority of voters to cast ballots for him.

Meanwhile, Herbert Hoover, the Republican nominee, seemed to offer the best of the "New Era." On election day, he polled 58.2 percent of the popular vote and carried 40 states for a total of 444 electoral votes—the Republicans' largest electoral triumph of the decade (see Map 23-1). Moreover, the Republicans increased their majorities in both the House and the Senate. The "New Era" would continue.

CHRONOLOGY

1913	Introduction of assembly line at Ford Motor Company
1919	Black Star Line founded by Marcus Garvey
1920	Beginning of recession Beginning of commercial radio broadcasting First season of the American Professional Football Association Warren G. Harding elected president
1921	Sheppard-Towner Maternity Act
1922	Fordney-McCumber Tariff Sinclair Lewis, *Babbitt*
1923	Death of Harding Calvin Coolidge succeeds as president
1924	Teapot Dome scandal Dawes Plan for German war reparations National Origins Act Calvin Coolidge elected president
1925	Founding of the Brotherhood of Sleeping Car Porters F. Scott Fitzgerald, *The Great Gatsby* Bruce Barton, *The Man Nobody Knows* Scopes trial
1926	Ernest Hemingway, *The Sun Also Rises* Gertrude Ederle's swim across the English Channel
1927	Charles Lindbergh's flight across the Atlantic Ocean First "talking picture," *The Jazz Singer*
1928	Kellogg-Briand Pact Herbert Hoover elected president

Conclusion

The Republicans' victory in 1928 underscored the limits of the resistance to the modern culture. Like the tides that confronted Gertrude Ederle in the English Channel, nativists, fundamentalists, and Klansmen could not beat back the many changes of the "New Era." As Hoover prepared to take over the White House, the triumph of the new culture and the new politics seemed assured. The appeal of the modern culture, rooted in the needs of the industrial economy, appeared undeniable. It offered a renewed sense of individual worth and possibility. It promised new freedom to women and youth. It held out an alluring vision of material pleasures—a life devoted to leisure and consumption—to all Americans.

Nevertheless, the modern culture and its Republican defenders were vulnerable. The political economic "New Era" of the 1920s was especially dependent on the state of the economy. Perhaps more than ever before in American history, the nation's dominant value system equated human happiness with the capacity to pay for pleasures. What would happen if Americans lost their jobs and their purchasing power? The new culture and the "New Era" had survived the dissent of alienated and excluded Americans in the 1920s. It would not survive the sudden end of prosperity.

Review Questions

1.   What were the causes of the transformation of the industrial economy in the 1910s and 1920s? How did that transformation benefit or harm different economic groups such as big business, workers, and farmers?

2.   What were the fundamental values of the modern culture that emerged by the 1920s? Why did this culture emerge?

3.   How did views of sexuality, gender, family, and youth change in the 1920s? Why was individualism so important to the modern culture?

4.   Why was there such a widespread backlash against the modern culture of the 1920s? Why did the backlash fail?

5.   Why did the Republican Party dominate the emerging political system of the 1920s? How did Republican policies reflect the economic and cultural changes of the decade?

Further Readings

Nancy F. Cott, *The Grounding of Modern Feminism* (1987). Cott's book is a perceptive exploration of feminist ideas and activism.

Lynn Dumenil, *The Modern Temper: American Culture and Society in the 1920s* (1995). Dumenil surveys key elements of the modern culture, including consumerism and changing gender roles, and emphasizes the importance of large-scale organization in American life.

Paula S. Fass, *The Damned and the Beautiful: American Youth in the 1920s* (1977). This monograph details the emergence of a distinctive youth culture during the decade.

Robert H. Ferrell, *The Presidency of Calvin Coolidge* (1998). Ferrell's book offers a balanced examination of the Republicans' use of power in the 1920s.

Robert S. Lynd and Helen Merrell Lynd, *Middletown: A Study in Contemporary American Culture* (1929). This pioneering sociological study of Muncie, Indiana, charts the spread of the modern culture in an American community.

Nancy MacLean, *Ku Klux Klan: The Making of the Second Ku Klux Klan* (1994). This study of Klan activity in a Georgia county stresses the importance of the Klansmen's hostility to the modern culture.

Roland Marchand, *Advertising the American Dream: Making Way for Modernity, 1920–1940* (1985). This study shows how the pioneering advertising men defined their profession and tried to shape popular tastes after World War I.

Michael E. McGerr, *The Decline of Popular Politics: The American North, 1865–1928* (1986). This monograph traces the cause of declining voter turnout to changes in political styles.

David Nasaw, *Going Out: The Rise and Fall of Public Amusements* (1993). Nasaw's book engagingly describes the evolution of movies, sports, and other amusements that helped to constitute the consumer culture of the 1920s.

George Sánchez, *Becoming Mexican American: Ethnicity, Culture, and Identity in Chicano Los Angeles, 1900–1945* (1993). A sensitive exploration of the Mexican encounter with life in the United States as the new consumer culture flourished.

History on the Internet

"The 1920s: Society, Fads, and Daily Life"

http://www.louisville.edu/~kprayb01/1920s-Society-1.html#AI

This site chronicles the changing popular culture of the 1920s in areas such as fashion, entertainment, and language.

"Prosperity and Thrift: The Coolidge Era and the Consumer Economy, 1921–1929"

http://memory.loc.gov/ammem/coolhtml/coolhome.html

This site is a compilation of numerous primary sources—from mass advertising and presidential addresses to short films. It tracks the nation's transition to a consumer society and examines the role of the government in that change. It also discusses life for those who did not enjoy the emerging fruits of the economy.

"Famous Trials in American History: *Tennessee vs. John Scopes:* **The Monkey Trial"**

http://www.law.umkc.edu/faculty/projects/ftrials/scopes/scopes.htm

This site details the famous legal battle, which testifies to the challenges to tradition that were prevalent in the 1920s. The site includes eyewitness accounts, excerpts from the trial, photographs, and more.

"Harlem: Mecca of the New Negro"

http://etext.lib.virginia.edu/harlem/index.html

The e-text of the historical 1925 *Survey Graphic,* a journal of social work, featured on this site is an example of one of the first attempts to understand the social, cultural, and political significance of the Harlem community in New York.

"The History of Mexican Americans in California: Revolution to Depression"

http://www.cr.nps.gov/history/online_books/5views/5views5c.htm

Explore the subject of immigration from Mexico to America. Through this site, learn about Mexican Americans' lives in the barrios in California and their struggle for a better life through mutual aid and work.

24

A GREAT DEPRESSION AND A NEW DEAL

1929-1940

OUTLINE

Sidney Hillman and the Search for Security

"The ideals of the labor movement" Sidney Hillman told radical members of his union in 1935, "must be security for every man and woman in the country." Hillman, leader of the Amalgamated Clothing Workers of America (ACWA), argued that the goal of socialism must be replaced by the less heady aim of a fairer, government-moderated capitalism. Throughout the 1930s he worked tirelessly with President Franklin Delano Roosevelt's New Deal to create this new political economy that would, he hoped, provide a greater measure of security to working people than ever before in American history.

Born in 1887 in Zagare, Lithuania, Hillman grew up in the closed community of a small Jewish village. In 1901 he was sent to Kovno to study to become a rabbi but soon embraced socialism and became involved in the revolutionary movements then challenging the Russian czar. In 1907, still committed to working for social causes, he emigrated to the United States and found work first as a clerk at Sears, Roebuck and then in the clothing industry.

In both positions Hillman came face to face with the terrifying insecurity faced by most working people and steeled his resolve to fight it.

In 1910 a massive strike in Chicago shaped Hillman's destiny. Begun by a small group of seamstresses angry at a wage cut, the walkout quickly expanded to over 40,000 workers and shut down clothing manufacture in the city for months. Hillman emerged during the strike as a practical leader who convinced his employer to recognize the union and to arbitrate the dispute.

In 1914 Hillman was offered the presidency of the ACWA, and the union spread rapidly through the industry. During World War I Hillman enlisted the help of the government to compel manufacturers of military clothing to abandon their opposition to the union. This move, and the overheated economy of wartime, expanded the ACWA's membership to nearly 140,000, making it the fourth largest union in the nation. And unlike most unions during the 1920s, Hillman's remained stable.

The advent of the Great Depression in 1929 put the whole enterprise in jeopardy. As the American economy tumbled, he struggled to keep his union together. The election of Franklin Roosevelt in 1932 opened the way for Hillman to once again work with the government to provide security for his organization and the working class as a whole. Hillman took a prominent role in the National Recovery Administration—Roosevelt's agency for industrial recovery—and used its provisions for business, government, and labor cooperation to stabilize the clothing industry. This endeavor failed for a variety of reasons, including the fact that workers in most industries remained unorganized.

Hillman decided to take action. He and others formed the Committee (later 'Congress') on Industrial Organizations (CIO), which quickly organized hundreds of thousands of workers in the steel, auto, electric, and rubber industries. At the same time, Hillman formed Labor's Non-Partisan League to support the re-election of F. D. R. Roosevelt's triumph in 1936 cemented a decades-

Sidney Hillman, one of the founders of the CIO, helped build the labor movement into a potent force in American politics.

long marriage of a revived labor movement with the Democratic Party.

By the time Hillman died in 1946, the New Deal had pushed America's political economy in the direction he had struggled for all of his life. The government now regulated the financial system in ways that helped prevent the kind of collapse that had taken place after 1929. Federal officials no longer stood as a bulwark against organized labor. Many of the nation's elderly and disabled were protected by a new system of social security. Unemployment insurance was available to millions of workers, and for the first time there was a minimum wage in many jobs. This was not socialism, but more in line with Hillman's dreams, it was capitalism made more stable and more socially responsible through the regulatory hand of the government. To be sure, Hillman spent his last years pushing for still further progressive reform. But by the late 1930s even he recognized that there were troubles brewing in Europe that would require Americans to turn their attention from domestic policy to foreign affairs. ∎

The Great Depression

In mid-October 1929 confidence in the continued growth of the stock market suddenly failed, sending tremors throughout the economy. By Thursday, October 24, panic had set in as investors rushed to unload their stocks. Prices rallied briefly, but on October 29, "Black Tuesday," stock values lost over 14 billion dollars, and within the month the market stood at only half its precrash worth. Hundreds of corporations and thousands of individuals were wiped out. On Wall Street, the central symbol of prosperity in the 1920s, mounted police had to hold angry mobs back from the doors of the stock exchange. Although the stock market crash did not cause the ensuing depression, it did expose the underlying weakness of the economy and shatter the confidence on which President Herbert Hoover had based his belief in the impending end of poverty. His optimistic speeches would echo hollowly over the ensuing years of widespread unemployment, hunger, and homelessness.

Causes of the Great Depression

There is no single factor that explains the onset and persistence of the Great Depression. No one among the politicians, bureaucrats, business leaders, and others responsible for addressing the problem had a clear idea of why things had gone so wrong. Indeed, today economists and historians still debate the issue. Yet, even if no definitive account can be given, it is clear that numerous flaws in the national and international economic structure along with ill-conceived government policies clearly bear a large degree of responsibility for causing the catastrophe (see Table 24-1).

In the 1920s the base of the economy had begun to shift. No longer was it driven by the production of steel, coal, textiles and the expansion of railroads and other infrastructure. Now, new industries that sold complex consumer goods like automobiles became the driving force. In addition to cars, sales of radios, clothing, processed foods, and a whole range of new products grew dramatically. This shift toward a vibrant new consumer-oriented economy was fueled by favorable business conditions, high rates of employment, and a new willingness to buy on credit that allowed consumers, mainly those in the relatively small middle class, to purchase more and more goods and services. The limits of this market had, however, been reached even before the Great Crash. When the stock market fell, the sudden collapse of purchasing power caused by mass unemployment and the loss of savings slowed the transition to the new economy.

A rickety credit and financial system added to the problems of the late 1920s. Even in the boom times earlier in the decade banks failed by the hundreds. For banks in rural areas these failures could be traced directly to the crisis in the farm economy. But all over America financial institutions suffered from inept and even criminal management. Banks were virtually free from effective regulation, and in the boom atmosphere of the 1920s

Crowds thronged Wall Street after the stock market crash in 1929. Here a huge group gathered in front of the Sub-Treasury building.

TABLE 24-1

Labor Force and Unemployment, 1929–1941 (Numbers in Millions)

Year	Labor Force	Unemployment	
		Number	% of Labor Force
1929	49.2	1.6	3.2
1930	49.8	4.3	8.7
1931	50.4	8.0	15.9
1932	51.0	12.1	23.6
1933	51.6	12.8	24.9
1934	52.2	11.3	21.7
1935	52.9	10.6	20.1
1936	53.4	9.0	16.9
1937	54.0	7.7	14.3
1938	54.6	10.4	19.0
1939	55.2	9.5	17.2
1940	55.6	8.1	14.6
1941	55.9	5.6	9.9

Source: United States Department of Commerce, Historical Statistics of the United States (1960), p. 70.

many of their executives invested their depositors' money in the shaky stock market or made large loans to investors. These practices magnified the impact of the crash by causing banks to fail. Many thousands lost money that they thought was safely saved.

Like the banks, the investment industry in the United States was free from regulation and given to misrepresentation, manipulation of stock prices, and corrupt inside deals. Few could be sure whether their money was going into sound companies or worthless paper. The corruption of the system became apparent after the crash and inhibited the ability of legitimate companies to raise money.

Government missteps and poor policies also had a role in causing the Depression. The Republican administrations of the 1920s were committed to reducing the interference of government in the economy, lowering taxes on the wealthy, and reducing the expenditures of government. As a result, little was done to counter the chaotic state of banks, address the problems of farmers, or redistribute wealth. The Federal Reserve might have done much to dampen speculation in stocks and force banks to adopt sounder policies or, after the Depression had begun, to expand the currency so as to promote growth. The Harding and Coolidge administrations and the Federal Reserve Board, acting on what were thought to be sound principles only made matters worse. Moreover, no part of the government had the fundamental data needed to understand and resolve the economic crisis.

The Great Depression was magnified by an international economic system still reeling from the effects of

World War I. Britain, France, and other allies had borrowed enormous sums from the United States to fight the war. Unable to repay their loans after the armistice, these nations had demanded large reparations from Germany and Austria. The United States had helped to reduce the burden of these reparations payments in the mid-1920s but refused to forgive the debts. All was well as long as the American economy boomed, because massive amounts of capital from the U. S. poured into Germany and Austria, flowed back through the Allied nations, and on to American vaults. This cycle was broken during the onset of depression in the United States. The European nations attempted to protect themselves by devaluing their currencies and raising trade barriers. The result was a steady decline in their economies that made payments on reparations or loans impossible. The whole cycle reached its breaking point in 1931, and the international financial system came crashing down bringing with it many more American banks and helping to further deepen the economic crisis.

The United States Descends Into Depression

The Great Depression was a year old when an unemployed worker in Pottstown, Pennsylvania, sat down and wrote a harsh letter to President Hoover. "I am one of the men out of work," he explained, "but the rich don't care so long as they have full and plenty." With winter coming on he pleaded with Hoover to speed up aid to "the struggling starving working class [of] under nourished men, women, and children." Such misery, he added, "really is alarming [in] this so called prosperous nation."

The statistics alone were alarming. Between 1929 and 1933 every index of economic activity showed a steadily worsening slide into depression. The Gross National Product shrank, from $104.4 billion in 1929 to $74.2 billion in 1933. In the same period the combined incomes of American workers fell by more than 40 percent. Bank failures increased, from 640 in 1928 to 2,294 in 1931. A *New York Times* index of business activity dropped from 114.8 in June of 1929 to 63.7 in March of 1933. Both exports and imports fell by more than two-thirds.

As business activity collapsed, joblessness skyrocketed. Periodic bouts of unemployment had always been a feature of capitalist economies even in good times. What distinguished the Great Depression was the extent and duration of unemployment. At the lowest point of the slump in the early 1930s, between 20 and 30 percent of wage earners were out of work. In some cities the jobless percentage was much higher, with Chicago and Detroit approaching 50 percent, Akron 60 percent, and Toledo a crushing 80 percent. In 1933, the Bureau of Labor Statistics estimated that as many as one in three workers, more than 12,600,000 Americans, were unemployed.

Behind the grim statistics lay the terrible human costs of the economic catastrophe. In the spring of 1930, as the

As the Depression deepened, breadlines appeared on the streets of cities all across America.

first Depression winter came to an end, breadlines appeared in major cities. In the fall apple peddlers crowded street corners hoping to earn a few nickels to replace some of their lost wages. The unemployed could be seen in the thousands, Sherwood Anderson wrote, "men who are heads of families creeping through the streets of American cities, eating from garbage cans; men turned out of houses and sleeping week after week on park benches, on the ground in parks, in the mud under bridges." Unemployed men and women stood in lines at factory gates desperately seeking work, at soup kitchens hoping for a meal, and at homeless shelters that were already overflowing.

The basic necessities—food, clothing, and shelter—were suddenly hard to get. "I have always been able to give my family a decent living," a struggling father in Seattle explained, "until economic conditions got so bad I was unable to make it go any longer." Schoolteachers began to report growing numbers of students listless from hunger. Big city hospitals began receiving patients with nutritional disorders including children suffering from rickets, a disease caused by a deficiency of vitamin D and niacin. Inadequate protein caused another disease, pellagra, to reappear in many parts of the South. *Fortune* magazine ran an article

on Americans who had actually starved to death. Embarrassed mothers sent children to school in rags. Men wrapped newspapers beneath their shirts as protection from the cold or put cardboard in their shoes to cover the holes. Desperate families, their savings gone, unable to pay the rent, "doubled up" by moving in with relatives. More and more tenants were evicted; more and more banks foreclosed on mortgages. Apartments stood vacant and homes went unsold, yet by 1932 more than a million homeless men, women, and children occupied shanty towns on the outskirts of towns and cities or slept in doorways and alleys. Hoboes appeared everywhere, traveling railroads and highways in a constant search for something to eat, somewhere to live, someplace to work.

Farmers faced a double catastrophe of economic and environmental disaster. Grain and cattle farmers in the plains states and the West aggressively increased production in the 1920s and then watched helplessly as the markets for corn, wheat, beef, and pork collapsed in the wake of the Great Crash. Between 1929 and 1932, the income of American farmers dropped by two-thirds. Then the drought struck. Between 1930 and 1936, the rains all but stopped in large parts of the South, the Southwest, and the

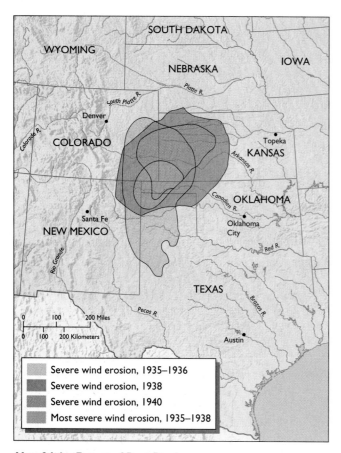

Map 24-1   Extent of Dust Bowl.
The "Dust Bowl" of the 1930s eventually spread across thousands of
square miles of the southern plains.

A dust storm threatens to swallow up this prairie home.

Great Plains. Exposed by decades of wasteful farming practices, the earth dried up and blew away (see Map 24-1). Spectacular dust storms carried topsoil hundreds of miles through the air, giving a new name—the **Dust Bowl**—to a large swath of the southern plains. Dust and depression ripped thousands of farm families from the land in Texas, Kansas, Oklahoma, and Arkansas, sending these "Okies," "Arkies," and "Texies" off to California in search of work.

The Great Depression affected nearly everyone in America, but it was most severe for those already disadvantaged in the American economy. While the environmental shock of the Dust Bowl affected many poor white farmers, the larger agricultural depression was even more devastating for vast numbers of African-American and white sharecroppers on the southern cotton lands, workers in the wheat fields of the Midwest, and the vast migrant labor pools that traveled up and down the East and West Coasts picking fruits and vegetables. In cities, African Americans, who held the least secure jobs, found themselves pushed from menial service tasks and unskilled work by desperate white workers.

By 1932 private charities, the major social safety net before the Depression, failed to meet the needs of desperate citizens. Economic losses reduced the resources of charities and the ability of the better-off to give. Ethnic organizations such as the Bohemian Charitable Association or Jewish Charities in Chicago had been a bulwark against adversity for members of their own groups. Now they found themselves overwhelmed by requests for aid. Summing up the state of charities of all kinds across the nation, Arthur T. Burns, the president of the Association of Community Chests and Councils, flatly declared that "the funds we have are altogether inadequate to meet the situation."

Public moneys were just as scarce. Only eight states provided any form of unemployment insurance; most of it meager. Such state welfare agencies as existed tended to be poorly funded in the best of times and were now stretched beyond their limits. Entire cities slid toward insolvency as their tax bases dwindled. Many states were expressly forbidden by their constitutions to borrow for social welfare expenditures. Frustrated politicians and citizens looked to the federal government for a solution, but beyond pensions for veterans, little existed in the way of a social welfare state. There was no social security for the elderly and

www.prenhall.com/boydston/dustbowl

web connection

Will History Repeat Itself?

New agriculture in the nineteenth century turned the "Great American Desert" into the "Great Plains," the breadbasket of America. By the 1930s, however, the constant digging of soil on a large scale, coupled with a prolonged drought, turned soil into a fine dust that scoured everything raw as it blew away and piled up in distant places. Midwestern farm families, unable to pay rent, mortgages, or taxes, left the plains by the thousands. Has the environment recovered from the "Dust Bowl?" Could it happen again?

disabled, no federal unemployment insurance for those who lost their jobs, and no food stamps to relieve hunger.

The federal government thus found itself under unprecedented pressure to do something, anything, to relieve the Depression. Labor leaders and farmers' spokesmen, even bankers and businessmen, abandoned their traditional resistance to a strong central government in the face of the crisis. The president of Columbia University suggested that a European-style dictatorship might provide more effective leadership. Others warned of social revolution if the government did not act swiftly. "I am as conservative as any man could be," A. N. Young, the president of the Wisconsin Farmers' Union, told a Senate committee, "but any economic system that has it in its power to set me and my wife in the streets, at my age—what else could I see but red."

Most of the pleas for federal action were aimed at the Hoover administration, and Herbert Hoover himself came to symbolize the failures of the federal government. The newspapers that jobless men wrapped themselves in were called "Hoover shirts." The shanty towns filled with the homeless were labeled "Hoovervilles." In the popular imagination, Herbert Hoover and the Great Depression became inseparable.

Hoover Responds to the Depression

In 1928 Herbert Hoover was widely considered the most qualified man in the country to be president. His early life exemplified the American dream. A relatively poor boy, orphaned at a young age, Hoover grew up in small-town America and worked hard to educate himself. Trained as an engineer at Stanford University, Hoover roamed the world to build and manage mining operations and had become a millionaire by his mid-twenties. Like many other young progressives of the age, Hoover sought to apply the skills gained in the business world to solving social problems. He won fame as the brilliant administrator who saved Europe from starvation after World War I and then as the powerful secretary of commerce during the booming 1920s.

Hoover came into the presidency with a well-developed theory on the role of the federal government in the American political economy. His vision centered on the belief that a complex, modern economy required accurate economic information, careful planning, and large-scale coordination. At the same time, Hoover rejected the idea that only a large and overbearing government could provide these services without crushing the creativity and flexibility essential to a capitalist economy. His political philosophy, termed **associationalism,** envisioned a federal government empowered to collect and disseminate information and structured to encourage voluntary cooperation among businesses but forbidden to intervene further. Government, he thought, should nourish useful associations without interfering in their work, thereby increasing the government's influence but not its size. This voluntarist dream fit well with the dominant ideology of America, and it was no surprise that Hoover easily won the presidency in 1928.

Once in office Hoover lost no time in implementing his ideas. One of the first achievements of his administration was the Agricultural Marketing Act of 1929, enacted months before the crash. Designed to alleviate the plight of American farmers, the bill established a Federal Farm Board, which brought together representatives of the various farming interests. The board helped establish agricultural cooperatives designed to purchase surplus crops and to make the distribution and sale of farm products more efficient, and it administered 500 million dollars in federal loans to help stabilize prices. The 1929 farming law did not, however, compel any reduction in production.

When the market crashed, Hoover's initial response was consistent with his overall vision. His goal was to get business to promise to cooperate to maintain wages and investment. In 1931, as banks were failing at a rate of 25 a week, he encouraged the formation of the National Credit Corporation, in which banks were urged to pool resources to stave off a general collapse.

Hoover approached relief for the unemployed in much the same way. He firmly opposed any government system of unemployment insurance or poor relief. Instead he organized first the President's Emergency Committee on Employment, which sought to convince companies not to lay off workers and cut wages. Next Hoover created the President's Organization on Unemployment Relief, which was designed to encourage private individuals and corporations to contribute to charities that were struggling to provide relief to the homeless and unemployed.

But the breadth and depth of the Depression overwhelmed all of Hoover's schemes. Crop prices fell so low that the Farm Board could not afford to continue buying staple crops above the market price. Instead the cooperatives began to dump their surpluses onto the market, further depressing prices and aggravating the plight of American farmers.

In September 1931, U. S. Steel cut wages across the board, and within 10 days countless other companies followed suit. Moreover, parts of Hoover's own administration refused to cooperate with his programs. In November, Treasury Secretary Andrew Mellon, a former banker, refused to support the National Credit Corporation's effort to save the Bank of Pittsburgh from going under. When banks failed, Mellon judged, "they deserved it." By the beginning of 1932, Hoover's approach to the Depression had come to nothing.

Hoover had never failed before in his life, and despite his reputation for indifference, he worked tirelessly to find a way to fight the Depression. By 1932, Hoover reluctantly conceded the need for more aggressive government programs, even at the risk of deficit spending. Recognizing that the National Credit Corporation could not save the banks, he proposed that Congress create the Reconstruction Finance Corporation (RFC). The RFC was authorized to loan two billion dollars to large corporations and financial institutions to stimulate investment. Other measures to increase government revenues and cut expenditures and to allow the Federal Farm Board to distribute its massive surpluses to the needy were also enacted. But it was too little too late. The Depression was three years old and showed no signs of lifting.

The Republican administration's policies did not simply fail to relieve the Depression, but rather increased its severity. Unable to control members of his own party, Hoover watched helplessly as Congress passed the Hawley-Smoot Tariff in 1930. The tariff raised import duties to their highest level in history, stifling any hope that international trade might help the economy and causing untold damage to the weak nations of Europe. Despite the

The Bonus Expeditionary Force, or Bonus Marchers, arrived in Washington, D.C., in the summer of 1932, the height of the Depression, asking that the government pay veteran's bonuses earlier than scheduled.

president's misgivings about the tariff, he signed the bill into law. At the same time Hoover opposed other measures that might have relieved poverty or stimulated recovery. He vetoed massive public works bills sponsored by congressional Democrats. Finally, Hoover's stubborn commitment to the gold standard, like his belief in a balanced budget, stifled economic growth and aggravated the effects of the Depression.

Hoover, whose popularity had plummeted as the Depression deepened, reinforced his reputation as a cold and aloof protector of the privileged classes by his response to the Bonus Marchers in 1932. In 1924 Congress had promised the veterans of World War I a "bonus" to be paid in 1945. But as the Depression threw millions out of work veterans asked to have their bonuses paid early. When the government declined, some veterans and their families refused to take no for an answer. A woman from Oil City, Pennsylvania, wrote to the president in December 1930 to explain how "desperate" she and her three children had become. Her husband, who "saw active service in the trenches," had applied for a pension and was turned down, "and that started me thinking," she wrote. Every day in school her children were asked to recite the words "Justice for All." "What a lie," she declared, "what a naked lie."

Such sentiments grew stronger among veterans as the Depression persisted, but Hoover and Congress continued to reject the demand for early payment. In the summer of 1932 the veterans formed a "Bonus Expeditionary Force" to march on Washington. Riding freight cars and buses, over 20,000 Bonus Marchers arrived and encamped on the Capitol grounds and the swamp lands across the Anacostia River. "Families were there galore, just couples and families with strings of kids," one marcher remembered. Hoover ordered the Army to remove the marchers from downtown Washington to their camp on the edge of the city. But General Douglas MacArthur exceeded his orders and attacked the marchers' encampment with tanks and mounted cavalry. Major George S. Patton, with sabre drawn, galloped through the encampment, setting fire to the miserable tents and shacks of the veterans. Among those he attacked was Joseph T. Angelino, who had won the Distinguished Service Cross in 1918 for saving Patton's life. Americans were shocked by photographs of MacArthur calmly sipping coffee while standing near a pool of blood. Hoover's silent support of MacArthur solidified the president's reputation for callousness.

As Congress struggled to devise policies to relieve unemployment and suffering, Hoover flatly dismissed the "futile attempt to cure poverty by the enactment of law." Arrogant and aloof, the president questioned the integrity and suspected the motives of everyone who disagreed with his policies. By the end of his presidency the "Great Humanitarian" had become sullen and withdrawn. It was a dispirited Republican Convention that met in Chicago to nominate Hoover for re-election in 1932.

The First New Deal

When the Democratic Convention chose its candidate for president in 1932, Franklin Delano Roosevelt flew from Albany, New York, to Chicago to accept the nomination in person, a dramatic gesture in an age new to air travel and personal politics. "I pledge myself," he told the enthusiastic crowd, "to a new deal for the American people." The phrase stuck and ever since the assortment of reforms enacted between 1933 and 1938 has come to be known as the New Deal. The programs came in two great waves commonly referred to as the "first" and "second" New Deals. The first commenced with the Hundred Days, a three month burst of executive and legislative activity following F. D. R.'s inauguration. The first New Deal continued through 1934.

The Election of 1932

The Depression reached its lowest depths as the 1932 election approached, and the Republicans seemed headed for disaster. Hoover had become an unpopular symbol of the government's failure. Republicans had lost their majority in the House of Representatives during the 1930 election and split evenly in the Senate. Their inability to develop a legislative program to attack the Depression made likely even greater losses in November 1932. But the Democrats had to overcome serious internal divisions if they were to take advantage of the situation.

Throughout the 1920s the Democratic Party had been split along cultural lines between the ethnically diverse, wet (i.e. anti-Prohibition), urban wing concentrated in the North and the East and the Anglo-Saxon Protestant rural southern and western wings. Ideological divisions on a whole range of issues separated northeastern business Democrats from western populists and urban progressives from southern conservatives.

The leading candidate for the Democratic nomination, New York's governor Franklin D. Roosevelt, had the background to overcome many of these divisions. Because F. D. R. came from an upstate rural district he was not associated with the machine politics of New York City. His interest in conservation endeared Roosevelt to many westerners. He had built strong ties to the southern Democrats while serving as Woodrow Wilson's assistant secretary of the Navy and, during the 1920s, as a sometime resident of Warm Springs, Georgia. As governor of New York Roosevelt had also built a strong record of support for progressive social reforms that appealed to urban liberals.

Roosevelt turned out to be the ideal candidate for the Democrats. As a distant cousin of Theodore Roosevelt, his name was widely recognized among the voters. F. D. R. also had immense personal charm. Despite having been crippled by polio since 1921 he proved a tireless campaigner and would go on to become one of the most visible of modern presidents. He was a born patrician, a blue-blooded member of the American aristocracy, raised in wealth and educated at Groton and Harvard. Yet he spoke in clear, direct language that ordinary Americans found persuasive and reassuring.

During the campaign, Roosevelt simultaneously embraced old orthodoxies and enticed reformers with hints of more radical changes. He campaigned for the presidency on a promise to cut government spending, balance the federal budget, and support the gold standard. Yet at the same time he promised more government relief for the poor. How he would finance such relief while also balancing the budget, F. D. R. declined to say. But it hardly mattered. In November 1932, the Republicans were swept out of office in a tide of popular repudiation (see Map 24-2). F. D. R. and the Democrats took control of the national government with the promise of "a new deal" for the American people.

Behind the scenes during the campaign, Roosevelt worked hard to develop a program to fight the Depression. While governor of New York, F. D. R. had surrounded himself with a particular group of intellectuals who provided him with an influential diagnosis of the Great Depression. Known as the "Brains Trust," they attempted to convince Roosevelt that the Depression was caused by the economy's fundamental defects. The core of the problem, they told F. D. R., was the maldistribution of wealth within the United States. Because the rich held onto too large a share of the profits of American industry, the economy was systematically producing much more than Americans could consume.

Despite the influence of intellectuals like the Brains Trust, however, Roosevelt never fully bought their ideas and never allowed any one group to dominate his thinking.

It was F. D. R.'s comfort with experimentation and chaos that would hold his administration together and make it capable of confronting the confusing persistence of the Depression. Where Hoover had retreated into dogmatism, F. D. R. endorsed "bold, persistent experimentation." Above all, he ordered his officials, "try something." And rather than trying to unite his followers behind a single idea or policy, Roosevelt seemed to enjoy watching his advisers feud. He acted as a dealmaker, arranging the final bargains and compromises for the exhausted combatants. The president, one adviser said, was "the boss, the dynamo, the works." F. D. R.'s goal, as he put it, was "to put at the head of the nation someone whose interests are not special but general, someone who can understand and treat with the country as a whole."

Roosevelt Takes Command

As the president-elect and his advisers discussed their approach to the Depression in the weeks before the inauguration the ailing American banking system took a sharp turn for the worse. In mid-February the governor of Michigan declared an eight-day bank holiday. In one of the nation's most important manufacturing states nearly a million depositors could not get their money. Stock prices dropped on the news, and the anxious rich began shipping their gold to safer countries. Panic struck and banks saw their funds fly out of the tellers' windows at an alarming rate. On the morning of the inauguration New York and Illinois, the two great centers of American finance, joined most of the other states in calling a bank holiday. The New York Stock Exchange and Illinois Board of Trade also closed. To many it seemed like the end of the American economy that had so recently been the envy of the world.

With commerce at a standstill the nation turned expectantly to the new president: Roosevelt did not disappoint. "First of all," he declared, "let me assert my firm belief that the only thing we have to fear is—fear itself, nameless, unreasoning, unjustified terror." In another time and place such words might have sounded like empty platitudes. But in the midst of a frightening financial collapse F. D. R.'s speech, delivered with verve and determination, transformed the mood of the nation almost overnight.

Roosevelt knew that reassuring words alone would not end the banking crisis. On the day he took office the new president declared a national bank holiday to last through the end of the week. He immediately instructed his new secretary of the Treasury to draft emergency legislation and

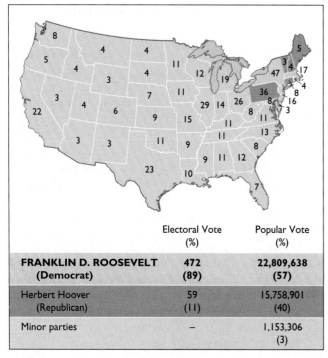

	Electoral Vote (%)	Popular Vote (%)
FRANKLIN D. ROOSEVELT (Democrat)	472 (89)	22,809,638 (57)
Herbert Hoover (Republican)	59 (11)	15,758,901 (40)
Minor parties	–	1,153,306 (3)

Map 24-2   The Presidential Election of 1932.
By November 1932 most American voters blamed the Depression on Hoover and the Republicans. The Democrats, led by F.D.R., swept into office by huge electoral margins.

called Congress into special session. When Congress convened on March 9 the drafting team had finished a bill, barely, and presented one pencil marked copy for its consideration. Congress was ready to act. Breaking all precedent, the House unanimously shouted its approval of the bill after less than one-half hour of debate; that evening the Senate voted to do the same with only seven dissents, and the president signed it into law that night. The Emergency Banking Act was a conservative bill aimed mainly at shoring up the existing banking system. Most importantly, it gave the Treasury secretary the power to determine which banks could safely reopen and which had to be reorganized first. It also enabled the Reconstruction Finance Corporation to shore up sound banks by buying their stocks. The act legitimized Roosevelt's national bank holiday and extended it through the weekend to give the Treasury time to decide which banks could open the following Monday.

On Sunday night, one week after taking office, F. D. R. went on national radio to deliver the first of his many "fireside chats." Sixty million people tuned their radios to hear Roosevelt explain, in his resonant, fatherly voice, his measures to address the banking crisis. He assured Americans that their money would be "safer in a reopened bank than under the mattress." This was a tremendous gamble because the government was not completely sure how solid most banks truly were, but it worked. The next day, 12,756 banks reopened, some in style. Five thousand customers of the Consolidated National Bank of Tucson, Arizona, were welcomed into a lobby decked with flowers and a band playing "Happy Days are Here Again." The run stopped and deposits began flowing back into the system. The immediate crisis was over.

Once the banking crisis had been resolved in March 1933, Roosevelt wanted to ensure that the financial system would remain sound in the long run. To this end,

within a few months the administration sponsored a number of bills to implement more enduring reforms. Over the objections of the bankers, the Glass-Steagall Banking Act of 1933 imposed conservative banking practices nationwide. Speculative loans, investments in the stock market, and shady business practices by banks were outlawed. In addition, the newly created Federal Deposit Insurance Corporation protected the savings of individual depositors. Two years later, the Banking Act of 1935 reorganized the Federal Reserve, bringing the entire system under more centralized and democratic control. Together, these laws established the credibility of the U. S. banking system.

One reason the banking system had become so vulnerable was its ties to the unregulated securities markets. The banking reforms prohibited such ties, but they left the stock market dangerously unregulated. So in 1933 the administration sponsored a Truth in Securities Act that required all companies issuing stock to file detailed financial reports with the Federal Trade Commission and to disclose accurate information about the stocks to all prospective buyers. The following year Congress passed the Securities and Exchange Act. Where the 1933 law regulated companies issuing stock, the 1934 legislation regulated the markets that sold stocks. It prohibited inside trading and other forms of stock manipulation. It gave the Federal Reserve Board the power to control how much credit was available for stock purchases. And it established the Securities and Exchange Commission, which quickly became one of the largest and most effective regulatory agencies in the country.

Federal Relief

Roosevelt's unemployment relief programs more sharply distinguished him from Hoover than had the banking and economy measures passed in his first days in office. In May, Congress passed a bill providing a half billion dollars for relief and creating the Federal Emergency Relief Administration (FERA) to oversee it. Lacking the organization to dispense money across the nation, the federal government passed on funds to existing local and state agencies. Headed by Harry Hopkins, a shrewd social worker and Roosevelt confidant from New York, FERA distributed money at a terrific rate. As winter came on, however, Hopkins convinced Roosevelt that only a massive new federal program could avert disaster. At F. D. R.'s request Congress created the Civil Works Administration (CWA), which employed, at its height, over four million men and women. During the winter, the CWA built or renovated over half a million miles of road, and tens of thousands of

F.D.R. used the radio to communicate directly with the American people, helping build confidence in New Deal programs to combat the Depression.

schools and other public buildings and paid the salaries of teachers. When spring came the CWA was eliminated—Roosevelt did not want the nation to get used to a federal welfare program—but FERA continued to run programs on a smaller scale.

Roosevelt generally came to relief only out of necessity, but he was enthusiastic about one program, the Civilian Conservation Corps (CCC). F. D. R. believed that life in the countryside and service to the nation would have a positive moral impact on the young men of the cities and those "wild boys" whom the Depression had compelled to roam the nation. The CCC employed these young men building roads and trails in the national parks. By the time the program was discontinued in 1942 it had dramatically transformed America's public lands and employed over three million teenagers and young adults.

This poster advertises the Civilian Conservation Corps, which put thousands of unemployed Americans to work on conservation projects across the country in the 1930s.

The New Deal Confronts the Farm Crisis

"I don't want on the relief if I can help it," a Louisiana farm woman wrote to the first lady, Eleanor Roosevelt, in the fall of 1935. "I want to work for my livin'." But she was desperate. She asked Mrs. Roosevelt to send her some money to save the family cow "for my little children to have milk." One of her children was sick and the doctor was no longer able to give her the medicine "unless we pay him some for he is in debt for it." The owner of the farm on which she and her family lived was threatening to evict them unless they got a mill plow, which they could not afford. She had turned to the first lady because of Mrs. Roosevelt's reputation for caring about the poor, but political realities would limit what the first lady, or her husband, could do to help people like this woman.

By the spring of 1933, farmers in many parts of the country were desperate. Prices of basic commodities like corn, cotton, wheat, and tobacco had fallen so low that it was not even worth the cost of harvesting them. The banking crisis left farmers without access to the necessary credit to continue, and millions faced the stark prospect of foreclosure and homelessness. To make matters worse, on the southern plains the Dust Bowl was churning up millions of acres of land. The crisis had reached such a level that in the Midwest the Farmers' Holiday Association was calling for a nationwide strike if Washington did not take immediate action.

New Deal efforts to reform the agricultural economy were contained in at least a half dozen major pieces of legislation, but they fell into three broad categories: (1) land-use planning and soil conservation, (2) the modernization of rural life, and (3) the effort to eradicate rural poverty.

The New Deal program that came closest to fulfilling each of these goals was Tennessee Valley Authority, or TVA. While campaigning for the presidency, Roosevelt had endorsed the proposal by Senator George Norris of Nebraska to develop the Muscle Shoals property along the Tennessee River. Norris' dream was realized when Congress created the TVA within the first Hundred Days. The TVA was a "corporation clothed with the power of government but possessed of the flexibility and initiative of a private enterprise." According to its administrator, it aimed to change the environment, the economy, the way of life, and the "habits, social, economic, and personal" of a region that spanned nine states.

One of the most ambitious projects of the entire New Deal, the TVA was also astonishingly successful. The dams eventually built by the TVA served many purposes. They controlled flooding in the Tennessee Valley, created reservoirs for irrigation, and provided cheap hydroelectric power to new factory complexes clustered around the dams (see Map 24-3). The TVA took responsibility for soil conservation, reforestation, improved navigation, and even the manufacture of fertilizer. During the course of the

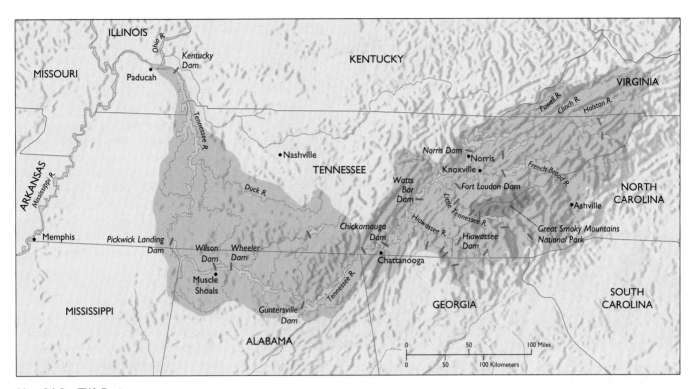

Map 24-3   TVA Projects.
The Tennessee Valley Authority (TVA) was one of the most ambitious of all New Deal projects. A network of dams provided electricity, irrigation, and flood control to many of the poorest regions of the South.

Roosevelt administration the poor, mountainous region along the Tennessee–North Carolina border went from growing cotton to manufacturing, among other things, components for nuclear weapons. The average income of the area's residents increased tenfold. As a comprehensive, centrally planned development scheme, the TVA came closest to the brains trusters' vision of how a modern political economy should work. But it was an exception among New Deal programs, which tended to be more fragmented and improvisational.

Inspired by the success of the TVA, the Roosevelt administration expanded its program of rural electrification. In 1935 the Rural Electrification Administration (REA) was established. By 1945 some 40 percent of America's farms had electricity, up from only 10 percent when the REA was founded. Electricity not only made life more comfortable for millions of farm families, it also made it possible for industry to move into new areas, thus bringing jobs to some of the poorest parts of the country.

In many other respects, however, the New Deal did little for the rural poor. Price supports and production controls were designed to help farmers who owned their own land. Similarly, soil conservation, irrigation, rural electrification, and various long-term reforms tended to benefit independent commercial farmers. These programs did not alleviate the poverty of subsistence farmers in the Ozarks or the mountains of eastern Kentucky and western

North Carolina. The landless poor—overwhelmingly Mexican migrant workers in the Far West, and tenants and sharecroppers, black and white, in the cotton South—did not benefit from New Deal programs. Indeed, one of the unintended consequences of the New Deal's reduction of production was to take work away from the poorest Americans even while their former bosses profited. The legacy of these programs was the rapid movement of these poor, often barely educated, people into the cities of the South and, with the advent of World War II, into the great metropolises of the North and West.

Native Americans suffered an especially severe form of rural poverty. Shunted onto reservations in the late nineteenth century, by 1930 the majority of American Indians were landless, miserably poor, and subjected to the corrupt paternalism of the Bureau of Indian Affairs. Alcoholism, crime, and infant mortality were all more common on reservations than they were even among the poorest whites. John Collier, F. D. R.'s Commissioner of Indian Affairs, was determined to correct the situation, and the Indian Reorganization Act of 1934 gave him the power to try. Collier reversed decades of federal attempts to force Indians to sell their lands and assimilate into the cultural mainstream. Under the New Deal, forced land sales were ended, and the reservations were actually enlarged. Tribal democracy replaced bureaucratic authority. In an effort to preserve traditional Indian cultures, Collier used the various agencies of the New Deal to build progressive schools

The Indian Reorganization Act of 1934 changed the political and economic structure of Indian reservations. Pictured here is Secretary of the Interior Harold L. Ickes accepting a new constitution for several Montana tribes.

dated that business, labor, and government officials negotiate a code of business conduct for each industry. The code would regulate trade practices, wages, hours, and production quotas. The hope was to raise prices by limiting production while simultaneously protecting the purchasing power of workers. Big businesses were granted exemptions from the antitrust laws if they signed onto the codes. Organized labor received protections from Section 7(a) of the act, which guaranteed unions the right of collective bargaining. Finally, 3.3 billion dollars were earmarked for jobs creation through a Public Works Administration.

The NRA was a bold idea, but it suffered from many of the same problems as Hoover's earlier schemes. It quickly brought together representatives from hundreds of industries to draw up their respective codes, but the process tended to be dominated by business. Few strong unions existed, and the government lacked the necessary reserve of personnel trained in industrial management. Smaller businesses were shut out, leaving America's largest corporations to write the codes in their interest. For a time in 1933 and 1934 the NRA's Blue Eagle, the symbol of compliance with the codes, flew proudly over the American economy. Soon, however, dissatisfaction with the program dampened enthusiasm, and by 1935 the eagle had come to roost atop a shaky and unpopular agency.

on the reservations. The same agencies also built hospitals and implemented soil conservation programs.

But the problems of Native Americans were too great even for someone as sympathetic and powerful as Collier. Congressional opponents, even western liberals, remained committed to the principle of forced assimilation and thus resented Collier's attempts to preserve traditional Indian culture. Even on its own terms Collier's plan could be only partially successful. What worked for the Pueblo Indians might not work for the Navajos, for example. And Indians themselves were divided over policies and goals. As a result, while the New Deal relieved some poverty among Native Americans, it did not develop a satisfactory solution to the long-term problem.

The Flight of the Blue Eagle

Farm problems may have seemed the most pressing to Roosevelt and his advisers, but reviving manufacturing was the key to ending the Depression. However, F. D. R. had no fixed plan for industrial recovery coming into office and preferred to wait until business interests could agree on one before acting. Congress, however, moved independently to pass a bill aimed at spreading employment by limiting the workweek to 30 hours. Heading off what he thought to be an ill-conceived plan, Roosevelt put forward his last proposal to become law in the first Hundred Days: the National Industrial Recovery Act. It created a National Recovery Administration and man-

The Second New Deal

The first Hundred Days had been extraordinary by any standard. Congress had given the president unprecedented power to regulate the economy. The financial system had been saved from collapse. Federal relief had been extended to the unemployed. The agricultural economy was given direct federal support. A "yardstick" for the nation's public utilities had been created by the TVA. And a bold experiment in industrial planning had been attempted. Almost everyone was dazzled by what had happened, but not everyone was pleased. Critics pointed out that much of this legislation was poorly drafted, overly conservative, or downright self-contradictory. If Hoover had been too rigid, F. D. R. struck even his admirers as hopelessly flexible. By 1935 the New Deal was besieged by critics from all directions. But rather than becoming demoralized, Roosevelt responded to political criticism and judicial setbacks by keeping Congress in session

Homeless sharecroppers shortly after being evicted from their farms by the landowners.

throughout the hot summer of 1935. The result was a another dramatic wave of reforms known as the second New Deal.

Critics Attack From All Sides

In May 1935 one of William Randolph Hearst's emissaries traveled to Washington to warn Roosevelt that the New Deal was becoming too radical. Hearst had long been one of the most powerful newspaper publishers in America, and like many businessmen he had "no confidence" in many of Roosevelt's advisers. But by 1935 Roosevelt was losing patience with the business community. Saving capitalism had always been one of Roosevelt's goals, but shortsighted businessmen and financiers never appreciated his efforts. They had their own reasons for detesting the New Deal, and in the long run they proved more potent critics than all of Roosevelt's radical opponents combined.

The fate of the Communist Party illustrates the difficulties radicals faced during the New Deal. On the one hand, the 1930s were "the heyday of American Communism." Jolted by the apparent collapse of the capitalist system, perhaps a quarter of a million Americans joined the Communist Party (CP) at some point during the decade. There were good reasons for doing so at the time. The Communists had proved themselves skillful grassroots organizers at a critical moment in the history of American labor unions. The CP also took the lead in de-

fending the Scottsboro Boys, a group of nine young African-American men falsely accused of raping two white women in Alabama. Yet the party's appeal was greatest after 1935 when, acting under a mandate from the Soviet Union, it adopted a "popular front" strategy of support for the New Deal. Thus the Communists were most popular when they were pragmatic rather than revolutionary. Furthermore, the party's appeal was diminished by its stifling ideological rigidity and its self-destructive deference to Soviet dictates. So while Americans joined the Communist Party by the tens of thousands, they also left it by the tens of thousands.

The Socialists fared even worse. Notwithstanding the appeal of its lively and intelligent standard-bearer, Norman Thomas, the Socialist Party actually lost ground during the 1930s. Thomas had won nearly 900,000 votes when he ran for president in 1932. Four years later he attracted fewer than 200,000. The reason was simple: Roosevelt had stolen the socialists' thunder. Although F. D. R. was openly committed to saving the capitalist system, he also believed that it was deeply flawed and needed to be reformed in fundamental ways. Socialists were skeptical as to just how much reform Roosevelt wanted. Asked whether he thought the president had carried out the socialist platform, Thomas replied: "on a stretcher."

More troublesome to Roosevelt were "Coughlinism," "Townsendism," and "Huey Longism." Father Charles Coughlin was a Catholic priest in Detroit who attracted listeners to his weekly radio show by blaming the Depression on international bankers and Wall Street. His solution was to nationalize the banking system and inflate the currency. F. D. R. was careful not to anger Coughlin, and at first the radio priest responded by attacking the New Deal while defending Roosevelt personally. The problem, according to Coughlin, was Communist and Jewish influence in Washington. But by 1935 Coughlin was openly critical of the president. He formed his own organization, the National Union for Social Justice, which pressured Congress to enact further reforms.

In California, meanwhile, Dr. Francis Townsend offered his own reform program that was especially popular among older Americans who were devastated by the Depression. The attractiveness of Townsend's plan rested in its simplicity: Through a transaction tax of two percent, the government would fund generous retirement pensions of $200 per month. By requiring the elderly retirees to spend all of their pensions each month, the program was supposed to pump money into the economy and thereby

ON TRIAL

The Scottsboro Boys

It began in 1931, when nine African-American youths, ranging in age from 12 to 20, were taken from a freight train in Scottsboro, Alabama, and charged with the rape of two young white women who were also aboard the train. The first trial, which lasted only three days, April 6 through 9, 1931, was little more than a lynching cloaked by judicial procedure. Thousands of angry white southerners poured into the otherwise sleepy town and were held back from the courthouse by more than 100 National Guardsmen. Without resources of their own, the defendants were provided with state-appointed legal counsel that was reluctant and barely competent. Victoria Price testified that she and her friend, Ruby Bates, had "lost consciousness" after having been "beaten up," "bruised," and raped by the nine young men. But a doctor who examined the victims immediately after the alleged attack testified that Price "was not lacerated at all. She was not bloody, neither was the other girl." A second doctor cast doubt on the charge that the girls had been raped. Nevertheless, an all-white jury quickly returned guilty verdicts. The courtroom broke into applause when the judge sentenced all but 12-year-old Roy Wright to death. "That courtroom was one big smiling white face," one defendant remembered.

At an earlier time this travesty of justice might never have come to national attention, but by 1931 America had begun to change. The verdicts produced a firestorm of protest in the North and, in New York City, thousands of black and white supporters marched in the streets of Harlem shouting "the Scottsboro Boys shall not die."

The National Association for the Advancement of Colored People (NAACP) initially hesitated to defend the "boys," but the Communist Party's International Labor Defense (ILD) took the case. The Communist Party had embraced the cause of racial equality for its own purposes, but it stood by African-American defendants convicted on shaky evidence when few other mainstream organizations would. The ILD's lawyers appealed the verdict on the grounds that the testimony and character of the two women were unreliable and that the defendants did not have competent legal counsel. In its landmark decision in

Powell v. Alabama the U. S. Supreme Court ruled that because the state-appointed defense attorneys had done almost nothing to protect the defendants the Scottsboro Boys' right to a fair trial had been denied. New trials were ordered.

The second set of trials lasted from March 27 to April 9, 1933. This time the ILD hired Samuel Leibowitz, a prominent New York lawyer, to defend the group. He proved himself a dedicated and intelligent courtroom advocate for the nine young men. Leibowitz had the trial moved out of Scottsboro, to Decatur, Alabama. He brought a scale model of the 42-car train into the courtroom and demonstrated that the accounts offered by Price and Bates were simply implausible. And he questioned the fairness of the proceeding itself on the grounds that African Americans were systematically excluded from Alabama juries. But the mere presence of an aggressive New Yorker in an Alabama courtroom stoked southern prejudices. "Show them," the prosecutor exhorted the jury, "that Alabama justice cannot be bought and sold with Jew money from New York."

The jurors followed the prosecutor's advice and ignored the evidence. They found Haywood Patterson, the first of the nine defendants, guilty as charged. But the prosecutor could not count on Judge James Edwin Horton to do the same thing. A doctor had told Horton in private that there was solid medical evidence that the girls had not been raped. Exercising an extraordinary amount of integrity and courage, Horton set the guilty verdict aside and ordered a new set of trials. His career on the bench was over.

Seventy-year-old Judge William Washington Callahan presided over the third set of trials, held between November 20 and December 6, 1933. Callahan had little of Horton's integrity. The new judge rejected Leibowitz' motion for acquittal on the grounds that African Americans had been systematically excluded from the jury pool. He prevented Leibowitz from introducing evidence that damaged the credibility of the two women. Callahan went on to instruct the jury that any sexual intercourse between

The Scottsboro Boys confer with their lawyer, Samuel Leibowitz, overseen by armed guards.

an African-American man and a white woman constituted rape, and until prodded by Leibowitz, he failed to inform the jury of how to render an acquittal. Nobody was surprised when the jury once again found the defendants guilty.

For the second time in this extraordinary case the U. S. Supreme Court reversed the guilty verdicts. In *Norris v. Alabama* the justices ruled that African Americans could not get a fair trial in any court that systematically excluded blacks from the jury pool. The high court thus struck a blow against the South's all-white justice system.

Infuriated Alabama officials proceeded to place token blacks onto the juries. In November 1935 a grand jury of 13 whites and one African American issued new indictments against the Scottsboro defendants. The fourth set of trials stretched over 18 months. The move revived attention to the case. The NAACP and numerous liberal groups worked independently of the ILD to condemn southern "justice" and attempt to free the accused young men. It was to no avail. Haywood Patterson was convicted again in January 1936 and sentenced to 75 years in prison. "I'd rather die," he said. Eighteen months later, in July, 1937, Clarence Norris was found guilty and sentenced to death, Andy Wright was convicted and sentenced to 99 years in prison, and Charlie Weems got 75 years. When Ozie Powell pleaded guilty to stabbing a deputy sheriff while in custody his rape charge was dropped, and he was sentenced to 20 years. At that point a new prosecutor, Thomas Lawson, took over the case and ended the shabby proceedings by abruptly dropping all the charges against the four remaining defendants.

The Supreme Court would not hear the case again, and the governor of Alabama refused to pardon those who were jailed. Three of the defendants—Weems, Wright, and Norris—were paroled in the 1940s, but Wright and Norris broke their parole and went back to prison. Wright was not released again until 1950. In 1948 Patterson escaped from prison and was later arrested in Detroit, but the governor of Michigan refused to extradite him back to Alabama. Clarence Norris, the last survivor, was finally pardoned in 1976 by the notorious segregationist governor of Alabama, George C. Wallace who, in a post-civil-rights-movement South, sought to atone for the sins of the past.

The Scottsboro case had a tragic outcome for the defendants, but it uncloaked the dirty secret of southern race relations and laid the groundwork for a much broader assault on the system. The case showed that the U. S. Supreme Court had ceased to turn a blind eye toward racial discrimination in the South. It also demonstrated that key groups in the nation, going well beyond the limited membership of the Communist Party, were once again willing to take a stand.

stimulate a recovery. Townsend's figures did not add up, but his following multiplied dramatically. Townsend clubs appeared all across the country. The *National Townsend Weekly* spread the word, and several dozen congressmen pledged their allegiance to the plan.

Huey Long's "Share Our Wealth" program was more comprehensive than Townsend's and more popular than Father Coughlin's. As governor of Louisiana, Long had amassed nearly dictatorial powers, which he used to drag his benighted state into the twentieth century. He built roads, hospitals, and schools; his programs reduced adult illiteracy, enhanced the quality of Louisiana State University, improved conditions in prisons and mental asylums, and established more rigorous training for doctors and nurses. In 1932 Long had played a crucial role in holding southern delegates for Roosevelt at the Chicago convention. Having moved from the governorship in Baton Rouge to the Senate in Washington, Long was a loyal but critical supporter of F. D. R. during the first Hundred Days. But he grew steadily more agitated by the administration's attempts to win support from the banking and business communities. By 1934 Long had broken with the president and was proposing his own alternative to the New Deal.

Long believed that the Depression was caused by the maldistribution of income. Consequently, his program for recovery called for the radical redistribution of wealth through confiscatory taxes on the rich and a guaranteed minimum income of $2,500 per year. Like Townsend's pension plan and Coughlin's proposal to nationalize the banks and inflate the currency, Long's "Share Our Wealth" program rested on a crucial kernel of truth about the condition of the American economy. Elderly Americans were indeed desperate. The currency did need to be inflated. And wealth was unequally distributed in the United States. Hence the reforms proposed by Townsend, Coughlin, and especially Long seemed plausible to millions of Americans.

The rising hostility of the business and financial communities was of concern to F. D. R.'s re-election campaign in 1936. These wealthy Americans rejected virtually all of the president's overtures. It would be several years before bankers would even admit that the New Deal had saved the financial system. Wall Street never admitted it. And after some initial gestures of cooperation, most industrialists became vocal critics of the NIRA.

As criticism of the New Deal grew, the conservative-dominated U. S. Supreme Court moved to strike down many of the key laws of the first Hundred Days. On May 27, 1935, the Court handed down a decision in *Schechter Poultry Corporation v. United States* that invalidated the National Industrial Recovery Act. The case had been brought by a small New York poultry company, but it was financed by larger companies interested in killing the NIRA. The justices ruled that the NIRA was unconstitutional and did so in a way that made it difficult for Congress to regulate the economy to any significant degree. Roosevelt was furious and feared that the demise of the NIRA portended the elimination of most of the achievements of the first New Deal. The president's fears were borne out in January 1936, when the Supreme Court overturned the Agricultural Adjustment Act, and continued through the spring until it seemed that the federal government was almost completely powerless to address the economic emergency.

Roosevelt Launches the Second Hundred Days

F. D. R. loved a good fight. No longer concerned about attracting the support of business Democrats, the president welcomed their criticism and shot right back. After 1935 the rhetoric flowing from the New Dealers became noticeably more radical. When the Supreme Court invalidated the NIRA, Roosevelt kept Congress in session through the sweltering Washington summer and forced through a raft of legislation in a "second Hundred Days," which marked the beginning of the second New Deal.

A few of the new proposals were designed to salvage important pieces of the NIRA. The Works Progress Administration (WPA), for example, revived the popular jobs program that Harry Hopkins had run under the old law. Similarly, the Wagner Act recovered and strengthened Section 7(a) of the NIRA, which had guaranteed workers the right to bargain collectively.

Other reforms of the second Hundred Days were designed to silence radical critics. Hoping to undermine the "crackpot ideas" of Huey Long, Roosevelt proposed a Revenue Act that would encourage a "wider distribution of the wealth." The Revenue Act raised estate and corporate taxes and pushed personal income taxes in the top bracket all the way up to 79 percent. Despite the political motives behind the bill, it made certain economic sense. Before the 1935 Revenue Act most New Deal programs had been financed by regressive sales and excise taxes. Thereafter programs were funded with progressive income taxes that fell most heavily on those best able to pay.

The Wheeler-Rayburn Act was another major achievement of the second New Deal. The law grew out of Roosevelt's concern about the concentrated power of holding companies in the nation's utility industry. In the face of a huge propaganda campaign against it, the administration pushed the law through Congress. It gave the Securities and Exchange Commission the power to break up utilities companies that made no geographic sense. It took many years for the SEC to rationalize the nation's power industry, but the results were actually beneficial to the industry itself. Forcing power companies to focus on specific regions made them more profitable in the long run.

The first New Deal had been preoccupied with the dire emergency of 1933. The second New Deal left a more enduring legacy. The administration put the finishing touches on its program to secure the long-term security of the nation's financial system and extend the relief programs that had helped so many to survive. It put in place a social security system that became the centerpiece of the American welfare state for the remainder of the century, and it allied itself with organized labor, thereby creating a new and powerful Democratic Party coalition. By the time Congress adjourned in late August 1935, the most important achievements of the New Deal were in place.

Social Security for Some

Bolstered by big Democratic gains in the 1934 elections, F. D. R. pursued a massive effort to fund work relief by sponsoring the Emergency Relief Appropriations Bill. Providing nearly five billion dollars, more than the entire 1932 federal budget, it was called by some members of his administration the "Big Bill." This appropriation breathed new life into the relief programs of the first New Deal and created a new Works Progress Administration (WPA), which was headed by Harry Hopkins. The WPA lasted for eight years, employing as many as 3.3 million Americans at one time. Two-thirds of WPA workers were unskilled, but the WPA hired people from all walks of life. It commis-

The WPA employed thousands of Americans, including the artists represented in this painting, c. 1938.

sioned artists to decorate post offices and write plays while WPA historians collected the stories of mill workers and former slaves. At Indiana University, the WPA paid undergraduates to build a student union. WPA lexicographers wrote a Hebrew-English dictionary. "There are rabbis who are broke," Hopkins explained. The program was hugely popular.

Critics complained with some justice that the WPA put people to work on meaningless "make-work" jobs or that many of the workers were incompetent to perform the jobs they were given. Political corruption was a more serious problem. WPA officials, especially at the local level, often used the agency as a patronage machine. Party regulars were sometimes favored with public-works projects, and individual jobs were awarded on the basis of party loyalty. Corruption was not rampant, but there was enough of it to provide ammunition to the WPA's opponents. Because the WPA was compelled to pay its workers the "prevailing" local wage, its effectiveness differed tremendously from one locale to another. In many states, particularly in the South, local officials openly discriminated against poor African Americans. Finally, the WPA was never funded adequately, and the funds it did secure were doled out unpredictably, making it all but impossible to plan public-works projects rationally.

In the face of all of these obstacles, however, the WPA did a remarkable job. New York City used WPA employees to transform its system of public parks into a model for recreational facilities nationwide. In Georgia the WPA built 145 new libraries, especially in isolated rural counties. Prompted by Eleanor Roosevelt, the WPA Women's and Professional Division hired hundreds of thousands of women. And the WPA's youth programs put hundreds of thousands of young men and women through high school and college. In many southern states employers began to complain that blacks preferred to work for the WPA because it paid better wages. The WPA was never able to employ all those who needed work in the Depression, but for millions of Americans it provided a critical source of immediate relief from the very real prospect of hunger and misery.

In addition to short-term relief, the New Deal created a permanent system of long-term economic security. In 1932 there were no national programs of unemployment insurance, workers' compensation, old-age pensions, or aid to needy children. The states were only slightly more able to care for citizens. As a result, most Americans had little or no protection from economic calamity.

The Social Security Act of 1935 took a critical first step toward providing such protection. It established matching grants to states that set up their own systems of workers' compensation, unemployment insurance, and aid to families with dependent children. Even more importantly, the federal government itself created a huge new social security system that guaranteed pensions to millions of elderly Americans. F. D. R. insisted that it be funded as an insurance plan with payroll taxes paid by employees and employers. He hoped that this would protect the system from the political attacks that welfare programs commonly encountered.

Most New Dealers had hoped to go much further. Secretary of Labor Frances Perkins wanted to include agricultural laborers and domestic servants, mostly women and African Americans, in the new Social Security system. But that would have provoked enough opposition from southern conservatives to kill the entire program. The administration also preferred federal rather than state programs of workers' compensation and unemployment insurance. There was, however, no federal bureaucracy in place that could have run such programs, and in any case there was fierce opposition to the idea of taking such programs away from the states.

Powerful conservative opposition thus limited the extent of the New Deal's plans for social welfare and economic security. As a result, welfare and insurance programs were weaker in the South than in the North and weaker for women and African Americans than for white men. Despite such strong opposition, the New Deal actually accomplished a great deal. By 1939 every state had established a program of unemployment insurance and assistance to the elderly. Welfare bureaucracies across the country were professionalized to meet the demands of the federal system. Almost overnight the Social Security system became the federal government's first huge social welfare bureaucracy. More Americans than ever before were thereby protected from the ravages of unemployment, disability, poverty, and old age.

Labor and the New Deal

The 1930s saw unions take a new role in America's political economy. During that decade the number of Americans organized in unions leaped by the millions, and by 1940 nearly one in four nonfarm workers was unionized. Labor organizations overcame resistance of employers to enroll workers in the economy's core industries including steel, rubber, electronics, and automobiles. Unions also became key players in the Democratic Party. None of the leading New Dealers, Roosevelt included, had anticipated this in 1932. Nevertheless, in critical ways the New Deal fostered the growth of organized labor and its inclusion in the Democratic electoral coalition.

The Roosevelt administration had never adopted the past government attitude of outright hostility toward unions. Rather, over the course of the 1930s F. D. R. moved from grudging acceptance to open support for organized labor. Section 7(a) of the NIRA, which had guaranteed workers the right to bargain collectively, was the first indi-

cation of this shift. Across the country workers sensed the change and responded with a spontaneous wave of strikes. Millworkers in the South launched remarkable, if ultimately doomed, strikes against textile manufacturers. Dockworkers in San Francisco managed to call a tremendously successful general strike throughout the city. At the same time, the NIRA inspired a talented group of national leaders, in particular John L. Lewis of the United Mine Workers, Sidney Hillman of the Amalgamated Clothing Workers, and David Dubinsky of the International Ladies' Garment Workers. All three took advantage of Section 7(a) to launch huge organizing drives.

Employers fought back against this new worker militancy. They used all the methods to intimidate workers—espionage, blacklisting, and armed assault—that had worked so well in earlier decades. But when it became clear that the federal government would now protect workers seeking to organize and bargain collectively, employers formed company unions to thwart independent action by workers themselves. By 1935 the employers seemed to be winning, particularly in May when the Supreme Court declared the NIRA, including Section 7(a), unconstitutional. In 1935 militancy among workers declined and the unionization drive seemed to be stalled. But the hopes of organized labor were kept alive by an influential and imaginative liberal senator from New York named Robert Wagner.

Wagner took the lead in expanding the limited protections of Section 7(a) into the National Labor Relations Act, also known as the Wagner Act. Although he had few ties to organized labor, Wagner believed that workers had a basic right to join unions. He also hoped that effective unions would stimulate the economy by raising workers' wages, thereby building consumer purchasing power. Like Section 7(a), the Wagner Act, as it came to be known, guaranteed workers the right to bargain collectively with their employers, but it also outlawed company unions, prohibited employers from firing workers after a strike, and restricted many of the other tactics traditionally used by companies to inhibit the formation of unions. Most importantly the Wagner Act created the National Labor Relations Board (NLRB) to enforce these provisions. In the summer of 1935 F. D. R., perhaps convinced that businessmen could not be counted on to support industrial planning, declared the Wagner Act "must" legislation, and the bill became law.

While Wagner and his colleagues moved in Congress, John L. Lewis and Sidney Hillman took another course. In 1935 they pressed the conservative leadership of the American Federation of Labor to accept the principle of industrial unions, which would organize workers in an entire sector of the economy such as steel manufacturing. The traditionalists of the AFL rejected the idea and held fast to the notion that workers should be organized by their crafts

Sitdown strikes at the General Motors Fisher Body plant in Flint, Michigan, in 1937. A sympathetic administration in Washington made union organization more successful than ever in the 1930s.

rather than by whole industries. Thwarted by the AFL leadership, Lewis, Hillman, and their allies formed a rival organization that eventually became the Congress of Industrial Organizations (CIO).

The CIO proceeded to organize some of the most powerful and prosperous industries in the country. Although none of these efforts depended on the Wagner Act for their initial success, the government's new attitude toward organized labor played an important role. For example, when the United Automobile Workers initiated a series of "sitdown strikes" against General Motors, neither F. D. R. nor the Democratic governor of Michigan sent in troops to remove workers from the factories that they were occupying. This sent a powerful message to the leaders of industry and helped to win the strike against the most powerful corporation in America. In addition, the NLRB protected the new unions from an employer counterattack during the recession that hit the economy in 1937.

Thus by the late 1930s a crucial political alliance had been formed. A newly vigorous labor movement had become closely associated with a reinvigorated national Democratic Party. Thanks to this alliance, American industrial workers entered a new era of prosperity and stability. Having won the ability to organize with the help of the government, industrial workers used their power to increase their wages, enhance their job security, improve their working conditions, and secure their retirements. Organized labor now had a new stake in preserving the system from economic collapse. As much as the banking and financial reforms of the first New Deal, the successful unionization of industrial workers helped stabilize American capitalism.

The New Deal Coalition and the Triumph of 1936

Franklin Roosevelt believed that to overcome his varied opposition and win his bid for re- election he had to create a Democratic coalition far broader than that of 1932. Roosevelt was not interested in building a cult of personality but in rebuilding the party system. "I'll be in the White House for eight years," he told a close adviser in 1932. "When those eight years are over, there'll be a Progressive Party, it may not be Democratic, but it will be Progressive." No such party in fact developed. But by 1936, under Roosevelt's charismatic leadership, the Democratic Party was transformed in fundamental ways. For the first time since the Civil War, a majority of voters identified themselves as Democrats, and the Democrats remained the majority party for decades to come. F. D. R. achieved this feat by forging a powerful coalition between the competing wings of the party. In the end, however, the same coalition that made the New Deal possible also limited its progressivism.

The rural South had been overwhelmingly Democratic for a century, and it remained a crucial part of the party's coalition. But Democrats became the majority because the New Deal accelerated the party's growing appeal to urban voters in the North. This shift was well under way during the 1920s, when Al Smith's two bids for the Democratic presidential nomination attracted the allegiance of ethnic blue-collar voters. Hard times and the New Deal confirmed their loyalty to the Democratic Party.

Both symbolism and substance attracted the urban working class to the New Deal. F. D. R. offered prominent ethnic Americans an unprecedented number of federal appointments. Jews and Catholics (Italian as well as Irish) served Roosevelt as advisers and cabinet officers. Many more accepted appointments to the federal judiciary. More importantly, thousands of working-class city dwellers found relief from the Depression through jobs with the CWA, the WPA, or the CCC. Those same New Deal programs generated a flood of patronage appointments that endeared Roosevelt to local Democratic machines. Finally, F. D. R.'s backing of the Wagner Act and his growing support for organized labor were reciprocated by the unions themselves. The CIO alone poured $600,000 into Roosevelt's campaign, replacing the money no longer forthcoming from the wealthy, and its members formed an army of volunteers to help get out the vote. Thus the Democratic Party became, by 1940, the party of the urban working class.

The New Deal's programs for the poor and unemployed help to explain the dramatic shift of allegiance among African-American voters. As they migrated from the rural South to the urban North, African Americans became an increasingly significant voting bloc.

Disfranchised by the Democrats in the South, African Americans originally brought their traditional allegiance to the Republicans—the party of Abraham Lincoln—with them to the North. But the Depression and the New Deal broke this historic pattern. By 1936 northern blacks voted overwhelmingly for F. D. R. and the Democrats. This was not because the Democrats had suddenly become the party of civil rights. On the contrary, the New Deal sponsored no legislation against discrimination, and F. D. R. himself sat silently as Congress rejected anti-lynching laws. New Deal programs frequently discriminated against African Americans, especially when southern whites controlled the programs in their own localities.

Nevertheless, northern blacks had reasons to switch their allegiances to the Democrats in the 1930s. New Deal agencies offered more assistance to poor, unemployed African Americans than any previous federal programs. And some New Dealers such as Harold Ickes, Harry Hopkins, and Will Alexander were consciously determined to run their agencies without discrimination. Mary McLeod Bethune, a prominent African-American educator and close friend of Eleanor Roosevelt, served the New Deal as director of the National Youth Administration's Office of Negro Affairs, which gave jobs and training to some 300,000 young African Americans. Besides controlling her own Special Negro Fund, Bethune successfully

pressured other New Deal administrators to open their programs to blacks. With perhaps a million African-American families depending on the WPA by 1939, black voters had solid economic reasons for joining the New Deal coalition.

A similar logic explains why prominent women reformers threw their support to the Democrats in the 1930s. Once again, F. D. R. had no feminist civil rights agenda, and New Deal programs discriminated against women by offering them lower pay, restricting them to stereotypical "female" jobs, and by terminating women's programs before all others. But as with African Americans, women benefited in unprecedented numbers from New Deal welfare and jobs programs. Through the first lady, Eleanor Roosevelt, a small but influential group of women suddenly gained the president's ear and assumed a prominent place in national politics. For the first time in American history a woman, Frances Perkins, was appointed to the cabinet. "At last," said Molly Dewson, director of the Women's Division of the Democratic National Committee, "women had their foot inside the door."

The most prominent female reformer associated with the New Deal was Eleanor Roosevelt. She was in many ways the last great representative of a woman's reform tradition that flourished in the late nineteenth and early twentieth centuries. She had worked in a settlement

New York Governor Herbert Lehman, Eleanor Roosevelt, and F.D.R. after a speech in which the president rejected charges that his administration promoted communism. In fact, F.D.R. was committed to saving capitalism by reforming it.

house and campaigned for suffrage and progressive causes. Eleanor and Franklin Roosevelt made a remarkable political couple. Millions of Americans read Eleanor's opinions in her weekly newspaper column, "My Day." She became for many Americans the conscience of the New Deal, the person closest to the president who spoke most forcefully for the downtrodden. Her well-deserved reputation for compassion protected her husband in at least two ways. Liberals who might have been more critical of the New Deal instead relied on Eleanor Roosevelt to push the president in the direction of more progressive reform. At the same time conservatives who were charmed by F. D. R.'s personality blamed all the faults of the New Deal on his wife. "It was very simple," one southern journalist explained. "Credit Franklin, better known as He, for all the things you like, and blame Eleanor, better known as She, or 'that woman,' for all the things you don't like. This way," southern conservatives reasoned, "He was cleared, She was castigated, and We were happy."

Although four years of the New Deal had not lifted the Depression, the economy was steadily improving. Jobs programs had put millions of Americans to work while helping stimulate recovery. The banking crisis was over. The rural economy had been stabilized. Based on this record and the backing of his powerful coalition of southern whites, northern urban voters, the labor movement, and many other Americans, F. D. R. won re-election by a landslide in 1936. He captured over 60 percent of the popular vote and, in the electoral college, defeated his Republican opponent Alf Landon in every state but Maine and Vermont. Landon, the governor of Kansas, even lost his home state. The new Democratic coalition also won sweeping command of the Congress. Seventy-six Democratic senators faced a mere 16 Republicans. In the House, the Democratic majority was even stronger, 333 to 89. Roosevelt now stood at the peak of his power.

Crisis of the New Deal

When the members of the new Congress took their seats in 1937 it seemed as if Roosevelt was unbeatable, but within a year the New Deal was all but paralyzed. A politically costly fight to "pack" the Supreme Court at last gave Roosevelt's conservative opponents a winning issue. A sharp recession further encouraged the New Deal's enemies and provoked an intellectual crisis within the administration itself. In 1938, when the Republicans regained much of their congressional strength, the reform energies of the New Deal were largely spent.

Within a year the nation turned its attention to rising threats from overseas.

Conservatives Launch a Counterattack

With conservative opponents seemingly vanquished, it seemed as if New Dealers could finish the job begun in 1933. Administration progressives like Frances Perkins hoped that the legislation hastily passed in the rush of the first Hundred Days, or in compromises with congressional conservatives, could now be strengthened.

F. D. R. himself appeared to be poised to launch the next great wave of New Deal reforms, but one apparently immovable barrier stood in the way: the U. S. Supreme Court. The court had already struck down the NIRA and the AAA, and recent rulings made it seem that neither the Social Security Act and the Wagner Act nor much else of the second Hundred Days would survive the scrutiny of the court's nine "old men." Before he went on, Roosevelt wanted to change the court. He had not yet had the opportunity to appoint any new justices, and pundits joked that the elderly judges not only refused to retire but refused to die. Sure that a constitutional amendment supporting his program would take too long or fail altogether, F. D. R. launched a reckless and unpopular effort to "reform" the Court. He proposed legislation that would allow the president to appoint a new justice for every sitting member of the court over 70 years of age. This "court packing" plan, as Roosevelt's opponents labeled it, would have given the president as many as six new appointments.

Conservatives smelled their chance. Ever since the first Hundred Days they had complained that Congress had given the president dangerously "dictatorial" powers to meet the economic crisis. As the years passed, conservatives argued, F. D. R. grew more and more heavy-handed in his use of that power. The court reform seemed to confirm their warnings. A president who had already ridden roughshod over Congress was now proposing to take control of the Supreme Court as well. Conservatives formed the National Committee to Uphold Constitutional Government. They skillfully cultivated congressional allies, allowing Democrats to take the lead in opposing the court reform. Even the New Deal's allies refused to campaign for the president's bill, and it took all of his political power and prestige to keep it before a hostile Congress. By the end of the summer of 1937, it was all over and the bill defeated.

Ironically, Roosevelt eventually won his point: The Supreme Court backed away from its narrow conception of the role of the federal government, and several of the justices soon retired, giving F. D. R. the critical appointments he needed to swing the court in the administration's favor. As a result, most of the New Deal legislation was protected from judicial assault.

Nevertheless, F. D. R.'s court reform plan proved a costly political mistake. The defeat of court reform was more than a stinging rebuke to the New Deal. It also emboldened the president's opponents. Critics who had remained silent for fear of presidential retribution now openly joined the opposition.

In November 1937 the administration's opponents gathered their forces and produced a Conservative Manifesto. In its call for balanced budgets, states' rights, lower taxes, and the defense of private property and the capitalist system, the manifesto heralded the themes around which conservatives would rally for the remainder of the century. In some cases opposition was purely a matter of interest-group pressure, but behind the Manifesto lay some hard political realities that drove the conservatives into opposition.

Southern congressmen, for example, were motivated by special regional concerns. Federal programs that offered an alternative to the bare subsistence wages of African-American and white agricultural workers fundamentally compromised the ruling political economy of the South. Southern conservatives began to complain and to blame the New Deal. "You ask any nigger in the street who's the greatest president in the world. Nine out of ten will tell you Franklin Roosevelt," one white southerner declared. "That's why I think he's so dangerous."

In the South and West there were growing fears that the New Deal was becoming too closely tied to the urban working class in the Northeast. To counteract this trend, conservatives appealed to the deeply rooted American suspicions of the central government. Still, the conservatives were not strong enough to block all New Deal legislation. As long as farm-state representatives needed Roosevelt's support, they fell back into the New Deal coalition. In late 1937 the administration succeeded in passing a Housing Act and a new Farm Tenancy bill. In 1938 Congress passed the Fair Labor Standards Act, the last of the major laws of the New Deal. It required the payment of overtime after 40 hours of work in a week, established a minimum wage, and eliminated child labor. Even a diminished New Deal passed, in one stroke, a bill that embodied some of the core reform ideas blocked during the progressive era.

However, the 1938 congressional elections gave the conservatives the strength they needed to bring New Deal reform to an end. The president tried to purge leading conservatives by campaigning actively against them, but the attempt failed miserably. Republicans gained 75 seats in the House and were now strong enough in the Senate to organize an effective anti-New Deal coalition with southern Democrats. By then, a jolting recession had created a crisis of confidence within the New Deal itself.

The "Roosevelt Recession" and the Liberal Crisis of Confidence

During the of 1936 campaign Roosevelt was stung by the conservative criticism of his failure to balance the budget. He had leveled the same charge against Hoover four years earlier, but the demands of the Depression made it difficult and dangerous to reduce government spending. Furthermore, deficit spending seemed to be helping to resuscitate the economy.

Hoping to silence his conservative critics after his reelection, Roosevelt ordered a sharp cutback in relief expenditures in 1937. On top of a bizarre contraction of the money supply ordered by the Federal Reserve and the removal of two billion dollars from the economy by the new Social Security taxes, Roosevelt's economy measure had a disastrous effect. Once again, the stock market crashed and industrial production plummeted. Even the relatively healthy automobile, rubber, and electrical industries were seriously hurt. Instead of being silenced, opponents carped about the "Roosevelt Recession" and accused the administration of destroying business confidence.

Among the president's advisers the competition between the budget balancers and the deficit spenders intensified. This was an important turning point in the intellectual history of the New Deal, as well as of twentieth-century American politics. Until 1938 the orthodoxy that associated economic health with balanced budgets was firmly entrenched in government and the business community. Experience with the recession of 1937–1938 converted most young New Dealers to the newer economic theories associated with John Maynard Keynes, the great English economist. During periods of economic stagnation, Keynes argued, the government needs to stimulate recovery through deficit spending. The goal of fiscal policy was no longer to encourage production, but rather to increase purchasing power among ordinary consumers. Roosevelt himself never fully embraced these theories, but more and more members of his administration found them attractive. Moreover, the massive inflow of government funds during World War II brought breathtaking economic revival and seemed to confirm the wisdom of **Keynesian economics.** Until the 1980s, presidents of both parties subscribed to Keynesian theory, although they differed on what kind of government programs federal spending should buy.

CHRONOLOGY

1928	Herbert Hoover elected president
1929	Stock market crash
1931	National Credit Corporation authorized
1932	Franklin Roosevelt elected president
1933	F. D. R. declares a bank holiday
	First Hundred Days
	Emergency Banking Act passed
	Economy Act passed
	Civilian Conservation Corps (CCC)
	U. S. goes off the gold standard
	Agricultural Adjustment Act (AAA)
	Emergency Farm Mortgage Act
	Tennessee Valley Authority (TVA)
	Truth in Securities Act
	Home Owners' Loan Act
	National Industrial Recovery Act (NIRA)
	Glass-Steagall Banking Act
	Farm Credit Act

1935	Second Hundred Days
	NIRA declared unconstitutional
	National Labor Relations Act
	Social Security Act
1936	AAA overturned
	Gone With the Wind published
	F. D. R. re-elected
1937	F. D. R. announces "court packing" plan
	Economy goes into recession
1938	Second Agricultural Adjustment Act
	Fair Labor Standards Act
	New Deal opponents win big in Congress
1939	Administrative Reorganization Act

Conclusion

The New Deal did not bring an end to the Great Depression, and this was undoubtedly its greatest failure. Nevertheless, Franklin Roosevelt achieved other important goals. "I want to save our system," he told a White House visitor in 1935, "the capitalistic system." By this standard, the New Deal was a smashing success. Still more impressive was the fact that the New Deal allowed Americans to survive the worst collapse in the history of capitalism while preserving the democratic political system. Perhaps most importantly, the New Deal created a system of security for the vast majority of American people. National systems of unemployment compensation, old-age pensions, and welfare programs grew from the stout sapling planted during the 1930s. Farm owners received new protections, as did the very soil of the nation. Workers were granted the right to organize, hours of labor were limited, child labor ended, and a floor was installed to hold wages above the bare minimum. Moreover, the financial system was stabilized and made more secure to the benefit of investors, depositors, and the economy as a whole.

America was a safer place at the end of the 1930s, but the world had become more dangerous. After 1938 the Roosevelt administration was increasingly preoccupied with the threatening behavior of nations that had responded poorly to the challenge of the Great Depression.

Review Questions

1. What were the causes of the Great Depression?

2. How did the policies of Hoover and Roosevelt differ?

3. How did the New Deal "save" capitalism?

4. What were the major achievements and failures of the New Deal?

5. How were party politics transformed by the New Deal?

Further Readings

Alan Brinkley, *The End of Reform* (1995). An intellectual history of the "internal crisis" of the New Deal.

Lizabeth Cohen, *Making a New Deal: Industrial Workers in Chicago, 1919–1939* (1990). This work successfully combines labor history with the history of popular culture.

James Goodman, *Stories of Scottsboro* (1994). A highly readable retelling of the Scottsboro incident through the eyes of various participants.

Ellis W. Hawley, *The New Deal and the Problem of Monopoly: A Study in Economic Ambivalence* (1966). One of the first scholarly critiques of the New Deal.

Eric Hobsbawm, *The Age of Extremes: A History of the World, 1914–1991* (1994). This text puts the Depression into a global context.

Richard Hofstadter, *The American Political Tradition* (1948). The highly critical chapter on F. D. R. is a classic that anticipated most later critiques.

David M. Kennedy, *Freedom From Fear: The American People in Depression and War* (1999). A strong recent synthesis of the period from 1933 to 1945.

William E. Leuchtenberg, *Franklin D. Roosevelt and the New Deal* (1963). Still the best short survey of the New Deal and the president who made it.

Arthur Schlesinger, Jr., *The Age of Roosevelt*, 3 vols (1957–1960). A literary and scholarly masterpiece of heroic history.

History on the Internet

"The Great Depression"

http://xroads.virginia.edu/g/1930s/PRINT/newdeal/intro3.html

This in-depth site examines all facets of the economic crisis, from its causes to the reactions in the U. S. and from the government to the populace.

"Fireside Chats of Franklin D. Roosevelt"

http://www.mhric.org/fdr/fdr.html

Learn about FDR's New Deal programs much like many Americans did in the 1930s through these radio addresses known as fireside chats. Read transcripts of these broadcasts that spanned from 1933–1944.

"Labor Unions During the Great Depression and the New Deal"

http://memory.loc.gov/ammem/ndlpedu/features/timeline/depwwii/depwar.html

In addition to an overview of the status of labor unions during the era, this site provides documents and interviews from Americans who belonged to these unions. The site discusses the importance of the New Deal to unionization and to workers' lives and also contains union songs and chants that reflect this period of unionization.

"We Have Got a Good Friend in John Collier: A Taos Pueblo Tries to Sell the Indian New Deal"

http://historymatters.gmu.edu/search.taf?_function=detail&layout_0uid1=32811&_UserReferA24A66F5FFD82CB6BFDCC596

In a letter to his friend John Collier, Taos Pueblo Indian Antonio Lunan writes to describe his progress in persuading the Indians to accept New Deal federal policy. He describes the Indians' questions and concerns.

"TVA: Electricity for All"

http://newdeal.feri.org/tva/index.htm

On this site, read the Tennessee Valley Authority Act, explore letters from the field that tell of the social and environmental impact of the expansive federal project, and learn about rural electrification.

25

THE SECOND WORLD WAR

1941-1945

OUTLINE

A. Philip Randolph

"Who is this guy Randolph?" Joseph Rauh asked. "What the hell has he got on the President of the U. S.?" It was June 1941 and Rauh, a government attorney, had just been instructed to draft a presidential executive order prohibiting discrimination on grounds of "race, color, creed, or national origin" in defense industries. It was a radical departure from decades of official support for legalized racism. It would use the economic muscle of the federal government to overturn job segregation nation-wide, and in the process make enemies for President Franklin Roosevelt. Rauh was enthusiastic about the order, but he couldn't understand why F. D. R., with his southern political base, would even consider it. The president was bending to pressure, Rauh learned, from a movement of African Americans led by a charismatic organizer named A. Philip Randolph.

Raised in Florida and educated at New York's City College, Randolph had founded the largest African-American labor union, the Brotherhood of Sleeping Car Porters, in 1925. Porters traveled the railroads as baggage handlers and valets, and during the Depression years Randolph's influence extended into every big-city station and small-town depot reached by the Brotherhood's magazine, the *Messenger*. According to the Federal Bureau of Investigation, which kept a secret file on Randolph's activities, he was a socialist. "Randolph believes race discrimination stems from the economic abuses of capi-talism," a Bureau informant reported, "he joined the Socialist Party because it advocates unconditional social, political, and economic equality for Negroes."

In 1941, it looked to Randolph like only a matter of months before the United States entered the war raging in Europe and Asia. President Franklin Roosevelt was sustaining Britain's struggle against Nazi Germany with weapons, food, and fuel, while Japan's drive into Southeast Asia threatened the U. S. colony in the Philippines. Randolph believed, according to his watchers, "that Negroes make most fundamental gains in periods of great social upheaval." War would create an opportunity to achieve equality, but only if African Americans demanded it. "The Negro sat by idly during the first world war thinking conditions would get better," he told an audience in Oklahoma City, "That won't be the procedure during the duration of this conflict."

In January 1941, Randolph called for African Americans to march to Washington to demand an end to job discrimination. "The administration leaders in Washington will never give the Negro justice," he declared, "until they see masses, ten, twenty, fifty thousand Negroes on the White House lawn." The March on Washington Movement (MOWM) was largely bluff. No buses were chartered, and there were no plans for where the thousands would sleep and eat, but Roosevelt and the FBI believed it enough to try to head it off.

A. Philip Randolph rejected the politics of petition by threatening to take protest to the streets. The March on Washington Movement foreshadowed the mass-action tactics of the civil rights movement of the 1950s.

A protest march would embarrass the government and disrupt mobilization. Roosevelt also had the power to accede to Randolph's demands. Using the leverage that he had over thousands of manufacturers who had received federal contracts in preparation for war, the president could desegregate a large portion of the economy without even asking Congress. He opened negotiations with Randolph through Eleanor Roosevelt. The organizers agreed to cancel the march in return for a presidential directive—Executive Order 8802—establishing a Fair Employment Practices Committee to assure fairness in hiring.

It was a victory for civil rights and for Randolph personally. If the Emancipation Proclamation had ended physical slavery, the New York *Amsterdam News*

declared, E. O. 8802 ended "economic slavery." Within a year, thousands of African Americans would be working at high-tech jobs in aircraft factories and arms plants.

Randolph had recognized that war created an opening for changing the economic and political rules of the game. The social upheaval of war touched all Americans. The armed forces sent millions, to serve and fight, everywhere from the arctic to the tropics. Millions of others left home to work in plants producing war materiel. Government stepped in to run the economy, and corporations, labor, the states, and universities fashioned new relationships to the federal government. The war stimulated revolutionary advances in science, industry, and agriculture. The United States itself became the foremost military and economic power in a world destroyed by war.

These changes enlarged the discretionary powers of the federal government and particularly the presidency. Americans willingly, even eagerly, accepted personal sacrifices and greater federal authority as part of the price of victory. As the March on Washington Movement proved, the president's enhanced powers could enlarge the freedoms and opportunities enjoyed by Americans, but they could also restrict individual liberties. Many Japanese Americans spent the war imprisoned in "relocation centers," and just six months after Roosevelt signed Executive Order 8802, the FBI placed Randolph's name on a list of persons to be placed in "custodial detention" in the event of a national emergency. The war unsettled the economy and society, enlisting all Americans in a global crusade, and arousing both idealism and fear. ▪

- The strategic and domestic issues at stake in the debate over American entry into the war

- The United States' balancing of its own interests with those of its allies in setting wartime strategy

- The war emergency increased the federal government's power over individuals and created a "mixed economy," in which government intervention was as important as market forces

- The war generated new economic opportunities for women and minorities, and wartime rhetoric highlighted issues of civil rights. War also bred fear that crushed individual rights and humanitarian impulses

Island in a Totalitarian Sea

Randolph's movement capitalized on a world crisis that reached back to the Versailles Peace Treaty that ended World War I. Global depression heightened international tensions, turning regional conflicts in Africa, Europe, and Asia into tests of ideology and power. In 1937 Japan attacked China. Two years later when Germany invaded Poland, France and Britain declared war, beginning World War II in Europe. As with the last war, Americans had time to reflect on the origins of the world crisis and its meaning before the crisis affected them directly. Most blamed the conflict on the failures of the Versailles Treaty and the desperation caused by the global Depression. Nations and empires were solving economic problems with military force.

Americans were divided, however, on how their country ought to respond to the growing threat. **Isolationists** believed the United States should stay out of war at all costs, marshaling its defenses to secure the Western Hemisphere against attack. In contrast, Roosevelt and other internationalists believed the United States had to support the nations fighting Germany and Japan while the war was still far from America's frontiers. The alternatives reflected different visions of America's role in the world and responsibilities at home. Internationalists saw a free-trading open-door world economy as a solution to international conflict and the United States' own economic problems. Isolationists worried about growing federal power and the ambitions of Britain and the Soviet Union. The threat of

fascism forced Americans to ask whether their own economy and government could measure up in the competition between nations.

Internationalists and isolationists both knew war would change American society. The future of world politics and the world economy would be shaped by America's choice of allies and war aims. In 1940, most Americans opposed aid to the enemies of fascism, fearing that giving such aid would lead the United States to become involved in the fighting. When France's defeat left Britain to fight alone, the polls shifted as more Americans saw aid to Britain as an alternative to U. S. involvement. Japan's attack on Pearl Harbor in December 1941 ended a debate that divided the nation.

A World of Hostile Blocs

In most of the world, economic growth in the 1920s had been less vigorous than in the United States. As demand for goods from Asia and Africa slackened, imperial authority relaxed and national independence movements flourished. Europe, the world's industrial center for more than a century, stagnated under the burdens imposed by the Versailles Treaty. Germany had to pay 33 billion dollars in war reparations to France and Britain, who in turn owed billions to the United States. The United States then loaned money back to Germany. Funds that could have created jobs, homes, and new industries went instead into this financial merry-go-round. One of the worst-hit economies was in Italy, where lingering unemployment contributed to the rise of Benito Mussolini's fascist government in 1922.

Like Italy, Japan was on the winning side of World War I, but its economy gained little from victory. Chinese consumers boycotted Japan to protest land grabs during the war. In 1923, an earthquake followed by fires and a tidal wave leveled Tokyo and Yokohama, killing 150,000 people. A series of financial panics toppled companies and prime ministers. The one bright spot was in the foreign market for silk. Ninety percent of Japan's silk went into the fashionable stockings worn by American women, and until 1930, that market seemed safe.

When the Depression hit, countries tied to a single commodity or to the American market suffered the most. After the crash, Americans stopped buying stockings, and the price of silk dropped by three-quarters. By the end of 1931, Japanese silk farmers were broke; by the next year they were starving. International prices for Australian wool, Cuban sugar, Canadian wheat, and Egyptian cotton plummeted. Brazil, unable to export coffee, used it to fuel locomotives. Everywhere, it seemed, the environment and the economy joined forces to destroy farmers. Those who survived bankruptcy succumbed to drought, floods, or famine.

Berlin Reichsbank officials carry baskets of devalued deutschmarks during the hyperinflation of 1923. Economic turbulence in Europe and Asia destroyed jobs and savings during the 1920s leaving democratic governments vulnerable.

In the industrial countries, jobless people stood in breadlines and built shanties near the centers of civilization and culture. More than two million workers were unemployed in Britain. American loans to Germany dried up in 1930, and by the end of the year more than six million Germans, 44 percent of the labor force, were out of work. This catastrophe, together with a hyperinflation that wiped out the savings of most of central Europe's middle class, silenced the voices of political moderates. This was the worst economic crisis in memory, and voters demanded extreme action.

The Depression destroyed the liberal international order based on free trade. For a century, governments around the world had favored policies that increased the movement of goods, people, and investment across borders. The steamship and telegraph accelerated that trend. In many respects, the world economy was more "globalized" before World War I than it is today. Asia, for example, produced a larger portion of the goods consumed by Americans in 1900 than it did in 1995. Movement toward an open-door world slowed during World War I and the 1920s, and then stopped completely with the Depression. World trade shrank from almost 3 billion dollars a year in 1929 to less than 1 billion dollars in 1933. Empires and nations began to restrict immigration, ration the flow of capital, and block the movement of goods with tariff walls. The gold standard, the symbol of free trade, had once allowed dollars, pesos, and francs to be exchanged freely. By 1936

Britain, the United States, and France had all abandoned the gold standard. Free trade had been replaced by **autarky,** the pursuit of national self-sufficiency.

Each country now looked out for itself, hoarding its scarce resources. Under nationalist leaders Getulio Vargas and Juan Perón, Brazil and Argentina restricted trade and steered investment into industry. The Soviet Union, already cut off from the capitalist world, built "socialism in one country." Japan merged its colonies in Taiwan, Korea, and Manchuria into the "Greater East Asia Co-Prosperity Sphere." The 1932 Ottawa Accords organized Britain, its empire, Canada, and Australia into a self-contained Sterling Bloc. France likewise attempted to insulate its empire from the effects of the Depression. To succeed, each bloc needed to have within its borders the ingredients of industrial growth—fuel, metals, skilled manpower, food—or it needed to take them from someone else.

In Germany, this policy was called *Grossraumwirtschaft*, the economics of large areas. It was the program of the National Socialist (Nazi) Party led by Adolf Hitler, who became chancellor in 1933. Hitler rose to power by playing on fears of economic chaos and resentment toward the Versailles Treaty. The harsh peace terms had been inflicted on Germany, he said, by a conspiracy of socialists and Jews. He promised to restore German greatness and carve out a German economic sphere in Eastern Europe and the Ukraine, but even before Hitler began to build his Third Reich, the world was breaking into rival economic units.

Autarky exacted heavy demands on citizens, requiring them to sacrifice prosperity, liberty, and lives for the nation. Efficiency was more important than democracy, and regimes around the world became more ruthless and less free. Colonized peoples suffered a new wave of repression. South Africa imposed restrictions on the residence and movement of blacks, a legal straitjacket known as *apartheid*. South American dictators strong-armed the press and labor unions. In Japan, secret groups within the army stalked and assassinated dissenting politicians. In Italy, Mussolini regimented the economy and outlawed opposition parties. Nazi ideology, in Hitler's words, placed "the good of the State before the good of the individual . . . with obedience going upward, authority going downward." Dictators pushed aside rights and religion and demanded fanatical, unquestioning allegiance. Americans began to use a new word, *totalitarian,* to describe fascist and Communist regimes that demanded complete loyalty and obedience.

Even to Americans, dictatorships had a high-tech, modern sheen. Sleekly streamlined Italian trains and warships were the most beautiful in the world. Japan built a glistening new capital atop Tokyo's ruins and rationalized its economy with Frederick Taylor's time and motion techniques. Fascist economies pulled quickly out of the Depression, cutting unemployment and earning admirers in the United States. Thousands of Italian Americans tuned in to Mussolini's weekly radio broadcasts from Rome. "If this country ever needed a Mussolini," Senator David A. Reed remarked, "it needs one now." In 1927, an Indiana automaker unveiled a new model coupe with a sleek, swept-back profile, the Studebaker Dictator.

Dictators enticed their followers with visions of imperial conquests and racial supremacy. Mussolini told Italians that they were descended from the Caesars and that he would build a new Roman Empire in Africa and the Mediterranean. Japanese schoolchildren learned that they belonged to a "Yamato race," purer and more virtuous than the inferior peoples they would one day rule. In Germany, Hitler built a state based on racism and brutality. Urging Germans to defend themselves against the *Untermenschen*, subhumans, in their midst—Jews, Gypsies, homosexuals—he suspended civil rights, purged non-Aryans from government and the professions, and compelled art, literature, and science to reflect the Nazi party's racial conception of the world. A secret police, the Gestapo, hunted down enemies of the regime, and a Nazi army, the SS, enforced party rule.

Jews were the main target of Nazi terror. In 1935, the Nuremberg Laws stripped Jews of citizenship and outlawed intermarriage with Germans to protect the purity of the "Aryan race." On the night of November 9, 1938, Nazi stormtroopers and ordinary citizens rampaged throughout Germany, burning synagogues, destroying Jewish shops, homes, and hospitals, killing 100 Jews and arresting 30,000

Mussolini and Hitler attracted followers with visions of economic security and imperial grandeur.

more. *Kristallnacht,* the "night of the broken glass," alerted Americans to the scale of the terror. Until then Franklin Roosevelt had believed international opinion would restrain Hitler. Now he was no longer sure.

The American president grew apprehensive as Germany, Italy, and Japan, together known as the Axis powers, sought to solve their economic problems through military conquest. Italy invaded Ethiopia in 1935. In July 1937, Japan attacked China. The following year, Hitler's troops marched into Austria. Roosevelt worried that the Axis would consolidate control of Europe and Asia, but American leaders had an even darker fear, one they scarcely breathed: that in a world of rival economic blocs, totalitarianism would outcompete democracy. Free markets and free labor might be no match for the ruthless, modern efficiency of the fascist states. The United States would be, Assistant Secretary of State Adolf Berle worried, "an old-fashioned general store in a town full of chain stores." It would have to regiment its own citizens just to keep up. "If Hitler destroys freedom everywhere else, it will perish here," *Fortune* magazine predicted. The United States would be "forced to become a great military power," to enlist industry, labor, and agriculture into a "state system, which, in its own defense, would have to take on the character of Hitler's system."

The Good Neighbor

Some Americans believed the United States ought to retreat into its own self-contained "dollar bloc," and in the early 1930s policy had briefly taken that direction. As American businessmen encountered hostility in foreign markets, they brought their investment capital back home. Industries and agriculture clamored for tariff protection. Historian Charles Beard in *The Idea of National Interest* (1934) urged Americans to seek self-sufficiency. Free trade had been a hallmark of American foreign policy since John Hay proclaimed the open door policy in 1899, but in the wake of the crash the United States took two steps toward closing the door to foreign trade: raising the tariff and dropping the gold standard. Congress set the Smoot-Hawley Tariff of 1930 high enough to block most imports. Critics warned that other countries would retaliate against American goods, and they did. Then, in April 1933, Roosevelt devalued the dollar. The move may have saved the banking system from collapse, but Roosevelt's own budget director called it "the end of Western civilization." One month after Roosevelt took office, the United States appeared to be moving toward autarky.

Within a year, Roosevelt reversed course and began pushing foreign trade as the answer to America's economic problems. He reacted partly to the failure of early New Deal programs but mainly to the vision of his single-minded secretary of state, Cordell Hull. A conservative former senator from Tennessee, Hull believed the open door was the answer to the problems of dictatorship and depression. Closed economic spheres bred repression and war. "If goods don't cross borders," he declared, "soldiers will." The best way to ensure peace, he argued, was to give all countries equal access to the world's markets. In a world of empires and blocs, Hull's formulation turned an old foreign-policy tradition, the open door, into a bold plan for building international peace and prosperity.

Using loans and the lure of the vast American market, Roosevelt and Hull slowly began to reopen markets in Latin America. The "Good Neighbor" policy—encouraging trade ties and renouncing the use of force in Latin America—had actually begun when Herbert Hoover renounced the Roosevelt Corollary in 1928. F. D. R. expanded the policy and made it his own. Hull surprised the Pan American Conference at Montevideo, Uruguay, in 1933 by voting in favor of a declaration that no nation had the right to intervene in the affairs of another. Good Neighbor policies undermined German and Japanese economic ventures, and Latin American governments allowed the FBI to track down Axis agents on their soil. Roosevelt tried to extend good neighborly policies to the rest of the world, urging peace-loving nations to "quarantine" aggressors, but the democracies were reluctant to join forces against the Axis powers.

In 1938, after absorbing Austria, Hitler demanded that Czechoslovakia cede part of its territory to Germany. Czechoslovakia's allies, Britain and France, agreed to negotiations, and in a meeting at Munich in September they yielded to Hitler's demands. F. D. R. cabled Hitler a last-minute appeal for restraint, but he accepted the final decision. The victors of World War I feared that a small war over Czechoslovakia would escalate into a larger one. After World War II, the term "Munich" came to symbolize the failure of attempts to appease aggressors, but in 1938 Americans were unsure how best to guard their freedoms and principles in a hostile world.

America First?

As the Axis threat grew, Roosevelt pushed for a buildup of U. S. forces, but Congress and the public had no enthusiasm for a showdown. Disillusioned by the results of the last war and anxious to concentrate on problems at home, Americans earnestly wanted to stay out of the conflicts in Europe and Asia, and they distrusted anyone who thought otherwise. Polls indicated that more than 70 percent of the public believed the United States had been tricked into World War I. Half a million students pledged that if another war came, they would refuse to serve. Senator Gerald P. Nye charged that the munitions industry was lobbying for war. Pacifists, economic nationalists, and veterans groups, backed by the *Chicago Tribune* and the Hearst newspapers, comprised a powerful **isolationist** constituency that aimed to prevent the United States from being drawn into hostilities.

In 1935 and 1936, Congress passed temporary Neutrality Acts that prohibited loans and credits to nations engaged in war. In 1937 the act became permanent, but some felt this was not enough. Representative Louis Ludlow of Indiana sponsored a constitutional amendment requiring a national referendum to declare war. The measure had a majority in the House but not the two-thirds it needed to pass. Congress deliberated against the backdrop of the Spanish Civil War. Fascist forces, aided by Germany and Italy, fought against democratic, loyalist forces aided by the Soviet Union. The war aroused passions in the United States, and some 3,000 Americans volunteered to fight with the Loyalists. Precisely for that reason, Congress decided to stay out of the conflict. The Neutrality Acts restricted the president's ability to aid the enemies of fascism just as Munich made the danger clear.

Between August 1939 and May 1940, Roosevelt watched his worst nightmare come true, as the United States became an island in a world dominated by force. The Soviet Union signed a nonaggression treaty with Germany. The full terms of the Nazi-Soviet pact were secret, leading diplomats to fear the worst, a totalitarian alliance stretching from the Rhine to the Pacific. In September 1939, German armies struck Poland, using tanks and dive-bombers to slice deep into the interior. Reporters used the new term *Blitzkrieg,* "lightning war," to describe the German tactics. Hitler and Soviet leader Josef Stalin split Poland between them. Britain and France declared war on Germany.

The following April, Nazi armies invaded Denmark and Norway. On May 10, Hitler launched an all-out offensive in the West. Tank columns pierced French lines in the Ardennes Forest and turned right toward the English Channel. France folded along with Belgium and the Netherlands. Britain stood alone against the German onslaught. "Someday the survivors of this generation will tell their grandchildren what it meant to live through a critical week in the world's history," Freda Kirchway wrote in the *New Republic.* "Worst of all they will say, was the feeling of helplessness."

Roosevelt now had to reckon with the possibility that Britain might collapse or surrender, placing the British fleet, control of the Atlantic, and possibly even Canada in Hitler's hands. Already the German air force, the *Luftwaffe,* was dueling for control of the skies over southern England. Determined to shore up this last line of defense, Roosevelt used his powers as commander in chief to bypass the Neutrality Acts. In June 1940, he submitted a bill to create the first peacetime draft in American history. He declared army weapons and supplies "surplus" so they could be sold to Britain. In September 1940, he traded Britain 50 old destroyers for leases to eight naval bases in Newfoundland, Bermuda, and the Caribbean. "If Mr. Roosevelt can do what he likes with our destroyers," Representative Frances Bolton declared, "and we give him our boys, God alone knows what he will do."

Congress grumbled, but the isolationists now found themselves isolated. The public watched the movement of armies as anxiously as the policymakers did. Rand McNally sold out of European maps. American broadcasters scrambled to put correspondents in the war zones. Sympathy for Britain grew as radio audiences heard the sounds of air attacks on London. Two-thirds of the public favored the draft, but isolationists were not ready to give up. In September 1940, the America First Committee, headed by the chairman of Sears and Roebuck, launched a new campaign that urged Americans to distance themselves from Europe and prepare for their own defense. Charles A. Lindbergh and Senator Burton Wheeler headlined America First rallies. The only reason for the United States to become involved, Lindbergh argued, "is because there are powerful elements in America who desire us to take part. They represent a small minority . . . but they control much of the machinery of influence and propaganda."

Roosevelt worried that the 1940 election would become a referendum on intervention. Isolationist Senator Robert Taft was a leading contender for the Republican nomination. Taft's radio spots told listeners that if war came, they could "blame yourself because you sent Franklin D. Roosevelt back to the White House." But the GOP convention chose Wendell L. Willkie, a Wall Street lawyer with internationalist views. In his acceptance speech, Willkie endorsed the draft and expressed sympathy for Britain's struggle. Willkie stood by his principles, but it was a tactical error. With defense and foreign policy issues off the table, the only thing Willkie had to offer was a younger, fresher face. The public was not buying it, and Roosevelt won an unprecedented third term by a five-million-vote margin.

Means Short of War

British Prime Minister Winston Churchill waited until after election day to broach the delicate but urgent issue of war finances. Britain had been buying American arms on a "cash and carry" basis, but the Exchequer had run out of funds. Britain had defaulted on its World War I loans, and the Neutrality Act prohibited new loans. Churchill knew the chances of securing credits from Congress were slim, but without funds the war would stop. F. D. R. gave his cabinet a weekend to come up with a plan, and the following Monday he produced the answer himself. Instead of loaning money, the United States would lend arms and equipment. Roosevelt compared the idea to lending a garden hose to a neighbor whose house is on fire. "There would be a gentleman's obligation to repay," but since there would be no loans, it would not violate the Neutrality Act. Lend-Lease, as the program came to be called, put the U. S. "arsenal of democracy" on Britain's side and granted F. D. R. unprecedented powers to extend aid in the nation's defense and to accept repayment "as the president deems satisfactory." The Lend-Lease bill, H. R. 1776, passed the Senate by a 2 to 1 margin in 1941.

Repayment took the form of economic concessions. Hull saw Lend-Lease as a chance to crack one of the largest autarkic blocs, the British Empire. He insisted that in return for Lend-Lease aid, Britain had to discard the Sterling Bloc and open its markets to American trade. Churchill's economic adviser, John Maynard Keynes, reluctantly agreed. Britain was now, at least formally, committed to the open door. Later that year Churchill and Roosevelt met aboard the cruisers *Augusta* and *Prince of Wales* off the Newfoundland coast to issue a declaration of war aims, the Atlantic Charter. It assured all nations "victor and vanquished" equal access to the trade and raw materials of the world.

In June 1941, Hitler stunned the world again by launching a lightning invasion of the Soviet Union. Three million men backed by 3,000 tanks slashed through the Soviet defenses with customary speed and rolled toward Moscow and Leningrad. Secretary of War Henry Stimson predicted that in three months Germany and Japan would control nearly all of Europe and Asia, but George C. Marshall, the Army's chief of staff, argued that if the Soviet Army could hold the area between Moscow and the Black Sea, the Germans would have a long winter ahead of them. Roosevelt shared his optimism. Soviet involvement took pressure off Britain and gave the Allies a real chance to defeat Hitler. Roosevelt extended Lend-Lease aid to Moscow. The German columns advanced without interruption, but to the dismay of Hitler's officers, Russian soldiers did not respond to *Blitzkrieg* as French and Polish soldiers had. "Even when encircled, the Russians stood their ground and fought," a Nazi general reported.

The German Navy concentrated on severing Britain's transatlantic lifelines. U-Boats and surface raiders sank half a million tons of shipping a month. To ease the burden on the British Navy, Roosevelt fought an undeclared naval war against Germany in the western Atlantic. The U. S. Navy convoyed merchant ships as far as Iceland, where British destroyers took over. F. D. R. said he was offering "all aid short of war," but it was not far short. Sparring between the American and German Navies became common, and in September a German U-Boat fired two torpedoes at the USS *Greer,* and the destroyer threw back depth charges. Roosevelt ordered aggressive patrols to expel German and Italian vessels from the western Atlantic. In the Battle of the Atlantic he had crossed the line from neutrality to belligerency, and he appeared to be seeking an incident that would make it official.

Japan, meanwhile, probed into Southeast Asia in an effort to encircle China. In 1939, Japanese militarists had adopted a "go south" strategy, planning to capture oilfields in the Netherlands East Indies and cut China's lifelines through French Indochina and Burma. Because the Philippines, a U. S. territory, lay across the invasion route, the question for the Japanese was not whether to declare war on the United States, but when. In July 1941, Japanese troops established bases in French Indochina. Roosevelt saw this as a clear threat, but preoccupied with the war in Europe, he wanted to forestall war in the Pacific. U. S. diplomats opened talks with Japan while Marshall, the army chief of staff, mobilized the Philippine Army and dispatched a fleet of B-17s in an attempt to deter an attack. When Japanese troop convoys moved into the South China Sea, Hull broke off negotiations and cut off Japan's

Japan's attack on the U. S. Navy's principal Pacific base at Pearl Harbor brought the United States into World War II. For Japan, it was the opening phase of a campaign to capture European and American colonies in Southeast Asia.

only source of oil. On November 27, Marshall warned Army and Navy commands in Hawaii and the Philippines to expect "an aggressive move by Japan" in the next few days. The Philippines, Thailand, and Malaya were the likely targets.

On Sunday afternoon, December 7, Americans listening to the radio heard the news that aircraft "believed to be from Japan" had attacked U. S. naval and air bases at Pearl Harbor in Hawaii. At 7:40 A.M. Hawaii time, 181 planes had bombed and strafed the airfields on Oahu, destroying or damaging more than 200 planes on the ground. Bombers then made a run at the 96 ships of the U. S. Pacific Fleet anchored next to each other. Three torpedoes struck the battleship *Oklahoma,* capsizing it with 400 crew members aboard. Alongside her the *Maryland* went down, spreading flaming oil over the shallow waters. A bomb exploded in the *Arizona*'s forward magazine, breaking the ship in half and killing over a thousand men. Hours later, more bad news came from the Philippines, where Japanese bombers also caught American planes on the ground. The following day, President Roosevelt appeared before Congress to ask for a declaration of war against Japan. Only one representative, Montana's Jeannette Rankin, voted no. On December 11, Germany honored its alliance with Japan and declared war on the United States.

Some historians have argued that Roosevelt knew of the approaching attack but withheld warnings, in order to draw the United States into war. In fact, naval authorities at Pearl Harbor anticipated an attack, but they expected it to come in the form of sabotage or harassing raids from the nearby Marianas islands. Relying partly on assumptions about the capabilities of Asians as a race, they doubted that Japan had the ability or audacity to project air and sea power across the Pacific in secrecy. When Japanese planes destroyed American aircraft on the ground in the Philippines nine hours after the Pearl Harbor attack, Douglas MacArthur observed that the bombers must have been flown by Germans. Such preconceptions blinded commanders to the warning signs and reinforced their assumption that the Japanese would strike elsewhere.

Turning the Tide

For the Allies there was only bad news in the first half of 1942. In January, New Yorkers watched from their beachfront homes while a German U-boat sank the tanker *Coimbra* off Long Island. Japanese invaders walked over the numerically superior British and Dutch armies in Malaya and the Netherlands East Indies and captured the American islands of Guam and Wake. In February, the "impregnable" fortress of Singapore surrendered, with most of the Australian and Indian armies still inside it.

Japan's Combined Fleet commanded the waters between Hawaii and India, striking at will. MacArthur declared Manila an open city and braced for an Alamo-style defense of the Bataan peninsula and the fortress island of Corregidor. "You're not running away are you?" a Filipino boy asked a Marine. "No sonny," the American replied. "Just retiring to prepared positions. That's all." Bataan held out until April 9; Corregidor until May 6 (see Map 25-1).

Few could see it, but the tide was beginning to turn against the Axis. The Soviets stopped the German advance in front of Moscow and held the line through the summer of 1942. On April 18, U. S. Colonel James Doolittle's B-25 bombers raided Tokyo, inflicting little damage but lifting American spirits. Just having the United States in the war elated Churchill. "Hitler's fate was sealed. Mussolini's fate was sealed," he rejoiced. "As for the Japanese, they would be ground to powder. All the rest was merely the proper application of overwhelming force." In Washington, leaders were trying to figure out how to come up with that overwhelming force and then how to use it once they had it. Roosevelt wanted to hold the line in the Pacific while coming to the aid of Britain and the Soviet Union as soon as possible. This meant stopping Japan's Combined Fleet, creating an American army, arming it, and putting it into action on the other side of the Atlantic. None of those jobs would prove to be easy.

Midway and Coral Sea

"We can run wild for six months or a year," Admiral Isoroku Yamamoto prophesied before designing the victorious attack on Pearl Harbor, "but after that I have utterly no confidence." Panic-stricken Americans imagined enemy landings on the California coast, but Japan's strategy was never so ambitious. It called for expelling the United States and Britain from the western Pacific and fortifying a defensive screen of islands to hold the Allies at bay until they sensibly sued for peace. After Pearl Harbor, the fleet turned west and south, raiding the coast of Australia and British bases in Ceylon, sinking thousands of tons of commercial shipping on the way. "The fact that the Japanese did not return to Pearl Harbor and complete the job was the greatest help for us," Chester Nimitz, the U. S. Pacific commander, later remembered, "for they left their principal enemy with time to catch his breath, restore his morale, and rebuild his forces."

After the Doolittle raid, the Japanese realized their error and laid plans to lure the U. S. Pacific Fleet into battle. The increase in Japanese radio traffic helped Commander Joseph Rochefort, who had already partly succeeded in breaking the Japanese naval codes. Each signal that could be captured was recorded on punch cards in Rochefort's basement office in Honolulu. In late April, he was confident enough to tell Nimitz that Japan was planning an attack on Port Moresby on the island of New Guinea.

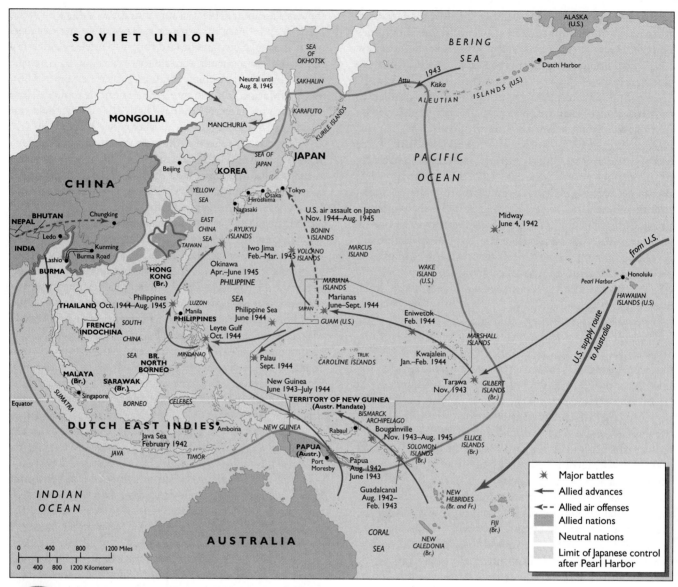

Map 25-1   World War II in the Pacific, 1942–1945.
Japan established a barrier of fortified islands across the western Pacific. U.S. forces penetrated it westward from Hawaii and from Australia northward through the Solomon Islands to the Philippines.

Nimitz dispatched two carriers, *Lexington* and *Yorktown*, to intercept the invasion convoy and its carrier escorts. The Japanese expected American interference, but not from two flattops. The battle of Coral Sea was the first engagement between carrier task forces in naval history. Sailors in the two fleets never saw the other's ships. Aircraft carried the battle to the enemy with devastating speed. Planes from *Yorktown* turned back the Japanese transports while *Lexington*'s dive bombers dispatched the carrier *Shoho*. The Japanese retaliated, damaging *Lexington* so badly that it had to be scuttled and ripping a hole in *Yorktown*'s flight deck. The two sides withdrew after fighting to a draw. Port Moresby was saved.

Yamamoto next chose to attack the American fleet directly. Sending a small force northward to mount a diversionary attack on the Aleutian Islands, he assembled a massive armada led by four carriers to assault Midway, the westernmost outpost of the Hawaiian chain. Both targets were vital to the Americans, and Yamamoto gambled that Nimitz would divide his forces, allowing the Combined Fleet to crush the remnant guarding Hawaii. Trusting Rochefort's codebreakers, Nimitz knew the real target was Midway. He also learned from Coral Sea that aircraft, not battleships, were the winning weapons. He hastily assembled task forces around the carriers *Hornet* and *Enterprise* and reinforced airfields on Midway and Oahu. Crews worked night and day to repair the *Yorktown* in time for the battle. The American fleet was still outnumbered, but this time surprise was on its side.

When Japanese aircraft encountered unexpectedly stiff resistance from Midway's flak gunners on the morning of June 4, they returned to their carriers and prepared for an unplanned second attack. With bombers, bombs, and aviation fuel littering their decks, the Japanese carriers were vulnerable. Defending Zeroes had been drawn down to the water by a U. S. torpedo bomber attack. At that moment dive bombers from *Yorktown* and *Enterprise* burst out of the clouds. They destroyed three carriers in a matter of minutes. Before being sunk by American bombs, the remaining carrier launched an attack against the unlucky *Yorktown*. The mighty Combined Fleet ceased to exist, and Japan's winning streak was over. Midway put Japan on the defensive and allowed the United States to concentrate on building an army and winning the war in Europe.

Gone With the Draft

In 1939, the United States had an army of less than 300,000 men, large enough to guard far-flung colonies against local insurrections, but not much else. The German Army that overran France in May 1940 consisted of 136 divisions. The United States could field only five. That same month, when the Army staged elaborate war games in Louisiana, it was still using horse cavalry. "Against Europe's total war," *Time* observed, "the U. S. Army looked like a few nice boys with BB guns."

Realizing that the United States could be drawn into war, Assistant Secretary of the Army John J. McCloy and leading military officials drew up plans for the creation of a ten-million-man force that would invade Europe in July 1943. As in World War I, the United States had to find ways to house, equip, and transport the Army, but this time it would be five times larger. After the Selective Service Act passed in September 1940, 16 million men registered for the draft and those selected began moving into the hastily constructed camps. By December 1941, two million men and 80,000 women had enlisted in the services. A year later the total exceeded five million. The draft revealed what a decade of Depression had done to the health and education of the country. The Army's standards were low—over 5 feet tall and 105 pounds, correctable vision, half of the natural teeth, and no flat feet, hernias, or VD. Still, half of the recruits were rejected in 1941, mostly for bad teeth and eyes, signs of malnutrition. A fifth were illiterate.

Buses rolled into the new camps and unloaded recruits in front of drill instructors who barked incomprehensible orders. Boot camp aimed to erase the civilian personality and replace it with an instinct for obedience and action. Selectees, as they were called, learned that there were three ways of doing things: the right way, the wrong way, and the Army way. Eugene Sledge left college to join the Marines and found himself standing in line at a camp in San Diego. "Your soul may belong to Jesus," his drill instructor bellowed, "but your ass belongs to the Marines." After 13 weeks of calisthenics, close-order drill, road marches, and rifle practice, he was assigned to the infantry. "I disliked him," Sledge said of his instructor, "but I respected him. He had made us Marines."

Recruits hungered for a weekend pass, but in base towns in the South and West, where many bases were located, there was little for them to do except loiter on street corners and look for trouble. The War Department joined several charities in creating the United Services Organization (USO), to provide recreation for the troops. USO halls offered a "home away from home" with meals, dances, movies, and wholesome entertainment. Overseas, the USO became famous for extravaganzas featuring entertainers like Bob Hope and Marlene Dietrich. Still, wherever there were large numbers of men on leave soldiers fought with each other and with the locals. Distinctions of apparel and race acted as stimuli for violence. Southerners lynched African-American soldiers for wearing their uniforms. In 1943, sailors idled in Los Angeles attacked Mexican-American youths—many of them employed in the Long Beach shipyards—who wore "zoot suits," a swing-era fashion combining a tailed jacket and pegged trousers favored by members of Chicano clubs known as *pachucos*. Aided by the Los Angeles police, the riot lasted for over a week, whereupon the city council passed an ordinance outlawing zoot suits. The problem for the council and for white southerners was not the clothes, but rather what they signified: the disintegration of the established social order, a process accelerated by the war.

The Army leadership struggled to preserve its racial traditions against the pressures of wartime expansion. "The army functions on racial lines," a newspaper reporter observed, "Officers talk race, not ability. The men discuss it all the time." Like the multiethnic imperial armies of Britain and France, the U. S. Army consisted of racially segregated units, some with special functions. The Japanese-American 442nd Regimental Combat Team and the Marines' Navajo "code talkers" became well known. African Americans served in the Army in segregated units, and until 1942 they were excluded from the Navy altogether. Roosevelt ordered the services to admit African Americans and appointed an African-American brigadier general, Benjamin O. Davis, but injustices remained. Even blood plasma was segregated in military hospitals.

Two issues aroused the most anger: the treatment African-American soldiers received on and around southern bases and exclusion from combat. In a letter to *Yank* magazine in 1944, Corporal Rapiered Trimmingham described how he and five other GIs in uniform had been refused service in a Texas lunchroom where German prisoners of war were being served. "I stood on the outside looking on, and could not help but ask myself why they are

The 99th Pursuit Squadron, known as the Black Eagles, trained at Tuskegee Institute and engaged the Luftwaffe in the skies over North Africa.

treated better than we are?" Mutinies and race riots erupted at bases in Florida, Alabama, and Louisiana where African-American soldiers were housed separately and denied furlough privileges. The Army responded by moving African-American GIs to the war theaters.

Though desperately short of infantrymen, the Army kept African Americans out of front-line units. Most were assigned to menial chores. Combat symbolized full citizenship to both whites and African Americans, and the NAACP pressed Roosevelt to create African-American fighting units. An African-American infantry division, the 92nd, went into battle in Italy; three air units—among them the 99th Pursuit Squadron, known as the Tuskegee Airmen—flew against the *Luftwaffe;* and one mechanized battalion, the 761st Tanks, received a commendation for action in the Ardennes. However, most African Americans went into the line as replacements when manpower was critically low, as during the Battle of the Bulge in late 1944. NAACP head Walter White observed that racially mixed units aroused few complaints in the field; resistance to desegregation came mainly from Washington.

With manpower in short supply, the armed forces hesitantly enlisted women to perform service roles. Congress passed legislation creating the Women's Army Corps (the WACs) in 1942. The Navy signaled its reluctance in the title of its auxiliary, the Women Accepted for Volunteer Emergency Service (WAVES). Eventually more than 100,000 women served as mechanics, typists, pilots, cooks, and nurses, but the unusual feature of women's service in the U. S. forces was not how many served, but how few. In nearly

Two enlistees take an oath to serve as WAVES. Some 11,275 women served in the Navy as stenographers, chauffeurs, air traffic controllers, and mechanics.

every other warring country women were fully mobilized for industry and combat. Women served as antiaircraft gunners in Britain and in the Soviet infantry. With women away, the state stepped in to perform traditionally female jobs, particularly caring for children, the sick, and the elderly, functions it continued to perform after the war. This "welfare state" came to be accepted and appreciated by the public in Europe, Canada, and Australia but not in the United States, where welfare continued to be associated with poor relief.

The Winning Weapons

Blitzkrieg and Pearl Harbor proved the value of modern military machinery, and during World War II weapons technology advanced with blinding speed. The quality of a nation's weapons, relative to the enemy's, often depended on how recently they had moved from the drafting table to mass production. Entering the war late, the United States gained a technological edge. American factories tooled up to produce models using the latest innovations, but many of these would not reach the fighting fronts until 1943 or later.

Until then, troops had to make do with weapons that were outclassed by their Axis counterparts. Marines went into action on Guadalcanal wearing World War I-era helmets and carrying the 1903 Springfield rifle. Japan's Zero was substantially faster and lighter than any American fighter. "When you fly a P-40 against a Zero," one pilot observed, "you can make one pass at him. Then, if you miss, you better get the hell out of there." Improved technique was able to compensate for poor equipment, and American pilots learned a weaving maneuver that gave them a better chance against the Zero, but it took a year for U. S. technology to catch up.

After 1943, the advantage began to pass to the Americans. The M-1 Garand rifle was the finest infantry weapon in the war. Artillery was precise and lethal, and American crews were skilled practitioners of the devastating "time-on-target" technique, which delivered shells onto a target from several directions simultaneously, leaving no place to hide. In the air, the elegant P-51 Mustang, a high-speed ultra-long-range fighter, could escort bomber groups from Britain as far as Berlin. It dominated the French skies after D-Day. American four-engine bombers—the B-17 Flying Fortress and the B-24 Liberator—were superior in range and capacity to German or Japanese air weapons. In 1944, the B-29 Superfortress, with its 141-foot wingspan, 10-ton bomb load, and awesome 4,200-mile range, took to the skies over the Pacific. Uniquely adapted to **city busting** raids against Japanese industrial targets (Boeing originally wanted to call it the Annihilator), the Superforts incinerated Japanese cities one after another. American tanks remained inferior to their German counterparts throughout the war, owing to the U. S. Army's failure to recognize the importance of this weapon.

Quantity was often a substitute for quality, however, and American designers sometimes cut corners to make a product that could be mass produced. The results were

A crew waits on a carrier flight deck as a torpedo bomber is set in a catapult for a raid on Wake Island. Carrier warfare was unique to the Pacific theater, where opposing fleets used aircraft to strike each other across vast expanses of ocean.

impressive. When Allied troops landed in France in 1944, they enjoyed a superiority of 20 to 1 in tanks and 25 to 1 in aircraft. When Roosevelt set a production target of 50,000 aircraft in 1940, the Germans considered it a bluff, but American factories turned out almost 300,000 planes during the war. Often, abundance resulted in "attrition" tactics that pitted American numbers against Axis skill. An American soldier in Salerno asked a captured German lieutenant why he had surrendered. "The Americans kept sending tanks down the road," the German replied. "Every time they sent a tank, we knocked it out. Finally, we ran out of ammunition, and the Americans didn't run out of tanks."

Americans also developed a number of "secret" weapons. The War Department funded defense laboratories at Johns Hopkins, MIT, Harvard and other universities, forging a permanent link between government, science, and military research. American and British scientists invented one of the first "smart" bombs, the proximity fuse, which set its own range by bouncing a radio signal off its target. To keep it from falling into Axis hands, it was used only for the air defense of London, on ships in the Pacific, and in the worst moments of the battles of Iwo Jima and the Bulge. Collaboration between American and British scientists produced improvements in sonar and radar, penicillin, and the atomic bomb.

The Manhattan Project that produced the atomic bomb was the war's largest military-scientific-industrial enterprise. In 1939, three scientists who had fled Nazi Europe—Leo Szilard, Eugene Wigner, and Edward Teller—urged the famous physicist Albert Einstein to warn Roosevelt that the Germans might invent a nuclear weapon. The National Academy of Sciences concluded that a weapon of "superlatively destructive power" could be built, and General Leslie R. Groves was put in charge of the project, which eventually employed 600,000 people and cost two billion dollars. World War II's marriage of technology and war changed warfare, and it also changed science. Researchers and inventors had once worked alone on problems of their own choosing. Now they worked in teams at government-funded laboratories on problems assigned by Washington.

The Second Front

To reassure Britain and the Soviet Union, F. D. R. adopted a "Europe First" strategy, holding the line against Japan while directing the main effort at defeating Nazi Germany. The Allies had little in common except that Hitler had chosen them as enemies. Britain was struggling to preserve its empire. The Soviet Union had once been allied with Germany and had a nonaggression pact with Japan. Roosevelt needed to keep this shaky coalition together long enough to defeat Hitler. His greatest fear was that one or both of the Allies would make a separate peace or be knocked out of the war before the American economy could be fully mobilized. Stalin and Churchill each had their own opinions about how to use American power, and their conflicting aims produced bitter disputes over strategy.

As the Nazis closed in on the Soviet oilfields during the 1942 summer offensive, Stalin pleaded with Britain and the United States to launch a cross-channel invasion of France. Roosevelt and Marshall also wanted a second front to relieve pressure on the Soviets. Since the Civil War, U. S. military doctrine had favored attacking the main body of the enemy's army on a wide **front**, which could be done only in northern Europe. Churchill, however, disagreed. To the British, the idea of a western front evoked the horrors of the trench warfare of World War I. Britain could not sustain those losses a second time in a century. Instead, Churchill wanted to encircle the Nazi empire, encourage insurrections, and finally invade when the enemy was caged, weakened, and bleeding. He proposed attacking the "soft underbelly" of the Axis from the Mediterranean (see Map 25-2).

Concerned about the safety of the North Atlantic sea lanes—still prowled by U-boats—and about the inexperience of American troops, F. D. R. reluctantly accepted Churchill's plan. A month after Pearl Harbor he had promised Stalin a second front "this year." In late 1942, he postponed it to the spring of 1943. Finally, in June 1943, he told Stalin it would not take place until 1944. "Need I speak of the dishearteningly negative expression," Stalin wrote to F. D. R., "that this fresh postponement of the second front . . . will produce in the Soviet Union?" He was being polite. The delays reinforced Stalin's suspicions that the capitalist powers were waiting for the U. S. S. R.'s defeat.

Instead of invading Europe, the British and American Combined Chiefs chose a softer target, North Africa, and American troops commanded by Lt. Gen. Dwight Eisenhower landed in Algeria and Morocco on the morning of November 8, 1942. They moved east to link up with British forces attacking into Tunisia. As Americans advanced on the mountainous Tunisian border in February, German Panzer divisions under General Erwin Rommel burst through the Kasserine Pass trapping American columns in the high, rocky terrain. Panicky troops surrendered or fled, blowing up their ammunition stores. American shells bounced off the Panzers' thick armor. One GI described them as "huge monsters, with a yellow tiger painted on their sides." Once through the pass, Rommel briefly had the chance to encircle and defeat the Allied forces in northern Tunisia, but his commanders ordered him to advance in another direction. The Americans and British regrouped for a counterattack.

Ernie Pyle, the popular war correspondent, reassured American readers that "even though they didn't do too well in the beginning, there was never at any time any question about the American bravery." Eisenhower was not so sure. He sacked the corps commander responsible for defending the Kasserine and replaced him with Maj. Gen. George S.

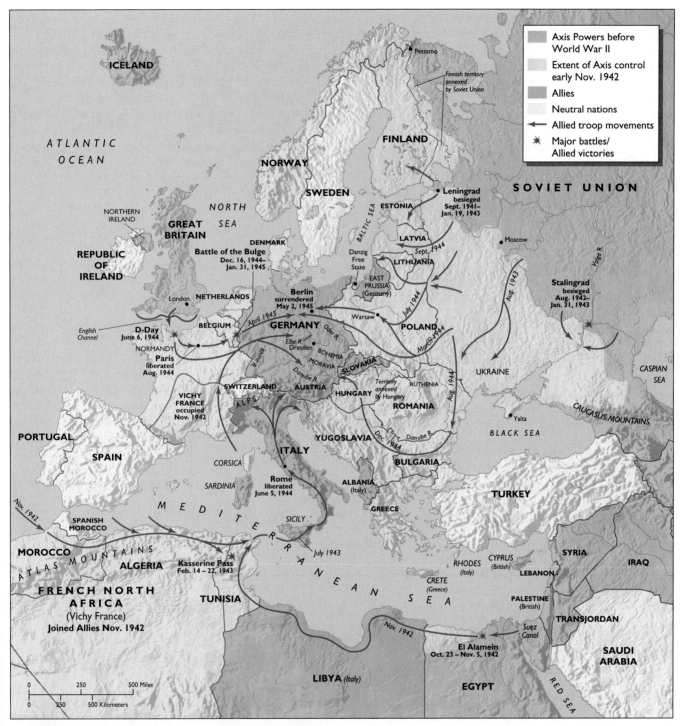

Axis Powers before World War II
Extent of Axis control early Nov. 1942
Allies
Neutral nations
Allied troop movements
Major battles/Allied victories

ICELAND

ATLANTIC OCEAN

NORTHERN IRELAND
GREAT BRITAIN
REPUBLIC OF IRELAND

NORWAY
SWEDEN
FINLAND
Petsamo
Finnish territory annexed by Soviet Union

SOVIET UNION

NORTH SEA
BALTIC SEA
ESTONIA
LATVIA
LITHUANIA
Danzig Free State
EAST PRUSSIA (Germany)

Leningrad besieged Sept. 1941–Jan. 19, 1943
• Moscow
Volga R.

Sept. 1944
July 1944
March 1944
Aug. 1943

Stalingrad besieged Aug. 1942–Jan. 31, 1943

DENMARK
Battle of the Bulge Dec. 16, 1944–Jan. 31, 1945

Berlin surrendered May 2, 1945
Warsaw •
POLAND
UKRAINE
CASPIAN SEA

London
NETHERLANDS
BELGIUM
April 1945
GERMANY
Elbe R.
Dresden •
Oder R.
BOHEMIA
MORAVIA
SLOVAKIA
Aug. 1944

English Channel
D-Day June 6, 1944
NORMANDY
Paris liberated Aug. 1944
Rhine R.
Danube R.
AUSTRIA
HUNGARY
Territory annexed by Hungary
RUTHENIA
ROMANIA
Yalta •
BLACK SEA
CAUCASUS MOUNTAINS

SWITZERLAND
VICHY FRANCE occupied Nov. 1942
ALPS
Danube R.
Dec. 1944

PORTUGAL
SPAIN
ITALY
YUGOSLAVIA
BULGARIA
TURKEY

CORSICA
SARDINIA
Rome liberated June 5, 1944
ALBANIA (Italy)
GREECE

MEDITERRANEAN SEA
SICILY
July 1943
CRETE (Greece)
RHODES (Italy)
CYPRUS (British)
SYRIA
LEBANON
IRAQ

Nov. 1942
SPANISH MOROCCO
MOROCCO
ATLAS MOUNTAINS
ALGERIA
Kasserine Pass Feb. 14–22, 1943
TUNISIA

FRENCH NORTH AFRICA (Vichy France) Joined Allies Nov. 1942

Nov. 1942
El Alamein Oct. 23–Nov. 5, 1942
PALESTINE (British)
Suez Canal
TRANSJORDAN
SAUDI ARABIA
RED SEA

LIBYA (Italy)
EGYPT

0   250   500 Miles
0   250   500 Kilometers

Map 25-2   World War II in Europe, 1942–1945.
While the Soviets reduced the main German force along the eastern front, the British and American allies advanced through Italy and France.

Patton. The Army increased basic training from 13 to 17 weeks and reviewed its doctrine and weapons. It was discovered that American tanks were too small and that artillery was not powerful enough. From that point forward armored divisions were to go into battle in full strength, instead of being committed "in driblets." For Patton, the Kasserine debacle showed that firepower, delivered by air, tanks, and artillery, was more reliable than infantry. His preference for technology over bravery became ingrained in American strategy after the war.

Allied forces captured Tunis and Bizerte on May 7, bagging 238,000 German and Italian prisoners. Rommel escaped to fight the Americans again in France a year later. At that time he would encounter a different American Army, larger, more experienced, and equipped with the newest weapons. As it mobilized to fight the Axis, the United States was changing too. Industry and people were shifting around. Government took on new functions, and industry shifted into high gear.

Organizing for Production

To defeat regimented, totalitarian enemies, Americans had to gear their political economy for war. They willingly, even gladly, concentrated power in business, government, and labor. Big was beautiful because it made possible the "miracle of production" that was both winning the war and raising living standards on the home front. During the height of the Depression, F. D. R. had never been bold enough to stoke up the economy by borrowing heavily (a technique economists call a "Keynesian stimulus"), but during the war, half of the money the federal government spent was borrowed, and nobody complained. The economy boomed. War contracts created 17 million new jobs. Industrial production doubled. The employment dial reached "full" in 1942 and stayed there until Japan surrendered. People had money to save, spend, or bet. In 1944, as much of Europe and Asia lay in ruins, Americans wagered a billion dollars on horse races. "People are crazy with money," a Philadelphia jeweler explained. "They don't care what they buy. They purchase things . . . just for the fun of spending."

The biggest spender, of course, was the military, and war industries worked by a new set of rules. Contractors depended on the government for financing, materials, and labor. New war plants, built at taxpayer expense, went up in towns that had seen little industry before. As industry moved, workers moved with it, changing jobs, migrating to the new boomtowns, and organizing themselves into a powerful political and economic force.

A Mixed Economy

"When Hitler put his war on wheels he ran it straight down our alley," General Brehon B. Somervell, the Army's chief of supply, declared. "He opened up a new battlefront, a front that we know well. It's called Detroit." Government planners were so enthusiastic about the potential for war production that military leaders felt a need to warn them against trying to beat Germany "by outproducing her" (see Figure 25-1). Undeterred, the Roosevelt administration added a layer of war mobilization agencies to control prices, assign labor, and gear up industry. It dusted off the tried and true methods from World War I—dollar-a-year-men and "cost plus" contracts—and added new incentives, such as tax breaks for retooling and federal loans and subsidies. "You have to let business make money out of the process," Secretary of War Henry Stimson explained, "or business won't work." Sometimes it still wouldn't, and the government seized at various times the steel industry, the railroads, the coal mines, and briefly, Montgomery Ward.

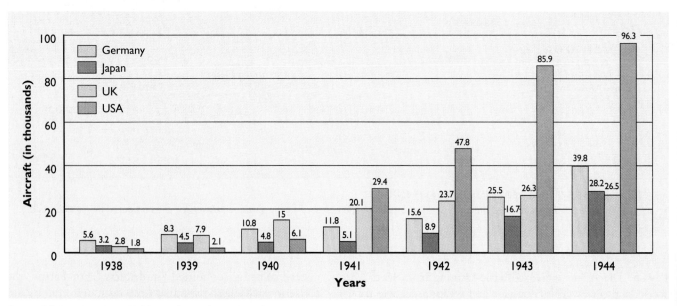

Figure 25-1   Number of Military Aircraft Produced.
U.S. production of military equipment lagged at first, but once in high gear it dwarfed the rest of the world.
Source: I.C.B. Dear, The Oxford Companion World War II (Oxford University Press, 1995), p. 22.

Output soared. At Willow Run, near Detroit, Michigan, Ford was turning out a fleet of B-24s larger than the whole *Luftwaffe*. Cargo ships, which took longer than a year to build in 1941, were coming out of the Kaiser Shipyards in an average of 56 days. Entirely new industries such as synthetic rubber (to replace natural rubber, grown in Japanese-controlled Southeast Asia) and lucite (a clear, hard plastic used for aircraft windshields) appeared overnight. Industrial techniques applied to agriculture—mechanization and chemical herbicides and pesticides—raised output by one-third while the number of farmers fell by 17 percent. Enterprising corporations patriotically increased their market share. Coca Cola's mobile bottling plants followed the front lines, creating a global thirst for their product. Wrigley added a stick of gum to each K-ration and made chewing gum a national habit.

Business leaders, denounced as "economic royalists" by F. D. R. himself only a few years earlier, regained the prestige they had lost during the Depression. Big business was now government's partner in the war effort. Major corporations like General Electric, Allis-Chalmers, and Westinghouse were even running parts of the super-secret Manhattan Project. "The Government supplies most, if

not all, of the capital, buys the goods produced, and generally controls operations, but with management in private hands," Edwin Witte, a member of the National War Labor Board explained. This produced "a mixed economy, which is not accurately described as either capitalism or socialism, as these terms have been used by the theorists." Witte was sure that "individual initiative, work, and thrift count as much as ever" in the new economy, but he could not say how.

Most business was still small; 97 percent of manufacturing, for example, came from firms with just a few hundred employees. During the war, however, Congress and the administration drew a line between the large high-tech firms, who were its partners in the business of national defense, and "small business" that had to be mollified with tax breaks and loans. Since the war, "small business" has been represented by its own federal agency, congressional subcommittees, and lobbying groups, while major corporations such as Lockheed-Martin and Archer Daniels Midland negotiate long-term contractual relationships with the federal government. World War II permanently divided the economy into separate "government" and "market" sectors, each with its own rules and ways of dealing with Washington.

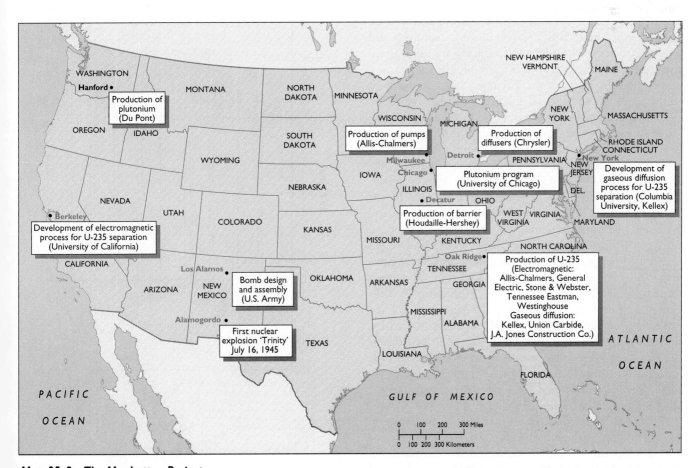

Map 25–3   The Manhattan Project.
The Manhattan Project created a new kind of collaboration between industry, government, and science. Much of the new infrastructure was located in the South and West.

Industry Moves South and West

Although Detroit got its share, the bulk of war contracts went to states in the South and Southwest and on the Pacific Coast, shifting industry's center of gravity down and to the left. Airplanes flown in World War I came from factories in Dayton, Ohio, and Buffalo, New York, but the B-29 Superfortress, the most technically advanced plane at the end of World War II, was manufactured in Seattle, Washington, Omaha, Nebraska, Wichita, Kansas, and Marietta, Georgia. Three of the Manhattan Project's largest facilities—the gaseous diffusion plant in Oak Ridge, Tennessee, DuPont's plutonium factory in Hanford, Washington, and the bomb design laboratory at Los Alamos, New Mexico—likewise broke the historic pattern that had concentrated high-tech industry in the Northeast and Midwest (see Map 25-3).

There were several reasons for this shift. Industries that needed power gravitated to the huge hydroelectric grids created by the New Deal. Aluminum plants went up during the war in the basins of the Tennessee and Columbia Rivers, to take advantage of abundant power from federal dams. The federal government also encouraged construction in the middle of the country to lessen the danger from enemy bombers. Corporations moved south and west to find low-wage nonunion workers. Powerful southern and western senators, who controlled military appropriations, also steered new factory development into their states.

The results were visible. The population of the West increased by 40 percent. Towns became cities overnight. The population of San Diego doubled in 1942. Los Angeles, Houston, Denver, Portland, Seattle, and Washington, D.C., became wartime boomtowns. While "old" industries such as automobiles and steel remained the mainstay of the economy above the Mason-Dixon line, the "sunbelt" states of the South and West became the home of the gleaming industries of the future: plastics, aluminum, aircraft, and nuclear power.

Few people objected to government direction of the economy when it meant new jobs and industry in regions that had been poor. Income taxes went up by 50 percent during the war, but there was little grumbling. A 1942 Gallup poll showed that two-thirds of Americans wanted the federal government to register all adults and assign them to war work as needed. The Office of Price Administration enlisted women consumers to enforce price ceilings, and thousands wrote in to inform on their local grocers. Citizens volunteered for scrap drives, bond drives, and blood drives, and they dug victory gardens.

The war effort was so popular that the administration did not worry much about propaganda. Compared to the elaborate censorship and public relations effort of World War I, the Office of War Information of the World War II era was a weak, indecisive outfit. Fears about the growth of government and its partnership with big corporations cer-

tainly existed, but they were seldom voiced. Americans recognized that running a war was a complex business that required supervision from a large bureaucracy. Roosevelt and other war managers—many of them former progressives—had learned a lesson from World War I: In gaining public support, inducements worked better than coercion.

New Jobs in New Places

The following advertisement appeared in a Chattanooga, Tennessee, newspaper in September 1942: "Wanted: Registered druggist; young or old, deaf or dumb. Must have license and walk without crutches. Apply Cloverleaf Drug Store." Labor was in such short supply that prisoners were considered model employees. Inmates at San Quentin made submarine nets, while felons at the federal pen in Puget Sound turned out Navy patrol boats. As it had during World War I, the need for workers pushed up wages, brought new employees into the work force, and set people on the move in search of better opportunities. It also swelled the ranks of organized labor from 10 million to almost 15 million between 1941 and 1945 (see Figure 25-2).

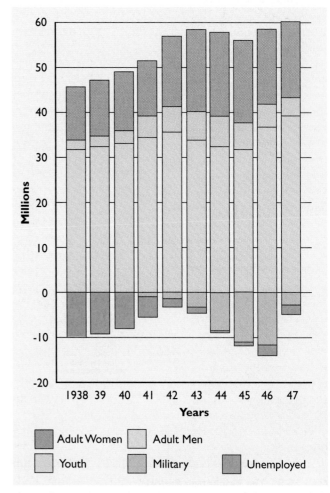

Figure 25-2   Make-up of U. S. Labor Force, 1938–1947.
Source: Dear, Oxford Companion World War II, p. 1182.

As it had with business, the federal government enlisted labor as a partner in the war effort. Unions grew because of a federally mandated "maintenance of membership" policy, by which new employees of unionized factories were automatically in the union unless they resigned within 15 days. Wartime inflation and resistance from management created tremendous pressure to strike, even in plants producing vital war supplies. Through the National Defense Mediation Board, the Roosevelt administration encouraged a cooperative bargaining relationship between unions and Washington, furthering a process begun by the New Deal. When wildcat locals of the United Auto Workers struck North American Aviation plants in Los Angeles in 1941, the NDMB first called upon the UAW leadership to mediate. When that failed, Stimson sent the Army to break the strike, but the NDMB then forced NAA's management to accept the union's wage demands. Through a combination of carrots and sticks, federal administrators encouraged a more collaborative, managerial style of union leadership. Unions did not have to struggle as much for membership or recognition; in return, they curbed militant locals and accepted federal oversight. Decision making moved from the one-story brick "locals" that dotted factory districts around the country to the marble headquarters of national unions in Washington, D. C.

People moved to jobs, rather than the other way around, and some four million workers, taking with them another five million family members, migrated as war mobilization redrew the map of economic opportunity. "Scarcely a section of the country or a community of any size escaped the impact of this great migration," according to an official report. Some 200,000 Mexican farm workers, known as *braceros,* crossed the border to harvest crops. As they had during World War I, African Americans from the South proved especially willing to move. San Francisco's African-American population doubled in a single year, 1944. At the peak of the migration, African Americans were arriving in Los Angeles at a rate of 300 to 400 a day. By leaving Mississippi to take a factory job in Los Angeles, a sharecropper could increase his salary six- or seven-fold. In war plants, workers were protected by antidiscrimination clauses, and wages were federally set. Salaries of African Americans rose twice as fast during the war as those of whites. African Americans moved into cities crowded with newcomers, families of overseas military personnel, ex-farmers seeking industrial jobs, and refugees from Europe. The migrants permanently changed the political complexion of their adopted hometowns and regions.

Workers were generally happy with higher wages, but many would have been glad to have a decent place to live. War Manpower Commissioner Paul V. McNutt complained that cities with plenty of housing, like New York, still suffered from unemployment while all the new factories were going to places with no housing to spare. There

were no rooms to rent within miles of Willow Run. In southern and western towns, workers "hot bedded," slept in shifts in boarding houses or lived in cars. Frustrations over the housing shortage sometimes boiled over into racial conflict. In 1943, when the federal government constructed a housing project with 1,000 units in Detroit along the border between Polish and African-American neighborhoods, mob violence erupted over who would take possession of the dwellings. After two days of rioting, federal troops occupied the city. Housing remained a chronic problem throughout the war and for several years afterward.

Women in Industry

"Rosie the Riveter," the image of the glamorous industrial worker laboring to bring her man home sooner, was largely a creation of the Office of War Information. Industry needed workers, and the OWI promised women that running heavy machinery was no more difficult than using kitchen appliances. Some 36 percent of the wartime labor force was female, but that was only marginally higher than the peacetime figure. Few women left housework to take a job in an aircraft factory solely for patriotic reasons. Instead, as it had with other workers, the war economy shifted women workers into new roles, allowing some to move from service or agricultural jobs into industry and allowing women with factory jobs to take better-paid and more highly skilled positions.

The number of manufacturing jobs for women grew from 12 million to 16.5 million, with many women moving into heavy industry as metalworkers, shipwrights, and assemblers of tanks and aircraft, jobs that had been off limits before. Employers had once refused to hire women for such heavy labor, but under the pressures of wartime they found that machinery could take away some of the physical strain and actually improve efficiency. Women worked

Women assemble aricraft rudders at a plant in Santa Monica, California.

coke ovens in the hottest parts of steel plants; they operated blast furnaces and rolling mills. For many women, the war offered the first real chance for occupational mobility.

Even so, employers did not offer women pay equal to that of men. Unions either refused women membership or expelled them when the war ended. Despite government encouragement, neither employers nor federal agencies offered much help for women trying to juggle job and family. Under the Lanham Act, which provided the first federal support for daycare, the government constructed 2,800 centers, but it was not nearly enough. Social workers occasionally found infants in cars parked outside factories. "Latch-key children," children left home alone while their mothers worked, were said to be a major problem. Government experts and social scientists saw female labor as necessary for the war effort but dangerous in the long run. "Many of them are rejecting their feminine roles," a social worker complained. "They wish to control their own fertility in marriage, and say they never wanted the children which had been thrust upon them." After the war, women were expected to yield their jobs to returning servicemen. They were blamed for neglecting their duties and encouraging juvenile delinquency, a backlash that had begun to build even before the war ended.

Between Idealism and Fear

In the movies Americans marched to war (and war plants) singing patriotic tunes by George M. Cohan, but in real life this war was noticeably free of high-minded idealism. A sentimental nationalism filled soldiers' letters in the Civil War and World War I, but GIs seldom wrote home to praise their leaders or their cause. Americans had already fought once to end all wars and keep the world safe for democracy. They were not ready to buy that bill of goods again quite yet. Journalist John Hersey asked marines on Guadalcanal what they were fighting for. "Scotch whiskey. Dames. A piece of blueberry pie. Music," they replied. Things were no clearer on the home front, where to writer Dwight Macdonald the war seemed to represent "the maximum of physical devastation accompanied by the minimum of human meaning." In one wartime advertisement, Goodyear Rubber Company asked "What can you say to those whose hearts bear the aching burden of this conflict? That their sons have died in a noble cause? That the nation mourns with them?" Obviously not.

To fill this moral vacuum, wartime leaders took idealistic hyperbole to new heights. Churchill spoke of the triumph of the "English-speaking peoples." Roosevelt said Americans were fighting for the Four Freedoms: freedom of speech; freedom of worship; freedom from want; and freedom from fear. Norman Rockwell's homey renderings of the four freedoms graced OWI posters and covers of the *Saturday Evening Post*.

web connection

Lies, Lies, Lies

www.prenhall.com/boydston/propaganda

Attacks on women. Babies on bayonets. Fearsome animal-like faces and bodies in enemy uniforms. These were recurring images, based on ignorance and fear, in the propaganda waged during World War II, on all sides. Propaganda has been described as a lie repeated often enough that it seems it must be true. During World War II in particular, racism permeated the propaganda crafted on every side and effectively terrorized civilians and made postwar relations especially difficult. What was the purpose of propaganda, and how did it work?

Americans did know what they were fighting against: totalitarianism, gestapos, and master races. Throughout the war and after, totalitarianism provided a powerful symbol of what America and Americans ought to oppose. The president of the U. S. Chamber of Commerce denounced the "bureaucratic capitalism" of the New Deal as "fascist" and "totalitarian." Labor unions and civil rights groups used the same words to brand their enemies. "You don't wanna be like Hitler, do ya?" Frank Sinatra asked in a wartime ad, rebuking a group of boys who had been picking on a Jewish classmate. Nobody did, and some groups facing injustice found they could shame the government into living up to its own rhetoric. Others found that in the face of wartime fears, the ideals voiced by leaders offered little protection.

Double V

African Americans improved their economic status in an atmosphere of seething racial hostility. Detroit was just one of many cities in which rapid economic growth touched off racial conflict. In Maryland, Michigan, New York, and Ohio white workers engaged in "hate strikes" to prevent the hiring of African-American workers. Over 3,000 white employees of a naval shipyard burned African-American neighborhoods in Beaumont, Texas, in June 1943 when rumors circulated that their jobs would be given to African Americans. Curfews, rumors of riots, and white citizen's committees kept many other cities on edge.

African Americans responded by linking their struggle for equal rights in the United States to the global war against fascism. Thurgood Marshall, chief counsel for the NAACP, compared the Detroit rioters to "the Nazi

Gestapo." "For years Negroes have felt that their position is isolated," NAACP leader Walter White observed, now "some of them are beginning to feel that dark people throughout the world will soon be on the march." African Americans branded racism as an alien ideology.

The nationwide African-American press and the blocs of African-American voters in northern cities made African Americans a more potent political force than they had been during World War I. In 1942, the *Pittsburgh Courier* launched the "Double V" campaign explicitly to join the struggles against racism and fascism in a fight for "victory at home as well as abroad." "Defeat Hitler, Mussolini, and Hirohito" it urged, "by Enforcing the Constitution and Abolishing Jim Crow." Membership in the NAACP grew tenfold during the war, and new groups that became household names during the civil rights movement of the 1960s began their work. African Americans and white liberals organized the Southern Regional Council to reform Jim Crow laws. In Chicago, students and activists inspired by the nonviolent tactics of Indian nationalist Mohandas Gandhi organized the Congress of Racial Equality (CORE), which desegregated restaurants and public facilities in the North. The NAACP won a legal victory in the Supreme Court case of *Smith v. Allwright* (1944), which invalidated all-white primary elections.

Along with other veterans, African-American soldiers received the benefits of the GI Bill. Many returned from the war determined not to accept discrimination any longer. Amzie Moore came back to Cleveland, Mississippi, after serving in the Army and was elected head of the local NAACP chapter. "Here I am being shipped overseas," he said of his service in the Pacific, "and I been segregated from this man who I might have to save or he save my life. I didn't fail to tell it." The war prepared Moore and a generation of African Americans for the struggle ahead.

Japanese Internment

Idealism was no match for fear, and in the days after Pearl Harbor, panicky journalists, politicians, and military authorities perpetrated an injustice on American citizens of Japanese descent. Ominous signs reading "Civilian Exclusion Order" went up in California and the Pacific Northwest in February 1942. They instructed "Japanese aliens and non-aliens" to report to relocation centers for removal from the Pacific coast "war zone." The Western Defense Command of Lt. Gen. John L. DeWitt and the *Los Angeles Times,* believing the Japanese planned to invade the West Coast, aroused the public against the Japanese "menace." FBI investigators found no suspicious plots and told the president so, but the press continued to print rumors of Japanese saboteurs. "The Pacific Coast is officially a combat zone," national columnist Walter Lippmann observed. "There is plenty of room elsewhere for [the Japanese] to exercise his rights." Responding to the press, DeWitt, and

the California congressional delegation, F. D. R. ordered the relocation.

At assembly centers, armed soldiers met the families, inspected the few belongings they were allowed to bring, and herded them onto trains. Some 112,000 Japanese Americans were moved to 10 barbed-wire enclosures in remote desert regions of the West and in the swamps of Arkansas. Rows of wooden barracks were surrounded by guard towers, high fences, and sentry posts with machine guns facing inward. The internees reacted differently to their imprisonment. Some wanted to show loyalty by cooperating, while others were unwilling to go along if it meant repudiating Japanese culture or refraining from protest. There were demonstrations and hunger strikes. Almost 6,000 second- and third-generation Americans renounced their citizenship and demanded to be deported to Japan.

In 1943, the War Relocation Authority allowed the release of some prisoners who gave positive answers to two questions: Are you willing to serve in the U. S. armed forces, and will you swear unqualified allegiance to the United States? They were tough questions to answer in light of what those being asked had experienced. "If my father is going to lose his only son it should be for some cause we respect," one man said, adding that he would have been happy to fight and die for the United States before he had been interned. "But my father can't feel the same after this evacuation and I can't either." Some 3,600 men from the camps did serve in the military, many in the highly decorated 442nd Regimental Combat Team.

Internees and civil-liberties lawyers challenged the legality of confining American citizens without charge or trial. Fred Korematsu, a welder from San Leandro, California, took a new name and had his face surgically altered in a futile attempt to stay out of the camps. When he was arrested, the American Civil Liberties Union used his case to challenge the exclusion order. Supreme Court Justice Hugo Black upheld the evacuation policy as justified by "military necessity." In January 1947, the Army's Western Defense Command applauded the fine record of the evacuation program and suggested that it could be used as a model for the treatment of suspect populations during the next national emergency.

No Shelter From the Holocaust

The United States might have saved more of the victims of Hitler's "final solution" had it chosen to do so. A combination of fear and anti-Semitism and a desire to avoid unwanted burdens led American leaders to dismiss the Holocaust as someone else's problem. In the years between *Kristallnacht* and Pearl Harbor, the United States could have provided a haven for the millions of Jews trying to flee Europe. Instead, the State Department, worried that spies and saboteurs would sneak in among the refugees, erected a paper wall of bureaucratic restrictions that kept the flow of immigrants to a trickle. Refugees found it easier to get a

WHERE THEY LIVED, WHERE THEY WORKED

Manzanar

Jeanne Wakatsuki's exile into internment began with a Greyhound bus ride from Los Angeles across the Mojave Desert. When the shades came up a mile from her destination, she saw "a yellow swirl across a blurred, reddish setting sun. The bus was being pelted by what sounded like splattering rain. It wasn't rain. This was my first look at something I would soon know very well, a billowing flurry of dust and sand churned up by the wind through Owens Valley." Its lakes and rivers emptied by the Los Angeles aqueduct, Owens Valley was a man-made desert.

Temperatures ranged from 115 degrees in summer to well below freezing in winter. On an alkali flat beneath the towering Inyo Range, workmen were building the Manzanar Relocation Camp, 600 wood and tarpaper barracks that would soon house more than 10,000 people. Each family received 20 square feet of floor space and an iron cot and army blanket for each member. Prisoners made the other furnishings themselves, filling burlap bags with straw for mattresses, making privacy screens from newspaper and chairs and tables from spare lumber.

At the Manzanar internment camp in Inyo County, California over 10,000 people spent the war in wooden barracks surrounded by barbed wire and machine guns. A 1982 presidential commission blamed "race prejudice, war hysteria, and a faliure of political leadership" for the incarceration.

Evacuees arrive in July 1942. There were ten "relocation centers," each located in remote areas of the West and South.

The prisoners fed themselves, tilling the dry soil and planting tomatoes, turnips, radishes, watermelons, and corn. They also raised cattle, pigs, and poultry, making the camp self-sufficient in both meat and vegetables. "People who lived in Owens Valley during the war still remember the flowers and lush greenery they could see from the highway as they drove past the main gate," Wakatsuki later wrote. Prisoners opened repair shops, laundries, a newspaper, a clinic, and a cemetery. They practiced medicine and law. The Manzanar Co-Op, which sold retail and mail-order goods, did one million dollars in business in 1944.

A young Nisei girl awaits evacuation. In 1988, Congress awarded a restitution of $20,000 to each of the surviving internees.

Manzanar was like a small city, except that it was surrounded by wire and armed guards. The camp administrators created a network of informants to spy on inmates. In December 1942, four prisoners beat up a man suspected of being an informant. When one was arrested, a group of prisoners demonstrated in front of the administration building to demand his release. Nervous guards fired into the crowd, killing two young men and wounding eight others. "You can't imagine how close we came to machine-gunning the whole bunch of them," a camp official explained. "The only thing that stopped us, I guess, were the effects such a shooting would have had on the Japs holding our boys in Manila and China."

It was the last "uprising" at the camp. Administrators censored the newspaper, prohibited expressions of Japanese culture, and required all meetings to be conducted in English. The community within the camp remained forever divided. Young men denounced their elders for respecting the law even when it was unjust. Administrators, with their persistent questionnaires, separated the angry from the docile and drew up blacklists.

Defiance was severely punished. Over eight thousand internees who would not renounce the emperor were separated from their families and sent to a camp at Tule Lake, California, and 263 young men who refused military service went to federal prison. Still, the majority of draft-eligible men in the camps served in the armed forces, many in intelligence and combat roles. The separation of the loyal from the disloyal, and the placement of so many in positions of trust, removed all justification for continuing to hold loyal Japanese Americans, apart from the political embarrassment their sudden release would cause.

Those who could—college students who gained admission to eastern universities, workers with contracts elsewhere, those who joined the armed forces—left, leaving only the very old and the very young. "What had to be endured was the climate, the confinement, the steady crumbling of family life," Wakatsuki wrote in her memoir, *Farewell to Manzanar*. "In such a narrowed world, in order to survive, you learn to contain your rage and your despair, and you try to re-create, as well as you can, your normality, some sense of things continuing."

visa from China than from the United States. In 1939, the *St. Louis* steamed from Hamburg with 930 Jewish refugees aboard. American immigration officials refused to let the refugees ashore because they lacked proper papers—papers that would have to be furnished by their Nazi persecutors. The ship and its passengers returned to Germany.

Once it began, Nazi Germany's systematic extermination of the Jews made news in the United States. Stories in the *New York Times* as early as 1942 described the deportations and concluded that "the greatest mass slaughter in history" was under way. Official reports by the Polish government in exile confirmed the scale of the atrocities. At Auschwitz, Poland, in the most efficient, high-tech death camp, 2,000 people an hour could be killed with Zyklon-B gas. Jewish leaders begged War Department officials to bomb the camp or the rail lines leading to it. The Army believed aerial bombardment could shut down industrial installations and that it regularly obliterated German war factories and rail junctions. The factory areas of Auschwitz were bombed twice in 1944, but John J. McCloy, the assistant secretary of war, refused to target the camp, dismissing it as a humanitarian matter of no concern to the Army. Roosevelt, who also knew of the Holocaust, might have rallied public support for Hitler's victims and made rescue a military priority, but he remained indifferent despite appeals from his wife, Eleanor. His inaction, according to historian David Wyman, was "the worst failure of his presidency."

When American soldiers penetrated Germany in 1945, they gained a new understanding of what they were fighting for and against. On April 15, Patton's Third Army liberated the Buchenwald death camp. Radio commentator Edward R. Murrow described the scene for listeners in the United States: the emaciated, skeletonlike survivors, the fetid piles of the dead, the ovens. "I pray you to believe what I have said about Buchenwald," he said. "I have reported what I saw." Eisenhower ordered photographs and films to be taken, and he brought German civilians from the surrounding communities to witness the mass burial, by bulldozer, of the corpses. Many GIs doubted that the things they had witnessed would be believed. "We got to talk about it, see?" one told reporter Martha Gellhorn, "We got to talk about it if anyone believes us or not."

Americans went into the First World War flushed with idealism and became disillusioned in victory's aftermath. The Second World War followed the reverse trajectory. Americans slowly came to see that their shopworn ideals offered what little protection there was against the hatred and bigotry that afflicted all nations, including their own. Rose Mclain of Washington state wrote her husband in the Pacific to promise "that our children will learn kindness, patience, and the depth of love . . . that they shall never know hate, selfishness and death from such [a war] as this has been."

Closing With the Enemy

"The Americans are so helpless," Joseph Goebbels, Hitler's propaganda minister, exclaimed in 1942, "that they must fall back again and again upon boasting about their matériel." After the North Africa campaign, the United States made good on its boasts. The American Army was small—only five million compared to Germany's nine million—but it was amply supplied and agile. Tactics emphasized speed and firepower, a combination suited to a nation so fond of the automobile. In 1944 and 1945 the United States carried the war to Japan and into the heart of Europe with a destructiveness never before witnessed. As the war drew to a close, Americans began to anticipate the difficulties of reconstructing the postwar world and to create institutions to structure a global economy at peace.

Taking the War to Europe

Using North Africa as a base, the Anglo-American Allies next attacked northward into Italy, knocking one of the Axis powers out of the war. In Sicily, where the Allies landed in July 1943, Patton applied the mobile, aggressive tactics he had advocated since 1940. Slicing the island in half with a thrust from Licata to Palermo and trapping a large part of the Italian Army, he swung east to Messina but arrived too late to block the Germans' escape. The defeat shook Italy. Strikes paralyzed the major cities, and Parliament deposed Mussolini and ordered his arrest. German troops took control and fiercely resisted the Allied landings at Salerno in September. Winter rains stopped the Anglo-American offensive south of Rome. "Vehicles were bogged above the axles," General Mark Clark grumbled, "the lowlands became seas of mud, and the German rearguard was cleverly entrenched in the hills."

To break the deadlock, Churchill ordered an amphibious assault behind German lines at Anzio in January. Catching the Germans by surprise, three Anglo-American divisions came ashore unopposed, but the Germans recovered quickly and surrounded the small beachhead, pinning down the Allies in a siege that lasted until May. The Germans sent glider bombs and remote-controlled tanks filled with explosives into the Allied lines. "Anzio was unique," American war cartoonist Bill Mauldin remembered, "It was a constant hellish nightmare, because when you weren't getting something you were expecting something, and it lasted for five months." American troops finally broke through to Rome on June 5, 1944.

The assault on France's Normandy coast the next day, D-Day, finally created the second front the Soviets had asked for in 1942. Early on the morning of June 6, 1944, the Allied invasion armada, thousands of supply and troopships and hundreds of warships, assembled off England's channel coast and began the run into beaches designated

Mitchell Jamieson, Burial Grounds *(1944). Wartime censors carefully spared the American audience from images of the anonymous, mass death of modern war, but scenes such as this one in Normandy always followed major battles.*

Juno, Gold, Sword, Utah, and Omaha. Hitler had fortified the beaches with an "Atlantic Wall" of mines, underwater obstacles, heavy guns, and cement forts. Americans waded ashore on the lightly held Utah Beach without much difficulty, but on Omaha the small boats headed straight into concentrated fire from shore batteries. The boats unloaded too soon, and men with full packs plunged into deep water. Floating tanks equipped with rubber skirts overturned and sank with crews inside. Commanders briefly considered calling off the attack, but soldiers in small groups began moving inland to outflank German firing positions. By the end of the day, they held the beach.

Eisenhower's greatest fear was another Anzio. The hedgerow country behind the beaches contained the most defensible terrain between the Channel and Germany. Each field and pasture was protected by earthen mounds topped with shrubs, natural walls that isolated troops. When a column of GIs crossed a hedgerow "the Germans could knock off the first one or two, cause the others to duck down behind the bank and then call for his own mortar support," according to one infantryman. "The German mortars were very, very efficient." However, just as had happened on Omaha Beach, the defects of the generals' strategy were compensated by the initiative of men at the lowest ranks of the Army. On their own, tankers experimented with devices to gouge holes through the hedgerows. Sergeant Curtis G. Culin crafted a set of tusks out of steel girders from a German roadblock. Thus equipped, "rhino" tanks could burst into an enemy-held enclosure and cover infantry following through the gap. By the end of the month the U. S. advance broke through the German defenses and captured the critical port city of Cherbourg.

Once in the open country, highly mobile American infantry chased the retreating enemy across France to the fortifications along the German border. There, in the Ardennes Forest, where panzers had pierced French lines in 1940, Hitler's armies rallied for a final desperate counterattack. Thirty divisions, supported by 1,000 aircraft, hit a lightly held sector of the American lines, broke through, and opened a "bulge" 40 miles wide and 60 miles deep in the Allied front. Two whole regiments were surrounded and forced to surrender, but the 101st Airborne, encircled and besieged at Bastogne, held onto a critical road junction, slowing the German advance and allowing the Allies to bring in reinforcements. The Battle of the Bulge lasted a month and resulted in more than 10,000 American dead and 47,000 wounded, but the German Army had lost the ability to resist.

Island Hopping in the Pacific

To get close enough to aim a knockout blow at Japan, the United States had to pierce the barrier of fortified islands stretching across the western Pacific from Alaska to Australia using only a fraction of the resources going to fight the war in Europe. The Army and the Navy each had a strategy, and the two services bickered over supplies and the shortest route to Tokyo. MacArthur favored a thrust northward from Australia through the Solomon Islands and New Guinea to retake the Philippines. Nimitz preferred a thrust across the central Pacific to seize islands that could be staging areas for an air and land assault on Japan.

By November 1943, MacArthur's American and Australian forces had advanced to Bougainville, the largest of the Solomon Islands and the nearest to the Japanese air and naval complex at Rabaul. Jungle fighting on these islands was especially vicious. Atrocity stories became self-fulfilling, as each side treated the other without mercy, killing prisoners and mutilating the dead. Both sides fought with "a brutish, primitive hatred," according to Eugene Sledge, whose Marine comrades kept gold teeth and skulls as trophies. Air attacks pulverized Rabaul's airfields and harbor in early 1944, opening the way for an advance into the southern Philippines.

Meanwhile, Nimitz launched a naval attack on Japan's island bases. With 11 new aircraft carriers, each holding 50 to 100 planes, the Fifth Fleet attacked Tarawa, a tiny atoll that contained 4,500 Japanese troops protected by log bunkers and hidden naval guns. Coral reefs snagged landing craft, forcing troops to wade ashore under heavy fire. Americans were shocked by the scale of the losses, more than 3,000 dead and wounded, for such a small piece of territory, but it was only one of many island battles. Tarawa provided a base for an invasion of the Marshall Islands, which in turn, allowed an advance into the Marianas. Following a strategy called "island hopping," American forces bypassed strongly held enemy islands and moved the battle lines closer to Japan.

The Allied capture of Saipan, Tinian, and Guam in July 1944 brought Japan within range of B-29 bombers. General Curtis LeMay brought his 21st Bomber Command to Saipan in January 1945 and began launching a new kind of air offensive against Japanese cities. LeMay experimented with low-level attacks using a mix of high explosives (to shatter houses and buildings) and incendiary bombs (to set fire to the debris). The proper mix could create a "firestorm," an inferno in which small fires coalesced into a flaming tornado hundreds of feet high pushed by hurricane-force winds. On the night of March 9, 1945, LeMay sent 334 bombers to Tokyo to light a fire that destroyed 267,000 buildings. The heat was so intense that the canals boiled, oxygen was burned from the air, and 83,000 people died from flames and suffocation. In the following months LeMay burned more than 60 percent of Japan's urban area. Americans felt city busting was justified, but, as historian Ronald Spector has written, bomber crews "smelling the smell of burning cities . . . probably realized that this was something new, something more terrible than even the normal awfulness of war."

Building a New World

As the war progressed across Europe and the Pacific, officials in Washington planned for the postwar future, and Allied leaders met to discuss their visions of the world after victory. Meeting in Casablanca in 1943, Roosevelt and Churchill agreed to demand the unconditional surrender of the Axis powers, to give the Allies a free hand to set the terms of peace. No country planned for peace as carefully or extensively as the United States did. The U. S. State, War, and Navy departments undertook a comprehensive survey of the world, examining each country and territory to determine its importance to the United States. The planners had only sketchy ideas about where future threats to peace would come from, but based on their own historical experience they believed that American security would depend on having a functioning international organization, a global system of free trade, and a worldwide network of American military bases.

Without the participation of the United States or the Soviet Union, the loosely organized League of Nations had stood little chance of maintaining the peace in the 1930s. Roosevelt envisioned a stronger organization led by the world's principal powers who would act as "policemen" within designated spheres of influence. Because imperial jealousies led to war, the new organization would work to disband empires, placing "trusteeships" over colonial territories preparing for self-government. The world after victory would be a world of nations, not empires or blocs. In September 1944, delegates from 39 nations met at the Dumbarton Oaks estate in Washington, D. C., and sketched out a plan for a United Nations organization comprised of a general assembly, in which all nations would be represented, and an executive council made up of the United States, China, the Soviet Union, Britain, and France.

To American leaders, the lesson of the 1930s had been that without prosperity there could be no peace. They wanted to create an open-door world, in which goods and money could move freely, eliminating the need or justification for conquest. In July 1944, 44 nations attended a conference at a mountain resort in Bretton Woods, New Hampshire, to make arrangements for global economic cooperation. The conferees created a system to manage and stabilize the international movement of money. The U. S. dollar would become an international currency, fixed against gold at the rate of 32 dollars an ounce. Other countries would fix or "peg" the value of their currencies against the dollar, making it easy and predictable to set prices on the world market. To rescue unstable currencies and lubricate deals, the delegates created an International Monetary Fund along with an International Bank for Reconstruction and Development (generally known as the World Bank).

Chairmen of delegations from 44 nations met at Bretton Woods, New Hampshire in July 1944.

The "Bretton Woods system" gave rise to the whole network of regional development banks and international aid agencies that govern international finance today.

Military planners were not ready to stake America's future security on trade or international organizations. Pearl Harbor had shown that the Atlantic and Pacific Oceans offered no protection against aggression. Military leaders could imagine aircraft and rockets striking deep into the American heartland suddenly and without warning. Beginning in 1943, they laid plans for a global system of military bases from the Azores to Algiers, Dhahran, Calcutta, Saigon, and Manila, encircling the vast Eurasian land mass. Planners could not say who the next enemy would be. Germany had bounced back once before and might again. Japan, the Soviet Union, and even Britain might present future threats. With such an extensive base network, the United States could act against any challenger before it could strike. The United States would deliver, not receive, the next Pearl Harbor. If the United States attacked *before and not after* a series of Munich conferences," one admiral explained, "the personal following of any future Hitler would be limited to a few would-be suicides." Britain and the Soviet Union looked upon this base system warily, suspecting they might be its targets, but American leaders were willing to take diplomatic risks to attain the security they felt they required.

The Fruits of Victory

Despite rumors of the president's failing health, Americans elected Franklin Roosevelt to a fourth term in 1944 by a margin of 53.5 percent to 46 percent for the challenger Thomas E. Dewey. On April 12, 1945, less than three months after his inauguration, Roosevelt died suddenly of a cerebral hemorrhage at Warm Springs, Georgia. "Mr. Roosevelt's body was brought back to Washington today for the last time," reporter I. F. Stone wrote on April 21, 1945. "Motorcycle police heralded the procession's approach. The marching men, the solemn bands, the armored cars, the regiment of Negro soldiers, the uniformed women's detachments . . . the coffin covered with a flag. . . . In that one quick look thousands of us said goodbye to a great and good man, and to an era." In Paris, French men and women offered condolences to American GIs. Flags flew at half staff on Guadalcanal, Kwajalein, and Tarawa. The president died just days before Allied troops in Europe achieved the great victory for which Roosevelt had struggled and planned. On April 25, American and Soviet troops shook hands at Torgau in Eastern Germany. On April 30, with Soviet soldiers just a few hundred yards away, Hitler committed suicide in his Berlin bunker. On May 8, all German forces surrendered unconditionally.

Harry S Truman, the new vice president and former senator from Missouri, was now commander in chief. Shortly after he took office, aides informed him that the Manhattan Project would soon test a weapon that might end the war in Asia. The first atomic explosion took place in the desert near Alamogordo, New Mexico, on July 16, 1945. Truman, meeting with Churchill and Stalin at Potsdam, Germany, was elated by the news. He informed Stalin while Churchill looked on, watching the expression of the Soviet leader. The bomb had been developed to be used against the Axis enemy, but by the time Truman learned about it, American leaders already saw it as a powerful instrument of postwar diplomacy. Henry Stimson, the secretary of war, called S-1, the code word for the atomic weapon, a "royal straight flush" and an "ace in the hole." Postwar relations with the Soviets would probably be tricky, but "over any such tangled weave of problems between the USA and the USSR the S-1 secret would be dominant." Stalin urged Truman to put the weapon to good use. Through intermediaries, Japanese diplomats had suggested an armistice on the condition that the emperor's life be spared, but Truman held out for unconditional surrender.

As American forces neared the Japanese home islands, defenders fought with suicidal ferocity. On Okinawa, soldiers and civilians retreated into caves and battled to the death. GIs feared the invasion of Japan's home islands, where resistance could only be worse. Then on August 6, a B-29 dropped an atomic bomb on Hiroshima. Two days later the Soviet Union declared war on Japan, and Soviet armies attacked deep into Manchuria, heartland of the Co-Prosperity Sphere (see

Map 25-4). On August 9, the United States dropped a second atomic bomb, this time on Nagasaki. It detonated 1,900 feet above Shima Hospital. In a fraction of a second, the hospital and nearly a square mile of the city center ignited. Bricks and granite melted in the nuclear fire. People were vaporized, some leaving shadows on the pavement. A few days later a French Red Cross worker saw the ruins of Hiroshima. "Not a bird or an animal to be seen anywhere. . . . On what remained of the station facade the hands of the clock had been stopped by the fire at 8:15. It was perhaps the first time in the history of humanity that the birth of a new era was recorded on the face of a clock."

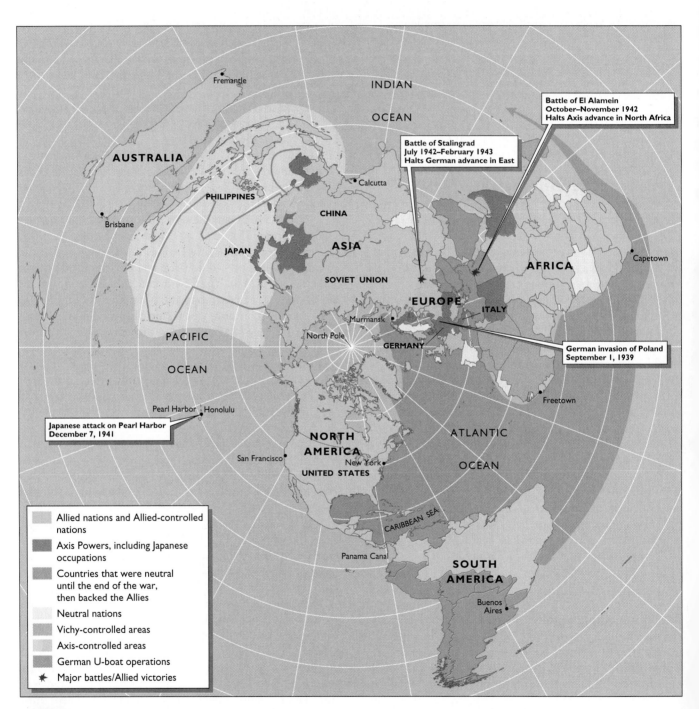

Map 25-4   A Global War.

Polar-projection maps such as this one became popular during the war and afterwards became the symbol of the United Nations. This perspective shows the war's geopolitical logic, the struggle on two fronts for control of the large central land mass of Eurasia.

Residents walk amid the ruins of Nagasaki, August 1945.

CHRONOLOGY

1930   Smoot-Hawley Tariff passed

1933   Hitler becomes chancellor of Germany
President Roosevelt devalues the dollar
The United States recognizes the Soviet Union

1934   Reciprocal Trade Act passed
Export-Import Bank created

1935   Congress passes first Neutrality Act

1937   War begins in Asia

1938   Mexico nationalizes oil fields
Munich agreement gives Hitler Sudetenland

1939   War begins in Europe

1940   Germany defeats France, Netherlands, Belgium
Destroyers-for-bases deal between the U. S. and
Britain

1941   Lend-Lease passed
Executive Order 8802 ends discrimination in
defense industries
Roosevelt and Churchill sign Atlantic Charter
Germany invades the Soviet Union
Japan attacks the United States at Pearl Harbor
U. S. declares war on Axis powers

1942   Philippines fall to Japan
Internment of Japanese Americans begins
Battles of Coral Sea and Midway turn the tide in
the Pacific
Allies land in North Africa

1943   Allies land in Sicily
Churchill and Roosevelt meet at Casablanca
U. S. troops advance to Bougainville
Marines capture Tarawa

1944   U. S. troops capture Rome
Allied landings in Normandy
U. S. troops capture Saipan
Bretton Woods Conference
Roosevelt re-elected for fourth term

1945   Roosevelt dies
Harry S Truman becomes president
Germany surrenders
Truman meets Churchill and Stalin at Potsdam
Atomic bombs dropped on Hiroshima and
Nagasaki
Japan surrenders

Conclusion

Emperor Hirohito announced Japan's unconditional surrender on August 14. In New York, crowds celebrated, but in most of the world there was silence and reflection. Thirty million people had been killed; great cities lay in ruins. At the end of the war, the United States' economic, scientific, and military mastery reached a pinnacle never attained by any of the great empires of history. Two-thirds of the world's gold was in American treasuries; half of the world's manufactured goods were made in the United States. At its height, Imperial Britain controlled 25 percent of the world's wealth. In 1945, the United States controlled 40 percent. America's air armada, almost 80,000 planes, 10 times the size of the *Luftwaffe,* dominated the skies; its naval fleet had more ships than the navies of all its enemies and allies combined. Senator Claude Pepper asked Navy Secretary James Forrestal where he intended to put all of the 1,200 warships at his disposal. "Wherever there's a sea," Forrestal replied. Then there was the atomic bomb. The rest of the world looked for signs of how the United States would use its formidable wealth and power.

Review Questions

1. How did Roosevelt's strategy for coping with the global depression differ from Britain's? From Japan's?

2. Which was more important to victory at Midway, planning or luck?

3. Why did the population of the West grow so rapidly during the war?

4. Thurgood Marshall worried about the emergence of "gestapo" in America. What did he mean?

5. According to American leaders, what caused World War II? How did their answers to that question affect their plans for the postwar world?

Further Readings

Thomas Childers, *Wings of Morning* (1995). A historian reconstructs the lives and war experiences of the last B-24 crew shot down over Germany.

I. C. B. Dear, *The Oxford Companion to World War II* (1995). Easily the best single-volume reference work on the war. Contains full descriptions of battles and campaigns, biographies of leading figures, chronologies, maps, and as many statistics as you could want.

Michael D. Doubler, *Closing With the Enemy: How GIs Fought the War in Europe, 1944–1945* (1994). World War II has been seen as a "general's war," but Doubler explains how the tactics that beat the Nazis came from the bottom up. The U. S. Army's ability to listen to the lowliest GIs was its best asset.

Doris Kearns Goodwin, *No Ordinary Time: Franklin and Eleanor Roosevelt: The Home Front in World War II* (1994). The story of the nation at war through the eyes of the family that led it.

E. B. Sledge, *With the Old Breed at Peleliu and Okinawa* (1990). A classic memoir, the story of a Marine infantryman's war in the Pacific told with candor and feeling.

Ronald H. Spector, *Eagle Against the Sun: The American War With Japan* (1985). A comprehensive history of the Pacific War from a leading military historian.

History on the Internet

"Rosie Pictures: Select Images Relating to American Women Workers During World War II"
http://lcweb.loc.gov/rr/print/126_rosi.html
See U. S. government-issued posters designed to encourage women to become defense workers. Some feature African-American women and speak to one of the earliest possibilities for women of color to work on production jobs in factories.

Japanese Internment, "Camp Harmony"
http://www.lib.washington.edu/exhibits/harmony/Exhibit/default.htm
This site tells the story of Seattle's "Camp Harmony" Japanese-American community, including information on housing, daily life in the camp, photographs, maps, and excerpts from the camp newsletter.

"Double Victory"
http://www.pbs.org/blackpress/educate_event/treason.html
and
http://www.pbs.org/blackpress/news_bios/index.html
Read about the "Double V" campaign and the African-American newspaper that started the campaign for freedom abroad and freedom at home for the nation's African-American citizens.

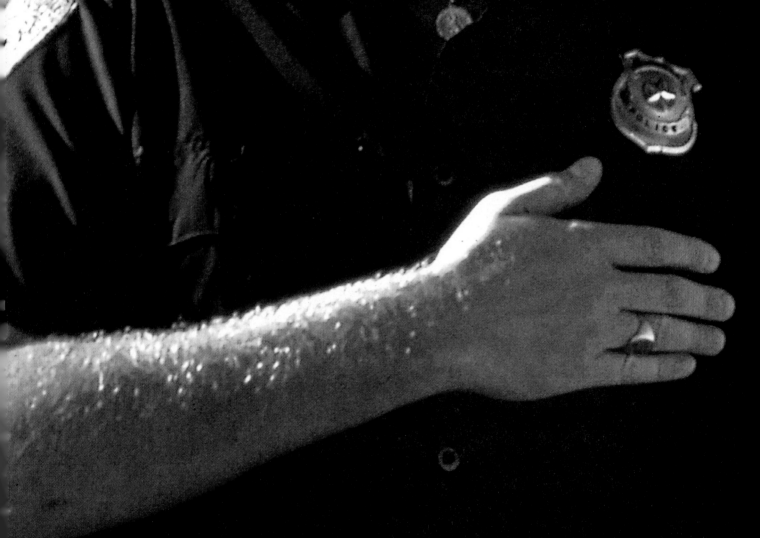

26

THE COLD WAR

1945-1952

OUTLINE

The Fall of Esther and Stephen Brunauer

Esther Caukin and Stephen Brunauer were an American success story. Born in California in 1901, Esther benefited from the increasing opportunities for women in the twentieth century. She graduated from Mills College, earned a doctoral degree from Stanford University, and became an administrator for the American Association of University Women. In 1931, she married Stephen Brunauer, a successful chemist who had come to the United States from Hungary in Eastern Europe.

The Brunauers were patriots who hated fascism. In the 1930s, Esther tried to educate Americans about the threat from Adolf Hitler's Germany. When World War II came, she went to work in the U. S. State Department. Stephen also worked for the government as an explosives expert in the Navy. After the war, he traveled to Hungary to gather scientific intelligence for the government and to help Hungarian scientists emigrate to the United States.

With fascism defeated and their careers well launched, the Brunauers had succeeded. Like most Americans, they could have looked forward to a happy, prosperous future. But then it all went wrong.

In 1947 a U. S. congressman accused Esther of being one of the "pro-Communist fellow travelers and muddle heads" in the State Department. One of her speeches, he said, was "echoing Soviet propaganda." That year, a federal agency refused to let Stephen attend a meeting about atomic energy because he had once, as a student in the 1920s, belonged to the Young Workers' League, a group with Communist ties. Somehow, even though they hated Communism as much as they hated fascism, the Brunauers found their patriotism questioned.

Then things got worse. On March 13, 1950, a U.S. Senator, Joseph R. McCarthy of Wisconsin, suggested to a Senate subcommittee that Esther and Stephen were supporting Communism. Esther, McCarthy testified, had engaged in "Communist-front activities"; Stephen had access "to some of the topmost secrets" of the U.S. military even though he may have told friends he was a member of the Communist Party. McCarthy demanded that the subcommittee subpoena federal records in order to find out whether the Brunauers were Communists who had betrayed their country. Stephen immediately denied he

743

had ever been a Communist. "I am a loyal American," Esther insisted.

Two weeks later Esther took the witness stand to defend herself and her husband before the subcommittee. Rejecting McCarthy's charges, she accused the Senator himself of betraying American values. His sudden and unfounded attack was, she said, "in violation of the traditions of fairness which are among our oldest heritages." Esther revealed how much McCarthy's accusations had already hurt her family. Since the thirteenth, they had

Esther Caukin Brunauer defends herself against Senator Joseph McCarthy's charges in March 1950. Two years later, she would lose her job.

received "anonymous telephone calls at all hours of the day and night, accompanied by threats and profanity." "Get out of this neighborhood, you Communists," one caller warned, "or you will be carried out in a box." "We are all upset and bewildered," Esther reported. "All of you who have families . . . how would you feel if it were happening in your home." Esther finished her testimony by offering letters of support from a Senator, a former Senator, and a college president. Dismissing McCarthy's charges, the college president, who was a brother of General Dwight D. Eisenhower, maintained that it was "un-American" to call Esther a "Communist sympathizer."

A majority of the subcommittee agreed. In July, the subcommittee's report concluded that McCarthy's charges against the Brunauers were "contemptible," "a fraud and a hoax." But the damage had been done. Despite the subcommittee report, there was some doubt whether Esther and Stephen were loyal, trustworthy Americans. The Brunauers' employers, the State Department and the Navy, were unwilling to take the risk of keeping such controversial people on the job. In 1951 the Navy suspended Stephen from his position, and the State Department suspended Esther from hers. Stephen gave up and quit his job that year. Esther tried to fight her suspension but found herself charged with "close and habitual association" with her husband. In 1952, the State Department fired her as a "security risk." The real reason for her dismissal, Esther told the press, was "political expediency." Their careers destroyed, the Brunauers left Washington to try to rebuild their lives out of the spotlight in Illinois.

How had it happened? How had the optimism of 1945 degenerated into trouble? Those were questions that most Americans could have asked in one way or another. At the

end of World War II, things had seemed so promising. Like the Brunauers, Americans lived in a country and a world that had been saved from ruin. At home, the economic boom of World War II had swept away the Great Depression. Abroad, the United States had helped to destroy the threat of fascism. Understandably, Americans could have expected the postwar world to be stable and safe.

Before two years had passed, however, the cold war, a tense peacetime confrontation with the Soviet Union, disrupted American life.

Stephen Bunauer, shown here in his naval uniform, was also accused of Communism and disloyalty by Senator McCarthy. A year later, he had quit his job.

Convinced that the Soviets intended to expand their power and spread Communism across Europe, U. S. leaders challenged their former allies. While the cold war developed, Americans also faced the task of maintaining prosperity in peacetime. Organized labor, women, and African Americans struggled to preserve and extend their rights and opportunities. President Harry Truman and the Democratic Party struggled as well to preserve their power and implement a liberal agenda.

However unsettling, the cold war was not an aberration. The confrontation with Communism was deeply rooted in the long-standing values and the new conditions of the American political economy at the close of World War II. Partly the product of the political economy, the cold war in turn deeply affected it. To contain Soviet expansion, the U. S. government took unprecedented peacetime actions— massive foreign aid, new alliances, a military buildup—that helped to transform the political economy in the 1940s and beyond.

Dramatic though they were, the new American policies did not prevent the cold war from widening and intensifying. By 1950, the nation was fighting a hot war on the other side of the world in Korea. By then, too, Americans knew that the Soviet Union had nuclear weapons that could conceivably devastate the United States. In turn, the Truman administration stepped up military spending and developed more powerful nuclear weapons. As the cold war seemed to spiral out of control, fear gripped American society. A frenzied search for Communist subversives at home threatened civil liberties and destroyed the careers of Esther and Stephen Brunauer. They suffered more than most people, but in one way or another, the cold war unsettled the lives of all Americans for years to come. ▪

The Origins of the Cold War

In the brief span of just two years, the United States and the Soviet Union went from a wartime alliance to the strained relations known as the cold war. The sweeping, long-term consequences of the cold war made it particularly important for Americans to understand the origins of the conflict. From the outset, the United States and the Soviet Union tried to pin the blame for the cold war on each other. For a long time, Americans wanted to believe that the Soviet Union, authoritarian and expansionist, was solely responsible. However, historians have gradually offered a more critical perspective, and they generally agree that both countries helped to start the cold war.

There is less agreement about the precise causes of the conflict. Ideological, political, military, and economic factors all clearly played a role. Ever since the founding of the Soviet Union toward the end of World War I, Soviets and Americans were ideological adversaries. They had essentially different political economies. The Soviet Union (the U. S. S. R.) was committed to Communism and socialism, the United States to democracy and capitalism. Despite their differences, the two countries fought together as allies in World War II. Wartime decisions, especially about the arrangement of the postwar world, laid the groundwork for animosity after 1945. In peacetime, the Soviet Union and the United States were the only countries strong enough to threaten each other. Moreover, they had quite different political, military, and economic interests. By 1947 those different interests produced open antagonism between the former allies. With the United States' vowing to combat the spread of Communism, the cold war was under way.

Ideological Adversaries

The Russian Revolution of 1917 that created the Soviet Union also committed the new nation to Communism. V. I. Lenin's Bolshevik revolutionaries installed a government dominated by the leadership of the Communist Party. They also installed a socialist economy in which the state—the government—owned property. At home, the Soviet Union limited individual rights, including freedom of speech and religion. Abroad, the new nation endorsed the revolutionary overthrow of capitalism.

The Soviets' Communist ideology obviously set them at odds with the political economy of the United States. The vast majority of Americans favored a capitalist economy, in which private citizens owned property. Americans celebrated individualism, freedom of speech, freedom of religion, and democratic government based on free elections. Although the United States did not always live up to these values, most Americans were sure that the "Red" Soviet Union never did and never would.

Nevertheless, open conflict between the two countries was not inevitable. While American leaders hated Communism, they could tolerate the existence of the Soviet Union. Fairly weak, the U. S. S. R. posed no military threat to the United States in the 1920s and 1930s. The Soviets could even be helpful to American interests. President Franklin Roosevelt, eager to promote U. S. trade and restrain Japanese expansion, officially recognized the Soviet Union in 1933.

Uneasy Allies

World War II demonstrated that the United States and the Soviet Union, despite their differences, could become allies. After the German invasion of the U. S. S. R. and the Japanese attack on Pearl Harbor, the United States and the Soviets were thrown together in the war against fascism in 1941. Still, the United States and the Soviet Union were uneasy allies at best. The wartime alliance also laid the groundwork for trouble. For many Americans, the lesson of the war was that the United States could not tolerate the appearance of fascism. No new dictator should ever be able to take over other European countries unopposed, as Adolf Hitler had in the 1930s. It would be easy to view authoritarian Soviet Communism as another kind of fascism and the brutal Soviet leader Josef Stalin as another Hitler. By 1945 some Americans already linked the Soviets with the Nazis by denouncing "Red Fascism."

Wartime decisions also promoted tensions between the United States and the Soviet Union. In 1943 the American government created ill feeling by excluding the Soviets from the surrender of Italy to the Allies. The delay of the Allied invasion of France until 1944 embittered the Soviets, who were desperately resisting the Germans at the cost of millions of lives. The American government further strained relations by sharing news of its secret atomic bomb project with the British but not with the Soviets.

Decisions about the postwar world led to trouble as well. At a conference in Yalta in the Soviet Union during February 1945, Franklin Roosevelt, Josef Stalin, and British Prime Minister Winston Churchill made plans that complicated relations in peacetime. Together, the three leaders promoted conflicting visions of the postwar world. On the one hand, the "Big Three" supported the self-determination of nations, the idea that countries should democratically decide their own future without interference from powerful outsiders. In a "Declaration of Liberated Europe," Roosevelt, Stalin, and Churchill stated that nations would be free and democratic. The "Big Three" also gave support to the idea that countries should act collectively to deal with world problems. They laid plans for the United Nations, an organization that would encourage states to cooperate in keeping the world free, safe, and secure.

Even as they promoted self-determination and collective action at Yalta, Roosevelt, Stalin, and Churchill undermined these principles. The Big Three obviously believed that powerful nations such as their own were each entitled to spheres of influence around the globe. In these areas, the United States, the Soviet Union, and Great Britain would exercise power independently and limit the self-determination of smaller states. Clearly, spheres of influence and unilateral action conflicted with democracy, self-determination, and collective action.

The conflict was made apparent when the three leaders dealt with the critical issue of the future of Poland, the Soviet Union's neighbor to the west. Despite the talk of self-determination and democracy, Stalin wanted to install a Polish government absolutely loyal to the Soviet Union. He could not risk an independent Poland that might be-

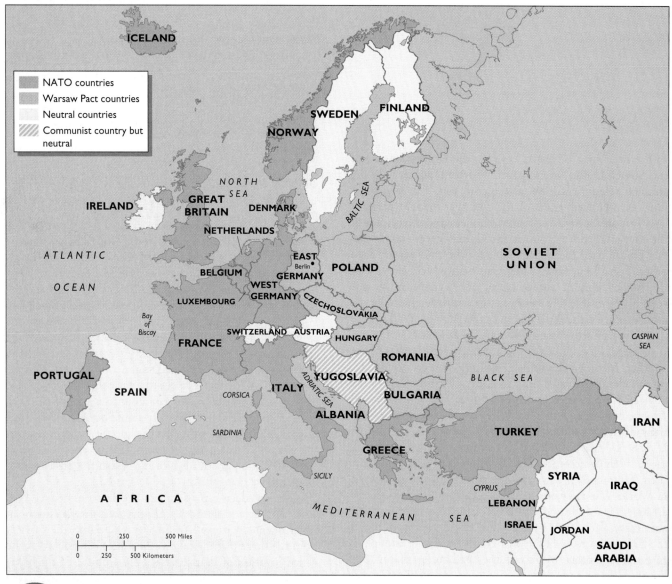

Map 26-1   Cold War in Europe, 1950.
Five years after World War II, the cold war had divided Europe into hostile camps, with NATO members allied to the United States and Warsaw Pact signers tied to the Soviet Union.

come the staging area for another invasion of the U. S. S. R. Churchill and Roosevelt, however, favored a self-governing Poland and backed a different Polish leadership group. Stalin agreed to elections, but seemingly felt that Roosevelt promised him a free hand in postwar Poland. This lack of clarity set the stage for future misunderstanding between the United States and the Soviet Union.

So did differences over the future of Germany. The United States wanted Germany, safely controlled by the Allies, to become a healthy part of the world economy. Stalin, determined never to be attacked by Germany again, wanted the country formally divided and weakened forever. In the end, the Big Three agreed that Germany would be temporarily divided into four separate zones of occupation. The United States, the U. S. S. R., Great Britain, and France would each administer one of the zones. Although Berlin, the German capital, lay within the Soviet zone, the four conquering powers would each control a section of the city. The Big Three also agreed that eventually Germany would be reunified, but they did not indicate when or how.

The uncertainties and contradictions of the Yalta meeting helped lead to Soviet-American disagreements even before the war ended. When Vice President Harry Truman succeeded Roosevelt in April 1945, the new president objected to the Soviets' attempt to take tight control of Poland. Promising to "stand up to the Russians," Tru-

man held a tense meeting in Washington with the Soviet Foreign Minister, V. M. Molotov. With "words of one syllable," the president "gave it to him straight 'one-two to the jaw.' " "I have never been talked to like that in my life," Molotov answered. "Carry out your agreements," snapped Truman, "and you won't get talked to like that."

When Truman met with Stalin and the British prime minister at the German city of Potsdam in July, relations were more cordial. But Truman reluctantly had to accept the realities of power. Because Soviet troops occupied most of Eastern Europe and much of Germany, there was little he could do about Stalin's actions there. Truman had to go along with Stalin's demand that some German territory be given to Poland. There was no progress on planning the future reunification of Germany. Sailing home to the United States, Truman privately called Stalin "an S. O. B." The president then concluded, "I guess he thinks I'm one too."

From Allies to Antagonists

After the war, the relationship between the United States and the Soviet Union eroded rapidly. The needs of the American and Soviet political economies diverged. With quite different visions of the postwar world, the two nations defined their national security interests in conflicting ways (see Map 26-1).

Cold-war leaders at Potsdam in July, 1945: The determined expressions of British Prime Minister Winston Churchill, U.S. President Harry Truman, and Soviet Premier Josef Stalin reveal the tensions that would produce confrontation after World War II.

Stalin and the Soviet leadership took a fairly cautious approach after the war. Although they were still committed to the ultimate overthrow of capitalism around the world, their immediate concern was the protection of the Soviet Union from another invasion. In addition to establishing a pro-Soviet Eastern Europe, Stalin wanted to make sure he could not be attacked from the south, through his neighbors Turkey and Iran. The Soviet leader also wanted to make sure that Germany and Japan never menaced his country again. Trying to rebuild the war-torn U. S. S. R., Stalin promoted national economic independence more than economic ties to other countries. As a result, the Soviets had little interest in encouraging speedy rebuilding and easy trade relations for other nations. Although the U. S. S. R. did not make a worldwide Communist revolution its first priority, it did not promote self-determination and democracy abroad either.

The leaders of the United States looked at the postwar world much differently. Unlike the Soviets, Truman and his associates did not have to worry about the immediate security of U. S. borders. American leaders did not fear any other military power in the short run. The United States, equipped with nuclear weapons, was clearly stronger than any rival, including the Soviet Union. But American lead-

ers feared that some other power might take advantage of economic weakness and political division around the world and eventually seize control of parts of Europe and Asia. Then the United States would be isolated and vulnerable. As the only major democracy in an authoritarian world, the nation would be cut off from the international economy and susceptible to attack.

To avoid this dismaying scenario, American leaders took nearly the opposite of the Soviet approach to the postwar world. Truman and other U. S. policymakers favored the quick reconstruction of nations, including Germany and Japan, that would participate in a world economy based on free trade. The United States needed these healthy trading partners in order to maintain prosperity at home. America also needed contented allies who would accept U. S. military bases on their soil. American policymakers felt that those bases would be crucial to keeping any future aggressor far from American shores.

The very different needs and interests of the Soviet and U. S. political economies soon translated into combative rhetoric. In February 1946 Stalin declared that capitalism and Communism were incompatible. A month later, Winston Churchill, no longer prime minister of Great Britain, came to speak at Fulton, Missouri. Introduced and applauded by Truman, Churchill ominously declared that "an Iron Curtain has descended across the Continent" of Europe. Central and Eastern Europe, the former prime minister warned, "lie in the Soviet sphere." In this menacing situation, Churchill called for an alliance of Great Britain and the United States. The rhetoric only made each side angrier. To Stalin, Churchill sounded like another Hitler ready to attack the Soviet Union. To an American Supreme Court justice, Stalin's statement amounted to "the Declaration of World War III."

As such language suggested, American leaders thought that Stalin wanted more than just safety from invasion. The Soviet Union, they concluded, aimed to expand further and further abroad. In February, George Kennan, an American diplomat in Moscow, sent back to the State Department in Washington a long telegram that both reflected and shaped the thinking of American policymakers. The Soviet leadership, explained Kennan, believed "there can be no permanent peaceful coexistence" between capitalism and socialism. Stalin and his regime were sure that capitalist nations, beset by internal problems, would attack socialist nations and one another. Acting on this unfounded fear, the U.S.S.R. would, Kennan insisted, try to destabilize capitalist nations, especially the United States. The Soviet "problem," Kennan optimistically contended, could be resolved without war, but the solution was, he conceded, "undoubtedly the greatest task our diplomacy has ever faced and probably . . . will ever have to face."

Truman's words and actions reflected Kennan's analysis. In 1946 the president tried to counter the apparent expansionism of the U. S. S. R. Declaring that he was "tired

"An iron curtain has descended." British Prime Minister Winston Churchill (seated) accepts the applause of President Harry Truman at Fulton, Missouri, in March 1946. Churchill's dark warning about the division of Europe helped set the tone of the cold war.

of babying the Soviets," Truman warned them against trying to increase their influence over Iran and Turkey. When the Soviets kept troops in Iran past the agreed-upon deadline for their withdrawal, Truman sent a battleship to the eastern Mediterranean and successfully pressed Moscow to remove its forces.

Relations between the United States and the Soviet Union deteriorated further in 1947. More concerned than ever about Stalin's behavior, Truman took aggressive steps to counter apparent Soviet expansionism in Turkey and Greece. The U. S. S. R. had been pressing for a role in Turkey for some time. In Greece, meanwhile, the monarchist regime was under attack from Communist guerrillas, seemingly aided by pro-Soviet eastern European nations. Great Britain had played the key role in supporting the Greek and Turkish governments, but by 1947 the British could no longer afford the cost of this aid. For Truman and his advisors, British withdrawal was disastrous. Control of Turkey would have given the Soviets access to the Indian Ocean and to the oil fields of the Middle East. A Communist victory in Greece could have given effective control of that Mediterranean nation to the Soviet Union. Worse, successes in Greece and Turkey could have helped Communism everywhere in Europe and the Middle East.

To prevent this disaster, the Truman administration wanted to take over for the British and provide 400 million dollars in aid to the Greek and Turkish governments, but such massive foreign aid was unprecedented in peacetime. To persuade Congress to appropriate the money, Truman knew he had to "scare hell out of the American people." So a somber president told a joint session of Congress on March 12, 1947, that the world once again faced a choice between freedom and totalitarianism. "The free peoples of the world look to us for support in maintaining their freedoms," Truman insisted. "If we falter in our leadership, we may endanger the peace of the world—and we shall surely endanger the welfare of this Nation." The president announced what became known as the "Truman Doctrine." "I believe," he said, "that it must be the policy of the United States to support free peoples who are resisting attempted subjugation by armed minorities or by outside pressures." The speech, observed *Life* magazine, was "[l]ike a bolt of lightning." Congress voted overwhelmingly to provide the aid to Greece and Turkey.

The crisis marked the turning point in the relationship between the United States and the Soviet Union. By 1947 the term "cold war" was being used to describe the American-Soviet confrontation. There was no formal declaration of war that marked the precise beginning of the cold war, but with the announcement of the Truman Doctrine, the confrontation had certainly begun. Dividing the world into good and evil, the United States was ready to support "free peoples" and oppose Communism. Former allies were now bitter antagonists.

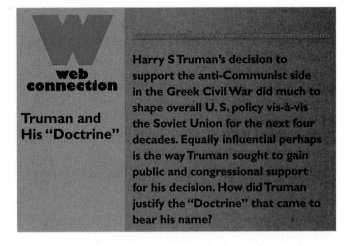

web connection

Truman and His "Doctrine"

Harry S Truman's decision to support the anti-Communist side in the Greek Civil War did much to shape overall U. S. policy vis-à-vis the Soviet Union for the next four decades. Equally influential perhaps is the way Truman sought to gain public and congressional support for his decision. How did Truman justify the "Doctrine" that came to bear his name?

Was the confrontation inevitable? There is no way for historians to prove whether events are inevitable or not, but it is difficult to see how the United States and the Soviet Union could have avoided some kind of antagonism after World War II. They had a history of tension and hostility, and they both possessed great military power. Most important, the two nations' political economies had produced clashing ideologies and needs, and so some kind of confrontation was highly likely.

It is much harder to say that the precise form of that confrontation, the cold war, was inevitable. The cold war was the product of human choices, such as Truman's decision to "scare hell out of the American people." The cold war was also the product of human mistakes, such as Kennan's erroneous conclusion that the Soviets were bent on continuing territorial expansion. Those choices and mistakes were certainly not inevitable. With good reason, Americans would wonder for decades whether the cold war could have been different.

Fighting the Cold War Abroad

The cold war intensified almost as soon as it started. In the late 1940s the United States implemented a strategy of containment to combat Soviet expansion. The Truman administration sought to hold back the U. S. S. R. with a combination of precedent-setting diplomatic, economic, and military initiatives. Moreover, the scope of the cold war quickly widened beyond Europe to include the entire world. In 1949 a Communist revolution engulfed China. In 1950, just five years after the end of World War II, the United States went to war again, this time to preserve the non-Communist regime of South Korea. As the cold war widened, it became more dangerous. When the Soviets exploded their own atomic bomb, the United States also dramatically stepped up military spending and built the hydrogen bomb. As the arms race spiraled, the cold war seemed frighteningly out of control.

The Strategy of Containment

Committed to opposing Soviet and Communist expansion, the Truman administration had to figure out just how to fight the cold war. Once again, the diplomat George Kennan helped give expression to American thinking about the confrontation with the Soviets. Writing under the pen name "X" in a journal article in 1947, Kennan argued "that the main element of any United States policy toward the Soviet Union must be that of a long-term, patient but firm and vigilant containment of Russian expansive tendencies."

The term **containment** aptly described American policy for the cold war. The United States worked to hold back the Soviets for the next 40 years, but "containment," as Kennan described it, was a broad, rather vague concept. Truman and his successors had to decide just where and when to contain the Soviet Union. They also had to decide what combination of diplomatic, economic, and military programs to hold back the Soviets.

One thing became clear quite quickly. Containment would not rely primarily on the United Nations. Like the United States, the Soviet Union had a veto over actions taken by the United Nations' powerful Security Council. From the beginning, the Soviets repeatedly used the veto to frustrate American efforts. Despite the U. S. role in creating this international institution, the Truman administration used the United Nations mainly as a place to score propaganda points, not as a major instrument of American policy.

To implement containment, Truman and his advisors revolutionized the American policies on foreign aid, overseas alliances, and national defense. Soon after the decision to help Greece and Turkey, the United States had to confront the slow recovery of war-ravaged Europe, which Winston Churchill described as "a rubble-heap, a charnel house, a breeding ground of pestilence and hate." Given their fears that an impoverished Europe would hurt the U. S. economy and embrace Communism, Truman and his advisors were determined to help the continent rebuild. In a speech at Harvard University in June 1947, Truman's new Secretary of State, General George C. Marshall, proposed a "European Recovery Plan" to help combat "hunger, poverty, desperation and chaos" and to promote "political and social conditions in which free institutions can exist." The Soviets, declining an invitation to join, refused to allow Eastern European countries to participate either, but 16 nations eagerly supported what became known as the "Marshall Plan." In the spring of 1948, Congress approved the plan with bipartisan support.

"The Marshall Plan saved Europe," Truman boasted. He exaggerated, but the aid program, the largest ever initiated by any nation, served its purposes remarkably well. From 1948 to 1952, 13 billion dollars from the United States went to restore agricultural production to prewar levels, boost industrial output beyond prewar rates, increase exports, and promote economic cooperation. Whole cities were rebuilt. By 1950, participating countries had already exceeded prewar production by 25 percent. Politically, the return of prosperity helped stabilize western European governments and weaken the region's Communist Parties. In the process, western European nations were bound more tightly to the United States. All these developments obviously served American economic and political interests. Because of the Marshall Plan, Communism seemed much less likely to spread into western Europe.

Containment required more than aid programs. It also demanded the kind of peacetime alliances that the United States had historically avoided. Such agreements, Americans had long believed, might drag the nation into unnecessary wars. But facing the unique challenge of the cold war, American leaders now saw alliances as a way of preventing, rather than provoking, armed conflict. By promising to defend other countries if they were attacked, the United States could make the Soviet Union think twice about pushing further into Europe.

This thinking led the Truman administration to a historic decision to forge the first peacetime military alliance with Europe. In 1949, the United States joined ten western European nations and Canada to form the North Atlantic Treaty Organization (NATO). Under the NATO agreement, an attack on any member nation would be treated as an attack on every member nation. The United States was pledged to go to war, subject to congressional approval. To strengthen the American commitment to western Europe, Congress appropriated 1.3 billion dollars in military aid for NATO countries, and Truman ordered American troops to the continent. General Dwight D. Eisenhower, the commander of the Allied invasion of France in World War II, agreed to become the supreme commander of NATO's combined military forces.

As these actions suggested, containment also depended on a strong military establishment in the United States. Reversing the rapid demobilization of the armed forces after World War II, the Truman administration pushed for the reorganization of the military. In 1947 Congress passed the National Security Act, which put the Army, Navy, and Air Force under a single cabinet secretary, the secretary of defense. This act also created both the Central Intelligence Agency (CIA) to gather and assess information on national security for the president and the National Security Council (NSC) to advise him on military, diplomatic, and other security matters. Before long, the CIA carried out covert psychological and political operations abroad, such as supporting anti-Communist politicians in Italy.

To build up the military, Congress passed a new Selective Service Act in 1948. The United States government once again had the right to draft men between 19 and 25 years of age into the armed services in peacetime. Finally, in 1949, Congress adopted another National Security Act, which brought together the Joint Chiefs of Staff, the heads of each of the armed services, to advise the president on military matters.

The Dangers of Containment

The strategy of **containment** exposed the United States to dangerous risks. There was always the chance that a confrontation with the Soviets could get out of hand and become a war. The dangers became clear in 1948 during a showdown over access to the German city of Berlin. That spring, the Americans, British, and French began to unify their zones of occupation in Germany into a single administrative unit. Faced with the prospect of a wealthy, unified, anti-Communist western Germany, Stalin took action in his own German zone of occupation. On June 24, the Soviets threw a blockade around Berlin, the German capital that was jointly occupied by all four former allies. Truman figured Stalin, unprepared for war, was bluffing. In any case, the United States could not let the Soviets weaken American prestige and power by taking control of Berlin. "We stay in Berlin, period," Truman snapped. But the 2.5 million people in the American, British, and French sections of Berlin were at risk of running out of food and coal. If the U. S. military tried to bring in supplies overland across the Soviet zone of Germany, there might be war.

An American transport plane airlifts supplies to the German city of Berlin, blockaded by the Soviets in 1948. The confrontation over control of the city, still damaged from World War II, underscored the dangers of containment.

Instead, the Truman administration sent relief to Berlin by air. American transport planes carried 2,500 tons of food and fuel a day to the people of Berlin. Along with this massive airlift, the Truman administration sent to Germany two squadrons of B-29 bombers, significantly, the kind of planes that had dropped the atomic bombs on Japan. In May 1949 the Soviets ended the blockade. Put to the test, the strategy of containment had worked. U. S. countermeasures had seemingly deterred Soviet expansion. But the risks were plain.

The dangers of containment became even greater for the United States later that year. In early September, American reconnaissance planes over the Pacific collected evidence that the Soviet Union had exploded an atomic bomb. The U. S. monopoly of nuclear weapons, which had boosted the nation's confidence, was over. Suddenly, the confrontation with the Soviets had potentially lethal consequences for the American people. As a Republican senator somberly observed, "[T]his is now a different world."

The Globalization of the Cold War

While the dangers of the cold war became frighteningly clear, the scope of the conflict widened. A confrontation that had begun in Europe soon spanned the world. Events in China played a key role in this globalization of the cold war.

At the end of World War II, the Chinese nationalist government of Jiang Jieshi, America's ally, faced a revolution led by the Communist Party of Mao Zedong. Hoping to save Jiang, Truman sent George Marshall on a mission in 1945 to promote a settlement between the nationalists and the Communists. The effort failed. Although Republicans strongly supported Jiang, the Truman administration concluded that the nationalist regime could not be saved. The president agreed to 2 billion dollars in aid for the nationalists from 1945 to 1949, but he refused to send American troops to China. In December 1949 the defeated nationalists fled the Chinese mainland for the island of Formosa, also known as Taiwan. "We . . . bet on a bad horse . . . ," Truman admitted. His conservative opponents were not as philosophical. They angrily blamed the administration for the "loss" of China.

The Chinese Revolution widened the cold war. Although Stalin did not direct the Chinese Communists, Americans readily saw Jiang's defeat as a victory for the Soviet Union. The Truman administration refused to recognize the new mainland Chinese regime, the People's Republic of China. Now Communism was not just a problem in Europe; it was apparently a threat in Asia, too.

By then, in fact, American policymakers believed that Communism was a potential threat in almost any part of the world. Long determined to keep European powers out of the Western Hemisphere, the United States moved to make sure that Communism did not spread to Latin

America. To implement containment in the hemisphere, the Truman administration relied on the same techniques it had used in Europe. At a conference in the Brazilian city of Rio de Janeiro in August 1947, the United States and 20 Latin American republics agreed to the Inter-American Treaty of Reciprocal Assistance. Under the terms of the agreement, known as the Rio Pact, the United States promised to train Latin American military leaders, regulate the flow of military supplies to its allies, and coordinate the defense of the region. In 1948 the United States joined with Latin American nations to create the Organization of American States (OAS). This body, with headquarters in Washington, D. C., promoted hemispheric solidarity and economic development and enforced the Rio Pact.

Even Africa, which was not critical to the defense of the United States, became a battlefield of the cold war. Although the United States favored self-determination and democracy abroad, the Truman administration hardly criticized its West European allies' continuing colonial rule over much of the continent. In 1948 Truman improved diplomatic relations with the white supremacist government of South Africa, partly because of its opposition to Communism and Soviet expansionism.

The Cold War Turns Hot in Korea

With the United States working to hold off Communism at so many points around the world, it was probably not surprising that the nation was drawn into war before long. Nevertheless, Americans were startled when their soldiers went into battle in South Korea in 1950, because the conflict came so soon after World War II and so far from the vital continent of Europe (see Map 26-2). But the Korean War was firmly rooted in the logic of the cold war.

The nation of Korea, a peninsula off of mainland China and southeast of a tip of the Soviet Union, had been liberated from the Japanese in 1945. American troops occupied the territory south of the 38th Parallel while Soviet troops occupied the territory to the north. Despite American policymakers' professed support for democracy and self-determination, they opposed a left-wing movement of Koreans who wanted their nation to become an independent "people's republic." Despite the policymakers' professed support for international cooperation, they acted unilaterally to prevent a Communist takeover from inside or outside the South. The Truman administration aided the anti-Communist government of Syngman Rhee in the South, while the Soviet Union promoted the regime of the Communist Kim Il Sung in the North. In 1948 the United States went along with the permanent division of Korea at the 38th Parallel. Then, in June 1950, after a series of incidents along the border, North Korea invaded the South.

The Korean invasion was the greatest crisis of Truman's presidency. By itself, South Korea was not strategically important to the United States, but the president and

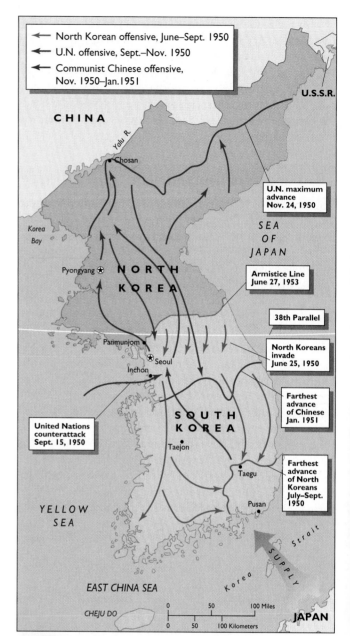

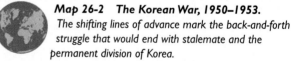

Map 26-2 The Korean War, 1950–1953.
The shifting lines of advance mark the back-and-forth struggle that would end with stalemate and the permanent division of Korea.

his advisors clearly believed that the Soviet Union was responsible for the North Korean attack. After the "loss" of China, the Truman administration could not afford to allow Communism to advance further in Asia. "By God," the president swore, "I am going to let them have it!" His administration secured approval from the United Nations for international action in Korea. Although troops from 15 countries eventually fought there for the United Nations, nine out of 10 United Nations soldiers came from the United States. America was at war then, or was it? Claiming that the conflict was only a "police action," Truman

The heat of the cold war: U.S. Marines move past the burning wreckage of a building after fighting with North Korean forces north of the 38th Parallel in Korea, October 1950.

never asked Congress for a declaration of war. For the first time, but not the last, a president committed troops to battle in the cold war without regard for the Constitution.

At first, the fighting did not go well. U. S. troops, unprepared and understrength, had to fall back before the North Korean Army. But in the summer, UN forces under the leadership of the American general Douglas MacArthur halted the North Koreans' advance. In September, American troops stormed ashore at Inchon on the west coast of South Korea, deep behind enemy lines. Within weeks of MacArthur's bold stroke, the South had been reclaimed.

Then Truman and his advisers made a fateful decision. Eager to do more than just contain Communism, they wanted to roll it back. Truman gave the order to invade North Korea and push for the reunification of the Korean peninsula. MacArthur, who privately thirsted for war with the Chinese Communists, pushed quickly northward, ever closer to China. Fearing an American invasion, the Chinese issued warnings, sent their forces into North Korea, and then, on November 25, unleashed a broad attack on UN troops. As MacArthur's army fled back south to the 38th Parallel, the general admitted it was an "entirely new war."

The Korean "police action" settled into a troubling stalemate. A frustrated MacArthur wanted to expand the war effort and fight back aggressively, but the chastened Truman administration, giving up on Korean reunification, was prepared to accept the old division at the 38th Parallel. That was too much for MacArthur, who broke the U. S. military's unwritten rule against public criticism of its civilian leadership. "There is no substitute for victory," MacArthur lectured in 1951. Truman, fed up, fired his popular general in April. Meanwhile, the war dragged on.

The Korean stalemate underscored some difficult realities of the cold war. The confrontation with Communism had the potential to sacrifice American lives in seemingly insignificant countries far away from the United States. American soldiers had to be prepared to fight in less noble circumstances than during World War II. They had to go into battle without a declaration of war. They also had to be prepared, as the saying went, to "die for a tie"—a less-than-total victory. Moreover, the American people had to watch with the knowledge that the fighting could easily spread into a wider war, perhaps even a nuclear war with the Soviet Union.

Escalating the U. S. Effort

The "loss" of China, the Soviet atomic bomb, and the Korean War had important consequences for American policy. The basic aims of containment never changed, but by the 1950s the Truman administration was prepared to go much further to carry them out. Escalating the U. S. effort, the Truman administration increased its support for anti-Communist causes, such as the French war in Southeast Asia.

Vietnam, along with Laos and Cambodia, made up Indochina, a southeast Asian colony of France. After losing Indochina to Japan during World War II, the French were ready to take over again in 1945. By then, however, many Vietnamese wanted their land to be free and independent. The Viet Minh, who had fought against the Japanese invaders, were now prepared to resist the French. Led by the Communist and nationalist Ho Chi Minh, the Viet Minh declared Vietnamese independence and appealed to the Truman administration for support in 1945 and 1946. Given its hostility to colonialism and its support for self-determination, the United States might well have been expected to support Vietnamese independence, but as in Africa, the United States refused to oppose the interests of a valued European ally. Truman did not even answer Ho's letters.

With some help from the Soviets and the Chinese Communists, the Viet Minh frustrated the French Army. By 1950, France needed help from the United States, and the Truman administration was willing to give that help. It was no longer just a matter of supporting a European ally. Now it was a matter of stopping further Communist expansion in Asia. So the United States gave military equipment and direct financial aid to the French war effort in Vietnam.

Another consequence of the events of 1949 and 1950 was the escalation of the arms race. In order to deploy troops around the world and to counter Soviet nuclear weapons, the United States had to strengthen its forces. In April 1950 the National Security Council approved a secret guideline for American policy known as NSC 68. Insisting that the Soviets were "seeking to create overwhelming military force," NSC 68 warned that "every individual faces the ever-present possibility of annihilation." America, vulnerable to Soviet attack, must develop "clearly superior overall power." Increased defense spending would require higher taxes and lower domestic expenditures, but it was an absolute necessity, and it might even stimulate the economy.

Truman worried about the cost of NSC 68, but the Korean War soon convinced him to push for its implementation. In September 1950, at the president's urging, Congress passed the Defense Production Act, which nearly doubled defense spending in a single year. By 1952, defense expenditures had nearly doubled again, to 44 billion dollars. Meanwhile, the armed forces grew from 1.5 million before the Korean War to 3.6 million in 1952 (see Figure 26-1).

The president had already made perhaps the most momentous decision of all. Early in 1950, over the objections of George Kennan and J. Robert Oppenheimer, the director of the atomic bomb project during World War II, Truman ordered the building of "the so-called hydrogen or superbomb." Successfully tested in November 1952, the atom-fusing, thermonuclear hydrogen bomb had far more explosive power than the atom-splitting atomic bomb, but that did not stop the arms race. Less than a year later, the U. S. S. R. had its own "H-bomb."

The spiraling arms race underscored the dramatic consequences of containment for the United States. The confrontation with Communism was transforming the American political economy. To fight the cold war, Americans accepted things they had long feared in peacetime: alliances, foreign aid, a massive standing army. Each of these innovations magnified the role of the federal government in the economy and society. The president, in charge of the CIA, an expanding military, and a growing nuclear arsenal, held more power in his hands than ever before. The federal

government, its budget swollen by military expenditures, had new power to shape the economy. The cold war affected American society in many other ways as well.

The Reconversion of American Society

While the cold war escalated, the United States confronted domestic challenges that tested the political economic arrangements created during the Depression and World War II. With the end of the war, Americans focused on **reconversion,** the restoration of the economy and society to a peacetime footing. Reconversion was a welcome process for a nation tired of war, but reconversion was also a cause for worry. Americans feared a return to the bleak economic conditions of the 1930s. Labor, women, and African Americans, especially, wanted to hold onto and extend wartime gains.

The Postwar Economy

As World War II ended, Americans wondered whether the economy would slide back into depression. Economists and policymakers worried that the end of the federal government's massive spending for the war effort would force businesses to lay off workers and cut investment. Americans questioned whether the economy could provide enough jobs for the millions of returning servicemen.

The economic disaster never came. Unemployment rose to almost four percent in the first few years after the war but never approached the double-digit rates of the 1930s. Despite brief downturns, the economy remained healthy.

This strong performance reflected several factors, including veterans' choices, the active role of the federal government, the gradual transformation of the industrial economy, and U. S. dominance of the world economy. Returning servicemen and women did not put excessive strain on the economy, partly because so many of them went back to school rather than look for work. Thanks to the generous provisions of the GI Bill of 1944, the federal government paid for up to three years of education for veterans. In all, half of the nation's 15.4 million returning veterans went to school or received technical training under the bill.

Spending by the federal government also helped to prevent a return to the economic conditions of the 1930s. With the end of World War II, federal expenditures decreased dramatically, but the government was still spending far more than it did during the 1930s. The GI Bill illustrated how that spending stimulated the economy. Pumping nearly 14.5 billion dollars into the educational system, the bill encouraged colleges and universities to ex-

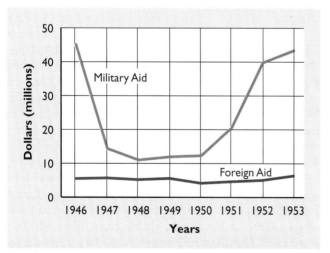

Figure 26-1   The Cost of the Cold War: U. S. Military and Foreign Aid Expenditures.

Source: Statistical Abstract of the United States, 1952, p. 199; 1953, pp. 225, 886; 1957, p. 879; Historical Statistics of the United States, II, p. 1124.

pand. As veterans swelled enrollments, institutions hired new faculty. Entire new educational systems, such as the State University of New York, were created.

Reconversion also went well because of the gradual transformation of the economy. In the late 1940s, the United States was still an industrial nation, with production centered in the Northeast and Midwest, but there were already signs of change. During and after the war, economic activity shifted toward the South and West. In the 1940s, the population of the western states grew by 50 percent while the population of the East grew by a comparatively modest 10 percent. The nature of the economy was changing, too. In 1945, coal provided more than half the nation's energy. Five years later oil and natural gas provided the majority. Spurred by the war, newer technologies and industries, such as plastics and aviation, were growing rapidly. This economic dynamism eased the process of reconversion.

Finally, the dominant role of the United States in the world economy facilitated reconversion. At the end of World War II, America was the only major industrial na-

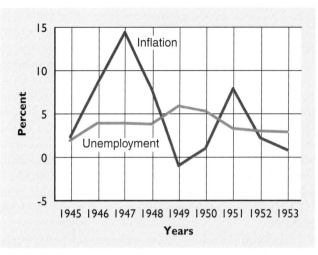

Figure 26-2   The Reconversion of the Economy: Inflation and Unemployment.
Despite the fears of economists and high inflation, the economy did not collapse after World War II.
Source: Historical Statistics of the United States, II, p. 1124.

tion whose economy had not been damaged by the conflict. No country's economy rivaled the size and productivity of the U. S. economy. As late as 1950, America, with only six percent of the world's population, accounted for a staggering 40 percent of the value of all the goods and services produced around the globe. The healthy demand for American exports helped to provide jobs for returning veterans and to sustain the economy.

Although the economy did not suffer from unemployment, it did confront inflation. The strong job market contributed to a rise in prices. With steady paychecks, Americans were eager to buy the appliances, cars, and houses that had been unavailable during the war. Supply could not keep up with consumer demand. Driven by shortages of houses and other goods, prices rose alarmingly in 1946. President Truman's veto terminated the wartime Office of Price Administration (OPA), which was supposed to control inflation, at the beginning of July. Although Truman reluctantly agreed to revive the OPA for another year, the consumer price index rose 14.4 percent in 1946. Ultimately production caught up with demand. By the late 1940s, inflation decreased, and an economic boom continued (see Figure 26-2).

The Challenge of Organized Labor

Reconversion posed special challenges for workers and the labor movement. Organized labor had never seemed more powerful. One-third of nonagricultural civilian workers belonged to unions. Those unions were politically influential. The Congress of Industrial Organizations (CIO) played a particularly significant role in the Democratic Party.

After pledging not to strike during World War II, organized labor was eager to test and expand its power in

Veterans happily leave military service for higher education. Helped by the G.I. Bill, millions of servicemen went back to school at Indiana University and other colleges and universities, thereby relieving pressure on the job market.

peacetime. The unions wanted wage increases to cope with inflation, make up for the loss of overtime pay at the end of the war, and reward workers for their contribution to booming corporate profits. Some unionists also wanted to claim more control over the way corporations did business. Not surprisingly, corporate executives were reluctant to give up any of their power or profits.

The result was a huge wave of strikes as soon as the war ended in August 1945. At the start of 1946, two million workers were on strike. Machinists in San Francisco, longshoremen in New York City, and other workers across the country called a record 4,985 strikes that year. "[L]abor has gone crazy," an anxious Truman told his mother.

The most dramatic and significant work stoppages took place in automobile factories, coal mines, and railroad yards. Late in 1945, the United Auto Workers (UAW) struck General Motors (GM) for a 30 percent raise in hourly wages, access to the company's account books, and more of a say in the company's decisions. UAW vice president Walter Reuther, known as "Walter Ruthless" to his enemies, insisted that the workers' demands would boost the economy without harming GM. Higher wages would stimulate consumption, Reuther maintained, without forcing the prosperous car company to raise prices; however, GM refused access to its books and rejected union interference in price setting and other management decisions. When the strike finally ended after 113 days in March 1946, the UAW won only some of its wage demands. The GM strike marked a turning point for American labor. Unions never again made such bold demands to participate in management. Instead, the labor movement focused more on questions of pay and benefits.

The coal and railroad strikes were even more contentious than the GM work stoppage. Members of the United Mine Workers (UMW) and the railway unions refused to accept arbitration by the federal government. As the coal supply dwindled, power systems suffered "brownouts," and railroad passengers were stranded. The situation tested the strong relationship between the liberal Democratic Party and organized labor forged in the New Deal. An angry President Truman ordered federal takeovers of both the mines and the railroads. "Let Truman dig coal with his bayonets," snarled John L. Lewis, leader of the UMW. But the strikes came to an end in May. When Lewis took the UMW out of the mines again in November, Truman took the UMW to court for violating a federal injunction against the strike. Forced to pay heavy fines, the union ended its walkout. Although angry unionists condemned Truman, much of the public applauded the president's action. Many Americans believed that Lewis, Reuther, and the other union leaders had become too powerful, arrogant, and demanding for the good of the country.

Counting on the public's unhappiness with unions, pro-business Republicans in Congress soon moved to limit the power of organized labor, which had been boosted so much by the Democratic New Deal. In 1947, a coalition of Republicans and conservative, mostly southern, Democrats passed the Taft-Hartley Act, a sweeping modification of federal labor law. The measure made it easier for employers to hire nonunion workers and to oppose the formation of unions. The bill also limited unions' right to organize supervisors, boycott employers, and engage in political activity. Most humiliating of all, it compelled union leaders to swear that they did not belong to the Communist Party. The Taft-Hartley Act, a Republican congressman declared, "puts the interest of John Q. Public above the interest of John L. Lewis." To angry unionists and their Democratic allies, the measure was the "Tuff-Heartless Act." Truman vetoed it, but Congress overrode him in June 1947.

The passage of the Taft-Hartley Act was not the end of organized labor's problems. "Operation Dixie," a drive to unionize the low-wage industries of the South, went poorly, in part because of divisions between white and African-American workers. Labor's attempts to force the repeal of Taft-Hartley all failed.

Despite these setbacks, workers and unions still prospered. Landmark contract negotiations between the UAW and GM offered a peaceful and lucrative model of labor relations. In 1948 the UAW won guaranteed cost-of-living adjustments, known as COLAs, and an annual wage increase tied to rises in worker productivity. In the so-called "Treaty of Detroit" signed in 1950, the UAW obtained other increases and a pension plan in an unusually long-term contract lasting five years. The UAW contracts replaced confrontation with cooperation and strikes with security. In return for pensions and protection against inflation, the autoworkers gave management stable, predictable labor relations over the long term.

The Treaty of Detroit ended a difficult period for organized labor. Reconversion had certainly not returned workers and unions to the conditions of the 1930s. Thanks to such lucrative contracts as the Treaty of Detroit, many workers were more secure than ever before, but reconversion also limited the power of organized labor in the American political economy. Aggressive strikes produced mixed results, public hostility, and government interference. Reconversion revealed the limits of the Democratic Party's support for labor as well. With the end of the strike wave, unions effectively abandoned their demand to participate in management in postwar America.

Opportunities for Women

Reconversion also posed special challenges to the status of American women. During World War II, the shortage of male civilian labor had expanded women's opportunities for employment outside the home. At the end of the war, most working women did not want to give up those op-

The postwar strike wave: Striking workers confront a driver attempting to cross their picket line in order to enter a Swift & Co. meatpacking plant.

portunities. They prized the income and the sense of satisfaction they gained from performing jobs traditionally monopolized by men. But there was a widespread belief that women should surrender jobs to returning servicemen. Despite the experience of World War II, American culture still assumed that women's ideal place was in the home.

Employers did tend to give away women's jobs—high-paying industrial positions, in particular—to male veterans. The number of women in the labor force dropped 13 percent from 1945 to 1946, but reconversion did not send displaced female workers home for good. Three-quarters of the women who wanted to stay at work after the war managed to find jobs.

Women's role in the postwar workplace was the product both of their desire and of financial necessity. Single, divorced, and widowed women needed to earn a living. Many families needed income from wives as well as husbands in order to make ends meet. By 1953 the number of women in the work force matched the level of 1945. A higher percentage of women were employed than had been the case before World War II. The number of women in nontraditional jobs increased, too. More women than ever before were skilled craftspersons, forepersons, physicians, and surgeons.

The number of married women in the postwar labor force was especially notable. The cultural prejudice against women's employment had always applied most strongly to married women. Traditionally, they were expected to devote themselves to husbands and children, not jobs and careers. Economic realities overcame cultural prejudices, however. In the late 1940s there was a shortage of single female workers because of the low birthrate before the war and the younger age at which women were marrying after the war. Increasingly, employers needed married women workers. By 1947 there were already more married women than single women in the wage labor force.

Women's experience in the military mirrored their experience in the civilian work force. The armed forces, like civilian employers, initially cut back the number of women in the ranks when the war ended, but reconversion did not cause a return to the prewar days when women had almost no place in the military. In 1947 Congress passed the Army-Navy Nurse Act, which granted women permanent status in the armed forces. The next year Congress merged the separate women's military organizations, such as the Women's Army Corps, into the regular armed services.

Despite these gains, women continued to face discrimination in the workplace. The vast majority of women workers had to settle for traditionally female, traditionally low-paying jobs in offices, stores, and factories. Because of persisting discrimination by employers, women's hourly pay rose only half as much as men's pay in the first years after the war. In the military, women were largely confined to traditionally female, noncombatant roles such as nursing. There were no women generals.

Women faced discrimination in the larger society as well. There was little interest in women's rights. After a meeting with female activists, Truman dismissed a constitutional amendment guaranteeing equal rights for women as a "lot of hooey." Most men and many women probably agreed.

Despite the lack of support for women's rights, women's opportunities were gradually expanding in the years after World War II; the combination of women's desires and the economy's needs was slowly promoting the feminization of the labor force.

Civil Rights for African Americans

Like women, African Americans had made significant gains during World War II. They had played new roles in the military, filled higher-paying jobs in the civilian econ-

Still on the job: Despite the return of servicemen to the U.S., American women continued to work in large numbers in offices and other settings after World War II.

omy, and aggressively pushed their demand for civil rights. Like women, African Americans wanted to preserve and extend their rights and opportunities in the postwar period. They, too, faced substantial resistance.

Several factors, including economic change, legal rulings, and wartime experiences, stimulated African Americans' drive for equal rights and opportunities after World War II. By the end of the war, the ongoing transformation of the southern economy was clearly undermining the old system of segregating African Americans and denying them the right to vote. As the mechanization of southern agriculture reduced the need for field hands, African Americans continued to leave farms for the region's growing cities and for the North and West. One of the fundamental rationales for segregation—the need for an inexpensive and submissive labor force to work the fields—was gradually disappearing. The developing southern economy also attracted white migrants from other regions of the country, people who had relatively little commitment to segregation and disfranchisement. Meanwhile, the African-American migrants to northern and western cities increased African-American votes and political influence in the nation.

During the 1940s, a series of decisions by the U. S. Supreme Court struck at racial discrimination and encouraged African Americans to challenge inequality. In *Smith v. Allwright* in 1944, the court had banned whites-only primary elections. In *Morgan v. Virginia* in 1946, the court ruled that interstate bus companies could not segregate passengers. In *Shelley v. Kraemer* in 1948, the court banned restrictive covenants, the private agreements between property owners not to sell houses to African Americans and other minorities. These and other court decisions made long-established forms of discrimination seem vulnerable. They also raised the possibility that African Americans might have a judicial ally in their struggle for justice.

African Americans' own experiences in wartime also encouraged them to demand more from the United States. African-American veterans, having fought for their country, now expected it to give them justice. Reconversion could not mean a return to the old days of discrimination. "Our people are not coming back with the idea of just taking up where they left off," an African-American private wrote. "We are going to have the things that are rightfully due us or else."

That kind of determination spurred civil rights activism after World War II. In the South, African Americans increasingly demanded the right to vote after *Smith v. Allwright*. The National Association for the Advancement of Colored People (NAACP), the oldest civil rights organization, set up citizenship schools in southern communities to show African-American voters how to register to vote. Across the South, local organizations such as the Atlanta All Citizens Registration Committee and the Mississippi Progressive Voters League emerged to challenge the disfranchisement of African Americans. The voting campaign was driven, too, by grassroots, often spontaneous action. In July 1946 Medgar Evers, a combat veteran who had just reached his twenty-first birthday, decided to try to vote in the Democratic Party's primary election in Decatur, Mississippi.

Such activism met resistance from the many southern whites who were still deeply committed to African-American disfranchisement and segregation. That day in 1946, a white mob kept Evers from voting. In Georgia, whites killed an African-American voter. More often, whites manipulated registration laws to disqualify would-be African-American voters. An African American who wanted to register might have to answer such questions as "How many bubbles are there in a bar of soap?" African-American voter registration in the South, only two percent in 1940, rose to 12 percent by 1947. With that increasing percentage came the election of a few African-American officials and better service from local government.

While the campaign for voting rights went forward in the South, civil rights activists fought segregation in all parts of the country. The interracial Congress of Racial Equality (CORE) took the lead in protesting public discrimination against African Americans. To test the Supreme Court's decision in *Morgan v. Virginia*, CORE sent an integrated team of 16 activists on a "journey of reconciliation," a two-week bus trip through the upper South in 1947. The activists' unsuccessful attempt to desegregate buses and bus terminals met with violence and arrests.

That year, an interracial CORE group did successfully force the integration of an amusement park in New Jersey. However, civil rights activists hardly dented legal segregation in the South in the 1940s. They had more success promoting antidiscrimination laws in the North. By 1953 fair-employment laws had been adopted in 30 cities and 12 states.

Activists also pressured President Truman to support civil rights. In the spring and summer of 1946, African-American and white pickets marched outside the White House with signs that read, "SPEAK, SPEAK, MR. PRESIDENT." Truman found himself in a position that would become familiar to other presidents during the cold war. Racial discrimination was an embarrassment for a nation claiming to represent freedom and democracy around the world, but support for civil rights was a political risk for a politician dependent on white support. Nevertheless, Truman took significant steps to fight discrimination.

In the fall of 1946, the president set up a Committee on Civil Rights. The next October, the committee's report, *To Secure These Rights*, called for strong federal action against discrimination, including the suppression of lynching, the protection of African-American voters, the enforcement of civil rights laws, the desegregation of the armed forces, and the promotion of equal employment opportunities. Admitting that "there is a serious gap between our ideals and some of our practices," Truman insisted "this gap must be closed." Furious white southern politicians and newspapers said Truman was "stabbing the South in the back."

"President Truman, We Need Your Help": African Americans picket the White House to demand justice for the black victim of a lynching in Georgia. The placards condemning powerful white southern Democrats—Senator Eugene Talmadge, Senator Theodore Bilbo, and Rep. John Rankin—are a reminder that Truman risked alienating white support if he responded to black demands for civil rights.

African Americans, meanwhile, kept the heat on Truman. To protest continuing discrimination in the military, A. Philip Randolph, the head of the Brotherhood of Sleeping Car Porters and the leader of the wartime Negro March on Washington Movement, proposed an African-American boycott of the draft. In July 1948 Truman responded with Executive Order 9981, which created the Committee on Equality of Treatment and Opportunity in the Armed Services. The committee moved vigorously to end discrimination in the military. At the same time, Truman established the Fair Employment Board, which moved more slowly against discrimination in federal hiring.

During the Truman years, the most publicized blow to racial inequality landed not in the White House or the courts, but rather on the baseball diamond. When the Brooklyn Dodgers called up infielder Jackie Robinson from the minor leagues in 1947, he became the first African-American man in decades to play in the majors. A strong, self-disciplined former soldier, Robinson took taunts and beanballs on the field and death threats in the mail. Fast, powerful, and exciting, he finished the season as the National League's Rookie of the Year. Robinson's success paved the way for increasing numbers of African-American players in the majors over the next several years.

Robinson's success also spelled the end of the Negro Leagues, the organizations created when African Americans were banned from the Major Leagues. As would sometimes be the case, integration undermined separate African-American institutions. Within a few years, the Negro Leagues lost customers to the Major Leagues and went out of business, but the achievements of Robinson, Larry Doby, and other pioneering African-American major leaguers sent a powerful message for civil rights. It was getting harder and harder to argue that African Americans were inferior and therefore deserving of inferior treatment.

The triumph of Jackie Robinson underscored the basic fact of African-American life during reconversion. On the whole, African Americans preserved and sometimes managed to expand their wartime gains. Nevertheless, African Americans still encountered injustice and inequality in almost every aspect of daily life. Legalized segregation and disfranchisement remained in place in the South. Though improving, the median income of African-American families was little more than half that of white families at the end of the 1940s. Life expectancy for African Americans was eight years less than for whites in the early 1950s. Moreover, most whites were not eager to redress these inequalities.

In one respect, at least, African Americans, women, and organized labor shared a common experience in the first years after World War II. For each of these groups, reconversion turned out to be better than feared and worse than hoped. African Americans, women, and workers all struggled to preserve and expand their rights and opportunities in the political economy of the late 1940s. They all confronted the limits of their power to change the society around them.

Jackie Robinson, star of the Brooklyn Dodgers and the first African American allowed to play in the Major Leagues since the nineteenth century. Robinson's smile conceals the determination it took to end segregation on the visible stage of big league baseball.

Society came through reconversion rather well. Instead of falling back into economic depression, America generally prospered. The political economic arrangements that had emerged from the Depression and World War II seemed to work well enough, but the difficulties of African Americans, women, and organized labor were reminders that reconversion had left much unfinished business. The United States grappled with that business for the next half century.

The Frustrations of Liberalism

While most Americans had no desire to go back to the conditions of the 1930s, liberal Democrats might have been tempted. During the Great Depression, liberalism, in the form of Franklin Roosevelt's New Deal, had reshaped the American political economy, thrusting the federal government more deeply than ever into economic and social life. But the liberal Democratic agenda, with its calls for further federal activism, had stalled during World War II. In the first years after the war, liberalism met with more frustration. Liberals and the Democratic Party struggled to prove that they had the answers for a nation no longer mired in the Depression. Harry Truman struggled to prove that he was a worthy successor to Roosevelt.

The Democrats' Troubles

An accidental president, Harry Truman naturally faced skepticism from many Americans. They wondered whether this unassuming man, a plain-spoken career politician, could take the place of Franklin Roosevelt, one of the great leaders of the twentieth century. Liberals wondered, too, whether Truman really shared their ideas. They were incensed when the president fired Secretary of Commerce Henry Wallace after the cabinet officer publicly criticized Truman's policy toward the U. S. S. R. in 1946.

At the same time, the president was handicapped by skepticism about the Democrats' liberal approach to the political economy. During the crisis of the Great Depression, Americans had been willing to endorse the liberals' faith in an activist government that intervened vigorously in the economy and ameliorated social problems, but in a fairly prosperous peacetime, people felt less need for government and more need for individual freedom.

The president embraced more of liberalism than the liberals expected. Shortly after he took office in 1945, Truman presented a twenty-one-point legislative program that included liberal proposals on education, employment, insurance, social security, and civil rights. Yet a Full Employment Bill, reflecting the liberal belief that the federal government should take more responsibility for increasing jobs and prosperity, met overwhelming conservative and moderate opposition. Watered down by Congress, the resulting Employment Act of 1946 created a Council of Economic Advisors for the president but did nothing to increase the role of the federal government in promoting employment.

Truman and the liberals suffered an even sharper defeat over the president's sweeping proposal for a compulsory national health insurance system that would guarantee medical care to all Americans. The plan considerably enhanced the power of the federal government, which would manage the insurance system and have the right to set doctors' and hospitals' fees. Conservatives and the medical profession promptly condemned Truman's proposal as "the kind of regimentation that led to totalitarianism in Germany." The bill embodying the president's plan failed to pass Congress. So did the rest of Truman's proposals.

Nevertheless, the federal government's role in national life continued to grow in cold-war America. Medical care offered a notable example. Even though national health insurance was defeated, federal intervention in the health-care system increased after World War II. The Veterans Administration established a vast network of federal hospitals to care for returning soldiers. In 1946 the Hill-Burton Act appropriated federal money for the construction of hospitals. That same year, Congress created the Communicable Disease Center (later called the Centers for Disease Control) in Atlanta, Georgia, to monitor infectious diseases. Congress also reorganized the National Institutes of Health in 1948 and established the National Institute of Mental Health in 1949.

While Truman struggled with domestic and foreign policy, he became increasingly unpopular. "To err is Truman," went the joke. The president looked weak and ineffective to some Americans, and tyrannical and overbearing to others. "Had Enough?" asked Republicans. Many Americans had. In the congressional elections in the fall of 1946, the voters gave the Republican Party a majority in both the House of Representatives and the Senate for the first time in 16 years.

Truman's Comeback

The 1946 elections seemed to point toward Truman's certain defeat in the presidential contest two years later, but the president managed a stunning comeback instead. The turnaround began with the victorious Republican majority of the Eightieth Congress that convened in 1947. Led by Senator Robert Taft of Ohio, the congressional Republicans hoped to beat back New Deal liberalism and substitute a different vision for the American political economy. Taft, the son of former president William Howard Taft, believed in limited government. Rather than "the corrupting idea that we can legislate prosperity, legislate equality, legislate opportunity," the senator known as "Mr. Republican" wanted "free Americans freely working out their destiny."

The Republicans did win passage of the Taft-Hartley Act, which was a blow to labor, liberals, and the president, but Taft and the Republicans found themselves hamstrung by Americans' ambivalence about liberalism. Many people did not appear to want bold new liberal programs such as national health insurance, but there was little sentiment to repeal the New Deal. Americans clearly wanted to hold on to the benefits they had received from the government in the Depression and World War II. Besides the Taft-Hartley Act, the Eightieth Congress did not accomplish much of the Republican agenda.

Nevertheless, things looked bleak for Harry Truman. By March 1948 only 35 percent of the people approved of his performance in office. Moreover, his party was splitting apart. On the left, his former Secretary of Commerce Henry Wallace was running for president as a "Progressive" appealing to liberals. On the right, Democratic Governor Strom Thurmond of South Carolina was running as a "Dixiecrat," appealing to white supporters of segregation. Losing Democratic votes to both Wallace and Thurmond, Truman seemed certain to lose the election in November.

His Republican opponent, Governor Thomas E. Dewey of New York, thought so. Too abrasive when he lost to Franklin Roosevelt in 1944, Dewey believed he

"Give 'em hell, Harry!" President Harry Truman speaks to a crowd from the back of his railroad car during the 1948 election campaign.

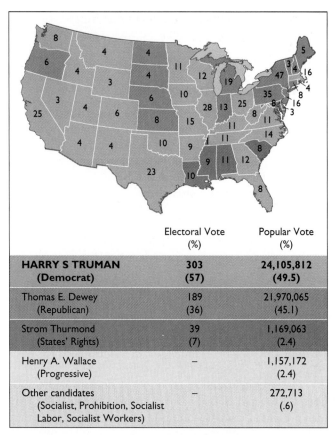

	Electoral Vote (%)	Popular Vote (%)
HARRY S TRUMAN (Democrat)	**303** **(57)**	**24,105,812** **(49.5)**
Thomas E. Dewey (Republican)	189 (36)	21,970,065 (45.1)
Strom Thurmond (States' Rights)	39 (7)	1,169,063 (2.4)
Henry A. Wallace (Progressive)	–	1,157,172 (2.4)
Other candidates (Socialist, Prohibition, Socialist Labor, Socialist Workers)	–	272,713 (.6)

Map 26-3   The 1948 Presidential Election.

could get away with a mild, uncontroversial campaign. But Truman worked hard to pull the Democratic New Deal majority back together. Climbing aboard his railway car, Truman visited more than half the states on an old-fashioned "whistle-stop" campaign. The president reached out to African Americans, labor, farmers, senior citizens, and other beneficiaries of New Deal liberalism. "Give 'em hell, Harry," the crowds shouted, and he did. Deriding the "do-nothing" Republican Congress, he hammered home the difference between the Democrats' and Republicans' visions of the political economy. "The Democratic Party puts human rights and human welfare first," he declared. "These Republican gluttons of privilege . . . want a return of the Wall Street economic dictatorship."

On election day, Wallace and Thurmond received only 1.1 millions votes each. Dewey attracted fewer votes than he had four years before. Holding together the New Deal coalition, Truman won the presidency in his own right with only 49.5 percent of the vote (see Map 26-3). Moreover, the Democrats recaptured the House and the Senate.

Truman's triumph did not last long. Like Taft two years before, he soon discovered that an election victory did not mean a mandate for his ideas. In his State of the Union address in January 1949, Truman declared that "every individual has a right to expect from our Government a fair deal." But the president's "Fair Deal" legislation made little head-

way in Congress. Despite Truman's comeback, the liberal vision of the political economy, so influential in the 1930s, could not command the politics of cold-war America.

Fighting the Cold War at Home

While conservatives and liberals battled back and forth over domestic policy, the cold war increasingly affected life in the United States. As the drafters of NSC 68 had hoped, the billions of dollars in defense expenditures eventually stimulated economic growth, but in the short run, the main domestic byproduct of the cold war was fear. Doubt and insecurity pervaded American culture in the late 1940s. Many Americans felt the new fear of nuclear weapons and the old fear of immigrants. Above all, American society succumbed to a largely irrational fear of Communist subversives inside the United States. To fight the cold war at home, anti-Communist crusaders such as Joe McCarthy hunted for disloyal Americans in important places—Washington, Hollywood, universities. By the 1950s, **McCarthyism** was a powerful force capable of destroying the lives of thousands of Americans, including Esther and Stephen Brunauer.

Doubts and Fears in the Atomic Age

Despite the U. S. triumph in World War II, American culture was surprisingly dark and pessimistic in the late 1940s. Victory did not wipe away the doubts created by the war itself. The rise of fascism, the Holocaust, and the bombings of Hiroshima and Nagasaki raised troubling questions about the inevitability of progress and the innate goodness of humankind. The cold war did nothing to calm those concerns. Even the welcome prosperity of the reconversion period did not soothe Americans' sense of doubt and anxiety. People felt small and less powerful in an age of giant corporations, big unions, big government, and super bombs.

Americans revealed their doubts and fears in a variety of ways. Not long after the announcement of the Truman Doctrine in 1947, people suddenly began seeing things in the sky. There were reports of "flying saucers" over 35 states and Canada. Some Americans even believed the federal government was covering up the truth about these unidentified flying objects.

Meanwhile, Hollywood films explored popular fears. In 1946 *The Best Years of Our Lives* traced the difficult, sometimes humiliating readjustment of three returning veterans. The same year, *It's a Wonderful Life* told the story of a small-town banker forced to accept the disappointment of his unfulfilled dreams. Both films expressed reservations about the morality of capitalism and the chances for Americans to enjoy economic independence. A new cinematic genre, *film noir,* offered an even darker view of individuals trapped in a confusing, immoral world. "I feel all dead inside," confessed the detective in *The Dark Corner* (1946). "I'm backed up in a dark corner and I don't know who's hitting me."

"Flying saucers" over the United States. Sightings of supposed UFOs were one indication of the strains of living in a cold-war America, menaced by the bomb and other anxieties.

Nuclear weapons were perhaps the greatest source of fear. The unprecedented power of the atomic bomb dominated the popular imagination. For many Americans, this was the Atomic Age. They dealt with their anxiety about the new age in a variety of ways. Some people tried dark attempts at humor. Americans drank "atomic cocktails" and danced to the "Atomic Polka." American women wore the new "bikini," the explosively scanty two-piece bathing suit named for the Pacific atoll where the U. S. staged nuclear tests. The Soviets' development of the atomic bomb and then the hydrogen bomb was impossible to laugh away.

Americans' fear was also reflected in the hardening of attitudes toward foreigners who wanted to live in the United States. At the end of World War II, a welcoming nation had eased the immigration process for the foreign wives of American servicemen by passing the War Brides Act of 1945, but as the cold war intensified, other potential migrants met a hostile reception. The Immigration and Nationality Act of 1952 continued tight restrictions on immigration, particularly from Asia. It also kept out Communists and homosexuals and allowed the deportation of American citizens suspected of disloyalty.

The Anti-Communist Crusade Begins

Americans may have feared disloyalty most of all. Many people believed the Soviet Union could not have become such a threat so quickly unless Communists inside America had betrayed their own country. The search for traitors quickly became a panicky "Red Scare," much like the one that followed the First World War.

Historians debate the origins of the second Red Scare as fervently as they debate the origins of the cold war. Some scholars trace the anti-Communist crusade to conservative Republican politicians. Others blame the Truman administration. The new Red Scare was not solely the creation of political leaders. Anti-Communism was already deeply rooted in American culture, but the powerful politicians of both major parties gave domestic anti-Communism its particularly dangerous form.

The crusaders had to search hard for Communism at home. Not surprisingly, there were few open Communists in cold-war America. The Communist Party of the United States of America (CPUSA), a legal political party, was losing followers. Infiltrated by the Federal Bureau of Investigation, the CPUSA was hardly a threat, never receiving more than a microscopic 0.3 percent of the popular vote in any presidential election. Nevertheless, the party became the target of persecution. In June 1948 the

ON TRIAL

The Hollywood Ten

With the passage of time, the enormity of the anti-Communist crusade becomes harder to understand. The search for Communist subversives seems fairly tame by the violent standards of the twentieth-century world. Little blood was shed. Relatively few people went to jail. Yet the anti-Communist crusade had a major impact on a supposedly free society. The case of the Hollywood Ten illustrates how the Red Scare managed to harm Americans who were not traitors. The case also shows how anti-Communists used the example of a handful of victims to intimidate many more Americans, including the leaders of powerful institutions.

The crusade rested on the authority of government. The case of the Hollywood Ten began when HUAC used its subpoena power to compel Edward Dmytryk, Dalton Trumbo, Ring Lardner, Jr., and the others to testify as so-called "unfriendly witnesses." The chair of the committee, J. Parnell Thomas of New Jersey, allowed only one of the Ten to read a prepared statement. Badgering the witnesses, Thomas did not allow the Ten to respond to accusations against them. He had three of them forcibly removed from the hearing room. He also insisted that each of the Ten answer what he called the "$64 question," "Are you now, or have you ever been a member of the Communist Party of the United States?" When the witnesses declined to answer directly, HUAC had all of them cited for contempt of Congress.

Along with the legal power of government, the anti-Communist crusade depended on the willing cooperation of many Americans. Movie stars such as Gary Cooper and Robert Montgomery appeared at the HUAC hearings as "friendly witnesses" to reveal the names of alleged Communists. Ronald Reagan, the president of the Screen Actors Guild and future president of the United States, cooperated with the anti-Communist crusade as well.

The Red Scare also depended on the help of powerful institutions. Faced with damaging publicity about Communism in Hollywood, the major movie studios quickly and ostentatiously joined the anti-Communist crusade. In November 1947 the studio heads issued a statement vowing not to rehire "any of the ten until such time as he is acquitted or has purged himself of contempt and declares under oath that he is not a Communist." The studios proceeded to discriminate against suspected Communists and to make safe films that could not possibly be considered pro-Communist. In this way, HUAC managed to reshape a powerful national institution without passing a law.

The anti-Communist crusade flourished because many Americans were afraid to speak out against it. The Hollywood Ten had some famous defenders in the film industry, including the actors Lauren Bacall and Humphrey Bogart, but few people were willing to risk accusations of Communism and disloyalty in order to support the "unfriendly witnesses."

Help from the judicial system was also essential to the Red Scare. The courts were willing to endorse or at least ignore the often unconstitutional treatment of suspected Communists. In the spring of 1948, the U. S. District Court in Washington, D. C., speedily convicted two of the Hollywood Ten, screenwriters John Howard Lawson and Dalton Trumbo, for contempt of Congress. When the U. S. Supreme Court refused to review their cases, the rest of the Ten were convicted in 1950. As the author E. B. White observed, "Ten men have been convicted, not of wrong-doing but of wrong thinking; that is . . . bad news."

The combination of government power, "friendly witnesses," discriminatory studios, intimidated supporters, and complaisant courts defeated the Hollywood Ten. In addition to their fines and jail sentences, they faced the blacklist. Only one of them, the director Edward Dmytryk, immediately denounced Communism and went back to work in Hollywood. Some of the rest wrote screenplays under pseudonyms, but they could not work openly in Hollywood until the 1960s, when the hysteria of the Red Scare had died down. In the meantime, HUAC had successfully used the example of the Hollywood Ten to intimidate the film industry and to send a powerful message to the rest of American society.

Truman administration charged 12 American Communist leaders with violations of the 1940 Smith Act, which had criminalized membership in "a group advocating . . . the overthrow of the government by force." The following year, 11 were convicted and sent to jail. In 1951 the Supreme Court upheld the convictions.

With so little open Communism, some Americans searched for secret Communists. The hunt was led by the House of Representatives' Committee on Un-American Activities. More often known as the House Un-American Activities Committee (HUAC), it had started out condemning Communism and the New Deal in 1938. In

Protesting the convictions of the "Hollywood 10," the eight screenwriters, a producer, and a director who refused to tell a congressional committee whether they belonged to the Communist Party. In the tense atmosphere of the cold war, the Hollywood 10 had few defenders.

1947 HUAC held hearings to lay bare a supposed Communist plot in Hollywood. Much of the film industry cooperated with HUAC, but eight screenwriters, a producer, and a director, who were Communists, cited their First Amendment rights and declined to testify about their political beliefs and activities. The "Hollywood Ten" were convicted of contempt of Congress and sent to jail for up to a year, with the eventual concurrence of the Supreme Court.

Hollywood got the message. Film studios "blacklisted," refused to hire, writers, directors, and actors even remotely suspected of Communist ties. Avoiding controversial subjects, the studios put out overwrought anti-Communist movies such as *The Red Menace* and *I Was a Communist for the FBI.*

Afraid of looking "soft" on Communism, the Truman administration helped promote the Red Scare, too. By word and action, the government encouraged the idea that there was a real problem with domestic Communism. "Communists," declared Truman's attorney general, Tom Clark, "are everywhere—in factories, offices, butcher shops, on street corners, in private businesses—and each carries with him the germs of death for society."

Late in 1946 the president set up a temporary committee to investigate "Employee Loyalty." The next year he created a permanent Federal Employee Loyalty Program. Any civil servant could lose his or her job by belonging to any of the "totalitarian, Fascist, Communist or subversive" groups listed by the attorney general. The loyalty program proceeded with little regard for due process. Presumed guilty, people accused of disloyalty could not confront their accusers, could be found guilty without evidence, and had to prove their own innocence. Although only about 300 employees were actually discharged for disloyalty, Truman's loyalty program helped create the impression that there must be a serious problem with Communism in Washington.

The Hunt for Soviet Spies

There was, in fact, spying going on inside the federal government. The Soviet Union, just like the United States, carried out espionage abroad. In 1945 an illegal raid by the Office of Strategic Services, the predecessor of the CIA, turned up secret U. S. government documents in the offices of *Amerasia,* a magazine that favored the Chinese Communists. That year, too, the Canadian government found evidence of a spy ring that had passed American atomic secrets to the Soviets during World War II.

Thanks to information from the Canadian case, the FBI began to suspect that Alger Hiss, an aide to the secretary of state, was a Soviet secret agent. Hiss was quietly eased out of his job. Then, in 1948, HUAC took testimony from Whittaker Chambers, an editor of *Time* magazine who claimed to have received secrets from the Roosevelt administration as a Soviet agent in the 1930s. Chambers accused Hiss of being a Communist. Educated at elite private schools and employed in the Agriculture Department in the 1930s, Hiss epitomized New Deal liberalism. Eminently respectable, he now ran the Carnegie Endowment for International Peace. Hiss denied the charge against him, said he had never even met Chambers, and sued the magazine editor for libel.

The suave Hiss appeared far more credible than the rumpled Chambers, who was an admitted perjurer, but congressman Richard Nixon of California, a Republican member of HUAC, forced Hiss to admit that he had in fact known Chambers under an alias. With help from HUAC and the FBI, Chambers charged that Hiss had given him

secret information in the 1930s. In front of reporters at Chambers' farm in Maryland, Chambers pulled rolls of microfilm out of a hollowed-out pumpkin. The film contained photographs of secret documents, some of which had apparently been typed on a typewriter belonging to Hiss' family. Hiss could not explain these "Pumpkin Papers." Under the statute of limitations, it was too late to try Hiss for spying, but it was not too late to indict him for lying to Congress. Hiss' perjury trial ended in a hung jury in 1949, but a second jury convicted him in January 1950. While Hiss sat in prison for almost four years, Chambers wrote a bestseller and Nixon became a senator. The case was a great triumph for Republicans and conservatives and a blow to Democrats and liberals.

As the Hiss case ended, another scandal stimulated Americans' fears. In early 1950, British authorities arrested Klaus Fuchs, a physicist who had worked at the U. S. nuclear research facility in Los Alamos, New Mexico. The investigation led eventually to David Greenglass, who had worked on the atomic bomb project during World War II. Greenglass admitted that he had passed information about the bomb to his brother-in-law, Julius Rosenberg. Julius, a former member of the Communist Party, and his wife Ethel were convicted in a controversial trial on charges of conspiracy to commit espionage. Though they had two young sons, both Rosenbergs were sentenced to death in April 1951. The Supreme Court refused to review the case. Ignoring millions of appeals for clemency from around the world, the federal government finally electrocuted the Rosenbergs in June 1953. The controversy over their guilt has continued down to the present day.

There now seems little disagreement over the reality of Soviet spying in the early years of the cold war. The U. S. S. R. clearly obtained some American nuclear secrets, but the impact of this spying was probably not as great as conservatives feared or as small as liberals insisted. Most likely, espionage sped up the Soviets' work on an atomic bomb that they would have eventually produced anyway.

The Rise of McCarthyism

Two weeks after Hiss' conviction, one week after Truman's announcement of the decision to build the hydrogen bomb, and just days after the arrest of Klaus Fuchs, Senator Joseph McCarthy of Wisconsin suddenly and spectacularly took command of the anti-Communist crusade. Speaking to the Republican women's club of Wheeling, West Virginia, the previously obscure senator claimed to have the names of 205 Communists working for the State Department. Truman responded that there was "not a word of truth" in the charge. In fact, McCarthy had no names of State Department Communists at all. Instead, he named other people as subversives, including Esther and Stephen Brunauer. A Democratic-controlled Senate subcommittee dismissed McCarthy's charges.

Nevertheless, McCarthy was instantly popular and powerful. Frightened by the developments of the last five years, many people believed his charges. Some Americans shared McCarthy's resentment of New Dealers and other privileged elites—the powerful figures he derided as "egg-sucking phony liberals" and "bright young men . . . born with silver spoons in their mouths." For some immigrant-stock Americans, support for McCarthy was a way to prove their loyalty to the United States. Republican leaders were happy to see their colleague hurt the Democratic Party with his charges.

Many Democrats hated what they called **McCarthyism,** but they were afraid to challenge such a powerful political force. Frightened Democratic legislators even helped Congress pass the Internal Security Act of 1950. This law forced the registration of Communist and Communist-front groups, allowed the internment of suspicious persons in national emergencies, provided for the deportation of allegedly subversive aliens, and barred Communists from defense jobs. Refusing to "put the Government of the United States in the thought control business," Truman vetoed the bill. Congress overrode his veto.

Eventually, McCarthy went too far. Angry that one of his aides, David Schine, had not received a draft deferment, the senator launched an investigation of supposed Communism in the United States Army. The secretary of the Army, Robert T. Stevens, refused to cooperate and claimed that McCarthy had pressured the service to take care of Schine. In April 1954 the Senate began hearings on the whole episode. Before a television audience of 20 million people, McCarthy failed to come up with evidence of treason in the Army. When he tried unjustifiably to smear one of the Army's young lawyers as a Communist, the senator was suddenly exposed. "Have you no sense of decency, sir, at long last?" asked the Army's chief counsel, Joseph Welch. It was an electric moment. The Senate hearings came to no judgment, but Americans did. McCarthy's popularity ratings dropped sharply. By the end of the year, the Senate finally had the courage to condemn him for "unbecoming conduct." Three years later he was dead.

The fall of McCarthy did not end McCarthyism. Americans were looking everywhere for Communists in the 1950s. Schools forced teachers to sign loyalty oaths. At several universities, faculty members lost their jobs. Communism had become a useful charge to hurl at anything

The harsh face of the anti-Communist crusade: Republican Senator Joseph R. McCarthy of Wisconsin forcibly makes a point.

that anybody might oppose—labor unions, civil rights, even modern art. Politicians and communities attacked nonrepresentational, abstract expressionist artists as "tools of the Kremlin" and "our enemies." To protect themselves, groups policed their own membership. Labor unions, led by Walter Reuther and other liberals, drove out Communist leaders and unions. The Cincinnati Reds renamed their team the "Redlegs" to make sure no one associated the world's oldest professional baseball team with Communism. Across the country, Americans became more careful about what they said out loud. Containment abroad seemed to have produced an uncontainable fear at home.

Conclusion

By the time Esther Brunauer lost her job in 1952, the cold war had deeply disrupted American life. To contain Communism, the United States had made unprecedented peacetime commitments that transformed the nation's political economy. Despite these changes, the cold war had widened and intensified. Just seven years after World War II, the

United States was at war again. Just seven years after dropping the first atomic bomb on the Japanese, Americans themselves lived with the threat of nuclear annihilation. They lived, too, with the frenzied search for domestic Communists. Amid the wild charges of McCarthyism, American society seemed to be out of control.

As Esther and Stephen Brunauer moved back to Illinois to find peace and rebuild their lives, other Americans needed peace as well. They wanted the fighting in Korea to end. Anxious to avoid a nuclear holocaust, they wanted the cold-war confrontation with the Soviets to stabilize. They also wanted some resolution to the hunt for Communism at home. Meanwhile, American society needed to focus on the unfinished business of reconversion, including the role of government and the rights and opportunities of labor, women, and African Americans. However, it would be impossible to avoid the consequences of the cold war.

CHRONOLOGY

1945   Yalta conference
Harry S. Truman's succession to the presidency
Potsdam conference
Beginning of postwar strike wave

1946   Winston Churchill's "Iron Curtain" speech
George Kennan's "long telegram" on Soviet expansionism
Employment Act of 1946
Morgan v. Virginia
Election of Republican majorities in House and Senate

1947   Announcement of "Truman Doctrine"
Beginning of Federal Employee Loyalty Program
CORE's "Journey of Reconciliation"
Integration of Major League baseball by Jackie Robinson
HUAC Hollywood hearings
Rio Pact
Taft-Hartley Act
National Security Act of 1947
Report by presidential Committee on Civil Rights, *To Secure These Rights*

1948   *Shelley v. Kraemer*
Congressional approval of Marshall Plan
Truman's Executive Order 9981
Beginning of Berlin crisis
Selective Service Act
Truman elected president

1949   Formation of North Atlantic Treaty Organization
Communist takeover of mainland China

1950   NSC 68
Alger Hiss' conviction for perjury
Joe McCarthy's speech in Wheeling, West Virginia
Treaty of Detroit
Beginning of Korean War
Internal Security Act of 1950

1951   Truman fires General Douglas MacArthur

1952   Immigration and Nationality Act
Test of hydrogen bomb

1953   Execution of Ethel and Julius Rosenberg

1954   Army-McCarthy Hearings

Review Questions

1.   How did ideological, political, military, and economic factors combine to produce the cold-war confrontation between the United States and the Soviet Union? Could the cold war have been avoided?

2.   How did reconversion affect American society? Did the return of peace after World War II help or hurt workers, women, and African Americans?

3.   Why did the liberal agenda falter after World War II?

4.   How did the United States fight the cold war? Was the American strategy effective?

5.   Why did the Red Scare become such a powerful force during the cold war? How did the search for domestic Communism affect American life?

Further Readings

Richard M. Fried, *Nightmare in Red: The McCarthy Era in Perspective* (1990). Provides a concise overview of the anti-Communist crusade.

William Graebner, *The Age of Doubt: American Thought and Culture in the 1940s* (1991). Probes the fears and insecurities that shaped American society during the cold war.

Alonzo L. Hamby, *Man of the People: A Life of Harry S. Truman* (1995). A full biography of the first cold-war president.

Melvyn P. Leffler, *A Preponderance of Power: National Security, the Truman Administration, and the Cold War* (1992). One of several important conflicting accounts of the origins of the cold war.

Nelson Lichtenstein, *The Most Dangerous Man in Detroit: Walter Reuther and the Fate of American Labor* (1995). Examines the hopes and frustrations of the labor movement after World War II.

David M. Oshinsky, *A Conspiracy So Immense: The World of Joe McCarthy* (1983). An engaging, even-handed biography of the most famous anti-Communist crusader.

Arnold Rampersad, *Jackie Robinson: A Biography* (1997). Explores the complicated man who integrated Major League Baseball.

Richard Rhodes, *Dark Sun: The Making of the Hydrogen Bomb* (1995). An engaging narrative account of a key development in the nuclear arms race.

Allen Weinstein, *Perjury: The Hiss-Chambers Case* (1978). Provides a thorough, controversial study of one of the most controversial episodes of the cold war.

History on the Internet

"Readings in the 1950s"

http://www.english.upenn.edu/~afilreis/50s/home.html

This site contains primary sources that reflect the anti-Communist ideology that permeated the cold-war era. Sources on the site include transcripts from testimony from anti-Communist hearings, magazine articles that address the cultural anxiety of nuclear threat, and numerous links to other sites.

"The Truman Doctrine"

http://www.yale.edu/lawweb/avalon/trudoc.htm

Read President Harry Truman's address before a joint session of Congress in which the "Truman Doctrine," or using U. S. economic power to ensure the freedom of all nations, was born.

"Korean War"

http://www.nps.gov/kwvm/war/korea.htm

On this site sponsored by the National Park Service, read about the origins of the Korean War, the conflict year by year, and the context of the homefront. It also features information on the war veterans' memorial.

27

THE CONSUMER SOCIETY

1950-1960

OUTLINE

E. J. Korvettes

At the end of World War II, Harry Ferkauf owned two luggage stores in midtown Manhattan in New York City. An immigrant Jewish man from eastern Europe, he haggled with customers over prices in the old way and made a decent living. He did not want or expect much more. After all, he had barely kept his business alive during the Great Depression.

Harry's son, Eugene, who managed one of the stores, was unwilling to accept the old ways and the old limits. After the war, when he returned from military service in the Pacific, Gene began offering discounts on luggage, watches, and other goods. Other neighborhood store-owners resented this low-priced competition. "The store is profitable enough as it is," Harry told his son. "Just leave me alone," Gene replied. Father and son argued frequently. Then, in 1948, Gene quit the business and put all his savings into his own discount store that would compete with the full-priced stores of the other merchants. "How could you do this to me?" Harry demanded.

By then, Gene was caught up in his vision of a new kind of store, where customers could buy appliances and other goods, without haggling, at low, fixed prices. Discounting his merchandise by a quarter and even a third, Gene could not make much money from a single sale. But if he sold enough televisions and refrigerators, he would earn more than his father ever had. With his family depending on him, Gene was frightened. He and his wife distributed thousands of cards announcing the new store on East 46th Street. On opening day, crowds filled the small shop and spent 3,000 dollars. Harry, who usually took in about 50 dollars a day, was impressed. "You've done it," he told Gene. In a year Harry was dead, and Gene was sure he had contributed to his father's death.

Still, Gene Ferkauf was on his way. In a few years, he had five successful discount stores in and around New York City. The business was called "E. J. Korvettes"— E for Eugene; J for his partner Joe Zwillenberg; and Korvettes after the small, quick Canadian warships of World War II. Korvettes appealed to a new generation, more optimistic than the older generation that had survived the Depression. These younger men and women were eager to buy televisions and other appliances. They

771

were unafraid to go into debt. Prosperous, they were leaving their parents' neighborhoods in the city for housing developments in new suburbs. Gene Ferkauf understood these people; he was one of them. He, too, moved from his small seventy-five-dollars-a-month urban apartment in Brooklyn to a 75,000 dollar suburban "mansion" in Jamaica, Queens.

In December 1953 Gene opened a vast new department store out on Westbury, Long Island, where farmland was giving way to new suburban housing developments. The crowds were so big that salesmen could not get back into the store after their lunch hours. The suburban store pulled in 138,000 dollars the first day, 2 million dollars the first month, and 28 million dollars the next year.

Riding the suburban wave, Gene Ferkauf had made it big. Korvettes expanded into suburbs in Connecticut, New Jersey, and Pennsylvania. By 1955 the business was so big and so demanding that Gene turned the partnership into a corporation. Sales had risen an astonishing 2,650 percent since 1950. Gene closed the stores in New York City and kept expanding into the suburbs. He had left his father's world behind.

Gene Ferkauf, satisfied founder of the E.J. Korvettes stores. The quick success of Korvettes reflected the spread of the suburbs and the final emergence of the consumer society after World War II.

Gene Ferkauf's success story reflected one of the central developments that shaped American society after World War II. Along with the cold war, economic prosperity transformed the nation in a host of ways. Like Gene Ferkauf, the United States broke with old customs and values during the affluent 1950s. Just as he left his father's world behind, American society left behind the sense of economic limits and constraints that marked the Great

Depression and the war. The 1950s marked the culmination of the nation's long transformation into a full-fledged consumer society. The explosive growth of E. J. Korvettes depended on this transformation. Gene Ferkauf profited because mainstream culture celebrated consumption and pleasure instead of work and self-restraint. He profited, too, because televisions and suburbs helped define the consumer lifestyle.

The emergence of the consumer society strongly affected the American political economy. The prosperous 1950s helped to produce a more homogeneous, seemingly more harmonious society, characterized by decreasing class differences, changing gender relations, and a baby boom. Enjoying the benefits of consumerism, American voters demanded less from the government. Twice, they overwhelmingly elected a cautious, reassuring president, Dwight Eisenhower, who tried to avoid major initiatives at home.

In later years, American culture would look back nostalgically at the 1950s—people would see those years as a prosperous golden age—but the consumer society had its conflicts, failures, and limits. In different ways, teenagers and some other Americans rebelled against the conformity and constraints of life in the 1950s. The benefits of the consumer society did not reach every group in the United States. Consumerism did not solve the problem of racial inequality or end the cold-war competition with the Soviets. By the close of the decade, many Americans worried about the inadequacies of the consumer society, even as they enjoyed its benefits. ∎

KEY TOPICS

- The creation of a consumer society based on economic prosperity, suburbanization, and new attitudes toward pleasure

- The survival of diversity and individuality despite the trend toward social conformity and homogeneity

- The cautious "Modern Republicanism" of President Dwight Eisenhower

- Challenges to the consumer society and mainstream politics from youth, beats, and African Americans

Living the Good Life

Consumerism was not a new development in the 1950s. Wealthy Americans had had the means to live well for centuries. Many middle-class Americans had been able to mimic the consumerism of the rich on a much smaller scale by the 1900s, but it was only in the 1950s that consumer values and habits finally dominated the American economy and culture. Never before had so many Americans had the chance to live the good life.

They tended to define that "good life" in economic terms. A dynamic, evolving economy provided more leisure and income. Sure of prosperity, Americans had the confidence to spend more of their time and money in the pursuit of pleasure. Millions of people lived the dream of homeownership in new suburbs. Even more Americans bought flashy automobiles, purchased their first televisions, and enjoyed a new openness about sex.

Economic Prosperity

Consumerism could not have flourished without prosperity. Despite three short recessions, the 1950s were a period of economic boom. The U. S. economy grew solidly over the course of the decade. The Gross National Product—the value of all the country's output of goods and services—grew at an average of 3.2 percent a year during the 1950s.

Several major factors spurred this economic growth. The shortage of consumer goods during and just after World War II had left Americans with money they were eager to spend. Because of the cold war, the federal government was also ready to spend money. Washington's expenditures for the defense build-up and foreign aid helped to stimulate the demand for American goods and services. At the same time, the industrial economy continued to evolve and develop. Traditional heavy manufacturing—the production of steel and automobiles—was still crucial to national prosperity. In the 1950s, however, newer industries became increasingly important: electronics, chemicals, plastics, aviation, and computers.

The new affluence: all the groceries consumed by a white-collar DuPont Chemical worker, his wife, and their two children in 1952.

The emergence of the computer business was especially significant for the long-term transformation of the economy. The United States led the way in the development of high-speed machines for processing information and performing calculations. The first successful mechanical computer, which used data recorded on punch cards, had appeared as early as 1888, but computers did not evolve rapidly until the end of World War II. In 1946, two engineers at the University of Pennsylvania, J. Presper Eckert, Jr., and John William Mauchly, completed the first fully electronic digital computer, loaded with hot bulky vacuum tubes. Known as ENIAC (Electronic Numerical Integrator and Computer), this pioneering machine weighed more than 30 tons and filled a large room. Then Eckert and Mauchly produced the UNIVAC 1 (Universal Automatic Computer), a more advanced machine that was used to count national census data in 1951 and presidential election returns in 1952.

Particularly as tiny solid-state transistors replaced vacuum tubes, computers became smaller, more powerful, and more common. By 1958, American companies were producing 1 billion dollars worth of computers a year. One of those companies—IBM (International Business Machines)—had become the world's leading computer manufacturer. Because computers were still so large and expensive, they were used mostly by big institutions, that is, universities, corporations, the Defense Department, and other agencies of the federal government. By 1961, there were already about 10,000 computers in use around the country. The nation was on the brink of the computer age.

Even as American industry continued to evolve, the nation's distribution and service sectors played a larger economic role than ever before. Businesses that sold goods or provided services to consumers flourished during the 1950s. While the number of manufacturing jobs barely changed, employment in retail stores like E. J. Korvettes increased 19 percent. Jobs in the service sector, such as restaurants, hotels, repair shops, hospitals, universities, and other businesses jumped 32 percent. Without much publicity, the United States had begun to develop a "post-industrial" economy, less dependent on production, and more dependent on service and consumption.

The prosperity of the 1950s also rested on relative labor peace. After the instability of the late 1940s, relations between workers and employers settled down in the 1950s. Unionized workers, their wages and benefits rising, seldom challenged employers. Strikes still occurred, of course, but they never threatened to disrupt the economy as they had in the 1940s.

Economic prosperity greatly benefited big business. In the 1950s, corporations loomed larger than ever before. New firms such as E. J. Korvettes emerged and grew. Thanks to a wave of mergers, established corporations became still larger. By 1960, corporations earned 18 times as much income as the rest of the nation's businesses combined.

Corporations enjoyed public approval as well as economic prosperity in the 1950s. After conspicuously serving their country during World War II, business executives now seemed to be leading the nation into an economic golden age. As a result, the popular suspicion of big business, so strong during the Depression, evaporated. Even liberals, once critical of corporate power, now celebrated the benefits of large-scale business enterprise. Not surprisingly, big businessmen exuded confidence in the 1950s. "What is good for the country is good for General Motors, and vice versa," Charles Wilson, the head of GM, is said to have announced.

American workers also benefited from the prosperity of the 1950s. During the decade, they enjoyed high employment, low inflation, and rising incomes. Typically, less than five percent of the work force was out of a job at one time. Wages rose dramatically. Factory workers' average hourly pay more than doubled between 1945 and 1960. Moreover, price rises did not eat up this increased income. After the painful inflation of the first postwar years, consumer prices rose less than two percent per year in the 1950s. The percentage of people living in poverty declined.

The economy also gave Americans more leisure time. "Never," observed a magazine in 1953, "have so many people had so much time on their hands—with pay—as today in the United States." By the 1950s, the forty-hour work week was commonplace in American factories. Many workers now looked forward to two- or three-week paid annual vacations. They also looked forward to retirement. As life expectancy increased and the economy boomed, more and more Americans could expect to retire at age 65 and then live comfortably off their pensions and Social Security. "American labor never had it so good," crowed a trade union leader.

Most Americans would probably have agreed. The impact of World War II and the cold war, the development of the industrial and service sectors, and stable labor relations had fostered a comfortable sense of economic well-being in the 1950s. Corporations and consumers alike had the means to live the good life.

The Suburban Dream

For growing numbers of people, the good life lay outside the city. In the 1950s, many urban and rural Americans dreamed of living in a house in the suburbs. American culture had long idealized homeownership, of course, and suburbs, developing since the nineteenth century, were nothing new. Yet the suburbs had been mainly for the well-to-do. Most Americans had never owned their own homes, but the dream of homeownership became a new reality for millions of people after World War II. Entrepreneurship, efficient construction methods, inexpensive land, and generous federal aid made possible a host of affordable housing developments outside the nation's cities. Along with Gene Ferkauf and his family, much of America moved to the suburbs in the 1950s. **Suburbanization** became critical to the consumer economy.

William J. Levitt's pioneering development, "Levittown," illustrated how the combination of entrepreneurship, low-priced land, and new construction techniques fueled a suburban housing boom. Like Gene Ferkauf, Levitt came back from military service in World War II with an optimistic vision of the future. Amid the postwar housing shortage, he wanted to make houses affordable for middle-class and working-class people. In the military, Levitt had learned to construct prefabricated houses quickly. Now, in 1947, drawing on the assembly-line techniques of automaker Henry Ford, he intended to build houses so efficiently that they could be sold at remarkably low prices. With his brother, Levitt bought a thousand acres of cheap farmland on New York's Long Island, not far from the site of Ferkauf's first suburban Korvettes store. The Levitts put up simple houses, with prefabricated parts, no basements, and low price tags. The original Cape Cod-style house cost 7,990 dollars—an appealing price for young couples buying their first homes.

Like Korvettes, Levittown quickly became a huge success. Buyers signed 1,400 contracts for houses on a single day in 1949. Named Levittown, his development grew to 17,500 dwellings housing 82,000 people. Levitt soon built another Levittown and then another. By then, he had imitators all around the country.

The Pursuit of Pleasure

The consumer society depended on Americans' eagerness to pursue pleasure. For prosperity to continue, consumers had to spend money not only on necessities, but also on enjoyments and luxuries. With more money and leisure time, many Americans were happy to do just that in the 1950s. Businesses made sure that nothing would prevent Americans from buying goods and services. If their wages and salaries were not enough, consumers could borrow money more easily than ever before. Along with federally guaranteed mortgage loans, people could now get credit cards. In 1950, the Diner's Club introduced the credit card for well-to-do New Yorkers. By the end of the decade, Sears Roebuck credit cards allowed over 10 million Americans to spend borrowed money. Like the shoppers who flocked to Gene Ferkauf's stores, optimistic Americans were unafraid to use their credit cards and go into debt. In 1945, Americans owed only 5.7 billion dollars for consumer goods other than houses. By 1960, they owed a stag-

Symbol of the consumer society: The first McDonald's fast-food restaurant, opened by the McDonald brothers in San Bernadino, California, in 1948.

gering 56.1 billion dollars. That nearly ten-fold increase in debt paid for a lot of pleasures.

Those pleasures were easier to find than ever before. In the 1950s, discount stores such as Korvettes made shopping seem simpler and more attractive, and so did another new creation, the shopping mall. In 1956, Southdale, the nation's first enclosed suburban shopping mall, opened outside Minneapolis, Minnesota. Consumers bought meals more easily, too. The first McDonald's fast-food restaurant opened in San Bernardino, California, in 1948. Taken over by businessman Ray Kroc, McDonald's began to grow into a national chain in the mid-1950s.

To get to McDonald's, the Southdale Mall, Korvettes, and Levittown, Americans needed cars. The automobile was essential to the suburban dream and the consumer economy. In the 1950s, cars reflected Americans' new sense of affluence and self-indulgence. Big, high-compression engines burning high-octane gasoline powered ever-bigger cars stuffed with new accessories—power steering, power brakes, power windows, and air conditioning. Unlike the drab autos of the Great Depression, the new models of the

WHERE THEY LIVED, WHERE THEY WORKED

Levittown, New York

For many Americans, the first Levittown epitomized the virtues and defects of suburbia and consumer society in post-World War II America. The Long Island suburb was atypical in some ways. Unlike most suburban developments, it was an entire, planned community built quickly from scratch by a single building company. Nevertheless, Levittown reflected and reinforced major social trends in the years after World War II, including the impulse toward social uniformity, the emphasis on domesticity, and the survival of individuality.

To many observers, the houses and streets of the new development all appeared to be the same. In fact, Levittown's first four-room Cape Cod houses came in only five models that differed very little from each other. William Levitt even admitted that he had once gotten lost in all the look-alike streets of his suburb.

The population of Levittown also seemed quite uniform. In the eyes of one critic, the development was a "one-class community." Most families had an annual income of about 3,500 to 4,000 dollars, just enough to afford the houses going up in Levittown. The male heads of households tended to be prosperous blue-collar workers, veterans of World War II reaching for middle-class status. The new homeowners were mainly between the ages of 25 and 45. Caught up in the postwar baby boom, they were having many babies. There were few teenagers or senior citizens in Levittown. There were hardly any African Americans, either.

The homogeneity of Levittown was no accident. The developer, William Levitt, planned it that way. The uniform style and cost of the houses ensured that the new development would attract only one class of residents. So-called restrictive covenants—special clauses in housing deeds—ensured that only whites could buy property in Levittown. Levitt also tried to impose uniform behavior on the residents. Community rules forbade putting up fences or hanging out the wash on weekends. Some of the residents themselves promoted conformity in Levittown. They wrote the local newspaper to attack neighbors who broke the rules. A nonconformist could expect to be labeled a "commie" or a "Russkie."

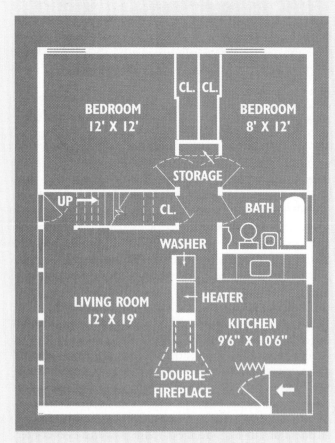

Figure 27-1   Blueprint of Levittown House.

Levittown from the air: At a distance, the houses seem to look alike, reinforcing a sense of conformity. Close up, the houses seemed more diverse as their owners made improvements.

In Levittown, as in the rest of America, there was a heavy emphasis on domesticity. The design of the community and its houses reflected the domestic values of the period. The small Cape Cod homes encouraged family "togetherness." With so little private space, family members congregated around the kitchen table or in front of the TV in the living room. The wives of Levittown were expected to spend weekdays doing domestic tasks at home, rather than working at a paying job. That was how Levitt could assume these women would not need to hang out laundry on the weekends. Because the kitchen was supposed to be the center of women's lives, that room was placed at the front of the Cape Cod houses in Levittown.

The design of Levittown also supported men's domestic role. Former apartment-dwellers found they had to spend time at home mowing their new lawns. Moreover, Levittown had few traditionally masculine public places—bars, fire-houses, ball fields, and the like. Instead, the community promoted family togetherness away from home with plenty of playgrounds and swimming pools for children and their parents. As the local property owners association concluded, "Levittown is a child-centered community."

Despite the power of conformity, Levittown also revealed the survival of individuality in America. With time, the suburb became less homogeneous. With each succeeding year, the Levitts offered houses with a bit more variety. In 1949, they replaced the Cape Cod model with new ranch-style houses. The following years saw new features such as car ports and other touches. As the 1950s wore on, residents gradually made houses into expressions of their individual tastes. They built garages and patios. They added rooms, gardens, signposts, and distinctive paint jobs. Despite the rules, they put up fences. "The houses take on the personalities of their owners," wrote a suburban resident.

In this way, as in others, Levittown was a product of 1950s America. This pioneering suburb revealed the power of domesticity and conformity. Levittown also demonstrated the persistence of individuality in the consumer society.

Levittown and the other suburban developments were made possible, in part, by the federal government. Potential buyers had to be able to get mortgage loans to pay for their houses. The federal government made that easier by guaranteeing loans to the millions of military veterans. To make homeownership more affordable for all Americans, the government allowed buyers to deduct mortgage interest payments from their federal income taxes. Naturally, new suburban homeowners still had to be able to travel to work, often miles away in the city. Here, too, the government helped. The National System of Defense Highways Act of 1956 encouraged the construction of freeways connecting cities and suburbs.

Under such favorable conditions, the United States quickly began to become a suburban nation. By 1950, American builders were putting up nearly two million houses a year, mostly in the suburbs. As the national rate of homeownership increased 20 percent between 1945 and 1960, the suburban population exploded. Before World War II, about one-fifth of Americans had lived in suburbs. By 1960, nearly one-third lived in places like Levittown. The suburban dream had become an everyday reality.

By then, the new suburbs were an integral part of the consumer economy. Economic prosperity, material abundance, entrepreneurship, and government aid had made the suburban developments possible. In turn, the suburbs spurred the consumer economy. The construction of new houses, schools, churches, stores, and roads created jobs for workers and profits for businesses. So did the purchase of backyard barbecues, new appliances, and all the other trappings of the suburban lifestyle. In the process, the suburbs had become one of the main symbols of American consumerism.

A suburban family stands proudly in front of a typical house in 1950 Levittown.

1950s rolled out in a blaze of color. They had "Passion Pink" and "Horizon Blue" interiors and two-tone and even three-tone exteriors studded with lots of shiny chrome.

Automakers used that chrome to solve one of the main problems of a consumer society—getting people, who already had plenty, to want to buy even more. How could Detroit persuade Americans to trade in old cars that were running just fine and purchase new ones? The answer was to make the new models look different from the old ones by throwing on more chrome, changing the colors, or adding tail fins. The Cadillac's fins began as a small bump on each rear fender of the 1948 model and developed year by year into the sharp-edged appendage that rose proudly three-and-a-half feet off the ground on the 1959 model. The result was what General Motor's chief designer called "dynamic obsolescence," the feeling that the old model with last year's fins was somehow inadequate. "We design a car to make a man unhappy with his 1957 Ford 'long about the end of 1958," boasted the head of styling at Ford (see Table 27-1).

More than ever, automakers offered cars as a reflection of a driver's identity. "The automobile tells us who we are and what we think we want to be," declared an observer. "It is a portable symbol of our personality and our position." The car of the 1950s clearly announced its owner's affluence. General Motors' line of cars rose carefully up the socioeconomic ladder, from the ordinary Chevrolet, to the more prosperous Pontiac, Oldsmobile, and Buick, all the way up to the ultimate symbol of success, the sumptuous Cadillac.

Automobiles also spoke to sexual identity. Detroit designed the interior of cars to appeal to women. Inside, the autos of the 1950s had to seem like comfortable or luxurious living rooms. The exterior offered men a combination of power and sexuality. Automakers tried to make men feel like they were flying supersonic jets. Oldsmobile put out the "Rocket 88" and Buick offered the "LeSabre," which was named after a U.S. Air Force fighter plane. While the back of a 1950s car looked like the winking afterburners of a jet, the front spoke to something else. The chrome protrusions on 1950s Cadillacs were known as "Dagmars" after the name of a large-breasted female television star. A car, as a Buick ad promised, "makes you feel like the man you are."

Eager to display their affluence and their identity, Americans flocked to buy cars. There were 25.8 million registered cars on the road in 1945. Fifteen years later, there were 61.7 million. "Dynamic obsolescence" seemed to be working just fine.

It was not remarkable that the chrome on a Cadillac would make Americans think of a television star. In the 1950s, television became a central part of American life. Invented in the 1920s, TV had its first commercial broadcast in the late 1930s. Yet by the end of World War II, there were just nine television stations and eight thousand television sets in the United States. Then technological advances made TV sets much less expensive. As sales boomed, there were new opportunities for broadcasters. By 1950, the Federal Communications Commission had licensed 104 TV stations, mostly in cities. Television was becoming a necessity. Bill Levitt included a free set in each new house in Levittown. By 1960, 90 percent of the nation's households had a television (see Table 27-2). In 15 years, TV had already become a part of everyday life.

From its early days, television reinforced the values of consumer society. Advertisements for consumer products

TABLE 27-1

Automobiles and Highways, 1945–1960

Year	Factory Sales (in 1,000s)	Registrations (in 1,000s)	Miles of Highway (in 1,000s)
1945	69.5	25,796.9	3,035
1946	2,148.6	28,217.0	5,057
1947	3,558.1	30,849.3	15,473
1948	3,909.2	33,355.2	21,725
1949	5,119.4	36,457.9	19,876
1950	6,665.8	40,339.0	19,876
1951	5,338.4	42,688.3	17,060
1952	4,320.7	43,823.0	22,147
1953	6,116.9	46,429.2	21,136
1954	5,558.8	48,468.4	20,548
1955	7,920.1	52,144.7	22,571
1956	5,816.1	54,210.9	23,609
1957	6,113.3	55,917.8	22,424
1958	4,257.8	56,890.5	28,137
1959*	5,591.2	59,453.9	32,633
1960	6,674.7	61,682.3	20,969

*Denotes first year for which figures include Alaska and Hawaii.
Historical Statistics of the United States, 1976, vol. 2, pp. 711, 716.

TABLE 27-2

Television, 1941–1960

Year	Television Stations	Households with Television Sets (in 1,000s)
1941	2	—
1945	9	—
1950	104	3,875
1955	458	30,700
1960	579	45,750

George Thomas Kurian, Datapedia (1994), Bernan Press (Lanham, MD), pp. 299–300.

The different tall tail fins of two late-1950s Cadillacs epitomized the gaudy "dynamic obsolescence" of the consumer society.

paid for television programming. That programming focused mainly on pleasure and diversion. Nightly national news broadcasts lasted only 15 minutes. There were operas, documentaries, and live, original dramas in what some critics consider television's "golden age," but most of the broadcast schedule was filled with variety shows, sports, Westerns, and situation comedies. The first big hit was Milton Berle's variety program, which often featured the host dressed up in women's clothes. The next hit was the situation comedy *I Love Lucy*, which showcased the predicaments of Lucille Ball and her bandleader husband, Desi Arnaz. Walt Disney's popular Western *Davey Crockett* fed nostalgia for America's vanished frontier. Disney's *Mickey Mouse Club* reached the growing audience of young children.

The popularity of TV undermined older forms of entertainment. Now that they could stay home and watch television, Americans were less likely to turn on their radios or go out to theaters and movies, but TV did not undermine the corporate economy. Corporations such as the Columbia Broadcasting System (CBS) and the National Broadcasting System (NBC) soon arranged television stations into networks and dominated the new industry.

It was also not surprising that the front end of a Cadillac would make some people think of a woman's breasts.

One of the hallmarks of American culture in the 1950s was a new openness about sexuality. To his surprise, Dr. Alfred C. Kinsey of Indiana University commanded enormous public attention with two pioneering academic studies—*Sexual Behavior in the Human Male* (1948) and *Sexual Behavior in the Human Female* (1953). To his readers' surprise, Kinsey reported that Americans were more sexually active outside of marriage than had been thought. Grace Metalious' novel *Peyton Place*, which suggested a seething cauldron of sexuality beneath the surface of a respectable New England town, became a big bestseller in 1956. The Supreme Court also contributed to sexual openness by overturning a ban on a film version of D. H. Lawrence's often-erotic novel, *Lady Chatterley's Lover*, in 1959.

The new candor about sexuality was probably best represented by *Playboy* magazine, first published by Hugh Hefner in December 1953. Hefner epitomized his generation's break with the past. The grandson of religious Nebraska farmers who would not smoke, drink, or swear, and the son of parents who would not display emotion, Hefner now ran pictures of bare-breasted women on the glossy pages of his magazine. The first issue of *Playboy* featured a centerfold photograph of the actress Marilyn Monroe. Hefner presented sex as one part of a hedonistic, consumer lifestyle complete with flashy cars, expensive stereos, and fine liquor.

The success of *Playboy,* along with the popularity of TV and tail fins, underscored how much American attitudes had changed from the Great Depression to the 1950s. Armed with money, leisure, and confidence, many Americans were ready to devote more of life to enjoyment. Business was ready to encourage them with credit cards, shopping malls, fast-food restaurants, and "dynamic obsolescence." Together, consumers and business dedicated America to the pursuit of pleasure. Before long, it became clear that many Americans could not afford to enjoy consumerism, but for a while at least, the nation seemed to be living the good life.

A Homogeneous Society?

The spread of consumerism reinforced a sense of sameness in America during the 1950s. It seemed as if the United States was becoming a homogeneous society whose members bought the same products, watched the same TV shows, worked for the same corporations, and dreamed the same dreams. Some observers worried that Americans had become conformists willing to sacrifice their individuality in order to be like one another. Declining class differences strengthened the feeling that people were becoming more alike, as did a rush to attend church and have children. Along with the renewed emphasis on religion and family, Americans faced pressure to conform to gender roles.

Nevertheless, the United States remained a heterogeneous society. While ethnic differences among whites decreased, race remained a powerful divider. The continuing dissimilarity of the states and the abundance of popular music styles underscored the persisting diversity of American society. Despite fears of conformity, the nation still encouraged difference and individuality.

The Discovery of Conformity

In the years after World War II, sociologists and other writers noticed a disturbing uniformity across American society. People, it seemed, were becoming increasingly alike, partly because they shared more and more experiences, such as consumerism and suburban lifestyles. Further, Americans appeared anxious to be like one another. Some commentators and social critics feared the loss of the personal freedom and individuality that seemed so basic to American life.

By the 1950s, a variety of factors promoted homogeneity in American life. During the frenzied search for domestic Communists, people did not want to risk accusations by appearing too different or unusual, and so, they participated in the same national consumer culture. Moreover, as corporations merged and small businesses disap-

web connection

How to Lie With Statistics

www.prenhall.com/boydston/statistics

The tumult of the 1960s flowed from the tension of the 1950s. Mistrust and rebellion later on were partly a response to the loss of a very deep trust. Later generations of Americans would wonder why the earlier generations seemed to believe everything they were told by churches, government, private industry, or anyone with a voice of authority. Yet trust made sense to many people who had lived through the Great Depression and World War II; they knew from experience that the country had survived due to concerted action, coordinated by government reliance on individual cooperation. Was the "disturbing uniformity" of the consumer society completely uniform, though? Darrell Huff's book, *How To Lie With Statistics* (1954), was one indication that critical thinking WAS going on.

peared, Americans worked for the same giant companies. The new suburbs intensified the sense of homogeneity. In 1957, one writer described suburbanites as "people whose age, income, number of children, problems, habits, conversations, dress, possessions, perhaps even blood types are almost precisely like yours."

To some observers, this similarity was more than a matter of shared experience. Americans, they believed, *wanted* to be like one other. In *The Lonely Crowd* (1950), sociologist David Riesman argued that people had become "other directed" rather than "inner directed." He suggested that instead of following their own internalized set of values, Americans adjusted their behavior to meet the expectations of the people around them. In *The Organization Man* (1956), William H. Whyte, Jr., described the conformist style of white-collar workers in big corporations. In the office or at home in the suburbs, the "organization man" was all too willing to go along with others. Whyte even suggested that the United States, supposedly dedicated to freedom, was becoming like the totalitarian Soviet Union. An American suburb, he concluded, was little more than "Russia with money."

The Decline of Class Differences

The homogeneity of American society was reinforced by the apparent decline of class differences. By the 1950s, the old upper class—the families of the Gilded-Age industrialists and financiers—had lost much wealth and power. With a few exceptions like the Fords and the Rockefellers, they no longer single-handedly controlled and managed America's big businesses. Thanks to the Great Depression, income and inheritance taxes, and sheer waste and mismanagement, the fortunes of the very wealthy were no longer quite so imposing. Many of the rich had given up their great mansions and astonishingly extravagant parties. A less-ostentatious generation of executives had a firm grip on America's corporations. In his book, *The Power Elite* (1956), sociologist C. Wright Mills argued that an interlocking military, political, and economic elite ran the country. However, this rather drab group did not have the bold, public swagger of the old, opulent upper class.

American farmers had also been disappearing for a long time, but not because of mismanagement. Since the late nineteenth century, the increasing efficiency of American agriculture, along with overseas competition, had meant the nation needed fewer farmers. The average farm worker, who supplied 15 people a year with food in 1945, produced enough food for 26 people by 1960. As a result, the number of American farms fell sharply from over six million in 1944 to just 3.7 million 15 years later.

In contrast, the working class remained large and apparently healthy. Manual and service workers, some 33 million strong, were still the nation's largest occupational group in 1960. About one-third of workers belonged to unions. The labor movement's size and power were underscored in 1955 when the American Federation of Labor (AFL) and the Congress of Industrial Organizations (CIO) merged to become the gigantic AFL-CIO.

Despite their numbers and organization, workers appeared to be a less aggressive and distinctive class in the 1950s. Well-paid blue-collar workers appeared content with American society and their role within it. Labor leaders endorsed consumerism and anti-Communism. Some observers argued that American workers had become essentially middle class in their buying habits and social values.

This apparent transformation, along with the decline of farmers and the upper class, made it easier to think of the United States as a classless society in the 1950s. Instead of fighting, different social groups were evidently becoming more middle class in their values and outlook. The middle class itself was burgeoning. By 1960, the white-collar sector made up 40 percent of the work force.

Even the ethnic differences that had once divided Americans no longer seemed so significant. Whites from different ethnic backgrounds mixed together in the new suburbs. The rate of intermarriage between ethnic groups increased. Anxious to prove their loyalty during the cold war, newer Americans were reluctant to emphasize their origins overseas. Ethnicity had apparently disappeared in the national melting pot of the consumer society.

Many Americans, especially powerful ones, had long wanted to believe that the United States was a unified society devoted to middle-class values. In the 1950s, there was probably more basis for this belief than ever before in the twentieth century. Nevertheless, prosperous Americans were ignoring some troublesome realities. The very poor remained concentrated in inner cities and remote rural areas. Social classes still differed significantly from each other in wealth, values, and power. The completely unified, classless society was an illusion, but, as so often happens in history, many people preferred illusion to reality.

The Resurgence of Religion and Family

The apparent homogeneity of American society in the 1950s was further promoted by a resurgence of religion and family in national life. Americans went back to church in the 1950s. Church membership doubled to 114 million between 1945 and 1960. The surge in attendance mostly benefited Christian denominations. By 1960, there were 64 million Protestants, 42 million Roman Catholics, and fewer than 6 million Jews. "Christian faith," observed *Time* magazine in 1954, "is back in the center of things" (see Table 27-3).

While the religious revival was somewhat difficult to explain, it apparently flowed from many sources. Millions of Americans clearly wanted reassurance and uplift in a society obsessed with consumerism and threatened with nuclear destruction. Some Americans no doubt attended church because that was what other people were doing.

Denominations encouraged the attendance boom by adapting religion to the consumer society. Naturally, they made use of television. Charismatic preachers such as Roman Catholic Bishop Fulton J. Sheen and evangelist Billy Graham became TV stars. To an extent, some religious denominations made church membership simpler and less demanding. *Reader's Digest* even published a shortened version of the *Bible*. The nation's political leaders encouraged the religious revival, too. Freedom of religion, they insisted, was one of the things that differentiated the United States from allegedly godless Communist nations. To underscore the national commitment to religion, the federal government even put the words "IN GOD WE TRUST" on all its currency.

American culture celebrated the family along with religion in the 1950s. Detroit presented its big automobiles as "family" cars. Manufacturers promoted television as a way of holding families together. More generally, American society venerated what *McCall's* magazine christened family "togetherness" in 1954.

"Togetherness" meant the nuclear family, with a mother, a father, and plenty of children. After decades of decline, the birth rate suddenly and unexpectedly rose during and after World War II. In 1943, more than three million babies were born for the first time since 1921. Beginning in 1954, Americans had more than four million babies a year. Thanks to new drugs, more of these babies survived.

TABLE 27-3

Religious Revival and Baby Boom, 1945–1960

Year	Membership of Religious Bodies (in 1,000s)	Live Births (in 1,000s)
1945[2]	71,700	2,858
1946[2]	73,673	3,411
1947	77,386	3,817
1948	79,436	3,637
1949	81,862	3,649
1950	86,830	3,632
1951	88,673	3,823
1952	92,277	3,913
1953	94,843	3,965
1954	97,483	4,078
1955	100,163	4,104
1956	103,225	4,218
1957	104,190	4,308
1958[1]	109,558	4,255
1959*	112,227	4,245
1960	114,449	4,258

*Denotes first year for which figures include Alaska and Hawaii.
[1]Includes Alaska
[2]Based on 50 percent sample for 1951–1954, 1956–1960.
Source: George Thomas Kurian, Datapedia (Lanham, MD: Beman Press, 1994), pp. 37, 146.

Antibiotics reduced the risk of diphtheria, typhoid fever, influenza, and other infections. The Salk and Sabin vaccines virtually wiped out the crippling disease of polio. As a result, the number of children per family went from 2.4 in 1945 up to 3.2 in 1957. By then, a third of the country was under the age of 15. Overall, in the 1950s, the American population grew by a record 29 million people to reach 179 million.

Like the religious revival, the "baby boom" of the 1940s and 1950s is somewhat difficult to explain. For more than 100 years, Americans had reduced the size of their families in order to ease burdens on mothers and family budgets and to provide more attention, education, and material resources to children. The economic prosperity of the cold-war era may have persuaded couples that they could afford to have more children. Prosperity alone did not explain why American culture became so much more child-centered during these years. In his *Common Sense Book of Baby and Child Care* (1946), pediatrician Benjamin Spock urged parents to raise their children with less severity and more attention, warmth, tenderness, and fun. *Baby and Child Care* outsold every other book in the 1950s except, not surprisingly, the *Bible*.

Together, the baby boom and the religious revival contributed to the growing sense of uniformity in American society during the 1950s. Along with television and suburbia, millions of Americans shared family "togetherness"

and religious attendance. There was conformity in the church and the nursery as well as on the job.

Maintaining Gender Roles

The baby boom helped heighten pressure on men and women to conform to traditional gender roles. In the 1950s, American culture strongly emphasized differences between the sexes: Women were expected to be homemakers and men, providers. The reality was more complicated. Women's roles, in particular, changed during the years after World War II. Nevertheless, they got little help in adapting to new demands. Both sexes, meanwhile, were warned against deviating from gender stereotypes.

American culture underscored the differences between genders in a variety of ways. This was the era that made blue the right color for boys and pink the right color for girls. Standards of beauty highlighted the physiological differences between women and men. Popular movie actresses such as Marilyn Monroe and Jayne Mansfield were large-hipped, large-breasted women like Dagmar. During the baby boom, women were expected more than ever to be helpful wives and devoted mothers. Men were still encouraged to define themselves primarily as money-earners who would provide for the family.

However, traditional gender roles evolved during the 1950s. Society stressed a man's domestic role more than before. While remaining the boss of his household, he was expected to be gentler and more involved with his family. Experts urged husbands to do some of the housework and to spend more time nurturing their children. Few men, however, lived up to the new ideal. According to one study, only two percent did any ironing at home.

Female roles evolved more dramatically. Women were not simply confined to the domestic sphere, to home, husband, and children, after World War II. In order to help pay for the consumer lifestyle, more and more wives had to go to work outside the home. Gene Ferkauf's wife, while taking care of their child, helped publicize the first Korvettes store. Other wives had to do much more to help family finances. By 1960, almost one married women in three held a job; and single, married, and widowed women made up more than one-third of the nation's labor force.

To a degree, American culture supported the expanding role of women outside the home. In the cold-war competition with the Soviets, Americans celebrated the supposedly greater freedom and opportunity for women in the United States. "You can do anything you want in life—anything—if you just try hard enough," a women's magazine told readers. Television featured situation comedies with feisty women, such as Lucy Ricardo in *I Love Lucy* and Alice Kramden in *The Honeymooners,* who got out of place sometimes and stood up to their men.

Nevertheless, women faced a difficult situation with relatively little help. While working outside the home, they

Marilyn Monroe, actress and symbol of the new sexual openness, strikes a provocative pose in the 1955 film, The Seven Year Itch.

were still expected to take care of husbands and children. Congress did vote an income tax deduction for child-care costs in 1954, but little first-class child care was available. At work, women were expected to watch men get ahead of them. Women's income was only 60 percent of men's in 1960. Men, not women, got most of the promotions, too. In all, women had new opportunities in the 1950s; they also had new burdens.

Women and men alike were expected to accept their social roles. American culture strongly condemned women and men who strayed outside conventional gender norms. *Modern Woman: The Lost Sex,* a 1947 bestseller by Marynia Farnham and Ferdinand Lundberg, censured feminism as the "deep illness" of "neurotically disturbed women" with "penis envy." *Deadly Is the Female* (1949), *Kiss Me Deadly* (1955), and other *film noir* movies dramatized the threat posed by independent women whose sexual charms could lure men to destruction. Psychologists and other experts demonized lesbians, who had become a more visible subculture during the 1940s, as "predatory prostitutes" and "psychopathic women homosexualists."

Like women, men faced condemnation if they failed to play conventional social roles. In the 1950s, unmarried men risked accusations of homosexuality. Along with gay women, gay men became targets of abuse during the cold war. Senator Joe McCarthy decried "sexual perverts." Around the country, police cracked down on gay bars. The message was clear: Men were supposed to be heterosexual; they were supposed to be husbands and fathers. Those roles, in turn, forced men to conform to social expectations. "Once a man has a wife and two young children," the writer Gore Vidal observed, "he will do what you tell him to."

Persisting Racial Differences

In spite of the many pressures toward conformity, American society was still quite heterogeneous in the 1950s. While ethnic differences among whites mattered less, racial differences still mattered a great deal. Society continued to segregate and discriminate against African Americans and Native Americans. The rapid growth of the Hispanic population helped to ensure that the United States would remain a multiracial nation.

Although suburbanization broke down ethnic differences among whites, it only intensified the racial divide between those whites and African Americans. The nation's suburbs were 95 percent white in 1950. As whites moved into Levittown and other suburbs, African Americans took their place in cities across the country. By 1960, more than half of the African-American population lived in cities. This *de facto* racial segregation reinforced the continuing *de jure* segregation of the South. By custom in the North and law in the South, African Americans were clearly set apart from white Americans in the 1950s.

Native Americans, living on their reservations, were also set apart. In 1953, Congress did try to "Americanize" the Indians by approving the termination of Indians' special legal status. "Termination" meant the end of federal aid to tribes and the end of many reservations. Supposedly more just and less expensive, the new policy was intended to turn Indians into full members of the consumer society.

It did not turn out that way. As reservations became counties, Indians had to sell valuable mineral rights and lands in order to pay taxes. Despite short-term profits from these deals, tribes faced poverty, unemployment, and social problems. Encouraged by the federal government's new Voluntary Relocation Program, about one in five Native Americans moved to cities. There, they found jobs and began to create new communities, but whether they lived on reservations or crowded city blocks, the nation's quarter of a million Indians remained largely separate and ignored in the 1950s. Like African Americans, Native Americans were set apart.

The increasing migration of Puerto Ricans also reinforced the multiracial character of American society. Beginning in the 1940s, large number of Puerto Ricans, who were already U. S. citizens, left their island hoping for more economic opportunity on the mainland. By 1960, the Puerto Rican population in the mainland United States had reached 887,000. Two-thirds concentrated in the East Harlem section of New York City, well uptown from the original E. J. Korvettes. These new migrants did find opportunities in the United States. They also found separation and discrimination.

Mexican immigration further contributed to the racial diversity of postwar America. After 1945, increasing numbers of Mexicans left their impoverished homeland for economic opportunity in the United States, particularly the booming Southwest. Congress, bowing to the needs of southwestern employers, continued the Bracero Program, the supposedly temporary wartime agreement with Mexico that had brought hundreds of thousands of laborers, *braceros* to the United States. Meanwhile, illegal Mexican migration increased dramatically after the war. Reflecting this increase, the number of undocumented Mexican migrants apprehended by the U. S. Immigration and Naturalization Service jumped from 29,000 in 1944 to nearly 200,000 in 1947.

Like other Mexican migrants before them, the *Chicanos* who successfully crossed the border into the United States met with an ambivalent reaction. As in the years before World War II, many Mexicans already living in the United States worried that the new arrivals would only compete for jobs, drive down wages, and feed Anglo prejudice. Many white Americans did indeed deride Chicanos as *mojados* or "wetbacks" because so many had supposedly swum the Rio Grande River to get into the United States illegally. Mexican Americans feared retaliation. They worried that the federal government would use the provisions of the Internal Security Act of 1950 and the Immigration and Nationality Act of 1952 to deport Mexican aliens unfairly back to Mexico and thereby break up many Mexican-American families. The government's intention became clear in 1954 with the launching of Operation Wetback, which supposedly sent more than one million immigrants back to Mexico in that year alone.

Despite the actions of the federal government, about 3.5 million Chicanos were living in the United States by 1960. The great majority of them worked for low wages in the cities and farms of the Southwest. Many Chicanos continued to live in *barrios* apart from whites. Because of Operation Wetback and other instances of prejudice, some Mexican Americans became more vocal about their circumstances and their rights by the end of the 1950s. The League of United Latin American Citizens (LULAC), long suspicious of new Chicano immigration, nevertheless denounced the impact of the Immigration and Nationality Act. More outspoken was the American G. I. Forum, an organization formed by Mexican-American veterans when a funeral parlor would not bury a deceased Chicano veteran in Three Rivers, Texas, in 1949. Ernesto Galarza, an official of the National Agricultural Workers' Union (NAWU), also spoke out eloquently about the plight of all Mexicans amid the Bracero Program and Operation Wetback. Such assertiveness made it all the harder for white Americans to ignore the presence of Chicanos in the consumer society.

The experiences of Hispanics, Native Americans, and African Americans underscored the continuing importance of race in the United States. While ethnicity mattered less to whites, racial differences continued to divide and structure American society. Mostly living apart, whites and non-whites faced different conditions and different futures. Prosperity and consumerism did not change that reality in the 1950s. By attracting Hispanic workers, the economy even promoted diversity. As long as race was such a potent factor in national life, the United States would never be a completely homogeneous society.

The Survival of Diversity

Along with race, a variety of forces ensured the survival of diversity in 1950s America. Despite the appearance of suburbs and discount stores all over the country, the states continued to differ from each other. As in the past, the migration of millions of Americans and the expansion of national boundaries promoted diversity. During the 1950s, more than 1.6 million people, many of them retired, moved to the warm climate of Florida. As a result, the state increasingly played a distinctive national role as a center for retirement and entertainment.

Meanwhile, millions more Americans moved westward. During the 1950s, California alone gained more than three million new residents. In some ways, the state's boom meant that it was becoming more like the rest of America. When the Dodgers left Brooklyn for Los Angeles and the Giants left New York for San Francisco after the 1957 season, California had the same major-league baseball that fans enjoyed in the East and Midwest. California also earned a reputation as the pioneer state of the consumer society, the home of the first Disneyland amusement park and the first McDonald's.

At the very end of the decade, the admission of two new states highlighted the continuing diversity of the United States. In 1959, Alaska and Hawaii became, respectively, the forty-ninth and fiftieth states in the union. Racially and culturally diverse, climatically and topographically distinctive, they helped make certain that America was not simply a land of corporations and Levittowns.

Popular music also exemplified the continuing diversity of the United States. The late 1940s and 1950s saw an almost bewildering proliferation of musical styles. Big swing bands gave way rapidly to such popular singers as Frank Sinatra and Patti Page. Jazz, which appealed to a multiracial audience, split into different camps—traditional, mainstream, and modern. The newly christened "country" music, which was rooted in white rural culture, also included different strains—cowboy songs, Western swing, honky-tonk, and bluegrass. During these years, a range of African-American musical forms, including blues, jazz, and vocal groups, became known as "rhythm and blues" or just "R and B." Meanwhile, Gospel music thrilled white and African-American audiences. All the while, Mexican Americans made Tejano music in Texas, Cajuns played Cajun music in Louisiana, and German and Polish Americans danced to polka bands in Illinois and Wisconsin.

Rhythm and blues collided with country music in the 1950s to create yet another powerful musical form: rock and roll. By 1952, the white disc jockey Alan Freed was playing R and B records on his radio show, "Moondog's Rock 'n' Roll Party," out of Cleveland. By 1954, a white country group, Bill Haley and the Comets, had recorded what may have been the first rock-and-roll hit, "Rock Around the Clock." Rock and roll produced both African-American and white heroes in its first years—Chuck Berry, Fats Domino, Jerry Lee Lewis, and Buddy Holly among others.

The biggest rock-and-roll sensation of all was a young white singer and guitar player, Elvis Presley. His life illustrated how the persisting diversity of American society made possible a strong sense of individuality. Born in Mississippi and raised in near poverty in Memphis, Tennessee, Presley grew up hearing a wide range of music from country to opera and from gospel to rhythm and blues. However, beginning with his first commercial record, "That's All Right, Mama," in 1954, Presley sang in a distinctive style that listeners could never quite pigeonhole. "Who do you sound like?" he was asked. "I don't sound like nobody," he said.

Because of Presley and other musicians, the sound of American popular music was anything but homogeneous. Because of the distinctiveness of Florida, California, Alaska, Hawaii, and other states, the United States was hardly monolithic. In these ways, at least, American society remained diverse after World War II. Amid all the worries about conformity, Americans, like Elvis Presley, could still "sound like nobody."

The Eisenhower Era at Home and Abroad

Prosperity encouraged Americans to demand less from government in the 1950s. In a period of rapid social change and continuing international tensions, most people wanted reassurance rather than boldness from Washington. The politics of the decade were dominated by President Dwight D. Eisenhower, a moderate leader well-suited to the times. This popular war hero reassured Americans that their country could cope with changes at home and challenges abroad. Elected president in 1952, Eisenhower easily won re-election in 1956. His middle-of-the-road domestic program, "Modern Republicanism," appealed to a prosperous electorate wary of governmental innovation. But Eisenhower's anti-Communist foreign policy did little to diminish popular anxieties about the cold war.

"Ike" and 1950s America

Dwight Eisenhower, a charismatic military hero with a bright, infectious grin, would have been an ideal public figure in almost any era of American history, but the man known affectionately by his boyhood nickname, Ike, was especially suited to the politics of 1950s America. The last president born in the nineteenth century, he had successfully accommodated the major changes of the twentieth. Throughout his life, Eisenhower managed to reconcile the old and the new. The man who led the very corporate America of the 1950s was a product of rural society. Born in Texas in 1890, Ike was raised on a farm in Abilene, Kansas. Although his parents were pacifists, Ike became a warrior. He graduated from West Point in 1915 and served in the Army, without getting a chance to fight, during World War I.

Mamie and Dwight Eisenhower. The first lady and the president were reassuring figures in the turbulent transition to the cold war and consumerism in the 1950s.

Raised on the individualistic values of the Midwest, Eisenhower adopted the bureaucratic style of modern organizations. He succeeded in the military after World War I, not because he was a great fighter or strategist, but because he was a great manager. A believer in harmonious teamwork, Eisenhower was the quintessential "Organization Man." As a commander in World War II, Eisenhower worked above all to keep sometimes fractious allies together. After the war, he deepened his organizational experience, first as president of Columbia University in New York City and then as the first commander of the armed forces of the North Atlantic Treaty Organization (NATO) in Europe.

Just as he accommodated the rise of big organizations, Eisenhower accommodated the extension of the nation's commitment abroad. Ike had grown up in the often isolationist Midwest, among people who feared American involvement in the world's problems. But his military career, from World War I to the cold war, rested on his acceptance of an activist role for the United States around the world.

Eisenhower easily fit the dominant culture of the 1950s. As gender ideals demanded, he was an involved, loving husband and father who liked to cook out for his family. In a society zealously pursuing pleasures, he was famous for his many hours on the golf course. His wife, Mamie, showed how women could respectably embrace consumerism. She eagerly wore the "New Look" fashions inspired by designer Christian Dior and avidly watched television soap operas.

With all his advantages, Eisenhower was a natural choice for the presidency. Nominated by the Republicans in 1952, he ran against Adlai Stevenson, the liberal Democratic governor of Illinois. Stevenson, witty and eloquent, was no match for Eisenhower. Running a moderate, conciliatory campaign, the former general avoided attacks on the liberal New Deal and promised to work for an end to the Korean War. Meanwhile, his running mate, Senator Richard Nixon of California, accused Stevenson of being soft on Communism. The Republican ticket won a big victory with 55 percent of the popular vote and 442 electoral votes. Thanks partly to Eisenhower's popularity, the Republican Party took control of the White House and both houses of Congress for the first time in 20 years.

"Modern Republicanism"

In office, Eisenhower advocated "Modern Republicanism" for the American political economy. This philosophy represented the president's attempt to steer a middle course between traditional Republican conservatism and Democratic liberalism. Modern Republicanism reflected Eisenhower's moderation and his understanding of the popular mood. With a conservative's faith in individual freedom, the president favored limited government and balanced budgets, but unlike most conservatives, Eisenhower the organization man believed that Washington had an important role to play in protecting individuals. Eisenhower the politician also recognized that most Americans did not want to give up such liberal programs as Social Security and farm subsidies.

Accordingly, the president took some steps to limit governmental control over the economy. The Eisenhower era produced tax cuts for the wealthy and decreased federal regulation of business. With the Submerged Lands Act of 1953, the federal government turned over offshore oil resources to the states for private exploitation. With the Atomic Energy Act of 1954, Washington allowed private firms for the first time to sell power produced by nuclear reactors.

Nevertheless, the Eisenhower administration did little to undermine the legacy of the New Deal and the Fair Deal. Despite his doubts about activist government, Eisenhower went along with increases in Social Security benefits and farm subsidies. Despite his belief in balanced budgets, his administration produced several budget deficits. During Eisenhower's presidency, Washington continued to play an active role in stimulating economic growth. Federal spending, including the highway program, helped fuel the booming consumer economy.

Modern Republicanism frustrated liberals who wanted a more eloquent leader and a more activist government. Eisenhower's philosophy also frustrated conservative "Old-Guard" Republicans who wanted to roll back liberalism, but many Americans appreciated the president's moderation. In the prosperous 1950s, there was not much popular demand for dramatic new federal programs. "The public loves Ike," a journalist observed. "The less he does the more they love him."

Eisenhower's popularity was confirmed at the polls in 1956. In a repeat of the 1952 election, the president once again headed the Republican ticket with Richard Nixon. Once again, the Democrats nominated Adlai Stevenson for president. This time Eisenhower won an even bigger victory with 58 percent of the popular vote and 457 electoral votes.

An Aggressive Approach to the Cold War

Like President Harry Truman before him, Eisenhower was fully committed to opposing Communism aggressively at home and around the world. Domestically, the president helped the crusade against alleged Communist subversives and tolerated its excesses. He refused to criticize the tactics of Senator Joseph R. McCarthy in public. Despite international protest, the president declined to stop the execution of the convicted atomic spies, Julius and Ethel Rosenberg, in 1953. The next year, Eisenhower denied the security clearance that J. Robert Oppenheimer, the former director of the Manhattan Project, needed to continue work on the government's top-secret nuclear projects. Even though Oppenheimer had not been proven disloyal, his career was shattered. Thousands of other alleged security risks also lost their federal jobs during the Eisenhower era.

Campaigning in 1952, Eisenhower and his advisers talked of rolling back Soviet power in Europe. Truman had pledged only to stop further Communist expansion with the policy of containment. Now Eisenhower spoke of the need to free already "captive peoples" from Communism. Presumably, that would mean contesting Soviet control of eastern Europe. Eisenhower's secretary of state, John Foster Dulles, even called for the "liberation" of eastern Europe. On the face of it, this assertive approach seemed more likely to lead to armed confrontation with the Soviets.

In office, Eisenhower and Dulles coupled their rhetoric with a new national security policy. Dulles threatened "instant, massive retaliation" with nuclear weapons in response to Soviet aggression, nonnuclear as well as nuclear. To support this threat, the U. S. military adopted the "New Look," a strategy named after Mamie Eisenhower's favorite fashions. De-emphasizing costly conventional armies, the military greatly increased its nuclear arsenal with new long-range bombers, missiles, and the first nuclear-powered submarines. Not surprisingly, **Massive Retaliation** and the "New Look" stirred fears at home and abroad of nuclear war.

The Eisenhower administration did not rely only on the public threat of "Massive Retaliation" and the "New Look" to stop Communist aggression. The president also used the Central Intelligence Agency to counter Communism by stealthier means. At the president's direction, the CIA carried out secret activities that were once considered unacceptable; however, as a presidential commission observed, the cold war was "a game" with "no rules." At home, the agency explored the possible uses of lysergic acid diethylamide—the dangerous hallucinogenic drug known as LSD—by using it on hundreds of unwitting Americans. Some of them went mad and at least one killed himself. Abroad, the agency gave secret aid to pro-American regimes and ran secret programs against seeming hostile governments. Most Americans had no idea what the CIA was doing.

The Eisenhower administration acted boldly in secret. In August 1953 a covert CIA operation, code-named "Ajax," orchestrated a coup that removed Mohammed Mossadeq, the nationalist prime minister of oil-rich Iran. Eisenhower and Dulles feared that this "madman," who had nationalized oil fields, would open the way for Communism and the Soviet Union. He was replaced by the young Shah Mohammed Reza Pahlavi, who gratefully accepted 45 million dollars in U. S. aid, turned his back on the Soviets, and made low-priced oil available to American companies.

The next year, "Pbsuccess," a secret CIA operation modeled on "Ajax," overthrew another foreign leader, this time much closer to home. Eisenhower and Dulles worried that a "Communist infection" in the Central-American nation of Guatemala could spread to the United States-controlled Panama Canal and further north to Mexico. In fact, the Soviet Union had made no effort to help Guatemala's new president, Jacob Arbenz Gúzman. Arbenz, heavily influenced by the Guatemalan Communist Party, supported the redistribution of land and threatened the interests of a powerful American corporation, the United Fruit Company. In June, "Pbsuccess" used misleading "disinformation," a small force of Guatemalan exiles, and CIA-piloted bombing raids to persuade Arbenz to resign.

The Eisenhower administration employed covert action elsewhere around the world. The CIA may even have played a role in the eventual assassination of the leaders of the Congo in Africa and the Dominican Republic in the Caribbean. Such covert activities, along with "Ajax" and "Pbsuccess," would prove highly controversial when they were discovered years later.

Avoiding War With the Communist Powers

Despite the tough talk about "liberation," "rollback," and "massive retaliation," the Eisenhower administration tried to avoid direct confrontation with the two major Communist powers, the People's Republic of China and the Soviet Union. Eisenhower knew he had to end the Korean conflict, the first hot war of the cold war. As he had promised in the 1952 campaign, Eisenhower traveled to Korea to observe conditions firsthand before his inauguration. Once in office, he pushed to end the military stalemate with North Korea and the People's Republic of China that ultimately killed 33,629 Americans. After much delay, a cease-fire agreement in July 1953 left the United States without a victory. Although America had wanted to reunify North and South Korea, the two nations remained divided. Nevertheless, the agreement ended a costly, difficult war that had brought the United States into battle against mainland China, the world's most populous Communist nation. It was, Eisenhower declared, "an acceptable solution."

Ending an old war with one Communist power, the Eisenhower administration avoided a new conflict with the other. In October 1956, Hungarians, spurred on by American propaganda broadcasts, rose up against their pro-Soviet government. Unwilling to tolerate independence for a neighboring country, the Soviet Union sent troops to break the rebellion. Despite all its talk of freeing captive peoples and using massive retaliation, the Eisenhower administration did not intervene to help the Hungarian rebels. The United States would not contest Soviet control of Eastern Europe after all.

More broadly, Eisenhower would not break with the Truman administration's fundamental approach to the

Vice President Richard Nixon upholds the virtues of the consumer society in his "Kitchen Debate" with Nikita Khrushchev at an exhibition in Moscow in 1959.

cold war. The president was cautious about military confrontation with the Soviets and the Chinese. Privately opposed to the use of the atomic bomb in 1945, Eisenhower declined to unleash nuclear weapons that would "destroy civilization" in the 1950s. Although he sent out CIA agents to conduct covert operations, the president was more reluctant than Truman to send American soldiers into open battle.

At the same time Eisenhower, like Truman, knew the cold war was an economic and political fight. The Eisenhower administration maintained foreign-aid programs and fought a propaganda war with the Soviets. In front of a model American kitchen in a Moscow exhibition in 1959, Vice President Richard Nixon and Soviet leader Nikita Khrushchev argued the merits of the their two systems. Not surprisingly Nixon turned this "Kitchen Debate" into a celebration of the prosperity and freedom of the consumer society. "Isn't it better," he asked the Soviet leader, "to be talking about the relative merits of our washing machines than of the relative strength of our rockets?"

While avoiding open conflict with the U. S. S. R., the Eisenhower administration took some modest steps to improve relations with the Soviets. After the death of the So-

viet leader, Josef Stalin, early in 1953, his successors signaled their desire for "peaceful coexistence" with the United States and the West. Responding cautiously, Eisenhower told the United Nations in December that he wanted to pursue disarmament and the peaceful use of atomic power with the Soviets. The president proposed an "Atoms for Peace" plan in which an international agency would experiment with nonmilitary uses for nuclear materials from the United States and the U. S. S. R. The Soviets, however, dragged their feet. Although the International Atomic Energy Agency was formed in 1957, the United States and the U. S. S. R. did not cooperate significantly to control the nuclear arms race during the Eisenhower years.

The president made another attempt at improving relations with the Soviets. In July 1955, Eisenhower joined the Soviet leader Nikita Khrushchev in Geneva, Switzerland, for the first meeting between an American president and Soviet rulers in the decade since World War II. At the Geneva summit, Eisenhower broached a plan for "Open Skies." According to this plan each side would be allowed to fly over the other and observe military installations. Although Khrushchev rejected the plan as a trick, the relatively amicable Geneva talks sparked some optimism about American-Soviet relations. That optimism effectively ended by May 1960, when the Soviets shot down an American spy plane, the U-2, flying high over the U. S. S. R. After the Eisenhower administration denied the entire affair, Khrushchev triumphantly produced the captured pilot, Francis Gary Powers, along with pieces of the plane.

In addition to embarrassing Eisenhower, the U-2 incident underscored the continuing rivalry between the United States and the major Communist powers. Despite "Open Skies" and "Atoms for Peace," the United States, the Soviet Union, and mainland China were still locked in a hostile confrontation. The Eisenhower administration refused even to recognize the Communist Chinese regime officially.

Crises in the Third World

Although Eisenhower worried most about the fate of Western Europe, his administration increasingly focused on the threat of Communist expansion in Africa, Asia, Latin America, and the Middle East. These regions, which made up the industrializing "Third World," were enmeshed in the confrontation between the "First World" of industrial, non-Communist nations and the "Second World" of industrial, Communist countries. Often plagued by poverty, violence, and civil war, many Third World societies struggled to break free from imperial domination. Their nationalist struggles against colonialism complicated American foreign policy during the Eisenhower era. In the Middle East and Southeast Asia in particular, the Eisenhower administration found itself caught up in explosive crises involving nationalism and Communism.

Under Khrushchev, the Soviet Union tried to exploit Third World discontent and conflict for its own purposes. Anxious to preserve America's influence and its access to natural resources, the Eisenhower administration stood ready to counter Soviet moves. The president made use of the well-established techniques of containment—aid, trade, and alliances. Eisenhower offered increased foreign aid to Third World countries and tried to stimulate trade with them. He also encouraged closer military ties. In the 1950s, the United States signed individual defense pacts with the Philippines, South Korea, and Taiwan.

Eisenhower's approach to the Third World was sorely tested in Southeast Asia. When he took office in 1953, the United States continued to support France's war to hold onto Vietnam and its other Southeast Asian colonies. The

president feared that a Communist victory in Vietnam would deprive the West of valuable raw materials and, more important, encourage the triumph of Communism elsewhere. Comparing the non-Communist nations of Asia and the Pacific to "a row of dominoes," Eisenhower explained that the fall of the first domino—Vietnam—would lead to the fall of the rest, including even Japan and Australia.

Despite vast American aid, the French could not defeat the nationalist forces of the Viet Minh, led by the Communist Ho Chi Minh and helped by the mainland Chinese. By 1954, the Viet Minh had surrounded French troops at Dienbienphu, near the border with Laos in northern Vietnam. Unwilling to fight another land war in Asia, Eisenhower refused to send American troops to save the French. The president also rejected the use of atomic bombs to drive the Viet Minh away from Dienbienphu. Without further help from the United States, France surrendered Dienbienphu in May.

Although the French defeat ended direct colonial control of Vietnam, the country was still not unified and fully independent. In 1954, peace talks at Geneva produced an agreement to cut Vietnam, like Korea, in half. Ho Chi Minh's forces would stay north of the 17th Parallel. His defeated, pro-French Vietnamese enemies would stay to the south of that line. The peace agreement stipulated that a popular election would unite the two halves of Vietnam in 1956. Certain that Ho Chi Minh and the Communists would win the election, the United States refused to sign the truce agreement.

Instead, the Eisenhower administration worked to create a permanent anti-Communist nation south of the 17th Parallel. To protect the new country of South Vietnam from Ho Chi Minh, the United States joined with Britain, France, Australia, New Zealand, Pakistan, Thailand, and the Philippines to create the South East Asian Treaty Organization (SEATO) in September 1954 (see Map 27-1). To ensure South Vietnam's loyalty, the Eisenhower administration backed Ngo Dinh Diem, a Roman Catholic anti-Communist who

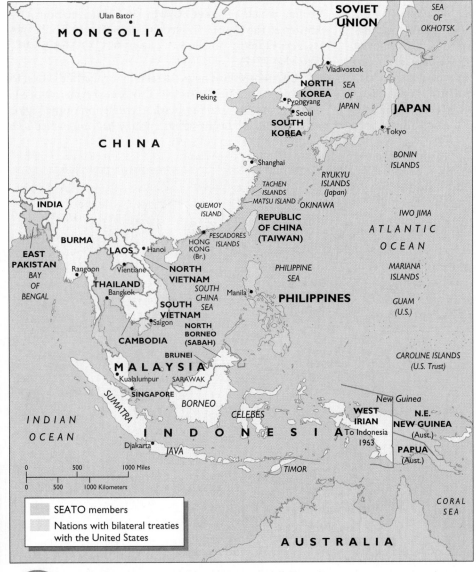

Map 27-1 America's Cold War Alliances in Asia.
Members of SEATO (the South East Asian Treaty Organization) and signers of other treaties with the United States. Through these pacts, the Eisenhower administration hoped to hold back the threat posed by Communist mainland China.

established a corrupt, repressive government. The United States sent military advisers and hundreds of millions of dollars to aid Diem.

By thwarting the Geneva Accords and establishing an unpopular regime in the South, Eisenhower had helped ensure that Vietnam would be torn by civil war in the years to come. Ho Chi Minh and many other Vietnamese would view the United States as an imperial enemy. In the short run, however, Eisenhower had avoided war and seemingly stopped the Asian dominoes from falling.

Eisenhower soon confronted another crisis in the Middle East. Gamal Abdel Nasser, who had seized power in Egypt in 1954, emerged as a forceful spokesman for Arab nationalism and Middle Eastern unity. Wrongly fearing that Nasser would open the way for Soviet power in the Middle East, John Foster Dulles withdrew an offer to aid the Egyptians. Nasser struck back by taking over the British- and French-owned Suez Canal in 1956. In retaliation, Britain and France, with Israel's cooperation, moved against Nasser. As Israeli troops fought their way into Egypt in October, Britain and France stood ready to take back the Suez Canal. Furious at the British and French, Eisenhower feared the invasion could give the Soviets an excuse to move into the Middle East. To force the British,

French, and Israelis to withdraw, the president threatened economic sanctions. Khrushchev, meanwhile, threatened to launch Soviet rockets in defense of the Egyptians. The British, French, and Israelis soon withdrew.

After the Suez crisis, in January 1957, the president announced what became known as the "Eisenhower Doctrine." The United States, he promised, would intervene to help any Middle Eastern nation threatened by armed aggression supported by international Communism. The next year, in an illustration of his doctrine, Eisenhower sent troops to Lebanon. The soldiers were not really needed in that Middle Eastern nation, but they did send a message about American power and resolve. The president underscored that message in 1959, when the United States encouraged the formation of another regional defense organization patterned after NATO. The new group, which included Turkey and other nations, was known as the Central Treaty Organization (CENTO) for its geographical position between NATO and SEATO (see Map 27-2).

Eisenhower had helped to stabilize the Middle East for a time, but the Suez crisis had also drawn America deeper than ever before into the swirling confusion of the region. As in Vietnam, the president's policy had intensified local

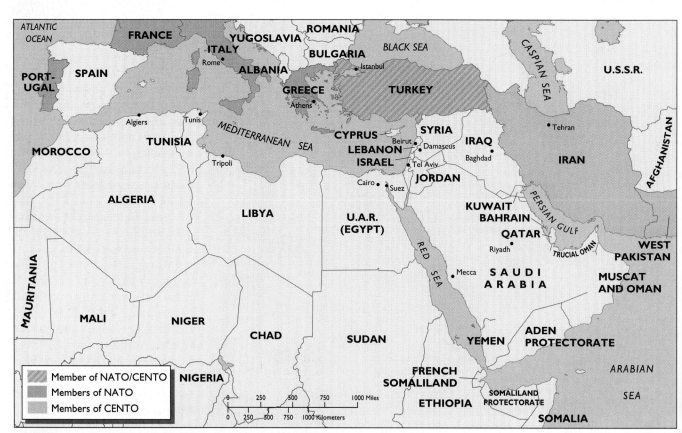

Map 27-2   America's Cold War Alliances in the Middle East.
Located between the members of NATO and SEATO, the members of CENTO (the Central Treaty Organization) joined with the United States to deter the threat of international Communism sponsored by the Soviet Union to the north.

divisions. Like his hostility to Ho Chi Minh, the president's distrust of Nasser made the United States seem like an opponent of nationalist independence for industrializing countries. The two Third World crises had been peacefully resolved temporarily, but Eisenhower's actions had increased the odds of future trouble in Southeast Asia, the Middle East, and other developing areas.

In the years to come, critics would charge that the president had bought short-term stability at the cost of long-term trouble. During the 1960s and 1970s, the United States would have to deal with Eisenhower's legacy in the Middle East, Vietnam, and the rest of the Third World.

Challenges to the Consumer Society

While the Eisenhower administration managed crises abroad, American society confronted challenges at home. In different ways, a rebellious youth culture, the alienated beat movement, and the divisive civil rights struggle upset the stability of the Eisenhower era. They showed that American society was not very homogeneous after all. They demonstrated, too, that consumerism had not solved all the nation's problems or won over all its citizens. Many Americans, in fact, were uneasy about the consumer society as the 1950s came to an end.

Rebellious Youth

"Never in our 180-year history," declared *Collier's* magazine in 1957, "has the United States been so aware of—or confused about—its teenagers." In the 1950s, the emergence of a distinct youth culture, built around such things as rock and roll, customized cars, comic books, and premarital sexual exploration, troubled many adults. No sudden development, the youth culture of the decade was the culmination of a trend apparent since the 1920s and 1930s. As more and more teenagers attended high school, they were, in effect, segregated in their own world. Within that world, they developed their own values and practices. In the 1950s, young people claimed rock and roll as their own music. They wore blue jeans; they read comic books and teen magazines. Expressing their individuality, boys modified standard Detroit cars into unique customized "hot rods." Teens were attracted to alienated and rebellious movie characters such as the troubled son played by James Dean in *Rebel Without a Cause* (1955) or the motorcycle gang leader played by Marlon Brando in *The Wild One* (1953). Worried adults feared that youth were copying the movies and defying authority. A wave of juvenile delinquency appeared to be sweeping the country.

Ironically, adults helped to create the youth culture. They had confronted teens with a rapidly changing society absorbed with sex, cars, and Communism, with new roles for mothers and fathers, with fears of conformity and dreams of individualism. Not surprisingly, uneasy young people tried to establish their own individuality. In the process, they created a distinctive culture. Adults, moreover, paid for this culture's trappings. The prosperous economy could afford to pay allowances to many children and to hire a growing minority of teenagers for part-time after-school jobs. As a result, business fully recognized young people as a distinct consumer market during the 1950s.

Many of these youth were rebellious, but not nearly as much as adults feared. Despite all the publicity, juvenile delinquency did not actually increase after World War II and neither did rates of sexual intercourse among teenagers. Girls, although restless and attracted to such

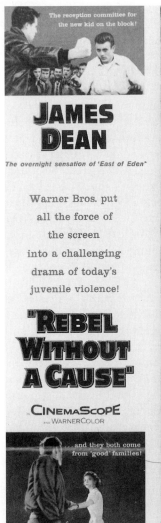

Films such as Rebel Without a Cause, *starring the brooding James Dean, played on adult fears about youthful rebellion in the 1950s.*

Elvis Presley delights a crowd—particularly its female members—in Long Beach, California, in June 1956.

supposedly "brain-washing" teenagers and leading them astray. In well-publicized hearings from 1954 to 1956, the Senate's Subcommittee to Investigate Juvenile Delinquency focused attention on the corrupting power of the mass media. Some critics claimed that comic books, rock and roll, and such teenage films as *Dragstrip Girl* were all part of a Communist plot against the United States.

The campaign against youth culture had little impact. A society devoted to free speech and consumerism was not going to restrict mass media or youthful consumers too much. Television networks, movie studios, record labels, and comic-book companies did not stop catering to teenagers with spending money. In addition, American society was ambivalent about youth culture. Many adults found teenagers' styles appealing. "We've stopped trying to teach them how to live," one magazine even claimed. "Instead, we're asking *them* how they think *we* should live."

figures as James Dean and Elvis Presley, never played a very visible role in the male-dominated youth culture of the 1950s. Most young people never questioned the political system. On the whole, youth culture exaggerated rather than rejected the values of adult, consumer society.

The early career of Elvis Presley illustrated the boundaries of youthful rebellion. Presley's appeal rested on an unsettling combination of rock and roll music and open sexuality that divided young and old. The very term "rock and roll," like "jazz," was a reference to sexual intercourse. Presley's style—his sensual mouth, disheveled "duck's ass" (DA) haircut, and gyrating hips—powerfully amplified the music's sexuality.

Despite his powerful appeal to teenagers, Presley remained relentlessly polite and soft-spoken, devoted to his parents, and deferential to interviewers. Buying a pink Cadillac and other luxury cars, he was as caught up in the consumer culture as other Americans were. Like Gene Ferkauf and millions of other Americans, Presley joined the suburban migration when he bought his house, "Graceland" on the outskirts of Memphis, Tennessee. Hardly a rebel, Presley was a new version of the old American dream of upward mobility.

Still, many grown-ups blamed Presley, rock and roll, and mass media for the spread of "dishonesty, violence, lust and degeneration" among young Americans. Some adults tried to censor or wipe out these apparent threats to youth. One popular television program first refused to bring on Presley and then showed him only from the waist up. To get rid of blue jeans and other teenage fashions, high schools imposed dress codes on their students. There was a crusade against comic books, teen magazines, and movies that were

The Beat Movement

A second group of rebels was smaller in numbers but a bit older and much more critical of American society. The beat movement, which emerged in New York City in the 1940s, expressed a sense of both alienation and hope. The term "beat" itself referred to a feeling of physical and emotional exhaustion and also to a state of transcendence, the "beatific." Worn down by contemporary culture, the beats searched hopefully for a way to get beyond it.

Uptown at Columbia University and downtown in Greenwich Village Allen Ginsberg, Jack Kerouac, John Clellon Holmes, William Burroughs, and others wanted, as one of them put it, "to emote, to soak up the world." Their quest would take them well beyond New York. Beats explored their sexuality, sampled mind-altering drugs, and investigated the spirituality of Far-Eastern religions. Kerouac captured the spirit of their odyssey in his novel about a trip across America, *On the Road,* (1957). Some of the beats did cross the country. San Francisco emerged as a center of beat culture during the decade. There, Allen Ginsberg published his long poem, *Howl* (1956), which evoked the beats' sense of alienation: "I saw the best minds of my generation destroyed/ by Madness, starving hysterical naked."

As Ginsberg's lines suggested, the beats had a dark vision of American society. Even more than teen culture, the beat movement was fascinated by outsiders and outcasts. Like the white-dominated teen culture, the beats were drawn to the culture of African Americans. But while teenagers danced to the relatively simple and upbeat sounds of African-American rhythm and blues, the beats embraced the rhythmically and harmonically challenging bop music of Charlie Parker and other African-American jazz musicians. Moreover, the beats were not nearly as positive about the consumer culture. In a society captivated by pink and other bright colors, "beatniks" declared their alienation from consumerism by wearing black. The beats were also angrier at the apparent meaninglessness of American politics in the Eisenhower era.

Other Americans reacted to the beats with a mixture of censure and curiosity. The publisher of *Howl* was tried on obscenity charges, but the public bought 100,000 copies of Ginsberg's poem. Magazines featured stories on the beats. Television shows parodied them.

Few in number, the beats sometimes seemed absurd, but the media's attention suggested just how important they were. The beat movement was a clear sign of budding dissatisfaction with consumer society, conventional sexual mores, and politics as usual.

The Struggle for Civil Rights

The African-American struggle for civil rights also challenged the political moderation of the Eisenhower era. By the 1950s, the system of segregation was under increasingly effective attack in the courts and on the streets. African Americans were inspired by the gains they had made in the 1940s and by the continuing discrimination they suffered in the 1950s.

As in the 1940s, the National Association for the Advancement of Colored People (NAACP) fought segregation in the courts. Focusing on public schools, the organization directly assaulted the discriminatory legacy of the Supreme Court's *Plessy v. Ferguson* ruling of 1896. In 1951 the NAACP's special counsel, Thurgood Marshall, combined five different lawsuits from four states and the District of Columbia, all aimed at segregation in the public schools. In one of these lawsuits, an African-American welder, Oliver Brown, challenged the constitutionality of a Kansas state law that allowed cities to segregate their schools. Because of the law, Brown's eight-year-old daughter, Linda, had to ride a bus 21 blocks to a "colored only" school even though there was a "white only" school just three blocks from home. When the Brown case reached the Supreme Court in December 1952, Thurgood Marshall attacked the *Plessy* argument that justified "separate but equal" facilities for whites and African Americans. As a result of segregation, Marshall maintained, Linda Brown and other African Americans received both an inferior education and a sense of their own inferiority. The lawyer concluded that segregation violated the citizenship rights guaranteed by the Fourteenth Amendment.

Marshall's arguments were persuasive. In May 1954, the court, led by new Chief Justice Earl Warren of California, handed down its ruling in *Brown v. Board of Education, Topeka, Kansas.* Warren, who believed the court should take a more active role in society, had carefully built a consensus among the justices. Overturning the *Plessy* decision, they ruled unanimously that public school segregation was in fact unconstitutional under the Fourteenth Amendment. "Separate but equal has no place," Warren announced. "Any language in *Plessy v. Ferguson* contrary to this finding is rejected." Warren's tenure as chief justice was one of the most important in the history of the court. No ruling of the Warren Court would prove more significant than the decision in the *Brown* case. African Americans and white liberals were jubilant. The ruling was, an African-American newspaper exulted, "a second emancipation proclamation." Marshall himself foresaw the dismantling of school segregation before the end of the decade (see Map 27-3).

It did not work out that way. The compromises Chief Justice Warren had made to gain a unanimous decision became clear when the court ruled on the enforcement of school desegregation in May 1955. The justices turned to local school boards, dominated by whites, to carry out the integration

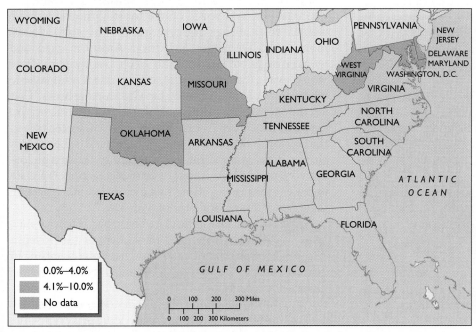

Map 27-3 *African Americans Attending Schools With White Students in Southern and Border States, 1954.*

The small percentages indicate just how successfully segregation had separated the races before the Supreme Court ruled in Brown v. Board of Education, Topeka, Kansas *in 1954.*

of the schools. Federal district courts were to oversee the process of desegregation, but that process, the justices explained, should occur with "all deliberate speed." In other words, school segregation had to end, but not right away.

Taking heart from this ruling, many whites refused to give up Jim Crow. The strongest opposition to the *Brown* ruling came from the South, where segregation was deeply entrenched in law and social custom. For some white southerners, as one put it, a "reasonable time" for the end of segregation would be "one or two hundred years." In 1956, 101 congressmen signed a "Southern Manifesto" calling on their home states to reject the *Brown* decision. Amid calls for **massive resistance** to desegregation, White Citizens' Councils formed in a number of southern states to prevent schools from integrating. Some states passed laws intended to stop school integration. There was violence, too. In 1955, white Mississippians killed Emmett Till, a fourteen-year-old African-American boy from Chicago, who had supposedly made advances to a white woman.

African Americans, encouraged by the court's action, were ready to fight even harder against segregation. After work on December 1, 1955, Rosa Parks, a forty-two-year-old, African-American tailor's assistant in Montgomery, Alabama, boarded a bus to go home. State law dictated segregation on city buses. Local custom required an African American like Parks to give up her seat to a white passenger and then move to the back of the bus, but when the bus driver told her to move, Parks would not get up. As she said, "my feet hurt." More than that, she wanted to find

A white student heckles an African-American student trying to integrate Central High School in Little Rock, Arkansas, in September 1957.

out "once and for all what rights I had as a human being and a citizen." The angry driver thought she had none; he had Parks arrested.

Local African-American leaders, who had encouraged her to test the law, seized on the arrest of this respectable woman to challenge segregation. On the cold, cloudy morning of December 5, African-American men and women began to boycott the city's bus system. They would walk, car pool, or take rides from sympathetic whites until the city modified Jim Crow on the buses. That afternoon, twenty-six-year-old Martin Luther King, Jr., pastor of the Dexter Avenue Baptist Church, agreed to lead the boycott. The son of a noted Atlanta preacher, King was already developing a brilliant oratorical style and a philosophy of nonviolent protest against segregation. "We are impatient for justice," King told a crowded mass meeting that night, "but we will protest with love."

The boycott met immediate resistance. The city outlawed car pools and indicted the leaders of the boycott. African-American homes and churches were bombed. In November 1956, however, the United States Supreme Court ruled Alabama's bus-segregation law unconstitutional. By then, the boycott had cost the bus company and downtown storeowners dearly. Montgomery's white community had lost the will to resist any longer. Instead of trying Rosa Parks, the city settled with the boycotters and agreed to integrate the buses. "We just rejoiced to-

The symbol of the Montgomery, Alabama, bus boycott: Rosa Parks, who refused to give up her bus seat to a white passenger in December 1955, being fingerprinted by a deputy sheriff.

gether," one of the boycotters remembered. "We had won self-respect."

Although other forms of segregation continued in Montgomery, the bus boycott was a crucial victory for the civil rights movement. Montgomery showed that a combination of local activism and federal intervention could overcome Jim Crow in southern communities. It established a charismatic new leader with a powerful message, and it soon brought forward a new civil rights organization, when King helped found the Southern Christian Leadership Conference in 1957. For one journalist, Montgomery "was the beginning of a flame that would go across America."

The flame did not travel easily. In 1957, the school board of Little Rock, Arkansas, accepted a federal court order to integrate the city's Central High School, but in September the state's segregationist governor, Orval Faubus, hoping for re-election, called out National Guard troops to stop the African-American students who wanted to enroll at Central. Even after meeting with President Eisenhower, Faubus would not order the troops away from the school. When he finally did remove the soldiers, an angry mob of whites surrounded Central High and made it impossible for the African-American students to stay. "Two, four, six, eight," cried the mob, "we ain't going to integrate."

Little Rock created a dilemma for the president. Not a believer in racial equality, Eisenhower wanted to avoid the divisive issue of civil rights. He privately opposed the *Brown* ruling and gave only mild support to the weak Civil Rights Act of 1957, which offered no real protection for African Americans' right to vote. The president knew, however, that his government was being defied in Little Rock and humiliated around the world. The Soviets, he complained, were "gloating over this incident and using it everywhere to misrepresent our whole nation." So Eisenhower sent in troops of the crack 101st Airborne of the U. S. Army. With that protection, nine African-American students went to Central High. Faubus tried unsuccessfully to turn the public schools into private all-white "academies," but integration proceeded again in Little Rock by 1959.

Like the Montgomery bus boycott, Little Rock demonstrated that a combination of federal action, however reluctant, and African-American courage could triumph over "massive resistance." The Central High crisis showed, too, how the cold war helped tip the balance against segregation. Competing with the Soviets for support from the multiracial Third World, no president could afford the embarrassment of racial inequality at home. The grassroots activism of African Americans and the decisions of federal courts made that embarrassment impossible to ignore, and segregation and discrimination would continue to upset the stability of Eisenhower's America. It was, the president concluded, "troublesome beyond imagination."

An Uneasy Mood

Youth culture, the beat movement, and the civil rights struggle contributed to an uneasy mood in America by the end of the 1950s. Even people who did not share the beats' values worried that the consumer society was flawed. Some intellectuals believed that "soft-headed high-living" had left the nation "cultureless." For the critic Lewis Mumford, modern automobiles were "fantastic and insolent chariots" and suburbs were "a low-grade uniform environment from which escape is impossible." Consumerism itself could seem like a trap for Americans. In his bestseller, *The Hidden Persuaders* (1957), Vance Packard played on the fears that advertisers were manipulating American consumers.

Americans were troubled, too, by signs of corruption in the consumer society. In 1958, they learned that record companies had paid Alan Freed and other disc jockeys to play particular records on the radio. This "payola" scandal destroyed Freed's career and damaged the reputation of rock and roll. The same year, Americans were shocked by revelations that contestants on popular TV quiz shows had secretly been given the answers to questions in advance. Some of the shows went off the air. Charles Van Doren, a

Cartoonist Herblock lampoons President Dwight Eisenhower's apparent lack of involvement in the nation's problems.

college professor much admired for his success on the show "Twenty-One," was convicted of perjury and lost his teaching job. In the process, television lost some of its innocent appeal.

While Americans worried about whether the consumer society was corrupt, they also had to wonder whether it could meet the challenge of the cold war. In October 1957, the Soviet Union sent *Sputnik,* the world's first satellite, into orbit around Earth. This unexpected accomplishment set off a wave of fear in the United States. If the Soviets could send up a satellite, they could be ahead in nuclear weapons and economic growth too. Americans felt suddenly more vulnerable.

Sputnik intensified concerns about the quality of American education. A diverse and growing student population, along with rising parental demands, had already put considerable strain on the nation's schools. Now Americans worried that the schools were not preparing children to compete with the Soviets in science and technology. In 1958, Congress, previously reluctant to provide aid to schools, passed the National Defense Education Act (NDEA). To win what Senator Lyndon Johnson called the "battle of brainpower," this wide-ranging measure promoted instruction in science, math, and foreign languages, supported construction of new schools, and offered loans and fellowships to students.

While Eisenhower did not want to overreact to the Soviets' success, *Sputnik* forced Washington to accelerate the American space program. The first U. S. satellite launch collapsed in flames—*Flopnik,* the world's press called it. At the end of January 1958, the government did successfully send up its first satellite, *Explorer I.* Later that year, Congress created the National Aeronautics and Space Administration (NASA) to coordinate America's exploration of space. These initiatives did not wipe away fears about the fate of a society caught up in consumerism and the cold war. "What we are really worried about," one magazine emphasized, "is that the whole kit and caboodle of our American way of life—missiles and toasters, our freedoms, fun, and foolishness—is about to go down the drain."

Eisenhower did little to change the national mood. Slowed by poor health, the president now struck more Americans as old and out of ideas. In 1960, he even had to create a Commission on National Goals to help figure out what the country should do. A few days before the end of his presidency in January 1961, Eisenhower fed the uncertain mood with a warning about the political economy in his farewell address. Noting that cold-war spending had built up the military and the defense industry, he warned against allowing this "military-industrial complex" to gain too much power. "We must never let the weight of this combination endanger our liberties or democratic processes," Eisenhower cautioned. It was a stunning admission that the cold war's transformation of the political economy might actually destroy rather than save democracy in America.

Eisenhower never became an unpopular president. Yet his difficulties were a sign of the new stresses on American society at the end of the 1950s. In different ways, youth culture, the beat movement, and the civil rights movement challenged the status quo. The great majority of Americans were not about to give up the benefits of the prosperous consumer economy, but clearly many people worried about whether consumerism and Modern Republicanism were enough to meet the challenges of the cold-war world.

Conclusion

Along with the cold war, the triumph of consumerism dramatically affected the United States in the 1950s. The booming consumer economy gave Gene Ferkauf and other Americans a new sense of security and affluence during the unsettling confrontation with Communism. Breaking with the past, they moved to the suburbs, had record numbers of children, bought televisions at E. J. Korvettes, and, more than ever before, defined life as the pursuit of material pleasures. Consumerism helped promote homogeneity and conformity in American society. It spurred the victory of Dwight Eisenhower and his moderate approach to the political economy.

For a moment, perhaps, it seemed as if America had achieved a kind of stability and harmony in a dangerous cold-war world, but that feeling did not last long. The United States was never as homogeneous as some Americans wanted to believe. The nation was still divided, above all, by race. As the rise of the youth culture and the beat movement suggested, consumerism itself spawned new divisions. At the end of the 1950s, many Americans questioned whether the consumer society could provide prosperity, equality, and security for all its citizens. The next decade, a tumultuous time, would give them an unsettling answer.

CHRONOLOGY

1946   Benjamin Spock, *Common Sense Book of Baby and Child Care*

1947   Opening of Levittown suburban development

1948   Opening of first McDonald's fast-food restaurant
Alfred Kinsey, *Sexual Behavior in the Human Male*

1950   Introduction of Diner's Club credit card

1951   UNIVAC 1 computer
Debut of *I Love Lucy*

1952   Dwight D. Eisenhower elected president

1953   Opening of first suburban E. J. Korvettes store
First issue of *Playboy* magazine
Beginning of Federal Termination policy for Native-American reservations
CIA Operation "Ajax" in Iran
Cease fire in Korea
Eisenhower "Atoms for Peace" proposal

1954   Atomic Energy Act
"Baby boom" birthrate over four million per year
Bill Haley and the Comets, "Rock Around the Clock"
Supreme Court school desegregation decision, *Brown v. Board of Education, Topeka, Kansas*
Federal "Operation Wetback"
Army-McCarthy Senate hearings
CIA Operation "Pbsuccess" in Guatemala
Creation of divided Vietnam in Geneva peace talks
Beginning of Senate hearings on Juvenile Delinquency

1955   Formation of AFL-CIO
Eisenhower "Open Skies" proposal
Beginning of bus boycott in Montgomery, Alabama

1956   National System of Defense Highways Act
William H. Whyte, Jr., *The Organization Man*
Opening of Southdale suburban shopping mall
Suez crisis
C. Wright Mills, *The Power Elite*
Re-election of President Eisenhower

1957   Announcement of Eisenhower Doctrine
Confrontation over school desegregation in Little Rock, Arkansas
Move of baseball Dodgers and Giants to California
Jack Kerouac, *On the Road*
Soviet *Sputnik* satellite launch

1958   National Defense Education Act
Rock and roll "payola" scandals
TV quiz show scandals

1959   Alaska and Hawaii statehood
Nixon-Khrushchev "Kitchen Debate" in Moscow

1960   President Eisenhower's Commission on National Goals
Soviet downing of U. S. U-2 spy plane

1961   Eisenhower's farewell address on "military-industrial complex"

Review Questions

1. Discuss the factors promoting consumerism in the years after World War II. Why were many Americans willing and able to participate in the consumer economy?

2. What forces promoted uniformity and conformity in 1950s America? Did the United States become a homogeneous society?

3. Why was Dwight Eisenhower such a popular public figure in the 1950s? How did he support consumerism?

4. How did President Eisenhower try to confront the threat of Communism around the world? Was his approach to the cold war successful?

5. Compare the youth culture, the beats, and the civil rights movement of the 1950s. Did any of them want radical change for the United States?

Further Readings

Stephen E. Ambrose, *Eisenhower*, 2 vols (1983–1984). Evenhandedly chronicles the life of the general and president.

David L. Anderson, *Trapped by Success: The Eisenhower Administration and Vietnam, 1953–1961* (1993). Examines the American decision to support South Vietnam after the French withdrawal.

Taylor Branch, *Parting the Waters: America in the King Years, 1954–1963* (1988). A lively narrative focusing on the role of Martin Luther King, Jr., in the civil rights struggle.

John P. Diggins, *The Proud Decades: America in War and in Peace, 1941–1960* (1988). Gives a broad overview of the postwar period.

Barbara M. Kelly, *Expanding the American Dream: Building and Rebuilding Levittown* (1993). Details the evolution of the quintessential suburban development.

Karal Ann Marling, *As Seen on TV: The Visual Culture of Everyday Life in the 1950s* (1994). Engagingly explores the emerging consumer culture.

Joanne Meyerowitz, ed., *Not June Cleaver: Women and Gender in Postwar America, 1945–1960* (1994). An important set of essays that collectively change our understanding of women in the postwar period.

Grace Palladino, *Teenagers: An American History* (1996). Persuasively describes the development of youth culture in the 1950s.

History on the Internet

"Levittown: Documents of an Ideal Suburb"

http://www.uic.edu/~pbhales/Levittown.html

Discover the cultural history of Levittown through contemporary photographs of the suburb and its inhabitants, construction of the houses, family life, and suburb-centered recreation.

"MLK Page"

www.umich.edu/politics/mlk

Consult this informative website for timelines of the American civil rights movement and learn more about pivotal events such as *Brown v. Board of Education* and the 1955 Montgomery bus boycott.

"Rebel Poets of the 1950s"

http://www.npg.si.edu/exh/rebels/poets.htm

Part of an exhibit on the beat movement, this site interprets the beats and their impact. Also, see paintings and photographs of beat poets.

"NSC68"

http://www.seattleu.edu/artsci/history/us1945/docs/nsc68-1.htm

This site features a National Security Council report ordered by President Eisenhower that examines U.S. programs for national defense, the risks of nuclear war, and Soviet preparedness.

28

THE RISE AND FALL OF THE NEW LIBERALISM

1960-1968

OUTLINE

"We Would Never Be Beaten": Vietnam, 1968

On the night of January 10, 1968, Second Lieutenant Fred Downs of the U. S. Army lay back on a sand dune and looked up at the stars over the coast of South Vietnam. Only 23, he was thousands of miles from the Indiana farm where he had grown up, and he was thousands of miles from the house where he lived with his wife and two little girls in Illinois. Why was Lieutenant Downs so far from home?

Downs' presence in South Vietnam reflected two factors that continued to shape American life after 1945: the cold war and prosperity. Downs was in South Vietnam because of the United States' ongoing opposition to the spread of Communism. His job was to lead a platoon of American soldiers in the war to protect South Vietnam's government from forces loyal to the North Vietnamese Communist, Ho Chi Minh. Downs was there, too, because of his country's great wealth. Only a rich, prosperous

society could afford to send Downs and several hundred thousand other military personnel to fight halfway around the world. Only such a society could surround Downs with an abundance of advanced weapons, from M-16 semi-automatic rifles to F-105 supersonic jets.

Downs' presence in South Vietnam also emphasized a critical change in the United States from the 1950s to the 1960s. During the 1950s the U. S. government had a cautious sense of the limits of American power and the dangers of fighting a war in Southeast Asia. President Dwight Eisenhower had avoided sending troops to fight in Vietnam, but American leaders in the 1960s, buoyed up by the prosperous economy, were more confident and more daring. Faced with the likely collapse of South Vietnam, the U. S. government had sent its troops to battle in 1965.

Fred Downs shared his leaders' confidence. "I knew we would never be beaten," he declared.

Still, the months in Vietnam had tested his confidence. The hot sun "cooked" him by day, the rain drenched him by night, and leeches sucked his blood. He worried about stepping on land mines and booby traps left by the enemy. He worried whether he could trust the South Vietnamese. He worried whether his country was fighting the war the right way. Too often, the Americans' advanced weapons didn't work: frighteningly, his M–16 rifle jammed in the middle of a fight.

Much of the time, Downs and his men went out hunting for the enemy on "Search and Destroy" missions. To his frustration, the Viet Cong and the North Vietnamese were hard to find. When he did get close to them, the result was a "deadly game of hide and seek." Downs shot and killed Viet Cong and North Vietnamese soldiers with his rifle. He stabbed a soldier to death in the throat with a bayonet. He killed women. He watched his own men die.

Downs himself was wounded four times. But the Army rewarded him with medals for his bravery and Downs put aside his worries. "My men thought I was invulnerable," he reported; "I did too." As he lay on that sand dune on the night of January 10, he saw "no clouds on my horizon." Downs was sure he would survive the war. "Nothing would happen to me," he believed.

The next morning, his platoon moved out. At 7:45, he went through a gate at the top of a hill and stepped on a mine. The mine—a "Bouncing Betty"—popped out of the ground and exploded waist-high. The explosion threw

American soldiers on patrol in South Vietnam. Like Lt. Fred Downs, these men were the visible and vulnerable agents of the United States' confident stand against Communism in Southeast Asia.

Downs into the air, ripped through his ear drums, tore away pieces of his legs and hips, mutilated his right hand, laid bare the bones of his right arm, and blew off his left arm at the elbow. Horrified, Downs looked at his wounds. "I felt," he recalled, "the total defeat of my life. . . . My body was sending so many pain signals to my brain that it was overloaded like an electrical circuit." Downs' men looked at him in despair: "Their invulnerable leader had been brought down."

Fred Downs' story mirrored the experience of his country in the 1960s. With growing confidence in its wealth, power, and wisdom, the United States tried bold projects during the decade. Americans turned for a time to a vigorous new liberalism that took a more activist approach to the political economy. The nation's leaders pledged both to fight Communism abroad and to reform life at home. By the mid-1960s, the federal government had gone to war in Vietnam and had begun to create a "Great Society" in the United States. The country that sent Fred Downs to fight on the other side of the world also tried to wipe out poverty, heal race relations, protect consumers and the environment, and improve education and health care. Fred Downs' fate reflected the fate of his nation. The great dreams ended in sobering realities. By 1968 the United States had to confront the limits of its power, just as Fred Downs had to confront the new limits of his life without an arm. ▮

KEY TOPICS

- How popular discontent spurred the emergence of a new liberalism characterized by faith in activist government, economic growth, and an emphasis on anti-Communism, racial equality, and quality of life for all Americans

- The influence of the new liberalism on American society through John Kennedy's "New Frontier" and Lyndon Johnson's "Great Society"

- The culmination of the nonviolent civil rights movement in the mid-1960s

- The ways in which the Vietnam War both reflected and damaged the liberalism of the Great Society

- The Great Society's inability to deal with the challenges of economic problems, the Black Power movement, the youth rebellion, and the women's movement

The Liberal Opportunity

Americans' uneasiness about their society, rather unfocused in the 1950s, became increasingly specific and passionate in the 1960s. During the new decade, more and more people realized that the prosperous consumer economy had left millions in poverty, damaged the environment, and threatened the health and welfare of all Americans. Meanwhile, the grassroots protests of African Americans dramatized the persistence of racial inequality in a wealthy and segregated nation.

These popular discontents created an opportunity for new ideas and new leaders in the 1960s. A fresh brand of liberalism promised to repair the defects of the consumer society with a new approach to the political economy. Confident that the federal government could keep the economy growing, liberals wanted an activist state to use more of the nation's increasing wealth to improve life at home and to confront the Communist challenge abroad. The election of 1960 produced a new Democratic president, John F. Kennedy, who was sympathetic to the ambitious new liberalism. Kennedy did not accomplish much of the liberal agenda before his tragic assassination in 1963, but his successor, Lyndon Johnson, was also committed to liberal ideas and policies. Johnson's landslide victory in the election of 1964 gave liberalism a powerful mandate to address the discontents of the consumer society.

Discontent in the Consumer Society

Despite the economic boom after World War II, the percentage of Americans living in poverty had hardly budged by 1960. Many millions of people lived the consumerist good life, but millions of others did not. By the standards of the day, about one in five people were poor. They lived in remote rural areas and crowded inner cities. They were young and old. They were African American, Hispanic American, Native American, and Caucasian. The majority of poor Americans, in fact, were white.

By the 1960s the rest of country found it harder and harder to ignore the poor. American society also found it harder to blame poverty on the failings of poor people themselves. In his influential book *The Other America* (1962), Michael Harrington publicized the plight of "the rejects of the affluent society," the poor people trapped in an "economic underworld . . . the invisible land of the other Americans." The poor, Harrington stressed, remained poor because of racism and a lack of opportunity, not because of personal shortcomings. Thanks in part to Harrington, more Americans began to ask why their affluent consumer society failed to provide decent housing, education, and jobs for all citizens.

At the same time, people were asking why the economy had to do so much ecological damage. By the 1960s, Americans were more concerned about the environment than at any time since the progressive era at the beginning of the twentieth century. The environmental threat was obvious in the cities. A well-publicized pall of smog seemed to hang perpetually over Los Angeles, so dependent on cars, instead of subways and trains, for transportation. Americans could no longer ignore the fact that their large, flashy automobiles, the symbol of the consumer society, were polluting the air.

The environmental threat was obvious in the countryside, too. Even as they moved into new suburban developments built on old farms, some Americans lamented the disappearance of undeveloped land. They began to criticize society's cavalier attitude toward the natural world. In the mid-1950s, environmentalists, led by the Sierra Club and the Wilderness Society, had successfully blocked the construction of the Echo Park Dam in the upper Basin of the Colorado River because the project would have inundated a national park, the Dinosaur National Monument. A new environmental movement, determined to protect wilderness lands from development, emerged from the battle over that dam. In the 1960s Americans became further sensitized to the threat that the consumer economy posed to the countryside. In her bestselling book *Silent Spring* (1962), marine biologist Rachel Carson emphasized the dangerous power that human beings held over the natural world. The use of chemical pesticides such as DDT, she argued, protected fruits and vegetables for American consumers but harmed insects, birds, and fish. Carson

Rachel Carson, whose bestseller Silent Spring *encouraged Americans' concerns about the environment in the 1960s.*

warned that environmental contamination, like nuclear weapons, threatened the survival of humankind.

In the 1960s, some Americans recognized that pollution was not the only threat to consumers. The uncritical approval of corporations in the 1950s gradually gave way to a more skeptical view of big business. As in the progressive era, Americans began to resent corporations' treatment of customers. In 1965, Ralph Nader, an intense young lawyer, published a disturbing book, *Unsafe at Any Speed,* about the automobile industry. The car manufacturers of Detroit, Nader charged, cared more about style and sales than the safety of drivers and passengers. American cars did not have safety features, such as seat belts, that could save lives. Moreover, Nader reported, executives at General Motors had known about safety defects in the Chevrolet Corvair but had refused to fix them. Faced with these revelations, General Motors seemed to confirm its arrogance by trying to discredit Nader rather than promising immediately to improve the Corvair.

Television, like the automobile, was one of the main pillars of the consumer society, and like the automobile, television came under fire in the 1960s. Already tarnished by the quiz show scandals of the 1950s, the television industry absorbed withering criticism from critics in the new decade. The most damaging blow came from Newton Minow, the Chairman of the Federal Communications Commission, who called television "a vast wasteland" in 1961. Like other critics, Minow belittled the low quality of television programs and condemned the "screaming, cajoling, and offending" commercials that paid for them. Like Rachel Carson, Minow offered an apocalyptic warning about the impact of consumer society on human life. "Just as history will decide whether the leaders of today's world employed the atom to destroy the world or to rebuild it for mankind's benefit," he declared, "so will history decide whether today's broadcasters employed their powerful voice to enrich the people or debase them."

The End of "Deliberate Speed"

In the early 1960s, Americans expressed their growing discontent with television, automobiles, and pollution largely through bestsellers and polite speeches. In contrast, the civil rights movement, building since the 1940s, increasingly protested racial inequality with bold action at the grassroots. A new, younger generation of African Americans was impatient with the slow "deliberate speed" of integration that the Supreme Court had mandated in *Brown v. Board of Education.* These men and women were ready to put an end to "deliberate speed" by confronting the system of segregation in the communities of the South. In 1960, the spirit of grassroots activism inspired a wave of sit-ins and then the formation of a new civil rights organization.

The sit-ins began in Greensboro, North Carolina. On February 1, 1960, four African-American, male students from North Carolina Agricultural and Technical College politely insisted on being served at the whites-only lunch counter of the local Woolworth's store. When the white waitress refused their order, the four students, who would become known as the Greensboro 4, stayed all afternoon. Returning the next day with about 30 male and female colleagues, the Greensboro 4 were again denied service. Soon hundreds of African-American students from North Carolina A & T and other campuses, along with some white students, were besieging Woolworth's. "I felt," concluded Franklin McCain, one of the Greensboro 4, "as though I had gained my manhood."

The lunch counter sit-in resembled the protests of the 1940s, but it had a far greater impact than the earlier demonstrations. Sit-ins spread across Greensboro and then to other southern and northern states. There were wade-ins at whites-only beaches, kneel-ins at whites-only churches, and even paint-ins at whites-only art galleries. In Greensboro, Woolworth's and other large stores allowed their lunch counters to serve African Americans. Elsewhere, the demonstrations forced reluctant whites to open up lunch counters and other facilities to African-American patrons. The demonstrations also helped produce a new civil rights organization, the Student Nonviolent Coordinating Committee. SNCC (pronounced "Snick") brought together both white and African-American young people, influenced by "Judaic-Christian traditions" and eager to create "a social order permeated by love."

The sit-ins illustrated the growing power of grassroots activism. Ordinary people, male and female, young and old, African American and white, were prepared to push courageously against the system of racial inequality. As in

Greensboro, their efforts forced some concessions from white southerners. The sit-ins also commanded the attention of white liberals across the country.

The Emergence of the New Liberalism

Out of power during the 1950s, liberal intellectuals and politicians, mostly Democrats, had been forced to reconsider their ideas and plans. By the 1960s, the liberals were offering a fresh agenda that responded to the discontents of the consumer society, to the civil right movement, and to the continuing cold-war confrontation with Communism.

The key to this new liberalism was a powerful faith in American economic growth. To meet its domestic and international challenges, the United States needed to expand its economy more rapidly. As one liberal economist observed, growth would provide "the resources needed to achieve great societies at home and grand designs abroad." However, the liberals charged, the Eisenhower administration had failed to expand the economy enough in the prosperous 1950s. Eisenhower's policies, declared another liberal economist, "have cost the United States its world leadership and gravely threatened its survival as a nation."

Liberal economists such as Leon Keyserling and John Kenneth Galbraith were confident that greater growth could be achieved in the 1960s. They believed the principles of the British economist John Meynard Keynes held the key to prosperity. By manipulating its budget, they reasoned, the federal government could keep the economy growing. The right amount of taxes and expenditures would ensure full employment, strong consumer demand, and a rising gross national product.

Growth alone would not make America great, the liberals cautioned. A society devoted mainly to piling up personal wealth and spending it on consumer goods was fundamentally flawed. Economic growth had to be used to create a better, more satisfying life for all Americans. Because the private sector could not solve pressing national problems, the federal government had to step in. The Eisenhower administration, liberals maintained, had neglected its duty to use government power to improve society. Now the federal government, making use of the country's wealth, needed to deal more actively with poverty, racial inequality, pollution, housing, education, world Communism, and other problems.

The new liberalism was partly an extension of the New Deal and the Fair Deal. Like the liberals of the 1930s and 1940s, liberals at the start of the 1960s believed in using government to correct problems created or ignored by the private sector. They also remained staunchly anti-Communist.

Nevertheless, the new liberalism differed from the old in important ways. New Dealers, faced with the worst economic depression in American history, had worried most of all about maintaining prosperity; the new liberals almost took prosperity for granted. They were sure that the economy could pay for a host of reforms. The old liberals had feared particularly that big business and class conflict posed dangers for the United States. Their successors, watching the civil rights struggle in places like Greensboro, generally saw racial divisions as the greatest domestic problem facing the country. Most of all, the new liberalism rested on a powerful feeling of confidence. Sure of America's prosperity and power, liberals in the 1960s felt they could intervene decisively in the problems of the nation and the world.

The Presidential Election of 1960

Out of power in the 1950s, liberals had a golden opportunity in the presidential election of 1960. The contest seemed to offer a clear choice between a vaguely liberal future and the status quo. On one side, the Democratic nominee, Senator John F. Kennedy of Massachusetts, was open to the liberals' agenda and shared their optimism. Only 42 when he announced his candidacy, Kennedy was youthful, energetic, and charismatic. Born to wealth and educated at Harvard University, he was the first Roman Catholic nominated for the presidency by a major party since Al Smith in 1928. As the captain of a Navy patrol torpedo boat in the Pacific, Kennedy had become a hero during World War II. Back home, he had won election first to the House of Representatives and then to the Senate. Although Kennedy compiled an undistinguished record in Congress, he promoted a sense of expectation. The candidate exuded, said one of his speechwriters, "the promise, almost limitless in dimensions, of enormous possibilities yet to come."

Kennedy gave voice to that promise during the campaign. Rejecting "the safe mediocrity of the past," he wanted to take the nation beyond the liberalism of the 1930s and 1940s, as well as beyond the Moderate Republicanism of the 1950s. Americans, he explained, stood "on the edge of a New Frontier—the frontier of the 1960s—a frontier of unknown opportunities and paths, a frontier of unfulfilled hopes and threats." On that frontier, the United States needed to foster economic growth, rebuild slums, end poverty, improve education for the young, and enhance retirement for the old.

In contrast, Kennedy's Republican opponent, Vice President Richard Nixon of California, seemed to live on the old frontier of the 1950s. He represented the cautious Eisenhower administration that favored balanced budgets and limited government rather than bold programs and dynamic economic growth. Like Kennedy, the Republican candidate aggressively opposed Communism, but Nixon did not talk about life on the "New Frontier." As a result, the campaign presented an apparent choice between maintaining the stability of the 1950s and exploring an exciting but unclear liberal future.

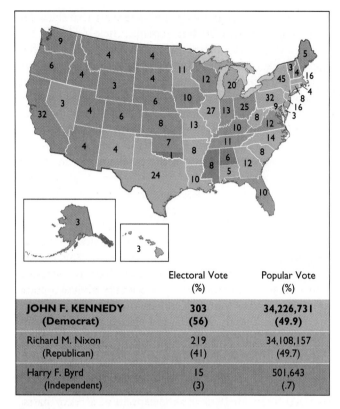

	Electoral Vote (%)	Popular Vote (%)
JOHN F. KENNEDY (Democrat)	**303** **(56)**	**34,226,731** **(49.9)**
Richard M. Nixon (Republican)	219 (41)	34,108,157 (49.7)
Harry F. Byrd (Independent)	15 (3)	501,643 (.7)

Map 28-1   The Presidential Election, 1960.
Democrat John F. Kennedy's clear margin in the electoral vote belies just how narrowly he outpolled Republican Richard M. Nixon in the popular vote.

Kennedy's stirring rhetoric did not produce a great victory in 1960. In fact the election was the closest presidential contest in history. Kennedy polled 49.7 percent of the vote to Nixon's 49.5 percent (see Map 28-1). Although Kennedy's Catholicism drove away some voters, he managed to keep much of the Democratic New Deal coalition of liberals, workers, and African Americans together. Still, Kennedy won by less than 120,000 votes. But as is often the case in presidential politics, a close election had large consequences. However narrowly, the voters had banished Nixon and the Eisenhower era. They had turned instead to a Democrat, influenced by liberal ideas, who was eager to explore the New Frontier.

Kennedy's Unfulfilled Promise

From the first moments of his presidency, Kennedy voiced the confident liberal faith in America's unlimited power and responsibility. "Let every nation know," he declared in his inaugural address in January 1961, "whether it wishes us well or ill, that we shall pay any price, bear any burden, meet any hardship, support any friend, oppose any foe to assure the survival and the success of liberty. This much we pledge—and more." Kennedy's extravagant promise per-

fectly captured the optimistic spirit of the early 1960s. So did the dramatic escalation of the space race.

The exploration of space, the ultimate frontier, seemed like an ideal occupation for confident Americans in the 1960s. Moreover, the space race allowed Kennedy to reject the cautious Eisenhower policies of the 1950s and to confront the Soviet challenge. As president, Eisenhower had opposed proposals to send an American spaceship to the moon. Meanwhile, the Soviet space program had continued to forge ahead. In April 1961 the Soviet Union sent up the first astronaut to orbit Earth. The next month the National Aeronautics and Space Administration (NASA) managed only to launch the astronaut Alan Shepard in the Mercury capsule *Freedom Seven* for a brief, suborbital flight. Once again Americans feared "that the wave of the future is Russian."

The Kennedy administration responded with dramatic rhetoric and the abundant resources of the growth economy. Insistent on "beating the Soviets," the president boldly pledged to land "a man on the moon . . . before the decade is out." With 60,000 workers and billions of dollars, the Apollo program began. In February 1962 astronaut John Glenn, aboard the Mercury capsule *Friendship Seven*, became the first American to orbit Earth. That year the United States launched Telstar, the first of a series of sophisticated communications satellites that would send and receive telephone calls and television pictures. In all, the space program mixed practical achievements such as Telstar with less practical, more symbolic gestures such as manned space flights.

That mixture of style and substance reflected the Kennedy administration as a whole. The president maintained a dynamic, energetic image, but his administration, hampered by a weak electoral mandate, did not venture too far out onto the liberal New Frontier.

How much Kennedy might have accomplished would never be known. On a trip to Texas, the president rode in an open limousine, past cheering crowds in Dallas, on Friday, November 22, 1963. As the motorcade drove by the Texas Book Depository building at 12:33, three shots rang out. Two bullets tore through Kennedy's throat and skull. Doctors pronounced him dead at a Dallas hospital half an hour later. That afternoon, police arrested Lee Harvey Oswald, a worker in the book depository, for the shootings. A quiet former Marine, Oswald had spent time in the Soviet Union and married a Soviet citizen. Two days later, as police transferred him from one jail to another, he was shot and killed at point-blank range by Jack Ruby, the troubled owner of a local nightclub.

Americans were shocked and numbed by the events that began on November 22nd and culminated with Kennedy's burial in Arlington National Cemetery on November 25th. For many it was inconceivable that so vigorous a man, representing such a powerful nation, could be killed. Some Americans could only believe the assassina-

The Kennedy assassination, November 22, 1963. Jacqueline Kennedy tries to help her mortally wounded husband, John F. Kennedy, as his motorcade drives through Dallas.

tion was the product of a dark conspiracy hatched by Cuban exiles, organized crime, conservative Texans, or even the CIA. There was never any proof of such a plot. A hurried investigation of the assassination, chaired by Chief Justice Earl Warren of the Supreme Court, concluded that Oswald had acted alone, but the Warren Commission never persuaded the many Americans who believed that Oswald could not possibly have fired all the shots that afternoon in Dallas.

The presidency of John Kennedy, little more than 1,000 days long, left a sad sense of unfulfilled promise. To many Americans, Kennedy's White House seemed like "Camelot," the royal seat of the mythical English King Arthur who led the Knights of the Round Table before his tragic death in battle. The reality of the New Frontier was less magical. Kennedy gave voice to the new liberalism, but he seldom translated liberal ideas into action. In the difficult, tumultuous years ahead, many Americans would suspect that things might have been different if Kennedy had lived, but Kennedy was a man of his party and of his time. It is hard to believe that he would have acted much differently from any other liberal Democratic leader in the heady, confident 1960s.

Lyndon Johnson's Mandate

In background and personality, the new president, Lyndon Johnson, seemed far different from his slain predecessor. Johnson was born into modest circumstances, not wealth. He made his own fortune, thanks largely to political con-

nections, instead of inheriting it from his father. Like Kennedy, Johnson served in the Navy during World War II, but he never became a war hero. A tall, powerful presence, Johnson was never an eloquent public speaker or a charismatic figure. His family lacked the polish and glamour of the Kennedys. He himself was often blunt and crude, rather than cool and suave, but the Texan did become an especially effective legislator, who knew better than Kennedy how to bully and cajole Senate colleagues into making a deal.

Despite the obvious differences in style and background, there were more fundamental similarities between Johnson and Kennedy. As president, Johnson stressed continuity with the Kennedy administration. He kept the slain president's cabinet officers. In fact, Johnson and Kennedy had much the same outlook. Both were members of the Democratic Party that engineered the New Deal, won World War II, and fought the cold war. Johnson, like Kennedy, shared the liberals' sense of limitless possibility for the United States. "We're the richest country in the world, the most powerful," Johnson declared. "We can do it all."

Johnson seemed to feel he could do it all after his landslide victory in the presidential election of 1964. The contest gave voters an unusually clear choice between competing visions of the American political economy. Johnson plainly stood for activist government, growth economics, and the rest of the new liberalism. His Republican opponent, Senator Barry Goldwater of Arizona, just as plainly stood for an emerging brand of conservatism. From 1936 to 1960 the Republican Party had chosen relatively moderate presidential candidates who had made an uncomfortable peace with the New Deal, but Goldwater flatly opposed liberal domestic policy, including civil rights and activist government. "We have gotten where we are," he declared, "not because of government, but in spite of government."

It was not much of a contest. Tanned, charismatic, and eloquent, Goldwater was too outspoken for many voters. The Johnson campaign portrayed him as a dangerous radical who would gut liberal programs and perhaps start a war. Johnson, in contrast, was supposed to be a statesman and a man of peace. The president managed a greater victory than Franklin Roosevelt had ever enjoyed. He won 61.1 percent of the popular vote, 44 states, and 486 electoral votes. Moreover, the Democrats increased their majorities in the House and Senate. Goldwater represented the wave of the future; by 1980 his views would not seem extreme. But in 1964 it was Johnson who appeared to speak for the mass of Americans.

Implementing the Liberal Agenda

In the 1960s the federal government attempted to create what Lyndon Johnson called the "Great Society," "a society of success without squalor, beauty without barrenness, works of genius without the wretchedness of poverty." With leadership from Kennedy and especially from Johnson, the Democratic-controlled Congress carried out most of the liberal agenda. A wave of new laws—the most important body of legislation since the New Deal—responded to the mounting discontents of the consumer society. The programs of the Great Society aimed to wipe out poverty and enhance the quality of life for all Americans. At the same time, the liberal majority on the Supreme Court afforded new protections for individual rights. By 1967 the principles of the new liberalism, turned into law, were transforming American government and society.

Declaring War on Poverty

The abolition of poverty was one of the most basic and ambitious goals of the Great Society. For liberals, the persistence of poverty amid prosperity stood as a chief failure of the consumer society and an embarrassment for the United States around the world.

Liberals argued that the poor needed help from the federal government. Because the private sector had failed to wipe out poverty, Washington had to step in. The government's main task was to help the poor become more productive workers who could contribute to economic growth. Increasing the productivity of the poor was not a simple matter, however. Liberals contended that the battle against poverty would have to include improved housing, education, health, and job opportunities, as well as job training.

Kennedy did support some modest antipoverty measures. In 1961 he signed into law the Area Redevelopment Act to help revive depressed areas such as the Appalachian countryside and the textile towns of New England. He also signed the Omnibus Housing Act to clear slum housing and bring urban renewal to inner cities. But, as Kennedy realized, these measures were not enough to wipe out poverty.

Declaring its "unconditional war on poverty," the Johnson administration embraced a much broader range of liberal programs. In 1964 it won congressional approval of the Economic Opportunity Act, which created an independent federal agency, the Office of Economic Opportunity (OEO), to spend nearly a billion dollars on a cluster of antipoverty programs. The OEO managed Volunteers in Service to America (VISTA), whose workers tried to teach literacy and other skills in impoverished areas. It ran

A triumphant President Lyndon B. Johnson shows off his signature on one of the floods of congressional bills that made up his ambitious reform program, the Great Society.

the Job Corps, a version of the New Deal's Civilian Conservation Corps, which taught necessary job skills to poor youth, and the OEO implemented Community Action Programs (CAPs), which encouraged the poor to organize themselves in American cities. By supporting the "maximum feasible participation" of the poor, the CAPs, unlike other poverty programs, had the potential to change the political economy by redistributing power away from local officials.

In 1965 and 1966 Congress continued the war on several fronts. To help feed the poor, the government established an expanded food stamp program. To help educate the poor, it created the Head Start Program, which provided both early schooling and meals and medical exams for impoverished preschool-aged children. To protect the rights of the poor, the Legal Services Program brought lawyers into slums. To improve urban life, the Model Cities Program targeted 63 cities for slum clearance and redevelopment. Congress also created the Department of Housing and Urban Development in 1965 and the Transportation Department in 1966 partly to help manage antipoverty programs.

The War on Poverty was at least a partial success. Mainly because of the ongoing economic boom, the percentage of people living below the poverty line decreased to 13 percent by 1970. But that meant that 25 million Americans were still poor, despite the expenditure of billions of dollars. Moreover, poverty was unevenly distributed. About a third of African Americans and a quarter of Americans of Spanish origin were impoverished as the 1970s began. Some programs of the War on Poverty were less successful than others. Some, like the CAPs, were controversial because they took power away from white political leaders in the cities. Still, the liberal War on Poverty made a significant, enduring difference in American life.

Improving the Quality of Life

Johnson wanted the Great Society to improve the quality of life for all Americans. Beginning in 1964, the president proposed and Congress enacted measures affecting health care, consumer protection, education, and culture. As liberals intended, these programs used the fruits of economic growth to furnish more security, opportunity, and cultural enrichment for the nation.

One of the fundamental commitments of New Deal liberalism was to provide greater security for Americans, to protect them from some of the shocks and uncertainties of capitalism. However, liberals had long been unable to win acceptance of federally subsidized health insurance that would guarantee medical care for all citizens. The Great Society took a major step toward national health insurance when Congress created Medicare in 1965. This program provided the elderly with insurance coverage for doctors' bills, surgery, and hospitalization. At the same time Congress created Medicaid, an antipoverty program that authorized the federal government to help the states provide medical care to welfare recipients and other members of the nonworking poor. As a result of Medicare and Medicaid, fewer Americans had to worry about their long-term access to health care.

To give Americans more security, the Johnson administration also dealt with the issue of consumer protection. Amid the uproar over Ralph Nader's revelations about the

Corvair, Congress passed the National Traffic and Motor Vehicle Safety Act of 1966, which set the first federal safety standards for automobiles. At the same time, Congress passed the Highway Safety Act, which required states to establish highway safety programs.

Along with more security, the Great Society tried to provide Americans with more opportunity. Members of the Johnson administration, like many people in American history, believed that education was essential for upward mobility. Like many leaders in the cold war, Johnson believed that improved education was essential, if the United States were to stay ahead of the Soviet Union. Accordingly, the president and Congress adopted the new liberals' belief in using the federal government to support education at all levels. The Elementary and Secondary School Act of 1965, the first major program of federal aid to public schools, channeled 1.3 billion dollars into school districts around the country. The Higher Education Act of 1965 encouraged youth to attend college by offering federally insured educational loans.

To encourage the "genius" and "beauty" that Johnson wanted for America, the Great Society included programs for cultural enrichment. In 1965 Congress established the National Endowment for the Arts to fund artists, musicians, dance companies, and theaters and the National Endowment for the Humanities to support the research and writing of scholars. In an attempt to improve the "vast wasteland" of commercial television, the Public Broadcasting Act of 1967 established a nonprofit corporation to support educational and cultural programming. Before long, the Corporation for Public Broadcasting would be giving money for such commercial-free television shows as "Sesame Street."

The Great Society's programs for cultural enrichment, education, consumer protection, and medical care added up to an impressive effort to enhance the quality of life for the broad range of Americans. These programs also added up to a major change in the American political economy. As liberals intended, government claimed more authority than ever to manage many Americans' daily lives. The Great Society brought a massive expansion of the size, cost, power, and intrusiveness of the federal government (see Table 28-1).

TABLE 28-1

Expanding the Federal Government, 1955–1970					
Year	**Civilian Employees (thous.)**	**Total Spending (millions)**	**Defense (millions)**	**Space (millions)**	**Health (millions)**	**Education & Manpower (millions)**
1955	2,397	$68,509	$40,245	$74	$271	$573
1960	2,399	$92,223	$45,908	$401	$756	$1,060
1965	2,528	$118,430	$49,578	$5,091	$1,704	$2,284
1970	2,982	$196,588	$80,295	$3,749	$12,907	$7,289

Source: Historical Statistics of the United States (1976), II, 1102, 1116.

web connection

Rachel Carson

www.prenhall.com/boydston/carson

Scientist Rachel Carson published *Silent Spring* in 1962, starting the late 20th-century's environmental movement by providing people with scientific information about the food they ate, the water they drank, and the air they breathed. In particular, Carson demonstrated the unintended effects of modern chemicals such as DDT on humans and every other part of the web of nature. By the time Lyndon Johnson was president (1963–1968), much of the public knew the research existed, and their demands led to increased government regulation of applied science. Many of those regulations continue today, and have been augmented by worldwide efforts to maintain human life and quality of life on planet Earth. What was the meaning of the term "silent spring," anyway? And how did Carson's work lead to such long-lasting effects?

That expansion would be controversial for years to come. Some Great Society measures—Medicare in particular—proved to be enormously expensive. Conservatives did not welcome an enlarged federal government that intruded on the arts, education, and medicine. Along with the conservatives, some corporations resented the government's regulation of business in the name of consumer protection. Despite these concerns, the various attempts to improve the quality of life represented some of the greatest successes of the new liberalism.

Protecting the Environment

Protection of the environment was a natural issue for liberals anxious to use federal power to improve the quality of life. Here was a problem, created by the booming consumer economy, that government could solve. Johnson and the Democratic-controlled Congress shared this view. During Johnson's presidency, more than 300 pieces of legislation led to the expenditure of over 12 billion dollars on environmental programs.

The Great Society used that money to minimize damage to air and water and to protect undeveloped land. In 1963 the Clean Air Act encouraged state and local governments to set up pollution control programs. Two years later, amendments to the act established the first pollution-emission standards for automobiles. The Air Quality Act of 1967 further strengthened federal authority to deal with air pollution. Meanwhile, the Water Quality Act of 1965 and the Clean Waters Restoration Act of 1966 enabled states and the federal government to fight water pollution. To promote natural beauty, Johnson acted to preserve wildlife and to develop national parks and recreation areas. The Wilderness Act of 1964 responded to environmentalists' calls for a system of wilderness lands protected from development. Johnson's wife, Lady Bird, campaigned to limit outdoor advertising and contribute to the beautification of the nation's highways.

Preserving Personal Freedom

The new liberalism contained a paradox. Even as liberals wanted to enhance the power of the federal government, they wanted to expand individual rights. Their concern for individual rights was apparent in their support for civil rights for African Americans and in a series of decisions by the Supreme Court. During the 1960s a liberal majority on the court, led by Chief Justice Earl Warren, acted to preserve a variety of individual rights for the American people.

Several rulings by the court protected the freedom to speak out and to live free from undue governmental interference. In *New York Times v. Sullivan* in 1964, the justices encouraged free speech by making it more difficult for public figures to sue news media for libel. In addition two important decisions protected the rights of people accused of crimes. In 1963 the court ruled in *Gideon v. Wainwright* that governments had to provide lawyers to poor defendants in felony cases. Three years later the majority opinion in *Miranda v. Arizona* required police to inform individuals of their rights, including the right to remain silent and the right to have an attorney, when they were arrested.

The Warren Court also tried to protect sexual and religious freedom. In 1965 the court's decision in *Griswold v. Connecticut* threw out a state law that banned the use of contraceptives. Affirming individuals' right to privacy, the justices in effect kept government out of the nation's bedrooms. In 1963 the court also acted to prohibit mandatory prayer in the nation's public schools. The decision in *School District of Abington Township v. Schempp* prohibited state and local governments from requiring public school students to say the Lord's Prayer or read the *Bible*.

The Supreme Court's rulings on school prayer and other issues of individual rights were controversial. Some people charged that the court was "driving God out" of the classroom. Other Americans believed that the court had gone too far to protect the rights of alleged criminals. Some conservatives demanded the impeachment of Chief Justice Warren. Their anger was a testimony to the effectiveness of the Warren Court. Through its rulings, the liberal majority on the court had substantially increased individual freedom during the 1960s. Few people had yet thought much about the tension between expanding both individual rights and government power.

The decisions of the Warren Court reinforced the triumph of the new liberalism. During the Kennedy and Johnson administrations, much of the liberal agenda had been accomplished. The Great Society, in particular, dealt with the key issues of the political economy—poverty, health care, consumer protection, education, culture, and environmental damage. The most significant body of legislation since the New Deal, Johnson's program vastly expanded the reach of the federal government and promised to change the lives of Americans in many ways. The impact of the Great Society would be felt for decades to come.

Winning Civil Rights

Of all the domestic challenges confronting the Great Society, none was more dramatic and more difficult than civil rights. The fervor of the grassroots civil rights movement helped spur the new liberalism in the 1960s. Yet, as a series of confrontations made clear, many white southerners were still determined to preserve the old racial order. Civil rights activists needed allies in the federal government, but the Kennedy administration was reluctant to commit its full power to African-American civil rights. Finally, however, the Great Society produced major legislation outlawing segregation and restoring African-American voting rights in the South. The potent combination of African-American activism and federal power had won civil rights—at least on paper.

White Resistance and Federal Reluctance

The civil rights movement did not win any easy victories in the South during the early 1960s. In one location after another, at-tempts to break down segregation and promote African-American voting met with stiff, often successful, resistance from some whites. The character of white resistance became evident during the "Freedom Rides" in the spring of 1961. After the Supreme Court outlawed the segregation of interstate bus terminals, the Congress of Racial Equality (CORE) sent a small group of African-American and white "Freedom Riders" south on two buses to test the decision. The Freedom Riders met with beatings from white citizens and harassment from local authorities. Only then did a reluctant Kennedy administration belatedly send federal marshals to protect the Freedom Riders.

White resistance could prove effective, especially if there were no federal marshals around. In 1961, when SNCC started a voter-registration drive in Mississippi, where very few African Americans could vote, some white people struck back. SNCC workers were beaten, and one activist was shot. Meanwhile, SNCC fought segregation and tried to register African-American voters in the small city of Albany, Georgia. Members of the Albany Movement, as it was called, were shot at, beaten, and arrested. Martin Luther King, Jr., leader of the Southern Christian Leadership Conference (SCLC) and veteran of the Montgomery bus boycott of 1955–1956, came to Albany and got arrested too. Although the movement continued into 1962, segregation still ruled Albany.

SNCC activists resented the lack of presidential support for their work in Mississippi and Georgia. President Kennedy found himself caught in a political bind. Like earlier cold-war presidents, Kennedy understood that

The price of civil rights: Freedom Riders outside their burning bus, which was set on fire by a white mob determined to stop the desegregation of southern bus terminals in May 1961.

racial inequality damaged the United States' image abroad, but the president also knew that the civil rights issue could split the Democratic Party. By supporting civil rights for African Americans, the president risked alienating white voters.

The defiance of southern whites gradually pushed Kennedy toward action. In 1962 the white governor of Mississippi, Ross Barnett, disregarded a federal court order by personally preventing an African-American student from enrolling at the all-white University of Mississippi. When federal marshals tried to escort the student, James Meredith, to school, white students pelted them with rocks and Molotov cocktails. The rioting killed two people and wounded more than 100 marshals. Only then did Kennedy call in 23,000 federal troops to stop the violence and allow Meredith to enroll.

Two confrontations in Alabama finally forced the president's hand in 1963. In April, Martin Luther King, Jr., and the SCLC led nonviolent protests to end segregation in the Southern steelmaking center, Birmingham, perhaps the most segregated city in America. The white majority

of Birmingham kept African Americans separate and unequal. African Americans were confined to inferior schools and to the lowest-paying jobs in the steel mills. Constituting more than 40 percent of the population, African Americans made up only about 10 percent of the city's registered voters. The city's Public Safety Commissioner, Eugene "Bull" Connor, was the incarnation of the stereotypical racist white southern law enforcement officer. To win a badly needed victory in this bastion of white supremacy, King and local allies in the civil rights movement planned to boycott department stores and overwhelm the jails with arrested protesters. Calling for the end of segregation, King laid down the gauntlet to Connor and the white community. "Here in Birmingham," King warned, "we have reached the point of no return."

In the next days, "Bull" Connor's officers arrested demonstrators by the hundreds. King ignored a judge's injunction against further protests and ended up in solitary confinement. In a powerful statement, *Letter from Birmingham Jail*, King responded to critics of the demonstrations. "We know through painful experience," he

Martin Luther King, Jr., and his wife Coretta Scott King at the front of the civil rights march from Selma, Alabama, on March 30, 1965. Male and female, old and young, black and white, the marchers illustrate the diversity of the coalition that walked with linked arms and determined faces to demand the right to vote for African Americans.

wrote, "that freedom is never voluntarily given by the oppressor; it must be demanded by the oppressed." King rejected further patience: "For years now I have heard the word 'Wait!' It rings in the ear of every Negro with a piercing familiarity. This 'Wait' has almost always meant 'Never.' We must come to see . . . that 'justice too long delayed is justice denied.'" Out on bail, King and the SCLC pushed harder for justice with a "children's crusade," demonstrations by thousands of young African-American students.

Goaded by the new protests, "Bull" Connor went too far in May. His officers turned fire hoses on young demonstrators, set dogs on them, and hit them with clubs. Shocking pictures of the scenes were shown around the world and increased the pressure on the white leadership of Birmingham and on President Kennedy. Some African Americans began to retaliate by flinging bricks and bottles at Connor's men. Within days mediators from Kennedy's Justice Department arranged for a deal in which the SCLC gave up the demonstrations and local businesses gave up segregation and promised to hire African Americans. King called it "the most magnificent victory for justice we've ever seen in the Deep South." However, soon thereafter the Ku Klux Klan marched outside the city and bombs went off at the home of King's brother and at SCLC headquarters. In response, African Americans rioted in the streets of Birmingham. The violent aftermath of King's "magnificent victory" forced Kennedy to send federal troops to keep the peace in Birmingham.

Then, in June, a second confrontation in Alabama drew the president still deeper into the civil rights struggle. That month, the state's white segregationist governor, George Wallace, tried unsuccessfully to defy federal officials and stop two African-American students from enrolling at the University of Alabama at Tuscaloosa. Only then did President Kennedy take an open stand on civil rights in an eloquent televised address. Admitting that the nation faced "a moral crisis," the president proposed sweeping civil rights legislation.

Two months later, on August 28, a march on Washington brought together a crowd of nearly 200,000 people, including 50,000 whites, at the Lincoln Memorial to commemorate the 100th anniversary of the Emancipation Proclamation and to demand "jobs and freedom." The crowd epitomized the growing national constituency for civil rights. Whites and African Americans, workers and students, singers and preachers joined hands to sing the stirring civil rights anthem, "We Shall Overcome." Martin Luther King, Jr., the best-known advocate of nonviolent integration, moved the nation with his vision of racial harmony. "I have a dream," he said, "that one day . . . little black boys and black girls will be able to join with little white boys and white girls as sisters and brothers." King looked forward to "that day when *all* God's children, black men and white men, Jews and Gentiles, Protestants and Catholics, will be able to join hands and sing in the words of the old Negro spiritual, 'Free at last! Free at last! Thank God Almighty, we are free at last!'"

Kennedy's address and the March on Washington marked a turning point in the civil rights struggle. The surging grassroots movement for racial equality, with the help of intransigent white opponents like "Bull" Connor, had created broad-based support for civil rights and finally forced the federal government to act.

The Death of Jim Crow

As 1963 ended, the battle for civil rights became still more intense. In the 10 weeks after the Birmingham confrontation, 758 "racial demonstrations" led to 14,733 arrests across the United States. When a bomb killed four African-American girls in a Baptist church in Birmingham in September, African-American rioters burned stores and destroyed cars, and the police killed two more children.

The violence continued the following year: CORE, SNCC, SCLC, and the National Association for the Advancement of Colored People (NAACP) had created the Council of Federated Organizations (COFO) to press for African-American voting rights in Mississippi. Robert Moses, an African-American schoolteacher inspired by the Greensboro sit-in, led the COFO crusade that united young African-American and white activists. In the fall of 1963, COFO had nominated an African-American candidate for governor and white candidate for lieutenant governor on a Freedom Democratic Party ticket. In 1964, Moses and COFO began a campaign with African-American and white volunteers to register African-American voters and started "Freedom Schools" for African-American children. The effort, known as "Freedom Summer," met hostility from whites, including the leadership of the state Democratic Party. In June two white activists, Michael Schwerner and Andrew Goodman, and one African-American activist, James Chaney, disappeared near Philadelphia, Mississippi. They were found a month later, shot to death gangland-style. Eventually a white deputy sheriff, a local Klan leader, and five other whites were convicted of "violating the rights" of Chaney, Goodman, and Schwerner.

The violence continued in Mississippi throughout the "Freedom Summer" of 1964. Homes and churches were burned. COFO workers were arrested, beaten, and shot at, and three more were killed. "It was the longest nightmare I have ever had, those three months," concluded Cleveland Sellers of COFO.

Lyndon Johnson could not escape the events in Mississippi. In the summer of 1964, the Mississippi Freedom Democratic Party (MFDP) sent a full delegation to the Democratic National Convention in Atlantic City, New Jersey. The MFDP delegates, including the eloquent Fannie Lou Hamer, hoped at least to share Mississippi's convention seats with the whites-only Democratic Party delegation. As television cameras filmed her testimony, Hamer, the daughter of sharecroppers, told the national Democratic Party's Credentials Committee the harrowing story of how she had been jailed and beaten for trying to register African-American voters. Afraid of alienating white southern voters for the upcoming presidential election, Johnson tried to stop the publicity for the MFDP and offered the delegates two seats in the convention. "We didn't come all this way for no two seats," Hamer retorted. The MFDP delegation went away empty-handed.

Johnson and the Democratic Party were clearly not ready to share power with African-American activists, but Johnson and his liberal allies were ready to end legalized segregation. In July, with Lyndon Johnson's prodding, Congress adopted the Civil Rights Act, which outlawed racial discrimination in the theaters, schools, restaurants, and other public places where Jim Crow had ruled. The measure also set up an Equal Employment Opportunity Commission (EEOC) to stop discrimination in hiring and promotion by most businesses. Even the schools gradually became integrated. In 1964 hardly any African-American students attended schools with white students. By 1972 nearly half of African-American school children attended integrated schools.

Despite the passage of the Civil Rights Act of 1964, the quest for racial equality was far from over. Across the South, the vast majority of African Americans still did not have the right to vote. In January 1965 the SCLC and SNCC tried to force the voting rights issue with protests in the city of Selma, Alabama. Predictably, the demonstrations produced violent white opposition in Selma and helpful publicity in the North. The sight of state troopers using tear gas, cattle prods, and clubs on peaceful marchers built quick support for voting rights.

Seizing the moment, Johnson called for the end of disfranchisement. In August, Congress passed the Voting Rights Act of 1965. This powerful measure forced southern states to give up literacy tests used to disfranchise African-American voters. It also empowered federal officials to intervene in elections to make sure that African-American men and women could register to vote. In three years, Mississippi, the site of determined opposition to African-American voting, saw African-American registration increase from six to 44 percent of eligible voters.

Together with the Civil Rights Act of 1964, the Voting Rights Act transformed the social and political landscape of the South. These twin achievements of the civil rights movement and the Great Society effectively doomed Jim Crow and laid a foundation for African-American political power. However, as would soon be clear, these quintessential features of the new liberalism did not end white racism or discrimination. The struggle for racial equality was far from over.

Fighting the Cold War

The new liberalism was staunchly anti-Communist. Kennedy and Johnson were as much cold warriors as Eisenhower and Truman before them, but the New Frontier and the Great Society modified the defense and foreign policies of the 1950s in important ways. More confident about American power and wisdom, the Kennedy administration increased the nation's defense spending and international commitments. A new defense strategy, Flexible Response, expanded U. S. military alternatives. A new emphasis on confronting Communism in the Third World encouraged U. S. intervention in Africa, Asia, and Latin America. Meanwhile, Kennedy and Johnson maintained the core American commitment to containing the Soviet Union. That commitment helped to produce dangerous crises in the early 1960s.

Flexible Response and the Third World

Although Kennedy shared President Eisenhower's commitment to containing Communism, his policies differed from Eisenhower's in several important ways. Kennedy believed the nation could afford to spend more money on the military. He also abandoned the doctrine of "Massive Retaliation," Eisenhower's threat to use nuclear weapons against any Soviet aggression, nonnuclear as well as nuclear. Kennedy and his advisers preferred **Flexible Response,** a defense strategy that made it easier for the president to choose different military options, not just nuclear weapons, in dealing with the Soviets. While spending generously on nuclear weapons, the Kennedy administration built up the country's conventional ground forces, the heavily armed soldiers who would be needed to beat back a Soviet invasion of western Europe. The president also built up Special Forces—the highly trained troops, known as "Green Berets," who could fight in Third World guerilla wars. With the implementation of Flexible Response, the United States was better prepared for challenges around the world.

Kennedy also differed from Eisenhower in his greater willingness to intervene in the affairs of the Third World. This was partly a reflection of Kennedy's characteristic confidence about American power and partly a response to Soviet actions. In January 1961 Nikita Khrushchev announced Soviet support for "wars of national liberation," insurgencies against established governments in Asia, Africa, and Latin America. In reply, Kennedy used different, even contradictory strategies to keep Communism out of the Third World in the 1960s. On the one hand, his administrations reflected a sometimes idealistic desire to encourage democracy and prosperity in developing countries. On the other hand, the United States frequently helped to thwart Third World independence and democracy in the name of anti-Communism.

To stop the spread of Communism, the Kennedy administration supported **modernization** in Africa, Asia, and Latin America; that is, policymakers wanted these continents to develop capitalist, democratic, independent, and anti-Communist regimes along the lines of the American political economy. To encourage modernization, the Kennedy administration created the Peace Corps in 1961. Under the leadership of Kennedy's brother-in-law, Sargent Shriver, thousands of young volunteers worked around the world to promote literacy, public health, and agriculture. The Peace Corps reflected

the idealism and anti-Communism of many Americans in the Kennedy years. It also reflected many Americans' arrogant sense of superiority. Not surprisingly, the organization was not always welcomed by the people it was supposed to help.

To promote the modernization of Latin America, Kennedy announced the formation of the Alliance for Progress in 1961. Over the next eight years, this venture provided 20 billion dollars for housing, health, education, and economic development for poorer countries in the Western Hemisphere. Partly because Latin American governments resisted social and political reforms, development proceeded slowly (see Map 28-2).

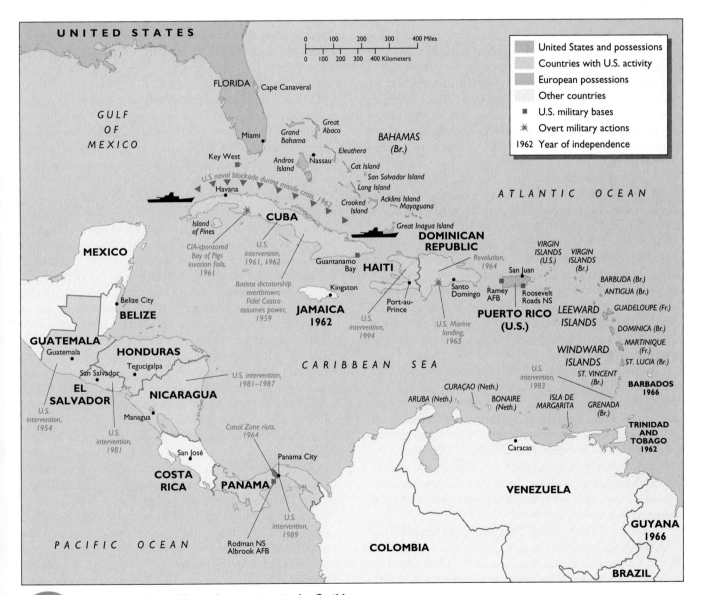

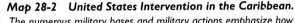

Map 28-2   United States Intervention in the Caribbean.
The numerous military bases and military actions emphasize how much the United States needed to shape Caribbean affairs during the 1960s and the whole cold war era from the 1950s to the 1980s.

The Kennedy administration did not always support independence, democracy, and development in the Third World. In some cases, the United States intervened in the domestic affairs of supposedly independent countries. In the former Belgian Congo, which became known as Zaire, the Kennedy administration used the CIA to engineer the election of an anti-Communist leader. The CIA secretly tried to manipulate elections in Chile as well. The United States also backed antidemocratic regimes if they were anti-Communist. In Argentina, Guatemala, Haiti, and Honduras, for instance, the Kennedy administration went along with the military overthrow of legitimate governments.

Cuba offered an especially dramatic example of U. S. intervention in the Third World. Taking office, Kennedy inherited a plan from the Eisenhower administration for a CIA-directed invasion of the island of Cuba by anti-Communist Cuban exiles. The president, eager to look strong, wanted to bring down Fidel Castro, the popular leader whose successful revolution was an example for the rest of Latin America. In an unsuccessful attempt to conceal U. S. responsibility, Kennedy canceled U. S. flights that would have protected the invasion. As a result, nearly all the 1,500 exiles who landed at the Bay of Pigs in April 1961 were killed or captured by Castro's well-armed troops. Embarrassed, Kennedy turned to the CIA, which launched "Operation Mongoose," an unsuccessful secret campaign to kill or depose Castro. The Cuban leader, aware of the American plot, declared himself a Communist and looked to the Soviets for help.

Kennedy's assassination made little difference for American defense and foreign policies. Despite their differences in personal style, Johnson and Kennedy looked at the world in much the same way. Like Kennedy, Johnson was a committed cold warrior. He, too, had an optimistic view of American power. Retaining most of Kennedy's key advisors, he kept Flexible Response in place in the mid-1960s.

Johnson was equally willing to undermine the independence of Third World countries. In April and May 1965, Johnson sent 22,000 American troops to the Dominican Republic to stop an increasingly violent struggle for political power. The United States had violated the sovereignty of this Caribbean nation because Johnson wanted "to prevent another Communist state in this hemisphere." The president acted without obtaining evidence of a Communist threat and without consulting Latin-American countries as required by treaty.

The U. S. intervention in the Dominican Republic and Cuba underscored the increased importance of the Third World for American policymakers in the 1960s. Anxious to stop the Soviets, the Kennedy and Johnson administrations were willing to ignore the sovereignty of Latin-American, African, and Asian countries. They were willing as well to ignore the more idealistic commitment to democracy and development reflected in the Peace Corps and the Alliance for Progress. As would become clear in Vietnam, the costs of the U. S. preoccupation with the Third World could be enormous.

Two Confrontations With the Soviets

While the United States tried to keep Communism out of the Third World, Kennedy faced two direct confrontations with the Soviet Union. The first occurred in 1961, when Khrushchev threatened to stop Western traffic into West Berlin, which was surrounded by Soviet-dominated East Germany. In response, the Kennedy administration called up reserve troops for service in West Germany, asked Congress to increase defense spending, and hinted at a preemptive nuclear strike against the Soviets. Khrushchev backed away from his threats, but in August the East German government quickly built a barbed-wire and concrete fence between East and West Berlin. By halting the embarrassing flight of East Germans to freedom in West Berlin, the so-called Berlin Wall defused the crisis. The wall also became a symbol of cold-war Europe, a visible "iron curtain" that separated Communists and non-Communists. In one of the celebrated moments of his presidency, in June 1963 Kennedy stood before the wall and pledged solidarity with the people of West Berlin. "Ich bin ein Berliner," he told the city: "I am a Berliner."

In October 1962 Kennedy entered a more dangerous confrontation with the Soviet Union. On October 15 photos from an American U-2 spy plane showed that the Soviets were building launch sites in Cuba for offensive nuclear missiles that could strike much of the United States. In secret meetings, Kennedy and his advisers debated how to force the Soviet Union to stop construction and withdraw the missiles. Rejecting an air attack, the president put ships in place on October 22 to intercept Soviet vessels bound for Cuba. That night, a somber Kennedy told a television audience about the Russian missiles and demanded their removal. Fearing a nuclear war, Americans waited for the Soviets' response. Khrushchev, unable to confront the United States in its own hemisphere, backed down. The Soviets withdrew their missiles in exchange for the removal of obsolete American missiles from Turkey.

The Cuban Missile Crisis both eased and intensified the cold war. On the one hand, the apparent close call with nuclear war sobered both sides. The Soviets and the Americans had a chance to think carefully about a nuclear conflict; neither found the prospect appealing, and the two countries sought to ease tensions. A teletype "hotline" was installed between the White House and the Kremlin so that the Soviet and American leaders could communicate quickly in another crisis. In 1963 the two powers also approved a Limited Test Ban Treaty halting tests of nuclear weapons anywhere but underground. On the other hand, the Cuban Missile Crisis made both the

The Brink of War? President Kennedy and his advisors ponder how to respond to the discovery that the Soviets were sending nuclear missiles to Cuba in October 1962.

Soviets and the Americans more determined to stand firm against each other.

The Berlin and Cuban crises were reminders that the heart of the cold war was the confrontation between the United States and the Soviet Union. That confrontation was as volatile in the 1960s as it had been in the 1940s and 1950s. The Test Ban Treaty may have marked the beginning of the end of the cold war, but the confrontation between the United States and the Soviet Union was still far from over.

The American War in Vietnam

The war in Vietnam was a decisive episode for the new liberalism and the nation in the 1960s. American participation in the conflict reflected the liberals' most basic values and assumptions—their determined anti-Communism and their almost limitless sense of national power and responsibility. Driven by these beliefs, Kennedy deepened the U. S. commitment to protect South Vietnam in the early 1960s. Picking up that commitment, Lyndon Johnson made the fateful decision to send American troops into battle in 1965, but the U. S. war effort did not go according to plan. As the fighting stretched on, the war powerfully affected the United States. Americans divided passionately over the conflict, and the economy faltered. By the end of 1967 the war, a product of liberalism, was beginning to destroy the liberals' Great Society.

Kennedy's Deepening Commitment

Kennedy inherited a deteriorating situation in South Vietnam in 1961. Ngo Dinh Diem's non-Communist government faced increasing attacks from the Viet Cong, the South Vietnamese guerrillas determined to overthrow his regime. Diem also faced a new political organization, the National Liberation Front, that was trying to mobilize his Communist and non-Communist opponents. He faced as well the continuing hostility of Ho Chi Minh's Communist government in North Vietnam. By the early 1960s, the North Vietnamese were sending soldiers and supplies over the well-concealed Ho Chi Minh Trail that ran through Laos and Cambodia into the heart of South Vietnam.

Like Eisenhower, Kennedy tried to shore up the Diem government. The United States provided Diem with plenty of advice and financial aid. Further, Kennedy sent more and more American advisers, including the Special Forces, to teach the South Vietnamese Army how to stop the Viet Cong insurgency. Before Kennedy took office, there were 900 American troops filling noncombat roles in South Vietnam. At his death, there were over 16,000.

Despite all this U. S. support, Diem's regime spiraled downward. His army could not stop the Viet Cong. A cold, unpopular ruler, he alienated his own people. In 1963 Americans were shocked by pictures of South Vietnamese Buddhists burning themselves to death with gasoline as a protest against the government. Losing confidence in Diem, the Kennedy administration did nothing to stop a military coup that resulted in the murder of the South Vietnamese leader at the beginning of November.

Having sent thousands of advisers and allowed the overthrow of Diem, the United States was more deeply involved in South Vietnam than ever before, but South Vietnam was weaker, not stronger. In the years after Kennedy's assassination, some Americans wanted to believe that the president would have kept the United States out of the Vietnam War if he had lived. Yet there was no compelling evidence that Kennedy intended to withdraw American troops in the months before his death. Instead, Kennedy's commitment had only made it more difficult for his successor to pull the United States out of Vietnam.

Johnson's Decision for War

At first, Johnson essentially followed Kennedy's policy. The new president could not tolerate the spread of Communism to South Vietnam. Like Eisenhower he believed in the domino theory, the idea that the fall of one country to Communism would lead to the fall of others. Like many Americans who witnessed the rise of Adolf Hitler in the 1930s, Johnson thought it was a mistake to tolerate any aggression. Finally, the president felt he could not turn his back on the commitments made by Kennedy, Eisenhower, and Truman. Johnson sent more aid and advisers to South Vietnam. He also stepped up American-directed covert action against the North.

It was this covert action that helped Johnson get congressional approval to act more aggressively. On August 2, 1964, a U. S. destroyer, the *Maddox,* was cruising a few miles off the coast of North Vietnam, in the Gulf of Tonkin, in order to monitor communications after a raid by the South Vietnamese Navy. When three North Vietnamese patrol torpedo boats unsuccessfully attacked the *Maddox,* the American ship sank two of the boats and damaged a third. Two days later the *Maddox,* along with a second U. S. destroyer, apparently fired mistakenly at a nonexistent North Vietnamese attack. Johnson ordered retaliatory strikes from U. S. aircraft carriers off the coast of South Vietnam and then asked Congress for the power to protect American military personnel. With only two dissenting votes, Congress approved what became known as the Tonkin Gulf Resolution, which gave the president the authority, without a declaration of war, to use military force to safeguard South Vietnam. Even though Johnson knew there had been no real threat to the United States, he had misled Congress to obtain a "blank check" to fight in Southeast Asia.

He needed it before long. While Johnson's star rose with the presidential election in November 1964, South Vietnam's fortunes continued to fall. After American soldiers were killed and wounded in a Viet Cong attack on a U. S. base in February 1965, the president authorized air strikes against North Vietnam itself. In March the U. S. began Operation Rolling Thunder, a continuing series of bombing raids on military targets in North Vietnam.

When the raids failed to deter the North Vietnamese and the Viet Cong, Johnson had a disagreeable but clear choice. If he wanted to save both South Vietnam and his reputation, he had to commit American ground troops to battle; if he did not take that drastic action, he would be blamed for the loss of South Vietnam to Communism. After a tense week of meetings with his advisers in July 1965, Johnson gave the order to send 180,000 soldiers to fight in South Vietnam. The president, armed with the Tonkin Gulf Resolution, did not ask for a congressional declaration of war.

Johnson's decision was the ultimate expression of the new liberalism. The president went to war not only because he opposed Communism, but also because he had such faith in American wealth and wisdom. Johnson believed that the United States could transform a weak, divided South Vietnam into a strong, united modern nation that could eventually survive on its own. Even though he was cautious about going to war, Johnson could not quite accept that the United States might actually lose. Moreover, he believed that the United States could afford to fight a war abroad and build a Great Society at home at the same time. "We are a rich nation," he reasoned, "and can afford to make progress at home while meeting obligations abroad." It was a fateful decision.

Fighting a Limited War

American policymakers intended to fight a limited war that would preserve an independent, non-Communist South Vietnam by the end of 1967, but the war did not go according to plan. Despite increasing U. S. casualties and troop commitments, the fighting continued as 1968 began.

Johnson and his advisers believed the United States did not need all its power to save South Vietnam (see Map 28-3). This was not intended to be another total war like World War II, in which the United States used nuclear weapons and attacked civilian targets. Instead, Vietnam was to be a limited war in which American forces led by General William Westmoreland would use conventional weapons against military targets. The goal was not to take over territory but rather to kill enough enemy soldiers to persuade the North Vietnamese and the Viet Cong to give up. The measure of American success would be the "body count," the number of dead North Vietnamese and Viet Cong. Relying on America's superior technology, Westmoreland expected the United States would prevail by the end of 1967.

It did not work out that way. Westmoreland's strategy turned out to be poorly suited to the realities of Vietnam. As Fred Downs discovered, the North Vietnamese and the Viet Cong usually escaped America's powerful forces by hiding in tunnels, fleeing through the jungle, fighting mainly at night, or retreating into Cambodia, Laos, and North Vietnam. Their strategy, as Downs realized, was to

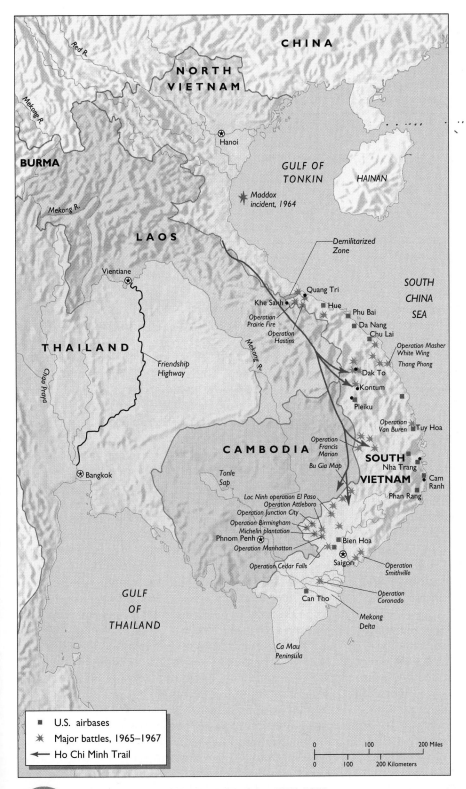

Map 28-3 America's War in Vietnam, 1965–1968.
The many military bases suggest how much power the United States had to commit to South Vietnam; the many major battles show how hard American troops had to fight to protect the South Vietnamese regime from the Viet Cong and from the North Vietnamese soldiers who traveled the Ho Chi Minh Trail.

live long enough for a frustrated U. S. military to leave South Vietnam.

Like Downs' men, American troops fought well. The body count was high, but at the close of 1967, when the war should have been ending, too many of the North Vietnamese and the Viet Cong were still alive and committed to the overthrow of South Vietnam. The American body count was high too. Over 9,000 U. S. troops died in 1967 alone. Even though there were now half a million troops in Westmoreland's command, he had not won the war. He had not lost the war, either; the United States had just about run out of time to fight (see Table 28-2).

The War's Impact at Home

The war in Vietnam had a major impact back home. An impassioned antiwar movement emerged to condemn American policy. The first opponents of American intervention in South Vietnam were pacifists who opposed all forms of war. Several even set themselves on fire, like the Buddhists in South Vietnam, to protest the war effort. Their sacrifice received little attention.

The protests of radicals, mostly students on college and university campuses, got much more notice. For these Americans, the Vietnam War epitomized the failings of the Great Society. Once again, the nation was supporting an antidemocratic regime in the name of anti-Communism. Communism in Southeast Asia, they believed, did not pose a real threat to the United States. Moreover, the war revealed how undemocratic America had become. Johnson, the radicals pointed out, had ignored the Constitution by sending troops into battle without a declaration of war. In addition, the selective-service law was forcing a repugnant choice on young men. They could either go through the draft and fight this illegal war or obtain student deferments to stay in school and prepare for empty lives in the consumer society.

TABLE 28-2

The Escalating War in Vietnam, 1960–1968

Year	U.S. Troops	U.S. Battle Deaths	S. Vietnamese Battle Deaths	N. Vietnamese & Viet Cong Battle Deaths (estimated)
1961	3,164	11	(three-year	12,000
1962	11,326	31	total =	21,000
1963	16,263	78	13,985)	21,000
1964	23,310	147	7,457	17,000
1965	184,000	1,369	11,403	35,382
1966	385,000	5,008	11,953	55,524
1967	486,000	9,378	12,716	88,104
1968	536,000	14,589	27,915	181,149

Sources: Michael Clodfelter, Vietnam in Military Statistics, 46, 57, 209 & 258; Fox Butterfield, ed., Vietnam War Almanac, 50, 54, 57, 64, 102, 132, 158, 192; Shelby Stanton, ed., Vietnam Order of Battle, 333.

Forced to rethink their basic assumptions about the United States and the cold war, a growing number of liberals and Democrats shared at least some of the radicals' analysis. These "Doves" acknowledged that the United States was backing an antidemocratic government in a brutal and apparently unnecessary war. South Vietnam was not, they admitted, vital to the economy or defense of the United States. Its fall would not lead to Communist victory elsewhere in the world, as the domino theory maintained. The conflict appeared to be a civil war among Vietnamese rather than some plot to expand Soviet or Chinese influence. Meanwhile, the war had shattered many liberals' and Democrats' overconfident view of the Great Society. The United States, confessed Senator J. William Fulbright of Arkansas in 1966, was a "sick society" suffering from an "arrogance of power." Unable to win the war, the federal government did not seem so wise and powerful, after all. For all its wealth and power, the nation apparently could not solve major problems as readily as the liberals had believed a few years earlier.

Some African Americans offered a different analysis of the war. For them, the conflict was a painful illustration of American racism. A disproportionate number of poor African Americans, unable to go to college and avoid the draft, were being expected to kill nonwhites abroad on behalf of a racist United States. First SNCC and then Martin Luther King, Jr., condemned the war. Refusing to be drafted, the boxer Muhammad Ali was sentenced to jail and stripped of his heavyweight championship in 1967. The U. S. Supreme Court then overturned his conviction for draft evasion in 1971, and he resumed his career.

The growing opposition to the war produced larger and angrier public demonstrations. In the spring of 1965 students and faculty staged "teach-ins" at college and university campuses to explore and question American policy in Vietnam. In April, 20,000 people gathered at the Washington Monument to protest the war. As the demonstrations continued, some young men risked jail by returning or burning their draft cards. On campuses, students protested the presence of recruiters trying to hire workers for defense contractors. In October 1967 the National Mobilization Committee, known as the "Mobe," staged Stop the Draft Week. As part of the protest, radicals in Oakland, California, tried to shut down an Army draft induction center, fought with police, and briefly took over a twenty-five-square-block area of the city. Meanwhile, nearly 100,000 people rallied in Washington, D. C., to protest the war.

Even as the antiwar movement developed, most Americans supported the war. To many people, the demonstrators were unpatriotic. "America—Love it or leave it," read a popular bumper sticker. "Hawks," mostly conservative Republicans and Democrats, wanted Johnson to fight harder. Nevertheless, more and more Americans had doubts about the bloody, costly war they saw on the television news. By October 1967 support for the war in one public opinion poll had fallen to 58 percent. According to the polls, only 28 percent of the people approved of Johnson's conduct of the war.

Bad economic news contributed to the public mood. Massive government spending for the war and the Great Society had overstimulated the economy. With jobs plentiful, Americans had plenty of money to spend. The strong consumer demand drove up prices, which in turn put upward pressure on wages. Anxious about inflation, the Federal Reserve contracted the money supply, which made it harder for businesses to get loans. When interest rates reached their highest levels since the 1920s, there were fears of a financial panic. The economy was no longer able to support both the Vietnam War and the Great Society. Despite liberal economic policies, the United States had not managed to create perpetual prosperity after all.

By the end of 1967 the war had put enormous stress on the Great Society. The antiwar movement was growing.

Many liberals had lost faith in the war and in some of their most cherished beliefs. The conflict undermined liberals' commitment to anti-Communism and their confidence in American power and wisdom. By dividing the nation, the conflict also undermined the support for Lyndon Johnson and the Great Society. By weakening the economy, furthermore, the Vietnam War made it harder to pay for the Great Society. The United States could not, as Johnson believed, "do it all." The new liberalism had reached its crisis.

The Great Society Comes Apart

Liberals attained power in the early 1960s because their agenda responded to popular discontent with the consumer society, but even as Congress enacted that agenda, many Americans were expressing new dissatisfactions and making new demands that liberalism could not easily accommodate. The Black Power movement, the youth rebellion, and a reborn women's movement exposed the limits of the liberal vision. In 1968 the strain of new demands, the Vietnam War, and economic realities tore apart the Great Society. That tumultuous year, marked by violence and upheaval, destroyed the fortunes of Lyndon Johnson and badly wounded the Democratic Party and the new liberalism.

The Emergence of Black Power

For many African Americans, the Great Society's response to racial inequality was too slow and too weak. As the previously described controversy over the MFDP delegation suggested, Johnson and many white Democrats were unwilling to share power with African Americans. Meanwhile, other events dramatized the gap between the promise of the Great Society and the reality of life in African America. Even as the civil rights movement reached its climax in the mid-1960s, a wave of race riots spread over the United States. When a white policeman shot a fifteen-year-old African American in the Harlem section of New York City in July 1964, angry African Americans burned and looted buildings. In August 1965 friction between white police and African-American citizens touched off a riot in the Watts section of Los Angeles, where 40 percent of the mostly African-American population lived in poverty. In five days more than 1,000 fires burned, and 34 people died. The wave of riots peaked in Detroit in July 1967 when 43 people died before U. S. Army paratroopers stopped the violence. All told, there were more than 300 race riots from 1964 to 1969 (see Map 28-4).

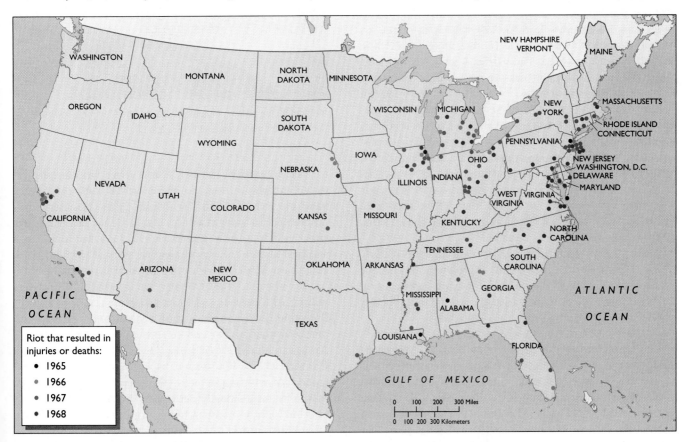

Map 28-4   Race Riots, 1965–1968.
The clusters of riots in the Northeast, Midwest, and California emphasize that race was not just a southern issue in the 1960s.
Source: Mark C. Carnes et al., Mapping America's Past, p. 217.

To many onlookers, the riots were, in the words of an official report on Watts, "senseless," but the disturbances flowed from the real frustrations of African Americans. Despite the civil rights movement's successful challenge to legalized segregation in the South, African Americans still lived with poverty and discrimination all across the country. Northern cities, the center of the riots, had been largely ignored by Martin Luther King, Jr., and other civil rights leaders. The riots signaled that the civil rights movement and the new liberalism, for all their accomplishments, had not addressed some of the most difficult problems of racial inequality.

When the civil rights movement used its standard tactics to deal with these problems, the results were disappointing. For years King and other activists had relied on nonviolent demonstrations and ties to white liberals to pursue the goal of integration, but that approach proved ineffective when King belatedly confronted racial injustice in the North. In 1965, the leader of the SCLC went north to confront "the Negro's repellent slum life" in Chicago. That summer, King joined marches protesting the de facto segregation of the city's educational system, which trapped African-American children in separate and unequal schools. King faced the determined opposition of the city's Democratic political boss, Mayor Richard Daley. Reluctant to challenge the powerful mayor, the Johnson administration would not give King real support. In 1966, King returned to lead the "Chicago Movement" to wipe out slums and win access to better housing in white neighborhoods. "Go back to Africa," white demonstrators chanted. At one protest march, white onlookers waved Confederate flags and yelled, "We want Martin Luther Coon." A rock hit King in the head. Daley accepted a compromise on fair housing but repudiated it as soon as King left town. Another King project, an attempt to promote equal economic opportunity, also foundered. Under the leadership of twenty-four-year-old Jesse Jackson, Operation Breadbasket threatened demonstrations and boycotts against businesses that refused to hire African Americans. The project produced few results. King's nonviolent tactics had failed.

The fate of the Chicago Movement and the MFDP, along with other episodes, led a growing number of African-American activists to question King's unwavering commitment to nonviolence, desegregation, and alliances with white liberals.

African Americans already had the example of a different approach to the problem of African-American/ white relations. The Nation of Islam, founded in Detroit in 1930 and headed for many years by Elijah Muhammad in Chicago, believed that whites are devils and African Americans are God's chosen people. The Black Muslims, as they were known, preached separation of the races and the self-reliance of African Americans. One of the Muslims' most powerful preachers was Malcolm X, a

Malcolm X, the militant Muslim preacher who called for black freedom "by any means necessary."

former pimp, drug pusher, and convict who angrily rejected integration and nonviolence. "If someone puts a hand on you," he said, "send him to the cemetery." He moderated his view of whites before being gunned down, apparently by Muslims, in Harlem in 1965, but Malcolm X was best known for his militant call "for the freedom of the 22 million Afro-Americans by any means necessary."

By the mid-1960s, many African Americans were willing to follow at least some of Malcolm X's example. Rejecting the longtime goal of integration, they now emphasized maintaining and celebrating a separate African-American identity. "Integration," charged Stokely Carmichael, a SNCC leader, "is a subterfuge for the maintenance of white supremacy [that] reinforces the idea that 'white' is automatically better and 'black' is by definition inferior." Now, many African Americans declared that "Black is beautiful." In asserting their distinctive identity, some African Americans accentuated their African heritage. They called themselves "Afro Americans" and

"African Americans," wore African robes and dashikis, explored African language and art, and observed the seven-day holiday Kwanzaa, based on an African harvest festival.

As they abandoned integration, African-American activists insisted on creating their own organizations. They argued that instead of working with white liberals and depending on the federal government, African-American people needed to go their own way. In 1966, SNCC and CORE ousted their white members. SNCC called particularly for the establishment of African-American businesses, schools, and political parties.

In rejecting nonviolence and integration, a number of African-American activists adopted a more militant stance that was encapsulated in the new slogan "Black Power." "The only way we gonna stop them white men from whuppin' us is to take over," Stokely Carmichael told a rally in Mississippi in June 1966. "What we gonna start saying now is Black Power!" And the crowd called back "Black Power!" The new slogan had different meanings for different people. The most radical interpretation came from the Black Panthers, who were first organized in Oakland, California, by Huey P. Newton and Bobby Seale. Dressed in black clothes and black berets, the Panthers armed themselves in order to protect their neighborhoods from white police. "The heirs of Malcolm X," Newton announced, "have picked up the gun. . . ." Newton, admiringly described by an associate as "the baddest mother-fucker ever to step foot inside of history," went to jail after a shootout with police. His successor, Eldridge Cleaver,

had to flee the country after his own police shootout. The Panthers also founded schools and promoted peaceful community activism, but they were best known in the media for their aura of violent militance.

Particularly because of the violent image of the Panthers, many Americans, African American and white, were hostile to the new slogan. For King and his allies, Black Power all too obviously meant repudiation of nonviolent integration and abandonment of the desegregationist partnership with white liberals. For many whites, Black Power stirred fears of violence. For white leaders like Richard Daley, Black Power meant giving up political authority to African Americans. For Lyndon Johnson, Black Power obviously meant a rejection of his Great Society.

The Youth Rebellion

In the 1960s many young people rebelled against adult authority and adult expectations. For most of them, the rebellion involved fairly mild demands for more freedom, particularly social and sexual freedom, on campus. For a minority of young people, the rebellion developed into an angry rejection of liberalism and the creation of an organized, radical **New Left.** For some young people, the rebellion meant replacing consumerism and conventional morality with a "counterculture," a new way of life. In all its forms, the youthful rebellion helped divide the Great Society.

By the early 1960s many students felt confined and oppressed in colleges and universities. The rapid growth of higher education after World War II had left many institutions overcrowded and impersonal. Moreover, these schools ordered students' lives through parietal rules that governed eating in dining halls, drinking alcohol, keeping cars on campus, and socializing in dorm rooms. Female students were subject to particularly strict rules, which typically included curfews.

Campuses across the country witnessed rebellions against parietal rules in the 1960s. Students were particularly impatient with the conventional sexual morality embedded in those rules. Demanding greater sexual freedom, students sharply criticized regulations that restricted the mixing of male and female students in dorms. By the end of the decade, students were even living together before marriage, to the consternation of college authorities and other adults.

Meanwhile, a much smaller number of students was beginning to see the shortcomings of colleges and universities as

"The heirs of Malcolm X have picked up the gun. . . .": armed Black Panthers stand outside a church burned by an arsonist.

symptoms of broader social problems. These youth created the New Left, a radical movement that attempted to confront liberalism and create a more democratic nation. The key organization of the New Left was Students for a Democratic Society (SDS), which emerged in 1960, as its first president observed, to produce "radical alternatives to the inadequate society of today."

During its national convention at Port Huron, Michigan, in 1962, SDS approved an "Agenda for a New Generation" that laid out the developing vision of youth troubled by racism, the cold war, and the threat of nuclear destruction. The "Port Huron Statement," as it became known, argued that American society denied people real choice and real power in their lives. The answer, SDS claimed, was "participatory democracy." The members of SDS did not believe that liberalism would promote real democracy in America. SDS did not expect much help from the old left of socialists and Communists, with their Marxist faith in the revolutionary power of the working class. Instead, the Port Huron Statement looked to students to lead the way by fighting for control of their schools.

The battle began at the University of California at Berkeley in 1964. That fall, the university's administration banned political speaking and organizing at Bancroft Way and Telegraph Avenue, the one strip of pavement where it had been allowed. When a civil rights activist was arrested for defying the ban in October, hundreds of students suddenly sat down around the police cars, effectively trapping the officers for 32 hours. After the stand-off, students created the Free Speech Movement (FSM) to deal with the administration. FSM's goal of greater student involvement in the educational process was essentially a demand for participatory democracy. When the university refused to accept that demand, students took over the main administration building. Although police arrested 773 students the next day, the administration succumbed to faculty protests and a student boycott of classes and agreed to new rules on free speech.

Americans in 1964 had never seen anything quite like the Berkeley protests. Here were privileged students, on their way to comfortable middle-class lives, condemning society, storming a building, and being dragged off by the police. Many people were infuriated; running for governor of California in 1966, the conservative former movie actor Ronald Reagan vowed to "clean up the mess at Berkeley," with all its "Beatniks, radicals and filthy speech advocates" and its "sexual orgies so vile I cannot describe them." Many younger Americans were inspired by the FSM; SDS membership rose from 2,500 in December 1964 to 10,000 in October 1965. By then, the New Left had found a perfect issue to dramatize the failings of liberalism—the Vietnam War. Student radicals became the backbone of the antiwar movement.

While the New Left flourished, young people were also creating the rebellious lifestyle that became known as the counterculture. Less politically oriented than the New Left, the counterculture challenged the conventional social values of the consumer society. By the mid-1960s, growing numbers of younger Americans were condemning conformity, careerism, materialism, and sexual repression. Not content just to attack parietal rules, youth groped toward an alternative lifestyle.

The counterculture rested on the enjoyment of rock music, drugs, and sexual freedom. Beginning in 1964, the "British Invasion," that is, the sudden popularity of the Beatles, the Rolling Stones, and other English groups, brought back a rebellious note to rock and roll. The Beatles' irreverent attitude toward authority, symbolized by their long hair, helped create "Beatlemania" in the United States. Young Americans loved the Beatles' first movie, *A Hard Day's Night* in 1964, because, a student wrote, "all the dreary old adults are mocked and brushed aside."

Rock also become more socially and politically conscious in the 1960s. Bob Dylan, Simon and Garfunkel, and other musicians rooted in folk music pushed rock music to deal with racism, nuclear weapons, and other issues. Dylan put the youthful challenge squarely to adult America: "Your sons and your daughters are beyond your command/ Your old road is rapidly aging./ Please get out of the new one/ If you can't lend a hand/ For the times they are a-changin'."

Rock music often sang the virtues of drugs and sex, two more elements of the counterculture. The use of marijuana, the hallucinogen LSD, and other drugs increased during the 1960s. Drugs appealed to the counterculture for two reasons. First, because most drugs were illegal, using them was a way of flouting adult convention. Second, drugs were a way of escaping everyday reality and finding some higher, more liberated consciousness. Sex offered a similar combination of pleasure and defiance. By celebrating and enjoying sexual intercourse outside marriage, young people could shock adults at the same time.

Many young people hoped that the counterculture would weave sex, drugs, and rock into a new lifestyle. The novelist Ken Kesey joined with his followers, the Merry Pranksters, to set up a commune outside San Francisco. Sex was part of the commune life. The commune had a lean-to known as the "Screw Shack." Drugs were part of it, too. The Merry Pranksters used drugs to synchronize with the cosmos and attain a state of ecstasy. By 1965 Kesey had created the "acid test," which fused drugs, rock, and light shows into a pioneering multimedia experience. The "acid test" helped establish the popularity of "acid rock," the "San Francisco sound" of the Jefferson Airplane and the Grateful Dead. The "acid test" also helped establish Kesey's notoriety. He soon had to flee to Mexico to avoid the law.

The purest form of the countercultural lifestyle was created by the hippies, who appeared around the nation

The counterculture comes together. The three dancers epitomize the joyful quest for freedom at the heart of the youth rebellion of the 1960s; the rest of the crowd is a reminder of how many young people sat and watched.

in the mid-1960s. Hippie culture centered especially in San Francisco where the beats had congregated in the 1950s. Rejecting materialism and consumerism, hippies celebrated free expression and free love. They wanted to replace competition and aggression with cooperation and community. One group of hippies, the Diggers, tried to transcend the consumer economy by giving away used clothes at their "free store" in Haight-Ashbury, handing out free food, and staging free concerts. By the beginning of 1967, hippie culture was in full flower. In January the Diggers held the first Human Be-In at Golden Gate Park to "shower the country with waves of ecstasy and purification." San Francisco, a newspaper concluded, had become "the love-guerrilla training school for drop-outs from mainstream America . . . where the new world, a human world of the 21st century is being constructed."

The "new world" of the hippies was not a complete departure from earlier rebellions or even from "mainstream America." The counterculture had obvious roots in the beat movement and the rebellious style of Elvis Presley and James Dean in the 1950s. The counterculture also had roots in the orthodox culture it attacked. By the close of the 1950s, adults themselves had already become ambivalent about consumerism and conventional morality. Sexual freedom for youth was encouraged partly by the greater sexual openness of mainstream culture, the Supreme Court's *Griswold* decision, and the introduction of the oral contraceptive (the "Pill") in 1960.

The counterculture also reflected a broad social unease with institutional and cultural constraints. For instance, Americans in the 1960s chafed at the authority of religious denominations. The "pop art" paintings of Andy Warhol and Roy Lichtenstein, the productions of the Living Theater, the essays of Susan Sontag, and the novels of Thomas Pynchon broke with formal, artistic conventions. In short, the counterculture formed in opposition to a mainstream, adult culture that was itself already changing. Moreover, that opposition could be exaggerated. The countercultural lifestyle itself became a form of consumerism, as young Americans flocked to buy the right clothes and record albums.

Nevertheless, the counterculture was a disruptive force in 1960s America. Like the Black Panthers, hippies were a small minority—not too many young people had the courage or the inclination to take LSD or to leave school for a commune. But like the Panthers and the other advocates of Black Power, the hippies and the counterculture deeply influenced young people and adults. The counterculture encouraged Americans to question conventional values and authority and to seek a new, less-constricted way of life.

By 1967, the New Left, the counterculture, and the other forms of youth rebellion were upsetting the Great Society. Lyndon Johnson was furious with the students who protested the Vietnam War. More generally, adults feared that young people were out of control. A society already divided by race was increasingly divided by generation.

GROWING UP IN AMERICA

Indiana University Students in the 1960s

The college students of the 1960s have been stereotyped as rebels, staging demonstrations and taking over buildings. Although radicalism flourished on such campuses as the University of California at Berkeley, the University of Wisconsin, and Columbia University, students at many schools, such as Indiana University, maintained fairly mainstream views.

Indiana University reflected the larger educational trends that encouraged radicalism. Like other schools, the school grew rapidly from 16,000 to nearly 30,000 students in the 1960s. The university also had a typically rigid set of parietal rules, including a dress code, a ban on student cars on campus, and a nightly curfew for female students.

This state of affairs did not produce much radicalism on the school's Bloomington campus. One night in 1966, 5,000 male students staged a panty raid and ran through every women's dormitory on campus, shouting, "We want panties!" A chapter of Students for a Democratic Society (SDS) formed in 1965, but there were never more than 200 or 300 activists on campus. Many Indiana students opposed the group's stand against the Vietnam War.

In 1965 the student government staged a "Bleed-In," so that students and faculty could give blood for wounded soldiers in Vietnam. When 200 radicals heckled Secretary of State Dean Rusk during a campus speech in October 1967, 14,000 students signed an apology.

SDS had more success when it promoted participatory democracy by campaigning against parietal rules. In 1967 an SDS leader beat out fraternity candidates to become student-body president with the slogan "Student Power Now." The broad-based movement against parietal rules progressed until the university finally abandoned the women's curfew in 1968. "The I.U. Chastity Belt is Withering," proclaimed the student paper.

A divided campus: a crowd of Indiana University students with some signs against U. S. intervention but at least one supporting the war effort.

Racial discrimination was another feature of student life. Representing only two or three percent of the student body, African Americans were an isolated minority on campus. Banned from white fraternities and sororities, African-American students had created three fraternities of their

The Rebirth of the Women's Movement

In the 1960s, the organized women's movement was reborn. Responding to their difficult, second-class roles in cold-war America, women pressed again for equal rights and opportunities. The New Frontier and the Great Society, however, barely addressed the issues raised by **second-wave feminism** in America. When their complaints produced little action, activist women created liberal and radical feminist organizations.

By the 1960s American women were reacting against the difficult social roles enforced on them after World War II. More women than ever went to college, but they were still not expected to use their education to pursue long-

"Victory": Indiana students demonstrate in support of U. S. war effort in Vietnam.

Sustaining the war effort: Indiana students line up to give blood for American soldiers in Vietnam.

own. Most African-American students did not want, as they said, to "be white," but they deeply resented the discrimina-tory practices of the university-sanctioned "Greek" system. African-American students were no exception to the fairly conservative culture of the university. SNCC had no

presence on the campus. In 1968, however, the Afro-American Students Association helped lead a sit-in at the university's annual "Little 500" student bicycle race that forced fraternities to give up their ban on African-American members.

term careers. More women than ever worked at least part time for wages outside the home, but they were still ex-pected to devote themselves to home and family. Women also had to put up with the continuing double standard of sexual behavior, which granted men more freedom to seek sexual gratification outside of marriage. As the new decade began, educated, relatively privileged, middle-class

women, in particular, began to question their second-class status. In part, they were inspired by the example of the civil rights movement.

Two best-selling books reflected these women's com-plaints. In *The Feminine Mystique* (1963), journalist Betty Friedan described "the problem that has no name," that is, the growing frustration of educated, middle-class wives and mothers who had subordinated their own aspirations for meaningful careers outside the home to the needs of men. Caught in "the housewife trap," these women had been conditioned by educators and experts to accept unsatisfying lives.

While Friedan criticized unequal career opportunities, the journalist Helen Gurley Brown rejected unequal sexual opportunities in her book, *Sex and the Single Girl* (1962). Brown did not challenge male sexual ethics, just as Friedan did not challenge male careerism. Instead, like Friedan, Brown wanted equal opportunity for women, both in and out of marriage. She explained, coyly, that "nice, single girls *do.*" To spread her female sexual philosophy, much as Hugh Hefner had spread his male version, Brown became the editor of the new *Cosmopolitan* magazine in 1965.

The complaints of Friedan, Brown, and other women received attention but little action from men. The Kennedy and Johnson administrations did not do much to solve "the problem that has no name." In 1961 Kennedy appointed the Presidential Commission on the Status of Women, chaired by Eleanor Roosevelt. The commission's cautious report, *American Women,* reaffirmed women's domestic role but also documented public gender discrimination. In 1963 Congress passed the Equal Pay Act, which mandated the same pay for men and women who did the same work, but the measure, full of loopholes, had little impact on women's comparatively low wages and salaries. A year later, Title VII, a little-noticed provision of the Civil Rights Act of 1964, prohibited employers from discriminating on the basis of sex in hiring and compensating workers. Yet the Equal Employment Opportunity Commission (EEOC) did little to enforce the law.

Male insensitivity and inaction soon pushed women to organize. In 1966 Betty Friedan and a handful of other women activists, angry at the EEOC, formed the National Organization for Women (NOW). Although frustrated with the Great Society, Friedan and the founders of NOW expressed essentially liberal values. They saw NOW as "a civil rights organization," a female version of the National Association for the Advancement of Colored People. NOW's "Bill of Rights" for women focused on government action to provide rights and opportunities. Although Friedan and other liberal feminists focused primarily on winning equal treatment for women in public, NOW also demanded access to contraception and abortion.

NOW's platform was too radical for many women and not radical enough for others. Some younger women, particularly activists in the civil rights movement and the New Left, wanted more than liberal solutions to their problems. They were inspired by the crusades for rights and democracy, and they were frustrated by the male members of these movements, who all too often consigned women to second-class status.

By the fall of 1967, activists were forming new groups dedicated to "women's liberation." These radical feminists took a stronger, more critical stance than the liberal women toward sexual inequality. Influenced by the New Left, some radicals blamed the capitalist system for the oppression of women, but a growing number of radicals saw men as the problem. "[F]or a time at least, men are the enemy," insisted a Florida feminist. Like African Americans in the Black Power movement, radical women talked less about rights and more about power. Their slogan was "Sisterhood Is Powerful!" Like the Black Power movement and the New Left, radical feminists were less interested in collaboration with male liberal politicians.

Fairly small in number, radical feminists nevertheless commanded a good deal of public attention. In September 1968 New York Radical Women organized a protest against the annual Miss America pageant in Atlantic City, New Jersey. Miss America, they insisted, was a "Degrading Mindless-Boob-Girlie Symbol." The pageant was an act of "Thought Control" intended "to further make women oppressed and men oppressors; to enslave us all the more in high-heeled, low-status roles." The protesters arranged to throw bras, girdles, make-up, and other "women-garbage" into a "Freedom Trash Can." Then they crowned a sheep "Miss America."

Radical feminism, like the rest of the reborn women's movement, was just emerging

Protesting the Miss America pageant in Atlantic City, New Jersey, in 1968: Radical feminists confront a male onlooker with the pageant's objectification of women.

in 1968, but it was already clear that activist women faced considerable hostility. Onlookers at the Miss America protest called the women "lesbians" and "screwy, frustrated women." Not surprisingly, men were generally uncomfortable with radical feminism, but even male liberals had not bothered to think much about NOW's liberal brand of feminism. Second-wave feminism, like Black Power and the New Left, did not fit comfortably within the political economy of white, male-dominated new liberalism.

1968: A Tumultuous Year

In 1968 the stresses and strains of the Great Society came together to produce the most tumultuous year in the United States since World War II. Unexpected military events in Vietnam forced Johnson to reduce the American war effort and give up his plans for re-election. Unable to pay for more Great Society programs, the president could not accommodate the demands of angry groups. The tensions in the country produced demonstrations, riots, and two stunning assassinations. Marking the end of the liberal ascendancy, Vice President Hubert Humphrey, the Democratic nominee, lost the presidential election in November.

While Fred Downs lay wounded in an Army hospital in Japan, the Viet Cong and North Vietnamese launched bold, sometimes suicidal attacks all over South Vietnam on the first day of Tet, the Vietnamese lunar new year. Although U. S. and South Vietnamese forces inflicted punishing losses on the attackers, the Tet Offensive shocked Americans. If the United States was winning the war, how could the North Vietnamese and the Viet Cong have struck so daringly in so many places, including the U. S. embassy in Saigon? Many Americans who had supported the decision to send troops into battle in South Vietnam now began to believe the war was unwinnable.

The Tet Offensive doomed Johnson's increasingly troubled administration. The president needed to send reinforcements to Vietnam, but he knew public opinion would oppose the move. As it was, he could not even pay for more troops. The economy would not support both the war and the Great Society any longer. The political situation was bad, too. On March 12 Senator Eugene McCarthy of Minnesota, an antiwar candidate with little money and seemingly no chance of success, nearly beat Johnson in New Hampshire's Democratic primary. Four days later, Senator Robert Kennedy of New York, the younger brother of John Kennedy, announced his own candidacy for the Democratic nomination. The charismatic Kennedy, opposed to the war, would be a formidable opponent for the president. Besieged by the war, the economy, and the presidential campaign, Johnson went on television the night of March 31. He told a surprised nation that he had ordered a halt to the bombing of much of North Vietnam. He also indicated his willingness to talk peace with the North Vietnamese. Then Johnson, drained by events, announced that he would not run again for president.

Johnson had painfully accepted the new limits on the war, the economy, and his own career. He had to accept limits on his Great Society, too. During 1968, congressional leaders forced him to agree to spending cuts for Great Society programs. Liberals were increasingly arguing that the federal government needed to guarantee a minimum income and not just training and opportunity to the poor, but Johnson did not have the money or the clout for major new welfare programs. He did not have the money for new initiatives to improve race relations; he did not have the money for the space program, that symbol of great liberal dreams, either. The president continued the Apollo program only at the cost of abandoning other space projects. The Great Society was coming back down to earth.

Meanwhile, the United States was torn by upheaval and violence. In the first six months of 1968, about 39,000 students carried out 221 demonstrations at 101 colleges and universities. In the spring, Martin Luther King, Jr., went to Memphis, Tennessee, to support striking African-

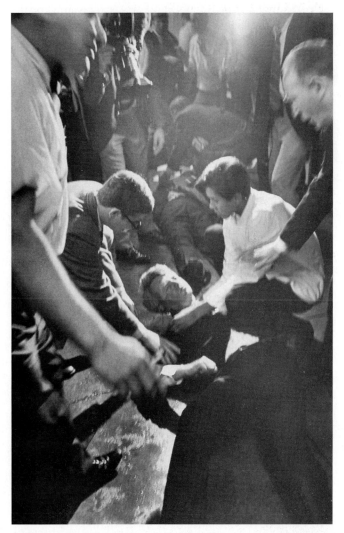

A violent society: Robert F. Kennedy lies dying from an assassin's bullet on the floor of a Los Angeles hotel on the night of his victory in the 1968 California presidential primary.

American and white sanitation workers. As King stood on the balcony of his motel on April 4, a white man, James Earl Ray, shot and killed him. King's assassination set off riots in more than 100 cities. It took 75,000 troops to quell the riots. Twenty-one thousand people were arrested. Forty-one African Americans and five whites died. African Americans "have had all they can stand," two African-American psychologists wrote.

The violence soon spread to the presidential campaign. After winning the California Democratic primary on the evening of June 5, Robert Kennedy was shot in a Los Angeles hotel by Sirhan Sirhan, a troubled Palestinian. Kennedy's death the next morning left Eugene McCarthy to contest the Democratic presidential nomination with Vice President Hubert Humphrey of Minnesota, who still supported the American war effort in Vietnam. Humphrey won the nomination at the Democratic convention in Chicago in August, but the party's deep division was obvious. Outside the convention hall, Mayor Daley's police battled in the streets with antiwar demonstrators.

Meanwhile, the Republican Party had given its presidential nomination to Richard Nixon, the man who lost to John Kennedy in 1960. A critic of the Great Society, Nixon promised to end the Vietnam War and unify the country. Nixon also tried to exploit the nation's social divisions with promises to speak for "the forgotten Americans, the nonshouters, the nondemonstrators." Running as a third-party candidate, the segregationist former governor of Alabama, George Wallace, reached out even more bluntly to middle- and working-class whites who increasingly resented African Americans and their liberal benefactors.

Like 1960, the 1968 election produced a narrow outcome with large consequences (see Map 28-5), but this time, Nixon was the winner. Although Humphrey gained in the polls by distancing himself from Johnson's Vietnam policy, the vice president could not overcome the troubles of the Democratic Party and the Great Society. Nixon attracted 43.4 percent of the popular vote to Humphrey's 42.7 and Wallace's 13.5. Running strongly in every region of the country, Nixon piled up 301 electoral votes. Although the Democrats retained control of the House and

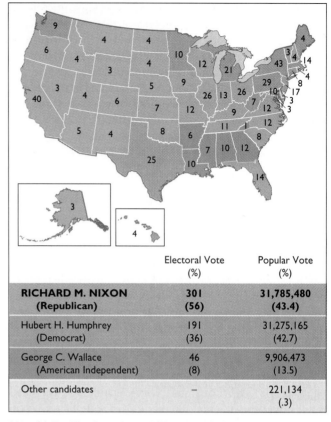

	Electoral Vote (%)	Popular Vote (%)
RICHARD M. NIXON (Republican)	**301** (56)	**31,785,480** (43.4)
Hubert H. Humphrey (Democrat)	191 (36)	31,275,165 (42.7)
George C. Wallace (American Independent)	46 (8)	9,906,473 (13.5)
Other candidates	–	221,134 (.3)

Map 28-5   The Presidential Election, 1968.
Like the 1960 election, this was another close contest with widespread consequences. But this time, former Vice President Richard M. Nixon was the winner.

Senate, the liberals' eight-year hold on the White House had been broken.

Nixon's victory ended a tumultuous year for the United States. Over the course of 1968, the new liberalism had finally lost its hold on the nation. The Johnson administration could not handle the demands of African Americans, youth, and women. It could not win the war in Vietnam or stabilize the economy. The violence of 1968 testified to the frustration of many Americans with the Great Society, as did the outcome of the presidential election.

Conclusion

In 1960 Nixon's defeat signaled the rise of the new liberalism. In 1968 his victory marked liberalism's fall. The end of liberal dominance was bound up in the end of illusions about limitless American power. John Kennedy's confident America—able to "pay any price, bear any burden, meet any hardship, support any friend, oppose any foe"— had vanished. By 1968 the American economy could no longer "pay any price." The United States could not suc-

cessfully support its friends in South Vietnam. It could not defeat the North Vietnamese and the Viet Cong. The government could not fulfill the ambitious plans of the New Frontier and the Great Society. Instead, the nation was deeply divided by generation, race, and gender. The assassinations of Robert Kennedy and Martin Luther King, Jr., dramatized the breakdown of the political system. These murders denied Americans the most fundamental democratic right, the right to choose their own leaders. The liberal approach to political economy depended on the state to reform and regulate society, but now the American state no longer seemed to work. The Great Society was certainly over. The buoyant sense of unlimited wealth, power, and wisdom that supported the new liberalism was gone.

Back in the United States in the spring of 1968, Fred Downs had to deal with his own losses. His left arm, his confidence, and his plans were gone. At a military hospital in Denver, he slowly and painfully remade his life within a new set of limits. He had to learn how to use a prosthetic arm, and he had to accept the break-up of his marriage. He had to learn how to deal with the divided, angry America of 1968. On the street one day, a man pointed to the hook sticking out of Downs' left sleeve. "Get that in Vietnam?" the man asked. Downs said he had. "Serves you right," the man snapped, and walked away. The United States, like that man, would have a difficult time coming to terms with the events of the 1960s.

CHRONOLOGY

1960 Lunch counter sit-ins at Greensboro, N. C.
Founding of Student Nonviolent Coordinating Committee (SNCC)
Formation of Students for a Democratic Society (SDS)
John Kennedy elected president

1961 Bay of Pigs invasion of Cuba
First U. S. suborbital space flight, by Alan Shepard
Freedom Rides
Beginning of SNCC voter-registration drive in Mississippi
Beginning of Albany Movement in Albany, Georgia
Erection of Berlin Wall
Creation of Peace Corps

1962 Michael Harrington, *The Other America*
Rachel Carson, *Silent Spring*
First U. S. orbital space flight, by John Glenn
Integration of University of Mississippi
Cuban Missile Crisis

1963 Betty Friedan, *The Feminine Mystique*
Clean Air Act
Limited Test Ban Treaty
Civil rights protests in Birmingham, Alabama
Civil rights march on Washington, D. C.
Assassination of Ngo Dinh Diem
Assassination of John Kennedy in Dallas
Lyndon B. Johnson succeeds to the presidency

1964 Beatlemania
Wilderness Act
Civil Rights Act of 1964
Announcement of Lyndon Johnson's "War on Poverty"

Economic Opportunity Act
Free Speech Movement
Harlem race riot
Tonkin Gulf incidents
Lyndon Johnson's landslide election as president

1965 Decision to send U. S. troops into battle in South Vietnam
Voting Rights Act of 1965
Creation of Medicare and Medicaid
Elementary and Secondary School Act
Water Quality Act
Watts race riot
Creation of Department of Housing and Urban Development
Creation of National Endowment for the Arts and National Endowment for the Humanities
Griswold v. Connecticut
Ralph Nader, *Unsafe at Any Speed*

1966 Founding of National Organization for Women (NOW)
Clean Waters Restoration Act
Miranda v. Arizona

1967 First "Be-In," Golden Gate Park
Air Quality Act
Public Broadcasting Act
Stop the Draft Week

1968 Tet Offensive in Vietnam
Assassination of Martin Luther King, Jr.
Assassination of Robert Kennedy
New York Radical Women's Miss America Protest
Richard Nixon elected president

Review Questions

1. What were the main values and goals of the new liberalism in the 1960s? How did 1960s liberalism differ from the liberalism of the New Deal and the Fair Deal?

2. What was the Great Society? How did its programs reflect liberal values?

3. What were the aims of the civil rights movement in the early 1960s? Was the movement successful?

4. Why did the United States go to war in Vietnam? How did the decision for war reflect liberal values?

5. Compare the Black Power movement, the New Left, and the counterculture. Did any of these want radical change for the United States?

Further Readings

Terry H. Anderson, *The Movement and the Sixties: Protest in America from Greensboro to Wounded Knee* (1995). A sweeping chronicle of the varieties of protest in the 1960s.

David Farber, *The Age of Great Dreams: America in the 1960s* (1994). Offers a readable account of the decade.

Betty Friedan, *The Feminine Mystique* (1963). Explores the plight of middle-class women that helped produce liberal feminism.

Samuel P. Hays, *Beauty, Health, and Permanence: Environmental Politics in the United States* (1987). A broad study of the emergence of the modern environmental movement.

George C. Herring, *America's Longest War: The United States and Vietnam, 1950–1975* (1996). A balanced overview of the war.

Allen J. Matusow, *The Unraveling of America: A History of Liberalism in the 1960s* (1984). Gives an incisive account of the aims and frustrations of the new liberalism.

Jim Miller, *"Democracy Is in the Streets": From Port Huron to the Siege of Chicago* (1987). Explores the SDS' efforts to define and promote "participatory democracy."

Howell Raines, *My Soul Is Rested: Movement Days in the Deep South Remembered* (1977). A moving collection of interviews that vividly recreate the struggle against segregation.

Tom Wolfe, *The Right Stuff* (1979). A wry evocation of the space program and the optimistic spirit of the early 1960s.

History on the Internet

"The Cuban Missile Crisis, 1962"

http://www.gwu.edu/~nsarchiv/nsa/cuba_mis_cri/cmcchron.html

This site provides an introduction and overview of events of the Cuban Missile Crisis. A glossary of terms includes military jargon and sketches of the key political actors involved. Photos on the site are available from the JFK Library.

"The Great Society Speech"

http://www.tamu.edu/scom/pres/speeches/lbjgreat.html

At this on-line speech archive, read Lyndon B. Johnson's "Great Society" speech and many other of his presidency.

"The History of NOW"

http://www.now.org/history/history.html

Visit the National Organization of Women's website and read about the group's founding, its involvement in the Equal Rights Amendment drive, and its advocacy for issues concerning working women. Also, read primary-source documents addressing women's liberation at Duke University's online collection "Documents from the Women's Liberation Movement" at

http://scriptorium.lib.duke.edu/wlm/.

29

LIVING WITH LESS

1968-1980

OUTLINE

"Panic at the Pump," 1973–1974

Across the country in the fall and winter of 1973–1974, frustrated drivers sat in their cars and waited in long lines to buy gasoline. Like most Americans, these men and women took for granted cheap, abundant energy. They were used to owning big cars, built in Detroit, that burned a lot of gas. They were also used to driving when and where they wanted. Suddenly, the price of gas had skyrocketed. Many service stations had little or no gas to sell. One news magazine reported "Panic at the Pump." Service-station attendants faced curses, threats, guns, and even a hand grenade. "You are going to give me gas," a motorist told an attendant, "or I will kill you." In New York City, frustrated drivers fought each other with fists and knives and then battled with police. Some gas-station owners, plagued by shortages and frightened by their customers, simply closed down.

The energy shortage and its effects spread well beyond gas stations. In the Northwest, big cars that used a lot of gas burned up in suspicious fires. In Pennsylvania, Ohio, and other states, truck drivers blockaded highways to protest the high cost of fuel and low speed limits. Governors ordered police and National Guard troops to haul the trucks off the highways. Lack of fuel grounded some commercial flights. Heating oil for homes and businesses was also in short supply. Particularly in the Northeast, Americans faced "the meanest winter of the century." Communities opened shelters for people who could not afford to heat their homes. "We are sitting on top of a disaster," confessed a state official in Massachusetts.

The crisis dramatized a fundamental turning point in American life. Beginning in the early 1960s, the United States had been unable to produce all the oil needed to run its industrial economy. By 1974, the nation had to import over a third of its oil from foreign countries, particularly from the Middle East. The energy needs of the United States and other western countries empowered the Organization of Petroleum Exporting Countries (OPEC), a group of Third World nations that had joined together to get higher prices for their oil. In October 1973 Arab members of OPEC refused to send petroleum to the United States and other nations that supported Israel. OPEC soon raised oil prices nearly 400 percent. The result was the "Panic at the Pump" in the United States.

The energy crisis: motorists line up for gas in Virginia.

Although the Arabs ended the oil embargo in March 1974, the underlying conditions that encouraged their boycott did not go away. After the soaring liberal hopes of the early 1960s, Americans confronted sobering new realities in the 1970s. The United States no longer seemed a land of unlimited possibilities. The nation did not have enough oil and other natural resources. Its economy, long so prosperous, was vulnerable to foreign nations. The federal government did not have enough power to challenge those nations and guarantee prosperity.

Americans' consumer lifestyle now seemed as impractical as the big cars built by Detroit. As a magazine concluded, the American people were "Learning to Live With Less."

It was not easy. The 1970s became a difficult, and not always successful, period of adjustment for the American political economy. Workers, employers, politicians, and families struggled with the consequences of limited resources and power. They puzzled over how to remake the relationship between the economy and government and between the nation and the world.

This task became still more difficult because of new demands for economic opportunity and political rights. Many disadvantaged Americans, who had already lived with less for too long, insisted on their fair share in the 1970s. Their demands troubled more fortunate Americans who worried about whether the political economy could meet everyone's needs in an age of dwindling resources. By the end of the decade, the United States had not solved the problem of equality and the other challenges of living with less. ∎

A New Crisis: Economic Decline

The crises of the 1960s had focused attention on the apparent weaknesses of American politics and government. Despite the programs of the Great Society, the federal government had not established racial harmony and equality. Despite its vast military power, the government had not won the Vietnam War. Many Americans, troubled by President Lyndon Johnson's lack of candor about the war, had begun to question the integrity of their leaders. After the assassinations of John F. Kennedy, Robert F. Kennedy, and Martin Luther King, Jr., Americans even wondered if their society was capable of democratic politics and peaceful change.

The 1970s did not end worries about the political system. In some respects, the events of the decade only intensified concerns about the capacity of government to achieve national goals and serve the people. The 1970s did increasingly focus Americans' attention on a new crisis—the economy. The oil embargo of 1973–1974 was only one sign of the developing weakness of the American economy. In the 1960s, many Americans had taken prosperity, like cheap energy, for granted. By the end of the 1970s, they wondered whether the economy, like the political system, would ever work smoothly again.

The Sources of Economic Decline

There were signs of economic decline almost everywhere by the 1970s. Although the economy continued to grow, the productivity of American workers peaked in 1966 and then began to fall. Corporate profits dropped off after the mid-1960s; the growth rate of the gross national product slowed; poverty remained, in spite of the Great Society; unemployment increased; inflation, which usually dropped when unemployment rose, also increased. In all, the economy seemed stagnant at best. The unprecedented combination of high unemployment and high inflation led to the coining of a new word—**stagflation**—to describe the nation's economic predicament (see Table 29-1).

There were several major reasons for American economic decline. Along with the energy crisis, the United States suffered from increasing international competition. From the end of World War II until the Vietnam War, the United States had been the world's greatest economic power. No other nation rivaled the size and productivity of the American economy. However, European industrial countries, devastated by the war, had rebuilt their economies, and so had Japan. Anxious to stop the spread of Communism in the 1940s and 1950s, American policy-makers had channeled billions of dollars in aid to these countries. The military protection provided by the United States had allowed Japan, West Germany, and other nations to save money on defense and concentrate resources on rebuilding. They now had efficient, up-to-date industries. As a result, these nations rivaled the United States, not only abroad but even in the American market.

The rise of Japan was the most dramatic illustration of these developments. Americans had derided Japanese goods—the words "Made in Japan" were synonymous with poor quality—but by the 1970s, Japan's modern factories turned out high-quality products that appealed to American consumers. Japanese televisions and other electronic goods filled American homes. Japanese cars—small, well made, and fuel-efficient—attracted American buyers worried about the high price of gas.

Because of such competition from Japan and other countries, the United States fell back in the international economic race. In 1950, the nation had accounted for 40 percent of the value of all the goods and services produced around the globe. By 1970 that figure was down to 23 percent. During these years, the American share of world trade dropped nearly 50 percent. Most stunning of all by the end of the 1970s, the United States was actually importing more manufactured goods than it was exporting.

American corporations also contributed to the nation's economic plight. Big businessmen had tended to maximize short-term profits at the cost of the long-term health of their companies. Some corporate leaders had not

TABLE 29-1

Year	Inflation %Change	Unemployment %Change	Combined* %Change
1970	5.9	4.9	10.8
1971	4.3	5.9	10.2
1972	3.3	5.6	8.9
1973	6.2	4.9	11.1
1974	11.0	5.6	16.6
1975	9.1	8.5	17.6
1976	5.8	7.7	13.5
1977	6.5	7.1	13.6
1978	7.7	6.1	13.8
1979	11.3	5.8	17.1
1980	13.5	7.1	20.6

*"Combined" means annual percentage changes of inflation and unemployment.
Source: Statistical Abstract of the United States, 1984, pp. 375–76, 463; tables 624–25, 760. (1971 inflation data from Statistical Abstract, 1973, p. 348, table 569).

plowed enough of their earnings back into research, development, and new equipment. As a result, American industries seemed unprepared for foreign competition. Detroit's automobiles, so attractive and advanced in the 1950s, now struck consumers as unglamorous, inefficient, and even poorly made. Ford's new Pinto sedan had to be recalled because its fuel tank was prone to explode.

Long an emblem of security and stability, American corporations suddenly appeared vulnerable. In 1970, the Penn Central Railroad became the largest corporation in American history to go bankrupt. That year, only massive aid from the federal government saved the giant Lockheed Aircraft company from going under as well. Meanwhile, other corporations thrived by becoming "multinationals," that is, firms that located factories and other facilities overseas. Although these companies kept their headquarters in the United States, they were directing jobs and dollars away from the American economy. The multinationals appeared to be strengthening themselves at the expense of the United States.

The federal government also played a part in the nation's economic predicament. Massive government spending, particularly for defense, had stimulated the economy from the 1940s to the 1960s, but by the 1970s defense spending did not have the same effect. Some analysts claimed that Washington had diverted too much of the nation's talent and resources from the private sector to military projects during the cold war. As a consequence, the American economy was unprepared for foreign competition. In addition, the government's huge expenditures for the Vietnam War promoted inflation.

Economists did not give federal policymakers much help. In the 1960s, the liberal followers of John Maynard Keynes had been confident that they understood the secret of maintaining prosperity. They believed the federal gov-

ernment could manipulate its budget in order to stabilize an economy about to stagnate due to low unemployment or overheat due to high prices. The economists were unprepared for the novel problem of stagflation. "The rules of economics," admitted the chairman of the Federal Reserve, "are not working quite the way they used to."

The Impact of Decline

Shaped by a broad range of factors, economic decline in turn began to reshape life in the United States. By the 1970s, it seemed as if the industrial revolution were being reversed. As corporations closed factories, Americans witnessed the "deindustrialization" of their country. Huge steel plants, the symbol of American industrial might, now stood empty. Electronics manufacturers switched the production of televisions to Canada, Japan, Taiwan, and Hong Kong. Food-processing companies moved their operations to Mexico. These developments intensified the trend, first evident in the 1950s, toward a service-centered economy. In the 1970s, most new jobs were in the sales and retail sectors. The United States, a union official lamented, was turning into "a nation of hamburger stands . . . a country stripped of industrial capacity and meaningful work . . . a service economy."

For American workers, the consequences of deindustrialization were difficult, even devastating. Heavy industry had been the stronghold of the labor movement; unions had not organized the service sector nearly as thoroughly. As a result, organized labor lost members, power, and influence. By the late 1970s, less than one in four workers belonged to a union.

The shift from unionized industrial jobs to unorganized service jobs eroded Americans' incomes. After rising from the 1950s into the 1960s, workers' spendable income began to drop by the mid-1970s. To keep up, more and more women took full-time jobs outside the home, but not all Americans could find work. As the huge baby-boom generation came of age, the economy did not produce enough jobs.

Economic decline accelerated the transformation of America's regions. People and power had been moving from north to south and east to west for a long time. The energy crisis and deindustrialization sped up that movement (see Map 29-1). With its cold, snowy winters, the North was especially vulnerable to the oil embargo and higher energy prices. America's "Snowbelt" now seemed a less attractive place to live and to do business. The Northeast and the Midwest, home to so many aging steel mills and auto plants, suffered especially. In the 1970s, the sight of empty, decaying factories made these regions America's "Rustbelt."

Fleeing deindustrialization, many northerners migrated south to the band of states ranging from Florida to California. This "Sunbelt" boomed in the 1970s. Farms

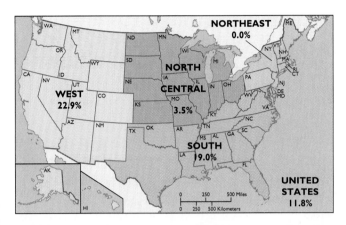

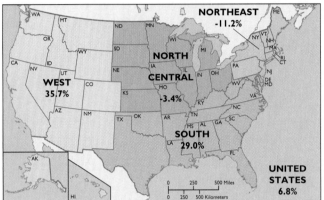

Map 29-1   Movement from Rustbelt to Sunbelt.
The percentages track the shift of population (top) and manufacturing jobs (bottom) from the Northeast and the Midwest to the South and West between 1970 and 1980.

Source: D.K. Adams et al., An Atlas of North American Affairs, 2d ed. (London and New York: Methuen).

turned into suburbs and cities such as Orlando, Houston, Dallas, Phoenix, San Diego, and Anaheim exploded in size and population.

With mild winters, the Sunbelt did not suffer so much from high oil prices. If anything, Texas and the southwestern states, rich in oil and natural gas reserves, profited from the energy crisis. The Sunbelt did not have such an aging industrial infrastructure either. Instead, it was home to newer, high-technology businesses, to thriving aerospace firms, electronics companies, and defense contractors. By 1970, one-quarter of U. S. military spending went to California and Texas alone; and the space program was centered in Texas and Florida. The Sunbelt was also at the cutting edge of the service economy, with its emphasis on leisure and consumption. More retirees moved to Florida than to any other state. Tourists flocked to the original Disneyland in California and the new Walt Disney World in Florida. They gambled their money in Las Vegas. The Vietnam War, social and political upheaval, and economic turmoil all touched the Sunbelt, of course, but somehow the outlook seemed a bit more optimistic there.

Confronting Decline: Nixon's Strategy

Richard Nixon was the first president to confront the decline of America's post-World War II prosperity and power. In some respects, he was well-suited to the task. Despite his long opposition to Communism and the New Deal, Nixon was not strongly committed to any particular ideology. A pragmatist, the new president was open to new realities and new approaches.

Nixon and his administration understood that the American political economy would, in fact, have to live with less. Better than many political leaders, the president learned some of the key lessons of the 1960s. He recognized that the failure of the war effort in Vietnam marked the end of America's cold-war pretensions. Nixon and his aides would not claim that the nation had unlimited power.

Nixon also recognized that the upheavals of the 1960s had weakened liberalism and its powerful supporters. According to the president, the troubles of Lyndon Johnson's Great Society demonstrated the failings of the activist, liberal approach to the political economy. He believed, too, that all the controversy over the Great Society, the Vietnam War, and other issues in the 1960s had fatally wounded the **establishment**—the largely Ivy-League educated, liberal, northeastern group who supposedly dominated Wall Street and Washington after World War II. Nixon probably exaggerated the cohesion of the "establishment" and the failure of liberalism, but he was right that the crises of the 1960s created opportunities for new people and new political economic approaches. Abroad and at home, the new president tried to take advantage of those opportunities.

A New Foreign Policy

The Nixon administration dealt most creatively with foreign policy for several reasons. First, the president was more interested in diplomacy than in domestic affairs. In addition, the Constitution and the cold war allowed him, as they had his predecessors, considerable freedom in military and diplomatic matters. With the help of his assistant for National Security affairs, Henry Kissinger, Nixon made bold use of that freedom.

The president and his national security advisor still regarded Communism as a menace, and the two men still saw the cold-war rivalry between the United States and the Soviet Union as the defining reality of the modern world. However, Nixon and Kissinger understood that the relative decline of American power dictated a new approach to the cold war. During Nixon's presidency, the United States pulled back from its promise to intervene around the world to stop the spread of Communism. Nixon moved to ease tensions with the Soviet Union and the People's

WHERE THEY LIVED, WHERE THEY WORKED

Youngstown, Ohio

For more than 75 years, workers made steel in the open-hearth furnaces at the Campbell Works of the Youngstown Sheet and Tube Company. Opened just after the start of the twentieth century, the huge mill was one of the plants that gave the community of Youngstown, in northeast Ohio, its reputation as a "Steel City." In exchange for hard labor, the Campbell Works also gave generations of Youngstown's workers a chance for prosperity. "Youngstown," a resident observed, "was a place in which the American Dream seemed to have come true for many working-class families."

The dream came to a sudden end in 1977. By then, the mill was an inefficient "antique" that made steel more slowly and expensively than new mills. On September 19 the parent company of Youngstown Sheet and Tube, Lykes Corporation, announced it was closing down the Campbell Works and transferring some production to a new facility in Illinois. As many as 5,000 workers would lose their jobs. Once a symbol of American industrial might, the Campbell Works had instantly become a symbol of deindustrialization and decline on that "Black Monday" in 1977.

The announcement of the shutdown stunned the mill's employees. To many, it was like another Pearl Harbor. Some workers realized right away that their way of life was gone. On the way home, they threw their hard hats and workboots into the Mahoning River.

Although many workers hoped that the Campbell Works could be saved, the Lykes Corporation refused to reopen the mill. The company claimed that the low price of foreign steel, especially from Japan, and the high cost of U. S. environmental regulations made it impossible to operate the mill at a profit. A coalition of workers and churches tried to buy the mill, but their plan fell through. Congress and President

Workers from Youngstown protest plant closings by blocking an escalator at the headquarters of U.S. Steel in Pittsburgh.

Republic of China. Amid great controversy, the president also moved to end American participation in the Vietnam War. By the end of Nixon's presidency, the United States's role in the world had changed considerably.

The twin pillars of the new foreign policy were the "Nixon Doctrine" and **détente**. In a speech on the Pacific island of Guam in July 1969, the president announced that the United States "cannot—and will not—conceive all the plans, design all the programs, execute all the decisions and undertake all the defense of the free nations of the world." America would continue to provide a nuclear umbrella for its "allies and friends," but they would have to defend themselves against rebellious insurgents and aggressive neighbors. This Nixon Doctrine amounted to a repudiation of the Truman Doctrine, President Harry Truman's promise in 1947 "to support free peoples who are resisting attempted subjugation by armed minorities or by outside pressures."

The landscape of deindustrialization: empty factories in the rustbelt.

Jimmy Carter, believing the Campbell Works was too inefficient to save, refused to help. Carter, an angry worker grumbled, "ought to run for president of Japan."

In the end, there was no way to save the Campbell Works. The workers lost their jobs, and much more. They felt cut off from their past and their future. "Our fathers worked here and our grandfathers worked here," said a union official. "Now I face the prospect of this turning into a ghost town." The optimistic future of the American Dream had disappeared. "They used to tell us: 'Get out of high school, get a job in a mill and you're fixed for life'," said a steelworker. "Now I know better."

Facing such bleak prospects, a quarter of the labor force at Campbell Works moved away from Youngstown. Many of them went to the booming Sunbelt. About half of the workers stayed on in Youngstown and found new jobs. Many of those jobs did not pay nearly as well as work at Youngstown Sheet and Tube. The remaining quarter of the work force also stayed on but found no work at all.

Other Youngstown residents also suffered because of the closing of the Campbell Works. Business dropped in the taverns where steelworkers had gone for a drink after the job. Other stores missed the steelworkers' patronage. "It will kill our business," a Youngstown storeowner lamented.

The shutdown at Youngstown Sheet and Tube was just the beginning of deindustrialization in Youngstown. By 1980, the "Steel City" was dotted with the decaying hulks of empty mills. Other communities feared they would be next. "There are going to be a few more Youngstowns before it's over," an economist predicted.

In addition to announcing a new relationship with its friends, the United States pursued a new relationship with its potential enemies, the Soviet Union and the People's Republic of China. Nixon and Kissinger wanted to lessen the cost and risks of America's tense rivalry with these two Communist nuclear powers. Separate agreements with the Soviet Union and China would, the American leaders hoped, keep those two nations from combining against the United States. With his unquestioned record of anti-Communism, Nixon believed he could persuade Americans to accept deals with the Soviets and the Chinese. He also believed the U. S. S. R. and China, now bitter enemies, would want to improve relations with the United States. So Nixon and Kissinger worked to establish what became known as "détente," a French term for the relaxation of tensions.

At the start of Nixon's presidency, the United States had still not recognized the legitimacy of the People's Republic of China. Instead, America supported the

Communists' bitter foes, the Nationalist Chinese regime on Taiwan. But Nixon soon signaled his eagerness to negotiate with the People's Republic. In a dramatic trip in February 1972, Nixon became the first American president to go to mainland China. He gave the Chinese leaders what they most wanted—a promise that the United States would eventually withdraw its troops from Taiwan. Without naming the U. S. S. R. the two sides made clear that they opposed any Soviet attempt to dominate Asia. His visit, exulted Nixon, "changed the world."

That was an overstatement. Nixon's Beijing trip did not so much change the world as bring American policy in line with the reality of the 1970s. The United States was no longer in a position to use troops to gets its way in Southeast Asia, but Nixon's trip underscored the gradual ending of anti-Communist hysteria back home in America. As Nixon intended, the trip also left the Soviets with the frightening possibility of a Chinese-American alliance.

The president had every reason to try to pressure the Soviet Union. After all, the U. S. S. R. was the one nation on earth that could destroy American society with nuclear weapons. Nixon did not want a confrontation with the Soviets. The United States no longer had clear military superiority. Instead, the president sought détente with the Soviet leadership. Above all, he wanted the Soviets to join with the United States in agreeing to limit their long-range or strategic nuclear arsenals. The Soviets also wished to reduce the expense and danger of the cold war. They needed

to counter Nixon's overture to the Chinese. Moreover, they badly needed American grain to help feed their own people.

Under these circumstances, the two sides began talks on the Strategic Arms Limitations Treaty (SALT I) in 1969. In May 1972, three months after his trip to China, Nixon became the first American president to travel to Moscow. The United States and the U. S. S. R. signed the SALT treaty limiting for five years the number of each nation's nuclear missiles. A second, Anti-Ballistic Missile (ABM) treaty sharply limited the number of defensive missiles that the two sides could deploy to protect their cities and nuclear missiles. Although they did not prevent the development of new weapons and the continuation of the arms race, the ABM and SALT treaties symbolized the American and Soviet agreement that "there is no alternative to . . . peaceful coexistence."

In that spirit, the United States soon agreed to sell grain to the Soviets. Although such gestures hardly ended the competition between the United States and the Soviet Union, détente seemed to promise that the competition would not turn deadly.

Ending the Vietnam War

Along with all the other motivations for détente, the Nixon administration sought better relations with the U. S. S. R. and the People's Republic of China in order to help end the

Richard Nixon, the first American president to visit mainland China, exchanges toasts with Premier Zhou Enlai. Nixon's 1972 trip heralded an easing of tensions with America's cold-war adversary.

Vietnam War. Nixon and Kissinger hoped the Soviets and the Chinese would pressure the North Vietnamese to accept a peace agreement.

The president needed such an agreement. By 1969, time had clearly run out for the American war effort. As Nixon knew, the United States could not win the Vietnam War. Meanwhile, the ongoing conflict divided the American people and undermined American prestige and power around the world. Anxious "not . . . to end up like" Lyndon Johnson, Nixon intended "to stop that war. Fast," but the president's peace plan turned out to be slow, controversial, and ultimately ineffective.

Nixon was caught in a dilemma. To appease public opinion, he began to bring American soldiers home in 1969. But without those soldiers, he had a hard time persuading North Vietnam to accept the continued existence of South Vietnam. The president attempted to resolve this dilemma with a policy known as "Vietnamization." In line with the Nixon Doctrine, the United States encouraged the South Vietnamese to take over their own defense. Although South Vietnam's armed forces became larger and better equipped with American aid, "Vietnamization" never did work. The South Vietnamese military alone could not beat back the Communists.

Accordingly, Nixon turned to U. S. airpower to support South Vietnamese troops and to intimidate the North Vietnamese into making a deal for peace. In March 1969, he authorized B-52 raids to wipe out North Vietnamese sanc-

tuaries in Cambodia. Because the bombing of this neutral country might outrage American and world opinion, the president kept the raids secret. However, the Cambodian operation did not force North Vietnam to make peace. Secret negotiations between Henry Kissinger and North Vietnamese diplomats also went nowhere.

Meanwhile, Nixon's actions angered many Americans. News of the secret bombings soon leaked out. In October, millions of Americans participated in "Moratorium Day," a dramatic break from business as usual, to protest the war. In November, over 250,000 people staged a "March Against Death" in Washington. That month, Americans finally learned about one of the most troubling episodes of the war. On March 16, 1968, United States soldiers had shot and killed between 200 and 500 unarmed South Vietnamese women, children, and old men in the hamlet of My Lai. This atrocity led to the 1970 court-martial and eventual conviction of Lt. William Calley, Jr., for mass murder. Some Americans thought Calley had been unfairly singled out. Others thought the My Lai Massacre symbolized the immorality of the American presence in Vietnam.

Demonstrations and public opinion did not stop the president from using violence to force a peace agreement. When General Lon Nol, the new pro-American leader of Cambodia, appealed for United States aid to stop a Communist insurgency, a joint United States-South Vietnamese force invaded Cambodia to look for North Vietnamese troops in April 1970. The Cambodian invasion never did

Death at Kent State University: The body of one of four students shot by the Ohio National Guard during protests over the U.S. invasion of Cambodia in 1970.

uncover many North Vietnamese troops, but it produced turmoil in the United States. Students demonstrated on campuses across the country; at least two demonstrations resulted in the loss of lives. On the afternoon of May 4, National Guard troops fired at an unarmed crowd of protesters at Kent State University in Ohio. Four students died; two of them had only been walking between classes. Ten days later, state police killed two African-American students at Jackson State College in Mississippi. These deaths intensified the outrage over the invasion of Cambodia. Students went out on strike at about 450 campuses. In some of these cases, protests also turned violent. Many ROTC offices exploded or burned. University presidents pleaded with Nixon to end the war. Union leaders spoke out against the invasion.

Some Americans, angered by the sight of demonstrating college students, mobilized in support of the president and the war effort. In New York City, 200 construction workers attacked student demonstrators. "The country is virtually on the edge of a spiritual—and perhaps physical—breakdown," the mayor of New York City lamented. "For the first time in a century, we are not sure there is a future for America."

As American troop withdrawals continued, the war and the peace negotiations dragged on. The Nixon administration received little good news in 1971. Vietnamization continued to founder. Meanwhile, the *New York Times* began publishing the so-called "Pentagon Papers," a massive secret history of the American involvement in Vietnam that had been authorized by former Secretary of Defense Robert McNamara. The documents, which made clear that the Johnson administration had misled the American people, further undermined public support for the war. The Nixon administration tried unsuccessfully to persuade the Supreme Court to block publication of the papers.

Unable to stop the Pentagon Papers or secure a peace agreement, Nixon stepped up his efforts to pressure North Vietnam into a settlement in 1972. When the North Vietnamese Army swept across the border into South Vietnam at the end of March, the president struck back with Operation Linebacker, a new aerial attack against North Vietnam. When negotiations stalled again, the president intensified the air raids in December. Nixon and Kissinger made exaggerated claims that these so-called "Christmas bombings" forced the North Vietnamese to accept peace terms. But on January 27, 1973, American, South Vietnamese, North Vietnamese, and Viet Cong negotiators did sign a peace agreement in Paris. For the United States, at least, the Vietnam War was over.

Campaigning for president in 1968, Nixon had promised "peace with honor" in Vietnam; his resolution of the U. S. involvement did not live up to his pledge. The United States had gone to war to preserve an anti-Communist South Vietnam, but the peace agreement did not guarantee South Vietnam's survival. Although North Vietnam

pledged to return American prisoners of war, it did not pledge to respect the existence of South Vietnam. Although the United States promised to withdraw its military forces, the agreement did not require the North Vietnamese to pull their own troops out of South Vietnam. Not surprisingly, the South Vietnamese balked at accepting a peace plan that so obviously threatened the future of their country. Nixon had to mix threats of punishment and pledges of support to force South Vietnam to go along with the agreement.

The cease fire came at a heavy cost. Twenty thousand more Americans had died since Nixon took office in 1969. More than 600,000 North and South Vietnamese soldiers had died in battle during the same period. The number of civilian casualties during these years will never be known. Nixon had accomplished an essential task of his new foreign policy—ending U. S. participation in the Vietnam war. But the president's critics would continue to wonder whether four more years of fighting had really been necessary, when the result was such a flawed peace agreement.

Chile and the Middle East

Détente was an important new approach to American foreign policy, but as events in Chile and the Middle East made clear, it did not end U. S. opposition to Communist successes and Soviet initiatives around the world. As those events also revealed, Nixon and Kissinger's policy did not suddenly restore American power abroad.

Nixon, like the presidents before him, refused to accept the establishment of a Communist regime in the Western Hemisphere. In 1970, he ordered the CIA to use "whatever means necessary" to block the election of Salvador Allende, a Marxist, as president of Chile. Allende was elected anyway. The CIA, with help from nongovernment groups, then destabilized Allende's regime by helping right-wing parties, driving up the price of bread, and encouraging demonstrations. When a military coup murdered Allende and thousands of his followers three years later, the United States denied responsibility and offered financial assistance to the new leader, Augusto Pincohet.

In the Middle East, the Nixon administration also displayed its hostility to Communism and its inability to shape events decisively. During the Six-Day War in 1967, Israel defeated Egyptian and Syrian forces and occupied territory along the Suez Canal in Egypt, the Golan Heights in Syria, and the West Bank of the Jordan River. Seeking revenge for this humiliating defeat, the Egyptians and Syrians attacked Israel in October 1973, on Yom Kippur, the holiest day of the Jewish calendar. When the United States defied Arab warnings and sent critical supplies to Israel, Arab countries responded with an oil embargo. Meanwhile, the Soviets supplied the Arabs and pressed for a role in the region. Determined to keep out the Soviet Union,

Nixon put American nuclear forces on alert. Kissinger deftly mediated between the combatants, who agreed to pull back their troops in January 1974. Although the embargo ended, American weakness was obvious. Supporting Israel, the United States still needed the Arabs' oil. Nixon and Kissinger were able to hold back the Soviet Union in the Middle East, but they could not bring peace to the region.

A Mixed Domestic Record

The Nixon administration responded less creatively to economic and governmental challenges at home. Domestic issues did not interest the president nearly as much as diplomacy, and the Constitution gave him less authority in domestic matters. Moreover, Nixon had to contend with a Congress controlled by Democrats. Whereas the president preferred a smaller and less active government, some liberal ideas and policies remained popular. As a result, Nixon had a mixed domestic record. In some areas, his administration shrank the federal government and the Great Society. In others, the Nixon White House accepted new liberal initiatives. Meanwhile, the president had little success in dealing with an ailing economy. The problem of decline, imaginatively addressed in Nixon's foreign policy, proved much more difficult to handle at home.

Nixon took office with some conventional Republican goals. He wanted the massive federal government to balance its budget and shed some of its power. In 1969, the president called for a "New Federalism," in which Washington would return "a greater share of control to state and local governments and to the people." As would become all too clear, Nixon believed a president had great authority; however, he was ready to create a less grandiose federal government.

During the Nixon years, there were spending cuts for some programs, including defense. The fate of the space program epitomized the new budgetary realities. On July 20, 1969, a lunar landing module, launched from the *Apollo 11* capsule, touched down on the moon. As astronaut Neil Armstrong became the first human to set foot on the surface, he proclaimed, "That's one small step for man, one giant leap for mankind." The United States had beaten the Soviets to the moon. This triumph suggested that there was still no limit to what Americans could do. There were, however, firm limits to what the space program could do. The administration slashed NASA's budget.

The "New Federalism" also put limits on Washington. In 1972 the administration persuaded Congress to pass a revenue-sharing plan that allowed state and local governments to spend funds collected by the federal government. But the president left largely intact the massive structure of New Deal and Great Society agencies and programs. By 1971, the unsettled economy and the cost of big government had produced a huge budget deficit.

The president did try to reform the federal welfare system first put in place by the New Deal. Like many conservatives, Nixon believed that welfare made the federal bureaucracy too large and the poor too dependent. During the president's first term, his administration tried to replace the largest federal welfare program, Aid to Families with Dependent Children (AFDC), with a controversial system inspired by presidential aide Daniel Patrick Moynihan, a Harvard sociologist. Moynihan's Family Assistance Plan (FAP) would have provided poor families with a guaranteed minimum annual income, but it also would have required the heads of poor households to accept any available jobs. Liberal critics opposed this "workfare" requirement. Conservative critics thought FAP did too much for the poor. As a result, the program failed to pass Congress.

Meanwhile, the Nixon administration went along with several liberal initiatives that sharply expanded the regulatory powers of the federal government. By the end of the 1960s, big business faced considerable criticism. The middle class in particular worried that corporations did not protect workers, consumers, or the environment. A grassroots environmental movement grew rapidly from the late 1960s into the 1970s. In April 1970 tens of millions of Americans participated in the first Earth Day ceremonies.

Liberals in Congress responded to popular opinion by establishing three new federal regulatory agencies to discipline business. The Environmental Protection Agency (EPA) and the Occupational Safety and Health Administration (OSHA) were authorized in 1970. The Consumer Product Safety Commission followed 2 years later. Along with the Equal Employment Opportunity Commission (EEOC) created during the Johnson administration, these agencies considerably enhanced the government's power over corporations. So did a series of measures to safeguard coastlines and endangered species and to limit the use of pesticides, the strip-mining of coal, and the pollution of air and water. Big business generally opposed these initiatives. Nixon did not like them either, but he followed public opinion and signed them into law.

An Uncertain Economic Policy

Nixon also reluctantly accepted liberal policies as he struggled with the economy. Inheriting inflation from Johnson, the Nixon administration soon had to deal with rising unemployment and falling corporate profits. The president, like most Republicans, believed government should not interfere much in the economy, but deteriorating economic conditions forced him to take a more active stand. Beginning in 1970, the president tried unsuccessfully to persuade business to hold the line on prices and organized labor to limit its wage demands.

The situation was complicated by the U. S. dollar's role in the international monetary system. Since the

One of the demonstrations around the nation marking the first Earth Day in April 1970.

Bretton Woods conference during World War II, the dollar had been, in effect, the world's currency. Many other nations tied the value of their own currencies to the American dollar. The value of the dollar, in turn, had been supported by the U. S. commitment to the gold standard. The federal government had promised to give an ounce of gold in return for 35 dollars. By the 1970s, however, that promise had become impossible. Strong European economies held too many dollars and the United States held too little gold. If other countries had become worried about the strength of the U. S. economy and demanded gold for their dollars, a panic could have followed.

In response, Nixon announced his "New Economic Policy" in August 1971. To prevent a gold crisis, the president took the United States off the gold standard by ending the exchange of gold for dollars. To strengthen the United States against foreign competition, Nixon lowered the value of the dollar and slapped new tariffs on imports. To slow down inflation, he authorized a freeze on wages and prices for 90 days followed by caps on future increases. The "New Economic Policy" marked a turning point for the United States. For the first time in American history, a president had resorted to a wage and price freeze in peacetime. The end of the gold standard may have helped U. S. goods sell more cheaply overseas, but it also underscored America's economic decline. For generations, people had said the dollar was as good as gold; that saying was no longer true.

Wage and price controls did not solve the underlying economic problems that caused inflation. The ongoing cost of the Vietnam War, along with the Arab oil embargo, continued to drive up prices. Nixon and his advisers had no solution to the problem of economic decline. There was no domestic counterpart to détente.

Refusing to Settle for Less: Struggles for Rights

In the late 1960s and 1970s, many Americans refused to settle for less. African Americans and women continued their struggles for rights and opportunities that they had long been denied in the American political economy. Their example and the optimistic promises of liberalism spurred other disadvantaged groups to demand recognition. Mexican Americans, Native Americans, and gays and lesbians organized and demonstrated for their causes. Other Americans, worried about preserving their own advantages in an era of limits, were often unwilling to support these new demands for rights and opportunities, but by the end of the 1970s, American society—however tentatively and reluctantly—was more committed to equality for women and minorities.

African Americans' Struggle for Racial Justice

After the assassination of Martin Luther King, Jr., in 1968, African Americans carried on their struggle for racial justice. The National Association for the Advancement of Colored People (NAACP), the Southern Christian Leadership Conference (SCLC), and other civil rights organizations continued to press for integration. Advocates of Black Power continued to advocate nationalism and separatism. At the local level, African Americans worked to control schools and win public office. By the 1970s, national attention focused on two relatively new and controversial means of promoting racial equality—affirmative action and mandatory school **busing**.

First ordered by the Johnson administration, affirmative action required businesses, universities, and other institutions receiving federal money to provide opportunities for women and nonwhites. Supporters viewed the policy as a way to make up for past and present discrimination against disadvantaged groups. Opponents argued that affirmative action was itself a form of discrimination that reduced opportunities for white people in general and white men in particular.

Nixon generally supported the principle of affirmative action. His administration developed the "Philadelphia Plan," which encouraged the construction industry to meet targets for hiring minority workers. In 1978, the Supreme Court offered qualified support for affirmative action with its decision in *Regents of the University of California v. Allan Bakke*. The justices ruled that the medical school of the University of California at Davis could not deny admission to Bakke, a white applicant who had better grades and test scores than some minority applicants accepted by the institution. While the court

barred schools from using fixed admissions quotas for different racial groups, it did allow educational institutions to use race as one of the criteria for admitting students. By the end of the 1970s, affirmative action had become an important means of increasing diversity in schools and other institutions.

School busing was even more controversial than affirmative action. By the late 1960s, the Supreme Court had become impatient with the delays in integrating the nation's schools. Even in the North, where there had been no *de jure* or legal segregation, there was still extensive *de facto* segregation. In *Swann v. Charlotte-Mecklenburg Board of Education* in 1971, the court upheld the mandatory busing of thousands of children in order to desegregate schools in the Charlotte, North Carolina, area. To its advocates, busing seemed to be the best way to insure equal education for African-American pupils. But many Americans opposed the policy, either because they did not want integration or because they did not want children taken out of neighborhood schools.

Nixon sided with the opponents of busing. He called the policy "a new evil . . . disrupting communities and imposing hardship on children—both black and white." Privately ordering his aides to enforce busing less vigorously, the president publicly called for a "moratorium" on new busing plans. Some communities implemented busing peacefully. Others faced protest and turmoil. In 1974, a federal court responding to a suit by African-American parents ordered busing to end *de facto* school segregation in Boston. When the white-dominated local school committee refused to comply, a federal judge imposed a busing plan on the community. While white liberals and African Americans generally supported the judge, many working-class and lower-middle-class whites did not. They formed Restore Our Alienated Rights (ROAR) and other organizations to protest plans to bus students between the predominantly African-American neighborhood of Roxbury and the largely Irish-American neighborhood of South Boston. In "Southie," whites taunted and injured African-American students arriving for school in September. The violence spread to Roxbury and continued through the fall. Although some white parents held their children out of school in the fall of 1975, the busing plan went into effect.

Busing came to Boston and other communities, but many white Americans were clearly reluctant to support new initiatives for African-American equality. With busing and affirmative action, the civil rights movement seemed to have reached its limits.

Police break up a crowd of demonstrators opposed to court-ordered busing to integrate public schools in Boston in 1974.

Women's Liberation

By the 1970s, the movement for women's liberation, the expression of feminism's second wave, was flourishing. Many women were coming together in "consciousness-raising" groups to discuss a broad range of issues in their lives. More generally, the media were focusing public attention on "women's lib." To commemorate the fiftieth anniversary of—the culmination of feminism's first wave, the ratification of the women's suffrage amendment to the Constitution—the Women's Strike for Equality took place across the country on August 26, 1970. Tens of thousands of women marched through the streets of Manhattan. In Los Angeles, marchers chanted, "Sisterhood is powerful, join us now." "It made all women feel beautiful," a marcher explained. "It made me feel 10 feet tall."

The women's liberation movement, like the struggle for African-American equality, was diverse. As in the 1960s, liberal feminists, such as women in the National Organization for Women (NOW), concentrated on equal public opportunities for women. Insisting that "The personal is the political," more radical feminists focused on a broader range of private as well as public issues. Oppression, they insisted, took place in the bedroom and the kitchen as well as the school and the workplace. Some radical feminists, influenced by the New Left, blamed women's plight on the inequalities of capitalism. Other radicals traced the oppression of women to men rather than capitalism, to gender rather than economics. Still others, sometimes labeled "cultural feminists," insisted that women's culture was different from and superior to male culture. To preserve themselves and their culture, they felt, women should concentrate on creating their own separate institutions, rather than on seeking formal equality with men. Some lesbian feminists, such as the Radicalesbians and the Furies, took this separatist logic one step further to argue that women should avoid heterosexual relationships altogether.

Linking the private and personal with the public and political, the women's movement necessarily fought on many fronts. Women's liberation was about names, magazines, and television shows as well as laws and court cases. By the 1970s, more women who married decided to keep their maiden names rather than adopt their husbands' surnames. Rather than identifying themselves by their marital status, many women abandoned the forms of address "Miss" or "Mrs." for "Ms."

Women's liberation made its mark on the media. In 1972, Gloria Steinem began to publish the feminist magazine *Ms*. On television, popular sit-coms portrayed independent women: The *Mary Tyler Moore Show*, for example, dealt with a single career woman who was not desperately seeking to marry and cook for a man. "You've got to make it on your own," the show's theme song declared. Another successful sit-com, *Maude*, approvingly portrayed an outspoken feminist, who, in one controversial episode, had an abortion. Meanwhile, some feminists condemned the availability of pornography, which, they argued, incited violence against women.

In the 1970s, women activists focused especially on three public issues—access to abortion, equal treatment in schools and workplaces, and passage of the Equal Rights Amendment to the Constitution (ERA). The abortion struggle was part of women's long-term effort to win control over their own bodies. Effectively outlawed for generations, abortions were generally unavailable and unsafe; in the 1970s, women went to court to challenge the law. In *Roe v. Wade* in 1973, the Supreme Court ruled a Texas antiabortion law unconstitutional on the grounds that it violated the "right to privacy" guaranteed by the Ninth and Fourteenth Amendments. With this decision, abortion began to become legally and widely available to American women.

Like the civil rights movement, the women's movement strongly demanded equal treatment in schools and workplaces in the 1970s. Women filed many complaints against discrimination by employers. At first reluctant, the Nixon administration moved to open up government employment to women and to press colleges and businesses to end discriminatory practices. In one notable case, the Equal Employment Opportunity Commission compelled the American Telephone and Telegraph corporation to initiate affirmative action and make payments to female and minority employees who had suffered discrimination. In 1972, Congress approved Title IX of the Higher Education Act, which required schools and universities receiving federal funds to give equal opportunities to women and men in admissions, athletics, and other programs.

The women's movement also continued the long-time struggle to enact the ERA. "Equality of rights under the law," the amendment read, "shall not be denied or abridged by the United States or by any State on account of sex." Only with this legal protection, many women believed, could they hope for real equality with men. In 1972 Congress finally passed the ERA. If 38 states had ratified the amendment within 7 years, it would have become the law of the land. Within a year, 28 states had endorsed ratification (see Map 29-2).

Despite this progress, the ERA and women's liberation encountered considerable opposition from men and even some women. To male critics, feminists were a "small band of bra-less bubbleheads" who suffered from "defeminization." Some women feared that equal rights would end their femininity and their protected legal status. "I'm against the whole equality thing," said a female typist. "I'm afraid of being drafted." Conservative women activists led a backlash against feminism and equal rights. In her book, *The Total Woman*, Marabel Morgan urged women to subordinate themselves to men's needs. Phyllis Schlafly organized an effective campaign against the ERA. Although

Map 29-2   *The Equal Rights Amendment (ERA).*
Despite substantial support in state legislatures across the country, the ERA faced crippling opposition in the mountain West and the South.

more states ratified the amendment, some rescinded their votes, and the ERA never became law.

The defeat of the amendment underscored the challenges that the women's movement faced at the end of the 1970s. Women still did not have full equality in American society. Nevertheless, women's liberation had led to major advances. Women had more control over their bodies, more access to education, and more opportunity in the workplace. The personal *had* become the political. Women's issues were at the center of American public life.

Mexican Americans and "Brown Power"

The different movements for African-American liberation inspired other racial and ethnic groups in the United States. In the 1960s and 1970s, Mexican Americans, the second-largest racial minority, developed a new self-consciousness. Proudly identifying themselves as "Chicanos," many Mexican Americans organized to protest poverty and discrimination. Like African Americans, Chicanos divided over goals and strategies, but the movements for "Brown Power" began to change the status of Mexican Americans in the United States.

Despite the federal efforts to keep out Mexican immigrants in the 1950s, the Mexican-American population grew rapidly. By 1980, at least 7 million Americans claimed Mexican heritage. The great majority lived in the southwestern states of Arizona, California, Colorado, New Mexico, and Texas. By the 1970s, most Chicanos lived in urban rather than rural areas. More than a million lived in the city of Los Angeles. Although Mexican Americans held an increasing percentage of skilled and white-collar jobs, Chicanos as a group earned substantially less than did Anglos (white Americans of non-Hispanic descent). One in four Mexican-American families lived in poverty in the mid-1970s.

Chicanos faced racism and discrimination. They were called "greasers," "spics," and "wetbacks." The media stereotyped them as lazy and shifty. Unlike African Americans, Chicanos did not have to confront *de jure* segregation, but they did face *de facto* segregation and discrimination just the same. Schools in Chicano neighborhoods were underfunded. In some California schools, Mexican-American children could not eat with Anglo children. California and Texas law prohibited teaching in Spanish. Chicano children were even punished for speaking Spanish.

Although Chicanos were not legally prevented from voting, gerrymandering diluted their political power. Despite its large Mexican-American population, Los Angeles had no Hispanic representative on the city council at the end of the 1960s. The justice system often treated Chicanos unfairly. "You are lower than animals and haven't the right to live in organized society—just miserable, lousy, rotten people," a judge told Chicano defendants in California. "Maybe Hitler was right."

The combination of poverty and discrimination marked Chicano life. Many Mexican Americans were crowded into *barrios*, rundown neighborhoods in the cities. In the countryside, many lived without hot water or toilets. Infant mortality was above average, and life expectancy was below average. Nationwide, almost half of the Mexican-American population was functionally illiterate. In Texas, nine out of 10 Chicanos had not finished high school.

Encouraged by the civil rights movement and the general optimism of the 1960s, Mexican Americans protested against poverty and injustice. The plight of migrant farm workers became a focus for Chicano activism. In the fertile San Joaquin Valley of California, the Mexican Americans who labored for powerful fruit-growers earned as little as 10 cents an hour and lived in miserable conditions. Unprotected by federal labor law, these agricultural workers were supposedly impossible to organize, but César Chávez, a former migrant worker influenced by Martin Luther King's nonviolent creed, helped them organize the National Farm Worker Association, which later became the United Farm Workers of America. In 1965 the union went out on strike or "huelga." The growers, accusing

Marchers' symbols display some of the diverse sources of Chicano activism: the United Farm Workers union, the Roman Catholic Virgin of Guadalupe, the American flag.

Chávez of Communist ties, called on police, strikebreakers, intimidation, and violence. Although the workers were united by their ethnic pride and Roman Catholic faith, the struggle took years. Chávez's nonviolent tactics, which included a twenty-five-day hunger strike in 1968, gradually appealed to liberals and other Americans. Chávez also initiated a successful nationwide consumer boycott against grapes. Under this pressure, the grape-growers began to settle with the union. It was, said Chávez, "the beginning of a new day."

While Chávez turned for inspiration to Martin Luther King, Jr., and the civil rights movement, other Chicanos responded to the nationalism of the Black Power movement. In New Mexico, Reies López "Tiger" Tijerina, a former preacher, favored separatism over integration, nationalism over assimilation. He created the Alianza Federal de Mercedes (Federal Alliance of Land Grants) to take back land that the United States had supposedly stolen from Mexicans. According to Tijerina, the return of the land would promote both cultural pride and economic independence. In 1967, Tijerina's raid on a courthouse and other militant acts earned him a jail sentence and a reputation as the "Robin Hood of New Mexico."

Chicano activism flourished in the late 1960s. In Denver, Colorado, Corky Gonzales started the Crusade for Justice, a pioneering Mexican-American civil rights group. In East Los Angeles, the Brown Berets, a paramilitary group, showed the influence of the Black Panthers. In California in 1969, college students began the Movimiento Estudiantil Chicano de Aztlán (Chicano Student Movement of Aztlán). The organization was known by its initials, MEChA, which spelled the word for "match" in the Spanish dialect of Mexican Americans. MEChA was meant to be the match that would kindle social change for Chicanos. In San Antonio, students created the Mexican American Youth Organization (MAYO). With cries of "Blow Out!," Chicano students in 1968 walked out of Lincoln High School in East Los Angeles to protest racism and unequal treatment. "Blowouts" soon spread across Los Angeles to other cities and states. The next year, a blowout in Crystal City, Texas, led to a boycott of Anglo businesses and to the formation of La Raza Unida, a political party, which won control of the local school board in 1970. Thousands of students marked September 16, 1969, Mexican Independence Day, with the First National Chicano Boycott of high schools.

All these protests and organizations reflected a strong sense of Chicano pride. "Brown is beautiful," Mexican Americans proclaimed. Their activism also reflected a deep desire to preserve the Chicano heritage. Protesters wanted bilingual education and Mexican-American studies in the schools. The protesters wanted equal opportunity and affirmative action in schools and workplaces as well. Most fundamentally, Mexican-American activism reflected the desire for empowerment, for what some called "Brown Power."

The Chicano movement did not have quite the impact of the African-American civil rights movement, but Mexican-American activists made some important local gains. On the national level, Congress prohibited state bans on teaching in Spanish. Yet white Americans, on the whole, paid less attention to the Brown Power movement than they did to the struggles of African Americans. Mexican Americans were themselves divided. Many middle-class Mexican Americans did not care for the term "Chicano" or for the separatism and revolutionary rhetoric of Tiger Tijerina. Nevertheless, the Brown Power movement had begun to change the status of Mexican Americans.

Asian-American Activism

Asian Americans also pressed for rights and recognition as the 1960s ended. Like Chicano activists, Chinese, Japanese, Filipino, and other Americans of Asian origin were inspired by the struggles of African Americans. Like Chicanos, Asian Americans confronted a history of discrimination in the United States. They, too, had to contend with denigrating stereotypes and hurtful epithets, such as "gooks," "Japs," and "Chinks." Asian-American activism was also driven by the Vietnam War. The United States' destructive violence in Southeast Asia raised troubling questions about white Americans' attitudes toward Asian peoples.

The size of the Asian-American population, much smaller than the Chicano population, limited organization and protest, but the provisions of the Immigration Act of 1965 had made possible increased Asian migration to the United States. From the 1960s through the 1970s, the war in Southeast Asia, political conditions in the Philippines, and beckoning opportunity in the United States spurred waves of Asian immigration. By 1980 America was home to more than three million Asian immigrants, including 812,000 Chinese, 781,000 Filipinos, and 716,000 Japanese. Overall, there were 3.7 million Americans of Asian descent. The majority of them lived in the Pacific states and in cities.

Asian-American activism followed the pattern of other minority movements. By the late 1960s, Asian Americans were demonstrating a new ethnic self-consciousness and pride. Such literary works as Maxine Hong Kingston's *Woman Warrior: A Memoir of a Girlhood Among Ghosts* (1976) explored the nature of Asian-American identity. Many Asian Americans saw themselves not only as Chinese or Japanese, inheritors of a particular national and ethnic heritage; they increasingly considered themselves members of a broader, pan-Asian group that united the different ethnic groups.

Like other minority groups, Asian Americans formed new organizations to press for rights and opportunities. In 1968, the Asian American Political Alliance (AAPA) emerged on the campus of the University of California at Berkeley to unite Chinese, Japanese, and Filipino students. Asian Americans pushed for Asian studies programs on college campuses. Beginning in 1969, Asian students went on strike at San Francisco State College and Berkeley to demand the introduction of Asian studies. By the end of the 1970s, a number of colleges and universities had responded to Asian-American students' demands for courses and programs.

Asian-American activism spread beyond campuses in the 1970s. In 1974 protests forced the hiring of Chinese-American workers to help build the Confucius Plaza complex in New York City's Chinatown. In San Francisco activists brought suit against the public-school system on behalf of 1,800 Chinese pupils. Ruling on the case in *Lau v. Nichols* in 1974, the Supreme Court declared that school systems had to provide bilingual instruction so that non-English-speaking students would have full educational opportunities. The decision was a significant gain for equal rights and cultural diversity.

Not all Asian-American activism was immediately successful. Japanese groups, including the Redress and Reparations Movement, demanded compensation for the U. S. government's internment of Japanese Americans during World War II. In 1976 Washington did rescind Executive Order 9066, the 1942 presidential directive that allowed internment to occur. But the federal government did not make a more comprehensive settlement with Japanese Americans until 1988. Some Asian-American activism was unsuccessful altogether. In the 1970s, there were protests to preserve the International Hotel in San Francisco's Manilatown, which had become a symbol of the Asian presence in that city's history, but the hotel, home to elderly Filipino men, was torn down nevertheless in 1977.

Asian Americans, like Chicanos, made only limited gains by 1980. Relatively small in number, the Asian-American population could not mount a massive protest movement around an issue that would command the sustained attention and sympathy of other Americans. However, Asian Americans had developed a new consciousness and new organizations; they had also forced real change at the local and national levels.

The Struggle for Native-American Rights

African-American activism also inspired Native Americans. Like African Americans and Mexican Americans, American Indians responded to poverty and discrimination. Native Americans' struggle also reflected their distinctive relationship with the federal government.

After many years of decline and stagnation, the Native-American population had grown rapidly since World War II (see Map 29-3). By 1970, there were nearly 800,000 Native Americans, most of whom lived west of the Mississippi. Nearly 300,000 Native Americans resided in just three states—Oklahoma, Arizona, and California. About half of all Native Americans still lived on reservations. Native Americans were divided into about 175 tribes and other groups, but, like Mexican Americans and African Americans, they were united by poor living conditions and persistent discrimination. Native Americans had the lowest average family income of any ethnic group in the United States. Reservations had especially high unemployment rates. Many Native-American children attended substandard schools. Television and other media stereotyped Native Americans as lazy and savage.

As always, Native-American life was shaped by Indians' unique relationship with the federal government. Many resented the Bureau of Indian Affairs (BIA), which had long patronized and exploited tribes. Like African-American and Mexican-American separatists, some Native Americans began to see themselves as a nation apart from the United States. Calling themselves "prisoners of war," these Native Americans struck an aggressive stance,

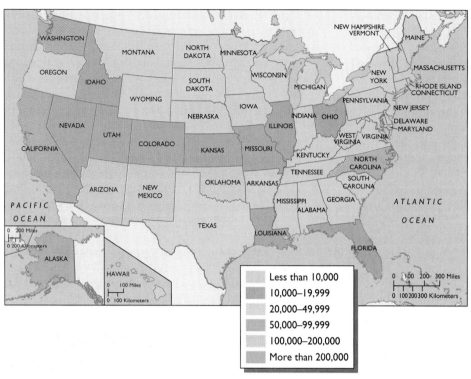

Map 29-3   Native-American Population, 1980.
After rapid growth in the years following World War II, the Native-American population remained largest west of the Mississippi River, and above all, across the Southwest. But there were substantial numbers of Native Americans in every region.

Source: Data from Statistical Abstract of the United States, 1984, pp. 375–76, 463, 760; and Statistical Abstract, 1973, p. 348.

planned to convert into a Native-American museum and center. In 1972, AIM took over and damaged the BIA headquarters in Washington. The next year, activists took over the BIA office in Wounded Knee, South Dakota, where federal troops had massacred Indians in 1890.

The Native-American rights movement made few gains in a society worried about limited resources and an uncertain future. A hostile Nixon administration worked to break up AIM. Through the Indian Self-determination Act of 1975, the federal government did allow Native Americans more chance for independence on the reservations. Still, Native Americans themselves were divided about their relationship to the government. Many tribal leaders wanted to continue selling off their lands through the BIA. AIM assailed Native Americans who accepted the BIA's authority as "Uncle Tomahawks" or "Apples"—red on the outside and white on the inside. On the other hand, a tribal leader referred to AIM as "bums." Despite such divisions, the movement had forced American society to confront the inequitable treatment of Native Americans more directly than at any time since the Great Depression.

expressed in such slogans as "Custer Had It Coming" and "Red Power." In his book *Custer Died for Your Sins* (1969), Vine Deloria, Jr., rejected assimilation by the "establishment." What Native Americans needed, Deloria argued, was "a cultural leave-us-alone-agreement."

Beginning in the 1960s, a Native-American movement emerged to protest federal policy, combat stereotypes, unite tribes, and perpetuate their cultures. Native Americans called for an end to employment discrimination and to the sale of Indian lands and resources to corporations. Activists staged "hunt-ins" and "fish-ins" to protest lost hunting and fishing rights. Native Americans also condemned the use of Indian symbols by schools and sports teams and demanded Indian-centered school curricula.

Some Indians favored more radical action. Copying the Black Panthers, a group of Native Americans in Minneapolis, Minnesota, formed an "Indian Patrol," clad in red berets and jackets, to defend against the police. The patrol evolved into the American Indian Movement (AIM), which spread to other cities. In 1969, AIM activists occupied the abandoned federal prison on Alcatraz Island in San Francisco Bay and told the authorities to leave. As thousands of Native Americans converged on Alcatraz, the occupiers unsuccessfully offered the government "$24 in glass beads and cloth" for the prison, which they

Homosexuals and "Gay Power"

Singled out for persecution in the McCarthy era, most gay men and women had learned to conceal their sexual identity in public. McCarthyism was over by the 1960s, but mainstream American culture still mercilessly ridiculed homosexuals as "faggots," "queers," and "dykes." The medical profession still treated homosexuality as an illness. "We are," said a gay writer, "the silent minority, the silenced minority—invisible women, invisible men." In the late 1960s, that began to change.

One catalyst was certainly the struggles of women, racial minorities, and students. Another was a police raid on the Stonewall Inn, a gay bar in New York City's Greenwich Village, one evening in June 1969. Such raids were commonplace, but this time, to the surprise of the police, gay men resisted. The next night, the police beat and arrested gay protesters, who yelled, "Gay Power!" and "I'm a faggot, and I'm proud of it!"

www.prenhall.com/boydston/AIM

web connection

The American Indian Movement

In America's popular culture, most references to American Indians seem to be as sports icons. The images are usually set in 18th- or 19th-century clothing and activities, as if Indian cultures froze at the moment of U.S. conquest of Indian nations. They are represented as tragic heroes, clueless goofs, or spiritual mystics who aid the conquerors. It took the American Indian Movement (AIM) and similar 20th-century social and political organizations to raise public consciousness to a level where it became apparent that American Indians exist today as human as anyone else, in cultures as dynamic and adaptive as every ethnic minority group must be. How did AIM help change the direction of public attention to Native North Americans in the 20th century?

Backlash: From Radical Action to Conservative Reaction

By the close of the 1960s, American society reverberated with demands to end the war in Vietnam and allow equal rights at home. Surrounded by protests, some hopeful activists believed the United States would be torn apart and remade. "The new American revolution has begun," a magazine concluded. But the revolution never came. Instead of merging, some radical movements squabbled and fell apart. Many Americans abandoned activism for their own private concerns; others angrily rejected protest movements. Encouraging this backlash, President Nixon won re-election in 1972. A decade that started with radical action ended with conservative reaction.

"The Movement" and the "Me-Decade"

Many activists believed that the struggles of women and minorities, along with student protest and the antiwar movement, were creating a single, great coalition, known simply as "the Movement." For a moment at the start of the 1970s, it seemed as if the Movement might in fact take shape, but that possibility faded quickly. The different protest groups sometimes cooperated, but they never merged, and they were often hostile to each other. The male members of Students for a Democratic Society (SDS) were slow to accept radical feminism. The Black Panthers derided SDS as "sissies" and women's lib as "pussy power." Heterosexual and lesbian feminists assailed each other.

In addition, key groups within the Movement fell apart. Much of the New Left never even made it to the 1970s. Plagued by internal divisions, SDS held its last convention in 1969. The Weathermen—a violent faction who took their name from the line of a song by Bob Dylan—called for "Days of Rage" in the "pig city" of Chicago in October 1969. Yet only a few hundred protesters showed up, smashed some windows, and got arrested. The hated "establishment" survived the attack. Transient radical groups bombed or burned corporate headquarters and other "establishment" targets but succeeded only in giving the New Left and the Movement a bad name. The Black Panthers did not hold on to their following in inner-city neighborhoods. The FBI secretly penetrated Panther chapters and worked to discredit the organization. Panther leaders fled the country, went to jail, or died at the hands of police. Radical feminist groups also declined as the 1970s wore on. Women's liberation increasingly focused on liberal demands, such as the ERA.

Stonewall became a rallying cry for gay activism. The Gay Liberation Front, the Student Homophile League, and other organizations appeared. Activists picketed companies that discriminated against gays, and homosexuals socialized more openly. On the first anniversary of Stonewall, 10,000 gay men and women paraded down New York's Sixth Avenue. "Two, four, six, eight!" marchers chanted. "Gay is just as good as straight!" "Homosexuals," *Time* magazine reported, "have never been so visible." Their movement began to have an effect on mainstream culture. In 1974, the American Psychiatric Association decided that homosexuality was not a "mental disorder" and that homosexuals deserved equal rights.

The emerging movements for gay, Native-American, and Chicano rights, along with the ongoing crusades of women and African Americans, made a deep impact on the 1970s. American society could not escape the burgeoning demands for equal rights and opportunities for all people. Women, gays, African Americans, Native Americans, and Chicanos did not win full equality, of course, but these groups made important gains when they refused to settle for less in the 1970s. As a result of this activism, American society was more fully committed to equal rights by the end of the decade.

The "new American revolution" never took place in part because some protest movements lost their targets. After the widespread demonstrations of 1970, the antiwar movement declined as it became clear that the U. S. was pulling out of Vietnam. The student movement declined, too, as young people lost some of their grievances. Around the country, colleges and universities were easing parietal rules and other regulations. In 1971, the states completed ratification of the Twenty-Sixth Amendment to the Constitution, which lowered the voting age to 18.

The "revolution" also failed to materialize because many people seemed to turn away from activism and political engagement in the 1970s. Some were disillusioned by the failure of the Great Society and the duplicity of the Johnson and Nixon administrations. Others were disappointed by the limited accomplishments of radical movements. Still others found themselves caught up in a variety of therapeutic and religious movements. Transcendental meditation, yoga, Zen, the occult, the Unification Church of the Reverend Sun Myung Moon, and other spiritual enterprises encouraged Americans to focus on their inner needs rather than on political change.

There were other forces at work, too. The 1970s, announced the writer Tom Wolfe, were "the Me-Decade." Wolfe and other observers believed Americans had become self-absorbed and narcissistic. The cause, explained the historian and social critic Christopher Lasch, was the crisis of capitalism in "an age of diminishing expectations." "Having no hope of improving their lives in any of the ways that matter," Lasch wrote in *The Culture of Narcissism,* "people have convinced themselves that what matters is psychic self-improvement." The fears about the self-absorbed "Me-Decade" were as exaggerated as the hopes for the revolutionary Movement. People did not suddenly stop hoping and working for change, but Wolfe and Lasch were basically correct. In a time of economic uncertainty and political disappointment, many Americans felt they could not afford the expansive liberal dreams of the 1960s. They had to look out for themselves.

The Plight of the White Ethnics

The "new American revolution" was a victim of anger as well as apathy. Many lower-middle-class and working-class whites rejected the Movement and much of what it represented. A newspaperman even suggested that these Americans were "on the edge of open, sustained, and possibly violent revolt" themselves. They felt abandoned by liberal politicians; they believed the Great Society did too little for them and too much for minorities; and they believed their neighborhoods were threatened by urban renewal projects and court-ordered busing. They resented the students and protesters who had avoided fighting in Vietnam, and many of them resented the women's movement. Most of all, they feared the consequences of economic decline. In a decade of deindustrialization, they faced the loss of their jobs and their standard of living. "I work my ass off," said an iron worker. "But I can't make it."

The media painted an unflattering portrait of these Americans. The popular television comedy *All in the Family* derided its main character, the conservative Archie Bunker, who was upset with his feminist daughter, his liberal son-in-law, and all the social change around him. He railed against "hebes," "spics," "spades," "fags," and "pinkos." Underneath Archie's outbursts was frustration over his disappointed expectations. "He'll never be more than what he is now," his wife Edith said sadly, "even though he had dreams once."

In reality, the white working and lower-middle classes were not so racist and forlorn. They took renewed pride in the ethnic heritage that set them apart from other Americans. These "white ethnics" were self-consciously German American or Irish American, like the opponents of busing in Boston. They were PIGS—Poles, Italians, Greeks, and Slovaks.

The white ethnics used their heritage to affirm an alternative set of values—their own counterculture—in 1970s America. For them, ethnicity meant a commitment to family, neighborhood, and religion in place of the individualistic American dream and the centralizing federal government. Francis Ford Coppola's Oscar-winning film, *The Godfather* (1972), emphasized ethnicity's powerful appeal. In the movie, a murderous Italian-American organized-crime "family" actually seemed attractive because of its commitment to ethnic values.

The ethnic revival did not appear to accomplish much. Like minority groups, the white ethnics lobbied for cultural recognition. Some colleges and universities responded by creating ethnic-studies programs. In 1972 Congress responded by passing the Ethnic Heritage Studies Act to "legitimatize ethnicity" and promote the study of immigrant cultures. Most important, perhaps, the white ethnics formed a large potential voting bloc, attractive to politicians.

The Conservative Counterattack

During the 1970s, the white ethnics became an important part of a conservative counterattack against radicalism, liberalism, and the Democratic Party. Assailing the Movement, Richard Nixon and the Republicans tried to put together a coalition of white ethnics in the North and white voters in the Sunbelt. That coalition rewarded Nixon with a landslide re-election in 1972.

The Nixon administration condemned radicalism and demonstrations. "Anarchy," the president fumed, "this is the way civilizations begin to die." Vice President Spiro

Marlon Brando in the title role of The Godfather, *the popular 1972 film that reflected key themes of white ethnicity in the post-Vietnam War era.*

Agnew attacked "malcontents, radicals, incendiaries, civil and uncivil disobedients among our young." He also assailed the "effete corps of impudent snobs who characterize themselves as intellectuals."

The Nixon administration used more than words against protesters. The president ordered Internal Revenue Service (IRS) investigations to harass liberal and antiwar figures. He employed the Federal Bureau of Investigation to infiltrate and disrupt the Black Power movement, the Brown Berets, and the New Left. He even made illegal domestic use of the CIA to obstruct the antiwar movement.

To oppose all the forces of disruption, Nixon also called for support from "the great silent majority of my fellow Americans." The president tried to insure some of that support with his so-called "Southern Strategy." He reached out to Sunbelt voters by opposing busing, rapid integration, crime, and radicalism. Nixon also tried to create a more conservative, less activist Supreme Court. In 1969, he named the cautious Warren Burger to succeed Earl Warren as chief justice. To fill another vacancy on the court, he nominated a conservative South Carolina judge,

Clement Haynsworth, who had angered civil rights and union leaders. The nomination failed in the Democratic-controlled Senate. Nixon followed with another conservative nominee, Judge G. Harrold Carswell of Florida, a weak jurist and a former avowed white supremacist. Carswell's nomination also failed, but the president had sent an unmistakable message to the "silent majority" in general and white southerners in particular.

The 1972 Election

The conservative counterattack paid off in the 1972 presidential election. Renominated, the Republican ticket of Nixon and Agnew faced a divided Democratic Party, torn apart by the turmoil of the 1960s. The president also benefited from some unforeseen occurrences in 1972. More than any other politician, George Wallace, the segregationist governor of Alabama, rivaled Nixon's appeal to the "silent majority." But Wallace's campaign for the Democratic nomination came to an end when a would-be assassin's bullet paralyzed him from the waist down. In addition, the Democratic vice presidential nominee, Senator Thomas Eagleton of Missouri, had to withdraw over revelations about his treatment for depression.

Nixon did not really need good luck in 1972. Moving to the left, the Democratic Party destroyed itself. The Democrats chose a strongly liberal senator, George McGovern of South Dakota, for president. McGovern's eventual running mate was another unabashed liberal, Sargent Shriver, a brother-in-law of the Kennedys. The liberal Democratic ticket, which endorsed busing and affirmative action and opposed the Vietnam War, alienated white ethnics, white southerners, and organized labor. McGovern's followers even produced new party rules that kept Mayor Richard Daley of Chicago, a symbol of the party's white ethnic base, out of the nominating convention.

Carrying 49 out of 50 states, Nixon easily won reelection in November 1972. With nearly 61 percent of the popular vote, the president had scored almost as big a triumph as Lyndon Johnson had in 1964, but Nixon's victory was deceptive. The election had not produced a partisan political realignment. Although the voters had rejected McGovern, they had not abandoned the Democratic Party. The Democrats still controlled both houses of Congress.

Nevertheless, the 1972 election was a vindication of the "Southern Strategy" and a sign that the traditional Democratic coalition was breaking up. More broadly, Nixon's triumph, along with the failure of the Movement, the rise of the white ethnics, and the self-absorption of the "Me-Decade," showed that the glory days of liberalism and radicalism were over. Democrats, liberals, women, and minorities continued to push their agendas in the 1970s, but they had to contend with a powerful conservative backlash.

Political Crisis: Three Troubled Presidencies

Nixon's triumph, the 1972 election, soon turned out to be his undoing. The discovery of illegal activities in the president's campaign led to the revelation of a host of other improprieties and, finally, to his resignation. Nixon's successors, Gerald Ford and Jimmy Carter, could not master the problems of a divided nation discovering the limits of its power. The troubled presidencies of Nixon, Ford, and Carter reinforced the sense of crisis in the United States. The 1970s ended like the 1960s, with Americans wondering whether their political system still worked.

Watergate: The Fall of Richard Nixon

Nixon's fall began when five men were caught breaking into the offices of the Democratic National Committee in the Watergate complex in Washington, D. C., just before 2:00 A.M. on June 17, 1972. The five burglars—four Cuban exiles and a former CIA agent—had ties to Nixon's campaign organization, the Committee to Re-Elect the President (CREEP). They were attempting to fix an electronic eavesdropping device that had been previously planted in the Democrats' headquarters. While George McGovern tried to draw attention to the Watergate break-in, Nixon's spokesman downplayed this "third-rate burglary attempt."

At first, **Watergate** had no impact on the president. He won re-election easily, but gradually, a disturbing story emerged. Two reporters for the *Washington Post,* Bob Woodward and Carl Bernstein, revealed money payments linking the five burglars to CREEP and even to Nixon's White House staff. The burglars went on trial with two other ex-CIA agents, G. Gordon Liddy and E. Howard Hunt, who had directed the break-in for CREEP. Faced with heavy sentences in March 1973, the burglars admitted that "higher-ups" had planned the break-in and then orchestrated a cover-up. One of those higher-ups, Nixon's presidential counsel John Dean, shortly revealed his role in the Watergate affair to a grand jury. The cover-up was unraveling: By the end of April, the president had to accept the resignations of his most trusted aides, H.R. "Bob" Haldeman and John Ehrlichman. To emphasize his commitment to justice, Nixon also named a special federal prosecutor, Archibald Cox, to investigate Watergate.

In the end, the president was trapped by his own words. A Senate committee, chaired by Sam Ervin of North Carolina, began hearings on Watergate in May 1973. Testifying before the committee, a White House aide revealed that a secret taping system routinely recorded conversations in the president's Oval Office in the White House. Claiming "executive privilege," Nixon refused to turn over tapes of his conversations after the break-in. When Archibald Cox continued to press for the tapes, Nixon ordered him fired on Saturday, October 20, 1973. Attorney General Elliott Richardson and a top aide refused to carry out the order and resigned. A third official finally discharged Cox. Nixon's "Saturday Night Massacre" set off a storm of public anger. Nixon had to name a new special prosecutor, Leon Jaworski. The Democratic-controlled House of Representatives began to explore articles of impeachment against the president. "I'm not a crook," Nixon insisted.

By 1974, "Watergate" had come to mean much more than the break-in at Democratic headquarters. The Nixon administration had engaged in a shocking range of improper and illegal behavior over the previous five years. Infuriated by news leaks in 1969, Henry Kissinger had ordered wiretaps on the phones of newspaper reporters and his own staff. Two years later, the White House had created the "Plumbers," a bumbling group of operatives led by Liddy and Hunt, to combat leaks, including the release of the Pentagon Papers by Daniel Ellsberg. Among other ventures, the Plumbers had broken into the offices of Ellsberg's psychiatrist. Anxious to win in 1972, Nixon's men had also engaged in "dirty tricks" to sabotage Democratic presidential aspirants. All this cost money. Nixon's personal lawyer had collected illegal political contributions, "laundered" the money to hide its source, and then transferred it to CREEP.

Nixon contributed directly to his administration's litany of scandals. The president had ordered the secret and illegal bombing of Cambodia. He had impounded—that is, refused to spend—money appropriated by Congress for programs he did not like. Two years earlier, consumed by anger and resentment, he had secretly approved John Dean's proposal to use federal agencies to hurt "our political enemies." Dean drew up an "Opponents List" of people who were to be hounded by the IRS. Ironically, Nixon himself fell afoul of the IRS. In April 1974 he had to pay back taxes and penalties when it became clear he had falsified his returns.

As a result of the Watergate break-in and other scandals, many of Nixon's associates had to leave office. No fewer than 26, including former Attorney General John Mitchell, went to jail. The law even caught up with Vice President Spiro Agnew, who was found to have accepted bribes as the governor of Maryland in the 1960s. In October 1973 Agnew accepted a plea bargain deal, pleaded "no contest" to a charge of tax evasion, and resigned as vice president. He was replaced by Republican Congressman Gerald R. Ford of Michigan.

Finally, the president himself had to leave office. Under growing pressure to release his tapes, Nixon tried to get away with publishing edited transcripts of some of his Oval Office conversations in the spring of 1974. Revealing a vulgar, rambling, and inarticulate president, the tran-

tion contributed to the feeling that the political system, like the economy, no longer seemed to work.

Gerald Ford and a Skeptical Nation

At first, Gerald Ford was a welcome relief for a nation stunned by the misdeeds of Richard Nixon. Modest and good-humored, the new president seemed unlikely to copy his predecessor and abuse the authority of the White House. But Ford also seemed stumbling and unimaginative in the face of the nation's declining prosperity and power. Lyndon Johnson suggested that Ford "had played football without a helmet too many times." Moreover, his administration had no real popular mandate. Ford was the first unelected vice president to succeed to the presidency. His vice president, former New York governor Nelson Rockefeller, had not been elected by the people either. The grandson of oil magnate John D. Rockefeller was confirmed by Congress in 1974.

Hounded by the Watergate scandal, President Richard Nixon, with family members behind him, announces his resignation from office in August 1974.

scripts only fed public disillusionment. In July the House Judiciary Committee voted to recommend to the full House of Representatives three articles of impeachment—obstruction of justice, abuse of power, and defiance of subpoenas.

Nixon still wanted to remain in office and fight the charges. But the Supreme Court ruled unanimously in early August that the president had to turn over his tapes to the special prosecutor. The tapes were a devastating "smoking gun." They showed that Nixon himself had participated in the cover-up of Watergate as early as June 23, 1972. The president had conspired to obstruct justice and had lied repeatedly to the American people. Support for Nixon disappeared immediately. Almost certain to be impeached, the president agreed to resign rather than face a trial in the Senate. He gave a disorganized, teary farewell address on the morning of August 9, 1974, and then left office in disgrace. "My fellow Americans, our long national nightmare is over," the new president, Gerald Ford, declared. "Our constitution works."

Few, if any, presidents have succeeded as grandly and failed as abjectly as Richard Nixon. This puzzling combination of greatness and weakness ensured that Nixon would remain the most controversial president of the twentieth century. He demonstrated real creativity in coming to terms with the new limits on American power, but in the end Nixon succumbed to his character flaws, to his consuming anger and insecurity. He also succumbed to the same temptation to abuse the vast power of the presidency that confronted each of his predecessors during the cold war. In some ways, Nixon helped solve the challenge of living with less in the 1970s. In others, he only intensified the sense of national decline. The scandals of his administra-

Ford had to govern a nation that had grown skeptical about politicians in general and the president in particular. Johnson's deceitful conduct of the Vietnam War and Nixon's scandals raised fears that the presidency had grown too powerful. To re-establish its authority, Congress passed the War Powers Act of 1973, which allowed the president to send troops to hostile situations overseas for no more than 60 days without obtaining congressional consent. If Congress were not to provide that consent, the troops would have to be returned to the United States within the following 30 days. In 1975 Congress conducted hearings on the secret operations of the CIA. Amid revelations about the agency's improper roles in domestic spying and the assassination of foreign leaders, the House and Senate created permanent committees to oversee what a leading Senator described as "a rogue elephant on the rampage." Ford had to ban the use of assassination in American foreign policy.

Soon after taking office, Ford himself fed public skepticism about the presidency. In September, he offered Nixon a full pardon for all crimes he may have committed as president. Critics charged, probably inaccurately, that Nixon and Ford had made a corrupt, secret deal. Ford's popularity dropped immediately. His presidency never fully recovered.

Ford's handling of economic issues did not make up for the pardon. A moderate Republican, the president did not want the federal government to take too active a role in managing the economy. But like Nixon, he could not stop some liberal initiatives. Congress, reflecting popular concern about corporations and the environment, strengthened the regulatory power of the Federal Trade Commission and extended the 1970 Clean Air Act.

Rejecting activist government, Ford could not do much about economic decline. His administration had no solutions for deindustrialization and stagflation. Believing inflation was the most serious problem, Ford did little to stop rising unemployment, which topped nine percent. His anti-inflation program, known as "WIN" for "Whip Inflation Now," mainly encouraged Americans to control price increases voluntarily. Ford wore a "WIN" button on his lapel, but inflation continued.

In foreign affairs, the president had to accept the limits on American power and on Nixon's policy of détente. Despite the 1973 cease-fire agreement, the fighting continued in Vietnam. Like Nixon before him, Ford promised to protect South Vietnam from North Vietnamese aggression, but Congress cut the administration's requests for monetary aid to the Saigon government. The commitment of American armed forces to South Vietnam was out of the question. When North Vietnamese troops invaded early in 1975, panicked civilians fled southward. Congress refused to give any more aid. As Saigon was overrun, the last Americans evacuated in helicopters. Thousands of loyal South Vietnamese fled with them, but many more were left behind. For more than 20 years, the United States had worked to preserve an independent, anti-Communist South Vietnam. Yet, on April 30, 1975, South Vietnam surrendered. There was nothing Ford could do to prevent the final, ignominious failure of America's Vietnam policy.

The president could also do nothing to save the pro-American government of Cambodia from Communist insurgents, the Khmer Rouge, earlier in April 1975. "I have only committed this mistake of believing in you, the Americans," said the leader of Cambodia before he was captured and beheaded. His government fell to the Khmer Rouge, who went on to murder countless numbers of Cambodian civilians. Ford did act the next month when the Khmer Rouge captured an American merchant ship, the *Mayaguez,* off Cambodia. At the cost of 41 deaths, United States marines rescued the thirty-nine-man crew. Ford temporarily soared in the popularity polls, but the *Mayaguez* incident hardly changed the fundamental reality. The United States no longer wielded much power in Southeast Asia.

The policy of détente with the Soviet Union was supposed to help America cope with its limited power, but détente was clearly in trouble during the Ford administration. The United States and the Soviets failed to agree to a second Strategic Arms Limitation Treaty, known as SALT II. American critics of détente, including Democratic Senator Henry Jackson of Washington, claimed that the policy sapped American defenses and overlooked human rights violations by the Soviets. In 1974, Jackson successfully added an amendment to a trade bill linking increased commerce to increased freedom for Soviet Jews to emigrate. The Jackson-Vanik Amendment helped sour the Soviets on détente. In turn, Ford further alienated American conservatives when he traveled to Helsinki, Finland, in 1975 to sign an agreement accepting the post-World War II boundaries of European nations. Critics believed the president had sold out Eastern Europe to the Soviets, but the president was only accepting reality. The United States could not roll back Communism in Eastern Europe.

Ford's troubles were reflected at the polls. The Democrats made large gains in the congressional elections in the fall of 1974. In 1976, the Nation's bicentennial, Ford won the Republican nomination for president, but he had to replace Rockefeller with a more conservative vice presidential nominee, Senator Robert Dole of Kansas. The Democrats' presidential choice was former Georgia governor Jimmy Carter, a far cry from the liberal George McGovern. Carter did choose a liberal runningmate, Senator Walter Mondale of Minnesota, but the Georgian ran as a moderate who could appeal to businessmen and white southerners. Carter promised efficiency rather than new reforms. Campaigning as an outsider who had never held office in Washington, he promised "a government as good as the American people."

A U.S. official pushes back a man trying to climb on an overloaded airplane evacuating South Vietnamese refugees as their country collapses in the spring of 1975.

Those people never got excited about the campaign. With low turnout at the polls, Carter won 50.1 percent of the vote to Ford's 48 percent. The Democrat won a majority in the electoral college by carrying much of the industrial Northeast and taking back almost all the South from the Republicans. The outcome was less an endorsement of Carter than a rejection of Ford, who became the first sitting president to lose an election since Herbert Hoover (see Map 29-4). Too many Americans agreed with a journalist that Ford "is an awfully nice man who isn't up to the presidency."

Why Not the Best?: Jimmy Carter

As he took office in 1977, Jimmy Carter seemed very different from Gerald Ford. The new Democratic president appeared capable and efficient. A graduate of the Naval Academy, he had served as an engineer in the Navy's nuclear submarine program. Then he had successfully taken over management of the family peanut farm before entering politics as a state legislator. Carter's commitment to perfectionism was captured in the title of his autobiography, *Why Not the Best?*.

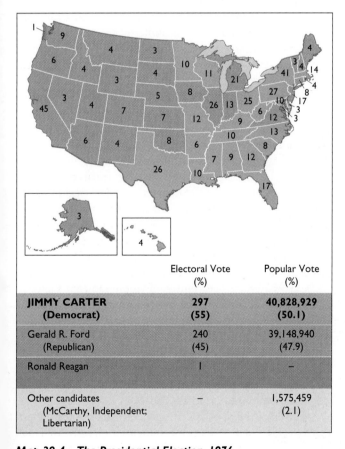

	Electoral Vote (%)	Popular Vote (%)
JIMMY CARTER (Democrat)	**297 (55)**	**40,828,929 (50.1)**
Gerald R. Ford (Republican)	240 (45)	39,148,940 (47.9)
Ronald Reagan	1	–
Other candidates (McCarthy, Independent; Libertarian)	–	1,575,459 (2.1)

Map 29-4 The Presidential Election, 1976.
Jimmy Carter managed to re-establish the Democratic party's appeal to white southerners.

In the next few years, Carter did respond more energetically and imaginatively than Ford had to the nation's problems. Unlike his predecessor, he had the advantage of working with a Congress controlled by his own party. But Carter came to be seen as a weak, uncertain leader who could neither manage Congress nor inspire the American people. Carter's shortcomings certainly contributed to his predicament. More important, he had to contend with the same intractable problems that had bedeviled Ford. In the 1970s, it seemed that no president could resolve the nation's economic, political, and diplomatic crises.

Like Ford, Carter had trouble putting to rest the recent past. Ford ran into trouble when he pardoned Nixon. Carter met angry criticism when he pardoned most American men who had resisted the draft during the Vietnam War. This controversial decision offended many veterans and conservatives and did not completely satisfy opponents of the war.

Carter also had to contend with increasing popular resentment of government. Many Americans believed that government regulation and taxation had gotten out of hand. They were upset when the provisions of the Endangered Species Act of 1973 forced a halt to the construction of a Tennessee dam because it threatened the survival of the snail darter, a small local fish. It seemed as if the federal government worried more about fish than about people's need for electricity and recreation.

The West was the stronghold of antigovernment sentiment in the 1970s. Many westerners objected to continuing federal ownership of vast tracts of land. The government actually owned more than half the land in each of six western states. Assailing the bureaucrats in Washington, D. C., the so-called "Sage Brush Rebellion" demanded state control over federal lands in the West. Businessmen in the West also wanted the government to allow more exploitation of oil, forests, and other resources on federal lands. Meanwhile, California became the center of an anti-tax movement in 1978. Angered by high taxes and government spending in their communities, California voters passed Proposition 13, which sharply reduced property taxes. As one of Carter's aides observed, the tax revolt was "a revolution against government."

As always, antigovernment sentiment was inconsistent. Many of the same people who attacked taxes and regulation expected aid and benefits from Washington. When the giant automaker Chrysler faced bankruptcy in 1979, the government had to save the company with a 1.5-billion-dollar loan guarantee. When Carter moved to cancel supposedly wasteful federal water projects in the West in 1977, he encountered a storm of protest from the heart of the Sage Brush Rebellion. Carter would not be the last politician who had to confront the contradictory demands of American voters.

Carter was most successful when he moved to limit rather than extend government. By the 1970s, some economists were advocating "deregulation" of businesses as a way to lower costs, increase competition, and improve services. The president, however, was not about to disturb broad regulatory agencies such as OSHA and the EPA. Instead, he aimed to lift federal regulation of specific industries, especially in transportation. In 1978, the government removed price controls on the airline industry. In the short run the move lowered fares, but in the long run it drove some airlines out of business.

Deregulation was a sign of a changing balance of political power. Big business, under attack since the 1960s, fought back in the late 1970s. Better organized than before, corporations lobbied effectively against regulation, organized labor, and taxes. Liberals, meanwhile, had lost influence. As a result, Congress never created the Consumer Protection Agency advocated by Ralph Nader and consumer activists. Legislation to make labor organization easier also failed. The Humphrey-Hawkins bill, which reasserted the government's responsibility to ensure full employment, was watered down in Congress. When Carter tried to raise taxes on business, Congress rebuffed him, cut taxes on capital gains, and added more loopholes to the tax law.

Carter attempted, with mixed results, to adjust the economy to the realities of living with less. His program of voluntary wage and price controls did not stop soaring inflation. After shortages of natural gas forced schools and businesses to close in the harsh winter of 1976–1977, Carter addressed the energy crisis. In April 1977, the president told Americans that "the energy shortage is permanent" and urged them to conserve. He proposed a complicated plan that included the establishment of the Department of Energy, taxes on gas-guzzling automobiles and large consumers of oil, tax incentives to stimulate production of oil and gas, and development of nuclear power. Carter called his plan "the moral equivalent of war," but too few Americans wanted to accept this call to arms. Conservatives thought the program expanded government authority. Liberals and environmentalists objected to its support for nuclear power and oil-company profits. The final plan, passed in 1978, was considerably weakened. The measure hardly solved the nation's energy problems, but it did encourage conservation.

Nuclear power, a key part of Carter's energy plan, soon lost much of its appeal. In March 1979 a nuclear reactor at Three Mile Island, downriver from Harrisburg, Pennsylvania, nearly suffered a catastrophic meltdown. As 100,000 frightened residents fled their homes, the reactor had to be permanently closed. Three Mile Island fed popular concerns about the safety of nuclear energy. Around the country, utilities scrapped plans for new nuclear power plants.

Three Mile Island also fed broader anxieties about the environmental damage caused by industrial capitalism. Americans wondered whether their neighborhoods would suffer the fate of Love Canal, near Niagara Falls, New York. There, hazardous waste buried by a chemical company had caused so many cases of cancer, miscarriages, birth defects, and other health problems that residents had to move away. Despite business concerns about regulation, the federal government did respond to environmental threats during the Carter years. Washington created a "superfund" of 1.6 billion dollars to clean up hazardous waste sites. The Carter administration also took control of 100 million acres of Alaska to prevent damage from economic development. That move was not enough for some environmentalists who began to argue that only strict limits on economic growth would preserve the United States and the world. Americans, they felt, might have to learn to live with a great deal less than they had imagined.

At first, Carter had more success with foreign policy than with domestic affairs. Continuing Nixon's de-escalation of the cold war, Carter announced that "we are now free of the inordinate fear of Communism." The president did not abandon Nixon's emphasis on détente with the Soviet Union, but the Democratic president focused more attention on supporting human rights and building harmony around the world. In 1978, Carter won Senate approval of a treaty yielding ownership of the Panama Canal to Panama at the end of the century. In keeping with its imperious attitude toward the Western Hemisphere, the United States had built and managed the canal with little regard for the rights of Panama. Now the treaty signaled a new and more respectful approach to Central and Latin America.

In 1978, Carter also mediated the first peace agreement between Israel and an Arab nation. Personally bringing together Israeli and Egyptian leaders at the Camp David presidential retreat, Carter helped forge a "Framework for Peace" that led to Israel's withdrawal from the Sinai Peninsula and the signing of an Israeli-Egyptian treaty. The agreement was vague; it did not settle the fate of the Israeli-occupied Golan Heights and Gaza Strip or the future of the Palestinian people. But it did establish a basis for future negotiations in a region torn by conflict for centuries. The negotiation of the Camp David peace accords was Carter's greatest achievement as president.

Carter viewed a commitment to human rights abroad as a way of recapturing the international respect that the United States had lost during the Vietnam War. In practice, however, his administration did not speak out consistently against the violation of rights around the world. Instead, Carter was supportive of American allies such as the rulers of Iran and the Philippines who clearly abused human rights in their own countries.

Carter's foreign policy also suffered from the eventual collapse of détente. The president did manage to reach agreement with the Soviets on the SALT II treaty, but the Senate, skeptical about Soviet intentions toward the

United States, was reluctant to ratify the agreement. Then, in December 1979, the Soviet Union invaded its southern neighbor, Afghanistan. Faced with this aggression, Carter withdrew the SALT II treaty, stopped grain shipments to the Soviet Union, forbade American athletes to compete in the 1980 Olympics in Moscow, and increased American military spending. These moves had no effect on the Soviet invasion, but détente was obviously over. Given Carter's uneven commitment to human rights, the direction of American foreign policy after Vietnam had become unclear.

By 1979, Carter was a deeply unpopular president. He had not stabilized the economy or set out a coherent foreign policy. Particular actions, such as the grain embargo and the Panama Canal Treaty, had alienated different groups of Americans. More important, Carter clearly had not established "a government as good as the American people." After pondering the situation at the Camp David retreat for 11 days in July, the president came back to shake up his cabinet and tell a television audience that the nation was suffering a "crisis of spirit." The president offered a number of proposals to deal with the energy crisis, but he spoke most strongly to the state of the nation. "All the legislation in the world can't fix what's wrong with America," Carter maintained. "What is lacking is confidence and a sense of community." Congress passed much of Carter's energy program, including a tax on oil companies' "windfall" profits, but his speech only seemed to alienate more Americans.

Carter became still more embattled when the Shah of Iran was overthrown by the followers of a religious leader, the Ayatollah Ruholla Khomeini, early in 1979. The Shah had long received lavish aid and praise from the United States. Now, the Iranian revolutionaries, eager to restore traditional Islamic values, condemned America for imposing the Shah and modern culture on their nation. The revolution in oil-rich Iran underscored the decline of American power. The United States could do nothing to prevent the fall of its ally, the Shah. In the wake of the revolution, oil prices rose. Once again, American had to contend with gas lines. Inflation spread through the economy.

The situation worsened when Khomeini condemned the United States—the "Great Satan"—for allowing the Shah to receive medical treatment in New York in October. On November 4, students loyal to Khomeini overran the United States embassy in Tehran, the Iranian capital, and took 60 Americans hostages. Carter froze Iranian assets in the United States, but he could not compel the release of all the hostages. As days passed, the United States seemed helpless. In the spring of 1980, the frustrated president ordered a secret military mission to rescue the remaining 52 hostages. On April 24, eight American helicopters left an aircraft carrier in the Persian Gulf and headed for a desert rendezvous with six transport planes carrying troops and supplies. When two helicopters broke down and another became lost, the mission had to be aborted. As the troops prepared to leave, a helicopter veered into a transport. Eight dead soldiers and four helicopters were left behind in the desert. The hostages remained in captivity.

A poster of President Jimmy Carter, carried in a demonstration near the American embassy in Tehran, mocks U.S. weakness in the Iranian hostage crisis in 1979.

CHRONOLOGY

1968   My Lai Massacre in South Vietnam
"Blowouts" by Chicano students at Lincoln
High School in East Los Angeles and other
schools
Founding of American Indian Movement
(AIM)

1969   Secret bombing of Cambodia ordered by
President Richard Nixon
Stonewall Riot in New York's Greenwich
Village
Apollo 11 moon landing
Announcement of Nixon Doctrine
Founding of Chicano student organization
MEChA
"Days of Rage" protests by Weathermen in
Chicago

1970   Bankruptcy of Penn Central Railroad
First Earth Day
Creation of Environmental
Protection Agency (EPA)
United States-South Vietnam invasion of
Cambodia
Killing of students at Kent State University and
Jackson State College
Women's Strike for Equality

1971   Conviction of Lt. William Calley, Jr., for role in
My Lai Massacre
Publication of Pentagon Papers by *New York
Times*
Nixon takes U. S. off gold standard
Ratification of Twenty-Sixth Amendment,
lowering voting age to 18
Supreme Court busing decision, *Swann v.
Charlotte-Mecklenburg Board of Education*

1972   President Nixon's trips to the People's Republic
of China and the Soviet Union

Strategic Arms Limitation Treaty (SALT I) and
Anti-Ballistic Missile (ABM) Treaty signed
Congressional passage of Equal Rights
Amendment
Operation Linebacker bombing raids on North
Vietnam
Watergate burglary
Re-election of President Nixon

1973   Peace agreement to end Vietnam War signed
Beginning of Arab oil embargo
Supreme Court abortion ruling, *Roe v. Wade*
Resignation of Vice President Agnew

1974   Beginning of struggle over busing in Boston
Resignation of President Nixon
Succession to presidency by Gerald Ford

1975   Surrender of South Vietnam to North Vietnam
Helsinki Agreement

1976   Announcement of the "Me-Decade" by Tom
Wolfe
Jimmy Carter elected president

1977   President Carter proposes energy plan

1978   Camp David peace accords
Supreme Court affirmative-action decision,
*Regents of the University of California v. Allan
Bakke*

1979   Accident at Three Mile Island nuclear power
plant
Iranian revolution

1980   Failed mission to rescue U.S. hostages in Iran

Conclusion

The failure of the rescue mission summed up the problems of the United States at the start of the 1980s. The nation was no longer strong enough to protect all its own citizens abroad. The American presidency seemed weak and inef-fectual. The American military seemed unable to project its power overseas. The American economy could not produce helicopters that worked. The nation had not yet adjusted to the challenges of living with less.

Review Questions

1. Discuss the causes of the economic troubles of the 1970s. How did economic decline affect the lives of Americans?

2. What was President Richard Nixon's strategy for helping Americans to live with less? Was that strategy successful?

3. Discuss the foreign policies of the Nixon administration, including détente and the Nixon Doctrine. How did these policies mark a departure from previous American approaches to the cold war?

4. Compare the movements for rights and recognition created by African Americans, Chicanos, Asian Americans, Native Americans, women, and gays. Were these movements different in important ways?

5. Why did a conservative backlash develop from the late 1960s through the 1970s? Did this conservative reaction have a major effect on American life?

6. Why did Richard Nixon, Gerald Ford, and Jimmy Carter have such troubled presidencies? Did these three presidents create their own problems, or did they face impossible situations?

Further Readings

Stephen E. Ambrose, *Nixon,* 3 vols (1987–1991). A readable narrative of Nixon's many triumphs and ultimate failure.

Terry H. Anderson, *The Movement and the Sixties: Protest in America From Greensboro to Wounded Knee* (1995). A sweeping chronicle of the many protests in both the 1960s and 1970s that created the "Movement."

Peter N. Carroll, *It Seemed Like Nothing Happened: The Tragedy and Promise of America in the 1970s* (1983). A fresh, journalistic account that is still the best general social history of the 1970s.

Ronald P. Formisano, *Boston Against Busing: Race, Class, and Ethnicity in the 1960s and 1970s* (1991). Nicely analyzes the white resistance to school desegregation.

Ignacio Garcia, *Chicanismo: The Forging of a Militant Ethos Among Mexican Americans* (2000). Offers a balanced account of the emerging Chicano rights movement.

Seymour Hersh, *The Price of Power: Kissinger in the Nixon White House* (1983). A harsh, fascinating study of the architect of détente.

Burton I. Kaufman, *The Presidency of James Earl Carter, Jr.* (1993). A fair-minded treatment of a troubled presidency.

Stanley I. Kutler, *The Wars of Watergate: The Last Crisis of Richard Nixon* (1990). A balanced, clear account of the scandal that brought down Richard Nixon.

Eric Marcus, *Making History: The Struggle for Gay and Lesbian Equal Rights, 1945–1980* (1992). Moving, candid oral histories that personalize the gay and lesbian liberation movement.

Winifred D. Wandersee, *On the Move: American Women in the 1970s* (1988). A detailed study of the different social and political phases of women's lib in the 1970s, including the fight for the Equal Rights Amendment.

History on the Internet

"The Wars of Vietnam: An Overview"

http://students.vassar.edu/~vietnam/overview.html

Offering an extensive overview of military conflicts in Vietnam from 1945 up through U. S engagement, this site offers full text of historical documents including the Tonkin Gulf Resolution and excerpts from American presidential speeches.

"May 4" Kent State

http://www.library.kent.edu/exhibits/4may95/index.html

Through their "May 4" collection, learn more about the Kent State student shootings. The site includes photos, links to various other sites, chronologies, and information on the aftermath of the incident.

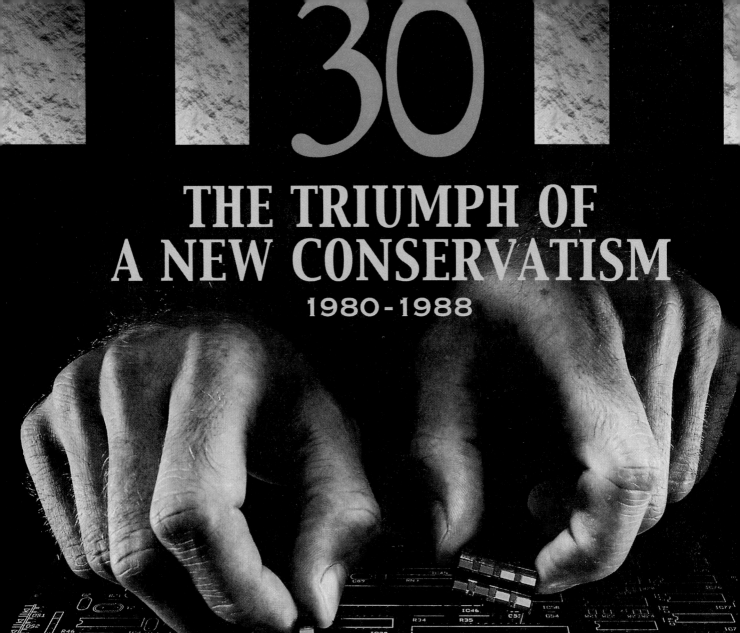

30

THE TRIUMPH OF
A NEW CONSERVATISM

1980-1988

OUTLINE

The Trumps' American Dream

In the 1980s Donald and Ivana Trump were one of the most famous couples in the United States. Rich, glamorous, and powerful, the Trumps appeared to prove that the American Dream could still come true.

Donald, the son of a prosperous real estate developer, seemed unaffected by recent history. As a young man, he ignored the rebellions of the 1960s and the economic troubles of the 1970s. At boarding school in the 1960s, he was "something of an alien," a writer explained. "His mind was on business when the minds of most of his peers were on pot, permissiveness, and hard rock music." Going into business in New York in the 1970s, Trump refused to be pessimistic about the city's depressed real estate market and uncertain finances. While the nation learned to live with less in a time of economic decline, Trump bought more and more. He aggressively acquired land and buildings at low prices. "I like beating my enemies to the ground," he boasted.

Trump's strategy paid off in the 1980s. By the time he turned 40 in 1986, Trump had accumulated one of the largest fortunes in America. He owned apartment houses and hotels. He built the posh Trump Tower on Fifth Avenue, complete with a five-story glass atrium and condominiums with price tags as high as 10 million dollars each. He had a glitzy gambling casino, Trump's Castle, in Atlantic City, New Jersey. He owned an airline, the Trump Shuttle. He owned a football team, the New Jersey Generals. He even had his own bestselling book, naturally titled *Trump.* Along with his three-story penthouse in the Trump Tower, he acquired a forty-seven-room hideaway in Connecticut and a seventeen-and-one-half-acre, 118-room estate in Palm Beach, Florida. He traveled in his own jet and his own helicopters. His twenty-nine-million-dollar yacht, the *Trump Princess,* had gold and onyx bathroom fixtures. "Who has done as much as I have?" he asked.

Trump's wife, Ivana, was a success story as well. She lived both an old dream for immigrants and a new dream for women. Born in Austria and raised in Czechoslovakia, she found riches and happiness in the United States. A modestly successful skier and model, Ivana married the man she called "The Donald" in New York in 1977 and became "a stunning prototype of the truly fashionable world-class billionairess."

Ivana's life with "The Donald" seemed to prove that a modern American woman could, in fact, have it all. After bearing three children she remained, an admiring biographer exclaimed, a "celebration of the body perfect." Ivana gracefully combined family and career. "She's not only a mother who sensibly but sensitively dotes on her good kids," her biographer maintained, "she's also a dynamo at the executive desk." Ivana helped supervise interior decoration for Donald's projects. Then she managed Trump's Casino. "I'm not tough, but I'm strong," Ivana explained. "You can't be a pussycat."

The Trumps faced a good deal of criticism. To some observers, their self-promoting lifestyle was flashy, excessive, and insubstantial. Donald's brash business methods seemed to trample ordinary people. Over the years, tenants accused him of cruel treatment. The U. S. Justice Department charged the Trump Organization with racial discrimination.

Ivana and Donald Trump, controversial symbols of materialism and conservatism in the 1980s.

Donald and Ivana survived the criticism, but the couple did not avoid personal and financial troubles by the end of the 1980s. Donald removed Ivana as manager of Trump's Casino in May 1988 because of lagging profits. Then she discovered his apparent affair with a model. In the course of a much-publicized break-up, Donald locked Ivana out of her office at the Trump Plaza. After their divorce, she confessed to "a tremendous sense of failure." She wondered, too, about the free-wheeling capitalism that had put the Trumps on top. "I'm not knocking the free enterprise system," she wrote, "but it can be a trap." Meanwhile, that system nearly destroyed Donald's empire. By 1990, he was deep in debt trying to fund his glitziest casino, the Trump Taj Mahal. To stave off bankruptcy, he had to sell the Trump Shuttle and other properties. His bankers put him on a monthly allowance.

Despite their troubles, the Trumps had not lost everything. No longer one of the few hundred richest men in America, Donald was still wealthy. Ivana came out of the divorce with the Connecticut mansion and 20 million dollars. In the next few years, she wrote romance novels and a how-to book on surviving divorce. Donald wrote his own defiant book, *Trump: Surviving at the Top.*

The Trumps' story reflected a central theme of the 1980s. Still coming to terms with the problems of economic and political decline, the United States turned toward an older, business-centered, conservative vision of the political economy. American culture once again celebrated businesspeople such as Donald Trump. Rejecting the pessimism of the 1970s, many Americans wanted to believe that success like the Trumps' was still possible. Downplaying the idealism of the 1960s, American culture once again exalted the material satisfactions of consumerism. Discounting the liberal faith in activist government, many people favored a more conservative state that promised to restore prosperity and left businesspeople like Donald Trump free to make a fortune.

The trend toward conservatism had wide-ranging consequences in the 1980s. A broad-based coalition elected a conservative Republican, Ronald Reagan, to the presidency. Eager to restore old social, economic, and political values, Reagan set out to recast the American political economy. At home, the "Reagan Revolution," as its supporters called it, aimed to cut taxes, reduce government regulation, and diminish union power in order to restore economic growth. Abroad, the Reagan Revolution meant the return to a foreign policy fiercely dedicated to confronting Communism. With Reagan's re-election in 1984, the new conservatism seemed triumphant.

Before the 1980s ended, however, many Americans wondered whether the conservative triumph, like the Trumps' fortune, was real after all. The conservatives' social agenda, embracing such issues as drugs, education, school prayer, abortion, and affirmative action, had met strong opposition. The nation's renewed prosperity seemed fragile and uneven. Like Donald's empire, the wealth of the 1980s depended on borrowed money and shaky deals. And, like Donald's tenants, some Americans found themselves ignored or exploited. By the close of the decade, ordinary people were learning Ivana's lesson: They could not have it all.

Nevertheless, the conservative resurgence was not an illusion. Americans did embrace more conservative values. The federal government did turn away from liberal policies. Economic decline did slow down. Like the Trumps' marriage and fortune, the conservative triumph was less than it seemed, but it was still real. ▪

A New Conservative Majority

By 1980, a new conservatism had emerged in the United States. This "New Right" drew strength from ongoing changes in the economy and in Americans' economic values. Religious change, especially the surging growth of evangelical Christianity, contributed to the new conservatism. So did the emergence of a conservative "counterestablishment,"—an infrastructure of political action groups, think tanks, and media. The rapid growth of a conservative coalition became clear in the 1980 presidential election, when a majority of voters elected Ronald Reagan to the White House.

The End of Economic Decline?

The decline of the American economy appeared to halt in the 1980s. The continuing growth of the Sunbelt fueled optimism. In the 1980s, people, jobs, and political power continued to flow from the North and East toward the economically vibrant South and West. Rustbelt industrial cities such as Pittsburgh, Detroit, and Gary, Indiana, lost population in the 1980s. Meanwhile, some counties in the Sunbelt states of Georgia, Florida, and Texas more than doubled in population. Growing rapidly, the Sunbelt remained a center of economic optimism. "The rest of the country can be a having a depression," a Texas oil man boasted, "but hell, you don't know it down here." The movement of population had political consequences, too. Reapportionment in 1980 gave more congressional seats and electoral votes to the relatively conservative states of the Sunbelt.

Across the country, technological innovations encouraged hopes for an economic revival. New products and services, introduced in the 1970s or even earlier, became wide-

spread in the 1980s. Microwave ovens, pocket calculators, compact disc players, cordless telephones, and fax machines were just a few features of a consumer electronics revolution. Video-cassette recorders, remote controls, satellites, and cable hook-ups transformed Americans' television viewing habits. By 1988, half of American households had cable television hook-ups and received at least 10 channels.

The most important new product was the microcomputer (see Figure 30-1). Along with other innovations, semiconductors—transistorized integrated circuits attached to small silicon crystals—allowed manufacturers to shrink the computer. By the late 1970s they could put the power of an old, room-sized mainframe computer into a metal box, with a keyboard and a television-like monitor, that would fit on a desk top. In 1977 a new company, Apple, offered its first microcomputer for sale. Four years later, the computing giant IBM introduced its first "personal computer" or PC. By the end of the 1980s, Americans were buying seven million microcomputers a year.

These explosive sales produced optimistic visions of the U. S. economy. Computers seemed to promise a way out of national economic decline. Whereas Asian manufacturers built most consumer-electronics products, American companies dominated the computer industry. Although many computer components were produced abroad, U. S. firms sold most assembled computers ("hardware") and the programs ("software") needed to run them. The microcomputer bolstered older companies such as IBM and created new companies such as Apple and Compaq. It made new entrepreneurs such as Steve Jobs, a

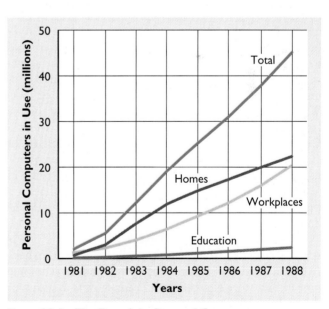

Figure 30-1 The Rise of the Personal Computer.
The rapid rise in the number of microcomputers in use in homes, workplaces, and schools in the 1980s inspired hopes that the nation's economic decline had ended.

Source: Statistical Abstract of the United States, 1989, p. 743; Statistical Abstract, 1993, p. 761.

founder of Apple, and Bill Gates, a founder of the leading software firm Microsoft, very wealthy. The microcomputer fed the growth of the Sunbelt. Compaq's headquarters were in Houston. Apple was one of many computer firms clustered in "Silicon Valley" just outside San Francisco. The microcomputer also seemed to be reviving parts of the Rustbelt. In Massachusetts, a string of vibrant computer companies stretched out from Boston along Route 128 to replace the textile mills and shoe factories that had long since left the state.

The growth of the computer industry rested on the seemingly limitless possibilities of the microcomputer. Observers wondered whether the computer revolution, like the industrial revolution before it, would take away jobs and make Americans lose control over their lives. For example, people feared that in the auto industry automated assembly lines, run by computers, might lead to layoffs of workers. The microcomputer also inspired utopian dreams of an "information" or "high-technology" society built on the production of knowledge rather than things. Promoting literacy and education, the computer would then lift up the poor and disadvantaged. Unlike the old, industrial economy, the smokeless, computerized economy could cut down on pollution and the consumption of raw materials. By enabling people to work at home, the microcomputer could eliminate commuting and relieve urban congestion.

While the 1980s pointed to a utopian future, the decade also recalled the cutthroat capitalism of the past. A wave of corporate takeovers and mergers, much like the consolidations at the turn of the twentieth century, swept across the economy. Aggressive investment bankers and entrepreneurs such as Michael Milken and Ivan Boesky used a variety of techniques to acquire companies. "Junk bonds," that is, high-risk, high-paying securities, were sold to finance takeovers. Executives agreed to sell their own companies in return for "golden parachutes," huge payments these executives received when they lost their jobs. With such tactics, enormous deals merged some of the largest and most famous American corporations. In 1985 General Electric bought RCA for six billion dollars. In 1986 alone there were more than 4,000 mergers worth a total of 190 billion dollars. The biggest deal of all came in 1988 when RJR Nabisco was sold for 25 billion dollars and the company's executives received a one-hundred-million-dollar golden parachute.

Like earlier mergers, the takeovers of the 1980s sparked criticism from Americans worried about expensive deals and the concentration of so much economic power. But other observers saw the takeovers as a sign of the vitality of the American economy. They argued that the mergers created larger and ultimately more efficient companies that could compete more successfully. These observers also praised Milken, Boesky, and other wealthy takeover artists as models of entrepreneurial energy and creativity.

The Rehabilitation of Business

The takeover wave, along with the growth of the Sunbelt and the computer industry, encouraged hopes for an economic revival. In turn, those hopes helped rehabilitate business and its values, which had been assailed in the 1960s and 1970s. The media enthusiastically reported the achievements and opinions of Donald Trump, Michael Milken, Ivan Boesky, Bill Gates, and Steve Jobs. *Dallas, Dynasty,* and other popular television shows told the fictional sagas of wealthy, free-wheeling businessmen and their families. Business was more respectable than at any time since the 1950s.

So was materialism. The Trumps and other business figures helped legitimize the pursuit and enjoyment of wealth. "Greed is all right," Boesky announced in 1985. "Everybody should be a little greedy. You shouldn't feel guilty." His message resonated in American culture. In one of her hit songs, pop-star Madonna joyfully proclaimed that she was a "Material Girl." There was renewed interest in luxurious living during the 1980s. A popular syndicated television show, *Lifestyles of the Rich and Famous,* detailed the material pleasures of wealthy Americans. "Thank goodness it's back," gushed the *New York Times,* "that lovely whipped cream of a word—luxury."

The baby-boom generation reflected the new appeal of business values. Abandoning social action, former 1960s radicals such as the Yippie leader Jerry Rubin took up business and other conventional careers. By 1983 the media were talking about the emergence of "yuppies" or "young urban professionals." Uninterested in reform, these self-centered baby boomers were supposedly eager to make lots of money and then spend it on BMW cars, Perrier water, and other consumer playthings. Although the yuppies received plenty of attention, they made up perhaps only five percent of the whole baby-boom generation. The transition from Yippies to yuppies was exaggerated. Observers overestimated both the idealism of the 1960s and the materialism of the 1980s. Nevertheless, the yuppie stereotype underscored the resurgence of business values. By the 1980s many Americans aspired to a more conservative, money-centered way of life.

The Rise of the Religious Right

At the same time American culture celebrated materialism, many Americans still turned to religion to find meaning in their lives. But the ongoing transformation of religious life also reinforced conservative values. As more liberal denominations grew slowly or even declined, conservative denominations, especially evangelical Christian churches, grew rapidly. Evangelical leaders and their allies took conservative stands on social and economic issues. By 1980 they had become a powerful political movement, the religious right.

GROWING UP IN AMERICA

Yuppies

Yuppies (young urban professionals) symbolized the conservative trend of the 1980s. Like Reagan, the Trumps, and other 1980s icons, the yuppies loved luxury and success. As the authors of a handbook on yuppies put it, "The name of the game is *the* best—buying it, owning it, using it, eating it, wearing it, growing it, cooking it, driving it, doing whatever with it." Yuppies also shared Reagan's optimistic belief that Americans did not have to live with less in the future. "They're rejecting this whole idea of limits, that somehow the pie is getting smaller," a pollster noted.

As symbols of conservatism, yuppies were highly controversial. Business leaders liked their work ethic and lavish consumer spending, but a chorus of commentators branded yuppies crass, materialistic young people. They were attacked for abandoning the idealism of the 1960s. They were attacked for "gentrifying" city neighborhoods by moving in, driving up the cost of housing, and thereby making it impossible for poor people to remain. They were called "the embodiment of selfishness to the point of decadence." They were denounced as "jerks."

Critics also insisted that yuppies were not typical of younger Americans. Most baby boomers, in fact, could not afford to be so optimistic about the future. Unlike the yuppies, they could not hope to live better than their parents. A college degree no longer seemed to produce the income, security, and prospects that baby boomers had expected. For many younger Americans, the lesson of the 1970s—the need to live with less—was still the lesson of the 1980s. After vainly looking for a job for months, a twenty-two-year-old graduate of Western Washington University summed it up. "You get the feeling," he said sadly, "that the potential for doing what you want is limited."

Dismissed as atypical and denounced as amoral, the yuppies died a quick death in the media. Before the 1980s had ended, yuppies had become unfashionable, and commentators had moved on to other subjects. However, the yuppie controversy told a great deal about the decade. Like the Reagan Revolution, yuppies were image as much as reality. As had happened so often in the past, Americans had projected their own desires and fears onto young people. The yuppie debate had allowed people to discuss the emerging conservative values of the Reagan era. Those values, embodied in the yuppie lifestyle, were clearly appealing for many Americans. But the abuse aimed at the yuppies was a clear indication that Americans had doubts about the new conservatism.

The yuppie lifestyle at home: An affluent young couple happily cooks together.

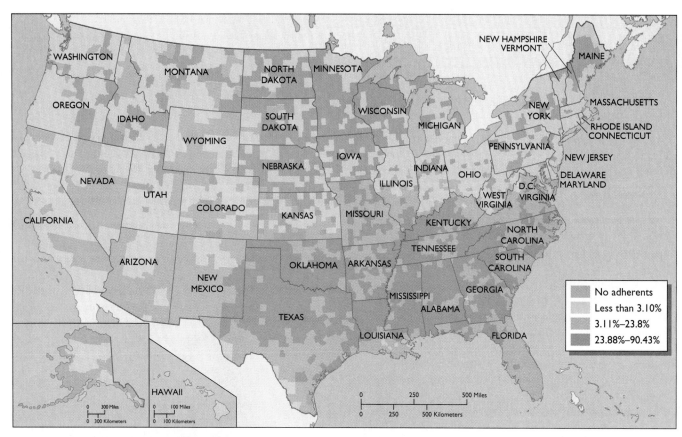

Map 30-1   The Growth of Evangelical Christianity.
The Southern Baptist Covention's share of the population, by county, reveals its gradual spread beyond its traditional base in the South by 1990.
Source: Peter L. Halvorson & William M. Newman, Atlas of Religious Change in America, 1952–1990 (1994), p. 120.

The rise of the religious right reflected a long-term trend in American religion. For many years, the so-called mainline churches—such Protestant denominations as the United Methodist Church, the Episcopal Church, the United Church of Christ, and the Presbyterian Church, USA—had suffered a relative decline. The percentage of church members who belonged to the mainline churches had been dropping sharply since at least 1940. Meanwhile, evangelical churches boomed (see Map 30-1). By the 1980s, the Southern Baptist Convention was the largest American Protestant denomination. Such smaller evangelical bodies as the Assemblies of God and the Church of God more than doubled in size from the 1960s to the 1980s.

The changing balance between mainline and evangelical churches had social and political consequences. The mainline denominations were relatively comfortable with secular society; they often took moderate or liberal positions on such social issues as civil rights and abortion. But the evangelical churches were much more likely to support conservative positions. Troubled by social change and emboldened by their own growth, evangelicals wanted to spread a conservative message aggressively across American culture and politics.

The emergence of so-called "televangelists" was the most obvious result of these efforts. From 1978 to 1989 the number of Christian broadcast ministries on television grew from 25 to 336. In addition to their own television shows, the most successful televangelists had their own networks, colleges, political groups, and even an amusement park. Pat Robertson, a born-again Baptist from Virginia, hosted "The 700 Club" and ran the Christian Broadcast Network. Jerry Falwell, a fundamentalist who believed in the literal interpretation of the *Bible,* hosted "The Old Time Gospel Hour" and founded Liberty Baptist College in Virginia. He also organized the Moral Majority, a political pressure group. A televangelist couple, Jim and Tammy Faye Bakker, started Heritage Park, USA, complete with a hotel and water park, in South Carolina.

Deeply conservative, the televangelists condemned many of the social changes of the 1960s and 1970s. They opposed women's liberation, abortion, gay rights, and the liberal programs of the Great Society. Anxious to "get God back in the classroom," they wanted prayer in public schools. Earning millions of dollars, they praised low taxes, limited government, and financial success. As materialistic as the Trumps, Jim and Tammy Faye Bakker proudly

The Reverend Jerry Falwell, fundamentalist and leader of the religious right.

showed off their six homes and their air-conditioned dog house. By 1980, the televangelists were moving into politics in order to win what Falwell called the "war against sin." Through their broadcasts, their organizations, and their fundraising, these evangelical leaders were creating a conservative political force, a religious right.

The Conservative Counter-establishment

Conservatives and Republicans had long despised the liberal "establishment," the elite of mostly northeastern, Ivy-League educated men who supposedly ran Wall Street and Washington after World War II. The "establishment" was never the powerful, tightly knit organization that President Richard Nixon and other critics imagined, but conservatives endeavored to stop the "establishment" by creating their own "counter-establishment."

Money helped build the conservative counter-establishment. Wealthy donors, such as the brewer Joseph Coors, contributed to conservative organizations and campaigns. Televangelists and such conservative fundraisers as Richard Viguerie collected small contributions from millions of less-wealthy Americans.

All this money helped to create and sustain a range of conservative institutions and activities. The John M. Olin Foundation and other philanthropic organizations, counterparts to the older and more liberal Ford and Carnegie foundations, supported conservative causes and initiatives. The National Conservative Political Action Committee (NCPAC) and other pressure groups lobbied for conservative legislation and supported conservative political candidates. Think tanks such as the Heritage Foundation and

the American Enterprise Institute, modeled on the liberal Brookings Institution, publicized conservative ideas and policies. Conservative magazines such as *The Public Interest* and *Human Events,* along with the older *National Review,* rivaled liberal publications such as the *New Republic.* The financial newspaper, the *Wall Street Journal,* offered a conservative alternative to the establishment daily paper, the *New York Times.*

Ideas as well as money built the conservative counter-establishment. A range of values and policies, some quite old, came together in the new conservatism and its vision of the American political economy. Like conservative businessmen and Republicans a century earlier, the New Right praised unrestricted free enterprise and minimal regulation of economic life. Like William F. Buckley, Barry Goldwater, and other cold-war conservatives, the New Right blended hostility to activist liberal government with a hatred of Communism. Many 1980s conservatives, especially evangelical Christians, wanted to use governmental power to enforce their views on such social issues as abortion, school prayer, and gay rights, but other conservatives, especially libertarians, believed government should leave people as free as possible. Despite these differences, the conservative counter-establishment offered a powerful cluster of ideas, deeply influenced by economic, social, religious, and political change since the 1960s.

The 1980 Presidential Election

The power of the new conservatism became evident in the presidential election of 1980. The Republican Party nominated a charismatic conservative candidate, Ronald Reagan. Confronting a divided Democratic Party and an unpopular president, Reagan won a stunning victory.

Reagan's life story reflected the rise of the Sunbelt and the new conservatism. Born into a lower-middle-class Irish-Catholic family in Illinois in 1911, Reagan left the Midwest during the Great Depression to make a new life in California. From the late 1930s through the early 1960s, he starred in movies and television shows in Hollywood. A staunch Democrat, he supported Franklin Roosevelt's New Deal and Harry Truman's cold war against Communism. Reagan then moved to the right as his acting career wound down in the 1950s and 1960s. Angry over high income taxes, he attacked big government while serving as a corporate spokesman for General Electric. As the New Frontier and the Great Society unfolded in the 1960s, Reagan became a Republican. His conservative views won him election as governor of California in 1966 and again in 1970.

The conservative tide carried Reagan along. Unable to defeat the moderate incumbent Gerald Ford for the Republican presidential nomination in 1976, Reagan easily earned the top spot on the ticket four years later. Although he chose a moderate running mate, George Bush of Texas, the Republican campaign offered a conservative vision of less government, lower taxes, and renewed military power for America. Genial and optimistic, Reagan reassured Democrats and independents that like himself they could find a home in the Republican Party.

Meanwhile, the Democratic nominee, incumbent President Jimmy Carter, could not overcome the double burdens of a weak economy and the ongoing hostage crisis in Iran. His moderate and sometimes conservative policies alienated Democratic liberals. His poor economic record alienated the party's white ethnics. Carter was not helped by the presidential campaign of the moderate Republican congressman, John Anderson of Illinois, who ran as an independent.

On election day, Reagan pulled off the rare feat of defeating an incumbent president. The Republican nominee swept all but four states and the District of Columbia (see Map 30-2). He managed only 50.7 percent of the popular vote, but his tally, combined with Anderson's 6.6 percent, suggested the extent of popular disaffection with Carter and the Democratic Party. The Democrats held on to the House of Representatives, but the Republicans took control of the Senate for the first time since the election of 1952. Sixteen years after Barry Goldwater's conservative candidacy had ended in a crushing defeat, the nation had turned sharply to the right. Reagan's victory marked the emergence of a conservative majority.

The Reagan Revolution at Home

Ronald Reagan probably shaped American life more decisively than any president since Franklin Roosevelt. Reagan's style—folksy and optimistic—made him a popular leader, but the Reagan years were more than a triumph of style. With some justice, his supporters believed that the president spurred a "Reagan Revolution," a sweeping conservative transformation of the American political economy.

At home, the Reagan Revolution meant a new approach to the federal government and the economy. Eager to decrease Washington's role in American life, the president moved to reduce federal functions and benefits. To restore economic growth, he moved to reduce taxes, regulation, and union power. The popularity of "Reaganomics," the president's economic policy, became clear at the polls. Reagan won re-election in a landslide in 1984.

The Reagan Style

The Reagan Revolution was partly a matter of the president's style. Despite the frustrations of the 1960s and 1970s, Reagan exuded optimism about the nation's future.

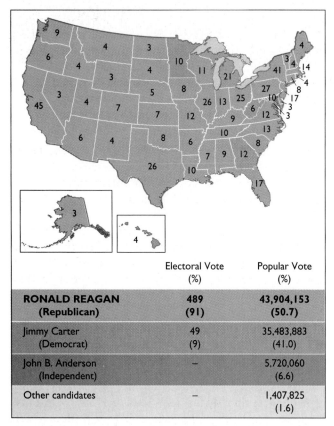

	Electoral Vote (%)	Popular Vote (%)
RONALD REAGAN (Republican)	**489** **(91)**	**43,904,153** **(50.7)**
Jimmy Carter (Democrat)	49 (9)	35,483,883 (41.0)
John B. Anderson (Independent)	–	5,720,060 (6.6)
Other candidates	–	1,407,825 (1.6)

Map 30-2   The Presidential Election, 1980.

The leader of the conservative "Reagan Revolution." President Ronald Reagan, with his wife, Nancy.

The end of the 1970s? Three of the former hostages who had been held in Iran celebrate their freedom, as they land at a U.S. airforce base in Germany on the day of Ronald Reagan's inauguration in 1981. The end of the hostage crisis seemed to promise new confidence for the United States after the frustration of the 1970s.

Rather than teach Americans how to live with less, he embraced luxury. Nevertheless, he managed to retain a common touch. After the troubled presidencies of the 1970s, Reagan made the job seem manageable again.

From the day of Reagan's inauguration in January 1981, his presidency signaled a confident, even opulent, new era for the United States. That morning, as if to mark the belated end of the frustrating 1970s, the Iranian government finally released its American hostages. In his inaugural address, Reagan firmly rejected pessimism about the nation's future. "We are not," the new president declared, "doomed to an inevitable decline." Rejecting limits, Reagan reveled in elegance. That night, he and his wife Nancy danced at a series of lavish balls. In all, the Reagan inaugural cost five times more than Jimmy Carter's inaugural four years earlier.

Even while the Reagans continued their lavish lifestyle in the White House, the president remained popular with many ordinary Americans. Reagan seemed warm, upbeat,

and unpretentious. After his career in movies and television, he knew how to speak simply and effectively to the American people. Although the president did not always master the details of issues, he became known as the "Great Communicator."

Reagan also appeared to enjoy and master his job. By the 1980s many Americans wondered whether the presidency was an impossible responsibility. Lyndon Johnson, tired and unpopular, had given up on re-election in 1968. Richard Nixon, caught in the Watergate scandals, had resigned in disgrace in 1974. His successors, Gerald Ford and Jimmy Carter, had not seemed up to the office. Reagan appeared to delight in the presidency; even though he took office as America's oldest president at the age of 69, Reagan projected an image of vigor and energy.

The president even managed to survive an assassination attempt. On March 30, 1981, John W. Hinckley, a troubled young loner eager to impress an actress, shot and wounded Reagan, his press secretary, and a policeman outside a Washington hotel. Reagan's chest wound was more serious than his spokesmen admitted, but the president met the situation with good humor. "Honey," he told his wife, "I forgot to duck." Many Americans admired Reagan's grace and strength. The president soared in opinion polls.

Shrinking Government

Reagan's administration was more than just a matter of style. The president offered a clear conservative alternative to the liberal policies of the New Deal and the Great Society. Above all, Reagan denied that a large, activist federal government could deal with the challenges of American life in the 1980s. "In this present crisis," Reagan insisted, "government is not the solution to our problem." Accordingly, he wanted to shrink the government's size and power. "Our government is too big," he observed, "and it spends too much."

Reagan's efforts to shrink the federal government met with mixed success. In his State of the Union address in January 1982, the president endorsed the "New Federalism," a plan to transfer some federal programs and tax revenues to the states. Reagan insisted the "New Federalism" would promote efficiency and economic growth, but many governors worried that their states would be saddled with expensive responsibilities. In the end, the federal government passed on only a few programs to the states.

In 1982 Reagan also created a commission, headed by business executive J. Peter Grace, to explore ways the federal government could save money. Reporting in 1984, the Grace Commission claimed that Washington could save more than 400 billion dollars over three years, partly by making it more difficult for Americans to qualify for welfare, pension, and other benefits. Congress was unwilling to make such potentially unpopular reforms. The commission also called for the line-item veto, which would allow a president to reject particular spending programs in the annual budget passed by Congress without having to veto the entire budget bill. Congress was not ready to give Reagan so much new power. Eventually passed in 1996, the line-item veto was declared unconstitutional by the Supreme Court two years later.

The president had more success when he attacked the broad range of social-welfare programs, one of the major functions of the federal government since the Great Depression. Along with many other conservatives, Reagan had particularly condemned antipoverty programs as an expensive waste of federal resources that sapped the work ethic and the morals of the poor. Reagan and his followers, like so many conservatives of earlier generations, believed that the political economy worked best when workers had to succeed or fail on their own. He wanted reductions in such programs as food stamps, school meal programs, and aid to cities. In response Congress cut appropriations for

urban public housing and eliminated job training for the unemployed.

Reagan found it nearly impossible to touch Medicare and Social Security, two expensive and popular programs that benefited not only the poor, but rather most Americans. The social security system, which provided pensions for retired workers and their dependents, proved especially difficult to cut. By the 1980s there was growing concern that workers' Social Security tax payments would eventually not be enough to cover the cost of benefits to retirees. Nevertheless, Reagan and Congress were unwilling to make significant cuts in Social Security. After a long struggle, they produced the Social Security Reform Act of 1983, which raised the minimum age for full benefits from 65 to 67 and made retirees pay taxes on some benefits. The measure did very little to reduce the total cost of Social Security. By 1984 the president was promising not to cut Social Security.

Despite his eagerness to reduce the size of government, Reagan did not tear down the federal system of welfare and other benefits. Expenditures for these programs continued to rise through the 1980s, but the Reagan administration did manage to slow the growth of welfare. Benefits did not expand dramatically in the 1980s. There were no costly new programs. As expenditures for national defense grew, welfare outlays made up a smaller proportion of the cost of government. They fell from 28 percent of the federal budget in 1980 to 22 percent by 1987. Reagan may not have succeeded in shrinking the federal government overall, but he did succeed in shrinking some parts of the government that he disliked.

Reaganomics

For Reagan and his followers, shrinking the government meant more than reducing federal expenditures for welfare and other programs. Conservatives wanted especially to decrease Washington's role in the economy. They argued that the nation prospered most when government left Americans as free as possible to manage their own businesses and keep their own earnings. Reflecting this conservative outlook, the Reagan administration worked to lower taxes, deregulate business, and cut federal support for unions. In all, "Reaganomics" substantially changed the American political economy by reducing the economic role of the federal government.

Reagan's economic policy drew on a relatively new theory known as **supply-side economics**. Beginning in the 1970s, economist Arthur Laffer and other conservatives had offered an alternative to the liberal, Keynesian economics that had guided federal policy since the New Deal. While Keynesians believed that increased consumer demand would spur economic growth, Laffer contended that an increased supply of goods and services was the key to growth. He rejected the Keynesian prescription for raising government spending in order to put more money in the hands of consumers. That approach, he maintained, actually hurt the economy: To pay for its spending, government raised taxes and thereby took money away from producers. To promote prosperity, he believed government should cut, rather than hike, taxes. By leaving more money in the hands of businesses, government would allow them to invest in more production of goods and services. The increase in supply would stimulate prosperity and even lead to more tax revenues for the government. The tax cut, Laffer concluded, would not even produce a federal **budget deficit**.

Supply-side economics was controversial. To liberal critics it seemed to be an excuse to let the rich keep more of their money, much like the Republican policies of the 1920s. Even some Republicans doubted that a cut in taxes would really end up producing more tax revenues for the government. While challenging Reagan for the Republican presidential nomination early in 1980, George Bush had dismissed Laffer's scheme as "voodoo economics," but the supply-side approach fit neatly with Reagan's conservative dislike for high taxes and big, active government.

Committed to supply-side economics, Reagan asked a joint session of Congress early in 1981 to cut taxes dramatically. Impressed by Reagan's popularity and the electorate's increasing conservatism, some congressional Democrats were prepared to go along with the president. As a result, the Democratic-controlled House joined the Republican-dominated Senate to pass the Economic Recovery Act of 1981 (known as the Kemp-Roth Bill, after its congressional sponsors). This measure cut federal income taxes five percent the first year and then 10 percent in each of the next two years. It especially benefited the wealthy by making the tax structure less progressive. The tax rate on the highest individual incomes and the taxes on large gifts and estates were all reduced. An important victory for Reagan, the Economic Recovery Act significantly weakened the government's long-standing support for the liberal policies of Keynesian economics and progressive taxation.

Reagan and his followers wanted the federal government not only to tax and spend less; they also wanted Washington to regulate less. Like other conservatives, Reagan believed that federal rules and requirements hamstrung American business and prevented economic growth. Accordingly, his administration stepped up the campaign for deregulation begun by Jimmy Carter. The government cut the budgets of such key regulatory agencies as the Environmental Protection Agency and the Occupational Safety and Health Administration. The Reagan administration also made sure that government officials did not strictly enforce regulatory rules and laws. Further, the administration deregulated the telephone industry. In 1982 the government broke up the giant American Telephone and Telegraph Company, which had monopolized long-distance service under federal supervision, into regional companies. New firms such as Sprint and MCI were allowed to compete for AT&T's long-distance business.

Reagan moved particularly to lift environmental restrictions on American businesses. He chose James G. Watt, a staunch conservative opponent of environmentalism and active government, to serve as secretary of the interior. Too controversial, Watt finally had to resign in 1983 after making derogatory comments about minority groups. Before that happened, however, the Reagan administration made it easier for timber and mining companies to exploit wilderness areas and allowed oil companies to drill for oil off the Pacific Coast. The administration also opposed environmentalists' demands for strong measures to protect against acid rain—the air pollution, caused by industrial emissions, that harmed lakes, forests, and crops especially in the Northeast and Canada.

Reaganomics also meant weakening the power of organized labor. Ironically, Reagan, once the head of the Screen Actors Guild, was the first former union official to

The "Reagan Revolution" confronts organized labor: President Reagan fires striking air traffic controllers in 1981.

serve as president. Like most conservatives, however, he believed that unions obstructed business and limited the freedom of individual workers. He believed as well that the federal government had done too much to encourage organized labor since the New Deal. Unions were already weakening when Reagan took office. Thanks mainly to **deindustrialization**, the number of unionized workers dropped from 21 million in 1970 to 17 million in 1986.

Reagan took steps to weaken the labor movement even further. Rather than describe unions as partners with business and government, the president criticized them as a selfish "special interest." Reagan made pro-business appointments to the National Labor Relations Board. Most important, he took a strong antiunion stance during a strike by the Professional Air Traffic Controllers Organization (PATCO) in 1981. Despite a law forbidding strikes by federal workers, PATCO walked out to protest unsafe conditions in the nation's air traffic control system. Unmoved, Reagan promptly fired the striking controllers, refused to hire them back, and replaced them with nonunion workers. The president's action encouraged business to take a hard line with employees. By the end of the 1980s, the union movement was weaker than at any time since the Great Depression.

The Reagan administration put Reaganomics in place with striking speed. The Economic Recovery Act, deregulation, and the PATCO strike considerably changed the federal government's role in the economy.

"Reaganomics" did not quite have the effect that its supporters anticipated. In the short run, Reagan's measures could not prevent a sharp recession, which began in the fall of 1981. As the Federal Reserve Bank tried to fight inflation by raising interest rates, the economy slowed, and unemployment increased. Reaganomics also increased the federal budget deficit. The supply-side theory that tax cuts would actually boost tax revenues and balance the budget proved incorrect.

By the spring of 1984, the recession had ended. Thanks largely to the Federal Reserve's monetary policy, the high inflation of the 1970s was over. The economy began a long period of growth and higher employment. Reagan's supporters gave the president credit for the renewed prosperity. His critics charged that the deficit rather than Reaganomics had produced the boom. Eventually, the critics contended, the deficit would hurt the economy. In the mid-1980s, however, Reaganomics appeared to be a success.

The 1984 Presidential Election

The unclear results of Reaganomics helped to shape national politics. In the depths of the recession, the Republicans lost 26 House seats in the midterm congressional elections of 1982. With the return of prosperity, and his popularity on the rise, the president was easily renomi-

nated by the party, along with Vice President Bush, in 1984. Reagan ran against a liberal Democratic nominee, former Vice President Walter Mondale of Minnesota. The Democrat, confronting a popular incumbent, had to make bold moves. Mondale chose the first female vice-presidential nominee of a major party, Representative Geraldine Ferraro of New York. To prove his honesty and openness, Mondale announced that he would raise taxes as president. Mondale could not overcome the problems of the Democratic Party. He was saddled with the disappointing record of the Carter administration and the alienation of white working- and middle-class Democrats.

In response, Reagan ran an optimistic campaign emphasizing the renewal of America. "Life is better, America is back," a Reagan commercial declared. "And people have a sense of pride they never felt they'd feel again." Mondale would jeopardize all that, the Reagan campaign charged, with tax increases and favors to such "special interests" as labor unions, feminists, and civil rights activists.

As Democrat Walter Mondale's runningmate in 1984, Geraldine Ferraro became the first woman chosen as the vice-presidential nominee for a major political party.

Election day revealed both the strength and the weakness of the Reagan Revolution. The contest was a personal triumph for the president. With his conservative message, Reagan polled 58.8 percent of the popular vote. Mondale, unapologetically liberal, drew only 40.6 percent. The popular vote translated into an electoral landslide for Reagan. The president lost only the District of Columbia and Mondale's home state of Minnesota. Reagan's big vote did not translate into a sweeping victory for his party. Holding on to the Senate, the Republicans failed to win a majority in the House of Representatives. The Reagan Revolution had not given the Republicans, the party of conservatism, complete control of the federal government.

The Reagan Revolution Abroad

Reagan's foreign policy, like his domestic policy, rested on old values. The president rejected the main diplomatic approaches of the 1970s—Richard Nixon's détente with the Soviet Union and Jimmy Carter's support for international human rights. Instead, the Reagan Revolution revived the strident anti-Communism of the 1940s and 1950s. The president moved to restore the nation's power in order to challenge the Soviet Union and stop Communism in the Western Hemisphere. Communism, however, had little or nothing to do with some difficult international issues including conflict in the Middle East, terrorism, and economic relations with Japan and developing nations. Nevertheless, the Reagan Revolution abroad plainly refocused American policy on the cold-war confrontation with Communism.

Restoring American Power

To carry out his anti-Communist foreign policy, the president needed to undo the legacy of the Vietnam War. After losing that conflict, the United States had cut back its armed forces and become reluctant to risk military confrontations abroad. The president set out to restore American power in the 1980s. Despite pressure from an international crusade against nuclear weapons, his administration succeeded in beefing up the nation's armed services.

Like most conservatives, the president did not believe that making cuts in government spending should include making cuts in the armed forces. Under Reagan, the nation's defense spending more than doubled, from 134 billion dollars in 1980 to more than 300 billion dollars by 1989. The president's administration built up all branches of the armed services and ordered development of controversial weapons systems. Construction of the B-1 strategic jet bomber, stopped by Jimmy Carter, resumed. Reagan began development of the B-2 "Stealth" bomber, an inno-

vative plane that could evade detection by enemy radar. He won Congressional approval for the MX "Peacekeeper," a nuclear missile with multiple warheads. He also persuaded Congress to authorize work on the neutron bomb, a nuclear weapon that could spread lethal radiation over a half-mile radius.

As he pursued his military build-up, Reagan had to confront a growing mass movement against nuclear weapons. In both Europe and the United States, millions of people, frightened by the horror of nuclear war, called for a "freeze," a halt to the introduction of new nuclear arms. In June 1982, a crowd of 700,000—perhaps the largest protest rally in American history—gathered in New York's Central Park to demand the freeze. The next year, the National Conference of Catholic Bishops supported the freeze and declared nuclear war immoral. Reagan flatly rejected the freeze movement as naïve and Communist-infiltrated. The best way to ensure peace, he believed, was to keep developing weapons. The nation's weapons programs continued.

A nuclear "freeze" rally in New York City in 1982. For a time, the movement to halt the introduction of new nuclear weapons challenged President Reagan's plans for an arms buildup.

The military buildup was a matter of attitudes as well as weapons and budgets. In the wake of the Vietnam War, many Americans seemed reluctant to endorse U. S. intervention abroad. They feared that the nation might become entrapped in another costly, losing battle overseas. This "Vietnam Syndrome" threatened the Reagan administration's foreign policy. The president could not afford to let other countries think the U. S. would not back up its words with action. Accordingly, Reagan used his speeches to stir up patriotic emotion. The president also tried to persuade Americans that the Vietnam War had been "a just cause," well worth supporting.

By the mid-1980s, Reagan had certainly succeeded in restoring much of America's military power. It remained to be seen, however, whether Americans were willing to use that power abroad.

Confronting the "Evil Empire"

The main purpose of the military buildup was to contain the Soviet Union. Suspicion of the Soviets and their Communist ideology was at the heart of Reagan's diplomacy. In the early 1980s, the United States aggressively challenged the U. S. S. R. Reagan's words set the tone of the new relationship with the Soviets. Using a term from the popular science fiction movie *Star Wars,* the president called the U. S. S. R. the "evil empire." He insisted that the Soviet Union and its Communist allies were doomed by failing economies and unpopular regimes. Communist ideology, Reagan declared, would end up "on the ash heap of history."

As these words suggested, the United States generally avoided cooperation with the Soviet Union. Reagan held no summit meetings with Soviet leaders during his first term. The president did end the embargo on grain sales, which Jimmy Carter had imposed after the Soviet invasion of Afghanistan, but the Reagan administration openly supported the mujahedeen, the Afghan rebels who were resisting the Soviets. The United States provided weapons and training to the mujahedeen. Reagan even met with their leaders.

More important, the president avoided arms-control agreements with the Soviets during his first term. Instead, he used the American military buildup to pressure the U. S. S. R. Reagan refused to submit the second Strategic Arms Limitation Treaty, signed by Jimmy Carter, to the Senate for ratification. New arms-control negotiations with the Soviets went nowhere. In response to the United States' deployment of new intermediate-range nuclear missiles in Western Europe, the Soviets walked out of the arms-control talks in 1983.

That year, Reagan put even more pressure on the U. S. S. R. when he announced plans for the Strategic Defense Initiative (SDI), a space-based missile-defense system. SDI would make use of lasers and other advanced technology to shoot down nuclear missiles launched at the United States. Although funded by Congress, SDI was a

long way from reality in 1983. Critics, convinced SDI was unrealistic science fiction, called the plan "Star Wars" after the movie.

The U. S. initiative pressed the U. S. S. R. in two ways. First, the Soviets would have to expend scarce resources in order to develop their own version of the SDI. Second, SDI seemingly made the U. S. S. R. more vulnerable to nuclear attack. Since the 1950s, the Americans and the Soviets had relied on the concept of "mutual assured destruction" as a deterrent to nuclear war, but SDI had the potential to enable the U. S. to survive a nuclear attack. The Soviets faced the frightening possibility that the United States, no longer facing assured destruction, might start a nuclear war with the U. S. S. R.

Although Reagan pressed the Soviet Union, he clearly wanted to avoid a confrontation with the major Communist powers. In 1983 a Soviet fighter plane shot down an unarmed Korean airliner, killing all 269 passengers and crew. Although a U. S. congressman was one of the victims, Reagan responded with restraint. Grain sales and arms negotiations continued. While the United States challenged the Soviets more aggressively, the Reagan administration did not confront the other major Communist power, the People's Republic of China. The Chinese, less

Armed with an automatic rifle, this young Nicaraguan Contra is one of the "freedom fighters" backed by the Reagan administration in its attempt to thwart Communism in Central America.

active in promoting Third-World Communism, seemed less of a threat than the Soviets. Instead, Reagan traded visits with China's premier in 1984 and encouraged cultural exchanges, economic cooperation, and a nuclear-weapons agreement.

Clearly, then, there were limits to the renewal of the cold war in the 1980s. But the Reagan administration had managed to turn back the clock. American foreign policy once again focused on challenging the Soviet Union.

The Reagan Doctrine in the Third World

The Reagan administration also changed American foreign policy toward the Third World. Jimmy Carter had wanted the United States to support human rights around the globe, but his successor preferred to support America's national security interests, including anti-Communism. The results of this "Reagan Doctrine" in the Caribbean, Central America, and Africa were controversial.

Reagan, along with other conservatives, had been impatient with the Carter administration's attempts to promote human rights abroad. The United States, conservatives believed, needed to back anti-Communist, pro-American governments, whether or not they fully respected human rights. Jeane J. Kirkpatrick, who became Reagan's ambassador to the United Nations, called for a distinction between "totalitarian" regimes hostile to the U. S. and "authoritarian" governments "friendly" to American national security interests. Critics claimed that this distinction was meaningless and insisted that the nation should not support antidemocratic governments. The administration adopted Kirkpatrick's view, which became known as the "Reagan Doctrine."

During the president's first term, his administration applied the Reagan Doctrine aggressively in Central America and the Caribbean (see Map 30-3). Determined to keep Communism out of the Western Hemisphere, the United States opposed the Marxist Sandinista government

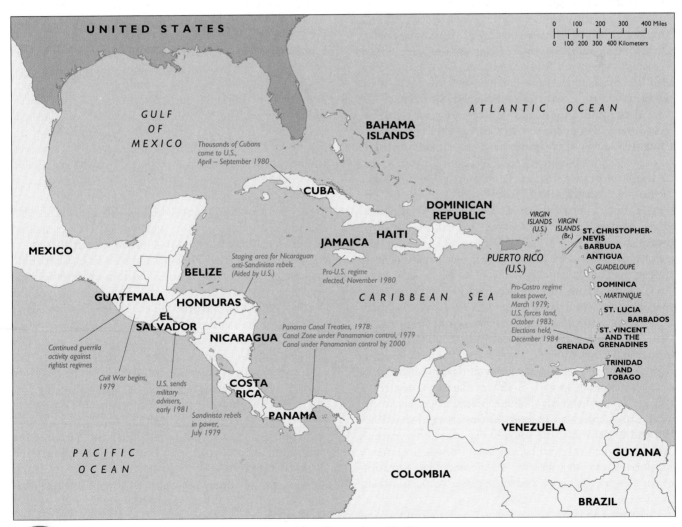

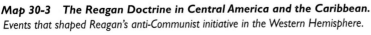

Map 30-3   The Reagan Doctrine in Central America and the Caribbean.
Events that shaped Reagan's anti-Communist initiative in the Western Hemisphere.

of Nicaragua and supported the repressive anti-Communist government of neighboring El Salvador.

The Nicaraguan regime had come to power in the late 1970s by overthrowing the dictatorship of Anastasio Somoza with the encouragement of the Carter administration. The Reagan administration believed the Sandinistas were too friendly to the Soviet Union and to leftist rebels trying to overthrow El Salvador's government. As a result, Reagan halted U. S. aid to Nicaragua in April 1981. At the president's direction, the CIA trained, armed, and supplied the Contra rebels who opposed the Sandinistas. Many of the Contras had ties to the oppressive Somoza government, but Reagan praised them as "freedom fighters" and even "the moral equivalent of our Founding Fathers."

Meanwhile, the president strongly backed the brutal right-wing government of El Salvador. Although the regime engaged in kidnapping and terror, Reagan did not want it to fall to pro-Sandinista and pro-Cuban rebels. El Salvador, the president explained, was "a textbook case of indirect armed aggression by Communist powers."

Despite such anti-Communist rhetoric, the Reagan administration could not persuade Congress to support its Central American policy fully. Congressional Democrats, like many Americans, did not want to risk another Vietnam War in Central America. They were skeptical about the Communist threat to El Salvador and Nicaragua. They were also troubled by the antidemocratic character of the Salvadoran government and the Contra rebels. In 1983 the Congress approved Reagan's Caribbean Basin Initiative, an economic development package for the Caribbean and Central America, but Reagan did not get the military aid he wanted for the Salvadoran government. Instead, in September 1982 Congress passed the Boland Amendment, which restricted aid to the Contras and banned efforts to topple the Sandinista regime. When the Reagan administration tried to circumvent the amendment, Congress strengthened it further.

The president applied the Reagan Doctrine more successfully in the Caribbean. On October 25, 1983, U. S. troops invaded the small West-Indian island of Grenada supposedly to protect about 1,000 Americans, mostly medical students, from a new militant Marxist regime. Reagan feared Grenada would become a Cuban or Soviet base close to U.S. shores. The invading force quickly secured the island and replaced the government with a pro-American regime. Critics charged that Reagan had undermined the sovereignty of another state in order to win an easy military victory. For the president's supporters, the invasion was a welcome demonstration of the Reagan Doctrine and an antidote to the Vietnam Syndrome.

The president also implemented the Reagan Doctrine in Africa. With its commitment to human rights, the Carter administration had condemned the long-standing policy of apartheid—racial separation—pursued by the white government of South Africa. Reagan would not take a similarly strong stance against apartheid. Rather than impose economic sanctions on the South African regime, the president endorsed only a mild policy of diplomatic discussions known as "constructive engagement."

From Africa to Central America, Reagan attempted to reorient U. S. policy toward the Third World. Given opposition at home, the president never fully implemented the Reagan Doctrine. Still, he largely displaced Carter's emphasis on human rights.

The Middle East and Terrorism

The Reagan Doctrine was not much help in dealing with the Middle East and with the growing problem of terrorism. Communism and the Soviet Union, the focus of Reagan's foreign policy, had little impact on Middle Eastern issues in the 1980s. As before, the United States wanted to ensure its supply of oil and to support its longtime ally, Israel. There was no new Arab oil embargo during the Reagan years, but the president's administration could not bring peace to the Middle East or end the threat of terrorism from the region. The Middle East remained a dangerous place for Americans in the 1980s.

Reagan found it difficult to build on the Camp David Accords between Israel and Egypt, which Jimmy Carter had negotiated. The Accords were supposed to lead to self-government for the Palestinian Arabs who lived in the Israeli-occupied West Bank and Gaza Strip. However, Israel and the Palestine Liberation Organization (PLO), the official representative of the Palestinians, remained at odds. The PLO continued to threaten Israel from bases in the neighboring country of Lebanon. In the spring of 1982, the Israelis invaded Lebanon, which was already convulsed by a civil war between the Muslims and Christians.

To end the Israeli invasion and to stabilize Lebanon, the United States sent Marines to join an international peacekeeping force in Beirut, the Lebanese capital. On October 23, 1983, a terrorist killed 241 Americans by driving a truck bomb into the four-story Marine headquarters at Beirut. The attack shocked Americans and marked a low point of Reagan's administration. The president did not want to reward terrorism by removing U. S. troops from Lebanon. Nevertheless, he pulled out the soldiers in 1984. There was still no peace in Lebanon and no agreement between the Israelis and the PLO.

The attack on the Marine headquarters illustrated the growing threat of terrorism against the United States and its allies. Reagan vowed to make terrorists "pay for their actions," but terrorism proved hard to stop. After Palestinians murdered an American passenger on a cruise ship in the Mediterranean in 1985, U. S. planes forced down the Egyptian airliner carrying the escaping terrorists. The Reagan administration believed that Muammar Qaddafi, leader of the North African nation of Libya, supported terrorism. In 1982 U. S. Navy fighter planes shot down two Libyan fighters off the Libyan coast. After American soldiers died in a terrorist bombing in West Germany in 1986, U. S. jets bombed Qaddafi's Libyan headquarters, killing one of his daughters. Qaddafi, whom Reagan called "the mad dog of the Middle East," seemed to become less critical of the United States, but the threat of terrorism did not go away.

Reagan also acted to safeguard America's oil supply. During a war between Iran and Iraq, the United States sent Navy ships to protect oil tankers in the Persian Gulf. As in Lebanon, American intervention was costly. In May 1987 Iraqi missiles struck the U. S. destroyer *Stark*, killing 37 of its crew. The Reagan administration, unwilling to help Iran, accepted Iraq's apology. In July 1988, the U. S. missile cruiser *Vincennes* accidentally shot down an Iranian airliner, killing 290 passengers. An American apology did little to quell Iranian anger, but the Iran-Iraq war soon ended, and with it the threat to America's oil supply.

The United States and the World Economy

Middle Eastern oil was only one of the economic factors shaping Reagan's foreign policy. During his administration, the president had to deal with strains on the world economy. After years of relative economic decline, the United States could not always impose its will on other nations. On the one hand, Reagan forced stern measures on debt-ridden Third-World countries. On the other hand, he could not compel Japan to improve trade relations with the United States.

By the end of the 1980s, the developing nations of the Third World owed foreign banks more than 1.2 trillion dollars in loan payments. Mexico, next door to the United States, was more than 100 billion dollars in debt. American banks stood to lose heavily if Mexico and other nations defaulted on loans. American producers stood to lose, too, if these countries could not afford to buy U. S. goods. The Reagan administration nevertheless refused to protect American banks from loan defaults. Instead, the government forced reluctant debtor countries to adopt austerity programs in return for new loans from the International Monetary Fund, the World Bank, and the United States. Although the debt crisis abated for a time, the fragility of the world economy was obvious.

The Reagan administration had much less power to dictate trade policy with Japan. As Japanese exports flowed into the United States, Americans increasingly resented Japan's domination of the Japanese home market. The U. S. Congress, believing the Japanese discriminated against American goods, pushed for retaliation. Under pressure from the Reagan administration, Japan placed voluntary quotas on its export of steel and automobiles to the United States. Although the Reagan administration de-

valued the dollar to make American goods cheaper, the trade imbalance with Japan continued. In 1988 the president signed the Omnibus Trade and Competitiveness Act, which allowed the government to place high tariffs on Japanese goods if Japan continued to discriminate against American goods. However, as long as Americans wanted to buy Japanese products, major U. S. retaliation was unlikely. By 1989 a Japanese car, the Honda Accord, had become the biggest-selling model in the United States for the first time.

The Japanese trade issue was a reminder of the constraints on the Reagan Revolution abroad. Nevertheless, the Reagan administration had altered the basic thrust of American diplomacy in the early 1980s. The nation's diplomacy was defined once again by cold-war anti-Communism.

The Battle Over Conservative Social Values

For all of Ronald Reagan's success in the early 1980s, the new conservatism met with considerable opposition. The conservatives' social values were especially controversial. Eager to combat the legacies of the 1960s, many conservatives wanted to restore supposedly traditional values and practices. In the 1980s conservatives labored to take control of the courts, promote school prayer, reform the schools, and combat drugs. The conservatives were also anxious to uphold older gender roles and sexual mores; they were reluctant to use government power to attack racial inequality. The conservative agenda collided head-on with one of the chief legacies of the 1960s—disadvantaged groups' demands for equal rights and opportunities. Moreover, many Americans were unwilling to abandon the social changes of the last generation. Faced with such opposition, conservatives failed to achieve much of their vision for American society.

Attacking the Legacy of the 1960s

The new conservatism was driven by a desire to undo the liberal and radical legacies of the 1960s. Conservatives blamed federal courts in general—and the Supreme Court of Chief Justice Earl Warren in particular—for much of the social change in the United States over the last generation. In the 1960s and 1970s liberal justices with an activist conception of the courts' role had supported defendants' rights, civil rights, affirmative action, busing, and abortion. Meanwhile, the courts had rejected such conservative causes as school prayer.

Determined to take control of the courts, President Reagan succeeded in appointing many staunch, relatively young conservatives to the federal bench. He also chose conservative nominees for the Supreme Court. In 1981 Sandra Day O'Connor, a fairly conservative judge from Arizona, became the court's first woman justice. When Chief Justice Warren Burger retired, Reagan replaced him with a more conservative colleague, William Rehnquist, in 1986. With the appointments of two more conservatives, Antonin Scalia and Anthony Kennedy, the Supreme Court seemed ready to turn away from liberalism.

It did not quite work out that way. In the 1980s the court followed conservative views in limiting the rights of defendants: Ruling in *United States v. Leon* and *Nix v. Williams* in 1984, the justices made it easier for prosecutors to use evidence improperly obtained by police. However, on a variety of other issues, the court took a surprisingly moderate stance. In *Wallace v. Jaffree* in 1985, the court disappointed evangelical Christians and other advocates of school prayer by invalidating an Alabama law that allowed schools to devote a minute each day to voluntary prayer or meditation.

Prayer was just one element of conservatives' broad plan to reform public education. They believed that the federal government had played too large a role in the schools since the 1960s. Parents, meanwhile, had too little say in the education of their children. Conservative educational reformers preferred to use market forces rather than government power to reform the schools. They wanted to dismantle the federal Department of Education. In addition, they wanted the government to enable parents to choose the best schools—public or private—for their children, and a system of federally funded vouchers or tax credits would help pay for this choice.

Because many Americans were worried about the quality of the schools, conservatives had a golden opportunity to promote their educational agenda. In 1983 a federal study, *A Nation at Risk,* documented American students' failure to match the accomplishments of students from other countries, especially in math and science. Despite such revelations, Congress refused to adopt the voucher system or to abolish the Department of Education.

Drug use was another issue that conservatives traced to the 1960s. In the early 1980s, drugs again became a major public concern with the spread of crack, a cheap but addictive form of cocaine. The sale and use of crack, especially in the cities, led to crime and violence. In 1986 the president and his wife, Nancy, announced a "national crusade" for a "drug-free" America. The campaign was an important cause for the first lady, who encouraged young people to "Just Say No" to drugs. Her husband, meanwhile, instituted drug testing for federal employees. At his urging, Congress twice appropriated funds for education about drugs and passed stiff penalties for their sale and use. The Reagans' "war on drugs" was controversial. Critics ridiculed the "Just Say No" slogan as naïve and ineffective. Despite the new penalties and expenditures, drug use did not appear to decrease appreciably.

Women's Rights and Abortion

One of the chief legacies of the 1960s was the women's rights movement. The new conservatism condemned feminism and lamented the changing role of women in America. Many conservatives, especially outspoken evangelical leaders, believed that women were undermining family life by leaving home for jobs and public positions. The conservatives tended to blame feminists and liberal government for encouraging women to abandon their traditional domestic roles. The conservative movement was especially determined to halt federal initiatives, such as affirmative-action programs and the proposed Equal Rights Amendment (ERA), that used government power to protect women's rights and opportunities. Women, many conservatives argued, did not need special protection.

The conservative agenda on women's rights met with mixed results in the 1980s. The unsuccessful campaign for the ERA effectively ended, but affirmative-action programs, designed to promote the hiring of women, continued around the country. So did women's push into the workplace and public life. As more and more American families needed two incomes, the number of wage-earning women continued to grow. By 1983 women made up half the paid work force. As their economic role expanded, American women received more recognition from the political system. Geraldine Ferraro's 1984 vice-presidential candidacy seemed to mark a turning point for women in American politics. Ironically, Reagan himself gave women new public prominence by choosing Jeane J. Kirkpatrick and Sandra Day O'Connor for important offices.

The conservative campaign against women's rights also lagged because of the many signs that women still did not enjoy equality in America. They were generally paid less than men doing the same sort of work, and they had less opportunity to break through the **glass ceiling** and win managerial jobs. Moreover, commentators had begun to note the "feminization" of poverty by the 1980s. Unmarried or divorced women, many with children, made up an increasing percentage of the poor. This suffering and inequality, liberals and feminists argued, disproved the conservative claim that women did not need special protection.

For many conservatives, abortion was the most troubling sign of the changed status of women. Along with religious activists and other Americans, conservatives condemned the right to abortion guaranteed by the Supreme Court's 1973 decision in *Roe v. Wade.* A growing "Right to Life" movement passionately denounced abortion as the murder of the unborn, practiced by selfish women who rejected motherhood and family.

Conservatives failed to narrow abortion rights significantly in the 1980s (see Map 30-4). Reagan did successfully urge Congress to stop the use of federal funds to pay for abortions, but a constitutional amendment outlawing abortion never passed the Senate during the Reagan ad-

Anti-abortion protestors, part of the Right to Life movement that challenged the legitimacy of the Supreme Court's Roe v. Wade *decision in the 1980s.*

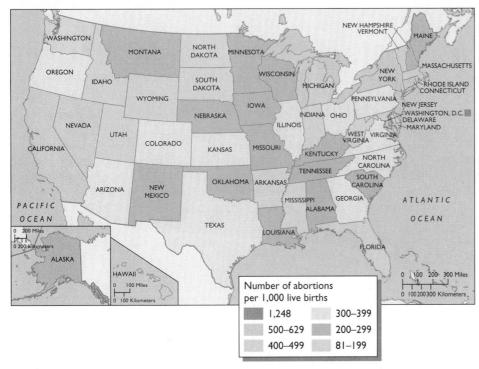

Map 30-4   Abortion in the 1980s.
The rate of abortions across the United States 14 years after the Supreme Court's decision legalizing abortion in Roe v. Wade.
Source: Timothy H. Fast & Cathy Carroll Fast, The Women's Atlas of the United States, rev. ed. (1995), p. 166.

Number of abortions
per 1,000 live births

1,248	300–399
500–629	200–299
400–499	81–199

ministration. In 1983 and 1986, the Supreme Court made rulings that upheld *Roe v. Wade.*

The Reagan years certainly did not witness major gains for women's rights, but this period did not mark the triumph of the conservative agenda for women, either. Women's public roles continued to expand in the 1980s. Meanwhile, women's right to abortion was essentially preserved.

Gays and the AIDS Crisis

The gay rights movement was another legacy of the 1960s that troubled many conservatives. By the end of the 1970s, the gay rights movement had met with considerable fear and hostility. A number of Americans, including such evangelical leaders as Jerry Falwell, condemned homosexuality on religious grounds. Some people believed that the public acceptance of equal rights for gay men and women would promote immorality and corrupt children. In 1977 Anita Bryant, a former Miss America, launched a national crusade, Save Our Children, to protest the passage of a gay rights ordinance in Dade County, Florida, where Miami is located. Voters soon repealed the measure. In San Francisco in 1978, Harvey Milk, the first avowedly gay member of the city's board of supervisors, was assassinated, along with the mayor, by a former supervisor. Many gays were shocked when the assassin received only a short jail sentence.

Despite such opposition, the gay rights movement made progress in the 1980s. By the end of the decade, most states had repealed sodomy laws that had long criminalized gay sex. In 1982 Wisconsin became the first state to pass a law protecting the rights of gay men and women.

The battle over gay rights took place against a tragic backdrop. In 1981 the Centers for Disease Control, the federal epidemiology agency, began reporting cases of acquired immune deficiency syndrome, or AIDS. This seemingly new disease destroyed the body's immune system, leaving it unable to fight off infections, rare cancers, and other afflictions. By the mid-1980s, researchers had traced AIDS to different forms of the human immunodeficiency virus (HIV) that were transmitted in semen and blood, but there was no cure for AIDS. By 1990 there were nearly 100,000 recorded deaths from the AIDS epidemic in the United States (see Figure 30-2).

Because 75 percent of the first victims were gay men, Americans initially considered AIDS a homosexual disease. Some people, including a number of evangelical leaders, believed this "gay cancer" was God's punishment for the alleged sin of homosexuality. As soon became clear, however, AIDS did not strike only men who engaged in anal sex. The disease could also be transmitted by heterosexual intercourse, by intravenous drug use that involved sharing needles, and by tainted blood transfusions.

Public understanding of AIDS and HIV gradually increased. Nevertheless, the specter of "gay cancer" promoted homophobia among Americans, and it slowed the public response to the disease. Gay activists pushed for government action. The AIDS Coalition to Unleash Power, known as ACT UP, and other organizations staged demonstrations and acts of civil disobedience to focus attention on the crisis. Nevertheless, the Reagan administration did not fund research on AIDS for several years. Meanwhile, the disease continued to spread.

A Gay Pride demonstration recalls the murder of Harvey Milk and protests the treatment of people with AIDS

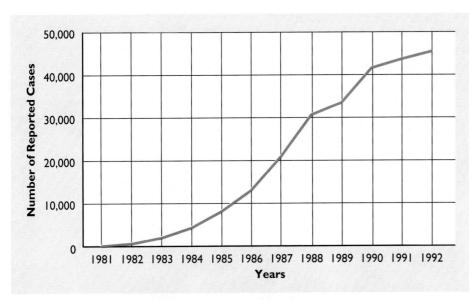

Figure 30-2   The Spread of AIDS.
Source: Statistical Abstract of the United States, 1989, p. 111; Statistical Abstract, 1993, p. 203.

The AIDS epidemic complicated the struggle over gay rights. For some Americans, the disease reinforced the conservative condemnation of homosexuality. For others, the suffering of AIDS victims engendered sympathy and compassion. As the 1980s ended, the conservative backlash against gay rights had not succeeded, but the AIDS epidemic continued.

African Americans and Racial Inequality

Conservatives were uneasy with still another legacy of the 1960s, the expansion of African-American civil rights and benefits guaranteed by the federal government. The new conservatism typically criticized the expansion of federal support for African-American civil rights and economic opportunity in the 1960s and 1970s. Conservatives believed that the liberal policies of the Great Society hurt, rather than helped, African-American people. True to their vision of the political economy, they maintained that individual initiative, and not government action, would promote racial equality. In keeping with these ideas, President Reagan opposed renewal of the Voting Rights Act, one of the key civil rights measures of the 1960s. He also condemned busing and affirmative action, the key civil rights initiatives of the 1970s. The president, like many Republicans, even opposed the creation of a national holiday marking the birthday of Martin Luther King, Jr.

The conservatives' tough stance came at a difficult time in the struggle for racial equality. Compared with the 1950s and 1960s, African Americans' crusade for justice and opportunity generally slowed in the 1970s and 1980s. Despite legal equality, African Americans faced persisting racism and discrimination from individuals and institutions. Disproportionately clustered in manual occupations, African Americans were particularly hurt by the deindustrialization and economic decline of the 1970s and 1980s. After years of improvement, African Americans' economic status relative to whites had stagnated or declined by most measures during the Reagan era. African Americans still made less money than whites did for comparable work. African Americans also had much less chance to climb the ladder to managerial positions.

Economic hardship and persistent discrimination did not affect all African Americans equally. In the 1980s the African-American middle class continued to thrive. Among college-educated Americans, the incomes of African-American men rose faster than those of whites into the mid-1980s. Middle-class African Americans could afford to move to better housing, often in suburbs and integrated areas. Meanwhile, working-class African Americans found their wages stagnating or falling compared with those of white workers. In the 1970s and 1980s, poverty rates rose faster among African Americans than among whites. By 1986, nearly one-third of African Americans lived in poverty. The "feminization" of poverty hit African-American families particularly hard. In 1985, 75 percent of poor African-American children lived in families headed by a single female. Observers feared that there was now a permanent African-American "underclass," segregated in inner-city neighborhoods with poor schools and widespread crime.

African Americans mobilized to fight for equality and opportunity in the 1980s. Across the country, the number of African-American elected officials increased markedly. Most notably, the Reverend Jesse Jackson, a protégé of Martin Luther King, Jr., won wide attention during the decade. Preaching self-esteem and economic self-help for African Americans, Jackson was the leader of Operation PUSH—People United to Save Humanity. In 1984 Jackson became the first prominent African-American presidential candidate when he challenged Walter Mondale for the Democratic nomination. Although Jackson lost, his campaign suggested how far American society had come in accepting African-American political participation.

African-American activism, exemplified by the Jackson campaign, made it difficult for Reagan and other conservatives to undo the civil rights revolution of the 1960s and 1970s, and so did the persistence of discrimination and inequality. Most Americans seemed to accept that some federal action was essential to redress the imbalance between races in America. Despite Reagan's opposition, in

The Reverand Jesse Jackson, whose activism emphasized economic opportunity as well as equality and political power for African Americans.

1982 Congress voted to extend the Voting Rights Act for 25 years. Reagan also lost when his administration supported the attempt by Bob Jones University, an evangelical institution, to retain its tax-exempt status even though it prohibited interracial dating and engaged in other forms of racial discrimination; in 1983 the Supreme Court ruled overwhelmingly against the university. The court also rejected the Reagan administration's bid to set aside local affirmative-action programs. In other decisions, the justices limited affirmative action somewhat, but this important liberal program survived the Reagan administration.

The battles over the rights of African Americans, gays, and women demonstrated that conservative social values remained controversial in the 1980s. Although many Americans were sympathetic with the conservative agenda, many others were not ready to undo the legacy of the 1960s. The result was a stalemate. Disadvantaged groups made relatively little progress in their struggle for equal rights and opportunities in the 1980s, but conservatives also made little progress in their own fights to stop affirmative action, gay rights, abortion, and drugs and to uphold school prayer, educational reform, and traditional gender roles.

The Limits of the New Conservatism

The stalemate over social values was not the only sign that there were limits to conservatism in the 1980s. Scandals plagued business and religious figures who had helped create the conservative climate of the decade. The Reagan administration was hurt by policy setbacks, economic woes, and its own scandals. For a time, the conservatives' triumph, like the Trumps' fortune, was seriously in doubt.

Business and Religious Scandals

In the late 1980s the new conservatism suffered from a series of scandals involving leading business and religious figures. Even before Donald Trump's fortunes declined in the late 1980s, other famous entrepreneurs were in trouble. In 1986 Ivan Boesky, the swaggering Wall Street deal maker, was indicted for insider trading, the illegal use of secret financial information. Rather than go to trial, he agreed to give up stock trading, inform on other law break-

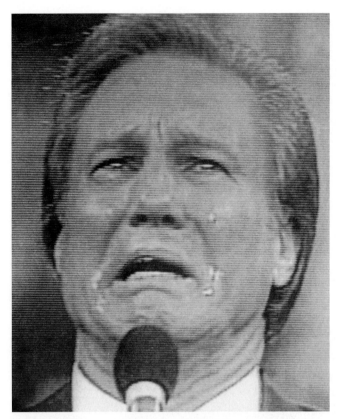

The face of religious scandal: Reverend Jimmy Swaggart confesses on television that he "had sinned."

ers, spend two years in jail, and pay a 100 million dollar fine. In 1987 Michael Milken, the junk-bond king, was indicted on fraud and racketeering charges. His eventual plea-bargain agreement included a ten-year jail sentence and a stunning 600 million dollar fine, the largest judgment against an individual in American history. In 1988 Leona Helmsley, a wealthy and well-publicized New York City hotel owner, was indicted for tax fraud. "We don't pay taxes," Helmsley had boasted. "The little people pay taxes." She wound up with her own jail sentence and a multimillion-dollar fine.

These scandals provoked second thoughts about the celebration of business and materialism in the early 1980s. Now critics censured the morals of businesspeople. Even Donald Trump called Helmsley "a disgrace to humanity." Critics pointed out that Boesky's and Milken's business methods had actually hurt the economy by saddling corporations with a great deal of debt and little cash to pay for it. Lavish lifestyles no longer seemed quite so attractive. As a former Helmsley employee noted, "Leona's unapologetic enjoyment of her wealth doesn't amuse us anymore."

Scandal touched religion as well as commerce during Reagan's second term. Leading televangelists, the spearheads of the conservative religious right, were caught in embarrassing predicaments. In 1987 Americans learned that Jim Bakker had defrauded investors in Heritage Park, USA, and paid hush money to hide his adulterous liaison with a church secretary. The scandal hurt the reputation of Jerry Falwell, who had taken over Bakker's organization. In 1988 Falwell resigned from his own Moral Majority. That year, the Pentecostal televangelist Jimmy Swaggart, a married father, admitted that he "had sinned" with prostitutes. Each of these scandals hurt the public standing of the religious right, which had done so much to support the Reagan Revolution.

Political Scandals

The Reagan administration had its own scandals. Almost from the start, some observers decried lax ethical standards, a so-called "sleaze factor," in the Reagan administration. Before the end of the president's first term, more than 20 officials of the Environmental Protection Agency, including its head, resigned or were fired over charges of favoritism toward lobbyists and polluters. In 1985 Secretary of Labor Raymond Donovan resigned after becoming the first cabinet officer ever indicted. He was acquitted on charges of fraud two years later. In 1988 Reagan's friend and attorney general, Edwin Meese III, resigned amid questions about his role in the corrupt awarding of government contracts to a defense firm. To critics of the administration, all this scandal stemmed from Reagan's conservative ideology. The president and his followers had supposedly encouraged fraud and corruption with their contemptuous attitude toward government and their eagerness to please business.

In his second term, Reagan faced much more damaging accusations. Early in October 1986, Sandinista soldiers in Nicaragua shot down a transport plane attempting to supply the Contra rebels. It soon became clear that the plane had been part of a secret effort by the Reagan administration to violate the Boland Amendment's ban on aid to the Contras. Then, early in November, a Lebanese magazine reported that the United States had traded arms to Iran. Despite denials from the president, the government had in fact sold the arms in order to win the release of American hostages held by terrorists in Lebanon. The Reagan administration had broken the president's pledge not to negotiate with terrorists and had violated a ban on arms sales to Iran. As if that were not bad enough, Americans soon learned that the arms deal and the Nicaraguan plane crash were connected. Government officials had illegally used proceeds from the sale to help pay for supplying the Contras.

The scandal that became known as the Iran-Contra affair had the potential to drive Reagan from office. If the president had ordered or known about the arms deal and the supply effort, he might have faced impeachment. The Reagan administration underwent three separate investigations by a special commission appointed by the president

At the center of the Iran-Contra Scandal: Marine Lieutenant Colonel Oliver North testifies passionately before a congressional committee in July 1987.

and headed by former Senator John Tower; by a special prosecutor appointed by the attorney general; and by a special congressional committee. These inquiries made clear that Reagan was probably deeply involved in the Iran-Contra affair, but none turned up enough evidence to impeach the president.

Nevertheless, the Iran-Contra affair badly damaged Reagan's reputation. Several of his associates left office and faced jail sentences. Former National Security Adviser Robert "Bud" McFarlane, who helped arrange the arms for hostages trade, pleaded guilty to withholding information from Congress. His successor, Rear Admiral John Poindexter, who helped divert the arms proceeds to the Contras, was allowed to resign. Poindexter's charismatic aide, Marine Lieutenant Colonel Oliver North, who played a key role in creating and then covering up the Iran-Contra operations, had to be fired. Tried and sentenced for their actions, both men had their convictions overturned on technical grounds. Meanwhile, the director of the CIA, William Casey, died in 1987, the day after testimony implicated him in the effort to aid the Contras. For conservatives, these men—the dashing North above all—were true American heroes, but their actions damaged Reagan's

standing in the eyes of many people. Much of the public concluded that the president must have known about his associates' dealings; his popularity dropped.

Setbacks for the Conservative Agenda

Against this backdrop of scandal, conservatives faced a series of policy setbacks during Reagan's second term. Despite the president's impressive victory in 1984, the conservative agenda did not dominate Washington. Even though Democrats controlled the House of Representatives, during his first term Reagan had usually persuaded Congress to back his conservative agenda. The Democrats were much less cooperative during his second term. Still in control of the House, Democratic legislators seemed much less afraid to oppose the president. The Democrats became even more combative after winning majorities in both the House and Senate in the congressional elections in the fall of 1986.

Accordingly, Reagan sometimes had to compromise with Congress. In 1985 the president called for a "Second American Revolution," a comprehensive overhaul of the income-tax system. But the Tax Reform Act, which passed

Congress in 1986, was a disappointment. The final measure did not lower and simplify income taxes nearly as much as the president had wanted.

Reagan also met outright defeat at the hands of Congress. In 1988, a coalition of Democrats and Republicans passed a bill compelling large companies to give workers 60 days' advance notice of plant closings and layoffs. Reagan opposed this liberal, pro-labor measure, but he knew that the bill's supporters had enough votes to override a presidential veto. Rather than fight, the president allowed the bill to become law without his signature.

The president faced repeated defeat on environmental policy. During the 1980s there was growing worldwide concern about environmental hazards. In December 1984 the subsidiary of a U. S. corporation accidentally allowed toxic gas to escape from a pesticide plant in Bhopal, India. The emission killed over 2,500 people and injured as many as 200,000. In April 1986 an explosion and fire allowed radioactive material to escape a nuclear power plant at Chernobyl in the U. S. S. R. The accident killed more than 30 people, injured over 200, exposed countless others to radioactivity, and caused extensive environmental damage.

In this alarming context, Reagan's conservative hostility to environmentalism was no longer so appealing. In 1986 the president had to accept the extension of the federal Superfund program to clean up hazardous waste in the United States. The next year, Congress overrode his veto of a bill renewing the Water Quality Control Act. In 1988, after years of avoiding action on acid rain, the Reagan administration signed an international agreement placing limits on certain emissions.

A Vulnerable Economy

Even the economy, the centerpiece of the Reagan Revolution, became a problem again during the president's second term. Despite conservative economic policies, inequality increased in the 1980s. During the decade, the gap between rich and poor widened sharply. While the average family income, after taxes, of the highest-paid tenth of Americans rose 27 percent from 1977 to 1988, the average family income of the poorest tenth actually fell 11 percent (see Figure 30-3). By the end of the 1980s, average family income, adjusted for inflation, was little more than it had been at the start of the 1970s. In the 1980s only the rich earned more and kept more. Other Americans faced economic stagnation or decline.

The falling incomes of the poorest Americans ensured the persistence of poverty in the Reagan years. Twenty-nine million Americans lived below the poverty line in 1980. Ten years later, that figure had grown to almost 37 million. Despite Reaganomics, the United States had one of the highest poverty rates among industrialized nations. Contrary to popular stereotypes, the typical poor American in the 1980s was white and female, not African American and male. A larger number of whites than African Americans lived in poverty.

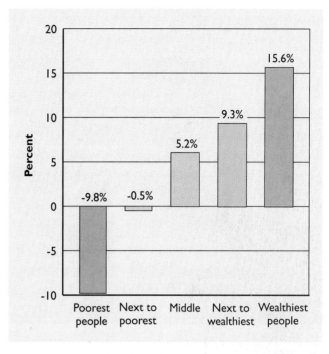

Figure 30-3   Changes in Families' Real Income, 1980–1990.
Source: Copyright © 1989 by the New York Times Co. Reprinted by Permission.

ican and male. A larger number of whites than African Americans lived in poverty.

One of the most visible consequences of poverty was homelessness. In the 1980s the number of homeless Americans, living in streets and shelters, increased markedly. In some cities, the homeless doubled from year to year. There were perhaps 30,000 homeless people in New York City by 1988. The sight of men and women, their belongings in shopping carts, sleeping on sidewalks, was common during the Reagan years.

Homelessness, poverty, and inequality produced a spirited debate in the 1980s. Democrats and liberals blamed these problems on Reaganomics. The president, they charged, had done nothing to stop the erosion of high-paying factory jobs. His welfare, housing, and job-training cuts hurt the poor, while his tax cuts and deregulation helped the rich. Supply-side economics, Reagan's critics concluded, had benefited only the wealthy.

In response, conservatives and Republicans pointed to what they saw as the harmful effects of the Great Society and other liberal policies. It was activist, liberal government, they maintained, that had hurt manufacturing and weakened the economy. Moreover, welfare programs caused poverty by destroying poor people's work ethic and making them dependent on handouts. The president and his followers felt no need to apologize for Reaganomics. "What I want to see above all," Reagan explained, "is that this remains a country where someone can always get rich."

web connection

Stagflation or The Rich Get Richer

www.prenhall.com/boydston/inequality

The gap between rich and poor grew in the 1980s, shrinking the middle class that had been growing. New jobs paid poorly, and tax changes benefited the well-to-do, with the result that net income (after taxes were paid) shot up by two-thirds for the 1 percent who had the most to begin with. Most Americans' after-tax incomes stagnated or shrank because real wages became lower, and consumer debt became higher. Why this shift in the way government distributed income? What did growing inequality mean for most citizens?

Not surprisingly, neither side persuaded the other in this debate. In reality, both liberal and conservative policies had produced flawed economic results. Lyndon Johnson's spending for the Great Society, along with the cost of the Vietnam War, had begun to undermine the economy in the 1960s. His antipoverty programs had been less effective than liberals wanted to admit, but the Reagan Revolution had offered no solution to poverty, either. While benefiting the rich and cutting inflation, Reaganomics did not reinvigorate manufacturing or boost middle-class incomes.

There were other signs of economic vulnerability by the mid-1980s. Despite the promises of Reaganomics, the federal budget deficit did not disappear. Instead, between 1981 and 1986, as the government cut taxes and increased defense spending, the deficit soared from 79 billion to 221 billion dollars—a staggering new record.

Like poverty and inequality, the deficit was a controversial subject: Some economists believed the deficit was a sign of great economic weakness; others believed it did not matter. Democrats and liberals blamed Reagan for the

Homeless Americans, huddled near the Mall in Washington, D.C., in the middle of a blizzard.

budgetary red ink. Some of the president's opponents even suggested that he created the deficits on purpose in order to force spending cuts in social programs. Reagan's supporters blamed Congress for failing to cut the budget.

In fact both the president and Congress were to blame. Neither Republicans nor Democrats wanted to reduce such popular benefits as Medicare and Social Security. Congress did enact the Balanced Budget and Emergency Deficit Control Act of 1985, known as the Gramm-Rudman Act, which promised automatic cuts to balance the budget by 1990. The next year a Supreme Court ruling critically weakened the measure. The deficit remained high during Reagan's last years in office. Under Reagan, the national debt—the total amount owed by the federal government to its creditors—reached 1 trillion dollars for the first time and then nearly tripled to 2.6 trillion dollars.

Along with this burgeoning debt, the Reagan years produced a growing international trade deficit. In 1980 the annual value of imports was 25.4 billion dollars greater than the value of the nation's exports. By 1986 that gap had grown to 145.1 billion dollars. American business was still not able to compete with foreign producers in the 1980s. Consumers at home and abroad found foreign goods, like the Honda Accord, more attractive than ever. Reaganomics had not solved the problem of America's relative decline in the world economy.

Doubts about Reagan's economic policy increased when the stock market plummeted unexpectedly on Monday, October 19, 1987. That day the Dow Jones Industrial Average lost 508 points—23 percent of its value. It was the biggest one-day decline since "Black Tuesday" in October 1929. For a moment, frightened Americans worried that this new crash would lead to another Great Depression. The market drop reflected underlying economic problems including the federal budget deficit, the trade deficit, and deindustrialization. It also stemmed from lax regulation of Wall Street by the Reagan administration.

The crash was one more economic blow to the Reagan Revolution. "What crashed was more than just the market," a journalist concluded. "It was the Reagan Illusion: the idea that there could be a defense buildup and tax cuts without a price, that the country could live beyond its means indefinitely." Moreover, Reaganomics had not halted the growth of poverty, inequality, homelessness, and trade deficits. In the late 1980s, the American economy, like Ivana Trump, apparently could not have it all.

Reagan's Comeback

By 1987 the Reagan presidency, beset by scandals and economic troubles, appeared to be in jeopardy. Reagan's accomplishments, like the Trumps' success, seemed uncertain. Americans, Donald Trump observed, "are beginning to question whether there's anything beneath that smile," but then the president began a comeback.

Reagan benefited from his political skills and his popularity with many Americans. Continuing economic growth overshadowed the stock market crash and other woes. Most important, perhaps, changes in the Soviet Union led to a dramatic easing of cold-war tensions. By the end of his presidency, Reagan had won back his popularity.

During his second term, Reagan showed a remarkable ability to withstand scandal and defeat. Opponents dubbed him the "Teflon president" because nothing seemed to stick to him. That was a tribute to Reagan's political skills. It was also a reflection of many Americans' real affection for him. After a series of disappointing presidencies since the 1960s, Americans seemed unwilling to let Reagan fail.

The economy also helped the president. Notwithstanding Americans' fears, the stock market crash did not lead to depression or even recession. The market soon recovered and began moving up again. The economy continued to grow. Despite poverty, deficits, and other problems, the nation was arguably more prosperous than during the 1970s.

Reagan's comeback was probably helped most of all by the transformation of the Soviet Union. By the mid-1980s the U.S.S.R. suffered from a weakening economy, an unpopular war in Afghanistan, and a costly arms race. At this critical juncture, Mikhail Gorbachev became general secretary of the Communist Party. After years of old and uninspired leaders, the dynamic and charismatic Gorbachev signaled a new era with a series of stunning reforms. At home, he called for restructuring the economy (*perestroika*) and tolerating more open discussion (*glasnost*). Abroad, he sought an easing of tensions with the United States and the West in order to slow the costly arms race and attract foreign investment.

Gorbachev's reforms, more audacious than Reagan's, gave the U.S. government a politically popular opportunity to thaw cold-war tensions. Initially the Reagan administration was unsure as to whether Gorbachev sincerely sought a new relationship, but Reagan met with the Soviet leader in a series of positive summits beginning in Geneva, Switzerland, in November 1985. Meanwhile, it became apparent that the Soviets were, in fact, changing their foreign policy. In 1988, they withdrew their troops from Afghanistan. The Soviets also began to ease their tight control over the Communist regimes of Eastern Europe.

As these developments unfolded, the United States and the Soviets made striking progress on arms control. In December 1987 Reagan and Gorbachev signed the Intermediate-Range Nuclear Forces Treaty (INF) at a summit in Washington, D.C. Under the terms of the treaty, the United States and the Soviet Union promised to destroy more than 2,500 intermediate-range nuclear missiles. For the first time, the two powers had agreed to give up a weapon altogether rather than just limit its numbers.

The INF treaty signaled a permanent easing of tensions between the United States and the Soviet Union. The cold war, so intense just a few years earlier, suddenly seemed to be ending. Reagan's supporters and critics argued over the cause. Conservatives and Republicans insisted that the president's defense buildup had forced the Soviets to capitulate. Democrats and liberals maintained that the buildup and the president's harsh rhetoric had actually slowed the thaw in U. S.-Soviet relations. In any event, the thaw had occurred. Asked in 1988 about calling the U. S. S. R. the "evil empire," Reagan replied, "I was talking about another time, another era."

As Reagan left office in January 1989, his comeback seemed complete. The economy was growing; the cold war was ending. He had the highest popularity rating of any president since the beginning of modern polling in the 1930s.

The confident leader of perestroika *in the Soviet Union: Mikhail Gorbachev, general secretary of the Communist Party, shown here in Moscow.*

CHRONOLOGY

1980   Ronald Reagan elected president

1981   Introduction of the IBM personal computer
Air traffic controllers' strike
Economic Recovery Act passes
Appointment of Sandra Day O'Connor to the
Supreme Court
AIDS cases first publicly reported

1982   Breakup of AT&T
Nuclear "freeze" rally in New York City
Passage of the Boland Amendment
Extension of the Voting Rights Act

1983   Announcement of Strategic Defense Initiative
Congress approves Caribbean Basin Initiative
Social Security Reform Act of 1983
U. S. invasion of Grenada
Terrorist attack on U. S. Marines in Lebanon
Publication of *A Nation at Risk*

1984   Report of the Grace Commission
Re-election of Ronald Reagan

1985   General Electric purchases RCA
Gramm-Rudman Act

1986   U. S. bombing of Libya
Nuclear power plant accident in Chernobyl,
U. S. S. R.
Tax Reform Act
Indictment of Ivan Boesky
Revelation of Iran-Contra affair

1987   Iraqi missile attack on U. S. destroyer *Stark*
Indictment of Michael Milken
Jim Bakker scandal
Stock market crash
Intermediate-Range Nuclear Forces Treaty

1988   Omnibus Trade and Competitiveness Act
U. S. accidentally shoots down Iranian airliner

Conclusion

Reagan's comeback emphasized the triumph of the new conservatism. Americans would debate the nature of that triumph for years to come. Certainly the conservative victory, like the Trumps' success, was never as great as it seemed in the heady days of the early 1980s. Americans did not embrace much of the conservative social agenda. They did not want to give up many of the benefits of liberal, activist government. The Reagan Revolution did not solve such basic economic problems as poverty. It made some problems, such as inequality and the budget deficit, even worse.

Nevertheless, the conservative triumph, like the Trumps' fortune, was real. In the 1980s American culture celebrated the wealth and values of Trump and other business figures. A new conservative coalition elected Reagan. The president, in turn, helped implement a conservative vision of the political economy that embraced reduced government, supply-side economics, and renewed cold war. Moreover, Reagan combated the sense of national decline that pervaded America in the 1970s.

The accomplishments of the new conservatism, as Reagan's troubled second term indicated, were fragile. The nation's economic revival was shaky, and so was the revival of its spirit. Americans were still worried about the future. "I think," Donald Trump concluded, "the '90s are going to be much trickier than the 1980s."

Review Questions

1. What were the main values and goals of the new conservatism in the 1980s? What role did business and religion play in shaping the conservative movement?

2. What was the Reagan Revolution in domestic policy? How did Reagan's domestic programs reflect conservative values?

3. Describe the aims of Reagan's foreign policy. How did his goals differ from those of earlier presidents during the cold war?

4. What groups resisted the conservative social agenda in the 1980s? How did the desire for equal rights and opportunities conflict with conservatism?

5. What factors limited the triumph of the new conservatism? Did conservatives really succeed in the 1980s?

Further Readings

Connie Bruck, *The Predators' Ball: The Inside Story of Drexel Burnham and the Rise of the Junk Bond Raiders* (1989). This work vividly describes some of the new, controversial business practices of the 1980s.

Theodore Draper, *A Very Thin Line: The Iran-Contra Affairs* (1991). A careful reconstruction of the major scandal of the Reagan presidency.

Susan Faludi, *Backlash: The Undeclared War Against American Women* (1991). Faludi's book captures the contentiousness surrounding gender issues in the 1980s.

Marshall Frady, *Jesse: The Life and Pilgrimage of Jesse Jackson* (1996). Frady presents a full biography of the most prominent African-American leader of the 1980s.

Paul Freiberger and Michael Swaine, *Fire in the Valley: The Making of the Personal Computer* (1974). An interesting anecdotal account of a critical development in the computer revolution.

Paul Gottfried, *The Conservative Movement* (1993). A balanced analysis, particularly strong on conservative ideas.

Haynes Johnson, *Sleepwalking Through History: America in the Reagan Years* (1991). A journalist's vivid chronicle of major developments in the 1980s.

William E. Pemberton, *Exit with Honor: The Life and Presidency of Ronald Reagan* (1997). One of the first full assessments of Reagan's career by a professional historian.

James M. Scott, *Deciding to Intervene: The Reagan Doctrine and American Foreign Policy* (1996). Scott's book focuses on the anti-Soviet aims of the Reagan administration.

Randy Shilts, *And the Band Played On: Politics, People, and the AIDS Epidemic* (1987). A moving account of the response to AIDS.

History on the Internet

"Possible Soviet Responses to the U. S. Strategic Defense Initiative"

http://www.fas.org/spp/starwars/offdocs/m8310017.htm

From the office of the Director of Central Intelligence, this report seeks to ascertain Soviet military strength and intentions during the Reagan era.

"Reagan"

http://www.pbs.org/wgbh/amex/reagan/filmmore/index.html

This comprehensive site contains information on the Iran-Contra affair, a timeline of Reagan's presidency, in-depth coverage of the 1982 recession and the Grenada invasion, and text copies of many of Reagan's presidential speeches. A companion site to a documentary on the president, this site also contains transcripts of interviews with scholars about the Reagan presidency.

31

A NEW AMERICA?

1989 -

OUTLINE

Felix Andreev and "The Blessing of America"

Felix Iosifovich Andreev felt trapped in the Soviet Union. He chafed under the restraints of the Communist political and economic system. A Jew, he resented the U. S. S. R.'s discrimination against his religion. For years, this magazine editor and former boxer had loved American movies, American books, and American jazz. The United States, Andreev believed, was a place of "liberty and generous people." However, for years he could not get there because Soviet immigration law made it impossible for him to leave. Then, in the late 1980s, the Soviet leader Mikhail Gorbachev loosened immigration restrictions as part of his attempt to reform the U. S. S. R. So, in 1989, Andreev moved with his wife and family to the Brighton Beach section of Brooklyn in New York City.

From the long perspective of American history, Andreev's story was not at all unusual. Immigrants, escaping oppression and seeking opportunity, had been migrating to America for centuries. In the late 1800s and early 1900s, many Russian Jews had come to live in

Brighton Beach. From another perspective, Andreev's arrival in Brooklyn was remarkable. For more than 40 years, the cold war had largely blocked migration between the Soviet Union and the United States. America's economic problems, especially the emerging crisis of de-industrialization in the 1970s, had made the nation a less obvious symbol of economic opportunity. Immigrants from Russia and other countries, once a large and visible presence in America, had played a less important role in national life since World War II.

As Felix Andreev's arrival in Brighton Beach suggested, things were changing. At the end of the 1980s, the cold war was coming to an end. The conflict between the United States and the Soviet Union, between capitalism and Communism, no longer defined American life. Instead, such forces as immigration were reshaping the nation as it approached the end of the century. Andreev was one of millions of immigrants from Russia, Asia, and Latin America who arrived in the United States in the

1980s and 1990s. Like immigrants before them, these new Americans both changed their adopted country and were changed by it.

Andreev's Brighton Beach showed the process at work. About half of the community's population of 50,000, the Russian immigrants were transforming this one-and-a-half-mile strip of Brooklyn. "Welcome to Siberia," read the sign on a nightclub. Restaurants and stores had signs written in Russia's distinctive Cyrillic alphabet. People spoke Russian in the streets. But Andreev and other immigrants did not want to recreate the Soviet Union they had left behind. They wanted to share what Andreev called "the blessing of America." Andreev's wife predicted that "the next generation will all be Americans."

It was hard to be so definite about the future. In the early 1990s the new Russian residents of Brighton Beach struggled to find jobs and make their way. As Andreev's wife admitted, the Russians "do not yet fit into" American society.

Brighton Beach symbolized the promise and the uncertainty of the nation as it ended one century and began another. Despite all the upheavals since the 1960s, the United States still represented the opportunity for

Signs of a new America: A rack of Russian-language newspapers, with their distinctive Cyrillic alphabet, for sale on an American street.

freedom and prosperity. That was why Felix Andreev and so many other immigrants came from around the world in the 1990s. The United States, however, like Andreev's new community, was plainly changing. An older nation, defined by the cold war, New Deal liberalism, and heavy industry, was disappearing. A new America had not yet taken its place. With the end of the cold war, the nation's role in the world was unclear. As the industrial revolution ran its course, the outlines of a **postindustrial economy** were still incomplete. Americans struggled to understand how their nation's global role and economic transformation were redefining the political economy.

Despite the conservative victories of the 1980s, neither Republicans nor Democrats dominated the politics of the 1990s. The old political labels—"liberal" and "conservative"—seemed less meaningful as the century ended. Battles for individual and group rights, a central feature of American life for half a century, were taking new forms. In the 1990s the United States was much like Felix Andreev. As a new millennium arrived, the nation had left behind much of its recent past but had not yet defined its future. ∎

A New Economy

Felix Andreev and other immigrants were drawn to the United States partly by the promise of its changing economy. As manufacturing played a smaller economic role, the United States continued to develop into a postindustrial society. More than ever, the service sector, led by computer companies and other high-technology firms, drove the economy. Like the industrial revolution before it, the computer revolution seemed to have the power to transform American life, but the nature of the new, postindustrial economy remained uncertain at the start of the twenty-first century. Some things were clear: The United States was increasingly enmeshed in the world economy. Global competition helped lead to **downsizing**—massive job layoffs intended to make American corporations leaner and more efficient. Partly because of downsizing and the computer revolution, the United States experienced sustained economic growth in the 1990s. Nevertheless, Americans remained uneasy about the economic future as a new century began.

Toward a Postindustrial Economy

Under way since the 1950s, the transition from an industrial to a postindustrial economy picked up momentum in the 1990s. Manufacturing played a smaller role in the economy. At the beginning of the decade, factories actually employed fewer production workers than in 1955. American corporations continued to move their manufacturing operations abroad in order to take advantage of lower wages and production costs. Consequently, workers had less chance to hold relatively high-wage jobs in the factories of smokestack America.

Those workers were increasingly likely to find employment in the service sector, the fastest-growing part of the economy. More and more Americans worked in restaurants, retail stores, and offices instead of factories. By 1994 the service sector accounted for about 70 percent of the nation's economic activity. The postindustrial economy had clearly arrived.

Many Americans believed that high technology would dominate the postindustrial economy. In the 1990s the ongoing electronics revolution continued to transform communications. More and more Americans carried pagers and cellular telephones. High-speed fiber-optic cables and new satellite dishes expanded the power and reach of telephone and television systems.

The most powerful symbol of the new economy was still the computer. As the century ended, the microcomputer revolution continued to unfold. Computers became smaller, faster, more powerful, and more common. Americans encountered computers almost everywhere—in grocery store checkout lines, in factories, under the hoods of cars, and at home. By 1999 more than half of the nation's households had at least one computer.

The most dramatic computing development in the 1990s was the explosive growth of the Internet, the communications network linking computer users around the nation and the world. Begun by the Department of Defense in the late 1960s, the Internet had spread through universities and across American society by the end of the century. Originally, people used the Internet to send and

Two drivers talk on their cellular telephones, one of the new technologies spurring optimistic visions of a new postindustrial economy at the end of the twentieth century.

receive e-mail (electronic messages), but by the middle of the 1990s millions of Americans began to explore the World Wide Web, a new and rapidly expanding segment of the Internet that blended text, graphics, audio, and video. The Internet and the Web quickly affected national life. Americans used this new "Information Superhighway" to communicate, to do research, to create and exhibit art, to listen to music, and to engage in **e-commerce,** buying and selling online.

These developments spurred the old utopian dream that the computer would define the postindustrial society, just as the factory had defined industrial America. Thanks to the computer and other electronic innovations, the dream held, Americans would process information instead of raw materials. They would produce knowledge and ideas instead of steel and cars. They would buy online instead of in stores. Postindustrial America would be a prosperous information society, sustained by the computerized e-commerce of an "Internet economy."

At the start of the twenty-first century, there were many reasons to believe this utopian dream was fast coming true. The computer revolution seemed to be repeating the industrial revolution. As in the late 1800s and early 1900s, a group of corporations, taking advantage of new technologies, was pushing to the forefront of American capitalism: software firms such as Microsoft and Oracle, hardware firms such as Dell Computer and Intel, e-commerce pioneers such as Amazon.com and eBay, and the Internet service provider, America Online. Established companies, meanwhile, rushed to do business online.

Like the industrial revolution, the computer revolution spurred a wave of corporate mergers and acquisitions. As communications, entertainment, and computing companies pushed to take advantage of the Internet and other

Microsoft founder Bill Gates appears on closed-circuit television during a press conference to answer questions about the federal antitrust suit aimed at his company.

electronics innovations, the number and value of mergers reached record levels in the last years of the 1990s. The ABC television network, already merged with Capital Cities Communications in the 1980s, was taken over by Walt Disney in 1995. That year, media giant Time-Warner, the product of a merger in 1989, bought out Turner Broadcasting. Then, in a sign of the growing importance of the Internet, America Online arranged to purchase Time-Warner in 2000.

The computer revolution also paralleled the industrial revolution by producing a new, hugely wealthy elite. In the 1990s Americans read about a host of multi-millionaires and billionaires, entrepreneurs whose fortunes had been created by computing. The most famous of this new corporate elite was Bill Gates, the co-founder of Microsoft, who became the wealthiest American since John D. Rockefeller, the co-founder of Standard Oil, nearly a century before.

Like the industrial revolution, the computer revolution also produced uncertainty and fear. At the end of the twentieth century, as at the beginning, many Americans worried about the economic and political power of giant new companies and new fortunes. Microsoft and Bill Gates became a lightning rod for these worries about the emerging postindustrial economy. To many critics, Gates seemed all too much like John D. Rockefeller—a grasping big businessman who used unfair tactics to drive competitors into the ground. Microsoft, like Standard Oil, became a symbol of monopoly power, and like Standard Oil, Microsoft became the target of state and federal prosecutors. In 2000, a federal judge ruled that Microsoft had violated the Sherman Anti-Trust Act by illegally forcing computer makers to use its software. The judge ordered that Microsoft, like Standard Oil, be broken up into smaller companies in order to restore competition.

The many parallels between the computer revolution and the industrial revolution seemed to prove that the **postindustrial economy** had indeed arrived at the start of the twenty-first century, but in some ways the computerized, "Internet economy" remained a dream. Few companies made substantial profits from "e-commerce." Many online companies quickly failed. Meanwhile, General Motors and Ford—old-fashioned manufacturing companies—remained the largest corporations in America. At the start of the twenty-first century, computers had not yet matched factories as a revolutionary force in American life. It was not even clear that computers, like machine tools and railroads before them, had boosted the productivity of workers.

Moreover, high-paying, high-technology jobs were not the only product of the growing service sector. In the 1990s most new service positions were low paying, involved limited technology, and required little education. The United States still employed many sales clerks and fry cooks who would never earn as much as the steel and auto

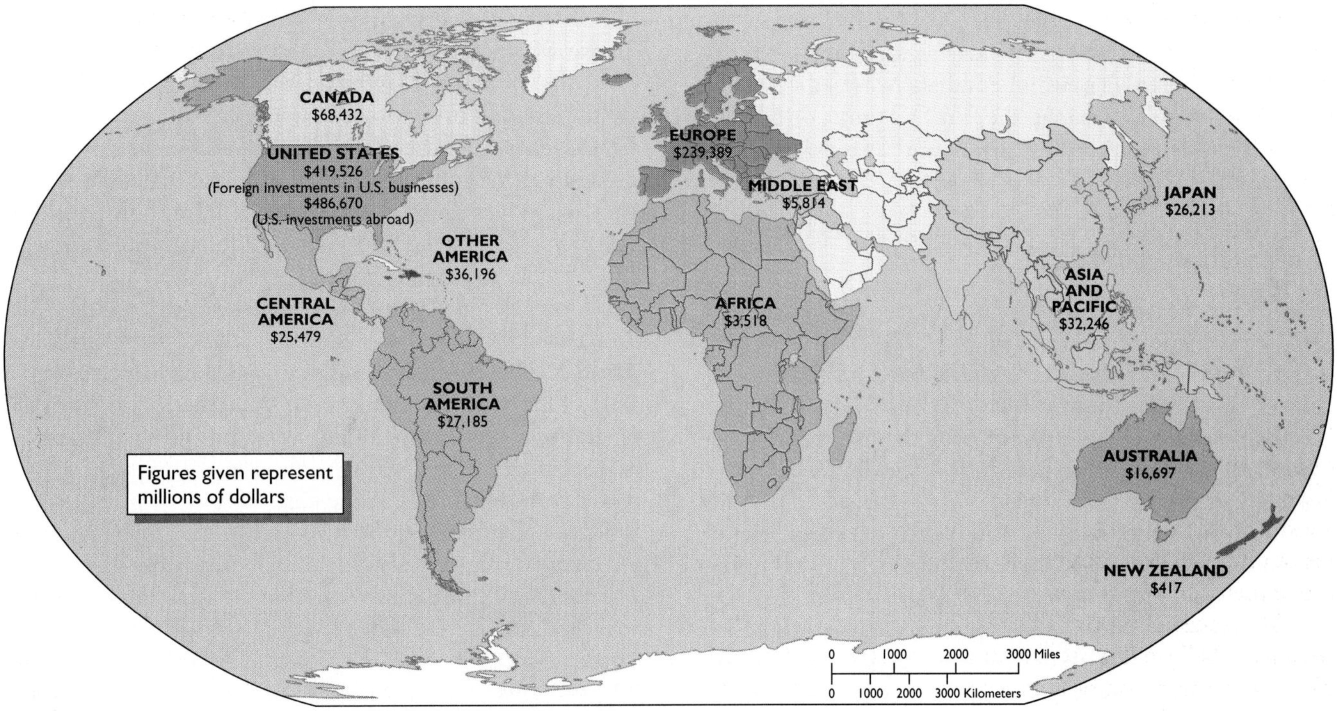

Map 31-1 The Globalization of the U.S. Economy.
The large worth of U.S. investment in other regions around the world was nearly equalled by the value of foreign investments in the U.S. in 1992.

workers of the old industrial economy. As a result, the growth of the service sector inspired fears of a low-tech future as well as dreams of a high-tech utopia.

At the start of the twenty-first century, no one could predict the outcome of America's ongoing economic transformation with much confidence. The postindustrial age had begun, but Americans could not be sure what it would bring.

Toward a Global Economy

There was at least one economic certainty at the start of the new century. The American economy was becoming ever more tightly bound up in a single global economy. Signs of economic globalization were everywhere at the end of the twentieth century. Americans owned more stock in foreign companies than ever before, and foreigners had more financial investments in the United States than ever before. U. S. exports and imports both jumped about 50 percent in the five years from 1990 to 1995 (see Map 31-1). Underscoring the growing importance of global commerce, the United States and more than 100 other countries changed the name of the international trade group known as GATT (the General Agreement on Tariffs and Trade) to the World Trade Organization in 1994.

International trade remained intensely competitive in the 1990s. Even though the United States still imported more than it exported, the nation seemed to fare better in its rivalry with other industrial nations. American corporations continued their efforts to become more efficient. By 1993 one study rated the United States, rather than Japan, the most competitive national economy in the world. A shift in auto sales symbolized the American resurgence. In 1992 the Ford Taurus replaced the Japanese Honda Accord as the bestselling car in the United States.

International competition involved governments as well as corporations. Since World War II, Western European nations had moved gradually toward economic and political cooperation. That trend, which had already produced the organization known as the Common Market, culminated with the formation of the European Union in 1993. Through the Union, such nations as France, Germany, and Great Britain planned to coordinate their economic and political policies and create a single vast economic unit. The member countries would then, it was believed, find it easier to trade with one another and prosper, and other countries, including the United States, might find it harder to compete in Europe.

The United States responded to the European threat by working with its neighbors to create an economic bloc in North America. In 1992 Canada, Mexico, and the United States announced the North American Free Trade Agreement (NAFTA), which established the world's largest and richest low-tariff trading zone to promote commerce among the three countries. NAFTA won considerable support from U. S. corporations, but organized labor feared that NAFTA would encourage those corporations to transfer even more jobs from the U. S. to Mexico. Environmentalists worried that the agreement would weaken the battle against industrial pollution. Despite this opposition, the Senate ratified the agreement in 1993.

Downsizing America

Global competition helped spur a wave of "downsizing" in the 1990s. Some of America's largest and most advanced corporations announced stunning cutbacks in their operations. For instance, the American Telephone and Telegraph Company (AT&T), long famous for the job security enjoyed by it workers, decided in 1996 to trim 40,000 positions over the next three years.

This and other corporate cutbacks were remarkable for a number of reasons: They came during a period of relative prosperity, they involved some of the largest and seemingly most stable American companies, and they affected many white-collar workers. Large corporations, quick to lay off assembly-line and other blue-collar employees, had traditionally been slow to cut loose white-collar workers. But now managers and professionals were vulnerable to unemployment as well.

Several factors helped produce this situation. Fundamentally, American businesses wanted to cut costs and increase profits. Despite the general prosperity, they worried about remaining efficient and competitive in the world economy. Also, the end of the cold war affected American corporations. As the federal government downsized the military, defense contractors lost business, and they too had to downsize.

Downsizing dramatically affected American workers. Those who lost their jobs faced an unsettling search for new employment. Many had to settle for lower-paying jobs. Most had to cope with a sense of failure and dislocation. Meanwhile, the remaining employees at downsized companies found themselves working harder than ever as they took over the responsibilities of laid-off co-workers. Realizing that they could lose their jobs at any time, employees felt less loyalty to corporations.

Downsizing particularly unsettled middle-class Americans, who had to abandon some of their cherished assumptions. In the 1990s the middle class realized what blue-collar workers had known since the 1970s: Even the largest corporations were not as stable and secure as they had seemed. Accordingly, middle-class status itself was not as stable and secure as in the past.

Not surprisingly, downsizing was controversial. Critics charged that downsizing actually made companies less efficient. The strategy left companies short-handed and deprived them of experienced workers' know-how. Downsizing, the critics concluded, was just "dumbsizing," but corporations insisted that downsizing was necessary to restore efficiency, competitiveness, and profits. The post-industrial economy was downsized as well as globalized.

An Uneasy Prosperity

Along with the pangs of downsizing, Americans experienced the exhilaration of sustained economic growth in the 1990s. The productivity of American workers and the vitality of the service sector helped keep the economy expanding for almost the whole decade. Partly because of international competition, corporate cost cutting, and low oil prices, inflation was negligible. Interest rates were low; unemployment rose during a recession early in the decade but then dropped off to record lows. Driven by excitement about computer-related companies, the stock market reached one record high after another in the 1990s. After passing 3,000 for the first time ever in 1991, the Dow Jones Industrial Average surpassed 4,000 and then 5,000 in 1995, and soared past 10,000 in 1999 (see Figure 31-1). The market crash of 1987 seemed long gone, as did Americans' sense of the need to live with less. Symbolically, Congress repealed the federal fifty-five-mile-per-hour speed limit for interstate highways in 1995.

Despite the good economic news of the 1990s, Americans remained uneasy at the start of the twenty-first century. Downsizing was one reason; falling wages were another. Allowing for inflation, the average

The impact of downsizing: unemployed white-collar workers wait anxiously for interviews at a job fair.

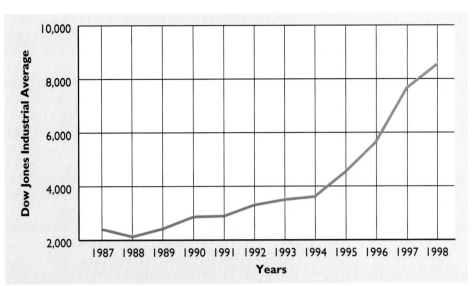

Figure 31-1   The Stock Market, 1987–1998.
The long, dramatic rise of the Dow Jones Industrial Average reflected the sustained growth of the U.S. economy in the 1990s.

Source: Phyllis S. Pierce, ed., The Dow Jones Averages, 1885–1995 (1996); World Almanac, 1998, p. 510; Standard and Poor's Daily Stock Price Record, NYSE, 1996, vol. 2, and 1997, vol. 2.

there would be more Americans over 65 and eligible for Social Security benefits than ever before (see Map 31-2). Many people believed there would not be enough money to pay the pensions of the baby-boom generation when it retired in the twenty-first century. Social Security needed reform, but the federal government was reluctant to act. On the one hand, political leaders did not want to pump more money into Social Security by imposing unpopular tax increases on American workers. On the other, they did not want to save money by cutting popular Social Security benefits. As a result, the threat to Social Security remained and even worsened. Americans continued to worry about their retirement.

weekly earnings of American workers in 1998 were less than in 1970. Several factors combined to keep those workers from making more money. The decline of manufacturing and the growth of the service sector meant the loss of relatively high-paying jobs. Employers were determined to hold down the growth of wages and salaries in the 1990s. Workers, facing the threats of downsizing and foreign competition, were reluctant to demand big wage increases, as were labor unions, which continued to have difficulty persuading workers to organize.

Americans also worried about whether they could afford the rapidly increasing costs of health care. The United States, almost alone among developed nations, had no national health insurance plan for its citizens. By the 1990s America was spending a greater proportion of its gross domestic product on health care than were the other developed nations. Nevertheless, perhaps 35 million Americans did not have health insurance in 1991. Millions more wondered whether their insurance would cover a catastrophic illness. The need for costly medical care would only increase as Americans' life expectancy continued to rise and the huge baby-boom generation aged. Amid calls for more federal control over health care, many Americans feared the government could not control medical costs without denying people the right to choose their own doctors. As a result, Congress failed to pass a proposal for sweeping health-care reform in 1993.

Americans feared, too, that they could not afford retirement. Since the 1980s experts and politicians had debated whether the social security system was headed for bankruptcy. With the aging of the baby-boom generation,

The Social Security and health-care issues, along with the corporate downsizing and falling wages, fostered an undertone of anxiety in the midst of prosperity. Even though the economy grew and the stock market flourished, Americans were unsure that the future would be prosperous. This uneasiness contributed to a broader uncertainty about the new economy. Leaving the industrial era behind, Americans were not yet sure what the postindustrial era would bring.

Political Deadlock

The economic dynamism at the start of the twenty-first century was accompanied by a pervasive sense of political deadlock. At the end of the 1980s, conservatives and Republicans believed that Ronald Reagan's presidency had revolutionized the American political economy. Much like Franklin Roosevelt's New Deal in the 1930s, the Reagan Revolution had, they expected, realigned politics, government, and the economy for years to come. Despite these hopes, the 1990s saw the end of the Reagan Revolution. Instead of a decisive shift to the right, the decade brought political moderation and uncertainty. Reagan's successors in the White House were unable to use the presidency as he had to move politics and government off center. Neither conservatism nor liberalism dominated the nation's politics and government. Although many Americans were unhappy with politics as usual, the political system remained largely unchanged. No party or philosophy seemed able to mold politics and government—a situation dramatized by a virtual dead heat in the presidential election of 2000.

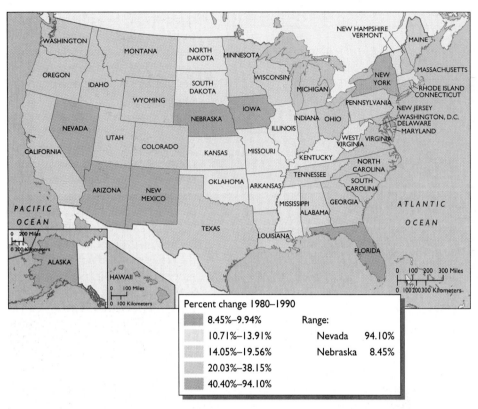

Percent change 1980–1990

8.45%–9.94%	Range:
10.71%–13.91%	Nevada 94.10%
14.05%–19.56%	Nebraska 8.45%
20.03%–38.15%	
40.40%–94.10%	

Map 31-2   Aging in America.
The increase in the percentage of the U.S. population age 65 and over from 1980 to 1990 helped fuel worries about health care and Social Security.
Source: Mattson, p. 38.

George Bush and the End of the Reagan Revolution

Conservatives were disappointed even before Reagan left office. The natural choice for his successor, Vice President George Bush of Texas, was not a conservative but a moderate willing to make political compromises. Moreover, Bush, the son of a Wall Street banker and U. S. senator from Connecticut, had attended elite schools and become part of the upper-class "Establishment" that many conservatives distrusted. Nevertheless, Bush had loyally served Reagan through two terms, and he had a broad background of government service, including stints as a congressman, ambassador to the United Nations, chair of the Republican Party, liaison to China, and director of the CIA.

Bush easily won the Republican presidential nomination and then the general election in 1988. Committing himself to Reagan's economic policy, Bush made a popular pledge never to raise taxes. "Read my lips," he vowed. "No new taxes." At the same time, Bush softened the image of the new conservatism by emphasizing his support for education and the environment. He easily defeated the Democratic nominee, former Governor Michael Dukakis of Massachusetts, who ran a colorless, ineffective campaign calling for efficient government, civil rights, and little more.

On election day, Bush polled 53 percent of the popular vote and carried 40 states for a total of 426 electoral votes.

Despite Bush's triumph, the election revealed the weak electoral impact of the Reagan Revolution. Once again, the Republicans had failed to break the Democrats' hold on the House and Senate. Despite Reagan's accomplishments, voters would not give his party full control in Washington.

The Republicans' limited victory in 1988 reinforced Bush's instinct for political moderation. Downplaying the conservative agenda, Bush promised a "kinder and gentler" presidency. He disappointed conservatives by signing the Clean Air Act of 1990, which attempted to reduce acid rain by cutting emissions from power plants and automobiles. He disappointed conservatives again by signing measures to increase federal funding for education. Above all, he alienated conservatives by abandoning his no-tax pledge and agreeing to a tax increase in 1990 to help decrease the federal budget deficit.

Bush's moderation did not ensure his popularity. The abandonment of his no-tax pledge reinforced the sense that he was a weak leader. Then an economic recession in 1991–1992 intensified Americans' dissatisfaction with the president.

The Rebellion Against Politics as Usual

Americans' unhappiness with George Bush was part of their broader dissatisfaction with politicians and government. By the 1990s there were signs of a brewing popular rebellion against politics as usual. As late as 1964, 76 percent of Americans had believed they could trust the government to do what was right always or most of the time. Then Lyndon Johnson's "credibility gap" and Richard Nixon's lies and cover-ups had shaken Americans' faith in presidents and politicians in the 1960s and 1970s. Politics in the 1980s, including the Iran-Contra scandal, had done little to restore that faith.

By 1994 only 19 percent of the people felt they could trust government. Politicians, Americans believed, were out of touch with ordinary citizens. That belief was reinforced by new ethical scandals that compelled the resignation of the speaker of the House in 1989 and the reprimand

Celebrating the "New World Order": President George Bush shakes hands with servicemen returning from the Gulf War.

of five senators in 1991. Americans were troubled by the feeling that politicians were ineffective as well as unethical. By the early 1990s commentators bemoaned the **gridlock** in Washington. During Bush's term, the president and Congress seemed unable to cooperate on critical issues; Bush vetoed legislation more than 40 times. Unable to agree on a budget with Congress, the president actually shut down "nonessential" government services over Columbus Day weekend in 1990. That episode epitomized many Americans' sense that the government no longer served their needs.

People were still more frustrated because politicians seemed unwilling to reform. By the 1990s there was widespread agreement that money played too large a role in elections. Politicians spent much of their time raising contributions for expensive campaigns. Americans feared that huge donations from special interest groups and wealthy individuals were corrupting politics. Although Congress and the president talked about the need for campaign finance reform, they could not bring themselves to change the system. Attempts to reform election spending failed repeatedly.

Americans tried other ways to reform Washington. There was considerable interest in passing laws that would limit the number of terms that officials could serve in Congress, but term limits, which could deny people the right to vote for the candidate of their choice, were too controversial. Americans settled instead for a more modest reform. For many years the states had not ratified the Twenty-Seventh Amendment to the Constitution, which would keep a congressional pay increase from taking effect until after the next election. Known as the "Madison Amendment" for its originator, President James Madison, the measure ensured that members of a Congress had to face the voters before getting a raise. Amid the popular anger at Congress, the amendment was finally ratified in 1992.

For a moment that year, it seemed as if popular disaffection was about to revolutionize American politics. Running a tired campaign for re-election in 1992, George Bush faced a sudden challenge from the strongest independent candidate in years, Ross Perot of Texas. A pugnacious, plain-spoken billionaire businessman, Perot played to Americans' unhappiness with the political system by promising to end gridlock, balance the budget, and reform campaign finances.

When voters began to wonder whether the quirky Perot could be an effective president, it was the Democratic

H. Ross Perot, the plain-spoken billionaire businessman whose presidential campaign in 1992 drew strength from Americans' desire to reform politics and government. Perot's ambition produced a new organization—United We Stand America, Inc. and the Reform Party— but no election victory.

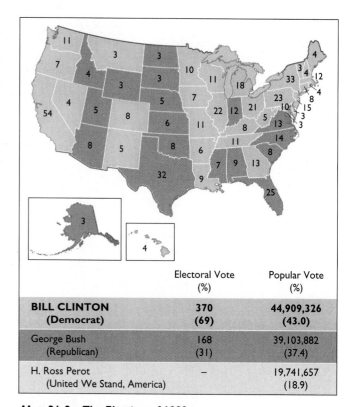

	Electoral Vote (%)	Popular Vote (%)
BILL CLINTON (Democrat)	370 (69)	44,909,326 (43.0)
George Bush (Republican)	168 (31)	39,103,882 (37.4)
H. Ross Perot (United We Stand, America)	–	19,741,657 (18.9)

Map 31-3   The Election of 1992.
Clinton won the presidency by reassembling a traditional Democratic coalition, strong in the industrial North and the West Coast, and competitive in the South.

nominee, Governor Bill Clinton of Arkansas, and not President Bush, who seemed to embody hopes for change. Calling himself a "New Democrat," the charismatic Clinton polled 43 percent of the popular vote to Bush's 37 percent and Perot's surprisingly strong 19 percent (see Map 31-3). Clinton managed to assemble the kind of voting coalition that had put Franklin Roosevelt and Harry Truman in the White House. Holding on to African-American support, the Arkansas governor won back many white southerners and workers, the so-called "Reagan Democrats." For the first time in 12 years, a Democrat occupied the White House. With the Democrats in control of the House and Senate as well, it seemed as if "gridlock" would come to an end.

Bill Clinton and the Disappointment of Reform

In some ways, Clinton's election marked a change in American political life. The first president born after World War II, Clinton was the first of the baby-boom generation to enter the White House. Clinton's rise from modest origins to become a Rhodes Scholar and then the nation's youngest governor reassured an unsettled America that upward mobility was still possible. His marriage to fellow lawyer Hillary Rodham was another hint of change. The new first lady was the first presidential wife with her own professional career outside the home.

Clinton did act like a "New Democrat" by balancing traditional liberal activism with more conservative efforts to shrink government. In 1993 he won congressional approval for a national service plan that provided college-tuition funds to young people who performed community service. He signed the Family and Medical Leave Act of 1993, which allowed government workers, as well as employees in most companies with 50 or more workers, to take up to 12 weeks of unpaid leave to deal with birth, adoption, or family illness.

Clinton was convinced that the federal government could not play an effective social role or maintain prosperity without balancing the budget. As part of a plan to "reinvent government," the president moved to cut the size of the federal work force. Through budget cuts and tax increases, Clinton and Congress managed to reduce the size of the federal deficit. By 1998 the government actually posted a budget surplus.

Nevertheless, the promise of the Clinton presidency was limited by the resurgent power of the Republican Party. Clinton's most sweeping liberal proposal, his plan for dramatically increasing the federal role in medical care,

President Bill Clinton addresses a 1993 town meeting in Michigan.

went down to defeat. In 1994 voters, disappointed by Clinton and the congressional Democrats, awarded control of the House of Representatives to Republicans for the first time in 40 years. Emboldened, the new Republican majority chose an outspoken conservative, Newt Gingrich of Georgia, as the Speaker of the House. The Republicans vowed to enact a conservative "Contract With America" that featured a balanced budget amendment to the Constitution, term limits, increased defense spending, welfare reform, and tax cuts. The Republicans never won enough popular support to enact key provisions of their "Contract," including the balanced budget amendment and term limits. Still, the Republican Party controlled both houses of Congress for the remainder of the decade.

The Republicans' strength forced Clinton to slight key liberal principles and make sometimes controversial compromises with conservatism. "The era of big government is over," he declared. The president accepted a bill limiting the federal government's authority to impose costly regulations and requirements, known as unfunded mandates, on the states.

Most important, Clinton signed a welfare bill in 1996 that significantly reduced federal support for the poor, especially children. Reflecting the conservative vision of political economy, the measure tried to minimize the role of the federal government in people's lives. The welfare bill replaced Aid to Families with Dependent Children (AFDC), which had long guaranteed federal payments to the poor, with grants to the states for use as they saw fit. To discourage dependence on government handouts, the bill limited welfare recipients to five years of assistance over their lifetime and required heads of households on welfare to find work within two years. To discourage extramarital pregnancies that supposedly threatened "family values," the bill imposed restrictions on unwed teenage mothers who were receiving benefits and offered bonuses for states with declining rates of illegitimate childbirth. Many Democrats and liberals angrily claimed that the president had betrayed the poor. Clinton's concessions to congressional Republicans made him seem less like a new kind of politician and more like the old breed ready to compromise principle in order to hold on to office.

Running for re-election in 1996, Clinton benefited from the strength of the economy and the weakness of his opponents. Ross Perot had created a new organization, the Reform Party, but his presidential candidacy could not rekindle the enthusiasm of 1992. The Republicans turned to moderate Bob Dole of Kansas, the Senate Majority

Members of the House Judiciary Committee review President Bill Clinton's taped testimony in the Paula Jones sexual harrassment lawsuit in December 1998. A majority of the committee soon approved articles of impeachment against Clinton.

alleged hotel-room encounter while he was governor of Arkansas.

Although these allegations had not prevented Clinton's re-election in 1996, scandal engulfed his second term. There were charges of illegal fundraising for the president's campaign. Expanding the Whitewater investigation, Kenneth Starr and a grand jury explored whether Clinton had obstructed justice in the Jones lawsuit by covering up an alleged sexual relationship with a young White House page, Monica Lewinsky. The president strongly denied such a relationship, but then the weight of the evidence, including a semen stain on one of Lewinksy's dresses, made it clear that the president had in fact had a sexual liaison with her. After months of denial, Clinton finally admitted to a grand jury in August 1998 that he had had "inappropriate intimate contact" with Lewinsky.

For a time, Clinton's presidency hung in the balance. In November 1998 the president settled Jones' suit by agreeing to pay her $500,000. In December the Republican-dominated House of Representatives voted two articles of impeachment charging Clinton with perjury and obstruction of justice. The following month, he became only the second president to go on trial in the Senate. Because the Constitution required a two-thirds majority to convict a president, the Republicans needed to persuade some Democrats to vote against the president, but Republican and Democratic senators alike were well aware that Clinton remained surprisingly popular. Most Americans, whatever they thought of Clinton's relationship with Lewinsky, seemed willing to separate the private and public lives of the president. Approving of Clinton's handling of his public duties as president, the majority of Americans did not want to see him removed from office. In February 1999, the Senate voted to acquit Clinton on both articles of impeachment.

Like Andrew Johnson in 1868, Clinton had held on to the presidency, but he had lost the opportunity to make a major impact on public policy in his second term. Clinton's legacy would rest on his shrewd management of the economy and on his attempts to chart a course between liberalism and conservatism. Although he had substantial accomplishments, Clinton's compromises and personal scandals ensured that his presidency would end with a sense of unfulfilled promise.

The Republicans, deeply frustrated by the failure of impeachment, almost failed to benefit from Clinton's public humiliation. Emphasizing the impeachment issue in the fall elections in 1998, the Republicans barely managed to

Leader, who seemed to epitomize the compromising career politician so many Americans distrusted. Never seriously threatened by Dole or Perot, Clinton won a clear victory with 49 percent of the popular vote. Dole attracted 41 percent of the popular vote and Perot only 8 percent.

Despite his re-election, Clinton no longer seemed like an agent of political change, as he had only four years earlier. Damaged by his compromises with conservatism, his reformist image was destroyed by a series of scandals. Soon after taking office, the president, along with the first lady, faced allegations that they had engaged in corrupt deals involving a real-estate project, the Whitewater Development Corporation, back in Arkansas in the 1970s and 1980s. Amid charges that the Clintons were trying to cover up **Whitewater,** Congress and a court-appointed independent counsel, Kenneth Starr, began to investigate the whole affair in 1994. Meanwhile, there were charges that the Clinton administration had improperly fired White House staff and obtained confidential FBI files on more than 600 people, including Republican officials. In 1994, moreover, Paula Corbin Jones filed a lawsuit charging Bill Clinton with unwanted sexual advances during an

hold on to their majority in the House of Representatives. In the aftermath of the elections, Speaker of the House Newt Gingrich, plagued by questions about his own ethics, decided to resign from Congress. Then his designated successor suddenly admitted extramarital affairs and left Congress as well.

Against this backdrop of frustration, the Republicans nominated George W. Bush, the governor of Texas, for president in 2000. The son of former president George Bush, the Republican nominee shared his father's moderation. Although critics questioned his experience and his ability, the younger Bush benefited from the unity and enthusiasm of Republicans eager to reclaim the White House. He benefited, too, from the decision of the Democratic nominee, Vice President Al Gore of Tennessee, to distance himself from the record of the Clinton administration.

The dull campaign suddenly became riveting on election night when the contest between these two cautious men turned out to be too close to call. As the vote counts stretched into days and then weeks without a clear result, there were fears of a constitutional crisis. The battle turned on the vote in Florida, where Bush held a fluctuating lead of a few hundred votes. Determined to overcome that lead, the Gore campaign called for recounts of the vote in key counties, where the votes of his supporters had supposedly been rejected or undercounted. Inevitably, the contest spilled into local courts, the Florida Supreme Court, and finally the United States Supreme Court. Risking their credibility, the justices of the nation's highest court settled the partisan battle with a close 5-to-4 ruling that effectively halted the recounts Gore needed. Certified the victor in Florida, George W. Bush became the president-elect.

It was nearly the closest presidential election in American history. Gore actually won the popular ballot with 550,000 more votes than Bush received, but Bush won the electoral college, and therefore the election, with 271 votes to Gore's 266. The narrow margin of victory and the narrow differences between the two candidates emphasized the persistence of political deadlock and uncertainty. Bush took the oath of office in January 2001 without a clear popular mandate. No party and no philosophy dominated American public life as the new century began.

After the Cold War

America's role in the world, so plainly fixed for nearly half a century, suddenly became uncertain at the close of the 1980s. The cold war ended surprisingly quickly with the collapse of Communist regimes in Eastern Europe and the Soviet Union. No longer preoccupied with the Soviet threat, Americans had to reconsider their needs and obligations as the only superpower in a changed world. For a moment in 1991, the American-led victory in the Persian Gulf War suggested that the United States might serve as an active international policeman in a "New World Order," but the moment passed. Americans were ambivalent about involvement in crises abroad. They were reluctant to maintain expensive military, intelligence, and foreign-aid programs. They were unsure, too, about the relative importance of supporting human rights and American economic interests abroad. At the start of the twenty-first century, no new principle had emerged to guide American foreign policy in the post-cold-war world.

With no clear winner in the presidential election of 2000, attention focused on the closely-contested state of Florida. Here, a judge and an observer try to decide how a voter's ballot should be counted in Broward County.

Victory in the Cold War

As President Ronald Reagan left office in 1989, the cold war continued to wind down. Fear and hatred no longer dominated relations between the United States and the Soviet Union. After more than 40 years of cold-war confrontations and crises, most Americans came to realize there was no worldwide Communist conspiracy threatening their country. Neither the United States nor the Soviet Union was likely to attack the other without provocation. Both sides recognized that the cold war was enormously expensive and potentially tragic.

Reflecting this understanding, Reagan's successor as president, George Bush, built cautiously on the initiatives of the second Reagan administration. In 1990 Bush and Soviet leader Mikhail Gorbachev signed an agreement to end production of chemical

The cold war ends: A man attacks the Berlin Wall, dividing East and West Germany, as onlookers cheer in 1989.

weapons and reduce existing stockpiles. The next year, Bush and Gorbachev signed the START (STrategic Arms Reduction Talks) Treaty, which called for the United States and the U. S. S. R. to cut back their arsenals of nuclear weapons by as much as 30 percent. Nuclear war seemed increasingly unlikely.

As in the Reagan years, Gorbachev was willing to cooperate with the United States in part because his regime had grown so weak. In 1989 the Soviet Union could do nothing to stop the collapse of its repressive Communist allies in Eastern Europe. That year, the unpopular Communist regime in Hungary, unable to reform a weak economy, had to agree to free elections. Accepting the transition to democracy, the Soviets announced the withdrawal of their troops. In Poland, the Communist regime also had to agree to free elections and economic reforms. Those elections led to the selection of a non-Communist premier before the year was over. Hard-line Communist regimes collapsed in Bulgaria, Czechoslovakia, and Rumania as well. Most dramatically, a new East German government agreed in November to allow travel through the Berlin Wall. Intended to keep East Berliners from escaping into non-Communist West Berlin, the Wall had long symbolized the cold-war division of Europe. As jubilant Berliners dismantled the wall, it symbolized the collapse of Communism in 1989.

Powerless to stop its allies from abandoning Communism, the Soviet leadership soon found that it could not save itself. Despite Gorbachev's attempts to improve life in the Soviet Union, many people, like Felix Andreev, were still unhappy with the low standard of living, an unpopular war in Afghanistan, and the repressiveness of Communism. Estonia, Latvia, Lithuania, and other republics chafed under Russia's domination of the U. S. S. R. In 1990 Russia itself chose a charismatic president, Boris Yeltsin, who quit the Communist Party, supported independence for the republics, and challenged Gorbachev. The next year, Gorbachev survived a failed coup by hard-line Communists but soon had to resign as party leader and president of the Soviet Union. The Soviet parliament suspended the Communist Party. As one republic after another declared its independence, the U. S. S. R. ceased to exist.

With the collapse of the Soviet Union, the cold war was over. Before 1991 had ended, President Bush took all American nuclear bombers off alert status. The United States and its allies had clearly won the cold war. As at the end of World War II, Americans witnessed the triumph of their principles and power. Around the world, capitalism and democracy seemed to be pushing back Communism. The United States now stood as the sole military superpower in the world. Nevertheless, Americans did not celebrate very much. The cold war had cost a great deal in money and lives. Many Americans wondered whether Communism had posed a mortal danger to the United States in the first place.

America's Role in a Changed World

With the cold war over, Americans had to reconsider their role in a changed world. Some Republicans called for a new, less internationalist foreign policy. Echoing conservatives of the 1940s and 1950s, they insisted that the United States should no longer provide so much aid and military protection to other countries, especially in Europe. They felt that American soldiers should risk their lives to protect the United States, not other countries.

In contrast, a broad range of internationalists in both the Democratic and Republican Parties believed the United States could protect itself and advance its political and economic interests only by participating actively in world affairs. Even though the cold war was over, America still faced a variety of challenges abroad. "We have slain a large dragon," CIA director James Woolsey testified in 1993, "but we live now in a jungle filled with a bewildering variety of poisonous snakes." The best way to kill those snakes, it appeared, was through the kind of international cooperation with NATO and the United Nations that some conservatives opposed.

The most powerful internationalist was President Bush. A naval aviator in World War II, Bush believed that American isolationism had encouraged fascist aggression in the 1930s and 1940s. American commitment to international freedom, the president understood, had won the war, preserved the peace, and sustained the nation's economy for so many years. Now, Bush argued, the United States had to maintain its overseas commitments. With the help of other powerful countries, he felt, America should use foreign aid, military strength, NATO, and the United Nations to maintain a stable international system, a "New World Order." Bush wanted "a world in which democracy is the norm, in which private enterprise, free trade, and prosperity enrich every nation—a world in which the rule of law prevails." Much like Woodrow Wilson and Harry Truman before him, Bush mixed together idealism and self-interest in his vision of the international political economy: A free world would be good both for other nations and for the United States. However, the president concluded, only American leadership could preserve that world.

The New World Order was a broad, vague concept. Bush and other internationalists had a hard time explaining just what overseas commitments America needed to make. Did the United States need to intervene everywhere that stability was threatened? It was also unclear whether the American people, still mindful of the costs of the Vietnam War, would endorse armed intervention abroad. Critics noted a tension between Bush's call for order and his support for democracy. Was the United States supposed to

web connection

A New World

www.prenhall.com/boydston/globalization

Globalization promises to change life in the United States—and the course of its history—as thoroughly and permanently as did the industrialization of the nineteenth century. The conclusion of the twentieth century was marked by fairly rapid expansion of global interaction in business, leisure travel, philanthropy, politics, social movements, and environmental interaction. The United States has become part—a large part, but just a part—of a "First World" society that now spans the planet. If the United States is now a service economy, where is production of goods taking place? Is this new way of looking at things an improvement? Does it matter if we think it is or not? What defines a nation besides a map, a passport, and the title of a history textbook?

protect antidemocratic countries in the name of international stability and national prosperity?

There was also a tension between Bush's commitment to international cooperation and the long-standing tendency for the United States to act alone in its own hemisphere. While the president spoke of the New World Order, he intervened unilaterally in the Central American nation of Panama in 1989. By then Bush had grown frustrated with General Manuel Noriega, the Panamanian leader who engaged in drug sales to the United States and other illegal activities. After Noriega thwarted democratic elections, Bush did not try to handle the situation through joint action with the Organization of American States or the United Nations. Instead, in 1989 he dispatched American troops, who captured Noriega and sent him to the United States for prosecution on drug charges. Bush's unilateral action, condemned by other Latin American countries, contradicted his rhetoric about international collaboration in the post-cold-war world.

Finally, the New World Order, like containment before it, would be expensive. Many Americans had looked forward to a "peace dividend" at the end of the cold war. They expected that money could now be saved on foreign aid and military expenditures and spent on domestic needs, but the New World Order abroad clearly jeopardized any "peace dividend" at home.

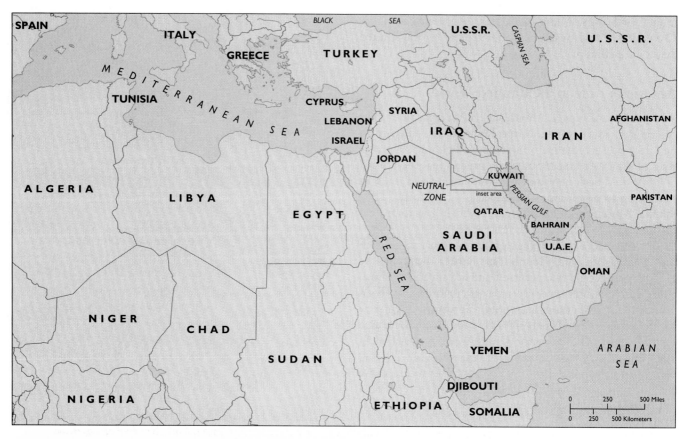

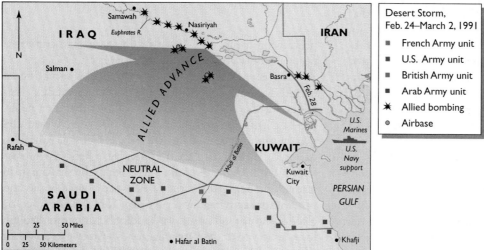

Map 31-4   The Persian Gulf War.
Operation Desert Storm, the allied attack on the forces of Iraq, tested President George Bush's vision of a "New World Order" in the oil-rich heart of the Middle East.

Source: Mark Carnes, Mapping America's Past (Henry Holt, 1996), p. 267; Hammond Atlas of the Twentieth Century (Time Books, 1996), p. 166.

The Persian Gulf War

The test of the New World Order came soon enough. On August 2, 1990, Iraq, led by President Saddam Hussein, overran Kuwait, its wealthy but defenseless neighbor to the south. Entrenched in Kuwait, Iraq now threatened its much larger western neighbor, oil-producing Saudi Arabia. Hussein's actions clearly jeopardized America's oil supply and its Saudi Arabian ally. The Kuwaiti invasion

also obviously challenged George Bush's calls for a stable New World Order of free nations.

The president reacted firmly. Comparing Hussein to Adolf Hitler, Bush created an international coalition opposing Iraq. By the end of 1990 more than half a million U. S. troops had joined with forces from more than 30 nations in Operation Desert Shield to protect Saudi Arabia (see Map 31-4). Meanwhile, the United Nations imposed

Troops of the U.S Marine First Division, wearing protection against Iraqi chemical weapons, advance to retake Kuwait from the forces of Saddam Hussein in the last phase of the Persian Gulf War in January 1991.

economic sanctions on Iraq. Convinced those sanctions were not enough to drive Hussein's soldiers out of Kuwait, the Bush administration successfully pressed the United Nations to authorize force if the Iraqis did not withdraw by January 15, 1991. The president also obtained congressional approval for the use of force.

When Hussein refused to pull back by the deadline, Operation Desert Shield became Operation Desert Storm. As television audiences watched around the world on the night of January 17, coalition forces began an intensive air attack against Iraq with planes and missiles. Unable to contest the air power of the coalition, Hussein struck back by launching Scud missile attacks against America's ally, Israel, hundreds of miles away. The missiles did little damage and failed to provoke Israeli retaliation that might have split the coalition. Instead, coalition forces, led by U. S. General Norman Schwarzkopf, began a ground attack against the Iraqi Army. There were fears that the coalition would suffer heavy casualties from Iraqi troops armed with chemical weapons, but in just 100 hours, Schwarzkopf's solders swept into Kuwait, devastated the Iraqis, and pushed on into Iraq. Impressed by the results, Bush called a halt before the invasion reached the Iraqi capital of Baghdad and toppled Hussein.

At first, the Persian Gulf War seemed like a great victory for the United States and the New World Order.

Coalition forces suffered only about 220 battle deaths. The United States lost only 148 troops while killing thousands of Iraqis. American technology appeared to work perfectly. U. S. Stealth bombers evaded Iraqi radar, and U. S. Patriot missiles knocked Iraqi Scuds out of the sky. Bush's popularity soared. The New World Order, at least for a moment, seemed like a practical reality. American leadership and American power had halted aggression and restored freedom abroad.

Americans' euphoria over the Gulf War did not last long, however. Studies showed that U. S. weapons had not worked quite so well, after all. Gulf War veterans began to suffer health problems possibly caused by exposure to Iraqi chemical weapons. Despite the slaughter of his forces, Saddam Hussein held on to power and hindered implementation of the agreement ending the war. His aircraft soon encroached on so-called "no-fly" zones over northern and southern Iraq, where they had been forbidden to fly and threaten Kurdish and Muslim minorities. As early as January 1993 U. S. forces launched missile attacks against Iraqi installations and shot down an Iraqi jet to counter these encroachments. Hussein also obstructed United Nations inspectors charged with searching for Iraqi chemical and nuclear weapons. In February 2001, the newly inaugurated George W. Bush ordered missile attacks against Iraqi forces in retaliation for violations of the no-fly zones. Despite his father's massive war effort, the goals of the New World Order had not been completely achieved. Hussein remained a threat to his neighbors and to American interests in the new century.

Retreating From the New World Order

In the years after the Persian Gulf War, the United States retreated from George Bush's vision of a New World Order. The American people were reluctant to accept the dangers of involvement abroad, especially where there was no obvious military or economic interest for the United States. That reluctance was apparent when violence followed the collapse of Communist rule in Yugoslavia in 1990. As this Eastern European country broke apart in the early 1990s, three major ethnic groups—Muslim Slavs, Serbs, and Croatians—fought a bitter civil war in the newly independent province of Bosnia-Herzegovina. The remnants of the old Yugoslavia, under the harsh leadership of Slobodan Milosevic, aided the Serbs as they carried out "ethnic cleansing," the forcible expulsion of Muslims and Croats from their homes. Faced with the worst mass brutality in Europe since World War II, first George Bush and then Bill Clinton were unwilling to risk military involvement in eastern Europe. Eventually, in 1994, American planes and missiles, operating in conjunction with NATO, began to attack Bosnian Serb forces from the air. The following year, the warring parties accepted a peace agreement brokered by the United States. The Clinton administration committed 20,000 troops to join a peacekeeping force, even though most Americans opposed the move.

Yugoslavia posed a challenge again when the Milosevic regime mistreated and attacked ethnic Albanians in the region of Kosovo. Humiliated by its inability to negotiate an end to the suffering in Kosovo, the Clinton administration finally supported a NATO air offensive against the Yugoslavian government in March 1999. The seventy-eight-day war that ended in June killed between two and five thousand people, badly damaged Yugoslavia's infrastructure, and forced Milosevic to accept a multinational peacekeeping force. There were no NATO casualties, in part because Clinton and other NATO leaders were unwilling to risk them.

There were other costs for the United States, however. Clinton's unwillingness to commit ground troops to battle made it clear that America was hesitant to pay a human price to intervene around the world. Ultimately, the United States had helped restore some peace to the regions of the former Yugoslavia. Yet, critics charged, millions had suffered and thousands had died before a cautious America had been willing to employ even a minimum of force.

The New World Order depended on maintaining the American power built up during the cold war, but a reluctance to spend money and make international commitments diminished that power in the 1990s. As their budget declined, military leaders cut troops, closed bases, and re-duced orders for new weapons. In 1993 the government officially abandoned the Strategic Defense Initiative or "Star Wars," Reagan's expensive project to create a space-based missile defense system. Meanwhile, the Central Intelligence Agency, the National Security Agency, and other intelligence operations struggled with tight budgets, low morale, and public criticism. With the Soviet confrontation over, many Americans no longer saw the need for so much spying. The federal government's foreign aid budget stagnated in the 1990s. Washington also failed to keep up its promised payments to support the work of the United Nations.

An Uncertain Foreign Policy

As the New World Order faded away, no single overarching principle emerged to direct the nation's diplomacy. After the cold war, anti-Communist passion no longer animated American foreign policy. For years, the United States had withheld diplomatic recognition of its former enemy, the Communist regime in the Socialist Republic of Vietnam, mainly because of the possibility that MIAs—American soldiers Missing in Action during the war—might still be held captive. However, by the 1990s, there was no evidence that MIAs remained alive in Southeast Asia. Eager for trade with Vietnam, President Clinton announced full diplomatic recognition of this Communist nation in 1995.

Economic interests helped shape policy toward another Asian Communist regime, the People's Republic of China. Although the Chinese leadership clearly violated the human rights of its people, first George Bush and then Bill Clinton proved unwilling to disrupt developing economic ties with the world's most populous country. Despite evidence of China's growing nuclear arsenal and its apparent spying on U. S. weapons programs, the Clinton administration pressed Congress to ease trade relations with the Asian nation.

As Clinton's policy toward China suggested, the American commitment to human rights was fairly weak. In the 1990s the U. S. government professed support for human rights around the world, but Clinton never made that support the centerpiece of American diplomacy, as President Jimmy Carter had in the 1970s. During Clinton's first term, he offended human rights advocates by sending boatloads of refugees back to an uncertain future in Haiti. Despite his professed commitment to human rights, the president would not anger voters in Florida and other states who objected to the cost of caring for the new immigrants.

Although Americans did not enthusiastically embrace the New World Order, anti-Communism, or human rights, they did not retreat into isolationism either. The United States was still prepared to act abroad where its interests seemed to be at stake. The Clinton administration pushed for peace between Israel and the Palestinian Liberation Organization in the Middle East despite terrorist bombings that killed American soldiers and civilians in Saudi Arabia in 1995 and 1996. In August 1998 bombs killed at least 190 people and wounded 5,000 at U.S. embassies in the African nations of Kenya and Tanzania. Blaming the embassy attacks on Islamic fundamentalist terrorists funded by Saudi businessman Osama bin Laden, the United States launched missile attacks on targets in Afghanistan and the Sudan linked to bin Laden.

Distressed by attacks overseas, Americans were shocked when Middle Eastern terrorism reached the United States itself. In February 1993 a car bomb exploded in the underground garage of one of the twin towers of New York City's giant office building complex, the World Trade Center. Six people were killed and more than a thousand injured in the first major international terrorist incident inside the United States. Investigators traced the attack to followers of a radical Islamic spiritual leader from Egypt, Sheikh Omar Abdel-Rahman, who lived in New Jersey. Rahman and over a dozen associates were convicted for the World Trade Center bombing and other plots. In 1996 another Muslim radical, charged with masterminding the Trade Center attack, was convicted with two other Muslims for plotting to blow up U.S. airliners over the Pacific Ocean.

As anger over the Trade Center attack faded in the United States, terrorist organizations apparently struck back to avenge the convictions of Rahman and other terrorists. On the morning of September 11, 2001, small groups of men hijacked four U.S. passenger jets soon after takeoff and aimed them at targets symbolizing American financial and military power in New York City and Washington, D.C. As onlookers watched in horror, two of the jets crashed into the upper floors of the Trade Center's twin towers. Within two hours, both towers collapsed in clouds of smoke and debris, killing and wounding thou-

As World Trade Tower I burns in the background after being hit by a hijacked jet airliner, a second hijacked plane roars toward a fiery collision with the second tower. Within hours, both towers would collapse, killing thousands.

sands of people. Meanwhile, the third jet crashed into the headquarters of the Defense Department at the Pentagon, killing and wounding hundreds, wrecking a section of the giant building and sending smoke into the sky above the nation's capitol city. The fourth jet, apparently intended for a target in or near Washington, crashed in western Pennsylvania. To stunned Americans, the attacks were a shocking revelation of their nation's vulnerability and even "another Pearl Harbor." The tragedy in New York, Washington, and Pennsylvania was also a reminder of the limits of the nation's power. When early evidence suggested that Osama bin Laden might well have organized the attacks, it was by no means clear that the United States could strike back effectively at his hiding place in Afghanistan.

The uncertainty after the destruction of the World Trade Center underscored the broader uncertainty over American foreign policy after the cold war. With the disappearance of the Communist threat, no single principle or interest guided U.S. diplomacy. At the start of the twenty-first century, the nation and the world waited to see whether the threat of terrorism would force Americans to overcome their reluctance to become more actively and forcefully involved around the globe.

Struggles Over Diversity and Rights

In the 1990s Americans continued to struggle with the diversity of their society. As in the past, people were profoundly aware of their differences. The wave of immigration made the nation even more heterogeneous than during the 1970s and 1980s. Not surprisingly, Americans debated the benefits of immigration and the treatment of immigrants. More broadly, people contested the value of diversity itself. Liberals and conservatives argued about whether too much diversity was destroying the family and the national culture.

The issue of diversity was so contentious, in part because individuals and groups had been asserting their rights vigorously since the 1940s. In the 1990s Americans still quarreled over the rights of African Americans, women, and homosexuals. The quest for rights also took new and sometimes disturbing forms during the decade. Some Americans demanded the right to die. Others demanded the right to live without government interference.

The Impact of Immigration

Felix Andreev was part of a wave of immigration that took shape in the 1980s and crested in the 1990s. Between 1990 and 1994 alone, 4.5 million immigrants came to the United States. By 1999 the immigrant population had reached 26.3 million, nearly 10 percent of the national total population, the largest percentage of immigrants since before World

Singer Gloria Estefan, whose "Miami sound" fused Latin rhythms and American pop music and made her a star.

War II. In the 1990s and beyond, immigration would play a greater role in American life than it had for many years.

The new immigrants were significant because of their origins as well as their numbers. Whereas in the 1950s two-thirds of immigrants still came from Europe, by the 1980s only 15 percent of immigrants were European. In the 1990s more than a quarter of the immigrant population came from Mexico alone. Large numbers of foreign-born Americans also migrated from the Philippines, China, Cuba, Jamaica, El Salvador, Poland, and the former East Germany.

The shift in immigrant origins should not have been surprising. With the rebuilding of their home economies after World War II, West Europeans were less likely to want to leave for America. The people of eastern Europe and the Third World, living with economic and political upheaval, had more reason to come to the United States. Still, Americans had not set out to encourage a mass migration, particularly by non-whites from less developed countries.

Drawn by a strong job market throughout the United States, the new immigrants settled in all sorts of communi-

ties, small and large, unlikely and likely. Mexican immigrants, for instance, came to stay in a host of small Midwestern towns and cities where semiskilled and unskilled jobs paid 10 and 15 times more than jobs in Mexico. At the edge of Kendallville, Indiana, a billboard beckoned to new Mexican arrivals, "Estamos Occupando"—We are hiring. In Columbus Junction, Iowa, Pedro Rodriguez and his friends arrived to take the hard, "stinky" jobs that native-born Americans did not want to do at the big IBP meat-packing plant. "We didn't see a lot of Spanish people," Rodriguez recalled, "and that's terrible. We had to go by sign language."

The new immigrants had their most publicized impact in a relative handful of states and major cities. The majority of immigrants settled in only six states—California, Florida, New York, Texas, Illinois, and New Jersey. These new Americans were likely to live in large cities such as Los Angeles, Miami, New York, Houston, and Chicago. As a result, the impact of the new immigration was highly concentrated and highly visible.

The effects of large, concentrated, nonwestern European immigration were especially evident in Miami, Florida, where newcomers mixed with earlier arrivals from Latin America. Since the 1960s, migration, particularly from nearby Cuba, had remade this formerly white-majority city. By the 1990s one-third of Miami's two million residents had Cuban origins. With substantial numbers of Colombians, Mexicans, Dominicans, and Peruvians as well, Miami had become the first major city with a Hispanic majority. That fact redefined city life. Miami was bilingual: Spanish was about as common as English. The city's economy depended heavily on trade and banking relations with Caribbean, Central American, and South American nations. The city's culture reflected the Hispanic majority. Miami was the home of singer Gloria Estefan, a Cuban immigrant who fused Latin rhythms with American pop music to create the popular "Miami sound." The new immigration put considerable strain on Miami. Its schools and hospitals were overcrowded, and many long-time residents resented the new arrivals. "We've become a Third World country," declared a white Miamian.

That was what some Americans believed would happen to the United States as a whole. In the new century Miami seemed to represent the future. The U. S. Census Bureau predicted that whites would make up a bare majority of the nation's population in 2050. By 2000, non-whites made up one-quarter of the population. Americans of Hispanic origin, both white and non-white, numbered some 35 million—almost 13 percent of the nation's population.

This was a disturbing prospect for some native-born Americans. Like other Americans before them, they worried that immigration would hurt the country. The critics of immigration were especially enraged by the millions of aliens who entered the country illegally, most of them by slipping across the Mexican border. By 1996 there were perhaps four million illegal aliens, most of whom apparently had fraudulent Social Security cards. In the short run, the critics of immigration charged, legal and illegal aliens would compete with the native-born population for jobs and drive down wages with their willingness to work cheaply. Particularly in California and Texas, native-born Americans complained that they had to keep paying higher taxes in order to provide health care, education, and welfare for poor immigrants. In the long run, some native-born Americans feared, Spanish would rival the English language, immigrant cultures would dilute the dominant culture, and whites would lose political power.

Other native-born Americans were not so fearful. Immigration, they believed, had made the United States great in the first place. Instead of undermining the economy, they felt, immigrants would improve it with their work ethic; as in the past, immigrants would invigorate rather than overwhelm the dominant culture. The United States would not become a Third-World country, the defenders of immigration concluded. Because of immigrants, the United States would remain a diverse, dynamic nation in the twenty-first century.

Inevitably, the disagreement over immigration spilled into politics. As in the past, some Americans wanted to restrict the rights of immigrants already in the United States and limit future immigration. This effort had already begun with the passage of the Immigration Reform and Control Act in 1986. Known as the Simpson-Mazzoli Act, the measure imposed harsher penalties on Americans who knowingly brought illegal aliens into the country and hired them. The measure also reflected pro-immigrant sentiment by offering amnesty to illegal aliens who had arrived since 1981.

The critics of immigration did not have much success when they tried to go beyond the Simpson-Mazzoli Act. In 1990 a revision of the federal immigration law actually raised the annual quota of immigrants who would be admitted. Illegal aliens were another matter. In 1994 California passed Proposition 187, a state referendum denying illegal aliens access to public education and other benefits.

In 1996 Congress appropriated more resources to stop the flow of illegal immigrants from Mexico.

Debating Diversity

Disagreements about diversity were at the heart of the immigration controversy. They also drove debates over two other charged issues: the status of the family and American culture. By the 1990s the ongoing transformation of the American family had become unmistakable. The supposedly "traditional" nuclear family of father, mother, and children no longer predominated in American households. Married couples with children, 40 percent of all households as late as 1970, made up only 25 percent by 1996 (see Table 31-1). There were proportionally fewer families because more Americans were living alone. The percentage of single-person households rose from 17 percent in 1970 to 25 percent in 1996. Families themselves were less likely to fit the traditional model, romanticized in the situation comedies of 1950s television. By 1996 27 percent of families with children contained one parent, usually a mother, rather than two.

A number of factors led to these changes in family structure. Americans were marrying later, having fewer children, and having them later in life. The divorce rate had doubled from 1960 to 1990. In the 1990s about half of all marriages were ending in divorce. As women's wages gradually rose, more women could afford to live alone or to head families by themselves.

Many conservatives and Republicans blamed these developments on the nation's moral decline. Allegedly, the counterculture of the 1960s, liberals, the media, feminists, gays, and others had undermined the nation's "family values." In 1992, for instance, Bush's vice president, Dan Quayle, attacked the TV sit-com *Murphy Brown* for supposedly denigrating fatherhood through its positive portrayal of the title character's decision to have a child out of wedlock. Some defenders of the family suggested that single mothers should receive fewer welfare benefits and that divorce should be made more difficult.

TABLE 31-1

The Changing American Family, 1960–1996*					
Year	Households	Families	Married-Couple Families	Single-Parent Families	One-Person Households
1960	52,799	44,905	23,358	3,332	6,917
1970	63,401	51,456	25,541	3,271	10,851
1980	80,776	58,426	24,961	6,061	18,296
1990	93,347	66,090	24,537	7,752	22,999
1996	99,627	69,594	24,920	9,284	24,900

Source: U.S. Census Bureau, Web Site, http://www.census.gov/population/socdemo/hhfam/rep86/96hh4.txt, http://www.bls.census.gov/population/socdemoc/hhfam/rep96/96hh1.txt and /96fml.txt
*Numbers given in thousands.

Liberals fought back by denying that conservatives spoke for real "family values." The conservatives, they claimed, did not understand that the family was not dying but simply adapting to change as it always had. The different forms of the family, like diversity in general, were supposedly a good thing.

While liberals and conservatives quarreled over the family, they also fought over the state of culture in America. Since the 1960s, the authority of the western literary, artistic, and philosophical heritage had been under attack from several directions. Literary critics and other advocates of "deconstruction" had argued that cultural products possessed no inherent, objective value, that western culture was revered not because of any intrinsic merit but because it reflected the interests of powerful Europeans and Americans. Other people, these critics felt, should be free to place a lesser value on western culture.

Beginning in the 1960s, several groups did just that. As they demanded rights, feminists, African Americans, gays, and other groups maintained that white heterosexual European men had not produced all important ideas and art. Society in general and schools in particular needed to recognize the cultural contributions of the disadvantaged and the oppressed. Instead of worshiping one culture, America needed to practice multiculturalism. At Stanford University in 1987, the Reverend Jesse Jackson joined students to protest a western culture course that excluded the accomplishments of women and minorities. "Hey hey, ho ho," the crowd chanted, "Western culture's got to go!"

That cry horrified such conservatives as William Bennett, who headed the National Endowment for the Humanities (NEH) in the 1980s. Western cultural values were, activists like Bennett insisted, vitally important for the well-being of American society. The conservatives charged that the multiculturalists were destroying the western heritage. Further, the multiculturalists were destroying free speech by making it impossible for anyone to question their positions. This coercive "political correctness" or "PC" was actually promoting conformity instead of diversity. On some college campuses, the conservatives noted, PC speech codes punished students for using language that might offend others. The conservatives also attacked the NEH and the National Endowment for the Arts (NEA). These federal agencies, they claimed, were displaying a liberal bias by funding politically correct academic and artistic projects that flouted western values.

Liberals, academics, artists, and others responded by defending the NEH, the NEA, campus speech codes, and multiculturalism. It was the conservatives, they asserted, who were trying to censor curricula and wipe out diversity.

In the end, the controversies over culture and the family did little to undermine the new diversity of American life. Although Congress cut the budgets of the NEH and the NEA, these agencies survived the conservative attack. States did virtually nothing to make divorce more difficult.

More broadly, the trends toward diverse households and multiculturalism had not halted at the turn of the century, but the controversies revealed just how deeply Americans were divided over diversity.

The Status of African Americans

While Americans debated diversity, individual groups continued to confront their unequal status in the 1990s. From the 1980s into the 1990s, African Americans made economic and political gains. The black middle class continued to grow. While African-American unemployment remained almost double the national average, it had reached its lowest level in a generation by 1995. African Americans also made progress in electoral politics: In 1992 more than 10,000 African Americans held public office nationwide. In 1989 David Dinkins became the first African-American mayor of New York, the nation's largest city.

These achievements hardly marked the end to racial injustice and conflict. During the 1990s three episodes, each involving the nation's legal system, dramatized the continuing unequal status of African Americans. In 1991 George Bush nominated an African-American judge, Clarence Thomas, to succeed Thurgood Marshall, the first African-American justice on the Supreme Court. Thomas' selection proved controversial because of his conservative views, his lack of distinguished credentials, and allegations of sexual harassment made against him by a former subordinate, Anita Hill. In televised congressional hearings, Hill, an African-American lawyer, claimed that Thomas had boasted of his sexual prowess, talked about pornography, and pressured her for dates. Angrily denying her story, Thomas denounced the hearings as "a high-tech lynching for uppity blacks." The Senate shortly confirmed his nomination to the court, but Americans were left to wonder whether Thomas had been singled out for public embarrassment because of his race.

Soon after the Thomas hearings, a second episode exposed the legal system's unequal treatment of African Americans, provoked a race riot, and left lingering questions about the general status of African Americans in the United States. In Los Angeles in 1991, white police stopped an African-American motorist, Rodney King, for drunk driving and then savagely beat him. Unknown to the officers, an onlooker had videotaped the beating. Despite the tape, an all-white jury acquitted four of the policemen of all charges in the affair on April 29, 1992. The stunning verdict set off rioting in the predominantly African-American community of South Central Los Angeles. Three days of violence left 51 people dead, 1,800 injured, and nearly 3,700 buildings burned.

In the aftermath, Americans debated whether the legal system offered justice to African Americans. They also argued over the cause of poverty and despair in South Cen-

"We will not rest." In the spring of 1992, rioters in South Central Los Angeles protest the acquittal of white police officers charged with beating an African-American driver, Rodney King.

tral Los Angeles and other African-American communities. The Bush administration seemed to blame the welfare policy and other liberal programs of the Great Society. Democrats pointed to the welfare cuts and other policies of the Reagan administration. Neither side had concrete solutions for South Central Los Angeles. In 1993 a federal court convicted two of the police for depriving King of his civil rights. The next year, another court awarded King $3.8 million in damages from the city of Los Angeles. The verdicts failed to wash away the basic messages of the King beating and its violent aftermath. African Americans were less likely than whites to receive fair treatment at the hands of the police and the courts. More broadly, society seemed to have no answer for the problems of African-American poverty and inequality.

Less than three months after the damage award to King, another criminal case in Los Angeles raised some of the same difficult questions about race and justice in America. In June 1994 Los Angeles police charged O.J. Simpson, a charismatic African-American actor, sports announcer, and former football star, with the stabbing murders of his white ex-wife and her male friend. During Simpson's criminal trial for the killings, his lawyers suggested that racist white police had lied and planted evidence to frame him. The mostly African-American jury

voted to acquit Simpson in October 1995, but in a civil trial in February 1997, a mostly white jury ordered Simpson to pay millions of dollars in damages to the families of the victims. The Simpson case laid bare deep differences in outlook between whites and African Americans. Most whites believed him guilty; most African Americans believed him innocent.

The Simpson case, the King beating, and the Thomas hearings provoked passionate debate but relatively little action. These episodes did help inspire the "Million Man March," a massive demonstration of African-American men organized by Minister Louis Farrakhan of the Nation of Islam. In October 1995 perhaps more than 800,000 African-American males converged on Washington, D. C., to dramatize their commitment to community, family, and personal responsibility. The march suggested the potential for mass action by African Americans, but that potential was largely unrealized in the 1990s.

The federal government did not take sweeping action to deal with African-American inequality. The administrations of both George Bush and Bill Clinton reflected Americans' apparent pessimism about race relations and government activism. In the 1990s few people seemed to believe that federal programs on the scale of the Great Society could secure equal rights for African Americans. As

ON TRIAL

The Simpson Criminal Trial

Observers immediately labeled the criminal trial of O. J. Simpson, for the murders of Nicole Brown Simpson and Ronald Goldman, "the trial of the century." There had been other highly publicized "trials of the century," but the Simpson trial made a powerful claim to the title because it touched on so many fundamental issues in American life. More than a lurid tale of murder among the famous and well-to-do, the case revealed a great deal about media, celebrity, gender, race, class, and justice in the United States.

The Simpson case received so much attention partly because of the development of communications media. From the beginning, the murders revealed the media's newfound ability to inundate Americans instantly with pictures and words. Helicopters and live satellite transmissions made it possible for a mesmerized television audience to watch as a Ford Bronco carrying a despondent O. J. Simpson led police on a strange, slow-speed highway chase five days after the killings. Cable networks gave viewers the rare chance to watch the ensuing trial live on television. Night after night, television offered an array of pundits and experts commenting on the trial. O. J. Simpson himself put out a book, an audio tape, and a video tape and maintained a 900 number.

Media alone did not create the avid public interest in the Simpson case. Americans were drawn to the case in part because of their fascination with wealth and celebrity. The murders took place against the affluent, fashionable backdrop of the Brentwood section of Los Angeles. O. J. Simpson moved in the glamorous worlds of sports, broadcasting, and Hollywood. Built on celebrity, the murder trial in turn made national celebrities out of previously obscure judges, lawyers, police, witnesses, and experts. Suddenly famous, they wrote books, turned up on talk shows, and hosted their own television programs.

For many Americans, the Simpson case was also about gender. They saw the murder of Nicole Brown Simpson as a symbol of male violence toward women. There was evidence that O. J. Simpson had abused his wife during their marriage and stalked her after their divorce. To feminists and other onlookers, Nicole's murder was the final act of abuse. In their view, O. J.'s acquittal dramatized the failure of the judicial system to protect women and give them justice.

To many Americans, the Simpson case certainly taught something about race relations, but what was the lesson? Race affected people's perception of O. J. Simpson. Whites tended to believe he was guilty of murder. Blacks tended to believe he was innocent. For some whites, Simpson's acquittal by a largely black jury proved that African Americans would not mete out justice to a member of their own race. For many African Americans, Simpson's arrest was one more example of the mistreatment that African Americans suffered at the hands of white police and prosecutors. Playing to this sentiment,

Flanked by his lawyers, O. J. Simpson hears he has been found "not guilty" of the murder of his former wife, Nicole Brown.

Simpson's attorneys argued that a racist Los Angeles police force had planted and fabricated evidence to frame their client.

The Simpson trial was about wealth and social class, too. To many Americans who believed that O. J. Simpson was guilty, his acquittal was a sign of the power of money. They complained that he, like other well-to-do Americans, had been able to hire the best attorneys and experts who then overwhelmed the prosecutors and won over the jury. In this view, the trial became a symbol of class inequality.

Finally, the Simpson criminal trial commanded attention because it mercilessly exposed strains on the American system of justice. In different ways money, race, gender, and media appeared to distort the outcome of the case. Justice was expensive: Like other people, O. J. Simpson used up his assets in order to pay for his defense. Watching the trial, Americans wondered whether juries could be fair and whether police could be trusted. They also wondered whether intense media coverage affected the performance of judges and lawyers. These concerns did not go away, even when Simpson was later convicted in the civil trial. If the Simpson criminal case was indeed the "trial of the century," it was because the case revealed so much about American justice at the end of the twentieth century.

a result, there was little pressure for federal action. Bush, like Reagan before him, disliked affirmative action, but affirmative action programs largely remained in place. The president did sign the Civil Rights Act of 1991, which helped workers to sue their employers for discrimination on the basis of race or sex. Although Clinton was supportive of affirmative action and civil rights, his administration did relatively little to deal with the problems dramatized by the Thomas, King, and Simpson episodes.

Contesting Women's Rights

The women's movement in the 1990s was in much the same position as the struggle for equal rights for African Americans. The economic gap between women and men continued to narrow during the decade. The percentage of adult women in the work force rose, as did the percentage of women in high-paying white-collar jobs. Women still did not make as much money as men did, but the disparity was growing smaller.

Women also played a larger role in government. After the 1992 elections, a record 53 women held seats in Congress, including the first female African-American Senator, Carol Moseley-Braun of Illinois. Clinton selected and the Senate confirmed the first female attorney general, Janet Reno, in 1993; the second female justice of the Supreme Court, Ruth Bader Ginsburg, in 1993; and the first female secretary of state, Madeleine Albright, in 1997. Despite criticism for Hillary Clinton's alleged role in her husband's scandals, the first lady won a seat in the United States Senate from New York in 2000.

Nevertheless, women faced continuing discrimination. A woman was likely to make less money than a man. She was also much more likely to live in poverty. Like African Americans, women were still underrepresented in Congress and other governmental bodies.

Controversies over sexual harassment also underscored the persistence of gender inequality in the 1990s. Several highly publicized incidents provoked widespread public discussion about the nature of relationships between men and women. As the sexes differed over what constituted harassment, many women complained that men "just don't get it." The Clarence Thomas confirmation hearings were not only about race; they were also about gender. For many Americans, Thomas' alleged treatment of Anita Hill dramatized the widespread harassment of women in the workplace. In 1995 that issue was raised again when Senator Robert Packwood of Oregon resigned after 10 women charged him with sexual harassment. President Clinton's affair with Monica Lewinsky further raised the issue of how men exploited their power over women.

As more women entered the military, the armed services also had to deal with the issue of harassment. In 1991, more than 80 women were harassed and sexually assaulted at the Las Vegas convention of the Tailhook Association, a group of past and present Naval aviators. This scandal, along with the Navy's attempt to cover it up, led to the early retirement of the service's top admiral and the resignation of its cabinet secretary. In 1996 and 1997, the Army was rocked by numerous allegations that drill sergeants had sexually harassed female recruits. Then, in 2000, the Army supported a claim by its highest-ranking woman general that she had been sexually harassed by a male general.

Despite such revelations, the organized feminist movement did not grow dramatically at the end of the twentieth century. Many Americans seemed to accept the expansion of women's rights but to reject feminism and feminists as too radical. Some observers argued that there was a concerted backlash against feminism by the end of the 1980s. At the least, feminists often found themselves defending earlier accomplishments, such as affirmative-action programs, rather than pushing for new objectives.

Abortion provided a case in point. From the 1980s into the 1990s the conservative Right to Life movement continued its passionate campaign against abortion. At the grassroots level, protesters picketed abortion clinics and tried to discourage pregnant women from having abortions. Some radicals resorted to violence, including the murder of clinic workers. Meanwhile, George Bush condemned abortion as "murder" and, like Reagan before him, named anti-abortion judges to the federal courts.

In spite of this assault, the right and practice of abortion continued in the 1990s. The Supreme Court declined to overturn its

Law professor Anita Hill testifies in the confirmation hearings of Supreme Court nominee Clarence Thomas.

Women's increasing role in government in the 1990s: Attorney General Janet Reno, with Bill Clinton; Supreme Court Justice Ruth Bader Ginsburg (top right); Senator Carol Mosley-Braun of Illinois (bottom right); and Secretary of State Madeleine Albright (bottom left).

decision in *Roe v. Wade* acknowledging the constitutional right to abortion. In *Planned Parenthood v. Casey* in 1992, the court did vote narrowly to uphold much of a Pennsylvania law limiting access to abortions. But the court also declared that a woman's right to choose an abortion was "a component of liberty we cannot renounce." Later that year, Bush's defeat at the hands of Clinton, a strongly prochoice Democrat, made abortion rights seem still more secure. Nevertheless, the struggle to shut down clinics and overturn *Roe v. Wade* continued.

Contesting Gay and Lesbian Rights

In a society struggling over diversity, homosexuality remained perhaps the most controversial difference of all. The rights of homosexuals, a significant public issue since the 1960s, remained unsettled at the start of the twenty-first century. Like women and African Americans, gay men and lesbian women had made real gains. During the Bush administration, the federal government committed more resources to AIDS research. The disease itself spread more slowly among the gay population. As heterosexuals contracted the disease, Americans seemed less likely to consider it the "gay cancer" or God's punishment of homosexuals. Meanwhile, gays became a more accepted presence in society. More television shows positively depicted homosexuality. Two openly gay men served in Congress. Many businesses, including Disneyland, welcomed gay customers. Leading corporations, including General Motors and Ford, began providing benefits to the partners of gay employees.

Nevertheless, homosexuals' calls for equal rights met with considerable opposition. Although most Americans believed businesses should not discriminate on the basis of sexual preference, a majority still believed that homosexuality was morally wrong. Every year, there were still hundreds of documented instances of violence against gays and lesbians. In a notorious case in 1998, Matthew Shepherd, a gay student at the University of Wyoming in Laramie, was beaten, robbed, tied to a fence, pistol whipped in the head, and left to die by two homophobic men who were later convicted of murder.

The resistance to gay rights was especially strong in the armed services. Officially barred from serving, homosexuals had long concealed their sexual orientation in order to remain in the military. By the 1990s, however, many gays called on the armed forces to allow openly homosexual officers and enlisted personnel. Deeply committed to a heterosexual definition of masculinity, the military would not change its rules. Then, in 1992 for the first time, a federal court ordered the Navy to reinstate an openly gay petty officer who had been discharged. Campaigning for president that year, Bill Clinton promised to lift the ban on gays in the armed services. Once in office, he met stiff resistance from military leaders who argued that tolerance of homosexuality would lower morale and hurt recruitment. Clinton compromised by instituting a "don't ask, don't tell" policy. The military would no longer ask recruits whether they were gay, and gays and lesbians would continue to conceal their sexual orientation. It was unclear how long this uneasy compromise would survive challenges in court.

There was no compromise in the struggle over legal protection for gay and lesbian rights in civilian life. In communities and states, homosexuals demanded laws that would prevent businesses from discriminating on the basis of sexual orientation. Conservatives, especially those concerned about the decline of "family values," moved to block gay and lesbian rights measures. In 1992 Colorado voters passed a state referendum forbidding communities to pass laws protecting gay rights, but the state's supreme court declared the referendum unconstitutional the next year. The issue did not rest there. In 1996 Congress joined the battle by passing the Defense of Marriage Act, which denied federal benefits to same-sex couples living together and allowed states to refuse to recognize same-sex marriages from other states. In 2000, the United States Supreme Court upheld the right of the Boy Scouts of America to dismiss a homosexual troop leader in New Jersey, despite the existence of a state gay rights law.

Two gay men exchange rings during a same-sex wedding ceremony in Hawaii.

New Demands for Rights

While old battles for rights continued throughout the 1990s, the decade also saw new and unsettling demands for rights. Some Americans insisted on the right to die—that is, the right of people dying or suffering great pain to end their lives. In 1990 a retired Michigan pathologist, Jack Kevorkian, helped a fifty-two-year-old woman in the early stages of Alzheimer's Disease to commit suicide. Over the next several years, Kevorkian admitted having assisted 130 men and women in ending their lives. Almost single-handedly, he sparked a passionate national debate about the right of terminally ill patients to commit suicide. Kevorkian's defenders argued that he was mercifully helping people to avoid prolonged suffering and die with dignity. Dubbing him "Dr. Death," his critics called Kevorkian a murderer who took advantage of emotionally distraught patients. In 1997 Congress banned the use of federal funds to support assisted suicide, but Oregon voters affirmed the right of doctors to prescribe lethal doses of drugs for terminally ill patients. In 1999 a Michigan court convicted Kevorkian of second degree murder for assisting in the death of a man suffering from Lou Gehrig's disease. Meanwhile, Americans continued to argue whether they had a right to die and how that right should be responsibly exercised.

By the 1990s a small number of Americans had claimed the right for religious or political reasons to live free from governmental authority. That claim inevitably brought them into conflict with the federal government. The result was a series of deadly episodes that raised difficult questions about the way Washington used its power.

In 1992 Randy Weaver, a white separatist who wanted to keep his family away from other races and government, failed to appear for a trial on weapons charges. Federal agents then converged on his remote cabin in Ruby Ridge, Idaho, to arrest him, but Weaver resisted. An eleven-day siege, punctuated by two gun battles, ended with the deaths of Weaver's wife, one of his sons, and a federal marshal. For some Americans, the Ruby Ridge confrontation demonstrated the arrogance and deceitfulness of the federal government. They felt vindicated in 1995 when Weaver was acquitted of assault and the U. S. Justice Department agreed to pay him a $3.1 million settlement. Five federal agents were then suspended for misconduct, and one was convicted of obstruction of justice.

In 1993 another tragic siege provoked more charges about the arrogance of federal power. David Koresh, the leader of the tiny Branch Davidian religious sect, had gathered about a hundred heavily armed followers in a compound outside Waco, Texas, to wait for the end of the world. When the federal Bureau of Alcohol, Tobacco, and Firearms (ATF) moved to arrest Koresh on weapons charges at the end of February, a fierce gun battle killed four agents and at least five Branch Davidians. Hundreds of law enforcement officers, including FBI agents, then surrounded the compound. The stand-off continued for 51 days, until April 19, when federal agents pumped tear gas into the compound and it burned down. At least 72 Branch Davidians, including Koresh and 17 children, died—some from bullets fired by members of the sect. For many Americans, the horrifying fire outside of Waco, carried live on television, had been caused by the insanity of Koresh, who considered himself the messiah. Other Americans blamed the tragedy on the federal government, which had refused to delay its assault even though there were children in the compound. For critics of the FBI and the Clinton administration, Waco stood as a symbol of Washington's intolerance of personal and religious freedom.

The Waco and Ruby Ridge incidents inspired thousands of people to take action. Around the country, right-wing paramilitary groups, known as "Patriots" and "civil

The impact of domestic terrorism: rescue workers and residents mourn the victims killed in the bombing of the Alfred P. Murrah Federal Building in Oklahoma City in 1995.

militias," trained with weapons to protect themselves from a supposedly hostile government. Some militia members and other antigovernment extremists believed that the federal government, secretly controlled by foreign countries, was planning to take away Americans' guns and freedom. Other extremists denied that local, state, or national government had the right to tax American citizens. Some Texans even claimed that their state was still legally an independent republic, as it had been in the nineteenth century.

A handful of antigovernment extremists apparently did more than train with guns and denounce Washington. On April 19, 1995—the second anniversary of the Waco tragedy—a car bomb exploded in front of a federal building in Oklahoma City, Oklahoma. Destroying much of the structure, the blast killed 169 people, including small children in a day-care center. Americans were stunned that the worst terrorist attack in the nation's history had occurred, not in a metropolitan center like New York City or Los Angeles, but in the nation's heartland. People were even more surprised when they learned the likely terrorists were not Middle Easterners but American-born critics of the federal government. In 1997 Timothy McVeigh, an Army veteran with ties to a right-wing militia group, was convicted of murdering victims of the bombing. A friend of McVeigh's confessed to a role in planning the bombing and another friend was convicted of conspiracy and manslaughter for his role.

The Oklahoma City attack was followed by other incidents that raised fears of domestic terrorism. In October 1995 sabotaged tracks derailed an Amtrak passenger train southwest of Phoenix, Arizona, killing one and injuring about a hundred. In July 1996 federal authorities arrested 12 members of a militia group in the Phoenix area on suspicion of plotting to blow up seven federal buildings. Later that month, during the Olympic games in Atlanta, Georgia, a bomb went off in a crowded park, killing one person. The leading suspect in the bombing, who had vague ties to white supremacist, antigovernment groups, may also have been responsible for two more bombings in Atlanta in 1997 and a bombing in Birmingham, Alabama, in 1998 that killed a police officer.

The sudden spread of domestic terrorism emphasized that Americans' sense of rights was unsettling and divisive. The right to die and the right to live free from government, like the right to equality for minority groups, would not be accepted immediately, if at all. The struggles over rights in a diverse society would continue.

Conclusion

At the start of the twenty-first century, Americans lived with uncertainty. An older nation, defined by the cold war, New Deal liberalism, and the industrial economy, was fading away, but the outlines of a new America remained indistinct. For Felix Andreev and other Americans, the United States still meant prosperity and freedom, but how would prosperity and freedom be maintained? There was no sure answer. The postindustrial economy was still evolving. America's role in the post-cold-war world was still undefined. There was little agreement about the rights of individuals and groups in an increasingly diverse society. American politics, caught somewhere between liberalism and conservatism, reflected all these uncertainties. Like so many people before them, Felix Andreev and the rest of the nation would work to define the meaning of America in a new century.

Review Questions

1. What were the main features of the postindustrial economy? Why were Americans anxious about the economy even though it was relatively strong?

2. What were the causes of the uncertain politics of the 1990s? How did popular discontent shape politics and government during the decade?

3. Why did the cold war come to an end? Did the United States win the cold war?

4. Describe the debates over the international role of the United States after the cold war. Why were Americans reluctant to support George Bush's vision of the New World Order?

5. Why was diversity such an important issue in the 1990s? How did the new immigration contribute to the concern about diversity?

6. How did the struggle for rights change in the 1990s? How did the spread of domestic terrorism reflect concern about rights?

CHRONOLOGY

1988   George Bush elected president

1989   Collapse of Communist regimes in eastern Europe
Invasion of Panama

1990   Clean Air Act of 1990 signed
First assisted suicide involving Jack Kevorkian
Partial shutdown of federal government

1991   START (STrategic Arms Reduction Talks) Treaty with Soviet Union
Persian Gulf War
Civil Rights Act of 1991
Clarence Thomas named to U. S. Supreme Court
Collapse of the Soviet Union
Dow Jones Industrial Average over 3,000 for first time

1992   Riot in Los Angeles after first Rodney King verdict
Ruling in *Planned Parenthood v. Casey*
Federal confrontation with Randy Weaver in Ruby Ridge, Idaho
Bill Clinton elected president
Ratification of Twenty-Seventh Amendment

1993   Car bombing of World Trade Center, New York City
Burning of Branch Davidian complex at Waco, Texas
Family and Medical Leave Act of 1993 signed
Cancellation of Strategic Defense Initiative ("Star Wars")
Ratification of North American Free Trade Agreement (NAFTA)

1994   Appointment of independent counsel Kenneth Starr in Whitewater affair
Accusation of sexual harassment against Bill Clinton by Paula Jones
Murder of Nicole Brown Simpson and Ronald Goldman
Election of Republican majority to House of Representatives
Adoption of Proposition 187 in California

1995   Bombing of federal building in Oklahoma City, Oklahoma
Peace treaty in Bosnia-Herzegovina civil war
U.S. diplomatic recognition of Socialist Republic of Vietnam
Repeal of federal 55-mile-an-hour speed limit
Million Man March

1996   Enactment of welfare reform
Re-election of Bill Clinton as president

1997   Dow Jones Industrial Average over 8,000 for first time

1998   Investigation of Bill Clinton's relationship with White House intern Monica Lewinsky

1999   Acquittal of Bill Clinton in Senate impeachment trial
NATO air war against Yugoslavia
Dow Jones Industrial Average over 10,000 for first time

2000   America Online acquisition of Time-Warner
Break-up of Microsoft ordered by federal court

2001   George W. Bush declared president

Further Readings

Stephanie Coontz, *The Way We Really Are: Coming to Terms With America's Changing Families* (1997). Coontz' book details family life in the 1990s.

Lawrence Freedman and Efraim Karsh, *The Gulf Conflict, 1990–1991: Diplomacy and War in the New World Order* (1993). This work carefully analyzes the international context of the Gulf War.

Raymond L. Garthoff, *The Great Transition: American-Soviet Relations and the End of the Cold War* (1994). A thorough narrative of the end of the U. S.-U. S. S. R. confrontation.

James Davison Hunter, *Culture Wars: The Struggle to Define America* (1991). Hunter thoughtfully studies some of the consequences of diversity.

Haynes Johnson and David S. Broder, *The System: The American Way of Politics at the Breaking Point* (1996). An exploration of the political discontents of the 1990s.

Jane Mayer and Jill Abramson, *Strange Justice: The Selling of Clarence Thomas* (1994). A journalistic account of the Hill-Thomas confrontation.

New York Times, ed., *The Downsizing of America* (1996). A detailed investigation of the social impact of corporate cutbacks.

Herbert S. Parmet, *George Bush: The Life of a Lone Star Yankee* (1997). The first scholarly biography of George H. Bush by a historian.

Sanford J. Ungar, *Fresh Blood: The New American Immigrants* (1995). A readable account, based on interviews, of the social and political aspects of the new immigration.

History on the Internet

"The History of GATT and the Structure of the WTO"
http://www.ljx.com/practice/internet.history.html

On this website, read more about the fundamental policies of the General Agreement of Tariffs and Trade (GATT), the 1947 economic policy intended to reduce trade barriers and regulate commerce.

"The History of Silicon Valley"
http://www.ocf.berklet.edu/~kenken/svhis.htm

This site details the beginnings of the information age through electronics. Read about the beginnings of Silicon Valley as a research center and how the industry was propelled by the revolutions of the personal computer and the World Wide Web.

"The Intermediate Nuclear Force Agreement (INF)"
http://www.state.gov/www/global/arms/treaties/infl.html

Read the full-text document of the INF agreement between the United States and the Soviet Union, an agreement that was the first true nuclear disarmament treaty.

"The Gulf War"
http://www/pbs.org/wgbh/pages/frontline/gulf/

Read about the Gulf War commanders, read testimony of American soldiers in combat, and learn about the events leading up to the invasion by consulting the timeline of events.

APPENDIX

The Declaration of Independence

When in the course of human events it becomes necessary for one people to dissolve the political bands which have connected them with another and to assume, among the powers of the earth, the separate and equal station to which the laws of nature and of nature's God entitle them, a decent respect to the opinions of mankind requires that they should declare the causes which impel them to the separation.

We hold these truths to be self-evident, that all men are created equal; that they are endowed by their Creator with certain unalienable rights; that among these are life, liberty, and the pursuit of happiness. That, to secure these rights, governments are instituted among men, deriving their just powers from the consent of the governed; that, whenever any form of government becomes destructive of these ends, it is the right of the people to alter or to abolish it, and to institute a new government, laying its foundation on such principles, and organizing its powers in such form, as to them shall seem most likely to effect their safety and happiness. Prudence, indeed, will dictate that governments long established should not be changed for light and transient causes; and, accordingly, all experience hath shown that mankind are more disposed to suffer, while evils are sufferable, than to right themselves by abolishing the forms to which they are accustomed. But when a long train of abuses and usurpations, pursuing invariably the same object, evinces a design to reduce them under absolute despotism, it is their right, it is their duty, to throw off such government and to provide new guards for their future security. Such has been the patient sufferance of these colonies, and such is now the necessity which constrains them to alter their former systems of government. The history of the present King of Great Britain is a history of repeated injuries and usurpations, all having, in direct object, the establishment of an absolute tyranny over these States. To prove this, let facts be submitted to a candid world:

He has refused his assent to laws the most wholesome and necessary for the public good.

He has forbidden his governors to pass laws of immediate and pressing importance, unless suspended in their operation till his assent should be obtained; and, when so suspended, he has utterly neglected to attend to them.

He has refused to pass other laws for the accommodation of large districts of people, unless those people would relinquish the right of representation in the legislature, a right inestimable to them and formidable to tyrants only.

He has called together legislative bodies at places unusual, uncomfortable, and distant from the depository of their public records, for the sole purpose of fatiguing them into compliance with his measures.

He has dissolved representative houses, repeatedly for opposing, with manly firmness, his invasions on the rights of the people.

He has refused, for a long time after such dissolutions, to cause others to be elected; whereby the legislative powers, incapable of annihilation, have returned to the people at large for their exercise; the state remaining, in the meantime, exposed to all the danger of invasion from without and convulsions within.

He has endeavored to prevent the population of these States; for that purpose, obstructing the laws for naturalization of foreigners, refusing to pass others to encourage their migration hither, and raising the conditions of new appropriations of lands.

He has obstructed the administration of justice by refusing his assent to laws for establishing judiciary powers.

He has made judges dependent on his will alone for the tenure of their offices and the amount and payment of their salaries.

He has erected a multitude of new offices and sent hither swarms of officers to harass our people and eat out their substance.

He has kept among us, in time of peace, standing armies, without the consent of our legislatures.

He has affected to render the military independent of, and superior to, the civil power.

He has combined with others to subject us to a jurisdiction foreign to our Constitution and unacknowledged by our laws, giving his assent to their acts of pretended legislation—

For quartering large bodies of armed troops among us;

For protecting them, by mock trial, from punishment for any murders which they should commit on the inhabitants of these States;

For cutting off our trade with all parts of the world;

For imposing taxes on us without our consent;

For depriving us, in many cases, of the benefit of trial by jury;

For transporting us beyond seas to be tried for pretended offences;

For abolishing the free system of English laws in a neighboring province, establishing therein an arbitrary government, and enlarging its boundaries, so as to render it at once an example and fit instrument for introducing the same absolute rule into these colonies;

For taking away our charters, abolishing our most valuable laws, and altering, fundamentally, the powers of our governments.

For suspending our own legislatures and declaring themselves invested with power to legislate for us in all cases whatsoever.

He has abdicated government here by declaring us out of his protection and waging war against us.

He has plundered our seas, ravaged our coasts, burnt our towns, and destroyed the lives of our people.

He is, at this time, transporting large armies of foreign mercenaries to complete the works of death, desolation, and tyranny already begun with circumstances of cruelty and perfidy scarcely paralleled in the most barbarous ages, and totally unworthy the head of a civilized nation.

He has constrained our fellow citizens, taken captive on the high seas, to bear arms against their country, to become the executioners of their friends and brethren, or to fall themselves by their hands.

He has excited domestic insurrections amongst us and has endeavored to bring on the inhabitants of our frontiers, the merciless Indian savages, whose known rule of warfare is an undistinguished destruction of all ages, sexes, and conditions.

In every stage of these oppressions, we have petitioned for redress in the most humble terms; our repeated petitions have been answered only by repeated injury. A prince whose character is thus marked by every act which may define a tyrant is unfit to be the ruler of a free people.

Nor have we been wanting in attention to our British brethren. We have warned them, from time to time, of attempts made by their legislature to extend an unwarrantable jurisdiction over us. We have reminded them of the circumstances of our emigration and settlement here. We have appealed to their native justice and magnanimity, and we have conjured them, by the ties of our common kindred, to disavow these usurpations, which would inevitably interrupt our connections and correspondence. They, too, have been deaf to the voice of justice and consanguinity. We must, therefore, acquiesce in the necessity which denounces our separation, and hold them, as we hold the rest of mankind, enemies in war, in peace, friends.

We, therefore, the representatives of the United States of America, in general Congress assembled, appealing to the Supreme Judge of the world for the rectitude of our intentions, do, in the name and by the authority of the good people of these colonies, solemnly publish and declare, that these united colonies are, and of right ought to be, free and independent states: that they are absolved from all allegiance to the British Crown, and that all political connection between them and the state of Great Britain is, and ought to be, totally dissolved; and that, as free and independent states, they have full power to levy war, conclude peace, contract alliances, establish commerce, and to do all other acts and things which independent states may of right do. And, for the support of this declaration, with a firm reliance on the protection of Divine Providence, we mutually pledge to each other our lives, our fortunes, and our sacred honor.

The Constitution of the United States of America

We the people of the United States, in order to form a more perfect union, establish justice, insure domestic tranquillity, provide for the common defense, promote the general welfare, and secure the blessings of liberty to ourselves and our posterity, do ordain and establish this Constitution for the United States of America.

Article I

SECTION 1. All legislative powers herein granted shall be vested in a Congress of the United States, which shall consist of a Senate and House of Representatives.

SECTION 2. 1. The House of Representatives shall be composed of members chosen every second year by the people of the several States, and the electors in each State shall have the qualifications requisite for electors of the most numerous branch of the State legislature.

2. No person shall be a representative who shall not have attained to the age of twenty-five years, and been seven years a citizen of the United States, and who shall not, when elected, be an inhabitant of that State in which he shall be chosen.

3. Representatives and direct taxes[1] shall be apportioned among the several States which may be included within this Union, according to their respective numbers, which shall be determined by adding to the whole number of free persons, including those bound to service for a term of years, and excluding Indians not taxed, three fifths of all other persons.[2] The actual enumeration shall be made within three years after the first meeting of the Congress of the United States, and within every subsequent term of ten years, in such manner as they shall be law direct. The number of representatives shall not exceed one for every thirty thousand, but each State shall have at least one representative; and until such enumeration shall be made, the State of New Hampshire shall be entitled to choose three, Massachusetts eight, Rhode Island and Providence Plantations one, Connecticut five, New York six, New Jersey four, Pennsylvania eight, Delaware one, Maryland six, Virginia ten, North Carolina five, South Carolina five, and Georgia three.

4. When vacancies happen in the representation from any State, the executive authority thereof shall issue writs of election to fill such vacancies.

5. The House of Representatives shall choose their speaker and other officers; and shall have the sole power of impeachment.

SECTION 3. 1. The Senate of the United States shall be composed of two senators from each State, chosen by the legislature thereof,[3] for six years; and each senator shall have one vote.

2. Immediately after they shall be assembled in consequence of the first election, they shall be divided as equally as may be into three classes. The seats of the senators of the first class shall be vacated at the expiration of the second year, of the second class at the expiration of the fourth year, and of the third class at the expiration of the sixth year, so that one third may be chosen every second year; and if vacancies happen by resignation, or otherwise, during the recess of the legislature of any State, the executive thereof may make temporary appointments until the next meeting of the legislature, which shall then fill such vacancies.[4]

3. No person shall be a senator who shall not have attained to the age of thirty years, and been nine years a citizen of the United States, and who shall not, when elected, be an inhabitant of that State for which he shall be chosen.

4. The Vice President of the United States shall be President of the Senate, but shall have no vote, unless they be equally divided.

5. The Senate shall choose their other officers, and also a president pro tempore, in the absence of the Vice President, or when he shall exercise the office of the President of the United States.

6. The Senate shall have the sole power to try all impeachments. When sitting for that purpose, they shall be on oath or affirmation. When the president of the United States is tried, the chief justice shall preside: and no person shall be convicted without the concurrence of two thirds of the members present.

7. Judgment in cases of impeachment shall not extend further than to removal from office, and disqualification to hold and enjoy any office of honor, trust or profit under the United States: but the party convicted shall nevertheless be liable and subject to indictment, trial, judgment and punishment, according to law.

SECTION 4. 1. The times, places, and manner of holding elections for senators and representatives, shall be prescribed in each State by the legislature thereof; but the Congress may at any time by law make or alter such regulations, except as to the places of choosing senators.

2. The Congress shall assemble at least once in every year, and such meeting shall be on the first Monday in December, unless they shall by law appoint a different day.

SECTION 5. 1. Each House shall be the judge of the elections, returns and qualifications of its own members, and a majority of each shall constitute a quorum to do business; but a smaller number may adjourn from day to day, and may be authorized to compel the attendance of absent members, in such manner, and under such penalties as each House may provide.

2. Each House may determine the rules of its proceedings, punish its members for disorderly behavior, and, with the concurrence of two thirds, expel a member.

3. Each House shall keep a journal of its proceedings, and from time to time publish the same, excepting such parts as may in their judgment require secrecy; and the yeas and nays of the members of either house on any question shall, at the desire of one fifth of those present, be entered on the journal.

4. Neither House, during the session of Congress, shall, without the consent of the other, adjourn for more than three days, nor to any other place than that in which the two Houses shall be sitting.

---

[1]See the Sixteenth Amendment.
[2]See the Fourteenth Amendment.
[3]See the Seventeenth Amendment.
[4]See the Seventeenth Amendment.

SECTION 6. 1. The senators and representatives shall receive a compensation for their services, to be ascertained by law, and paid out of the Treasury of the United States. They shall in all cases, except treason, felony, and breach of the peace, be privileged from arrest during their attendance at the session of their respective Houses, and in going to and returning from the same; and for any speech or debate in either House, they shall not be questioned in any other place.

2. No senator or representative shall, during the time for which he was elected, be appointed to any civil office under the authority of the United States, which shall have been created, or the emoluments whereof shall have been increased, during such time; and no person holding any office under the United States shall be a member of either House during his continuance in office.

SECTION 7. 1. All bills for raising revenue shall originate in the House of Representatives; but the Senate may purpose or concur with amendments as on other bills.

2. Every bill which shall have passed the House of Representatives and the Senate, shall, before it become a law, be presented to the President of the United States; if he approves he shall sign it, but if not he shall return it, with his objections, to that House in which it shall have originated, who shall enter the objections at large on their journal, and proceed to reconsider it. If after such reconsideration two thirds of that House shall agree to pass the bill, it shall be sent, together with the objections, to the other House, by which it shall likewise be reconsidered, and if approved by two thirds of that House, it shall become a law. But in all such cases the votes of both Houses shall be determined by yeas and nays, and the names of the persons voting for and against the bill shall be entered on the journal of each House respectively. If any bill shall not be returned by the President within ten days (Sundays excepted) after it shall have been presented to him, the same shall be a law, in like manner as if he had signed it, unless the Congress by their adjournment prevent its return, in which case it shall not be a law.

3. Every order, resolution, or vote to which the concurrence of the Senate and the House of Representatives may be necessary (except on a question of adjournment) shall be presented to the President of the United States; and before the same shall take effect, shall be approved by him, or being disapproved by him, shall be repassed by two thirds of the Senate and House of Representatives, according to the rules and limitations prescribed in the case of a bill.

SECTION 8. The Congress shall have the power

1. To lay and collect taxes, duties, imposts, and excises, to pay the debts and provide for the common defense and general welfare of the United States; but all duties, imposts, and excises shall be uniform throughout the United States.

2. To borrow money on the credit of the United States;

3. To regulate commerce with foreign nations, and among the several States, and with the Indian tribes;

4. To establish a uniform rule of naturalization, and uniform laws on the subject of bankruptcies throughout the United States;

5. To coin money, regulate the value thereof, and of foreign coin, and fix the standard of weights and measures;

6. To provide for the punishment of counterfeiting the securities and current coin of the United States;

7. To establish post offices and post roads;

8. To promote the progress of science and useful arts, by securing for limited times to authors and inventors the exclusive right to their respective writings and discoveries;

9. To constitute tribunals inferior to the Supreme Court;

10. To define and punish piracies and felonies committed on the high seas, and offenses against the law of nations;

11. To declare war, grant letters of marque and reprisal, and make rules concerning captures on land and water;

12. To raise and support armies, but no appropriation of money to that use shall be for a longer term than two years;

13. To provide and maintain a navy;

14. To make rules for the government and regulation of the land and naval forces;

15. To provide for calling forth the militia to execute the laws of the Union, suppress insurrections and repel invasions;

16. To provide for organizing, arming, and disciplining the militia, and for governing such part of them as may be employed in the service of the United States, reserving to the States respectively, the appointment of the officers, and the authority of training the militia according to the discipline prescribed by Congress;

17. To exercise exclusive legislation in all cases whatsoever, over such district (not exceeding ten miles square) as may, by cession of particular States, and the acceptance of Congress, become the seat of the government of the United States, and to exercise like authority over all places purchased by the consent of

the legislature of the State in which the same shall be, for the erection of forts, magazines, arsenals, dockyards, and other needful buildings; and

18. To make all laws which shall be necessary and proper for carrying into execution the foregoing powers, and all other powers vested by this Constitution in the government of the United States, or any department or officer thereof.

SECTION 9. 1. The migration or importation of such persons as any of the States now existing shall think proper to admit, shall not be prohibited by the Congress prior to the year one thousand eight hundred and eight, but a tax or duty may be imposed on such importation, not exceeding ten dollars for each person.

2. The privilege of the writ of habeas corpus shall not be suspended, unless when in cases of rebellion or invasion the public safety may require it.

3. No bill of attainder or ex post facto law shall be passed.

4. No capitation, or other direct, tax shall be laid, unless in proportion to the census or enumeration herein-before directed to be taken.[5]

5. No tax or duty shall be laid on articles exported from any State.

6. No preference shall be given by any regulation of commerce or revenue to the ports of one State over those of another: nor shall vessels bound to, or from, one State be obliged to enter, clear, or pay duties in another.

7. No money shall be drawn from the treasury, but in consequence of appropriations made by law; and a regular statement and account of the receipts and expenditures of all public money shall be published from time to time.

8. No title of nobility shall be granted by the United States: and no person holding any office of profit or trust under them, shall, without the consent of the Congress, accept of any present, emolument, office, or title, of any kind whatever, from any king, prince, or foreign State.

SECTION 10. 1. No State shall enter into any treaty, alliance, or confederation; grant letters of marque and reprisal; coin money; emit bills of credit; make any thing but gold and silver coin a tender in payment of debts; pass any bill of attainder, ex post facto law, or law impairing the obligation of contracts, or grant, any title of nobility.

2. No State shall, without the consent of the Congress, lay any imposts or duties on imports or exports, except what may be absolutely necessary for executing its inspection laws: and the net produce of all duties and imposts laid by any State on imports or exports, shall be for the use of the treasury of the United States; and all such laws shall be subject to the revision and control of the Congress.

3. No State shall, without the consent of Congress, lay any duty of tonnage, keep troops, or ships of war in time of peace, enter into any agreement or compact with another State, or with a foreign power, or engage in war, unless actually invaded, or in such imminent danger as will not admit of delay.

Article II

SECTION 1. 1. The executive power shall be vested in a President of the United States of America. He shall hold his office during the term of four years, and, together with the Vice President, chosen for the same term, be elected, as follows:

2. Each State shall appoint, in such manner as the legislature thereof may direct, a number of electors, equal to the whole number of senators and representatives to which the State may be entitled in the Congress: but no senator or representative, or person holding any office of trust or profit under the United States, shall be appointed an elector.

The electors shall meet in their respective States, and vote by ballot for two persons, of whom one at least shall not be an inhabitant of the same State with themselves. And they shall make a list of all the persons voted for, and of the number of votes for each; which list they shall sign and certify, and transmit sealed to the seat of the government of the United States, directed to the president of the Senate. The president of the Senate shall, in the presence of the Senate and House of Representatives, open all the certificates, and the votes shall then be counted. The person having the greatest number of votes shall be the President, if such number be a majority of the whole number of electors appointed; and if there be more than one who have such majority, and have an equal number of votes, then the House of Representatives shall immediately choose by ballot one of them for President; and if no person have a majority, then from the five highest on the list the said House shall in like manner choose the President. But in choosing the President, the votes shall be taken by States, the representation from each State having one vote; a quorum for this purpose shall consist of a member or members from two thirds of the States, and a majority of all the States shall be necessary to a choice. In every case after the choice of the President, the person having the greatest number of votes of the electors shall be the

---

[5]See the Sixteenth Amendment.

Vice President. But if there should remain two or more who have equal votes, the Senate shall choose from them by ballot the Vice President.[6]

3. The Congress may determine the time of choosing the electors, and the day on which they shall give their votes; which day shall be the same throughout the United States.

4. No person except a natural born citizen, or a citizen of the United States, at the time of the adoption of this Constitution, shall be eligible to the office of President; neither shall any person be eligible to the office who shall not have attained to the age of thirty-five years, and been fourteen years a resident within the United States.

5. In case of the removal of the President from office, or of his death, resignation, or inability to discharge the powers and duties of the said office, the same shall devolve on the Vice President, and the Congress may by law provide for the case of removal, death, resignation or inability, both of the President and Vice President, declaring what officer shall then act as President, and such officer shall act accordingly until the disability be removed, or a President shall be elected.

6. The President shall, at stated times, receive for his services a compensation which shall neither be increased nor diminished during the period for which he shall have been elected, and he shall not receive within that period any other emolument from the United States, or any of them.

7. Before he enter on the execution of his office, he shall take the following oath or affirmation:—"I do solemnly swear (or affirm) that I will faithfully execute the office of president of the United States, and will to the best of my ability, preserve, protect and defend the Constitution of the United States."

SECTION 2. 1. The President shall be commander in chief of the army and navy of the United States, and of the militia of the several States, when called into the actual service of the United States; he may require the opinion in writing, of the principal officer in each of the executive departments, upon any subject relating to the duties of their respective offices, and he shall have power to grant reprieves and pardons for offenses against the United States, except in cases of impeachment.

2. He shall have power, by and with the advice and consent of the Senate, to make treaties, provided two thirds of the senators present concur; and he shall nominate, and by and with the advice and consent of

the Senate, shall appoint ambassadors, other public ministers and consuls, judges of the Supreme Court, and all other officers of the United States, whose appointments are not herein otherwise provided for, and which shall be established by law; but the Congress may by law vest the appointment of such inferior officers, as they think proper, in the President alone, in the courts of laws, or in the heads of departments.

3. The President shall have power to fill up all vacancies that may happen during the recess of the Senate, by granting commissions which shall expire at the end of their next session.

SECTION 3. He shall from time to time give to the Congress information of the state of the Union, and recommend to their consideration such measures as he shall judge necessary and expedient; he may, on extraordinary occasions, convene both houses, or either of them, and in case of disagreement between them with respect to the time of adjournment, he may adjourn them to such time as he shall think proper; he shall receive ambassadors and other public ministers; he shall take care that the laws be faithfully executed, and shall commission all the officers of the United States.

SECTION 4. The President, Vice President, and all civil officers of the United States, shall be removed from office on impeachment for, and conviction of, treason, bribery, or other high crimes and misdemeanors.

Article III

SECTION 1. The judicial power of the United States shall be vested in one Supreme Court, and in such inferior courts as the Congress may from time to time ordain and establish. The judges, both of the Supreme and inferior courts, shall hold their offices during good behavior, and shall, at stated times, receive for their services, a compensation, which shall not be diminished during their continuance in office.

SECTION 2. 1. The judicial power shall extend to all cases, in law and equity, arising under this Constitution, the laws of the United States, and treaties made, or which shall be made, under their authority;—to all cases of admiralty and maritime jurisdiction;—to controversies to which the United States shall be a party;[7]—to controversies between two or more States;—between a State and citizens of another State;—between citizens of different States;—between citizens of the same State claiming lands under grants of different States, and between a State, or the citizens thereof, and foreign States, citizens or subjects.

---

[6]Superseded by the Twelfth Amendment.

[7]See the Eleventh Amendment.

2. In all cases affecting ambassadors, other public ministers and consuls, and those in which a State shall be party, the Supreme Court shall have original jurisdiction. In all the other cases before mentioned, the Supreme Court shall have appellate jurisdiction, both as to law and fact, with such exceptions, and under such regulations as the Congress shall make.

3. The trial of all crimes, except in cases of impeachment, shall be by jury; and such trial shall be held in the State where the said crimes shall have been committed; but when not committed within any State, the trial shall be such place or places as the Congress may by law have directed.

SECTION 3. 1. Treason against the United States shall consist only in levying war against them, or in adhering to their enemies, giving them aid and comfort. No person shall be convicted of treason unless on the testimony of two witnesses to the same overt act, or on confession in open court.

2. The Congress shall have power to declare the punishment of treason, but no attainder of treason shall work corruption of blood, or forfeiture except during the life of the person attained.

Article IV

SECTION 1. Full faith and credit shall be given in each State to the public acts, records, and judicial proceedings of every other State. And the Congress may by general laws prescribe the manner in which such acts, records and proceedings shall be proved, and the effect thereof.

SECTION 2. 1. The citizens of each State shall be entitled to all privileges and immunities of citizens in the several States.[8]

2. A person charged in any State with treason, felony, or other crime, who shall flee from justice, and be found in another State, shall on demand of the executive authority of the State from which he fled, be delivered up to be removed to the State having jurisdiction of the crime.

3. No person held to service or labor in one State under the laws thereof, escaping into another, shall, in consequence of any law or regulation therein, be discharged from such service or labor, but shall be delivered up on claim of the party to whom such service or labor may be due.[9]

SECTION 3. 1. New States may be admitted by the Congress into this Union; but no new State shall be formed or erected within the jurisdiction of any other State, nor any State be formed by the junction of two or more States, or parts of States, without the consent of the legislatures of the States concerned as well as of the Congress.

2. The Congress shall have power to dispose of and make all needful rules and regulations respecting the territory or other property belonging to the United States; and nothing in this Constitution shall be so construed as to prejudice any claims of the United States, or of any particular State.

SECTION 4. The United States shall guarantee to every State in this Union a republican form of government, and shall protect each of them against invasion; and on application of the legislature, or of the executive (when the legislature cannot be convened) against domestic violence.

Article V

The Congress, whenever two thirds of both Houses shall deem it necessary, shall propose amendments to this Constitution, or, on the application of the legislatures of two thirds of the several States, shall call a convention for proposing amendments, which in either case shall be valid to all intents and purposes, as part of this Constitution, when ratified by the legislatures of three fourths of the several States, or by conventions in three fourths thereof, as the one or the other mode of ratification may be proposed by the Congress; Provided that no amendment which may be made prior to the year one thousand eight hundred and eight shall in any manner affect the first and fourth clauses in the ninth section of the first article; and that no State, without its consent, shall be deprived of its equal suffrage in the Senate.

Article VI

1. All debts contracted and engagements entered into, before the adoption of this Constitution, shall be as valid against the United States under this Constitution, as under the Confederation.[10]

2. This Constitution, and the laws of the United States which shall be made in pursuance thereof; and all treaties made, or which shall be made, under the authority of the United States, shall be the supreme law of the land; and the judges in every State shall be bound thereby, any thing in the Constitution or laws of any State to the contrary notwithstanding.

3. The senators and representatives before mentioned, and the members of the several State legislatures, and all executive and judicial officers, both

---

[8]See the Fourteenth Amendment, Sec. 1.
[9]See the Thirteenth Amendment.

[10]See the Fourteenth Amendment, Sec. 4.

of the United States and of the several States, shall be bound by oath or affirmation to support this Constitution; but no religious test shall ever be required as a qualification to any office or public trust under the United States.

Article VII

The ratification of the conventions of nine States shall be sufficient for the establishment of this Constitution between the States so ratifying the same.

Done in Convention by the unanimous consent of the States present the seventeenth day of September in the year of our Lord one thousand seven hundred and eighty-seven, and of the independence of the United States of America the twelfth. In witness whereof we have hereunto subscribed our names.

Articles in addition to, and amendment of, the Constitution of the United States of America, proposed by Congress, and ratified by the legislatures of the several States, pursuant to the fifth article of the original Constitution.

Amendment I

[First ten amendments ratified December 15, 1791]
Congress shall make no law respecting an establishment of religion, or prohibiting the free exercise thereof; or abridging the freedom of speech, or of the press; or the right of the people peaceably to assemble, and to petition the government for a redress of grievances.

Amendment II

A well regulated militia, being necessary to the security of a free State, the right of the people to keep and bear arms, shall not be infringed.

Amendment III

No soldier shall, in time of peace be quartered in any house, without the consent of the owner, nor in time of war, but in a manner to be prescribed by law.

Amendment IV

The right of the people to be secure in their persons, houses, papers, and effects, against unreasonable searches and seizures, shall not be violated, and no warrants shall issue, but upon probable cause, supported by oath or affirmation, and particularly describing the place to be searched, and the persons or things to be seized.

Amendment V

No person shall be held to answer for a capital or otherwise infamous crime, unless on a presentment or indictment of a grand jury, except in cases arising in the land or naval forces, or in the militia, when in actual service in time of war or public danger; nor shall any person be subject for the same offense to be twice put in jeopardy of life or limb; nor shall be compelled in any criminal case to be a witness against himself, nor be deprived of life, liberty, or property, without due process of law; nor shall private property be taken for public use, without just compensation.

Amendment VI

In all criminal prosecutions, the accused shall enjoy the right to a speedy and public trial, by an impartial jury of the State and district wherein the crime shall have been committed, which district shall have been previously ascertained by law, and to be informed of the nature and cause of the accusation; to be confronted with the witnesses against him; to have compulsory process for obtaining witnesses in his favor, and to have the assistance of counsel for his defense.

Amendment VII

In suits at common law, where the value in controversy shall exceed twenty dollars, the right of trial by jury shall be preserved, and no fact tried by a jury shall be otherwise reexamined in any court of the United States, than according to the rules of the common law.

Amendment VIII

Excessive bail shall not be required, nor excessive fines imposed, nor cruel and unusual punishments inflicted.

Amendment IX

The enumeration in the Constitution of certain rights shall not be construed to deny or disparage others retained by the people.

Amendment X

The powers not delegated to the United States by the Constitution, nor prohibited by it to the States, are reserved to the States respectively, or to the people.

Amendment XI [January 8, 1798]

The judicial power of the United States shall not be construed to extend to any suit in law or equity, commended or prosecuted against one of the United States by citizens of another State, or by citizens or subjects of any foreign State.

Amendment XII [September 25, 1804]

The electors shall meet in their respective States, and vote by ballot for President and Vice President, one of whom, at least, shall not be an inhabitant of the same State with themselves; they shall name in their ballots the person voted for as President, and in distinct ballots, the person voted for as Vice President, and they shall make distinct lists of all persons voted for as President and of all persons voted for as Vice President, and of the number of votes for each, which lists they shall sign and certify, and transmit sealed to the seat of the government of the United States, directed to the President of the Senate;—The President of the Senate shall, in the presence of the Senate and House of Representatives, open all the certificates and the votes shall then be counted;—The person having the greatest number of votes for President, shall be the President, if such number be a majority of the whole number of electors appointed; and if no person have such majority, then from the persons having the highest numbers not exceeding three on the list of those voted for as President, the House of Representatives shall choose immediately, by ballot, the President. But in choosing the President, the votes shall be taken by States, the representation from each State having one vote; a quorum for this purpose shall consist of a member or members from two thirds of the States, and a majority of all the States shall be necessary to a choice. And if the House of Representatives shall not choose a President whenever the right of choice shall devolve upon them, before the fourth day of March next following, then the Vice President shall act as President, as in the case of the death or other constitutional disability of the President. The person having the greatest number of votes as Vice President shall be the Vice President, if such number be a majority of the whole number of electors appointed, and if no person have a majority, then from the two highest numbers on the list, the Senate shall choose the Vice President; a quorum for the purpose shall consist of two thirds of the whole number of Senators, and a majority of the whole number shall be necessary to a choice. But no person constitutionally ineligible to the office of president shall be eligible to that of Vice President of the United States.

Amendment XIII [December 18, 1865]

SECTION 1. Neither slavery nor involuntary servitude, except as punishment for crime whereof the party shall have been duly convicted, shall exist within the United States, or any place subject to their jurisdiction.

SECTION 2. Congress shall have power to enforce this article by appropriate legislation.

Amendment XIV [July 28, 1868]

SECTION 1. All persons born or naturalized in the United States, and subject to the jurisdiction thereof, are citizens of the United States and of the State wherein they reside. No State shall make or enforce any law which shall abridge the privileges or immunities of citizens of the United States; nor shall any State deprive any person of life, liberty, or property, without due process of law; nor deny to any person within its jurisdiction the equal protection of the laws.

SECTION 2. Representatives shall be apportioned among the several States according to their respective numbers, counting the whole number of persons in each State, excluding Indians not taxed. But when the right to vote at any election for the choice of electors for President and Vice President of the United States, representatives in Congress, the executive and judicial officers of a State, or the members of the legislature thereof, is denied to any of the male inhabitants of such State, being twenty-one years of age, and citizens of the United States, or in any way abridged, except for participating in rebellion, or other crime, the basis of representation there shall be reduced in the proportion which the number of such male citizens shall bear to the whole number of male citizens twenty-one years of age in such State.

SECTION 3. No person shall be a senator or representative in Congress, or elector of President and Vice President, or hold any office, civil or military, under the United States, or under any State, who having previously taken an oath, as a member of Congress, or as an officer of the United States, or as a member of any State legislature, or as an executive or judicial officer of any State, to support the Constitution of the United States, shall have engaged in insurrection or rebellion against the same, or given aid or comfort to the enemies thereof. But Congress may by a vote of two thirds of each House, remove such disability.

SECTION 4. The validity of the public debt of the United States, authorized by law, including debts incurred for payment of pensions and bounties for services in suppressing insurrection or rebellion; shall not be questioned. But neither the United States nor any State shall assume or pay any debt or obligation incurred in aid of insurrection or rebellion against the United States, or any claim for the loss or emancipation of any slave; but all such debts, obligations, and claims shall be held illegal and void.

SECTION 5. The Congress shall have the power to enforce, by appropriate legislation, the provisions of this article.

Amendment XV [March 30, 1870]

SECTION 1. The right of citizens of the United States to vote shall not be denied or abridged by the United States or by any State on account of race, color, or previous condition of servitude.

SECTION 2. The Congress shall have power to enforce this article by appropriate legislation.

Amendment XVI [February 25, 1913]

The Congress shall have power to lay and collect taxes on incomes, from whatever source derived, without apportionment among the several States, and without regard to any census or enumeration.

Amendment XVII [May 31, 1913]

The Senate of the United States shall be composed of two senators from each State, elected by the people thereof, for six years; and each senator shall have one vote. The electors in each State shall have the qualifications requisite for electors of the most numerous branch of the State legislature.

When vacancies happen in the representation of any State in the Senate, the executive authority of such State shall issue writs of election to fill such vacancies: *Provided,* That the legislature of any State may empower the executive thereof to make temporary appointments until the people fill the vacancies by election as the legislature may direct.

This amendment shall not be so construed as to affect the election or term of any senator chosen before it becomes valid as part of the Constitution.

Amendment XVIII[11] [January 29, 1919]

After one year from the ratification of this article, the manufacture, sale, or transportation of intoxicating liquors within, the importation thereof into, or the exportation thereof from the United States and all territory subject to the jurisdiction thereof for beverage purposes is thereby prohibited.

The Congress and the several States shall have concurrent power to enforce this article by appropriate legislation.

This article shall be inoperative unless it shall have been ratified as an amendment to the Constitution by the legislatures of the several States, as provided in the Constitution, within seven years from the date of the submission hereof to the States by Congress.

Amendment XIX [August 26, 1920]

The right of citizens of the United States to vote shall not be denied or abridged by the United States or by any State on account of sex.

Congress shall have the power to enforce this article by appropriate legislation.

Amendment XX [January 23, 1933]

SECTION 1. The terms of the President and Vice President shall end at noon on the 20th day of January and the terms of Senators and Representatives at noon on the 3d day of January, of the years in which such terms would have ended if this article had not been ratified; and the terms of their successors shall then begin.

SECTION 2. The Congress shall assemble at least once in every year, and such meeting shall begin at noon on the 3d day of January, unless they shall by law appoint a different day.

SECTION 3. If, at the time fixed for the beginning of the term of president, the President-elect shall have died, the Vice President-elect shall become President. If a President shall not have been chosen before the time fixed for the beginning of his term, or if the President-elect shall have failed to qualify, then the Vice President-elect shall act as president until a President shall have qualified; and the Congress may by law provide for the case wherein neither a President-elect nor a Vice President-elect shall have qualified, declaring who shall then act as President, or the manner in which one who is to act shall be selected, and such person shall act accordingly until a President or Vice President shall have qualified.

SECTION 4. The Congress may by law provide for the case of the death of any of the persons from whom, the House of Representatives may choose a President whenever the right of choice shall have devolved upon them, and for the case of the death of any of the persons from whom the Senate may choose a Vice President whenever the right of choice shall have devolved upon them.

SECTION 5. Sections 1 and 2 shall take effect on the 15th day of October following the ratification of this article.

SECTION 6. This article shall be inoperative unless it shall have been ratified as an amendment to the Constitution by the legislatures of three-fourths of the several States within seven years from the date of its submission.

Amendment XXI [December 5, 1933]

SECTION 1. The Eighteenth Article of amendment to the Constitution of the United States is hereby repealed.

SECTION 2. The transportation or importation into any State, Territory, or possession of the United States for delivery or use therein of intoxicating liquors in violation of the laws thereof, is hereby prohibited.

SECTION 3. This article shall be inoperative unless it shall have been ratified as an amendment to the Constitution by conventions in the several States, as provided in the Consitution, within seven years from the date of the submission thereof to the States by the Congress.

---

[11]Repealed by the Twenty-first Amendment.

Amendment XXII [March 1, 1951]

No person shall be elected to the office of the President more than twice, and no person who has held the office of President, or acted as President, for more than two years of a term to which some other person was elected President shall be elected to the office of the President more than once.

But this article shall not apply to any person holding the office of President when this article was proposed by the Congress, and shall not prevent any person who may be holding the office of President, or acting as President, during the term within which this article becomes operative from holding the office of President or acting as President during the remainder of such term.

This article shall be inoperative unless it shall have been ratified as an amendment to the Constitution by the legislatures of three-fourths of the several States within seven years from the date of its submission to the States by the Congress.

Amendment XXIII [March 29, 1961]

SECTION 1. The District constituting the seat of Government of the United States shall appoint in such manner as the Congress may direct.

A number of electors of President and Vice President equal to the whole number of Senators and Representatives in Congress to which the District would be entitled if it were a State, but in no event more than the least populous State; they shall be in addition to those appointed by the States, but they shall be considered, for the purposes of the election of President and Vice Present, to be electors appointed by a State; and they shall meet in the District and perform such duties as provided by the twelfth article of amendment.

SECTION 2. The Congress shall have power to enforce this article by appropriate legislation.

Amendment XXIV [January 23, 1964]

SECTION 1. The right of citizens of the United States to vote in any primary or other election for President or Vice President, for electors for President or Vice President, or for Senator or Representative in Congress, shall not be denied or abridged by the United States or any State by reason of failure to pay any poll tax or other tax.

SECTION 2. The Congress shall have power to enforce this article by appropriate legislation.

Amendment XXV [February 10, 1967]

SECTION 1. In case of the removal of the President from office or of his death or resignation, the Vice President shall become President.

SECTION 2. Whenever there is a vacancy in the office of the Vice President, the President shall nominate a Vice President who shall take office upon confirmation by a majority of both Houses of Congress.

SECTION 3. Whenever the President transmits to the President pro tempore of the Senate and the Speaker of the House of Representatives his written declaration that he is unable to discharge the powers and duties of his office, and until he transmits to them a written declaration to the contrary, such powers and duties shall be discharged by the Vice President as Acting President.

SECTION 4. Whenever the Vice President and a majority of either the principal officers of the executive departments or of such other body as Congress may by law provide, transmit to the President pro tempore of the Senate and the Speaker of the House of Representatives their written declaration that the President is unable to discharge the powers and duties of his office, the Vice President shall immediately assume the powers and duties of the office as Acting President.

Thereafter, when the President transmits to the President pro tempore of the Senate and the Speaker of the House of Representatives his written declaration that no inability exists, he shall resume the powers and duties of his office unless the Vice President and a majority of either the principal officers of the executive departments or of such other body as Congress may by law provide, transmit within four days to the President pro tempore of the Senate and the Speaker of the House of Representatives their written declaration that the President is unable to discharge the powers and duties of his office. Thereupon Congress shall decide the issue, assembling within forty-eight hours for that purpose if not in session. If the Congress, within twenty-one days after receipt of the latter written declaration, or, if Congress is not in session, within twenty-one days after Congress is required to assemble, determines by two-thirds vote of both houses that the President is unable to discharge the powers and duties of his office, the Vice President shall continue to discharge the same as Acting President; otherwise, the President shall resume the powers and duties of his office.

Amendment XXVI [June 30, 1971]

SECTION 1. The right of citizens of the United States who are eighteen years of age or older to vote shall not be denied or abridged by the United States or by any State on account of age.

SECTION 2. The Congress shall have power to enforce this article by appropriate legislation.

Presidents and Vice Presidents

1. George Washington (1789)
   John Adams (1789)

2. John Adams (1797)
   Thomas Jefferson (1797)

3. Thomas Jefferson (1801)
   Aaron Burr (1801)
   George Clinton (1805)

4. James Madison (1809)
   George Clinton (1809)
   Elbridge Gerry (1813)

5. James Monroe (1817)
   Daniel D. Tompkins (1817)

6. John Quincy Adams (1825)
   John C. Calhoun (1825)

7. Andrew Jackson (1829)
   John C. Calhoun (1829)
   Martin Van Buren (1833)

8. Martin Van Buren (1837)
   Richard M. Johnson (1837)

9. William H. Harrison (1841)
   John Tyler (1841)

10. John Tyler (1841)

11. James K. Polk (1845)
    George M. Dallas (1845)

12. Zachary Taylor (1849)
    Millard Fillmore (1849)

13. Millard Fillmore (1850)

14. Franklin Pierce (1853)
    William R. King (1853)

15. James Buchanan (1857)
    John C. Breckinridge (1857)

16. Abraham Lincoln (1861)
    Hannibal Hamlin (1861)
    Andrew Johnson (1865)

17. Andrew Johnson (1865)

18. Ulysses S. Grant (1869)
    Schuyler Colfax (1869)
    Henry Wilson (1873)

19. Rutherford B. Hayes (1877)
    William A. Wheeler (1877)

20. James A. Garfield (1881)
    Chester A. Arthur (1881)

21. Chester A. Arthur (1881)

22. Grover Cleveland (1885)
    T. A. Hendricks (1885)

23. Benjamin Harrison (1889)
    Levi P. Morton (1889)

24. Grover Cleveland (1893)
    Adlai E. Stevenson (1893)

25. William McKinley (1897)
    Garret A. Hobart (1897)
    Theodore Roosevelt (1901)

26. Theodore Roosevelt (1901)
    Charles Fairbanks (1905)

27. William H. Taft (1909)
    James S. Sherman (1909)

28. Woodrow Wilson (1913)
    Thomas R. Marshall (1913)

29. Warren G. Harding (1921)
    Calvin Coolidge (1921)

30. Calvin Coolidge (1923)
    Charles G. Dawes (1925)

31. Herbert C. Hoover (1929)
    Charles Curtis (1929)

32. Franklin D. Roosevelt (1933)
    John Nance Garner (1933)
    Henry A. Wallace (1941)
    Harry S Truman (1945)

33. Harry S Truman (1945)
    Alben W. Barkley (1949)

34. Dwight D. Eisenhower (1953)
    Richard M. Nixon (1953)

35. John F. Kennedy (1961)
    Lyndon B. Johnson (1961)

36. Lyndon B. Johnson (1963)
    Hubert H. Humphrey (1965)

37. Richard M. Nixon (1969)
    Spiro T. Agnew (1969)
    Gerald R. Ford (1973)

38. Gerald R. Ford (1974)
    Nelson A. Rockefeller (1974)

39. James E. Carter Jr. (1977)
    Walter F. Mondale (1977)

40. Ronald W. Reagan (1981)
    George H. W. Bush (1981)

41. George H. W. Bush (1989)
    James D. Quayle III (1989)

42. William J. B. Clinton (1993)
    Albert Gore (1993)

43. George W. Bush (2001)
    Richard Cheney (2001)

Presidential Elections

Year	Number of States	Candidates	Party	Popular Vote*	Electoral Vote[†]	Percentage of Popular Vote
1789	11	GEORGE WASHINGTON	No party designations		69	
		John Adams			34	
		Other Candidates			35	
1792	15	GEORGE WASHINGTON	No party designations		132	
		John Adams			77	
		George Clinton			50	
		Other Candidates			5	
1796	16	JOHN ADAMS	Federalist		71	
		Thomas Jefferson	Democratic Republican		68	
		Thomas Pinckney	Federalist		59	
		Aaron Burr	Democratic Republican		30	
		Other Candidates			48	
1800	16	THOMAS JEFFERSON	Democratic Republican		73	
		Aaron Burr	Democratic Republican		73	
		John Adams	Federalist		65	
		Charles C. Pinckney	Federalist		64	
		John Jay	Federalist		1	
1804	17	THOMAS JEFFERSON	Democratic Republican		162	
		Charles C. Pinckney	Federalist		14	
1808	17	JAMES MADISON	Democratic Republican		122	
		Charles C. Pinckney	Federalist		47	
		George Clinton	Democratic Republican		6	
1812	18	JAMES MADISON	Democratic Republican		128	
		DeWitt Clinton	Federalist		89	
1816	19	JAMES MONROE	Democratic Republican		183	
		Rufus King	Federalist		34	
1820	24	JAMES MONROE	Democratic Republican		231	
		John Quincy Adams	Independent Republican		1	
1824	24	JOHN QUINCY ADAMS		108,740	84	30.5
		Andrew Jackson		153,544	99	43.1
		William H. Crawford		46,618	41	13.1
		Henry Clay		47,136	37	13.2
1828	24	ANDREW JACKSON	Democrat	647,286	178	56.0
		John Quincy Adams	National Republican	508,064	83	44.0
1832	24	ANDREW JACKSON	Democrat	687,502	219	55.0
		Henry Clay	National Republican	530,189	49	42.4
		William Wirt	Anti-Masonic	33,108	7	2.6
		John Floyd	National Republican		11	

*Percentage of popular vote given for any election year may not total 100 percent because candidates receiving less than 1 percent of the popular vote have been omitted.

[†]Prior to the passage of the Twelfth Amendment in 1904, the electoral college voted for two presidential candidates; the runner-up became Vice-President. Data from Historical Statistics of the United States, Colonial Times to 1957 (1961), pp. 682–683, and The World Almanac.

Presidential Elections
(continued)

Year	Number of States	Candidates	Party	Popular Vote	Electoral Vote	Percentage of Popular Vote
1836	26	MARTIN VAN BUREN	Democrat	765,483	170	50.9
		William H. Harrison	Whig		73	
		Hugh L. White	Whig		26	
		Daniel Webster	Whig	739,795	14	49.1
		W. P. Mangum	Whig		11	
1840	26	WILLIAM H. HARRISON	Whig	1,274,624	234	53.1
		Martin Van Buren	Democrat	1,127,781	60	46.9
1844	26	JAMES K. POLK	Democrat	1,338,464	170	49.6
		Henry Clay	Whig	1,300,097	105	48.1
		James G. Birney	Liberty	62,300		2.3
1848	30	ZACHARY TAYLOR	Whig	1,360,967	163	47.4
		Lewis Cass	Democrat	1,222,342	127	42.5
		Martin Van Buren	Free Soil	291,263		10.1
1852	31	FRANKLIN PIERCE	Democrat	1,601,117	254	50.9
		Winfield Scott	Whig	1,385,453	42	44.1
		John P. Hale	Free Soil	155,825		5.0
1856	31	JAMES BUCHANAN	Democrat	1,832,955	174	45.3
		John C. Frémont	Republican	1,339,932	114	33.1
		Millard Fillmore	American ("Know Nothing")	871,731	8	21.6
1860	33	ABRAHAM LINCOLN	Republican	1,865,593	180	39.8
		Stephen A. Douglas	Democrat	1,382,713	12	29.5
		John C. Breckinridge	Democrat	848,356	72	18.1
		John Bell	Constitutional Union	592,906	39	12.6
1864	36	ABRAHAM LINCOLN	Republican	2,206,938	212	55.0
		George B. McClellan	Democrat	1,803,787	21	45.0
1868	37	ULYSSES S. GRANT	Republican	3,013,421	214	52.7
		Horatio Seymour	Democrat	2,706,829	80	47.3
1872	37	ULYSSES S. GRANT	Republican	3,596,745	286	55.6
		Horace Greeley	Democrat	2,843,446	*	43.9
1876	38	RUTHERFORD B. HAYES	Republican	4,036,572	185	48.0
		Samuel J. Tilden	Democrat	4,284,020	184	51.0
1880	38	JAMES A. GARFIELD	Republican	4,453,295	214	48.5
		Winfield S. Hancock	Democrat	4,414,082	155	48.1
		James B. Weaver	Greenback-Labor	308,578		3.4
1884	38	GROVER CLEVELAND	Democrat	4,879,507	219	48.5
		James G. Blaine	Republican	4,850,293	182	48.2
		Benjamin F. Butler	Greenback-Labor	175,370		1.8
		John P. St. John	Prohibition	150,369		1.5
1888	38	BENJAMIN HARRISON	Republican	5,447,129	233	47.9
		Grover Cleveland	Democrat	5,537,857	168	48.6
		Clinton B. Fisk	Prohibition	249,506		2.2
		Alson J. Streeter	Union Labor	146,935		1.3

Because of the death of Greeley, Democratic electors scattered their votes.

Presidential Elections
(continued)

Year	Number of States	Candidates	Party	Popular Vote	Electoral Vote	Percentage of Popular Vote
1892	44	GROVER CLEVELAND	Democrat	5,555,426	277	46.1
		Benjamin Harrison	Republican	5,182,690	145	43.0
		James B. Weaver	People's	1,029,846	22	8.5
		John Bidwell	Prohibition	264,133		2.2
1896	45	WILLIAM MCKINLEY	Republican	7,102,246	271	51.1
		William J. Bryan	Democrat	6,492,559	176	47.7
1900	45	WILLIAM MCKINLEY	Republican	7,218,491	292	51.7
		William J. Bryan	Democrat; Populist	6,356,734	155	45.5
		John C. Woolley	Prohibition	208,914		1.5
1904	45	THEODORE ROOSEVELT	Republican	7,628,461	336	57.4
		Alton B. Parker	Democrat	5,084,223	140	37.6
		Eugene V. Debs	Socialist	402,283		3.0
		Silas C. Swallow	Prohibition	258,536		1.9
1908	46	WILLIAM H. TAFT	Republican	7,675,320	321	51.6
		William J. Bryan	Democrat	6,412,294	162	43.1
		Eugene V. Debs	Socialist	420,793		2.8
		Eugene W. Chafin	Prohibition	253,840		1.7
1912	48	WOODROW WILSON	Democrat	6,296,547	435	41.9
		Theodore Roosevelt	Progressive	4,118,571	88	27.4
		William H. Taft	Republican	3,486,720	8	23.2
		Eugene V. Debs	Socialist	900,672		6.0
		Eugene W. Chafin	Prohibition	206,275		1.4
1916	48	WOODROW WILSON	Democrat	9,127,695	277	49.4
		Charles E. Hughes	Republican	8,533,507	254	46.2
		A. L. Benson	Socialist	585,113		3.2
		J. Frank Hanly	Prohibition	220,506		1.2
1920	48	WARREN G. HARDING	Republican	16,143,407	404	60.4
		James M. Cox	Democrat	9,130,328	127	34.2
		Eugene V. Debs	Socialist	919,799		3.4
		P. P. Christensen	Farmer-Labor	265,411		1.0
1924	48	CALVIN COOLIDGE	Republican	15,718,211	382	54.0
		John W. Davis	Democrat	8,385,283	136	28.8
		Robert M. La Follette	Progressive	4,831,289	13	16.6
1928	48	HERBERT C. HOOVER	Republican	21,391,993	444	58.2
		Alfred E. Smith	Democrat	15,016,169	87	40.9
1932	48	FRANKLIN D. ROOSEVELT	Democrat	22,809,638	472	57.4
		Herbert C. Hoover	Republican	15,758,901	59	39.7
		Norman Thomas	Socialist	881,951		2.2
1936	48	FRANKLIN D. ROOSEVELT	Democrat	27,752,869	523	60.8
		Alfred M. Landon	Republican	16,674,665	8	36.5
		William Lemke	Union	882,479		1.9
1940	48	FRANKLIN D. ROOSEVELT	Democrat	27,307,819	449	54.8
		Wendell L. Willkie	Republican	22,321,018	82	44.8
1944	48	FRANKLIN D. ROOSEVELT	Democrat	25,606,585	432	53.5
		Thomas E. Dewey	Republican	22,014,745	99	46.0

Presidential Elections
(continued)

Year	Number of States	Candidates	Party	Popular Vote	Electoral Vote	Percentage of Popular Vote
1948	48	HARRY S TRUMAN	Democrat	24,105,812	303	49.5
		Thomas E. Dewey	Republican	21,970,065	189	45.1
		J. Strom Thurmond	States' Rights	1,169,063	39	2.4
		Henry A. Wallace	Progressive	1,157,172		2.4
1952	48	DWIGHT D. EISENHOWER	Republican	33,936,234	442	55.1
		Adlai E. Stevenson	Democrat	27,314,992	89	44.4
1956	48	DWIGHT D. EISENHOWER	Republican	35,590,472	457*	57.6
		Adlai E. Stevenson	Democrat	26,022,752	73	42.1
1960	50	JOHN F. KENNEDY	Democrat	34,227,096	303†	49.9
		Richard M. Nixon	Republican	34,108,546	219	49.6
1964	50	LYNDON B. JOHNSON	Democrat	42,676,220	486	61.3
		Barry M. Goldwater	Republican	26,860,314	52	38.5
1968	50	RICHARD M. NIXON	Republican	31,785,480	301	43.4
		Hubert H. Humphrey	Democrat	31,275,165	191	42.7
		George C. Wallace	American Independent	9,906,473	46	13.5
1972	50	RICHARD M. NIXON‡	Republican	47,165,234	520	60.6
		George S. McGovern	Democrat	29,168,110	17	37.5
1976	50	JIMMY CARTER	Democrat	40,828,929	297	50.1
		Gerald R. Ford	Republican	39,148,940	240	47.9
		Eugene McCarthy	Independent	739,256		0.9
1980	50	RONALD REAGAN	Republican	43,201,220	489	50.9
		Jimmy Carter	Democrat	34,913,332	49	41.2
		John B. Anderson	Independent	5,581,379		6.6
1984	50	RONALD REAGAN	Republican	53,428,357	525	59.0
		Walter F. Mondale	Democrat	36,930,923	13	41.0
1988	50	GEORGE H. W. BUSH	Republican	48,901,046	426	53.4
		Michael Dukakis	Democrat	41,809,030	111	45.6
1992	50	BILL CLINTON	Democrat	43,728,275	370	43.2
		George Bush	Republican	38,167,416	168	37.7
		H. Ross Perot	United We Stand, America	19,237,247		19.0
1996	50	BILL CLINTON	Democrat	45,590,703	379	49.0
		Bob Dole	Republican	37,816,307	159	41.0
		H. Ross Perot	Reform	7,866,284		8.0
2000	50	GEORGE W. BUSH	Republican	50,456,169	271	48.0
		Al Gore	Democrat	50,996,116	266	48.0
		Ralph Nader	Green	2,767,176	0	3.0

*Walter B. Jones received 1 electoral vote.

†Harry F. Byrd received 15 electoral votes.

‡Resigned August 9, 1974: Vice President Gerald R. Ford became President.

Admission of States into the Union

State	Date of Admission	State	Date of Admission
1. Delaware	December 7, 1787	26. Michigan	January 26, 1837
2. Pennsylvania	December 12, 1787	27. Florida	March 3, 1845
3. New Jersey	December 18, 1787	28. Texas	December 29, 1845
4. Georgia	January 2, 1788	29. Iowa	December 28, 1846
5. Connecticut	January 9, 1788	30. Wisconsin	May 29, 1848
6. Massachusetts	February 6, 1788	31. California	September 9, 1850
7. Maryland	April 28, 1788	32. Minnesota	May 11, 1858
8. South Carolina	May 23, 1788	33. Oregon	February 14, 1859
9. New Hampshire	June 21, 1788	34. Kansas	January 29, 1861
10. Virginia	June 25, 1788	35. West Virginia	June 20, 1863
11. New York	July 26, 1788	36. Nevada	October 31, 1864
12. North Carolina	November 21, 1789	37. Nebraska	March 1, 1867
13. Rhode Island	May 29, 1790	38. Colorado	August 1, 1876
14. Vermont	March 4, 1791	39. North Dakota	November 2, 1889
15. Kentucky	June 1, 1792	40. South Dakota	November 2, 1889
16. Tennessee	June 1, 1796	41. Montana	November 8, 1889
17. Ohio	March 1, 1803	42. Washington	November 11, 1889
18. Louisiana	April 30, 1812	43. Idaho	July 3, 1890
19. Indiana	December 11, 1816	44. Wyoming	July 10, 1890
20. Mississippi	December 10, 1817	45. Utah	January 4, 1896
21. Illinois	December 3, 1818	46. Oklahoma	November 16, 1907
22. Alabama	December 14, 1819	47. New Mexico	January 6, 1912
23. Maine	March 15, 1820	48. Arizona	February 14, 1912
24. Missouri	August 10, 1821	49. Alaska	January 3, 1959
25. Arkansas	June 15, 1836	50. Hawaii	August 21, 1959

DEMOGRAPHICS OF THE UNITED STATES

Population Growth

Year	Population	Percent Increase
1630	4,600	
1640	26,600	478.3
1650	50,400	90.8
1660	75,100	49.0
1670	111,900	49.0
1680	151,500	35.4
1690	210,400	38.9
1700	250,900	19.2
1710	331,700	32.2
1720	466,200	40.5
1730	629,400	35.0
1740	905,600	43.9
1750	1,170,800	29.3
1760	1,593,600	36.1
1770	2,148,100	34.8
1780	2,780,400	29.4
1790	3,929,214	41.3
1800	5,308,483	35.1
1810	7,239,881	36.4
1820	9,638,453	33.1
1830	12,866,020	33.5
1840	17,069,453	32.7
1850	23,191,876	35.9
1860	31,443,321	35.6
1870	39,818,449	26.6
1880	50,155,783	26.0
1890	62,947,714	25.5
1900	75,994,575	20.7
1910	91,972,266	21.0
1920	105,710,620	14.9
1930	122,775,046	16.1
1940	131,669,275	7.2
1950	150,697,361	14.5
1960	179,323,175	19.0
1970	203,235,298	13.3
1980	226,545,805	11.5
1990	248,709,873	9.8
2000	281,421,906	9.0

Source: *Historical Statistics of the United States* (1975); *Statistical Abstract of the United States* (1991); Population Estimates Program, Population Division, U.S. Census Bureau, April 2001.
Note: Figures for 1630–1780 include British colonies within limits of present United States only; Native-American population included only in 1930 and thereafter.

Immigration, by origin
(in thousands)

Period	Europe	Americas	Asia
1820–30	106	12	—
1831–40	496	33	—
1841–50	1,597	62	—
1851–60	2,453	75	42
1861–70	2,065	167	65
1871–80	2,272	404	70
1881–90	4,735	427	70
1891–1900	3,555	39	75
1901–10	8,065	362	324
1911–20	4,322	1,144	247
1921–30	2,463	1,517	112
1931–40	348	160	16
1941–50	621	355	32
1951–60	1,326	997	150
1961–70	1,123	1,716	590
1971–80	800	1,983	1,588
1981–90	762	3,616	2,738
1991–2000	1,100	3,800	2,200

Source: *Historical Statistics of the United States* (1975); *Statistical Abstract of the United States* (1991); Population Estimates Program, Population Division, U.S. Census Bureau, April 2001.

Racial Composition of the Population
(in thousands)

Year	White	Black	Indian	Hispanic	Asian
1790	3,172	757	(NA)	(NA)	(NA)
1800	4,306	1,002	(NA)	(NA)	(NA)
1820	7,867	1,772	(NA)	(NA)	(NA)
1840	14,196	2,874	(NA)	(NA)	(NA)
1860	26,923	4,442	(NA)	(NA)	(NA)
1880	43,403	6,581	(NA)	(NA)	(NA)
1900	66,809	8,834	(NA)	(NA)	(NA)
1910	81,732	9,828	(NA)	(NA)	(NA)
1920	94,821	10,463	(NA)	(NA)	(NA)
1930	110,287	11,891	(NA)	(NA)	(NA)
1940	118,215	12,866	(NA)	(NA)	(NA)
1950	134,942	15,042	(NA)	(NA)	(NA)
1960	158,832	18,872	(NA)	(NA)	(NA)
1970	178,098	22,581	(NA)	(NA)	(NA)
1980	194,713	26,683	1,420	14,609	3,729
1990	208,704	30,483	2,065	22,354	7,458
2000	226,861	35,470	2,448	31,387	11,279

Source: *U.S. Bureau of the Census, U.S. Census of Population: 1940, vol. II, part 1, and vol. IV, part 1; 1950, vol. II, part 1; 1960, vol. I, part 1; 1970, vol. I, part B; and Current Population Reports, P25-1095 and P25-1104; and unpublished data*; Population Estimates Program, Population Division, U.S. Census Bureau, January 2001.

Work Force

Year	Total Number Workers (1000s)	Farmers as % of Total	Women as % of Total	% Workers in Unions
1810	2,330	84	(NA)	(NA)
1840	5,660	75	(NA)	(NA)
1860	11,110	53	(NA)	(NA)
1870	12,506	53	15	(NA)
1880	17,392	52	15	(NA)
1890	23,318	43	17	(NA)
1900	29,073	40	18	3
1910	38,167	31	21	6
1920	41,614	26	21	12
1930	48,830	22	22	7
1940	53,011	17	24	27
1950	59,643	12	28	25
1960	69,877	8	32	26
1970	82,049	4	37	25
1980	108,544	3	42	23
1990	117,914	3	45	16
2000	140,900	5.5	47	18.6

Source: *Historical Statistics of the United States* (1975); *Statistical Abstract of the United States* (1991 and 1996); Population Estimates Program, Population Division, U.S. Census Bureau, April 2001.

Vital Statistics
(in thousands)

Year	Births	Deaths	Marriages	Divorces
1800	55	(NA)	(NA)	(NA)
1810	54.3	(NA)	(NA)	(NA)
1820	55.2	(NA)	(NA)	(NA)
1830	51.4	(NA)	(NA)	(NA)
1840	51.8	(NA)	(NA)	(NA)
1850	43.3	(NA)	(NA)	(NA)
1860	44.3	(NA)	(NA)	(NA)
1870	38.3	(NA)	9.6 (1867)	0.3 (1867)
1880	39.8	(NA)	9.1 (1875)	0.3 (1875)
1890	31.5	(NA)	9.0	0.5
1900	32.3	17.2	9.3	0.7
1910	30.1	14.7	10.3	0.9
1920	27.7	13.0	12.0	1.6
1930	21.3	11.3	9.2	1.6
1940	19.4	10.8	12.1	2.0
1950	24.1	9.6	11.1	2.6
1960	23.7	9.5	8.5	2.2
1970	18.4	9.5	10.6	3.5
1980	15.9	8.8	10.6	5.2
1990	16.7	8.6	9.8	4.7
2000	14.8	8.8	8.5	4.1

Source: *Historical Statistics of the United States* (1975); *Statistical Abstract of the United States* (1999) CDC 2000 National Vital Statistics Report, Vol. 49, No. 6, 8/22/01.

The Economy and Federal Spending

Year	Gross National Product (GNP) (in billions)	Foreign Trade (in millions)			Federal Budget (in billions)	Federal Surplus/Deficit (in billions)	Federal Debt (in billions)
		Exports	Imports	Balance of Trade			
1790	(NA)	$ 20	$ 23	$ −3	$ 0.004	$+0.00015	$ 0.076
1800	(NA)	71	91	−20	0.011	+0.0006	0.083
1810	(NA)	67	85	−18	0.008	+0.0012	0.053
1820	(NA)	70	74	−4	0.018	−0.0004	0.091
1830	(NA)	74	71	+3	0.015	+0.100	0.049
1840	(NA)	132	107	+25	0.024	−0.005	0.004
1850	(NA)	152	178	−26	0.040	+0.004	0.064
1860	(NA)	400	362	+38	0.063	−0.01	0.065
1870	$ 7.4	451	462	−11	0.310	+0.10	2.4
1880	11.2	853	761	+92	0.268	+0.07	2.1
1890	13.1	910	823	+87	0.318	+0.09	1.2
1900	18.7	1,499	930	+569	0.521	+0.05	1.2
1910	35.3	1,919	1,646	+273	0.694	−0.02	1.1
1920	91.5	8,664	5,784	+2,880	6.357	+0.3	24.3
1930	90.7	4,013	3,500	+513	3.320	+0.7	16.3
1940	100.0	4,030	7,433	−3,403	9.6	−2.7	43.0
1950	286.5	10,816	9,125	+1,691	43.1	−2.2	257.4
1960	506.5	19,600	15,046	+4,554	92.2	+0.3	286.3
1970	992.7	42,700	40,189	+2,511	195.6	−2.8	371.0
1980	2,631.7	220,783	244,871	−24,088	590.9	−73.8	907.7
1990	5,524.5	394,030	494,042	−100,012	1,251.8	−220.5	3,233.3
2000	9,860.8	773,304	1,222,772	−449,468	1,765.7	+117.3	5,686.0

Source: *U.S. Office of Management and Budget, Budget of the United States Government, annual; Statistical Abstract of the United States, 2000.*

GLOSSARY

Arminianism Religious doctrine developed by the Dutch theologian Jacobus Arminius that argued that men and women had free will and suggested that hence they could earn their way into heaven by good works.

Armistice A cessation of hostilities by agreement among the opposing sides; a cease-fire.

Associationalism President Herbert Hoover's preferred method of responding to the depression. Rather than have the government directly involve itself in the economy, Hoover hoped to use the government to bring together "associations" of businessmen to cooperate with one another in responding to the economic crisis.

Autarky At the height of the world depression, industrial powers sought to isolate their economies within self-contained spheres, generally governed by rigid national (or imperial) economic planning. Japan's Co-Prosperity Sphere, the Soviet Union, and the British Empire each comprised a more or less closed economic unit. The goal of these autarkies was to build an internal market while reducing trade with the outside world.

Benevolent Empire The loosely affiliated network of charitable reform associations that emerged in the United States (especially in urban areas) in response to widespread revivalism of the early nineteenth century.

Berdache In Indian societies, a man who dressed and adopted the mannerisms of women and had sex only with other men. In Native American culture, the *berdache*, half man and half woman, symbolized cosmic harmony.

Budget deficit The failure of tax revenues to pay for annual federal spending on military, welfare, and other programs. The resulting budget deficits forced Washington to borrow money to cover its costs. The growing budget deficits were controversial, in part because the government's borrowing increased both its long-term debt and the amount of money it had to spend each year to pay for the interest on loans.

Busing The controversial, court-ordered practice of sending children by bus to public schools outside their neighborhoods in order to promote racial integration in the schools.

Calvinism Religious doctrine developed by the theologian John Calvin that argued that God alone determines who will receive salvation and hence, men and women cannot earn their own salvation or even be certain about their final destinies.

Carpetbagger A derogatory term referring to northern whites who moved to the South after the Civil War. Stereotyped as corrupt and unprincipled, "carpetbaggers" were in fact a diverse group motivated by a variety of interests and beliefs.

Charter colony Colony established by a trading company or other group of private entrepreneurs who received a grant of land and the right to govern it from the king. The charter colonies included Virginia, Plymouth, Massachusetts Bay, Rhode Island, and Connecticut.

City busting As late as the 1930s, President Roosevelt and most Americans regarded attacking civilians from the air as an atrocity, but during World War II cities became a primary target for U.S. warplanes. The imprecise nature of bombardment, combined with racism and the belief that Japanese and German actions justified retaliation, led American air commanders to follow a policy of systematically destroying urban areas, particularly in Japan.

Communist Member of the Communist Party or follower of the doctrines of Karl Marx. The term (or accusation) was applied more broadly in the twentieth century to brand labor unionists, progressives, civil rights workers, and other reformers as agents of a foreign ideology.

Communitarians Individuals who supported and/or took up residence in separate communities created to embody improved plans of social, religious, and/or economic life.

Commutation The controversial policy of allowing potential draftees to pay for a replacement to serve in the Army. The policy was adopted by both the Union and Confederate governments during the Civil War, and in both cases opposition to commutation was so intense that the policy was abandoned.

Consent One of the key principles of liberalism, which held that people could not be subject to laws to which they had not given their consent. This principle is reflected in both the Declaration of Independence and the preamble to the Constitution, which begins with the famous words, "We the people of the United States, in order to form a more perfect union."

Constitutionalism A loose body of thought that developed in Britain and the colonies and was used by the colonists to justify the Revolution by claiming that it was in accord with the principles of the British Constitution. Constitutionalism had two main elements. One was the rule of law, and the other, the principle of consent, that one cannot be subjected to laws or taxation except by duly elected representatives. Both were rights that had been won through struggle with the monarch.

Consumer revolution A slow and steady increase over the course of the eighteenth century in the demand for, and purchase of, consumer goods. The consumer revolution of the eighteenth century was closely related to the *industrious revolution.*

Consumerism The emerging ideology that defined the purchase of goods and services as basic to individual identity and essential to the national economy. Increasingly powerful by the 1920s and dominant by the 1950s, consumerism urged people to find happiness in the pursuit of leisure and pleasure more than in the work ethic.

Containment The basic U.S. strategy for fighting the cold war. Used by diplomat George Kennan in a 1947 magazine article, "containment" referred to the combination of diplomatic, economic, and military programs necessary to hold back Soviet expansionism after World War II.

Cooperationists Those southerners who opposed immediate secession after the election of Abraham Lincoln in 1860. Cooperationists argued instead that secessionists should wait to see if the new president was willing to "cooperate" with the South's demands.

Copperhead A northerner who sympathized with the South during the Civil War.

Deindustrialization The reverse of industrialization, as factory shutdowns decreased the size of the manufacturing sector. Plant closings began to plague the American economy in the 1970s, prompting fears that the nation would lose its industrial base.

Democratic Republicans One of the two parties to make up the first American party system. Following the fiscal and political views of Jefferson and Madison, Democratic Republicans generally advocated a weak federal government and opposed federal intervention in the economy of the nation.

Détente This French term for the relaxation of tensions was used to describe the central foreign policy innovation of the Nixon administration—a new, less-confrontational relationship with Communism. In addition to opening a dialogue with the People's Republic of China, Nixon sought a more stable, less confrontational relationship with the Soviet Union.

Diffusion The controversial theory that the problem of slavery would be resolved if the slave economy was allowed to expand, or "diffuse," into the western territories. Southerners developed this theory as early as the 1820s in response to northerners who hoped to restrict slavery's expansion.

Disfranchisement   The act of depriving a person or group of voting rights. In the nineteenth century the right to vote was popularly known as the franchise. The Fourteenth Amendment of the Constitution affirmed the right of adult male citizens to vote, but state-imposed restrictions and taxes deprived large numbers of Americans—particularly African Americans—of the vote from the 1890s until the passage of the Voting Rights Act of 1964.

Downsizing   American corporations' layoffs of both blue- and white-collar workers in an attempt to become more efficient and competitive. Downsizing was one of the factors that made Americans uneasy about the economy, despite the impressive surge of the stock market in the 1990s.

Dust Bowl   Across much of the Great Plains decades of wasteful farming practices combined with several years of drought in the early 1930s to produce a series of massive dust storms that blew the topsoil across hundreds of miles. The expansive area afflicted by these storms became known as the Dust Bowl.

E-commerce   Short for "electronic commerce," this was the term for the internet-based buying and selling that was one of the key hopes for the computer-driven postindustrial economy. The promise of e-commerce was still unfulfilled at the start of the twenty-first century.

Encomienda   A new system of labor developed by the Spanish in the New World in which Spanish settlers (*encomenderos*) compelled groups of Native Americans to work for them. The *encomendero* owned neither the land nor the Indians who worked for him, but had the unlimited right to compel a particular group of Indians to work for him. This system was unique to the New World; nothing precisely like it had existed in Spain or elsewhere in Europe.

"Establishment"   The elite of mainly Ivy-League educated, Anglo-Saxon Protestant, male, liberal, northeasterners that supposedly dominated Wall Street and Washington after World War II. The Establishment's support for corporations, activist government, and containment engendered hostility from opposite poles of the political spectrum—from conservatives and Republicans like Richard Nixon at one end and from the New Left and the Movement at the other. Although many of the post-World War II leaders of the United States did tend to share common origins and ideologies, this elite was never as powerful, self-conscious, or unified as its opponents believed.

Eugenics   The practice of attempting to solve social problems through the control of human reproduction. Drawing on the authority of evolutionary biology, eugenists enjoyed considerable influence in the United States, especially on issues of corrections and public health, from the turn of the century through World War II. Applications of this pseudoscience included the identification of "born" criminals by physical characteristics and "better baby" contests at county fairs.

Federalists   One of the two parties to make up the first American party system. Following the fiscal and political policies proposed by Alexander Hamilton, Federalists generally advocated the importance of a strong federal government, including federal intervention in the economy of the new nation.

Feminism   An ideology insisting on the fundamental equality of women and men. The feminists of the 1960s differed over how to achieve that equality: While liberal feminists mostly demanded equal rights for women in the workplace and in politics, radical feminists more thoroughly condemned the capitalist system and male oppression and demanded equality in both private and public life.

Feudalism   A social and political system that developed in Europe in the Middle Ages under which powerful lords offered less powerful noblemen protection in return for their loyalty. Feudalism also included the economic system of *manorialism,* under which dependent serfs worked on the manors controlled by those lords.

Fire-eaters   Militant southerners who pushed for secession in the 1850s.

Flexible Response   The defense doctrine of the Kennedy and Johnson administrations. Abandoning the Eisenhower administration's heavy emphasis on nuclear weapons, Flexible Response stressed the buildup of the nation's conventional and special forces so that the president had a range of military options in response to communist aggression.

Front   Early twentieth-century mechanized wars were fought along a battle line or "front" separating the opposing sides. By World War II, tactical innovations—*blitzkreig,* parachute troops, gliders, and amphibious landings—aimed to break through, disrupt, or bypass the front, which became a more fluid boundary than the fortified trench lines of World War I. The term also acquired a political meaning, particularly for labor and the left. A coalition of parties supporting (or opposing) an agreed-upon line could be called a "popular front."

Gentility   A term without a precise meaning that represented all that was polite, civilized, refined, and fashionable. It was everything that vulgarity, its opposite, was not. Because the term had no precise meaning, it was always subject to negotiation, striving, and anxiety as Americans, beginning in the eighteenth century, tried to show others that they were *genteel* through their manners, their appearance, and their styles of life.

"Glass ceiling"   The invisible barrier of discrimination that prevented female white-collar workers from rising to top executive positions in corporations.

Greenbackers   Those who advocated currency inflation by keeping the money printed during the Civil War, known as "greenbacks," in circulation.

Gridlock   The political traffic jam that tied up the federal government in the late 1980s and 1990s. Gridlock developed from the inability of either major party to control both the presidency and Congress for any extended period of time. More fundamentally, gridlock reflected the inability of any party or president to win a popular mandate for a bold legislative program.

Horizontal integration   More commonly known as "monopoly." An industry was "horizontally integrated" when a single company took control of virtually the entire market for a specific product. John D. Rockefeller's Standard Oil came close to doing this.

Humanism   A Renaissance intellectual movement that focused upon the intellectual and artistic capacities and achievements of humankind. Under the patronage of Queen Isabel, Spain became a center of European humanism.

Immediatism   The variant of antislavery sentiment that demanded immediate (as opposed to gradual) personal and federal action against the institution of slavery. This approach is most closely associated with William Lloyd Garrison and is dated from the publication of Garrison's newspaper, the *Liberator,* in January 1831.

Imperialism   A process of extending dominion over territories beyond the national boundaries of a state. In the eighteenth century, Britain extended imperial control over North America through settlement, but in the 1890s imperial influence was generally exercised through indirect rule. Subject peoples retained some local authority while the imperial power controlled commerce and defense. Few Americans went to the Philippines as settlers, but many passed through as tourists, missionaries, business executives, officials, and soldiers.

Individualism   The social and political philosophy celebrating the central importance of the individual human being in society. Insisting on the rights of the individual in relationship to the group, individualism was one of the intellectual bases of capitalism and democracy. The resurgent individualism of the 1920s, with its emphasis on each American's freedom and fulfillment, was a critical element of the decade's emergent consumerism and Republican dominance.

Industrious revolution   Beginning in the late seventeenth century in Western Europe and extending to the North American colonies in the eighteenth century, a fundamental change in the way that people worked, as they worked harder and organized their households to produce goods that could be sold, so that they would have money to pay for the new consumer goods that they wanted.

Initiative, recall, and referendum First proposed by the People's Party's Omaha platform (1892), along with the direct election of senators and the secret ballot, as measures to subject corporate capitalism to democratic controls. Progressives, chiefly in western and midwestern states, favored them as a check on the power of state officials. The *initiative* allows legislation to be proposed by petition. The *recall* allows voters to remove public officials, and the *referendum* places new laws or constitutional amendments on the ballot for the direct approval of the voters.

Interest group An association whose members organize to exert political pressure on officials or the public. Unlike political parties, whose platforms and slates cover nearly every issue and office, an interest group focuses on a narrower list of concerns reflecting the shared outlook of its members. With the decline of popular politics around the turn of the twentieth century, business, religious, agricultural, women's, professional, neighborhood, and reform associations created a new form of political participation.

Isolationist Between World War I and World War II, the United States refused to join the League of Nations, scaled back its military commitments abroad, and sought to maintain its independence of action on foreign affairs. These policies were called isolationist, although some historians prefer the term "independent internationalist" in recognition of the United States's continuing global influence. In the late 1930s, isolationists favored policies aimed at distancing the United States from European affairs and building a national defense based on air power and hemispheric security.

Joint-stock company a form of business organization that was the forerunner to the modern corporation. The joint-stock company was used to raise both capital and labor for New World ventures. Shareholders contributed either capital or their labor for a period of years.

Judicial nationalism The use of the judiciary to assert the primacy of the national government over state and local government and the legal principle of contract over principles of local custom.

Keynesian Economics The theory, named after the great English economist John Maynard Keynes, that advocated the use of "countercyclical" fiscal policy. This meant that during good times the government should pay down the debt so that, during bad times, it could afford to stimulate the economy with deficit spending.

Liberalism A body of political thought that traces its origins to John Locke and whose chief principles are consent, freedom of conscience, and property. Liberalism held that people could not be governed except by their own consent and that the purpose of government was to protect people, as well as their property.

Linked economic development A form of economic development that ties together a variety of enterprises so that development in one stimulates development in others, for example those that provide raw materials, parts, or transportation.

Manifest Destiny A term first coined in 1845 by journalist John O'Sullivan to express the belief, widespread among antebellum Americans, that the United States was destined to expand across the North American continent to the Pacific and had an irrefutable right to the lands involved in this expansion. This belief was frequently justified on the grounds of claims to political and racial superiority.

Market revolution The term used to designate the period of the early nineteenth century, roughly 1815–1830, during which internal dependence on cash markets and wages became widespread.

Mass production A system of efficient, high volume manufacturing based on division of labor into repetitive tasks, simplification and standardization of parts, increasing use of specialized machinery, and careful supervision. Emerging since the nineteenth century, mass production

reached a critical stage of development with Henry Ford's introduction of the moving assembly line at his Highland Park automobile factory. Mass production drove the prosperity of the 1920s and helped make consumerism possible.

Massive resistance The rallying cry of southern segregationists who pledged to oppose the integration of the schools ordered by the U.S. Supreme Court in *Brown v. Board of Education* in 1954. The tactics of massive resistance included legislation, demonstrations, and violence.

Massive retaliation The defense doctrine of the Eisenhower administration, which promised "instant, massive retaliation" with nuclear weapons in response to Soviet aggression.

McCarthyism The hunt for communist subversion in the United States in the first years of the cold war. Democrats in particular used the term, a reference to the sometimes disreputable tactics of Republican Senator Joseph R. McCarthy of Wisconsin, in order to question the legitimacy of the conservative anti-Communist crusade.

Mercantilism An economic theory developed in early-modern Europe to explain and guide the growth of European nation-states. Its goal was to strengthen the state by making the economy serve its interests. According to the theory of mercantilism, the world's wealth, measured in gold and silver, was fixed; that is, it could never be increased. As a result, each nation's chief economic objective must be to secure as much of the world's wealth as possible. One nation's gain was necessarily another's loss. Colonies played an important part in the theory of mercantilism. Their role was to serve as sources of raw materials and as markets for manufactured goods for the mother country alone.

Middle ground The region between European and Indian settlements in North America that was neither fully European nor fully Indian, but rather a new world created out of two different traditions. The middle ground came into being every time Europeans and Indians met, needed each other, and could not (or would not) achieve what they wanted through the use of force.

Millennialism A strain of Protestant belief that holds that history will end with the thousand-year reign of Christ (the millennium). Some Americans saw the Great Awakening, the French and Indian War, and the Revolution as signs that the millennium was about to begin in America, and this belief infused Revolutionary thought with an element of optimism. Millennialism was also one aspect of a broad drive for social perfection in nineteenth-century America.

Modernization The process by which developing countries in the Third World were to become more like the United States—i.e., capitalist, independent, and anti-Communist. Confidence about the prospects for modernization was one of the cornerstones of liberal foreign policy in the 1960s.

Moral suasion The strategy of using persuasion (as opposed to legal coercion) to convince individuals to alter their behavior. In the antebellum years, moral suasion generally implied an appeal to religious values.

Mutual Aid Societies Organizations through which people of relatively meager means pooled their resources for emergencies. Usually, individuals paid small amounts in dues and were able to borrow larger amounts in times of need. In the early nineteenth century, mutual aid societies were especially common among workers and in free African-American communities.

National Republicans Over the first twenty years of the nineteenth century, the Republican Party gradually abandoned its Jeffersonian animosity toward an activist federal government and industrial development and became a strong proponent of both of these positions. Embodied in the American system, these new views were fully captured in the party's designation of itself as National Republicans by 1824.

Nativism A bias against anyone not born in the United States and in favor of native-born Americans. This attitude assumes the superior culture and political virtue of white Americans of Anglo-Saxon descent, or of individuals assumed to have this lineage. During the period 1820–1850, Irish immigrants became the particular targets of nativist attitudes.

New Left   The radical student movement that emerged in opposition to the new liberalism in the 1960s. The New Left condemned the cold war and corporate power and called for the creation of a true "participatory democracy" in the United States. Placing its faith in the radical potential of young, middle-class students, the New Left differed from the "Old Left" of the late nineteenth and early twentieth centuries, which believed workers would lead the way to socialism.

Patriotism   Love of country. Ways of declaring and displaying national devotion underwent a change from the nineteenth to the twentieth century. Whereas politicians were once unblushingly called patriotic, after World War I the title was appropriated to describe the sacrifices of war veterans. Patriotic spectacle in the form of public oration and electoral rallies gave way to military-style commemorations of Armistice Day and the nation's martial heritage.

Political virtue   In the political thought of the early republic, the personal qualities required in citizens if the republic was to survive.

Polygyny   Taking more than one wife. Indian tribes such as the Hurons practiced polygyny, and hence they did not object when French traders who already had wives in Europe took Indian women as additional wives.

Popular sovereignty   A solution to the slavery controversy espoused by leading northern Democrats in the 1850s. It held that the inhabitants of western territories should be free to decide for themselves whether or not they wanted to have slavery. In principle, popular sovereignty would prevent Congress from either enforcing or restricting slavery's expansion into the western territories.

Postindustrial economy   The service- and computer-based economy that was succeeding the industrial economy, which had been dominated by manufacturing, at the end of the twentieth century.

Principle of Judicial Review   The principle of law that recognizes in the judiciary the power to review and rule on the constitutionality of laws. First established in *Marbury v. Madison* (1803) under Chief Justice John Marshall.

Producers ideology   The belief that all those who lived by producing goods shared a common political identity in opposition to those who lived off financial speculation, rent, or interest.

Proprietary colony   Colony established by a royal grant to an individual or family. The proprietary colonies included Maryland, New York, New Jersey, Pennsylvania, and the Carolinas.

Public opinion   Not quite democracy or consent, public opinion was a new way of understanding the influence of the citizenry on political calculations. Freudian psychology and the new mass media encouraged a view of the public as both fickle and powerful. Whereas the popular will (a nineteenth-century concept) was steady and rooted in national traditions, public opinion was variable and based on attitudes that could be aroused or manipulated by advertising.

Realism   A major artistic movement of the late nineteenth century that embraced writers, painters, critics and photographers. Realists strove to avoid sentimentality and to depict human life "realistically."

Reconversion   The economic and social transition from the war effort to peacetime. Americans feared that reconversion might bring a return to the depression conditions of the 1930s.

Re-export trade   Maritime trade between two foreign ports, with an intermediate stop in a port of the ship's home nation. United States shippers commonly engaged in the re-export trade during the European wars of the late eighteenth and early nineteenth centuries, when England and France tried to prevent each other from shipping or receiving goods. United States shippers claimed that the intermediate stop in the United States made their cargoes neutral.

Republicanism   A set of doctrines rooted in classical antiquity that held that power is always grasping and dangerous and presents a threat to liberty. Republicanism supplied constitutionalism with a motive by explaining how a balanced constitution could be transformed into tyranny as grasping men used their power to encroach upon the liberty of the citizens. In addition, republicanism held that people achieved fulfillment only through participation in public life, as citizens in a republic. Republicanism required the individual to display *virtue* by sacrificing his (or her) private interest for the good of the republic.

***Requerimiento* (the Requirement)**   A document issued by the Spanish Crown in 1513 in order to clarify the legal bases for the enslavement of hostile Indians. Each *conquistador* was required to read a copy of the *Requerimiento* to each group of Indians he encountered. The *Requerimiento* promised friendship to all Indians who accepted Christianity, but threatened war and enslavement for all those who resisted.

Safety-valve theory   An argument commonly made in the nineteenth century that the abundance of western land spared the United States from the social upheavals common to capitalist societies in Europe. In theory, as long as eastern workers had the option of migrating west and becoming independent farmers they could not be subjected to European levels of exploitation. Thus the West was said to provide a "safety-valve" against the social pressures caused by capitalist development.

Scalawag   A derogatory term referring to southern whites who sympathized with the Republicans during Reconstruction.

Second-wave feminism   The reborn women's movement of the 1960s and 1970s that reinterpreted the first wave of nineteenth- and early twentieth-century feminists' insistence.

Separation of powers   One of the chief innovations of the Constitution and a distinguishing mark of the American form of democracy, in which the executive, legislative, and judicial branches of government are separated so that they can check and balance each other.

Slave power   In the 1850s northern Republicans explained the continued economic and political strength of slavery by claiming that a "slave power" had taken control of the federal government and used its authority to artificially keep slavery alive.

Slave society   A society in which slavery is central to the economy and political structure, in contrast to a *society with slaves,* in which the presence of slaves does not alter the fundamental structures of the society.

Social Darwinism   Darwin's theory of natural selection transferred from biological evolution to human history. Social Darwinists argued that some individuals and groups, particularly racial groups, were better able to survive in the "race of life."

Stagflation   The unusual combination of stagnant growth and high inflation that plagued the American economy in the 1970s.

Strict constructionism   The view that the Constitution has a fixed, explicit meaning which can be altered only through formal amendment. Loose constructionism is the view that the Constitution is a broad framework within which various specific interpretations and applications are possible without formal amendment.

Suburbanization   The spread of suburban housing developments and, more broadly, of the suburban ideal.

Supply-side economics   The controversial theory, associated with economist Arthur Laffer, that drove "Reaganomics," the conservative economic policy of the Reagan administration. In contrast to liberal economic theory, supply-side economics emphasized that producers—the "supply side" of the economic equation—drove economic growth, rather than consumers—the "demand side." To encourage producers to invest more in new production, Laffer and other supply-siders called for massive tax cuts.

Tariff   A tax on goods moving across an international boundary. Because the Constitution allows tariffs only on imports, as a political issue the tariff question has chiefly concerned the protection of domestic manufactures from foreign competition. Industries producing mainly for American consumers have preferred a higher tarriff, while farmers and industries aimed at global markets have typically favored reduced tariffs. Prior to the Civil War, the tariff was a symbol of diverging political economies in the North and South. The North advocated high tariffs to protect growing domestic manufacturing ("protective tariffs") and the South opposed high tariffs on the grounds that they increased the cost of imported manufactured goods.

Taylorism   A method for maximizing industrial efficiency by systematically reducing the time and motion involved in each step of the production process. This "scientific" system was designed by Frederick Taylor and explained in his book *The Principles of Scientific Management* (1911).

Universalism   Enlightenment belief that all people are by their nature essentially the same.

Vertical integration   The practice of taking control of every aspect of the production, distribution and sale of a commodity. For example, Andrew Carnegie vertically integrated his steel operations by purchasing the mines that produced the ore, the railroads that carried the ore to the steel mills, the mills themselves, and the distribution system that carried the finished steel to customers.

Virtual representation   British doctrine that said that all Britons, even those who did not vote, were represented by Parliament, if not "actually," by representatives they had chosen, then "virtually," because each member of Parliament was supposed to act on behalf of the entire realm, not only his constituents or even those who had voted for him.

Voluntarism   A style of political activism that took place largely outside of electoral politics. Voluntarism emerged in the nineteenth century, particularly among those Americans who were not allowed to vote. Thus women formed voluntary associations that pressed for social and political reforms, even though women were excluded from electoral politics.

Waltham System   Named after the system used in early textile mills in Waltham, Massachusetts, the term refers to the practice of bringing all elements of production together in a single factory setting with the application of nonhuman powered machinery.

Watergate   The name of the Washington, D.C., office and apartment complex where five men with ties to the presidential campaign of Richard Nixon were caught breaking into the headquarters of the Democratic National Committee in June 1972. "Watergate" became the catchall term for the wide range of illegal practices of Nixon and his followers that were uncovered in the aftermath of the break-in.

Whig Party   The political party founded by Henry Clay in the mid-1830s. The name derived from the seventeenth- and eighteenth-century British anti-monarch position and was intended to suggest that the Jacksonian Democrats (and Jackson in particular) sought despotic powers. In many ways the heirs of National Republicans, the Whigs supported economic expansion, but they also believed in a strong federal government to control the dynamism of the market. The Whig Party attracted many moral reformers.

Whitewater   With its echo of Richard Nixon's "Watergate" scandals in the 1970s, "Whitewater" became the catchall term for the scandals that plagued Bill Clinton's presidency in the 1990s. The term came from the name of a real estate development company in Arkansas. Clinton and his wife Hillary supposedly had corrupt dealings with the Whitewater Development Corporation in the 1970s and 1980s that they purportedly attempted to cover up in the 1990s.

Woman's Rights Movement   The antebellum organizing efforts of women on their own behalf, in the attempt to secure a broad range of social, civic, and political rights. This movement is generally dated from the convention at Seneca Falls in 1848. Only after the Civil War would woman's rights activism begin to confine its efforts to suffrage.

BIBLIOGRAPHY

This Bibliography contains a selected listing of the extensive body of literature available on American History. It is compiled chapter-by-chapter, enabling the reader to easily find additional references in a given area, and offers an expanded compilation of literature for students who wish to explore topics in fuller detail.

CHAPTER 1

Blackburn, Robin, *The Making of New World Slavery: From the Baroque to the Modern 1492–1800* (1997). Bethell, Leslie, ed., *The Cambridge History of Latin America, Vol. I* (1984). Boucher, Philip P., *Cannibal Encounters: Europeans and Island Caribs, 1492–1763* (1992). Boxer, Charles, *The Portuguese Seaborne Empire: 1415–1825* (1969). Bray, Warwick, ed., *The Meeting of Two Worlds: Europe and the Americas, 1492–1650* (1993). Burkholder, Mark A., and Lyman Johnson, *Colonial Latin America* (2000). Canny, Nicholas, and Anthony Pagden, *Colonial Identity in the Atlantic World, 1500–1800* (1987). Casas, Bartolome de las, *A Short Account of the Destruction of the Indies*, with an introduction by Anthony Pagden (1992). Chaplin, Joyce E., *Subject Matter: Technology, The Body, and Science on the Anglo-Amercian Frontier, 1500–1676.* (2001). Clayton, Lawrence A., et al., eds., *The De Soto Chronicles: The Expedition of Hernando de Soto to North America in 1539–1543*, 2 vols. (1993). Coe, Michael, Dean Snow, and Elizabeth Benson, *Atlas of Ancient America* (1986). Crosby, Alfred W., Jr., *Ecological Imperialism: The Biological Expansion of Europe, 900–1900* (1986). Denevan, William M., ed., *The Native Population of the Americas in 1492* (1992). Diaz, Bernal, *The Conquest of New Spain* (1963). Dobyns, Henry F., *Their Number Become Thinned: Native American Population Dynamics in Eastern North America* (1983). Dunn, Oliver, and James E. Kelley, Jr., eds., *The Diario of Christopher Columbus's First Voyage to America, 1492–1493* (1989). Elliott, J. H., *Spain and Its World, 1500–1700* (1989). Fagan, Brian M., *Ancient North America: The Archeology of a Continent* (1991). Fage, J. D., *A History of Africa* (1988). Fernandez-Armesto, Felipe, *Columbus* (1991).

Gibson, Charles, *Spain in America* (1966). Gutierrez, Ramon, *When Jesus Came the Corn Mothers Went Away: Marriage, Sexuality, and Power in New Mexico, 1500–1846* (1991). Hanke, Lewis, *The Spanish Struggle for Justice in the Conquest of America* (1965). Hoffman, Paul, *A New Andalucia and a Way to the Orient* (1990). Hulme, Peter, and Neil L. Whitehead, eds., *Wild Majesty* (1992). Jennings, Francis, *The Founders of America* (1993). Kartunnen, Frances, *Between Worlds: Interpreters, Guides, and Survivors* (1994). Klein, Herbert S., *African Slavery in Latin America and the Caribbean* (1986). Kupperman, Karen O., ed., *America in European Consciousness, 1493–1750* (1995). Leon-Portilla, Miguel, ed., *The Broken Spears: The Aztec Account of the Conquest of Mexico* (1990). Liss, Peggy K., *Isabel: The Queen* (1992). Lockhart, James, and Stuart B. Schwartz, *Early Latin America* (1983). Lunenfeld, Marvin, ed., *1492: Discovery, Invasion, Encounter* (1991).

Milanich, Jerald T., and Susan Milanich, eds., *First Encounters: Spanish Explorations in the Caribbean and the United States, 1492–1570* (1989). _____, and Charles Hudson, *Hernando de Soto and the Indians of Florida* (1993). Morison, Samuel Eliot, *The European Discovery of America: The Southern Voyages, 1492–1616* (1974). _____, *Journals and Other Documents on the Life and Voyages of Christopher Columbus* (1963). Nabokov, Peter, ed., *Native American Testimony, 1492–1992* (1999). Oliver, Roland, *The African Experience: Major Themes in African History from Earliest Times to the Present* (1991). Pagden, Anthony, ed., *European Encounters with the New World* (1993). _____, *Lords of All the World: Ideologies of Empire in Spain, Britain and France, c. 1500–1800* (1995). Parry, J. H., *The Age of Reconnaissance: Discovery, Exploration and Settlement 1450–1650* (1963). _____, *The Spanish Seaborne Empire* (1966). Peters, Edward, *Inquisition* (1988). Phillips, J. R. S., *The Medieval Expansion of Europe* (1988). Quinn, David B., *North America From Earliest Discovery to First Settlements* (1975). Rouse, Irving, *The Tainos* (1992). Ruiz, Ramon Eduardo, *Triumphs and Tragedy: A History of the Mexican People* (1992).

Scammell, G. V., *The World Encompassed: The First European Maritime Empires, c. 800–1650* (1981). Solow, Barbara L., *Slavery and the Rise of the Atlantic System* (1991). Trigger, Bruce G., and Wilcomb Washburn, eds., *The Cambridge History of the Native Peoples of the Americas, Vol. 1* (1996).

CHAPTER 2

Allen, John Logan, ed., *North American Exploration: A New World* (1997). Anderson, Karen, *Chain Her by One Foot: The Subjugation of Native Women in Seventeenth-Century New France* (1991). Canny, Nicholas P., *The Elizabethan Conquest of Ireland: A Pattern Established, 1565–1576* (1976). Dechêne, Louise, *Habitants and Merchants in Seventeenth-Century Montreal* (1992). Delâge, Denys, *Bitter Feast: Amerindians and Europeans in Northeastern America, 1600–1664* (1993). Dennis, Matthew, *Cultivating a Landscape of Peace: Iroquois-European Encounters in Seventeenth-Century America* (1993). Dickason, Olive Patricia, *Canada's First Nations: A History of Founding Peoples from Earliest Times* (1992). Eccles, W. J., *The Canadian Frontier* (1974). _____, *Essays on New France* (1987).

Gleach, Frederic W., *Powhatan's World and Colonial Virginia: A Conflict of Cultures* (1997). Hoffman, Paul, *A New Andalucia and a Way to the Orient* (1990). Hume, Ivor Noël, *The Virginia Adventure: Roanoke to James Towne: An Archaeological and Historical Odyssey* (1994). Inikori, Joseph, and Stanley L.

Engerman, eds., *The Atlantic Slave Trade: Effects on Economies, Societies, and Peoples in Africa, The Americas, and Europe* (1992). Jaenen, Cornelius J., *Friend and Foe: Aspects of French-Amerindian Cultural Contact in the Sixteenth and Seventeenth Centuries* (1976). Jennings, Francis, *The Ambiguous Iroquois Empire: The Covenant Chain Confederation of Indian Tribes with English Colonies* (1984). Klein, Herbert, *African Slavery in Latin America and the Caribbean* (1986). Kupperman, Karen Ordahl, *Settling with the Indians: The Meeting of English and Indian Cultures in America, 1580–1640* (1980).

Merwick, Donna, *Possessing Albany, 1630–1710: The Dutch and English Experience* (1990). Morgan, Edmund S., *American Slavery, American Freedom: The Ordeal of Colonial Virginia* (1975). Morison, Samuel Eliot, *Samuel de Champlain: Father of New France* (1972). Peckham, Howard, and Charles Gibson, eds., *Attitudes of Colonial Powers Toward the American Indian* (1969). Quinn, David B., ed., *America From Concept to Discovery: Early Explorations of North America* (1979). _____, *North America From Earliest Discovery to First Settlements: The Norse Voyages to 1612* (1977). _____, *Set Fair for Roanoke: Voyages and Colonies, 1584–1606* (1995). Richter, Daniel K., and James H. Merrell, *Beyond the Covenant Chain: The Iroquois and Their Neighbors in Indian North America, 1600–1800* (1987). Rink, Oliver A., *Holland on the Hudson: An Economic and Social History of Dutch New York* (1986). Rountree, Helen C., ed., *Powhatan Foreign Relations* (1993).

Scammell, G. V., *The World Encompassed: The First European Maritime Empires* (1981). Trigger, Bruce, *Natives and Newcomers: Canada's "Heroic Age" Reconsidered* (1985). _____, and Wilcomb E. Washburn, eds., *The Cambridge History of the Native Peoples of the Americas, Vol. I* (1996). Wallace, Anthony F. C., *The Death and Rebirth of the Seneca* (1970). Weber, David, *The Spanish Frontier in North America* (1992). White, Richard, *The Middle Ground: Indians, Empires, and Republics in the Great Lakes Region, 1650–1815* (1991). White, Shane, *Somewhat More Independent: The End of Slavery in New York City, 1770–1810* (1991).

CHAPTER 3

Allen, David Grayson, *In English Ways: The Movement of Societies and the Transferral of English Local Law and Custom to Massachusetts Bay in the Seventeenth Century* (1981). Anderson, Virginia DeJohn, *New England's Generation: The Great Migration and the Formation of Society and Culture in the Seventeenth Century* (1991). Barbour, Philip L., ed., *The Complete Works of John Smith* (1986). _____, *Pocahontas and Her World* (1969). Bernhard, Virginia, "Men, Women and Children at Jamestown: Population and Gender in Early Virginia, 1607–1610," *Journal of Southern History*, LVIII (1992). Blackburn, Robin, *The Making of New World Slavery: From the Baroque to the Modern, 1402–1800* (1997). Bradford, William, *Of Plymouth Plantation, 1620–1647,* ed. Samuel Eliot Morison (1952). Breen, Timothy H., and Stephen Innes, *"Myne Owne Ground": Race and Freedom on Virginia's Eastern Shore, 1640–1676* (1980). Bremer, Francis J., *The Puritan Experiment: New England Society from Bradford to Edwards* (1976). Carr, Lois Green, et al., eds., *Colonial Chesapeake Society* (1988). Delbanco, Andrew, *The Puritan Ordeal* (1989). Demos, John,

ed., *Remarkable Providences: Readings on Early American History* (1991). Foster, Stephen, *The Long Argument: English Puritanism and the Shaping of New England Culture, 1570–1700* (1991). _____, *Their Solitary Way: The Puritan Social Ethic in the First Century of Settlement in New England* (1971). Freedman, Estelle B., and John D'Emilio, *Intimate Matters: A History of Sexuality in America* (1988).

Gleach, Frederic W., *Powhatan's World and Colonial Virginia: A Conflict of Cultures* (1997). Greene, Jack P., *Pursuits of Happiness: The Social Development of Early Modern British Colonies and the Formation of American Culture* (1988). Greven, Philip J., *Four Generations: Population, Land, and Family in Colonial Andover, Massachusetts* (1970). _____, *The Protestant Temperament: Patterns of Childrearing, Religious Experience, and the Self in Early America* (1977). Hambrick-Stowe, Charles, *The Practice of Piety: Puritan Devotional Disciplines in Seventeenth-century New England* (1982). Horn, James, *Adapting to a New World: English Society in the Seventeenth-Century Chesapeake* (1994). Jordan, Winthrop D., *White over Black: American Attitudes Toward the Negro, 1550–1812* (1968). Karlsen, Carol, *The Devil in the Shape of a Woman: Witchcraft in Colonial New England* (1987). Kolchin, Peter, *American Slavery, 1619–1877* (1993). Kupperman, Karen Ordahl, *Providence Island, 1630–1641: The Other Puritan Colony* (1993). _____, *Settling with the Indians: The Meeting of English and Indian Cultures in America, 1580–1640* (1980). Langdon, George D., Jr., *Pilgrim Colony: A History of New Plymouth, 1620–1691* (1966). Lockridge, Kenneth A., *A New England Town, The First Hundred Years: Dedham, Massachusetts 1636–1736* (rev. ed., 1985).

McCusker, John J., and Russell R. Menard, *The Economy of British America, 1607–1789* (1991). McGiffert, Michael, ed., "Constructing Race," *William and Mary Quarterly*, 3d Ser., LIV (1997). Miller, Perry, ed., *The American Puritans: Their Prose and Poetry* (1956). _____, *The New England Mind: The Seventeenth Century* (1939). Morgan, Edmund S., *The Puritan Dilemma: The Story of John Winthrop* (1958). _____, *Visible Saints: The History of a Puritan Idea* (1963). Norton, Mary Beth, *Founding Mothers and Fathers: Gendered Power and the Forming of American Society* (1996). Potter, Stephen R., *Commoners, Tribute, and Chiefs: The Development of Algonquian Culture in the Potomac Valley* (1993). Powell, Sumner Chilton, *Puritan Village: The Formation of a New England Town* (1963). Quinn, David Beers, *North America From Earliest Discovery to First Settlements: The Norse Voyages to 1612* (1975). Rountree, Helen, *Pocahontas's People: The Powhatan Indians of Virginia Through Four Centuries* (1990). _____, ed., *Powhatan Foreign Relations, 1500–1722* (1993). _____, *The Powhatan Indians of Virginia: Their Traditional Culture* (1989). Rutman, Darrett B., *Winthrop's Boston: A Portrait of a Puritan Town* (1965).

Salisbury, Neal, *Manitou and Providence: Indians, Europeans, and the Making of New England, 1500–1643* (1982). _____, "Squanto: Last of the Patuxets," in Gary B. Nash and David W. Sweet, eds., *Struggle and Survival in Colonial America* (1981). Stannard, David E., *The Puritan Way of Death: A Study in Religion, Culture, and Social Change* (1977). Stone, Lawrence, *The Family, Sex, and Marriage in England, 1500–1800* (1977). Stout, Harry S., *The New England Soul: Preaching and*

Religious Culture in Colonial New England (1986). Tate, Thad, and David Ammerman, eds., *The Chesapeake in the Seventeenth Century: Essays on Anglo-American Society and Politics* (1979). Thomas, M. Halsey, ed., *The Diary of Samuel Sewall, 1674–1708* (1973.) Ulrich, Laurel Thatcher, *Good Wives: Image and Reality in the Lives of Women in Northern New England, 1650–1750* (1982). Vaughan, Alden T., *New England Frontier: Puritans and Indians, 1620–1675* (1994). _____, ed., *The Puritan Tradition in America, 1620–1730* (1972). Wood, Peter H., Gregory A. Waselkov, and M. Thomas Halsey, eds., *Powhatan's Mantle: Indians in the Colonial Southeast* (1989). Woodward, Grace Steele, *Pocahontas* (1969). Zuckerman, Michael, *Peaceable Kingdoms: New England Towns in the Eighteenth Century* (1970). _____, "Pilgrims in the Wilderness: Community, Modernity, and the Maypole at Merry Mount," *New England Quarterly*, L (1977).

CHAPTER 4

Appleby, Joyce, *Economic Thought and Ideology in Seventeenth-Century England* (1978). _____, *Liberalism and Republicanism in the Historical Imagination* (1992). Bailyn, Bernard, and Philip D. Morgan, eds., *Strangers Within the Realm: Cultural Margins of the First British Empire* (1991). Berlin, Ira D., *Many Thousands Gone: The First Two Centuries of Slavery in North America* (1998). Bonomi, Patricia U., *A Factious People: Politics and Society in Colonial New York* (1971). Boyer, Paul, and Stephen Nissenbaum, *Salem Possessed: The Social Origins of Witchcraft* (1972). _____, ed. *Salem Village Witchcraft: A Documentary Record of Local Conflict in Colonial New England* (1972). Breen, T. H., *Puritans and Adventurers: Change and Persistence in Early America* (1980). Breslaw, Elaine G., *Tituba, Reluctant Witch of Salem: Devilish Indians and Puritan Fantasies* (1996). Crane, Verner, *The Southern Frontier, 1670–1732*, with a new preface by Peter H. Wood (1981). Craven, Wesley Frank, *White, Red, and Black: The Seventeenth-Century Virginian* (1971). Degler, Carl N., *Out of Our Past: The Forces that Shaped Modern America*, 3rd. ed. (1984). Dunn, Richard S., *Sugar and Slaves: The Rise of the Planter Class in the English West Indies* (1972). Eccles, W. J., *France in America* (1990). Eltis, David, *The Rise of African Slavery in the Americas* (2000). Espinosa, J. Manuel, *The Pueblo Indian Revolt of 1696 and the Franciscan Mission in New Mexico* (1988).

Goodfriend, Joyce, *Before the Melting Pot: Society and Culture in Colonial New York City, 1664–1692* (1992). Greene, Jack P., ed., *Great Britain and the American Colonies, 1606–1763* (1970). Hall, David D., ed., *Witch-Hunting in Seventeenth-Century New England: A Documentary History, 1638–1692* (1991). _____, *Worlds of Wonder, Days of Judgment: Popular Religious Belief in Early New England* (1989). Hall, Gwendolyn Midlo, *Africans in Colonial Louisiana: The Development of Afro-Creole Culture in the Eighteenth Century* (1992). Hammond, George P., and Agapito Reys, eds., *Don Juan de Oñate: Colonizer of New Mexico, 1595–1628* (1953). Hoffer, Peter Charles, *The Devil's Disciples: Makers of the Salem Witchcraft Trials* (1996). Illick, Joseph, *Colonial Pennsylvania: A History* (1976). Jennings, Francis, *The Ambiguous Iroquois Empire: The Covenant Chain Confederation of Indian Tribes with English Colonies* (1984). Johnson, Richard R., *Adjustment to Empire: The New England Colonies, 1665–1715* (1981). Kammen, Michael, *Colonial New York: A History* (1975). Karlsen, Carol, *The Devil in the Shape of a Woman: Witchcraft in Colonial New England* (1987). Klein, Herbert S., *African Slavery in Latin America and the Caribbean* (1986). Kishlansky, Mark, *A Monarchy Transformed: Britain, 1603–1714* (1996). Knaut, Andrew L., *The Pueblo Revolt of 1680: Conquest and Resistance in Seventeenth–Century New Mexico* (1995). Kolchin, Peter, *American Slavery, 1619–1877* (1993). Konig, David Thomas, *Law and Society in Puritan Massachusetts: Essex County, 1629–1692* (1979). Kupperman, Karen Ordahl, ed., *Major Problems in American Colonial History* (2000). Landers, Jane, *Black Society in Spanish Florida* (1999). Leach, Douglas Edward, *Arms for Empire: A Military History of the British Colonies of North America, 1607–1763* (1973). Lefler, Hugh T., and William S. Powell, *Colonial North Carolina: A History* (1973). Locke, John, *Two Treatises of Government; A Critical Edition with an Introduction*, ed., Peter Laslett (1960). Lovejoy, David S., *The Glorious Revolution in America* (1972).

Malone, Patrick M., *The Skulking Way of War: Technology and Tactics Among the New England Indians* (1991). Melvoin, Richard I., *The New England Outpost: War and Society in Colonial Deerfield* (1989). Merrell, James H., *The Indians' New World: Catawbas and their Neighbors from European Contact Through the Era of Removal* (1989). Merwick, Donna, *Possessing Albany, 1630–1710: The Dutch and English Experiences* (1990). Middlekauff, Robert, *The Mathers: Three Generations of Puritan Intellectual, 1596–1728* (1971). Middleton, Richard, *Colonial America: A History, 1585–1776* (1996). Miller, Perry, *Errand into the Wilderness* (1956). Nash, Gary B., *Quakers and Politics: Pennsylvania, 1681–1726* (1996). _____, *Red, White, and Black: The Peoples of Early America*, 2nd ed. (1982). _____, *Urban Crucible: Social Change, Political Consciousness, and the Origins of the American Revolution* (1979). _____ and Jean Soderlund, *Freedom by Degrees: Emancipation in Pennsylvania and Its Aftermath* (1991). Nobles, Gregory H., *American Frontiers: Cultural Encounters and Continental Conquest* (1997). Nylander, Jane, *Our Own Snug Firesides: Images of the New England Home, 1760–1860* (1993). Oakes, James, *Slavery and Freedom: An Interpretation of the Old South* (1990). Patterson, Orlando, *Slavery and Social Death: A Comparative Study* (1982). Pope, Robert G., *The Half-Way Covenant: Church Membership in Puritan New England* (1986). Quinn, David B., ed., *Early Maryland in a Wider World* (1982). Richter, Daniel K., *The Ordeal of the Longhouse: The Peoples of the Iroquois League in the Era of European Colonization* (1992). Ritchie, Robert C., *The Duke's Province: A Study of New York Politics and Society, 1664–1691* (1977). Robinson, W. Stitt, *The Southern Colonial Frontier, 1607–1763* (1979). Rose, Willie Lee, ed., *A Documentary History of Slavery in North America* (1976). Rosenthal, Bernard, *Salem Story: Reading the Witch Trials of 1692* (1993). Rountree, Helen, *Pocahontas's People: The Powhatan Indians of Virginia Through Four Centuries* (1990).

Simmons, Marc, *The Last Conquistador: Juan de Oñate and the Settling of the Far Southwest* (1991). Sirmans, M. Eugene, *Colonial South Carolina: A Political History, 1663–1763* (1966). Slotkin, Richard, and James K. Folson, eds., *So Dreadfull a Judgment: Puritan Responses to King Philip's War, 1676–1677*

(1978). Usner, Daniel H., Jr., *Indians, Settlers, and Slaves in a Frontier Exchange Economy: The Lower Mississippi Valley before 1783* (1992). Vaughan, Alden T., ed., *The Puritan Tradition in America, 1620–1730* (1972). Webb, Stephen Saunders, *1676: The End of American Independence* (1984). Weber, David, *The Spanish Frontier in North America* (1992). White, Richard, *The Middle Ground: Indians, Empires, and Republics in the Great Lakes Region, 1650–1815* (1991). Wooten, David, ed., *The Political Writings of John Locke* (1993). Wright, J. Leitch, Jr., *The Only Land They Knew: The Tragic Story of the American Indians in the Old South* (1981).

CHAPTER 5

Ahlstrom, Sydney E., *A Religious History of the American People* (1972). Allison, Robert J., ed., *The Interesting Narrative of the Life of Olaudah Equiano* (1995). Bailyn, Bernard, "The Peopling of British North America: An Introduction," in *Perspectives in American History*, Vol. 2 (1985). _____, *Voyagers to the West: A Passage in the Peopling of America on the Eve of the Revolution* (1986). _____, and Philip D. Morgan, eds., *Strangers within the Realm: Cultural Margins of the First British Empire* (1991). Berlin, Ira, *Many Thousands Gone: The First Two Centuries of Slavery in North America* (1998). _____, and Philip D. Morgan, eds., *Cultivation and Culture: Labor and the Shaping of Slave Life in the Americas* (1993). Bonomi, Patricia, *Under the Cope of Heaven: Religion, Society, and Politics in Colonial America* (1986). Boorstin, Daniel J., *The Lost World of Thomas Jefferson* (1948). Boydston, Jeanne, *Home and Work: Housework, Wages, and the Ideology of Labor in the Early Republic* (1990). Breen, T. H., *Puritans and Adventurers: Change and Persistence in Early America* (1980). Brewer, John, and Roy Porter, eds., *Consumption and the World of Goods* (1993). Bullock, Steven C., *Revolutionary Brotherhood: Freemasonry and the Transformation of the American Social Order, 1730–1840,* (1996). Bushman, Richard, *The Refinement of America: Persons, Houses, Cities* (1992). Butler, Jon, *Awash in a Sea of Faith: Christianizing the American People* (1990). _____, *Becoming American: The Revolution before 1776* (2000). Coleman, Kenneth, *Colonial Georgia: A History* (1976). Conroy, David W., *In Public Houses: Drink and the Revolution of Authority in Colonial Massachusetts* (1987). Cott, Nancy F., et al., eds., *Root of Bitterness: Documents of the Social History of American Women* (1996). Davis, Harold E., *The Fledgling Province: Social and Cultural Life in Colonial Georgia* (1976). Duffy, John, *Epidemics in Colonial America* (1971). Engerman, Stanley L., and Robert E. Gallman, eds., *The Cambridge Economic History of the United States* (1996). Fiering, Norman S., *Jonathan Edwards's Moral Thought and Its British Context* (1981). Franklin, Benjamin, *Writings* (1987).

Gallay, Alan, *The Formation of a Planter Elite: Jonathan Bryan and the Southern Colonial Frontier* (1989). Gilje, Paul A., *The Road to Mobocracy: Popular Disorder in New York City, 1763–1834* (1987). Gordon, Michael, ed., *The American Family in Social-Historical Perspective* (1983). Greene, Jack P., *Pursuits of Happiness: The Social Development of Early Modern British Colonies and the Formation of American Culture* (1988). _____, *The Quest for Power: The Lower Houses of Assembly in the Southern Royal Colonies, 1689–1776* (1976). _____, and

J. R. Pole, eds., *Colonial British America: Essays in the New History of the Early Modern Era* (1984). Gross, Robert A. *The Minutemen and Their World* (1976). Hancock, David, *Citizens of the World: London Merchants and the Integration of the British Atlantic Community, 1735–1785* (1995). Heimert, Alan, *Religion and the American Mind, from the Great Awakening to the Revolution* (1968). _____, and Perry Miller, eds., *The Great Awakening: Documents Illustrating the Crisis and Its Consequences* (1967). Henretta, James A., and Gregory H. Nobles, *Evolution and Revolution: American Society, 1600–1820* (1987). Hoffman, Ronald, et al., eds., *Through a Glass Darkly: Reflections on Personal Identity in Early America* (1997). Innes, Stephen A., *Creating the Commonwealth: The Economic Culture of Puritan New England* (1995). _____, ed., *Work and Labor in Early America* (1988). Kammen, Michael, *Colonial New York: A History* (1975). Klein, Herbert, *The Atlantic Slave Trade* (1999). Koch, Adrienne, and William Peden, eds., *The Life and Selected Writings of Thomas Jefferson* (1944). Kulikoff, Allan, *Tobacco and Slaves: The Development of Southern Cultures in the Chesapeake, 1680–1800* (1986). Lambert, Frank, *"Pedlar in Divinity": George Whitefield and the Transatlantic Revivals* (1994). Landers, Jane, "El Gracia de Santa Teresa de Mose: A Free Black Town in Spanish Colonial Florida," *American Historical Review,* 95 (1991). Lewis, Jan, *The Pursuit of Happiness: Family and Values in Jefferson's Virginia* (1983).

Mancall, Peter, *Deadly Medicine: Indians and Alcohol in Early America* (1995). May, Henry F., *The Enlightenment in America* (1976). Matson, Cathy, *Merchants and Empire: Trading in Colonial New York* (1998). McCusker, John J., and Russell R. Menard, *The Economy of British America, 1607–1789* (1985). Middlekauff, Robert, *The Mathers: Three Generations of Puritan Intellectuals* (1971). Middleton, Richard, *Colonial America: A History, 1585–1776* (1996). Morgan, Philip D., "Slave Life in Eighteenth-Century Charleston," *Perspectives in American History,* Vol. I (1984). _____, "Work and Culture: The Task System and the World of Lowcountry Blacks, 1700–1800," *William and Mary Quarterly,* 3d Ser., XXXIX (1982). Mullin, Michael, *Africa in America: Slave Acculturation and Resistance in the American South and the British Caribbean, 1736–1831* (1992). Oberg, Barbara B., and Harry S. Stout, eds., *Benjamin Franklin, Jonathan Edwards, and the Representation of American Culture* (1993). Olwell, Robert, *Masters, Slaves, and Subjects: The Culture of Power in the South Carolina Low Country, 1740–1790* (1998). Paine, Thomas, *Collected Writings* (1995). Rawley, James A., *The Transatlantic Slave Trade: A History* (1981). Rediker, Marcus B., *Between the Devil and the Deep Blue Sea: Merchant Seamen, Pirates, and the Anglo-American Maritime World, 1700–1750* (1987).

Sobel, Mechal, *The World they Made Together: Black and White Values in Eighteenth-Century Virginia* (1987). Spalding, Phinizy, *Oglethorpe in America* (1977). Stout, Harry S., *The Divine Dramatist: George Whitefield and the Rise of Modern Evangelicalism* (1991). Thornton, John K., "African Dimensions of the Stono Rebellion," *American Historical Review,* 91 (1994). Ulrich, Laurel Thatcher, *Good Wives; Image and Reality in the Lives of Women in Northern New England, 1650–1750* (1980). Vickers, Daniel, *Farmers and Fishermen: Two Centuries of Work in Essex County, Massachusetts, 1630–1850* (1994). Warner,

Michael, *The Letters of the Republic: Publication and the Public Sphere in Eighteenth-Century America* (1990). Whitefield, George, *Sketches of the Life and Labors of the Rev. George Whitefield* (n.d.). Wolf, Stephanie Grauman, *As Various as Their Land: The Everyday Lives of Eighteenth-Century Americans* (1993). Wright, Esmond, *Franklin of Philadelphia* (1986). Zabin, Serena, "Places of Exchange: New York City, 1700–1763," Ph.D. diss., Rutgers University (2000).

CHAPTER 6

Anderson, Fred, *A People's Army: Massachusetts Soldiers and Society in the Seven Years' War* (1984). Bailyn, Bernard, *The Origins of American Politics* (1968). Barrow, Thomas C., *Trade and Empire: The British Customs Service in Colonial America, 1660–1775* (1967). Braund, Kathleen E. Holland, *Deerskins and Duffels: Creek Indian Trade with Anglo-America, 1685–1815* (1993). Breen, T. H., "Narrative of Commercial Life: Consumption, Ideology, and Community on the Eve of the American Revolution," *William and Mary Quarterly*, 3rd Ser., L (1993). Brewer, John, *Party, Ideology, and Popular Politics at the Accession of George II* (1976). Bushman, Richard, *King and People in Provincial Massachusetts* (1985). Dowd, Gregory E., *A Spirited Resistance: The North American Indian Struggle for Unity, 1745–1815* (1992). Draper, Theodore, *A Struggle for Power: The American Revolution* (1996). Eccles, W. J., *France in America* (1990). Ferling, John E., *A Wilderness of Miseries: War and Warriors in Early America* (1980). Flexner, James Thomas, *George Washington: The Forge of Experience, 1732–1775* (1965). _____, *Lord of the Mohawks: A Biography of Sir William Johnson* (1979). Franklin, Benjamin, *Benjamin Franklin: Writings* (1987).

Gilje, Paul A., *Rioting in America* (1996). _____, *The Road to Mobocracy: Popular Disorder in New York City, 1763–1834* (1987). Gipson, Lawrence H., *The British Empire before the American Revolution*, 15 vols (1936–1972). Greene, Jack P., *Peripheries and Center: Constitutional Development in the Extended Policies of the British Empire and the United States* (1987). _____, *The Quest for Power: The Lower Houses of Assembly in the Southern Royal Colonies* (1963). Hamilton, Milton W., *Sir William Johnson: Colonial American, 1715–1763* (1976). Hinderacker, Eric, *Elusive Empires: Constructing Colonialism in the Ohio Valley, 1673–1800* (1997). Hoerder, Dirk, *Crowd Action in Revolutionary Massachusetts, 1765–1780* (1977). Holton, Woody, *Forced Founders: Indians, Debtors, Slaves & the Making of the American Revolution in Virginia* (1999). Jefferson, Thomas, *Thomas Jefferson: Writings* (1984). Jennings, Francis, *The Ambiguous Iroquois Empire: The Covenant Chain Confederation of Indian Tribes with English Colonies* (1984.) _____, *Empire of Fortune: Crowns, Colonies, and Tribes in the Seven Years War in America* (1988). Johnson, Susannah Willard, *A Narrative of the Captivity of Mrs. Johnson* (1990). Labaree, Benjamin Woods, *The Boston Tea Party* (1964). Leach, Douglas Edward, *Roots of Conflict: British Armed Forces and Colonial Americans, 1677–1763* (1986).

Maier, Pauline, *From Resistance to Revolution: Colonial Radicals and the Development of American Opposition to Britain, 1765–1776* (1972). McConnell, Michael N., *A Country Between: The Upper Ohio Valley and Its Peoples, 1724–1774* (1992). Melvoin, Richard I., *New England Outpost: War and Society in Colonial Deerfield* (1989). Middlekauff, Robert, *Benjamin Franklin and His Enemies* (1996). _____, *The Glorious Cause: The American Revolution, 1763–1789* (1982). Morgan, Edmund S. and Helen M., *The Stamp Act Crisis: Prologue to Revolution* (1953). Nash, Gary, *The Urban Crucible: Social Change, Political Consciousness, and the Origins of the American Revolution* (1979). Nobles, Gregory H., *American Frontiers: Cultural Encounters and Continental Conquest* (1997). Peckham, Howard H., *Pontiac and the Indian Uprising* (1947). Pencak, William, *War, Politics, and Revolution in Provincial Massachusetts* (1981). _____, "Warfare and Political Change in Mid-Eighteenth-Century Massachusetts," *The Journal of Imperial and Commonwealth History*, 8 (1980), 51–73. Robinson, W. Stitt, *The Southern Frontier, 1607–1763* (1979).

Sosin, Jack M., *The Revolutionary Frontier, 1763–1783* (1967). Steele, Ian K., *Warpaths: Invasions of North America* (1994). Ulrich, Laurel Thatcher, *Good Wives: Image and Reality in the Lives of Women in Northern New England, 1650–1750* (1982). Vaughan, Alden T., *Roots of American Racism: Essays on the Colonial Experience* (1995). Walton, Gary M., and James F. Shepherd, *The Economic Rise of Early America* (1979). Warden, G. B., *Boston, 1689–1776* (1970). Wood, Gordon S., *The Creation of the American Republic, 1776–1787* (1966). _____, *The Rising Glory of America, 1760–1820* (1990). Wright, Esmond, *Franklin of Philadelphia* (1986). Zobel, Hiller, *The Boston Massacre* (1970).

CHAPTER 7

Alden, John R., *A History of the American Revolution* (1975). Aron, Stephen, *How the West Was Lost: The Transformation of Kentucky from Daniel Boone to Henry Clay* (1996). Bailyn, Bernard, *Faces of Revolution: Personalities and Times in the Struggle for American Independence* (1990). Bailyn, Bernard, ed., *The Debate on the Constitution*, 2 vols (1993). Beeman, Richard, Stephen Botein, and Edward C. Carter II, *Beyond Confederation: Origins of the Constitution and American National Identity* (1987). Berlin, Ira, and Ronald Hoffman, eds., *Slavery and Freedom in the Age of the American Revolution* (1983). Bernstein, Richard, *Are We to Be a Nation? The Making of the Constitution* (1987). Bloch, Ruth, "The Gendered Meanings of Virtue in Revolutionary America," *Signs*, 13 (1987), 37–58. Bonwick, Colin, *The American Revolution* (1991). Calloway, Colin, *The American Revolution in Indian Country: Crisis and Diversity in Native American Communities* (1995). Carp, E. Wayne, *To Starve the Army at Pleasure: Continental Army Administration and American Political Culture, 1775–1783* (1984). Cooke, Jacob E., ed., *The Federalist* (1961). Countryman, Edward, *The American Revolution* (1985). _____, *A People in Revolution: The American Revolution and Political Society in New York, 1760–1790* (1981). Crow, Jeffrey, and Larry Tise, eds., *The Southern Experience in the American Revolution* (1978). Doerflinger, Thomas M., *A Vigorous Spirit of Enterprise: Merchants and Economic Development in Revolutionary Philadelphia* (1986). Egnal, Marc, *A Mighty Empire: The Origins of the American Revolution* (1988). Engerman, Stanley L., and Robert Gallman, eds., *The*

Cambridge Economic History of the United States, Vol I (1996). Farrand, Max, ed., *The Records of the Federal Convention of 1787*, 4 vols (1966). Fischer, David Hackett, *Paul Revere's Ride* (1994). Flexner, James Thomas, *George Washington and the New Nation (1783–1793)* (1970). _____, *George Washington in the American Revolution (1775–1783)* (1968). Fliegelman, Jay, *Declaring Independence: Jefferson, Natural Language, and the Culture of Performance* (1993). Foner, Eric, *Tom Paine and Revolutionary America* (1976).

Greene, Jack P., *Colonies to Nation, 1763–1789* (1967). _____, and J. R. Pole, eds., *The Blackwell Encyclopedia of the American Revolution* (1991). Gross, Robert A., ed., *In Debt to Shays: The Bicentennial of an Agrarian Rebellion* (1993). _____, *The Minutemen and Their World* (1976). Gruber, Ira D., *The Howe Brothers and the American Revolution* (1972). Higginbotham, Don, *The War of American Independence: Military Attitudes, Policies, and Practice, 1763–1789* (1971). Hoffman, Ronald, and Peter J. Albert, eds., *The Transforming Hand of Revolution: Reconsidering the American Revolution as a Social Movement* (1995). _____, *Women in the Age of the American Revolution* (1989). Hoffman, Ronald, et al., eds., *The Economy of Early America: The Revolutionary Period, 1763–1790* (1988). Jensen, Merrill, *The Articles of Confederation: An Interpretation of the Social-Constitutional History of the American Revolution, 1774–1781* (1970). Jordan, Winthrop D., *White Over Black: American Attitudes Toward the Negro, 1550–1812* (1968). Kaminski, John, and Richard Leffler, eds., *Federalists and Antifederalists: The Debate Over the Ratification of the Constitution* (1989). Ketcham, Ralph, *James Madison: A Biography* (1971). Klein, Rachel N., *Unification of a Slave State: Planter Class in the South Carolina Backcountry, 1760–1808* (1990). Koistinen, Paul A. C., *Beating Plowshares into Swords: The Political Economy of American Warfare, 1606–1865* (1996). Konig, David Thomas, ed., *Devising Liberty: Preserving and Creating Freedom in the New American Republic* (1995). Kurtz, Stephen G., and James H. Hudson, eds., *Essays on the American Revolution* (1973). Lee, Jean B., *The Price of Nationhood: The American Revolution in Charles County* (1994). Lewis, Jan, "The Republican Wife: Virtue and Seduction in the Early Republic," *William and Mary Quarterly*, 3d Ser., XLIV (1987), 689–721. Lockridge, Kenneth A. "Social Change and the Meaning of the American Revolution," *Journal of Social History*, 6 (1973), 403–39.

Mackesy, Piers, *The War for America, 1775–1783* (1965). Maier, Pauline, *American Scripture: Making the Declaration of Independence* (1997). _____, *The Old Revolutionaries: Political Lives in the Age of Samuel Adams* (1980). Main, Jackson Turner, *The Sovereign States* (1973). Martin, Joseph Plumb, *Private Yankee Doodle Dandy* (1962). Matson, Cathy D., and Peter S. Onuf, *A Union of Interests: Political and Economic Thought in Revolutionary America* (1990). Merrell, James H., "Declarations of Independence: Indian-White Relations in the New Nation," in Jack P. Greene, ed., *The American Revolution: Its Character and Limits* (1987), 197–223. Middlekauff, Robert, *The Glorious Cause: The American Revolution, 1763–1789* (1982). Miller, Perry, "From the Covenant to the Revival," in James Ward Smith and A. Leland Jamison, eds., *The Shaping of American Religion* (1961), 322–68.

Morris, Richard B., *The Forging of the Union, 1781–1789* (1987). _____, *Seven Who Shaped Our Destiny: The Founding Fathers as Revolutionaries* (1973). Nash, Gary B., *Race and Revolution* (1990). _____, *The Urban Crucible: Social Change, Political Consciousness, and the Origins of the American Revolution* (1979). Norton, Mary Beth, *The British-Americans: The Loyalist Exiles in England, 1774–1789* (1972). _____, *Liberty's Daughters: The Revolutionary Experience of American Women, 1750–1800* (1980). Onuf, Peter S., "The Origins and Early Development of State Legislatures," in Joel H. Silbey, ed., *Encyclopedia of the American Legislative System* (1994), 175–94. _____, *The Origins of the Federal Republic: Jurisdictional Controversies in the United States, 1775–1787* (1983). _____, *Statehood and Union: A History of the Northwest Ordinance* (1987). Paine, Thomas, *Collected Writings* (1995). Perkins, Bradford, *The Cambridge History of American Foreign Relations, Vol I: The Creation of a Republican Empire, 1776–1865* (1993). Rakove, Jack N., *The Beginnings of National Politics: An Interpretive History of the Continental Congress* (1979).

Smith, Barbara Clark, "Food Rioters and the American Revolution," *William and Mary Quarterly*, 3d Ser., LI (1994), 3–38. Storing, Herbert J., *The Complete Antifederalist*, 7 vols (1981). Syrett, Harold C., ed., *The Papers of Alexander Hamilton*, 27 vols (1961–1987). Szatmary, David P., *Shays' Rebellion: The Making of an Agrarian Insurrection* (1980). Taylor, Alan, *William Cooper's Town: Power and Persuasion on the Frontier of the Early American Republic* (1995). Wallace, Anthony F. C., *The Death and Rebirth of the Seneca* (1969). Washburn, Wilcomb E., ed., *History of Indian-White Relations* (1988). Weigley, Russell F., *Morristown: Official National Park Handbook* (1983). _____, *The Partisan War: The South Carolina Campaign of 1780–1782* (1970). Wills, Garry, *Inventing America: Jefferson's Declaration of Independence* (1978). Wood, Gordon S., *The Radicalism of the American Revolution* (1992). Young, Alfred F., ed., *The American Revolution* (1976). _____, *Beyond the American Revolution: Explorations in the History of American Radicalism* (1993).

CHAPTER 8

Appleby, Joyce Oldham, *Capitalism and a New Social Order: The Republican Vision of the 1790s* (1983). Banning, Lance, *The Jeffersonian Persuasion: Evolution of a Party Ideology* (1978). _____, *The Sacred Fire of Liberty: James Madison and the Founding of the Federal Republic* (1995). Beeman, Richard B., *The Evolution of the Southern Backcountry: A Case Study of Lunenburg County, Virginia, 1746–1832* (1984). Bemis, Samuel F., *Jay's Treaty: A Study in Commerce and Diplomacy* (1962). Berkhofer, Robert F., Jr., *Salvation and the Savage: An Analysis of Protestant Missions and American Indian Response, 1787–1862* (1965). Berlin, Ira, *Many Thousands Gone: The First Two Centuries of Slavery in North America* (1998). Buel, Richard, Jr., *Securing the Revolution: Ideology in American Politics, 1789–1815* (1972). Calloway, Colin G., *Crown and Calumet: British-Indian Relations, 1783–1815* (1987). Cole, Arthur H., ed., *Industrial and Commercial Correspondence of Alexander Hamilton* (1928). Cox, Tench, *A View of the United States of America* (1794). Cunningham, Noble E., *The*

Jeffersonian Republicans: The Formation of Party Organization, 1789–1801 (1957). Dillon, Merton L., *Slavery Attacked: Southern Slaves and their Allies, 1619–1865* (1990). Dorfman, Joseph, *The Economic Mind in American Civilization,* 2 vols (1946). Edmunds, R. David, *Tecumseh: The Quest for Indian Leadership* (1984). Elkins, Stanley, and Eric McKitrick, *The Age of Federalism: The Early American Republic, 1788–1800* (1993).

Hamilton, Alexander, *The Papers of Alexander Hamilton,* ed. Harold C. Syrett et al. 27 vols (1961–67). _____, *The Reports of Alexander Hamilton,* ed. Jacob E. Cooke (1964). Hartz, Louis, *The Liberal Tradition in America: An Interpretation of American Political Thought since the Revolution* (1955). Henretta, James A., *The Evolution of American Society, 1700–1815: An Interdisciplinary Analysis* (1973). Heyrman, Christine Leigh, *Southern Cross: The Beginnings of the Bible Belt* (1997). Hoffman, Ronald, and Peter J. Albert, eds., *Women in the Age of the American Revolution* (1989). Horsman, Reginald, *Expansionism and American Indian Policy* (1967). Jefferson, Thomas, *Notes on the State of Virginia* (1964). _____, *The Papers of Thomas Jefferson,* ed. Julian P. Boyd, 20 vols (1950). Jordan, Winthrop D., *White Over Black: American Attitudes Toward the Negro, 1550–1812* (1968). Kerber, Linda, *Women of the Republic: Intellect and Ideology in Revolutionary America* (1980). Ketcham, Ralph L., *James Madison: A Biography* (1971). Lee, Jean B., *The Price of Nationhood: The American Revolution in Charles County* (1994).

Malone, Dumas, *Jefferson and His Time* (1948–1981). Marris, Kenneth C., *The Historical Atlas of Political Parties in the United States, 1789–1989* (1988). McCoy, Drew, *The Elusive Republic: Political Economy in Jeffersonian America* (1984). Miller, John C., *The Federalist Era, 1789–1801* (1960). Mittell, Sherman F., ed., *The Federalist: A Commentary on the Constitution of the United States being a Collection of Essays Written in Support of the Constitution agreed upon September 17, 1787, by The Federal Convention* (1937). Nabakov, Peter, ed., *Native American Testimony: I Chronicle of Indian-White Relations from Prophecy to the Present, 1492–1992* (1991). Nelson, John R., Jr., *Liberty and Property: Political Economy and Policy Making, 1789–1812* (1987). Nettels, Curtis P., *The Emergence of a National Economy, 1775–1815* (1962). North, Douglass C., *The Economic Growth of the United States, 1790–1860* (1966). Norton, Mary Beth, *Liberty's Daughters: The Revolutionary Experience of American Women, 1750–1800* (1980). Perdue, Theda, *Slavery and the Evolution of Cherokee Society, 1540–1866* (1979). Peterson, Merrill D., *Thomas Jefferson and the New Nation* (1970). Risjord, Norman K., *Thomas Jefferson* (1994). Rorabaugh, W. J., *The Craft Apprentice, from Franklin to the Machine Age in America* (1986).

Shalhope, Robert E., "Toward a Republican Synthesis: The Emergence of an Understanding of Republicanism in American Historiography," *William and Mary Quarterly,* 3rd Ser. XXXIX (April 1982), 334–56. Sharp, James Roger, *American Politics in the Early Republic: The New Nation in Crisis* (1993). Sheehan, Bernard W., *Seeds of Extinction: Jeffersonian Philanthropy and the American Indian* (1973). Skemp, Sheila L., *Judith Sargent Murray: A Brief Biography with Documents* (1988). Sloan, Herbert, *Principle and Interest: Thomas Jefferson and the Problem of Debt* (1994). Smyth, Albert Henry, ed., *The Writings of Benjamin Franklin* (1907). Sword, Wiley, *President Washington's Indian War* (1985). Taylor, Alan, *Liberty Men and Great Proprietors: The Revolutionary Settlement on the Maine Frontier, 1760–1820* (1990). Ulrich, Laurel Thatcher, *A Midwife's Tale: The Life of Martha Ballard, Based on her Diary, 1785–1812* (1990). Wallace, Anthony F. C., *The Death and Rebirth of the Seneca* (1970). Watts, Stephen, *The Republic Reborn: War and the Making of Liberal America, 1790–1820* (1987). White, Richard, *The Middle Ground: Indians, Empires, and Republics in the Great Lakes Region, 1650–1815* (1991). Wood, Gordon, *The Creation of the American Republic 1776–1787* (1969). Wright, Donald R., *African Americans in the Early Republic, 1789–1831* (1993). Wright, J. Leitch, Jr., *Creeks and Seminoles: The Destruction and Regeneration of the Muscogulge People* (1986). Yenne, Bill, *The Encyclopedia of North American Indian Tribes: A Comprehensive Study of Tribes from the Abitibi to the Zuni* (1986). Young, Alfred E., *The Democratic Republicans of New York: The Origins, 1763–1797* (1967). Zagarri, Rosemarie, *A Woman's Dilemma: Mercy Otis Warren and the American Revolution* (1995). Zverper, John, *Political Philosophy and Rhetoric: A Study of the Origins of American Party Politics* (1977).

CHAPTER 9

Ambrose, Stephen, *Undaunted Courage: Meriwether Lewis, Thomas Jefferson and the Opening of the American West* (1996). Banning, Lance, *The Jeffersonian Persuasion: Evolution of a Party Ideology* (1978). Beeman, Richard B., *The Evolution of the Southern Backcountry: A Case Study of Lunenburg County, Virginia, 1746–1832* (1984). Bergon, Frank, ed., *The Journals of Lewis and Clark* (1989). Berkhofer, Robert F., Jr., *Salvation and the Savage: An Analysis of Protestant Missions and American Indian Response, 1787–1862* (1965). Berlin, Ira, "Time, Space, and the Transformation of Afro-American Society in the United States: 1770–1820" in Elise Marienstras and Barbara Karsky, eds., *Autre Temps, Autre Espace/An Other Time, An Other Place: Études sur l'Amérique pré-Industrielle* (1986). Boles, John B., *Black Southerners, 1619–1869* (1983). _____, *The Great Revival, 1787–1805: The Origins of the Southern Evangelical Mind* (1972). Boyd, Julian P., ed., *The Papers of Thomas Jefferson* (1950). Bruce, Dickson D., Jr., *And They All Sang Hallelujah: Plain-Folk Camp-Meeting Religion, 1800–1845* (1974). Butler, Jon, *Awash in a Sea of Faith: Christianizing the American People* (1972). Cawelti, John G., *Apostles of the Self-Made Man: Changing Concepts of Success in America* (1965). Conklin, Paul K., *Cane Ridge: America's Pentecost* (1990). Curry, Leonard P., *The Free Black in Urban America, 1800–1850: The Shadow of a Dream* (1981). Dillon, Merton L., *Slavery Attacked: Southern Slaves and their Allies, 1619–1865* (1990). Dowd, Gregory Evans, *A Spirited Resistance: The North American Indian Struggle for Unity, 1745–1815* (1992). Edmunds, R. David, *Tecumseh: The Quest for Indian Leadership* (1984). Egerton, Douglas R., *Gabriel's Rebellion: The Virginia Slave Conspiracies* (1993). Foner, Philip S., *History of Black Americans: Volume One: From Africa to the Emergence of the Cotton Kingdom* (1975).

Henretta, James A., *The Evolution of American Society, 1700–1815: An Interdisciplinary Analysis* (1973). Horsman, Reginald, *Expansionism and American Indian Policy* (1967). Horton, James Oliver, and Lois E. Horton, *In Hope of Liberty: Culture, Community, and Protest among Northern Free Blacks, 1700–1860* (1997). Jordan, Winthrop D., *White Over Black: American Attitudes Toward the Negro, 1550–1812* (1968). Litwack, Leon F., *North of Slavery: The Negro in the Free States, 1790–1860* (1961).

Mahon, John K., *The War of 1812* (1972). Malone, Dumas, *Jefferson and His Time* (1948–1981). Marris, Kenneth C., *The Historical Atlas of Political Parties in the United States, 1789–1989* (1988). McCoy, Drew, *The Elusive Republic: Political Economy in Jeffersonian America* (1984). McLoughlin, William G., *Cherokee Renascence in the New Republic* (1986). _____, "Thomas Jefferson and the Beginning of Cherokee Nationalism, 1806–1809," *William and Mary Quarterly*, 3rd Ser., XXXII (1975), 547–80. Melish, Joanne Pope, *Disowning Slavery: Gradual Emancipation and "Race" in New England, 1780–1860* (1998). Nash, Gary B., *Forging Freedom: The Formation of Philadelphia's Black Community, 1720–1840* (1988). Nelson, John R., Jr., *Liberty and Property: Political Economy and Policy Making, 1789–1812* (1987). Nettels, Curtis P., *The Emergence of a National Economy, 1775–1815* (1962). North, Douglass C., *The Economic Growth of the United States, 1790–1860* (1966; First published 1961). Peterson, Merrill D., *Thomas Jefferson and the New Nation* (1970). Risjord, Norman K., *Thomas Jefferson* (1994). Rock, Howard B., *Artisans of the New Republic: the Tradesmen of New York City in the Age of Jefferson* (1984). Rorabaugh, W. J., *The Craft Apprentice, from Franklin to the Machine Age in America* (1986). Ryan, Mary P., *Cradle of the Middle Class: The Family in Oneida County, New York, 1790–1865* (1981).

Scott, Anne Firor, *Natural Allies: Women's Associations in American History* (1992). Shalhope, Robert E., "Toward a Republican Synthesis: The Emergence of an Understanding of Republicanism in American Historiography," *William and Mary Quarterly*, 3rd Ser., XXXIX (1982), 334–56. Sharp, James Roger, *American Politics in the Early Republic: The New Nation in Crisis* (1993). Sheehan, Bernard W., *Seeds of Extinction: Jeffersonian Philanthropy and the American Indian* (1973). Sidbury, James, *Ploughshares into Swords: Race, Rebellion, and Identity in Gabriel's Virginia, 1730–1810* (1997). Sloan, Herbert, *Principle and Interest: Thomas Jefferson and the Problem of Debt* (1994). Smelser, Marshall, *The Democratic Republic, 1801–1815* (1968). Smith, Rogers M., *Civic Ideals: Conflicting Visions of Citizenship in U. S. History* (1997). Stansell, Christine, *City of Women: Sex and Class in New York, 1780–1860* (1986). Stone, Barton W., "A Short History of the Life of Barton W. Stone," in James R. Rogers, *The Cane Ridge Meeting House, to which is Appended the Autobiography of B. W. Stone* (1910). Taylor, Alan, *Liberty Men and Great Proprietors: The Revolutionary Settlement on the Maine Frontier, 1760–1820* (1990). Tucker, Robert W., and David C. Hendrickson, *Empire of Liberty: the Statecraft of Thomas Jefferson* (1990). Ulrich, Laurel Thatcher, *A Midwife's Tale: The Life of Martha Ballard, Based on her Diary, 1785–1812* (1990). Wallace, Anthony F. C., *Jefferson and the Indians: The Tragic Fate of the First Americans*

(1999). Watts, Stephen, *The Republic Reborn: War and the Making of Liberal America, 1790–1820* (1987). White, Shane, *Somewhat More Independent: The End of Slavery in New York City* (1991). Wiebe, Robert H., *The Opening of American Society: From the Adoption of the Constitution to the Eve of Disunion* (1984). Wilentz, Sean, *Chants Democratic: New York City and the Rise of the American Working Class, 1788–1850* (1984). Wright, Donald R., *African Americans in the Early Republic, 1789–1831* (1993).

CHAPTER 10

Aaron, Daniel, *Cincinnati, Queen City of the West, 1819–1838* (1992). Ashworth, John, *Slavery, Capitalism, and Politics in the Antebellum Republic, Vol. 1: Commerce and Compromise, 1820–1850* (1995). Berlin, Ira, *Slaves without Masters: The Free Negro in the Antebellum South* (1974). Blackmar, Elizabeth, *Manhattan for Rent, 1785–1850* (1989). Blassingame, John W., *The Slave Community: Plantation Life in the Antebellum South* (1972). Bleser, Carol, *In Joy and Sorrow: Women, Family, and Marriage in the Victorian South, 1830–1900* (1991). Bolton, Charles C., *Poor Whites of the Antebellum South: Tenants and Laborers in Central North Carolina and Northeastern Mississippi* (1994). Brent, Linda [Harriet Jacobs], *Incidents in the Life of a Slave Girl*, ed. L. Maria Child (1973). Butler, Jon, *Awash in a Sea of Faith: Christianizing the American People* (1990). Carby, Hazel V., *Reconstructing Womanhood: The Emergence of the Afro-American Woman Novelist* (1987). Clark, Christopher, *The Roots of Rural Capitalism: Western Massachusetts, 1780–1860* (1990). Clinton, Catherine, *The Plantation Mistress: Woman's World in the Old South* (1982). Collins, Bruce, *White Society in the Antebellum South* (1985). Conklin, Paul K., *The Uneasy Center: Reformed Christianity in Antebellum America* (1995). Curry, Leonard P., *The Free Black in Urban America, 1800–1850: The Shadow of the Dream* (1981). Dangerfield, George, *The Era of Good Feelings* (1952). Davis, David Brion, *The Problem of Slavery in the Age of Revolution, 1770–1823* (1975). Douglass, Frederick, *Narrative of the Life of Frederick Douglass, an American Slave, Written by Himself*, ed. Benjamin Quarles (1960). Dowd, Gregory, *A Spirited Resistance: The North American Indian Struggle for Unity* (1992). Dublin, Thomas, *Farm to Factory: Women's Letters, 1830–1860*, 2nd ed. (1993). Duncan, John M., *Travels through Part of the United States and Canada in 1818 and 1819*, 2 vols (1823). Escott, Paul D., *Slavery Remembered: A Record of Twentieth-Century Slave Narratives* (1979). Faust, Drew, *James Henry Hammond and the Old South* (1982). Fields, Barbara Jeanne, *Slavery and Freedom on the Middle Ground: Maryland During the Nineteenth Century* (1985). Fox-Genovese, Elizabeth, *Within the Plantation Household: Black and White Women in the Old South* (1988).

Gates, Paul W., *The Farmer's Age: Agriculture, 1815–1860* (1960). Gutman, Herbert G., *The Black Family in Slavery and Freedom, 1750–1925* (1976). Hahn, Steven, and Jonathan Prude, eds., *The Countryside in the Age of Capitalist Transformation: Essays in the Social History of Rural America* (1985). Harris, J. William, ed., *Society and Culture in the Slave South* (1992). Hudson, Winthrop S., *Religion in America: An Historical Account of the Development of American Religious Life* (1965). Jones, Jacqueline, *Labor of Love, Labor of Sorrow: Black*

Women, Work, and the Family from Slavery to the Present (1985). Kolchin, Peter, *American Slavery, 1619–1877* (1993). *Letters of John Pintard to his Daughter Eliza Noel Pontard Davidson, 1816–1833,* 4 vols (1940). Licht, Walter, *Industrializing America: The Nineteenth Century* (1995). Loewenberg, Bert James, and Ruth Bogin, eds., *Black Women in Nineteenth-Century American Life: Their Words, Their Thoughts, Their Feelings* (1976).

McCurry, Stephanie, *Masters of Small Worlds: Yeoman Households, Gender Relations, and the Political Culture of the Antebellum South Carolina Low Country* (1995). Morris, Christopher, *Becoming Southern: The Evolution of a Way of Life, Warren County and Vicksburg, Mississippi, 1770–1860* (1995). Morrison, John H., *History of American Steam Navigation* (1958). Oakes, James, *The Ruling Race: A History of American Slaveholders* (1982). Riley, Glenda, *The Female Frontier: A Comparative View of Women on the Prairie and the Plains* (1988). Rock, Howard B., *Artisans of the New Republic: The Tradesmen of New York in the Age of Jefferson* (1979).

Sellers, Charles, *The Market Revolution: Jacksonian America, 1815–1846* (1991). Shammas, Carole, "Black Women's Work and the Evolution of Plantation Society in Virginia," *Labor History,* 26/1 (Winter 1985), 5–28. Sheriff, Carol, *The Artificial River: The Erie Canal and the Paradox of Progress, 1817–1862* (1996). Stansell, Christine, *City of Women: Sex and Class in New York, 1780–1860* (1986). Tadman, Michael, *Speculators and Slaves: Masters, Traders and Slaves in the Old South* (1989). White, Deborah Gray, *Ar'n't I a Woman? Female Slaves in the Plantation South* (1985). Wilentz, Sean, *Chants Democratic: New York City and the Rise of the American Working Class, 1788–1850* (1984). Wishart, David J., *The Fur Trade of the American West, 1807–1840: A Geographical Synthesis* (1979).

CHAPTER 11

Address of the Republican General Committee of Young Men of the City and County of New-York Friendly to the Election of Gen: Andrew Jackson to the Presidency to The Republican Electors of the State of New-York (1828). Baxter, Maurice G., *Henry Clay and the American System* (1995). Bellows, Barbara L., *Benevolence Among Slaveholders: Assisting the Poor in Charleston, 1670–1860* (1993). Benson, Lee, *The Concept of Jacksonian Democracy* (1961). Bestor, Arthur, *Backwoods Utopias: The Sectarian Origins and the Owenite Phase of Communitarian Socialism in America, 1663–1829,* 2nd ed. (1970). Butler, Diana Hochstedt, *Standing Against the Whirlwind: Evangelical Episcopalians in Nineteenth-Century America* (1995). Cawelti, John G., *Apostles of the Self-Made Man: Changing Concepts of Success in America* (1965). Clay, Henry, *An Address of Henry Clay, to the Public; Containing Certain Testimony in Refutation of the Charges Against Him, Made by Gen. Andrew Jackson, Touching the Last Presidential Election* (1818). Cole, Donald B., *The Presidency of Andrew Jackson* (1993). Conklin, Paul K., *The Uneasy Center: Reformed Christianity in Antebellum America* (1995). Cott, Nancy F., *The Bonds of Womanhood: "Woman's Sphere" in New England, 1780–1835* (1977). Cross, Whitney, *The Burned-Over District* (1950). Curry, Leonard P., *The Free Black in Urban America, 1800–1850: the Shadow of a Dream* (1981). Feller, Daniel, *The Jacksonian Promise: America, 1815–1840* (1995). _____, *The Public Lands in Jacksonian Politics* (1984). Finney, Charles G[randison], *Autobiography* [Originally Entitled *Memoirs of Charles Grandison Finney*] (1876). Formisano, Ronald P., *The Birth of Mass Political Parties* (1971). Foster, Lawrence, *Women, Family, and Utopia: Communal Experiments of the Shakers, the Oneida Community, and the Mormons* (1991).

Gaustad, Edwin Scott, *A Religious History of America,* Rev. ed. (1966). Ginzberg, Lori D., *Women and the Work of Benevolence: Morality, Politics, and Class in the Nineteenth-Century United States* (1991). Goodrich, Carter, *Government Promotion of American Canals and Railroads, 1800–1890* (1960). Hagan, William T., *The Sac and Fox Indians* (1958). Hall, Thomas Cuming, *The Religious Background of American Culture* (1930). Holt, Michael F., "The Anti-Masonic and Know Nothing Parties," in Arthur M. Schlesinger, Jr., ed., *History of United States Political Parties,* 4 vols (1973). _____, *The Political Crisis of the 1850s* (1978). Horsman, Reginald, *Race and Manifest Destiny: The Origins of American Racial Anglo-Saxonism* (1981). Jackson, Donald, ed., *Black Hawk: An Autobiography* (1955). Johnson, Paul E., *A Shopkeeper's Millennium* (1978). _____, and Sean Wilentz, *The Kingdom of Matthias: The Story of Sex and Salvation in Nineteenth-Century America* (1994). Licht, Walter, *Industrialization in America: The Nineteenth Century* (1995). Litwack, Leon F., *North of Slavery: The Negro in the Free States, 1790–1860* (1961). Loewenberg, Bert James, and Ruth Bogin, eds., *Black Women in Nineteenth-Century American Life: Their Words, Their Thoughts, Their Feelings* (1976).

Matthews, Donald G., "The Second Great Awakening as an Organizing Process, 1780–1830," *American Quarterly,* XXI (1969), 23–43. McCormick, Richard P., *The Second American Party System* (1966). McLoughlin, William G., *Cherokee Renascence in the New Republic* (1986). Mintz, Stephen, *Moralizers and Modernizers: America's Pre-Civil War Reformers* (1995). Nash, Gary B., *Forging Freedom: The Formation of Philadelphia's Black Community, 1720–1840* (1988). Nordhoff, Charles, *The Communistic Societies of the United States: From Personal Observations* (1966). Pollack, Queena, *Peggy Eaton: Democracy's Mistress* (1931). Prucha, Francis P., *The Great Father: The United States Government and the Indians,* 2 vols (1984). _____, *Sword of the Republic: The United States Army on the Frontier, 1783–1846* (1969). Remini, Robert V., *Andrew Jackson and the Course of American Democracy, 1833–1845* (1984). _____, *Andrew Jackson and the Course of American Empire, 1767–1821* (1977). _____, *Andrew Jackson and the Course of American Freedom, 1822–1832* (1981). Roediger, David, *The Wages of Whiteness: Race and the Making of the American Working Class* (1991). Rosenberg, Carroll Smith, *Religion and the Rise of the American City: The New York City Mission Movement, 1812–1870* (1971). Rowe, David, *Thunder and Trumpets: Millerites and Dissenting Religion in Upstate New York, 1800–1850* (1985). Rugoff, Milton, *The Beechers: An American Family of the Nineteenth Century* (1981). Ryan, Mary P., *Cradle of the Middle Class: The Family in Oneida County, New York, 1790–1865* (1981).

Satz, Ronald D., *American Indian Policy in the Jacksonian Era* (1977). Saxton, Alexander, *The Rise and Fall of the White Republic: Class Politics and Mass Culture in Nineteenth-Century America* (1990). Schlesinger, Arthur M., Jr., *The Age of Jackson* (1947). Sellers, Charles, *The Market Revolution: Jacksonian America, 1815–1846* (1991). Smith, Sam B., and Harriet Chappell Owsley, eds., *The Papers of Andrew Jackson*, 6 vols (1980). Spellman, Peter W., and Thomas A. Askew, *The Churches and the American Experience: Ideals and Institutions* (1984). Stansell, Christine, *City of Women: Sex and Class in New York, 1789–1860* (1986). Tanner, Helen Hornbeck, ed., *Atlas of Great Lakes Indian History* (1987). Taylor, George Rogers, ed., *Jackson Versus Biddle: The Struggle over the Second Bank of the United States* (1949). Van Deusen, Glendon G., *The Jacksonian Era, 1828–1848* (1959). Wallace, Anthony F. C., "Prelude to Disaster: The Course of Indian-White Relations Which Led to the Black Hawk War of 1832," in Ellen M. Whitney, ed., *The Black Hawk War, 1831–1832* (Published as vols 35–38, Collections of the Illinois State Historical Library 1970–1978.) I, 1–51. Walter, Ronald G., *American Reformers, 1815–1860* (1978). Ward, John William, *Andrew Jackson—Symbol for an Age* (1953). Watson, Harry L., *Liberty and Power: The Politics of Jacksonian America* (1990). Weddle, David L., *The Law as Gospel: Revival and Reform in the Theology of Charles G. Finney* (1985). Wilburn, Jean Alexander, *Biddle's Bank: The Crucial Years* (1967). Wilentz, Sean, *Chants Democratic: New York City and the Rise of the American Working Class, 1788–1850*. New York, 1984.

CHAPTER 12

Billington, Ray Allen, *The Protestant Crusade, 1800–1860: A Study of the Origins of American Nativism* (1938). Blackmar, Elizabeth, *Manhattan for Rent, 1785–1850* (1989). Blumin, Stuart M., *The Emergence of the Middle Class: Social Experience in the American City, 1760–1900* (1989). Boydston, Jeanne, *Home and Work: Housework, Wages, and the Ideology of Labor in the Early Republic* (1990). Carlton, Frank Tracy, *Economic Influences upon Educational Progress in the United States, 1820–1850* (1965). Cawelti, John G., *Apostles of the Self-Made Man: Changing Concepts of Success in America* (1965). Child, Mrs. [Lydia Maria], *The American Frugal Housewife*, 12th ed., (1833). Cole, Donald B., *The Presidency of Andrew Jackson* (1993). Cott, Nancy F., *The Bonds of Womanhood: "Woman's Sphere" in New England, 1780–1835* (1977). Curry, Leonard P., *The Free Black in Urban America, 1800–1850: The Shadow of a Dream* (1981). Davis, David Brion, "The Emergence of Immediatism in British and American Antislavery Thought," *Mississippi Valley Historical Review*, XLIX (September 1962), 209–30. Dew, Thomas R., *Review of the Debate in the Virginia Legislature of 1831 and 1832* (1832). Duberman, Martin, ed., *The Antislavery Vanguard: New Essays on the Abolitionists* (1965). Dudley, William, ed., *Slavery: Opposing Views* (1992). Feller, Daniel, *The Jacksonian Promise: America, 1815–1840* (1995). Foner, Philip S., *From Colonial Times to the Founding of the American Federation of Labor. Volume One: History of the Labor Movement in the United States* (1947). _____, *Women and the American Labor Movement: From the First Trade Unions to the Present* (1979). Freyer, Tony A., *Producers versus Capitalists: Constitutional Conflict in Antebellum America*

(1994). Friedman, Lawrence J., *Gregarious Saints: Self and Community in American Abolitionism, 1830–1870* (1982).

Ginzberg, Lori D., "'The Hearts of Your Readers Will Shudder': Fanny Wright, Infidelity, and American Free Thought," *American Quarterly*, Vol 46, No. 2 (June 1994), 195–226. Griffin, Clifford S., *Their Brothers' Keepers: Moral Stewardship in the United States, 1800–1865* (1960). Jackson, Sidney L., *America's Struggle for Free Schools: Social Tension and Education in New England and New York, 1827–42* (1965). Kaestle, Carl F., *Pillars of the Republic: Common Schools and American Society, 1780–1860* (1983). Katz, Michael B., *The Irony of Early School Reform: Educational Innovation in Mid-Nineteenth Century Massachusetts* (1968). Lazerow, Jama, *Religion and the Working Class in Antebellum America* (1995).

Mintz, Stephen, *Moralizers and Modernizers: America's Pre-Civil War Reformers* (1995). North, Douglass C., *The Economic Growth of the United States, 1790–1860* (1966. First published 1961). Pease, William H., and Jane H. Pease, *The Web of Progress: Private Values and Public Styles in Boston and Charleston, 1828–1843* (1985). Remini, Robert V., *Andrew Jackson and the Course of American Democracy, 1833–1845* (1984). _____, *Andrew Jackson and the Course of American Empire, 1767–1821* (1977). _____, *Andrew Jackson and the Course of American Freedom, 1822–1832* (1981). _____, *The Election of Andrew Jackson* (1963). Roediger, David R., *Towards the Abolition of Whiteness: Essays on Race, Politics, and Working Class History* (1994). _____, *The Wages of Whiteness: Race and the Making of the American Working Class* (1991). Rosenberg, Carroll Smith, *Religion and the Rise of the American City: The New York City Mission Movement, 1812–1870* (1971). Rudolph, Frederick, ed., *Essays on Education in the Early Republic* (1965). Ryan, Mary P., *Cradle of the Middle Class: The Family in Oneida County, New York, 1790–1865* (1981).

Saxton, Alexander, *The Rise and Fall of the White Republic: Class Politics and Mass Culture in Nineteenth-Century America* (1990). Schlesinger, Arthur M., Jr., *The Age of Jackson* (1947). Scott, Anne Firor, *Natural Allies: Women's Associations in American History* (1992). Smith, Sam B., and Harriet Chappell Owsley, eds., *The Papers of Andrew Jackson*, 6 vols (1980). Stansell, Christine, *City of Women: Sex and Class in New York, 1789–1860* (1986). Vassar, Rena L., ed., *Social History of American Education: Volume One: Colonial Times to 1860* (1965). Walker, David, *David Walker's Appeal to the Coloured Citizens of the World* (1995). Walters, Ron, *American Reformers, 1815–1860* (1978). Welter, Rush, *Popular Education and Democratic Thought in America* (1962). Wilentz, Sean, *Chants Democratic: New York City and the Rise of the American Working Class, 1788–1850* (1984). Yellin, Jean Fagan, and John C. Van Horne, eds., *The Abolitionist Sisterhood: Women's Political Culture in Antebellum America* (1994).

CHAPTER 13

Ballantine, Betty, and Ian Ballantine, eds., *The Native Americans: An Illustrated History* (1993). Bauer, K. Jack, *The Mexican War, 1846–1848* (1974). Bergeron, Paul H., *The Presidency of James K. Polk* (1987). Binkley, William C., *The Texas Revolution* (1952). Blue, Frederick J., *The Free Soilers:*

Third Party Politics (1973). Brack, Gene M., Mexico Views Manifest Destiny (1976). Butruille, Susan G., Women's Voices from the Oregon Trail (1993). Campbell, Randolph B., An Empire for Slavery: The Peculiar Institution in Texas (1989). Clark, Christopher, The Communitarian Moment: the Radical Challenge of the Northampton Association (1995). Clark, Malcolm, Jr., Eden Seekers: The Settlement of Oregon, 1818–1862 (1981). Clayton, Lawrence R., and Joseph E. Chance, eds., The March to Monterrey: The Diary of Lt. Rankin Dilworth (1966). Dawley, Alan, Class and Community: The Industrial Revolution in Lynn (1976). Dillon, Merton L., Slavery Attacked: Southern Slaves and Their Allies, 1618–1685 (1990). Faragher, John Mack, Women and Men on the Overland Trail (1979). Faust, Drew Gilpin, ed., The Ideology of Slavery: Proslavery Thought in the Antebellum South, 1830–1860 (1981). Foster, Lawrence, Women, Family, and Utopia: Communal Experiments of the Shakers, the Oneida Community, and the Mormons (1991).

Ginzberg, Lori D., Women and the Work of Benevolence: Morality, Politics, and Class in the Nineteenth-Century United States (1990). Graebner, Norman A., Empire on the Pacific: A Study in American Continental Expansion (1955). Holloway, Mark, Heavens on Earth: Utopian Communities in America, 1680–1880, 2nd ed. (1966). Horsman, Reginald, Race and Manifest Destiny: The Origins of American Racial Anglo-Saxonism (1981). Isenberg, Nancy, Sex and Citizenship in Antebellum America (1998). Jeffrey, Julie Roy, Converting the West: A Biography of Narcissa Whitman (1991). Johannsen, Robert W., To the Halls of Montezumas: The Mexican War in the American Imagination (1985). Johnson, Paul E., and Sean Wilentz, The Kingdom of Matthias: A Story of Sex and Salvation in Nineteenth-Century America (1994). Kohl, Lawrence Frederick, The Politics of Individualism: Parties and the American Character in the Jacksonian Era (1989).

Maffly-Kipp, Laurie F., Religion and Society in Frontier California (1994). Marquis, Thomas B., The Cheyennes of Montana, ed. Thomas D. Weist (1978). Matovina, Timothy M., Tejano Religion and Ethnicity: San Antonio, 1821–1860 (1995). McCaffrey, James M., Army of Manifest Destiny: The American Soldier in the Mexican War, 1846–1848 (1992). Miller, Robert Ryan, ed., The Mexican War Journal and Letters of Ralph W. Kirkham (1991). Mintz, Steven, Moralists and Modernizers: America's Pre-Civil War Reformers (1995). Monaghan, Jay, The Overland Trail (1971). Montejano, David, Anglos and Mexicans in the Making of Texas, 1836–1986 (1987). Morrison, Michael A., Slavery and the American West: The Eclipse of Manifest Destiny and the Coming of the Civil War (1997). Parker, Theodore, The Slave Power (1969). Peterson, Norma Lois, The Presidencies of William Henry Harrison and John Tyler (1989). Prude, Jonathan, The Coming of the Industrial Order: Town and Factory Life in Rural Massachusetts, 1810–1860 (1983). Reidy, Joseph, From Slavery to Agrarian Capitalism in the Cotton Plantation South: Central Georgia, 1800–1880 (1992). Remini, Robert, Martin Van Buren and the Making of the Democratic Party (1959).

Schroeder, John H., Mr. Polk's War: American Opposition and Dissent, 1846–1848 (1973). Seager, Robert, II, And Tyler Too: A Biography of John and Julia Gardiner Tyler (1963). Sellers,

Charles, James K. Polk, Continentalist: 1843–1846 (1966). _____, James K. Polk, Jacksonian: 1795–1843 (1957). Sloan, Irving J., ed., Martin van Buren, 1782–1862 (1969). Smith-Rosenberg, Carroll, Disorderly Conduct: Visions of Gender in Victorian America (1985). Stansell, Christine, City of Women: Sex and Class in New York, 1789–1860 (1986). Stephanson, Anders, Manifest Destiny: American Expansion and the Empire of Right (1995). Tijerina, Andrés, Tejanos and Texas under the Mexican Flag, 1821–1836 (1994). Weber, David, The Mexican Frontier, 1821–1846. The American Southwest under Mexico (1982). White, Richard, "It's Your Misfortune and None of My Own"; A History of the American West (1991). Wilentz, Sean, Chants Democratic: New York City and the Rise of the American Working Class, 1788–1850 (1984). Wilson, Major L., The Presidency of Martin Van Buren (1984).

CHAPTER 14

Barney, William, The Road to Secession: A New Perspective on the Old South (1972). Blumin, Stuart, The Emergence of the Middle Class: Social Experience in the American City, 1790–1900 (1989). Campbell, Stanley, The Slave Catchers (1970). Cooper, William J., Jr., The South and the Politics of Slavery, 1828–1856 (1978). Craven, Avery, The Coming of the Civil War, 2nd ed. (1957). Fehrenbacher, Don E., Prelude to Greatness: Lincoln in the 1850s (1952). Fehrenbacher, Don, The Slaveholding Republic: An Account of the United States Government's Relations to Slavery (2001). Fishlow, Albert, American Railroads and the Transformation of the Antebellum Economy (1965). Fogel, Robert, Without Consent or Contract: The Rise and Fall of American Slavery (1989).

Genovese, Eugene D., The Political Economy of Slavery: Studies in the Economy and Society of the Slave South (1965). Greenstone, David J., The Lincoln Persuasion: Remaking American Liberalism (1993). Hamilton, Holman, Prologue to Conflict: The Crisis and Compromise of 1850 (1970). Holt, Michael F., The Rise and Fall of the American Whig Party: Jacksonian Politics and the Onset of the Civil War (1999). Huston, James, The Panic of 1857 and the Coming of the Civil War (1987). Jaffa, Harry V., Crisis of the House Divided: An Interpretation of the Lincoln-Douglas Debates (1959). Johannsen, Robert W., Stephen A. Douglas (1973). Johnson, Walter, Soul By Soul: Life Inside the Antebellum Slave Market (1999).

May, Robert E., The Southern Dream of a Caribbean Empire, 1854–1861 (1973). McCardell, John, The Idea of a Southern Nation: Southern Nationalists and Southern Nationalism, 1830–1860 (1979). Morrison, Chaplain W., Democratic Politics and Sectionalism: The Wilmot Proviso Controversy (1967). Nevins, Allan, Ordeal of the Union, 4 vols (1947–1950). Nichols, Roy F., The Disruption of American Democracy (1948). Niven, John, The Coming of the Civil War, 1837–1861 (1990). Oakes, James, Slavery and Freedom: An Interpretation of the Old South (1990). Potter, David M., The South and the Sectional Conflict (1969).

Sewell, Richard B., Ballots for Freedom: Antislavery Politics in the United States, 1837–1860 (1976). Stampp, Kenneth M., America in 1857: A Nation on the Brink (1990). Summers, Mark W., The

Plundering Generation: Corruption and the Crisis of the Union, 1849–1861 (1987). Tadman, Michael, *Speculators and Slaves: Masters, Traders, and Slaves in the Old South* (1996 ed.). Takaki, Ronald, *A Pro-Slavery Crusade: The Agitation to Reopen the African Slave Trade* (1971). Wright, Gavin, *The Political Economy of the Cotton South: Households, Markets and Wealth in the Nineteenth Century* (1978). Zarefsky, David, *Lincoln, Douglas, and Slavery: The Crucible of Public Debate* (1990).

CHAPTER 15

Ball, Douglas B., *Financial Failure and Confederate Defeat* (1990). Barney, William L., *The Secessionist Impulse: Alabama and Mississippi in 1860* (1974). Bernstein, Iver, *The New York City Draft Riots: Their Significance for American Society and Politics in the Age of the Civil War* (1990). Catton, Bruce, *This Hallowed Ground* (1956). _____, *Glory Road* (1952). _____, *Mr. Lincoln's Army* (1951). _____, *A Stillness at Appomattox* (1953). Channing, Steven A., *Crisis of Fear: Secession in South Carolina* (1970). Clinton, Catherine, and Nina Silber, eds., *Divided Houses: Gender and the Civil War* (1992). Connelly, Thomas L., *The Marble Man: Robert E. Lee and His Image in American Society* (1977). Cooper, William J., Jr. *Jefferson Davis: American* (2000). Cornish, Dudley T., *The Sable Arm: Negro Troops in the Union Army* (1977). Current, Richard, *Lincoln and the First Shot* (1963). _____, ed., *Why the North Won the Civil War* (1960). Eaton, Clement, *A History of the Southern Confederacy* (1954). Escott, Paul D., *After Secession: Jefferson Davis and the Failure of Confederate Nationalism* (1978). Faust, Drew Gilpin, *The Creation of Confederate Nationalism* (1988). _____, *Mothers of Invention: Women of the Slaveholding South in the American Civil War* (1996). Fredrickson, George M., *The Inner Civil War: Northern Intellectuals and the Crisis of the Union* (1965).

Glatthaar, Joseph T., *Forged in Battle: the Civil War Alliance of Black Soldiers and White Officers* (1990). Guelzo, Allen C., *Abraham Lincoln: Redeemer President* (1999). Hettle, Wallace, *The Peculiar Democracy: Southern Democrats in Peace and Civil War* (2001). Jaffa, Harry V., *A New Birth of Freedom: Abraham Lincoln and the Coming of the Civil War* (2000). Jones, Howard, *The Union in Peril: The Crisis over British Intervention in the Civil War* (1992). Linderman, Gerald, *Embattled Courage: The Experience of Combat in the American Civil War* (1987).

McPherson, James M., *For Cause and Comrades: Why Men Fought in the Civil War* (1997). _____, *The Negro's Civil War: How American Negroes Felt and Acted During the War for the Union* (1965). _____, *The Struggle for Equality: Abolitionists and the Negro in the Civil War and Reconstruction* (1964). _____, *What They Fought For, 1861–1865* (1994). Mitchell, Reid, *Civil War Soldiers* (1988). _____, *The Vacant Chair: The Northern Soldier Leaves Home* (1993). Neely, Mark E., Jr., *The Fate of Liberty: Abraham Lincoln and Civil Liberties* (1990). Nevins, Allan, *The War for the Union*, 4 vols (1959–1971). Nolan, Alan T., *Lee Considered: General Robert E. Lee and Civil War History* (1991). Oates, Steven B., *A Woman of Valor: Clara Barton and the Civil War* (1994). Paludan, Phillip S., *Victims: A True Story of the Civil War* (1981). Potter, David M.,

Lincoln and His Party in the Secession Crisis (1942). Quarles, Benjamin, *The Negro in the Civil War* (1953). Rable, George C., *Civil Wars: Women and the Crisis of Southern Nationalism* (1989). Roark, James L., *Masters Without Slaves: Southern Planters in the Civil War and Reconstruction* (1977).

Thomas, Emory, *Robert E. Lee: A Biography* (1995). Vinovskis, Maris A., ed., *Toward a Social History of the American Civil War* (1990). Voegli, V. Jacques, *Free But Not Equal: The Midwest and the Negro during the Civil War* (1967). Wiley, Bell Irwin, *The Life of Billy Yank* (1952). _____, *The Life of Johnny Reb* (1943). Wilson, Douglas, *Honor's Voice: The Transformation of Abraham Lincoln* (1998).

CHAPTER 16

Belz, Herman, *Emancipation and Equal Rights: Politics and Constitutionalism in the Civil War Era* (1978). _____, *Reconstructing the Union: Theory and Policy during the Civil War* (1969). Benedict, Michael Les, *A Compromise of Principle: Congressional Republicans and Reconstruction* (1974). Brock, W. R., *An American Crisis: Congress and Reconstruction, 1865–1867* (1963). Cox, LaWanda, *Lincoln and Black Freedom: A Study in Presidential Leadership* (1981). Current, Richard, *Those Terrible Carpetbaggers* (1988). Donald, David, *The Politics of Reconstruction, 1864–1867* (1967). DuBois, Ellen Carol, *Feminism and Suffrage: The Emergence of an Independent Women's Movement in America, 1848–1869* (1978). Edwards, Laura, *Gendered Strife and Confusion: The Political Culture of Reconstruction* (1977). Fields, Barbara Jeanne, *Slavery and Freedom on the Middle Ground: Maryland during the Nineteenth Century* (1985). Foner, Eric, *Freedom's Lawmakers: A Directory of Black Officeholders during Reconstruction* (1993). _____, *Nothing But Freedom: Emancipation and Its Legacy* (1983).

Gillette, William, *Retreat from Reconstruction, 1869–1879* (1979). Hermann, Janet Sharp, *The Pursuit of a Dream* (1981). Holt, Thomas G., *Black over White: Negro Political Leadership in South Carolina during Reconstruction* (1977). Hyman, Harold, *A More Perfect Union: The Impact of the Civil War and Reconstruction on the Constitution* (1973). Jaynes, Gerald David, *Branches Without Roots: Genesis of the Black Working Class in the American South, 1862–1882* (1986).

McCrary, Peyton, *Abraham Lincoln and Reconstruction: The Louisiana Experiment* (1978). McFeely, William S., *Grant: A Biography* (1981). _____, *Yankee Stepfather: General O. O. Howard and the Freedmen* (1968). McGerr, Michael, *The Decline of Popular Politics: The American North, 1865–1928* (1986). McKitrick, Eric L., *Andrew Johnson and Reconstruction* (1960). Montgomery, David, *Beyond Equality: Labor and the Radical Republicans, 1861–1872* (1967). Morgan, Lynda J., *Emancipation in Virginia's Tobacco Belt, 1850–1870* (1992). Nieman, Donald L., *To Set the Law in Motion: The Freedmen's Bureau and Legal Rights for Blacks, 1865–1869* (1979). Perman, Michael, *Reunion Without Compromise: The South and Reconstruction, 1865–1879* (1973). _____, *The Road to Redemption: Southern Politics, 1868–1879* (1984). Powell, Lawrence N., *New Masters: Northern Planters during the Civil War and Reconstruction* (1980).

Rabinowitz, Howard N., *Race Relations in the Urban South, 1865–1890* (1978). Rose, Willie Lee, *Rehearsal for Reconstruction: The Port Royal Experiment* (1964). Royce, Edward, *The Origins of Southern Sharecropping* (1993).

Saville, Julie, *The Work of Reconstruction: From Slave to Wage Laborer in South Carolina, 1860–1870* (1994). Sproat, John G., *"The Best Men": Liberal Reformers in a Gilded Age* (1968). Summers, Mark, *Railroads, Reconstruction and the Gospel of Prosperity: Aid Under the Radical Republicans, 1865–1877* (1984). Trelease, Allen W., *White Terror: The Ku Klux Klan Conspiracy and Southern Reconstruction* (1971). Wayne, Michael, *The Reshaping of Plantation Society: The Natchez District, 1860–1880* (1983). Wiener, Jonathan, *Social Origins of the New South: Alabama, 1860–1885* (1978). Williamson, Joel, *After Slavery: The Negro in South Carolina during Reconstruction, 1861–1877* (1965). Wright, Gavin, *Old South, New South: Revolutions in the Southern Economy Since the Civil War* (1986).

CHAPTER 17

Ayres, Edward L., *The Promise of the New South: Life after Reconstruction* (1992). Bledstein, Burton J., *The Culture of Professionalism: The Middle Class and the Development of Higher Education in America* (1976). Bodnar, John E., *The Transplanted: A History of Immigrants in Urban America* (1985). Brody, David, *Steelworkers in America: The Nonunion Era* (1960). Cochran, Thomas, and William Miller, *The Age of Enterprise: A Social History of Industrial America* (1942). Dubofsky, Melvin, *Industrialism and the American Worker* (1975). Dykstra, Robert R., *The Cattle Towns* (1968). Fite, Gilbert C., *The Farmer's Frontier* (1963).

Goldfield, David, and Blaine Brownell, *Urban America: A History*, 2d. ed. (1990). Gutman, Herbert G., *Work, Culture and Society in Industrialising America* (1976). Handlin, Oscar, *The Uprooted: The Epic Story of the Great Migrations that Made the American People* (1951, 1973). Hearnden, Patrick H., *Independence and Empire: The New South's Cotton Mill Campaign, 1865–1901* (1982). Jackson, Kenneth T., *Crabgrass Frontier: The Suburbanization of the United States* (1985). Jeffrey, Julie Roy, *Frontier Women* (1979). Johnson, Susan Lee, *Roaring Camp: The Social World of the California Gold Rush* (2000). Josephson, Matthew, *The Robber Barons: The Great American Capitalists, 1861–1901* (1934). Limerick, Patricia Nelson, *Legacy of Conquest: The Unbroken Past of the American West* (1987). Lingenfelter, Richard, *The Hardrock Miners: A History of the Mining Labor Movement in the American West, 1863–1893* (1974).

Montgomery, David, *Workers' Control in America: Studies in the History of Work, Technology, and Labor Struggles* (1979). Rabinowitz, Howard, *Race Relations in the Urban South, 1865–1890* (1978).

Slotkin, Richard, *The Fatal Environment: The Myth of the Frontier in the Age of Industrialization* (1985). Taylor, Philip A. M., *The Distant Magnet: European Emigration to the U.S.A.* (1971). Teaford, Jon C., *City and Suburb: The Political Fragmentation of Metropolitan America, 1850–1970* (1979). Thernstrom, Stephen, *The Other Bostonians: Poverty and Progress in the American Metropolis, 1880–1970* (1973). Utley, Robert M., *The Indian Frontier of the American West, 1846–1890* (1984). Wiebe, Robert, *The Search for Order, 1877–1920* (1967). Wyman, Mark, *Hard Rock Epic: Western Miners and the Industrial Revolution, 1860–1910* (1979).

CHAPTER 18

Addams, Jane, *Twenty Years at Hull House* (1910). Archdeacon, Thomas, *Becoming American: An Ethnic History* (1981). Banner, Lois, *American Beauty* (1981). Barth, Gunther, *City People: The Rise of Modern City Culture in Nineteenth Century America* (1980). Beisel, Nicola Kay, *Imperiled Innocents: Anthony Comstock and Family Reproduction in Victorian America* (1997). Bodnar, John, *The Transplanted: A History of Immigrants in Urban America* (1985). Boorstin, Daniel J., *The Americans: The Democratic Experience* (1973). Boyer, Paul S., *Purity in Print: The Vice-society Movement and Book Censorship in America* (1968). Danly, Susan, and Cheryl Leibold, et al., *Eakins and the Photograph* (1994). Fabian, Ann, *Card Sharps and Bucket Shops: Gambling in Nineteenth-Century America* (1999). Fredrickson, George, *The Black Image in the White Mind: The Debate on Afro-American Character and Destiny, 1817–1914* (1971).

Gilfoyle, Timothy, *City of Eros: New York City, Prostitution, and the Commercialization of Sex, 1820–1920* (1992). Gorn, Elliot J., *The Manly Art: Bare-knuckle Prize Fighting in America* (1986). Graff, Gerald, *Professing Literature: An Institutional History* (1987). Green, Harvey, *Fit for America: Health, Fitness, Sport, and American Society* (1986). Harris, Neil, *Cultural Excursions: Marketing Appetites and Cultural Tastes in Modern America* (1990). Hawkins, Mike, *Social Darwinism in European and American Thought, 1860–1945: Nature as Model and Nature as Threat* (1997). Higham, John, *Send These To Me: Jews and Other Immigrants in Urban America* (1984). Hofstadter, Richard, *Social Darwinism in American Thought* (1992). Lears, T. J. Jackson, *No Place of Grace: Antimodernism and the Transformation of American Culture, 1880–1920* (1981). Lott, Eric, *Love and Theft: Blackface Minstrelsy and the American Working Class* (1993). Lucie-Smith, Edward, *American Realism* (1994).

May, Henry, *Protestant Churches and Industrial America* (1949 and 1963). Mintz, Steven, *A Prison of Expectations: The Family in Victorian Culture* (1983). Nasaw, David, *Going Out: The Rise and Fall of Public Amusements* (1993). Novak, Barbara, *American Painting of the Nineteenth Century: Realism, Idealism, and the American Experience*, 2nd ed. (1979). Rodgers, Daniel, *The Work Ethic in Industrial America, 1850–1920* (1970). Rothman, Sheila M., *Woman's Proper Place: A History of Changing Ideals and Practices, 1870 to the Present* (1978). Rydell, Robert, *All the World's A Fair: Visions of Empire at American International Expositions, 1876–1916* (1984).

Sollors, Werner, *Beyond Ethnicity: Consent and Descent in American Culture* (1986). Toll, Robert, *On With The Show: The First Century of Show Business in America* (1976). Trachtenberg, Alan, *Reading American Photographs: Images as History, Mathew Brady to Walker Evans* (1989).

CHAPTER 19

Baker, Paula C., *The Moral Frameworks of Public Life: Gender, Politics, and the State in Rural New York, 1870–1930* (1991). Beatty, Bess, *A Revolution Gone Backward: The Black Response to National Politics, 1876–1896* (1987). Beisner, Robert L., *From the Old Diplomacy to the New, 1865–1900* (1975). Bordin, Ruth, *Frances Willard: A Biography* (1986). Brock, William R., *Investigation and Responsibility: Public Responsibility in the United States, 1865–1900* (1984). Buhle, Mary Jo, *Women and American Socialism, 1870–1920* (1981). Campbell, Ballard, *Representative Democracy: Public Policy and Midwestern Legislatures in the Late Nineteenth Century* (1980). Campbell, Charles S., *The Transformation of American Foreign Relations, 1865–1900* (1976).

Garraty, John A., *The New Commonwealth, 1877–1890* (1968). Gould, Lewis L., *The Presidency of William McKinley* (1980). Hays, Samuel P., *The Response to Industrialism, 1885–1914*, 2nd ed. (1995). Jensen, Richard J., *The Winning of the Midwest: Social and Political Conflict, 1888–1896* (1971). Keller, Morton, *Affairs of State: Public Life in Late Nineteenth Century America* (1977). Kleppner, Paul J., *The Cross of Culture: A Social Analysis of Midwestern Politics, 1850–1900* (1970).

McCormick, Richard L., *The Party Period and Public Policy: American Politics from the Age of Jackson to the Progressive Era* (1986). McMath, Robert C., Jr., *The Populist Vanguard: A History of the Southern Farmers' Alliance* (1975). Mink, Gwendolyn, *Old Labor and New Immigrants in American Political Development: Union, Party, and the State, 1875–1920* (1986). Morgan, H. Wayne, *From Hayes to McKinley: National Politics, 1877–1896* (1969). Nugent, Walter T. K., *Money and American Society, 1865–1880,* (1968). Orren, Karen, *Belated Feudalism: Labor, the Law, and Liberal Development in the United States* (1991). Painter, Nell Irvin, *Standing at Armageddon: The United States, 1877–1919* (1987). Peskin, Allan, *Garfield: A Biography* (1978). Reeves, Thomas C., *Gentleman Boss: The Life of Chester Alan Arthur* (1975).

Skowronek, Stephen, *Building A New American State: The Expansion of National Administration Capacities, 1877–1920* (1982). Socolofsky, Homer Edward, and Allan B. Spetter, *The Presidency of Benjamin Harrison* (1987). Teaford, Jon C., *The Unheralded Triumph: City Government in America, 1870–1900* (1984). Terrill, Tom E., *The Tariff, Politics and American Foreign Policy, 1874–1900* (1973). Tomsich, John, *A Genteel Endeavor: American Culture and Politics in the Gilded Age* (1971). Unger, Irwin, *The Greenback Era: A Social and Political History of American Finance, 1865–1879* (1964). Weinstein, Allen, *Prelude to Populism: Origins of the Silver Issue, 1867–1878* (1970). Welch, Richard E., Jr., *The Presidencies of Grover Cleveland* (1988). Wiebe, Robert H., *The Search for Order, 1877–1920* (1967).

CHAPTER 20

Adams, Henry, *The Education of Henry Adams* (1918). Ayers, Edward L., *The Promise of the New South: Life After Reconstruction* (1992). Bailey, Thomas A., *A Diplomatic History of the American People* (1958). Brands, H. W., *The Reckless Decade: America in the 1890s* (1995). Chernow, Ron, *The House of Morgan: An American Banking Dynasty and the Rise of Modern Finance* (1990). Cochran, Thomas C., and William Miller, *The Age of Enterprise: A Social History of Industrial America* (1961). Dulles, Foster Rhea, *Labor in America: A History* (1960).

Gilbert, James B., *Perfect Cities: Chicago's Utopias of 1893* (1991). Ginger, Ray, *Age of Excess: The United States from 1877 to 1914* (1965). _____, *Altgeld's America: The Lincoln Ideal Versus Changing Realities* (1958). Kanigel, Robert, *The One Best Way: Frederick Winslow Taylor and the Enigma of Efficiency* (1997). Karnow, Stanley, *In Our Image: America's Empire in the Philippines* (1989). Lewis, David L., *W. E. B. Du Bois: Biography of a Race, 1868–1919* (1993).

McCloskey, Robert Green, *American Conservatism in the Age of Enterprise, 1865–1910* (1951). McCormick, Richard L., *The Party Period and Public Policy* (1986). McCormick, Thomas J., *China Market: America's Quest for Informal Empire, 1893–1901* (1967). McDougall, Walter A., *Let the Sea Make a Noise: A History of the North Pacific From Magellan to MacArthur* (1993). McGerr, Michael E., *The Decline of Popular Politics: The American North, 1865–1928* (1986). Montgomery, David, *The Fall of the House of Labor: The Workplace, the State, and American Labor Activism, 1865–1925* (1987). Musicant, Ivan, *Empire by Default: The Spanish American War and the Dawn of the American Century* (1998). Richardson, Dorothy, *The Long Day: The Story of a New York Working Girl* (1990). Rosenberg, Emily S., *Spreading the American Dream: American Economic and Cultural Expansion, 1890–1945* (1982).

Salvatore, Nick, *Eugene V. Debs: Citizen and Socialist* (1982). Schirmer, Daniel B., *Republic or Empire: American Resistance to the Philippine War* (1972). Slotkin, Richard, *Gunfighter Nation: The Myth of the Frontier in Twentieth Century America* (1993). Strouse, Jean, *Morgan: American Financier* (1999). Trask, David F., *The War with Spain in 1898* (1981).

CHAPTER 21

Brands, H. W., *T. R.: The Last Romantic* (1997). Bringhurst, Bruce, *Antitrust and the Oil Monopoly: The Standard Oil Cases, 1890–1911* (1979). Clark, Norman H., *Deliver Us From Evil: An Interpretation of American Prohibition* (1976). Cooper, John Milton, Jr., *The Warrior and the Priest: Theodore Roosevelt and Woodrow Wilson in American Politics* (1983). Crichon, Judy, *America 1900: The Turning Point* (1998). Diner, Steven J., *A Very Different Age: Americans in the Progressive Era* (1998). Dulles, Foster Rhea, *Labor in America* (1955). Faulkner, Harold Underwood, *The Quest for Social Justice, 1898–1914* (1931). Filene, Peter G., "Narrating Progressivism: Unitarians v. Pluralists v. Students," *Journal of American History,* 79 (1993) 4, 1546–61.

Gould, Lewis L., *The Presidency of Theodore Roosevelt* (1991). Harbaugh, William H., *Power and Responsibility: The Life and Times of Theodore Roosevelt* (1961). Kessler-Harris, Alice, *Out to Work: A History of Wage Earning Women* (1982). Lewis, David Levering, *W. E. B. Du Bois: Biography of a Race,*

1868–1919 (1993). Lukas, J. Anthony, *Big Trouble: A Murder in a Small Western Town Sets Off a Struggle for the Soul of America* (1997).

McGerr, Michael E., *The Decline of Popular Politics* (1986). McMurry, Linda O., *To Keep the Waters Troubled: The Life of Ida B. Wells* (1998). Ninkovich, Frank, *Modernity and Power: A History of the Domino Theory in the Twentieth Century* (1994). Rodgers, Daniel T., "In Search of Progressivism," *Reviews in American History*, 10 (1982) 4, 113–32. Rosen, Ruth, *The Lost Sisterhood: Prostitution in America, 1900–1918* (1982).

Salvatore, Nick, *Eugene V. Debs: Citizen and Socialist* (1982). Schiesl, Martin J., *The Politics of Efficiency: Municipal Administration and Reform in America, 1800–1920* (1977). Scully, Eileen P., "Taking the Low Road to Sino-American Relations: 'Open Door' Expansionists and the Two China Markets," *Journal of American History*, 82 (1995) 1, 62–83. Shannon, David A., *The Socialist Party of America: A History* (1955). Sklar, Kathryn Kish, *Florence Kelley and the Nation's Work: The Rise of Women's Political Culture, 1830–1900* (1995). Starr, Kevin, *Inventing the Dream: California Through the Progressive Era* (1985). Thelen, David, *Robert M. La Follette and the Insurgent Spirit* (1976). Weibe, Robert H., "The Anthracite Strike of 1902: A Record of Confusion," *Mississippi Valley Historical Review*, 48 (1961) 2, 229–51. _____, *The Search for Order, 1877–1920* (1967).

CHAPTER 22

Bailey, Thomas A., "The Sinking of the Lusitania," *The American Historical Review*, 41 (1935) 1, 54–73. Bird, Kai, *The Chairman: John J. McCloy, The Making of the American Establishment* (1992). Butler, Gregory S., "Visions of a Nation Transformed: Modernity and Ideology in Wilson's Political Thought," *Journal of Church and State*, 39 (Winter 1997) 1, 37–51. Chatfield, Charles, "World War I and the Liberal Pacifist in the United States," *American Historical Review*, 75 (1970) 7, 1920–37. Clark, Norman H., *Deliver Us From Evil: An Interpretation of American Prohibition* (1976). Clifford, John Garry, *The Citizen Soldiers: The Plattsburg Training Camp Movement, 1919–1920* (1972). Davis, Richard Harding, "The Plattsburg Idea," *Collier's* (October 9, 1915) 7–9. Ferrell, Robert H., *Woodrow Wilson and World War I, 1917–1921* (1985).

Horne, Alistair, *The Price of Glory* (1964). Katz, Freidrich, "Pancho Villa and the Attack on Columbus, New Mexico," *American Historical Review*, 83 (1978) 1, 101–30. _____, *The Secret War in Mexico: Europe, the United States, and the Mexican Revolution* (1981). Levin, N. Gordon, Jr., *Woodrow Wilson and World Politics* (1968).

Miles, Lewis W., "Plattsburgh," *Sewanee Review*, 24 (January 1916) 1, 19–23. Miller, William D., *Pretty Bubbles in the Air: America in 1919* (1991). Page, Ralph W., "What I Learned at Plattsburg," *World's Work* (November 1915), 105–08. Perry, Ralph Barton, "Impressions of a Plattsburg Recruit," *New Republic* (October 2, 1915), 229–31. Rudwick, Elliott M., *Race Riot in East Saint Louis, July 2, 1917* (1964). Russell, Francis, *Tragedy in Dedham: The Story of the Sacco-Vanzetti Case* (1962).

Schaffer, Ronald, *America in the Great War: The Rise of the War Welfare State* (1991). Schoonover, Thomas D., "To End All Social Reform: A Progressive's Search for International Order," *Reviews in American History*, 21 (1993), 647–54. Tuchman, Barbara, *The Guns of August* (1976). Ward, Robert D., "The Origin and Activities of the National Security League, 1914–1919," *Mississippi Valley Historical Review*, 47 (January 1960) 1, 51–65. Wynn, Neil A., *From Progressivism to Prosperity: World War I and American Society* (1986).

CHAPTER 23

Barron, Hal S., *Mixed Harvest: The Second Great Transformation in the Rural North, 1870–1930* (1997). Blee, Kathleen M., *Women of the Klan: Racism and Gender in the 1920s* (1991). Burner, David, *Herbert Hoover: A Public Life* (1979). _____, *The Politics of Provincialism: The Democratic Party in Transition, 1918–1932* (1968). Chandler, Alfred D., Jr., *Strategy and Structure* (1962). Coben, Stanley, *Rebellion Against Victorianism: The Impetus for Change in 1920s America* (1991). Cohen, Warren I., *Empire Without Tears: America's Foreign Relations, 1921–1933* (1987). De Benedetti, Charles, *Origins of the Modern American Peace Movement: 1915–1929* (1978). D'Emilio, John, and Estelle Freedman, *Intimate Matters: A History of Sexuality in America* (1988). Douglas, Ann, *Terrible Honesty: Mongrel Manhattan in the 1920s* (1995). Douglas, Susan J., *Inventing American Broadcasting, 1899–1922* (1987).

Gordon, Linda, *Woman's Body, Woman's Right: A Social History of Birth Control in America* (1977). Griswold, Robert, *Fatherhood in America: A History* (1993). Gutierrez, David, *Walls and Mirrors: Mexican Americans, Mexican Immigrants, and the Politics of Ethnicity* (1995). Hawley, Ellis W., *The Great War and the Search for a Modern Order: A History of the American People and Their Institutions, 1917–1933* (1992). _____, ed., *Herbert Hoover as Secretary of Commerce: Studies in New Era Thought and Practice* (1981). Hogan, Michael J., *Informal Entente: The Private Structure of Cooperation in Anglo-American Economy, 1918–1929* (1977). Hounshell, David A., *From the American System to Mass Production, 1800–1932: The Development of Manufacturing Technology in the United States* (1984). Huggins, Nathan I., *Harlem Renaissance* (1971). Jackson, Kenneth T., *The Ku Klux Klan in the City, 1915–1930* (1967). Kennedy, J. Gerald, *Imagining Paris: Exile, Writing and American Identity* (1993). Kern, Stephen, *The Culture of Time and Space, 1880–1918* (1983). Koszarski, Richard, *An Evening's Entertainment: The Age of the Silent Feature Picture, 1915–1928* (1990). Ladd-Taylor, Molly, *Mother-Work: Women, Child Welfare, and the State, 1890–1930* (1994). Lears, Jackson, *Fables of Abundance: A Cultural History of Advertising in America* (1994). Leffler, Melvyn P., *The Elusive Quest: America's Pursuit of European Stability and French Security, 1919–1933* (1979). Lemons, J. Stanley, *The Woman Citizen: Social Feminism in the 1920s* (1973). Lichtman, Alan J., *Prejudice and the Old Politics: The Presidential Election of 1928* (1979).

Marsden, George M., *Fundamentalism and American Culture: The Shaping of Twentieth-Century Evangelicalism, 1870–1925* (1980). Meyerowitz, Joanne J., *Women Adrift: Independent Wage Earners in Chicago, 1880–1930* (1988). Montgomery,

David, *The Fall of the House of Labor: The Workplace, the State, and American Labor Activism, 1865–1925* (1987). Moore, Leonard J., *Citizen Klansmen: The Ku Klux Klan in Indiana, 1921–1928* (1991). Peretti, Burton W., *The Creation of Jazz: Music, Race, and Culture in Urban America* (1992).

Schlesinger, Arthur M., Jr., *The Crisis of the Old Order: 1919–1933* (1957). Seymour, Harold, *Baseball: The Golden Age* (1971). Singal, Daniel Joseph, *The War Within: From Victorian to Modernist Thought in the South, 1919–1945* (1982). Trani, Eugene P., and David L. Wilson, *The Presidency of Warren G. Harding* (1977). Zunz, Olivier, *Making America Corporate, 1870–1920* (1990).

CHAPTER 24

Badger, Anthony J., *The New Deal: The Depression Years, 1933–1940* (1989). Bernstein, Irving, *The Lean Years* (1960). _____, *The Turbulent Years* (1970). Bernstein, Michael A., *The Great Depression: Delayed Recovery and Economic Change in America, 1929–1939* (1987). Bird, Caroline, *The Invisible Scar* (1966). Brinkley, Alan, *Liberalism and Its Discontents* (1998). _____, *Voices of Protest* (1982). Burns, James MacGregor, *Roosevelt: The Lion and the Fox* (1956). Carnegie, Dale, "Grab Your Bootstraps," *Colliers*, March 5, 1938, 14–15. Carter, Dan T., *Scottsboro: A Tragedy of the American South* Rev ed (1979). Cooke, Blanche Wiesen, *Eleanor Roosevelt* 2 vol (1992–1999). Daniels, Roger, *The Bonus March* (1971). Denning, Michael, *The Cultural Front: The Laboring of American Culture in the Twentieth Century* (1997). Edwards, Anne, *Road to Tara* (1983). Eichengreen, Barry, *Golden Fetters: The Gold Standard and the Great Depression, 1919–1939* (1995). Ellis, Edward Robb, *A Nation in Torment: The Great American Depression, 1929–1939* (1970). Fraser, Steve, *Labor Will Rule: Sidney Hillman and the Rise of American Labor* (1991). _____, and Gary Gerstle, *The Rise and Fall of the New Deal Order, 1930–1980* (1989).

Galbraith, John Kenneth, *The Great Crash: 1929* (1961). Gourevitch, Peter, *Politics in Hard Times: Comparative Responses to International Economic Crises* (1986). Granberry, Edward, "The Private Life of Margaret Mitchell," *Colliers*, March 13, 1937, 22–24. Greenberg, Cheryl Lynn, *"Or Does it Explode?": Black Harlem in the Great Depression* (1991). Gregory, James, *American Exodus: The Dust Bowl Migration and Okie Culture in California* (1989). Harriman, Margaret Case, "He Sells Hope," *Saturday Evening Post*, August 14, 1937, 12–34. Hofstadter, Richard, *The Age of Reform* (1956). Kelley, Robin D. G., *Hammer and Hoe: Alabama Communists During the Great Depression* (1990). Kennedy, David M., *Freedom From Fear: The American People in Depression and War* (1999). Kindelberger, Charles, *The World in Depression* (1973). Kirby, John B., *Black Americans in the Roosevelt Era* (1980). Klehr, Harvey, *The Heyday of American Communism: The Depression Decade* (1984). Leuchtenberg, William E., *Franklin D. Roosevelt and the New Deal* (1963).

Manchester, William, *The Glory and the Dream* (1973). McElvaine, Robert S., *The Great Depression: America, 1929–1941* (1984). Nelson, Bruce, *Workers on the Waterfront: Seamen, Longshoremen, and Unionism in the 1930s* (1988).

Patterson, James, *Congressional Conservatism and the New Deal* (1967). _____, *The New Deal and the States* (1969). Pells, Richard, *Radical Visions and American Dreams: Culture and Social Thought in the Depression Years* (1973). Plotke, David, *Building a Democratic Political Order: Reshaping American Liberalism in the 1930s and 1940s* (1996). Pyron, Darden Asbury, *Southern Daughter* (1991).

Schulman, Bruce J., *From Cotton Belt to Sunbelt: Federal Policy, Economic Development, and the Transformation of the South, 1938–1980* (1991). Sitkoff, Harvard, *A New Deal for Blacks* (1978). Temin, Peter, *Lessons from the Great Depression* (1996). Watkins, T. H., *The Hungry Years* (1999). Williams, T. Harry, *Huey Long: A Biography* (1969). Wilson, Joan Hoff, *Herbert Hoover: Forgotten Progressive* (1975). Worster, Donald, *The Dust Bowl: The Southern Plains in the 1930s* (1979).

CHAPTER 25

Adams, Michael C. C., *The Best War Ever: America and World War II* (1994). Alperovitz, Gar, *The Decision to Use the Atomic Bomb and the Architecture of an American Myth* (1995). Ambrose, Stephen, *American Heritage New History of World War II* (1997). _____, *Citizen Soldiers* (1997). Bendiner, Elmer, *The Fall of Fortresses* (1980). Bergerud, Eric, *Touched With Fire: The Land War in the South Pacific* (1996). Blum, John Morton, *V Was for Victory* (1976). Blumenson, Martin, *Kasserine Pass* (1966). Deighton, Len, *Blood, Tears and Folly: An Objective Look at World War II* (1993). Dower, John W., *War Without Mercy* (1986). Feingold, Henry L., *The Politics of Rescue: The Roosevelt Administration and the Holocaust, 1938–1945* (1970). Finkle, Lee, "The Conservative Aims of Militant Rhetoric: Black Protest During World War II," *Journal of American History*, 60 (December 1973) 3, 692–713. Flower, Desmond, and James Reeves, eds., *The War, 1939–1945: A Documentary History* (1997). Fussell, Paul, *Wartime* (1989).

Harris, William H., "A. Philip Randolph as a Charismatic Leader, 1925–1941," *Journal of Negro History*, 64 (Autumn 1979) 4, 301–315. Heinrichs, Waldo, *Threshold of War* (1988). Hobsbawm, Eric, *The Age of Extremes* (1994). Houston, Jeanne Wakatsuki, and James D. Houston, *Farewell to Manzanar* (1973). Hynes, Samuel, *Flights of Passage* (1988). Kennedy, Paul, *The Rise and Fall of the Great Powers* (1987). Kimball, Warren F., *The Juggler: Franklin Roosevelt as Wartime Statesman* (1991). Leffler, Melvyn P., *The Specter of Communism* (1994).

Manchester, William, *The Glory and the Dream: A Narrative History of America, 1932–1972* (1973). Milward, Alan S., *War, Economy and Society 1939–1945* (1977). Morison, Samuel Eliot, *Coral Sea, Midway and Submarine Actions* (1949). _____, *The Two-Ocean War* (1963). O'Neill, William L., *A Democracy at War* (1993). Perrett, Geoffrey, *Days of Sadness, Years of Triumph* (1973). Pogue, Forrest C., *George C. Marshall: Ordeal and Hope, 1939–1942* (1965). Prange, Gordon W., *Miracle at Midway* (1982). Rosenberg, Emily S., *Spreading the American Dream: American Economic and Cultural Expansion, 1890–1945* (1982).

Sitkoff, Harvard, "Racial Militancy and Interracial Violence in the Second World War," *Journal of American History*, 58

(December 1971) 3, 661–81. Spickard, Paul R., *Japanese Americans: The Formation and Transformations of an Ethnic Group* (1996). United States, Federal Bureau of Investigation, "FBI File: A. Philip Randolph" (1990). Weighley, Russell F., *Eisenhower's Lieutenants* (1981). Wright, Gordon, *The Ordeal of Total War, 1939–1945* (1997).

CHAPTER 26

Blackwelder, Julia Kirk, *Now Hiring: The Feminization of Work in the United States, 1900–1995* (1997). Boyer, Paul, *By the Bomb's Early Light: American Thought and Culture at the Dawn of the Atomic Age* (1985). Cumings, Bruce, *The Origins of the Korean War*, 2 vols (1981–1990). Dalfiume, Richard, *Desegregation of the U.S. Armed Forces: Fighting on Two Fronts, 1939–1953* (1969). Donovan, Robert J., *Conflict and Crisis: The Presidency of Harry S Truman, 1945–1948* (1977). _____, *Tumultuous Years: The Presidency of Harry S Truman, 1948–1953* (1982). Egerton, John, *Speak Now Against the Day: The Generation Before the Civil Rights Movement in the South* (1994). Fried, Richard M., *The Russians Are Coming! the Russians Are Coming!: Pageantry and Patriotism in Cold-War America* (1999).

Gaddis, John Lewis, *The United States and the Origins of the Cold War, 1941–1947* (1972). _____, *We Now Know: Rethinking Cold War History* (1997). Hamby, Alonzo L., *Beyond the New Deal: Harry S. Truman and American Liberalism* (1973). Hartmann, Susan M., *The Home Front and Beyond: American Women in the 1940s* (1982). _____, *Truman and the 80th Congress* (1971). Heller, Francis H., ed., *Economics and the Truman Administration* (1981). Hogan, Michael J., *The Marshall Plan: America, Britain, and the Reconstruction of Western Europe, 1947–1952* (1987). Knox, Donald, *The Korean War: An Oral History*, 2 vols (1985–1988). Lacey, Michael J., ed., *The Truman Presidency* (1989). LaFeber, Walter, *America, Russia, and the Cold War, 1945–1992* (1993). Lawson, Steven M., *Black Ballots: Voting Rights in the South, 1944–1969* (1976).

May, Lary, ed., *Recasting America: Culture and Politics in the Age of Cold War* (1989). McCoy, Donald, and Richard Ruetten, *Quest and Response: Minority Rights and the Truman Administration* (1973). Meier, August, and Elliott Rudwick, *CORE: A Study in the Civil Rights Movement, 1942–1968* (1973). Merrill, Dennis, ed., *Documentary History of the Truman Presidency*, 20 vols (1995–1997). Nadel, Alan, *Containment Culture: American Narratives, Postmodernism, and the Atomic Age* (1995). Navasky, Victor S., *Naming Names* (1989). Patterson, James T., *Mr. Republican: A Biography of Robert A. Taft* (1972). Poen, Monte M., *Harry S. Truman Versus the Medical Lobby: The Genesis of Medicare* (1979). Polan, Dana, *Power and Paranoia: History, Narrative, and the American Cinema, 1940–1950* (1986). Radosh, Ronald, and Joyce Milton, *The Rosenberg File: A Search for the Truth* (1984). Renshaw, Patrick, *American Labor and Consensus Capitalism, 1935–1990* (1991).

Stueck, William, *The Korean War: An International History* (1995). Sugrue, Thomas J., *The Origins of the Urban Crisis: Race and Inequality in Postwar Detroit* (1996). Weiner, Lynn Y., *From Working Girl to Working Mother: The Female Labor Force in the United States, 1820–1980* (1985). Whitfield, Stephen J., *The Culture of the Cold War* (1991).

CHAPTER 27

Baughman, James L., *The Republic of Mass Culture: Journalism, Filmmaking and Broadcasting in America since 1941* (1991). Beschloss, Michael R., *Mayday: Eisenhower, Khrushchev and the U-2 Affair* (1991). Bowie, Robert R., and Richard H. Immerman, *Waging Peace: How Eisenhower Shaped an Enduring Cold War Strategy* (2000). Breines, Wini, *Young, White, and Miserable: Growing Up Female in the Fifties* (1992). Broadwater, Jeff, *Eisenhower and the Anti-Communist Crusade* (1992). Burk, Robert Fredrick, *The Eisenhower Administration and Black Civil Rights, 1953–1961* (1984). Cullather, Nick, *Illusions of Influence: The Political Economy of United States-Philippines Relations, 1942–1960* (1994). Divine, Robert, *The Sputnik Challenge* (1993). Dockrill, Saki, *Eisenhower's New-Look National Security Policy, 1953–1961* (1996). Dudziak, Mary, *Cold War Civil Rights: Race and the Image of American Democracy* (2000). Foreman, Joel, ed., *The Other Fifties: Interrogating Midcentury American Icons* (1997). Fried, Richard M., *Nightmare in Red: The McCarthy Era in Perspective* (1990).

Gardner, Lloyd C., *Approaching Vietnam: From World War II through Dienbienphu* (1988). Gartman, David, *Auto Opium: A Social History of American Automobile Design* (1994). Graebner, William, *Coming of Age in Buffalo: Youth and Authority in the Postwar Era* (1990). Guralnick, Peter, *Last Train to Memphis: The Rise of Elvis Presley* (1994). Gutierrez, David, *Walls and Mirrors: Mexican Americans, Mexican Immigrants, and the Politics of Ethnicity* (1995). Horowitz, Daniel, ed., *American Social Classes in the 1950s: Selections from Vance Packard's The Status Seekers* (1995). Jackson, Kenneth, *Crabgrass Frontier: The Suburbanization of the United States* (1985). Jones, Gerard, *Honey, I'm Home! Sitcoms: Selling the American Dream* (1992). Karabell, Zachary, *Architects of Intervention: The United States, the Third World, and the Cold War, 1946–1962* (1999). Kluger, Richard, *Simple Justice: The History of Brown v. Board of Education and Black America's Struggle for Equality* (1977). Korrol, Virginia Sanchez, *From Colonia to Community: The History of Puerto Ricans in New York City* (1994). Kunz, Diane B., *The Economic Diplomacy of the Suez Crisis* (1991). Lhamon, Ward T., *Deliberate Speed: The Origins of a Cultural Style in the American 1950s* (1990).

May, Elaine Tyler, *Homeward Bound: American Families in the Cold War Era* (1988). Meier, Matt S., and Feliciano Ribera, *Mexican Americans, American Mexicans: from Conquistadors to Chicanos* (1993). O'Neill, William L., *American High: The Years of Confidence, 1945–1960* (1986). Pach, Chester J., and Elmo Richardson, *The Presidency of Dwight D. Eisenhower* (1991). Raines, Howell, *My Soul Is Rested: Movement Days in the Deep South Remembered* (1977). Ramos, Henry A. J., *The American G.I. Forum: In Pursuit of the Dream, 1948–1993* (1998). Rawls, James J., *Chief Red Fox Is Dead: A History of Native Americans Since 1945* (1996). Rupp, Leila J., *Survival in the Doldrums: The American Women's Rights Movement, 1945 to the 1960s* (1987).

Takeyh, Ray, *The Origins of the Eisenhower Doctrine: The US, Britain, and Nasser's Egypt, 1953–57* (2000). Watson, Steven, *The Birth of the Beat Generation: Visionaries, Rebels, and Hipsters, 1944–1960* (1995).

CHAPTER 28

Appy, Christian G., *Working-Class War: American Combat Soldiers & Vietnam* (1993). Beschloss, Michael, *The Crisis Years: Kennedy and Khrushchev, 1960–1963* (1991). Blum, John Morton, *Years of Discord: American Politics and Society, 1961–1974* (1991). Brands, H. W., *The Wages of Globalism: Lyndon Johnson and the Limits of American Power* (1995). Brick, Howard, *Age of Contradiction: American Thought and Culture in the 1960s* (2000). Burner, David, *John F. Kennedy and a New Generation* (1988). Carson, Clayborne, *In Struggle: SNCC and the Black Awakening of the 1960s* (1981). Chafe, William H., *Civilities and Civil Rights: Greensboro, North Carolina, and the Black Struggle for Freedom* (1980). Dallek, Robert, *Flawed Giant: Lyndon Johnson and His Times, 1961–1973* (1991). Davies, Gareth, *From Opportunity to Entitlement: The Transformation and Decline of Great Society Liberalism* (1996). Dickstein, Morris, *Gates of Eden: American Culture in the Sixties* (1977). Dittmer, John, *Local People: The Struggle for Civil Rights in Mississippi* (1994). Douglas, Susan J., *Where the Girls Are: Growing Up Female with the Mass Media* (1994). Downs, Frederick, *The Killing Zone: My Life in the Vietnam War* (1978). Evans, Sara, *Personal Politics: The Roots of Women's Liberation in the Civil Rights Movement & the New Left* (1979). Farber, David, ed., *The Sixties: From Memory to History* (1994).

Garrow, David J., *Bearing the Cross: Martin Luther King, Jr., and the Southern Christian Leadership Conference* (1986). Giglio, James N., *The Presidency of John F. Kennedy* (1991). Halberstam, David, *The Best and the Brightest* (1972). Haley, Alex, *The Autobiography of Malcolm X* (1966). Harrison, Cynthia, *On Account of Sex: The Politics of Women's Issues, 1945–1968* (1988). Harvey, Mark W. T., *A Symbol of Wilderness: Echo Park and the American Conservation Movement* (1994). Hodgson, Godfrey, *America in Our Time: From World War II to Nixon* (1976). Hoffman, Elizabeth Cobbs, *All You Need Is Love: The Peace Corps and the Spirit of the 1960s* (1998). Horne, Gerald, *Fire This Time: The Watts Uprising and the 1960s* (1996). Horowitz, Daniel, *Betty Friedan and the Making of the Feminine Mystique: The American Left, the Cold War, and Modern Feminism* (1998). Jeffreys-Jones, Rhodri, *Peace Now!: American Society and the Ending of the Vietnam War* (1999). Kahin, George McT., *Intervention: How America Became Involved in Vietnam* (1986). Kaiser, David E., *American Tragedy: Kennedy, Johnson, and the Origins of the Vietnam War* (2000). Krepinevich, Andrew F., Jr., *The Army and Vietnam* (1986). Linden-Ward, Blanche, & Carol Hurd Green, *Changing the Future: American Women in the 1960s* (1993).

Macedo, Stephen, ed., *Reassessing the Sixties: Debating the Political and Cultural Legacy* (1997). McAdam, Doug, *Freedom Summer* (1988). McDougall, Walter A., *. . . the Heavens and the Earth: A Political History of the Space Age* (1985). Moïse, Edwin E., *Tonkin Gulf and the Escalation of the Vietnam War* (1996).

Paterson, Thomas G., ed., *Kennedy's Quest for Victory: American Foreign Policy, 1961–1963* (1989). Payne, Charles M., *I've Got the Light of Freedom: The Organizing Tradition and the Mississippi Freedom Struggle* (1995). Pearson, Hugh, *The Shadow of the Panther: Huey Newton and the Price of Black Power in America* (1994). Ralph, James R., Jr., *Northern Protest: Martin Luther King, Jr., Chicago, and the Civil Rights Movement* (1993). Rorabaugh, W. J., *Berkeley at War: The 1960s* (1989). Rothman, Hal K., *The Greening of a Nation: Environmentalism in the United States Since 1945* (1998).

Schlesinger, Arthur M., Jr., *Robert Kennedy and His Times* (1978). Schwartz, Bernard, *Super Chief: Earl Warren and His Supreme Court* (1983). Steigerwald, David, *The Sixties and the End of Modern America* (1995). Summer, Harry G., Jr., *On Strategy: A Critical Analysis of the Vietnam War* (1982). Szatmary, David P., *Rockin' in Time: A Social History of Rock-and-Roll* (1997). Van Deburg, William L., *New Day in Babylon: The Black Power Movement and American Culture, 1965–1975* (1992). Wells, Tom, *The War Within: America's Battle Over Vietnam* (1996).

CHAPTER 29

Adam, Barry D., *The Rise of a Gay and Lesbian Movement*, Rev. ed. (1995). Barnet, Richard J., and Ronald E. Müller, *Global Reach: The Power of the Multinational Corporations* (1974). Bartley, Numan V., *The New South, 1945–1980: The Story of the South's Modernization, 1945–1980* (1995). Bernstein, Carl, and Bob Woodward, *All the President's Men* (1974). Bernstein, Michael A., and David E. Adler, eds., *Understanding American Economic Decline* (1994). Bill, James A., *The Eagle and the Lion: The Tragedy of American-Iranian Relations* (1988). Brands, H. W., *Since Vietnam: The United States in World Affairs, 1973–1995* (1996). Campisi, Jack, *The Mashpee Indians: Tribe on Trial* (1991). Carter, Dan T., *The Politics of Rage: George Wallace, the Origins of the New Conservatism, and the Transformation of American Politics* (1995). Chan, Sucheng, *Asian Americans: An Interpretive History* (1990). D'Emilio, John, *Sexual Politics, Sexual Communities: The Making of a Homosexual Minority in the United States, 1940–1970* (1983). Duberman, Martin, *Stonewall* (1993). Engelhardt, Tom, *The End of Victory Culture: Cold War America and the Disillusioning of a Generation* (1995). Espiritu, Yen Le, *Asian American Panethnicity: Bridging Institutions and Identities* (1992). Ford, Daniel F., *Three Mile Island: Thirty Minutes to Meltdown* (1982). Frye, Gaillard, *The Dream Long Deferred* (1988).

Garrow, David J., *Liberty and Sexuality: The Right to Privacy and the Making of* Roe v. Wade (1994). Garthoff, Raymond L., *Détente and Confrontation: American-Soviet Relations from Nixon to Reagan* (1994). Gartman, David, *Auto Opium: A Social History of American Automobile Design* (1994). Greene, John Robert, *The Limits of Power: The Nixon and Ford Administrations* (1992). Isaacs, Arnold R., *Without Honor: Defeat in Vietnam and Cambodia* (1983). Isaacson, Walter, *Kissinger: A Biography* (1992). Jones, Charles O., *The Trusteeship Presidency: Jimmy Carter and the United States Congress* (1988). Kimball, Jeffrey P., *Nixon's Vietnam War* (1998). LaFeber, Walter, *The Panama Canal Crisis in Historical*

Perspective (1989). Lasch, Christopher, *The Culture of Narcissism: American Life in an Age of Diminishing Expectations* (1979). Lawson, Steven F., *Running for Freedom: Civil Rights and Black Politics in America Since 1941* (1997).

Marin, Marguerite V., *Social Protest in an Urban Barrio: A Study of the Chicano Movement, 1966–1974* (1991). Nagel, Joanne, *American Indian Ethnic Renewal: Red Power and the Resurgence of Identity and Culture* (1996). Rieder, Jonathan, *Canarsie: The Jews and Italians of Brooklyn Against Liberalism* (1985). Rosen, Ellen Israel, *Bitter Choices: Blue-Collar Women in and out of Work* (1987). Ryan, Paul B., *The Iranian Rescue Mission and Why It Failed* (1986).

Sale, Kirkpatrick, *Power Shift: The Rise of the Southern Rim and Its Challenge to the Eastern Establishment* (1975). Schlesinger, Arthur M., Jr., *The Imperial Presidency* (1973). Schulman, Bruce J., *From Cotton Belt to Sun Belt: Federal Policy, Economic Development, and the Transformation of the South, 1938–1980* (1991). Schur, Edwin, *The Awareness Trap: Self-Absorption instead of Social Change* (1976). Small, Melvin, *The Presidency of Richard Nixon* (1999). Smith, Gaddis, *Morality, Reason, and Power: American Diplomacy in the Carter Years* (1986). Stern, Kenneth S., *Loud Hawk: The United States versus the American Indian Movement* (1994). Szasz, Andrew, *EcoPopulism: Toxic Waste and the Movement for Environmental Justice* (1994). Takaki, Ronald, *Strangers from a Different Shore: A History of Asian Americans* (1989). Thurow, Lester, *The Zero-Sum Society: Distribution and the Possibilities for Economic Change* (1980). Vigil, Ernesto, *The Crusade for Justice: Chicano Militancy and the Government's War on Dissent*. Wei, William, *The Asian American Movement* (1993). Wicker, Tom, *One of Us: Richard Nixon and the American Dream* (1991). Wilkinson, J. Harvie, III, *From Brown to Bakke: The Supreme Court and School Integration, 1954–1978* (1979). Wolfe, Alan, *America's Impasse: The Rise and Fall of the Politics of Growth* (1981).

CHAPTER 30

Adam, Barry D., *The Rise of a Gay and Lesbian Movement Rev. ed.* (1995). Anderson, Martin, *Revolution: The Reagan Legacy* (1988). Berman, William C., *America's Right Turn: From Nixon to Bush* (1994). Blumenthal, Sidney, *The Rise of the Counter-Establishment: From Conservative Ideology to Political Power* (1986). Campbell-Kelly, Martin, and William Aspray, *Computer: A History of the Information Machine* (1996). Cannon, Lou, *Ronald Reagan: The Role of a Lifetime* (1991). Davis, Flora, *Moving the Mountain: The Women's Movement in America since 1960* (1991). Ferree, Myra Marx, and Beth B. Hess, *Controversy and Coalition: The New Feminist Movement Across Three Decades of Change* (1994). Friedman, Benjamin M., *Day of Reckoning: The Consequences of American Economic Policy under Reagan and After* (1988).

Gallagher, John, *Perfect Enemies: The Religious Right, the Gay Movement, and the Politics of the 1990s* (1996). Garthoff, Raymond L., *Détente and Confrontation: American-Soviet Relations from Nixon to Reagan* (1994). _____, *The Great Transition: American-Soviet Relations and the End of the Cold War* (1994). Gillon, Steven M., *The Democrats' Dilemma: Walter*

F. Mondale and the Liberal Legacy (1992). Hill, Dilys M., et al., *The Reagan Presidency: An Incomplete Revolution?* (1990). Hodgson, Godfrey, *The World Turned Right Side Up: A History of the Conservative Ascendancy in America* (1996). Hoeveler, J. David, *Watch on the Right: Conservative Intellectuals in the Reagan Era* (1991). Hurt, Harry, *The Lost Tycoon: The Many Lives of Donald J. Trump* (1993). Jaynes, Gerald David, and Robin M. Williams, Jr., eds., *A Common Destiny: Blacks and American Society* (1989). Fitzgerald, Frances, *Way Out There in the Blue: Reagan and Star Wars and the End of the Cold War* (2000). Jeffords, Susan, *Hard Bodies: Hollywood Masculinity in the Reagan Era* (1994). Jorstad, Erling, *Holding Fast/Pressing On: Religion in America in the 1980s* (1990). Lewis, Michael, *Liar's Poker: Rising Through the Wreckage on Wall Street* (1989). Lofland, John, *Polite Protesters: The American Peace Movement of the 1980s* (1993).

Martin, William C., *With God on Our Side: The Rise of the Religious Right in America* (1996). McGirr, Lisa, *Suburban Warriors: The Origins of the New American Right* (2001). Meyer, Jane, and Doyle McManus, *Landslide: The Unmaking of the President, 1984–1988* (1988). Murray, Charles, *Losing Ground: American Social Policy, 1950–1980* (1984). Noonan, Peggy, *What I Saw at the Revolution: A Political Life in the Reagan Era* (1990). Phillips, Kevin P., *The Politics of Rich and Poor: Wealth and the American Electorate in the Reagan Aftermath* (1990). Rayack, Elton, *Not So Free to Choose: The Political Economy of Milton Friedman and Ronald Reagan* (1987). Reed, Adolph L., *The Jesse Jackson Phenomenon: The Crisis of Purpose in Afro-American Politics* (1986).

Schaller, Michael, *Reckoning with Reagan: America and Its President in the 1980s* (1992). Scheer, Robert, *With Enough Shovels: Reagan, Bush, and Nuclear War* (1982). Taylor, John, *Circus of Ambition: The Culture of Wealth and Power in the Eighties* (1989). Thelen, David P., *Becoming Citizens in the Age of Television: How Americans Challenged the Media and Seized Political Initiative During the Iran-Contra Debate* (1996). Thompson, Mark, ed., *Long Road to Freedom: The Advocate History of the Gay and Lesbian Movement* (1994). Wolters, Raymond, *Right Turn: William Bradford Reynolds, the Reagan Administration, and Black Civil Rights* (1996).

CHAPTER 31

Abramson, Jeffrey, ed., *Postmortem: The O. J. Simpson Case: Justice Confronts Race, Domestic Violence, Lawyers, Money, and the Media* (1996). Beschloss, Michael R., and Strobe Talbott, *At the Highest Levels: The Inside Story of the End of the Cold War* (1993). Bingham, Clara, *Women on the Hill: Challenging the Culture of Congress* (1997). Button, James W., et al., *Private Lives, Public Conflicts: Battles Over Gay Rights in American Communities* (1997). Campbell, Colin, and Bert A. Rockman, eds., *The Clinton Presidency: First Appraisals* (1996). Dertouzos, Michael L., *What Will Be: How the New World of Information Will Change Our Lives* (1998). Drew, Elizabeth, *Showdown: The Struggle Between the Gingrich Congress and the Clinton White House* (1996). Duignan, Peter, and L. H. Gann, eds., *The Debate in the United States Over Immigration* (1998). Dunnigan, James F., and Austin Bay, *From Shield to Storm:*

High-Tech Weapons, Military Strategy, & Coalition Warfare in the Persian Gulf (1992).

Gitlin, Todd, *The Twilight of Common Dreams: Why America Is Wracked by Culture Wars* (1995). Gordon, Avery, and Christopher Newfield, eds., *Mapping Multiculturalism* (1996). Green, John C., et al., eds., *Religion and the Culture Wars: Dispatches from the Front* (1996). Greenberg, Stanley B., *Middle Class Dreams: The Politics and Power of the New American Majority* (1995). Greene, John Robert, *The Presidency of George Bush* (2000). Haas, Richard N., *The Reluctant Sheriff: The United States After the Cold War* (1997). Hafner, Katie, and Matthew Lyon, *Where Wizards Stay Up Late: The Origins of the Internet* (1998). Hogan, Michael, ed., *The End of the Cold War: Its Meanings and Implications* (1992). Lind, Michael, *The Next American Nation: The New Nationalism and the Fourth American Revolution* (1995). Lowi, Theodore J., and Benjamin Ginsberg, *Embattled Democracy: Politics and Policy in the Clinton Era* (1995).

Maraniss, David, *First in His Class: A Biography of Bill Clinton* (1995). Matteo, Sherri, ed., *American Women in the Nineties: Today's Critical Issues* (1993). McGuckin, Frank, ed., *Terrorism in the United States* (1997). Morris, Roger, *Partners in Power: The Clintons and Their America* (1996). Newman, Katherine S., *Declining Fortunes: The Withering of the American Dream* (1993). Nolan, James L., Jr., ed., *The American Culture Wars: Current Contests and Future Prospects* (1996). Phillips, Kevin P., *The Politics of Rich and Poor: Wealth and the American Electorate in the Reagan Aftermath* (1990). Posner, Gerald L., *Citizen Perot: His Life and Times* (1996). Ripley, Randall B., and James M. Lindsay, eds., *U.S. Foreign Policy After the Cold War* (1997). Rivlin, Gary, *The Plot to Get Bill Gates* (1999). Rubin, Lillian B., *Families on the Fault Line: America's Working Class Speaks about the Family, the Economy, Race, and Ethnicity* (1994).

Skocpol, Theda, *Boomerang: Clinton's Health Security Effort and the Turn Against Government in U. S. Politics* (1996). Slessarev, Helene, *The Betrayal of the Urban Poor* (1991). Spain, Daphne, and Suzanne M. Bianchi, *Balancing Act: Motherhood, Marriage, and Employment Among American Women* (1996). Stern, Kenneth S., *A Force Upon the Plain: The American Militia Movement and the Politics of Hate* (1996). Stewart, James B., *Blood Sport: The President and His Adversaries* (1996). Thomas, Evan, et al., *Back from the Dead: How Clinton Survived the Republican Revolution* (1997). Toobin, Jeffrey, *A Vast Conspiracy: The Real Story of the Sex Scandal That Nearly Brought Down a President* (2000). Wray, Matt, and Annalee Newitz, eds., *White Trash: Race and Class in America* (1997).

PHOTO CREDITS

INDEX

Y

Z